# The Pegans
# of Martic Township, Pennsylvania
# and Their Descendants in America

*Vol. 2 Collateral Lines*

# By Ann (PeGan) Miller Carr

# Pegan Family History

Ann "PeGan" Miller Carr

ISBN: 978-1-60414-949-4

Published by
Fideli Publishing, Inc.

www.FideliPublishing.com

# Dedication

For my wonderful husband, David Allen Carr, who encouraged and supported me every step of the way; and my grandsons, Reuben Anthony Miller and Sidney Grayson Miller (and any siblings who may join them).

# TABLE OF CONTENTS

# Descendants of Alexander Pagan

1. **Alexander² Pagan** (*James¹*) was born about 1714 in Dumfries or Gallaway, Scotland or Ulster, Ireland. He was the son of James Pagan and Unknown Unknown. Alexander died in Fishing Creek, Chester Co., South Carolina?, after 1763. It is possible that the elder Alexander Pagan did not come to America around 1737 with his father James I and brothers Archibald, James II and Andrew I, but arrived later, perhaps in the 1750s. The are no deeds for this Alexander Pagan in Lancaster County, nor does he appear on the Martic Twp., Lancaster Co., Pennsylvania tax lists in 1751, 1754, or from 1756-1759, but at that time only men who owned land were taxed. He also is not listed from 1769 on. (The tax assessments from 1752-1754, 1755, and from 1759-1769 are not extent.)[1]

The *Heritage History of Chester County, South Carolina, Vol. II* says that family records state that three brothers, Alexander, James and Archibald Pagan, together with their father, who is not named, emigrated from County Antrim, Ireland, to Lancaster County, Pennsylvania. From there, Alexander Pagan moved to the Fishing Creek section of Chester County, South Carolina, getting a land grant for 200 acres in 1765 (recorded in Mecklenburg Co., North Carolina, since this was several years before the border demarcation).[2] The same information is found in Glenda Pagan Hibdon's The Pagan, Hunt and Sanderson genealogies.[3]

Alexander Pagan may have moved to South Carolina with a great number of Muddy Run Presbyterian Church members from Martic Twp., Lancaster Co., Pennsylvania to South Carolina. This move is mentioned in *The History of Lancaster Co., Pennsylvania:*

> "The church history of Martic township commences with the Muddy Run Presbyterian Church. The land upon which the church stands was taken up or patented in 1742 by David Jones, John Marshall and William Andrews, and a log house built the same year. There are no records to show who was the first pastor, as some years after its erection nearly all of the settlers left, on account of a difficulty with the Indians, and moved to South Carolina."[4]

This migration from southern Lancaster County to Chester County, South Carolina happened in the early 1760s, about the time of the French and Indian War.[3]

Alexander's sons settled in the Rocky Creek section of Chester County. James raised a large family. Captain Alexander Pegan II died in the Battle of Fishing Creek in the Revolutionary War; he was married and had three children, the last of whom was born after Alexander II's death.[5, 6] Archibald Pagan may have lived in Chester County for a short time, but later records place him in Charleston, Charleston Co., South Carolina. It is not known for certain if he married or had children, but it is believed that he never married.

Descendants of Alexander Pagan continued to spell the surname "Pagan" down through the generations and still do today. Information on Alexander Pagan's descendants is from internet sources, and they cannot be documented or fully outlined in this book without further intensive research in South Carolina and other states.

Alexander married **Unknown Mills?** before 1735. They had three sons.

Sons of Alexander Pagan and Unknown Mills?:

+ 2 m I. **James³ Pagan** was born in County Antrim, Ireland, before 1736. He died in Rocky Creek, Chester Co., South Carolina, between 1810 and 1815.

1

+ 3   m   II.   **Alexander[3] Pagan II** was born in County Antrim, Ireland, about 1736. He died in Fishing Creek, Chester Co., South Carolina, on August 18, 1780.[5, 6]

+ 4   m   III.   **Archibald[3] Pagan** was born in County Antrim, Ireland, after 1736. He died in Charleston, Charleston Co., South Carolina, in May 1809.[7]

# 3rd Generation

**2. James³ Pagan** (*Alexander²*, *James¹*) was born before 1736 in County Antrim, Ireland. He was the son of Alexander Pagan (1) and Unknown Mills? James died in Rocky Creek, Chester Co., South Carolina, between 1810 and 1815. James Pagan is said to have been a Revolutionary War veteran, serving, as his brother Alexander Pagan did, in the campaign against the infamous British Colonel Bannestare Tarleton.

James Pagan in mentioned in his brother Alexander's will; Alexander wills his land to his two brothers, James and Archibald.[8]

> 1815, August 17 - Abraham Gill of Chester Dist. bought from William Stringfellow, Chester Dist., for $275, 48 acres on Rocky Creek, had belonged to the estate of James Pagan decd, the part allotted to Peggy Pagan, alias Peggy Kelsey. Witnesses were R.W. Gill and W. W. Bradford.[9]

> 1816, Feb. 17 - Robert W. Gill, administrator of the estate of Abraham Gill, decd, of Chester Dist. bought from Carson Pagan, Chester Dist., for $250, 66 acres on Rocky Cr., part of estate of James Pagan allotted to Carson Pagan. Start near Foxes Spring, N 86 E 18 poles, N 4 W 35 poles, E 17 N 17 poles, S 10 E 35 poles to start. Witnesses were John Kelsey Sen. and Wm. Pagan.[10]

James Pegan witnesses the administrative bond for his cousin-in-law John Downing's estate in Fishing Creek, Chester Co., South Carolina. John Downing was married to Mary Pegan/Pagan Downing, daughter of Andrew Pegan/Pagan Sr., brother of Alexander Pagan Sr.[11]

Information on this James Pagan's descendants is from internet sources, and they cannot be documented or fully outlined for this book without further intensive research in South Carolina and other states.

James married **Mary Carson?** before 1800. They had ten children.

Children of James Pagan and Unknown Carson?:

+ 5 m I. **William⁴ Pagan** was born before 1775.

+ 6 m II. **Carson⁴ Pagan** was born before 1775.

+ 7 f III. **Margaret⁴ Pagan** was born before 1784. She was also known as **Peggy.**

+ 8 f IV. **Daughter One⁴ Pagan** was born before 1784.

+ 9 m V. **Son One⁴ Pagan** was born before 1784.

+ 10 m VI. **Son Two⁴ Pagan** was born before 1784.

+ 11 m VII. **Son Three⁴ Pagan** was born between 1785 and 1790.

+ 12 f VIII. **Daughter Two⁴ Pagan** was born between 1785 and 1790.

+ 13 f IX. **Daughter Three⁴ Pagan Pagan** was born between 1785 and 1790.

+ 14 m X. **Son Four⁴ Pagan** was born between 1790 and 1800.

**3. Alexander³ Pagan II** (*Alexander²*, *James¹*) was born about 1736 in County Antrim, Ireland. He was the son of Alexander Pagan (1) and Unknown Mills? Alexander lived in 1765 in Fishing Creek, Chester Co., South Carolina. Alexander died in Fishing Creek, Chester Co., South Carolina, on August 18, 1780, at age 44.[4] He has a commemorative gravestone in Fishing Creek Presbyterian Cemetery, Chester, Chester Co., South Carolina.[5]

According to Ann Pickens Collins in the *History of Chester County, South Carolina, Vol. II*, Pagan family records state that three brothers, Alexander, James and Archibald Pagan, together with their father, emigrated from County Antrim, Ireland, to Lancaster County, Pennsylvania. From there, Alexander Pagan moved to the Fishing Creek section of Chester County, South Carolina, getting a land grant for 200 acres in 1765 (recorded in Mecklenburg Co., North Carolina, since this was several years before the border demarcation).[2]

Alexander may have moved to South Carolina with a great number of Muddy Run Presbyterian

Church members from Martic Twp., Lancaster Co., Pennsylvania to South Carolina. This move is mentioned in *The History of Lancaster Co., Pennsylvania:*

> "The church history of Martic township commences with the Muddy Run Presbyterian Church. The land upon which the church stands was taken up or patented in 1742 by David Jones, John Marshall and William Andrews, and a log house built the same year. There are no records to show who was the first pastor, as some years after its erection nearly all of the settlers left, on account of a difficulty with the Indians, and moved to South Carolina."[3]

His brothers settled in the Rocky Creek section of Chester County. James raised a large family. Little is known of Archibald Pagan who later removed to Charleston, Charleston Co., South Carolina.

Elizabeth F. Ellet, in her book, *The Women of the American Revolution, Vol. III,* mentions that Capt. Alexander Pagan was killed at the Battle of Fishing Creek on August 20, 1780 while rallying his men.[4]

Alexander Pagan/Pegan left a will:

> "Will of Alexander Pegan of Fishing Creek in the County of Craven & South Carolina, Planter, being in Good Health. 1 June 1778.
>
> To Jennet my Dear beloved Wife, the third part of my whole personal Estate with her living of the place during her Widowhood To my Daughter Agnes Pegan, the other two thirds of said Estate, likewise if it should please providence to give me a son by my wife Jennet Pegan now being Pregnant, I bequeath to him my whole real Estate, only Agnes to have if Living to the years of Maturity, One Hundred or the value thereof from said Estate. But on the other Hand it being a female Child, my two Daughters to be Coequal sharers in the whole … And lastly these my Children dying all in none age, I Bequeath my Land to my Brothers James & Archibald Pegan and their Heirs, them paying my Wife Jennet Pegan two hundred Pound Currency of said Province. My Loving Uncle Robert Gill and Uncle John Mills my Executor."[7, 12]

Alexander Pegan II mentions two uncles, Robert Gill and John Mills, as executors of his estate. Robert Gill married Elinor Kelso, who was the aunt of Alexander II's wife Jennet Kelso Pegan. But it seems that John Mills did not marry a relative of Jennet's... so was John Mill's the brother of Alexander I's wife and Alexander II's mother?

Information on Alexander Pagan II's descendants is from internet sources and they cannot be fully documented or outlined in this book without further intensive research in South Carolina and other states.

Alexander married **Jannette Kelso** about 1770 in Chester Co., South Carolina. They had three children. Jannette Kelso was born in County Antrim, Ireland, in 1751 and died in Chester Co., South Carolina, after April 5, 1826.

Children of Alexander Pagan II and Janet or Jannette Kelsey or Kelso:

+ 15 f I.     **Agnes⁴ Pagan** was born in Fishing Creek, Chester Co., South Carolina, in 1773. She was also known as **Nancy.** Agnes died after 1810.

+ 16 f II.    **Susannah⁴ Pagan** was born in Fishing Creek, Chester Co., South Carolina, in 1778. She died in Shelby Co., Tennessee, in 1863.

+ 17 m III.   **Alexander⁴ Pagan III** was born in Fishing Creek, Chester Co., South Carolina, in 1780. He died in York Co., South Carolina, on April 12, 1862.

4. **Archibald³ Pagan** (*Alexander²*, *James¹*) was born after 1736 in County Antrim, Ireland. He was the son of Alexander Pagan (1) and Unknown Mills? Archibald died in Charleston, Charleston Co., South Carolina, in May 1809.[8]

Archibald Pagan was mentioned in his brother Alexander Pagan's will. Alexander bequeathed his land to his brothers James and Archibald.[6, 7]

From the *Charleston (SC) Courier*, published May 28, 1807:

Ranaway on the 27th ult.

The subscriber's servant, William about 25 years of age, 5 feet 8 inches high, marked with the small pox. He carried with him two cloth coatees, one blue and the other brown; a pair of black velvet, and a pair of mixed cassimere pantaloons. When he is spoken to he has a down look. He is well known, being much employed about the city in playing the tamboureen.

A reward of Fifty Dollars will be paid on proof to conviction of his being harboured by a white person; and Ten Dollars, on his being secured in the Work-House.

Archibald Pagan, 131 King-street

May 7.[13]

This Archibald Pegan was listed as a subscriber in Charleston, Charleston Co., South Carolina to *Sermons on Practical Subjects,* published sermons by the Rev. Joseph Washburn of the Farmington, Connecticut Congregationalist Church.[14]

Archibald Pagan moved to the Rocky Creek, Chester Co., South Carolina area with his father Alexander and two brothers, Alexander II and James Pagan, by 1763. But there are no deeds or records on Archibald in Chester County. It seems that he may have moved to Charleston shortly after coming to Chester County.

According to an abstract of an 1809 Charleston, South Carolina estate, a John Bohannon, administrator of outstanding goods and property of a Meinrad Greiner, deceased, says that Archibald Pagan was the original administrator of Greiner's estate, and was in possession of the administration when Archibald himself died in 1808. Bohannon states that Archibald Pagan never reported to the court on an accounting of Greiner's assets, even though Archibald was collecting on debts owed to Greiner, hired out Greiner's four slaves, and sold goods and merchandise belonging to Greiner's estate. Bohannon further claims that Greiner's property and other assets have now become listed as part of Archibald Pagan's estate, and he demanded that Archibald Pagan's administrator be summoned before the court to surrender all of Greiner's assets and property.[15]

No evidence of a marriage or children for Archibald Pagan has been found.

# 4ᵗʰ Generation

5. **William⁴ Pagan** (*James³, Alexander², James¹*) was born before 1775. He was the son of James Pagan (2) and Unknown Carson?

6. **Carson⁴ Pagan** (*James³, Alexander², James¹*) was born before 1775. He was the son of James Pagan (2) and Unknown Carson?

7. **Margaret⁴ Pagan** (*James³, Alexander², James¹*) was born before 1784. She was also known as **Peggy.** She was the daughter of James Pagan (2) and Unknown Carson?

Margaret married **Unknown Kelsey or Kelso** before 1815.

8. **Daughter One⁴ Pagan** (*James³, Alexander², James¹*) was born before 1784. She was the daughter of James Pagan (2) and Unknown Carson?

9. **Son One⁴ Pagan** (*James³, Alexander², James¹*) was born before 1784. He was the son of James Pagan (2) and Unknown Carson?

10. **Son Two⁴ Pagan** (*James³, Alexander², James¹*) was born before 1784. He was the son of James Pagan (2) and Unknown Carson?

11. **Son Three⁴ Pagan** (*James³, Alexander², James¹*) was born between 1785 and 1790. He was the son of James Pagan (2) and Unknown Carson?

12. **Daughter Two⁴ Pagan** (*James³, Alexander², James¹*) was born between 1785 and 1790. She was the daughter of James Pagan (2) and Unknown Carson?

13. **Daughter Three⁴ Pagan** (*James³, Alexander², James¹*) was born between 1785 and 1790. She was the daughter of James Pagan (2) and Unknown Carson?

14. **Son Four⁴ Pagan** (*James³, Alexander², James¹*) was born between 1790 and 1800. He was the son of James Pagan (2) and Unknown Carson?

15. **Agnes⁴ Pagan** (*Alexander³, Alexander², James¹*) was born in 1773 in Fishing Creek, Chester Co., South Carolina. She was also known as **Nancy.** She was the daughter of Alexander Pagan II (3) and Jannette Kelso. Agnes died after 1810.

She married **Leonard Jones.** They had six children. Leonard Jones was born about 1770.

Children of Agnes Pagan and Leonard Jones:

+ 18 m I. **Son One⁵ Jones** was born between 1800 and 1810.

+ 19 m II. **Son Two⁵ Jones** was born between 1800 and 1810.

+ 20 m III. **Son Three⁵ Jones** was born between 1800 and 1810.

+ 21 m IV. **Son Four⁵ Jones** was born between 1800 and 1810.

+ 22 f V. **Daughter One⁵ Jones** was born between 1800 and 1810.

+ 23 f VI. **Daughter Two⁵ Jones** was born between 1800 and 1810. She died after 1810.

16. **Susannah⁴ Pagan** (*Alexander³, Alexander², James¹*) was born in 1778 in Fishing Creek, Chester Co., South Carolina. She was the daughter of Alexander Pagan II (3) and Jannette Kelso. Susannah died in Shelby Co., Tennessee, in 1863 at age 85. She was buried in Wherry Cemetery, Lakeland, Shelby Co., Tennessee.[16]

Susannah married **Thomas Wherry** before 1804. They had seven children. Thomas Wherry was born in Chester Co., South Carolina, on March 3, 1779. Thomas reached age 79 and died in Shelby Co., Tennessee, on July 7, 1858. He was buried in Wherry Cemetery, Lakeland, Shelby Co., Tennessee.[15]

Children of Susannah Pagan and Thomas Wherry:

+ 24 f I. **Mary⁵ Wherry** was born in York Co., South Carolina, on May 1, 1804. She died in York Co., South Carolina, on May 12, 1806.

+ 25 m II. **John⁵ Wherry** was born in York Co., South Carolina, on March 20, 1807. He died in Rusk Co., Texas, on April 6, 1871.[17]

+ 26 f III. **Elizabeth Chambers⁵ Wherry** was born in York Co., South Carolina, on July 16, 1809. She died in Shelby Co., Tennessee, in 1882.[15]

+ 27  m  IV.  **Samuel Alexander Pagan⁵ Wherry** was born in North Carolina on October 18, 1811. He died in Shelby Co., Tennessee, on September 4, 1842.[15]

+ 28  m  V.  **Andrew Jackson⁵ Wherry** was born in North Carolina on October 25, 1815. He died in Shelby Co., Tennessee, in 1875.[15]

+ 29  m  VI.  **Wyatt Alonzo⁵ Wherry** was born in Catawba, York Co., South Carolina, on March 1, 1818. He died in Elsie, Clatsop Co., Oregon, on September 26, 1900.

+ 30  m  VII.  **Willis⁵ Wherry** was born in Shelby Co., Tennessee, on September 13, 1820. He died in Shelby Co., Tennessee, before 1840.

17. **Alexander⁴ Pagan III** (*Alexander³*, *Alexander²*, *James¹*) was born in 1780 in Fishing Creek, Chester Co., South Carolina. He was the son of Alexander Pagan II (3) and Jannette Kelso. Alexander died in York Co., South Carolina, on April 12, 1862, at age 82.

Alexander married **Mary Gill Mills** before 1805. They had fourteen children. Mary Gill Mills was born in Chester Co., South Carolina, on April 20, 1789. Mary Gill reached age 62 and died in Chester Co., South Carolina, on March 9, 1852.

Children of Alexander Pagan III and Mary Gill Mills:

+ 31  m  I.  **John Mills⁵ Pagan** was born in Fishing Creek, Chester Co., South Carolina, on April 10, 1805. He died in Bradley Co., Arkansas, on April 15, 1895.

+ 32  f  II.  **Mary Clarke⁵ Pagan** was born in Fishing Creek, Chester Co., South Carolina, on April 22, 1807. She

died in Fishing Creek, Chester Co., South Carolina, before 1810.

+ 33  m  III.  **James⁵ Pagan** was born in Fishing Creek, Chester Co., South Carolina, on April 22, 1809. He died in Shelton, Fairfield Co., South Carolina, on November 25, 1898.[18]

+ 34  f  IV.  **Infant Susannah Eleanor⁵ Pagan** was born in Fishing Creek, Chester Co., South Carolina, in 1808. She died in Fishing Creek, Chester Co., South Carolina, before 1829.

+ 35  m  V.  **Infant Alexander Robert⁵ Pagan III** was born in Fishing Creek, Chester Co., South Carolina, in 1810. He died in Fishing Creek, Chester Co., South Carolina, before 1814.

+ 36  m  VI.  **Thomas Sumpter⁵ Pagan** was born in Fishing Creek, Chester Co., South Carolina, in 1811. He died in Bradley Co., Arkansas, on September 25, 1861.

+ 37  m  VII.  **Alexander Lawrens⁵ Pagan** was born in Fishing Creek, Chester Co., South Carolina, on February 6, 1814. He died in Fishing Creek, Chester Co., South Carolina, on October 16, 1817.

+ 38  m  VIII.  **George Bonder⁵ Pagan** was born in Fishing Creek, Chester Co., South Carolina, on July 28, 1816. He died in Millcreek, Winston Co., Mississippi, on July 25, 1901.[19]

+ 39  f  IX.  **Rebecca Irvine Fayssoux⁵ Pagan** was born in Fishing Creek, Chester Co., South Carolina, on January 11, 1819. She died in Crandall, Kaufman Co., Texas, on June 15, 1901.[20]

+ 40  m  X.  **Archibald Gill⁵ Pagan** was born in Fishing Creek, Chester Co., South Carolina, on July 13, 1823.

He died in Fishing Creek, Chester Co., South Carolina, on July 10, 1857.[5]

+ 41 f XI. **Mary Jeanette⁵ Pagan** was born in Fishing Creek, Chester Co., South Carolina, on February 2, 1825. She was also known as **Jeanette.** Mary Jeanette died in York, York Co., Pennsylvania, on June 17, 1910.[21]

+ 42 f XII. **Charlotte Clarke⁵ Pagan** was born in Chester Co., South Carolina, on February 15, 1826. She died in Chester Co., South Carolina, on July 15, 1842.[5]

+ 43 f XIII. **Susan Eleanor⁵ Pagan**_was born in Fishing Creek, Chester Co., South Carolina, in 1829. She died in York, York Co, South Carolina?, on May 20, 1912.[20]

+ 44 f XIV. **Sarah Agnes⁵ Pagan** was born in Fishing Creek, Chester Co., South Carolina, in 1832. She died in Fishing Creek, Chester Co., South Carolina, on February 25, 1858.[5]

# 5th Generation

**18. Son One⁵ Jones** (*Agnes⁴ Pagan, Alexander³, Alexander², James¹*) was born between 1800 and 1810. He was the son of Leonard Jones and Agnes Pagan (15).

**19. Son Two⁵ Jones** (*Agnes⁴ Pagan, Alexander³, Alexander², James¹*) was born between 1800 and 1810. He was the son of Leonard Jones and Agnes Pagan (15).

**20. Son Three⁵ Jones** (*Agnes⁴ Pagan, Alexander³, Alexander², James¹*) was born between 1800 and 1810. He was the son of Leonard Jones and Agnes Pagan (15).

**21. Son Four⁵ Jones** (*Agnes⁴ Pagan, Alexander³, Alexander², James¹*) was born between 1800 and 1810. He was the son of Leonard Jones and Agnes Pagan (15).

**22. Daughter One⁵ Jones** (*Agnes⁴ Pagan, Alexander³, Alexander², James¹*) was born between 1800 and 1810. She was the daughter of Leonard Jones and Agnes Pagan (15).

**23. Daughter Two⁵ Jones** (*Agnes⁴ Pagan, Alexander³, Alexander², James¹*) was born between 1800 and 1810. She was the daughter of Leonard Jones and Agnes Pagan (15). Daughter Two died after 1810.

**24. Mary⁵ Wherry** (*Susannah⁴ Pagan, Alexander³, Alexander², James¹*) was born on May 1, 1804, in York Co., South Carolina. She was the daughter of Thomas Wherry and Susannah Pagan (16). Mary died in York Co., South Carolina, on May 12, 1806.

**25. John⁵ Wherry** (*Susannah⁴ Pagan, Alexander³, Alexander², James¹*) was born on March 20, 1807, in York Co., South Carolina. He was the son of Thomas Wherry and Susannah Pagan (16). John died in Rusk Co., Texas, on April 6, 1871.

John married **Margaret Yeary** on October 25, 1832, in Shelby Co., Tennessee. They had one daughter. Margaret Yeary was born in Tennessee on November 15, 1813. Margaret reached age 78 and died in Kaufman Co., Texas, on November 12, 1892.

Daughter of John Wherry and Margaret Yeary:

+ 45 f I.   **Mary Ann⁶ Wherry** was born in Shelby Co., Tennessee, on August 3, 1833. She died in Kemp, Kaufman Co., Texas, in 1920.

**26. Elizabeth Chambers⁵ Wherry** (*Susannah⁴ Pagan, Alexander³, Alexander², James¹*) was born on July 16, 1809, in York Co., South Carolina. She was the daughter of Thomas Wherry and Susannah Pagan (16). Elizabeth Chambers died in Shelby Co., Tennessee, in 1882 at age 72. She was buried in Wherry Cemetery, Lakeland, Shelby Co., Tennessee.[15]

Never married.

**27. Samuel Alexander Pagan⁵ Wherry** (*Susannah⁴ Pagan, Alexander³, Alexander², James¹*) was born on October 18, 1811, in North Carolina. He was the son of Thomas Wherry and Susannah Pagan (16). Samuel Alexander Pagan died in Shelby Co., Tennessee, on September 4, 1842, at age 30. He was buried in Wherry Cemetery, Lakeland, Shelby Co., Tennessee.[15]

Never married.

**28. Andrew Jackson⁵ Wherry** (*Susannah⁴ Pagan, Alexander³, Alexander², James¹*) was born on October 25, 1815, in North Carolina. He was the son of Thomas Wherry and Susannah Pagan (16). Andrew Jackson died in Shelby Co., Tennessee, in 1875 at age 59. He was buried in Wherry Cemetery, Lakeland, Shelby Co., Tennessee.[15]

Never married.

**29. Wyatt Alonzo⁵ Wherry** (*Susannah⁴ Pagan, Alexander³, Alexander², James¹*) was born on March 1, 1818, in Catawba, York Co., South Carolina. He was the son of Thomas Wherry and Susannah Pagan (16). Wyatt Alonzo died in Elsie, Clatsop Co., Oregon, on September 26, 1900, at age 82.

He married **Rowena Josephine Howard.** Rowena Josephine Howard was born in Dyersburg, Dyer Co., Tennessee, on March 26, 1829. Rowena Josephine reached age 84 and died in Wapato, Yakima Co., Washington, on September 21, 1913.

30. **Willis⁵ Wherry** (*Susannah⁴ Pagan, Alexander³, Alexander², James¹*) was born on September 13, 1820, in Shelby Co., Tennessee. He was the son of Thomas Wherry and Susannah Pagan (16). Willis died in Shelby Co., Tennessee, before 1840.

31. **John Mills⁵ Pagan** (*Alexander⁴, Alexander³, Alexander², James¹*) was born on April 10, 1805, in Fishing Creek, Chester Co., South Carolina. He was the son of Alexander Pagan III (17) and Mary Gill Mills. John Mills died in Bradley Co., Arkansas, on April 15, 1895, at age 90.

John Mills married **Rebecca Elizabeth McDaniel** on December 11, 1836. They had 10 children. Rebecca Elizabeth McDaniel was born in South Carolina in 1815. Rebecca Elizabeth reached age 40 and died in Noxubee Co., Mississippi, on March 9, 1855.

John Mills Pagan married **Nancy Permelia Joiner** on December 2, 1857, in Bradley Co., Arkansas. They had one daughter.

Children of John Mills Pagan and Rebecca Elizabeth McDaniel:

+ 46   f   I.   **Infant Mary Ann⁶ Pagan** was born in Fishing Creek, Chester Co., South Carolina, in 1837. She died in Fishing Creek, Chester Co., South Carolina, in 1837.

+ 47   f   II.   **Sarah Elizabeth⁶ Pagan** was born in Fishing Creek, Chester Co., South Carolina, on February 6, 1839. She died in Bradley Co., Arkansas?, on July 16, 1858.

+ 48   f   III.   **Julia Viola⁶ Pagan** was born in Fishing Creek, Chester Co., South Carolina, on November 4, 1840. She died in Bradley Co., Arkansas, on April 25, 1871.[22]

+ 49   f   IV.   **Charlotte Louisa⁶ Pagan** born in Fishing Creek, Chester Co., South Carolina, on August 2, 1842. She died in Fishing Creek, Chester Co., South Carolina, on August 2, 1844.

+ 50   m   V.   **John McDaniel⁶ Pagan** was born in Noxubee Co., Mississippi, in November 1844. He died in Bradley Co., Arkansas, on November 23, 1924.[21]

+ 51   f   VI.   **Susannah Mahalia⁶ Pagan** was born in Noxubee Co., Mississippi, in 1846. She died in Kaufman Co., Texas, between 1876–1880.

+ 52   f   VII.   **Mary Ann Rebecca⁶ Pagan** was born in Noxubee Co., Mississippi, on September 11, 1848. She was also known as **Mollie.** Mary Ann Rebecca died in Kaufman Co., Texas, on May 31, 1899.[19]

+ 53   m   VIII.   **Alexander Daniel⁶ Pagan** was born in Noxubee Co., Mississippi, in February 1851. He died in November 1924.

+ 54   m   IX.   **John J.⁶ Pagan** was born in Noxubee Co., Mississippi, in 1853. He died in Bradley Co., Arkansas, on August 26, 1867.

+ 55   m   X.   **George M.C.⁶ Pagan** was born in Noxubee Co., Mississippi, about March 9, 1855. He died in Marion, Bradley Co., Arkansas, on November 1, 1881.

Daughter of John Mills Pagan and Nancy Permelia Joiner:

+ 56   f   I.   **Catherine⁶ Pagan** was born in Bradley Co., Arkansas, in 1859.

32. **Mary Clarke⁵ Pagan** (*Alexander⁴, Alexander³, Alexander², James¹*) was born on April 22, 1807, in Fishing Creek, Chester Co., South Carolina. She was the daughter of Alexander Pagan III (17) and Mary Gill Mills. Mary Clarke died in Fishing Creek, Chester Co., South Carolina, before 1810.

**33. James$^{5}$ Pagan** (*Alexander$^{4}$, Alexander$^{3}$, Alexander$^{2}$, James$^{1}$*) was born on April 22, 1809, in Fishing Creek, Chester Co., South Carolina. He was the son of Alexander Pagan III (17) and Mary Gill Mills. James died in Shelton, Fairfield Co., South Carolina, on November 25, 1898, at age 89. He was buried in Saint John's Episcopal Cemetery, Winnsboro, Fairfield Co., South Carolina.[17]

James married **Anne Callender Fayssoux** in 1843 in Philadelphia Co., Pennsylvania. They had five children. Anne Callender Fayssoux was born in Fishing Creek, Chester Co., South Carolina, on September 18, 1816. Anne Callender reached age 82 and died in Winnsboro, Fairfield Co., South Carolina, on February 12, 1899. She was buried in Saint John's Episcopal Cemetery, Winnsboro, Fairfield Co., South Carolina.[17]

Children of James Pagan and Anne Callender Fayssoux:

+ 57 m I. **Edwards Fayssoux$^{6}$ Pagan** was born in Chester Co., South Carolina, on January 7, 1846. He died in Great Falls, Chester Co., South Carolina, on October 10, 1923.[17]

+ 58 f II. **Mary Nacreid$^{6}$ Pagan** was born in Chester Co., South Carolina, on February 18, 1847. She died in Chester Co., South Carolina, on August 23, 1872.[23]

+ 59 f III. **Annie Irvine$^{6}$ Pagan** was born in Chester Co., South Carolina, on March 28, 1848. She died in Lincolnton, Lincoln Co., North Carolina, on June 28, 1890.[24]

+ 60 m IV. **Irvine Fayssoux$^{6}$ Pagan** was born in Chester Co., South Carolina, in December 1849. He died in Shelton, Fairfield Co., South Carolina, in 1912.[17]

+ 61 f V. **Rebecca Armstrong$^{6}$ Pagan** was born in Chester Co., South Carolina, on August 22, 1852. She was also known as **Beckie.** Rebecca Armstrong died in Columbia, Richland Co., South Carolina, on October 14, 1921.[25]

**34. Infant Susannah Eleanor$^{5}$ Pagan** (*Alexander$^{4}$, Alexander$^{3}$, Alexander$^{2}$, James$^{1}$*) was born in 1808 in Fishing Creek, Chester Co., South Carolina. She was the daughter of Alexander Pagan III (17) and Mary Gill Mills. Infant Susannah Eleanor died in Fishing Creek, Chester Co., South Carolina, before 1829.

**35. Infant Alexander Robert$^{5}$ Pagan III** (*Alexander$^{4}$, Alexander$^{3}$, Alexander$^{2}$, James$^{1}$*) was born in 1810 in Fishing Creek, Chester Co., South Carolina. He was the son of Alexander Pagan III (17) and Mary Gill Mills. Infant Alexander Robert died in Fishing Creek, Chester Co., South Carolina, before 1814.

**36. Thomas Sumter$^{5}$ Pagan** (*Alexander$^{4}$, Alexander$^{3}$, Alexander$^{2}$, James$^{1}$*) was born in 1811 in Fishing Creek, Chester Co., South Carolina. He was the son of Alexander Pagan III (17) and Mary Gill Mills. Thomas Sumter died in Bradley Co., Arkansas, on September 25, 1861, at age 50.

Thomas Sumter married **Elizabeth Eveline Gill** on March 9, 1837. They had four children. Elizabeth Eveline Gill was born in York Co., South Carolina, on October 21, 1821. Elizabeth Eveline reached age 54 and died in Prescott, Nevada Co., Arkansas, on May 4, 1876.

Children of Thomas Sumter Pagan and Elizabeth Eveline Gill:

+ 62 f I. **Anne Rebecca King$^{6}$ Pagan** was born in York, York Co., South Carolina, on February 2, 1838. She died in Prescott, Nevada Co., Arkansas, on June 2, 1876.

+ 63 m II. **James Alexander$^{6}$ Pagan** was born in York, York Co., South Carolina, on December 12, 1841. He died in Prescott, Nevada Co., Arkansas?, on July 10, 1913.[26]

+ 64 f III. **Mary Cloud$^{6}$ Pagan** was born in York, York Co., South Carolina, on

July 21, 1844. She died in Prescott, Nevada Co., Arkansas?, on February 22, 1937.[27]

+ 65 m IV. **John Gill⁶ Pagan** was born in York, York Co., South Carolina, on August 10, 1856. He died in Arkansas on December 18, 1864.

**37. Alexander Laurens⁵ Pagan** (*Alexander⁴, Alexander³, Alexander², James¹*) was born on February 6, 1814, in Fishing Creek, Chester Co., South Carolina. He was the son of Alexander Pagan III (17) and Mary Gill Mills. Alexander Laurens died in Fishing Creek, Chester Co., South Carolina, on October 16, 1817, at age three. He is buried in Fishing Creek Cemetery, Chester, Chester Co., South Carolina.[5]

**38. George Bonder⁵ Pagan** (*Alexander⁴, Alexander³, Alexander², James¹*) was born on July 28, 1816, in Fishing Creek, Chester Co., South Carolina. He was the son of Alexander Pagan III (17) and Mary Gill Mills. George Bonder died in Millcreek, Winston Co., Mississippi, on July 25, 1901, at age 84. He was buried in Liberty Universalist Church Cemetery, Millcreek, Winston Co., Mississippi.[18]

George Bonder married **Martha Elizabeth Joiner** before 1847. They had five children. Martha Elizabeth Joiner was born in Fairfield Co., South Carolina, in 1822. Martha Elizabeth reached age 36 and died in Noxubee Co., Mississippi, about 1858.

George Bonder Pagan married **Lorinda Love** in 1861. They had two children. Lorinda Love was born in South Carolina in 1829.

Children of George Bonder Pagan and Martha Elizabeth Joiner:

+ 66 f I. **Charlotte⁶ Pagan** was born in Chester Co., South Carolina, on January 31, 1847. She died on September 18, 1910.[18]

+ 67 m II. **George Gill⁶ Pagan II** was born in Noxubee Co., Mississippi, on June 24, 1852. He died on December 4, 1929.

+ 68 m III. **John Mills⁶ Pagan** was born in Noxubee Co., Mississippi, in 1854.

+ 69 f IV. **Marian⁶ Pagan** was born in Noxubee Co., Mississippi, in 1856.

+ 70 m V. **Harry⁶ Pagan** was born in Noxubee Co., Mississippi, in 1858.

Children of George Bonder Pagan and Lorinda Love:

+ 71 m I. **Milton⁶ Pagan** was born in Noxubee Co., Mississippi, in 1861.

+ 72 f II. **Sallie⁶ Pagan** was born in Noxubee Co., Mississippi, in 1866.

**39. Rebecca Irvine Fayssoux⁵ Pagan** (*Alexander⁴, Alexander³, Alexander², James¹*) was born on January 11, 1819, in Fishing Creek, Chester Co., South Carolina. She was the daughter of Alexander Pagan III (17) and Mary Gill Mills. Rebecca Irvine Fayssoux died in Crandall, Kaufman Co., Texas, on June 15, 1901, at age 82. She was buried in Crandall Cemetery, Crandall, Kaufman Co., Texas.[19]

Rebecca Irvine Fayssoux married **James Harvey Crawford** in South Carolina. They had five children. James Harvey Crawford was born in Chester Co., South Carolina, on November 17, 1816. James Harvey reached age 52 and died in Johnsville, Bradley Co., Arkansas, on November 29, 1868. He was buried in Calvary Cemetery, Johnsville, Bradley Co., Arkansas.[21]

Children of Rebecca Irvine Fayssoux Pagan and James Harvey Crawford:

+ 73 m I. **John Alexander⁶ Crawford**.
+ 74 m II. **James Pagan⁶ Crawford**.
+ 75 f III. **Mary Gill⁶ Crawford**.
+ 76 m IV. **George Harvey⁶ Crawford**.
+ 77 m V. **Edward Gordon⁶ Crawford**.

**40. Archibald Gill⁵ Pagan** (*Alexander⁴, Alexander³, Alexander², James¹*) was born on July 13, 1823, in Fishing Creek, Chester Co., South Carolina. He was the son of Alexander Pagan III (17) and Mary Gill

Mills. Archibald Gill died in Fishing Creek, Chester Co., South Carolina, on July 10, 1857, at age 33. He was buried in Fishing Creek Presbyterian Cemetery, Chester, Chester Co., South Carolina.[5]

Archibald Gill married **Cicily Atkinson** before 1857. They had one son.

Son of Archibald Gill Pagan and Cicily Atkinson:

+ 78    m    I.    **James Atkinson**[6] **Pagan** was born in Chester Co., South Carolina?, on February 18, 1853. He died in White City, St. Lucie Co., Florida, on July 31, 1932.

41. **Mary Jeanette**[5] **Pagan** (*Alexander*[4], *Alexander*[3], *Alexander*[2], *James*[1]) was born on February 2, 1825, in Fishing Creek, Chester Co., South Carolina. She was also known as **Jeanette**. She was the daughter of Alexander Pagan III (17) and Mary Gill Mills. Mary Jeanette died in York, York Co., South Carolina, on June 17, 1910, at age 85. She was buried in Bethesda Presbyterian Church Cemetery, York, York Co., South Carolina.[20]

Mary Jeanette married **Samuel Moore Hanna** on May 13, 1859, in Chester Co., South Carolina. They had three sons. Samuel Moore Hanna was born in York Co., South Carolina, on August 22, 1831. Samuel Moore lived in 1900 in Bethesda, York Co., South Carolina. He reached age 72 and died in York, York Co, South Carolina, on November 10, 1903. Samuel Moore was buried in Bethesda Presbyterian Church Cemetery, York, York Co., South Carolina.[20]

Sons of Mary Jeanette Pagan and Samuel Moore Hanna:

+ 79    m    I.    **Alexander**[6] **Hanna**.

+ 80    m    II.    **Robert S.**[6] **Hanna**.

+ 81    m    III.    **Thomas**[6] **Hanna**.

42. **Charlotte Clarke**[5] **Pagan** (*Alexander*[4], *Alexander*[3], *Alexander*[2], *James*[1]) was born on February 15, 1826, in Chester Co., South Carolina. She was the daughter of Alexander Pagan III (17) and Mary Gill Mills. Charlotte Clarke died in Chester Co.,

South Carolina, on July 15, 1842, at age 16. She was buried in Fishing Creek Presbyterian Cemetery, Chester, Chester Co., South Carolina.[5]

43. **Susan Eleanor**[5] **Pagan** (*Alexander*[4], *Alexander*[3], *Alexander*[2], *James*[1]) was born in 1829 in Fishing Creek, Chester Co., South Carolina. She was the daughter of Alexander Pagan III (17) and Mary Gill Mills. Susan Eleanor died in York, York Co, South Carolina?, on May 20, 1912, at age 83. She was buried in Bethesda Presbyterian Church Cemetery, York, York Co., South Carolina.[20]

Susan Eleanor married **William Mansfield Gordon** about 1857. They had five sons. William Mansfield Gordon was born in York Co., South Carolina, in 1831. William Mansfield reached age 42 and died in York Co., South Carolina?, on March 7, 1873. He was buried in Bethesda Presbyterian Church Cemetery, York, York Co., South Carolina.[20]

Sons of Susan Eleanor Pagan and William Mansfield Gordon:

+ 82    m    I.    **Alex Pagan**[6] **Gordon** was born in York Co., South Carolina, on March 6, 1859. He died in York Co., South Carolina, on September 6, 1869.[20]

+ 83    m    II.    **William**[6] **Gordon II** was born in York Co., South Carolina, in 1861.

+ 84    m    III.    **Mansfield**[6] **Gordon** was born in York Co., South Carolina, in 1863.

+ 85    m    IV.    **Calvin Sandifor**[6] **Gordon** was born in York Co., South Carolina, on August 1, 1866. He died in York, York Co, South Carolina?, on January 6, 1935.[28]

+ 86    m    V.    **Clement F.**[6] **Gordon** was born in York Co., South Carolina, in 1868.

44. **Sarah Agnes**[5] **Pagan** (*Alexander*[4], *Alexander*[3], *Alexander*[2], *James*[1]) was born in 1832 in Fishing Creek, Chester Co., South Carolina. She was the daughter of Alexander Pagan III (17) and Mary Gill Mills. Sarah Agnes died in Fishing Creek, Chester Co., South Carolina, on February 25, 1858, at age

26. She was buried in Fishing Creek Presbyterian Cemetery, Chester, Chester Co., South Carolina.[5]

Childless.

She married **Samuel Moore Hanna.** Samuel Moore Hanna was born in York Co., South Carolina, on August 22, 1831. Samuel Moore lived in 1900 in Bethesda, York Co., South Carolina. He reached age 72 and died in York, York Co, South Carolina, on November 10, 1903. Samuel Moore was buried in Bethesda Presbyterian Church Cemetery, York, York Co., South Carolina.[20]

# 6<sup>th</sup> Generation

**45. Mary Ann⁶ Wherry** (*John⁵, Susannah⁴ Pagan, Alexander³, Alexander², James¹*) was born on August 3, 1833, in Shelby Co., Tennessee. She was the daughter of John Wherry (25) and Margaret Yeary. Mary Ann died in Kemp, Kaufman Co., Texas, in 1920 at age 86.

She married **Weaver Alexander Cotton.**

**46. Infant Mary Ann⁶ Pagan** (*John Mills⁵, Alexander⁴, Alexander³, Alexander², James¹*) was born in 1837 in Fishing Creek, Chester Co., South Carolina. She was the daughter of John Mills Pagan (31) and Rebecca Elizabeth McDaniel. Infant Mary Ann died in Fishing Creek, Chester Co., South Carolina, in 1937 at age 100.

**47. Sarah Elizabeth⁶ Pagan** (*John Mills⁵, Alexander⁴, Alexander³, Alexander², James¹*) was born on February 6, 1839, in Fishing Creek, Chester Co., South Carolina. She was the daughter of John Mills Pagan (31) and Rebecca Elizabeth McDaniel. Sarah Elizabeth died in Bradley Co., Arkansas?, on July 16, 1858, at age 19.

**48. Julia Viola⁶ Pagan** (*John Mills⁵, Alexander⁴, Alexander³, Alexander², James¹*) was born on November 4, 1840, in Fishing Creek, Chester Co., South Carolina. She was the daughter of John Mills Pagan (31) and Rebecca Elizabeth McDaniel. Julia Viola died in Bradley Co., Arkansas, on April 25, 1871, at age 30. She was buried in Calvary Cemetery, Johnsville, Bradley Co., Arkansas.[21]

Never married.

**49. Charlotte Louisa⁶ Pagan** (*John Mills⁵, Alexander⁴, Alexander³, Alexander², James¹*) was born on August 2, 1842, in Fishing Creek, Chester Co., South Carolina. She was the daughter of John Mills Pagan (31) and Rebecca Elizabeth McDaniel. Charlotte Louisa died in Fishing Creek, Chester Co., South Carolina, on August 2, 1844, at age two.

**50. John McDaniel⁶ Pagan** (*John Mills⁵, Alexander⁴, Alexander³, Alexander², James¹*) was born in November 1844 in Noxubee Co., Mississippi. He was the son of John Mills Pagan (31) and Rebecca Elizabeth McDaniel. John McDaniel died in Bradley Co., Arkansas, on November 23, 1924, at age 80. He was buried in Calvary Cemetery, Johnsville, Bradley Co., Arkansas.[21]

Childless.

John McDaniel married **Sarah Ellen Thomas** in 1873. Sarah Ellen Thomas was born in Chester Co., South Carolina, on May 29, 1854. Sarah Ellen reached age 80 and died in Johnsville, Bradley Co., Arkansas, on March 10, 1935. She was buried in Calvary Cemetery, Johnsville, Bradley Co., Arkansas.[21]

**51. Susannah Mahalia⁶ Pagan** (*John Mills⁵, Alexander⁴, Alexander³, Alexander², James¹*) was born in 1846 in Noxubee Co., Mississippi. She was the daughter of John Mills Pagan (31) and Rebecca Elizabeth McDaniel. Susannah Mahalia died in Kaufman Co., Texas, between 1876 and 1880.

Susannah Mahalia married **William A. Mooreland** on September 10, 1867, in Bradley Co., Arkansas. They had three children. William A. Mooreland was born in Virginia in 1842. William A. died after 1870.

Children of Susannah Mahalia Pagan and William A. Mooreland:

f I. **Catherine⁷ Mooreland** was born in Marion Twp., Bradley Co., Arkansas, in 1868.

m II. **John⁷ Mooreland** was born in Marion Twp., Bradley Co., Arkansas, in 1870.

f III. **Mary Virginia⁷ Mooreland** was born in Texas on November 6, 1876. She died in Crandall, Kaufman Co., Texas, on February 12, 1948.

**52. Mary Ann Rebecca⁶ Pagan** (*John Mills⁵, Alexander⁴, Alexander³, Alexander², James¹*) was born on September 11, 1848, in Noxubee Co., Mississippi. She was also known as **Mollie**. She was the daughter of John Mills Pagan (31) and Rebecca Elizabeth McDaniel. Mary Ann Rebecca died in Kaufman

Co., Texas, on May 31, 1899, at age 50. She was buried in Crandall Cemetery, Crandall, Kaufman Co., Texas.[19]

Mary Ann Rebecca married **James Pagan Crawford** on April 19, 1866, in Bradley Co., Arkansas. They had seven children. James Pagan Crawford was born in York Co., South Carolina, on June 1, 1842. James Pagan reached age 73 and died in Kaufman Co., Texas, in October 1915. He was buried in Crandall Cemetery, Crandall, Kaufman Co., Texas.[19]

Children of Mary Ann Rebecca Pagan and James Pagan Crawford:

f    I.    **Nancy Rebecca**[7] **Crawford** was born in Bradley Co., Arkansas, on January 20, 1867. She died in Forney, Kaufman Co., Texas, on September 18, 1884. [29]

f    II.   **Charlotte**[7] **Crawford** was born in Bradley Co., Arkansas, in 1869.

m   III.  **James A.**[7] **Crawford** was born in Oklahoma in 1875.

f    IV.   **Willa Jennie**[7] **Crawford** was born in Oklahoma in 1878. She died in Brownwood, Brown Co., Texas, in 1900 at age 22.[30]

m   V.    **George McDonald**[7] **Crawford** was born in Kaufman Co., Texas, on June 4, 1882. He died in Shelby Co., Texas, on August 6, 1947.[31]

m   VI.   **Gordon**[7] **Crawford** was born in Kaufman Co., Texas, in 1885.

     VII.  **Gillie**[7] **Crawford** was born in Kaufman Co., Texas, in 1890.

**53. Alexander Daniel**[6] **Pagan** (*John Mills*[5], *Alexander*[4], *Alexander*[3], *Alexander*[2], *James*[1]) was born in February 1851 in Noxubee Co., Mississippi. He was the son of John Mills Pagan (31) and Rebecca Elizabeth McDaniel. Alexander Daniel died in November 1924 at age 73.

Alexander Daniel married **Mary Malinda Irwin** on September 1, 1870, in Bradley Co., Arkansas. They had five children. Mary Malinda Irwin was born in Palestine, Bradley Co., Arkansas, in February 1852. Mary Malinda died after 1920.

Children of Alexander Daniel Pagan and Mary Malinda Irwin:

f    I.    **Lilly V.**[7] **Pagan** was born in Bradley Co., Arkansas, in 1871. She died after 1880.

m   II.   **James McDonald**[7] **Pagan** was born in Oklahoma on April 6, 1874. He died in Hermleigh, Scurry Co., Texas, on December 16, 1935.[32]

m   III.  **John D.**[7] **Pagan** was born in Marion, Bradley Co., Arkansas, in 1877. He died after 1880.

m   IV.   **George Alexander**[7] **Pagan** was born in Marion, Bradley Co., Arkansas, on September 20, 1882. He lived between 1920 and 1940 in Midland, Midland Co., Texas. George Alexander died in Los Angeles, Los Angeles Co., California, on June 29, 1961.

m   V.    **Henry Alford**[7] **Pagan** was born in Goldthwaite, Mills Co., Texas, on June 13, 1891. He lived in 1968 in Odessa, Ector Co., Texas. Henry Alfred died in Midland, Midland Co., Texas, on June 13, 1968.[33]

**54. John J.**[6] **Pagan** (*John Mills*[5], *Alexander*[4], *Alexander*[3], *Alexander*[2], *James*[1]) was born in 1853 in Noxubee Co., Mississippi. He was the son of John Mills Pagan (31) and Rebecca Elizabeth McDaniel. John J. died in Bradley Co., Arkansas, on August 26, 1867, at age 14.

**55. George M.C.**[6] **Pagan** (*John Mills*[5], *Alexander*[4], *Alexander*[3], *Alexander*[2], *James*[1]) was born about March 9, 1855 in Noxubee Co., Mississippi. He was the son of John Mills Pagan (31) and Rebecca Elizabeth McDaniel. George M.C. died in Marion, Bradley Co., Arkansas, on November 1, 1881, at age 26.

Never married.

**56. Catherine⁶ Pagan** (*John Mills⁵, Alexander⁴, Alexander³, Alexander², James¹*) was born in 1859 in Bradley Co., Arkansas. She was the daughter of John Mills Pagan (31) and Nancy Permelia Joiner.

**57. Edwards Fayssoux⁶ Pagan** (*James⁵, Alexander⁴, Alexander³, Alexander², James¹*) was born on January 7, 1846, in Chester Co., South Carolina. He was the son of James Pagan (33) and Anne Callender Fayssoux. Edwards Fayssoux died in Great Falls, Chester Co., South Carolina, on October 10, 1923, at age 77. He was buried in Saint John's Episcopal Cemetery, Winnsboro, Fairfield Co., South Carolina.[17]

Edwards Fayssoux married **Sally DeWitt McCollough** in 1870. They had six children. Sally DeWitt McCollough was born in Spartanburg, Spartanburg, South Carolina, on July 30, 1849. Sally DeWitt reached age 78 and died in Great Falls, Chester Co., South Carolina, on December 20, 1927. She was buried in Saint John's Episcopal Cemetery, Winnsboro, Fairfield Co., South Carolina.[17]

Children of Edwards Fayssoux Pagan and Sally DeWitt McCollough:

   f   I.   **Harriett Hart⁷ Pagan** was born in Spartanburg, Spartanburg Co., South Carolina, on August 15, 1871. She died in Ridgeway, Fairfield Co., South Carolina, on August 4, 1940.[34]

   m   II.   **John McCollough⁷ Pagan** was born in South Carolina on August 8, 1875. He died in Great Falls, Chester Co., South Carolina, on May 25, 1949.[35]

   m   III.   **Calender Irvine⁷ Pagan** was born in Fairfield Co., South Carolina, on January 15, 1879. He died in Chester Co., South Carolina?, on October 19, 1933.[34]

   m   IV.   **Sumpter Means⁷ Pagan** was born in Fairfield Co., South Carolina,

in 1882. He died in Spartanburg, Spartenburg Co., South Carolina, in 1913.[17]

   f   V.   **Mary Nacreid⁷ Pagan** was born in South Carolina on January 24, 1885. She died on May 21, 1976.[34]

   m   VI.   **Ben Hart⁷ Pagan** was born in Liberty Hill, Kershaw Co., South Carolina, on August 10, 1887. He died in Great Falls, Chester Co., South Carolina, on January 18, 1939.[34]

**58. Mary Nacreid⁶ Pagan** (*James⁵, Alexander⁴, Alexander³, Alexander², James¹*) was born on February 18, 1847, in Chester Co., South Carolina. She was the daughter of James Pagan (33) and Anne Callender Fayssoux. Mary Nacreid died in Chester Co., South Carolina, on August 23, 1872, at age 25. She was buried in Evergreen Cemetery, Chester, Chester Co., South Carolina.[22]

She married **James McKnight Brawley**. They had one son. James McKnight Brawley was born in Chester Co., South Carolina, on March 14, 1846. James McKnight lived in 1901 in Chester, Chester Co., South Carolina. He reached age 54 and died in Charleston, Charleston Co., South Carolina, on January 8, 1901. James McKnight was buried in Evergreen Cemetery, Chester, Chester Co., South Carolina.[22]

Son of Mary Nacreid Pagan and James McKnight Brawley:

   m   I.   **James Pagan⁷ Brawley** was born in Chester Co., South Carolina, on August 23, 1872. He died in Raleigh, Wake Co., North Carolina, on February 25, 1932.[36]

**59. Annie Irvine⁶ Pagan** (*James⁵, Alexander⁴, Alexander³, Alexander², James¹*) was born on March 28, 1848, in Chester Co., South Carolina. She was the daughter of James Pagan (33) and Anne Callender Fayssoux. Annie Irvine died in Lincolnton, Lincoln Co., North Carolina, on June 28, 1890, at age 42. She was buried in Saint Luke's Episcopal Church Cemetery, Lincolnton, Lincoln Co., North Carolina.[23]

She married **William Lee Davidson.** They had eight children. William Lee Davidson was born in Mecklenburg Co., North Carolina, on February 10, 1825. William Lee reached age 74 and died in Chester, Chester Co., South Carolina, on August 13, 1899. He was buried in Saint Luke's Episcopal Church Cemetery, Lincolnton, Lincoln Co., North Carolina.[23]

Children of Annie Irvine Pagan and William Lee Davidson:

|   |      |                                         |
|---|------|-----------------------------------------|
| m | I.   | **James Latta[7] Davidson.**            |
| f | II.  | **Mary Pagan[7] Davidson.**             |
| m | III. | **Zeb Vance[7] Davidson.**              |
| f | IV.  | **Bessie Irvine[7] Davidson.**          |
| m | V.   | **Annie Lee[7] Davidson.**              |
| f | VI.  | **Leila Fayssoux[7] Davidson.**         |
| m | VII. | **William Lee[7] Davidson II.**         |
| m | VIII.| **Robert Malcolm[7] Davidson.**         |

**60. Irvine Fayssoux[6] Pagan** (*James[5], Alexander[4], Alexander[3], Alexander[2], James[1]*) was born in December 1849 in Chester Co., South Carolina. He was the son of James Pagan (33) and Anne Callender Fayssoux. Irvine Fayssoux died in Shelton, Fairfield Co., South Carolina, in 1912 at age 62. He was buried in Saint John's Episcopal Cemetery, Winnsboro, Fairfield Co., South Carolina.[17]

Irvine Fayssoux married **Mary Stark McCollough** in 1894 in South Carolina. They had one daughter. Mary Stark McCollough was born in Winnsboro, Fairfield Co., South Carolina, on July 30, 1857. Mary Stark reached age 77 and died in Jacksonville, Duval Co., Florida, on December 19, 1934. She was buried in Saint John's Episcopal Cemetery, Winnsboro, Fairfield Co., South Carolina.[17]

Daughter of Irvine Fayssoux Pagan and Mary Stark McCollough:

|   |    |                                                        |
|---|----|--------------------------------------------------------|
| f | I. | **Mary[7] Pagan** was born in June 1896.               |

**61. Rebecca Armstrong[6] Pagan** (*James[5], Alexander[4], Alexander[3], Alexander[2], James[1]*) was born on August 22, 1852, in Chester Co., South Carolina. She was also known as **Beckie.** She was the daughter of James Pagan (33) and Anne Callender Fayssoux. Rebecca Armstrong died in Columbia, Richland Co., South Carolina, on October 14, 1921, at age 69. She was buried in First Presbyterian Churchyard Cemetery, Columbia, Richland Co., South Carolina.[24]

Rebecca Armstrong married **James Quentin Davis** in 1877. They had three sons. James Quentin Davis was born in Fairfield Co., South Carolina, on March 23, 1851. James Quentin reached age 74 and died in Columbia, Richland Co., South Carolina, on January 10, 1926. He was buried in First Presbyterian Churchyard Cemetery, Columbia, Richland Co., South Carolina.[24]

Sons of Rebecca Armstrong Pagan and James Quentin Davis:

|   |      |                                          |
|---|------|------------------------------------------|
| m | I.   | **Clement Fayssoux[7] Davis.**           |
| m | II.  | **James Quentin[7] Davis II.**           |
| m | III. | **John Bratton[7] Davis.**               |

**62. Anne Rebecca King[6] Pagan** (*Thomas Sumter[5], Alexander[4], Alexander[3], Alexander[2], James[1]*) was born on February 2, 1838, in York, York Co., South Carolina. She was the daughter of Thomas Sumter Pagan (36) and Elizabeth Eveline Gill. Anne Rebecca King died in Prescott, Nevada Co., Arkansas, on June 2, 1876, at age 38.

Anne Rebecca King married **Daniel George O'Leary** before 1867 in South Carolina. They had two children. Daniel George O'Leary was born in South Carolina in 1830. Daniel George died in York, York Co., South Carolina, after 1880.

Children of Anne Rebecca King Pagan and Daniel George O'Leary:

|   |    |                                                                                                      |
|---|----|------------------------------------------------------------------------------------------------------|
| m | I. | **James Dan George[7] O'Leary** was born in Beech Creek, Clark Co., Arkansas?, on May 9, 1867. He    |

died in York, York Co., South Carolina, on May 26, 1891.[27]

f II. **Annis Rebecca**[7] **O'Leary** was born in Prescott, Nevada Co., Arkansas, on July 27, 1875. She lived in 1947 in York, York Co., South Carolina. Annis Rebecca died in a hospital in Spartanburg, Spartanburg Co., South Carolina, on November 11, 1947.[27]

63. **James Alexander**[6] **Pagan** (*Thomas Sumter*[5], *Alexander*[4], *Alexander*[3], *Alexander*[2], *James*[1]) was born on December 12, 1841, in York, York Co., South Carolina. He was the son of Thomas Sumter Pagan (36) and Elizabeth Eveline Gill. James Alexander died in Prescott, Nevada Co., Arkansas?, on July 10, 1913, at age 71. He was buried in Liberty Cemetery, Redland, Nevada Co., Arkansas.[25]

James Alexander married **Mary Catherine McClelland** about 1867 in Arkansas. They had five children. Mary Catherine McClelland was born in Arkansas in 1845. She was also known as **Mollie.** Mary Catherine reached age 67 and died in Prescott, Nevada Co., Arkansas?, on July 31, 1912. She was buried in Liberty Cemetery, Redland, Nevada Co., Arkansas.[25] Buried under the name Mollie McClelland Pagan.

James Alexander Pagan married **Roena Sullivan** on February 2, 1913, in Nevada Co., Arkansas. Roena Sullivan was born in Arkansas on October 26, 1862. Roena reached age 72 and died on April 20, 1935. She was buried in Woodlawn Cemetery, Texarkana, Miller Co., Arkansas.[37] Roena Sullivan Fitzhughes Parish Dykes Holder Pagan was married five times.

Children of James Alexander Pagan and Mary Catherine McClelland:

f I. **Sidney Elizabeth**[7] **Pagan** was born in Missouri Twp., Hempstead Co., Arkansas, on October 20, 1868. She died in Van Buren, Crawford Co., Arkansas, in 1946.

m II. **William A.**[7] **Pagan** was born in Missouri Twp., Hempstead Co., Arkansas, on January 12, 1871. He died in Clark Co., Arkansas, on December 12, 1948.

f III. **Hannah Rebecca**[7] **Pagan** was born in Missouri Twp., Nevada Co., Arkansas, on April 16, 1873. She died in Lindsay Twp., Garvin Co., Oklahoma, on March 12, 1946.

f IV. **Mary Cloud Isibella**[7] **Pagan** was born in Missouri Twp., Nevada Co., Arkansas, on September 5, 1875. She died on January 5, 1878.

f V. **Maud**[7] **Pagan** was born on August 20, 1878. She died on July 4, 1880.

64. **Mary Cloud**[6] **Pagan** (*Thomas Sumter*[5], *Alexander*[4], *Alexander*[3], *Alexander*[2], *James*[1]) was born on July 21, 1844, in York, York Co., South Carolina. She was the daughter of Thomas Sumter Pagan (36) and Elizabeth Eveline Gill. Mary Cloud died in Prescott, Nevada Co., Arkansas?, on February 22, 1937, at age 92. She was buried in De Ann Cemetery, Prescott, Nevada Co., Arkansas.[26]

Mary Cloud married **John Waller Adams** on December 4, 1866, in Hempstead Co., Arkansas. They had three sons. John Waller Adams was born in Kentucky on April 20, 1843. John Waller reached age 78 and died in Prescott, Nevada Co., Arkansas?, on January 26, 1922. He was buried in De Ann Cemetery, Prescott, Nevada Co., Arkansas.[26]

Sons of Mary Cloud Pagan and John Waller Adams:

m I. **Rufus G.**[7] **Adams** was born in Pleasant Hill, Big Creek Twp., Cass Co., Missouri, on September 10, 1867. He died in St Louis, St. Louis Co., Missouri, on December 23, 1934.[38]

m II. **Robert H.**[7] **Adams** was born in Pleasant Hill, Big Creek Twp., Cass Co., Missouri, on August 23,

1870. He died in Missouri Twp., Nevada Co., Arkansas, on March 7, 1920.[26]

m  III.  **James Victor[7] Adams** was born in Missouri Twp., Nevada Co., Arkansas, on March 4, 1879. He died in Nevada Co., Arkansas, on October 18, 1941.

65. **John Gill[6] Pagan** (*Thomas Sumter[5], Alexander[4], Alexander[3], Alexander[2], James[1]*) was born on August 10, 1856, in York, York Co., South Carolina. He was the son of Thomas Sumter Pagan (36) and Elizabeth Eveline Gill. John Gill died in Arkansas on December 18, 1864, at age eight.

66. **Charlotte[6] Pagan** (*George Bonder[5], Alexander[4], Alexander[3], Alexander[2], James[1]*) was born on January 31, 1847, in Chester Co., South Carolina. She was the daughter of George Bonder Pagan (38) and Martha Elizabeth Joiner. Charlotte died on September 18, 1910, at age 63. She was buried in Liberty Universalist Church Cemetery, Millcreek, Winston Co., Mississippi.[18]

She married **Jacob Feaster Coleman.** Jacob Feaster Coleman was born on March 17, 1845. Jacob Feaster reached age 75 and died on July 6, 1920. He was buried in Liberty Universalist Church Cemetery, Millcreek, Winston Co., Mississippi.[18]

67. **George Gill[6] Pagan II** (*George Bonder[5], Alexander[4], Alexander[3], Alexander[2], James[1]*) was born on June 24, 1852, in Noxubee Co., Mississippi. He was the son of George Bonder Pagan (38) and Martha Elizabeth Joiner. George Gill died on December 4, 1929, at age 77.

68. **John Mills[6] Pagan** (*George Bonder[5], Alexander[4], Alexander[3], Alexander[2], James[1]*) was born in 1854 in Noxubee Co., Mississippi. He was the son of George Bonder Pagan (38) and Martha Elizabeth Joiner.

He married **Julia Amanda Hull.**

69. **Marian[6] Pagan** (*George Bonder[5], Alexander[4], Alexander[3], Alexander[2], James[1]*) was born in 1856 in Noxubee Co., Mississippi. She was the daughter of George Bonder Pagan (38) and Martha Elizabeth Joiner.

70. **Harry[6] Pagan** (*George Bonder[5], Alexander[4], Alexander[3], Alexander[2], James[1]*) was born in 1858 in Noxubee Co., Mississippi. He was the son of George Bonder Pagan (38) and Martha Elizabeth Joiner.

71. **Milton[6] Pagan** (*George Bonder[5], Alexander[4], Alexander[3], Alexander[2], James[1]*) was born in 1861 in Noxubee Co., Mississippi. He was the son of George Bonder Pagan (38) and Lorinda Love.

72. **Sallie[6] Pagan** (*George Bonder[5], Alexander[4], Alexander[3], Alexander[2], James[1]*) was born in 1866 in Noxubee Co., Mississippi. She was the daughter of George Bonder Pagan (38) and Lorinda Love.

73. **John Alexander[6] Crawford** (*Rebecca Irvine Fayssoux[5] Pagan, Alexander[4], Alexander[3], Alexander[2], James[1]*). He is the son of James Harvey Crawford and Rebecca Irvine Fayssoux Pagan (39).

74. **James Pagan[6] Crawford** (*Rebecca Irvine Fayssoux[5] Pagan, Alexander[4], Alexander[3], Alexander[2], James[1]*). He is the son of James Harvey Crawford and Rebecca Irvine Fayssoux Pagan (39).

75. **Mary Gill[6] Crawford** (*Rebecca Irvine Fayssoux[5] Pagan, Alexander[4], Alexander[3], Alexander[2], James[1]*). She is the daughter of James Harvey Crawford and Rebecca Irvine Fayssoux Pagan (39).

She married **Henry Alfred Atkinson.**

76. **George Harvey[6] Crawford** (*Rebecca Irvine Fayssoux[5] Pagan, Alexander[4], Alexander[3], Alexander[2], James[1]*). He is the son of James Harvey Crawford and Rebecca Irvine Fayssoux Pagan (39).

77. **Edward Gordon[6] Crawford** (*Rebecca Irvine Fayssoux[5] Pagan, Alexander[4], Alexander[3], Alexander[2], James[1]*). He is the son of James Harvey Crawford and Rebecca Irvine Fayssoux Pagan (39).

78. **James Atkinson[6] Pagan** (*Archibald Gill[5], Alexander[4], Alexander[3], Alexander[2], James[1]*) was born on February 18, 1853, in Chester Co., South Carolina? He was the son of Archibald Gill Pagan (40) and Cicily Atkinson. James Atkinson died in White City, St. Lucie Co., Florida, on July 31, 1932, at age 79.

79. **Alexander[6] Hanna** (*Mary Jeanette[5] Pagan, Alexander[4], Alexander[3], Alexander[2], James[1]*). He is the son of Samuel Moore Hanna and Mary Jeanette Pagan (41).

80. **Robert S.**[6] **Hanna** (*Mary Jeanette*[5] *Pagan, Alexander*[4], *Alexander*[3], *Alexander*[2], *James*[1]). He is the son of Samuel Moore Hanna and Mary Jeanette Pagan (41).

81. **Thomas**[6] **Hanna** (*Mary Jeanette*[5] *Pagan, Alexander*[4], *Alexander*[3], *Alexander*[2], *James*[1]). He is the son of Samuel Moore Hanna and Mary Jeanette Pagan (41).

82. **Alex Pagan**[6] **Gordon** (*Susan Eleanor*[5] *Pagan, Alexander*[4], *Alexander*[3], *Alexander*[2], *James*[1]) was born on March 6, 1859, in York Co., South Carolina. He was the son of William Mansfield Gordon and Susan Eleanor Pagan (43). Alex Pagan died in York Co., South Carolina, on September 6, 1869, at age 10. He was buried in Bethesda Presbyterian Church Cemetery, York, York Co., South Carolina.[20]

83. **William**[6] **Gordon II** (*Susan Eleanor*[5] *Pagan, Alexander*[4], *Alexander*[3], *Alexander*[2], *James*[1]) was born in 1861 in York Co., South Carolina. He was the son of William Mansfield Gordon and Susan Eleanor Pagan (43).

84. **Mansfield**[6] **Gordon** (*Susan Eleanor*[5] *Pagan, Alexander*[4], *Alexander*[3], *Alexander*[2], *James*[1]) was born in 1863 in York Co., South Carolina. He was the son of William Mansfield Gordon and Susan Eleanor Pagan (43).

85. **Calvin Sandifor**[6] **Gordon** (*Susan Eleanor*[5] *Pagan, Alexander*[4], *Alexander*[3], *Alexander*[2], *James*[1]) was born on August 1, 1866, in York Co., South Carolina. He was the son of William Mansfield Gordon and Susan Eleanor Pagan (43). Calvin Sandifor died in York, York Co, South Carolina?, on January 6, 1935, at age 68. He was buried in Rose Hill Cemetery, York, York Co., South Carolina.[27]

Childless.

He married **Anna Kittie Lindsay.** Anna Kittie Lindsay was born in South Carolina in 1870. Anna Kittie reached age 64 and died in York, York Co, South Carolina?, on December 31, 1934. She was buried in Rose Hill Cemetery, York, York Co., South Carolina.[27]

86. **Clement F.**[6] **Gordon** (*Susan Eleanor*[5] *Pagan, Alexander*[4], *Alexander*[3], *Alexander*[2], *James*[1]) was born in 1868 in York Co., South Carolina. He was the son of William Mansfield Gordon and Susan Eleanor Pagan (43).

# Endnotes

1   Pagan/Pegan entries, 1750-1810, Lancaster County tax records. Microfilm, Roll #23. Genealogy Center, Allen County Public Library, Fort Wayne, 900 Library Plaza, Fort Wayne, IN.

2   Collins, Anne Pickens, *Heritage History of Chester County, South Carolina, Vol. II,* ed. by Louise Gill Knox. Chester County, South Carolina: Chester County Historical Society; 1982, pg. 199. Genealogy Center, Allen County Public Library, Fort Wayne, 900 Library Plaza, Fort Wayne, IN.

3   Hibdon, Glenda Pagan, *The Pagan, Hunt and Sanderson genealogies.* Knoxville, Tennessee: Tennessee Valley Publishing; 1994. Genealogy Center, Allen County Public Library, Fort Wayne, 900 Library Plaza, Fort Wayne, IN.

4   Ellis, Frank and Samuel Evans*, History of Lancaster County, Pennsylvania: with biographical sketches of its pioneers and prominent men.* Philadelphia: Everts & Peck; 1883, pg. 974. Mishawaka Heritage Center, Mishawaka Penn-Harris Public Library, 209 Lincolnway East, Mishawaka, IN.

5   Ellet, Elizabeth F., *The Women of the American Revolution, Vol. III*. New York: Baker & Scribner; 1850, pg. 280. Archive.org., Online database: https://archive.org/stream/womenofamericanr03elle/womenofamericanr03elle_djvu.txt

6   Find A Grave—Fishing Creek Presbyterian Cemetery, Chester, Chester Co., South Carolina, Find A Grave.com, Alexander Pagan, Find A Grave Memorial #11197710.

7        South Carolina, Wills and Probate Records, 1670-1980, Ancestry.com, Charleston County, Letters of Administration, Vol. Tt, Archibald Pagan, pg.82.

8   South Carolina, Wills and Probate Records, 1670-1980, Ancestry.com, Kershaw County, Index and Will, Vol. 1, Book C, A1, 1770-1841, Alexander Pagan, pg. 48.

9   Chester County, South Carolina, Deed Records R:220, Chester County Clerk of Courts, Register of Deeds Office, Chester, South Carolina.

10  Chester County, South Carolina, Deed Records R:307, Chester County Clerk of Courts, Register of Deeds Office, Chester, South Carolina.

11  South Carolina, Wills and Probate Records, 1670-1980, Ancestry.com, Chester County, Probate Files, John Downing, File #14, Pack 341.

12  "Early Wills of the Camden District", South Carolina Magazine of Ancestral Research, Vol. II, Spring 1974, No. 2, pg. 97.

    South Carolina, Wills and Probate Records, 1670-1980, Ancestry.com, Chester County, Probate Files, John

13  "Slave Ads Taken from the Charleston Courier", South Carolina. South Carolina Genealogy Trails, Online database: http://genealogytrails.com/scar/slave_ads.htm, captured 1/30/2017.

14  Washburn, Rev. Joseph and Asahel Hooker, *Sermons on Practical Subjects*. Hartford, Connecticut: Lincoln & Green, 1807. Original from the University of California, Digitized Nov 20, 2007.

15  South Carolina Department of Archives and History, Columbia, South Carolina. Records of the Equity Court, Bills, Document Number 1809—26, Microfilm #86, Reel D1268, PAR Number 21380904; Race and Slavery Petitions Project, #21380904, http://library.uncg.edu/slavery/petitions/pDetailsNew.aspx?pID=66545&s=2.

16  Find A Grave—Wherry Cemetery, Lakeland, Shelby Co., Tennessee, Find A Grave.com.

17  Find A Grave—Pine Grove Cumberland Presbyterian Cemetery, Pinehill, Rusk Co., Texas, Find A Grave.com.

18  Find A Grave—Saint John's Episcopal Cemetery, Winnsboro, Fairfield Co., South Carolina, Find A Grave.com.

19  Find A Grave—Liberty Universalist Church Cemetery, Millcreek, Winston Co., Mississippi, Find A Grave.com.

20  Find A Grave—Crandall Cemetery, Crandall, Kaufman Co., Texas, Find A Grave.com.

21  Find A Grave—Bethesda Presbyterian Church Cemetery, York, York Co., South Carolina, Find A Grave.com.

22  Find A Grave—Calvary Cemetery, Johnsville, Bradley Co., Arkansas, Find A Grave.com.

23  Find A Grave—Evergreen Cemetery, Chester, Chester Co., South Carolina, Find A Grave.com.

24  Find A Grave—Saint Luke's Episcopal Church Cemetery, Lincolnton, Lincoln Co., North Carolina, Find A Grave.com.

25  Find A Grave—First Presbyterian Churchyard Cemetery, Columbia, Richland Co., South Carolina, Find A Grave.com.

26  Find A Grave—Liberty Cemetery, Redland, Nevada Co., Arkansas, Find A Grave.com.

27  Find A Grave—De Ann Cemetery, Prescott, Nevada Co., Arkansas, Find A Grave.com.

28  Find A Grave—Rose Hill Cemetery, York, York Co., South Carolina, Find A Grave.com.

29  Find A Grave—Hillcrest Cemetery, Forney, Kaufman Co., Texas, Find A Grave.com.

30  Find A Grave—Elkins Cemetery, Brownwood, Brown Co., Texas, Find A Grave.com.

31  Find A Grave—Chapel Hill Cemetery, San Augustine Co., Texas, Find A Grave.com.

32  Find A Grave—Pyron Cemetery, Hermleigh, Scurry Co., Texas, Find A Grave.com.

33  Find A Grave—Kermit Cemetery, Kermit, Winkler Co., Texas, Find A Grave.com.

34  Find A Grave—Saint Stephen's Episcopal Church Cemetery, Ridgeway, Fairfield Co., South Carolina, Find A Grave.com.

35  Find A Grave—Greenlawn Cemetery, Great Falls, Chester Co., South Carolina, Find A Grave.com.

36  Find A Grave—Oakwood Cemetery, Raleigh, Wake Co., North Carolina, Find A Grave.com.

37  Find A Grave—Woodlawn Cemetery, Texarkana, Miller Co., Arkansas, Find A Grave.com.

38  Find A Grave—Oak Grove Cemetery, Bel Nor, St. Louis Co., Missouri, Find A Grave.com.

# Descendants of Archibald Pagan

1. **Archibald[2] Pagan** (*James[1]*) was born in 1717 in Dumfries or Gallaway, Scotland or Ulster, Ireland.[1] He was the son of James Pagan and Unknown Unknown. Archibald died in Martic Twp., Lancaster Co., Pennsylvania, on November 20, 1749, at age 32.[1] He was buried in Old Chestnut Level Presbyterian Lower Cemetery, Drumore Twp., Lancaster Co., Pennsylvania. [1, 2]

Archibald married **Agnes Unknown** before 1748. They had one son. Agnes died in Pennsylvania? after 1749.

In his will dated November 17, 1749, Archibald Pagan mentions his wife "Agness" and his "only beloved son James Pagan". Archibald states his wish that his son James "when he is four years of age to go to brother Andrew Pagan & he to keep him until James reaches fifteen years of age. Andrew to teach him to read and write".[3]

The executor and one of the witnesses was James Pagan. The registrar of wills stated, "... appeared before me...one of his Majesties justices Hon. James Pagen and John Duncan...". We do not know which James Pagan was a witness to this will, but it was probably James II, the brother to Archibald and Andrew.[3]

Archibald Pagan's grave in the Old Chestnut Level Presbyterian Cemetery, Drumore Twp., Lancaster Co., Pennsylvania is the oldest known Pegan family grave in America. His original slate gravestone was still standing and legible in July 2013.[1].

His son, believed to be the "James Pagan/Pegan the miller" found in Lancaster County, Pennsylvania tax records (freeman lists), seems to have never married.[4]

Son of Archibald Pagan and Agnes Unknown:

+ 2   m   I.   **James[3] Pagan** was born in Lancaster Co. Pennsylvania? before 1749. He died in Martic Twp., Lancaster Co., Pennsylvania?, after 1800.

# 3<sup>rd</sup> Generation

2. **James[3] Pagan** (*Archibald[2]*, *James[1]*) was born before 1749 in Lancaster Co. Pennsylvania? He was the son of Archibald Pagan (1) and Agnes Unknown. James died in Martic Twp., Lancaster Co., Pennsylvania?, after 1800.

Never married.

James Pagan or Pegan, son of Archibald, seems to have been an infant, or at most a very small boy, when his father died. In his will, his father Archibald appoints his brother, and James' uncle, Andrew as James' guardian. [3]

James Pagan/Pegan appears on the Martic Twp., Lancaster Co., Pennsylvania "freeman" tax lists for unmarried men of age as "James Pagan the miller."[4] He may have been apprenticed in this trade per instructions in his father Archibald's will.[3] He may have operated the sawmill which, according to an article, "The History of Martic Township" by Larry Hess, was on the land claimed and squatted on, but never owned, by Andrew Pegan/Pegan Sr. Mr. Hess, however, mistakenly cites Andrew Pagan's name as "Adam" Pagan in the article. There is no record of any Adam Pagan in Lancaster County or in Pennsylvania, or in the other 12 American colonies in that era. [5]

This James Pegan seems to have never married, as his name is consistently on the "freeman's" tax list from 1773-1800.[4] He is not found in the 1790 census, as the other two James Pagans who are, James III, the son of James II, listed as James Sr., and James, the son of Andrew I, listed as James Jr., both have descendants in their households.

He is listed as "James the Miller" on the Martic Township., Pennsylvania Revolutionary War militia lists.[6]

James Pagan, the miller, ward of Andrew Pegan/Pagan Sr., is not mentioned in Andrew Sr.'s will.[7]

# Endnotes

1  Find-A-Grave--Old Chestnut Level Presbyterian Cemetery, Find-A-Grave.com, Archibald Pegan, Find A Grave Memorial #159014964.

2  Southern Lancaster County, Pennsylvania Historical Society, P.O. Box 33 Quarryville Pa 17566.

3  Archibald Pagan will (1749), Lancaster County, Pennsylvania Will Book J, Vol. 1: 163. Lancaster County, Pennsylvania Archives, Lancaster County, Pennsylvania.

4  Pagan/Pegan entries, 1851-1831, Lancaster County, Pennsylvania tax records, Microfilm, Lancaster County, Roll #23, Genealogy Center, Allen County Public Library, Fort Wayne, Indiana.

5  Hess, Larry, "The History of Martic Township", *Millersville-Penn Manor Community History*; ed. by Robert E. Coley, James A. Jolly, Carole L. Slotter. Millersville, Pennsylvania: Produced by the Research Committee of the Millersville-Penn Manor Bicentennial Committee, 1776, pg. 80. Conestoga Historical Society, 51 Kendig Road, Conestoga, PA.

6  *Pennsylvania, Published Archive Series, Fifth Series, 1743-1785, Vol. VII*, Pennsylvania Archives, Harrisburg: Pennsylvania: Pennsylvania State Archives; 1906, pg. 581. Family History Library, 35 North West Temple, Salt Lake City, UT.

7  Andrew Pegan will (1788), Lancaster County, Pennsylvania Will Book F: Vol. 1: 84-86. Lancaster County, Pennsylvania Archives, 150 North Queen Street, Lancaster County, PA.

# Descendants of James Pagan II

1. **James[2] Pagan II** (*James[1]*) was born about 1726 in Dumfries or Gallaway, Scotland or Ulster, Ireland. He was the son of James Pagan and Unknown Unknown. James died in Mifflin Twp., Allegheny Co., Pennsylvania?, after 1787. James Pagan/Pegan II immigrated with his father and brothers Archibald and Andrew to Martic Twp., Lancaster Co., Pennsylvania from County Antrim, Ireland, around 1742 with other Scots-Irish Covenanters.[1]

(Note: The 1740-1742 date is considered too late now, as two historians at the Lancaster County Historical Society in Lancaster, Pennsylvania told this author in July 2013).

James married **Unknown Unknown** before 1748. They had three sons.

His name, along with his brother Andrew's, appears on the first extent Martic Township, Lancaster County, Pennsylvania tax list in 1751[2]

James Pegan bought 200 acres of land in Martic Twp., Lancaster Co., Pennsylvania, in 1763 from a Benjamin Arnold.[3] This James Pegan's land was confiscated for tax debt in 1787.[4]

From Edward Wevadou's "Abstracts of Lancaster County Deed Records":

> "II-533: Sheriff James Ross re. to Paul Zantzinger, merchant, of Lancaster Bourough 200 a Martic tp: History: On 11 Aug 1787, the Court of Common Please ordered the sheriff to seize the real estate of James Pagan, yeoman, of Lancaster County, due to unpaid debts owing to George Hess & Margaret Graham [the executors of John Graham]. The sheriff duly seized 200a Martic tp., which he later sold at public venue to Paul Zanzinger, the party hereto.
>
> 3 Jun 1789: R.W. Ball & Jacob Graeff (Note: The auctioneers)"[5]

James Pegan II is not found in Martic Twp. after 1787 according to the tax lists.[2] He seems to have removed to Allegheny County, Pennsylvania,where his sons settled.

He left no will.

According to Martic Township tax lists, and the process of elimination using his brother Andrew Pagan/Pegan Sr.'s will, his James Pagan/Pegan had three known sons: John, Archibald and James III.[2] He may have also had daughters, but of these there are no records. Information about his descendants is from internet research, and they cannot be fully documented or outlined in this book without additional extensive research in Pennsylvania and other possibly other states.

Sons of James Pagan II and Unknown Unknown:

+ 2 m I. **John[3] Pegan** was born in Martic Twp., Lancaster Co., Pennsylvania, in 1748. He died in Mifflin Twp., Allegheny Co., Pennsylvania, between 1810 and 1820.

+ 3 m II. **James[3] Pegan III** was born in Martic Twp., Lancaster Co., Pennsylvania, about 1750. He died in Martic Twp., Lancaster Co., Pennsylvania?, between 1793 and 1800.

+ 4 m III. **Archibald[3] Pegan** was born in Martic Twp., Lancaster Co., Pennsylvania, about 1753. He died in Versailles Twp., Allegheny Co., Pennsylvania, about 1832.

# 3<sup>rd</sup> Generation

2. **John**<sup>3</sup> **Pegan** (*James*<sup>2</sup> *Pagan II*, *James*<sup>1</sup>) was born in 1748 in Martic Twp., Lancaster Co., Pennsylvania. He was the son of James Pagan II (1) and Unknown Unknown. He died in Mifflin Twp., Allegheny Co., Pennsylvania, between 1810 and 1820.

In the Martic Twp., Lancaster Co., Pennsylvania tax records, John Pagan, son of James, was known as "John Pagan Sr." to differentiate him from John, the son of Andrew Pagan, who was known as "John Pagan Jr." This John Pagan first shows in the tax records for Martic Twp. as "James Pagan and son John" in 1772.[2]

John Pegan is listed on the Martic Twp., Lancaster Co., Pennsylvania militia roll for the Revolutionary War.[6]

This John Pegan married Jean Wherry/Wharry, as "my daughter Jean, wife of John Pegan" in Thomas Wherry/Wharry's will.[7]

From the History of Erie County, Pennsylvania:

In 1798 came to Erie, William Wallace; to Wayne Township, William Smith and David Findley; to Elk Creek Township, John Dietz and George Haybarger; to Union Township, John Wilson, John Pagan, John Welsh, and Jacob Shepard; to Springfield Township, …"[8]

This John Pegan/Pagan later joins his brother Archibald in Mifflin Twp., Allegheny Co., Pennsylvania by 1810 *(Census Place: Mifflin, Allegheny, Pennsylvania; Roll: 44; Page: 155; Image: 00085).* John Pegan/Pagan is more than 45 years old, as is his wife, whose name is unknown. He has one son under age 10 and two sons (?) between the ages of 16-25 and two daughters age 10-16.

John and **Jean Wharry/Wherry** Pegan married before 1788 in Lancaster Co., Pennsylvania. They had five children. Jean Wherry/ Wharry was born in Martic Twp., Lancaster Co., Pennsylvania?, about 1760. She died in Mifflin Twp., Allegheny Co., Pennsylvania?, after 1810.

Children of John Pegan and Jean Wharry or Wherry:

+ 5 m I. **John**<sup>4</sup> **Pagan II** was born in Martic Twp., Lancaster Co., Pennsylvania, about 1785. He died in Mifflin Twp., Allegheny Co., Pennsylvania, before 1820.

+ 6 m II. **James**<sup>3</sup> **Pegan** was born in Martic Twp., Lancaster Co., Pennsylvania, about 1787. He died in Mifflin Twp., Allegheny Co., Pennsylvania, after 1830.

+ 7 f III. **Daughter One**<sup>3</sup> **Pegan** was born in Pennsylvania between 1795 and 1800.

+ 8 f IV. **Daughter Two**<sup>3</sup> **Pegan** was born in Pennsylvania between 1795 and 1800.

+ 9 m V. **Son Three**<sup>3</sup> **Pegan** was born in Erie Co., Pennsylvania?, in 1800.

3. **James**<sup>3</sup> **Pegan III** (*James*<sup>2</sup> *Pagan II*, *James*<sup>1</sup>) was born about 1750 in Martic Twp., Lancaster Co., Pennsylvania. He was the son of James Pagan II (1) and Unknown Unknown. James died in Martic Twp., Lancaster Co., Pennsylvania?, between 1793 and 1800.

James "Pagin" marries a Mary "Pagin" at St. James Episcopal Church in Lancaster, Lancaster Co., Pennsylvania on August 2, 1771.[9] They had three children. Mary died after 1790.

Was it this James Pegan, or his uncle James Pagan, who may have been marrying for the second time? And was Mary Pagan her maiden name, and was she a cousin (she would have to be the daughter of Alexander, the son of James I), or, more likely, was she perhaps a widow of another Pegan man (such as Alexander Pegan, the son of Andrew, who may have been married briefly before he died?)

Like his brothers John and Archibald and other Pegan cousins, James Pegan III served in the

Revolutionary War. He was a member of the Martic Township Militia.[6]

This James Pegan is enumerated as "Jams Pegan" in the 1790 U.S. Census in Martic Twp., Lancaster Co., Pennsylvania. (*Census Place: Martick, Lancaster, Pennsylvania; Series: M637; Roll: 8; Page: 58; Image: 748.*) There are two males more than 16 years old and three females. One female may be James' wife, the others may be daughters, female relatives or perhaps one may be a maid.

His name is found on the 1793 Martic Twp., Lancaster Co., tax list, but he is not found in the 1800 U.S. Census.[2] He may have died in Martic Twp. Between 1793-1800, or perhaps joined his father James and brothers Archibald and John in Mifflin Twp., Allegheny Co., Pennsylvania and died there. He left no will.

(Note: In addition to James Pegan, the son of Andrew Pegan Sr., on the 1800 Martic Township tax list, there is a "James Pegan, the miller" listed. But this James was the son of Archibald Pagan. Archibald Pagan was a brother to James II, Andrew I and Alexander Pagan I.)[2]

Children of James Pegan III and Mary Pagan?:

+ 10 m I. **John Jacob Pegan or[4] Pagan II** was born in Martic Twp., Lancaster Co., Pennsylvania, in 1773. He died in Wheeling, Ohio Co., (West) Virginia, after 1840.

+ 11 f II. **Daughter One[4] Pagan.**

+ 12 f III. **Daughter Two[4] Pagan.**

4. **Archibald[3] Pagan** (*James[2], James[1]*) was born about 1753 in Martic Twp., Lancaster Co., Pennsylvania. He was the son of James Pagan II (1) and Unknown Unknown. Archibald lived in 1786 in Martic Twp., Lancaster Co., Pennsylvania. He died in Versailles Twp., Allegheny Co., Pennsylvania, about 1832 at age 79.

Archibald married **Unknown Unknown** about 1782 in Lancaster Co., Pennsylvania. They had one daughter. Unknown Unknown was born between 1756 and 1774. His wife died in Versailles Twp., Allegheny Co., Pennsylvania?, after 1820.

As late as 1786, Archibald Pegan/Pagan resided in Martic Twp., Lancaster Co., Pennsylvania.[2] He may have moved to Versailles Twp., Allegheny Co., Pennsylvania by 1790, but he was not recorded in that census.

According to Allegheny Co. land and deed records, Archibald Pagan/Pegan never owned property. However, he did enlist in the Pennsylvania militia during the American Revolution, along with the other Pegans.[6]

For his service, Archibald was later granted a pension by the Pennsylvania legislature:

> ...50. An act for the relief of sundry soldiers and widows of soldiers of the revolutionary war. That the state treasurer is hereby authorized to pay to John Davis of Armstrong county...Archibald Pagan of Allegheny count..., forty dollars each, immediately, and an annuity of forty dollars each, payable half yearly during life, to commence on 1 Jan 1827.[10]

In 1800, Archibald Pagan, enumerated as "Archibauld Pagon", is listed in Versailles Twp., Allegheny Co., Pennsylvania. There is a one in col. 5, a one in col. 8 and a two in col. 9 (one male more than age 45; one female age 16-25 and two females 26-44). (*Census Place: Versailles, Allegheny, Pennsylvania; Series: M32; Roll: 35; Page: 43; Image: 73.*)

Archibald Pagan continues to live in Versailles Twp., Allegheny Co., Pennsylvania in 1810 and 1820. In 1810, there is a one in col. 5 and a 2 in col. 10. (*Census Place: Versailles, Allegheny, Pennsylvania; Roll: 44; Page: 338; Image: 00177.*) In 1820, there is a one in col. 6 and a 2 in col. 11 (in both censuses, one male more than 45 years old and two females more than 45 years old). (*Census Place: Versailles, Allegheny, Pennsylvania; Page: 192; NARA Roll: M33_97; Image: 108.*)

In 1800, 1810 and 1820, the older females in the same age group are his wife and perhaps either his or her sister.

Archibald Pagan's name does not appear in the 1830 census, but his pension seems to have ended in 1832. He was probably living in someone else's household, possibly, if his daughter lived, in hers under her also unknown married name.

Daughter of Archibald Pagan and Unknown Unknown:

+ 13 f I. **Daughter**[4] **Pagan** was born in Pennsylvania between 1775 and 1784. She died in Allegheny Co., Pennsylvania?, after 1800.

# 4th Generation

5. **John[4] Pagan II** (*John[3] Pegan, James[2] Pagan II, James[1]*) was born about 1785 in Martic Twp., Lancaster Co., Pennsylvania. He was the son of John Pegan (2) and Jean Wharry or Wherry. John died in Mifflin Twp., Allegheny Co., Pennsylvania, before 1820. This John Pagan is referred to by his brother, James Pagan in James' testimony in a land ownership dispute involving a former neighbor in Mifflin Twp., Allegheny Co., Pennsylvania, John Wood, against John Farmare and Robert Davis in 1826 in Allegheny Cou[n]ty. In the original 1826 court case, James refers to "his brother John, " who allegedly was with him when James' witnessed an action. James then says his brother John is deceased.[11]

6. **James[4] Pagan** (*John[3] Pegan, James[2] Pagan II, James[1]*) was born about 1787 in Martic Twp., Lancaster Co., Pennsylvania. He was the son of John Pegan (2) and Jean Wharry or Wherry. James died in Mifflin Twp., Allegheny Co., Pennsylvania, after 1830. This James Pegan gives testimony in a land ownership case involving John Wood against John Farmare and Robert Davis in 1826 in Allegheny Co., Pennsylvania.[11]

James Pagan married **Unknown Unknown**. They had one daughter. His wife was born between 1790 and 1800 and died after 1820.

According to the 1830 census, this James Pagan may have had one daughter, born between 1816-1820, as there is a female of that age enumerated in his household, along with a wife born between 1790-1800. He is enumerated as "James Paggin" (*Census Place: Mifflin, Allegheny, Pennsylvania; Series: M19; Roll: 144; Page: 242*).

Daughter of James Pagan and Unknown Unknown:

+ 14   f   I.   **Daughter[5] Pagan** was born in Mifflin Twp., Allegheny Co., Pennsylvania, between 1816 and 1820 and died after 1840.

7. **Daughter One[4] Pegan** (*John[3], James[2] Pagan II, James[1]*) was born between 1795 and 1800 in Pennsylvania. She was the daughter of John Pegan (2) and Jean Wharry or Wherry.

8. **Daughter Two[4] Pegan** (*John[3], James[2] Pagan II, James[1]*) was born between 1795 and 1800 in Pennsylvania. She was the daughter of John Pegan (2) and Jean Wharry or Wherry.

9. **Son Three[4] Pegan** (*John[3], James[2] Pagan II, James[1]*) was born in 1800 in Erie Co., Pennsylvania?. He was the son of John Pegan (2) and Jean Wharry or Wherry.

10. **John Jacob Pegan or[4] Pagan II** (*James[3] Pegan III, James[2] Pagan II, James[1]*) was born in 1773 in Martic Twp., Lancaster Co., Pennsylvania. He was the son of James Pegan III (3) and Mary Pagan?. He died in Wheeling, Ohio Co., (West) Virginia, after 1840.

John Jacob Pagan/Pegan married **Unknown Unknown**. They seem to have had one daughter. His wife was born between 1770 and 1780 and died in Wheeling, Ohio Co., (West) Virginia?, after 1840.

John Jacob Pagan is not found in the 1830 U.S. Federal Census. However, he is found on Ohio chattel tax lists from 1829-1833 in Knox Twp., Columbiana Co., Ohio.[12]

John Jacob Pegan is enumerated in the 1840 census in Wheeling, (West) Virginia. (*Census Place: Wheeling Ward 1, Ohio, Virginia; Roll: 571; Page: 50; Image: 6890*. There is one male more than 45 years old, one female more than 45 years old, and one female between 15-20 years old. The younger female could be a daughter or a servant.

John Jacob Pegan may have been a lawyer. A John Jacob Pegan seems to have represented his younger cousin, William Louis ("Lewis") Pagan, the plaintiff in a scandalous slander suit in Montgomery County, Ohio in 1834. A few months later, the Pagans/Pegans withdrew the charges in this civil suit against the defendant, whom the Pegans/Pagans first claimed defamed young William Louis, then a minor, by saying he committed sodomy with a local minister. This minister had earlier been dismissed from a church in Pittsburgh, Pennsylvania for unspecified reasons.[13]

Daughter of John Jacob Pegan or Pagan II and Unknown Unknown:

+  15   f   I.   **Daughter⁵ Pagan** was born between 1820 and 1825.

**11. Daughter One⁴ Pegan** (*James³ Pegan III, James² Pagan II, James¹*). She is the daughter of James Pegan III (3) and Mary Pagan?.

**12. Daughter⁴ Two Pegan** *James³ Pegan III, James² Pagan II, James¹*). She is the daughter of James Pegan III (3) and Mary Pagan?.

**13. Daughter⁴ Pagan** (*Archibald³, James², James¹*) was born between 1775 and 1784 in Pennsylvania. She was the daughter of Archibald Pagan (4) and Unknown Unknown. Daughter died in Allegheny Co., Pennsylvania?, after 1800. We are assuming that young woman 16-25 years of age in Archibald Pagan's household in 1800 is his daughter. We do not know her name. She either died or married before 1810. As there are no civil records available for Pennsylvania before the 1880s, and church records in this area of Pennsylvania were scarce at the time, no marriage record is found for her.

# 5th Generation

14. **Daughter⁵ Pagan** (*James⁴, John³ Pegan, James² Pagan II, James¹*) was born between 1816 and 1820 in Mifflin Twp., Allegheny Co., Pennsylvania. She was the daughter of James Pagan (6) and Unknown Unknown. In 1840, she is living with her father James Pagan. She is either a widow or separated/divorced from a husband and she has a son between ages five and nine.

15. **Daughter⁵ Pagan** (*John Jacob Pegan or⁴ Pagan II, James³ Pegan III, James² Pagan II, James¹*) was born between 1820 and 1825. She was the daughter of John Jacob Pegan or Pagan II (10) and Unknown Unknown. This person, who appears in John Jacob Pagan's household in 1840, may have been either his daughter or a servant.

# Endnotes

1    Ellis, Frank and Samuel Evans, *History of Lancaster County, Pennsylvania: with biographical sketches of its pioneers and prominent men*, Philadelphia: Everts & Peck, 1883, pg. 680. Mishawaka Heritage Center, Mishawaka Penn-Harris Public Library, 209 Lincolnway East, Mishawaka, IN

2    Pagan/Pegan entries, Lancaster County, Pennsylvania. Tax Records. Martic Township, 1751-1831, microfilm, Lancaster County, Roll #23. Genealogy Center, Allen County Public Library, Fort Wayne, IN.

3    Benjamin Arnold to James Pegan, Lancaster County, Pennsylvania Deed Book C: 436-438. Lancaster County, Pennsylvania Archives, 150 North Queen Street, Lancaster, PA.

4    Lancaster County, Pennsylvania Deeds, Sheriff James E. Ross of Lancaster County, Pennsylvania to Paul Zanzinger, Lancaster County, Pennsylvania Deeds, Book G: 436 (03 Jun 1789). Lancaster County, Pennsylvania Archives, 150 North Queen Street, Lancaster, PA.

5    *Abstracts of Lancaster County Deed Records.* Compiled by Edward Wevadou. Apollo Pennsylvania: Closson Press; 2003, pg. 33. Family History Library, 35 North West Temple, Salt Lake City, UT.

6    *Pennsylvania Archives, Fifth Series, Vol. VII,* 1906, pg. 581. Pennsylvania State Archives, 350 North Street, Harrisburg, PA. Family History Library, 35 North West Temple, Salt Lake City, UT.

7    Thomas Wherry will (1788), Lancaster County, Pennsylvania Will Book E: Vol. 1: 468-69. Lancaster County, Pennsylvania Archives, 150 North Queen Street, Lancaster, PA.

8    Bates, Samuel P., Benjamin Whitman, N.W. Brown, R.C. Weakley, F.E. Warner, *History of Erie County, Pennsylvania.* Chicago: Beers & Co., 1884, pg. 237. Genealogy Center, Allen County Public Library, Fort Wayne, IN.

9    Nathan Zipfel, PA-Roots, "Marriages, St. James Church, Lancaster, PA, 1755-1856. James Pagin to Mary Pagin; Online database: http://www.pa-roots.com/index.php/pacounties/lancaster-county/295-birth-death-marriage-records-lancaster-county/999-marriages-st-james-church-lancaster-pa-1755-1856.

10   *Laws of the Commonwealth of Pennsylvania, Pennsylvania State Legislature, 1826-27.* Harrisburg, Pennsylvania: Commonwealth of Pennsylvania, 1827, pg. 89. Carnegie Library of Pittsburgh, 4400 Forbes Avenue, Pittsburgh, PA.

11   Watts, Frederick, ed. By William Wister Jr., *Reports of Cases Argued and Adjudged in the Supreme Court of Pennsylvania, Vol. X, July-September 1840.* Philadelphia: Kay & Brother; 1882, pg. 198-9. Kresge Law Library, Biolchini Hall of Law, 1100 Eck Hall of Law, 725 Howard Street, University of Notre Dame, Notre Dame, IN.

12   Ohio Tax Records, 1800-1850, FamilySearch.org, Entries for John J. Pagan, 1829-1833, Knox Township, Columbiana County, Ohio.

13   Lewis Pegan by his Next Friend John Jacob Pegan vs. David Winters, Montgomery County, Ohio Common Pleas Court Records, September Term 1839, Book N, pg. 515. Montgomery County, Ohio Records Center and Archives, 117 South Main Street, 6th Floor, Dayton, OH.

# Descendants of Jane Pagan Lusk

1. **Jane³ Pagan** (*Andrew² Pagan, James¹*) was born about 1743 in Martic Twp., Lancaster Co., Pennsylvania. She was the daughter of Andrew Pagan and Ann McDowell?. Jane died in York, York Co, South Carolina, about January 1821 at age 77.

Jane Pagan married **Robert Lusk** about 1760 in Lancaster Co., Pennsylvania. They had ten children. Robert Lusk was born in Pennsylvania or Ireland before 1746. Robert died in York, York Co, South Carolina, about January 1797.

Robert and Jane Pagan Lusk left with Jane's uncle Alexander Pagan I and his family and others from Martic Twp., Lancaster Co., Pennsylvania around 1765-6 and removed to Fishing Creek, Chester Co., South Carolina. From *Early Records of Fishing Creek Presbyterian Church: Chester County South Carolina 1799-1859*...

> "Fishing Creek Presbyterian Church was organized about 1770. Its first bench of elders consisted of Samuel Neely, John Latta, Robert Walker and Robert Lusk...".[2]

Robert Lusk died intestate. His probate was filed on February 7, 1797 in York Co., South Carolina. His estate administrators were his wife Jane Pagan Lusk and his son Robert Lusk, Jr. But the only papers in the file, other than the administration letter are his inventory documents. No information on descendants is found.[1]

Robert Lusk is enumerated in the 1790 census in York Co., South Carolina (*Census Place: York, South Carolina; Series: M637; Roll: 11; Page: 193; Image: 125*). There are five males more than 16 years old and seven females.

Jane Pegan Lusk is not found in the 1800 or 1810 U.S. Federal Censuses.

In the 1820 census, Jane Lusk is enumerated as the head of household in York, York Co., South Carolina. Sons Robert II, Andrew and James, all more than age 45, and both her daughters Martha and Margaret, both between the ages of 26-44, are living with her (*Census Place: York, York, South Carolina; Page: 167; NARA Roll: M33_121; Image: 311*). All her children seem to be single, as documented in Jane's will.

In her will, dated March 27, 1820, none of her surviving children--Robert II, James, Andrew, Martha or Margaret, were married or had issue. Her two daughters, according to the estate papers, were unmarried and son James died before the will was probated on January 19, 1821. One of the witnesses to an administration document was nephew William Downing, son of Jane's sister Mary Pagan Downing. The lawyer who administered most of the estate was Thomas Reid, husband of Mary Lusk Reid, Jane Pagan Lusk's niece by marriage.[3]

Her other alleged children, Elizabeth, Mary, Ann, Jane and Samuel, probably died in childhood or young adulthood.

No graves are known for any of Jane Pagan Lusk's family.

In 1830, her daughter Margaret Lusk, still spouseless, is recorded in the census with a male age 60-69 (probably her brother Robert), a female 30-39 and a female 20-29 in York Co., South Carolina (*Census Place: York, South Carolina; Series: M19; Roll: 173; Page: 344*). It is highly unlikely that the women are giving their true ages, as their mother Jane would have been too old to bear them in 1790 or 1800.

Little else is known about Jane Pagan Lusk's line. Information about her descendants is scarce. Indeed, she may not have had any past her own children. No Lusks are enumerated in subsequent U.S. Federal Censuses before 1910 in York Co., South Carolina.

Descendants, if any, cannot be fully documented or outlined further without extensive research in South Carolina and other states.

Children of Jane Pagan and Robert Lusk:

+ 2 m I. **Robert⁴ Lusk II** was born before 1770 in Lancaster Co., Pennsylvania.

+ 3 f II. **Elizabeth⁴ Lusk** Elizabeth died before March 27, 1820.

+ 4 f III. **Martha⁴ Lusk** was born about 1778 in York, York Co, South Carolina, about 1777. She died after March 27, 1820.

+ 5 f IV. **Mary⁴ Lusk** Mary died before March 27, 1820.

+ 6 m V. **Samuel⁴ Lusk** Samuel died before March 27, 1820.

+ 7 m VI. **James⁴ Lusk** was born before 1774. He died between March 27, 1820 and January 19, 1821.

+ 8 m VII. **Andrew⁴ Lusk** was born before 1774. He died after March 27, 1820.

+ 9 f VIII. **Margaret⁴ Lusk** was born in York, York Co, South Carolina, between 1776 and 1794. She died after 1830.

+ 10 f IX. **Ann⁴ Lusk** Ann died before March 27, 1820.

+ 11 f X. **Jane⁴ Lusk** Jane died before March 27, 1820.

# 2nd Generation

2. **Robert**[4] **Lusk II** (*Jane*[3] *Pagan, Andrew*[2] *Pagan, James*[1]) was born before 1770 in Lancaster Co., Pennsylvania. He was the son of Robert Lusk and Jane Pagan (1). Robert died after 1830.

3. **Elizabeth**[4] **Lusk** (*Jane*[3] *Pagan, Andrew*[2] *Pagan, James*[1]). She was the daughter of Robert Lusk and Jane Pagan (1). Elizabeth died before March 27, 1820.

4. **Martha**[4] **Lusk** (*Jane*[3] *Pagan, Andrew*[2] *Pagan, James*[1]) was born about 1777 in York, York Co, South Carolina. She was the daughter of Robert Lusk and Jane Pagan (1). Martha died after March 27, 1820.

5. **Mary**[4] **Lusk** (*Jane*[3] *Pagan, Andrew*[2] *Pagan, James*[1]). Mary was born about 1778. She was the daughter of Robert Lusk and Jane Pagan (1). Mary died before March 27, 1820.

6. **Samuel**[4] **Lusk** (*Jane*[3] *Pagan, Andrew*[2] *Pagan, James*[1]). He was the son of Robert Lusk and Jane Pagan (1). Samuel died before March 27, 1820.

7. **James**[4] **Lusk** (*Jane*[3] *Pagan, Andrew*[2] *Pagan, James*[1]) was born before 1774. He was the son of Robert Lusk and Jane Pagan (1). James died between March 27, 1820 and January 19, 1821.

8. **Andrew**[4] **Lusk** (*Jane*[3] *Pagan, Andrew*[2] *Pagan, James*[1]) was born before 1774. He was the son of Robert Lusk and Jane Pagan (1). Andrew died after March 27, 1820.

9. **Margaret**[4] **Lusk** (*Jane*[3] *Pagan, Andrew*[2] *Pagan, James*[1]) was born between 1776 and 1794 in York, York Co, South Carolina. She was the daughter of Robert Lusk and Jane Pagan (1). Margaret died after 1830.

10. **Ann**[4] **Lusk** (*Jane*[3] *Pagan, Andrew*[2] *Pagan, James*[1]). She was the daughter of Robert Lusk and Jane Pagan (1). Ann died before March 27, 1820.

11. **Jane**[4] **Lusk** (*Jane*[3] *Pagan, Andrew*[2] *Pagan, James*[1]). She was the daughter of Robert Lusk and Jane Pagan (1). Jane died before March 27, 1820.

# Endnotes

1    Robert Lusk estate (1797), York County, South Carolina Estate Record Book Case #59, File #2-677. York County, South Carolina Probate Court, 2 South Congress Street, York, SC.

2    *Early Records of Fishing Creek Presbyterian Church: Chester County, South Carolina, 1799-1859, with Appendices of the visitation list of Rev. John Simpson, 1774-1776, and the Cemetery roster, 1762-1979*, compiled by Brett H. Holcomb and Elmer O. Parker. Greenville, South Carolina: A Press, Inc.; 1980, pg. 1. Genealogy Center, Allen County Public Library, 900 Library Plaza, Fort Wayne, IN.

3    Jane Lusk will (1820), York County, South Carolina Will Book G: 41, Case #27, File #441. York County, South Carolina Probate Court, 2 South Congress Street, York, SC.

# Descendants of Mary Pagan Downing

1. **Mary³ Pagan** (*Andrew²*, *James¹*) was born in early 1746 in Martic Twp., Lancaster Co., Pennsylvania. She was the daughter of Andrew Pagan and Ann McDowell? Mary died in Fishing Creek, Chester Co., South Carolina, on March 19, 1832, at age 86. She was buried in Fishing Creek Presbyterian Cemetery, Chester, Chester Co., South Carolina.[1]

Mary married **John William Downing** on March 13, 1764, in Lancaster Co., Pennsylvania.[2] They had 10 children. John William Downing was born in County Down, Ireland, about 1740. He died in Fishing Creek, Chester Co., South Carolina, in May 1802. John William was buried in Fishing Creek Presbyterian Cemetery, Chester, Chester Co., South Carolina.[1]

In *Wayne County, Tennessee 1817-1995: History & Families,* on page 199, Misha Stegall Stanford says John Downing was born in Ireland in 1740 (Note: Could vary to 1744) and immigrated to America about 1760 with his father and other family.[3]

John and Mary Pegan Downing were married at the St. James Episcopal Church in Philadelphia.[2]

According to the Martic Township, Lancaster Co., Pennsylvania tax records, John Downing was a weaver.[4]

John and Mary Pegan Downing removed from Martic Twp., Lancaster Co., Pennsylvania with Mary's sister Jane Pegan Lusk and her husband Robert, Mary's cousins, James, Archibald and Alexander Pagan, and other descendants of the Scotch-Irish Covenanters, members of Muddy Run Presbyterian Church, around 1765-1767 because of Indian skirmishes in the area.[5]

"John Combest, planter, of St. Marks Parish, Craven Co., to John Downing, weaver, for L 140 currency, 150 a. on Fishing Creek, in St. Marks Parish, bounding on all sides on vacant land; granted 1 Feb. 1768 by Gov. Charles Greville (Lord) Montagu to Daniel Kelly; who on 24 Apr. 1768 sold to John Combest. See Aud. Book I-O, p. 69,5 Sept. 1768. Witnesses: Samuel Porter, James Hanna. Before Zaer Isbell, J.P., on 25 Apr. 1769. Recorded 19 June 1769"[6]

From the *South Carolina Magazine of Ancestral Research* (SCMAR), 1979:

Some Early Settlers on Fishing Creek…

John Downing… a plantation or tract of Land Containing 250 Acres of Land Situate in Craven County W. of fishing Creek … on James Lusk's line … on Robert Lusk's Line … on Wm Boyd's Line … on Robert Gill's Line … on vacant Land … Survey Certified 16th March 1772 & Granted the 26th Sepr 1772 to the Mem'st … (sworn) the 23d of Novr 1772 (signed) James Pinkerton, D.S. del'd May 27th, 1773 to Hugh White (vol. 11, p. 514)."[7]

John Downing was a Quartermaster in Colonel George Gill's regiment of South Carolina Militia during the Revolutionary War:

"John Downing served in the militia under Lt. Thomas Black and Col. Neel and was in the Briar Creek Expedition. From 1 Nov to 21 Dec. 1780, he served as a quartermaster under Capt. Mills at Lacy's Fort. In June of 1781, he was under Captain Hugh Knox at Congaree Fort and in Nov. 1781, he was a quartermaster under a Lt. Kelley at Orangeburg. He served under Lt. Archibald Gill during 1782 and was at Four Holes and Fork of Edisto". Based on supporting documents, a collection of claims for provisions and services made to the legislature after the war, it appears that John served as a quartermaster, a horseman, a footman, and a soldier during 196 days of total service in five separate 'campaigns.'"[8]

John Downing is enumerated in the 1790 census in Chester Co., South Carolina *(Census Place: Chester, South Carolina; Series: M637; Roll: 11; Page: 179; Image: 117)*. There are two males age 16 or older, two males younger than 16, and six females. Son Andrew, allegedly born in 1771, has already established his own household and lives close to his father. Daughter Elizabeth is already married. As John and Mary Pagan Downing are said to have had nine children, there is an extra female in the home.

In 1800, John Downing is again living in Chester Co., South Carolina *(Year: 1800; Census Place: Chester, South Carolina; Series: M32; Roll: 47; Page: 92; Image: 184)*. This time, there are three males between ages 16-25 and a male 45 years old or older; three females age 10-15, two females age 16-25, and a female age 45 or older. Again, this shows an extra female between the age of 10-15. It seems that the Downings may have had another daughter, perhaps born abt. 1787, who died unmarried before 1811 when her father's land was sold.

John Downing dies in May 1802. Administration bond for his estate in Chester Co., South Carolina is in File 14, Pack 341, with bond dated September 1802. The administration bond was granted to his wife, Mary Downing. The papers are signed by Mary Downing and witnessed by James Pagan (Mary Pagan Downing's first cousin, son of Alexander Pagan I) and John Downing II.[9]

The widowed Mary Pagan Downing is enumerated in the 1810 census in Chester Co., South Carolina *(Census Place: Chester, Chester, South Carolina; Roll: 60; Page: 520; Image: 00271)*. There is one male age 16-25, one male age 26-44, one female age 10-15, one female age 16-25 and one female age 45 or older.

Mary Pagan Downing is not found under her own name after the 1810 census.

A deed on January 12, 1811 and recorded on March 19, 1814 names John Downing's wife, Mary, and their surviving children/spouses: Johnathan (sic) Jones (Elizabeth), Ann Downing, Andrew Downing,

John Downing, John Gill (Mary), Robert Downing, William Gilmore (Jane), Sally Downing:

A land deed to William Downing for 529 3/4 acres, being a grant made to John Downing, dec'd, in the year 1772; and the said dec'd, John Downing, being the husband and father of said conveyors; and the land has such boundries (sic) as appears by plat hereto annexed. $598.62 William Johns Jr. (witness) Leander Downing (witness) Signed by Mary, Jonathan Jones and Betsey his wife (her mark), John, John Gill and Polly his wife (her mark), Robert, and Sally. (William Gilmore, the husband of Jane Downing, never signed, although a space was left for his name).[10]

Mary was "readmitted" to the Fishing Creek, South Carolina Presbyterian Church sometime between April 1812 and April 1813.[11]

A full inclusion of all the descendants of Mary Pagan Downing and her husband John Downing would be too numerous for this book. Much information on this line can be found online and in some lineage books, including *The Pagan, Hunt Sanderson genealogies* by Glenda Pagan Hibdon and *Early Records of Fishing Creek Presbyterian Church, Chester County, South Carolina, 1799-1859…*, a compilation by Brent H. Holcomb and Elmer O. Parker.[11, 12]

Also, the descendants of John and Mary Pagan Downing are very active in documenting the family history, and several letters sent among family members from about 1826-7 exist, as does the bible of John and Mary's son Andrew.[13, 14]

Only a few generations are included here to help those interested in this line connect with the immigrant ancestor James Pagan. A complete family line would require intensive research in South Carolina, Tennessee, Arkansas, Ohio, Michigan, Indiana, Illinois, Missouri and other states.

Children of Mary Pagan and John William Downing:

+ 2    f    I.    **Elizabeth**[4] **Downing** was born in Martic Twp., Lancaster Co., Pennsylvania, in 1765. She was also known as **Betsey**. Elizabeth died in Carroll Co., Tennessee, on August 13, 1855. She was buried in Furgerson Cemetery, Cedar Grove, Carroll Co., Tennessee.[15]

+ 3   f   II.   **Ann**[4] **Downing** was born in Fishing Creek, Chester Co., South Carolina, in 1767. She died in Chester Co., South Carolina?, on December 4, 1843.

+ 4   m   III.   **William**[4] **Downing** was born in Fishing Creek, Chester Co., South Carolina, in 1768. He died in Chester Co., South Carolina?, after 1827.

+ 5   m   IV.   **Andrew Pagan**[4] **Downing** was born in Fishing Creek, Chester Co., South Carolina, on April 5, 1771.[14] He died in Houston, Wayne Co., Tennessee, on April 21, 1844. Andrew Pagan was buried in Mount Hebron Cemetery, Houston, Wayne Co., Tennessee.[16]

+ 6   m   V.   **John**[4] **Downing II** was born in Fishing Creek, Chester Co., South Carolina, on December 31, 1776. He died in Harrison Twp., Darke Co., Ohio, on May 17, 1870. John was buried in Hill Cemetery, New Madison, Harrison Twp., Darke Co., Ohio.[17]

+ 7   f   VI.   **Mary**[4] **Downing** was born in Fishing Creek, Chester Co., South Carolina, in 1778. She was also known as **Polly.** Mary died in Fishing Creek, Chester Co., South Carolina, in 1826.

+ 8   m   VII.   **Robert Gill**[4] **Downing** was born in Fishing Creek, Chester Co., South Carolina, about 1782. He died in New Madison, Harrison Twp., Darke Co., Ohio, on May 17, 1870.

+ 9   f   VIII.   **Jane**[4] **Downing** was born in Fishing Creek, Chester Co., South Carolina, in 1785. She died after 1820.

+ 10   f   IX.   **Daughter**[4] **Downing** was born in Chester Co., South Carolina, about 1787. She died in Chester Co., South Carolina, before 1811.

+ 11   f   X.   **Sarah**[4] **Downing** was born in Fishing Creek, Chester Co., South Carolina, in 1790. She was also known as **Sally.** Sarah died in Mountain View, Stone Co., Arkansas, in 1854. She was buried in Flatwoods Cemetery, Mountain View, Stone Co., Arkansas.[18]

# 4th Generation

**2. Elizabeth⁴ Downing** (*Mary³ Pagan, Andrew², James¹*) was born in 1765 in Martic Twp., Lancaster Co., Pennsylvania. She was also known as **Betsey.** She was the daughter of John William Downing and Mary Pagan (1). Elizabeth died in Carroll Co., Tennessee, on August 13, 1855, at age 90. She was buried in Furgerson Cemetery, Cedar Grove, Carroll Co., Tennessee.[15]

Elizabeth married **Jonathan Jones** on March 7, 1787, in Chester Co., South Carolina. They had nine children. Jonathan Jones was born in Fishing Creek, Chester Co., South Carolina, on May 8, 1757. Jonathan reached age 78 and died in Chester Co., South Carolina, on August 4, 1835. He was buried in Fishing Creek Presbyterian Cemetery, Chester, Chester Co., South Carolina.[1]

Children of Elizabeth Downing and Jonathan Jones:

+ 12  m  I.  **William H.⁵ Jones** was born in Fishing Creek, Chester Co., South Carolina, in 1788. He died in Carroll Co., Tennessee, in 1850.

+ 13  m  II.  **James⁵ Jones** was born in Fishing Creek, Chester Co., South Carolina, in 1790. He died in Chester Co., South Carolina?, on January 25, 1835.

+ 14  f  III.  **Mary⁵ Jones** was born in Fishing Creek, Chester Co., South Carolina, on March 7, 1792. She died in Carroll Co., Tennessee, on July 18, 1866. Mary was buried in Furgerson Cemetery, Cedar Grove, Carroll Co., Tennessee.[15]

+ 15  f  IV.  **Catherine⁵ Jones** was born in Fishing Creek, Chester Co., South Carolina, on May 20, 1794. She died in Carroll Co., Tennessee, on February 18, 1870. Catherine was buried in Furgerson Cemetery, Cedar Grove, Carroll Co., Tennessee.[15]

+ 16  f  V.  **Elizabeth⁵ Jones** was born in Fishing Creek, Chester Co., South Carolina, on October 5, 1796. She was also known as **Betsey.** Elizabeth died in Chester Co., South Carolina, on May 5, 1895. She was buried in Fishing Creek Presbyterian Cemetery, Chester, Chester Co., South Carolina.[1]

+ 17  f  VI.  **Jennett Simpson⁵ Jones** was born in Fishing Creek, Chester Co., South Carolina, on May 15, 1799. She died in 1877.

+ 18  f  VII.  **Sarah Carson⁵ Jones** was born in Fishing Creek, Chester Co., South Carolina, on June 14, 1801. She died in Carroll Co., Tennessee, in 1874. Sarah Carson was buried in Robeson Cemetery, Cedar Grove, Carroll Co., Tennessee.[19]

+ 19  f  VIII.  **Ann⁵ Jones** was born in Fishing Creek, Chester Co., South Carolina, on July 28, 1803. She died in Carroll Co., Tennessee, on February 27, 1862. Ann was buried in Furgerson Cemetery, Cedar Grove, Carroll Co., Tennessee.[15]

+ 20  m  IX.  **John Downing⁵ Jones** was born in Fishing Creek, Chester Co., South Carolina, on January 20, 1808. He died in Carroll Co., Tennessee, on September 1, 1847. John Downing was buried in Furgerson Cemetery, Cedar Grove, Carroll Co., Tennessee.[15]

**3. Ann⁴ Downing** (*Mary³ Pagan, Andrew², James¹*) was born in 1767 in Fishing Creek, Chester Co., South Carolina. She was the daughter of John William Downing and Mary Pagan (1). Ann died in Chester Co., South Carolina?, on December 4, 1843, at age 76.

Never married.

4. **William**[4] **Downing** (*Mary*[3] *Pagan, Andrew*[2], *James*[1]) was born in 1768 in Fishing Creek, Chester Co., South Carolina. He was the son of John William Downing and Mary Pagan (1). William died in Chester Co., South Carolina?, after 1827.

William married **Unknown Unknown** about 1801. They had four children. Unknown Unknown was born between 1776 and 1794. Unknown died in Chester Co., South Carolina, about 1825.

Children of William Downing and Unknown Unknown:

+ 21 m I.     **Son One**[5] **Downing** was born in Chester Co., South Carolina, about 1803.

+ 22 m II.     **Son Two**[5] **Downing** was born in Chester Co., South Carolina, between 1805 and 1810.

+ 23 m III.     **Son Three**[5] **Downing** was born in Chester Co., South Carolina, between 1810 and 1820.

+ 24 f IV.     **Daughter**[5] **Downing** was born in Chester Co., South Carolina, between 1810 and 1820.

5. **Andrew Pagan**[4] **Downing** (*Mary*[3] *Pagan, Andrew*[2], *James*[1]) was born on April 5, 1771, in Fishing Creek, Chester Co., South Carolina.[4] He was the son of John William Downing and Mary Pagan (1). Andrew Pagan died in Houston, Wayne Co., Tennessee, on April 21, 1844, at age 73. He was buried in Mount Hebron Cemetery, Houston, Wayne Co., Tennessee.[16]

Andrew Pagan married **Elizabeth Jones** about 1789 in Chester Co., South Carolina? They had eleven children. Elizabeth Jones was born in Chester Co., South Carolina, on April 14, 1772. Elizabeth reached age 74 and died in Houston, Wayne Co., Tennessee, on March 12, 1847. She was buried in Mount Hebron Cemetery, Houston, Wayne Co., Tennessee.[16]

Children of Andrew Pagan Downing and Elizabeth Jones:

+ 25 f I.     **Mary**[5] **Downing** was born in Chester Co., South Carolina, on July 6, 1791. She died in Wayne Co., Tennessee, on April 21, 1857. Mary was buried in Mount Hebron Cemetery, Houston, Wayne Co., Tennessee.[16]

+ 26 f II.     **Katherine**[5] **Downing** was born in Chester Co., South Carolina, on August 6, 1793.

+ 27 m III.     **John**[5] **Downing** was born in Chester Co., South Carolina, on December 3, 1796. He died in Houston, Texas Co., Missouri, on September 24, 1863.

+ 28 f IV.     **Ann**[5] **Downing** was born in Chester Co., South Carolina, on August 12, 1799. She died in Tennessee in 1855.

+ 29 m V.     **Alexander**[5] **Downing** was born in Chester Co., South Carolina, on October 11, 1801. He died in Millersburg, Rutherford Co., Tennessee, between 1860 and 1870.

+ 30 m VI.     **William**[5] **Downing** was born in Chester Co., South Carolina, on January 2, 1803. He died in Hardin Co., Tennessee, in 1872. William was buried in Patterson Cemetery, Hardin Co., Tennessee.[20]

+ 31 f VII.     **Elizabeth**[5] **Downing** was born in Chester Co., South Carolina, on June 13, 1805. She died in Chester Co., South Carolina, on July 18, 1808.

+ 32 m VIII.     **James**[5] **Downing** was born in Chester Co., South Carolina, on May 6, 1808.

+ 33 f IX.     **Sarah**[5] **Downing** was born in Wayne Co., Tennessee, on August 13, 1811. She died in Centerville,

Faulkner Co., Arkansas, on February 8, 1881. Sarah was buried in Woolley Cemetery, Centerville, Faulkner Co., Arkansas.[21]

+ 34  m  X.  **Andrew Pagan⁵ Downing II** was born in Wayne Co., Tennessee, on June 6, 1813. He died in Wayne Co., Tennessee, on October 31, 1815.

+ 35  m  XI.  **Jonathan Jones⁵ Downing** was born in Wayne Co., Tennessee, on August 11, 1816. He died in Lavinia, Carroll Co., Tennessee, on March 11, 1885.

6.  **John⁴ Downing II** (*Mary³ Pagan, Andrew², James¹*) was born on December 31, 1776, in Fishing Creek, Chester Co., South Carolina. He was the son of John William Downing and Mary Pagan (1). John died in Harrison Twp., Darke Co., Ohio, on May 17, 1870, at age 93. He was buried in Hill Cemetery, New Madison, Harrison Twp., Darke Co., Ohio. [17] John Downing was a resident of Harrison Twp., Darke Co., Ohio by 1820. (*1820 U S Census; Census Place: Harrison, Darke, Ohio; Page: 142; NARA Roll: M33_89; Image: 87*).

John married **Margaret Ferris or Faris** on April 24, 1804, in Chester Co., South Carolina. They had six children. Margaret Ferris or Faris was born in Ireland on August 4, 1783. Margaret Ferris or reached age 80 and died in Harrison Twp., Darke Co., Ohio, on February 13, 1864. She was buried in Hill Cemetery, New Madison, Harrison Twp., Darke Co., Ohio.[17]

Children of John Downing II and Margaret Ferris or Faris:

+ 36  m  I.  **Samuel⁵ Downing** was born in Chester, Chester Co., South Carolina, on April 6, 1805. He died in Sebewa Twp., Ionia Co., Michigan, on July 7, 1871. Samuel was buried in George Washington Hoover-Allensville Cemetery, Jackson Twp., Randolph Co., Indiana.[22]

+ 37  f  II.  **Elvira⁵ Downing** was born in Chester Co., South Carolina, on January 17, 1807. She died in Hollansburg, Harrison Twp., Darke Co., Ohio, on February 28, 1837. Elvira was buried in Hill Cemetery, New Madison, Harrison Twp., Darke Co., Ohio.[17]

+ 38  f  III.  **Minerva Jane⁵ Downing** was born in Chester, Chester Co., South Carolina, on December 7, 1808. She died in German Twp., Darke Co., Ohio, on November 4, 1893. Minerva Jane was buried in Hollansburg Cemetery, Hollansburg, Harrison Twp., Darke Co., Ohio.[23]

+ 39  m  IV.  **Jason L.⁵ Downing** was born in Chester Co., South Carolina, on April 4, 1811. He died in New Madison, Harrison Twp., Darke Co., Ohio, in 1901. Jason L. was buried in Green Mound Cemetery, New Madison, Harrison Twp., Darke Co., Ohio.[24]

+ 40  m  V.  **John Edward⁵ Downing II** was born in Chester Co., South Carolina, on January 19, 1813. He died in New Madison, Harrison Twp., Darke Co., Ohio, on October 27, 1872. John Edward was buried in First Universalist Church Cemetery, New Madison, Harrison Twp., Darke Co., Ohio.[25]

+ 41  m  VI.  **Robert J.⁵ Downing** was born in Bourbon Co., Kentucky, on June 10, 1815. He died in Harrison Twp., Darke Co., Ohio, on December 4, 1888. Robert J. was buried in Hollansburg Cemetery, Hollansburg, Harrison Twp., Darke Co., Ohio.[23]

7.  **Mary⁴ Downing** (*Mary³ Pagan, Andrew², James¹*) was born in 1778 in Fishing Creek, Chester Co.,

South Carolina. She was also known as **Polly.** She was the daughter of John William Downing and Mary Pagan (1). Mary died in Fishing Creek, Chester Co., South Carolina, in 1826 at age 48.

Mary married **John Gill** before 1811. John Gill was born in Fishing Creek, Chester Co., South Carolina, in 1783. John reached age 43 and died in Fishing Creek, Chester Co., South Carolina, in 1826.

8. **Robert Gill⁴ Downing** (*Mary³ Pagan, Andrew², James¹*) was born about 1782 in Fishing Creek, Chester Co., South Carolina. He was the son of John William Downing and Mary Pagan (1). Robert Gill lived in 1850 in Funks Grove Twp., McLean Co., Illinois. He died in New Madison, Harrison Twp., Darke Co., Ohio, on May 17, 1870, at age 88.

He married **Sarah Unknown.** They had seven children. Sarah Unknown was born in South Carolina in 1786. Sarah died in Harrison Twp., Darke Co., Ohio, after 1870. Some undocumented sources say Sarah's last name was Hill.

Children of Robert Gill Downing and Sarah Unknown:

+ 42 f I. **Sarah⁵ Downing** was born in White Co., Tennessee?, on July 21, 1807. She died in Indiana on March 26, 1845.

+ 43 f II. **Mary Ann⁵ Downing** was born in White Co., Tennessee?, in 1813.

+ 44 m III. **Andrew Jackson⁵ Downing** was born in White Co., Tennessee, in 1815. He died in Maple Hill, Wabaunsee Co., Kansas?, after 1880.

+ 45 f IV. **Amanda Jane⁵ Downing** was born in White Co., Tennessee, on January 25, 1817. She died in Darke Co., Ohio, on February 13, 1872.

+ 46 m V. **Joseph Herr⁵ Downing** was born in White Co., Tennessee, in 1822. He died in Washington Twp., Putnam Co., Indiana?, after 1860.

+ 47 m VI. **Robert⁵ Downing II** was born in White Co., Tennessee, in 1828. He died in Washington Twp., Putnam Co., Indiana?, after 1860.

+ 48 f VII. **Esther Eleanor⁵ Downing** was born in White Co., Tennessee.

9. **Jane⁴ Downing** (*Mary³ Pagan, Andrew², James¹*) was born in 1785 in Fishing Creek, Chester Co., South Carolina. She was the daughter of John William Downing and Mary Pagan (1). Jane died after 1820.

Jane married **William Gilmore** on May 10, 1809, in York Co., South Carolina. William died in York, York Co, South Carolina?, after 1820.

10. **Daughter⁴ Downing?** (*Mary³ Pagan, Andrew², James¹*) was born about 1787 in Chester Co., South Carolina. She was the daughter of John William Downing and Mary Pagan (1). Daughter died in Chester Co., South Carolina, before 1811.

11. **Sarah⁴ Downing** (*Mary³ Pagan, Andrew², James¹*) was born in 1790 in Fishing Creek, Chester Co., South Carolina. She was also known as **Sally.** She was the daughter of John William Downing and Mary Pagan (1). Sarah died in Mountain View, Stone Co., Arkansas, in 1854 at age 64. She was buried in Flatwoods Cemetery, Mountain View, Stone Co., Arkansas.[18]

Sarah married **William Hinkle** about 1812 in Chester Co., South Carolina. They had seven children. William Hinkle was born in Chester, Chester Co., South Carolina, on December 7, 1792. William reached age 74 and died in Mountain View, Stone Co., Arkansas, on April 15, 1867. He was buried in Flatwoods Cemetery, Mountain View, Stone Co., Arkansas.[18]

Children of Sarah Downing and William Hinkle:

+ 49 m I. **Jesse⁵ Hinkle** was born in Chester, Chester Co., South Carolina, on June 10, 1814. He died in Lunenburg, Izard Co., Arkansas, on May 22, 1891.

+ 50    m    II.    **John Downing[5] Hinkle** was born in Wayne Co., Tennessee, on June 26, 1816. He died in Melbourne, Izard Co., Arkansas, on September 1, 1852.

+ 51    m    III.    **Andrew J.[5] Hinkle** was born in Wayne Co., Tennessee, on February 24, 1818. He died in Mountain View, Stone Co., Arkansas, in 1870. Andrew J. was buried in Flatwoods Cemetery, Mountain View, Stone Co., Arkansas.[18]

+ 52    f    IV.    **Catherine[5] Hinkle** was born in Madison Co., Alabama, on December 26, 1819. She died in Mountain View, Stone Co., Arkansas, on November 11, 1863. Catherine was buried in Flatwoods Cemetery, Mountain View, Stone Co., Arkansas.[18]

+ 53    f    V.    **Mary Jane[5] Hinkle** was born in Wayne Co., Tennessee, on June 14, 1821. She died in Irons Point, Izard Co., Arkansas, on June 3, 1877. Mary Jane was buried in Flatwoods Cemetery, Mountain View, Stone Co., Arkansas.[18]

+ 54    f    VI.    **Francis M.[5] Hinkle** was born in Madison Co., Alabama, on November 18, 1826. She died in Blue Mountain, Stone Co., Arkansas, on September 12, 1870. Francis M. was buried in Flatwoods Cemetery, Mountain View, Stone Co., Arkansas.[18]

+ 55    m    VII.    **William Riley[5] Hinkle** was born in Wayne Co., Tennessee, on October 7, 1828. He died in Blue Mountain, Stone Co., Arkansas, on February 25, 1902.

# 5th Generation

**12. William H.[5] Jones** (*Elizabeth[4] Downing, Mary[3] Pagan, Andrew[2], James[1]*) was born in 1788 in Fishing Creek, Chester Co., South Carolina. He was the son of Jonathan Jones and Elizabeth Downing (2). William H. died in Carroll Co., Tennessee, in 1850 at age 62.

William H. married **Juliet Granville Porter** in 1808 in South Carolina. They had two children. Juliet Granville Porter was born in Fishing Creek, Chester Co., South Carolina, in 1788. Juliet Granville reached age 67 and died in Carroll Co., Tennessee, in 1855.

Children of William H. Jones and Juliet Granville Porter:

+ 56 f I. **Mary[6] Jones.**

+ 57 m II. **Samuel[6] Jones.**

**13. James[5] Jones** (*Elizabeth[4] Downing, Mary[3] Pagan, Andrew[2], James[1]*) was born in 1790 in Fishing Creek, Chester Co., South Carolina. He was the son of Jonathan Jones and Elizabeth Downing (2). James died in Chester Co., South Carolina?, on January 25, 1835, at age 45.

**14. Mary[5] Jones** (*Elizabeth[4] Downing, Mary[3] Pagan, Andrew[2], James[1]*) was born on March 7, 1792, in Fishing Creek, Chester Co., South Carolina. She was the daughter of Jonathan Jones and Elizabeth Downing (2). Mary died in Carroll Co., Tennessee, on July 18, 1866, at age 74. She was buried in Furgerson Cemetery, Cedar Grove, Carroll Co., Tennessee.[15]

She married **Robert Brownfield Porter.** They had nine children. Robert Brownfield Porter was born in South Carolina on December 3, 1791. Robert Brownfield reached age 74 and died in Carroll Co., Tennessee, on May 7, 1866. He was buried in Furgerson Cemetery, Cedar Grove, Carroll Co., Tennessee.[15]

Children of Mary Jones and Robert Brownfield Porter:

+ 58 f I. **Eliza Katherine[6] Porter.**

+ 59 f II. **Mary H.[6] Porter.**

+ 60 m III. **James Jones[6] Porter.**

+ 61 m IV. **David Brownfield[6] Porter.**

+ 62 m V. **William S.[6] Porter.**

+ 63 f VI. **Amanda Jane[6] Porter.**

+ 64 f VII. **Juliet Ann[6] Porter.**

+ 65 f VIII. **Sarah A.[6] Porter.**

+ 66 f IX. **Martha Louise[6] Porter.**

**15. Catherine[5] Jones** (*Elizabeth[4] Downing, Mary[3] Pagan, Andrew[2], James[1]*) was born on May 20, 1794, in Fishing Creek, Chester Co., South Carolina. She was the daughter of Jonathan Jones and Elizabeth Downing (2). Catherine died in Carroll Co., Tennessee, on February 18, 1870, at age 75. She was buried in Furgerson Cemetery, Cedar Grove, Carroll Co., Tennessee.[15]

Never married.

**16. Elizabeth[5] Jones** (*Elizabeth[4] Downing, Mary[3] Pagan, Andrew[2], James[1]*) was born on October 5, 1796, in Fishing Creek, Chester Co., South Carolina. She was also known as **Betsey.** She was the daughter of Jonathan Jones and Elizabeth Downing (2). Elizabeth died in Chester Co., South Carolina, on May 5, 1895, at age 98. She was buried in Fishing Creek Presbyterian Cemetery, Chester, Chester Co., South Carolina.[1]

She married **John Dunlap.** They had five children. John Dunlap was born in Chester Co., South Carolina, on June 20, 1794. John reached age 67 and died in Chester Co., South Carolina, on January 4, 1862. He was buried in Fishing Creek Presbyterian Cemetery, Chester, Chester Co., South Carolina.[1]

Children of Elizabeth Jones and John Dunlap:

+ 67 f I. **Mary[6] Dunlap.**

+ 68 f II. **Catherine[6] Dunlap**

+ 69 f III. **Anna[6] Dunlap**

+ 70    f    IV.    **Sarah⁶ Dunlap**

+ 71    m    V.    **John⁶ Dunlap II.**

**17. Jennett Simpson⁵ Jones** (*Elizabeth⁴ Downing, Mary³ Pagan, Andrew², James¹*) was born on May 15, 1799, in Fishing Creek, Chester Co., South Carolina. She was the daughter of Jonathan Jones and Elizabeth Downing (2). Jennett Simpson died in 1877 at age 77.

**18. Sarah Carson⁵ Jones** (*Elizabeth⁴ Downing, Mary³ Pagan, Andrew², James¹*) was born on June 14, 1801, in Fishing Creek, Chester Co., South Carolina. She was the daughter of Jonathan Jones and Elizabeth Downing (2). Sarah Carson died in Carroll Co., Tennessee, in 1874 age 72. She was buried in Robeson Cemetery, Cedar Grove, Carroll Co., Tennessee.[19]

She married **George Montgomery.** They had nine children. George Montgomery was born in South Carolina in 1795. George reached age 82 and died in Carroll Co., Tennessee, in 1877. He was buried in Robeson Cemetery, Cedar Grove, Carroll Co., Tennessee.[19]

Children of Sarah Carson Jones and George Montgomery:

+ 72    m    I.    **William O.⁶ Montgomery.**

+ 73    m    II.    **Thomas VanBuren⁶ Montgomery.**

+ 74    f    III.    **Jane C.⁶ Montgomery.**

+ 75    f    IV.    **Caroline Jeanette⁶ Montgomery.**

+ 76    f    V.    **Sarah E.⁶ Montgomery.**

+ 77    m    VI.    **Samuel Johnson⁶ Montgomery.**

+ 78    f    VII.    **Rebecca⁶ Montgomery.**

+ 79    m    VIII.    **George W.⁶ Montgomery II.**

+ 80    f    IX.    **Mary A.⁶ Montgomery.**

**19. Ann⁵ Jones** (*Elizabeth⁴ Downing, Mary³ Pagan, Andrew², James¹*) was born on July 28, 1803, in Fishing Creek, Chester Co., South Carolina. She was the daughter of Jonathan Jones and Elizabeth Downing (2). Ann died in Carroll Co., Tennessee, on February 27, 1862, at age 58. She was buried

in Furgerson Cemetery, Cedar Grove, Carroll Co., Tennessee.[15]

She married **William Montgomery.** They had six children. William Montgomery was born in South Carolina in 1797. William died in Carroll Co., Tennessee, after 1870.

Children of Ann Jones and William Montgomery:

+ 81    f    I.    **Adalise⁶ Montgomery.**

+ 82    f    II.    **Mary E.⁶ Montgomery.**

+ 83    m    III.    **Samuel Granville⁶ Montgomery.**

+ 84    m    IV.    **William H.⁶ Montgomery II.**

+ 85    m    V.    **Thomas P.⁶ Montgomery.**

+ 86    m    VI.    **John L.⁶ Montgomery.**

**20. John Downing⁵ Jones** (*Elizabeth⁴ Downing, Mary³ Pagan, Andrew², James¹*) was born on January 20, 1808, in Fishing Creek, Chester Co., South Carolina. He was the son of Jonathan Jones and Elizabeth Downing (2). John Downing died in Carroll Co., Tennessee, on September 1, 1847, at age 39. He was buried in Furgerson Cemetery, Cedar Grove, Carroll Co., Tennessee.[15]

He married **Ann McDowell.** They had five sons. Ann McDowell was born in Ireland in 1816. Ann reached age 84 and died in Carroll Co., Tennessee?, in 1900. She was buried in Furgerson Cemetery, Cedar Grove, Carroll Co., Tennessee.[15] Her name at death was Ann McDowell Jones Moore.

Sons of John Downing Jones and Ann McDowell:

+ 87    m    I.    **William Downing⁶ Jones** was born in Fishing Creek, Chester Co., South Carolina, in 1836.

+ 88    m    II.    **Thomas Edwin⁶ Jones** was born in Carroll Co., Tennessee, in 1839.

+ 89    m    III.    **James⁶ Jones** was born in Carroll Co., Tennessee, in 1842.

+ 90    m    IV.    **John R.⁶ Jones** was born in Carroll Co., Tennessee, in 1844.

+ 91 m V. **J. Harve⁶ Jones** was born in Carroll Co., Tennessee, in 1847.

**21. Son One⁵ Downing** (*William⁴, Mary³ Pagan, Andrew², James¹*) was born about 1803 in Chester Co., South Carolina. He was the son of William Downing (4) and Unknown Unknown.

**22. Son Two⁵ Downing** (*William⁴, Mary³ Pagan, Andrew², James¹*) was born between 1805 and 1810 in Chester Co., South Carolina. He was the son of William Downing (4) and Unknown Unknown.

**23. Son Three⁵ Downing** (*William⁴, Mary³ Pagan, Andrew², James¹*) was born between 1810 and 1820 in Chester Co., South Carolina. He was the son of William Downing (4) and Unknown Unknown.

**24. Daughter⁵ Downing** (*William⁴, Mary³ Pagan, Andrew², James¹*) was born between 1810 and 1820 in Chester Co., South Carolina. She was the daughter of William Downing (4) and Unknown Unknown.

**25. Mary⁵ Downing** (*Andrew Pagan⁴, Mary³ Pagan, Andrew², James¹*) was born on July 6, 1791, in Chester Co., South Carolina. She was the daughter of Andrew Pagan Downing (5) and Elizabeth Jones. Mary died in Wayne Co., Tennessee, on April 21, 1857. She was buried in Mount Hebron Cemetery, Houston, Wayne Co., Tennessee.[16]

Never married.

**26. Katherine⁵ Downing** (*Andrew Pagan⁴, Mary³ Pagan, Andrew², James¹*) was born on August 6, 1793, in Chester Co., South Carolina. She was the daughter of Andrew Pagan Downing (5) and Elizabeth Jones.

**27. John⁵ Downing** (*Andrew Pagan⁴, Mary³ Pagan, Andrew², James¹*) was born on December 3, 1796, in Chester Co., South Carolina. He was the son of Andrew Pagan Downing (5) and Elizabeth Jones. John died in Houston, Texas Co., Missouri, on September 24, 1863.

John married **Elizabeth Hinkle** about 1819 in Madison Co., Alabama. They had six children. Elizabeth Hinkle was born in South Carolina? on January 9, 1794. Elizabeth reached age 34 and died in Wayne Co., Tennessee, on December 17,

1828. She was buried in Mount Hebron Cemetery, Houston, Wayne Co., Tennessee.[16]

John Downing married **Aly Unknown** after 1828. They had two children.

Children of John Downing and Elizabeth Hinkle:

+ 92 m I. **Andrew Porter⁶ Downing.**

+ 93 f II. **Frances⁶ Downing.**

+ 94 m III. **Jesse⁶ Downing.**

+ 95 f IV. **Elizabeth⁶ Downing.**

+ 96 m V. **Jonathan J.⁶ Downing.**

+ 97 f VI. **William Alexander⁶ Downing.**

Children of John Downing and Aly Unknown:

+ 98 m I. **John G.⁶ Downing II.**

+ 99 f II. **Eliza C.⁶ Downing.**

**28. Ann⁵ Downing** (*Andrew Pagan⁴, Mary³ Pagan, Andrew², James¹*) was born on August 12, 1799, in Chester Co., South Carolina. She was the daughter of Andrew Pagan Downing (5) and Elizabeth Jones. Ann died in Tennessee in 1855 age 55.

Ann married **Baltis Hinkle** on January 3, 1820, in Madison Co., Alabama. They had five children. Baltis Hinkle was born in South Carolina in 1797. Baltis reached age 33 and died in Wayne Co., Tennessee?, about 1830.

Ann Downing Hinkle married **Tyrance Emerson** after 1830. Tyrance Emerson was born in Chatham Co., North Carolina, about 1789. Tyrance died after 1830.

Children of Ann Downing and Baltis Hinkle:

+ 100 m I. **William⁶ Hinkle.**

+ 101 m II. **John⁶ Hinkle.**

+ 102 m III. **Alexander⁶ Hinkle.**

+ 103 f IV. **Catherine⁶ Hinkle.**

+ 104 m V. **Baltis D.⁶ Hinkle II.**

**29. Alexander⁵ Downing** (*Andrew Pagan⁴, Mary³ Pagan, Andrew², James¹*) was born on October 11, 1801, in Chester Co., South Carolina. He was the son of Andrew Pagan Downing (5) and Elizabeth Jones. Alexander died in Millersburg, Rutherford Co., Tennessee, between 1860 and 1870.

He married **Elizabeth Robinson?** They had eleven children. Elizabeth Robinson? was born in Tennessee in 1814. Elizabeth died in Rutherford Co., Tennessee?, after 1880.

Children of Alexander Downing and Elizabeth Robinson?:

| | | | |
|---|---|---|---|
| + | 105 | m | I. | **William⁶ Downing.** |
| + | 106 | f | II. | **Sarah⁶ Downing.** |
| + | 107 | m | III. | **Lafayette⁶ Downing.** |
| + | 108 | m | IV. | **Son⁶ Downing.** |
| + | 109 | m | V. | **John⁶ Downing.** |
| + | 110 | f | VI. | **Elizabeth⁶ Downing.** |
| + | 111 | m | VII. | **Robinson⁶ Downing.** |
| + | 112 | f | VIII. | **Harriet⁶ Downing.** |
| + | 113 | m | IX. | **Alexander⁶ Downing II.** |
| + | 114 | m | X. | **George B.⁶ Downing.** |
| + | 115 | m | XI. | **James M.⁶ Downing.** |

**30. William⁵ Downing** (*Andrew Pagan⁴, Mary³ Pagan, Andrew², James¹*) was born on January 2, 1803, in Chester Co., South Carolina. He was the son of Andrew Pagan Downing (5) and Elizabeth Jones. William died in Hardin Co., Tennessee, in 1872 at age 68. He was buried in Patterson Cemetery, Hardin Co., Tennessee.[20]

He married **Effa Patterson.** They had seven children. Effa Patterson was born in South Carolina? in 1809. Effa died in Hardin Co., Tennessee, after 1880. She was buried in Patterson Cemetery, Hardin Co., Tennessee? In the 1850-1880 censuses, Effa Patterson Downing's age and birthplace vary. She was born bet. 1805-1809 in either North or South Carolina.

Children of William Downing and Effa Patterson:

| | | | |
|---|---|---|---|
| + | 116 | m | I. | **John A.⁶ Downing.** |
| + | 117 | m | II. | **Peter Patterson⁶ Downing.** |
| + | 118 | m | III. | **Francis M.⁶ Downing.** |
| + | 119 | f | IV. | **Elizabeth⁶ Downing.** |
| + | 120 | f | V. | **Catherine⁶ Downing.** |
| + | 121 | f | VI. | **Mary⁶ Downing.** |
| + | 122 | f | VII. | **Flora J.⁶ Downing.** |

**31. Elizabeth⁵ Downing** (*Andrew Pagan⁴, Mary³ Pagan, Andrew², James¹*) was born on June 13, 1805, in Chester Co., South Carolina. She was the daughter of Andrew Pagan Downing (5) and Elizabeth Jones. Elizabeth died in Chester Co., South Carolina, on July 18, 1808, at age three.

**32. James⁵ Downing** (*Andrew Pagan⁴, Mary³ Pagan, Andrew², James¹*) was born on May 6, 1808, in Chester Co., South Carolina. He was the son of Andrew Pagan Downing (5) and Elizabeth Jones.

**33. Sarah⁵ Downing** (*Andrew Pagan⁴, Mary³ Pagan, Andrew², James¹*) was born on August 13, 1811, in Wayne Co., Tennessee. She was the daughter of Andrew Pagan Downing (5) and Elizabeth Jones. Sarah died in Centerville, Faulkner Co., Arkansas, on February 8, 1881, at age 69. She was buried in Woolley Cemetery, Centerville, Faulkner Co., Arkansas.[21]

Sarah married **William Riley Woolley** on December 29, 1829, in Wayne Co., Tennessee. They had eight children. William Riley Woolley was born in Kentucky on March 18, 1812. He was also known as **Riley.** William Riley reached age 46 and died in Greenbrier, Faulkner Co., Arkansas, on January 10, 1859. He was buried in Woolley Cemetery, Centerville, Faulkner Co., Arkansas.[21]

Children of Sarah Downing and William Riley Woolley:

| | | | |
|---|---|---|---|
| + | 123 | m | I. | **Albert⁶ Woolley.** |
| + | 124 | f | II. | **Elizabeth⁶ Woolley.** |
| + | 125 | m | III. | **Jonathan⁶ Woolley.** |

+ 126  m  IV.  **Andrew⁶ Woolley.**

+ 127  m  V.  **John⁶ Woolley.**

+ 128  m  VI.  **James⁶ Woolley.**

+ 129  f  VII.  **Mary⁶ Woolley.**

+ 130  f  VIII.  **Sarah⁶ Woolley.**

**34. Andrew Pagan⁵ Downing II** (*Andrew Pagan⁴, Mary³ Pagan, Andrew², James¹*) was born on June 6, 1813, in Wayne Co., Tennessee. He was the son of Andrew Pagan Downing (5) and Elizabeth Jones. Andrew Pagan died in Wayne Co., Tennessee, on October 31, 1815, at age two.

**35. Jonathan Jones⁵ Downing** (*Andrew Pagan⁴, Mary³ Pagan, Andrew², James¹*) was born on August 11, 1816, in Wayne Co., Tennessee. He was the son of Andrew Pagan Downing (5) and Elizabeth Jones. Jonathan Jones died in Lavinia, Carroll Co., Tennessee, on March 11, 1885, at age 68.

Jonathan Jones married **Flora Teresa Porter** on December 14, 1840, in Carroll Co., Tennessee. Flora Teresa Porter was born in South Carolina in 1815. Flora Teresa reached age 50 and died in Wayne Co., Tennessee, in 1865.

Jonathan Jones Downing married **Emily Jane Moore** after 1865. They had one son. Emily Jane Moore was born in Tennessee in 1827. She was also known as **Jane.** Emily Jane reached age 53 and died in Lavinia, Carroll Co., Tennessee, in 1880.

Son of Jonathan Jones Downing and Emily Jane Moore:

+ 131  m  I.  **James Madison⁶ Downing** was born in Carroll Co., Tennessee, on February 9, 1872. He died in Humboldt, Carroll Co., Tennessee, on December 4, 1958.

**36. Samuel⁵ Downing** (*John⁴, Mary³ Pagan, Andrew², James¹*) was born on April 6, 1805, in Chester, Chester Co., South Carolina. He was the son of John Downing II (6) and Margaret Ferris or Faris. Samuel died in Sebewa Twp., Ionia Co., Michigan, on July 7, 1871, at age 66. He was buried in George Washington Hoover-Allensville Cemetery, Jackson Twp., Randolph Co., Indiana.[22] In 1870, Samuel and Elizabeth Baird Downing are living in Sebewa Twp., Ionia Co., Michigan.

Samuel married **Elizabeth Baird** on September 10, 1829, in Darke Co., Ohio. They had nine children. Elizabeth Baird was born in Pennsylvania on July 17, 1808. Elizabeth reached age 75 and died in Sebewa Twp., Ionia Co., Michigan, on May 21, 1884. She was buried in Alderman Cemetery, Ionia, Ionia Twp., Ionia Co., Michigan.[26]

Children of Samuel Downing and Elizabeth Baird:

+ 132  m  I.  **John⁶ Downing** was born in Darke Co., Ohio, on July 19, 1832. He died in South Salem, Wayne Twp., Randolph Co., Indiana, on November 10, 1862. John was buried in George Washington Hoover-Allensville Cemetery, Jackson Twp., Randolph Co., Indiana.[22]

+ 133  m  II.  **Samuel Walker⁶ Downing II** was born on March 28, 1847. He died on May 14, 1935.

+ 134  f  III.  **Sarah⁶ Downing.**

+ 135  f  IV.  **Margaret Caroline⁶ Downing.**

+ 136  f  V.  **Rebecca Leona⁶ Downing.**

+ 137  m  VI.  **James Leander⁶ Downing.**

+ 138  m  VII.  **Thomas Hurst⁶ Downing.**

+ 139  m  VIII.  **Jason Jackson⁶ Downing.**

+ 140  f  IX.  **Catherine Elizabeth⁶ Downing.**

**37. Elvira⁵ Downing** (*John⁴, Mary³ Pagan, Andrew², James¹*) was born on January 17, 1807, in Chester Co., South Carolina. She was the daughter of John Downing II (6) and Margaret Ferris or Faris. Elvira died in Hollansburg, Harrison Twp., Darke Co., Ohio, on February 28, 1837, at age 30. She was buried in Hill Cemetery, New Madison, Harrison Twp., Darke Co., Ohio.[17]

She married **Ludlow Spencer.** They had two children. Ludlow Spencer was born in Greenville Twp.,

Darke Co., Ohio, on December 3, 1808. Ludlow reached age 65 and died in Harrison Twp., Darke Co., Ohio, on November 19, 1874. He was buried in Spencer Cemetery, New Madison, Harrison Twp., Darke Co., Ohio.[27]

Children of Elvira Downing and Ludlow Spencer:

+  141  m  I.    **Clark**[6] **Spencer.**

+  142  f   II.   **Margaret**[6] **Spencer.**

**38. Minerva Jane**[5] **Downing** (*John*[4], *Mary*[3] *Pagan, Andrew*[2], *James*[1]) was born on December 7, 1808, in Chester, Chester Co., South Carolina. She was the daughter of John Downing II (6) and Margaret Ferris or Faris. Minerva Jane died in German Twp., Darke Co., Ohio, on November 4, 1893, at age 84. She was buried in Hollansburg Cemetery, Hollansburg, Harrison Twp., Darke Co., Ohio.[23]

Minerva Jane married **Harvey Harrison** on August 2, 1827, in Darke Co., Ohio. They had eight children. Harvey Harrison was born in Barren Co., Kentucky, on March 16, 1804. Harvey reached age 60 and died in German Twp., Darke Co., Ohio, on February 19, 1865. He was buried in Hollansburg Cemetery, Hollansburg, Harrison Twp., Darke Co., Ohio.[12]

Children of Minerva Jane Downing and Harvey Harrison:

+  143  m  I.    **John Edward**[6] **Harrison** was born in German Twp., Darke Co., Ohio, on September 25, 1830. He died in Converse, Jackson Twp., Miami Co., Indiana, on November 28, 1911. John Edward was buried in Converse Cemetery, Converse, Richland Twp., Grant Co., Indiana.[28]

+  144  m  II.   **James M.**[6] **Harrison** was born in German Twp., Darke Co., Ohio, on April 26, 1833. He died in Greensfork Twp., Randolph Co.,

+  145  f   III.  **Mary A.**[6] **Harrison** was born in German Twp., Darke Co., Ohio, in 1835. She died after 1850.

Indiana, in 1887. James M. was buried in Hollansburg Cemetery, Hollansburg, Harrison Twp., Darke Co., Ohio.[23]

+  146  m  IV.   **Samuel J.**[6] **Harrison** was born in German Twp., Darke Co., Ohio, in 1838. He died after 1860.

+  147  m  V.    **Harvey Alexander**[6] **Harrison** was born in German Twp., Darke Co., Ohio, on October 3, 1841. He was also known as **Harry.** Harvey Alexander died in Union City, Wayne Twp., Randolph Co., Indiana, on February 3, 1917. He was buried in Union City Cemetery, Union City, Wayne Twp., Randolph Co., Indiana.[29]

+  148  m  VI.   **Wesley Leander**[6] **Harrison** was born in German Twp., Darke Co., Ohio, on June 5, 1844. He died in Greenville, Greenville Twp., Darke Co., Ohio, on March 1, 1911. Wesley Leander was buried in Greenville Union Cemetery, Greenville, Greenville Twp., Darke Co., Ohio.[30]

+  149  f   VII.  **Elizabeth**[6] **Harrison** was born in German Twp., Darke Co., Ohio, in 1847. She died after 1870.

+  150  m  VIII. **William Addison**[6] **Harrison** was born in German Twp., Darke Co., Ohio, on March 7, 1850. He died in Liberty Twp., Darke Co., Ohio, on April 20, 1929. William Addison was buried in Hollansburg Cemetery, Hollansburg, Harrison Twp., Darke Co., Ohio.[23]

**39. Jason L.**[5] **Downing** (*John*[4], *Mary*[3] *Pagan, Andrew*[2], *James*[1]) was born on April 4, 1811, in Chester Co., South Carolina. He was the son of John Downing II (6) and Margaret Ferris or Faris. Jason L. died in New Madison, Harrison Twp., Darke Co., Ohio, in 1901 at age 89. He was buried in Green Mound

Cemetery, New Madison, Harrison Twp., Darke Co., Ohio.[24]

Jason L. married **Rebecca Jane Baird** on December 16, 1841, in Darke Co., Ohio. They had six children. Rebecca Jane Baird was born in Butler Twp., Darke Co., Ohio, on August 29, 1822. Rebecca Jane reached age 67 and died in New Madison, Harrison Twp., Darke Co., Ohio, on August 12, 1890. She was buried in Green Mound Cemetery, New Madison, Harrison Twp., Darke Co., Ohio.[24]

Children of Jason L. Downing and Rebecca Jane Baird:

+ 151  m  I.    **Robert Fulton⁶ Downing.**

+ 152  m  II.   **Samuel⁶ Downing.**

+ 153  f   III.  **Margaret J.⁶ Downing.**

+ 154  m  IV.   **George W.⁶ Downing.**

+ 155  f   V.    **Sarah C.⁶ Downing.**

+ 156  f   VI.   **Fannie Elizabeth⁶ Downing.**

40. **John Edward⁵ Downing II** (*John⁴, Mary³ Pagan, Andrew², James¹*) was born on January 19, 1813, in Chester Co., South Carolina. He was the son of John Downing II (6) and Margaret Ferris or Faris. John Edward died in New Madison, Harrison Twp., Darke Co., Ohio, on October 27, 1872, at age. He was buried in First Universalist Church Cemetery, New Madison, Harrison Twp., Darke Co., Ohio.[25]

John Edward married **Jane White** in 1837 in Darke Co., Ohio. Jane died before 1842.

John Edward Downing II married **Sarah Mordah Morrison** about 1842. They had five children. Sarah Mordah Morrison was born in South Carolina in 1815. Sarah Mordah died after 1870.

Children of John Edward Downing II and Sarah Mordah Morrison:

+ 157  f   I.    **Louisa⁶ Downing.**

+ 158  f   II.   **Mary⁶ Downing.**

+ 159  f   III.  **Melissa⁶ Downing.**

+ 160  m  IV.   **James L.⁶ Downing.**

+ 161  f   V.    **Margaret⁶ Downing.**

41. **Robert J.⁵ Downing** (*John⁴, Mary³ Pagan, Andrew², James¹*) was born on June 10, 1815, in Bourbon Co., Kentucky. He was the son of John Downing II (6) and Margaret Ferris or Faris. Robert J. died in Harrison Twp., Darke Co., Ohio, on December 4, 1888, at age 73. He was buried in Hollansburg Cemetery, Hollansburg, Harrison Twp., Darke Co., Ohio.[23]

Robert J. married **Indiana Baird** on June 12, 1836, in Darke Co., Ohio. They had ten children. Indiana Baird was born in Indiana on October 6, 1817. Indiana reached age 60 and died in New Madison, Harrison Twp., Darke Co., Ohio, on October 2, 1878. She was buried in First Universalist Church Cemetery, New Madison, Harrison Twp., Darke Co., Ohio.[25]

Children of Robert J. Downing and Indiana Baird:

+ 162  f   I.    **Elizabeth⁶ Downing.**

+ 163  m  II.   **Andrew J.⁶ Downing.**

+ 164  m  III.  **John M.⁶ Downing.**

+ 165  f   IV.   **Margaret⁶ Downing.**

+ 166  f   V.    **Demaris A.⁶ Downing.**

+ 167  f   VI.   **Amanda Ellen⁶ Downing.**

+ 168  m  VII.  **Jason L.⁶ Downing.**

+ 169  f   VIII. **Elvira A.⁶ Downing.**

+ 170  f   IX.   **Melissa⁶ Downing.**

+ 171  f   X.    **Lilla⁶ Downing.**

42. **Sarah⁵ Downing** (*Robert Gill⁴, Mary³ Pagan, Andrew², James¹*) was born on July 21, 1807, in White Co., Tennessee? She was the daughter of Robert Gill Downing (8) and Sarah Unknown. Sarah died in Indiana on March 26, 1845, at age 37.

43. **Mary Ann⁵ Downing** (*Robert Gill⁴, Mary³ Pagan, Andrew², James¹*) was born in 1813 in White Co., Tennessee? She was the daughter of Robert Gill Downing (8) and Sarah Unknown.

**44. Andrew Jackson⁵ Downing** (*Robert Gill⁴, Mary³ Pagan, Andrew², James¹*) was born in 1815 in White Co., Tennessee. He was the son of Robert Gill Downing (8) and Sarah Unknown. Andrew Jackson lived in 1850 in Bloomington, McLean Co., Illinois. He also resided in 1860 in Bonham, Fannin Co., Texas. Andrew Jackson was living in 1870 in Jefferson, Marion Co., Texas. He died in Maple Hill, Wabaunsee Co., Kansas?, after 1880.

Andrew Jackson married **Mary Rodgers** on February 8, 1836, in Vigo Co., Indiana. They had ten children. Mary Rodgers was born in New York in 1817. Mary died in Texas? after 1870.

Children of Andrew Jackson Downing and Mary Rodgers:

+  172  m  I.      **Watts⁶ Downing.**

+  173  f  II.     **Ann⁶ Downing.**

+  174  f  III.    **Emma⁶ Downing.**

+  175  f  IV.     **Mary⁶ Downing.**

+  176  f  V.      **Laura⁶ Downing.**

+  177  m  VI.     **Andrew J.⁶ Downing II.**

+  178  m  VII.    **George⁶ Downing.**

+  179  f  VIII.   **Lida⁶ Downing.**

+  180  f  IX.     **Margaret⁶ Downing.**

+  181  f  X.      **Josephine⁶ Downing.**

**45. Amanda Jane⁵ Downing** (*Robert Gill⁴, Mary³ Pagan, Andrew², James¹*) was born on January 25, 1817, in White Co., Tennessee. She was the daughter of Robert Gill Downing (8) and Sarah Unknown. Amanda Jane died in Darke Co., Ohio, on February 13, 1872, at age 55.

Amanda Jane married **Milton Hill** on November 14, 1839, in Darke Co., Ohio. They had eight children. Milton Hill was born in Harrison Twp., Darke Co., Ohio?, on February 10, 1820.

Children of Amanda Jane Downing and Milton Hill:

+  182  m  I.      **Alfred⁶ Hill.**

+  183  m  II.     **Joseph⁶ Hill.**

+  184  m  III.    **Asa⁶ Hill.**

+  185  f  IV.     **Sarah⁶ Hill.**

+  186  f  V.      **Melinda⁶ Hill.**

+  187  m  VI.     **Ezra⁶ Hill.**

+  188  f  VII.    **Martha⁶ Hill.**

+  189  f  VIII.   **Mary Ella⁶ Hill.**

**46. Joseph Herr⁵ Downing** (*Robert Gill⁴, Mary³ Pagan, Andrew², James¹*) was born in 1822 in White Co., Tennessee. He was the son of Robert Gill Downing (8) and Sarah Unknown. Joseph Herr died in Washington Twp., Putnam Co., Indiana?, after 1860.

He married **Elisabeth Unknown.** They had five children. Elisabeth Unknown was born in Ohio in 1831. Elisabeth died after 1860.

Children of Joseph Herr Downing and Elisabeth Unknown:

+  190  m  I.      **Alexander⁶ Downing.**

+  191  f  II.     **Mary A.⁶ Downing.**

+  192  f  III.    **Sarah E.⁶ Downing.**

+  193  f  IV.     **Emma⁶ Downing.**

+  194  m  V.      **William⁶ Downing.**

**47. Robert⁵ Downing II** (*Robert Gill⁴, Mary³ Pagan, Andrew², James¹*) was born in 1828 in White Co., Tennessee. He was the son of Robert Gill Downing (8) and Sarah Unknown. Robert lived in 1850 in Funks Grove Twp., McLean Co., Illinois. He died in Washington Twp., Putnam Co., Indiana?, after 1860.

Robert married **Barbara Shaffer** on March 18, 1847, in Owen Co., Indiana. They had five children. Barbara Shaffer was born in Indiana in 1829. Barbara died after 1860.

Children of Robert Downing II and Barbara Shaffer:

+  195  f  I.      **Amanda Jane⁶ Downing.**

+ 196  m  II.  **William J.⁶ Downing.**

+ 197  f  III.  **Sarah S.⁶ Downing.**.

+ 198  f  IV.  **Emma A.⁶ Downing.**

+ 199  m  V.  **Andrew R.⁶ Downing.**

**48. Esther Eleanor⁵ Downing** (*Robert Gill⁴, Mary³ Pagan, Andrew², James¹*) was born in White Co., Tennessee. She is the daughter of Robert Gill Downing (8) and Sarah Unknown.

**49. Jesse⁵ Hinkle** (*Sarah⁴ Downing, Mary³ Pagan, Andrew², James¹*) was born on June 10, 1814, in Chester, Chester Co., South Carolina. He was the son of William Hinkle and Sarah Downing (11). Jesse died in Lunenburg, Izard Co., Arkansas, on May 22, 1891, at age 76.

**50. John Downing⁵ Hinkle** (*Sarah⁴ Downing, Mary³ Pagan, Andrew², James¹*) was born on June 26, 1816, in Wayne Co., Tennessee. He was the son of William Hinkle and Sarah Downing (11). John Downing died in Melbourne, Izard Co., Arkansas, on September 1, 1852, at age 36.

**51. Andrew J.⁵ Hinkle** (*Sarah⁴ Downing, Mary³ Pagan, Andrew², James¹*) was born on February 24, 1818, in Wayne Co., Tennessee. He was the son of William Hinkle and Sarah Downing (11). Andrew J. died in Mountain View, Stone Co., Arkansas, in 1870 at age 51. He was buried in Flatwoods Cemetery, Mountain View, Stone Co., Arkansas.[18]

Andrew J. married **Mary Majors** on September 14, 1845. Mary Majors was born in November 1819. Mary reached age 90 and died on November 2, 1909. She was buried in Flatwoods Cemetery, Mountain View, Stone Co., Arkansas.[18]

**52. Catherine⁵ Hinkle** (*Sarah⁴ Downing, Mary³ Pagan, Andrew², James¹*) was born on December 26, 1819, in Madison Co., Alabama. She was the daughter of William Hinkle and Sarah Downing (11). Catherine died in Mountain View, Stone Co., Arkansas, on November 11, 1863, at age 43. She was buried in Flatwoods Cemetery, Mountain View, Stone Co., Arkansas.[18]

She married **Joshua Mayberry Beckham.** Joshua Mayberry Beckham was born in Orange Co, North Carolina, on May 14, 1815. Joshua Mayberry reached age 72 and died in Mountain View, Stone Co., Arkansas, on February 3, 1888. He was buried in Flatwoods Cemetery, Mountain View, Stone Co., Arkansas.[18]

**53. Mary Jane⁵ Hinkle** (*Sarah⁴ Downing, Mary³ Pagan, Andrew², James¹*) was born on June 14, 1821, in Wayne Co., Tennessee. She was the daughter of William Hinkle and Sarah Downing (11). Mary Jane died in Irons Point, Izard Co., Arkansas, on June 3, 1877, at age 55. She was buried in Flatwoods Cemetery, Mountain View, Stone Co., Arkansas.[18]

She married **Tinsley Dill Martin.** They had six children. Tinsley Dill Martin was born in Tennessee on April 11, 1825. Tinsley Dill reached age 75 and died in Mountain View, Stone Co., Arkansas, on May 4, 1900. He was buried in Flatwoods Cemetery, Mountain View, Stone Co., Arkansas.[18]

Children of Mary Jane Hinkle and Tinsley Dill Martin:

+ 200  f  I.  **Permelia⁶ Martin.**

+ 201  m  II.  **William Taylor⁶ Martin.**

+ 202  f  III.  **Sarah Frances⁶ Martin.**

+ 203  m  IV.  **John Dill⁶ Martin.**

+ 204  f  V.  **Amanda⁶ Martin.**

+ 205  m  VI.  **Owen Hunt⁶ Martin.**

**54. Francis M.⁵ Hinkle** (*Sarah⁴ Downing, Mary³ Pagan, Andrew², James¹*) was born on November 18, 1826, in Madison Co., Alabama. She was the daughter of William Hinkle and Sarah Downing (11). Francis M. died in Blue Mountain, Stone Co., Arkansas, on September 12, 1870, at age 43. She was buried in Flatwoods Cemetery, Mountain View, Stone Co., Arkansas.[18]

Never married.

**55. William Riley⁵ Hinkle** (*Sarah⁴ Downing, Mary³ Pagan, Andrew², James¹*) was born on October 7, 1828, in Wayne Co., Tennessee. He was the son of William Hinkle and Sarah Downing (11). William Riley died in Blue Mountain, Stone Co., Arkansas, on February 25, 1902, at age 73.

He married **Frances Melissa Majors.** They had four children. Frances Melissa Majors was born in Tennessee on December 3, 1835. Frances Melissa reached age 41 and died in Blue Mountain, Stone Co., Arkansas, on September 14, 1877. She was buried in Flatwoods Cemetery, Mountain View, Stone Co., Arkansas.[18]

William Riley Hinkle married **Mary F. Taylor** before 1846. They had one daughter. Mary F. Taylor was born on November 30, 1826. Mary F. reached age 29 and died in Blue Mountain, Izard Co., Arkansas?, on October 28, 1856. She was buried in Flatwoods Cemetery, Mountain View, Stone Co., Arkansas.[18]

William Riley Hinkle married **Nancy L. Byler** before 1880. Nancy L. Byler was born in Tennessee on December 10, 1833. Nancy L. reached age 70 and died in Blue Mountain, Stone Co., Arkansas, on November 9, 1904. She was buried in Flatwoods Cemetery, Mountain View, Stone Co., Arkansas.[18]

Children of William Riley Hinkle and Frances Melissa Majors:

+  206  m  I.    **Jesse[6] Hinkle.**

+  207  m  II.   **Joshua[6] Hinkle.**

+  208  m  III.  **Andrew[6] Hinkle.**

+  209  f  IV.   **Cora Dell[6] Hinkle.**

Daughter of William Riley Hinkle and Mary F. Taylor:

+  210  f  I.    **Catherine[6] Hinkle.** was born in Tennessee in 1846.

## 6th Generation

**56. Mary**[6] **Jones** (*William H.*[5], *Elizabeth*[4] *Downing, Mary*[3] *Pagan, Andrew*[2], *James*[1]). She was the daughter of William H. Jones (12) and Juliet Granville Porter.

**57. Samuel**[6] **Jones** (*William H.*[5], *Elizabeth*[4] *Downing, Mary*[3] *Pagan, Andrew*[2], *James*[1]). He was the son of William H. Jones (12) and Juliet Granville Porter.

**58. Eliza Katherine**[6] **Porter** (*Mary*[5] *Jones, Elizabeth*[4] *Downing, Mary*[3] *Pagan, Andrew*[2], *James*[1]). She was the daughter of Robert Brownfield Porter and Mary Jones (14).

**59. Mary H.**[6] **Porter** (*Mary*[5] *Jones, Elizabeth*[4] *Downing, Mary*[3] *Pagan, Andrew*[2], *James*[1]). She was the daughter of Robert Brownfield Porter and Mary Jones (14).

**60. James Jones**[6] **Porter** (*Mary*[5] *Jones, Elizabeth*[4] *Downing, Mary*[3] *Pagan, Andrew*[2], *James*[1]). He was the son of Robert Brownfield Porter and Mary Jones (14).

**61. David Brownfield**[6] **Porter** (*Mary*[5] *Jones, Elizabeth*[4] *Downing, Mary*[3] *Pagan, Andrew*[2], *James*[1]). He was the son of Robert Brownfield Porter and Mary Jones (14).

**62. William S.**[6] **Porter** (*Mary*[5] *Jones, Elizabeth*[4] *Downing, Mary*[3] *Pagan, Andrew*[2], *James*[1]). He was the son of Robert Brownfield Porter and Mary Jones (14).

**63. Amanda Jane**[6] **Porter** (*Mary*[5] *Jones, Elizabeth*[4] *Downing, Mary*[3] *Pagan, Andrew*[2], *James*[1]). She was the daughter of Robert Brownfield Porter and Mary Jones (14).

**64. Juliet Ann**[6] **Porter** (*Mary*[5] *Jones, Elizabeth*[4] *Downing, Mary*[3] *Pagan, Andrew*[2], *James*[1]). She was the daughter of Robert Brownfield Porter and Mary Jones (14).

**65. Sarah A.**[6] **Porter** (*Mary*[5] *Jones, Elizabeth*[4] *Downing, Mary*[3] *Pagan, Andrew*[2], *James*[1]). She was the daughter of Robert Brownfield Porter and Mary Jones (14).

**66. Martha Louise**[6] **Porter** (*Mary*[5] *Jones, Elizabeth*[4] *Downing, Mary*[3] *Pagan, Andrew*[2], *James*[1]). She was the daughter of Robert Brownfield Porter and Mary Jones (14).

**67. Mary**[6] **Dunlap** (*Elizabeth*[5] *Jones, Elizabeth*[4] *Downing, Mary*[3] *Pagan, Andrew*[2], *James*[1]). She was the daughter of John Dunlap and Elizabeth Jones (16).

**68. Catherine**[6] **Dunlap** (*Elizabeth*[5] *Jones, Elizabeth*[4] *Downing, Mary*[3] *Pagan, Andrew*[2], *James*[1]). She was the daughter of John Dunlap and Elizabeth Jones (16).

**69. Anna**[6] **Dunlap** (*Elizabeth*[5] *Jones, Elizabeth*[4] *Downing, Mary*[3] *Pagan, Andrew*[2], *James*[1]). She was the daughter of John Dunlap and Elizabeth Jones (16).

**70. Sarah**[6] **Dunlap** (*Elizabeth*[5] *Jones, Elizabeth*[4] *Downing, Mary*[3] *Pagan, Andrew*[2], *James*[1]). She was the daughter of John Dunlap and Elizabeth Jones (16).

**71. John**[6] **Dunlap II** (*Elizabeth*[5] *Jones, Elizabeth*[4] *Downing, Mary*[3] *Pagan, Andrew*[2], *James*[1]). He was the son of John Dunlap and Elizabeth Jones (16).

**72. William O.**[6] **Montgomery** (*Sarah Carson*[5] *Jones, Elizabeth*[4] *Downing, Mary*[3] *Pagan, Andrew*[2], *James*[1]). He was the son of George Montgomery and Sarah Carson Jones (18).

**73. Thomas VanBuren**[6] **Montgomery** (*Sarah Carson*[5] *Jones, Elizabeth*[4] *Downing, Mary*[3] *Pagan, Andrew*[2], *James*[1]). He was the son of George Montgomery and Sarah Carson Jones (18).

**74. Jane C.**[6] **Montgomery** (*Sarah Carson*[5] *Jones, Elizabeth*[4] *Downing, Mary*[3] *Pagan, Andrew*[2], *James*[1]). She was the daughter of George Montgomery and Sarah Carson Jones (18).

**75. Caroline Jeanette**[6] **Montgomery** (*Sarah Carson*[5] *Jones, Elizabeth*[4] *Downing, Mary*[3] *Pagan, Andrew*[2], *James*[1]). She was the daughter of George Montgomery and Sarah Carson Jones (18).

**76. Sarah E.**[6] **Montgomery** (*Sarah Carson*[5] *Jones, Elizabeth*[4] *Downing, Mary*[3] *Pagan, Andrew*[2], *James*[1]). She was the daughter of George Montgomery and Sarah Carson Jones (18).

77. **Samuel Johnson⁶ Montgomery** (*Sarah Carson⁵ Jones, Elizabeth⁴ Downing, Mary³ Pagan, Andrew², James¹*). He was the son of George Montgomery and Sarah Carson Jones (18).

78. **Rebecca⁶ Montgomery** (*Sarah Carson⁵ Jones, Elizabeth⁴ Downing, Mary³ Pagan, Andrew², James¹*). She was the daughter of George Montgomery and Sarah Carson Jones (18).

79. **George W.⁶ Montgomery II** (*Sarah Carson⁵ Jones, Elizabeth⁴ Downing, Mary³ Pagan, Andrew², James¹*). He was the son of George Montgomery and Sarah Carson Jones (18).

80. **Mary A.⁶ Montgomery** (*Sarah Carson⁵ Jones, Elizabeth⁴ Downing, Mary³ Pagan, Andrew², James¹*). She was the daughter of George Montgomery and Sarah Carson Jones (18).

81. **Adalise⁶ Montgomery** (*Ann⁵ Jones, Elizabeth⁴ Downing, Mary³ Pagan, Andrew², James¹*). She was the daughter of William Montgomery and Ann Jones (19).

82. **Mary E.⁶ Montgomery** (*Ann⁵ Jones, Elizabeth⁴ Downing, Mary³ Pagan, Andrew², James¹*). She was the daughter of William Montgomery and Ann Jones (19).

83. **Samuel Granville⁶ Montgomery** (*Ann⁵ Jones, Elizabeth⁴ Downing, Mary³ Pagan, Andrew², James¹*). He was the son of William Montgomery and Ann Jones (19).

84. **William H.⁶ Montgomery II** (*Ann⁵ Jones, Elizabeth⁴ Downing, Mary³ Pagan, Andrew², James¹*). He was the son of William Montgomery and Ann Jones (19).

85. **Thomas P.⁶ Montgomery** (*Ann⁵ Jones, Elizabeth⁴ Downing, Mary³ Pagan, Andrew², James¹*). He was the son of William Montgomery and Ann Jones (19).

86. **John L.⁶ Montgomery** (*Ann⁵ Jones, Elizabeth⁴ Downing, Mary³ Pagan, Andrew², James¹*). He was the son of William Montgomery and Ann Jones (19).

87. **William Downing⁶ Jones** (*John Downing⁵, Elizabeth⁴ Downing, Mary³ Pagan, Andrew², James¹*) was born in 1836 in Fishing Creek, Chester Co., South Carolina. He was the son of John Downing Jones (20) and Ann McDowell.

88. **Thomas Edwin⁶ Jones** (*John Downing⁵, Elizabeth⁴ Downing, Mary³ Pagan, Andrew², James¹*) was born in 1839 in Carroll Co., Tennessee. He was the son of John Downing Jones (20) and Ann McDowell.

89. **James⁶ Jones** (*John Downing⁵, Elizabeth⁴ Downing, Mary³ Pagan, Andrew², James¹*) was born in 1842 in Carroll Co., Tennessee. He was the son of John Downing Jones (20) and Ann McDowell.

90. **John R.⁶ Jones** (*John Downing⁵, Elizabeth⁴ Downing, Mary³ Pagan, Andrew², James¹*) was born in 1844 in Carroll Co., Tennessee. He was the son of John Downing Jones (20) and Ann McDowell.

91. **J. Harve⁶ Jones** (*John Downing⁵, Elizabeth⁴ Downing, Mary³ Pagan, Andrew², James¹*) was born in 1847 in Carroll Co., Tennessee. He was the son of John Downing Jones (20) and Ann McDowell.

92. **Andrew Porter⁶ Downing** (*John⁵, Andrew Pagan⁴, Mary³ Pagan, Andrew², James¹*). He was the son of John Downing (27) and Elizabeth Hinkle.

93. **Frances⁶ Downing** (*John⁵, Andrew Pagan⁴, Mary³ Pagan, Andrew², James¹*). She was the daughter of John Downing (27) and Elizabeth Hinkle.

94. **Jesse⁶ Downing** (*John⁵, Andrew Pagan⁴, Mary³ Pagan, Andrew², James¹*). He was the son of John Downing (27) and Elizabeth Hinkle.

95. **Elizabeth⁶ Downing** (*John⁵, Andrew Pagan⁴, Mary³ Pagan, Andrew², James¹*). She was the daughter of John Downing (27) and Elizabeth Hinkle.

96. **Jonathan J.⁶ Downing** (*John⁵, Andrew Pagan⁴, Mary³ Pagan, Andrew², James¹*). He was the son of John Downing (27) and Elizabeth Hinkle.

97. **William Alexander⁶ Downing** (*John⁵, Andrew Pagan⁴, Mary³ Pagan, Andrew², James¹*). She was the daughter of John Downing (27) and Elizabeth Hinkle.

98. **John G.⁶ Downing II** (*John⁵, Andrew Pagan⁴, Mary³ Pagan, Andrew², James¹*). He was the son of John Downing (27) and Aly Unknown.

99. **Eliza C.**[6] **Downing** (*John*[5], *Andrew Pagan*[4], *Mary*[3] *Pagan, Andrew*[2], *James*[1]). She was the daughter of John Downing (27) and Aly Unknown.

100. **William**[6] **Hinkle** (*Ann*[5] *Downing, Andrew Pagan*[4], *Mary*[3] *Pagan, Andrew*[2], *James*[1]). He was the son of Baltis Hinkle and Ann Downing (28).

101. **John**[6] **Hinkle** (*Ann*[5] *Downing, Andrew Pagan*[4], *Mary*[3] *Pagan, Andrew*[2], *James*[1]). He was the son of Baltis Hinkle and Ann Downing (28).

102. **Alexander**[6] **Hinkle** (*Ann*[5] *Downing, Andrew Pagan*[4], *Mary*[3] *Pagan, Andrew*[2], *James*[1]). He was the son of Baltis Hinkle and Ann Downing (28).

103. **Catherine**[6] **Hinkle** (*Ann*[5] *Downing, Andrew Pagan*[4], *Mary*[3] *Pagan, Andrew*[2], *James*[1]). She was the daughter of Baltis Hinkle and Ann Downing (28).

104. **Baltis D.**[6] **Hinkle II** (*Ann*[5] *Downing, Andrew Pagan*[4], *Mary*[3] *Pagan, Andrew*[2], *James*[1]). He was the son of Baltis Hinkle and Ann Downing (28).

105. **William**[6] **Downing** (*Alexander*[5], *Andrew Pagan*[4], *Mary*[3] *Pagan, Andrew*[2], *James*[1]). He was the son of Alexander Downing (29) and Elizabeth Robinson?

106. **Sarah**[6] **Downing** (*Alexander*[5], *Andrew Pagan*[4], *Mary*[3] *Pagan, Andrew*[2], *James*[1]). She was the daughter of Alexander Downing (29) and Elizabeth Robinson?

107. **Lafayette**[6] **Downing** (*Alexander*[5], *Andrew Pagan*[4], *Mary*[3] *Pagan, Andrew*[2], *James*[1]). He was the son of Alexander Downing (29) and Elizabeth Robinson?

108. **Son**[6] **Downing** (*Alexander*[5], *Andrew Pagan*[4], *Mary*[3] *Pagan, Andrew*[2], *James*[1]). He was the son of Alexander Downing (29) and Elizabeth Robinson?

109. **John**[6] **Downing** (*Alexander*[5], *Andrew Pagan*[4], *Mary*[3] *Pagan, Andrew*[2], *James*[1]). He was the son of Alexánder Downing (29) and Elizabeth Robinson?

110. **Elizabeth**[6] **Downing** (*Alexander*[5], *Andrew Pagan*[4], *Mary*[3] *Pagan, Andrew*[2], *James*[1]). She was the daughter of Alexander Downing (29) and Elizabeth Robinson?

111. **Robinson**[6] **Downing** (*Alexander*[5], *Andrew Pagan*[4], *Mary*[3] *Pagan, Andrew*[2], *James*[1]). He was the son of Alexander Downing (29) and Elizabeth Robinson?

112. **Harriet**[6] **Downing** (*Alexander*[5], *Andrew Pagan*[4], *Mary*[3] *Pagan, Andrew*[2], *James*[1]). She was the daughter of Alexander Downing (29) and Elizabeth Robinson?

113. **Alexander**[6] **Downing II** (*Alexander*[5], *Andrew Pagan*[4], *Mary*[3] *Pagan, Andrew*[2], *James*[1]). He was the son of Alexander Downing (29) and Elizabeth Robinson?

114. **George B.**[6] **Downing** (*Alexander*[5], *Andrew Pagan*[4], *Mary*[3] *Pagan, Andrew*[2], *James*[1]). He was the son of Alexander Downing (29) and Elizabeth Robinson?

115. **James M.**[6] **Downing** (*Alexander*[5], *Andrew Pagan*[4], *Mary*[3] *Pagan, Andrew*[2], *James*[1]). He was the son of Alexander Downing (29) and Elizabeth Robinson?

116. **John A.**[6] **Downing** (*William*[5], *Andrew Pagan*[4], *Mary*[3] *Pagan, Andrew*[2], *James*[1]). He was the son of William Downing (30) and Effa Patterson.

117. **Peter Patterson**[6] **Downing** (*William*[5], *Andrew Pagan*[4], *Mary*[3] *Pagan, Andrew*[2], *James*[1]). He was the son of William Downing (30) and Effa Patterson.

118. **Francis M.**[6] **Downing** (*William*[5], *Andrew Pagan*[4], *Mary*[3] *Pagan, Andrew*[2], *James*[1]). He was the son of William Downing (30) and Effa Patterson.

119. **Elizabeth**[6] **Downing** (*William*[5], *Andrew Pagan*[4], *Mary*[3] *Pagan, Andrew*[2], *James*[1]). She was the daughter of William Downing (30) and Effa Patterson.

120. **Catherine**[6] **Downing** (*William*[5], *Andrew Pagan*[4], *Mary*[3] *Pagan, Andrew*[2], *James*[1]). She was the daughter of William Downing (30) and Effa Patterson.

121. **Mary**[6] **Downing** (*William*[5], *Andrew Pagan*[4], *Mary*[3] *Pagan, Andrew*[2], *James*[1]). She was the daughter of William Downing (30) and Effa Patterson.

122. **Flora J.**[6] **Downing** (*William*[5], *Andrew Pagan*[4], *Mary*[3] *Pagan, Andrew*[2], *James*[1]). She was the daughter of William Downing (30) and Effa Patterson.

123. **Albert**[6] **Woolley** (*Sarah*[5] *Downing, Andrew Pagan*[4], *Mary*[3] *Pagan, Andrew*[2], *James*[1]). He was the son of William Riley Woolley and Sarah Downing (33).

124. **Elizabeth**[6] **Woolley** (*Sarah*[5] *Downing, Andrew Pagan*[4], *Mary*[3] *Pagan, Andrew*[2], *James*[1]). She was the daughter of William Riley Woolley and Sarah Downing (33).

125. **Jonathan**[6] **Woolley** (*Sarah*[5] *Downing, Andrew Pagan*[4], *Mary*[3] *Pagan, Andrew*[2], *James*[1]). He was the son of William Riley Woolley and Sarah Downing (33).

126. **Andrew**[6] **Woolley** (*Sarah*[5] *Downing, Andrew Pagan*[4], *Mary*[3] *Pagan, Andrew*[2], *James*[1]). He was the son of William Riley Woolley and Sarah Downing (33).

127. **John**[6] **Woolley** (*Sarah*[5] *Downing, Andrew Pagan*[4], *Mary*[3] *Pagan, Andrew*[2], *James*[1]). He was the son of William Riley Woolley and Sarah Downing (33).

128. **James**[6] **Woolley** (*Sarah*[5] *Downing, Andrew Pagan*[4], *Mary*[3] *Pagan, Andrew*[2], *James*[1]). He was the son of William Riley Woolley and Sarah Downing (33).

129. **Mary**[6] **Woolley** (*Sarah*[5] *Downing, Andrew Pagan*[4], *Mary*[3] *Pagan, Andrew*[2], *James*[1]). She was the daughter of William Riley Woolley and Sarah Downing (33).

130. **Sarah**[6] **Woolley** (*Sarah*[5] *Downing, Andrew Pagan*[4], *Mary*[3] *Pagan, Andrew*[2], *James*[1]). She was the daughter of William Riley Woolley and Sarah Downing (33).

131. **James Madison**[6] **Downing** (*Jonathan Jones*[5], *Andrew Pagan*[4], *Mary*[3] *Pagan, Andrew*[2], *James*[1]) was born on February 9, 1872, in Carroll Co., Tennessee. He was the son of Jonathan Jones Downing (35) and Emily Jane Moore. James Madison died in Humboldt, Carroll Co., Tennessee, on December 4, 1958, at age 86.

132. **John**[6] **Downing** (*Samuel*[5], *John*[4], *Mary*[3] *Pagan, Andrew*[2], *James*[1]) was born on July 19, 1832, in Darke Co., Ohio. He was the son of Samuel Downing (36) and Elizabeth Baird. John died in South Salem, Wayne Twp., Randolph Co., Indiana, on November 10, 1862, at age 30. He was buried in George Washington Hoover-Allensville Cemetery, Jackson Twp., Randolph Co., Indiana.[22]

John married **Sarah Gullett** on March 14, 1853, in Ionia Co., Michigan. They had four children. Sarah Gullett was born in Ohio on August 15, 1828. Sarah reached age 83 and died in Sebewa Twp., Ionia Co., Michigan, on June 22, 1912. She was buried in West Sebewa Cemetery, Lake Odessa, Odessa Twp., Ionia Co., Michigan.[31]

Children of John Downing and Sarah Gullett:

+ 211  f  I.  **Florence Lucille**[7] **Downing** was born in Wayne Twp., Randolph Co., Indiana, on May 22, 1854. She died in Tremain's corners, Orange Twp., Ionia Co., Michigan, on March 24, 1904. Florence Lucille was buried in Letts Cemetery, Ionia, Ionia Twp., Ionia Co., Michigan.[32]

+ 212  f  II.  **Alpharetta L.**[7] **Downing** was born in Wayne Twp., Randolph Co., Indiana, on August 20, 1857. She died in Belding, Otisco Twp., Ionia Co., Michigan, on March 12, 1939. Alpharetta L. was buried in West Sebewa Cemetery, Lake Odessa, Odessa Twp., Ionia Co., Michigan.[31]

+ 213  m  III.  **Samuel M.**[7] **Downing** was born in South Salem, Wayne Twp., Randolph Co., Indiana, in August 1859. He died in Ionia, Ionia Twp., Ionia Co., Michigan, on March 13, 1933. Samuel M. was buried in West Sebewa Cemetery, Lake Odessa, Odessa Twp., Ionia Co., Michigan.[31]

+ 214  m  IV.  **Ezekiel John**[7] **Downing** was born in South Salem, Wayne Twp., Randolph Co., Indiana, on January 3, 1861. He died in Lake Odessa, Odessa Twp., Ionia Co., Michigan, in December 1951.

133. **Samuel Walker**[6] **Downing II** (*Samuel*[5], *John*[4], *Mary*[3] *Pagan, Andrew*[2], *James*[1]) was born on March 28, 1847. He was the son of Samuel Downing (36) and Elizabeth Baird. Samuel Walker died on May 14, 1935, at age 88.

**134. Sarah⁶ Downing** (*Samuel⁵, John⁴, Mary³ Pagan, Andrew², James¹*). She was the daughter of Samuel Downing (36) and Elizabeth Baird.

She married **Unknown Williams.**

**135. Margaret Caroline⁶ Downing** (*Samuel⁵, John⁴, Mary³ Pagan, Andrew², James¹*). She was the daughter of Samuel Downing (36) and Elizabeth Baird.

She married **Unknown Peacock.**

**136. Rebecca Leona⁶ Downing** (*Samuel⁵, John⁴, Mary³ Pagan, Andrew², James¹*). She was the daughter of Samuel Downing (36) and Elizabeth Baird.

She married **Enos Polly.**

**137. James Leander⁶ Downing** (*Samuel⁵, John⁴, Mary³ Pagan, Andrew², James¹*). He was the son of Samuel Downing (36) and Elizabeth Baird.

**138. Thomas Hurst⁶ Downing** (*Samuel⁵, John⁴, Mary³ Pagan, Andrew², James¹*). He was the son of Samuel Downing (36) and Elizabeth Baird.

**139. Jason Jackson⁶ Downing** (*Samuel⁵, John⁴, Mary³ Pagan, Andrew², James¹*). He was the son of Samuel Downing (36) and Elizabeth Baird.

**140. Catherine Elizabeth⁶ Downing** (*Samuel⁵, John⁴, Mary³ Pagan, Andrew², James¹*). She was the daughter of Samuel Downing (36) and Elizabeth Baird.

She married **Unknown Peacock.**

**141. Clark⁶ Spencer** (*Elvira⁵ Downing, John⁴, Mary³ Pagan, Andrew², James¹*). He was the son of Ludlow Spencer and Elvira Downing (37).

**142. Margaret⁶ Spencer** (*Elvira⁵ Downing, John⁴, Mary³ Pagan, Andrew², James¹*). She was the daughter of Ludlow Spencer and Elvira Downing (37).

**143. John Edward⁶ Harrison** (*Minerva Jane⁵ Downing, John⁴, Mary³ Pagan, Andrew², James¹*) was born on September 25, 1830, in German Twp., Darke Co., Ohio. He was the son of Harvey Harrison and Minerva Jane Downing (38). John Edward died in Converse, Jackson Twp., Miami Co., Indiana, on November 28, 1911, at age 81. He was buried in Converse Cemetery, Converse, Richland Twp., Grant Co., Indiana.[28]

He married **Harriet Benson.** They had two daughters. Harriet Benson was born in Harrison Twp., Darke Co., Ohio, on March 14, 1838. Harriet reached age 76 and died in Peru, Peru Twp., Miami Co., Indiana, on March 19, 1914. She was buried in Converse Cemetery, Converse, Richland Twp., Grant Co., Indiana.[28]

Daughters of John Edward Harrison and Harriet Benson:

+ 215 f I. **Minerva Ida⁷ Harrison** was born in Harrison Twp., Darke Co., Ohio, on March 25, 1856. She was also known as **Ida.** Minerva Ida died in Converse, Jackson Twp., Miami Co., Indiana, on January 27, 1890. She was buried in Converse Cemetery, Converse, Richland Twp., Grant Co., Indiana.[28]

+ 216 f II. **Nora J.⁷ Harrison** was born in Harrison Twp., Darke Co., Ohio, on June 14, 1867. She died in Peru, Peru Twp., Miami Co., Indiana, on June 27, 1935. Nora J. was buried in Mount Hope Cemetery, Peru, Peru Twp., Miami Co., Indiana.[33]

**144. James M.⁶ Harrison** (*Minerva Jane⁵ Downing, John⁴, Mary³ Pagan, Andrew², James¹*) was born on April 26, 1833, in German Twp., Darke Co., Ohio. He was the son of Harvey Harrison and Minerva Jane Downing (38). James M. died in Greensfork Twp., Randolph Co., Indiana, in 1887 at age 53. He was buried in Hollansburg Cemetery, Hollansburg, Harrison Twp., Darke Co., Ohio.[23]

James M. married **Emily E. French** on December 9, 1855. They had six children. Emily E. French was born in Virginia on May 19, 1834. Emily E. reached age 69 and died in Greensfork Twp., Randolph Co., Indiana, in 1904. She was buried in Hollansburg Cemetery, Hollansburg, Harrison Twp., Darke Co., Ohio.[23]

Children of James M. Harrison and Emily E. French:

+ 217 f I. **Aurelia A.[7] Harrison** was born in Greensfork Twp., Randolph Co., Indiana, on January 1, 1857. She died after 1882.

+ 218 f II. **Lavina J.[7] Harrison** was born in Greensfork Twp., Randolph Co., Indiana, on March 20, 1858. She died in Greensfork Twp., Randolph Co., Indiana, on January 30, 1878. Lavina J. was buried in Hollansburg Cemetery, Hollansburg, Harrison Twp., Darke Co., Ohio.[23]

+ 219 m III. **Francis M.[7] Harrison** was born in Greensfork Twp., Randolph Co., Indiana, on December 29, 1859. He died in Greensfork Twp., Randolph Co., Indiana, on March 7, 1876. Francis M. was buried in Hollansburg Cemetery, Hollansburg, Harrison Twp., Darke Co., Ohio.[23]

+ 220 m IV. **William H.[7] Harrison** was born in Greensfork Twp., Randolph Co., Indiana, on October 12, 1865. He died in Greensfork Twp., Randolph Co., Indiana, in 1886. William H. was buried in Hollansburg Cemetery, Hollansburg, Harrison Twp., Darke Co., Ohio.[23]

+ 221 f V. **Emma E.[7] Harrison** was born in Greensfork Twp., Randolph Co., Indiana, on November 23, 1872. She died after 1882.

+ 222 VI. **Samuel J.[7] Harrison** was born in Greensfork Twp., Randolph Co., Indiana, on December 12, 1863. He or she died in Greensfork Twp., Randolph Co., Indiana, on April 20, 1864. Samuel J. was buried in Hollansburg Cemetery, Hollansburg, Harrison Twp., Darke Co., Ohio.[23]

145. **Mary A.[6] Harrison** (*Minerva Jane[5] Downing, John[4], Mary[3] Pagan, Andrew[2], James[1]*) was born in 1835 in German Twp., Darke Co., Ohio. She was the daughter of Harvey Harrison and Minerva Jane Downing (38). Mary A. died after 1850.

146. **Samuel J.[6] Harrison** (*Minerva Jane[5] Downing, John[4], Mary[3] Pagan, Andrew[2], James[1]*) was born in 1838 in German Twp., Darke Co., Ohio. He was the son of Harvey Harrison and Minerva Jane Downing (38). Samuel J. died after 1860.

147. **Harvey Alexander[6] Harrison** (*Minerva Jane[5] Downing, John[4], Mary[3] Pagan, Andrew[2], James[1]*) was born on October 3, 1841, in German Twp., Darke Co., Ohio. He was also known as **Harry.** He was the son of Harvey Harrison and Minerva Jane Downing (38). Harvey Alexander lived in 1880 in Harrison Twp., Franklin Co., Kansas. He died in Union City, Wayne Twp., Randolph Co., Indiana, on February 3, 1917, at age 75. Harvey Alexander was buried in Union City Cemetery, Union City, Wayne Twp., Randolph Co., Indiana.[29]

Harvey Alexander married **Mahala Tillson** in 1864. They had five children. Mahala Tillson was born in Harrison Twp., Darke Co., Ohio, on June 8, 1845. Mahala reached age 58 and died in Union City, Wayne Twp., Randolph Co., Indiana, on November 9, 1903. She was buried in Union City Cemetery, Union City, Wayne Twp., Randolph Co., Indiana.[29]

Children of Harvey Alexander Harrison and Mahala Tillson:

+ 223 m I. **Thaddeus V.[7] Harrison** was born in Hollansburg, Harrison Twp., Darke Co., Ohio, on May 10, 1867. He died in Chicago, Cook Co., Illinois, on October 7, 1900. Thaddeus V. was buried in Union City Cemetery, Union City, Wayne Twp., Randolph Co., Indiana.[29]

+ 224 f II. **Minnie L.[7] Harrison** was born in Hollansburg, Harrison Twp., Darke Co., Ohio, on November 8, 1868. She died in Winchester, White

River Twp., Randolph Co., Indiana, on September 15, 1951. Minnie L. was buried in Fountain Park Cemetery, Winchester, White River Twp., Randolph Co., Indiana.[34]

+ 225 m III. **David F.**[7] **Harrison** was born in Hollansburg, Harrison Twp., Darke Co., Ohio, on December 27, 1871. He died in El Paso, El Paso Co., Texas, on January 19, 1924. David F. was buried in Union City Cemetery, Union City, Wayne Twp., Randolph Co., Indiana.[29]

+ 226 f IV. **Edith Ann**[7] **Harrison** was born in Hollansburg, Harrison Twp., Darke Co., Ohio, on July 23, 1875. She died in Union City, Wayne Twp., Randolph Co., Indiana, on August 27, 1955. Edith Ann was buried in Union City Cemetery, Union City, Wayne Twp., Randolph Co., Indiana.[29]

+ 227 m V. **William Edward**[7] **Harrison** was born in Union City, Wayne Twp., Randolph Co., Indiana, on August 1, 1878. He died in Union City, Wayne Twp., Randolph Co., Indiana, on August 29, 1949. William Edward was buried in Union City Cemetery, Union City, Wayne Twp., Randolph Co., Indiana.[29]

**148. Wesley Leander**[6] **Harrison** (*Minerva Jane*[5] *Downing, John*[4]*, Mary*[3] *Pagan, Andrew*[2]*, James*[1]) was born on June 5, 1844, in German Twp., Darke Co., Ohio. He was the son of Harvey Harrison and Minerva Jane Downing (38). Wesley Leander died in Greenville, Greenville Twp., Darke Co., Ohio, on March 1, 1911, at age 66. He was buried in Greenville Union Cemetery, Greenville, Greenville Twp., Darke Co., Ohio.[30]

Wesley Leander married **Catherine M. Dickey** on November 17, 1867, in Darke Co., Ohio. They had six children. Catherine M. Dickey was born in Preble Co., Ohio, on March 28, 1847. Catherine

M. reached age 79 and died in Hamilton, Butler Co., Ohio, on August 23, 1926. She was buried in Greenville Union Cemetery, Greenville, Greenville Twp., Darke Co., Ohio.[30]

Children of Wesley Leander Harrison and Catherine M. Dickey:

+ 228 m I. **Albert Dickey**[7] **Harrison** was born in Neave Twp., Darke Co., Ohio, on April 15, 1869. He died in Grand Rapids, Grand Rapids Twp., Kent Co., Michigan, on December 18, 1949.

+ 229 f II. **Lillian**[7] **Harrison** was born in Neave Twp., Darke Co., Ohio, on February 2, 1871. She died in Troy, Concord Twp., Miami Co., Ohio, on September 10, 1952. Lillian was buried in New Carlisle Cemetery, New Carlisle, Bethel Twp., Clark Co., Ohio.[35]

+ 230 f III. **Florence**[7] **Harrison** was born in Neave Twp., Darke Co., Ohio, on July 3, 1873. She died in Hamilton, Butler Co., Ohio, on February 9, 1961. Florence was buried in Greenwood Cemetery, Hamilton, Butler Co., Ohio.[36]

+ 231 m IV. **Leander Everett**[7] **Harrison** was born in Neave Twp., Darke Co., Ohio, in March 1875. He died in Greenville, Greenville Twp., Darke Co., Ohio, on July 2, 1925. Leander Everett was buried in Greenville Union Cemetery, Greenville, Greenville Twp., Darke Co., Ohio.[30]

+ 232 f V. **Edna**[7] **Harrison** was born in Neave Twp., Darke Co., Ohio, on July 22, 1883. She died in Hamilton, Butler Co., Ohio, on July 24, 1965. Edna was buried in Greenville Union Cemetery, Greenville, Greenville Twp., Darke Co., Ohio.[30]

+ 233 m VI. **Benjamin L.**[7] **Harrison** was born in Greenville, Greenville Twp., Darke Co., Ohio, on March 14, 1894. He died in Greenville, Greenville Twp., Darke Co., Ohio, on August 21, 1933. Benjamin L. was buried in Greenville Union Cemetery, Greenville, Greenville Twp., Darke Co., Ohio.[30]

**149. Elizabeth**[6] **Harrison** (*Minerva Jane*[5] *Downing, John*[4], *Mary*[3] *Pagan, Andrew*[2], *James*[1]) was born in 1847 in German Twp., Darke Co., Ohio. She was the daughter of Harvey Harrison and Minerva Jane Downing (38). Elizabeth died after 1870.

**150. William Addison**[6] **Harrison** (*Minerva Jane*[5] *Downing, John*[4], *Mary*[3] *Pagan, Andrew*[2], *James*[1]) was born on March 7, 1850, in German Twp., Darke Co., Ohio. He was the son of Harvey Harrison and Minerva Jane Downing (38). William Addison died in Liberty Twp., Darke Co., Ohio, on April 20, 1929, at age 79. He was buried in Hollansburg Cemetery, Hollansburg, Harrison Twp., Darke Co., Ohio.[23]

He married **Lurena Spencer.** They had one daughter. Lurena Spencer was born in German Twp., Darke Co., Ohio, on March 7, 1860. Lurena reached age 78 and died in Richmond, Wayne Twp., Wayne Co., Indiana, on September 22, 1938. She was buried in Hollansburg Cemetery, Hollansburg, Harrison Twp., Darke Co., Ohio.[23]

Daughter of William Addison Harrison and Lurena Spencer:

+ 234 f I. **Olive H.**[7] **Harrison** was born in Liberty Twp., Darke Co., Ohio, on August 12, 1881. She died in Fountain City, New Garden Twp., Wayne Co., Indiana, on January 4, 1943.

**151. Robert Fulton**[6] **Downing** (*Jason L.*[5], *John*[4], *Mary*[3] *Pagan, Andrew*[2], *James*[1]). He was the son of Jason L. Downing (39) and Rebecca Jane Baird.

**152. Samuel**[6] **Downing** (*Jason L.*[5], *John*[4], *Mary*[3] *Pagan, Andrew*[2], *James*[1]). He was the son of Jason L. Downing (39) and Rebecca Jane Baird.

**153. Margaret J.**[6] **Downing** (*Jason L.*[5], *John*[4], *Mary*[3] *Pagan, Andrew*[2], *James*[1]). She was the daughter of Jason L. Downing (39) and Rebecca Jane Baird.

**154. George W.**[6] **Downing** (*Jason L.*[5], *John*[4], *Mary*[3] *Pagan, Andrew*[2], *James*[1]). He was the son of Jason L. Downing (39) and Rebecca Jane Baird.

**155. Sarah C.**[6] **Downing** (*Jason L.*[5], *John*[4], *Mary*[3] *Pagan, Andrew*[2], *James*[1]). She was the daughter of Jason L. Downing (39) and Rebecca Jane Baird.

**156. Fannie Elizabeth**[6] **Downing** (*Jason L.*[5], *John*[4], *Mary*[3] *Pagan, Andrew*[2], *James*[1]). She was the daughter of Jason L. Downing (39) and Rebecca Jane Baird.

**157. Louisa**[6] **Downing** (*John Edward*[5], *John*[4], *Mary*[3] *Pagan, Andrew*[2], *James*[1]). She was the daughter of John Edward Downing II (40) and Sarah Mordah Morrison.

**158. Mary**[6] **Downing** (*John Edward*[5], *John*[4], *Mary*[3] *Pagan, Andrew*[2], *James*[1]). She was the daughter of John Edward Downing II (40) and Sarah Mordah Morrison.

**159. Melissa**[6] **Downing** (*John Edward*[5], *John*[4], *Mary*[3] *Pagan, Andrew*[2], *James*[1]). She was the daughter of John Edward Downing II (40) and Sarah Mordah Morrison.

**160. James L.**[6] **Downing** (*John Edward*[5], *John*[4], *Mary*[3] *Pagan, Andrew*[2], *James*[1]). He was the son of John Edward Downing II (40) and Sarah Mordah Morrison.

**161. Margaret**[6] **Downing** (*John Edward*[5], *John*[4], *Mary*[3] *Pagan, Andrew*[2], *James*[1]). She was the daughter of John Edward Downing II (40) and Sarah Mordah Morrison.

**162. Elizabeth**[6] **Downing** (*Robert J.*[5], *John*[4], *Mary*[3] *Pagan, Andrew*[2], *James*[1]). She was the daughter of Robert J. Downing (41) and Indiana Baird.

**163. Andrew J.**[6] **Downing** (*Robert J.*[5], *John*[4], *Mary*[3] *Pagan, Andrew*[2], *James*[1]). He was the son of Robert J. Downing (41) and Indiana Baird.

**164. John M.**[6] **Downing** (*Robert J.*[5], *John*[4], *Mary*[3] *Pagan*, *Andrew*[2], *James*[1]). He was the son of Robert J. Downing (41) and Indiana Baird.

**165. Margaret L.**[6] **Downing** (*Robert J.*[5], *John*[4], *Mary*[3] *Pagan*, *Andrew*[2], *James*[1]). She was the daughter of Robert J. Downing (41) and Indiana Baird.

**166. Demaris A.**[6] **Downing** (*Robert J.*[5], *John*[4], *Mary*[3] *Pagan*, *Andrew*[2], *James*[1]). She was the daughter of Robert J. Downing (41) and Indiana Baird.

**167. Amanda Ellen**[6] **Downing** (*Robert J.*[5], *John*[4], *Mary*[3] *Pagan*, *Andrew*[2], *James*[1]). She is the daughter of Robert J. Downing (41) and Indiana Baird.

**168. Jason L.**[6] **Downing** (*Robert J.*[5], *John*[4], *Mary*[3] *Pagan*, *Andrew*[2], *James*[1]). He was the son of Robert J. Downing (41) and Indiana Baird.

**169. Elvira A.**[6] **Downing** (*Robert J.*[5], *John*[4], *Mary*[3] *Pagan*, *Andrew*[2], *James*[1]). She was the daughter of Robert J. Downing (41) and Indiana Baird.

**170. Melissa**[6] **Downing** (*Robert J.*[5], *John*[4], *Mary*[3] *Pagan*, *Andrew*[2], *James*[1]). She was the daughter of Robert J. Downing (41) and Indiana Baird.

**171. Lilla**[6] **Downing** (*Robert J.*[5], *John*[4], *Mary*[3] *Pagan*, *Andrew*[2], *James*[1]). She was the daughter of Robert J. Downing (41) and Indiana Baird.

**172. Watts**[6] **Downing** (*Andrew Jackson*[5], *Robert Gill*[4], *Mary*[3] *Pagan*, *Andrew*[2], *James*[1]). He was the son of Andrew Jackson Downing (44) and Mary Rodgers.

**173. Ann**[6] **Downing** (*Andrew Jackson*[5], *Robert Gill*[4], *Mary*[3] *Pagan*, *Andrew*[2], *James*[1]). She was the daughter of Andrew Jackson Downing (44) and Mary Rodgers.

**174. Emma**[6] **Downing** (*Andrew Jackson*[5], *Robert Gill*[4], *Mary*[3] *Pagan*, *Andrew*[2], *James*[1]). She was the daughter of Andrew Jackson Downing (44) and Mary Rodgers.

**175. Mary**[6] **Downing** (*Andrew Jackson*[5], *Robert Gill*[4], *Mary*[3] *Pagan*, *Andrew*[2], *James*[1]). She was the daughter of Andrew Jackson Downing (44) and Mary Rodgers.

**176. Laura**[6] **Downing** (*Andrew Jackson*[5], *Robert Gill*[4], *Mary*[3] *Pagan*, *Andrew*[2], *James*[1]). She was the daughter of Andrew Jackson Downing (44) and Mary Rodgers.

**177. Andrew J.**[6] **Downing II** (*Andrew Jackson*[5], *Robert Gill*[4], *Mary*[3] *Pagan*, *Andrew*[2], *James*[1]). He was the son of Andrew Jackson Downing (44) and Mary Rodgers.

**178. George**[6] **Downing** (*Andrew Jackson*[5], *Robert Gill*[4], *Mary*[3] *Pagan*, *Andrew*[2], *James*[1]). He was the son of Andrew Jackson Downing (44) and Mary Rodgers.

**179. Lida**[6] **Downing** (*Andrew Jackson*[5], *Robert Gill*[4], *Mary*[3] *Pagan*, *Andrew*[2], *James*[1]). She was the daughter of Andrew Jackson Downing (44) and Mary Rodgers.

**180. Margaret**[6] **Downing** (*Andrew Jackson*[5], *Robert Gill*[4], *Mary*[3] *Pagan*, *Andrew*[2], *James*[1]). She was the daughter of Andrew Jackson Downing (44) and Mary Rodgers.

**181. Josephine**[6] **Downing** (*Andrew Jackson*[5], *Robert Gill*[4], *Mary*[3] *Pagan*, *Andrew*[2], *James*[1]). She was the daughter of Andrew Jackson Downing (44) and Mary Rodgers.

**182. Alfred**[6] **Hill** (*Amanda Jane*[5] *Downing*, *Robert Gill*[4], *Mary*[3] *Pagan*, *Andrew*[2], *James*[1]). He was the son of Milton Hill and Amanda Jane Downing (45).

**183. Joseph**[6] **Hill** (*Amanda Jane*[5] *Downing*, *Robert Gill*[4], *Mary*[3] *Pagan*, *Andrew*[2], *James*[1]). He was the son of Milton Hill and Amanda Jane Downing (45).

**184. Asa**[6] **Hill** (*Amanda Jane*[5] *Downing*, *Robert Gill*[4], *Mary*[3] *Pagan*, *Andrew*[2], *James*[1]). He was the son of Milton Hill and Amanda Jane Downing (45).

**185. Sarah**[6] **Hill** (*Amanda Jane*[5] *Downing*, *Robert Gill*[4], *Mary*[3] *Pagan*, *Andrew*[2], *James*[1]). She was the daughter of Milton Hill and Amanda Jane Downing (45).

**186. Melinda**[6] **Hill** (*Amanda Jane*[5] *Downing*, *Robert Gill*[4], *Mary*[3] *Pagan*, *Andrew*[2], *James*[1]). She was the daughter of Milton Hill and Amanda Jane Downing (45).

**187. Ezra**[6] **Hill** (*Amanda Jane*[5] *Downing*, *Robert Gill*[4], *Mary*[3] *Pagan*, *Andrew*[2], *James*[1]). He was the son of Milton Hill and Amanda Jane Downing (45).

188. **Martha⁶ Hill** (*Amanda Jane⁵ Downing, Robert Gill⁴, Mary³ Pagan, Andrew², James¹*). She was the daughter of Milton Hill and Amanda Jane Downing (45).

189. **Mary Ella⁶ Hill** (*Amanda Jane⁵ Downing, Robert Gill⁴, Mary³ Pagan, Andrew², James¹*). She was the daughter of Milton Hill and Amanda Jane Downing (45).

190. **Alexander⁶ Downing** (*Joseph Herr⁵, Robert Gill⁴, Mary³ Pagan, Andrew², James¹*). He was the son of Joseph Herr Downing (46) and Elisabeth Unknown.

191. **Mary A.⁶ Downing** (*Joseph Herr⁵, Robert Gill⁴, Mary³ Pagan, Andrew², James¹*). She was the daughter of Joseph Herr Downing (46) and Elisabeth Unknown.

192. **Sarah E.⁶ Downing** (*Joseph Herr⁵, Robert Gill⁴, Mary³ Pagan, Andrew², James¹*). She was the daughter of Joseph Herr Downing (46) and Elisabeth Unknown.

193. **Emma⁶ Downing** (*Joseph Herr⁵, Robert Gill⁴, Mary³ Pagan, Andrew², James¹*). She was the daughter of Joseph Herr Downing (46) and Elisabeth Unknown.

194. **William⁶ Downing** (*Joseph Herr⁵, Robert Gill⁴, Mary³ Pagan, Andrew², James¹*). He was the son of Joseph Herr Downing (46) and Elisabeth Unknown.

195. **Amanda Jane⁶ Downing** (*Robert⁵, Robert Gill⁴, Mary³ Pagan, Andrew², James¹*). She was the daughter of Robert Downing II (47) and Barbara Shaffer.

196. **William J.⁶ Downing** (*Robert⁵, Robert Gill⁴, Mary³ Pagan, Andrew², James¹*). He was the son of Robert Downing II (47) and Barbara Shaffer.

197. **Sarah S.⁶ Downing** (*Robert⁵, Robert Gill⁴, Mary³ Pagan, Andrew², James¹*). She was the daughter of Robert Downing II (47) and Barbara Shaffer.

198. **Emma A.⁶ Downing** (*Robert⁵, Robert Gill⁴, Mary³ Pagan, Andrew², James¹*). She was the daughter of Robert Downing II (47) and Barbara Shaffer.

199. **Andrew R.⁶ Downing** (*Robert⁵, Robert Gill⁴, Mary³ Pagan, Andrew², James¹*). He was the son of Robert Downing II (47) and Barbara Shaffer.

200. **Permelia⁶ Martin** (*Mary Jane⁵ Hinkle, Sarah⁴ Downing, Mary³ Pagan, Andrew², James¹*). She was the daughter of Tinsley Dill Martin and Mary Jane Hinkle (53).

201. **William Taylor⁶ Martin** (*Mary Jane⁵ Hinkle, Sarah⁴ Downing, Mary³ Pagan, Andrew², James¹*). He was the son of Tinsley Dill Martin and Mary Jane Hinkle (53).

202. **Sarah Frances⁶ Martin** (*Mary Jane⁵ Hinkle, Sarah⁴ Downing, Mary³ Pagan, Andrew², James¹*). She was the daughter of Tinsley Dill Martin and Mary Jane Hinkle (53).

203. **John Dill⁶ Martin** (*Mary Jane⁵ Hinkle, Sarah⁴ Downing, Mary³ Pagan, Andrew², James¹*). He was the son of Tinsley Dill Martin and Mary Jane Hinkle (53).

204. **Amanda⁶ Martin** (*Mary Jane⁵ Hinkle, Sarah⁴ Downing, Mary³ Pagan, Andrew², James¹*). She was the daughter of Tinsley Dill Martin and Mary Jane Hinkle (53).

205. **Owen Hunt⁶ Martin** (*Mary Jane⁵ Hinkle, Sarah⁴ Downing, Mary³ Pagan, Andrew², James¹*). He was the son of Tinsley Dill Martin and Mary Jane Hinkle (53).

206. **Jesse⁶ Hinkle** (*William Riley⁵, Sarah⁴ Downing, Mary³ Pagan, Andrew², James¹*). He was the son of William Riley Hinkle (55) and Frances Melissa Majors.

207. **Joshua⁶ Hinkle** (*William Riley⁵, Sarah⁴ Downing, Mary³ Pagan, Andrew², James¹*). He was the son of William Riley Hinkle (55) and Frances Melissa Majors.

208. **Andrew⁶ Hinkle** (*William Riley⁵, Sarah⁴ Downing, Mary³ Pagan, Andrew², James¹*). He was the son of William Riley Hinkle (55) and Frances Melissa Majors.

209. **Cora Dell⁶ Hinkle** (*William Riley⁵, Sarah⁴ Downing, Mary³ Pagan, Andrew², James¹*). She was the daughter of William Riley Hinkle (55) and Frances Melissa Majors.

210. **Catherine⁶ Hinkle** (*William Riley⁵, Sarah⁴ Downing, Mary³ Pagan, Andrew², James¹*) was born in 1846 in Tennessee. She was the daughter of William Riley Hinkle (55) and Mary F. Taylor.

# 7th Generation

**211. Florence Lucille[7] Downing** (*John[6], Samuel[5], John[4], Mary[3] Pagan, Andrew[2], James[1]*) was born on May 22, 1854, in Wayne Twp., Randolph Co., Indiana. She was the daughter of John Downing (132) and Sarah Gullett. Florence Lucille died in Tremain's corners, Orange Twp., Ionia Co., Michigan, on March 24, 1904, at age 49. She was buried in Letts Cemetery, Ionia, Ionia Twp., Ionia Co., Michigan.[32]

She married **James Luke LeLonge.** They had one son. James Luke LeLonge was born in 1850. He was also known as **Luke.** James Luke reached age 78 and died in Tremain's corners, Orange Twp., Ionia Co., Michigan, on December 24, 1928. He was buried in Letts Cemetery, Ionia, Ionia Twp., Ionia Co., Michigan.[32]

Son of Florence Lucille Downing and James Luke LeLonge:

+ 236 m I.   **Alvatus[8] LeLonge** was born in December 1873. He died in Berlin Twp., Ionia Co., Michigan, on March 22, 1949. Alvatus was buried in Letts Cemetery, Ionia, Ionia Twp., Ionia Co., Michigan.[32]

**212. Alpharetta L.[7] Downing** (*John[6], Samuel[5], John[4], Mary[3] Pagan, Andrew[2], James[1]*) was born on August 20, 1857, in Wayne Twp., Randolph Co., Indiana. She was the daughter of John Downing (132) and Sarah Gullett. Alpharetta L. died in Belding, Otisco Twp., Ionia Co., Michigan, on March 12, 1939, at age 81. She was buried in West Sebewa Cemetery, Lake Odessa, Odessa Twp., Ionia Co., Michigan.[31]

Alpharetta L. married **Robert F. Barry** on August 9, 1878, in Ionia Co., Michigan. They had two daughters. Robert F. Barry was born in Orange Twp., Ionia Co., Michigan, on January 7, 1857. Robert F. reached age 58 and died in Belding, Otisco Twp., Ionia Co., Michigan, on November 24, 1915. He was buried in West Sebewa Cemetery, Lake Odessa, Odessa Twp., Ionia Co., Michigan.[31]

Daughters of Alpharetta L. Downing and Robert F. Barry:

+ 237 f I.   **Sarah Olive[8] Barry** was born in Sebewa Corners, Sebewa Twp., Ionia Co., Michigan, on June 16, 1879. She was also known as **Olive.** Sarah Olive died in Smyrna, Otisco Twp., Ionia Co., Michigan, on November 18, 1958. She was buried in Smyrna Cemetery, Smyrna, Otisco Twp., Ionia Co., Michigan.[37]

+ 238 f II.   **Nettie L.[8] Barry** was born in Sebewa Corners, Sebewa Twp., Ionia Co., Michigan, on July 3, 1884. She died in Sebewa Corners, Sebewa Twp., Ionia Co., Michigan, on July 6, 1884. Nettie L. was buried in West Sebewa Cemetery, Lake Odessa, Odessa Twp., Ionia Co., Michigan.[31]

**213. Samuel M.[7] Downing** (*John[6], Samuel[5], John[4], Mary[3] Pagan, Andrew[2], James[1]*) was born in August 1859 in South Salem, Wayne Twp., Randolph Co., Indiana. He was the son of John Downing (132) and Sarah Gullett. Samuel M. died in Ionia, Ionia Twp., Ionia Co., Michigan, on March 13, 1933, at age 73. He was buried in West Sebewa Cemetery, Lake Odessa, Odessa Twp., Ionia Co., Michigan.[31]

Samuel M. married **Lucia Emma Carter** on August 7, 1880, in Ionia Co., Michigan. They had one daughter. Lucia Emma Carter was born in Mississinawa Twp., Darke Co., Ohio, in 1857. She was also known as **Emma.** Lucia Emma reached age 34 and died in Sebewa Twp., Ionia Co., Michigan, in 1891. She was buried in West Sebewa Cemetery, Lake Odessa, Odessa Twp., Ionia Co., Michigan.[31]

Samuel M. Downing married **Emma Snyder** on April 3, 1895, in Ionia Co., Michigan. Emma Snyder was born in Ada, Ada Twp., Kent Co.,

Michigan, on December 27, 1857. Emma reached age 79 and died in Ionia, Ionia Twp., Ionia Co., Michigan, on September 19, 1937. She was buried in West Sebewa Cemetery, Lake Odessa, Odessa Twp., Ionia Co., Michigan.[31]

Daughter of Samuel M. Downing and Lucia Emma Carter:

+ 239 f I. **Bertha**[8] **Downing** was born in Sebewa Twp., Ionia Co., Michigan, in February 1886. She died after 1900.

**214. Ezekiel John**[7] **Downing** (*John*[6], *Samuel*[5], *John*[4], *Mary*[3] *Pagan*, *Andrew*[2], *James*[1]) was born on January 3, 1861, in South Salem, Wayne Twp., Randolph Co., Indiana. He was the son of John Downing (132) and Sarah Gullett. Ezekiel John died in Lake Odessa, Odessa Twp., Ionia Co., Michigan, in December 1951 at age 90.

Ezekiel John married **Maud Estep** on November 10, 1886, in Ionia Co., Michigan. They had six children. Maud Estep was born in Sebewa Twp., Ionia Co., Michigan, on November 18, 1866. Maud reached age 65 and died in Sebewa Twp., Ionia Co., Michigan, on March 24, 1932. She was buried in West Sebewa Cemetery, Lake Odessa, Odessa Twp., Ionia Co., Michigan.[31]

Children of Ezekiel John Downing and Maud Estep:

+ 240 f I. **Ethelyn**[8] **Downing** was born in Sebewa Twp., Ionia Co., Michigan, on December 7, 1892. She died in Sebewa Twp., Ionia Co., Michigan, on February 19, 1893. Ethelyn was buried in West Sebewa Cemetery, Lake Odessa, Odessa Twp., Ionia Co., Michigan.[31]

+ 241 f II. **Evelyn Rebecca**[8] **Downing** was born in Sebewa Twp., Ionia Co., Michigan, on February 19, 1893. She died in Sunfield, Sunfield Twp., Eaton Co., Michigan, on October 20, 1977. Evelyn Rebecca was bur-

ied in West Sebewa Cemetery, Lake Odessa, Odessa Twp., Ionia Co., Michigan.[31]

+ 242 m III. **Vernon Ezekiel**[8] **Downing** was born in Sebewa Twp., Ionia Co., Michigan, on September 25, 1894. He died in Grand Rapids, Grand Rapids Twp., Kent Co., Michigan, on October 9, 1961. Vernon Ezekiel was buried in West Sebewa Cemetery, Lake Odessa, Odessa Twp., Ionia Co., Michigan.[31]

+ 243 f IV. **Ione L.**[8] **Downing** was born in Sebewa Twp., Ionia Co., Michigan, on July 23, 1898. She died in Grand Rapids, Grand Rapids Twp., Kent Co., Michigan, on April 21, 1950. Ione L. was buried in West Sebewa Cemetery, Lake Odessa, Odessa Twp., Ionia Co., Michigan.[31]

+ 244 f V. **Ilah Leona**[8] **Downing** was born in Sebewa Twp., Ionia Co., Michigan, on July 23, 1898. She died in Bakersfield, Kern Co., California, on February 25, 1990.

+ 245 m VI. **Homer Herman**[8] **Downing** was born in Orange Twp., Ionia Co., Michigan, on February 10, 1901. He died in Sebewa Twp., Ionia Co., Michigan, on February 14, 1984. Homer Herman was buried in East Sebewa Cemetery, Sunfield, Sebewa Twp., Ionia Co., Michigan.[38]

**215. Minerva Ida**[7] **Harrison** (*John Edward*[6], *Minerva Jane*[5] *Downing*, *John*[4], *Mary*[3] *Pagan*, *Andrew*[2], *James*[1]) was born on March 25, 1856, in Harrison Twp., Darke Co., Ohio. She was also known as **Ida.** She was the daughter of John Edward Harrison (143) and Harriet Benson. Minerva Ida died in Converse, Jackson Twp., Miami Co., Indiana, on January 27, 1890, at age 33. She was buried in Converse Cemetery, Converse, Richland Twp., Grant Co., Indiana.[28]

Minerva Ida married **Winfield Scott Street** on August 20, 1879, in Miami Co., Indiana. They had one daughter. Winfield Scott Street was born in Eaton, Washington Twp., Preble Co., Ohio, in October 1852. He was also known as **Scott**. Winfield Scott reached age 58 and died in Clinton Twp., Cass Co., Indiana, on August 22, 1911. He was buried in Converse Cemetery, Converse, Richland Twp., Grant Co., Indiana.[28]

Daughter of Minerva Ida Harrison and Winfield Scott Street:

+ 246 f  I.  **Nora M.**[8] **Street** was born in Converse, Jackson Twp., Miami Co., Indiana, on December 9, 1884. He died in Converse, Jackson Twp., Miami Co., Indiana, on August 18, 1885. Nora M. was buried in Converse Cemetery, Converse, Richland Twp., Grant Co., Indiana.[28]

**216. Nora J.**[7] **Harrison** (*John Edward*[6], *Minerva Jane*[5] *Downing, John*[4], *Mary*[3] *Pagan, Andrew*[2], *James*[1]) was born on June 14, 1867, in Harrison Twp., Darke Co., Ohio. She was the daughter of John Edward Harrison (143) and Harriet Benson. Nora J. died in Peru, Peru Twp., Miami Co., Indiana, on June 27, 1935, at age 68. She was buried in Mount Hope Cemetery, Peru, Peru Twp., Miami Co., Indiana.[33]

Nora J. Harrison Lieurance had a son with **Unknown Unknown.**

Nora J. married Otto Lieurance on December 22, 1898, in Grant Co., Indiana. They had one daughter. Otto Lieurance was born in Peru, Peru Twp., Miami Co., Indiana, on March 29, 1870. Otto reached age 69 and died in Peru, Peru Twp., Miami Co., Indiana, on February 4, 1940. He was buried in Mount Hope Cemetery, Peru, Peru Twp., Miami Co., Indiana..[33]

Son of Nora J. Harrison and Unknown Unknown:

+ 247 m  I.  **Russel**[8] **Harrison** was born in Converse, Jackson Twp., Miami Co., Indiana, on January 20, 1891. He died in Grand Haven, Ottawa Co., Michigan?, in November 1964. Russel was buried in Mount Hope Cemetery, Peru, Peru Twp., Miami Co., Indiana.[33]

Daughter of Nora J. Harrison and Otto Lieurance:

+ 248 f  I.  **Ruth Elizabeth**[8] **Lieurance** was born in Peru, Peru Twp., Miami Co., Indiana, on April 11, 1904. She died in a facility in Franklin, Johnson Co., Indiana, on September 17, 1969. Ruth Elizabeth was buried in Mount Hope Cemetery, Peru, Peru Twp., Miami Co., Indiana.[33]

**217. Aurelia A.**[7] **Harrison** (*James M.*[6], *Minerva Jane*[5] *Downing, John*[4], *Mary*[3] *Pagan, Andrew*[2], *James*[1]) was born on January 1, 1857, in Greensfork Twp., Randolph Co., Indiana. She was the daughter of James M. Harrison (144) and Emily E. French. Aurelia A. died after 1882.

**218. Lavina J.**[7] **Harrison** (*James M.*[6], *Minerva Jane*[5] *Downing, John*[4], *Mary*[3] *Pagan, Andrew*[2], *James*[1]) was born on March 20, 1858, in Greensfork Twp., Randolph Co., Indiana. She was the daughter of James M. Harrison (144) and Emily E. French. Lavina J. died in Greensfork Twp., Randolph Co., Indiana, on January 30, 1878, at age 19. She was buried in Hollansburg Cemetery, Hollansburg, Harrison Twp., Darke Co., Ohio.[23]

**219. Francis M.**[7] **Harrison** (*James M.*[6], *Minerva Jane*[5] *Downing, John*[4], *Mary*[3] *Pagan, Andrew*[2], *James*[1]) was born on December 29, 1859, in Greensfork Twp., Randolph Co., Indiana. He was the son of James M. Harrison (144) and Emily E. French. Francis M. died in Greensfork Twp., Randolph Co., Indiana, on March 7, 1876, at age 16. He was buried in Hollansburg Cemetery, Hollansburg, Harrison Twp., Darke Co., Ohio.[23]

**220. William H.**[7] **Harrison** (*James M.*[6], *Minerva Jane*[5] *Downing, John*[4], *Mary*[3] *Pagan, Andrew*[2], *James*[1]) was born on October 12, 1865, in Greensfork Twp., Randolph Co., Indiana. He was the son of James M. Harrison (144) and Emily E. French. William H. died in Greensfork Twp., Randolph Co., Indiana, in 1886 at age 20. He was buried in Hollansburg Cemetery, Hollansburg, Harrison Twp., Darke Co., Ohio.[23]

**221. Emma E.**[7] **Harrison** (*James M.*[6], *Minerva Jane*[5] *Downing, John*[4], *Mary*[3] *Pagan, Andrew*[2], *James*[1]) was born on November 23, 1872, in Greensfork Twp., Randolph Co., Indiana. She was the daughter of James M. Harrison (144) and Emily E. French. Emma E. died after 1882.

**222. Samuel J.**[7] **Harrison** (*James M.*[6], *Minerva Jane*[5] *Downing, John*[4], *Mary*[3] *Pagan, Andrew*[2], *James*[1]) was born on December 12, 1863, in Greensfork Twp., Randolph Co., Indiana. He or she was a child of James M. Harrison (144) and Emily E. French. Samuel J. died in Greensfork Twp., Randolph Co., Indiana, on April 20, 1864. He or she was buried in Hollansburg Cemetery, Hollansburg, Harrison Twp., Darke Co., Ohio.[23]

**223. Thaddeus V.**[7] **Harrison** (*Harvey Alexander*[6], *Minerva Jane*[5] *Downing, John*[4], *Mary*[3] *Pagan, Andrew*[2], *James*[1]) was born on May 10, 1867, in Hollansburg, Harrison Twp., Darke Co., Ohio. He was the son of Harvey Alexander Harrison (147) and Mahala Tillson. Thaddeus V. died in Chicago, Cook Co., Illinois, on October 7, 1900, at age 33. He was buried in Union City Cemetery, Union City, Wayne Twp., Randolph Co., Indiana.[29]

Thaddeus V. married **Ada L. Elzroth** on June 21, 1889, in Miami Co., Indiana. They had one son. Ada L. Elzroth was born in Waltz Twp., Wabash Co., Indiana, on May 4, 1871. Ada L. reached age 84 and died in Los Angeles, Los Angeles Co., California, on May 9, 1955.

Son of Thaddeus V. Harrison and Ada L. Elzroth:

+ 249 m I. **Thaddeus Glenn**[8] **Harrison II** was born in Chicago, Cook Co., Illinois, in 1891. He was also known as **Glenn**. Thaddeus Glenn died in

St. Paul, Ramsey Co., Minnesota?, after 1955.

**224. Minnie L.**[7] **Harrison** (*Harvey Alexander*[6], *Minerva Jane*[5] *Downing, John*[4], *Mary*[3] *Pagan, Andrew*[2], *James*[1]) was born on November 8, 1868, in Hollansburg, Harrison Twp., Darke Co., Ohio. She was the daughter of Harvey Alexander Harrison (147) and Mahala Tillson. Minnie L. died in Winchester, White River Twp., Randolph Co., Indiana, on September 15, 1951, at age 82.[23] She was buried in Fountain Park Cemetery, Winchester, White River Twp., Randolph Co., Indiana.[34]

Minnie L. married **Thomas Corwin Hiatt** on May 15, 1894, in Randolph Co., Indiana. They had two children. Thomas Corwin Hiatt was born in Franklin Twp., Randolph Co., Indiana, in February 1868. Thomas Corwin reached age 36 and died in Indianapolis, Marion Co., Indiana, on March 30, 1904. He was buried in Fountain Park Cemetery, Winchester, White River Twp., Randolph Co., Indiana.[34]

Children of Minnie L. Harrison and Thomas Corwin Hiatt:

+ 250 f I. **Edith M.**[8] **Hiatt** was born in Franklin Twp., Randolph Co., Indiana, in May 1895. She died after 1920.

+ 251 m II. **Howard Jackson**[8] **Hiatt** was born in Franklin Twp., Randolph Co., Indiana, on July 15, 1902. He died in Indianapolis, Marion Co., Indiana, on April 27, 1994. Howard Jackson was buried in Washington Park East Cemetery, Indianapolis, Warren Twp., Marion Co., Indiana.[39]

**225. David F.**[7] **Harrison** (*Harvey Alexander*[6], *Minerva Jane*[5] *Downing, John*[4], *Mary*[3] *Pagan, Andrew*[2], *James*[1]) was born on December 27, 1871, in Hollansburg, Harrison Twp., Darke Co., Ohio. He was the son of Harvey Alexander Harrison (147) and Mahala Tillson. David F. lived in 1924 in Union City, Wayne Twp., Randolph Co.,

Indiana. He died in El Paso, El Paso Co., Texas, on January 19, 1924, at age 52. David F. was buried in Union City Cemetery, Union City, Wayne Twp., Randolph Co., Indiana.[29]

Childless.

He married **Maud Ladd.** Maud Ladd was born in Union Twp., Randolph Co., Indiana, in 1871. Maud reached age 53 and died in Union City, Wayne Twp., Randolph Co., Indiana?, in 1924. She was buried in Union City Cemetery, Union City, Wayne Twp., Randolph Co., Indiana.[29]

**226. Edith Ann**[7] **Harrison** (*Harvey Alexander*[6], *Minerva Jane*[5] *Downing, John*[4], *Mary*[3] *Pagan, Andrew*[2], *James*[1]) was born on July 23, 1875, in Hollansburg, Harrison Twp., Darke Co., Ohio. She was the daughter of Harvey Alexander Harrison (147) and Mahala Tillson. Edith Ann died in Union City, Wayne Twp., Randolph Co., Indiana, on August 27, 1955, at age 80. She was buried in Union City Cemetery, Union City, Wayne Twp., Randolph Co., Indiana.[29]

Childless.

Edith Ann married **Irvin Stump** on November 3, 1920, in Randolph Co., Indiana. Irvin Stump was born in Wayne Twp., Randolph Co., Indiana, in November 1882. Irvin reached age 59 and died in Dayton, Montgomery Co., Ohio, on July 14, 1942. He was buried in Union City Cemetery, Union City, Wayne Twp., Randolph Co., Indiana.[29]

**227. William Edward**[7] **Harrison** (*Harvey Alexander*[6], *Minerva Jane*[5] *Downing, John*[4], *Mary*[3] *Pagan, Andrew*[2], *James*[1]) was born on August 1, 1878, in Union City, Wayne Twp., Randolph Co., Indiana. He was the son of Harvey Alexander Harrison (147) and Mahala Tillson. William Edward died in Union City, Wayne Twp., Randolph Co., Indiana, on August 29, 1949, at age 71. He was buried in Union City Cemetery, Union City, Wayne Twp., Randolph Co., Indiana.[29]

William Edward married **Martha Ellen Starbuck** on March 2, 1916, in Randolph Co., Indiana. Martha Ellen Starbuck was born in 1889. Martha Ellen reached age 79 and died in 1968. She was

buried in Union City Cemetery, Union City, Wayne Twp., Randolph Co., Indiana.[29]

**228. Albert Dickey**[7] **Harrison** (*Wesley Leander*[6], *Minerva Jane*[5] *Downing, John*[4], *Mary*[3] *Pagan, Andrew*[2], *James*[1]) was born on April 15, 1869, in Neave Twp., Darke Co., Ohio. He was the son of Wesley Leander Harrison (148) and Catherine M. Dickey. Albert Dickey died in Grand Rapids, Grand Rapids Twp., Kent Co., Michigan, on December 18, 1949, at age 80.

**229. Lillian**[7] **Harrison** (*Wesley Leander*[6], *Minerva Jane*[5] *Downing, John*[4], *Mary*[3] *Pagan, Andrew*[2], *James*[1]) was born on February 2, 1871, in Neave Twp., Darke Co., Ohio. She was the daughter of Wesley Leander Harrison (148) and Catherine M. Dickey. Lillian lived in 1952 in New Carlisle, Bethel Twp., Clark Co., Ohio. She died in Troy, Concord Twp., Miami Co., Ohio, on September 10, 1952, at age 81. Lillian was buried in New Carlisle Cemetery, New Carlisle, Bethel Twp., Clark Co., Ohio.[35]

Lillian married **Osborn Wilson** on September 12, 1905, in Darke Co., Ohio. They had one son. Osborn Wilson was born in Greenville, Greenville Twp., Darke Co., Ohio, on November 2, 1869. Osborn reached age 94 and died in New Carlisle, Bethel Twp., Clark Co., Ohio, on July 11, 1964. He was buried in New Carlisle Cemetery, New Carlisle, Bethel Twp., Clark Co., Ohio.[35]

Son of Lillian Harrison and Osborn Wilson:

+ 252 m I.   **Harrison Auguston**[8] **Wilson** was born in Greenville, Greenville Twp., Darke Co., Ohio, on June 30, 1906. He lived in 1983 in Meigs Co., Ohio. Harrison Auguston died in Gallipolis, Gallipolis Twp., Gallia Co., Ohio, on October 20, 1983. He was buried in New Carlisle Cemetery, New Carlisle, Bethel Twp., Clark Co., Ohio.[35]

**230. Florence**[7] **Harrison** (*Wesley Leander*[6], *Minerva Jane*[5] *Downing, John*[4], *Mary*[3] *Pagan, Andrew*[2], *James*[1]) was born on July 3, 1873, in Neave Twp., Darke Co., Ohio. She was the daughter of Wesley Leander Harrison (148) and Catherine M. Dickey.

Florence died in Hamilton, Butler Co., Ohio, on February 9, 1961, at age 87. She was buried in Greenwood Cemetery, Hamilton, Butler Co., Ohio.[36]

Childless.

Florence married **Harry Woolford** on June 8, 1910, in Darke Co., Ohio. Harry Woolford was born in Middletown, Butler Co., Ohio, on March 14, 1872. Harry reached age 72 and died in Hamilton, Butler Co., Ohio, on January 18, 1945. He was buried in Greenwood Cemetery, Hamilton, Butler Co., Ohio.[36]

**231. Leander Everett⁷ Harrison** (*Wesley Leander⁶, Minerva Jane⁵ Downing, John⁴, Mary³ Pagan, Andrew², James¹*) was born in March 1875 in Neave Twp., Darke Co., Ohio. He was the son of Wesley Leander Harrison (148) and Catherine M. Dickey. Leander Everett died in Greenville, Greenville Twp., Darke Co., Ohio, on July 2, 1925, at age 50. He was buried in Greenville Union Cemetery, Greenville, Greenville Twp., Darke Co., Ohio.[30]

He married **Unknown Unknown.**

**232. Edna⁷ Harrison** (*Wesley Leander⁶, Minerva Jane⁵ Downing, John⁴, Mary³ Pagan, Andrew², James¹*) was born on July 22, 1883, in Neave Twp., Darke Co., Ohio. She was the daughter of Wesley Leander Harrison (148) and Catherine M. Dickey. Edna died in Hamilton, Butler Co., Ohio, on July 24, 1965, at age 82. She was buried in Greenville Union Cemetery, Greenville, Greenville Twp., Darke Co., Ohio.[30]

Although her gravestone says she was born in 1882, census records indicate Edna Harrison Wright was born in 1883.

Edna married **Clarence L. Wright** on June 8, 1908, in Darke Co., Ohio. They divorced between 1920 and 1930. They had one son. Clarence L. Wright was born in Caldwell, Olive Twp., Noble Co., Ohio, on October 9, 1883. He lived in 1920 in Huntington, Cabell Co., West Virginia. Clarence L. reached age 59 and died in Columbus, Franklin Co., Ohio, on March 22, 1943. He was

buried in Union Cemetery, Columbus, Franklin Co., Ohio.[40]

Son of Edna Harrison and Clarence L. Wright:

+ 253 m I. **Clyde⁸ Wright** was born in Greenville, Greenville Twp., Darke Co., Ohio, in 1909. He died in Hamilton, Butler Co., Ohio, on February 1, 1963. Clyde was buried in Greenville Union Cemetery, Greenville, Greenville Twp., Darke Co., Ohio.[30]

**233. Benjamin L.⁷ Harrison** (*Wesley Leander⁶, Minerva Jane⁵ Downing, John⁴, Mary³ Pagan, Andrew², James¹*) was born on March 14, 1894, in Greenville, Greenville Twp., Darke Co., Ohio. He was the son of Wesley Leander Harrison (148) and Catherine M. Dickey. Benjamin L. died in Greenville, Greenville Twp., Darke Co., Ohio, on August 21, 1933, at age 39. He was buried in Greenville Union Cemetery, Greenville, Greenville Twp., Darke Co., Ohio.[30]

He married **Blanch Smith.**

**234. Olive H.⁷ Harrison** (*William Addison⁶, Minerva Jane⁵ Downing, John⁴, Mary³ Pagan, Andrew², James¹*) was born on August 12, 1881, in Liberty Twp., Darke Co., Ohio. She was the daughter of William Addison Harrison (150) and Lurena Spencer. Olive H. died in Fountain City, New Garden Twp., Wayne Co., Indiana, on January 4, 1943, at age 61. He was buried in Hollansburg Cemetery, Hollansburg, Harrison Twp., Darke Co., Ohio.[23]

Childless.

She married **Carl W. Thompson.** Carl W. Thompson was born in Greensfork Twp., Randolph Co., Indiana, on October 10, 1879. Carl W. reached age 78 and died in Phoenix, Maricopa Co., Arizona, on July 12, 1958. He was buried in Hollansburg Cemetery, Hollansburg, Harrison Twp., Darke Co., Ohio.[23]

# Endnotes

1   Find A Grave—Fishing Creek Presbyterian Cemetery, Chester, Chester Co., South Carolina, Find A Grave.com.

2   Pennsylvania Church Records—Adams, Berks and Lancaster Counties, 1729-1881, Ancestry.com, St. James Episcopal Church, Philadelphia, John Downing and Mary Pagan.

3   Wayne County Historical Society, Wayne County, Tennessee 1817-1995: History & Families. Waynesboro, Tennessee: Rose Publishing Company; 1995, pg. 199. Genealogy Center, Allen County Public Library, 900 Library Plaza, Fort Wayne, IN.

4   John Downing entries, Lancaster County, Pennsylvania Tax Lists, 1751-1800, Microfilm, Roll #23, Genealogy Center, Allen County Public Library, Fort Wayne, IN.

5   Ellis, Franklin and Samuel Evans, *History of Lancaster County, Pennsylvania, with biographical sketches of many of the pioneers and prominent men.* Philadelphia: Everts & Peck; 1883, pg. 974. Mishawaka Heritage Center, Mishawaka Penn-Harris Public Library, 209 Lincolnway East, Mishawaka, IN.

6   Chester County, South Carolina Deeds, John Combest to John Downing, Chester County, South Carolina Deed Old Book N-3:252. Chester County Clerk of Courts, Recorders Office, 313 West Market Street, Chester, SC.

7   "Some Early Residents of Fishing Creek", The South Carolina Magazine of Ancestral Research (SCMAR): Volume VII, Volume VII, Winter 1979, No. 1, p.8. Genealogy Center, Allen County Public Library 900 Library Plaza, Fort Wayne, IN.

8   Moss, Bobby Gilmer, *Roster of South Carolina Patriots in the American Revolution.* Baltimore: Genealogical Publishing Co. Inc.; 1985, pg. 265. Huntington City-Township Public Library, 255 West Park Drive, Huntington, IN.

9   Chester County, South Carolina Probate Files, John Downing estate file, Case #239, File #14, Pack #341. Chester County, South Carolina Clerk of Probate Court, 140 Main Street, Chester, SC.

10  Chester County, South Carolina Deeds, Mary Downing, et. al., to William Downing, Chester County, South Carolina Old Deed Book Q: 281. Chester County Clerk of Courts, Recorders Office, 313 West Market Street, Chester, SC.

11  *Early Records of Fishing Creek Presbyterian Church: Chester County, South Carolina, 1799-1859, with Appendices of the visitation list of Rev. John Simpson, 1774-1776, and the Cemetery roster, 1762-1979*; compiled by Brett H. Holcomb and Elmer O. Parker. Greenville, South Carolina: A Press, Inc.; 1980, pg. 30. Genealogy Center, Allen County Public Library, 900 Library Plaza, Fort Wayne, IN.

12  Hibdon, Glenda Pagan, *The Pagan, Hunt and Sanderson genealogies.* Knoxville, Tennessee: Tennessee Valley Publishing, 1994. Genealogy Center, Allen County Public Library, 900 Library Plaza, Fort Wayne, IN.

13  Emails from Nan Roose, Lancaster, Pennsylvania, Ann Miller Carr, author, 2012-2013.

14  Family Data: Andrew Downing bible, biblerecords.com, DOWNING BIBLE, Submitted by Gary Geiger; Online database: http://www.biblerecords.com/downing.html

15  Find A Grave—Furgerson Cemetery, Cedar Grove, Carroll Co., Tennessee, Find A Grave.com.

16  Find A Grave—Mount Hebron Cemetery, Houston, Wayne Co., Tennessee, Find A Grave.com.

17  Find A Grave—Hill Cemetery, New Madison, Harrison Twp., Darke Co., Ohio, Find A Grave.com.

18  Find A Grave—Flatwoods Cemetery, Mountain View, Stone Co., Arkansas, Find A Grave.com.

19  Find A Grave—Robeson Cemetery, Cedar Grove, Carroll Co., Tennessee, Find A Grave.com.

20  Find A Grave—Patterson Cemetery, Hardin Co., Tennessee, Find A Grave.com.

21  Find A Grave—Woolley Cemetery, Centerville, Faulkner Co., Arkansas, Find A Grave.com.

22  Find A Grave—George Washington Hoover-Allensville Cemetery, Jackson Twp., Randolph Co., Indiana, Find A Grave.com.

23  Find A Grave—Hollansburg Cemetery, Hollansburg, Harrison Twp., Darke Co., Ohio, Find A Grave.com.

24  Find A Grave—Green Mound Cemetery, New Madison, Harrison Twp., Darke Co., Ohio, Find A Grave.com.

25  Find A Grave—First Universalist Church Cemetery, New Madison, Harrison Twp., Darke Co., Ohio, Find A Grave.com.

26  Find A Grave—Alderman Cemetery, Ionia, Ionia Twp., Ionia Co., Michigan, Find A Grave.com.

27  Find A Grave—Spencer Cemetery, New Madison, Harrison Twp., Darke Co., Ohio, Find A Grave.com.

28  Find A Grave—Converse Cemetery, Converse, Richland Twp., Grant Co., Indiana, Find A Grave.com.

29  Find A Grave—Union City Cemetery, Union City, Wayne Twp., Randolph Co., Indiana, Find A Grave.com.

30  Find A Grave—Greenville Union Cemetery, Greenville, Greenville Twp., Darke Co., Ohio, Find A Grave.com.

31  Find A Grave—West Sebewa Cemetery, Lake Odessa, Odessa Twp., Ionia Co., Michigan, Find A Grave.com.

32  Find A Grave—Letts Cemetery, Ionia, Ionia Twp., Ionia Co., Michigan, Find A Grave.com.

33  Find A Grave—Mount Hope Cemetery, Peru, Peru Twp., Miami Co., Indiana, Find A Grave.com.

34  Find A Grave—Fountain Park Cemetery, Winchester, White River Twp., Randolph Co., Indiana, Find A Grave.com.

35   Find A Grave—New Carlisle Cemetery, New Carlisle, Bethel Twp., Clark Co., Ohio, Find A Grave.com.

36   Find A Grave—Greenwood Cemetery, Hamilton, Butler Co., Ohio, Find A Grave.com, Mary Jane Stubbs, Find A Grave Memorial #155791805.

37   Find A Grave—Smyrna Cemetery, Smyrna, Otisco Twp., Ionia Co., Michigan, Find A Grave.com.

38   Find A Grave—East Sebewa Cemetery, Sunfield, Sebewa Twp., Ionia Co., Michigan, Find A Grave.com.

39   Find A Grave—Washington Park East Cemetery, Indianapolis, Warren Twp., Marion Co., Indiana, Find A Grave.com.

40   Find A Grave—Union Cemetery, Columbus, Franklin Co., Ohio, Find A Grave.com.

# Descendants of Margaret Pagan Herrin/Herran/Herron

**1. Margaret[3] Pagan** (*Andrew[2] Pagan, James[1]*) was born before 1754 in Martic Twp., Lancaster Co., Pennsylvania. She was the daughter of Andrew Pagan and Ann McDowell?. Margaret died after 1790.

Margaret married **John Herrin/Herran/Herron** on Tuesday, July 26, 1774, in Lancaster Co., Pennsylvania. They had one daughter. John Herrin or Herran or Herron was born in Ireland? before 1753. John Herrin or Herran or lived in 1790 in Hopewell Twp., York Co., Pennsylvania?. He died in Hopewell Twp., York Co., Pennsylvania?, after 1790.

The surname is seen as Herron, Heron, Herrin, Herran, and more spellings.

John and Margaret "Pagen" Herron were married at the St. James Episcopal Church in Lancaster, Pennsylvania on 26 Jul 1774.[1][1]

He could be the John Herron who was appointed to the board of managers overseeing the construction of a new Guinston Presbyterian Church building in 1774 in Hopewell Twp., York Co., Pennsylvania.[2]

They may be the "John Herrin" family, with one male more than 16 years old and two females, in Hopewell Twp., York Co., Pennsylvania in the 1790 census (*Census Place: Hopewell, York, Pennsylvania; Series: M637; Roll: 9; Page: 333; Image: 182*).

They are known to have had at least one child, Ann, who is mentioned, along with her mother, as "granddaughter Ann Herran" in her grandfather Andrew Pegan/Pagan Sr.'s Lancaster County, Pennsylvania will in 1787.[3]

After 1790, John Herrin/Herran/Herron is hard to trace. He may have died before 1800, and Margaret may have remarried. Their daughter, Ann Herron (etc.) is not found in any records either. What happened to them is unknown, although there are Herrons found in Washington County, Pennsylvania in the early 1800s near her brother Andrew Pegan II and his family.

Daughter of Margaret Pegan and John Herrin/Herran/Herron:

+ 2   f   I.   **Ann[4] Herran** was born in Lancaster Co. or York Co., Pennsylvania, between 1775 and 1787. She died after 1790.

# 4th Generation

2.  **Ann⁴ Herran** (*Margaret³ Pegan, Andrew² Pagan, James¹*) was born between 1775 and 1787 in Lancaster Co. or York Co., Pennsylvania. She was the daughter of John Herrin or Herran or Herron and Margaret Pegan (1). Ann died after 1788. Ann "Herran" is mentioned in her grandfather, Andrew Pagan Sr.'s will.[3]

# Endnotes

1    Wright, F. Edward, *The Lancaster County, Pennsylvania church records of the 18th century, Vol. 3*. Westminster, Maryland: Family Line Publications; 1994, pg. 116. Genealogy Center, Allen County Public Library, 900 Library Plaza, Fort Wayne, IN.

2    Prowell, George R. *History of York County:Pennsylvania, in 2 Vols., Vol. 1*. Chicago: Beers & Co.; 1907, pg. 944. Genealogy Center, Allen County Public Library, 900 Library Plaza, Fort Wayne, IN.

3    Andrew Pegan will (1788), Lancaster County, Pennsylvania Will Books, Book F: Vol. 1: 84-86. Lancaster County, Pennsylvania Archives, 150 North Queen Street, Lancaster, Pennsylvania.

# Descendants of James Pegan, Son of Andrew I

**1**   **James[3] Pegan** (*Andrew[2] Pagan, James[1]*) was born in 1752 in Martic Twp., Lancaster Co., Pennsylvania. He was the son of Andrew Pagan and Ann McDowell? James died in Martic Twp., Lancaster Co., Pennsylvania, on January 20, 1834, at age 82. He was buried in Old Chestnut Level Presbyterian Lower Cemetery, Drumore Twp., Lancaster Co., Pennsylvania.[1, 2]

James Pegan married **Sarah Brannon** before 1787. They had eight children. Sarah Brannon was born in Martic Twp., Lancaster Co., Pennsylvania, in 1754. Sarah reached age 78 and died in Martic Twp., Lancaster Co., Pennsylvania, on March 3, 1832. She was buried in Old Chestnut Level Presbyterian Lower Cemetery, Drumore Twp., Lancaster Co., Pennsylvania.[1, 2]

James Pegan "inherited" his father's land in Martic Twp., Pennsylvania, according to Andrew Sr.'s will.[3] James became the heir after his elder brother, Alexander, Andrew I's eldest son according to the Martic Township tax records, died, seemingly unmarried and without property, about 1773-4.[4]

That Andrew Pagan/Pegan's land was inherited by his son James Pagan/Pegan is evident in a deed for land belonging to the late John Long of Drumore Twp., Lancaster Co., Pennsylvania. The deed, drawn up on April 2, 1800 and recorded on 17 May 1803 to settle John Long's will, was between the grantors "Hugh Long and Others, " the children of John Long, and grantee Peter Baughman. The deed mentions the land is in Martic Township adjacent to "the land of Andrew Pagan" which was now in the hands of "James Pagan":

> "Whereas, Thomas and Richard Penn, Proprietaries and Governors of Pennsylvania, Patent dated September 8,1769, granted unto John Long, of Drumore township, Lancaster County, aforesaid. All that certain tract of land in Martick township, Coxanty

of Lancaster, in the then Province of Pennsylvania, bounded and described as follows, Beginning at a marked maple tree, thence by lands of Andrew Pagan, now James Pagan... Said Patent recorded in Patent Book AA, Vol, II, page 118..."[5]

However, there was a catch—Andrew never legally owned the land. No deed of purchase exists, although the land is credited as Andrew Pagan/Pegan Sr.'s on maps in other deeds, warrants and patents entered by his neighboring landowners. After intensive searching for any paper trail on the property, this author contacted the historians at the Pennsylvania State Archives in 2015. They confirmed her theory that Andrew Sr. was a squatter and never the legal landowner.[6] James Pegan takes out a warrant application for 100 acres in Martic Township on November 11, 1795, saying that his family has lived on this land for about 10 years.[7]

Perhaps, somehow, James discovered that his father had no legal claim to the land and took steps to rectify this. According to the patent index, James finally is granted a patent on the land on February 6, 1810, and names the homestead as "Pegan's Fancy".[6] For some reason, the "History of Martic Township" in Evan's *History of Lancaster County, Pennsylvania* says that James' eldest son Andrew takes out the patent, but this is not what the patent index states.[8] The Pennsylvania State Archive historians confirmed that this warrant and patent was for the same 100 acres accredited to Andrew Pagan/Pegan Sr. shown in his neighbors' deeds, and warrant surveys.[6]

From the "History of Martic Township" chapter in *History of Lancaster County...*:

> "James Pegan, grandfather of the present family of Pegans in Martic township, came to Lancaster County prior to 1757, and settled upon a tract of land in Martic township, near the village of Bethesda. This tract was

known as "Pegan's Fancy". A patent for this land was issued to Andrew Pegan, bearing date 1810. James Pegan, above mentioned, had three sons, namely, James, Andrew, and Henry, and three daughters, Margaret, Ann, and Jane. Andrew Pegan, who received the patent already mentioned, was the father of seven children, three sons and four daughters. His sons were James, Alexander, and Andrew. Two of these reside at present (1883) in Martic township, James near the village of Bethesda, and Alexander near the village of Mount Nebo. Margaret (deceased), the oldest of the daughters, was married to George Nimlow. Two of her descendants, namely, Hannah Margaret, wife of Isaac Walton, merchant, and Anna Mary, wife of James Akens, shoemaker, reside at present (1883) in the village of Mount Nebo. A son, James Andrew, is a tobacco merchant in the city of Lancaster, and Sarah Jane is married to Hugh Kilgore, of York County. James Pegan has been postmaster at Bethesda from 1863 to the present time (1883). Alexander Pegan has held the same office at Mount Nebo (with occasional interruptions) for a number of years. James Pegan, the grandfather of the present family, served as a soldier in the Continental army during the struggle of the colonies for national independence."[9]

According to an article, "The History of Martic Township" by Larry Hess, the land also contained a sawmill. Mr. Hess, however, mistakenly cites Andrew Pagan's name as "Adam" Pagan in the article.[10]

This tract, "Pegan's Fancy", stays in James Pegan's line, for generations. Roy D. Pegan, a descendant of James and Sarah Brannon who was a family historian for this line, left a file of family information and pictures of a house, built in the mid-1800s, which another descendant built on the land. James' descendants held an annual reunion there for decades through the 1950s.[2]

But in the late 1960s, when the Susquehanna Electric Company, now a division of Excelon Generation, claimed the land as part of a new dam project on the Susquehanna River. The electric company constructed a 250-foot high, 4800-foot long rock-filled dam on the Muddy Run, a small tributary of the Susquehanna

River which flowed through "Pegan's Fancy" or very near it, forming the Muddy Run Reservoir.[11]

According to Robert L. Pegan, one of the few descendants of James and Sarah Brannon Pegan who bears the family surname, says the entire land tract, including the home, is now underwater in the Muddy Run Reservoir, in Muddy Run Park, about 100 feet from the water's edge. Robert Pegan believes that part of the foundation from Andrew Pagan/Pegan Sr.'s sawmill still existed when the land was flooded.[12]

Roy D. Pegan kept detailed records of the births, deaths and marriages in this family. This chapter relied much on Roy's records, augmented by online research. However, Roy D. Pegan says in his file that his ancestor James Pegan who married Sarah Brannon was the son of James Pegan II, son of James I and brother to Andrew Sr. But this is incorrect. James Pegan's warrant and survey and the other aforementioned surveys clearly show that the James Pegan who took out the warrant and patent was the son of Andrew Pagan/Pegan Sr., although he is referred to on the 1790 census as "James Pagan, Jr." We know this James is the son of Andrew because his land bordered that of Patrick Campbell, as Andrew Sr.'s had, according to a warrant survey from the Pennsylvania State Archives.[2, 6]

James may have been cited as a "Jr." because his much older cousin, James Pagan III, was still a resident of Martic Twp. (In this era, often two men with the same name were differentiated with "Sr." or "Jr." on documents and in the census, whether they were father and son, uncle and nephew, or cousins. The designation only refers to which one was older and which was younger.) His 1790 census seems to be in error, as there was one male more than age 16, three males under age 16, and two females in the household. From other data, the correct enumeration should have been one male more than age 16, two males under age 16, and three females *(Census Place: Martick, Lancaster, Pennsylvania; Series: M637; Roll: 8; Page: 59; Image: 749).*

"James Pegan Sr." left a will in Martic Twp., Lancaster Co., Pennsylvania, which was proven on March 5, 1834 In the will he mentions his daughter Jean Pegan, then unmarried, son James III, daughter Margaret

Pegan Miller, and grandchildren Sarah Pegan Robinson, Agnes Robinson, Margaret Robinson and Thomas James Robinson, children of his late daughter Ann Pegan Robinson.[13]

James Pegan and Sarah Brannon's gravestones still stand and are near that of his uncle, Archibald Pagan, in Old Chestnut Level Presbyterian Cemetery in Drumore Township, Lancaster County, Pennsylvania. As aforementioned, they have only a handful of male descendants that bear the Pegan surname in the present day. But there are legions of descendants through the females in the family. Unlike his siblings' descendants, who migrated throughout the U.S., very few of James' progeny ventured away from the area—the vast majority still live in Lancaster and York counties, Pennsylvania, in the very northern part of Maryland, and northern Delaware (although Ann Pegan Robinson's progeny have not been located).

Children of James Pegan and Sarah Brannon:

+ 2  f  I.  **Ann**[4] **Pegan** was born in Martic Twp., Lancaster Co., Pennsylvania, before 1787. She died before 1830.

+ 3  m  II.  **Andrew**[4] **Pegan** was born in Martic Twp., Lancaster Co., Pennsylvania, in 1788. He died in Martic Twp., Lancaster Co., Pennsylvania, in 1830. Andrew was buried in Old Chestnut Level Presbyterian Lower Cemetery, Drumore Twp., Lancaster Co., Pennsylvania.[2]

+ 4  m  III.  **John**[4] **Pegan** was born in Martic Twp., Lancaster Co., Pennsylvania, before 1790. He died in Martic Twp., Lancaster Co., Pennsylvania, before 1810.

+ 5  f  IV.  **Margaret**[4] **Pegan** was born in Martic Twp., Lancaster Co., Pennsyl-

vania, on April 16, 1787. She died in Peach Bottom Twp., York Co., Pennsylvania, on March 16, 1867. Margaret was buried in Chanceford Presbyterian Cemetery, Airville, Lower Chanceford Twp., York Co., Pennsylvania.[14]

+ 6  m  V.  **Henry**[4] **Pegan** was born in Martic Twp., Lancaster Co., Pennsylvania, in March 1790. He died in Martic Twp., Lancaster Co., Pennsylvania, on November 28, 1809. Henry was buried in Old Chestnut Level Presbyterian Lower Cemetery, Drumore Twp., Lancaster Co., Pennsylvania.[1, 2]

+ 7  f  VI.  **Sarah**[4] **Pegan** was born in Martic Twp., Lancaster Co., Pennsylvania, in July 1794. She died in Martic Twp., Lancaster Co., Pennsylvania, on September 19, 1814. Sarah was buried in Old Chestnut Level Presbyterian Lower Cemetery, Drumore Twp., Lancaster Co., Pennsylvania.[1, 2]

+ 8  m  VII.  **James**[4] **Pegan II** was born in Martic Twp., Lancaster Co., Pennsylvania, on July 27, 1796. He died in Martic Twp., Lancaster Co., Pennsylvania, on April 6, 1875. James was buried in Muddy Run Presbyterian Cemetery, Martic Twp., Lancaster Co., Pennsylvania.[2, 15]

+ 9  f  VIII.  **Jane**[4] **Pegan** was born in Martic Twp., Lancaster Co., Pennsylvania, in 1800. She died in Martic Twp., Lancaster Co., Pennsylvania, after 1834.

# 4th Generation

**2. Ann⁴ Pegan** (*James³, Andrew² Pagan, James¹*) was born before 1787 in Martic Twp., Lancaster Co., Pennsylvania. She was the daughter of James Pegan (1) and Sarah Brannon. Ann died before 1830. Ann Pegan, is mentioned in her grandfather Andrew Pegan Sr.'s will and cited as the daughter of James Pegan. Her married surname was Robinson, but she died before her father James Pegan II (known as James Pegan Sr.) wrote his will. All four of her children are mentioned in James' will.

Ann married **Unknown Robinson** before 1820. They had four children.

Children of Ann Pegan and Unknown Robinson:

+ 10  f   I.     **Sarah Pegan⁵ Robinson.**

+ 11  f   II.    **Agnes⁵ Robinson.**

+ 12  f   III.   **Margaret⁵ Robinson.**

+ 13  m  IV.   **Thomas James⁵ Robinson.**

**2. Andrew⁴ Pegan** (*James³, Andrew² Pagan, James¹*) was born in 1788 in Martic Twp., Lancaster Co., Pennsylvania. He was the son of James Pegan (1) and Sarah Brannon. Andrew died in Martic Twp., Lancaster Co., Pennsylvania, in 1830 at age 42. He was buried in Old Chestnut Level Presbyterian Lower Cemetery, Drumore Twp., Lancaster Co., Pennsylvania.[2]

This Andrew Pegan/Pagan/Pegon received the land patent for the tract of family land, "Pegan's Fancy", near the village of Bethesda in southwestern Lancaster Co., Pennsylvania in 1810.

Andrew married **Jane Leiper or Leeper** before 1815. They had seven children. Jane Leiper or Leeper was born in Martic Twp., Lancaster Co., Pennsylvania? on March 29, 1793.[16] Jane Leiper or reached age 85 and died in Martic Twp., Lancaster Co., Pennsylvania, on December 10, 1878. She was buried in Mount Nebo Cemetery (Presbyterian Graveyard), White Oak, Martic Twp., Lancaster Co., Pennsylvania.[2, 16]

Jane Leeper Pegan is listed as "Pegan, Jane, wid. of Andrew" in the 1869-70 Lancaster County, Pennsylvania directory.[17]

Children of Andrew Pegan and Jane Leiper or Leeper:

+ 14  f   I.     **Margaret⁵ Pegan** was born in Martic Twp., Lancaster Co., Pennsylvania, on September 26, 1815. She died in Martic Twp., Lancaster Co., Pennsylvania, on August 31, 1878. Margaret was buried in Mount Nebo Cemetery (Presbyterian Graveyard), White Oak, Martic Twp., Lancaster Co., Pennsylvania.[16]

+ 15  m  II.    **James Henry⁵ Pegan** was born in Martic Twp., Lancaster Co., Pennsylvania, on August 8, 1818. He died in Bethesda, Martic Twp., Lancaster Co., Pennsylvania, on January 11, 1898. James Henry was buried in Mount Nebo Cemetery (Presbyterian Graveyard), White Oak, Martic Twp., Lancaster Co., Pennsylvania.[2, 16]

+ 16  f   III.   **Anna⁵ Pegan** was born in Martic Twp., Lancaster Co., Pennsylvania, on December 12, 1820. She died in Lower Chanceford Twp., York Co., Pennsylvania, on February 6, 1900. Anna was buried in Chanceford Presbyterian Cemetery, Airville, Lower Chanceford Twp., York Co., Pennsylvania.[2, 14]

+ 17  f   IV.   **Sarah Jane⁵ Pegan** was born in Martic Twp., Lancaster Co., Pennsylvania, on April 7, 1823.[2, 3] She died in Lower Chanceford Twp., York Co. Pennsylvania, on September 13, 1911 Sarah Jane was buried in Chanceford Presbyterian Cemetery, Airville, Lower Chanceford Twp., York Co., Pennsylvania.[14]

+ 18 f V. **Mary S.⁵ Pegan** was born in Martic Twp., Lancaster Co., Pennsylvania, on June 16, 1825. She died in Martic Twp., Lancaster Co., Pennsylvania, on September 2, 1869. Mary S. was buried in Mount Nebo Cemetery (Presbyterian Graveyard), White Oak, Martic Twp., Lancaster Co., Pennsylvania.[2, 16]

+ 19 m VI. **Alexander L.⁵ Pegan** was born in Martic Twp., Lancaster Co., Pennsylvania, in January 1828. He died in Lancaster, Lancaster Co., Pennsylvania, in 1901. Alexander L. was buried in Lancaster Cemetery, Lancaster, Lancaster Co., Pennsylvania.[2, 18]

+ 20 m VII. **Andrew A.⁵ Pegan II** was born in Martic Twp., Lancaster Co., Pennsylvania, on March 2, 1831. He died in Manor Twp., Lancaster Co., Pennsylvania, on August 25, 1916. Andrew A. was buried in Green Mount Cemetery, Highville, Manor Twp., Lancaster Co., Pennsylvania.[19]

4. **John⁴ Pegan** (*James³, Andrew² Pagan, James¹*) was born before 1790 in Martic Twp., Lancaster Co., Pennsylvania. He was the son of James Pegan (1) and Sarah Brannon. John died in Martic Twp., Lancaster Co., Pennsylvania, before 1810.

5. **Margaret⁴ Pegan** (*James³, Andrew² Pagan, James¹*) was born on April 16, 1787, in Martic Twp., Lancaster Co., Pennsylvania. She was the daughter of James Pegan (1) and Sarah Brannon. Margaret died in Peach Bottom Twp., York Co., Pennsylvania, on March 16, 1867, at age 79. She was buried in Chanceford Presbyterian Cemetery, Airville, Lower Chanceford Twp., York Co., Pennsylvania.[14]

She married **Allen Miller** before 1814. They had eight children. Allen Miller was born in Chanceford Twp., York Co., Pennsylvania, on October 19, 1783. Allen reached age 74 and died in Peach Bottom Twp., York Co., Pennsylvania, on April 26,

1858. He was buried in Chanceford Presbyterian Cemetery, Airville, Lower Chanceford Twp., York Co., Pennsylvania.[14]

Children of Margaret Pegan and Allen Miller:

+ 21 m I. **Robert⁵ Miller** was born in Peach Bottom Twp., York Co., Pennsylvania, about 1815. He died in Peach Bottom Twp., York Co., Pennsylvania, between 1830 and 1840.

+ 22 f II. **Sarah Jane⁵ Miller** was born in Peach Bottom Twp., York Co., Pennsylvania, on November 5, 1816. She died in Peach Bottom Twp., York Co., Pennsylvania, on July 16, 1888. Sarah Jane was buried in Slate Ridge Cemetery, Delta, Peach Bottom Twp., York Co., Pennsylvania.[20]

+ 23 f III. **Mary Ann⁵ Miller** was born in Peach Bottom Twp., York Co., Pennsylvania, on January 23, 1818. She died in Peach Bottom Twp., York Co., Pennsylvania, on April 20, 1863. Mary Ann was buried in Chanceford Presbyterian Cemetery, Airville, Lower Chanceford Twp., York Co., Pennsylvania.[14]

+ 24 f IV. **Elizabeth⁵ Miller** was born in Peach Bottom Twp., York Co., Pennsylvania, on June 6, 1821. She died in Peach Bottom Twp., York Co., Pennsylvania, on March 10, 1823. Elizabeth was buried in Chanceford Presbyterian Cemetery, Airville, Lower Chanceford Twp., York Co., Pennsylvania.[14]

+ 25 m V. **James⁵ Miller** was born in Peach Bottom Twp., York Co., Pennsylvania, on October 17, 1825. He died in Peach Bottom Twp., York Co., Pennsylvania, on May 17,

1868. James was buried in Chanceford Presbyterian Cemetery, Airville, Lower Chanceford Twp., York Co., Pennsylvania.[14]

+ 26 f VI. **Margaret Elizabeth⁵ Miller** was born in Peach Bottom Twp., York Co., Pennsylvania, on December 29, 1828. She was also known as **Elizabeth**. Margaret Elizabeth died in Peach Bottom Twp., York Co., Pennsylvania, on August 5, 1902. She was buried in Chanceford Presbyterian Cemetery, Airville, Lower Chanceford Twp., York Co., Pennsylvania.[14]

+ 27 f VII. **Agnes⁵ Miller** was born in Peach Bottom Twp., York Co., Pennsylvania, on May 30, 1830. She died in Lower Chanceford Twp., York Co., Pennsylvania, on December 29, 1917. Agnes was buried in Chanceford Presbyterian Cemetery, Airville, Lower Chanceford Twp., York Co., Pennsylvania.[14]

+ 28 f VIII. **Martha Ellen⁵ Miller** was born in Peach Bottom Twp., York Co., Pennsylvania, on November 6, 1833. She died in Peach Bottom Twp., York Co., Pennsylvania, on February 5, 1913. Martha Ellen was buried in Chanceford Presbyterian Cemetery, Airville, Lower Chanceford Twp., York Co., Pennsylvania.[14]

6. **Henry⁴ Pegan** (*James³, Andrew² Pagan, James¹*) was born in March 1790 in Martic Twp., Lancaster Co., Pennsylvania. He was the son of James Pegan (1) and Sarah Brannon. Henry died in Martic Twp., Lancaster Co., Pennsylvania, on November 28, 1809, at age 19. He was buried in Old Chestnut Level Presbyterian Lower Cemetery, Drumore Twp., Lancaster Co., Pennsylvania.[1, 2]

Never married.

7. **Sarah⁴ Pegan** (*James³, Andrew² Pagan, James¹*) was born in July 1794 in Martic Twp., Lancaster Co., Pennsylvania. She was the daughter of James Pegan (1) and Sarah Brannon. Sarah died in Martic Twp., Lancaster Co., Pennsylvania, on September 19, 1814, at age 20. She was buried in Old Chestnut Level Presbyterian Lower Cemetery, Drumore Twp., Lancaster Co., Pennsylvania.[1, 2]

8. **James⁴ Pegan II** (*James³, Andrew² Pagan, James¹*) was born on July 27, 1796, in Martic Twp., Lancaster Co., Pennsylvania. He was the son of James Pegan (1) and Sarah Brannon. James died in Martic Twp., Lancaster Co., Pennsylvania, on April 6, 1875, at age 78. He was buried in Muddy Run Presbyterian Cemetery, Martic Twp., Lancaster Co., Pennsylvania.[2, 15]

James married **Mary Jane Gowen** in 1827 in Lancaster Co., Pennsylvania. They had six children. Mary Jane Gowen was born in Lancaster Co., Pennsylvania? on March 19, 1802. She was also known as **Jane**. Mary Jane reached age 78 and died in Chanceford Twp., York Co., Pennsylvania, on August 11, 1880. She was buried in Old Guinston Church Cemetery, Airville, Chanceford Twp., York Co., Pennsylvania.[2, 21]

Although Roy D. Pegan refers to Mary Jane Gowen as "Mary Jean Gowen", and there is an internet marriage record with the latter name, her gravestone, census records, and her daughter Mary Ann Pegan's obituary all refer to her as "Jane".

Children of James Pegan II and Mary Jane Gowen:

+ 29 m I. **James Jonas⁵ Pegan III** was born in Martic Twp., Lancaster Co., Pennsylvania, in 1828. He died in Martic Twp., Lancaster Co., Pennsylvania, in 1840.

30 f II. **Mary Ann⁵ Pegan** was born in Martic
+ Twp., Lancaster Co., Pennsylvania, in 1831. She died in Chanceford Twp., York Co., Pennsylvania, on March 31, 1896. Mary Ann was buried in

Old Guinston Church Cemetery, Airville, Chanceford Twp., York Co., Pennsylvania.[22]

+ 31 m III. **Henry⁵ Pegan** was born in Martic Twp., Lancaster Co., Pennsylvania, on December 8, 1833. He died in Lancaster, Lancaster Co., Pennsylvania, on February 16, 1911. Henry was buried in Spring Grove Cemetery, Jackson Twp., York Co., Pennsylvania. [23, 24]

+ 32 f IV. **Sarah Eliza⁵ Pegan** was born in Martic Twp., Lancaster Co., Pennsylvania, on December 19, 1835. She died in East Hopewell Twp., York Co., Pennsylvania, on August 26, 1914. Sarah Eliza was buried in Old Guinston Church Cemetery, Airville, Chanceford Twp., York Co., Pennsylvania.[2]

+ 33 m V. **Isaac A.⁵ Pegan** was born in Martic Twp., Lancaster Co., Pennsylvania, on August 4, 1837. He died in Martic Twp., Lancaster Co., Pennsylvania, on August 12, 1849. Isaac A. was buried

in Muddy Run Presbyterian Cemetery, Martic Twp., Lancaster Co., Pennsylvania.[15]

+ 34 f VI. **Margaret Jane⁵ Pegan** was born in Martic Twp., Lancaster Co., Pennsylvania, on November 8, 1844. She was also known as **Maggie**. Margaret Jane died in York, York Co., Pennsylvania, on November 12, 1923. She was buried in Old Guinston Church Cemetery, Airville, Chanceford Twp., York Co., Pennsylvania.[2]

9. **Jane⁴ Pegan** (*James³, Andrew² Pagan, James¹*) was born in 1800 in Martic Twp., Lancaster Co., Pennsylvania. She was the daughter of James Pegan (1) and Sarah Brannon. The Roy D. Pegan file and the Martic Township section in the History of Lancaster County, Pennsylvania name her as Jane. But she is referred to as Jean Pegan in her father James' will. Jane/Jean Pegan was still single at the time of her father James Pegan death. There are no further records on her. She may have died unmarried and childless.

# 5th Generation

**10. Sarah Pegan⁵ Robinson** (*Ann⁴ Pegan, James³, Andrew² Pagan, James¹*). She is the daughter of Unknown Robinson and Ann Pegan (2).

**11. Agnes⁵ Robinson** (*Ann⁴ Pegan, James³, Andrew² Pagan, James¹*). She is the daughter of Unknown Robinson and Ann Pegan (2).

**12. Margaret⁵ Robinson** (*Ann⁴ Pegan, James³, Andrew² Pagan, James¹*). She is the daughter of Unknown Robinson and Ann Pegan (2).

**13. Thomas James⁵ Robinson** (*Ann⁴ Pegan, James³, Andrew² Pagan, James¹*). He is the son of Unknown Robinson and Ann Pegan (2).

**14. Margaret⁵ Pegan** (*Andrew⁴, James³, Andrew² Pagan, James¹*) was born on September 26, 1815, in Martic Twp., Lancaster Co., Pennsylvania. She was the daughter of Andrew Pegan (3) and Jane Leiper or Leeper. Margaret died in Martic Twp., Lancaster Co., Pennsylvania, on August 31, 1878, at age 62. She was buried in Mount Nebo Cemetery (Presbyterian Graveyard), White Oak, Martic Twp., Lancaster Co., Pennsylvania.[16]

Margaret married **George Nimlow** before 1843. They had seven children. George Nimlow was born in Maryland on January 1, 1813. George reached age 51 and died in Martic Twp., Lancaster Co., Pennsylvania, on June 29, 1864. He was buried in Mount Nebo Cemetery (Presbyterian Graveyard), White Oak, Martic Twp., Lancaster Co., Pennsylvania.[16]

Children of Margaret Pegan and George Nimlow:

+ 35 m I.    **James Andrew⁶ Nimlow** was born in Fulton Twp., Lancaster Co., Pennsylvania, on November 21, 1843. He died in Lancaster, Lancaster Co., Pennsylvania, on April 30, 1927. James Andrew was buried in Greenwood Cemetery, Lancaster, Lancaster Co., Pennsylvania.[2, 25]

+ 36 f II.    **Hannah Margaret⁶ Nimlow** was born in Fulton Twp., Lancaster Co., Pennsylvania, on July 2, 1844. She died in Martic Twp., Lancaster Co., Pennsylvania, on February 18, 1916. Hannah Margaret was buried in Mount Nebo Cemetery (Presbyterian Graveyard), White Oak, Martic Twp., Lancaster Co., Pennsylvania.[16]

+ 37 m III.    **Alexander Leiper or Leeper⁶ Nimlow** was born in Fulton Twp., Lancaster Co., Pennsylvania, in 1845. He died in Boise, Ada Co., Idaho, on September 7, 1908.[26] Alexander Leiper or Leeper was buried in Boise Barracks National Cemetery, Boise, Ada Co., Idaho.[27]

+ 38 f IV.    **Anna Mary⁶ Nimlow** was born in Fulton Twp., Lancaster Co., Pennsylvania, in June 1849. She died in Lancaster, Lancaster Co., Pennsylvania, on February 2, 1902. Anna Mary was buried in Mount Nebo Cemetery (Presbyterian Graveyard), White Oak, Martic Twp., Lancaster Co., Pennsylvania.[2, 16]

+ 39 m V.    **George⁶ Niblock (Nimlow II)** was born in Fulton Twp., Lancaster Co., Pennsylvania, on July 7, 1851. He died in Conoy Twp., Lancaster Co., Pennsylvania, on October 28, 1923. George Niblock was buried in Mount Tunnel Cemetery, Elizabethtown, Mt. Joy Twp., Lancaster Co., Pennsylvania.[28]

+ 40 m VI.    **Miller K.⁶ Nimlow** was born in Martic Twp., Lancaster Co., Pennsylvania, on April 4, 1854. He died in Mt. Nebo, Martic Twp., Lancaster Co., Pennsylvania, on July 22, 1870. Miller K. was buried in Mount Nebo Cemetery (Presbyterian Graveyard), White

Oak, Martic Twp., Lancaster Co., Pennsylvania.[16]

+ 41 f VII. **Ida Jane**[6] **Nimlow** was born in Martic Twp., Lancaster Co., Pennsylvania, on December 25, 1859. She died in Martic Twp., Lancaster Co., Pennsylvania, on February 16, 1861. Ida Jane was buried in Mount Nebo Cemetery (Presbyterian Graveyard), White Oak, Martic Twp., Lancaster Co., Pennsylvania.[16]

15. **James Henry**[5] **Pegan** (*Andrew*[4], *James*[3], *Andrew*[2] *Pagan, James*[1]) was born on August 8, 1818, in Martic Twp., Lancaster Co., Pennsylvania. He was the son of Andrew Pegan (3) and Jane Leiper or Leeper. He died in Bethesda, Martic Twp., Lancaster Co., Pennsylvania, on January 11, 1898, at age 79. James Henry was buried in Mount Nebo Cemetery (Presbyterian Graveyard), White Oak, Martic Twp., Lancaster Co., Pennsylvania.[2, 16]

James Henry married **Harriet Ankrim** on January 15, 1854, in Lancaster Co., Pennsylvania. They had one son. Harriet Ankrim was born in Martic Twp., Lancaster Co., Pennsylvania? on April 28, 1825.[16] Harriet reached age 49 and died in Martic Twp., Lancaster Co., Pennsylvania, on May 20, 1874. She was buried in Mount Nebo Cemetery (Presbyterian Graveyard), White Oak, Martic Twp., Lancaster Co., Pennsylvania.[2, 16]

James Henry Pegan married **Mary E. Markley** about 1881. They had one daughter. Mary E. Markley was born in York, York Co., Pennsylvania, on August 23, 1845. Mary E. reached age 81 and died in Lancaster, Lancaster Co., Pennsylvania, on January 10, 1927. She was buried in Mount Nebo Cemetery (Presbyterian Graveyard), White Oak, Martic Twp., Lancaster Co., Pennsylvania.[2, 16]

Son of James Henry Pegan and Harriet Ankrim:

+ 42 m I. **Samuel A.**[6] **Pegan** was born in Martic Twp., Lancaster Co., Pennsylvania,

on November 28, 1854. He died in Sunnyburn, Lower Chanceford Twp., York Co., Pennsylvania, on December 13, 1908. Samuel A. was buried in Greenwood Cemetery, Lancaster, Lancaster Co., Pennsylvania.[2, 25]

Daughter of James Henry Pegan and Mary E. Markley:

+ 43 f I. **Myra S.**[6] **Pegan** was born in Martic Twp., Lancaster Co., Pennsylvania, on December 29, 1882. She died in Atlanta, DeKalb Co., Georgia, on October 3, 1937. Myra S. was buried in Greenwood Cemetery, Lancaster, Lancaster Co., Pennsylvania.[2, 25]

16. **Anna**[5] **Pegan** (*Andrew*[4], *James*[3], *Andrew*[2] *Pagan, James*[1]) was born on December 12, 1820, in Martic Twp., Lancaster Co., Pennsylvania. She was the daughter of Andrew Pegan (3) and Jane Leiper or Leeper. Anna died in Lower Chanceford Twp., York Co., Pennsylvania, on February 6, 1900, at age 79. She was buried in Chanceford Presbyterian Cemetery, Airville, Lower Chanceford Twp., York Co., Pennsylvania.[2, 14]

Never married.

Anna was living with her brother-in-law and sister, Hugh and Sarah Ann Pegan Kilgore, in Lower Chanceford Twp., York Co., Pennsylvania in 1880.

17. **Sarah Jane**[5] **Pegan** (*Andrew*[4], *James*[3], *Andrew*[2] *Pagan, James*[1]) was born on April 7, 1823, in Martic Twp., Lancaster Co., Pennsylvania.[3, 2] She was the daughter of Andrew Pegan (3) and Jane Leiper or Leeper. Sarah Jane died in Lower Chanceford Twp., York Co., Pennsylvania, on September 13, 1911, at age 88. She was buried in Chanceford Presbyterian Cemetery, Airville, Lower Chanceford Twp., York Co., Pennsylvania.[14]

Sarah Jane married **Hugh William Kilgore** about 1845. They had eight children. Hugh William Kilgore was born in Lower Chanceford Twp., York Co., Pennsylvania, on May 3, 1813. Hugh William reached age 73 and died in Lower Chanceford Twp., York Co., Pennsylvania, on November 20, 1886. He was buried in Chanceford Presbyterian

Cemetery, Airville, Lower Chanceford Twp., York Co., Pennsylvania.[2, 14]

Children of Sarah Jane Pegan and Hugh William Kilgore:

+ 44 m I. **Alvin Levi**[6] **Kilgore** was born in Lower Chanceford Twp., York Co., Pennsylvania, on October 17, 1846. He died in Lower Chanceford Twp., York Co., Pennsylvania, on October 5, 1916. Alvin Levi was buried in Chanceford Presbyterian Cemetery, Airville, Lower Chanceford Twp., York Co., Pennsylvania.[2, 14]

+ 45 m II. **James Ankrim**[6] **Kilgore** was born in Lower Chanceford Twp., York Co., Pennsylvania, on September 6, 1848. He died in Lower Chanceford Twp., York Co., Pennsylvania, on December 6, 1914. James Ankrim was buried in Chanceford Presbyterian Cemetery, Airville, Lower Chanceford Twp., York Co., Pennsylvania.[14]

+ 46 f III. **Laura Clinda**[6] **Kilgore** was born in Lower Chanceford Twp., York Co., Pennsylvania, on November 2, 1850. She died in Lower Chanceford Twp., York Co., Pennsylvania, on October 24, 1894. Laura Clinda was buried in Chanceford Presbyterian Cemetery, Airville, Lower Chanceford Twp., York Co., Pennsylvania.[2]

+ 47 m IV. **William Ramsey**[6] **Kilgore** was born in Lower Chanceford Twp., York Co., Pennsylvania, in August 1853. He died in York, York Co., Pennsylvania? in 1917.[2]

+ 48 f V. **Anna Margaret**[6] **Kilgore** was born in Lower Chanceford Twp., York Co., Pennsylvania, on October 17, 1857. She was also known as **Maggie** and **Margaret**. Anna Margaret died in Lower Chanceford Twp., York Co., Pennsylvania, on May 13, 1938. She was buried in Old Guinston Church Cemetery, Airville, Chanceford Twp., York Co., Pennsylvania.[2, 21]

+ 49 m VI. **Emory Milton**[6] **Kilgore** was born in Lower Chanceford Twp., York Co., Pennsylvania, on September 17, 1860. He was also known as **Milton**. Emory Milton died in Lower Chanceford Twp., York Co., Pennsylvania, on June 29, 1949. He was buried in Chanceford Presbyterian Cemetery, Airville, Lower Chanceford Twp., York Co., Pennsylvania.[2, 14]

+ 50 f VII. **Luella Jane**[6] **Kilgore** was born in Lower Chanceford Twp., York Co., Pennsylvania, on March 24, 1863. She was also known as **Ella**. Luella Jane died in Delta, Peach Bottom Twp., York Co., Pennsylvania, on April 2, 1943. She was buried in Salem United Methodist Church Cemetery, Delta, Peach Bottom Twp., York Co., Pennsylvania.[2]

+ 51 f VIII. **Janetta**[6] **Kilgore** was born in Lower Chanceford Twp., York Co., Pennsylvania, in 1868. She died in Lower Chanceford Twp., York Co., Pennsylvania, in 1868. Janetta was buried in Chanceford Presbyterian Cemetery, Airville, Lower Chanceford Twp., York Co., Pennsylvania.[2]

**18. Mary S.**[5] **Pegan** (*Andrew*[4], *James*[3], *Andrew*[2] *Pagan*, *James*[1]) was born on June 16, 1825, in Martic Twp., Lancaster Co., Pennsylvania. She was the daughter of Andrew Pegan (3) and Jane Leiper or Leeper. Mary S. died in Martic Twp., Lancaster Co., Pennsylvania, on September 2, 1869, at age 44. She was buried in Mount Nebo Cemetery (Presbyterian Graveyard), White Oak, Martic Twp., Lancaster Co., Pennsylvania.[2, 16]

Never married.

**19. Alexander L.⁵ Pegan** (*Andrew⁴, James³, Andrew²Pagan, James¹*) was born in January 1828 in Martic Twp., Lancaster Co., Pennsylvania. He was the son of Andrew Pegan (3) and Jane Leiper or Leeper. Alexander L. worked as a Postmaster of Mt. Nebo, Martic Twp., Lancaster Co., Pennsylvania in 1883. He died in Lancaster, Lancaster Co., Pennsylvania, in 1901 at age 73. Alexander L. was buried in Lancaster Cemetery, Lancaster, Lancaster Co., Pennsylvania.[2, 18]

Alexander L. married **Ruthanna Appleton** on October 28, 1849, in Lancaster Co., Pennsylvania. They had seven children. Ruthanna Appleton was born in Martic Twp., Lancaster Co., Pennsylvania, on October 6, 1833. Ruthanna reached age 82 and died in Lancaster, Lancaster Co., Pennsylvania, on June 17, 1916. She was buried in Lancaster Cemetery, Lancaster, Lancaster Co., Pennsylvania.[18]

Children of Alexander L. Pegan and Ruthanna Appleton:

+ 52 f I.　　**Harriet Jane⁶ Pegan** was born in Martic Twp., Lancaster Co., Pennsylvania, on March 24, 1850. She died in Martic Twp., Lancaster Co., Pennsylvania, on March 1, 1873. Harriet Jane was buried in Mount Nebo Cemetery (Presbyterian Graveyard), White Oak, Martic Twp., Lancaster Co., Pennsylvania.[16]

+ 53 m I.　　**Lewis Cass⁶ Pegan** was born in Martic Twp., Lancaster Co., Pennsylvania, on May 28, 1852. He died in Lancaster, Lancaster Co., Pennsylvania, on August 1, 1929. Lewis Cass was buried in Greenwood Cemetery, Lancaster, Lancaster Co., Pennsylvania.[25]

+ 54 f II.　　**Sarah⁶ Pegan** was born in Martic Twp., Lancaster Co., Pennsylvania, on November 23, 1854. She died in Lancaster, Lancaster Co., Pennsylvania, on March 10, 1922. Sarah was buried in Greenwood Cemetery, Lancaster, Lancaster Co., Pennsylvania.[25]

+ 55 m III.　　**William H.⁶ Pegan** was born in Martic Twp., Lancaster Co., Pennsylvania, on September 20, 1857. He died in Martic Twp., Lancaster Co., Pennsylvania, on June 7, 1939. William H. was buried in Riverview Burial Park Cemetery, Lancaster, Lancaster Co., Pennsylvania.[29]

+ 56 m IV.　　**James Calvin⁶ Pegan** was born in Martic Twp., Lancaster Co., Pennsylvania, on December 22, 1859. He died in Pittsburgh, Allegheny Co., Pennsylvania, on January 7, 1915. James Calvin was buried in Chartiers Cemetery, Carnegie, Scott Twp., Allegheny Co., Pennsylvania.[30]

+ 57 f V.　　**Anna Mary⁶ Pegan** was born in Martic Twp., Lancaster Co., Pennsylvania, on November 4, 1864. She died in East Lampeter Twp., Lancaster Co., Pennsylvania, on August 4, 1950. Anna Mary was buried in Zion Lutheran Cemetery, Leola, Upper Leacock Twp., Lancaster Co., Pennsylvania.[31]

+ 58 m VI.　　**Elmer Elsworth⁶ Pegan** was born in Martic Twp., Lancaster Co., Pennsylvania, on January 2, 1863. He died in Wilmington, New Castle Co., Delaware, on January 13, 1939. Elmer Ellsworth James was buried in Silverbrook Cemetery, Wilmington, New Castle Co., Delaware.[32]

+ 59 f VII.　　**Effie May⁶ Pegan** was born in Martic Twp., Lancaster Co., Pennsylvania, on December 10, 1868. She died in Lancaster, Lancaster Co., Pennsylvania, on December 23, 1938. Effie May was buried in Riverview Burial Park Cemetery, Lancaster, Lancaster Co., Pennsylvania.[29].

**20. Andrew A.⁵ Pegan II** (*Andrew⁴, James³, Andrew²Pagan, James¹*) was born on March 2, 1831, in Martic Twp., Lancaster Co., Pennsylvania. He was the son of Andrew Pegan (3) and Jane Leiper or

Leeper. Andrew A. died in Manor Twp., Lancaster Co., Pennsylvania, on August 25, 1916, at age 85. He was buried in Green Mount Cemetery, Highville, Manor Twp., Lancaster Co., Pennsylvania.[19]

He married **Louisa Bailey**. They had three children. Louisa Bailey was born in Shrewsbury Twp., York Co., Pennsylvania, on February 6, 1839. Louisa reached age 56 and died in Conestoga Twp., Lancaster Co., Pennsylvania, on February 11, 1895. She was buried in Green Mount Cemetery, Highville, Manor Twp., Lancaster Co., Pennsylvania.[19]

Children of Andrew A. Pegan II and Louisa Bailey:

+ 60 f I. **Bertha⁶ Pegan** was born in Martic Twp., Lancaster Co., Pennsylvania, on April 21, 1868. She died in Manor Twp., Lancaster Co., Pennsylvania, on August 27, 1957. Bertha was buried in Grace United Methodist Church Cemetery, Millersville, Manor Twp., Lancaster Co., Pennsylvania.[33]

+ 61 m II. **Harry Franklin⁶ Pegan** was born in Bethesda, Martic Twp., Lancaster Co., Pennsylvania, on September 25, 1870. Harry Franklin died in Lancaster, Lancaster Co., Pennsylvania, on June 23, 1939. He was buried in Woodward Hill Cemetery, Lancaster, Lancaster Co., Pennsylvania.[34]

+ 62 m III. **Roy David⁶ Pegan** was born in East Drumore Twp., Lancaster Co., Pennsylvania, on January 1, 1873. He died in East Lampeter Twp., Lancaster Co., Pennsylvania, on May 5, 1958.

**21. Robert⁵ Miller** (*Margaret⁴ Pegan, James³, Andrew² Pagan, James¹*) was born about 1815 in Peach Bottom Twp., York Co., Pennsylvania. He was the son of Allen Miller and Margaret Pegan (5). Robert died in Peach Bottom Twp., York Co., Pennsylvania, between 1830 and 1840.

**22. Sarah Jane⁵ Miller** (*Margaret⁴ Pegan, James³, Andrew² Pagan, James¹*) was born on November 5, 1816, in Peach Bottom Twp., York Co., Pennsylvania. She was the daughter of Allen Miller and Margaret Pegan (5). Sarah Jane died in Peach Bottom Twp., York Co., Pennsylvania, on July 16, 1888, at age 71. She was buried in Slate Ridge Cemetery, Delta, Peach Bottom Twp., York Co., Pennsylvania.[20]

Sarah Jane married **David Fulton** on June 29, 1839, in York Co., Pennsylvania. They had six children. David Fulton was born in Peach Bottom Twp., York Co., Pennsylvania, on May 12, 1816. David reached age 78 and died in Peach Bottom Twp., York Co., Pennsylvania, on April 29, 1895. He was buried in Slate Ridge Cemetery, Delta, Peach Bottom Twp., York Co., Pennsylvania.[20]

Children of Sarah Jane Miller and David Fulton:

+ 63 f I. **Martha Ann⁶ Fulton** was born in Peach Bottom Twp., York Co., Pennsylvania, on June 13, 1840. She died in Peach Bottom Twp., York Co., Pennsylvania, on November 13, 1916. Martha Ann was buried in Slate Ridge Cemetery, Delta, Peach Bottom Twp., York Co., Pennsylvania.[2, 20]

+ 64 m II. **John Henry⁶ Fulton** was born in Peach Bottom Twp., York Co., Pennsylvania, on June 14, 1842. He died in Peach Bottom Twp., York Co., Pennsylvania, on September 23, 1932. John Henry was buried in Slate Ridge Cemetery, Delta, Peach Bottom Twp., York Co., Pennsylvania.[2, 20]

+ 65 f III. **Margaret A.⁶ Fulton** was born in Peach Bottom Twp., York Co., Pennsylvania, on March 13, 1845. She died in Fulton Twp., Lancaster Co., Pennsylvania, on December 5, 1884. Margaret A. was buried in Slate Ridge Cemetery, Delta, Peach Bottom Twp., York Co., Pennsylvania.[2]

+ 66 f IV. **Elizabeth Jane⁶ Fulton** was born in Peach Bottom Twp., York Co.,

Pennsylvania, on November 19, 1848. She was also known as **Lizzie**. Elizabeth Jane died in Peach Bottom Twp., York Co., Pennsylvania, on June 13, 1936. She was buried in Slate Ridge Cemetery, Delta, Peach Bottom Twp., York Co., Pennsylvania.[2, 20]

+ 67 m V.   **Robert Allen**[6] **Fulton** was born in Peach Bottom Twp., York Co., Pennsylvania, on June 11, 1852. He died in Peach Bottom Twp., York Co., Pennsylvania, on July 19, 1907. Robert Allen was buried in Slate Ridge Cemetery, Delta, Peach Bottom Twp., York Co., Pennsylvania.[2, 20]

+ 68 f VI.   **Agnes Miller**[6] **Fulton** was born in Peach Bottom Twp., York Co., Pennsylvania, on October 28, 1854. She died in Peach Bottom Twp., York Co., Pennsylvania, on July 22, 1909. Agnes Miller was buried in Slate Ridge Cemetery, Delta, Peach Bottom Twp., York Co., Pennsylvania.[2, 20]

**23. Mary Ann**[5] **Miller** (*Margaret*[4] *Pegan, James*[3]*, Andrew*[2] *Pagan, James*[1]) was born on January 23, 1818, in Peach Bottom Twp., York Co., Pennsylvania. She was the daughter of Allen Miller and Margaret Pegan (5). Mary Ann died in Peach Bottom Twp., York Co., Pennsylvania, on April 20, 1863, at age 45. She was buried in Chanceford Presbyterian Cemetery, Airville, Lower Chanceford Twp., York Co., Pennsylvania.[14]

Never married.

Mary Ann Miller's tombstone gives her age at death as 44 years, three months and 16 days, which would be January 14, 1819. But since her sister Elizabeth Miller Barton was born on September 17, 1819, Mary Ann was probably born in 1818.

**24. Elizabeth**[5] **Miller** (*Margaret*[4] *Pegan, James*[3]*, Andrew*[2] *Pagan, James*[1]) was born on June 6, 1821, in Peach Bottom Twp., York Co., Pennsylvania. She was the daughter of Allen Miller and Margaret Pegan (5). Elizabeth died in Peach Bottom Twp., York Co.,

Pennsylvania, on March 10, 1823, at age one. She was buried in Chanceford Presbyterian Cemetery, Airville, Lower Chanceford Twp., York Co., Pennsylvania.[14]

**25. James**[5] **Miller** (*Margaret*[4] *Pegan, James*[3]*, Andrew*[2] *Pagan, James*[1]) was born on October 17, 1825, in Peach Bottom Twp., York Co., Pennsylvania. He was the son of Allen Miller and Margaret Pegan (5). James died in Peach Bottom Twp., York Co., Pennsylvania, on May 17, 1868, at age 42. He was buried in Chanceford Presbyterian Cemetery, Airville, Lower Chanceford Twp., York Co., Pennsylvania.[14]

Never married.

**26. Margaret Elizabeth**[5] **Miller** (*Margaret*[4] *Pegan, James*[3]*, Andrew*[2] *Pagan, James*[1]) was born on December 29, 1828, in Peach Bottom Twp., York Co., Pennsylvania. She was also known as **Elizabeth**. She was the daughter of Allen Miller and Margaret Pegan (5). Margaret Elizabeth died in Peach Bottom Twp., York Co., Pennsylvania, on August 5, 1902, at age 73. She was buried in Chanceford Presbyterian Cemetery, Airville, Lower Chanceford Twp., York Co., Pennsylvania.[14]

Childless.

Margaret Elizabeth married **Jarrett Barton** in 1868. Jarrett Barton was born in Harford Co., Maryland? on December 17, 1821. Jarrett reached age 66 and died in Peach Bottom Twp., York Co., Pennsylvania, on March 2, 1888. He was buried in Slate Ridge Cemetery, Delta, Peach Bottom Twp., York Co., Pennsylvania.[20]

Although some sources claim that Jarrett Barton married an "Elizabeth Jones", Roy D. Pegan writes in his James and Sarah Brannon Pegan family history that Elizabeth Miller, daughter of Allen and Margaret Pegan Miller, was Jarret Barton's wife. Also, her gravestone names her as Margaret E. Barton, daughter of Allen and Margaret Miller and wife of Jarrett Barton.[2, 14]

**27. Agnes**[5] **Miller** (*Margaret*[4] *Pegan, James*[3]*, Andrew*[2] *Pagan, James*[1]) was born on May 30, 1830, in Peach Bottom Twp., York Co., Pennsylvania. She was the daughter of Allen Miller and Margaret Pegan (5). Agnes died in Lower Chanceford Twp., York

Co., Pennsylvania, on December 29, 1917, at age 87. She was buried in Chanceford Presbyterian Cemetery, Airville, Lower Chanceford Twp., York Co., Pennsylvania.[14]

Never married.

28. **Martha Ellen⁵ Miller** (*Margaret⁴ Pegan, James³, Andrew² Pagan, James¹*) was born on November 6, 1833, in Peach Bottom Twp., York Co., Pennsylvania. She was the daughter of Allen Miller and Margaret Pegan (5). Martha Ellen died in Peach Bottom Twp., York Co., Pennsylvania, on February 5, 1913, at age 79. She was buried in Chanceford Presbyterian Cemetery, Airville, Lower Chanceford Twp., York Co., Pennsylvania.[14]

Martha Ellen married **William J. Mitchell** about 1858. They had two daughters. William J. Mitchell was born in Fawn Twp., York Co., Pennsylvania? on February 13, 1838. William J. reached age 55 and died in Peach Bottom Twp., York Co., Pennsylvania, on May 3, 1893. He was buried in Chanceford Presbyterian Cemetery, Airville, Lower Chanceford Twp., York Co., Pennsylvania.[14]

Daughters of Martha Ellen Miller and William J. Mitchell:

+ 69  f  I.  **Sarah Ann⁶ Mitchell** was born in Peach Bottom Twp., York Co., Pennsylvania. She died in Peach Bottom Twp., York Co., Pennsylvania, on July 31, 1859. She died in Mansfield, Madison Twp., Richland Co., Ohio on November 28, 1928. She was buried in Lexington Cemetery, Lexington, Troy Twp., Richland Co., Ohio.[35]

+ 70  f  II.  **Margaret Rosa⁶ Mitchell** was born in Peach Bottom Twp., York Co., Pennsylvania, on August 10, 1866. She was also known as **Maggie or Rosa**. Margaret Rosa died in Lower Chanceford Twp., York Co., Pennsylvania, on December 31, 1917. She was buried in Chanceford Presbyterian Cemetery, Airville, Lower

Chanceford Twp., York Co., Pennsylvania.[14]

29. **James Jonas⁵ Pegan III** (*James⁴, James³, Andrew² Pagan, James¹*) was born in 1828 in Martic Twp., Lancaster Co., Pennsylvania. He was the son of James Pegan II (8) and Mary Jane Gowen. James Jonas died in Martic Twp., Lancaster Co., Pennsylvania, in 1840 at age 12.

30. **Mary Ann⁵ Pegan** (*James⁴, James³, Andrew² Pagan, James¹*) was born in 1831 in Martic Twp., Lancaster Co., Pennsylvania. She was the daughter of James Pegan II (8) and Mary Jane Gowen. Mary Ann died in Chanceford Twp., York Co., Pennsylvania, on March 31, 1896, at age 65. She was buried in Old Guinston Church Cemetery, Airville, Chanceford Twp., York Co., Pennsylvania.[21]

Never married.

31. **Henry⁵ Pegan** (*James⁴, James³, Andrew² Pagan, James¹*) was born on December 8, 1833, in Martic Twp., Lancaster Co., Pennsylvania. He was the son of James Pegan II (8) and Mary Jane Gowen. Henry died in Lancaster, Lancaster Co., Pennsylvania, on February 16, 1911, at age 77. He was buried in Spring Grove Cemetery, Jackson Twp., York Co., Pennsylvania.[23, 24]

Henry and Mary Matilda Penny Pegan were separated in 1860, as Henry was living with his parents and Mary Matilda and their two daughters were living with hers, according to census data. They must have reconciled in the early 1860s, as their third daughter, Mary Lena, was born in 1864.

Henry married **Mary Matilda Penny** on April 23, 1855, in Lancaster Co., Pennsylvania. They had three daughters. Mary Matilda Penny was born in Drumore Twp., Lancaster Co., Pennsylvania? on August 24, 1836. She reached age 31 and died in Drumore Twp., Lancaster Co., Pennsylvania, on October 14, 1867. Mary Matilda was buried in New Chestnut Level Presbyterian Church Cemetery, Drumore Twp., Lancaster Co., Pennsylvania.[36]

Henry Pegan married **Elizabeth Ann Neel** in 1870. They had two children. Elizabeth Ann Neel was born in Drumore Twp., Lancaster Co.,

Pennsylvania, on September 5, 1839. She was also known as **Lizzie Ann**. Elizabeth Ann reached age 66 and died in Jackson Twp., York Co., Pennsylvania, on January 31, 1906. She was buried in Spring Grove Cemetery, Jackson Twp., York Co., Pennsylvania.[24]

Daughters of Henry Pegan and Mary Matilda Penny:

+ 71 f I. **Ida Melissa⁶ Pegan** was born in Drumore Twp., Lancaster Co., Pennsylvania, on November 21, 1858. She died in York Twp., York Co., Pennsylvania, on December 15, 1922. Ida Melissa was buried in Old Guinston Church Cemetery, Airville, Chanceford Twp., York Co., Pennsylvania.[21]

+ 72 f II. **Alice Eva⁶ Pegan** was born in Drumore Twp., Lancaster Co., Pennsylvania, on February 29, 1860. She was also known as **Eva**. Alice Eva died in Lower Chanceford Twp., York Co., Pennsylvania, on September 21, 1896. "Eve Alice" is buried in Old Guinston Church Cemetery, Airville, Chanceford Twp., York Co., Pennsylvania.[21]

+ 73 f III. **Mary Lena⁶ Pegan** was born in Drumore Twp., Lancaster Co., Pennsylvania, on July 2, 1864. She was also known as **Lena**. Mary Lena died in Coatesville, Valley Twp., Chester Co., Pennsylvania, on May 9, 1943. She was buried in Oxford Cemetery, Oxford, Chester Co., Pennsylvania.[37]

Children of Henry Pegan and Elizabeth Ann Neel:

+ 74 f I. **Luella M.⁶ Pegan** was born in Drumore Twp., Lancaster Co., Pennsylvania, on May 19, 1871. She died in Harrisburg, Dauphin Co., Pennsylvania, on February 9, 1963. Luella M. was buried in Prospect Hill Cemetery, Harrisburg, Dauphin Co., Pennsylvania.[38]

+ 75 m II. **Harry Hutton⁶ Pegan** was born in Drumore Twp., Lancaster Co., Pennsylvania, on February 10, 1873. He died in Spring Grove, Jackson Twp., York Co., Pennsylvania, on October 26, 1962. Harry Hutton was buried in Spring Grove Cemetery, Jackson Twp., York Co., Pennsylvania.[24]

32. **Sarah Eliza⁵ Pegan** (*James⁴, James³, Andrew² Pagan, James¹*) was born on December 19, 1835, in Martic Twp., Lancaster Co., Pennsylvania. She was the daughter of James Pegan II (8) and Mary Jane Gowen. Sarah Eliza died in East Hopewell Twp., York Co., Pennsylvania, on August 26, 1914, at age 78. She was buried in Old Guinston Church Cemetery, Airville, Chanceford Twp., York Co., Pennsylvania.[21]

Sarah Eliza married **Samuel Isaac Adams** on June 17, 1869, in York Co., Pennsylvania. They had three children. Samuel Isaac Adams was born in Co. Armagh, Ireland, in April 1823. Samuel Isaac reached age 89 and died in East Hopewell Twp., York Co., Pennsylvania, on January 18, 1913. He was buried in Old Guinston Church Cemetery, Airville, Chanceford Twp., York Co., Pennsylvania.[21]

According to the Roy D. Pegan genealogy of James and Sarah Brannon Pegan's descendants, Samuel Jamieson and Sarah Eliza Pegan Adams also had a daughter named Sarah Adams who married a Lennie B. Michael. However, in the 1900 and 1910 censuses, Sarah Eliza Pegan Adams says she has borne only three children. (In 1900, all three were alive, in 1910, only two were surviving.) Also, there is no record of a Lennie and Sarah Adams Michael of appropriate age.[2]

Children of Sarah Eliza Pegan and Samuel Isaac Adams:

+ 76 f I. **Jennie Elizabeth⁶ Adams** was born in Fawn Twp., York Co., Pennsylvania, on April 23, 1870. She was also known as **Jennie**. Jennie Elizabeth died in East Hopewell Twp., York

Co., Pennsylvania, on March 9, 1947. She was buried in Round Hill Presbyterian Church Cemetery, Cross Roads, East Hopewell Twp., York Co., Pennsylvania.[39]

+ 77 f II. **Mary Margaret⁶ Adams** was born in Fawn Twp., York Co., Pennsylvania, on February 22, 1872. She was also known as **Margie**. Mary Margaret died in Fawn Twp., York Co., Pennsylvania, on February 27, 1906. She was buried in Old Guinston Church Cemetery, Airville, Chanceford Twp., York Co., Pennsylvania.[21]

+ 78 m III. **Samuel Jamieson⁶ Adams II** was born in Fawn Twp., York Co., Pennsylvania, on February 6, 1875. He was also known as **Jamieson**. Samuel Jamieson died in Bel Air, Harford Co., Maryland, on July 31, 1969. He was buried in Old Guinston Church Cemetery, Airville, Chanceford Twp., York Co., Pennsylvania.[21]

**33. Isaac A.⁵ Pegan** (*James⁴, James³, Andrew² Pagan, James¹*) was born on August 4, 1837, in Martic Twp., Lancaster Co., Pennsylvania. He was the son of James Pegan II (8) and Mary Jane Gowen. Isaac A. died in Martic Twp., Lancaster Co., Pennsylvania, on August 12, 1849, at age 12. He was buried in Muddy Run Presbyterian Cemetery, Martic Twp., Lancaster Co., Pennsylvania.[15]

**34. Margaret Jane⁵ Pegan** (*James⁴, James³, Andrew² Pagan, James¹*) was born on November 8, 1844, in Martic Twp., Lancaster Co., Pennsylvania. She was also known as **Maggie**. She was the daughter of James Pegan II (8) and Mary Jane Gowen. Margaret Jane died in York, York Co., Pennsylvania, on November 12, 1923, at age 79. She was buried in Old Guinston Church Cemetery, Airville, Chanceford Twp., York Co., Pennsylvania.[2]

Margaret Jane married **David Barber Grove** before 1882. They had two sons. David Barber Grove was born in Chanceford Twp., York Co., Pennsylvania, on June 1, 1855. David Barber reached age 67 and died in Chanceford Twp., York Co., Pennsylvania, on October 22, 1922. He was buried in Old Guinston Church Cemetery, Airville, Chanceford Twp., York Co., Pennsylvania.[2]

Sons of Margaret Jane Pegan and David Barber Grove:

+ 79 m I. **James Pegan⁶ Grove** was born in Chanceford Twp., York Co., Pennsylvania, on July 18, 1882. He died in a hospital in Springettsbury Twp., York Co., Pennsylvania, on January 22, 1964. James Pegan was buried in Mount Rose Cemetery, Spring Garden Twp., York Co., Pennsylvania.[40]

+ 80 m II. **Vinton Lemmon⁶ Grove** was born in Chanceford Twp., York Co., Pennsylvania, on April 23, 1885. He died in Chanceford Twp., York Co., Pennsylvania, on May 27, 1922. Vinton Lemmon was buried in Old Guinston Church Cemetery, Airville, Chanceford Twp., York Co., Pennsylvania.[21]

# 6th Generation

**35. James Andrew**[6] **Nimlow** (*Margaret*[5] *Pegan, Andrew*[4]*, James*[3]*, Andrew*[2] *Pagan, James*[1]) was born on November 21, 1843, in Fulton Twp., Lancaster Co., Pennsylvania. He was the son of George Nimlow and Margaret Pegan (14). He died in Lancaster, Lancaster Co., Pennsylvania, on April 30, 1927, at age 83. James Andrew was buried in Greenwood Cemetery, Lancaster, Lancaster Co., Pennsylvania.[2, 25]

Childless.

James Andrew married **Susan Clayman** about 1873. Susan Clayman was born in Providence Twp., Lancaster Co., Pennsylvania, on June 12, 1846. Susan reached age 66 and died in Martic Twp., Lancaster Co., Pennsylvania, on January 14, 1913. She was buried in Greenwood Cemetery, Lancaster, Lancaster Co., Pennsylvania.[2, 25]

James Andrew Nimlow married **Carrie Goodling** after 1913. Carrie Goodling was born in York, York Co., Pennsylvania, in 1856. Carrie reached age 86 and died in York, York Co., Pennsylvania, in 1942. She was buried in Prospect Hill Cemetery, York Twp., York Co., Pennsylvania.[2]

**36. Hannah Margaret**[6] **Nimlow** (*Margaret*[5] *Pegan, Andrew*[4]*, James*[3]*, Andrew*[2] *Pagan, James*[1]) was born on July 2, 1844, in Fulton Twp., Lancaster Co., Pennsylvania. She was the daughter of George Nimlow and Margaret Pegan (14). Hannah Margaret died in Martic Twp., Lancaster Co., Pennsylvania, on February 18, 1916, at age 71. She was buried in Mount Nebo Cemetery (Presbyterian Graveyard), White Oak, Martic Twp., Lancaster Co., Pennsylvania.[16]

Hannah Margaret married **Isaac Walton** in 1868. They had two children. Isaac Walton was born in Martic Twp., Lancaster Co., Pennsylvania, on August 19, 1835. Isaac reached age 77 and died in Martic Twp., Lancaster Co., Pennsylvania? on January 24, 1913. He was buried in Mount Nebo Cemetery (Presbyterian Graveyard), White Oak, Martic Twp., Lancaster Co., Pennsylvania.[16]

Children of Hannah Margaret Nimlow and Isaac Walton:

+ 81 m I. **Elmer**[7] **Walton** was born in Martic Twp., Lancaster Co., Pennsylvania, on December 6, 1869. He died in Martic Twp., Lancaster Co., Pennsylvania, on April 27, 1944. Elmer was buried in Bethesda United Methodist Cemetery, Bethesda, Martic Twp., Lancaster Co., Pennsylvania.[2, 41]

+ 82 f II. **Anna Margie**[7] **Walton** was born in Martic Twp., Lancaster Co., Pennsylvania, on June 15, 1876. She was also known as **Margie**. Anna Margie died in Martic Twp., Lancaster Co., Pennsylvania, on September 3, 1881. She was buried in Mount Nebo Cemetery (Presbyterian Graveyard), White Oak, Martic Twp., Lancaster Co., Pennsylvania.[16]

**37. Alexander Leiper or Leeper**[6] **Nimlow** (*Margaret*[5] *Pegan, Andrew*[4]*, James*[3]*, Andrew*[2] *Pagan, James*[1]) was born in 1844 in Fulton Twp., Lancaster Co., Pennsylvania. He was the son of George Nimlow and Margaret Pegan (14). Alexander Leiper or Leeper died in Boise, Ada Co., Idaho, on September 7, 1908, at age 64.[26] He was buried in Boise Barracks National Cemetery, Boise, Ada Co., Idaho.[27]

Seems not to have married.

"Leeber" Nimlow's Idaho death certificate says he was age 64 and single when he died.

**38. Anna Mary**[6] **Nimlow** (*Margaret*[5] *Pegan, Andrew*[4]*, James*[3]*, Andrew*[2] *Pagan, James*[1]) was born in June 1849 in Fulton Twp., Lancaster Co., Pennsylvania. She was the daughter of George Nimlow and Margaret Pegan (14). Anna Mary died in Lancaster, Lancaster Co., Pennsylvania, on February 2, 1902, at age 52. She was buried in Mount Nebo Cemetery (Presbyterian Graveyard), White Oak, Martic Twp., Lancaster Co., Pennsylvania.[2, 16]

Anna Mary married **James Isaac Akins** about 1873. They had four children. James Isaac Akins was born in Sadsbury Twp., Lancaster Co., Pennsylvania, in 1844. James Isaac lived in 1883 in Mt. Nebo, Martic Twp., Lancaster Co., Pennsylvania. He reached age 55 and died in Lancaster, Lancaster Co., Pennsylvania, on October 23, 1899. James Isaac was buried in Mount Nebo Cemetery (Presbyterian Graveyard), White Oak, Martic Twp., Lancaster Co., Pennsylvania.[2, 16]

Children of Anna Mary Nimlow and James Isaac Akins:

+ 83  f  I. **Margaret**[7] **Akins** was born in Martic Twp., Lancaster Co., Pennsylvania, in 1874. She was also known as **Maggie**. Margaret died in Martic Twp., Lancaster Co., Pennsylvania, before 1900. She was buried in Mount Nebo Cemetery (Presbyterian Graveyard), White Oak, Martic Twp., Lancaster Co., Pennsylvania.[2]

+ 84  f  II. **Ida**[7] **Akins** was born in Martic Twp., Lancaster Co., Pennsylvania, on January 16, 1881. She died in Manor Twp., Lancaster Co., Pennsylvania, on August 7, 1917. Ida was buried in Washington Boro Cemetery, Manor Twp., Lancaster Co., Pennsylvania.[42]

+ 85  m  III. **Earl Isaac**[7] **Akins** was born in Martic Twp., Lancaster Co., Pennsylvania, on November 18, 1882. He died in York, York Co., Pennsylvania, on April 20, 1957. Earl Isaac was buried in Prospect Hill Cemetery, York Twp., York Co., Pennsylvania.[2, 43]

+ 86  IV. **Child**[7] **Akins** was born in Martic Twp., Lancaster Co., Pennsylvania, between 1875 and 1900. He or she died in Martic Twp., Lancaster Co., Pennsylvania, between 1875 and 1900.

**39. George Niblock**[6] (**Nimlow II**) (*Margaret*[5] *Pegan, Andrew*[4], *James*[3], *Andrew*[2] *Pagan, James*[1]) was born on July 7, 1851, in Fulton Twp., Lancaster Co., Pennsylvania. He was the son of George Nimlow and Margaret Pegan (14). George Niblock died in Conoy Twp., Lancaster Co., Pennsylvania, on October 28, 1923, at age 72. He was buried in Mount Tunnel Cemetery, Elizabethtown, Mt. Joy Twp., Lancaster Co., Pennsylvania.[28]

According to Roy D. Pegan, George Nimlow II changed the surname to Nimblock.[2] But his death certificate says George Niblock.[44]

George Niblock married **Rebecca Smith** about 1880. They had three children. Rebecca Smith was born in Cecil Co., Maryland? on September 10, 1861. Rebecca reached age 39 and died in Elizabethtown, Mt. Joy Twp., Lancaster Co., Pennsylvania, on February 15, 1901. She was buried in Mount Tunnel Cemetery, Elizabethtown, Mt. Joy Twp., Lancaster Co., Pennsylvania.[28]

Children of George Niblock (Nimlow II) and Rebecca Smith:

+ 87  m  I. **Clarence Watson**[7] **Niblock** was born in Cecil Co., Maryland? on September 25, 1881. He died in Conoy Twp., Lancaster Co., Pennsylvania, on March 22, 1940. Clarence Watson was buried in Bainbridge Public Cemetery, Conoy Twp., Lancaster Co., Pennsylvania.[45]

+ 88  f  II. **Genevieve Mae**[7] **Niblock** was born in Delaware on February 14, 1887. She was also known as **Jennie**. Genevieve Mae died in Elizabethtown, Mt. Joy Twp., Lancaster Co., Pennsylvania, in May 1970.

+ 89  f  III. **Gertrude**[7] **Niblock** was born in Elizabethtown, Mt. Joy Twp., Lancaster Co., Pennsylvania, in 1894. She died in Elizabethtown, Mt. Joy Twp., Lancaster Co., Pennsylvania, in 1897. Gertrude was buried in Mount Tunnel Cemetery, Elizabethtown, Mt. Joy Twp., Lancaster Co., Pennsylvania.[28]

**40. Miller K.**[6] **Nimlow** (*Margaret*[5] *Pegan, Andrew*[4], *James*[3], *Andrew*[2] *Pagan, James*[1]) was born on April 4, 1854, in Martic Twp., Lancaster Co., Pennsylvania.

He was the son of George Nimlow and Margaret Pegan (14). Miller K. died in Mt. Nebo, Martic Twp., Lancaster Co., Pennsylvania, on July 22, 1870, at age 16. He was buried in Mount Nebo Cemetery (Presbyterian Graveyard), White Oak, Martic Twp., Lancaster Co., Pennsylvania.[16]

41. **Ida Jane**[6] **Nimlow** (*Margaret*[5] *Pegan, Andrew*[4]*, James*[3]*, Andrew*[2] *Pagan, James*[1]) was born on December 25, 1859, in Martic Twp., Lancaster Co., Pennsylvania. She was the daughter of George Nimlow and Margaret Pegan (14). Ida Jane died in Martic Twp., Lancaster Co., Pennsylvania, on February 16, 1861, at age one. She was buried in Mount Nebo Cemetery (Presbyterian Graveyard), White Oak, Martic Twp., Lancaster Co., Pennsylvania.[16]

42. **Samuel A.**[6] **Pegan** (*James Henry*[5]*, Andrew*[4]*, James*[3]*, Andrew*[2] *Pagan, James*[1]) was born on November 28, 1854, in Martic Twp., Lancaster Co., Pennsylvania. He was the son of James Henry Pegan (15) and Harriet Ankrim. Samuel A. died in Sunnyburn, Lower Chanceford Twp., York Co., Pennsylvania, on December 13, 1908, at age 54. He was buried in Greenwood Cemetery, Lancaster, Lancaster Co., Pennsylvania.[2, 25]

Samuel A. married **Alice Amanda Kilgore** in 1877. They had one son. Alice Amanda Kilgore was born in Lower Chanceford Twp., York Co., Pennsylvania, on February 2, 1860. She was also known as **Amanda**. Alice Amanda reached age 74 and died in Lancaster, Lancaster Co., Pennsylvania, on December 23, 1934. She was buried in Greenwood Cemetery, Lancaster, Lancaster Co., Pennsylvania.[2, 25]

Son of Samuel A. Pegan and Alice Amanda Kilgore:

+ 90 m I. **Chester Clyde**[7] **Pegan** was born in Martic Twp., Lancaster Co., Pennsylvania, on August 20, 1879. He died in Lancaster, Lancaster Co., Pennsylvania, on March 7, 1905. Chester Clyde was buried in Greenwood Cemetery, Lancaster, Lancaster Co., Pennsylvania.[2, 25]

43. **Myra S.**[6] **Pegan** (*James Henry*[5]*, Andrew*[4]*, James*[3]*, Andrew*[2] *Pagan, James*[1]) was born on December 29, 1882, in Martic Twp., Lancaster Co., Pennsylvania.

She was the daughter of James Henry Pegan (15) and Mary E. Markley. Myra S. died in Atlanta, DeKalb Co., Georgia, on October 3, 1937, at age 54. She was buried in Greenwood Cemetery, Lancaster, Lancaster Co., Pennsylvania.[2, 25]

Myra S. married **Alfred Emmanuel Urban** on September 14, 1904, in Lancaster Co., Pennsylvania. They had two daughters. Alfred Emmanuel Urban was born in Columbia, West Hempfield Twp., Lancaster Co., Pennsylvania, on March 8, 1871. Alfred Emmanuel reached age 55 and died in Lancaster, Lancaster Co., Pennsylvania, on February 3, 1927. He was buried in Greenwood Cemetery, Lancaster, Lancaster Co., Pennsylvania.[2, 25]

Daughters of Myra S. Pegan and Alfred Emmanuel Urban:

+ 91 f I. **Mary Amanda**[7] **Urban** was born in Lancaster, Lancaster Co., Pennsylvania, in 1905. She died in College Park, Prince George's Co., Maryland? after 1965.

+ 92 f II. **Lillian Virginia**[7] **Urban** was born in Lancaster, Lancaster Co., Pennsylvania, on October 21, 1909. She died in Lima, Ottawa Twp., Allen Co., Ohio, on July 6, 1965. Lillian Virginia was buried in Memorial Park Mausoleum Cemetery, Lima, Ottawa Twp., Allen Co., Ohio.[46]

44. **Alvin Levi**[6] **Kilgore** (*Sarah Jane*[5] *Pegan, Andrew*[4]*, James*[3]*, Andrew*[2] *Pagan, James*[1]) was born on October 17, 1846, in Lower Chanceford Twp., York Co., Pennsylvania. He was the son of Hugh William Kilgore and Sarah Jane Pegan (17). Alvin Levi died in Lower Chanceford Twp., York Co., Pennsylvania, on October 5, 1916, at age 69. He was buried in Chanceford Presbyterian Cemetery, Airville, Lower Chanceford Twp., York Co., Pennsylvania.[2, 14]

Alvin Levi married **Eliza Amanda McCalla** about 1876. They had three children. Eliza Amanda McCalla was born in Lower Chanceford Twp., York Co., Pennsylvania, on May 23, 1848. She was also known as **Amanda**. Eliza Amanda reached age 42 and died in Lower Chanceford Twp., York

Co., Pennsylvania, on February 23, 1891. She was buried in Chanceford Presbyterian Cemetery, Airville, Lower Chanceford Twp., York Co., Pennsylvania.[2, 14]

Alvin Levi Kilgore married **Caroline Gallagher** or **Galligher** about 1907. Caroline Gallagher was born in Bryansville, Peach Bottom Twp., York Co., Pennsylvania, on August 2, 1862. Caroline reached age 72 and died in Peoria, Peoria Twp., Peoria Co., Illinois on August 18, 1934. She was buried in Springdale Cemetery, Peoria, Peoria Twp., Peoria Co., Illinois.[47]

Children of Alvin Levi Kilgore and Eliza Amanda McCalla:

+ 93 f I.   **Grace Anna**[7] **Kilgore** was born in Lower Chanceford Twp., York Co., Pennsylvania, on February 24, 1878. She died in Airville, Lower Chanceford Twp., York Co., Pennsylvania, in June 1969. Grace Anna was buried in Chanceford Presbyterian Cemetery, Airville, Lower Chanceford Twp., York Co., Pennsylvania.[14]

+ 94 m II.   **Samuel Ralph**[7] **Kilgore** was born in Lower Chanceford Twp., York Co., Pennsylvania, on November 13, 1879. He was also known as **Ralph**. Samuel Ralph died in Hillsdale, Hillsdale Twp., Hillsdale Co., Michigan, in 1953. He was buried in Portage Cemetery, Portage, Wood Co., Ohio.[48]

+ 95 m III.   **William**[7] **Kilgore** was born in Lower Chanceford Twp., York Co., Pennsylvania, between 1880 and 1891. He died in Lower Chanceford Twp., York Co., Pennsylvania, between 1880 and 1891.[2]

**45. James Ankrim**[6] **Kilgore** (*Sarah Jane*[5] *Pegan, Andrew*[4], *James*[3], *Andrew*[2] *Pagan, James*[1]) was born on September 6, 1848, in Lower Chanceford Twp., York Co., Pennsylvania. He was the son of Hugh William Kilgore and Sarah Jane Pegan (17). James

Ankrim died in Lower Chanceford Twp., York Co., Pennsylvania, on December 6, 1914, at age 66. He was buried in Chanceford Presbyterian Cemetery, Airville, Lower Chanceford Twp., York Co., Pennsylvania.[14]

James Ankrim married **Rebecca Reed** in 1875. They had four children. Rebecca Reed was born in Chanceford Twp., York Co., Pennsylvania, on September 7, 1848. Rebecca reached age 78 and died in Peach Bottom Twp., York Co., Pennsylvania, on January 29, 1927. She was buried in Chanceford Presbyterian Cemetery, Airville, Lower Chanceford Twp., York Co., Pennsylvania.[14]

Children of James Ankrim Kilgore and Rebecca Reed:

+ 96 m I.   **Hugh Whiteford**[7] **Kilgore** was born in Lower Chanceford Twp., York Co., Pennsylvania, on January 6, 1876. He died in East Nottingham Twp., Chester Co., Pennsylvania, on May 17, 1960. Hugh Whiteford was buried in Slateville Presbyterian Church Cemetery, Delta, Peach Bottom Twp., York Co., Pennsylvania.[49]

+ 97 m II.   **Samuel Reed**[7] **Kilgore** was born in Lower Chanceford Twp., York Co., Pennsylvania, on August 31, 1877. He was also known as **Reed**. Samuel Reed died in Peach Bottom Twp., York Co., Pennsylvania, on March 4, 1943. He was buried in Slate Ridge Cemetery, Delta, Peach Bottom Twp., York Co., Pennsylvania.[20]

+ 98 f III.   **Sarah Jane**[7] **Kilgore** was born in Lower Chanceford Twp., York Co., Pennsylvania, on November 27, 1879. She was also known as **Sadie**. Sarah Jane died in Peach Bottom Twp., York Co., Pennsylvania? on December 9, 1964. She was buried in Chanceford Presbyterian Cemetery, Airville, Lower Chanceford Twp., York Co., Pennsylvania.[14]

+ 99 m IV.   **Chester W.**[7] **Kilgore** was born in Lower Chanceford Twp., York Co.,

Pennsylvania, on August 15, 1886. He died in Lawrence, Douglas Co., Kansas, in September 1968. Chester W. was buried in Memorial Park Cemetery, Lawrence, Douglas Co., Kansas.[50]

**46. Laura Clinda⁶ Kilgore** (*Sarah Jane⁵ Pegan, Andrew⁴, James³, Andrew² Pagan, James¹*) was born on November 2, 1850, in Lower Chanceford Twp., York Co., Pennsylvania. She was the daughter of Hugh William Kilgore and Sarah Jane Pegan (17). Laura Clinda died in Lower Chanceford Twp., York Co., Pennsylvania, on October 24, 1894, at age 43. She was buried in Chanceford Presbyterian Cemetery, Airville, Lower Chanceford Twp., York Co., Pennsylvania.[14]

Laura Clinda married **John Veasey Chandlee** on October 10, 1878. They had three sons. John Veasey Chandlee was born in Lower Chanceford Twp., York Co., Pennsylvania, on January 7, 1844. John Veasey reached age 57 and died in Lower Chanceford Twp., York Co., Pennsylvania, on December 18, 1901. He was buried in Chanceford Presbyterian Cemetery, Airville, Lower Chanceford Twp., York Co., Pennsylvania.[14]

Sons of Laura Clinda Kilgore and John Veasey Chandlee:

+ 100 m I. **Ira Whiteford⁷ Chandlee** was born in Lower Chanceford Twp., York Co., Pennsylvania, on October 28, 1879. He died in Delta, Peach Bottom Twp., York Co., Pennsylvania? on November 7, 1965. Ira Whiteford was buried in Pine Grove Presbyterian Church Cemetery, Lower Chanceford Twp., York Co., Pennsylvania.[51]

+ 101 m II. **Walter Veasey⁷ Chandlee** was born in Lower Chanceford Twp., York Co., Pennsylvania, on November 30, 1881. He died in Red Lion, York Twp., York Co., Pennsylvania, on March 15, 1942. Walter Veasey Chandlee was buried in Chance-

ford Presbyterian Cemetery, Airville, Lower Chanceford Twp., York Co., Pennsylvania.[14]

+ 102 m III. **William⁷ Chandlee** was born in Lower Chanceford Twp., York Co., Pennsylvania, on October 24, 1884. He died in Lower Chanceford Twp., York Co., Pennsylvania, on September 24, 1910. William was buried in Pine Grove Presbyterian Church Cemetery, Lower Chanceford Twp., York Co., Pennsylvania.[51]

**47. William Ramsey⁶ Kilgore** (*Sarah Jane⁵ Pegan, Andrew⁴, James³, Andrew² Pagan, James¹*) was born in August 1853 in Lower Chanceford Twp., York Co., Pennsylvania. He was the son of Hugh William Kilgore and Sarah Jane Pegan (17). William Ramsey died in York, York Co., Pennsylvania? in 1917 at age 63.[2]

The Roy D. Pegan file says that William Ramsey Kilgore died in 1917 in York, York Co., Pennsylvania.[2] But no online death certificate is found for him. He may be buried in Chanceford Presbyterian Cemetery, Lower Chanceford Twp., York Co., Pennsylvania with his wife, Mary Caroline Cunningham Kilgore.

William Ramsey married **Mary Caroline Cunningham** before 1885. They had one son. Mary Caroline Cunningham was born in Peach Bottom Twp., York Co., Pennsylvania, on April 21, 1856. Mary Caroline reached age 58 and died in York, York Co., Pennsylvania, on June 30, 1914. She was buried in Chanceford Presbyterian Cemetery, Airville, Lower Chanceford Twp., York Co., Pennsylvania.[14]

Son of William Ramsey Kilgore and Mary Caroline Cunningham:

+ 103 m I. **Walter Stephen⁷ Kilgore** was born in York, York Co., Pennsylvania, on July 16, 1885. He died in Chicago, Cook Co., Illinois, on May 2, 1919.

Walter Stephen was buried in Chanceford Presbyterian Cemetery, Airville, Lower Chanceford Twp., York Co., Pennsylvania.[14]

**48. Anna Margaret[6] Kilgore** (*Sarah Jane[5] Pegan, Andrew[4], James[3], Andrew[2] Pagan, James[1]*) was born on October 17, 1857, in Lower Chanceford Twp., York Co., Pennsylvania. She was also known as **Maggie** and **Margaret**. She was the daughter of Hugh William Kilgore and Sarah Jane Pegan (17). Anna Margaret died in Lower Chanceford Twp., York Co., Pennsylvania, on May 13, 1938, at age 80. She was buried in Old Guinston Church Cemetery, Airville, Chanceford Twp., York Co., Pennsylvania.[2, 21]

Anna Margaret married **Alexander Martin** about 1885. They had one daughter. Alexander Martin was born in Lower Chanceford Twp., York Co., Pennsylvania, on November 9, 1853. Alexander reached age 86 and died in Lower Chanceford Twp., York Co., Pennsylvania, on August 9, 1940. He was buried in Old Guinston Church Cemetery, Airville, Chanceford Twp., York Co., Pennsylvania.[2, 21]

Daughter of Anna Margaret Kilgore and Alexander Martin:

+ 104 f I. **Cora[7] Martin** was born in Lower Chanceford Twp., York Co., Pennsylvania, on August 24, 1886. She died in Lower Chanceford Twp., York Co., Pennsylvania? in September 1964.

**49. Emory Milton[6] Kilgore** (*Sarah Jane[5] Pegan, Andrew[4], James[3], Andrew[2] Pagan, James[1]*) was born on September 17, 1860, in Lower Chanceford Twp., York Co., Pennsylvania. He was also known as **Milton**. He was the son of Hugh William Kilgore and Sarah Jane Pegan (17). Emory Milton died in Lower Chanceford Twp., York Co., Pennsylvania, on June 29, 1949, at age 88. He was buried in Chanceford Presbyterian Cemetery, Airville, Lower Chanceford Twp., York Co., Pennsylvania.[2, 14]

Emory Milton married **Rebecca Martin Dougherty** before 1885. They had three children. Rebecca Martin Dougherty was born in Lebanon, North Lebanon Twp., Lebanon Co., Pennsylvania, on October 29, 1868. She was also known as **Martie.**

Rebecca Martin reached age 98 and died in Airville, Lower Chanceford Twp., York Co., Pennsylvania, on September 25, 1967. She was buried in Chanceford Presbyterian Cemetery, Airville, Lower Chanceford Twp., York Co., Pennsylvania.[2, 14]

Children of Emory Milton Kilgore and Rebecca Martin Dougherty:

+ 105 f I. **Gertrude[7] Kilgore** was born in Lower Chanceford Twp., York Co., Pennsylvania, on April 7, 1895. She died in Oxford, Chester Co., Pennsylvania, on July 1, 1995. Gertrude was buried in Chanceford Presbyterian Cemetery, Airville, Lower Chanceford Twp., York Co., Pennsylvania.[14]

+ 106 m II. **Dale Dougherty[7] Kilgore** was born in Lower Chanceford Twp., York Co., Pennsylvania, on September 24, 1897. He died in Airville, Lower Chanceford Twp., York Co., Pennsylvania, on October 15, 1980. Dale Dougherty was buried in Chanceford Presbyterian Cemetery, Airville, Lower Chanceford Twp., York Co., Pennsylvania.[14]

+ 107 m III. **Emory[7] Kilgore II** was born in Lower Chanceford Twp., York Co., Pennsylvania, on January 13, 1903. He died in Airville, Lower Chanceford Twp., York Co., Pennsylvania, on August 30, 2002. Emory was buried in Chanceford Presbyterian Cemetery, Airville, Lower Chanceford Twp., York Co., Pennsylvania.[14]

**50. Luella Jane[6] Kilgore** (*Sarah Jane[5] Pegan, Andrew[4], James[3], Andrew[2] Pagan, James[1]*) was born on March 24, 1863, in Lower Chanceford Twp., York Co., Pennsylvania. She was also known as **Ella**. She was the daughter of Hugh William Kilgore and Sarah Jane Pegan (17). Luella Jane died in Delta, Peach Bottom Twp., York Co., Pennsylvania, on April 2, 1943, at age 80. She was buried in Salem United

Methodist Church Cemetery, Delta, Peach Bottom Twp., York Co., Pennsylvania.[2]

Luella Jane married **Martin Luther Hess** before 1888. They had three children. Martin Luther Hess was born in Lower Chanceford Twp., York Co., Pennsylvania, on December 10, 1859. He was also known as **Luther**. Martin Luther reached age 78 and died in Lower Chanceford Twp., York Co., Pennsylvania, on January 16, 1938. He was buried in Salem United Methodist Church Cemetery, Delta, Peach Bottom Twp., York Co., Pennsylvania.[2, 52]

Children of Luella Jane Kilgore and Martin Luther Hess:

+ 108 f I. **Daisy Mae[7] Hess** was born in Lower Chanceford Twp., York Co., Pennsylvania, on September 14, 1888. She died in Red Lion, York Twp., York Co., Pennsylvania, on May 29, 1957, at age 68. Daisy Mae was buried in Salem United Methodist Church Cemetery, Delta, Peach Bottom Twp., York Co., Pennsylvania.[52]

+ 109 f II. **Sarah Margaret[7] Hess** was born in Lower Chanceford Twp., York Co., Pennsylvania, on October 21, 1891. She died in Chattanooga, Hamilton Co., Tennessee, on November 2, 1985. Sarah Margaret was buried in Hamilton Memorial Gardens, Hixon, Hamilton Co., Tennessee.[53]

+ 110 m III. **Harry Lyle[7] Hess** was born in Lower Chanceford Twp., York Co., Pennsylvania, on May 24, 1897. He was also known as **Lyle**. Harry Lyle died in Delta, Peach Bottom Twp., York Co., Pennsylvania, on September 8, 1980. He was buried in Salem United Methodist Church Cemetery, Delta, Peach Bottom Twp., York Co., Pennsylvania.[52]

**51. Janetta[6] Kilgore** (*Sarah Jane[5] Pegan, Andrew[4], James[3], Andrew[2] Pagan, James[1]*) was born in 1868 in Lower Chanceford Twp., York Co., Pennsylvania. She was the daughter of Hugh William Kilgore and Sarah Jane Pegan (17). Janetta died in Lower Chanceford Twp., York Co., Pennsylvania, in 1868. She was buried in Chanceford Presbyterian Cemetery, Airville, Lower Chanceford Twp., York Co., Pennsylvania.[2]

**52. Harriet Jane[6] Pegan** (*Alexander L.[5], Andrew[4], James[3], Andrew[2] Pagan, James[1]*) was born on March 24, 1850, in Martic Twp., Lancaster Co., Pennsylvania. She was the daughter of Alexander L. Pegan (19) and Ruthanna Appleton. Harriet Jane died in Martic Twp., Lancaster Co., Pennsylvania, on March 1, 1873, at age 22. She was buried in Mount Nebo Cemetery (Presbyterian Graveyard), White Oak, Martic Twp., Lancaster Co., Pennsylvania.[16]

Never married. Find A Grave entry says her gravestone has her mother as "Beth Jane". This is an error.

**53. Lewis Cass[6] Pegan** (*Alexander L.[5], Andrew[4], James[3], Andrew[2] Pagan, James[1]*) was born on May 28, 1852, in Martic Twp., Lancaster Co., Pennsylvania. He was the son of Alexander L. Pegan (19) and Ruthanna Appleton. Lewis Cass died in Lancaster, Lancaster Co., Pennsylvania, on August 1, 1929, at age 77. He was buried in Greenwood Cemetery, Lancaster, Lancaster Co., Pennsylvania.[25]

Lewis Cass married **Catherine McMullen** about 1874. She was also known as **Katie**. They had three children. Catherine McMullen was born in Pennsylvania in 1859. Catherine died in Martic Twp., Lancaster Co., Pennsylvania, between 1882 and 1900. She is possibly buried in Mount Nebo Cemetery (Presbyterian Graveyard), White Oak, Martic Twp., Lancaster Co., Pennsylvania.[2]

Lewis Cass Pegan married **Elizabeth R. Musser** on November 22, 1905, in Lancaster Co., Pennsylvania. Elizabeth R. Musser was born in Pennsylvania on July 9, 1870. Elizabeth R. reached age 46 and died in Lancaster, Lancaster Co., Pennsylvania, on November 22, 1916. She was buried in Greenwood Cemetery, Lancaster, Lancaster Co., Pennsylvania.[25]

Children of Lewis Cass Pegan and Catherine McMullen:

+ 111  f  I.  **Cora I.**[7] **Pegan** was born in Martic Twp., Lancaster Co., Pennsylvania, on December 7, 1875. She died in Lancaster, Lancaster Co., Pennsylvania, on April 4, 1962. Cora I. was buried in Riverview Burial Park Cemetery, Lancaster, Lancaster Co., Pennsylvania.[29]

+ 112  f  II.  **Harriet Jane**[7] **Pegan** was born in Martic Twp., Lancaster Co., Pennsylvania, on February 7, 1880. She died in Lancaster, Lancaster Co., Pennsylvania, on May 3, 1936. Harriet Jane was buried in Riverview Burial Park Cemetery, Lancaster, Lancaster Co., Pennsylvania.[29]

+ 113  m  III.  **Harlan Appleton**[7] **Pegan** was born in Martic Twp., Lancaster Co., Pennsylvania, on January 24, 1882. He died in Mountville, Lancaster Co., Pennsylvania, on June 22, 1956. Harlan Appleton was buried in Greenwood Cemetery, Lancaster, Lancaster Co., Pennsylvania.[25]

**54. Sarah**[6] **Pegan** (*Alexander L.*[5], *Andrew*[4], *James*[3], *Andrew*[2] *Pagan*, *James*[1]) was born on November 23, 1854, in Martic Twp., Lancaster Co., Pennsylvania. She was the daughter of Alexander L. Pegan (19) and Ruthanna Appleton. Sarah died in Lancaster, Lancaster Co., Pennsylvania, on March 10, 1922, at age 67. She was buried in Greenwood Cemetery, Lancaster, Lancaster Co., Pennsylvania.[25]

Sarah married **Isaac Barton** before 1879. They had two sons. Isaac Barton was born in Martic Twp., Lancaster Co., Pennsylvania, on June 25, 1851. Isaac reached age 48 and died in Lancaster, Lancaster Co., Pennsylvania, on May 8, 1900. He was buried in Greenwood Cemetery, Lancaster, Lancaster Co., Pennsylvania.[25]

Sarah Pegan Barton married **David Keeports**. David Keeports was born in Union Twp., Adams Co., Pennsylvania, on February 8, 1841. David reached age 79 and died in Lancaster, Lancaster Co.,

Pennsylvania, on February 20, 1920. He was buried in Lancaster Cemetery, Lancaster, Lancaster Co., Pennsylvania.[18]

Sons of Sarah Pegan and Isaac Barton:

+ 114  m  I.  **Ralph Alexander**[7] **Barton** was born in Lancaster, Lancaster Co., Pennsylvania, on September 7, 1879. He died in Lancaster, Lancaster Co., Pennsylvania, on November 27, 1949. Ralph Alexander was buried in Greenwood Cemetery, Lancaster, Lancaster Co., Pennsylvania.[25]

+ 115  m  II.  **Elmer Isaac**[7] **Barton** was born in Lancaster, Lancaster Co., Pennsylvania, on June 18, 1884. He died in Boston, Suffolk Co., Massachusetts, in 1937. Elmer Isaac was buried in Mount Calvary Cemetery, Roslindale, Suffolk Co., Massachusetts.[54]

**55. William H.**[6] **Pegan** (*Alexander L.*[5], *Andrew*[4], *James*[3], *Andrew*[2] *Pagan*, *James*[1]) was born on September 20, 1857, in Martic Twp., Lancaster Co., Pennsylvania. He was the son of Alexander L. Pegan (19) and Ruthanna Appleton. William H. died in Martic Twp., Lancaster Co., Pennsylvania, on June 7, 1939, at age 81. He was buried in Riverview Burial Park Cemetery, Lancaster, Lancaster Co., Pennsylvania.[29]

Childless.

William H. married **Eleanor M. Gibson** in 1884. Eleanor M. Gibson was born in Martic Twp., Lancaster Co., Pennsylvania? on February 8, 1838. Eleanor M. reached age 77 and died in Martic Twp., Lancaster Co., Pennsylvania, on March 28, 1915. She was buried in Mount Nebo Cemetery (Presbyterian Graveyard), White Oak, Martic Twp., Lancaster Co., Pennsylvania.[16]

**56. James Calvin**[6] **Pegan** (*Alexander L.*[5], *Andrew*[4], *James*[3], *Andrew*[2] *Pagan*, *James*[1]) was born on December 22, 1859, in Martic Twp., Lancaster Co., Pennsylvania. He was the son of Alexander L. Pegan (19) and Ruthanna Appleton. James Calvin died in Pittsburgh, Allegheny Co., Pennsylvania, on January 7, 1915, at age 55. He was buried in Chartiers Cemetery, Carnegie, Scott Twp., Allegheny Co., Pennsylvania.[30]

James Calvin married **Mary Jane Laird** about 1880. They had six children. Mary Jane Laird was born in Martic Twp., Lancaster Co., Pennsylvania, in December 1859. She was also known as **Mamie**. Mary Jane reached age 44 and died in Pittsburgh, Allegheny Co., Pennsylvania, on February 7, 1904. She was buried in Chartiers Cemetery, Carnegie, Scott Twp., Allegheny Co., Pennsylvania.[30]

Children of James Calvin Pegan and Mary Jane Laird:

+ 116 m I. **Ira Calvin**[7] **Pegan** was born in Elliott Twp., Allegheny Twp., Pennsylvania, in 1881. He died in Elliott Twp., Allegheny Twp., Pennsylvania, in 1896. Ira Calvin was buried in Chartiers Cemetery, Carnegie, Scott Twp., Allegheny Co., Pennsylvania.[30]

+ 117 f II. **Laura Etta**[7] **Pegan** was born in Elliott Twp., Allegheny Twp., Pennsylvania, on November 9, 1884. She died in Carnegie, Scott Twp., Allegheny Co., Pennsylvania, on January 9, 1978. Laura Etta was buried in Jefferson Memorial Park Cemetery, Pleasant Hills, Allegheny Co., Pennsylvania.[55]

+ 118 f III. **Effie P.**[7] **Pegan** was born in Elliott Twp., Allegheny Twp., Pennsylvania, on October 9, 1887. She died in Pittsburgh, Allegheny Co., Pennsylvania, on September 24, 1971. Effie P. was buried in Jefferson Memorial Park Cemetery, Pleasant Hills, Allegheny Co., Pennsylvania.[55, 56]

+ 119 f IV. **Ruth Ann**[7] **Pegan** was born in Elliott Twp., Allegheny Twp., Pennsylvania, on August 14, 1889. She died in Pittsburgh, Allegheny Co., Pennsylvania, on December 20, 1970. Ruth

Ann was buried in Jefferson Memorial Park Cemetery, Pleasant Hills, Allegheny Co., Pennsylvania. [55, 56]

+ 120 f V. **Mabel**[7] **Pegan** was born in Elliott Twp., Allegheny Twp., Pennsylvania, in 1894. She died in Elliott Twp., Allegheny Twp., Pennsylvania, in 1895. Mabel was buried in Chartiers Cemetery, Carnegie, Scott Twp., Allegheny Co., Pennsylvania.[30]

+ 121 f VI. **Margaret**[7] **Pegan** was born in Elliott Twp., Allegheny Twp., Pennsylvania, in May 1899. She died in Elliott Twp., Allegheny Twp., Pennsylvania, in 1900. Margaret was buried in Chartiers Cemetery, Carnegie, Scott Twp., Allegheny Co., Pennsylvania.[30]

**57. Anna Mary**[6] **Pegan** (*Alexander L.*[5], *Andrew*[4], *James*[3], *Andrew*[2] *Pagan, James*[1]) was born on November 4, 1864, in Martic Twp., Lancaster Co., Pennsylvania. She was the daughter of Alexander L. Pegan (19) and Ruthanna Appleton. Anna Mary died in East Lampeter Twp., Lancaster Co., Pennsylvania, on August 4, 1950, at age 85. She was buried in Zion Lutheran Cemetery, Leola, Upper Leacock Twp., Lancaster Co., Pennsylvania.[31]

Anna Mary married **Ambrose Kirkwood** on May 9, 1890, in Lancaster Co., Pennsylvania. They had one son. Ambrose Kirkwood was born in Drumore Twp., Lancaster Co., Pennsylvania, in 1857. Ambrose reached age 36 aand died in Lancaster, Lancaster Co., Pennsylvania, on March 30, 1893. He was buried in Lancaster Cemetery, Lancaster, Lancaster Co., Pennsylvania.[18]

Anna Mary Pegan Kirkwood married **Adam L. Miller** about 1902. They had two children. Adam L. Miller was born in Bareville, Upper Leacock Twp., Lancaster Co., Pennsylvania, on March 10, 1850. Adam L. reached age 76 and died in East Lampeter Twp., Lancaster Co., Pennsylvania, on November 6, 1926. He was buried in Zion Lutheran Cemetery, Leola, Upper Leacock Twp., Lancaster Co., Pennsylvania.[31]

Son of Anna Mary Pegan and Ambrose Kirkwood:

+ 122 m I. **Son**[7] **Kirkwood** was born in Lancaster Co., Pennsylvania, about October 18, 1890. He died in Lancaster Co., Pennsylvania or Chatham Co., North Carolina, on October 18, 1890. Son was buried in Lancaster Cemetery, Lancaster, Lancaster Co., Pennsylvania.[18]

Children of Anna Mary Pegan and Adam L. Miller:

+ 123 f I. **Loretta**[7] **Miller** was born in East Lampeter Twp., Lancaster Co., Pennsylvania, on December 28, 1903. She died in Haverford Twp., Delaware Co., Pennsylvania, on November 1, 1970. Loretta was buried in Saint Paul's Lutheran Cemetery, Ardmore, Lower Merion Twp., Montgomery Co., Pennsylvania.[57]

+ 124 m II. **Sherwood A.**[7] **Miller** was born in East Lampeter Twp., Lancaster Co., Pennsylvania, on July 28, 1905. He died in Brownstown, West Earl Twp., Lancaster Co., Pennsylvania, on November 26, 1981. Sherwood A. was buried in Zion Lutheran Cemetery, Leola, Upper Leacock Twp., Lancaster Co., Pennsylvania.[31]

**58. Elmer Ellsworth James**[6] **Pegan** (*Alexander L.*[5], *Andrew*[4], *James*[3], *Andrew*[2] *Pagan*, *James*[1]) was born on January 2, 1863, in Martic Twp., Lancaster Co., Pennsylvania. He was the son of Alexander L. Pegan (19) and Ruthanna Appleton. Elmer Ellsworth James died in Wilmington, New Castle Co., Delaware, on January 13, 1939, at age 76. He was buried in Silverbrook Cemetery, Wilmington, New Castle Co., Delaware.[32]

Elmer Ellsworth James married **Estella Rachel Scott** in 1890. They had nine children. Estella Rachel Scott was born in Ogleton, New Castle Co., Delaware, on February 18, 1863. She was

also known as **Stella**. Estella Rachel reached age 58 and died in Wilmington, New Castle Co., Delaware, on September 15, 1921. She was buried in Silverbrook Cemetery, Wilmington, New Castle Co., Delaware.[32]

Children of Elmer Ellsworth James Pegan and Estella Rachel Scott:

+ 125 m I. **William Henry**[7] **Pegan** was born in Wilmington, New Castle Co., Delaware, on August 31, 1891. He died in Delaware City, New Castle Co., Delaware, on September 21, 1950. William Henry was buried in Silverbrook Cemetery, Wilmington, New Castle Co., Delaware.[32]

+ 126 m II. **Harry Oliver**[7] **Pegan** was born in Rockland, New Castle Co., Delaware, on June 22, 1893. He died in Philadelphia, Philadelphia Co., Pennsylvania, on September 23, 1959. Harry Oliver was buried in All Saints Cemetery, Wilmington, New Castle Co., Delaware.[58]

+ 127 f III. **Adelaide or Adeline**[7] **Pegan** was born in Wilmington, New Castle Co., Delaware, on August 5, 1895. She was also known as **Addie**. Adelaide or Adeline died in Wilmington, New Castle Co., Delaware, on March 28, 1966.

+ 128 m IV. **Samuel**[7] **Pegan** was born in Wilmington, New Castle Co., Delaware, on February 23, 1897. He died in a hospital in Philadelphia, Philadelphia Co., Pennsylvania, on June 18, 1947. Samuel was buried in Silverbrook Cemetery, Wilmington, New Castle Co., Delaware.[32]

+ 129 m V. **Harvey**[7] **Pegan** was born in Wilmington, New Castle Co., Delaware, on March 16, 1897. He died in Springfield, Delaware

Co., Pennsylvania, in October 1966.

+ 130 m VI. **Son One**[7] **Pegan** was born in Wilmington, New Castle Co., Delaware, on November 1, 1901. He died in Wilmington, New Castle Co., Delaware, on November 1, 1901.

+ 131 m VII. **Raymond**[7] **Pegan** was born in Wilmington, New Castle Co., Delaware, on October 20, 1903. He died in Wilmington, New Castle Co., Delaware, in December 1969. Raymond was buried in Gracelawn Memorial Park Cemetery, Farmhurst, New Castle Co., Delaware.[59]

+ 132 m VIII. **Everett**[7] **Pegan** was born in Wilmington, New Castle Co., Delaware, on March 18, 1905. He died in New Castle Co., Delaware, on October 7, 1959. Everett was buried in Gracelawn Memorial Park, Farmhurst, New Castle Co., Delaware.[59]

+ 133 m IX. **Son Two**[7] **Pegan** was born in Wilmington, New Castle Co., Delaware, on September 23, 1910. He died in Wilmington, New Castle Co., Delaware, on September 23, 1910.

**59. Effie May**[6] **Pegan** (*Alexander L.*[5], *Andrew*[4], *James*[3], *Andrew*[2] *Pagan, James*[1]) was born on December 10, 1868, in Martic Twp., Lancaster Co., Pennsylvania. She was the daughter of Alexander L. Pegan (19) and Ruthanna Appleton. Effie May died in Lancaster, Lancaster Co., Pennsylvania, on December 23, 1938, at age 70. She was buried in Riverview Burial Park Cemetery, Lancaster, Lancaster Co., Pennsylvania.[29]

Childless.

Effie May married **Henry A. Kuhn** on March 8, 1891, in Lancaster Co., Pennsylvania. Henry

A. Kuhn was born in Hanover Twp., York Co., Pennsylvania, in August 1866. He was also known as **Harry**. Henry A. died in Lancaster, Lancaster Co., Pennsylvania, between 1900 and 1910.

Effie May Pegan Kuhn married **Aldus Hackman Goss** after 1910. They divorced. Aldus Hackman Goss was born in Conestoga Twp., Lancaster Co., Pennsylvania, on March 25, 1876. He reached age 75 and died in Pequa Twp., Lancaster Co., Pennsylvania, on July 2, 1951. Aldus Hackman was buried in Byerland Mennonite Cemetery, Pequa Twp, Lancaster Co., Pennsylvania.[60]

**60. Bertha**[6] **Pegan** (*Andrew A.*[5], *Andrew*[4], *James*[3], *Andrew*[2] *Pagan, James*[1]) was born on April 21, 1868, in Martic Twp., Lancaster Co., Pennsylvania. She was the daughter of Andrew A. Pegan II (20) and Louisa Bailey. Bertha died in Manor Twp., Lancaster Co., Pennsylvania, on August 27, 1957, at age 89. She was buried in Grace United Methodist Church Cemetery, Millersville, Manor Twp., Lancaster Co., Pennsylvania.[33]

Bertha married **Martin Luther Urban** on April 28, 1889, in Lancaster Co., Pennsylvania. They had three sons. Martin Luther Urban was born in Conestoga Twp., Lancaster Co., Pennsylvania, on February 12, 1868. Martin Luther reached age 70 and died in Manor Twp., Lancaster Co., Pennsylvania, on May 24, 1938. He was buried in Grace United Methodist Church Cemetery, Millersville, Manor Twp., Lancaster Co., Pennsylvania.[33]

Sons of Bertha Pegan and Martin Luther Urban:

+ 134 m I. **Arthur Allen**[7] **Urban** was born in Manor Twp., Lancaster Co., Pennsylvania, on July 22, 1889. He died in Lancaster, Lancaster Co., Pennsylvania, on November 26, 1967. Arthur Allen was buried in Millersville Mennonite Cemetery, Millersville, Manor Twp., Lancaster Co., Pennsylvania.[61]

+ 135 m II. **Phares Pegan**[7] **Urban** was born in Manor Twp., Lancaster Co., Pennsylvania, on March 6, 1893.

He died in Washington Boro, Manor Twp., Lancaster Co., Pennsylvania, in January 1976. Phares Pegan was buried in Grace United Methodist Church Cemetery, Millersville, Manor Twp., Lancaster Co., Pennsylvania.[33]

+ 136 m III. **Ralph Martin**[7] **Urban** was born in Manor Twp., Lancaster Co., Pennsylvania, on September 1, 1901. He died in Lancaster, Lancaster Co., Pennsylvania, on July 31, 1981. Ralph Martin was buried in Millersville Mennonite Cemetery, Millersville, Manor Twp., Lancaster Co., Pennsylvania.[61]

**61. Harry Franklin**[6] **Pegan** (*Andrew A.*[5], *Andrew*[4], *James*[3], *Andrew*[2] *Pagan, James*[1]) was born on September 25, 1870, in Bethesda, Martic Twp., Lancaster Co., Pennsylvania. He was also known as **Harry**. He was the son of Andrew A. Pegan II (20) and Louisa Bailey. Harry Franklin died in Lancaster, Lancaster Co., Pennsylvania, on June 23, 1939, at age 68. He was buried under the name Harry Pegan in Woodward Hill Cemetery, Lancaster, Lancaster Co., Pennsylvania.[34]

Childless.

He married **Mary H. Waltz**. Mary H. Waltz was born in West Hempfield Twp., Lancaster Co., Pennsylvania, in July 1876. Mary H. reached age 95 and died in Lancaster, Lancaster Co., Pennsylvania, in 1972. She was buried in Woodward Hill Cemetery, Lancaster, Lancaster Co., Pennsylvania.[34]

**62. Roy David**[6] **Pegan** (*Andrew A.*[5], *Andrew*[4], *James*[3], *Andrew*[2] *Pagan, James*[1]) was born on January 1, 1873, in East Drumore Twp., Lancaster Co., Pennsylvania. He was the son of Andrew A. Pegan II (20) and Louisa Bailey. Roy David died in East Lampeter Twp., Lancaster Co., Pennsylvania, on May 5, 1958, at age 85. He was buried in Millersville Mennonite Cemetery, Millersville, Manor Twp., Lancaster Co., Pennsylvania.[61]

Childless.

Roy David married **Christina Ehrhart** on April 3, 1903, in Lancaster Co., Pennsylvania. Christina Ehrhart was born in Manor Twp., Lancaster Co., Pennsylvania, on July 12, 1869. Christina reached age 66 and died in Lancaster, Lancaster Co., Pennsylvania, on March 4, 1936. She was buried in Millersville Mennonite Cemetery, Millersville, Manor Twp., Lancaster Co., Pennsylvania.[61]

Roy David Pegan was a family historian who kept notes on the James and Sarah Brannon Pegan line. He donated his research to the Lancaster Historical Society archives.[2]

**63. Martha Ann**[6] **Fulton** (*Sarah Jane*[5] *Miller, Margaret*[4] *Pegan, James*[3], *Andrew*[2] *Pagan, James*[1]) was born on June 13, 1840, in Peach Bottom Twp., York Co., Pennsylvania. She was the daughter of David Fulton and Sarah Jane Miller (22). Martha Ann died in Peach Bottom Twp., York Co., Pennsylvania, on November 13, 1916, age 76. She was buried in Slate Ridge Cemetery, Delta, Peach Bottom Twp., York Co., Pennsylvania.[2, 20]

Martha Ann married **Samuel Parke Johnson** on December 7, 1869, in York Co., Pennsylvania. They had four children. Samuel Parke Johnson was born in Peach Bottom Twp., York Co., Pennsylvania, on July 20, 1845. Samuel Parke reached age 81 and died in Peach Bottom Twp., York Co., Pennsylvania, on July 7, 1927. He was buried in Slate Ridge Cemetery, Delta, Peach Bottom Twp., York Co., Pennsylvania.[2, 20]

Children of Martha Ann Fulton and Samuel Parke Johnson:

+ 137 f I. **Sarah**[7] **Johnson** was born in Peach Bottom Twp., York Co., Pennsylvania, on August 6, 1871. [8] She died in Lower Chanceford Twp., York Co., Pennsylvania, on February 25, 1950. Sarah was buried in Slate Ridge Cemetery, Delta, Peach Bottom Twp., York Co., Pennsylvania.[2, 20]

+ 138 m II. **James**[7] **Johnson** was born in Peach Bottom Twp., York Co., Pennsylvania, in 1874. He died in Peach Bottom Twp., York Co., Pennsylvania, in 1891.

+  139  f  III.  **Grace Anna**[7] **Johnson** was born in Peach Bottom Twp., York Co., Pennsylvania, on November 27, 1876. She died in Delta, Peach Bottom Twp., York Co., Pennsylvania, on September 1, 1961. Grace Anna was buried in Slate Ridge Cemetery, Delta, Peach Bottom Twp., York Co., Pennsylvania.[20]

+  140  m  IV.  **Samuel Fulton**[7] **Johnson II** was born in Peach Bottom Twp., York Co., Pennsylvania, on October 9, 1880. He was also known as **Fulton** and **S. Fulton**. Samuel Fulton died in Peach Bottom Twp., York Co., Pennsylvania, on January 6, 1941. He was buried in Slate Ridge Cemetery, Delta, Peach Bottom Twp., York Co., Pennsylvania.[20]

**64. John Henry**[6] **Fulton** (*Sarah Jane*[5] *Miller, Margaret*[4] *Pegan, James*[3], *Andrew*[2] *Pagan, James*[1]) was born on June 14, 1842, in Peach Bottom Twp., York Co., Pennsylvania. He was the son of David Fulton and Sarah Jane Miller (22). John Henry died in Peach Bottom Twp., York Co., Pennsylvania, on September 23, 1932, at age 90. He was buried in Slate Ridge Cemetery, Delta, Peach Bottom Twp., York Co., Pennsylvania.[2, 20]

John Henry married **Mary Eleanor Anderson** before 1877. They had four children. Mary Eleanor Anderson was born in Hopewell Twp., York Go., Pennsylvania, on February 17, 1842. She was also known as **Ellen**. Mary Eleanor reached age 79 and died in Peach Bottom Twp., York Co., Pennsylvania, on November 29, 1921. She was buried in Slate Ridge Cemetery, Delta, Peach Bottom Twp., York Co., Pennsylvania.[2, 20]

Children of John Henry Fulton and Mary Eleanor Anderson:

+  141  m  I.  **David Edgar**[7] **Fulton** was born in Peach Bottom Twp., York Co., Pennsylvania, on March 1, 1877. He died in Peach Bottom Twp., York Co., Pennsylvania, on October 10, 1960. David Edgar was buried in Slate Ridge Cemetery, Delta, Peach Bottom Twp., York Co., Pennsylvania.[20]

+  142  f  II.  **Mary Janetta**[7] **Fulton** was born in Peach Bottom Twp., York Co., Pennsylvania, on February 21, 1881. She died in Delta, Peach Bottom Twp., York Co., Pennsylvania, in November 1967. Mary Janetta was buried in Slate Ridge Cemetery, Delta, Peach Bottom Twp., York Co., Pennsylvania.[20]

+  143  m  III.  **James Anderson**[7] **Fulton** was born in Peach Bottom Twp., York Co., Pennsylvania, on May 24, 1883. He died in Peach Bottom Twp., York Co., Pennsylvania, on December 7, 1938. James Anderson was buried in Slate Ridge Cemetery, Delta, Peach Bottom Twp., York Co., Pennsylvania.[20]

+  144  m  IV.  **Samuel J.**[7] **Fulton** was born in Peach Bottom Twp., York Co., Pennsylvania, on May 29, 1886. He died in Peach Bottom Twp., York Co., Pennsylvania, on February 2, 1923. Samuel J. was buried in Slate Ridge Cemetery, Delta, Peach Bottom Twp., York Co., Pennsylvania.[20]

**65. Margaret A.**[6] **Fulton** (*Sarah Jane*[5] *Miller, Margaret*[4] *Pegan, James*[3], *Andrew*[2] *Pagan, James*[1]) was born on March 13, 1845, in Peach Bottom Twp., York Co., Pennsylvania. She was the daughter of David Fulton and Sarah Jane Miller (22). Margaret A. died in Fulton Twp., Lancaster Co., Pennsylvania, on December 5, 1884, at age 39. She was buried in Slate Ridge Cemetery, Delta, Peach Bottom Twp., York Co., Pennsylvania.[2]

Margaret A. married **John Thomas Gregg** on September 23, 1869. They had two children. John Thomas Gregg was born in Drumore Twp., Lancaster

Co., Pennsylvania, on December 8, 1844 or 1845. He was also known as **Thomas**. John Thomas reached age 66 and died in Fulton Twp., Lancaster Co., Pennsylvania, on January 8, 1911. He was buried in Slate Ridge Cemetery, Delta, Peach Bottom Twp., York Co., Pennsylvania.[2, 20]

John Thomas Gregg's death certificate says he was born on December 8, 1845.[62] But other records and his tombstone, which indicates he died at age 66 years and six months on January 8, 1911, which would mean he was born on December 8, 1844.[20, 63, 64]

Children of Margaret A. Fulton and John Thomas Gregg:

+ 145 f I. **Mabel A.**[7] **Gregg** was born in Fulton Twp., Lancaster Co., Pennsylvania, on October 1, 1871. She died in Lancaster, Lancaster Co., Pennsylvania, in March 1968. Mabel A. was buried in New Chestnut Level Presbyterian Church Cemetery, Drumore Twp., Lancaster Co., Pennsylvania.[36]

+ 146 m II. **William Fulton**[7] **Gregg** was born in Fulton Twp., Lancaster Co., Pennsylvania, on February 24, 1875. He died in Columbia City, Columbia Co., Oregon, on July 28, 1925.

66. **Elizabeth Jane**[6] **Fulton** (*Sarah Jane*[5] *Miller, Margaret*[4] *Pegan, James*[3]*, Andrew*[2] *Pagan, James*[1]) was born on November 19, 1848, in Peach Bottom Twp., York Co., Pennsylvania. She was also known as **Lizzie**. She was the daughter of David Fulton and Sarah Jane Miller (22). Elizabeth Jane died in Peach Bottom Twp., York Co., Pennsylvania, on June 13, 1936, at age 87. She was buried in Slate Ridge Cemetery, Delta, Peach Bottom Twp., York Co., Pennsylvania.[2, 8]

Elizabeth Jane married **George Geiger** before 1877. They had three children. George Geiger was born in York Co., Pennsylvania? in 1830. George reached age 53 and died in Peach Bottom Twp., York Co., Pennsylvania, in 1883. He was buried in Slate Ridge Cemetery, Delta, Peach Bottom Twp., York Co., Pennsylvania.[2, 20]

Children of Elizabeth Jane Fulton and George Geiger:

+ 147 m I. **George Fulton**[7] **Geiger II** was born in Peach Bottom Twp., York Co., Pennsylvania, on January 31, 1877. He died in Peach Bottom Twp., York Co., Pennsylvania, on July 28, 1926. George Fulton was buried in Slate Ridge Cemetery, Delta, Peach Bottom Twp., York Co., Pennsylvania.[20]

+ 148 f II. **Infant Daughter One**[7] **Geiger**. Infant Daughter One was buried in Slate Ridge Cemetery, Delta, Peach Bottom Twp., York Co., Pennsylvania.[20]

+ 149 f III. **Infant Daughter Two**[7] **Geiger**. Infant Daughter Two was buried in Slate Ridge Cemetery, Delta, Peach Bottom Twp., York Co., Pennsylvania.[20]

67. **Robert Allen**[6] **Fulton** (*Sarah Jane*[5] *Miller, Margaret*[4] *Pegan, James*[3]*, Andrew*[2] *Pagan, James*[1]) was born on June 11, 1852, in Peach Bottom Twp., York Co., Pennsylvania. He was the son of David Fulton and Sarah Jane Miller (22). Robert Allen died in Peach Bottom Twp., York Co., Pennsylvania, on July 19, 1907, at age 55. He was buried in Slate Ridge Cemetery, Delta, Peach Bottom Twp., York Co., Pennsylvania.[2, 20]

Robert Allen married **Rachel E. Davis** between 1880 and 1882. They had four children. Rachel E. Davis was born in Stearns, Harford Co., Maryland, on April 18, 1856. Rachel E. reached age 66 and died in Peach Bottom Twp., York Co., Pennsylvania, on November 24, 1922. She was buried in Slate Ridge Cemetery, Delta, Peach Bottom Twp., York Co., Pennsylvania[2, 20]

According to the Roy D. Pegan genealogy of James and Sarah Brannon Pegan's descendants, Robert Allen and Rachel Davis Fulton had daughters named Elizabeth and Eleanor. But census records say one of their daughters was named Annie B. Fulton. The other daughter was born and died in 1893 and may have been named Eleanor Elizabeth.[2]

Children of Robert Allen Fulton and Rachel E. Davis:

+ 150 m I. **William Davis[7] Fulton** was born in Peach Bottom Twp., York Co., Pennsylvania, on September 27, 1883. He died in Baltimore, Baltimore Co., Maryland, after 1942.

+ 151 m II. **Ross David[7] Fulton** was born in Peach Bottom Twp., York Co., Pennsylvania, on December 20, 1885. He died in Peach Bottom Twp., York Co., Pennsylvania, on April 10, 1910. Ross David was buried in Slate Ridge Cemetery, Delta, Peach Bottom Twp., York Co., Pennsylvania.[20]

+ 152 f III. **Annie B.[7] Fulton** was born in Peach Bottom Twp., York Co., Pennsylvania, on May 5, 1890. She died in Peach Bottom Twp., York Co., Pennsylvania, on May 4, 1912. Annie B. was buried in Slate Ridge Cemetery, Delta, Peach Bottom Twp., York Co., Pennsylvania.[20]

+ 153 f IV. **Eleanor Elizabeth[7] Fulton** was born in Peach Bottom Twp., York Co., Pennsylvania, in 1893. She died in Peach Bottom Twp., York Co., Pennsylvania, in 1893.[2]

**68. Agnes Miller[6] Fulton** (*Sarah Jane[5] Miller, Margaret[4] Pegan, James[3], Andrew[2] Pagan, James[1]*) was born on October 28, 1854, in Peach Bottom Twp., York Co., Pennsylvania. She was the daughter of David Fulton and Sarah Jane Miller (22). Agnes Miller died in Peach Bottom Twp., York Co., Pennsylvania, on July 22, 1909, at age 54. She was buried in Slate Ridge Cemetery, Delta, Peach Bottom Twp., York Co., Pennsylvania.[2, 20]

Never married.

**69. Sarah Ann[6] Mitchell** (*Martha Ellen[5] Miller, Margaret[4] Pegan, James[3], Andrew[2] Pagan, James[1]*) was born in Peach Bottom Twp., York Co., Pennsylvania on July 31, 1859. She was the daughter of William J. Mitchell and Martha Ellen Miller (28). Sarah Ann died in Mansfield, Madison Twp., Richland Co., Ohio on November 28, 1928 at age 69. She was buried in Lexington Cemetery, Lexington, Troy Twp., Richland Co., Ohio.[34]

Sarah Ann married **William Franklin Douglass** before 1885. He was also known as **Frank**. William Franklin Mitchell was born on June 14, 1861 in Troy Twp., Richland Co., Ohio. He reached age 57 and died in Mansfield, Madison Twp., Richland Co., Ohio?, on September 4, 1918. William Franklin was buried in Lexington Cemetery, Lexington, Troy Twp., Richland Co., Ohio.[34]

Children of Sarah Ann Mitchell and William Franklin Douglass:

+ 154 m I. **Willie S.W. Douglass** was born in Lexington, Troy Twp., Richland Co., Ohio, on July 29, 1885. Willie S.W. died in Mansfield, Madison Twp., Richland Co., Ohio, on April 28, 1899. He was buried in Lexington Cemetery, Lexington, Troy Twp., Richland Co., Ohio.[34]

+ 155 f II. **Ada Mae[7] Douglass** was born in Lexington, Troy Twp., Richland Co., Ohio, on May 29, 1889.[65] She was also **Mae**. She died in Mansfield, Madison Twp., Richland Co., Ohio on May 7, 1972.[66]

**70. Margaret Rosa[6] Mitchell** (*Martha Ellen[5] Miller, Margaret[4] Pegan, James[3], Andrew[2] Pagan, James[1]*) was born on August 10, 1866, in Peach Bottom Twp., York Co., Pennsylvania. She was also known as **Maggie or Rosa**. She was the daughter of William J. Mitchell and Martha Ellen Miller (28). Margaret Rosa died in Lower Chanceford Twp., York Co., Pennsylvania, on December 31, 1917, at age 51. She was buried in Chanceford Presbyterian

Cemetery, Airville, Lower Chanceford Twp., York Co., Pennsylvania.[14]

Margaret Rosa married **George Brinton Kilgore** about 1890. They had three children. George Brinton Kilgore was born in Lower Chanceford Twp., York Co., Pennsylvania, on December 4, 1861. George Brinton reached age 82 and died in Lower Chanceford Twp., York Co., Pennsylvania, on April 28, 1944. He was buried in Chanceford Presbyterian Cemetery, Airville, Lower Chanceford Twp., York Co., Pennsylvania.[14]

Children of Margaret Rosa Mitchell and George Brinton Kilgore:

+ 156 m I.   **James Mitchell**[7] **Kilgore** was born in Lower Chanceford Twp., York Co., Pennsylvania, on February 3, 1892. He was also known as **Mitchell**. James Mitchell died in Mansfield, Madison Twp., Richland Co., Ohio, on June 6, 1945. He was buried in Mansfield Cemetery, Ontario, Madison Twp., Richland Co., Ohio.[67]

+ 157 f II.   **Ula Agnes Ellen**[7] **Kilgore** was born in Lower Chanceford Twp., York Co., Pennsylvania, on October 28, 1893. She was also known as **Agnes**. Ula Agnes Ellen died in Red Lion, York Twp., York Co., Pennsylvania, on January 14, 1962. She was buried in Pine Grove Presbyterian Church Cemetery, Lower Chanceford Twp., York Co., Pennsylvania.[51]

+ 158 f III.   **Nora Eliza**[7] **Kilgore** was born in Lower Chanceford Twp., York Co., Pennsylvania, on March 5, 1904. She died in Brogue, Chanceford Twp., York Co., Pennsylvania, on March 23, 1984. Nora Eliza was buried in Mount Olivet United Methodist Church Cemetery, Fawn Grove, Fawn Twp., York Co., Pennsylvania[68]

**71. Ida Melissa**[6] **Pegan** (*Henry*[5], *James*[4], *James*[3], *Andrew*[2] *Pagan, James*[1]) was born on November 21, 1858, in Drumore Twp., Lancaster Co., Pennsylvania. She was the daughter of Henry Pegan (31) and Mary Matilda Penny. Ida Melissa died in York Twp., York Co., Pennsylvania, on December 15, 1922, at age 64. She was buried in Old Guinston Church Cemetery, Airville, Chanceford Twp., York Co., Pennsylvania.[21]

Ida Melissa married **Samuel Adams Grove** on December 26, 1878. They had eleven children. Samuel Adams Grove was born in Lower Chanceford Twp., York Co., Pennsylvania, on December 28, 1855. Samuel Adams reached age 75 and died in York Twp., York Co., Pennsylvania, on July 23, 1931. He was buried in Old Guinston Church Cemetery, Airville, Chanceford Twp., York Co., Pennsylvania.[21]

Children of Ida Melissa Pegan and Samuel Adams Grove:

+ 159 m I.   **Child**[7] **Grove** was born in York Co., Pennsylvania, between 1878 and 1900. He died in York Co., Pennsylvania, between 1878 and 1900.

+ 160 m II.   **John Evelyn**[7] **Grove** was born in Lower Chanceford Twp., York Co., Pennsylvania, on May 25, 1879. He was also known as **Evelyn**. John Evelyn died in Sunnyburn, Lower Chanceford Twp., York Co., Pennsylvania, on May 19, 1906. He was buried in Salem United Methodist Church Cemetery, Delta, Peach Bottom Twp., York Co., Pennsylvania.[52]

+ 161 m III.   **Francis Henry**[7] **Grove** was born in Lower Chanceford Twp., York Co., Pennsylvania, on January 1, 1885. He was also known as **Frank**. Francis Henry died in Peach Bottom Twp., York Co., Pennsylvania, on December 11, 1960. He was bur ied in Slate Ridge Cemetery, Delta, Peach Bottom Twp., York Co., Pennsylvania.[20]

+ 162 m IV.   **Wayne Penny**[7] **Grove** was born in Lower Chanceford Twp., York

Co., Pennsylvania, on March 17, 1886. Wayne Penny died in York Twp., York Co., Pennsylvania, on January 13, 1972. He was buried in Mount Rose Cemetery, Spring Garden Twp., York Co., Pennsylvania.[40]

+ 163 m V. **William Allison**[7] **Grove** was born in Chanceford Twp., York Co., Pennsylvania, on October 24, 1887. He was also known as **Allison**. William Allison died in Detroit, Wayne Co., Michigan, on March 25, 1933.[69] He was buried in Woodmere Cemetery, Detroit, Wayne Co., Michigan.[70]

+ 164 m VI. **Claire Jamieson**[7] **Grove** was born in Chanceford Twp., York Co., Pennsylvania, on December 4, 1888. He died in York, York Co., Pennsylvania, on September 15, 1987. Claire Jamison was buried in Longstown United Methodist Cemetery, York Twp., York Co., Pennsylvania.[71]

+ 165 f VII. **Anna Matilda**[7] **Grove** was born in Peach Bottom Twp., York Co., Pennsylvania, on June 17, 1891. She died in Springettsbury Twp., York Co., Pennsylvania, on February 24, 1963. Anna Matilda was buried in Longstown United Methodist Cemetery, York Twp., York Co., Pennsylvania.[71]

+ 166 m VIII. **Infant Samuel M.**[7] **Grove** was born in Peach Bottom Twp., York Co., Pennsylvania, on February 13, 1893. He died in Peach Bottom Twp., York Co., Penn sylvania, on October 4, 1893. Infant Samuel M. was buried in Old Guinston Church Cemetery, Airville, Chanceford Twp., York Co., Pennsylvania.[21]

+ 167 f IX. **Sara Mary**[7] **Grove** was born in Peach Bottom Twp., York Co., Pennsylvania, on September 13, 1894. She died in York, York Co., Pennsylvania, about May 17, 1973. Sara Mary was buried in Mount Rose Cemetery, Spring Garden Twp., York Co., Pennsylvania.[40]

+ 168 m X. **James Russell**[7] **Grove** was born in Peach Bottom Twp., York Co., Pennsylvania, on March 13, 1897. He was also known as **Russell**. James Russell died in York, York Co., Pennsylvania, on November 1, 1977. He was buried in Freysville Cemetery, Windsor Twp., York Co., Pennsylvania.[72]

+ 169 m XI. **Samuel Gail**[7] **Grove II** was born in Peach Bottom Twp., York Co., Pennsylvania, on May 20, 1898. He died in York, York Co., Pennsylvania, in May 1978. He was buried in Stony Brook Mennonite Cemetery, York, York Co., Pennsylvania.[73]

**72. Alice Eva**[6] **Pegan** (*Henry*[5], *James*[4], *James*[3], *Andrew*[2] *Pagan, James*[1]) was born on February 29, 1860, in Drumore Twp., Lancaster Co., Pennsylvania. She was also known as **Eva**. She was the daughter of Henry Pegan (31) and Mary Matilda Penny. Alice Eva died in Lower Chanceford Twp., York Co., Pennsylvania, on September 21, 1896, at age 36. "Eve Alice" is buried in Guinston Presbyterian Church Cemetery, Airville, Lower Chanceford Twp., York Co., Pennsylvania.[21]

Alice Eva married **William Wilkins Grove** on November 23, 1893, in York Co., Pennsylvania. They had one son. William Wilkins Grove was born in Lower Chanceford Twp., York Co., Pennsylvania? on December 7, 1862. William Wilkins reached age 79 and died in Red Lion, York Twp., York Co., Pennsylvania, on December 22, 1941. He was buried in Old Guinston Church Cemetery, Airville,

Chanceford Twp., York Co., Pennsylvania.[21] Buried under the name W. Wilkins Grove.

Son of Alice Eva Pegan and William Wilkins Grove:

+ 170 m I. **John Paul**[7] **Grove** was born in Lower Chanceford Twp., York Co., Pennsylvania, on December 29, 1894. He was also known as **Paul**. John Paul died in York, York Co., Pennsylvania, on April 16, 1963. He was buried in Old Guinston Church Cemetery, Airville, Chanceford Twp., York Co., Pennsylvania.[21]

**73. Mary Lena**[6] **Pegan** (*Henry*[5], *James*[4], *James*[3], *Andrew*[2] *Pagan*, *James*[1]) was born on July 2, 1864, in Drumore Twp., Lancaster Co., Pennsylvania. She was also known as **Lena**. She was the daughter of Henry Pegan (31) and Mary Matilda Penny. Mary Lena died in Coatesville, Valley Twp., Chester Co., Pennsylvania, on May 9, 1943, at age of 78. She was buried in Oxford Cemetery, Oxford, Chester Co., Pennsylvania.[37]

Mary Lena married **Robert Ellsworth Wickersham** on December 24, 1892, in York Co., Pennsylvania. They had two children. Robert Ellsworth Wickersham was born in Upper Oxford Twp., Chester Co., Pennsylvania, on April 30, 1864. Robert Ellsworth lived in 1885 in Chester Co., Pennsylvania. He reached age 76 and died in Coatesville, Valley Twp., Chester Co., Pennsylvania, on March 15, 1941. Robert Ellsworth was buried in Oxford Cemetery, Oxford, Chester Co., Pennsylvania.[37]

Children of Mary Lena Pegan and Robert Ellsworth Wickersham:

+ 171 m I. **J. Clyde**[7] **Wickersham** was born in Russellville, Upper Oxford Twp., Chester Co., Pennsylvania, on April 28, 1894. He died in Russellville, Upper Oxford Twp., Chester Co., Pennsylvania, on November 3, 1967. J. Clyde was buried in Oxford Cemetery, Oxford, Chester Co., Pennsylvania.[37]

+ 172 f II. **Mary Adelaide**[7] **Wickersham** was born in Russellville, Upper Oxford Twp., Chester Co., Pennsylvania, on June 8, 1904. She died in Contoocook, Merrimack Co., New Hampshire, on October 12, 1997. Mary Adelaide was buried in Upper Octarara Church Cemetery, Parkesburg, Sadbury Twp., Chester Co., Pennsylvania.[74]

**74. Luella M.**[6] **Pegan** (*Henry*[5], *James*[4], *James*[3], *Andrew*[2] *Pagan*, *James*[1]) was born on May 19, 1871, in Drumore Twp., Lancaster Co., Pennsylvania. She was the daughter of Henry Pegan (31) and Elizabeth Ann Neel. Luella M. died in Harrisburg, Dauphin Co., Pennsylvania, on February 9, 1963, at age 91. She was buried in Prospect Hill Cemetery, Harrisburg, Dauphin Co., Pennsylvania.[38]

Childless.

Luella M. married **John O. Love** on April 24, 1902, in York Co., Pennsylvania. John O. Love was born in Conestoga Twp., Lancaster Co., Pennsylvania, on August 22, 1868. John O. reached age 81 and died in Harrisburg, Dauphin Co., Pennsylvania, on August 1, 1950. He was buried in Prospect Hill Cemetery, Harrisburg, Dauphin Co., Pennsylvania.[38]

**75. Harry Hutton**[6] **Pegan** (*Henry*[5], *James*[4], *James*[3], *Andrew*[2] *Pagan*, *James*[1]) was born on February 10, 1873, in Drumore Twp., Lancaster Co., Pennsylvania. He was the son of Henry Pegan (31) and Elizabeth Ann Neel. Harry Hutton died in Spring Grove, Jackson Twp., York Co., Pennsylvania, on October 26, 1962, at age 89. He was buried in Spring Grove Cemetery, Jackson Twp., York Co., Pennsylvania.[24]

Harry Hutton married **Lizzie Ann Bailey** on June 21, 1897, in York Co., Pennsylvania. They had three children. Lizzie Ann Bailey was born in Manchester Twp., York Co., Pennsylvania? on September 25, 1863. She was also known as **Lizzie**. Lizzie Ann reached age 70 and died in Spring Grove, Jackson Twp., York Co., Pennsylvania, on May 20, 1934. She was buried in Spring Grove Cemetery, Jackson Twp., York Co., Pennsylvania.[24]

Lizzie Ann Bailey Pegan's death certificate says her parents were George and Julia Beck Bailey, but these may have been her grandparents.[75] In the 1870 U.S. Federal Census, she was living in the home of John and Catherine Drayer in Manchester Twp., York Co., Pennsylvania, who said she was nine years old (she was seven).

Children of Harry Hutton Pegan and Lizzie Ann Bailey:

+ 173  f  I.  **Ruth Estella**[7] **Pegan** was born in Spring Grove, Jackson Twp., York Co., Pennsylvania, on January 6, 1899. She died in Spring Grove, Jackson Twp., York Co., Pennsylvania, in August 1974. Ruth Estella was buried in Spring Grove Cemetery, Jackson Twp., York Co., Pennsylvania.[24]

+ 174  m  II.  **Philip Eugene**[7] **Pegan** was born in Spring Grove, Jackson Twp., York Co., Pennsylvania, on January 20, 1900. He died in York, York Co., Pennsylvania, in May 1970. Philip Eugene was buried in Spring Grove Cemetery, Jackson Twp., York Co., Pennsylvania.[24]

+ 175  m  III.  **Nathan Neil Pegan** was born in Spring Grove, Jackson Twp., York Co., Pennsylvania, on August 29, 1902. He died in Spring Grove, Jackson Twp., York Co., Pennsylvania, on February 6, 1974. Nathan Neil was buried in Spring Grove Cemetery, Jackson Twp., York Co., Pennsylvania.[24]

**76. Jennie Elizabeth**[6] **Adams** (*Sarah Eliza*[5] *Pegan, James*[4], *James*[3], *Andrew*[2] *Pagan, James*[1]) was born on April 23, 1870, in Fawn Twp., York Co., Pennsylvania. She was also known as **Jennie**. She was the daughter of Samuel Isaac Adams and Sarah Eliza Pegan (32). Jennie Elizabeth died in East Hopewell Twp., York Co., Pennsylvania, on March 9, 1947, at age 76. She was buried in Round Hill Presbyterian Church Cemetery, Cross Roads, East Hopewell Twp., York Co., Pennsylvania.[39]

Jennie Elizabeth married **Samuel Smith Manifold** on October 3, 1901, in York Co., Pennsylvania. They had four children. Samuel Smith Manifold was born in Hopewell Twp., York Co., Pennsylvania, on December 26, 1858.[25] Samuel Smith reached age 75 and died in East Hopewell Twp., York Co., Pennsylvania, on September 29, 1934. He was buried in Round Hill Presbyterian Church Cemetery, Cross Roads, East Hopewell Twp., York Co., Pennsylvania.[39]

Children of Jennie Elizabeth Adams and Samuel Smith Manifold:

+ 176  f  I.  **Jessie Eliza**[7] **Manifold** was born in East Hopewell Twp., York Co., Pennsylvania, on July 11, 1903. She died in Stewartstown, Hopewell Twp., York Co., Pennsylvania, on November 17, 1978. Jessie Eliza was buried in Round Hill Presbyterian Church Cemetery, Cross Roads, East Hopewell Twp., York Co., Pennsylvania.[39]

+ 177  m  II.  **Samuel Benjamin**[7] **Manifold** was born in East Hopewell Twp., York Co., Pennsylvania, on December 31, 1904. He was also known as **Benjamin**. Samuel Benjamin died in Stewartstown, Hopewell Twp., York Co., Pennsylvania, in April 1987. He was buried in Round Hill Presbyterian Church Cemetery, Cross Roads, East Hopewell Twp., York Co., Pennsylvania.[39]

+ 178  f  III.  **Margaret Eleanor**[7] **Manifold** was born in East Hopewell Twp., York Co., Pennsylvania, on November 3, 1908. She died in a hospital in York, York Co., York Co., Pennsylvania, on May 9, 2009. Margaret Eleanor was buried in Stewartstown Cemetery, Stewartstown, Hopewell Twp., York Co., Pennsylvania.[76]

+ 179  f  IV.  **Elizabeth L.**[7] **Manifold** was born in East Hopewell Twp., York Co., Pennsylvania, on November 18,

1911. She died in Woodbridge, Prince William Co., Virginia, on January 18, 2007. Elizabeth L. was buried in Round Hill Presbyterian Church Cemetery, Cross Roads, East Hopewell Twp., York Co., Pennsylvania.[39]

**77. Mary Margaret⁶ Adams** (*Sarah Eliza⁵ Pegan, James⁴, James³, Andrew² Pagan, James¹*) was born on February 22, 1872, in Fawn Twp., York Co., Pennsylvania. She was also known as **Margie**. She was the daughter of Samuel Isaac Adams and Sarah Eliza Pegan (32). Mary Margaret died in Fawn Twp., York Co., Pennsylvania, on February 27, 1906, at age 34. She was buried in Old Guinston Church Cemetery, Airville, Chanceford Twp., York Co., Pennsylvania.[21]

Never married.

**78. Samuel Jamieson⁶ Adams II** (*Sarah Eliza⁵ Pegan, James⁴, James³, Andrew² Pagan, James¹*) was born on February 6, 1875, in Fawn Twp., York Co., Pennsylvania. He was also known as **Jamieson**. He was the son of Samuel Isaac Adams and Sarah Eliza Pegan (32). Samuel Jamieson died in Bel Air, Harford Co., Maryland, on July 31, 1969, at age 94. He was buried as S. Jamieson Adams in Old Guinston Church Cemetery, Airville, Chanceford Twp., York Co., Pennsylvania.[21]

He married **Ella Margaret Grove**. They had three children. Ella Margaret Grove was born in Chanceford Twp., York Co., Pennsylvania, on November 13, 1881. Ella Margaret reached age 87 and died in Cardiff, Harford Co., Maryland? on February 16, 1969. She is buried in Old Guinston Church Cemetery, Airville, Chanceford Twp., York Co., Pennsylvania.[21]

Children of Samuel Jamieson Adams II and Ella Margaret Grove:

+ 180 m I. **Son⁷ Adams** was born in High Rock, Lower Chanceford Twp., York Co., Pennsylvania, on March 25, 1908. He died in High Rock, Lower Chanceford Twp.,

York Co., Pennsylvania, on March 25, 1908. Son was buried in Old Guinston Church Cemetery, Airville, Chanceford Twp., York Co., Pennsylvania.[9]

+ 181 f II. **Gladys Grove⁷ Adams** was born in Chanceford Twp., York Co., Pennsylvania, on July 10, 1909. She died in Bel Air, Harford Co., Maryland, on November 14, 2000.

+ 182 f III. **Sara Agnes⁷ Adams** was born in Chanceford Twp., York Co., Pennsylvania, on October 30, 1911. She died in Winchester, Frederick Co., Virginia, on January 17, 1994. Sara Agnes was buried in Shenandoah Memorial Park Cemetery, Winchester, Frederick Co., Virginia.[77]

**79. James Pegan⁶ Grove** (*Margaret Jane⁵ Pegan, James⁴, James³, Andrew² Pagan, James¹*) was born on July 18, 1882, in Chanceford Twp., York Co., Pennsylvania. He was the son of David Barber Grove and Margaret Jane Pegan (34). James Pegan lived in 1964 in Conewego Twp., York Co., Pennsylvania. He died in a hospital in Springettsbury Twp., York Co., Pennsylvania, on January 22, 1964, at age 81. James Pegan was buried in Mount Rose Cemetery, Spring Garden Twp., York Co., Pennsylvania.[40]

James Pegan married **Sarah Blanche Jamieson** before 1909. They had one son. Sarah Blanche Jamieson was born in Lower Chanceford Twp., York Co., Pennsylvania, on August 12, 1881. She was also known as **Blanche**. Sarah Blanche reached age 71 and died in Conewego Twp., York Co., Pennsylvania, on February 16, 1953. She was buried in Mount Rose Cemetery, Spring Garden Twp., York Co., Pennsylvania.[40]

Son of James Pegan Grove and Sarah Blanche Jamieson:

+ 183 m I. **David Earl⁷ Grove** was born in York, York Co., Pennsylvania, on December 17, 1909. He was also known as

**Earl**. David Earl died in York, York Co., Pennsylvania, on December 29, 1994. He was buried in Mount Rose Cemetery, Spring Garden Twp., York Co., Pennsylvania.[40]

80. **Vinton Lemmon**[6] **Grove** (*Margaret Jane*[5] *Pegan, James*[4], *James*[3], *Andrew*[2] *Pagan, James*[1]) was born on April 23, 1885, in Chanceford Twp., York Co., Pennsylvania. He was the son of David Barber Grove and Margaret Jane Pegan (34). Vinton Lemmon died in Chanceford Twp., York Co., Pennsylvania, on May 27, 1922, at age 37. He was buried in Old Guinston Church Cemetery, Airville, Chanceford Twp., York Co., Pennsylvania.[21]

Vinton Lemmon married **Elsie May Boyd** before 1914. They had two children. Elsie May Boyd was born in North Hopewell Twp., York Co., Pennsylvania, on January 8, 1894. Elsie May reached age 68 and died in York, York Co., Pennsylvania, on March 6, 1962. She was buried in Fairview Cemetery, York Twp., York Co., Pennsylvania.[78]

Children of Vinton Lemmon Grove and Elsie May Boyd:

+ 184 f I. **Lulu**[7] **Grove** was born in Chanceford Twp., York Co., Pennsylvania, in 1914. She died in Chanceford Twp., York Co., Pennsylvania, in 1915. Lulu was buried in Old Guinston Church Cemetery, Airville, Chanceford Twp., York Co., Pennsylvania.[21]

+ 185 m II. **Emory**[7] **Grove** was born in Chanceford Twp., York Co., Pennsylvania, on August 29, 1921. He died in Red Lion, York Twp., York Co., Pennsylvania, on June 18, 1999. Emory was buried in Red Lion Cemetery, Red Lion, York Twp., York Co., Pennsylvania.[79, 80]

# 7th Generation

**81. Elmer**[7] **Walton** (*Hannah Margaret*[6] *Nimlow, Margaret*[5] *Pegan, Andrew*[4]*, James*[3]*, Andrew*[2] *Pagan, James*[1]) was born on December 6, 1869, in Martic Twp., Lancaster Co., Pennsylvania. He was the son of Isaac Walton and Hannah Margaret Nimlow (36). Elmer died in Martic Twp., Lancaster Co., Pennsylvania, on April 27, 1944, at age 74. He was buried in Bethesda United Methodist Cemetery, Bethesda, Martic Twp., Lancaster Co., Pennsylvania.[2, 41]

Elmer married **Harriet Jane Appleton** in 1891. They had three children. Harriet Jane Appleton was born in Martic Twp., Lancaster Co., Pennsylvania, on June 27, 1871. Harriet Jane reached age 82 and died in Martic Twp., Lancaster Co., Pennsylvania? on May 7, 1954. She was buried in Bethesda United Methodist Cemetery, Bethesda, Martic Twp., Lancaster Co., Pennsylvania.[2, 41]

Children of Elmer Walton and Harriet Jane Appleton:

+  186  m  I.  **Luther Maurice**[8] **Walton** was born in Mt. Nebo, Martic Twp., Lancaster Co., Pennsylvania, on January 15, 1892. He died in Reading, Berks Co., Pennsylvania, on October 25, 1950. Luther Maurice was buried in Morris Cemetery, Phoenixville, Schuylkill Twp., Chester Co., Pennsylvania.[81]

+  187  f  II.  **Mary Margaret**[8] **Walton** was born in Mt. Nebo, Martic Twp., Lancaster Co., Pennsylvania, on January 31, 1894. She died in Holtwood, Martic Twp., Lancaster Co., Pennsylvania, on October 26, 1963. Mary Margaret was buried in Mount Nebo United Methodist Church Cemetery, Pequea, Pequea Twp., Lancaster Co., Pennsylvania.[82]

+  188  f  III.  **Luella A.**[8] **Walton** was born in Lancaster, Lancaster Co., Pennsylvania, on September 17, 1897

She died in Lancaster, Lancaster Co., Pennsylvania, on February 14, 1920. Luella A. was buried in Greenwood Cemetery, Lancaster, Lancaster Co., Pennsylvania.[2, 25]

**82. Anna Margie**[7] **Walton** (*Hannah Margaret*[6] *Nimlow, Margaret*[5] *Pegan, Andrew*[4]*, James*[3]*, Andrew*[2] *Pagan, James*[1]) was born on June 15, 1876, in Martic Twp., Lancaster Co., Pennsylvania. She was also known as **Margie**. She was the daughter of Isaac Walton and Hannah Margaret Nimlow (36). Anna Margie died in Martic Twp., Lancaster Co., Pennsylvania, on September 3, 1881, at age five. She was buried in Mount Nebo Cemetery (Presbyterian Graveyard), White Oak, Martic Twp., Lancaster Co., Pennsylvania.[16]

**83. Margaret**[7] **Akins** (*Anna Mary*[6] *Nimlow, Margaret*[5] *Pegan, Andrew*[4]*, James*[3]*, Andrew*[2] *Pagan, James*[1]) was born in 1874 in Martic Twp., Lancaster Co., Pennsylvania. She was also known as **Maggie**. She was the daughter of James Isaac Akins and Anna Mary Nimlow (38). Margaret died in Martic Twp., Lancaster Co., Pennsylvania, before 1900. She was buried in Mount Nebo Cemetery (Presbyterian Graveyard), White Oak, Martic Twp., Lancaster Co., Pennsylvania.[2]

**84. Ida**[7] **Akins** (*Anna Mary*[6] *Nimlow, Margaret*[5] *Pegan, Andrew*[4]*, James*[3]*, Andrew*[2] *Pagan, James*[1]) was born on January 16, 1881, in Martic Twp., Lancaster Co., Pennsylvania. She was the daughter of James Isaac Akins and Anna Mary Nimlow (38). Ida died in Manor Twp., Lancaster Co., Pennsylvania, on August 7, 1917, at age 36. She was buried in Washington Boro Cemetery, Manor Twp., Lancaster Co., Pennsylvania.[42]

Ida married **Winfield Scott Ortman** in 1900. They had two daughters. Winfield Scott Ortman was born in Manor Twp., Lancaster Co., Pennsylvania, on November 18, 1880. Winfield Scott lived in 1920 in Reading, Berks Co., Pennsylvania. He reached age 54 and died in Paradise Twp., York Co., Pennsylvania, on May 20, 1935. Winfield Scott was buried in Washington Boro Cemetery, Manor Twp., Lancaster Co., Pennsylvania.[42]

Daughters of Ida Akins and Winfield Scott Ortman:

+ 189  f  I.  **Violet⁸ Ortman** was born in Manor Twp., Lancaster Co., Pennsylvania, on October 24, 1901. She died in East Vincent Twp., Chester Co., Pennsylvania, on October 16, 1918. Violet was buried in Washington Boro Cemetery, Manor Twp., Lancaster Co., Pennsylvania.[42]

+ 190  f  II.  **Minerva Mae⁸ Ortman** was born in Manor Twp., Lancaster Co., Pennsylvania, on September 18, 1908. She died in New Oxford Twp., Adams Co., Pennsylvania or Hanover, York Co., Pennsylvania, on March 7, 1997.

**85. Earl Isaac⁷ Akins** (*Anna Mary⁶ Nimlow, Margaret⁵ Pegan, Andrew⁴, James³, Andrew² Pagan, James¹*) was born on November 18, 1882, in Martic Twp., Lancaster Co., Pennsylvania. He was the son of James Isaac Akins and Anna Mary Nimlow (38). Earl Isaac died in York, York Co., Pennsylvania, on April 20, 1957, at age 74. He was buried in Prospect Hill Cemetery, York Twp., York Co., Pennsylvania.[2, 43]

Childless.

Earl Isaac married **Ellen Rostetter** before 1910. They divorced before 1940. Ellen Rostetter was born in Spring Garden Twp., York Co., Pennsylvania, on December 5, 1879. She was also known as **Ellen**. Ellen reached age 69 and died in Susquehanna Twp., Dauphin Co., Pennsylvania, on January 12, 1949. She was buried in Prospect Hill Cemetery, York Twp., York Co., Pennsylvania.[2, 43]

Ellen Rostetter's baptismal record at Aldersgate United Methodist Church in York Co., Pennsylvania states she was born on December 5, 1879.[83] Her Pennsylvania death certificate at Harrisburg State Hospital in Susquehanna Twp., Dauphin Co., Pennsylvania says her maiden name was "Hostetter"

and that she was born on May 5, 1878.[84] Census records indicate the 1879 date is correct.

**86. Child⁷ Akins** (*Anna Mary⁶ Nimlow, Margaret⁵ Pegan, Andrew⁴, James³, Andrew² Pagan, James¹*) was born between 1875 and 1900 in Martic Twp., Lancaster Co., Pennsylvania. He or she was a child of James Isaac Akins and Anna Mary Nimlow (38). Child One died in Martic Twp., Lancaster Co., Pennsylvania, between 1875 and 1900.

**87. Clarence Watson⁷ Niblock** (*George Niblock⁶ (Nimlow II), Margaret⁵ Pegan, Andrew⁴, James³, Andrew² Pagan, James¹*) was born on September 25, 1881, in Cecil Co., Maryland? He was the son of George Niblock (Nimlow II) (39) and Rebecca Smith. Clarence Watson died in Conoy Twp., Lancaster Co., Pennsylvania, on March 22, 1940, at age 58. He was buried in Bainbridge Public Cemetery, Conoy Twp., Lancaster Co., Pennsylvania.[45]

He married **Bertha Viola McCord**. They had three children. Bertha Viola McCord was born in Eden Twp., Lancaster Co., Pennsylvania, on September 21, 1883. Bertha Viola reached age 88 and died in Conoy Twp., Lancaster Co., Pennsylvania, in 1972. She was buried in Bainbridge Public Cemetery, Conoy Twp., Lancaster Co., Pennsylvania.[45]

For some reason, Clarence Watson Niblock is not listed in the Roy D. Pegan genealogy of the James and Sarah Brannon Pegan family, although his parents George and Rebecca McCord Niblock and his sisters Jennie Niblock Gilbert and Gertrude Niblock are.[2]

Children of Clarence Watson Niblock and Bertha Viola McCord:

+ 191  m  I.  **Lloyd⁸ Niblock** was born in Conoy Twp., Lancaster Co., Pennsylvania, in 1905. He died in Conoy Twp., Lancaster Co., Pennsylvania? in 1972. Lloyd was buried in Bainbridge Public Cemetery, Conoy Twp., Lancaster Co., Pennsylvania.[45]

+ 192  f  II.  **Bertha Viola⁸ Niblock** was born in Conoy Twp., Lancaster Co., Pennsylvania, on July 22, 1907. She was also known as **Viola**. Bertha Viola died in Conoy Twp., Lancaster Co., Pennsylvania, on June 20, 1921. She was buried in Bainbridge Public Cemetery, Conoy Twp., Lancaster Co., Pennsylvania.[45]

+  193  f  III.  **Dorothy Everda⁸ Niblock** was born in Nine Points, Bart Twp., Lancaster Co., Pennsylvania, on December 27, 1910. She died in Lancaster, Lancaster Co., Pennsylvania, on June 4, 1991. Dorothy Everda was buried in Goods Mennonite Church Cemetery, Elizabethtown, Mt. Joy Twp., Lancaster Co., Pennsylvania.[85]

**88. Genevieve Mae⁷ Niblock** (*George Niblock⁶ (Nimlow II), Margaret⁵ Pegan, Andrew⁴, James³, Andrew² Pagan, James¹*) was born on February 14, 1887, in Delaware. She was also known as **Jennie**. She was the daughter of George Niblock (Nimlow II) (39) and Rebecca Smith. Genevieve Mae died in Elizabethtown, Mt. Joy Twp., Lancaster Co., Pennsylvania, in May 1970 at age 83.

Genevieve Mae married **Benjamin F. Gilberg or Gilbert** on August 20, 1910, in Dauphin Co., Pennsylvania.[86] They divorced before 1940. They had two children. Benjamin F. Gilberg or Gilbert was born in Bainbridge, Conoy Twp., Lancaster Co., Pennsylvania? on March 8, 1892. He reached age 58 and died in Philadelphia, Philadelphia Co., Pennsylvania, on July 9, 1950.

His surname on his marriage record and the 1910 census is Gilberg.[86] He changed it to Gilbert before the 1920 census.

Children of Genevieve Mae Niblock and Benjamin F. Gilberg or Gilbert:

+  194  m  I.  **Melvin Benjamin⁸ Gilbert** was born in Conoy Twp., Lancaster Co., Pennsylvania, on November 24, 1911. He died in Winchester,

Frederick Co., Virginia, on July 12, 1976. Melvin Benjamin was buried in Arlington National Cemetery, Arlington, Virginia.[87]

+  195  f  II.  **Theo G.⁸ Gilbert** was born in Conoy Twp., Lancaster Co., Pennsylvania, in 1915. She died after 1930.

**89. Gertrude⁷ Niblock** (*George Niblock⁶ (Nimlow II), Margare\t⁵ Pegan, Andrew⁴, James³, Andrew² Pagan, James¹*) was born in 1894 in Elizabethtown, Mt. Joy Twp., Lancaster Co., Pennsylvania. She was the daughter of George Niblock (Nimlow II) (39) and Rebecca Smith. Gertrude died in Elizabethtown, Mt. Joy Twp., Lancaster Co., Pennsylvania, in 1897 at age three. She was buried in Mount Tunnel Cemetery, Elizabethtown, Mt. Joy Twp., Lancaster Co., Pennsylvania.[28]

**90. Chester Clyde⁷ Pegan** (*Samuel A.⁶, James Henry⁵, Andrew⁴, James³, Andrew² Pagan, James¹*) was born on August 20, 1879, in Martic Twp., Lancaster Co., Pennsylvania. He was the son of Samuel A. Pegan (42) and Alice Amanda Kilgore. Chester Clyde died in Lancaster, Lancaster Co., Pennsylvania, on March 7, 1905, at age 25. He was buried in Greenwood Cemetery, Lancaster, Lancaster Co., Pennsylvania.[2, 25]

Chester Clyde married **Ida Jane Groff** on September 3, 1902, in Lancaster Co., Pennsylvania. They had one son. Ida Jane Groff was born in Lancaster, Lancaster Co., Pennsylvania, on December 31, 1877.[2, 25] Ida Jane reached age 29 and died in Lancaster, Lancaster Co., Pennsylvania, on December 21, 1907. She was buried in Greenwood Cemetery, Lancaster, Lancaster Co., Pennsylvania.[25]

Son of Chester Clyde Pegan and Ida Jane Groff:

+  196  m  I.  **James Groff⁸ Pegan** was born in Lancaster, Lancaster Co., Pennsylvania, on June 23, 1903.[2, 25] He died in Lancaster, Lancaster Co., Pennsylvania, on March 23, 1904. James Groff was buried in Greenwood Cemetery, Lancaster, Lancaster Co., Pennsylvania.[25]

**91. Mary Amanda**[7] **Urban** (*Myra S.*[6] *Pegan, James Henry*[5], *Andrew*[4], *James*[3], *Andrew*[2] *Pagan, James*[1]) was born in 1905 in Lancaster, Lancaster Co., Pennsylvania. She was the daughter of Alfred Emmanuel Urban and Myra S. Pegan (43). Mary Amanda lived in 1937 in Atlanta, DeKalb Co., Georgia. She died in College Park, Prince George's Co., Maryland? after 1965.

Never married.

**92. Lillian Virginia**[7] **Urban** (*Myra S.*[6] *Pegan, James Henry*[5], *Andrew*[4], *James*[3], *Andrew*[2] *Pagan, James*[1]) was born on October 21, 1909, in Lancaster, Lancaster Co., Pennsylvania. She was the daughter of Alfred Emmanuel Urban and Myra S. Pegan (43). Lillian Virginia died in Lima, Ottawa Twp., Allen Co., Ohio, on July 6, 1965, at age 55. She was buried in Memorial Park Mausoleum Cemetery, Lima, Ottawa Twp., Allen Co., Ohio.[46]

Lillian Virginia married **Paul Simpson Hamer** about 1938. They had two sons. Paul Simpson Hamer was born in McKeesport, Allegheny Co., Pennsylvania, on September 30, 1909. Paul Simpson reached age 86 and died in Lima, Ottawa Twp., Allen Co., Ohio, on December 23, 1995. He was buried in Memorial Park Mausoleum Cemetery, Lima, Ottawa Twp., Allen Co., Ohio.[46]

Sons of Lillian Virginia Urban and Paul Simpson Hamer:

+ 197 m II. **Robert Urban**[8] **Hamer** was born in Athens, Athens Twp., Athens Co., Ohio, on September 18, 1936. He died in Dayton, Montgomery Co., Ohio, on November 12, 1984.

+ 198 m I. **Paul**[8] **Hamer II** was born in Wapakoneta, Duchonquet Twp., Auglaize Co., Ohio, in December 1939. He died in Wapakoneta, Duchonquet Twp., Auglaize Co., Ohio, on February 10, 1940. Paul was buried in Greenlawn Cemetery, Wapakoneta, Duchonquet Twp., Auglaize Co., Ohio.[88]

**93. Grace Anna**[7] **Kilgore** (*Alvin Levi*[6], *Sarah Jane*[5] *Pegan, Andrew*[4], *James*[3], *Andrew*[2] *Pagan, James*[1]) was born on February 24, 1878, in Lower Chanceford Twp., York Co., Pennsylvania. She was the daughter of Alvin Levi Kilgore (44) and Eliza Amanda McCalla. Grace Anna died in Airville, Lower Chanceford Twp., York Co., Pennsylvania, in June 1969 at age 91. She was buried in Chanceford Presbyterian Cemetery, Airville, Lower Chanceford Twp., York Co., Pennsylvania.[14]

Grace Anna married **James Andrew Glenn** on July 29, 1896. They had five children. James Andrew Glenn was born in Lower Chanceford Twp., York Co., Pennsylvania, on March 18, 1856. James Andrew reached age 75 and died in Lower Chanceford Twp., York Co., Pennsylvania, on May 22, 1931. He was buried in Chanceford Presbyterian Cemetery, Airville, Lower Chanceford Twp., York Co., Pennsylvania.[14]

Children of Grace Anna Kilgore and James Andrew Glenn:

+ 199 m I. **Purdy Lester**[8] **Glenn** was born in Lower Chanceford Twp., York Co., Pennsylvania, on August 15, 1898. He died in Delta, Peach Bottom Twp., York Co., Pennsylvania, on May 27, 1984. Purdy Lester was buried in Pine Grove Presbyterian Church Cemetery, Lower Chanceford Twp., York Co., Pennsylvania.[51]

+ 200 m II. **James Earl**[8] **Glenn II** was born in Lower Chanceford Twp., York Co., Pennsylvania, on May 1, 1902. He was also known as **Earl**. James Earl died in Airville, Lower Chanceford Twp., York Co., Pennsylvania, in March 1983. He was buried in Salem United Methodist Church Cemetery, Delta, Peach Bottom Twp., York Co., Pennsylvania.[52]

+ 201 m III. **Alvin Huber**[8] **Glenn** was born in Lower Chanceford Twp., York Co.,

Pennsylvania, on January 20, 1906. He died in Delta, Peach Bottom Twp., York Co., Pennsylvania, in May 1977. Alvin Huber was buried in Salem United Methodist Church Cemetery, Delta, Peach Bottom Twp., York Co., Pennsylvania.[52]

+ 202 f IV. **Lida Maxwell**[8] **Glenn** was born in Lower Chanceford Twp., York Co., Pennsylvania, on December 2, 1907. She died in Airville, Lower Chanceford Twp., York Co., Pennsylvania, in November 1980.

+ 203 f V. **Nora**[8] **Glenn** was born in Lower Chanceford Twp., York Co., Pennsylvania, on January 16, 1913. She died in Holtwood, Martic Twp., Lancaster Co., Pennsylvania, on November 27, 2000.

**94. Samuel Ralph**[7] **Kilgore** (*Alvin Levi*[6], *Sarah Jane*[5] *Pegan, Andrew*[4]*, James*[3]*, Andrew*[2] *Pagan, James*[1]) was born on November 13, 1879, in Lower Chanceford Twp., York Co., Pennsylvania. He was also known as **Ralph**. He was the son of Alvin Levi Kilgore (44) and Eliza Amanda McCalla. Samuel Ralph died in Hillsdale, Hillsdale Twp., Hillsdale Co., Michigan, in 1953 at age 73. He was buried in Portage Cemetery, Portage, Wood Co., Ohio.[48]

Samuel Ralph married **Mary Ann Hess** on February 19, 1903, in Wood Co., Ohio. They had four children. Mary Ann Hess was born in Lower Chanceford Twp., York Co., Pennsylvania, on June 18, 1879. Mary Ann reached age 48 and died in Portage, Wood Co., Ohio, on November 30, 1927. She was buried in Portage Cemetery, Portage, Wood Co., Ohio.[48]

Children of Samuel Ralph Kilgore and Mary Ann Hess:

+ 204 f I. **Nina Amanda**[8] **Kilgore** was born in Mummasburg, Franklin Twp., Adams Co., Pennsylvania, on August 13, 1904. She died in Hill-

sdale, Hillsdale Twp., Hillsdale Co., Michigan, on March 30, 1957. Nina Amanda was buried in Portage Cemetery, Portage, Wood Co., Ohio.[48]

+ 205 m II. **Kenneth W.**[8] **Kilgore** was born in Portage, Liberty Twp., Wood Co., Ohio, on July 15, 1907. He died in Livonia, Wayne Co., Michigan, on May 20, 1981. Kenneth W. was buried in Portage Cemetery, Portage, Wood Co., Ohio.[48]

+ 206 m III. **Don Woodrow**[8] **Kilgore** was born in Portage, Liberty Twp., Wood Co., Ohio, on August 11, 1916. He died in Dearborn, Wayne Co., Michigan, on March 13, 1988. Don Woodrow was buried in Portage Cemetery, Portage, Wood Co., Ohio.[48]

+ 207 m IV. **Martin Leonard**[8] **Kilgore** was born in Portage, Liberty Twp., Wood Co., Ohio, on March 16, 1919. He died on October 13, 2017 in Spring Arbor, Spring Arbor Twp., Jackson Co., Michigan.

**95. William**[7] **Kilgore** (*Alvin Levi*[6]*, Sarah Jane*[5] *Pegan, Andrew*[4]*, James*[3]*, Andrew*[2] *Pagan, James*[1]) was born between 1880 and 1891 in Lower Chanceford Twp., York Co., Pennsylvania. He was the son of Alvin Levi Kilgore (44) and Eliza Amanda McCalla. William died in Lower Chanceford Twp., York Co., Pennsylvania, between 1880 and 1891.

**96. Hugh Whiteford**[7] **Kilgore** (*James Ankrim*[6]*, Sarah Jane*[5] *Pegan, Andrew*[4]*, James*[3]*, Andrew*[2] *Pagan, James*[1]) was born on January 6, 1876, in Lower Chanceford Twp., York Co., Pennsylvania. He was the son of James Ankrim Kilgore (45) and Rebecca Reed. Hugh Whiteford died in East Nottingham Twp., Chester Co., Pennsylvania, on May 17, 1960, at age 84. He was buried in Slateville Presbyterian Church Cemetery, Delta, Peach Bottom Twp., York Co., Pennsylvania.[49]

Hugh Whiteford married **Alice Emma Dunlap** before 1906. They had five children. Alice Emma Dunlap was born in Fawn Twp., York Co., Pennsylvania, on December 24, 1875. She was also known as **Emma**. Alice Emma reached age 97 and died in Peach Bottom Twp., York Co., Pennsylvania, on March 15, 1973. She was buried in Slateville Presbyterian Church Cemetery, Delta, Peach Bottom Twp., York Co., Pennsylvania.[49]

Children of Hugh Whiteford Kilgore and Alice Emma Dunlap:

+ 208 m I. **Clarence H.**[8] **Kilgore** was born in Peach Bottom Twp., York Co., Pennsylvania, on February 28, 1906. He died in Airville, Lower Chanceford Twp., York Co., Pennsylvania, on December 6, 1995. Clarence H. was buried in Slateville Presbyterian Church Cemetery, Delta, Peach Bottom Twp., York Co., Pennsylvania.[49]

+ 209 f II. **Sarah Angeline**[8] **Kilgore** was born in Peach Bottom Twp., York Co., Pennsylvania, on January 9, 1908. She was also known as **Angie**. Sarah Angeline died in East Nottingham Twp., Chester Co., Pennsylvania, on July 12, 1995. She was buried in Nottingham Cemetery, East Nottingham Twp., Chester Co., Pennsylvania.[89]

+ 210 m III. **Kenneth Dunlap**[8] **Kilgore** was born in Peach Bottom Twp., York Co., Pennsylvania, on October 1, 1909. He died in Camp Hill, Cumberland Co., Pennsylvania, in April 1986. Kenneth Dunlap was buried in Slateville Presbyterian Church Cemetery, Delta, Peach Bottom Twp., York Co., Pennsylvania.[49]

+ 211 f IV. **Mary E.**[8] **Kilgore** was born in Peach Bottom Twp., York Co., Pennsylvania, on October 27, 1911. She died in Stuart, Martin Co., Florida, on January 6, 2002. Mary E. was buried in Conestoga Memorial Park Cemetery, Lancaster Twp., Lancaster Co., Pennsylvania.[90]

+ 212 f V. **Eunice**[8] **Kilgore** was born in Peach Bottom Twp., York Co., Pennsylvania, on February 17, 1913. She died in North East, Cecil Co., Maryland, on July 21, 1988.

**97. Samuel Reed**[7] **Kilgore** (*James Ankrim*[6], *Sarah Jane*[5] *Pegan, Andrew*[4], *James*[3], *Andrew*[2] *Pagan, James*[1]) was born on August 31, 1877, in Lower Chanceford Twp., York Co., Pennsylvania. He was also known as **Reed**. He was the son of James Ankrim Kilgore (45) and Rebecca Reed. Samuel Reed died in Peach Bottom Twp., York Co., Pennsylvania, on March 4, 1943, at age 65. He was buried in Slate Ridge Cemetery, Delta, Peach Bottom Twp., York Co., Pennsylvania.[20]

Samuel Reed married **Rebecca Dinsmore** on January 15, 1908. They had five children. Rebecca Dinsmore was born in Peach Bottom Twp., York Co., Pennsylvania, on April 28, 1880. Rebecca reached age 33 and died in Peach Bottom Twp., York Co., Pennsylvania, on March 15, 1914. She was buried in Slate Ridge Cemetery, Delta, Peach Bottom Twp., York Co., Pennsylvania.[20]

Children of Samuel Reed Kilgore and Rebecca Dinsmore:

+ 213 m I. **James Robert**[8] **Kilgore** was born in Peach Bottom Twp., York Co., Pennsylvania, on December 9, 1908. He died in Nazareth, Northampton Co., Pennsylvania, on July 5, 1991.

+ 214 m II. **Charles Gilbert**[8] **Kilgore** was born in Peach Bottom Twp., York Co., Pennsylvania, in 1910.[2] He was also known as **Gilbert**. Charles Gilbert died in Peach Bottom Twp., York Co., Pennsylvania, in 1926.[2]

+ 215 m III. **Joseph Dinsmore<sup>8</sup> Kilgore** was born in Peach Bottom Twp., York Co., Pennsylvania, on September 21, 1911. He died in Delta, Peach Bottom Twp., York Co., Pennsylvania, on February 12, 2000.

+ 216 m IV. **Philip Reed<sup>8</sup> Kilgore** was born in Peach Bottom Twp., York Co., Pennsylvania, on October 24, 1912. He died in York, York Co., Pennsylvania, on March 5, 1999. Philip Reed was buried in Fawn Grove Methodist Church Cemetery, Fawn Grove, Fawn Grove Twp., York Co., Pennsylvania.[91]

+ 217 f V. **Dorothy Nelson<sup>8</sup> Kilgore** was born in Peach Bottom Twp., York Co., Pennsylvania, on November 5, 1913. She died in Delta, Peach Bottom Twp., York Co., Pennsylvania, on January 10, 2012. Dorothy Nelson was buried in Slate Ridge Cemetery, Delta, Peach Bottom Twp., York Co., Pennsylvania.[20]

**98. Sarah Jane<sup>7</sup> Kilgore** (*James Ankrim<sup>6</sup>, Sarah Jane<sup>5</sup> Pegan, Andrew<sup>4</sup>, James<sup>3</sup>, Andrew<sup>2</sup> Pagan, James<sup>1</sup>*) was born on November 27, 1879, in Lower Chanceford Twp., York Co., Pennsylvania. She was also known as **Sadie**. She was the daughter of James Ankrim Kilgore (45) and Rebecca Reed. Sarah Jane died in Peach Bottom Twp., York Co., Pennsylvania? on December 9, 1964, at age 85. She was buried in Chanceford Presbyterian Cemetery, Airville, Lower Chanceford Twp., York Co., Pennsylvania.[14]

Never married.

**99. Chester W.<sup>7</sup> Kilgore** (*James Ankrim<sup>6</sup>, Sarah Jane<sup>5</sup> Pegan, Andrew<sup>4</sup>, James<sup>3</sup>, Andrew<sup>2</sup> Pagan, James<sup>1</sup>*) was born on August 15, 1886, in Lower Chanceford Twp., York Co., Pennsylvania. He was the son of James Ankrim Kilgore (45) and Rebecca Reed. Chester W. died in Lawrence, Douglas Co., Kansas, in September 1968 at age 82. He was buried in Memorial Park Cemetery, Lawrence, Douglas Co., Kansas.[34]

Chester W. married **Minnie Victoria Robinson** before 1925. They had one daughter. Minnie Victoria Robinson was born in Logan Co., Oklahoma, in 1885. Minnie Victoria reached age 89 and died in Lawrence, Douglas Co., Kansas, in 1974. She was buried in Memorial Park Cemetery, Lawrence, Douglas Co., Kansas.[50]

Daughter of Chester W. Kilgore and Minnie Victoria Robinson:

+ 218 f I. **Minnie May<sup>8</sup> Kilgore** was born in Lawrence, Douglas Co., Kansas, on August 17, 1924. She died in Lawrence, Douglas Co., Kansas, on July 8, 2002. Minnie May was buried in Memorial Park Cemetery, Lawrence, Douglas Co., Kansas.[50]

**100. Ira Whiteford<sup>7</sup> Chandlee** (*Laura Clinda<sup>6</sup> Kilgore, Sarah Jane<sup>5</sup> Pegan, Andrew<sup>4</sup>, James<sup>3</sup>, Andrew<sup>2</sup> Pagan, James<sup>1</sup>*) was born on October 28, 1879, in Lower Chanceford Twp., York Co., Pennsylvania. He was the son of John Veasey Chandlee and Laura Clinda Kilgore (46). Ira Whiteford died in Delta, Peach Bottom Twp., York Co., Pennsylvania? on November 7, 1965, at age 86. He was buried in Pine Grove Presbyterian Church Cemetery, Lower Chanceford Twp., York Co., Pennsylvania.[51]

Ira Whiteford married **Lucy Mary Ringland** before 1915. They had two children. Lucy Mary Ringland was born in Lower Chanceford Twp., York Co., Pennsylvania, on September 17, 1892. Lucy Mary reached age 97 and died in York, York Co., Pennsylvania, on February 20, 1990. She was buried in Pine Grove Presbyterian Church Cemetery, Lower Chanceford Twp., York Co., Pennsylvania.[51]

Children of Ira Whiteford Chandlee and Lucy Mary Ringland:

+ 219 m I. **Thomas Warren<sup>8</sup> Chandlee** was born in Lower Chanceford Twp.,

York Co., Pennsylvania, on February 4, 1915. He was also known as **Warren**. Thomas Warren died in Elkton, Cecil Co., Maryland? on July 26, 1992. He was buried in Pine Grove Presbyterian Church Cemetery, Lower Chanceford Twp., York Co., Pennsylvania.[51]

+ 220 f II. **Margaret**[8] **Chandlee** was born in Lower Chanceford Twp., York Co., Pennsylvania, on November 14, 1927.

101. **Walter Veasey**[7] **Chandlee** (*Laura Clinda*[6] *Kilgore, Sarah Jane*[5] *Pegan, Andrew*[4]*, James*[3]*, Andrew*[2] *Pagan, James*[1]) was born on November 30, 1881, in Lower Chanceford Twp., York Co., Pennsylvania. He was the son of John Veasey Chandlee and Laura Clinda Kilgore (46). Walter Veasey died in Red Lion, York Twp., York Co., Pennsylvania, on March 15, 1942, at age 60. He was buried in Chanceford Presbyterian Cemetery, Airville, Lower Chanceford Twp., York Co., Pennsylvania.[14]

Walter Veasey married **Pearl Gemmel** before 1910. They had one daughter. Pearl Gemmel was born in Chanceford Twp., York Co., Pennsylvania, on June 1, 1881. Pearl reached age 87 and died in Red Lion, York Twp., York Co., Pennsylvania, in July 1968. She was buried in Chanceford Presbyterian Cemetery, Airville, Lower Chanceford Twp., York Co., Pennsylvania.[14]

Daughter of Walter Veasey Chandlee and Pearl Gemmel:

+ 221 f I. **Marian L.**[8] **Chandlee** was born in Lower Chanceford Twp., York Co., Pennsylvania, on July 4, 1910. She died in Red Lion, York Twp., York Co., Pennsylvania, on October 7, 1992. Marian L. was buried in Red Lion Cemetery, Red Lion, York Twp., York Co., Pennsylvania.[80]

102. **William**[7] **Chandlee** (*Laura Clinda*[6] *Kilgore, Sarah Jane*[5] *Pegan, Andrew*[4]*, James*[3]*, Andrew*[2] *Pagan, James*[1]) was born on October 24, 1884, in Lower Chanceford Twp., York Co., Pennsylvania. He was the son of John Veasey Chandlee and Laura Clinda Kilgore (46). William died in Lower Chanceford Twp., York Co., Pennsylvania, on September 24, 1910, at tage 25. He was buried in Pine Grove Presbyterian Church Cemetery, Lower Chanceford Twp., York Co., Pennsylvania.[51]

Never married.

103. **Walter Stephen**[7] **Kilgore** (*William Ramsey*[6]*, Sarah Jane*[5] *Pegan, Andrew*[4]*, James*[3]*, Andrew*[2] *Pagan, James*[1]) was born on July 16, 1885, in York, York Co., Pennsylvania. He was the son of William Ramsey Kilgore (47) and Mary Caroline Cunningham. Walter Stephen died in Chicago, Cook Co., Illinois, on May 2, 1919, at age 33. He was buried in Chanceford Presbyterian Cemetery, Airville, Lower Chanceford Twp., York Co., Pennsylvania.[14]

Walter Stephen married **Mabel Pearl Sinclair** before 1906. They had two children. Mabel Pearl Sinclair was born in Wiarton, Bruce Co., Ontario, Canada, on August 8, 1883. Mabel Pearl reached age 25 and died in Baltimore, Baltimore Co., Maryland, in October 1908.

Walter Stephen Kilgore married **Lena Unknown** after 1910. Lena Unknown was born in Maryland in 1887. Lena died after 1919.

Children of Walter Stephen Kilgore and Mabel Pearl Sinclair:

+ 222 m I. **Ernest W.**[8] **Kilgore** was born in Baltimore, Baltimore Co., Maryland? on June 16, 1906. He died in Oak Lawn, Cook Co., Illinois, on August 16, 1985.

+ 223 f II. **Minnie**[8] **Kilgore** was born in Baltimore, Baltimore Co., Maryland, in October 1908. She died in Baltimore, Baltimore Co., Maryland, in October 1908.

104. **Cora**[7] **Martin** (*Anna Margaret*[6] *Kilgore, Sarah Jane*[5] *Pegan, Andrew*[4]*, James*[3]*, Andrew*[2] *Pagan, James*[1]) was born on August 24, 1886, in Lower Chanceford Twp., York Co., Pennsylvania. She was the daugh-

ter of Alexander Martin and Anna Margaret Kilgore (48). Cora died in Lower Chanceford Twp., York Co., Pennsylvania? in September 1964 at age 78.

Cora married **Raymond Scott** before 1910. They had seven children. Raymond Scott was born in Lower Chanceford Twp., York Co., Pennsylvania, on March 17, 1890. Raymond reached age 90 and died in Delta, Peach Bottom Twp., York Co., Pennsylvania, in May 1980.

Children of Cora Martin and Raymond Scott:

+ 224 m I. **Kenneth**[8] **Scott** was born in Lower Chanceford Twp., York Co., Pennsylvania, on May 18, 1910. He died in York, York Co., Pennsylvania, in July 1986.

+ 225 m II. **Robert M.**[8] **Scott** was born in Lower Chanceford Twp., York Co., Pennsylvania, on July 12, 1911. He died in Delta, Peach Bottom Twp., York Co., Pennsylvania? on March 18, 1996.

+ 226 m III. **J. Ray**[8] **Scott** was born in Delta, Peach Bottom Twp., York Co., Pennsylvania, on April 28, 1913. He was also known as **Ray**. J. Ray died in York, York Co., Pennsylvania, on July 8, 2004. He was buried in McKendree United Methodist Cemetery, Airville, Lower Chanceford Twp., York Co., Pennsylvania.[92]

+ 227 m IV. **Harold Edwin**[8] **Scott** was born in Delta, Peach Bottom Twp., York Co., Pennsylvania, on May 15, 1915. He died in York, York Co., Pennsylvania, on September 26, 2011. Harold Edwin was buried in Saint Paul's Wolf's Evangelical Covenant Cemetery, West York Twp., York Co., Pennsylvania.[93]

+ 228 f V. **Sarah Margaret**[8] **Scott** was born in Delta, Peach Bottom Twp., York Co., Pennsylvania, on August 17, 1917. She died in Elmira, Chemung Co., New York, on August 30, 2003. Sarah Margaret was buried in Woodlawn Cemetery, Elmira, Chemug Co., New York.[94]

+ 229 f VI. **Esther E.**[8] **Scott** was born in Delta, Peach Bottom Twp., York Co., Pennsylvania, on November 24, 1919. She died in Bel Air, Harford Co., Maryland, on September 16, 2015. Esther E. was buried in Pine Grove Presbyterian Church Cemetery, Lower Chanceford Twp., York Co., Pennsylvania.[51]

+ 230 m VII. **Charles Arthur**[8] **Scott** was born in Lower Chanceford Twp., York Co., Pennsylvania, on August 17, 1922. He died in Baltimore, Baltimore Co., Maryland, in March 1984.

**105. Gertrude**[7] **Kilgore** (*Emory Milton*[6], *Sarah Jane*[5] *Pegan, Andrew*[4], *James*[3], *Andrew*[2] *Pagan, James*[1]) was born on April 7, 1895, in Lower Chanceford Twp., York Co., Pennsylvania. She was the daughter of Emory Milton Kilgore (49) and Rebecca Martin Dougherty. Gertrude died in Oxford, Chester Co., Pennsylvania, on July 1, 1995, at age 100. She was buried in Chanceford Presbyterian Cemetery, Airville, Lower Chanceford Twp., York Co., Pennsylvania.[14]

Never married.

**106. Dale Dougherty**[7] **Kilgore** (*Emory Milton*[6], *Sarah Jane*[5] *Pegan, Andrew*[4], *James*[3], *Andrew*[2] *Pagan, James*[1]) was born on September 24, 1897, in Lower Chanceford Twp., York Co., Pennsylvania. He was the son of Emory Milton Kilgore (49) and Rebecca Martin Dougherty. Dale Dougherty died in Airville, Lower Chanceford Twp., York Co., Pennsylvania, on October 15, 1980, at age 83. He was buried in Chanceford Presbyterian Cemetery, Airville, Lower Chanceford Twp., York Co., Pennsylvania.[14]

Dale Dougherty married **Ruth Hepp** before 1923. They had three children. Ruth Hepp was born in Lititz, Lancaster Co., Pennsylvania, on October 3, 1899. Ruth reached age 82 and died in Airville, Lower Chanceford Twp., York Co., Pennsylvania, on August 9, 1982. She was buried in Chanceford Presbyterian Cemetery, Airville, Lower Chanceford Twp., York Co., Pennsylvania.[14]

Children of Dale Dougherty Kilgore and Ruth Hepp:

+ 231   f   I.   **Janet Marie⁸ Kilgore** was born in Lower Chanceford Twp., York Co., Pennsylvania, on January 27, 1923. She died in Dover Twp., York Co., Pennsylvania, on March 2, 1992.

+ 232   m   II.   **Donald Emory⁸ Kilgore** was born in Lower Chanceford Twp., York Co., Pennsylvania, on March 20, 1927.

+ 233   m   III.   **Robert L.⁸ Kilgore** was born in Lower Chanceford Twp., York Co., Pennsylvania, in 1931.

**107. Emory⁷ Kilgore II** (*Emory Milton⁶, Sarah Jane⁵ Pegan, Andrew⁴, James³, Andrew² Pagan, James¹*) was born on January 13, 1903, in Lower Chanceford Twp., York Co., Pennsylvania. He was the son of Emory Milton Kilgore (49) and Rebecca Martin Dougherty. Emory died in Airville, Lower Chanceford Twp., York Co., Pennsylvania, on August 30, 2002, at age 99. He was buried in Chanceford Presbyterian Cemetery, Airville, Lower Chanceford Twp., York Co., Pennsylvania.[14]

Emory married **Mabel Jenness** before 1933. They had two sons. Mabel Jenness was born in Dublin, Harford Co., Maryland, on February 8, 1905. Mabel reached age 96 and died in Airville, Lower Chanceford Twp., York Co., Pennsylvania, on January 29, 2002. She was buried in Chanceford Presbyterian Cemetery, Airville, Lower Chanceford Twp., York Co., Pennsylvania.[14]

Sons of Emory Kilgore II and Mabel Jenness:

+ 234   m   I.   **Eugene M.⁸ Kilgore** was born in Lower Chanceford Twp., York Co., Pennsylvania, in 1933.

+ 235   m   II.   **William⁸ Kilgore** was born in 1940.

**108. Daisy Mae⁷ Hess** (*Luella Jane⁶ Kilgore, Sarah Jane⁵ Pegan, Andrew⁴, James³, Andrew² Pagan, James¹*) was born on September 14, 1888, in Lower Chanceford Twp., York Co., Pennsylvania. She was the daughter of Martin Luther Hess and Luella Jane Kilgore (50). Daisy Mae died in Red Lion, York Twp., York Co., Pennsylvania, on May 29, 1957, at age 68. She was buried in Salem United Methodist Church Cemetery, Delta, Peach Bottom Twp., York Co., Pennsylvania.[52]

Daisy Mae married **Harry Melvin Anderson** on April 6, 1911. They had six children. Harry Melvin Anderson was born in Lower Chanceford Twp., York Co., Pennsylvania, on October 5, 1888. Harry Melvin reached age 69 and died in Red Lion, York Twp., York Co., Pennsylvania, on June 14, 1958. He was buried in Salem United Methodist Church Cemetery, Delta, Peach Bottom Twp., York Co., Pennsylvania.[52]

Children of Daisy Mae Hess and Harry Melvin Anderson:

+ 236   f   I.   **Edna⁸ Anderson** was born in Lower Chanceford Twp., York Co., Pennsylvania, on May 29, 1912. She died in Red Lion, York Twp., York Co., Pennsylvania, on February 3, 2010.

+ 237   f   II.   **Marian L.⁸ Anderson** was born in Lower Chanceford Twp., York Co., Pennsylvania, on July 11, 1913. She died in Red Lion, York Twp., York Co., Pennsylvania, in September 1983. Marian L. was buried in Bethel United Methodist Church Cemetery, Shenks Ferry, Chanceford Twp., York Co., Pennsylvania.[95]

+ 238   m   III.   **Clair⁸ Anderson** was born in Lower Chanceford Twp., York Co., Pennsylvania, in 1918. He died in Lower-

Chanceford Twp., York Co., Pennsylvania, before 1920.

+ 239 m IV. **Harvey Donald**[8] **Anderson** was born in Lower Chanceford Twp., York Co., Pennsylvania, on November 1, 1920. He was also known as **Donald**. Harvey Donald died in York Co., Pennsylvania, on March 29, 2002.

+ 240 m V. **Philip Ernest**[8] **Anderson** was born in Lower Chanceford Twp., York Co., Pennsylvania, on September 4, 1925. He died in Red Lion, York Twp., York Co., Pennsylvania, on November 9, 1997. Philip Ernest was buried in Susquehanna Memorial Gardens Cemetery, York, York Co., Pennsylvania.[96]

+ 241 f VI. **Betty Sue**[8] **Anderson** was born in Lower Chanceford Twp., York Co., Pennsylvania, in 1938.

109. **Sarah Margaret**[7] **Hess** (*Luella Jane*[6] *Kilgore, Sarah Jane*[5] *Pegan, Andrew*[4], *James*[3], *Andrew*[2] *Pagan, James*[1]) was born on October 21, 1891, in Lower Chanceford Twp., York Co., Pennsylvania. She was the daughter of Martin Luther Hess and Luella Jane Kilgore (50). Sarah Margaret died in Chattanooga, Hamilton Co., Tennessee, on November 2, 1985, at age 94. She was buried in Hamilton Memorial Gardens, Hixon, Hamilton Co., Tennessee.[53]

Sarah Margaret married **Alwyn Murat Anderson** before 1918. They had five sons. Alwyn Murat Anderson was born in Lower Chanceford Twp., York Co., Pennsylvania, on October 9, 1889. Alwyn Murat lived in 1940 in Norris, Anderson Co., Tennessee. He reached age 65 and died in Chattanooga, Hamilton Co., Tennessee, on August 15, 1955. Alwyn Murat was buried in Hamilton Memorial Gardens, Hixon, Hamilton Co., Tennessee.[53]

Sons of Sarah Margaret Hess and Alwyn Murat Anderson:

+ 242 m I. **Roger Scott**[8] **Anderson** was born in Lower Chanceford Twp., York Co.,

Pennsylvania, on October 31, 1918. He died in Knoxville, Knox Co., on May 30, 2009. Roger Scott was buried in Greenwood Cemetery, Knoxville, Knox Co., Tennessee.[97]

+ 243 m II. **Robert Alwyn**[8] **Anderson** was born in Lower Chanceford Twp., York Co., Pennsylvania, on May 30, 1920. He died in Chattanooga, Hamilton Co., Tennessee, on January 27, 1991. Robert Alwyn was buried in Hamilton Memorial Gardens, Hixon, Hamilton Co., Tennessee.[53]

+ 244 m III. **Richard Clayton**[8] **Anderson** was born in Lower Chanceford Twp., York Co., Pennsylvania, on December 15, 1921. He died in Knoxville, Knox Co., Tennessee, on December 26, 2000. Richard Clayton was buried in Lynnhurst Cemetery, Knoxville, Knox Co., Tennessee.[98]

+ 245 m IV. **Harold Luther**[8] **Anderson** was born in Lower Chanceford Twp., York Co., Pennsylvania, on February 21, 1924. He died in Knoxville, Knox Co., Tennessee, on April 20, 2000. Harold Luther was buried in Lynnhurst Cemetery, Knoxville, Knox Co., Tennessee.[98]

+ 246 m V. **John**[8] **Anderson** was born in Lower Chanceford Twp., York Co., Pennsylvania, in 1927.

110. **Harry Lyle**[7] **Hess** (*Luella Jane*[6] *Kilgore, Sarah Jane*[5] *Pegan, Andrew*[4], *James*[3], *Andrew*[2] *Pagan, James*[1]) was born on May 24, 1897, in Lower Chanceford Twp., York Co., Pennsylvania. He was also known as **Lyle**. He was the son of Martin Luther Hess and Luella Jane Kilgore (50). Harry Lyle died in Delta, Peach Bottom Twp., York Co., Pennsylvania, on September 8, 1980, at age 83. He was buried in Salem United Methodist Church Cemetery, Delta, Peach Bottom Twp., York Co., Pennsylvania.[52]

Harry Lyle married **Mary Ella Thompson** before 1920. They had three sons. Mary Ella Thompson was born in Peach Bottom Twp., York Co., Pennsylvania, on October 25, 1896. She was also known as **Ella**. Mary Ella reached age 94 and died in Dallastown, Windsor Twp., York Co., Pennsylvania, on December 17, 1990. She was buried in Salem United Methodist Church Cemetery, Delta, Peach Bottom Twp., York Co., Pennsylvania.[52]

Sons of Harry Lyle Hess and Mary Ella Thompson:

+ 247 m I.    **Gerald Lyle⁸ Hess** was born in Lower Chanceford Twp., York Co., Pennsylvania, on June 5, 1921. He died in Wheat Ridge, Jefferson Co., Colorado? on March 18, 1999.

+ 248 m II.   **Ramsey Martin⁸ Hess** was born in Lower Chanceford Twp., York Co., Pennsylvania, on July 28, 1924. He was also known as **Martin** and **Bill**. Ramsey Martin died in Elizabethtown, Mt. Joy Twp., Lancaster Co., Pennsylvania, on January 2, 2008. He was buried in Slateville Presbyterian Church Cemetery, Delta, Peach Bottom Twp., York Co., Pennsylvania.[49]

+ 249 m III.  **Robert D.⁸ Hess** was born in Lower Chanceford Twp., York Co., Pennsylvania, on September 16, 1928.

**111. Cora I.⁷ Pegan** (*Lewis Cass⁶, Alexander L.⁵, Andrew⁴, James³, Andrew² Pagan, James¹*) was born on December 7, 1875, in Martic Twp., Lancaster Co., Pennsylvania. She was the daughter of Lewis Cass Pegan (53) and Catherine McMullen. Cora I. died in Lancaster, Lancaster Co., Pennsylvania, on April 4, 1962, at age 86. She was buried in Riverview Burial Park Cemetery, Lancaster, Lancaster Co., Pennsylvania.[29]

Cora I. married **Thomas Carl Stouch** on April 5, 1896, in Lancaster Co., Pennsylvania. They had seven children. Thomas Carl Stouch was born in Green Twp., Ashland Co., Ohio, on December 2, 1869. Thomas Carl reached age 86 and died in Lancaster, Lancaster Co., Pennsylvania, on October 7, 1956. He was buried in Riverview Burial Park Cemetery, Lancaster, Lancaster Co., Pennsylvania.[29]

Thomas Carl Stouch was a professional baseball player with the Louisville Colonels for one year (1898). He played second base.

Children of Cora I. Pegan and Thomas Carl Stouch:

+ 250 f I.    **Ruth Emeline⁸ Stouch** was born in Lancaster Co., Pennsylvania, on September 28, 1896. She died in Seneca, Oconee Co., South Carolina, on July 3, 1989. Ruth Emeline was buried in Church of the Holy Apostles Episcopal Cemetery, Barnwell, Barnwell Co., South Carolina.[99]

+ 251 f II.   **Anna C.⁸ Stouch** was born in Georgia on October 18, 1903. She died in Tacoma, Pierce Co., Washington, on May 2, 1988. Anna C. was buried in Mountain View Cemetery, Tacoma, Pierce Co., Washington.[100]

+ 252 m III.  **Thomas Carl⁸ Stouch II** was born in Greenville, Greenville Co., South Carolina, on December 2, 1908. He died in Paradise Twp., Lancaster Co., Pennsylvania, on November 4, 2001. Thomas Carl was buried in Rancks United Methodist Church Cemetery, New Holland, Earl Twp., Lancaster Co., Pennsylvania.[101]

+ 253 m IV.  **Lewis⁸ Stouch** was born in Greenville, Greenville Co., South Carolina, on September 5, 1910. He died in Mannheim Twp., Lancaster Co., Pennsylvania? on October 20, 1994.

+ 254 f V.   **Julia M.⁸ Stouch** was born in Greenville, Greenville Co., South Carolina, on October 1, 1912 She. died in Lancaster, Lancaster Co., Pennsylvania, on February 19, 2005 Julia M. was buried in St. Joseph's

New Roman Catholic Cemetery, Bausman, Lancaster Twp., Lancaster Co., Pennsylvania.[102]

+ 255 f VI. **Elizabeth Frances**[8] **Stouch** was born in Greenville, Greenville Co., South Carolina, on December 5, 1914. She died in Chestertown, Kent Co., Maryland, on June 1, 1996. Elizabeth Frances was buried in Westminster Presbyterian Cemetery, Mifflintown, Juniata Co., Pennsylvania.[103]

+ 256 m VII. **John Wingard**[8] **Stouch** was born in Lancaster, Lancaster Co., Pennsylvania, on January 23, 1920. He died in Lititz, Lancaster Co., Pennsylvania, on February 4, 2004. John Wingard was buried in Riverview Burial Park Cemetery, Lancaster, Lancaster Co., Pennsylvania.[29]

**112. Harriet Jane**[7] **Pegan** (*Lewis Cass*[6], *Alexander L.*[5], *Andrew*[4], *James*[3], *Andrew*[2] *Pagan, James*[1]) was born on February 7, 1880, in Martic Twp., Lancaster Co., Pennsylvania. She was the daughter of Lewis Cass Pegan (53) and Catherine McMullen. Harriet Jane died in Lancaster, Lancaster Co., Pennsylvania, on May 3, 1936, at age 56. She was buried in Riverview Burial Park Cemetery, Lancaster, Lancaster Co., Pennsylvania.[29]

Harriet Jane married **John Wesley Gilgore II** on February 19, 1905, in Lancaster Co., Pennsylvania. They had four children. John Wesley Gilgore II was born in Lancaster, Lancaster Co., Pennsylvania, on November 22, 1879. John Wesley reached age 58 and died in Lancaster, Lancaster Co., Pennsylvania, on February 18, 1938. He was buried in Riverview Burial Park Cemetery, Lancaster, Lancaster Co., Pennsylvania.[29]

Children of Harriet Jane Pegan and John Wesley Gilgore II:

+ 257 m I. **Harlan Edgar**[8] **Gilgore** was born in Lancaster, Lancaster Co., Penn-

sylvania, on December 7, 1905. He died in Lancaster, Lancaster Co., Pennsylvania, on December 29, 1976. Harlan Edgar was buried in Lancaster Cemetery, Lancaster, Lancaster Co., Pennsylvania.[18]

+ 258 f II. **Dorothy**[8] **Gilgore** was born in Lancaster, Lancaster Co., Pennsylvania, on June 16, 1907. She died in Lititz, Lancaster Co., Pennsylvania, on August 7, 2001. Dorothy was buried in Millersville Mennonite Cemetery, Millersville, Manor Twp., Lancaster Co., Pennsylvania.[61]

+ 259 m III. **William**[8] **Gilgore** was born in Lancaster, Lancaster Co., Pennsylvania, on July 29, 1911. He died in Lancaster, Lancaster Co., Pennsylvania, in December 1971.

+ 260 m IV. **Robert Claire**[8] **Gilgore** was born in Mannheim Twp., Lancaster Co., Pennsylvania, on July 31, 1916. He died in Lititz, Lancaster Co., Pennsylvania, on December 11, 1998. Robert Claire was buried in Riverview Burial Park Cemetery, Lancaster, Lancaster Co., Pennsylvania.[29]

**113. Harlan Appleton**[7] **Pegan** (*Lewis Cass*[6], *Alexander L.*[5], *Andrew*[4], *James*[3], *Andrew*[2] *Pagan, James*[1]) was born on January 24, 1882, in Martic Twp., Lancaster Co., Pennsylvania. He was the son of Lewis Cass Pegan (53) and Catherine McMullen. Harlan Appleton died in Mountville, Lancaster Co., Pennsylvania, on June 22, 1956, at age 74. He was buried in Greenwood Cemetery, Lancaster, Lancaster Co., Pennsylvania.[25]

Harlan Appleton married **Edith Keeler** on December 8, 1908, in York Co., Pennsylvania. They divorced before 1940. They had four children. Edith Keeler was born in Lancaster, Lancaster Co., Pennsylvania, on February 27, 1886. She reached age 86 and died in Lancaster, Lancaster

Co., Pennsylvania, on December 1, 1972. Edith was buried in Greenwood Cemetery, Lancaster, Lancaster Co., Pennsylvania.[25]

Children of Harlan Appleton Pegan and Edith Keeler:

+ 261 f I. **Anna V.**[8] **Pegan** was born in Lancaster, Lancaster Co., Pennsylvania, on October 3, 1908. She died in Cornwall, Lebanon Co., Pennsylvania, on August 17, 1998. Anna V. was buried in Susquehanna Memorial Gardens Cemetery, York, York Co., Pennsylvania.[96]

+ 262 f II. **Daughter**[8] **Pegan** was born in Lancaster, Lancaster Co., Pennsylvania, on August 5, 1910. She died in Lancaster, Lancaster Co., Pennsylvania, on August 5, 1910. Daughter was buried in Lancaster Cemetery, Lancaster, Lancaster Co., Pennsylvania.[18]

+ 263 m III. **Lewis Casper**[8] **Pegan** was born in Martic Twp., Lancaster Co., Pennsylvania, on March 8, 1912. He died in Seminole, Pinellas Co., Florida, on January 16, 2004. Lewis Casper was buried in Bay Pines National Cemetery, Bay Pines, Pinellas Co., Florida.[104, 105]

+ 264 f IV. **Dorothy Elizabeth**[8] **Pegan** was born in Martic Twp., Lancaster Co., Pennsylvania, on March 24, 1916. She died in Lancaster, Lancaster Co., Pennsylvania, on March 28, 1997. Dorothy Elizabeth was buried in St. Anthony's Roman Catholic Cemetery, Lancaster, Lancaster Co., Pennsylvania.[106]

**114. Ralph Alexander**[7] **Barton** (*Sarah*[6] *Pegan, Alexander L.*[5], *Andrew*[4], *James*[3], *Andrew*[2] *Pagan, James*[1]) was born on September 7, 1879, in Lancaster, Lancaster Co., Pennsylvania. He was the son of Isaac Barton and Sarah Pegan (54). Ralph Alexander died in Lancaster, Lancaster Co., Pennsylvania, on November 27, 1949, at age 70. He was buried in Greenwood Cemetery, Lancaster, Lancaster Co., Pennsylvania.[25]

Childless.

Ralph Alexander married **Mabel Trissler** before 1910. Mabel Trissler was born in Lancaster, Lancaster Co., Pennsylvania, on January 29, 1881. Mabel reached age 76 and died in Lancaster, Lancaster Co., Pennsylvania, on June 17, 1957. She was buried in Greenwood Cemetery, Lancaster, Lancaster Co., Pennsylvania.[25]

**115. Elmer Isaac**[7] **Barton** (*Sarah*[6] *Pegan, Alexander L.*[5], *Andrew*[4], *James*[3], *Andrew*[2] *Pagan, James*[1]) was born on June 18, 1884, in Lancaster, Lancaster Co., Pennsylvania. He was the son of Isaac Barton and Sarah Pegan (54). Elmer Isaac died in Boston, Suffolk Co., Massachusetts, in 1937 at age 52. He was buried in Mount Calvary Cemetery, Roslindale, Suffolk Co., Massachusetts.[54]

Elmer Isaac married **Jessie Harvey** about 1905. They divorced. They had two children. Jessie Harvey was born in Lancaster, Lancaster Co., Pennsylvania, on September 28, 1888. She reached age 86 and died in Lancaster, Lancaster Co., Pennsylvania, on March 21, 1975. Jessie was buried in Riverview Burial Park Cemetery, Lancaster, Lancaster Co., Pennsylvania.[29]

Elmer Isaac Barton married **Anna L. Gookin** in 1920. They had three children. Anna L. Gookin was born in Massachusetts in July 1888. Anna L. reached age 69 and died in Boston, Suffolk Co., Massachusetts, in 1958. She was buried in Mount Calvary Cemetery, Roslindale, Suffolk Co., Massachusetts.[54]

In 1900, Anna L. Gookin's age was listed as 11, born Jul 1888. In 1910, her year of birth was about 1891; in 1920, 1894. After her marriage, the 1930 census lists her year of birth as approx. 1897. The year on her gravestone is 1895, but the 1888 date is probably right.

Children of Elmer Isaac Barton and Jessie Harvey:

+ 265 m I. **Elmer L.**[8] **Barton II** was born in Lancaster, Lancaster Co., Pennsylvania, on June 5, 1905. He died in Lancaster, Lancaster Co., Pennsylvania? on December 4, 1974. Elmer L. was buried in Riverview Burial Park Cemetery, Lancaster, Lancaster Co., Pennsylvania.[29]

+ 266 f II. **Helen⁸ Barton** was born in Lancaster, Lancaster Co., Pennsylvania, on February 18, 1907. She died in Lancaster, Lancaster Co., Pennsylvania, on November 29, 1932. Helen was buried in Greenwood Cemetery, Lancaster, Lancaster Co., Pennsylvania.[25]

Children of Elmer Isaac Barton and Anna L. Gookin:

+ 267 m I. **Elmer Francis⁸ Barton II** was born in Boston, Suffolk Co., Massachusetts, on August 7, 1922. He died in Walpole, Norfolk Co., Massachusetts? on August 23, 2012.

+ 268 f II. **Colombiere Mabel⁸ Barton** was born in West Roxbury, Suffolk Co., Massachusetts, on August 13, 1924. She was also known as **Louise**. Colombiere Mabel died in Malden, Middlesex Co., Massachusetts, on March 14, 1996.

+ 269 f III. **Carolyn Martha⁸ Barton** was born in Boston, Suffolk Co., Massachusetts, on June 30, 1927. She died in Mesa, Maricopa Co., Arizona, on October 7, 2013. Carolyn Martha was buried in Forest Dale Cemetery, Malden, Middlesex Co., Massachusetts.[107]

**116. Ira Calvin⁷ Pegan** (*James Calvin⁶, Alexander L.⁵, Andrew⁴, James³, Andrew² Pagan, James¹*) was born in 1881 in Elliott Twp., Allegheny Twp., Pennsylvania. He was the son of James Calvin Pegan (56) and Mary Jane Laird. Ira Calvin died in Elliott Twp., Allegheny Twp., Pennsylvania, in 1896 at age 15. He was buried in Chartiers

Cemetery, Carnegie, Scott Twp., Allegheny Co., Pennsylvania.[30]

**117. Laura Etta⁷ Pegan** (*James Calvin⁶, Alexander L.⁵, Andrew⁴, James³, Andrew² Pagan, James¹*) was born on November 9, 1884, in Elliott Twp., Allegheny Twp., Pennsylvania. She was the daughter of James Calvin Pegan (56) and Mary Jane Laird. Laura Etta died in Carnegie, Scott Twp., Allegheny Co., Pennsylvania, on January 9, 1978, at age 93. She was buried in Jefferson Memorial Park Cemetery, Pleasant Hills, Allegheny Co., Pennsylvania.[55]

Laura Etta married **Donald Neff Davis** on January 29, 1911. They had four children. Donald Neff Davis was born in Cairo Twp., Allen Co., Ohio, on September 20, 1879. Donald Neff reached age 47 and died in Pittsburgh, Allegheny Co., Pennsylvania, on July 20, 1927. He was buried in Chartiers Cemetery, Carnegie, Scott Twp., Allegheny Co., Pennsylvania.[30]

Children of Laura Etta Pegan and Donald Neff Davis:

+ 270 f I. **Esther Ann⁸ Davis** was born in Pittsburgh, Allegheny Co., Pennsylvania, on May 7, 1912. She died in Pittsburgh, Allegheny Co., Pennsylvania, on August 3, 1988. Esther Ann was buried in Chartiers Cemetery, Carnegie, Scott Twp., Allegheny Co., Pennsylvania.[30]

+ 271 m II. **Robert Pegan⁸ Davis II** was born in Crafton, Allegheny Co., Pennsylvania, on January 27, 1914. He died in Ionia, Ionia Twp., Ionia Co., Michigan, on May 3, 1980. Robert Pegan was buried in Balcom Cemetery, Berlin Center, Berlin Twp., Ionia Co., Michigan.[108]

+ 272 m III. **William Laird⁸ Davis** was born in Crafton, Allegheny Co., Pennsylvania, on July 4, 1916. He was also known as **Laird**. William Laird died in Oakdale, Allegheny Co., Pennsylvania, on December

3, 2002. He was buried in Jefferson Memorial Park Cemetery, Pleasant Hills, Allegheny Co., Pennsylvania.[55]

+ 273 f IV. **Betty Jane⁸ Davis** was born in Crafton, Allegheny Co., Pennsylvania, on June 24, 1921. She died in Clio, Vienna Twp., Genessee Co., Michigan, on September 3, 2014. Betty Jane was buried in National Cemetery of the Alleghenies, Cecil Twp., Washington Co., Pennsylvania.[109]

**118. Effie P.⁷ Pegan** (*James Calvin⁶, Alexander L.⁵, Andrew⁴, James³, Andrew² Pagan, James¹*) was born on October 9, 1887, in Elliott Twp., Allegheny Twp., Pennsylvania. She was the daughter of James Calvin Pegan (56) and Mary Jane Laird. Effie P. died in Pittsburgh, Allegheny Co., Pennsylvania, on September 24, 1971, at age 83. She was buried in Jefferson Memorial Park Cemetery, Pleasant Hills, Allegheny Co., Pennsylvania.[55, 56]

Childless.

Effie P. married **Frank D. Hill** after 1930 in Allegheny Co., Pennsylvania. Frank D. Hill was born in Hollidaysburg, Blari Twp., Blair Co., Pennsylvania? on March 22, 1891. Frank D. reached age 75 and died in Pittsburgh, Allegheny Co., Pennsylvania, on June 28, 1966. He was buried in Jefferson Memorial Park Cemetery, Pleasant Hills, Allegheny Co., Pennsylvania.[55, 56]

**119. Ruth Ann⁷ Pegan** (*James Calvin⁶, Alexander L.⁵, Andrew⁴, James³, Andrew² Pagan, James¹*) was born on August 14, 1889, in Elliott Twp., Allegheny Twp., Pennsylvania. She was the daughter of James Calvin Pegan (56) and Mary Jane Laird. Ruth Ann died in Pittsburgh, Allegheny Co., Pennsylvania, on December 20, 1970, at age 81. She was buried in Jefferson Memorial Park Cemetery, Pleasant Hills, Allegheny Co., Pennsylvania.[55, 56]

She married **George Henry Dettling**. They had two children. George Henry Dettling was born in Allegheny, Allegheny Co., Pennsylvania, on February 4, 1887. George Henry reached age 87 and died in Pittsburgh, Allegheny Co., Pennsylvania, on September 5, 1974. He was buried in Jefferson Memorial Park Cemetery, Pleasant Hills, Allegheny Co., Pennsylvania.[55, 56]

Children of Ruth Ann Pegan and George Henry Dettling:

+ 274 f I. **Ruth Ann⁸ Dettling** was born in Pittsburgh, Allegheny Co., Pennsylvania, on August 29, 1915. She died in Bellevue, King Co., Washington, on July 27, 2008.

+ 275 m II. **George Henry⁸ Dettling II** was born in Mt. Lebanon, Allegheny Co., Pennsylvania, on January 9, 1925. He died in Ann Arbor, Ann Arbor Twp., Washtenaw Co., Michigan, on February 14, 1991. George Henry was buried in Jefferson Memorial Park Cemetery, Pleasant Hills, Allegheny Co., Pennsylvania.[55, 56]

**120. Mabel⁷ Pegan** (*James Calvin⁶, Alexander L.⁵, Andrew⁴, James³, Andrew² Pagan, James¹*) was born in 1894 in Elliott Twp., Allegheny Twp., Pennsylvania. She was the daughter of James Calvin Pegan (56) and Mary Jane Laird. Mabel died in Elliott Twp., Allegheny Twp., Pennsylvania, in 1895 at age one. She was buried in Chartiers Cemetery, Carnegie, Scott Twp., Allegheny Co., Pennsylvania.[30]

**121. Margaret⁷ Pegan** (*James Calvin⁶, Alexander L.⁵, Andrew⁴, James³, Andrew² Pagan, James¹*) was born in May 1899 in Elliott Twp., Allegheny Twp., Pennsylvania. She was the daughter of James Calvin Pegan (56) and Mary Jane Laird. Margaret died in Elliott Twp., Allegheny Twp., Pennsylvania, in 1900. She was buried in Chartiers Cemetery, Carnegie, Scott Twp., Allegheny Co., Pennsylvania.[30]

**122. Son⁷ Kirkwood** (*Anna Mary⁶ Pegan, Alexander L.⁵, Andrew⁴, James³, Andrew² Pagan, James¹*) was born about October 18, 1890 in Lancaster Co., Pennsylvania. He was the son of Ambrose

Kirkwood and Anna Mary Pegan (56). Son died in Lancaster Co., Pennsylvania or Chatham Co., North Carolina, on October 18, 1890. He was buried in Lancaster Cemetery, Lancaster, Lancaster Co., Pennsylvania.[34]

**123. Loretta**[7] **Miller** (*Anna Mary*[6] *Pegan, Alexander L.*[5], *Andrew*[4], *James*[3], *Andrew*[2] *Pagan, James*[1]) was born on December 28, 1903, in East Lampeter Twp., Lancaster Co., Pennsylvania. She was the daughter of Adam L. Miller and Anna Mary Pegan (57). Loretta died in Haverford Twp., Delaware Co., Pennsylvania, on November 1, 1970, at age 66. She was buried in Saint Paul's Lutheran Cemetery, Ardmore, Lower Merion Twp., Montgomery Co., Pennsylvania.[57]

Loretta married **Harold Marcus Geiges** before 1928. They had one son. Harold Marcus Geiges was born in Camden, Camden Co., New Jersey, on April 20, 1902. Harold Marcus reached age 89 and died in Orando, Orange Co., Florida, on February 18, 1992.

Son of Loretta Miller and Harold Marcus Geiges:

+ 276 m I. **Charles Kirkwood**[8] **Geiges** was born in Haverford Twp., Delaware Co., Pennsylvania, on June 21, 1928. He died in Havertown, Haverford Twp., Delaware Co., Pennsylvania, on September 28, 1991. Charles Kirkwood was buried in Valley Forge Gardens Cemetery, King of Prussia, Upper Merion Twp., Montgomery Co., Pennsylvania.[110]

**124. Sherwood A.**[7] **Miller** (*Anna Mary*[6] *Pegan, Alexander L.*[5], *Andrew*[4], *James*[3], *Andrew*[2] *Pagan, James*[1]) was born on July 28, 1905, in East Lampeter Twp., Lancaster Co., Pennsylvania. He was the son of Adam L. Miller and Anna Mary Pegan (57). Sherwood A. died in Brownstown, West Earl Twp., Lancaster Co., Pennsylvania, on November 26, 1981, at age 76. He was buried in Zion Lutheran Cemetery, Leola, Upper Leacock Twp., Lancaster Co., Pennsylvania.[31]

Sherwood A. married **Evelyn Marie Howard** before 1930. They had two children. Evelyn Marie Howard was born in Columbia, Manor Twp., Lancaster Co., Pennsylvania, on July 26, 1906. Evelyn Marie reached age 72 and died in Brownstown, West Earl Twp., Lancaster Co., Pennsylvania, on November 4, 1978. She was buried in Zion Lutheran Cemetery, Leola, Upper Leacock Twp., Lancaster Co., Pennsylvania.[31]

Sherwood A. Miller married **Mildred Mearig** after 1978. Mildred Mearig was born in Upper Leacock Twp., Lancaster Co., Pennsylvania, on January 30, 1915. Mildred reached age 92 and died in Lancaster, Lancaster Co., Pennsylvania, on January 24, 2008. She was buried in Zion Lutheran Cemetery, Leola, Upper Leacock Twp., Lancaster Co., Pennsylvania.[31]

Children of Sherwood A. Miller and Evelyn Marie Howard:

+ 277 f I. **Joanne E.**[8] **Miller** was born in East Lampeter Twp., Lancaster Co., Pennsylvania, in 1931.

+ 278 m II. **Sherwood Howard**[8] **Miller II** was born in East Lampeter Twp., Lancaster Co., Pennsylvania, in 1936.

**125. William Henry**[7] **Pegan** (*Elmer Ellsworth James*[6], *Alexander L.*[5], *Andrew*[4], *James*[3], *Andrew*[2] *Pagan, James*[1]) was born on August 31, 1891, in Wilmington, New Castle Co., Delaware. He was the son of Elmer Ellsworth James Pegan (58) and Estella Rachel Scott. William Henry died in Delaware City, New Castle Co., Delaware, on September 21, 1950, at age 59. He was buried in Silverbrook Cemetery, Wilmington, New Castle Co., Delaware.[32]

Childless.

William Henry married **Alva Myrtle Cavender** on January 27, 1912, in New Castle Co., Delaware[111] Alva Myrtle Cavender was born in Glasgow, New Castle Co., Delaware, on May 30, 1891. Alva Myrtle reached age 82 and died in Wilmington, New Castle Co., Delaware, in September 1973.

Probably buried in Silverbrook Cemetery in Wilmington, New Castle Co., Delaware.

**126. Harry Oliver**[7] **Pegan** (*Elmer Ellsworth James*[6], *Alexander L.*[5], *Andrew*[4], *James*[3], *Andrew*[2] *Pagan*, *James*[1]) was born on June 22, 1893, in Rockland, New Castle Co., Delaware. He was the son of Elmer Ellsworth James Pegan (58) and Estella Rachel Scott. Harry Oliver died in Philadelphia, Philadelphia Co., Pennsylvania, on September 23, 1959, at age 66. He was buried in All Saints Cemetery, Wilmington, New Castle Co., Delaware.[58]

Childless.

Harry Oliver married **Mary Ethel Mitchell** on April 14, 1920, in New Castle Co., Delaware. Mary Ethel Mitchell was born in New Jersey on October 9, 1896. Mary Ethel reached age 98 and died in Wilmington, New Castle Co., Delaware, on September 19, 1995. She was buried in All Saints Cemetery, Wilmington, New Castle Co., Delaware.[58]

**127. Adelaide or Adeline**[7] **Pegan** (*Elmer Ellsworth James*[6], *Alexander L.*[5], *Andrew*[4], *James*[3], *Andrew*[2] *Pagan*, *James*[1]) was born on August 5, 1895, in Wilmington, New Castle Co., Delaware. She was also known as **Addie**. She was the daughter of Elmer Ellsworth James Pegan (58) and Estella Rachel Scott. Adelaide or Adeline died in Wilmington, New Castle Co., Delaware, on March 28, 1966, at age 70.

Adelaide or Adeline married **Thomas Daniel Gentry** on September 30, 1915, in New Castle Co., Delaware.[86] They had three children. Thomas Daniel Gentry was born in Greene Co., Virginia, on December 14, 1893. Thomas Daniel reached age 62 and died in Wilmington, New Castle Co., Delaware, on December 23, 1955.

Children of Adelaide or Adeline Pegan and Thomas Daniel Gentry:

+ 279 m I. **Ellsworth James**[8] **Gentry** was born in Wilmington, New Castle Co., Delaware, on August 25, 1916. He died in Wilmington, New Castle Co., Delaware, on May 12, 1984.

Ellsworth James was buried in Silver brook Cemetery, Wilmington, New Castle Co., Delaware.[32]

+ 280 f II. **Adeline Blair**[8] **Gentry** was born in Wilmington, New Castle Co., Delaware, on December 12, 1917. She died in Wilmington, New Castle Co., Delaware, on December 14, 1920.

+ 281 m III. **Thomas Daniel**[8] **Gentry II** was born in Wilmington, New Castle Co., Delaware, on March 25, 1919. He died in Wilmington, New Castle Co., Delaware, on February 21, 1993.

**128. Samuel**[7] **Pegan** (*Elmer Ellsworth James*[6], *Alexander L.*[5], *Andrew*[4], *James*[3], *Andrew*[2] *Pagan*, *James*[1]) was born on February 23, 1897, in Wilmington, New Castle Co., Delaware. He was the son of Elmer Ellsworth James Pegan (58) and Estella Rachel Scott. Samuel lived in 1947 in Wilmington, New Castle Co., Delaware. He died in a hospital in Philadelphia, Philadelphia Co., Pennsylvania, on June 18, 1947, at age 50. Samuel was buried in Silverbrook Cemetery, Wilmington, New Castle Co., Delaware.[32]

Samuel married **Mollie R. Tubbs** about 1921. They had one son. Mollie R. Tubbs was born in Newark, Worcester Co., Maryland, on March 7, 1900. Mollie R. reached age 70 and died in Wilmington, New Castle Co., Delaware, in October 1970. Probably buried in Silverbrook Cemetery, Wilmington, New Castle Co., Delaware.

Son of Samuel Pegan and Mollie R. Tubbs:

+ 282 m I. **Elmer Thomas**[8] **Pegan** was born in Wilmington, New Castle Co., Delaware, on March 26, 1923. He died in Wilmington, New Castle Co., Delaware, in April 1981.

**129. Harvey**[7] **Pegan** (*Elmer Ellsworth James*[6], *Alexander L.*[5], *Andrew*[4], *James*[3], *Andrew*[2] *Pagan*, *James*[1]) was born on March 16, 1897, in Wilmington, New

Castle Co., Delaware. He was the son of Elmer Ellsworth James Pegan (58) and Estella Rachel Scott. Harvey died in Springfield, Delaware Co., Pennsylvania, in October 1966 at age 69.

Harvey married **Mary Stevens** before 1915. They had one daughter. Mary Stevens was born in East Bradford, Chester Co., Pennsylvania, on June 3, 1897. Mary reached age 77 and died in Ardmore, Delaware Co., Pennsylvania, in December 1974.

Daughter of Harvey Pegan and Mary Stevens:

+ 283   f   I.   **Dorothy Elizabeth⁸ Pegan** was born in Lower Merion Twp., Montgomery Co., Pennsylvania? in 1915. She died after 1940.

**130. Son⁷ Pegan** (*Elmer Ellsworth James⁶, Alexander L.⁵, Andrew⁴, James³, Andrew² Pagan, James¹*) was born on November 1, 1901, in Wilmington, New Castle Co., Delaware. He was the son of Elmer Ellsworth James Pegan (58) and Estella Rachel Scott. Son died in Wilmington, New Castle Co., Delaware, on November 1, 1901.

**131. Raymond⁷ Pegan** (*Elmer Ellsworth James⁶, Alexander L.⁵, Andrew⁴, James³, Andrew² Pagan, James¹*) was born on October 20, 1903, in Wilmington, New Castle Co., Delaware. He was the son of Elmer Ellsworth James Pegan (58) and Estella Rachel Scott. Raymond died in Wilmington, New Castle Co., Delaware, in December 1969 at age 66. He was buried in Gracelawn Memorial Park Cemetery, Farmhurst, New Castle Co., Delaware.[59]

Raymond married **Mae Shortt** before 1926. They had two children. Mae Shortt was born in Newark, Worchester Co., Maryland, on March 26, 1910. Mae reached age 75 and died in Wilmington, New Castle Co., Delaware, in May 1985. She was buried in Gracelawn Memorial Park, Farmhurst, New Castle Co., Delaware.[59]

Children of Raymond Pegan and Mae Shortt:

+ 284   m   I.   **Raymond⁸ Pegan II** was born in Wilmington, New Castle Co., Delaware, on November 14, 1926.[112]

He died in Wilmington, New Castle Co., Delaware, on June 24, 1971.[87] Raymond was buried in All Saints Cemetery, Wilmington, New Castle Co., Delaware.[59]

+ 285   f   II.   **Stella Kathleen⁸ Pegan** was born in Wilmington, New Castle Co., Delaware, on March 10, 1928. She was also known as **Kathleen**. Stella died in Wilmington, New Castle Co., Delaware, on February 24, 1987. She was buried in Gracelawn Memorial Park, Farmhurst, New Castle Co., Delaware.[59]

**132. Everett⁷ Pegan** (*Elmer Ellsworth James⁶, Alexander L.⁵, Andrew⁴, James³, Andrew² Pagan, James¹*) was born on March 18, 1905, in Wilmington, New Castle Co., Delaware. He was the son of Elmer Ellsworth James Pegan (58) and Estella Rachel Scott. Everett died in New Castle Co., Delaware, on October 7, 1959, at age 54. He was buried in Gracelawn Memorial Park, Farmhurst, New Castle Co., Delaware.[59]

Everett married **Sarah Elizabeth Maxwell** on April 11, 1925, in New Castle Co., Delaware.[86] They had one daughter. Sarah Elizabeth Maxwell was born in Wilmington, New Castle Co., Delaware, on December 22, 1905. Sarah Elizabeth reached age 51 and died in Wilmington, New Castle Co., Delaware, on April 1, 1957. She was buried in Gracelawn Memorial Park, Farmhurst, New Castle Co., Delaware.[59]

Daughter of Everett Pegan and Sarah Elizabeth Maxwell:

+ 286   f   I.   **Mildred Jennie⁸ Pegan** was born in Wilmington, New Castle Co., Delaware, on August 9, 1925. She died after 2015.

**133. Son Two⁷ Pegan** (*Elmer Ellsworth James⁶, Alexander L.⁵, Andrew⁴, James³, Andrew² Pagan, James¹*) was born on September 23, 1910, in Wilmington, New Castle Co., Delaware. He was the son of Elmer Ellsworth James Pegan (58) and Estella

Rachel Scott. Son Two died in Wilmington, New Castle Co., Delaware, on September 23, 1910.

**134. Arthur Allen⁷ Urban** (*Bertha⁶ Pegan, Andrew A.⁵, Andrew⁴, James³, Andrew² Pagan, James¹*) was born on July 22, 1889, in Manor Twp., Lancaster Co., Pennsylvania. He was the son of Martin Luther Urban and Bertha Pegan (60). Arthur Allen died in Lancaster, Lancaster Co., Pennsylvania, on November 26, 1967, at age 78. He was buried in Millersville Mennonite Cemetery, Millersville, Manor Twp., Lancaster Co., Pennsylvania.[61]

Arthur Allen married **Alice Witmer** before 1920. They had three children. Alice Witmer was born in Manor Twp., Lancaster Co., Pennsylvania, on October 20, 1881. Alice reached age 64 and died in Lancaster, Lancaster Co., Pennsylvania, on October 19, 1946. She was buried in Millersville Mennonite Cemetery, Millersville, Manor Twp., Lancaster Co., Pennsylvania.[61]

Children of Arthur Allen Urban and Alice Witmer:

+ 287 m I. **Earl Witmer⁸ Urban** was born in Manor Twp., Lancaster Co., Pennsylvania, on January 11, 1920. He died in Hudson, Pasco Co., Florida, on March 19, 1988.

+ 288 f II. **Erma Elizabeth⁸ Urban** was born in Manor Twp., Lancaster Co., Pennsylvania, on October 17, 1924. She died in Neffsville, Manheim Twp., Lancaster Co., Pennsylvania on September 30, 2014. Erma Elizabeth was buried in Millers Millersville, Manor Twp., Lancaster Co., Pennsylvania.[61]

+ 289 f III. **Ruth Arlene⁸ Urban** was born in Manor Twp., Lancaster Co., Pennsylvania, in 1928. She died in Manor Twp., Lancaster Co., Pennsylvania, in 1931. Ruth Arlene was buried in Millersville Mennonite Cemetery, Millersville, Manor Twp., Lancaster Co., Pennsylvania.[61]

**135. Phares Pegan⁷ Urban** (*Bertha⁶ Pegan, Andrew A.⁵, Andrew⁴, James³, Andrew² Pagan, James¹*) was born on March 6, 1893, in Manor Twp., Lancaster Co., Pennsylvania. He was the son of Martin Luther Urban and Bertha Pegan (60). Phares Pegan died in Washington Boro, Manor Twp., Lancaster Co., Pennsylvania, in January 1976 at age 82. He was buried in Grace United Methodist Church Cemetery, Millersville, Manor Twp., Lancaster Co., Pennsylvania.[33]

Phares Pegan married **Grace Benedict** before 1922. They had three children. Grace Benedict was born in Conestoga Twp., Lancaster Co., Pennsylvania, on August 8, 1899. Grace reached age 86 and died in Lancaster, Lancaster Co., Pennsylvania, in May 1986.

Children of Phares Pegan Urban and Grace Benedict:

+ 290 f I. **Jean⁸ Urban** was born in Manor Twp., Lancaster Co., Pennsylvania, on June 19, 1922. She died in Columbia, Lancaster Co., Pennsylvania, on August 23, 2015. Jean was buried in Millersville Mennonite Cemetery, Millersville, Manor Twp., Lancaster Co., Pennsylvania.[61]

+ 291 m II. **Robert Benedict⁸ Urban** was born in Manor Twp., Lancaster Co., Pennsylvania, on October 22, 1923. He died in Lancaster Co., Pennsylvania, on November 25, 1968. Robert Benedict was buried in Conestoga Memorial Park Cemetery, Lancaster Twp., Lancaster Co., Pennsylvania.[90]

+ 292 m III. **Phares⁸ Urban II** was born in Manor Twp., Lancaster Co., Pennsylvania, on January 27, 1928. He died in Holtwood, Martic Twp., Lancaster Co., Pennsylvania, on May 17, 2007.

**136. Ralph Martin⁷ Urban** (*Bertha⁶ Pegan, Andrew A.⁵, Andrew⁴, James³, Andrew² Pagan, James¹*) was born on September 1, 1901, in Manor Twp., Lancaster Co., Pennsylvania. He was the son of Martin Luther Urban and Bertha Pegan (60). Ralph Martin died in Lancaster, Lancaster Co., Pennsylvania, on July 31, 1981, at age 79. He was buried in Millersville Mennonite Cemetery, Millersville, Manor Twp., Lancaster Co., Pennsylvania.[61]

Ralph Martin married **Gertrude Sneath** before 1929. They had two children. Gertrude Sneath was born in Manor Twp., Lancaster Co., Pennsylvania, on March 28, 1903. Gertrude reached age 60 and died in Lancaster, Lancaster Co., Pennsylvania, on October 27, 1963. She was buried in Millersville Mennonite Cemetery, Millersville, Manor Twp., Lancaster Co., Pennsylvania.[61]

Children of Ralph Martin Urban and Gertrude Sneath:

+ 293 f I. **Elaine Madeline[8] Urban** was born in Lancaster, Lancaster Co., Pennsylvania, on August 14, 1929. She died in Lancaster, Lancaster Co., Pennsylvania, on August 11, 2001. Elaine Madeline was buried in Millersville Mennonite Cemetery, Millersville, Manor Twp., Lancaster Co., Pennsylvania.[61]

+ 294 m II. **Ralph Kenneth[8] Urban II** was born in Lancaster, Lancaster Co., Pennsylvania, on January 15, 1931. He was also known as **Kenneth**. Ralph Kenneth died in Lancaster, Lancaster Co., Pennsylvania? on April 3, 1969. He was buried in Millersville Mennonite Cemetery, Millersville, Manor Twp., Lancaster Co., Pennsylvania.[61]

**137. Sarah[7] Johnson** (*Martha Ann[6] Fulton, Sarah Jane[5] Miller, Margaret[4] Pegan, James[3], Andrew[2] Pagan, James[1]*) was born on August 6, 1871, in Peach Bottom Twp., York Co., Pennsylvania.[8] She was the daughter of Samuel Parke Johnson and Martha Ann Fulton (63). Sarah died in Lower Chanceford Twp., York Co., Pennsylvania, on February 25, 1950, at age 78. She was buried in Slate Ridge Cemetery, Delta, Peach Bottom Twp., York Co., Pennsylvania.[2, 20]

Sarah married **Elmer Ramsey Wiley** before 1891. They divorced. They had four children. Elmer Ramsey Wiley was born in Peach Bottom Twp., York Co., Pennsylvania, in July 1867. He reached age 58 and died in Lower Chanceford Twp., York Co., Pennsylvania, on February 6, 1926. Elmer Ramsey was buried in Slateville Presbyterian Church Cemetery, Delta, Peach Bottom Twp., York Co., Pennsylvania.[49]

Children of Sarah Johnson and Elmer Ramsey Wiley:

+ 295 m I. **James Howard[8] Wiley** was born in Lower Chanceford Twp., York Co., Pennsylvania, on September 5, 1891. He was also known as **Howard** and **Joseph Howard Wiley**. James Howard died in Dayton, Montgomery Co., Ohio, on November 5, 1964. He was buried in Miami Valley Memorial Gardens Cemetery, Springboro, Clearcreek Twp., Warren Co., Ohio.[113]

+ 296 m II. **Samuel Johnson[8] Wiley** was born in Lower Chanceford Twp., York Co., Pennsylvania, on July 23, 1893. He died in Fulton Twp., Lancaster Co., Pennsylvania, on May 10, 1966. Samuel Johnson was buried in Little Britain Presbyterian Church Cemetery, Fulton Twp., Lancaster Co., Pennsylvania.[114]

+ 297 m III. **Elmer Crawford[8] Wiley II** was born in Lower Chanceford Twp., York Co., Pennsylvania, on May 28, 1897. He died in Delta, Peach Bottom Twp., York Co., Pennsylvania, in September 1974.

+ 298 f IV. **Louise[8] Wiley** was born in Lower Chanceford Twp., York Co., Pennsylvania, on November 2, 1900. She died in Airville, Lower Chanceford Twp., York Co., Pennsylvania, in November 1985.

**138. James⁷ Johnson** (*Martha Ann⁶ Fulton, Sarah Jane⁵ Miller, Margaret⁴ Pegan, James³, Andrew² Pagan, James¹*) was born in 1874 in Peach Bottom Twp., York Co., Pennsylvania. He was the son of Samuel Parke Johnson and Martha Ann Fulton (63). James died in Peach Bottom Twp., York Co., Pennsylvania, in 1891 at age 17.

**139. Grace Anna⁷ Johnson** (*Martha Ann⁶ Fulton, Sarah Jane⁵ Miller, Margaret⁴ Pegan, James³, Andrew² Pagan, James¹*) was born on November 27, 1876, in Peach Bottom Twp., York Co., Pennsylvania. She was the daughter of Samuel Parke Johnson and Martha Ann Fulton (63). Grace Anna died in Delta, Peach Bottom Twp., York Co., Pennsylvania, on September 1, 1961, at age 84. She was buried in Slate Ridge Cemetery, Delta, Peach Bottom Twp., York Co., Pennsylvania.[20]

Grace Anna married **Nelson Caldwell Dinsmore** before 1909. They had four children. Nelson Caldwell Dinsmore was born in Peach Bottom Twp., York Co., Pennsylvania, on September 11, 1874. Nelson Caldwell reached age 68 and died in West York, York Co., Pennsylvania, on April 22, 1943. He was buried in Slate Ridge Cemetery, Delta, Peach Bottom Twp., York Co., Pennsylvania.[20]

Children of Grace Anna Johnson and Nelson Caldwell Dinsmore:

+ 299 m I. **Robert Fulton⁸ Dinsmore** was born in Peach Bottom Twp., York Co., Pennsylvania, on February 1, 1909. He died in Dade Co., Florida, in November 1967.

+ 300 m II. **Samuel Nelson⁸ Dinsmore** was born in Peach Bottom Twp., York Co., Pennsylvania, in 1910. He died in 1955. Samuel Nelson was buried in Slate Ridge Cemetery, Delta, Peach Bottom Twp., York Co., Pennsylvania.[20]

+ 301 f III. **Minna Marie⁸ Dinsmore** was born in Peach Bottom Twp., York Co., Pennsylvania, in 1912. She was also known as **Marie**. Minna Marie died in Wilmington, New Castle, Delaware? in 1973. She was buried in Slate Ridge Cemetery, Delta, Peach Bottom Twp., York Co., Pennsylvania.[20]

+ 302 m IV. **James Alexander⁸ Dinsmore** was born in Peach Bottom Twp., York Co., Pennsylvania, on December 20, 1915. He died in Peach Bottom Twp., York Co., Pennsylvania, on September 1, 1973. James Alexander was buried in Slate Ridge Cemetery, Delta, Peach Bottom Twp., York Co., Pennsylvania.[20]

**140. Samuel Fulton⁷ Johnson II** (*Martha Ann⁶ Fulton, Sarah Jane⁵ Miller, Margaret⁴ Pegan, James³, Andrew² Pagan, James¹*) was born on October 9, 1880, in Peach Bottom Twp., York Co., Pennsylvania. He was also known as **Fulton** and **S. Fulton**. He was the son of Samuel Parke Johnson and Martha Ann Fulton (63). Samuel Fulton died in Peach Bottom Twp., York Co., Pennsylvania, on January 6, 1941, at age 60. He was buried in Slate Ridge Cemetery, Delta, Peach Bottom Twp., York Co., Pennsylvania.[20]

Never married.

**141. David Edgar⁷ Fulton** (*John Henry⁶, Sarah Jane⁵ Miller, Margaret⁴ Pegan, James³, Andrew² Pagan, James¹*) was born on March 1, 1877, in Peach Bottom Twp., York Co., Pennsylvania. He was the son of John Henry Fulton (64) and Mary Eleanor Anderson. David Edgar died in Peach Bottom Twp., York Co., Pennsylvania, on October 10, 1960, at age 83. He was buried in Slate Ridge Cemetery, Delta, Peach Bottom Twp., York Co., Pennsylvania.[20]

David Edgar married **Lena Kohlbus** before 1906. They had one son. Lena Kohlbus was born in Street, Harford Co., Maryland, on March 8, 1888. Lena reached age 100 and died in Peach Bottom Twp.,

York Co., Pennsylvania, on February 2, 1989. She was buried in Slate Ridge Cemetery, Delta, Peach Bottom Twp., York Co., Pennsylvania.[20]

Son of David Edgar Fulton and Lena Kohlbus:

+ 303  m  I.  **Lewis Price**[8] **Fulton** was born in Peach Bottom Twp., York Co., Pennsylvania, on July 12, 1906. He died in Peach Bottom Twp., York Co., Pennsylvania, on December 25, 1914. Lewis Price was buried in Slate Ridge Cemetery, Delta, Peach Bottom Twp., York Co., Pennsylvania. [20]

142. **Mary Janetta**[7] **Fulton** (*John Henry*[6], *Sarah Jane*[5] *Miller, Margaret*[4] *Pegan, James*[3]*, Andrew*[2] *Pagan, James*[1]) was born on February 21, 1881, in Peach Bottom Twp., York Co., Pennsylvania. She was the daughter of John Henry Fulton (64) and Mary Eleanor Anderson. Mary Janetta died in Delta, Peach Bottom Twp., York Co., Pennsylvania, in November 1967 at age 86. She was buried in Slate Ridge Cemetery, Delta, Peach Bottom Twp., York Co., Pennsylvania.[20]

Mary Janetta married **Bunyan Hess Wise** before 1907. They had seven children. Bunyan Hess Wise was born in Peach Bottom Twp., York Co., Pennsylvania, on February 12, 1879. Bunyan Hess reached age 49 and died in Peach Bottom Twp., York Co., Pennsylvania, on September 7, 1928. He was buried in Slate Ridge Cemetery, Delta, Peach Bottom Twp., York Co., Pennsylvania.[20]

Children of Mary Janetta Fulton and Bunyan Hess Wise:

+ 304  m  I.  **John F.**[8] **Wise** was born in Peach Bottom Twp., York Co., Pennsylvania, on May 12, 1907. He died in York, York Co., Pennsylvania, on September 24, 1990. John F. was buried in Slate Ridge Cemetery, Delta, Peach Bottom Twp., York Co., Pennsylvania.[20]

+ 305  m  II.  **Samuel A.**[8] **Wise** was born in Peach Bottom Twp., Pennsyl-vania, on September 21, 1910. He died in York, York Co., Pennsylvania, on May 11, 1999. Samuel A. was buried in Slate Ridge Cemetery, Delta, Peach Bottom Twp., York Co., Pennsylvania.[20]

+ 306  m  III.  **Ralph Anderson**[8] **Wise** was born in Peach Bottom Twp., York Co., Pennsylvania, on March 25, 1913. He died in Delta, Peach Bottom Twp., York Co., Pennsylvania, on April 15, 1995. Ralph Anderson was buried in Bryansville Cemetery, Bryansville, Peach Bottom Twp., York Co., Pennsylvania.[115]

+ 307  f  IV.  **Mary Eleanor**[8] **Wise** was born in Peach Bottom Twp., York Co., Pennsylvania, on June 2, 1915. She died in York, York Co., Pennsylvania, on December 10, 2001. Mary Eleanor was buried in Fawn Grove Methodist Church Cemetery, Fawn Grove, Fawn Grove Twp., York Co., Pennsylvania.[91]

+ 308  f  V.  **Grace Anna**[8] **Wise** was born in Peach Bottom Twp., York Co., Pennsylvania, on September 16, 1917. She died after 2015.

+ 309  f  VI.  **Infant Daughter**[8] **Wise** was born in Peach Bottom Twp., York Co., Pennsylvania, on January 15, 1922. She died in Peach Bottom Twp., York Co., Pennsylvania, on January 15, 1922.

+ 310  f  VII.  **Bertha M.**[8] **Wise** was born in Peach Bottom Twp., York Co., Pennsylvania, on February 7, 1923.

143. **James Anderson**[7] **Fulton** (*John Henry*[6], *Sarah Jane*[5] *Miller, Margaret*[4] *Pegan, James*[3]*, Andrew*[2] *Pagan, James*[1]) was born on May 24, 1883, in Peach Bottom Twp., York Co., Pennsylvania. He was the son of John Henry Fulton (64) and Mary Eleanor Anderson. James Anderson died

in Peach Bottom Twp., York Co., Pennsylvania, on December 7, 1938, at age 55. He was buried in Slate Ridge Cemetery, Delta, Peach Bottom Twp., York Co., Pennsylvania.[20]

James Anderson married **Elizabeth Jane Parry** before 1912. They had three children. Elizabeth Jane Parry was born in Cardiff, Harford Co., Maryland, on January 21, 1886. Elizabeth Jane reached age 68 and died in Peach Bottom Twp., York Co., Pennsylvania, on January 28, 1954. He was buried in Slate Ridge Cemetery, Delta, Peach Bottom Twp., York Co., Pennsylvania.[20]

Children of James Anderson Fulton and Elizabeth Jane Parry:

+ 311 f I. **Daughter**[8] **Fulton** was born in Peach Bottom Twp., York Co., Pennsylvania, on October 19, 1912. She died in Peach Bottom Twp., York Co., Pennsylvania, on October 19, 1912. Daughter was buried in Slate Ridge Cemetery, Delta, Peach Bottom Twp., York Co., Pennsylvania.[20]

+ 312 f II. **Margaret Eleanora**[8] **Fulton** was born in Peach Bottom Twp., York Co., Pennsylvania, on July 24, 1914. She died in Peach Bottom Twp., York Co., Pennsylvania, on June 23, 1920. Margaret Eleanora was buried in Slate Ridge Cemetery, Delta, Peach Bottom Twp., York Co., Pennsylvania.[20]

+ 313 m III. **James Anderson**[8] **Fulton II** was born in Peach Bottom Twp., York Co., Pennsylvania, on October 16, 1918. He died in Stevens, Ephrata Twp., Lancaster Co., Pennsylvania, on December 17, 1998. James Anderson was buried in Memory Gardens Cemetery, East Cocalico Twp., Lancaster Co., Pennsylvania.[116]

**144. Samuel J.**[7] **Fulton** (*John Henry*[6], *Sarah Jane*[5] *Miller, Margaret*[4] *Pegan, James*[3], *Andrew*[2] *Pagan, James*[1]) was born on May 29, 1886, in Peach Bottom Twp., York Co., Pennsylvania. He was the son of John Henry Fulton (64) and Mary Eleanor Anderson. Samuel J. died in Peach Bottom Twp., York Co., Pennsylvania, on February 2, 1923, at age 36. He was buried in Slate Ridge Cemetery, Delta, Peach Bottom Twp., York Co., Pennsylvania.[20]

Samuel J. married **Grace W. Hughes** before 1912. They had one son. Grace W. Hughes was born in Delta, Peach Bottom Twp., York Co., Pennsylvania, on November 6, 1888. Grace W. reached age 66 and died in York, York Co., Pennsylvania, on June 28, 1955. She was buried in Slate Ridge Cemetery, Delta, Peach Bottom Twp., York Co., Pennsylvania.[20]

Son of Samuel J. Fulton and Grace W. Hughes:

+ 314 m I. **John Henry**[8] **Fulton** was born in Peach Bottom Twp., York Co., Pennsylvania, on July 17, 1912. He died in York, York Co., Pennsylvania, on January 1, 1991. John Henry was buried in Mount Rose Cemetery, Spring Garden Twp., York Co., Pennsylvania.[40]

**145. Mabel A.**[7] **Gregg** (*Margaret A.*[6] *Fulton, Sarah Jane*[5] *Miller, Margaret*[4] *Pegan, James*[3], *Andrew*[2] *Pagan, James*[1]) was born on October 1, 1871, in Fulton Twp., Lancaster Co., Pennsylvania. She was the daughter of John Thomas Gregg and Margaret A. Fulton (65). Mabel A. died in Lancaster, Lancaster Co., Pennsylvania, in March 1968 at age 96. She was buried in New Chestnut Level Presbyterian Church Cemetery, Drumore Twp., Lancaster Co., Pennsylvania.[36]

Childless.

Mabel A. married **George O. Wilson** on August 5, 1911, in Dauphin Co., Pennsylvania. George O. Wilson was born in Fulton Twp., Lancaster Co., Pennsylvania? on April 29, 1859. George O. reached age 60 and died in Philadelphia, Philadelphia Co., Pennsylvania, on April 2, 1920. He was buried in Penn Hill (Friends) Burial Ground, Penn Hill, Fulton Twp., Lancaster Co., Pennsylvania.[117]

Mabel A. Gregg Wilson married **Hiram Christian Miller** between 1920 and 1930. Hiram Christian Miller was born in West Hempfield Twp., Lancaster Co., Pennsylvania, on September 29, 1864. Hiram Christian reached age 82 and died in Lancaster, Lancaster Co., Pennsylvania, on July 26, 1947. He was buried in New Chestnut Level Presbyterian Church Cemetery, Drumore Twp., Lancaster Co., Pennsylvania.[36]

**146. William Fulton[7] Gregg** (*Margaret A.[6] Fulton, Sarah Jane[5] Miller, Margaret[4] Pegan, James[3], Andrew[2] Pagan, James[1]*) was born on February 24, 1875, in Fulton Twp., Lancaster Co., Pennsylvania. He was the son of John Thomas Gregg and Margaret A. Fulton (65). William Fulton lived in 1910 in Westport, Clatsop Co., Oregon. He also resided in 1920 in Rainier, Columbia Co., Oregon. William Fulton died in Columbia City, Columbia Co., Oregon, on July 28, 1925, at age 50.

William Fulton married **Euretta Irwin** about 1908. They had one daughter. Euretta Irwin was born in Maryland in 1874. Euretta reached age 55 and died in Portland, Multnomah Co., Oregon, on February 3, 1929.

Daughter of William Fulton Gregg and Euretta Irwin:

+ 315 f I. **Mildred[8] Gregg** was born in Astoria, Clatsop Co., Oregon, on June 4, 1909. She died in Astoria, Clatsop Co., Oregon, on June 5, 1909. Mildred was buried in Astoria, Clatsop Co., Oregon.

**147. George Fulton[7] Geiger II** (*Elizabeth Jane[6] Fulton, Sarah Jane[5] Miller, Margaret[4] Pegan, James[3], Andrew[2] Pagan, James[1]*) was born on January 31, 1877, in Peach Bottom Twp., York Co., Pennsylvania. He was the son of George Geiger and Elizabeth Jane Fulton (66). George Fulton died in Peach Bottom Twp., York Co., Pennsylvania, on July 28, 1926, at age 49. He was buried in Slate Ridge Cemetery, Delta, Peach Bottom Twp., York Co., Pennsylvania.[20]

Never married.

**148. Infant Daughter One[7] Geiger** (*Elizabeth Jane[6] Fulton, Sarah Jane[5] Miller, Margaret[4] Pegan, James[3], Andrew[2] Pagan, James[1]*). She was the daughter of George Geiger and Elizabeth Jane Fulton (66). Infant Daughter One was buried in Slate Ridge Cemetery, Delta, Peach Bottom Twp., York Co., Pennsylvania.[20]

**149. Infant Daughter Two[7] Geiger** (*Elizabeth Jane[6] Fulton, Sarah Jane[5] Miller, Margaret[4] Pegan, James[3], Andrew[2] Pagan, James[1]*). She was the daughter of George Geiger and Elizabeth Jane Fulton (66). Infant Daughter Two was buried in Slate Ridge Cemetery, Delta, Peach Bottom Twp., York Co., Pennsylvania.[20]

**150. William Davis[7] Fulton** (*Robert Allen[6], Sarah Jane[5] Miller, Margaret[4] Pegan, James[3], Andrew[2] Pagan, James[1]*) was born on September 27, 1883, in Peach Bottom Twp., York Co., Pennsylvania. He was the son of Robert Allen Fulton (67) and Rachel E. Davis. William Davis died in Baltimore, Baltimore Co., Maryland, after 1942.

He married **Grace Terrell**. They had one son. Grace Terrell was born in Whiteford, Harford Co., Maryland, on August 6, 1889. Grace died in Baltimore, Baltimore Co., Maryland, after 1942.

Son of William Davis Fulton and Grace Terrell:

+ 316 m I. **William Terrell[8] Fulton II** was born in Baltimore, Baltimore Co., Maryland, on May 9, 1921. He died in Lutherville, Timonium Twp., Baltimore Co., Maryland, on April 14, 2008.

**151. Ross David[7] Fulton** (*Robert Allen[6], Sarah Jane[5] Miller, Margaret[4] Pegan, James[3], Andrew[2] Pagan, James[1]*) was born on December 20, 1885, in Peach Bottom Twp., York Co., Pennsylvania. He was the son of Robert Allen Fulton (67) and Rachel E. Davis. Ross David died in Peach Bottom Twp., York Co., Pennsylvania, on April 10, 1910, at age 24. He was buried in Slate Ridge Cemetery, Delta, Peach Bottom Twp., York Co., Pennsylvania.[20]

**152. Annie B.⁷ Fulton** (*Robert Allen⁶, Sarah Jane⁵ Miller, Margaret⁴ Pegan, James³, Andrew² Pagan, James¹*) was born on May 5, 1890, in Peach Bottom Twp., York Co., Pennsylvania. She was the daughter of Robert Allen Fulton (67) and Rachel E. Davis. Annie B. died in Peach Bottom Twp., York Co., Pennsylvania, on May 4, 1912, at age 21. She was buried in Slate Ridge Cemetery, Delta, Peach Bottom Twp., York Co., Pennsylvania.[20]

**153. Eleanor Elizabeth⁷ Fulton** (*Robert Allen⁶, Sarah Jane⁵ Miller, Margaret⁴ Pegan, James³, Andrew² Pagan, James¹*) was born in 1893 in Peach Bottom Twp., York Co., Pennsylvania. She was the daughter of Robert Allen Fulton (67) and Rachel E. Davis. Eleanor Elizabeth died in Peach Bottom Twp., York Co., Pennsylvania, in 1893.[2] Probably buried in Slate Ridge Cemetery, Delta, Peach Bottom Twp., York Co., Pennsylvania.

**154. Willie S.W.⁷ Douglass** (*Sarah Ann⁶ Mitchell, Martha Ellen⁵ Miller, Margaret⁴ Pegan, James³, Andrew² Pagan, James¹*) was born on July 29, 1885, in Lexington, Troy Twp., Richland Co., Ohio. He was the son of William Franklin Douglass and Sarah Anne Mitchell (69). Willie S.W. died in Mansfield, Madison Twp., Richland Co., Ohio, on April 28, 1899, at age 13. He was buried in Lexington Cemetery, Lexington, Troy Twp., Richland Co., Ohio.[35]

**155. Ada Mae⁷ Douglass** (*Sarah Ann⁶ Mitchell, Martha Ellen⁵ Miller, Margaret⁴ Pegan, James³, Andrew² Pagan, James¹*) was born on May 29, 1899, in Lexington, Troy Twp., Richland Co., Ohio. She was also known as **Mae**. She was the daughter of William Franklin Douglass and Sarah Anne Mitchell (69). Ada Mae died in Mansfield, Madison Twp., Richland Co., Ohio in May 7, 1972 at age 82. She is probably buried in Lexington Cemetery, Lexington, Troy Twp., Richland Co., Ohio.

Never married.

**156. James Mitchell⁷ Kilgore** (*Margaret Rosa⁶ Mitchell, Martha Ellen⁵ Miller, Margaret⁴ Pegan, James³, Andrew² Pagan, James¹*) was born on February 3, 1892, in Lower Chanceford Twp., York Co., Pennsylvania. He was also known as **Mitchell**. He was the son of George Brinton Kilgore and Margaret Rosa Mitchell (70). James Mitchell died in Mansfield, Madison Twp., Richland Co., Ohio, on June 6, 1945, at age 53. He was buried in Mansfield Cemetery, Ontario, Madison Twp., Richland Co., Ohio.[67]

James Mitchell married **Hannah Jane McNeil** about 1913. They had five sons. Hannah Jane McNeil was born in Fawn Twp., York Co., Pennsylvania, on February 19, 1892. Hannah Jane reached age 53 and died in Mansfield, Madison Twp., Richland Co., Ohio, on August 17, 1945. She was buried in Mansfield Cemetery, Ontario, Madison Twp., Richland Co., Ohio.[67]

Sons of James Mitchell Kilgore and Hannah Jane McNeil:

+ 317 m I. **James Clarence⁸ Kilgore II** was born in Lower Chanceford Twp., York Co., Pennsylvania, on March 17, 1915. He died in Mansfield, Madison Twp., Richland Co., Ohio, on February 6, 1998. James Clarence was buried in Mansfield Memorial Park Cemetery, Ontario, Madison Twp., Richland Co., Ohio.[118]

+ 318 m II. **Willis Leroy⁸ Kilgore** was born in Mansfield, Madison Twp., Richland Co., Ohio, on April 20, 1917. He died in San Antonio, Bexar Co., Texas, on July 10, 1963. Willis Leroy was buried in Fort Sam Houston National Cemetery, San Antonio, Bexar Co., Texas.[119]

+ 319 m III. **George Franklin⁸ Kilgore** was born in Mansfield, Madison Twp., Richland Co., Ohio, on October 1, 1918. He died in Mansfield, Madison Twp., Richland Co., Ohio, on February 13, 1985. George Franklin was buried in Windsor Park Cemetery, Mansfield, Madison Twp., Richland Co., Ohio.[120]

+ 320 m IV. **John Harvey⁸ Kilgore** was born in Mansfield, Madison Twp., Richland Co., Ohio, on June 24, 1921. He died in Mansfield, Madison Twp., Richland Co., Ohio, on July 8, 2010. John Harvey was buried in Mansfield Memorial Park Cemetery, Ontario, Madison Twp., Richland Co., Ohio.[67]

+ 321 m V.   **Joseph Raymond[8] Kilgore** was born in Mansfield, Madison Twp., Richland Co., Ohio, on September 18, 1927. He died in Fort Myers, Lee Co., Florida, on February 17, 1989.

**157. Ula Agnes Ellen[7] Kilgore** (*Margaret Rosa[6] Mitchell, Martha Ellen[5] Miller, Margaret[4] Pegan, James[3], Andrew[2] Pagan, James[1]*) was born on October 28, 1893, in Lower Chanceford Twp., York Co., Pennsylvania. She was also known as **Agnes**. She was the daughter of George Brinton Kilgore and Margaret Rosa Mitchell (70). Ula Agnes Ellen died in Red Lion, York Twp., York Co., Pennsylvania, on January 14, 1962, at age 68. She was buried in Pine Grove Presbyterian Church Cemetery, Lower Chanceford Twp., York Co., Pennsylvania.[51]

Ula Agnes Ellen married **David Elwood Burkins** before 1913. They had four children. David Elwood Burkins was born in Fawn Twp., York Co., Pennsylvania, on November 6, 1890. David Elwood reached age 69 and died in Red Lion, York Twp., York Co., Pennsylvania? on January 9, 1960. He was buried in Pine Grove Presbyterian Church Cemetery, Lower Chanceford Twp., York Co., Pennsylvania.[51]

Children of Ula Agnes Ellen Kilgore and David Elwood Burkins:

+ 322 m I.   **Charles B.[8] Burkins** was born in Peach Bottom Twp., York Co., Pennsylvania, on January 9, 1913. He died in York Springs, Adams Co., Pennsylvania, on April 6, 1998. Charles B. was buried in Salem Union Cemetery, Jacobus, York Co., Pennsylvania.[121]

+ 323 f II.   **Ida R.[8] Burkins** was born in Peach Bottom Twp., York Co., Pennsylvania, on August 28, 1914. She died in York, York Co., Pennsylva nia, on September 8, 1941. Ida R. was buried in Bethany United Methodist Church Cemetery, Felton, Chanceford Twp., York Co., Pennsylvania.[122]

+ 324 m III.   **Ross[8] Burkins** was born in Peach Bottom Twp., York Co., Pennsylvania, on August 11, 1916. He died in Red Lion, York Twp., York Co., Pennsylvania, on November 1, 2005. Ross was buried in Zion United Methodist Church Cemetery, Red Lion, York Twp., York Co., Pennsylvania.[123]

+ 325 m IV.   **Infant Son[8] Burkins** was born in Peach Bottom Twp., York Co., Pennsylvania, on November 19, 1928. He died in Peach Bottom Twp., York Co., Pennsylvania, on November 19, 1928. Infant Son was buried in Pine Grove Presbyterian Church Cemetery, Lower Chanceford Twp., York Co., Pennsylvania.[51]

**158. Nora Eliza[7] Kilgore** (*Margaret Rosa[6] Mitchell, Martha Ellen[5] Miller, Margaret[4] Pegan, James[3], Andrew[2] Pagan, James[1]*) was born on March 5, 1904, in Lower Chanceford Twp., York Co., Pennsylvania. She was the daughter of George Brinton Kilgore and Margaret Rosa Mitchell (70). Nora Eliza died in Brogue, Chanceford Twp., York Co., Pennsylvania, on March 23, 1984, at age 80. She was buried in Mount Olivet United Methodist Church Cemetery, Fawn Grove, Fawn Twp., York Co., Pennsylvania.[68]

Nora Eliza married **Harry Wilson Burns** before 1922. They had eight children. Harry Wilson Burns was born in Fawn Twp., York Co., Pennsylvania, on September 12, 1901. He was also known as **Wilson**. Harry Wilson reached age 79 and died in Brogue, Chanceford Twp., York Co., Pennsylvania, on October 17, 1980. He was buried in Mount Olivet United Methodist Church Cemetery, Fawn Grove, Fawn Twp., York Co., Pennsylvania.[68]

Children of Nora Eliza Kilgore and Harry Wilson Burns had eight children, including:

+ 326 m I. **George William**[8] **Burns** was born in Peach Bottom Twp., York Co., Pennsylvania, on September 22, 1922. He died in Lower Chanceford Twp., York Co., Pennsylvania, on October 7, 1927. George William was buried in Mount Olivet United Methodist Church Cemetery, Fawn Grove, Fawn Twp., York Co., Pennsylvania.[68]

+ 327 f II. **Maggie Ruth**[8] **Burns** was born in Goram, Lower Chanceford Twp., York Co., Pennsylvania, on March 14, 1924. She died in Dallastown, Windsor Twp., York Co., Pennsylvania, on August 30, 2006. Maggie Ruth was buried in Saint Luke's Evangelical Lutheran Cemetery, New Bridgeville, Chanceford Twp., York Co., Pennsylvania.[124]

+ 328 m III. **Harry Wilson**[8] **Burns II** was born in Peach Bottom Twp., York Co., Pennsylvania, on August 15, 1926. He died in Lower Chanceford Twp., York Co., Pennsylvania, on August 27, 1929. Harry Wilson was buried in Mount Olivet United Methodist Church Cemetery, Fawn Grove, Fawn Twp., York Co., Pennsylvania.[68]

+ 329 m IV. **Joseph Milton**[8] **Burns** was born in Lower Chanceford Twp., York Co., Pennsylvania, on September 26, 1928. He was also known as **Milton**. Joseph Milton died in Dallastown, Windsor Twp., York

Co., Pennsylvania, on July 15, 2015.

+ 330 m V. **Charles W.**[8] **Burns** was born in Lower Chanceford Twp., York Co., Pennsylvania, on August 16, 1960. He died in Columbia, Lancaster Co., Pennsylvania, on October 21, 2016. Charles W. was buried in Mount Zion Baptist Church Cemetery, Brogue, Chanceford Twp., York Co., Pennsylvanai.[125]

+ 331 m VI. **Clyde**[8] **Burns** was born in Lower Chanceford Twp., York Co., Pennsylvania, in 1933.

+ 332 m VII. **J. Harold**[8] **Burns** was born in Lower Chanceford Twp., York Co., Pennsylvania, in 1935.

**159. Child**[7] **Grove** (*Ida Melissa*[6] *Pegan, Henry*[5]*, James*[4]*, James*[3]*, Andrew*[2] *Pagan, James*[1]) was born between 1878 and 1900 in York Co., Pennsylvania. He was the son of Samuel Adams Grove and Ida Melissa Pegan (71). Child died in York Co., Pennsylvania, between 1878 and 1900.

**160. John Evelyn**[7] **Grove** (*Ida Melissa*[6] *Pegan, Henry*[5]*, James*[4]*, James*[3]*, Andrew*[2] *Pagan, James*[1]) was born on May 25, 1879, in Lower Chanceford Twp., York Co., Pennsylvania. He was also known as **Evelyn**. He was the son of Samuel Adams Grove and Ida Melissa Pegan (71). John Evelyn died in Sunnyburn, Lower Chanceford Twp., York Co., Pennsylvania, on May 19, 1906, at age 26. He was buried in Salem United Methodist Church Cemetery, Delta, Peach Bottom Twp., York Co., Pennsylvania.[52]

Childless.

John Evelyn married **Elizabeth Ellen Zealor** between 1900 and 1906. Elizabeth Ellen Zealor was born in Lower Chanceford Twp., York Co., Pennsylvania, on September 23, 1882. Elizabeth Ellen reached age 70 and died in Havre de Grace, Harford Co., Maryland, on April 21, 1953. She was buried in Angel Hill Cemetery, Harve de Grace, Harford Co., Maryland.[126]

Her name was Elizabeth Galloway when she died.

**161. Francis Henry[7] Grove** (*Ida Melissa[6] Pegan, Henry[5], James[4], James[3], Andrew[2] Pagan, James[1]*) was born on January 1, 1885, in Lower Chanceford Twp., York Co., Pennsylvania. He was also known as **Frank**. He was the son of Samuel Adams Grove and Ida Melissa Pegan (71). Francis Henry died in Peach Bottom Twp., York Co., Pennsylvania, on December 11, 1960, at age 75. He was buried in Slate Ridge Cemetery, Delta, Peach Bottom Twp., York Co., Pennsylvania.[20]

Francis Henry married **Mary P. McLaughlin** before 1905. They had three children. Mary P. McLaughlin was born in Peach Bottom Twp., York Co., Pennsylvania, on June 25, 1884. Mary P. lived in 1960 in Peach Bottom Twp., York Co., Pennsylvania. She reached age 76 and died in a facility in Columbia, Lancaster Co., Pennsylvania, on September 29, 1960. Mary P. was buried in Slate Ridge Cemetery, Delta, Peach Bottom Twp., York Co., Pennsylvania.[20]

Children of Francis Henry Grove and Mary P. McLaughlin:

+ 333 f I. **Marian E.[8] Grove** was born in Peach Bottom Twp., York Co., Pennsylvania, on May 15, 1905. She died in Delta, Peach Bottom Twp., York Co., Pennsylvania, on June 4, 1991. Marian E. was buried in Slate Ridge Cemetery, Delta, Peach Bottom Twp., York Co., Pennsylvania.[20]

+ 334 f II. **Mary Evelyn[8] Grove** was born in Bryansville, Peach Bottom Twp., York Co., Pennsylvania, on February 24, 1909. She was also known as **Evelyn**. Mary Evelyn died in York, York Co., Pennsylvania, on August 5, 1984. She was buried in Prospect Hill Cemetery, York Twp., York Co., Pennsylvania.[43]

+ 335 m III. **Samuel Francis[8] Grove** was born in Peach Bottom Twp., York Co., Pennsylvania, in 1912. He died in Peach Bottom Twp., York Co., Pennsylvania, in 1913. Samuel Francis was buried in Slate Ridge Cemetery, Delta, Peach Bottom Twp., York Co., Pennsylvania.[20]

**162. Wayne Penny[7] Grove** (*Ida Melissa[6] Pegan, Henry[5], James[4], James[3], Andrew[2] Pagan, James[1]*) was born on March 17, 1886, in Lower Chanceford Twp., York Co., Pennsylvania. He was also known as **Wayne**. He was the son of Samuel Adams Grove and Ida Melissa Pegan (71). Wayne Penny died in York Twp., York Co., Pennsylvania, on January 13, 1972, at age 85. He was buried in Mount Rose Cemetery, Spring Garden Twp., York Co., Pennsylvania.[40]

Wayne Penny married **Hanna M. McCleary** on June 6, 1912, in York Co., Pennsylvania. They had seven children. Hanna M. McCleary was born in Fawn Twp., York Co., Pennsylvania, on June 29, 1885. Hanna M. reached age 87 and died in York Twp., York Co., Pennsylvania, on May 9, 1973. She was buried in Mount Rose Cemetery, Spring Garden Twp., York Co., Pennsylvania.[40]

Children of Wayne Penny Grove and Hanna M. McCleary:

+ 336 m I. **Wayne Kenneth[8] Grove II** was born in York Twp., York Co., Pennsylvania, on March 26, 1913. He died in York Twp., York Co., Pennsylvania, on August 17, 1978. Wayne Kenneth was buried in Prospect Hill Cemetery, York Twp., York Co., Pennsylvania.[43]

+ 337 f II. **Anita Mae[8] Grove** was born in York Twp., York Co., Pennsylvania, on August 8, 1915. She died in York Twp., York Co., Pennsylvania, on April 6, 2001. Anita Mae was buried in Mount Rose Cemetery, Spring Garden Twp., York Co., Pennsylvania.[40]

+ 338 f III. **Louise E.⁸ Grove** was born in York Twp., York Co., Pennsylvania, on September 18, 1917. She died in Thomasville, Jackson Twp., York Co., Pennsylvania, on December 6, 2000. Louise E. was buried in Rest Haven Cemetery, Hanover Twp., York Co., Pennsylvania.[127]

+ 339 m IV. **Dale W.⁸ Grove** was born in York Twp., York Co., Pennsylvania, on April 28, 1919. He died in York, York Co., Pennsylvania, on January 9, 2015. Dale W. was buried in Susquehanna Memorial Gardens Cemetery, York, York Co., Pennsylvania.[96]

+ 340 m V. **Herbert Adams⁸ Grove** was born in York Twp., York Co., Pennsylvania, on September 24, 1920. He died in Long Beach, Los Angeles Co., California, on January 5, 2011.

+ 341 m VI. **Carl Warren⁸ Grove** was born in York Twp., York Co., Pennsylvania, on August 19, 1922. He was also known as **Grovie**. Carl Warren died in York, York Co., Pennsylvania, on October 3, 2013. He was buried in Prospect Hill Cemetery, York Twp., York Co., Pennsylvania.[43]

+ 342 m VII. **Leonard Allison⁸ Grove** was born in York Twp., York Co., Pennsylvania, on August 20, 1927. He died in York, York Co., Pennsylvania, on January 10, 2017. Leonard Allison was buried in Prospect Hill Cemetery, York Twp., York Co., Pennsylvania.[43]

**163. William Allison⁷ Grove** (*Ida Melissa⁶ Pegan, Henry⁵, James⁴, James³, Andrew² Pagan, James¹*)

was born on October 24, 1887, in Chanceford Twp., York Co., Pennsylvania. He was also known as **Allison**. He was the son of Samuel Adams Grove and Ida Melissa Pegan (71). William Allison died in Detroit, Wayne Co., Michigan, on March 25, 1933, at age 45.[69] He was buried in Woodmere Cemetery, Detroit, Wayne Co., Michigan.[70]

William Allison married **Fannie Irene Alexander** before 1911. They had one son. Fannie Irene Alexander was born in York, York Co., Pennsylvania, in December 1886. She was also known as **Irene**. Fannie Irene reached age 35 and died in Phoenix, Maricopa Co., Arizona, on July 1, 1922. She was buried in Los Angeles, Los Angeles Co., California.[128]

Fanny Irene Alexander Grove's death certificate does not indicate which cemetery she is buried in, it only says she was buried in Los Angeles, California.

Son of William Allison Grove and Fannie Irene Alexander:

+ 343 m I. **Alexander Allison⁸ Grove** was born in Detroit, Wayne Co., Michigan, in 1911. He was also known as **Alex**. Alexander Allison died after 1930.

**164. Claire Jamison⁷ Grove** (*Ida Melissa⁶ Pegan, Henry⁵, James⁴, James³, Andrew² Pagan, James¹*) was born on December 4, 1888, in Chanceford Twp., York Co., Pennsylvania. He was the son of Samuel Adams Grove and Ida Melissa Pegan (71). Claire Jamison died in York, York Co., Pennsylvania, on September 15, 1987, at age 98. He was buried in Longstown United Methodist Cemetery, York Twp., York Co., Pennsylvania.[71]

Claire Jamison married **Blanche Gertrude Gable** before 1917. They had one daughter. Blanche Gertrude Gable was born in York, York Co., Pennsylvania, on November 13, 1892. Blanche Gertrude reached age 76 and died in York, York Co., Pennsylvania, in September 1969. She was buried in Longstown United Methodist Cemetery, York Twp., York Co., Pennsylvania.[71]

Daughter of Claire Jamison Grove and Blanche Gertrude Gable:

+ 344 f I. **Gertrude Melissa**[8] **Grove** was born in York, York Co., Pennsylvania, on September 20, 1917. She died in Monterey, Monterey Co., California, on November 1, 1972.

**165. Anna Matilda**[7] **Grove** (*Ida Melissa*[6] *Pegan, Henry*[5]*, James*[4]*, James*[3]*, Andrew*[2] *Pagan, James*[1]) was born on June 17, 1891, in Peach Bottom Twp., York Co., Pennsylvania. She was the daughter of Samuel Adams Grove and Ida Melissa Pegan (71). Anna Matilda died in Springettsbury Twp., York Co., Pennsylvania, on February 24, 1963, at age 71. She was buried in Longstown United Methodist Cemetery, York Twp., York Co., Pennsylvania.[71]

Anna Matilda married **Melvin Benjamin Franklin Horn** on March 20, 1913, in York Co., Pennsylvania. They had four children. Melvin Benjamin Franklin Horn was born in Springettsbury Twp., York Co., Pennsylvania, on May 22, 1891. Melvin Benjamin Franklin reached age 75 and died in York, York Co., Pennsylvania, on December 11, 1966. He was buried in Longstown United Methodist Cemetery, York Twp., York Co., Pennsylvania.[71]

Children of Anna Matilda Grove and Melvin Benjamin Franklin Horn:

+ 345 m I. **Earnest Benjamin**[8] **Horn** was born in Springettsbury Twp., York Co., Pennsylvania, on March 12, 1915. He died in Springettsbury Twp., York Co., Pennsylvania, on March 12, 1915. Earnest Benjamin was buried in Longstown United Methodist Cemetery, York Twp., York Co., Pennsylvania.[71]

+ 346 f II. **Sarah Esther**[8] **Horn** was born in Springettsbury Twp., York Co., Pennsylvania, on May 22, 1916. She was also known as **Esther**. Sarah Esther died in York Twp., York Co., Pennsylvania, on January 22, 1994. She was buried in Longstown United Methodist Cemetery, York Twp., York Co., Pennsylvania.[71]

+ 347 m III. **Rodger Melvin**[8] **Horn** was born in Springettsbury Twp., York Co., Pennsylvania, on October 26, 1919. He died in Dallastown, Windsor Twp., York Co., Pennsylvania, on July 10, 2009. Rodger Melvin was buried in Mount Rose Cemetery, Spring Garden Twp., York Co., Pennsylvania.[40]

+ 348 f IV. **Romaine Grove**[8] **Horn** was born in Springettsbury Twp., York Co., Pennsylvania, on October 31, 1921. She died in York Twp., York Co., Pennsylvania, on May 3, 2004. Romaine Grove was buried in Prospect Hill Cemetery, York Twp., York Co., Pennsylvania.[43]

**166. Infant Samuel M.**[7] **Grove** (*Ida Melissa*[6] *Pegan, Henry*[5]*, James*[4]*, James*[3]*, Andrew*[2] *Pagan, James*[1]) was born on February 13, 1893, in Peach Bottom Twp., York Co., Pennsylvania. He was the son of Samuel Adams Grove and Ida Melissa Pegan (71). Infant Samuel M. died in Peach Bottom Twp., York Co., Pennsylvania, on October 4, 1893. He was buried in Old Guinston Church Cemetery, Airville, Chanceford Twp., York Co., Pennsylvania.[21]

**167. Sara Mary**[7] **Grove** (*Ida Melissa*[6] *Pegan, Henry*[5]*, James*[4]*, James*[3]*, Andrew*[2] *Pagan, James*[1]) was born on September 13, 1894, in Peach Bottom Twp., York Co., Pennsylvania. She was the daughter of Samuel Adams Grove and Ida Melissa Pegan (71). Sara Mary died in York, York Co., Pennsylvania, about May 17, 1973 at age 78. She was buried in Mount Rose Cemetery, Spring Garden Twp., York Co., Pennsylvania.[40]

Childless.

Sara Mary married **Benjamin Harrison Sinclair** about 1925. Benjamin Harrison Sinclair was born in Lower Chanceford Twp., York Co., Pennsylvania, on October 2, 1888. He was also known as **Harry**. Benjamin Harrison reached age 74 and died in York, York Co., Pennsylvania, on March 2, 1963. He was buried in Mount Rose Cemetery, Spring Garden Twp., York Co., Pennsylvania.[40]

168. **James Russell**[7] **Grove** (*Ida Melissa*[6] *Pegan, Henry*[5], *James*[4], *James*[3], *Andrew*[2] *Pagan, James*[1]) was born on March 13, 1897, in Peach Bottom Twp., York Co., Pennsylvania. He was also known as **Russell**. He was the son of Samuel Adams Grove and Ida Melissa Pegan (71). James Russell died in York, York Co., Pennsylvania, on November 1, 1977, at age 80. He was buried in Freysville Cemetery, Windsor Twp., York Co., Pennsylvania.[72]

Childless.

James Russell married **Helen May Sentz** on November 12, 1919, in York Co., Pennsylvania. Helen May Sentz was born in Windsor Twp., York Co., Pennsylvania, on January 25, 1898. Helen May reached age 66 and died in York, York Co., Pennsylvania, on June 9, 1964. She was buried in Freysville Cemetery, Windsor Twp., York Co., Pennsylvania.[72]

169. **Samuel Gail**[7] **Grove II** (*Ida Melissa*[6] *Pegan, Henry*[5], *James*[4], *James*[3], *Andrew*[2] *Pagan, James*[1]) was born on May 20, 1898, in Peach Bottom Twp., York Co., Pennsylvania. He was the son of Samuel Adams Grove and Ida Melissa Pegan (71). Samuel Gail died in York, York Co., Pennsylvania, in May 1978 at age 79. He was buried in Stony Brook Mennonite Cemetery, York, York Co., Pennsylvania.[73]

Samuel Gail married **Ada Irene Witmer** about 1921. They had one son. Ada Irene Witmer was born in Springettsbury Twp., York Co., Pennsylvania, on July 20, 1899. Ada Irene reached age 92 and died in York, York Co., Pennsylvania? in August 1991. She was buried in Stony Brook Mennonite Cemetery, York, York Co., Pennsylvania.[73]

Son of Samuel Gail Grove II and Ada Irene Witmer:

+ 349 m I. **Donald W.**[8] **Grove** was born in Windsor Twp., York Co., Pennsylvania, on October 11, 1923. He died in Mesa, Maricopa Co., Arizona on April 2, 1973. Donald W. is buried in Stony Brook Mennonite Cemetery, York, York Co., Pennsylvania.[73]

170. **John Paul**[7] **Grove** (*Alice Eva*[6] *Pegan, Henry*[5], *James*[4], *James*[3], *Andrew*[2] *Pagan, James*[1]) was born on December 29, 1894, in Lower Chanceford Twp., York Co., Pennsylvania. He was also known as **Paul**. He was the son of William Wilkins Grove and Alice Eva Pegan (72). John Paul died in York, York Co., Pennsylvania, on April 16, 1963, at age 68. He was buried in Old Guinston Church Cemetery, Airville, Chanceford Twp., York Co., Pennsylvania.[21]

John Paul married **Ida Mae Workinger** before 1920. They had two daughters. Ida Mae Workinger was born in East Hopewell Twp., York Co., Pennsylvania, on April 26, 1895. Ida Mae reached age 43 and died in Lower Chanceford Twp., York Co., Pennsylvania, on August 28, 1938. She was buried in Old Guinston Church Cemetery, Airville, Chanceford Twp., York Co., Pennsylvania.[21]

John Paul Grove married **Pauline Odessa Ruff** after 1940. They had one daughter. Pauline Odessa Ruff was born in Airville, Chanceford Twp., York Co., Pennsylvania, on October 10, 1909. Pauline Odessa reached age 95 and died in Red Lion, York Twp., York Co., Pennsylvania, on March 14, 2005. She was buried in Old Guinston Church Cemetery, Airville, Chanceford Twp., York Co., Pennsylvania.[21]

Daughters of John Paul Grove and Ida Mae Workinger:

+ 350 f I. **E. Jean**[8] **Grove** was born in High Rock, Lower Chanceford Twp., York Co., Pennsylvania, on November 27, 1920. She was also known as **Jean**. E. Jean died in Windsor

Twp., York Co., Pennsylvania, on June 30, 2016.

+ 351 f II. **Bernice Elanora[8] Grove** was born in High Rock, Lower Chanceford Twp., York Co., Pennsylvania, on July 21, 1927. She died in Norristown, Montgomery Co., Pennsylvania, on November 15, 1998.

**171. J. Clyde[7] Wickersham** (*Mary Lena[6] Pegan, Henry[5], James[4], James[3], Andrew[2] Pagan, James[1]*) was born on April 28, 1894, in Russellville, Upper Oxford Twp., Chester Co., Pennsylvania. He was the son of Robert Ellsworth Wickersham and Mary Lena Pegan (73). J. Clyde died in Russellville, Upper Oxford Twp., Chester Co., Pennsylvania, on November 3, 1967, at age 73. He was buried in Oxford Cemetery, Oxford, Chester Co., Pennsylvania.[37]

May have never married.

**172. Mary Adelaide[7] Wickersham** (*Mary Lena[6] Pegan, Henry[5], James[4], James[3], Andrew[2] Pagan, James[1]*) was born on June 8, 1904, in Russellville, Upper Oxford Twp., Chester Co., Pennsylvania. She was the daughter of Robert Ellsworth Wickersham and Mary Lena Pegan (73). Mary Adelaide died in Contoocook, Merrimack Co., New Hampshire, on October 12, 1997, at age 93. She was buried in Upper Octarara Church Cemetery, Parkesburg, Sadbury Twp., Chester Co., Pennsylvania.[74]

Mary Adelaide married **Edgar Drew Miller** before 1933. They had one son. Edgar Drew Miller was born in Paradise Twp., Lancaster Co., Pennsylvania, on March 8, 1902. Edgar Drew reached age 86 and died in Downingtown, Chester Co., Pennsylvania, on October 11, 1988. He was buried in Upper Octarara Church Cemetery, Parkesburg, Sadbury Twp., Chester Co., Pennsylvania.[74]

Son of Mary Adelaide Wickersham and Edgar Drew Miller:

+ 352 m I. **Robert Wayne[8] Miller** was born in Coatesville, Valley Twp., Chester Co., Pennsylvania, on September 23, 1933. He was also known as **Wayne; R. Wayne Miller**. Robert Wayne died in Hopkinton, Merrimack Co., New Hampshire, on February 7, 1994. He was buried in Upper Octarara Church Cemetery, Parkesburg, Sadbury Twp., Chester Co., Pennsylvania.[74]

**173. Ruth Estella[7] Pegan** (*Harry Hutton[6], Henry[5], James[4], James[3], Andrew[2] Pagan, James[1]*) was born on January 6, 1899, in Spring Grove, Jackson Twp., York Co., Pennsylvania. She was the daughter of Harry Hutton Pegan (75) and Lizzie Ann Bailey. Ruth Estella died in Spring Grove, Jackson Twp., York Co., Pennsylvania, in August 1974 at age 75. She was buried in Spring Grove Cemetery, Jackson Twp., York Co., Pennsylvania.[24]

Never married.

Ruth E. Pegan and her brother Philip E. Pegan operated the Spring Grove News Service in Spring Grove, Pennsylvania.

**174. Philip Eugene[7] Pegan** (*Harry Hutton[6], Henry[5], James[4], James[3], Andrew[2] Pagan, James[1]*) was born on January 20, 1900, in Spring Grove, Jackson Twp., York Co., Pennsylvania. He was the son of Harry Hutton Pegan (75) and Lizzie Ann Bailey. Philip Eugene died in York, York Co., Pennsylvania, in May 1970 at age 70. He was buried in Spring Grove Cemetery, Jackson Twp., York Co., Pennsylvania.[24]

Never married.

Philip Eugene Pegan and his sister Ruth E. Pegan were partners in the Spring Grove News Service in Spring Grove, Jackson Twp., York Co., Pennsylvania for many years.

**175. Nathan Neil[7] Pegan** (*Harry Hutton[6], Henry[5], James[4], James[3], Andrew[2] Pagan, James[1]*) was born on August 29, 1902, in Spring Grove, Jackson Twp., York Co., Pennsylvania. He was the son of Harry Hutton Pegan (75) and Lizzie Ann Bailey. Nathan Neil died in Spring Grove, Jackson Twp., York Co., Pennsylvania, on February 6, 1974, at age 71. He was buried in Spring Grove Cemetery, Jackson Twp., York Co., Pennsylvania.[24]

He married **Bessie Sue Gunnet** bef. 1919. They had two daughters. Bessie Sue Gunnet was born in North Codorus Twp., York Co., Pennsylvania, on February 14, 1901. Bessie Sue reached age 78 and died in Spring Grove, Jackson Twp., York Co., Pennsylvania, on April 15, 1979. She was buried in Spring Grove Cemetery, Jackson Twp., York Co., Pennsylvania.[24]

Daughters of Nathan Neil Pegan and Bessie Sue Gunnet:

+ 353 f  I.  **Evelyn R.**[8] **Pegan** was born in Spring Grove, Jackson Twp., York Co., Pennsylvania, on August 30, 1919. She died in Spring Grove Jackson Twp., York Co., Pennsylvania, on May 19, 1972.,

+ 354 f  II.  **Ethel Virginia**[8] **Pegan** was born in Spring Grove, Jackson Twp., York Co., Pennsylvania, in 1926. She was also known as **Etts**.

**176. Jessie Eliza**[7] **Manifold** (*Jennie Elizabeth*[6] *Adams, Sarah Eliza*[5] *Pegan, James*[4]*, James*[3]*, Andrew*[2] *Pagan, James*[1]) was born on July 11, 1903, in East Hopewell Twp., York Co., Pennsylvania. She was the daughter of Samuel Smith Manifold and Jennie Elizabeth Adams (76). Jessie Eliza died in Stewartstown, Hopewell Twp., York Co., Pennsylvania, on November 17, 1978. She was buried in Round Hill Presbyterian Church Cemetery, Cross Roads, East Hopewell Twp., York Co., Pennsylvania.[39]

Jessie Eliza married **Harold Manifold Trout** before 1938. They had two children. Harold Manifold Trout was born in East Hopewell Twp., York Co., Pennsylvania, on October 22, 1903. Harold Manifold reached age 91 and died in Stewartstown, Hopewell Twp., York Co., Pennsylvania, on February 24, 1995. He was buried in Round Hill Presbyterian Church Cemetery, Cross Roads, East Hopewell Twp., York Co., Pennsylvania.[39]

Children of Jessie Eliza Manifold and Harold Manifold Trout:

+ 355 f  I.  **Karen Marie**[8] **Trout** was born in East Hopewell Twp., York Co., Pennsylvania, in 1938.

+ 356 m  II.  **Son**[8] **Trout** was born in East Hopewell Twp., York Co., Pennsylvania, on September 5, 1941. He died in East Hopewell Twp., York Co., Pennsylvania, on September 5, 1941. Son was buried in Round Hill Presbyterian Church Cemetery, Cross Roads, East Hopewell Twp., York Co., Pennsylvania.[39]

**177. Samuel Benjamin**[7] **Manifold** (*Jennie Elizabeth*[6] *Adams, Sarah Eliza*[5] *Pegan, James*[4]*, James*[3]*, Andrew*[2] *Pagan, James*[1]) was born on December 31, 1904, in East Hopewell Twp., York Co., Pennsylvania. He was also known as **Benjamin**. He was the son of Samuel Smith Manifold and Jennie Elizabeth Adams (76). Samuel Benjamin died in Stewartstown, Hopewell Twp., York Co., Pennsylvania, in April 1987 at age 82. He was buried in Round Hill Presbyterian Church Cemetery, Cross Roads, East Hopewell Twp., York Co., Pennsylvania.[39]

Samuel Benjamin married **Grace Veach** before 1930. They had five children. Grace Veach was born in East Hopewell Twp., York Co., Pennsylvania, on April 28, 1906. Grace reached age 90 and died in York, York Co., Pennsylvania, on December 19, 1996. She was buried in Round Hill Presbyterian Church Cemetery, Cross Roads, East Hopewell Twp., York Co., Pennsylvania.[39]

Samuel Benjamin Manifold and Grace Veach had five children, including:

+ 357 f  I.  **Grace Elaine**[8] **Manifold** was born in East Hopewell Twp., York Co., Pennsylvania, in 1930. She was also known as **Elaine**. Grace Elaine died after 2015.

+ 358 m II. **Benjamin Eugene**[8] **Manifold** was born in East Hopewell Twp., York Co., Pennsylvania, on February 28, 1933. He was also known as **Eugene**. Benjamin Eugene died in Stewartstown, Hopewell Twp., York Co., Pennsylvania, on July 28, 1997. He was buried in Round Hill Presbyterian Church Cemetery, Cross Roads, East Hopewell Twp., York Co., Pennsylvania.[39]

+ 359 f III. **Betty Lou**[8] **Manifold** was born in Chanceford Twp., York Co., Pennsylvania, in 1938.

+ 360 f I. **Daughter**[8] **Manifold**.

**178. Margaret Eleanor**[7] **Manifold** (*Jennie Elizabeth*[6] *Adams, Sarah Eliza*[5] *Pegan, James*[4]*, James*[3]*, Andrew*[2] *Pagan, James*[1]) was born on November 3, 1908, in East Hopewell Twp., York Co., Pennsylvania. She was the daughter of Samuel Smith Manifold and Jennie Elizabeth Adams (76). Margaret Eleanor lived before 2009 in Shrewsbury, Shrewsbury Twp., York Co., Pennsylvania. She died in a hospital in York, York Co., Pennsylvania, on May 9, 2009, at age 100. Margaret Eleanor was buried in Stewartstown Cemetery, Stewartstown, Hopewell Twp., York Co., Pennsylvania.[76]

Margaret Eleanor married **Gemmill Weist Lanius** on January 19, 1935, in York Co., Pennsylvania. They had three children. Gemmill Weist Lanius was born in Hopewell Twp., York Co., Pennsylvania, on September 5, 1907. Gemmill Weist reached age 63 and died in Stewartstown, Hopewell Twp., York Co., Pennsylvania, on January 18, 1971. He was buried in Stewartstown Cemetery, Stewartstown, Hopewell Twp., York Co., Pennsylvania.[76]

The Roy D. Pegan file says Gemmill and Margaret Eleanor Manifold Lanius had three children, but he named only their son Richard Weist Lanius. The other two children, a boy and a girl, probably died in infancy but there are no Pennsylvania death certificates or cemetery records for them. They are not mentioned in Margaret Eleanor Manifold Lanius Schuman's obituary.[2]

Margaret Eleanor Manifold Lanius married **Curvin B. Schuman** on May 24, 1973. Curvin B. Schuman was born in Mannheim Twp., York Co., Pennsylvania, on October 20, 1906. Curvin B. reached age 91 and died in Shrewsbury, Shrewsbury Twp., York Co., Pennsylvania, on November 15, 1997. He was buried in Saint Jacobs Stone Church Cemetery, Glenville, Codorus Twp., York Co., Pennsylvania.[129]

Children of Margaret Eleanor Manifold and Gemmill Weist Lanius:

+ 361 m I. **Richard Weist**[8] **Lanius** was born in Hopewell Twp., York Co., Pennsylvania, on August 29, 1935. He was also known as **Zeke**. Richard Weist died in a hospital in Lebanon, North Lebanon Twp.,Lebanon Co., Pennsylvania, on November 22, 1983. He was buried in Stewartstown Cemetery, Stewartstown, Hopewell Twp., York Co., Pennsylvania.[76]

+ 362 m II. **Infant Son**[8] **Lanius** was born after 1935 and probably died young.

+ 363 f III. **Infant Daughter**[8] **Lanius** was born after 1935 and probably died young.

**179. Elizabeth L.**[7] **Manifold** (*Jennie Elizabeth*[6] *Adams, Sarah Eliza*[5] *Pegan, James*[4]*, James*[3]*, Andrew*[2] *Pagan, James*[1]) was born on November 18, 1911, in East Hopewell Twp., York Co., Pennsylvania. She was the daughter of Samuel Smith Manifold and Jennie Elizabeth Adams (76). Elizabeth L. died in Woodbridge, Prince William Co., Virginia, on January 18, 2007, at age 95. She was buried in Round Hill Presbyterian Church Cemetery, Cross Roads, East Hopewell Twp., York Co., Pennsylvania.[39]

Childless.

Elizabeth L. married **Charles Frederick Stier** on June 20, 1936. They had one son. Charles Frederick

Stier was born in Philadelphia, Philadelphia Co., Pennsylvania, on December 25, 1909. Charles Frederick reached age 85 and died in Alexandria, Virginia, on May 21, 1995. He was buried in Round Hill Presbyterian Church Cemetery, Cross Roads, East Hopewell Twp., York Co., Pennsylvania.[39]

**180. Son⁷ Adams** (*Samuel Jamieson⁶, Sarah Eliza⁵ Pegan, James⁴, James³, Andrew² Pagan, James¹*) was born on March 25, 1908, in High Rock, Lower Chanceford Twp., York Co., Pennsylvania. He was the son of Samuel Jamieson Adams II (78) and Ella Margaret Grove. Son died in High Rock, Lower Chanceford Twp., York Co., Pennsylvania, on March 25, 1908. He was buried in Old Guinston Church Cemetery, Airville, Chanceford Twp., York Co., Pennsylvania.[21]

**181. Gladys Grove⁷ Adams** (*Samuel Jamieson⁶, Sarah Eliza⁵ Pegan, James⁴, James³, Andrew² Pagan, James¹*) was born on July 10, 1909, in Chanceford Twp., York Co., Pennsylvania. She was the daughter of Samuel Jamieson Adams II (78) and Ella Margaret Grove. Gladys Grove died in Bel Air, Harford Co., Maryland, on November 14, 2000, at age 91.

Gladys Grove married **McClellan F. Baxter** before 1934. They had two sons. McClellan F. Baxter was born in Baltimore, Baltimore Co., Maryland, on May 5, 1910. McClellan F. reached age 86 and died in Bel Air, Harford Co., Maryland, on April 25, 1997.

Sons of Gladys Grove Adams and McClellan F. Baxter:

+ 364 m I. **Gerard⁸ Baxter** was born in Cardiff, Harford Co., Maryland, in 1934.

+ 365 m II. **Dennis⁸ Baxter** was born in Baltimore, Baltimore Co., Maryland, in 1939.

**182. Sara Agnes⁷ Adams** (*Samuel Jamieson⁶, Sarah Eliza⁵ Pegan, James⁴, James³, Andrew² Pagan, James¹*) was born on October 30, 1911, in Chanceford Twp., York Co., Pennsylvania. She was the daughter of Samuel Jamieson Adams II (78) and Ella Margaret Grove. Sara Agnes died in Winchester, Frederick Co., Virginia,

on January 17, 1994, at age 82. She was buried in Shenandoah Memorial Park Cemetery, Winchester, Frederick Co., Virginia.[77]

Sara Agnes married **Lennie B. Michael** before 1940. Lennie B. Michael was born in Ukraine, Russia, on August 3, 1910. Lennie B. lived in Middletown Twp., Delaware Co., Pennsylvania. He reached age 82 and died in Winchester, Frederick Co., Virginia, on February 12, 1993. Lennie B. was buried in Shenandoah Memorial Park Cemetery, Winchester, Frederick Co., Virginia.[77]

**183. David Earl⁷ Grove** (*James Pegan⁶, Margaret Jane⁵ Pegan, James⁴, James³, Andrew² Pagan, James¹*) was born on December 17, 1909, in York, York Co., Pennsylvania. He was also known as **Earl**. He was the son of James Pegan Grove (79) and Sarah Blanche Jamieson. David Earl died in York, York Co., Pennsylvania, on December 29, 1994, at age 85. He was buried in Mount Rose Cemetery, Spring Garden Twp., York Co., Pennsylvania.[40]

David Earl married **Margaret Arlene Boring** about 1929. They divorced. They had one daughter. Margaret Arlene Boring was born in North York, York Co., Pennsylvania, on April 9, 1909. Margaret Arlene reached age 83 and died in York, York Co., Pennsylvania, on March 7, 1993.

Daughter of David Earl Grove and Margaret Arlene Boring:

+ 366 f I. **Carolyn⁸ Grove** was born in York Co., Pennsylvania, in 1931.

**184. Lulu⁷ Grove** (*Vinton Lemmon⁶, Margaret Jane⁵ Pegan, James⁴, James³, Andrew² Pagan, James¹*) was born in 1914 in Chanceford Twp., York Co., Pennsylvania. She was the daughter of Vinton Lemmon Grove (80) and Elsie May Boyd. Lulu died in Chanceford Twp., York Co., Pennsylvania, in 1915 at age one. She was buried in Old Guinston Church Cemetery, Airville, Chanceford Twp., York Co., Pennsylvania.[20]

**185. Emory⁷ Grove** (*Vinton Lemmon⁶, Margaret Jane⁵ Pegan, James⁴, James³, Andrew² Pagan, James¹*) was born on August 29, 1921, in Chanceford Twp., York Co., Pennsylvania. He was the son of

Vinton Lemmon Grove (80) and Elsie May Boyd. Emory died in Red Lion, York Twp., York Co., Pennsylvania, on June 18, 1999, at age 77. He was buried in Red Lion Cemetery, Red Lion, York Twp., York Co., Pennsylvania.[79, 80]

Emory married **Helen Janette Richardson** before 1944. They had two children. Helen Janette Richardson was born in Lower Chanceford Twp., York Co., Pennsylvania, on January 21, 1923. She was also known as **Janette**. Helen Janette reached age 79 and died in Red Lion, York Twp., York Co., Pennsylvania, on September 1, 2002. She was buried in Red Lion Cemetery, Red Lion, York Twp., York Co., Pennsylvania.[80]

# 8th Generation

**186. Luther Maurice⁸ Walton** (*Elmer⁷, Hannah Margaret⁶ Nimlow, Margaret⁵ Pegan, Andrew⁴, James³, Andrew² Pagan, James¹*) was born on January 15, 1892, in Mt. Nebo, Martic Twp., Lancaster Co., Pennsylvania. He was the son of Elmer Walton (81) and Harriet Jane Appleton. Luther Maurice died in Reading, Berks Co., Pennsylvania, on October 25, 1950, at age 58. He was buried in Morris Cemetery, Phoenixville, Schuylkill Twp., Chester Co., Pennsylvania.[81]

Luther Maurice married **Katherine Mae Hutchinson** in 1916. They had one daughter. Katherine Mae Hutchinson was born in Reading, Berks Co., Pennsylvania, on October 2, 1892. Katherine Mae reached age 50 and died in Reading, Berks Co., Pennsylvania, on November 8, 1942. She was buried in Charles Evans Cemetery, Reading, Berks Co., Pennsylvania.[130]

Daughter of Luther Maurice Walton and Katherine Mae Hutchinson:

+ 367 f I. **Margaret⁹ Walton** was born in Philadelphia, Philadelphia Co., Pennsylvania, on April 7, 1920. She died in Alexandria, Porter Twp., Huntingdon Co., Pennsylvania, on May 25, 2002. Margaret was buried in Morris Cemetery, Phoenixville, Schuylkill Twp., Chester Co., Pennsylvania.[81]

**187. Mary Margaret⁸ Walton** (*Elmer⁷, Hannah Margaret⁶ Nimlow, Margaret⁵ Pegan, Andrew⁴, James³, Andrew² Pagan, James¹*) was born on January 31, 1894, in Mt. Nebo, Martic Twp., Lancaster Co., Pennsylvania. She was the daughter of Elmer Walton (81) and Harriet Jane Appleton. Mary Margaret died in Holtwood, Martic Twp., Lancaster Co., Pennsylvania, on October 26, 1963, at age 69. She was buried in Mount Nebo United Methodist Church Cemetery, Pequea, Pequea Twp., Lancaster Co., Pennsylvania.[82]

Mary Margaret married **Emerson Douts** in 1915. They had five children. Emerson Douts was born in Martic Twp., Lancaster Co., Pennsylvania, on June 20, 1890. Emerson reached age 87 and died in Holtwood, Martic Twp., Lancaster Co., Pennsylvania, on August 19, 1977. He was buried in Mount Nebo United Methodist Church Cemetery, Pequea, Pequea Twp., Lancaster Co., Pennsylvania.[59]

Children of Mary Margaret Walton and Emerson Douts:

+ 368 f I. **Rebecca Walton⁹ Douts** was born in Martic Twp., Lancaster Co., Pennsylvania, on May 1, 1917. She died in Quarryville, East Drumore Twp., Lancaster Co., Pennsylvania, on August 4, 2006. Rebecca Walton was buried in Mount Nebo United Methodist Church Cemetery, Pequea, Pequea Twp., Lancaster Co., Pennsylvania.[82]

+ 369 m II. **John Luther⁹ Douts** was born in Martic Twp., Lancaster Co., Pennsylvania, on March 15, 1920. He died in Minot, Ward Co., North Dakota, on March 23, 2006. John Luther was buried in Bethel Cemetery, Battleview, Burke Co., North Dakota.[131]

+ 370 m III. **Henry Elmer⁹ Douts** was born in Martic Twp., Lancaster Co., Pennsylvania, on January 19, 1922. He was also known as **Elmer**. Henry Elmer died in Saint Thomas, Franklin Co., Pennsylvania, on September 25, 2001. He was buried in Mount Nebo United Methodist Church Cemetery, Pequea, Pequea Twp., Lancaster Co., Pennsylvania.[82]

+ 371 f IV. **Anna Jane[9] Douts** was born in Martic Twp., Lancaster Co., Pennsylvania, on June 7, 1923. She was also known as **Jane**.

+ 372 m V. **Charles Emerson[9] Douts** was born in Martic Twp., Lancaster Co., Pennsylvania, on November 4, 1926. He died in Washington Boro, Manor Twp., Lancaster Co., Pennsylvania, on November 2, 2016. Charles Emerson was buried in Washington Boro Cemetery, Manor Twp., Lancaster Co., Pennsylvania.[42]

**188. Luella A.[8] Walton** (*Elmer[7], Hannah Margaret[6] Nimlow, Margaret[5] Pegan, Andrew[4], James[3], Andrew[2] Pagan, James[1]*) was born on September 17, 1897, in Lancaster, Lancaster Co., Pennsylvania. She was the daughter of Elmer Walton (81) and Harriet Jane Appleton. Luella A. died in Lancaster, Lancaster Co., Pennsylvania, on February 14, 1920, at age 22. She was buried in Greenwood Cemetery, Lancaster, Lancaster Co., Pennsylvania.[2, 25]

Luella A. married **James Arthur Norris** about 1917. They had one son. James Arthur Norris was born in Lancaster, Lancaster Co., Pennsylvania, on March 31, 1897. He was also known as **Arthur**. James Arthur reached age 84 and died in Lancaster, Lancaster Co., Pennsylvania, on November 4, 1981. He was buried in Greenwood Cemetery, Lancaster, Lancaster Co., Pennsylvania.[25]

Son of Luella A. Walton and James Arthur Norris:

+ 373 m I. **James Lawrence[9] Norris II** was born in Lancaster, Lancaster Co., Pennsylvania, on December 12, 1918. He died in Boothbay Harbor, Lincoln Co., Maine, on July 15, 1988. James Lawrence was buried in Bergstrasse Cemetery, Ephrata, Ephrata Twp., Lancaster Co., Pennsylvania.[132]

**189. Violet[8] Ortman** (*Ida[7] Akins, Anna Mary[6] Nimlow, Margaret[5] Pegan, Andrew[4], James[3], Andrew[2] Pagan, James[1]*) was born on October 24, 1901, in Manor Twp., Lancaster Co., Pennsylvania. She was the daughter of Winfield Scott Ortman and Ida Akins (84). Violet died in East Vincent Twp., Chester Co., Pennsylvania, on October 16, 1918, at age 16. She was buried in Washington Boro Cemetery, Manor Twp., Lancaster Co., Pennsylvania.[42]

Violet, although clearly the daughter of Winfield Scott and Ida Akins Ortman, is not listed by Roy D. Pegan in his genealogy of James and Sarah Brannon Pegan and their descendants.[2]

**190. Minerva Mae[8] Ortman** (*Ida[7] Akins, Anna Mary[6] Nimlow, Margaret[5] Pegan, Andrew[4], James[3], Andrew[2] Pagan, James[1]*) was born on September 18, 1908, in Manor Twp., Lancaster Co., Pennsylvania. She was the daughter of Winfield Scott Ortman and Ida Akins (84). Minerva Mae died in New Oxford Twp., Adams Co., Pennsylvania or Hanover, York Co., Pennsylvania, on March 7, 1997, at age 88.

Minerva Mae married **Norman Lloyd Grimm** in 1927. They had four children. Norman Lloyd Grimm was born in Paradise Twp., York Co., Pennsylvania, on March 18, 1907. Norman Lloyd died in McSherrystown, Adams Co., Pennsylvania? between 1944 and 1956.

Minerva Mae Ortman Grimm married **Unknown Reaver** after 1944.

Children of Minerva Mae Ortman and Norman Lloyd Grimm:

+ 374 f I. **Alberta[9] Grimm** was born in Paradise Twp., York Co., Pennsylvania, in 1928.

+ 375 f II. **Norma Jean[9] Grimm** was born in York, York Co., Pennsylvania, in 1933.

+ 376 m III. **Earl D.[9] Grimm** was born in Pennsylvania on July 13, 1940.

+ 377 m IV. **Phillip Lee[9] Grimm** was born in McSherrystown, Adams Co., Pennsylvania, on January 27, 1943.

He died in West Manheim Twp., York Co., Pennsylvania, on July 15, 1961. Phillip Lee was buried in Rest Haven Cemetery, Hanover Twp., York Co., Pennsylvania.[126]

**191. Lloyd⁸ Niblock** (*Clarence Watson⁷, George Niblock⁶ (Nimlow II), Margaret⁵ Pegan, Andrew⁴, James³, Andrew² Pagan, James¹*) was born in 1905 in Conoy Twp., Lancaster Co., Pennsylvania. He was the son of Clarence Watson Niblock (87) and Bertha Viola McCord. Lloyd died in Conoy Twp., Lancaster Co., Pennsylvania? in 1972 at age 67. He was buried in Bainbridge Public Cemetery, Conoy Twp., Lancaster Co., Pennsylvania.[45]

May have never married.

**192. Bertha Viola⁸ Niblock** (*Clarence Watson⁷, George Niblock⁶ (Nimlow II), Margaret⁵ Pegan, Andrew⁴, James³, Andrew² Pagan, James¹*) was born on July 22, 1907, in Conoy Twp., Lancaster Co., Pennsylvania. She was also known as **Viola**. She was the daughter of Clarence Watson Niblock (87) and Bertha Viola McCord. Bertha Viola died in Conoy Twp., Lancaster Co., Pennsylvania, on June 20, 1921, at age 13. She was buried in Bainbridge Public Cemetery, Conoy Twp., Lancaster Co., Pennsylvania.[45]

**193. Dorothy Everda⁸ Niblock** (*Clarence Watson⁷, George Niblock⁶ (Nimlow II), Margaret⁵ Pegan, Andrew⁴, James³, Andrew² Pagan, James¹*) was born on December 27, 1910, in Nine Points, Bart Twp., Lancaster Co., Pennsylvania. She was the daughter of Clarence Watson Niblock (87) and Bertha Viola McCord. Dorothy Everda died in Lancaster, Lancaster Co., Pennsylvania, on June 4, 1991, at age 80. She was buried in Goods Mennonite Church Cemetery, Elizabethtown, Mt. Joy Twp., Lancaster Co., Pennsylvania.[85]

She married **James S. Reisinger** before 1928. They had three children. James S. Reisinger was born in Tyrone Twp., Perry Co., Pennsylvania, on December 20, 1902. James S. reached age 54 and died in Bainbridge, Conoy Twp., Lancaster Co., Pennsylvania, on January 31, 1957. He was buried in Goods Mennonite Church Cemetery, Elizabethtown, Mt. Joy Twp., Lancaster Co., Pennsylvania.[85]

Dorothy Everda Niblock Reisinger married **Charles T. Kuhn** after 1957. Charles T Kuhn was born in Brown Twp., Mifflin Co., Pennsylvania, on August 7, 1908. Charles T reached age 67 and died in Lancaster, Lancaster Co., Pennsylvania, on February 2, 1976. He was buried in Manor Church Cemetery, Lancaster, Lancaster Co., Pennsylvania.[133]

Children of Dorothy Everda Niblock and James S. Reisinger:

+ 378  f  I.  **Dorothy V.⁹ Reisinger** was born in Bainbridge, Conoy Twp., Lancaster Co., Pennsylvania, on May 28, 1928.

+ 379  f  II.  **Natalie Arlene⁹ Reisinger** was born in Bainbridge, Conoy Twp., Lancaster Co., Pennsylvania, on July 3, 1930. She was also known as **Arlene**. Natalie Arlene died in Mount Joy Twp., Lancaster Co., Pennsylvania, on June 20, 2001.

+ 380  m  III.  **James Elwood⁹ Reisinger** was born in Bainbridge, Conoy Twp., Lancaster Co., Pennsylvania, on January 5, 1933. He died in Lebanon, North Lebanon Twp., Lebanon Co., Pennsylvania, on November 10, 1998. James Elwood was buried in Goods Mennonite Church Cemetery, Elizabethtown, Mt. Joy Twp., Lancaster Co., Pennsylvania.[85]

**194. Melvin Benjamin⁸ Gilbert** (*Genevieve Mae⁷ Niblock, George Niblock⁶ (Nimlow II), Margaret⁵ Pegan, Andrew⁴, James³, Andrew² Pagan, James¹*) was born on November 24, 1911, in Conoy Twp., Lancaster Co., Pennsylvania. He was the son of Benjamin F. Gilberg or Gilbert and Genevieve Mae Niblock (88). Melvin Benjamin died in Winchester, Frederick Co., Virginia, on July

12, 1976, at age 64. He was buried in Arlington National Cemetery, Arlington, Virginia.[87]

Childless.

He married **Evelyn Lathrop** in 1939. Evelyn Lathrop was born in Tumwater, Thurston Co., Washington? on July 22, 1914. Evelyn reached age 75 and died in Chicago, Cook Co., Illinois, on March 5, 1990.

**195. Theo G.[8] Gilbert** (*Genevieve Mae[7] Niblock, George Niblock[6] (Nimlow II), Margaret[5] Pegan, Andrew[4], James[3], Andrew[2] Pagan, James[1]*) was born in 1915 in Conoy Twp., Lancaster Co., Pennsylvania. She was the daughter of Benjamin F. Gilberg or Gilbert and Genevieve Mae Niblock (88). Theo G. died after 1930.

**196. James Groff[8] Pegan** (*Chester Clyde[7], Samuel A.[6], James Henry[5], Andrew[4], James[3], Andrew[2] Pagan, James[1]*) was born on June 23, 1903, in Lancaster, Lancaster Co., Pennsylvania.[2, 25] He was the son of Chester Clyde Pegan (90) and Ida Jane Groff. James Groff died in Lancaster, Lancaster Co., Pennsylvania, on March 23, 1904. He was buried in Greenwood Cemetery, Lancaster, Lancaster Co., Pennsylvania.[25]

**197. Robert Urban[8] Hamer** (*Lillian Virginia[7] Urban, Myra S.[6] Pegan, James Henry[5], Andrew4, James3, Andrew[2] Pagan, James[1]*) was born in Athens, Athens Twp., Athens Co., Ohio, on September 18, 1936. He was the son of Paul Simpson Hamer and Lillian Virginia Urban (92). He died in Dayton, Montgomery Co., Ohio, on November 12, 1984, at age 48.

Robert Urban married **Ann Unknown**. They divorced. They had two children.

**198. Paul[8] Hamer II** (*Lillian Virginia[7] Urban, Myra S.[6] Pegan, James Henry[5], Andrew[4], James[3], Andrew[2] Pagan, James[1]*) was born in December 1939 in Wapakoneta, Duchonquet Twp., Auglaize Co., Ohio. He was the son of Paul Simpson Hamer and Lillian Virginia Urban (92). Paul died in Wapakoneta, Duchonquet Twp., Auglaize Co., Ohio, on February 10, 1940. He was buried in Greenlawn Cemetery, Wapakoneta, Duchonquet Twp., Auglaize Co., Ohio.[88]

**199. Purdy Lester[8] Glenn** (*Grace Anna[7] Kilgore, Alvin Levi[6], Sarah Jane[5] Pegan, Andrew[4], James[3], Andrew[2] Pagan, James[1]*) was born on August 15, 1898, in Lower Chanceford Twp., York Co., Pennsylvania. He was the son of James Andrew Glenn and Grace Anna Kilgore (93). Purdy Lester died in Delta, Peach Bottom Twp., York Co., Pennsylvania, on May 27, 1984, at age 85. He was buried in Pine Grove Presbyterian Church Cemetery, Lower Chanceford Twp., York Co., Pennsylvania.[51]

Purdy Lester married **Ethel Kilgore** on May 21, 1919. They had four daughters. Ethel Kilgore was born in Lower Chanceford Twp., York Co., Pennsylvania, on December 25, 1896. Ethel reached age 79 and died in Delta, Peach Bottom Twp., York Co., Pennsylvania, on May 31, 1976. She was buried in Pine Grove Presbyterian Church Cemetery, Lower Chanceford Twp., York Co., Pennsylvania.[51]

Daughters of Purdy Lester Glenn and Ethel Kilgore:

+ 381 f I. **Hope[9] Glenn** was born in Lower Chanceford Twp., York Co., Pennsylvania, in 1921.

+ 382 f II. **Grace[9] Glenn** was born in Lower Chanceford Twp., York Co., Pennsylvania, in 1923.

+ 383 f III. **Mary Ellen[9] Glenn** was born in Lower Chanceford Twp., York Co., Pennsylvania, in 1927.

+ 384 f IV. **Alice Clair[9] Glenn** was born in Delta, Peach Bottom Twp., York Co., Pennsylvania, on September 30, 1937. She died in Fawn Grove Twp., York Co., Pennsylvania? on September 23, 1998.

**200. James Earl[8] Glenn II** (*Grace Anna[7] Kilgore, Alvin Levi[6], Sarah Jane[5] Pegan, Andrew[4], James[3], Andrew[2] Pagan, James[1]*) was born on May 1, 1902, in Lower Chanceford Twp., York Co., Pennsylvania. He was also known as **Earl**. He was the son of James Andrew Glenn and Grace Anna Kilgore (93). James Earl died in Airville, Lower Chanceford Twp., York Co., Pennsylvania, in

March 1983 at age 80. He was buried in Salem United Methodist Church Cemetery, Delta, Peach Bottom Twp., York Co., Pennsylvania.[52]

Childless.

James Earl married **Olive Barton** in 1941. Olive Barton was born in Peach Bottom Twp., York Co., Pennsylvania, on September 20, 1904. Olive reached age 98 and died in Airville, Lower Chanceford Twp., York Co., Pennsylvania, on April 28, 2003. She was buried in Salem United Methodist Church Cemetery, Delta, Peach Bottom Twp., York Co., Pennsylvania.[52]

**201. Alvin Huber⁸ Glenn** (*Grace Anna⁷ Kilgore, Alvin Levi⁶, Sarah Jane⁵ Pegan, Andrew⁴, James³, Andrew² Pagan, James¹*) was born on January 20, 1906, in Lower Chanceford Twp., York Co., Pennsylvania. He was the son of James Andrew Glenn and Grace Anna Kilgore (93). Alvin Huber died in Delta, Peach Bottom Twp., York Co., Pennsylvania, in May 1977 at age 71. He was buried in Salem United Methodist Church Cemetery, Delta, Peach Bottom Twp., York Co., Pennsylvania.[52]

Alvin Huber married **Nellie Salome Almoney** on April 6, 1929. They had three children. Nellie Salome Almoney was born in Fawn Twp., York Co., Pennsylvania, on June 2, 1911. Nellie Salome reached age 74 and died in Delta, Peach Bottom Twp., York Co., Pennsylvania, in May 1986. She was buried in Salem United Methodist Church Cemetery, Delta, Peach Bottom Twp., York Co., Pennsylvania.[52]

Children of Alvin Huber Glenn and Nellie Salome Almoney:

+ 385 f I. **Alice Jean⁹ Glenn** was born in Lower Chanceford Twp., York Co., Pennsylvania, in 1929.

+ 386 f II. **Phyllis E.⁹ Glenn** was born in Lower Chanceford Twp., York Co., Pennsylvania, on March 1, 1934.

+ 387 m III. **Alvin Huber⁹ Glenn II** was born in Lower Chanceford Twp., York Co., Pennsylvania, on November 6, 1937.

**202. Lida Maxwell⁸ Glenn** (*Grace Anna⁷ Kilgore, Alvin Levi⁶, Sarah Jane⁵ Pegan, Andrew⁴, James³, Andrew² Pagan, James¹*) was born on December 2, 1907, in Lower Chanceford Twp., York Co., Pennsylvania. She was the daughter of James Andrew Glenn and Grace Anna Kilgore (93). Lida Maxwell died in Airville, Lower Chanceford Twp., York Co., Pennsylvania, in November 1980 age 72.

Lida Maxwell married **James Paul Brown** on October 24, 1931, in Dauphin Co., Pennsylvania. They had one son. James Paul Brown was born in Harford Co., Maryland, in 1909. James Paul reached age 61 and died in Airville, Lower Chanceford Twp., York Co., Pennsylvania, in February 1970.

Son of Lida Maxwell Glenn and James Paul Brown:

+ 388 m I. **Gary Elmer⁹ Brown** was born in Lower Chanceford Twp., York Co., Pennsylvania, on July 7, 1935. He died in a hospital in York, York Co., Pennsylvania, on June 15, 1998. Gary Elmer was buried in Susquehanna Memorial Gardens Cemetery, York, York Co., Pennsylvania.[96]

**203. Nora⁸ Glenn** (*Grace Anna⁷ Kilgore, Alvin Levi⁶, Sarah Jane⁵ Pegan, Andrew⁴, James³, Andrew² Pagan, James¹*) was born on January 16, 1913, in Lower Chanceford Twp., York Co., Pennsylvania. She was the daughter of James Andrew Glenn and Grace Anna Kilgore (93). Nora died in Holtwood, Martic Twp., Lancaster Co., Pennsylvania, on November 27, 2000, at age 87.

Nora married **Ralph Leon Kilgore** about 1934. They had four children. Ralph Leon Kilgore was born in Lower Chanceford Twp., York Co., Pennsylvania, on June 10, 1910. He was also known as **Leon**. Ralph Leon reached age 79 and died in Airville, Lower Chanceford Twp., York Co., Pennsylvania, on August 4, 1989.

Children of Nora Glenn and Ralph Leon Kilgore:

+ 389 m I. **Leon⁹ Kilgore** was born in Lower Chanceford Twp., York Co., Pennsylvania, in 1935.

+ 390 m II. **Carl⁹ Kilgore** was born in Lower Chanceford Twp., York Co., Pennsylvania, in 1937.

+ 391 f III. **Hazel⁹ Kilgore** was born in Lower Chanceford Twp., York Co., Pennsylvania, in 1939.

+ 392 m IV. **Infant Son⁹ Kilgore** was born in Lower Chanceford Twp., York Co., Pennsylvania, in 1943. He died in Lower Chanceford Twp., York Co., Pennsylvania, in 1943. Son was buried in Pine Grove Presbyterian Church Cemetery, Lower Chanceford Twp., York Co., Pennsylvania.[35]

**204. Nina Amanda⁸ Kilgore** (*Samuel Ralph⁷, Alvin Levi⁶, Sarah Jane⁵ Pegan, Andrew⁴, James³, Andrew² Pagan, James¹*) was born on August 13, 1904, in Mummasburg, Franklin Twp., Adams Co., Pennsylvania. She was the daughter of Samuel Ralph Kilgore (94) and Mary Ann Hess. Nina Amanda died in Hillsdale, Hillsdale Twp., Hillsdale Co., Michigan, on March 30, 1957, at age 52. She was buried in Portage Cemetery, Portage, Wood Co., Ohio.[32]

Nina Amanda married **Thurman Clarence Dietrich** before 1935. They had one son. Thurman Clarence Diethrich was born in Bloomdale, Bloom Twp., Wood Co., Ohio? on March 18, 1901. Thurman Clarence reached age 87 and died in Plant City, Hillsborough Co., Florida, on June 5, 1988. He was buried in Grace Memorial Gardens Cemetery, Hudson, Pasco Co., Florida.[134]

Son of Nina Amanda Kilgore and Thurman Clarence Dietrich:

+ 393 m I. **Edward B.⁹ Dietrich** was born in Toledo, Lucas Co., Ohio, on August 6, 1935.

**205. Kenneth W.⁸ Kilgore** (*Samuel Ralph⁷, Alvin Levi⁶, Sarah Jane⁵ Pegan, Andrew⁴, James³, Andrew² Pagan, James¹*) was born on July 15, 1907, in Portage, Liberty Twp., Wood Co., Ohio. He was the son of Samuel Ralph Kilgore (94) and Mary Ann Hess. Kenneth W. died in Livonia, Wayne Co., Michigan, on May 20, 1981, at age 73. He was buried in Portage Cemetery, Portage, Wood Co., Ohio.[48]

Kenneth W. married **Helen Madonna Killian** on July 6, 1929, in Oakland Co., Michigan. They had one son. Helen Madonna Killian was born in Warren, Salamonie Twp., Huntington Co., Indiana, on February 10, 1908. Helen Madonna reached age 92 and died in Moneta, Bedford Co., Virginia, on January 23, 2001. She was buried in Portage Cemetery, Portage, Wood Co., Ohio.[48]

**206. Don Woodrow⁸ Kilgore** (*Samuel Ralph⁷, Alvin Levi⁶, Sarah Jane⁵ Pegan, Andrew⁴, James³, Andrew² Pagan, James¹*) was born on August 11, 1916, in Portage, Liberty Twp., Wood Co., Ohio. He was the son of Samuel Ralph Kilgore (94) and Mary Ann Hess. Don Woodrow died in Dearborn, Wayne Co., Michigan, on March 13, 1988, at age 71. He was buried in Portage Cemetery, Portage, Wood Co., Ohio.[48]

**207. Martin Leonard⁸ Kilgore** (*Samuel Ralph⁷, Alvin Levi⁶, Sarah Jane⁵ Pegan, Andrew⁴, James³, Andrew² Pagan, James¹*) was born on March 17, 1919, in Portage, Liberty Twp., Wood Co., Ohio. He was the son of Samuel Ralph Kilgore (94) and Mary Ann Hess. Martin Leonard died in Spring Arbor, Spring Arbor Twp., Jackson Co., Michigan on October 17, 2017.

Martin Leonard married **Erlene E. Emans** on January 29, 1942, in Allen Co., Indiana. They had two sons. Erlene E. Emans was born in Mendon, Union Twp., Mercer Co., Ohio, on September 8, 1918.

**208. Clarence H.⁸ Kilgore** (*Hugh Whiteford⁷, James Ankrim⁶, Sarah Jane⁵ Pegan, Andrew⁴, James³, Andrew² Pagan, James¹*) was born on February 28, 1906, in Peach Bottom Twp., York Co., Pennsylvania. He was the son of Hugh Whiteford Kilgore (96) and Alice Emma Dunlap. Clarence

H. died in Airville, Lower Chanceford Twp., York Co., Pennsylvania, on December 6, 1995, at age 89. He was buried in Slateville Presbyterian Church Cemetery, Delta, Peach Bottom Twp., York Co., Pennsylvania.[49]

Clarence H. married **Nellie Susan Pierson** about 1930. They divorced. They had three children. Nellie Susan Pierson was born in Oxford, Chester Co., Pennsylvania, on August 30, 1911. She reached age 49 and died in Peach Bottom Twp., York Co., Pennsylvania, on December 4, 1960. Nellie Susan was buried in Slate Ridge Cemetery, Delta, Peach Bottom Twp., York Co., Pennsylvania.[20]

Buried under the name of Nellie Susan Proctor.

Clarence H. Kilgore married **Jodie E. Tooel** after 1938. They had two children. Jodie E. Tooel was born in Searles, Tuscaloosa Co., Alabama, on March 27, 1906. Jodie E. reached age 78 and died in Airville, Lower Chanceford Twp., York Co., Pennsylvania, on March 5, 1985. She was buried in Slateville Presbyterian Church Cemetery, Delta, Peach Bottom Twp., York Co., Pennsylvania.[49]

Children of Clarence H. Kilgore and Nellie Susan Pierson:

+ 394 m  I.  **Victor Boyd⁹ Kilgore** was born in Peach Bottom Twp., York Co., Pennsylvania, on January 4, 1932. He died in Broadway, Lee Co., North Carolina, on September 15, 2013. Victor Boyd was buried in Pine Grove Presbyterian Church Cemetery, Lower Chanceford Twp., York Co., Pennsylvania.[51]

+ 395 m  II.  **Hugh F.⁹ Kilgore** was born in Peach Bottom Twp., York Co., Pennsylvania, on February 18, 1933. He died in Peach Bottom Twp., York Co., Pennsylvania, on August 6, 1933. Hugh F. was buried in Slateville Presbyterian Church Cemetery, Delta, Peach Bottom Twp., York Co., Pennsylvania.[49]

+ 396 f  III.  **Harriet⁹ Kilgore** was born in Peach Bottom Twp., York Co., Pennsylvania, on August 28, 1938.

**209. Sarah Angeline⁸ Kilgore** (*Hugh Whiteford⁷, James Ankrim⁶, Sarah Jane⁵ Pegan, Andrew⁴, James³, Andrew² Pagan, James¹*) was born on January 9, 1908, in Peach Bottom Twp., York Co., Pennsylvania. She was also known as **Angie**. She was the daughter of Hugh Whiteford Kilgore (96) and Alice Emma Dunlap. Sarah Angeline died in East Nottingham Twp., Chester Co., Pennsylvania, on July 12, 1995, at age 87. She was buried in Nottingham Cemetery, East Nottingham Twp., Chester Co., Pennsylvania.[89]

Sarah Angeline married **Frederick E. Boyd** before 1935. They had two children. Frederick E. Boyd was born in East Nottingham Twp., Chester Co., Pennsylvania, on December 23, 1905. Frederick E. reached age 81 and died in East Nottingham Twp., Chester Co., Pennsylvania, in July 1987. He was buried in Nottingham Cemetery, East Nottingham Twp., Chester Co., Pennsylvania.[89]

Children of Sarah Angeline Kilgore and Frederick E. Boyd:

+ 397 m  I.  **Frederick F.⁹ Boyd II** was born in East Nottingham Twp., Chester Co., Pennsylvania, in 1935.

+ 398 f  II.  **Jane Yvonne⁹ Boyd** was born in East Nottingham Twp., Chester Co., Pennsylvania, in 1937.

**210. Kenneth Dunlap⁸ Kilgore** (*Hugh Whiteford⁷, James Ankrim⁶, Sarah Jane⁵ Pegan, Andrew⁴, James³, Andrew² Pagan, James¹*) was born on October 1, 1909, in Peach Bottom Twp., York Co., Pennsylvania. He was the son of Hugh Whiteford Kilgore (96) and Alice Emma Dunlap. Kenneth Dunlap died in Camp Hill, Cumberland Co., Pennsylvania, in April 1986 at age 76. He was buried in Slateville Presbyterian Church Cemetery, Delta, Peach Bottom Twp., York Co., Pennsylvania.[33]

Kenneth Dunlap married **Kathryn Rebecca Drumond** before 1933. They had two children. Kathryn Rebecca Drumond was born in Washington, District of Columbia, on March 27, 1906. Kathryn Rebecca reached age 95 and died in Mechanicsburg, Cumberland Co., Pennsylvania, on August 24, 2001. She was buried in Slateville Presbyterian Church Cemetery, Delta, Peach Bottom Twp., York Co., Pennsylvania.[49]

Children of Kenneth Dunlap Kilgore and Kathryn Rebecca Drumond:

+ 399  m  I.   **James**[9] **Kilgore** was born in Havre de Grace, Harford Co., Maryland, in 1933.

+ 400  f  II.  **Emma**[9] **Kilgore** was born in Havre de Grace, Harford Co., Maryland, in 1935.

**211. Mary E.**[8] **Kilgore** (*Hugh Whiteford*[7], *James Ankrim*[6], *Sarah Jane*[5] *Pegan*, *Andrew*[4], *James*[3], *Andrew*[2] *Pagan*, *James*[1]) was born on October 27, 1911, in Peach Bottom Twp., York Co., Pennsylvania. She was the daughter of Hugh Whiteford Kilgore (96) and Alice Emma Dunlap. Mary E. died in Stuart, Martin Co., Florida, on January 6, 2002, at age 90. She was buried in Conestoga Memorial Park Cemetery, Lancaster Twp., Lancaster Co., Pennsylvania.[90]

Mary E. married **Ivan Ellsworth Cochran** before 1936. They had one son. Ivan Ellsworth Cochran was born in Lower Chanceford Twp., York Co., Pennsylvania, on March 23, 1910. Ivan Ellsworth reached age 87 and died in Fort Lauderdale, Broward Co., Florida, on September 30, 1997. He was buried in Conestoga Memorial Park Cemetery, Lancaster Twp., Lancaster Co., Pennsylvania.[90]

Son of Mary E. Kilgore and Ivan Ellsworth Cochran:

+ 401  m  I.   **Ronald**[9] **Cochran** was born in Martic Twp., Lancaster Co., Pennsylvania, in 1936.

**212. Eunice**[8] **Kilgore** (*Hugh Whiteford*[7], *James Ankrim*[6], *Sarah Jane*[5] *Pegan*, *Andrew*[4], *James*[3], *Andrew*[2] *Pagan*, *James*[1]) was born on February 17, 1913, in Peach Bottom Twp., York Co., Pennsylvania. She was the daughter of Hugh Whiteford Kilgore (96) and Alice Emma Dunlap. Eunice died in North East, Cecil Co., Maryland, on July 21, 1988, at age 75.

Eunice married **Charles Boyd** before 1934. They had three sons. Charles Boyd was born in West Nottingham Twp., Chester Co., Pennsylvania, on January 8, 1909. Charles reached age 86 and died in Spring Grove, Jackson Twp., York Co., Pennsylvania, on November 25, 1995.

Sons of Eunice Kilgore and Charles Boyd:

+ 402  m  I.   **Robert K.**[9] **Boyd** was born in West Nottingham Twp., Chester Co., Pennsylvania, in 1934.

+ 403  m  II.  **Samuel**[9] **Boyd** was born in West Nottingham Twp., Chester Co., Pennsylvania, in 1938.

+ 404  m  III. **Hughjene**[9] **Boyd.**

**213. James Robert**[8] **Kilgore** (*Samuel Reed*[7], *James Ankrim*[6], *Sarah Jane*[5] *Pegan*, *Andrew*[4], *James*[3], *Andrew*[2] *Pagan*, *James*[1]) was born on December 9, 1908, in Peach Bottom Twp., York Co., Pennsylvania. He was the son of Samuel Reed Kilgore (97) and Rebecca Dinsmore. James Robert died in Nazareth, Northampton Co., Pennsylvania, on July 5, 1991, at age 82.

James Robert married **Mabel Ella Daniel** before 1946. They had two daughters. Mabel Ella Daniel was born in Nazareth, Northampton Co., Pennsylvania, on February 29, 1912. Mabel Ella reached age 86 and died in Nazareth, Northampton Co., Pennsylvania, on April 1, 1998.

**214. Charles Gilbert**[8] **Kilgore** (*Samuel Reed*[7], *James Ankrim*[6], *Sarah Jane*[5] *Pegan*, *Andrew*[4], *James*[3], *Andrew*[2] *Pagan*, *James*[1]) was born in 1910 in Peach Bottom Twp., York Co., Pennsylvania.[2] He was also known as **Gilbert**. He was the son of Samuel Reed Kilgore (97) and Rebecca Dinsmore. Charles Gilbert died in Peach Bottom Twp., York Co., Pennsylvania, in 1926 at age 16.[2]

**215. Joseph Dinsmore⁸ Kilgore** (*Samuel Reed⁷, James Ankrim⁶, Sarah Jane⁵ Pegan, Andrew⁴, James³, Andrew² Pagan, James¹*) was born on September 21, 1911, in Peach Bottom Twp., York Co., Pennsylvania. He was the son of Samuel Reed Kilgore (97) and Rebecca Dinsmore. Joseph Dinsmore died in Delta, Peach Bottom Twp., York Co., Pennsylvania, on February 12, 2000, at age 88.

**216. Philip Reed⁸ Kilgore** (*Samuel Reed⁷, James Ankrim⁶, Sarah Jane⁵ Pegan, Andrew⁴, James³, Andrew² Pagan, James¹*) was born on October 24, 1912, in Peach Bottom Twp., York Co., Pennsylvania. He was the son of Samuel Reed Kilgore (97) and Rebecca Dinsmore. Philip Reed died in York, York Co., Pennsylvania, on March 5, 1999, at age 86. He was buried in Fawn Grove Methodist Church Cemetery, Fawn Grove, Fawn Grove Twp., York Co., Pennsylvania.[91]

Philip Reed married **J. Elizabeth Webb** before 1940. J. Elizabeth Webb was born in Bart Twp., Lancaster Co., Pennsylvania, in 1913. She was also known as **Elizabeth**. J. Elizabeth reached age 69 and died in Fawn Grove Twp., York Co., Pennsylvania, in 1982. She was buried in Fawn Grove Methodist Church Cemetery, Fawn Grove, Fawn Grove Twp., York Co., Pennsylvania.[91]

**217. Dorothy Nelson⁸ Kilgore** (*Samuel Reed⁷, James Ankrim⁶, Sarah Jane⁵ Pegan, Andrew⁴, James³, Andrew² Pagan, James¹*) was born on November 5, 1913, in Peach Bottom Twp., York Co., Pennsylvania. She was the daughter of Samuel Reed Kilgore (97) and Rebecca Dinsmore. Dorothy Nelson died in Delta, Peach Bottom Twp., York Co., Pennsylvania, on January 10, 2012, at age 98. She was buried in Slate Ridge Cemetery, Delta, Peach Bottom Twp., York Co., Pennsylvania.[20]

Never married.

**218. Minnie May⁸ Kilgore** (*Chester W.⁷, James Ankrim⁶, Sarah Jane⁵ Pegan, Andrew⁴, James³, Andrew² Pagan, James¹*) was born on August 17, 1924, in Lawrence, Douglas Co., Kansas. She was the daughter of Chester W. Kilgore (99) and Minnie Victoria Robinson. Minnie May died in Lawrence, Douglas Co., Kansas, on July 8, 2002, at age 77. She was buried in Memorial Park Cemetery, Lawrence, Douglas Co., Kansas.[50]

Minnie May married **Lee Jackson Clevenger II** on April 20, 1951, in Alameda Co., California. They had three children. Lee Jackson Clevenger II was born in Kansas City, Wyandotte Co., Kansas? on June 4, 1929. He was also known as **Jack**. Lee Jackson reached age 86 and died in Lawrence, Douglas Co., Kansas, on September 15, 2015. He was buried in Memorial Park Cemetery, Lawrence, Douglas Co., Kansas.[50]

**219. Thomas Warren⁸ Chandlee** (*Ira Whiteford⁷, Laura Clinda⁶ Kilgore, Sarah Jane⁵ Pegan, Andrew⁴, James³, Andrew² Pagan, James¹*) was born on February 4, 1915, in Lower Chanceford Twp., York Co., Pennsylvania. He was also known as **Warren**. He was the son of Ira Whiteford Chandlee (100) and Lucy Mary Ringland. Thomas Warren died in Elkton, Cecil Co., Maryland? on July 26, 1992, at age 77. He was buried in Pine Grove Presbyterian Church Cemetery, Lower Chanceford Twp., York Co., Pennsylvania.[51]

**220. Margaret⁸ Chandlee** (*Ira Whiteford⁷, Laura Clinda⁶ Kilgore, Sarah Jane⁵ Pegan, Andrew⁴, James³, Andrew² Pagan, James¹*) was born on November 14, 1927, in Lower Chanceford Twp., York Co., Pennsylvania. She is the daughter of Ira Whiteford Chandlee (100) and Lucy Mary Ringland.

She married **Charles William Sidwell** after 1940. Charles William Sidwell was born in Delta, Peach Bottom Twp., York Co., Pennsylvania, on October 24, 1924.

**221. Marian L.⁸ Chandlee** (*Walter Veasey⁷, Laura Clinda⁶ Kilgore, Sarah Jane⁵ Pegan, Andrew⁴, James³, Andrew² Pagan, James¹*) was born on July 4, 1910, in Lower Chanceford Twp., York Co., Pennsylvania. She was the daughter of Walter Veasey Chandlee (101) and Pearl Gemmel. Marian L. died in Red Lion, York Twp., York Co., Pennsylvania, on October 7, 1992, at age 82. She was buried in Red Lion Cemetery, Red Lion, York Twp., York Co., Pennsylvania.[80]

Marian L. married **Herbert Arthur Workinger** before 1940. Herbert Arthur Workinger was born in Chanceford Twp., York Co., Pennsylvania, on

August 30, 1908. Herbert Arthur reached age 41 and died in Red Lion, York Twp., York Co., Pennsylvania, on April 21, 1950. He was buried in Red Lion Cemetery, Red Lion, York Twp., York Co., Pennsylvania.[80]

**222. Ernest W.**[8] **Kilgore** (*Walter Stephen*[7], *William Ramsey*[6], *Sarah Jane*[5] *Pegan, Andrew*[4], *James*[3], *Andrew*[2] *Pagan, James*[1]) was born on June 16, 1906, in Baltimore, Baltimore Co., Maryland? He was the son of Walter Stephen Kilgore (103) and Mabel Pearl Sinclair. Ernest W. died in Oak Lawn, Cook Co., Illinois, on August 16, 1985, at age 79.

Childless

He married **Margaret Jean Renno**. Margaret Jean Renno was born in Chicago, Cook Co., Illinois, on October 31, 1907. Margaret Jean reached age 87 and died in Oak Lawn, Cook Co., Illinois, on November 10, 1994.

**223. Minnie**[8] **Kilgore** (*Walter Stephen*[7], *William Ramsey*[6], *Sarah Jane*[5] *Pegan, Andrew*[4], *James*[3], *Andrew*[2] *Pagan, James*[1]) was born in October 1908 in Baltimore, Baltimore Co., Maryland. She was the daughter of Walter Stephen Kilgore (103) and Mabel Pearl Sinclair. Minnie died in Baltimore, Baltimore Co., Maryland, in October 1908.

**224. Kenneth**[8] **Scott** (*Cora*[7] *Martin, Anna Margaret*[6] *Kilgore, Sarah Jane*[5] *Pegan, Andrew*[4], *James*[3], *Andrew*[2] *Pagan, James*[1]) was born on May 18, 1910, in Lower Chanceford Twp., York Co., Pennsylvania. He was the son of Raymond Scott and Cora Martin (104). Kenneth died in York, York Co., Pennsylvania, in July 1986 at age 76.

**225. Robert M.**[8] **Scott** (*Cora*[7] *Martin, Anna Margaret*[6] *Kilgore, Sarah Jane*[5] *Pegan, Andrew*[4], *James*[3], *Andrew*[2] *Pagan, James*[1]) was born on July 12, 1911, in Lower Chanceford Twp., York Co., Pennsylvania. He was the son of Raymond Scott and Cora Martin (104). Robert M. died in Delta, Peach Bottom Twp., York Co., Pennsylvania? on March 18, 1996, at age 84.

**226. J. Ray**[8] **Scott** (*Cora*[7] *Martin, Anna Margaret*[6] *Kilgore, Sarah Jane*[5] *Pegan, Andrew*[4], *James*[3], *Andrew*[2] *Pagan, James*[1]) was born on April 28, 1913, in Delta, Peach Bottom Twp., York Co., Pennsylvania. He was also known as **Ray**. He was the son of Raymond Scott

and Cora Martin (104). J. Ray died in York, York Co., Pennsylvania, on July 8, 2004, at age 91. He was buried in McKendree United Methodist Cemetery, Airville, Lower Chanceford Twp., York Co., Pennsylvania.[92]

He married **Mildred Wambaugh a**fter 1940. They had two children. Mildred Wambaugh was born in Lower Chanceford Twp., York Co., Pennsylvania? on April 13, 1915. Mildred reached age 72 and died in Delta, Peach Bottom Twp., York Co., Pennsylvania? in September 1987. She was buried in McKendree United Methodist Cemetery, Airville, Lower Chanceford Twp., York Co., Pennsylvania.[92]

**227. Harold Edwin**[8] **Scott** (*Cora*[7] *Martin, Anna Margaret*[6] *Kilgore, Sarah Jane*[5] *Pegan, Andrew*[4], *James*[3], *Andrew*[2] *Pagan, James*[1]) was born on May 15, 1915, in Delta, Peach Bottom Twp., York Co., Pennsylvania. He was the son of Raymond Scott and Cora Martin (104). Harold Edwin died in York, York Co., Pennsylvania, on September 26, 2011, at age 96. He was buried in Saint Paul's Wolf's Evangelical Covenant Cemetery, West York Twp., York Co., Pennsylvania.[93]

Harold Edwin married **Louise Stough Heilman** on December 9, 1948. They had two children. Louise Stough Heilman was born in York, York Co., Pennsylvania, on April 22, 1917. Louise Stough reached age 92 and died in York, York Co., Pennsylvania, on August 9, 2009. She was buried in Saint Paul's Wolf's Evangelical Covenant Cemetery, West York Twp., York Co., Pennsylvania.[93]

Harold Edwin Scott and Louise Stough Heilman had two children, including:

+ 405 m I. **Dale R.**[9] **Scott** was born in York, York Co., Pennsylvania, on September 4, 1949. He died in York, York Co., Pennsylvania, on August 1, 2005. Dale R. was buried in Saint Paul's Wolf's Evangelical Covenant Cemetery, West York Twp., York Co., Pennsylvania.[93]

**228. Sarah Margaret**[8] **Scott** (*Cora*[7] *Martin, Anna Margaret*[6] *Kilgore, Sarah Jane*[5] *Pegan, Andrew*[4],

*James*[3], *Andrew*[2] *Pagan, James*[1]) was born on August 17, 1917, in Delta, Peach Bottom Twp., York Co., Pennsylvania. She was the daughter of Raymond Scott and Cora Martin (104). Sarah Margaret died in Elmira, Chemung Co., New York, on August 30, 2003, at age 86. She was buried in Woodlawn Cemetery, Elmira, Chemug Co., New York.[94]

Sarah Margaret married **Curtis Elmore Shappee** before 1940. Curtis Elmore Shappee was born in Elmira, Chemung Co., New York, on August 17, 1917. Curtis Elmore reached age 78 and died in Elmira, Chemung Co., New York, on March 26, 1996. He was buried in Woodlawn Cemetery, Elmira, Chemug Co., New York.[94]

229. **Esther E.**[8] **Scott** (*Cora*[7] *Martin, Anna Margaret*[6] *Kilgore, Sarah Jane*[5] *Pegan, Andrew*[4], *James*[3], *Andrew*[2] *Pagan, James*[1]) was born on November 24, 1919, in Delta, Peach Bottom Twp., York Co., Pennsylvania. She was the daughter of Raymond Scott and Cora Martin (104). Esther E. lived in 2015 in Forest Hill, Harford Co., Maryland. She died in Bel Air, Harford Co., Maryland, on September 16, 2015, at age 95. Esther E. was buried in Pine Grove Presbyterian Church Cemetery, Lower Chanceford Twp., York Co., Pennsylvania.[51]

She married **John Robert Wayne** after 1940. They had three children. John Robert Wayne was born in Slate Hill, Peach Bottom Twp., York Co., Pennsylvania, on June 15, 1919. John Robert reached age 72 and died in Bel Air, Harford Co., Maryland, on March 21, 1992.

230. **Charles Arthur**[8] **Scott** (*Cora*[7] *Martin, Anna Margaret*[6] *Kilgore, Sarah Jane*[5] *Pegan, Andrew*[4], *James*[3], *Andrew*[2] *Pagan, James*[1]) was born on August 17, 1922, in Lower Chanceford Twp., York Co., Pennsylvania. He was the son of Raymond Scott and Cora Martin (104). Charles Arthur died in Baltimore, Baltimore Co., Maryland, in March 1984 at age 61.

231. **Janet Marie**[8] **Kilgore** (*Dale Dougherty*[7], *Emory Milton*[6], *Sarah Jane*[5] *Pegan, Andrew*[4], *James*[3], *Andrew*[2] *Pagan, James*[1]) was born on January 27, 1923, in Lower Chanceford Twp., York Co., Pennsylvania. She was the daughter of Dale Dougherty Kilgore (106) and Ruth Hepp. Janet Marie died in Dover Twp., York Co., Pennsylvania, on March 2, 1992, at age 69.

Janet Marie married **Lawrence Dennis Rinehart** in 1944. Lawrence Dennis Rinehart was born in North Codorus Twp., York Co., Pennsylvania, on November 29, 1918. Lawrence Dennis reached age 93 and died in Dover Twp., York Co., Pennsylvania, on December 7, 2011.

232. **Donald Emory**[8] **Kilgore** (*Dale Dougherty*[7], *Emory Milton*[6], *Sarah Jane*[5] *Pegan, Andrew*[4], *James*[3], *Andrew*[2] *Pagan, James*[1]) was born on March 20, 1927, in Lower Chanceford Twp., York Co., Pennsylvania. He is the son of Dale Dougherty Kilgore (106) and Ruth Hepp.

233. **Robert L.**[8] **Kilgore** (*Dale Dougherty*[7], *Emory Milton*[6], *Sarah Jane*[5] *Pegan, Andrew*[4], *James*[3], *Andrew*[2] *Pagan, James*[1]) was born in 1931 in Lower Chanceford Twp., York Co., Pennsylvania. He is the son of Dale Dougherty Kilgore (106) and Ruth Hepp.

234. **Eugene M.**[8] **Kilgore** (*Emory*[7], *Emory Milton*[6], *Sarah Jane*[5] *Pegan, Andrew*[4], *James*[3], *Andrew*[2] *Pagan, James*[1]) was born in 1933 in Lower Chanceford Twp., York Co., Pennsylvania. He is the son of Emory Kilgore II (107) and Mabel Jenness.

235. **William**[8] **Kilgore** (*Emory*[7], *Emory Milton*[6], *Sarah Jane*[5] *Pegan, Andrew*[4], *James*[3], *Andrew*[2] *Pagan, James*[1]) was born in 1940. He is the son of Emory Kilgore II (107) and Mabel Jenness.

236. **Edna**[8] **Anderson** (*Daisy Mae*[7] *Hess, Luella Jane*[6] *Kilgore, Sarah Jane*[5] *Pegan, Andrew*[4], *James*[3], *Andrew*[2] *Pagan, James*[1]) was born on May 29, 1912, in Lower Chanceford Twp., York Co., Pennsylvania. She was the daughter of Harry Melvin Anderson and Daisy Mae Hess (108). Edna died in Red Lion, York Twp., York Co., Pennsylvania, on February 3, 2010, at age 97.

She married **Luther O. Shelly** after 1940. They had two daughters. Luther O. Shelly was born in Dallastown, Windsor Twp., York Co., Pennsylvania, on September 4, 1912. Luther O. reached age 91 and died in Red Lion, York Twp., York Co., Pennsylvania, on January 19, 2004.

**237. Marian L.⁸ Anderson** (*Daisy Mae⁷ Hess, Luella Jane⁶ Kilgore, Sarah Jane⁵ Pegan, Andrew⁴, James³, Andrew² Pagan, James¹*) was born on July 11, 1913, in Lower Chanceford Twp., York Co., Pennsylvania. She was the daughter of Harry Melvin Anderson and Daisy Mae Hess (108). Marian L. died in Red Lion, York Twp., York Co., Pennsylvania, in September 1983 at age 70. She was buried in Bethel United Methodist Church Cemetery, Shenks Ferry, Chanceford Twp., York Co., Pennsylvania.[95]

She married **Clair William Krewson** abt. 1940. They had one daughter. Clair William Krewson was born in Chanceford Twp., York Co., Pennsylvania, on March 21, 1916. Clair William reached age 74 and died in Red Lion, York Twp., York Co., Pennsylvania? on March 5, 1991. He was buried in Bethel United Methodist Church Cemetery, Shenks Ferry, Chanceford Twp., York Co., Pennsylvania.[95]

Daughter of Marian L. Anderson and Clair William Krewson:

+ 406 f I. **Carol E.⁹ Krewson** was born in Chanceford Twp., York Co., Pennsylvania, on October 13, 1941. She died in Windsor Twp., York Co., Pennsylvania, on January 2, 2012. Carol E. was buried in Bethel United Methodist Church Cemetery, Shenks Ferry, Chanceford Twp., York Co., Pennsylvania.[95]

**238. Clair⁸ Anderson** (*Daisy Mae⁷ Hess, Luella Jane⁶ Kilgore, Sarah Jane⁵ Pegan, Andrew⁴, James³, Andrew² Pagan, James¹*) was born in 1918 in Lower Chanceford Twp., York Co., Pennsylvania. He was the son of Harry Melvin Anderson and Daisy Mae Hess (108). Clair died in Lower Chanceford Twp., York Co., Pennsylvania, before 1920.

**239. Harvey Donald⁸ Anderson** (*Daisy Mae⁷ Hess, Luella Jane⁶ Kilgore, Sarah Jane⁵ Pegan, Andrew⁴, James³, Andrew² Pagan, James¹*) was born on November 1, 1920, in Lower Chanceford Twp., York Co., Pennsylvania. He was also known as **Donald**. He was the son of Harry Melvin Anderson and Daisy

Mae Hess (108). Harvey Donald died in York Co., Pennsylvania, on March 29, 2002, at age 81.

**240. Philip Ernest⁸ Anderson** (*Daisy Mae⁷ Hess, Luella Jane⁶ Kilgore, Sarah Jane⁵ Pegan, Andrew⁴, James³, Andrew² Pagan, James¹*) was born on September 4, 1925, in Lower Chanceford Twp., York Co., Pennsylvania. He was the son of Harry Melvin Anderson and Daisy Mae Hess (108). Philip Ernest died in Red Lion, York Twp., York Co., Pennsylvania, on November 9, 1997, at age 72. He was buried in Susquehanna Memorial Gardens Cemetery, York, York Co., Pennsylvania.[96]

He married **Eunice A. Parthree** after 1940. They had two children. Eunice A. Parthree was born in Delta, Peach Bottom Twp., York Co., Pennsylvania, on May 2, 1926. Eunice A. lived before 2016 in Red Lion, York Twp., York Co., Pennsylvania. She reached age 90 and died in Middletown, Dauphin Co., Pennsylvania, on July 4, 2016. Eunice A. was buried in Susquehanna Memorial Gardens Cemetery, York, York Co., Pennsylvania.[96]

**241. Betty Sue⁸ Anderson** (*Daisy Mae⁷ Hess, Luella Jane⁶ Kilgore, Sarah Jane⁵ Pegan, Andrew⁴, James³, Andrew² Pagan, James¹*) was born in 1938 in Lower Chanceford Twp., York Co., Pennsylvania. She was the daughter of Harry Melvin Anderson and Daisy Mae Hess (108). Betty Sue died after 1940.

Seems to have died in childhood.

**242. Roger Scott⁸ Anderson** (*Sarah Margaret⁷ Hess, Luella Jane⁶ Kilgore, Sarah Jane⁵ Pegan, Andrew⁴, James³, Andrew² Pagan, James¹*) was born on October 31, 1918, in Lower Chanceford Twp., York Co., Pennsylvania. He was the son of Alwyn Murat Anderson and Sarah Margaret Hess (109). Roger Scott died in Knoxville, Knox Co., Tennessee, on May 30, 2009, at age 90. He was buried in Greenwood Cemetery, Knoxville, Knox Co., Tennessee.[97]

Roger Scott married **Marian Anatlas Pace** on October 26, 1944, in Anderson Co., Tennessee. They had two daughters. Marian Anatlas Pace was born in Asheboro, Randolph Co., North Carolina, on December 22, 1918. She was also known as **Anatlas**. Marian Anatlas reached age 82 and died in Knoxville, Knox Co., Tennessee, on December

21, 2001. She was buried in Greenwood Cemetery, Knoxville, Knox Co., Tennessee.[97]

**243. Robert Alwyn⁸ Anderson** (*Sarah Margaret⁷ Hess, Luella Jane⁶ Kilgore, Sarah Jane⁵ Pegan, Andrew⁴, James³, Andrew² Pagan, James¹*) was born on May 30, 1920, in Lower Chanceford Twp., York Co., Pennsylvania. He was the son of Alwyn Murat Anderson and Sarah Margaret Hess (109). Robert Alwyn died in Chattanooga, Hamilton Co., Tennessee, on January 27, 1991, at age 70. He was buried in Hamilton Memorial Gardens, Hixon, Hamilton Co., Tennessee.[53]

He married **Helen Catherine Morgan**. Helen was born on 24 May 1927. Helen reached age 71 and died in Chattanooga, Hamilton Co., Tennessee, on abt. February 13, 1998. She was buried in Hamilton Memorial Gardens, Hixon, Hamilton Co., Tennessee.[53]

**244. Richard Clayton⁸ Anderson** (*Sarah Margaret⁷ Hess, Luella Jane⁶ Kilgore, Sarah Jane⁵ Pegan, Andrew⁴, James³, Andrew² Pagan, James¹*) was born on December 15, 1921, in Lower Chanceford Twp., York Co., Pennsylvania. He was the son of Alwyn Murat Anderson and Sarah Margaret Hess (109). Richard Clayton died in Knoxville, Knox Co., Tennessee, on December 26, 2000, at age 79. He was buried in Lynnhurst Cemetery, Knoxville, Knox Co., Tennessee.[98]

Richard Clayton married **Valda D. Ferguson** on June 1, 1942, in Knox Co., Tennessee. They had two children. Valda D. Ferguson was born on October 11, 1921.

**245. Harold Luther⁸ Anderson** (*Sarah Margaret⁷ Hess, Luella Jane⁶ Kilgore, Sarah Jane⁵ Pegan, Andrew⁴, James³, Andrew² Pagan, James¹*) was born on February 21, 1924, in Lower Chanceford Twp., York Co., Pennsylvania. He was the son of Alwyn Murat Anderson and Sarah Margaret Hess (109). Harold Luther died in Louden, Louden Co., Tennessee, on April 20, 2000, at age 76. He was buried in Lynnhurst Cemetery, Knoxville, Knox Co., Tennessee.[98]

Harold Luther married **Merriem Reva McGaha** on May 27, 1947, in Cocke Co., Tennessee. Merriem

Reva McGaha was born in Newport, Cocke Co., Tennessee, on December 13, 1922.

**246. John⁸ Anderson** (*Sarah Margaret⁷ Hess, Luella Jane⁶ Kilgore, Sarah Jane⁵ Pegan, Andrew⁴, James³, Andrew² Pagan, James¹*) was born in 1927 in Lower Chanceford Twp., York Co., Pennsylvania. He is the son of Alwyn Murat Anderson and Sarah Margaret Hess (109).

John married **Lucina Pless** on December 29, 1951, in Anderson Co., Tennessee.

**247. Gerald Lyle⁸ Hess** (*Harry Lyle⁷, Luella Jane⁶ Kilgore, Sarah Jane⁵ Pegan, Andrew⁴, James³, Andrew² Pagan, James¹*) was born on June 5, 1921, in Lower Chanceford Twp., York Co., Pennsylvania. He was the son of Harry Lyle Hess (110) and Mary Ella Thompson. Gerald Lyle died in Wheat Ridge, Jefferson Co., Colorado? on March 18, 1999, at age 77.

Gerald Lyle married **Marion Elizabeth Rhodes** before 1952. Marion Elizabeth Rhodes was born in Houston, Harris Co., Texas, on September 10, 1923. Marion Elizabeth reached age 48 and died in Wichita, Sedgwick Co., Kansas? about December 28, 1971. She was buried in Valley View Cemetery, Garden City, Finney Co., Kansas.[135]

**248. Ramsey Martin⁸ Hess** (*Harry Lyle⁷, Luella Jane⁶ Kilgore, Sarah Jane⁵ Pegan, Andrew⁴, James³, Andrew² Pagan, James¹*) was born on July 28, 1924, in Lower Chanceford Twp., York Co., Pennsylvania. He was also known as **Martin** and **Bill**. He was the son of Harry Lyle Hess (110) and Mary Ella Thompson. Ramsey Martin died in Elizabethtown, Mt. Joy Twp., Lancaster Co., Pennsylvania, on January 2, 2008, at age 83. He was buried in Slateville Presbyterian Church Cemetery, Delta, Peach Bottom Twp., York Co., Pennsylvania.[49]

He married **Mary Charlotte Boyd** after 1940. They had one daughter. Mary Charlotte Boyd was born in Peach Bottom Twp., York Co., Pennsylvania, on October 2, 1928. Mary Charlotte reached age 63 and died in Delta, Peach Bottom Twp., York Co., Pennsylvania? on May 3, 1992. She was buried in Slateville Presbyterian Church Cemetery, Delta, Peach Bottom Twp., York Co., Pennsylvania.[49]

Ramsey Martin Hess married **Emma Elizabeth Miller** after 1992. They had at least one daughter. Emma Elizabeth Miller was born in Fawn Grove Twp., York Co., Pennsylvania, on June 23, 1922. She was also known as **Elizabeth**. Emma Elizabeth reached age 78 and died in Delta, Peach Bottom Twp., York Co., Pennsylvania, on May 4, 2001. She was buried in Slate Ridge Cemetery, Delta, Peach Bottom Twp., York Co., Pennsylvania.[8]

**249. Robert D.[8] Hess** (*Harry Lyle[7], Luella Jane[6] Kilgore, Sarah Jane[5] Pegan, Andrew[4], James[3], Andrew[2] Pagan, James[1]*) was born on September 16, 1928, in Lower Chanceford Twp., York Co., Pennsylvania. He is the son of Harry Lyle Hess (110) and Mary Ella Thompson.

Robert D. married **Doris Marie Tarbert (Mount)** on September 25, 1948. They had two sons. Doris Marie (Tarbert) Mount was born in Delta, Peach Bottom Twp., York Co., Pennsylvania, on January 6, 1929. Doris Marie (Tarbert) reached age 87 and died in Dallastown, Windsor Twp., York Co., Pennsylvania, on February 26, 2016. She was buried in Pine Grove Presbyterian Church Cemetery, Lower Chanceford Twp., York Co., Pennsylvania.[51]

Before her marriage, Doris preferred to use her stepfather's surname, Mount.

**250. Ruth Emeline[8] Stouch** (*Cora I.[7] Pegan, Lewis Cass[6], Alexander L.[5], Andrew[4], James[3], Andrew[2] Pagan, James[1]*) was born on September 28, 1896, in Lancaster Co., Pennsylvania. She was the daughter of Thomas Carl Stouch and Cora I. Pegan (111). Ruth Emeline died in Seneca, Oconee Co., South Carolina, on July 3, 1989, at age 92. She was buried in Church of the Holy Apostles Episcopal Cemetery, Barnwell, Barnwell Co., South Carolina.[99]

Ruth Emeline married **Wingard Williams Carter** on December 29, 1914, in Greenville Co., South Carolina. They had three children. Wingard Williams Carter was born in Erhart, Bamberg Co., South Carolina, on November 23, 1892. He was also known as **William**. Wingard Williams reached age 67 and died in Barnwell, Barnwell Co., South Carolina, on October 18, 1960. He was buried in

Church of the Holy Apostles Episcopal Cemetery, Barnwell, Barnwell Co., South Carolina.[98]

Children of Ruth Emeline Stouch and Wingard Williams Carter:

+ 407   f   I.   **Ida Ruth[9] Carter** was born in Varnville, Hampton Co., South Carolina, on June 3, 1920. She died in Seneca, Oconee Co., South Carolina, on December 5, 1984. Ida Ruth was buried in Oconee Memorial Park Cemetery and Mausoleum, Seneca, Oconee Co., South Carolina.[136]

+ 408   m   II.   **Wingard William[9] Carter II** was born in Varnville, Hampton Co., South Carolina, on August 22, 1922. He died in Rock Hill, York Co., South Carolina, on February 26, 1978. Wingard William was buried in Grandview Memorial Park Cemetery, Rock Hill, York Co., South Carolina.[137]

+ 409   f   III.   **Daughter[9] Carter** was born in Varnville, Hampton Co., South Carolina, in 1923. She died in Varnville, Hampton Co., South Carolina, in 1923. Daughter was buried in Church of the Holy Apostles Episcopal Cemetery, Barnwell, Barnwell Co., South Carolina.[73]

**251. Anna C.[8] Stouch** (*Cora I.[7] Pegan, Lewis Cass[6], Alexander L.[5], Andrew[4], James[3], Andrew[2] Pagan, James[1]*) was born on October 18, 1903, in Georgia. She was the daughter of Thomas Carl Stouch and Cora I. Pegan (111). Anna C. died in Tacoma, Pierce Co., Washington, on May 2, 1988, at age 84. She was buried in Mountain View Cemetery, Tacoma, Pierce Co., Washington.[74]

Anna C. married **Robert H. Liller** before 1930. They had three daughters. Robert H. Liller was born in Lancaster, Lancaster Co., Pennsylvania? on October 17, 1903. Robert H. reached age 71 and died in Tacoma, Pierce Co., Washington, on

May 14, 1975. He was buried in Mountain View Cemetery, Tacoma, Pierce Co., Washington.[74]

Daughters of Anna C. Stouch and Robert H. Liller:

+ 410 f I. **Nancy⁹ Liller** was born in Lancaster, Lancaster Co., Pennsylvania, in 1930.

+ 411 f II. **Gloria Ann⁹ Liller** was born in Lancaster, Lancaster Co., Pennsylvania, in 1934.

+ 412 f III. **Helen Roberta⁹ Liller** was born in Lancaster, Lancaster Co., Pennsylvania, in 1938.

**252. Thomas Carl⁸ Stouch II** (*Cora I.⁷ Pegan, Lewis Cass⁶, Alexander L.⁵, Andrew⁴, James³, Andrew² Pagan, James¹*) was born on December 2, 1908, in Greenville, Greenville Co., South Carolina. He was the son of Thomas Carl Stouch and Cora I. Pegan (111). Thomas Carl died in Paradise Twp., Lancaster Co., Pennsylvania, on November 4, 2001, at age 92. He was buried in Rancks United Methodist Church Cemetery, New Holland, Earl Twp., Lancaster Co., Pennsylvania.[101]

Thomas Carl married **Ethel I. Usner** on March 31, 1934, in Dauphin Co., Pennsylvania. Ethel I. Usner was born in New Holland, Earl Twp., Lancaster Co., Pennsylvania, on June 10, 1911. They divorced and had no children. Ethel I. reached age 87 and died in Lancaster, Lancaster Co., Pennsylvania, on February 14, 1999. She was buried in Rancks United Methodist Church Cemetery, New Holland, Earl Twp., Lancaster Co., Pennsylvania.[101]

Thomas Carl Stouch II married **Edna Trout** aft. 1940. They had one daughter. Edna Trout was born in Paradise Twp., Lancaster Co., Pennsylvania, on September 23, 1910. Edna reached age 87 and died in Paradise Twp., Lancaster Co., Pennsylvania, on August 30, 1998. She was buried in Rancks United Methodist Church Cemetery, New Holland, Earl Twp., Lancaster Co., Pennsylvania.[101]

**253. Lewis⁸ Stouch** (*Cora I.⁷ Pegan, Lewis Cass⁶, Alexander L.⁵, Andrew⁴, James³, Andrew² Pagan, James¹*) was born on September 5, 1910, in Greenville, Greenville Co., South Carolina. He was the son of Thomas Carl Stouch and Cora I. Pegan (111). Lewis died in Mannheim Twp., Lancaster Co., Pennsylvania? on October 20, 1994, at age 84.

He married **Marion Ross**. They had three children. Marion Ross was born in Lancaster, Lancaster Co., Pennsylvania, on April 3, 1914. Marion reached age 61 and died in Brevard Co., Florida, on May 23, 1975.

Children of Lewis Stouch and Marion Ross:

+ 413 f I. **Phyllis⁹ Stouch** was born in Lancaster, Lancaster Co., Pennsylvania, in 1933.

+ 414 m II. **Lewis⁹ Stouch II** was born in Mannheim Twp., Lancaster Co., Pennsylvania? in 1936.

+ 415 m III. **Thomas⁹ Stouch** was born in Mannheim Twp., Lancaster Co., Pennsylvania? in 1937.

**254. Julia M.⁸ Stouch** (*Cora I.⁷ Pegan, Lewis Cass⁶, Alexander L.⁵, Andrew⁴, James³, Andrew² Pagan, James¹*) was born on October 1, 1912, in Greenville, Greenville Co., South Carolina. She was the daughter of Thomas Carl Stouch and Cora I. Pegan (111). Julia M. died in Lancaster, Lancaster Co., Pennsylvania, on February 19, 2005, at age 92. She was buried in St. Joseph's New Roman Catholic Cemetery, Bausman, Lancaster Twp., Lancaster Co., Pennsylvania.[102]

Julia M. married **Daniel L. Roschel** in 1930. They had six children. Daniel L. Roschel was born in Lancaster Twp., Lancaster Co., Pennsylvania, in 1903. Daniel L. reached age 62 and died in Lancaster, Lancaster Co., Pennsylvania, in 1965. He was buried in St. Joseph's New Roman Catholic Cemetery, Bausman, Lancaster Twp., Lancaster Co., Pennsylvania.[102]

Children of Julia M. Stouch and Daniel L. Roschel:

+ 416  f  I.   **Doris R.**$^9$ **Roschel** was born in Lancaster, Lancaster Co., Pennsylvania, on October 19, 1930.

+ 417  m  II.  **Daniel L.**$^9$ **Roschel II** was born in Lancaster, Lancaster Co., Pennsylvania, on August 4, 1934.

+ 418  m  III. **Charles H.**$^9$ **Roschel** was born in Lancaster, Lancaster Co., Pennsylvania, on April 12, 1940.

**255. Elizabeth Frances**$^8$ **Stouch** (*Cora I.*$^7$ *Pegan, Lewis Cass*$^6$*, Alexander L.*$^5$*, Andrew*$^4$*, James*$^3$*, Andrew*$^2$ *Pagan, James*$^1$) was born on December 5, 1914, in Greenville, Greenville Co., South Carolina. She was the daughter of Thomas Carl Stouch and Cora I. Pegan (111). Elizabeth Frances died in Chestertown, Kent Co., Maryland, on June 1, 1996, at age 81. She was buried in Westminster Presbyterian Cemetery, Mifflintown, Juniata Co., Pennsylvania.[103]

Elizabeth Frances married **Chester Irvin Knight** before 1934. They had two sons. Chester Irvin Knight was born in Delaware Twp., Juniata Co., Pennsylvania, on April 16, 1911. Chester Irvin reached age 74 and died in Mifflintown, Juniata Co., Pennsylvania, in September 1985. He was buried in Westminster Presbyterian Cemetery, Mifflintown, Juniata Co., Pennsylvania.[103]

Sons of Elizabeth Frances Stouch and Chester Irvin Knight:

+ 419  m  I.   **Chester Irvin**$^9$ **Knight II** was born in Mannheim Twp., Lancaster Co., Pennsylvania, in 1934.

+ 420  m  II.  **James Leroy**$^9$ **Knight** was born in Mannheim Twp., Lancaster Co., Pennsylvania, in 1936.

**256. John Wingard**$^8$ **Stouch** (*Cora I.*$^7$ *Pegan, Lewis Cass*$^6$*, Alexander L.*$^5$*, Andrew*$^4$*, James*$^3$*, Andrew*$^2$ *Pagan, James*$^1$) was born on January 23, 1920, in Lancaster, Lancaster Co., Pennsylvania. He was the son of Thomas Carl Stouch and Cora I. Pegan (111). John Wingard died in Lititz, Lancaster Co., Pennsylvania, on February 4, 2004, at age 84. He was buried in Riverview Burial Park Cemetery, Lancaster, Lancaster Co., Pennsylvania.[29]

Childless.

He married **Polly M. Dayton** after 1940. Polly M. Dayton was born in Huntsdale, Rockingham Co., North Carolina, on October 14, 1912. Polly M. reached age 88 and died in Lititz, Lancaster Co., Pennsylvania, on December 9, 2000. She was buried in Riverview Burial Park Cemetery, Lancaster, Lancaster Co., Pennsylvania.[29]

**257. Harlan Edgar**$^8$ **Gilgore** (*Harriet Jane*$^7$ *Pegan, Lewis Cass*$^6$*, Alexander L.*$^5$*, Andrew*$^4$*, James*$^3$*, Andrew*$^2$ *Pagan, James*$^1$) was born on December 7, 1905, in Lancaster, Lancaster Co., Pennsylvania. He was the son of John Wesley Gilgore II and Harriet Jane Pegan (112). Harlan Edgar died in Lancaster, Lancaster Co., Pennsylvania, on December 29, 1976, at age 71. He was buried in Lancaster Cemetery, Lancaster, Lancaster Co., Pennsylvania.[18]

May have been childless.

Harlan Edgar married **Nora Brown** before 1940. Nora Brown was born in Honey Brook, Chester Co., Pennsylvania, on March 17, 1909. Nora reached age 93 and died in Lancaster, Lancaster Co., Pennsylvania, on September 29, 2002. She was buried in Lancaster Cemetery, Lancaster, Lancaster Co., Pennsylvania.[18]

**258. Dorothy**$^8$ **Gilgore** (*Harriet Jane*$^7$ *Pegan, Lewis Cass*$^6$*, Alexander L.*$^5$*, Andrew*$^4$*, James*$^3$*, Andrew*$^2$ *Pagan, James*$^1$) was born on June 16, 1907, in Lancaster, Lancaster Co., Pennsylvania. She was the daughter of John Wesley Gilgore II and Harriet Jane Pegan (112). Dorothy died in Lititz, Lancaster Co., Pennsylvania, on August 7, 2001, at age 94. She was buried in Millersville Mennonite Cemetery, Millersville, Manor Twp., Lancaster Co., Pennsylvania.[61]

Childless.

She married **William G. Pontz**. William G. Pontz was born in Lancaster, Lancaster Co., Pennsylvania, on July 2, 1905. William G. reached age 73 and died in Lancaster, Lancaster Co., Pennsylvania, in April 1979. He was buried in Millersville Mennonite Cemetery, Millersville, Manor Twp., Lancaster Co., Pennsylvania.[61]

**259. William⁸ Gilgore** (*Harriet Jane⁷ Pegan, Lewis Cass⁶, Alexander L.⁵, Andrew⁴, James³, Andrew² Pagan, James¹*) was born on July 29, 1911, in Lancaster, Lancaster Co., Pennsylvania. He was the son of John Wesley Gilgore II and Harriet Jane Pegan (112). William died in Lancaster, Lancaster Co., Pennsylvania, in December 1971 at age 60.

William married **Helen Raum** before 1940. They had one son. Helen Raum was born in Lancaster, Lancaster Co., Pennsylvania, on May 12, 1912. Helen reached age 88 and died in Lancaster, Lancaster Co., Pennsylvania, on September 4, 2000.

Son of William Gilgore and Helen Raum:

+ 421 m I.    **Joseph W.⁹ Gilgore** was born in Lancaster, Lancaster Co., Pennsylvania, on September 6, 1941. He died in Lancaster, Lancaster Co., Pennsylvania, on October 27, 1941. Joseph W. was buried in Riverview Cemetery, Lancaster, Lancaster Co., Pennsylvania.[138]

**260. Robert Claire⁸ Gilgore** (*Harriet Jane⁷ Pegan, Lewis Cass⁶, Alexander L.⁵, Andrew⁴, James³, Andrew² Pagan, James¹*) was born on July 31, 1916, in Mannheim Twp., Lancaster Co., Pennsylvania. He was the son of John Wesley Gilgore II and Harriet Jane Pegan (112). Robert Claire died in Lititz, Lancaster Co., Pennsylvania, on December 11, 1998, at age 82. He was buried in Riverview Burial Park Cemetery, Lancaster, Lancaster Co., Pennsylvania.[29]

Childless.

Robert Claire married **Violet M. McCracken** before 1940. They divorced. Violet M. McCracken was born in Columbia, West Hempfield Twp., Lancaster Co., Pennsylvania, on November 15, 1910. She reached age 75 and died in Columbia, West Hempfield Twp., Lancaster Co., Pennsylvania, on June 11, 1986. Violet M. was buried in Laurel

Hill Memorial Gardens Cemetery, Columbia, West Hempfield Twp., Lancaster Co., Pennsylvania.[139]

Violet's second marriage was to Harvey Dale Kilgore and she died and was buried under the name Violet M. Kilgore.

**261. Anna V.⁸ Pegan** (*Harlan Appleton⁷, Lewis Cass⁶, Alexander L.⁵, Andrew⁴, James³, Andrew² Pagan, James¹*) was born on October 3, 1908, in Lancaster, Lancaster Co., Pennsylvania. She was the daughter of Harlan Appleton Pegan (113) and Edith Keeler. Anna V. died in Cornwall, Lebanon Co., Pennsylvania, on August 17, 1998, at age 89. She was buried in Susquehanna Memorial Gardens Cemetery, York, York Co., Pennsylvania.[96]

Childless.

Anna V. married **James Ralph Singleton** after 1940. James Ralph Singleton was born in Slate Hill, York Co., Pennsylvania, on October 6, 1910. James Ralph reached age 75 and died in Nokomis, Sarasota Co., Florida, on January 7, 1986. He was buried in Susquehanna Memorial Gardens Cemetery, York, York Co., Pennsylvania.[96]

**262. Daughter⁸ Pegan** (*Harlan Appleton⁷, Lewis Cass⁶, Alexander L.⁵, Andrew⁴, James³, Andrew² Pagan, James¹*) was born on August 5, 1910, in Lancaster, Lancaster Co., Pennsylvania. She was the daughter of Harlan Appleton Pegan (113) and Edith Keeler. Daughter died in Lancaster, Lancaster Co., Pennsylvania, on August 5, 1910. She was buried in Lancaster Cemetery, Lancaster, Lancaster Co., Pennsylvania.[18]

**263. Lewis Casper⁸ Pegan** (*Harlan Appleton⁷, Lewis Cass⁶, Alexander L.⁵, Andrew⁴, James³, Andrew² Pagan, James¹*) was born on March 8, 1912, in Martic Twp., Lancaster Co., Pennsylvania. He was the son of Harlan Appleton Pegan (113) and Edith Keeler. Lewis Casper died in Seminole, Pinellas Co., Florida, on January 16, 2004, at age 91. He was buried in Bay Pines National Cemetery, Bay Pines, Pinellas Co., Florida.[104, 105]

Lewis Casper married **Lucille A. Zhorski** after 1940. They had three children. Lucille A. Zhorski was born in Jersey City, Hudson Co., New Jersey, on August 19, 1919. Lucille A. reached age 92 and died in Seminole, Pinellas Co., Florida, on March 8, 2012. She was buried in Holy Cross Cemetery, North Arlington, Bergen Co., New Jersey.[140]

264. **Dorothy Elizabeth⁸ Pegan** (*Harlan Appleton⁷, Lewis Cass⁶, Alexander L.⁵, Andrew⁴, James³, Andrew² Pagan, James¹*) was born on March 24, 1916, in Martic Twp., Lancaster Co., Pennsylvania. She was the daughter of Harlan Appleton Pegan (113) and Edith Keeler. Dorothy Elizabeth died in Lancaster, Lancaster Co., Pennsylvania, on March 28, 1997, at age 81. She was buried in St. Anthony's Roman Catholic Cemetery, Lancaster, Lancaster Co., Pennsylvania.[106]

Childless.

Elizabeth married **John Robert Groff** on April 27, 1940, in Alexandria, Virginia.[141] They divorced. John Robert Groff was born in Parkesburg, Chester Co., Pennsylvania, on February 29, 1908. He reached age 72 and died in Paoli, Chester Co., Pennsylvania, on September 21, 1980. John Robert was buried in Upper Octorara Church Cemetery, Parkesburg, Sadbury Twp., Chester Co., Pennsylvania.[74]

Dorothy Elizabeth Pegan Groff married **Unknown Mirto** before 1944.

Dorothy Elizabeth Pegan Groff Mirto married **Henry M. Stauffer** on October 22, 1955. Henry M. Stauffer was born in Ephrata, Lancaster Co., Pennsylvania, on July 13, 1919. Henry M. reached age 95 and died in a facility in Lititz, Lancaster Co., Pennsylvania, on May 25, 2015.

265. **Elmer L.⁸ Barton II** (*Elmer Isaac⁷, Sarah⁶ Pegan, Alexander L.⁵, Andrew⁴, James³, Andrew² Pagan, James¹*) was born on June 5, 1905, in Lancaster, Lancaster Co., Pennsylvania. He was the son of Elmer Isaac Barton (115) and Jessie Harvey. Elmer L. died in Lancaster, Lancaster Co., Pennsylvania? on December 4, 1974, at age 69. He was buried in Riverview Burial Park Cemetery, Lancaster, Lancaster Co., Pennsylvania.[29]

He married **Mary Kemp** before 1955. They may have divorced. Mary Kemp was born in New Castle, Lawrence Co., Pennsylvania? in 1905. Mary died after 1955.

266. **Helen⁸ Barton** (*Elmer Isaac⁷, Sarah⁶ Pegan, Alexander L.⁵, Andrew⁴, James³, Andrew² Pagan, James¹*) was born on February 18, 1907, in Lancaster, Lancaster Co., Pennsylvania. She was the daughter of Elmer Isaac Barton (115) and Jessie Harvey. Helen died in Lancaster, Lancaster Co., Pennsylvania, on November 29, 1932, at age 25. She was buried in Greenwood Cemetery, Lancaster, Lancaster Co., Pennsylvania.[25] Helen Barton Robinson is buried under the name Helen Barton.

Helen married **William John Robison II** in 1931. William John Robison II was born in Lancaster, Lancaster Co., Pennsylvania, on November 2, 1912. William John reached age 90 and died in Lancaster, Lancaster Co., Pennsylvania, on February 3, 2003. He was buried in First Reformed Church Memorial Garden Cemetery, Lancaster, Lancaster Co., Pennsylvania.[142]

267. **Elmer Francis⁸ Barton** (*Elmer Isaac⁷, Sarah⁶ Pegan, Alexander L.⁵, Andrew⁴, James³, Andrew² Pagan, James¹*) was born on August 7, 1922, in Boston, Suffolk Co., Massachusetts. He was the son of Elmer Isaac Barton (115) and Anna L. Gookin. Elmer Francis died in Walpole, Norfolk Co., Massachusetts? on August 23, 2012, at age 90.

268. **Colombiere Mabel⁸ Barton** (*Elmer Isaac⁷, Sarah⁶ Pegan, Alexander L.⁵, Andrew⁴, James³, Andrew² Pagan, James¹*) was born on August 13, 1924, in West Roxbury, Suffolk Co., Massachusetts. She was also known as **Louise**. She was the daughter of Elmer Isaac Barton (115) and Anna L. Gookin. Colombiere Mabel lived in 1995 in Greenwood, Greenwood Co., South Carolina. She died in Malden, Middlesex Co., Massachusetts, on March 14, 1996, at age 71.

She used Louise as her preferred name in later life.

Colombiere Mabel married **Unknown Poirier** in 1955.

Colombiere Mabel Barton Poirier married **Angelo E. Provitola** before 1960. They divorced. They had one son. Angelo E. Provitola was born in Malden, Middlesex Co., Massachusetts, on February 1, 1921. He reached age 87 and died in Malden, Middlesex Co., Massachusetts, on January 3, 2009.

**269. Carolyn Martha⁸ Barton** (*Elmer Isaac⁷, Sarah⁶ Pegan, Alexander L.⁵, Andrew⁴, James³, Andrew² Pagan, James¹*) was born on June 30, 1927, in Boston, Suffolk Co., Massachusetts. She was the daughter of Elmer Isaac Barton (115) and Anna L. Gookin. Carolyn Martha lived in 1988 in Malden, Middlesex Co., Massachusetts. She died in Mesa, Maricopa Co., Arizona, on October 7, 2013, at age 86. Carolyn Martha was buried in Forest Dale Cemetery, Malden, Middlesex Co., Massachusetts.[107]

Carolyn Martha married **Francis William Heft** in 1950 in Suffolk Co., Massachusetts. They had four children. Francis William Heft was born in Chelsea, Suffolk Co., Massachusetts, on May 1, 1922. Francis William reached age 51 and died in Malden, Middlesex Co., Massachusetts, on January 11, 1974. He was buried in Forest Dale Cemetery, Malden, Middlesex Co., Massachusetts.[107]

**270. Esther Ann⁸ Davis** (*Laura Etta⁷ Pegan, James Calvin⁶, Alexander L.⁵, Andrew⁴, James³, Andrew² Pagan, James¹*) was born on May 7, 1912, in Pittsburgh, Allegheny Co., Pennsylvania. She was the daughter of Donald Neff Davis and Laura Etta Pegan (117). Esther Ann died in Pittsburgh, Allegheny Co., Pennsylvania, on August 3, 1988, at age 76. She was buried in Chartiers Cemetery, Carnegie, Scott Twp., Allegheny Co., Pennsylvania.[30]

Esther Ann married **James Barr Vogel** on July 17, 1940, in Allegheny Co., Pennsylvania. James Barr Vogel was born in Pittsburgh, Allegheny Co., Pennsylvania, on September 3, 1911. James Barr reached age 79 and died in Pittsburgh, Allegheny Co., Pennsylvania, on November 12, 1990. He was buried in Chartiers Cemetery, Carnegie, Scott Twp., Allegheny Co., Pennsylvania.[30]

**271. Robert Pegan⁸ Davis II** (*Laura Etta⁷ Pegan, James Calvin⁶, Alexander L.⁵, Andrew⁴, James³, Andrew² Pagan, James¹*) was born on January 27, 1914, in Crafton, Allegheny Co., Pennsylvania. He was the son of Donald Neff Davis and Laura Etta Pegan (117). Robert Pegan died in Ionia, Ionia Twp., Ionia Co., Michigan, on May 3, 1980, at age 66. He was buried in Balcom Cemetery, Berlin Center, Berlin Twp., Ionia Co., Michigan.[108]

Robert Pegan married **Mildred L. Unknown** after 1940. Mildred L. Unknown was born on January 25, 1909. Mildred L. reached age 69 and died in Ionia, Ionia Twp., Ionia Co., Michigan, on May 11, 1978. She was buried in Balcom Cemetery, Berlin Center, Berlin Twp., Ionia Co., Michigan.[108]

**272. William Laird⁸ Davis** (*Laura Etta⁷ Pegan, James Calvin⁶, Alexander L.⁵, Andrew⁴, James³, Andrew² Pagan, James¹*) was born on July 4, 1916, in Crafton, Allegheny Co., Pennsylvania. He was also known as **Laird**. He was the son of Donald Neff Davis and Laura Etta Pegan (117). William Laird died in Oakdale, Allegheny Co., Pennsylvania, on December 3, 2002, at age 86. He was buried in Jefferson Memorial Park Cemetery, Pleasant Hills, Allegheny Co., Pennsylvania.[55]

William Laird married **Elizabeth Jean Hawe** on February 6, 1948, in Allegheny Co., Pennsylvania. They had two daughters. Elizabeth Jean Hawe was born in Wilkinsburg, Allegheny Co., Pennsylvania, on October 2, 1918. She was also known as **Jean**. Elizabeth Jean reached age 85 and died in Carnegie, Scott Twp., Allegheny Co., Pennsylvania, on December 27, 2003. She was buried in Jefferson Memorial Park Cemetery, Pleasant Hills, Allegheny Co., Pennsylvania.[55]

**273. Betty Jane⁸ Davis** (*Laura Etta⁷ Pegan, James Calvin⁶, Alexander L.⁵, Andrew⁴, James³, Andrew² Pagan, James¹*) was born on June 24, 1921, in Crafton, Allegheny Co., Pennsylvania. She was the daughter of Donald Neff Davis and Laura Etta Pegan (117). Betty Jane lived before 2010 in Crafton, Allegheny Co., Pennsylvania. She died in Clio, Vienna Twp., Genessee Co., Michigan, on September 3, 2014, at age 93. Betty Jane was buried in National Cemetery of the Alleghenies, Cecil Twp., Washington Co., Pennsylvania.[109]

Betty Jane married **Harry Graham Follett II** in 1940 in Brooke Co. West Virginia. They had three sons. Harry Graham Follett II was born in Thornburg, Ingram Twp., Allegheny Co.,

Pennsylvania, on January 18, 1918. He was also known as **Bud**. Harry Graham reached age 78 and died in Crafton, Allegheny Co., Pennsylvania, on July 13, 1996. He was buried in National Cemetery of the Alleghenies, Cecil Twp., Washington Co., Pennsylvania.[109]

**274. Ruth Ann⁸ Dettling** (*Ruth Ann⁷ Pegan, James Calvin⁶, Alexander L.⁵, Andrew⁴, James³, Andrew² Pagan, James¹*) was born on August 29, 1915, in Pittsburgh, Allegheny Co., Pennsylvania. She was the daughter of George Henry Dettling and Ruth Ann Pegan (119). Ruth Ann died in Bellevue, King Co., Washington, on July 27, 2008, at age 92.

Ruth Ann married **Frank Lloyd Matson II** on June 15, 1940, in Allegheny Co., Pennsylvania. Frank Lloyd Matson II was born in Church Twp., Wetzel Co., West Virginia, on June 26, 1912. Frank Lloyd reached age 81 and died in Bellevue, King Co., Washington, on July 30, 1993.

**275. George Henry⁸ Dettling II** (*Ruth Ann⁷ Pegan, James Calvin⁶, Alexander L.⁵, Andrew⁴, James³, Andrew² Pagan, James¹*) was born on January 9, 1925, in Mt. Lebanon, Allegheny Co., Pennsylvania. He was the son of George Henry Dettling and Ruth Ann Pegan (119). George Henry died in Ann Arbor, Ann Arbor Twp., Washtenaw Co., Michigan, on February 14, 1991, at age 66. He was buried in Jefferson Memorial Park Cemetery, Pleasant Hills, Allegheny Co., Pennsylvania.[55, 56]

He married **Sellie Seiler Hemple**. They had one daughter.

Daughter of George Henry Dettling II and Sellie Seiler Hemple:

+ 422 f I. **Dana Laird⁹ Dettling** was born in Pittsburgh, Allegheny Co., Pennsylvania, on July 27, 1956. She died in Pittsburgh, Allegheny Co., Pennsylvania, on July 28, 1956. Dana Laird was buried in Jefferson Memorial Park Cemetery, Pleasant Hills, Allegheny Co., Pennsylvania.[55, 56]

**276. Charles Kirkwood⁸ Geiges** (*Loretta⁷ Miller, Anna Mary⁶ Pegan, Alexander L.⁵, Andrew⁴, James³, Andrew² Pagan, James¹*) was born on June 21, 1928, in Haverford Twp., Delaware Co., Pennsylvania. He was the son of Harold Marcus Geiges and Loretta Miller (123). Charles Kirkwood died in Havertown, Haverford Twp., Delaware Co., Pennsylvania, on September 28, 1991, at age 63. He was buried in Valley Forge Gardens Cemetery, King of Prussia, Upper Merion Twp., Montgomery Co., Pennsylvania.[110]

**277. Joanne E.⁸ Miller** (*Sherwood A.⁷, Anna Mary⁶ Pegan, Alexander L.⁵, Andrew⁴, James³, Andrew² Pagan, James¹*) was born in 1931 in East Lampeter Twp., Lancaster Co., Pennsylvania. She is the daughter of Sherwood A. Miller (124) and Evelyn Marie Howard.

**278. Sherwood Howard⁸ Miller II** (*Sherwood A.⁷, Anna Mary⁶ Pegan, Alexander L.⁵, Andrew⁴, James³, Andrew² Pagan, James¹*) was born in 1936 in East Lampeter Twp., Lancaster Co., Pennsylvania. He is the son of Sherwood A. Miller (124) and Evelyn Marie Howard.

Sherwood Howard married **Joyce Ann Heff** on August 27, 1956, in Lancaster Co. Pennsylvania.

**279. Ellsworth James⁸ Gentry** (*Adelaide or Adeline⁷ Pegan, Elmer Ellsworth James⁶, Alexander L.⁵, Andrew⁴, James³, Andrew² Pagan, James¹*) was born on August 25, 1916, in Wilmington, New Castle Co., Delaware. He was the son of Thomas Daniel Gentry and Adelaide or Adeline Pegan (127). Ellsworth James died in Wilmington, New Castle Co., Delaware, on May 12, 1984, at age 67. He was buried in Silverbrook Cemetery, Wilmington, New Castle Co., Delaware.[32]

Ellsworth James married **Dorothy P. Pierce** on October 27, 1934, in New Castle Co., Delaware. They had eight children. Dorothy P. Pierce was born in Wilmington, New Castle Co., Delaware, on May 14, 1917. Dorothy P. reached age 90 and died in Wilmington, New Castle Co., Delaware, on February 11, 2008. She was buried in Silverbrook Cemetery, Wilmington, New Castle Co., Delaware.[32]

Ellsworth James Gentry and Dorothy P. Pierce had eight children, including:

+ 423 f I. **Dorothy**[9] **Gentry** was born in Gordon Heights, New Castle Co., Delaware, in 1935.

+ 424 m II. **Ellsworth James**[9] **Gentry II** was born in Gordon Heights, New Castle Co., Delaware, on September 23, 1936. He died in Wilmington, New Castle Co., Delaware, on November 15, 1992.

+ 425 m III. **John E.**[9] **Gentry** was born in Gordon Heights, New Castle Co., Delaware, on November 23, 1939. He died in July 1968.

+ 426 m V. **Thomas Daniel**[9] **Gentry** was born in Gordon Heights, New Castle Co., Delaware, in 1942. He died in Wilmington, New Castle Co., Delaware, on August 23, 1947.

+ 427 m VI. **Douglas Gary**[9] **Gentry** was born in Wilmington, New Castle Co., Delaware, in 1949. He died in Wilmington, New Castle Co., Delaware, on December 11, 2014. Douglas Gary was buried in Silverbrook Cemetery, Wilmington, New Castle Co., Delaware.[32]

**280. Adeline Blair**[8] **Gentry** (*Adelaide or Adeline*[7] *Pegan, Elmer Ellsworth James*[6], *Alexander L.*[5], *Andrew*[4], *James*[3], *Andrew*[2] *Pagan, James*[1]) was born on December 12, 1917, in Wilmington, New Castle Co., Delaware. She was the daughter of Thomas Daniel Gentry and Adelaide or Adeline Pegan (127). Adeline Blair died in Wilmington, New Castle Co., Delaware, on December 14, 1920, at age three.

**281. Thomas Daniel**[8] **Gentry II** (*Adelaide or Adeline*[7] *Pegan, Elmer Ellsworth James*[6], *Alexander L.*[5], *Andrew*[4], *James*[3], *Andrew*[2] *Pagan, James*[1]) was born on March 25, 1919, in Wilmington, New Castle Co., Delaware. He was the son of Thomas Daniel Gentry and Adelaide or Adeline Pegan (127).

Thomas Daniel died in Wilmington, New Castle Co., Delaware, on February 21, 1993, at age 73.

May have never married.

**282. Elmer Thomas**[8] **Pegan** (*Samuel*[7], *Elmer Ellsworth James*[6], *Alexander L.*[5], *Andrew*[4], *James*[3], *Andrew*[2] *Pagan, James*[1]) was born on March 26, 1923, in Wilmington, New Castle Co., Delaware. He was the son of Samuel Pegan (128) and Mollie R. Tubbs. Elmer Thomas died in Wilmington, New Castle Co., Delaware, in April 1981 at age 58.

Elmer Thomas married **Betty Jane Heister** on January 16, 1943, in New Castle Co., Delaware. Betty Jane Heister was born in Kingston, Luzerne Co., Pennsylvania, on March 23, 1924. Betty Jane died after 1943.

Elmer Thomas Pegan married **Helen Reba Alford** on August 21, 1948, in New Castle Co., Delaware, Helen Reba Alford was born in Edgemoor, New Castle Co., Delaware, on September 22, 1921. Helen Reba reached age 55 and died in Wilmington, New Castle Co., Delaware, in March 1977.

**283. Dorothy Elizabeth**[8] **Pegan** (*Harvey*[7], *Elmer Ellsworth James*[6], *Alexander L.*[5], *Andrew*[4], *James*[3], *Andrew*[2] *Pagan, James*[1]) was born in 1915 in Lower Merion Twp., Montgomery Co., Pennsylvania? She was the daughter of Harvey Pegan (129) and Mary Stevens. Dorothy Elizabeth died after 1940.

**284. Raymond**[8] **Pegan II** (*Raymond*[7], *Elmer Ellsworth James*[6], *Alexander L.*[5], *Andrew*[4], *James*[3], *Andrew*[2] *Pagan, James*[1]) was born on November 14, 1926, in Wilmington, New Castle Co., Delaware.[112] He was the son of Raymond Pegan (131) and Mae Shortt. Raymond died in Wilmington, New Castle Co., Delaware, on June 24, 1971, at age 44.[112] He was buried in All Saints Cemetery, Wilmington, New Castle Co., Delaware.[58]

Raymond married **Nancy Patricia Nennstiehl** on September 20, 1949, in New Castle Co., Delaware. They had one daughter. Nancy Patricia Nennstiehl was born in Christana, New Castle Co., Delaware, on April 19, 1929.[112] Nancy Patricia reached age 82 and died in South Bethany, Sussex Co., Delaware, on March 11, 2012.[112] She was buried in All Saints Cemetery, Wilmington, New Castle Co., Delaware.[58]

**285. Stella Kathleen⁸ Pegan** (*Raymond⁷, Elmer Ellsworth James⁶, Alexander L.⁵, Andrew⁴, James³, Andrew² Pagan, James¹*) was born on March 10, 1928, in Wilmington, New Castle Co., Delaware. She was also known as **Kathleen**. She was the daughter of Raymond Pegan (131) and Mae Shortt. Stella died in Wilmington, New Castle Co., Delaware, on February 24, 1987, at age 58. She was buried in Gracelawn Memorial Park, Farmhurst, New Castle Co., Delaware.[59]

Stella married **George Hudson Downey** on January 24, 1948, in New Castle Co., Delaware. George Hudson Downey was born in Chester, Delaware Co., Pennsylvania? on December 30, 1924. George Hudson reached age 50 and died in Wilmington, New Castle Co., Delaware, on April 24, 1975. He was buried in Gracelawn Memorial Park, Farmhurst, New Castle Co., Delaware.[59]

**286. Mildred Jennie⁸ Pegan** (*Everett⁷, Elmer Ellsworth James⁶, Alexander L.⁵, Andrew⁴, James³, Andrew² Pagan, James¹*) was born on August 9, 1925, in Wilmington, New Castle Co., Delaware. She was the daughter of Everett Pegan (132) and Sarah Elizabeth Maxwell.

Mildred Jennie married **Francis Paul Pedelini** in 1952. They had three children. Francis Paul Pedelini was born in Wilmington, New Castle Co., Delaware, on October 26, 1927. Francis Paul reached age 83 and died in Wilmington, New Castle Co., Delaware, on March 14, 2011. He was buried in All Saints Cemetery, Wilmington, New Castle Co., Delaware.[58]

Mildred Jennie Pegan and Francis Paul Pedelini had three children, including:

+ 428 m III. **Frank Paul Pedelini** was born in Wilmington, New Castle Co., Delaware, on December 10, 1955. He died in Merlin, Josephine Co., Oregon, on April 2, 2006.

**287. Earl Witmer⁸ Urban** (*Arthur Allen⁷, Bertha⁶ Pegan, Andrew A.⁵, Andrew⁴, James³, Andrew² Pagan,*

*James¹*) was born on January 11, 1920, in Manor Twp., Lancaster Co., Pennsylvania. He was the son of Arthur Allen Urban (134) and Alice Witmer. Earl Witmer died in Hudson, Pasco Co., Florida, on March 19, 1988, at age 68.

**288. Erma Elizabeth⁸ Urban** (*Arthur Allen⁷, Bertha⁶ Pegan, Andrew A.⁵, Andrew⁴, James³, Andrew² Pagan, James¹*) was born on October 17, 1924 in Manor Twp., Lancaster Co., Pennsylvania. She was the daughter of Arthur Allen Urban (134) and Alice Witmer. Erma Elizabeth died on September 30, 2014 in Neffsville, Manheim Twp., Lancaster Co., Pennsylvania. She was buried in Millersville Mennonite Cemetery, Millersville, Manor Twp., Lancaster Co., Pennsylvania.[61]

She married **Claire Eugene Underkoffler**. They had four children. daughter. Clair E. Underkoffler was born in Hopeland, Clay Twp., Lancaster Co., Pennsylvania on December 21, 1923. He reached age 49 died on August 27, 1973 in Lancaster, Lancaster Co., Pennsylvania. Clair Eugene is buried in Millersville Mennonite Cemetery, Millersville, Manor Twp., Lancaster Co., Pennsylvania.[61]

Erma Elizabeth Urban and Claire Eugene Underkoffler had four children, including:

+ 429 m I. **Infant Daughter⁹ Underkoffler** was born in Lancaster, Lancaster Co., Pennsylvania, on March 27, 1948. She died in Lancaster, Lancaster Co., Pennsylvania, on March 27, 1948 in Lancaster Co., Pennsylvania.[143]

+ 430 m I. **Carol Ann⁹ Underkoffler** was born in Lancaster, Lancaster Co., Pennsylvania, on February 15, 1949. She died in Leola Lancaster, Lancaster Co., Pennsylvania, on August 9, 2010. Carol Ann was buried in Millersville Mennonite Cemetery, Millersville, Manor Twp., Lancaster Co., Pennsylvania.[61]

**289. Ruth Arlene⁸ Urban** (*Arthur Allen⁷, Bertha⁶ Pegan, Andrew A.⁵, Andrew⁴, James³, Andrew² Pagan, James¹*) was born on November 8, 1930 in Manor Twp., Lancaster Co., Pennsylvania. She was the daughter of Arthur Allen Urban (134) and Alice Witmer. Ruth Arlene died in Manor Twp., Lancaster Co., Pennsylvania, on February 15, 1931. She was buried in Millersville Mennonite Cemetery, Millersville, Manor Twp., Lancaster Co., Pennsylvania.[61]

**290. Jean**[8] **Urban** (*Phares Pegan*[7], *Bertha*[6] *Pegan, Andrew A.*[5], *Andrew*[4], *James*[3], *Andrew*[2] *Pagan, James*[1]) was born on June 19, 1922, in Manor Twp., Lancaster Co., Pennsylvania. She was the daughter of Phares Pegan Urban (135) and Grace Benedict. Jean died in Columbia, Lancaster Co., Pennsylvania, on August 23, 2015, at age 93. She was buried in Millersville Mennonite Cemetery, Millersville, Manor Twp., Lancaster Co., Pennsylvania.[61]

Jean married **Amos Funk** on April 8, 1944. They had three sons. Amos Funk was born in Manor Twp., Lancaster Co., Pennsylvania, on December 14, 1920. Amos reached age 84 and died in West Hempfield Twp., Lancaster Co., Pennsylvania, on February 9, 2005. He was buried in Millersville Mennonite Cemetery, Millersville, Manor Twp., Lancaster Co., Pennsylvania.[61]

**291. Robert Benedict**[8] **Urban** (*Phares Pegan*[7], *Bertha*[6] *Pegan, Andrew A.*[5], *Andrew*[4], *James*[3], *Andrew*[2] *Pagan, James*[1]) was born on October 22, 1923, in Manor Twp., Lancaster Co., Pennsylvania. He was the son of Phares Pegan Urban (135) and Grace Benedict. Robert Benedict died in Lancaster Co., Pennsylvania, on November 25, 1968, at age 45. He was buried in Conestoga Memorial Park Cemetery, Lancaster Twp., Lancaster Co., Pennsylvania.[90]

He married **Linda Unknown**.

**292. Phares**[8] **Urban II** (*Phares Pegan*[7], *Bertha*[6] *Pegan, Andrew A.*[5], *Andrew*[4], *James*[3], *Andrew*[2] *Pagan, James*[1]) was born on January 27, 1928, in Manor Twp., Lancaster Co., Pennsylvania. He was the son of Phares Pegan Urban (135) and Grace Benedict. Phares died in Holtwood, Martic Twp., Lancaster Co., Pennsylvania, on May 17, 2007, at age 79.

He married **Mary Alice Nicodemus**. Mary Alice Nicodemus was born about 1937.

**293. Elaine Madeline**[8] **Urban** (*Ralph Martin*[7], *Bertha*[6] *Pegan, Andrew A.*[5], *Andrew*[4], *James*[3], *Andrew*[2] *Pagan, James*[1]) was born on August 14, 1929, in Lancaster, Lancaster Co., Pennsylvania. She was the daughter of Ralph Martin Urban (136) and Gertrude Sneath. Elaine Madeline died in Lancaster, Lancaster Co., Pennsylvania, on August 11, 2001, at age 71. She was buried in Millersville Mennonite Cemetery, Millersville, Manor Twp., Lancaster Co., Pennsylvania.[61]

She is buried under her maiden name, Elaine M. Urban.

She married **John Michael Vogrin**(?). They divorced. They had two sons.

**294. Ralph Kenneth**[8] **Urban II** (*Ralph Martin*[7], *Bertha*[6] *Pegan, Andrew A.*[5], *Andrew*[4], *James*[3], *Andrew*[2] *Pagan, James*[1]) was born on January 15, 1931, in Lancaster, Lancaster Co., Pennsylvania. He was also known as **Kenneth**. He was the son of Ralph Martin Urban (136) and Gertrude Sneath. Ralph Kenneth died in Lancaster, Lancaster Co., Pennsylvania? on April 3, 1969, at age 38. He was buried in Millersville Mennonite Cemetery, Millersville, Manor Twp., Lancaster Co., Pennsylvania.[45]

He is buried under the name of R. Kenneth Urban.

He married **Unknown Unknown**. They had two sons.

**295. James Howard**[8] **Wiley** (*Sarah*[7] *Johnson, Martha Ann*[6] *Fulton, Sarah Jane*[5] *Miller, Margaret*[4] *Pegan, James*[3], *Andrew*[2] *Pagan, James*[1]) was born on September 5, 1891, in Lower Chanceford Twp., York Co., Pennsylvania. He was also known as **Howard** and **Joseph Howard Wiley**. He was the son of Elmer Ramsey Wiley and Sarah Johnson (137). James Howard lived in 1940 in Layman, Montgomery Co., Virginia. He died in Dayton, Montgomery Co., Ohio, on November 5, 1964, at age 73. James Howard was buried in Miami Valley Memorial Gardens Cemetery, Springboro, Clearcreek Twp., Warren Co., Ohio.[113]

Family legend says James Howard Wiley, who had aliases of Howard Wiley and Joseph Howard Wiley, was a "fall guy" for a bootlegging and smuggling operation during Prohibition. Also, his first marriage to Jessie Nancy Barnett allegedly disintegrated because he thought that son Warren Dunlap Wiley was not his child. James Howard Wiley declared Jessie was unfaithful, deserted his family, and moved to North Carolina. Jessie also left, taking baby Hazel with her and leaving William J. and Emma Wiley with their uncle Samuel Wiley to raise. Elmer Wiley, James Howard Wiley's other brother, also helped raise them.

James Howard married **Jessie Nancy Barnett** on February 28, 1912. They divorced. They had five children. Jessie Nancy Barnett was born in Peach Bottom Twp., York Co., Pennsylvania, on February 6, 1891. She reached age 85 and died in Elizabethtown, Mt. Joy Twp., Lancaster Co., Pennsylvania, in July 1976. May have married a Coulter after 1940.

James Howard Wiley married **Pencie Miller Ridinger** before 1925. They had one daughter. Pencie Miller Ridinger was born in Court House, Floyd Co., Virginia, on January 6, 1901. Pencie Miller reached age 25 and died in Court House, Floyd Co., Virginia, on January 21, 1926. She was buried in Floyd Cemetery, Floyd, Floyd Co., Virginia.[144]

James Howard Wiley married **Stella May Reid** on February 8, 1926, in Rockingham Co., North Carolina. They divorced before 1940. They had five children. Stella May Reid was born in Floyd, Floyd Co., Virginia, on April 29, 1904. She reached age 71 and died in Blacksburg, Montgomery Co., Virginia, on May 11, 1975. Stella May was buried in Roselawn Memorial Gardens Cemetery, Christiansburg, Montgomery Co., Virginia.[145]

James Howard Wiley married **Barbara Unknown** after 1940 in Anderson Co., Tennessee?

James Howard Wiley married **Unknown Unknown**.

Children of James Howard Wiley and Jessie Nancy Barnett:

+ 431 m I. **William James⁹ Wiley** was born in Fulton Twp., Lancaster Co. Pennsylvania, on September 4, 1913. He died in Paradise Twp. Lancaster Co., Pennsylvania, on January 8, 1978. William James was buried in Old Leacock Presbyterian Cemetery, Intercourse, Leacock Twp., Lancaster Co., Pennsylvania.[146]

+ 432 f II. **Emma Rae⁹ Wiley** was born in Fulton Twp., Lancaster Co., Pennsylvania, on October 5, 1916. She died in Elkton, Cecil Co., Maryland, on March 25, 2003.

+ 433 m III. **Joseph Howard⁹ Wiley** was born in Fulton Twp., Lancaster Co., Pennsylvania, on August 8, 1918. He died in Fulton Twp., Lancaster Co., Pennsylvania, on April 20, 1920. Joseph Howard was buried in Mt. Nebo Church Cemetery, Peach Bottom Twp., York Co., Pennsylvania.[147]

+ 434 m IV. **Warren Dunlap⁹ Wiley** was born in Fulton Twp., Lancaster Co., Pennsylvania, on August 3, 1920. He died in a hospital in Lancaster, Lancaster Co., Pennsylvania, on November 20, 1920. Warren Dunlap was buried in Mt. Nebo Church Cemetery, Peach Bottom Twp., York Co., Pennsylvania.[147]

+ 435 f V. **Hazel Marion⁹ Wiley** was born in Delta, Peach Bottom Twp., York Co., Pennsylvania, on August 15, 1921. She died in a hospital in Marion, Marion Twp., Willliamson Co., Illinois, on March 5, 2007. Hazel Marion was buried in Saint Mary's Orthodox Cemetery, Royalton, Osage Twp., Franklin Co., Illinois.[148]

Daughter of James Howard Wiley and Pencie Miller Ridinger:

+ 436 f I. **Mary Sue⁹ Wiley** was born in Court House, Floyd Co., Virginia, on November 30, 1925. She died in Springvale, York Co., Maine, on February 17, 1991. Mary Sue was buried in Roselawn Memorial Gardens Cemetery, Christiansburg, Montgomery Co., Virginia.[145]

Children of James Howard Wiley and Stella May Reid:

+ 437 f I. **Lillian Howard**[9] **Wiley** was born in Floyd, Floyd Co., Virginia, on November 2, 1926. She was also known as **Pat**. Lillian Howard died in a hospital in Newark, New Castle Co., Delaware, on November[j] 28, 1997. She was buried in Delaware Veterans Memorial Cemtery, Bear, New Castle Co., Delaware.[149]

+ 438 m II. **James Howard**[9] **Wiley II** was born in Blacksburg, Montgomery Co., Virginia, on July 18, 1928.

+ 439 f III. **Dorothy Louise**[9] **Wiley** was born in Blacksburg, Montgomery Co., Virginia, on June 25, 1930. She died in Newark, New Castle Co., Delaware? on July 15, 1989.

+ 440 f IV. **Rebecca Jean**[9] **Wiley** was born in Blacksburg, Montgomery Co., Virginia, in 1932. She died before 1940.

+ 441 f V. **Agnes Caroline**[9] **Wiley** was born in Blacksburg, Montgomery Co., Virginia, in 1934.

**296. Samuel Johnson**[8] **Wiley** (*Sarah*[7] *Johnson, Martha Ann*[6] *Fulton, Sarah Jane*[5] *Miller, Margaret*[4] *Pegan, James*[3]*, Andrew*[2] *Pagan, James*[1]) was born on July 23, 1893, in Lower Chanceford Twp., York Co., Pennsylvania. He was the son of Elmer Ramsey Wiley and Sarah Johnson (137). Samuel Johnson died in Fulton Twp., Lancaster Co., Pennsylvania, on May 10, 1966, at age 72. He was buried in Little Britain Presbyterian Church Cemetery, Fulton Twp., Lancaster Co., Pennsylvania.[114]

Samuel Johnson married **Mabel Chambers** before 1919. They had three sons. Mabel Chambers was born in Fulton Twp., Lancaster Co., Pennsylvania, on January 13, 1896. Mabel reached age 81 and died in Peach Bottom Twp., York Co., Pennsylvania, in February 1977.

Sons of Samuel Johnson Wiley and Mabel Chambers:

+ 442 m I. **Infant Son**[9] **Wiley** was born in Fulton Twp., Lancaster Co., Pennsylvania, in 1919. He died in Fulton Twp., Lancaster Co., Pennsylvania, in 1919.

+ 443 m II. **Elmer R.**[9] **Wiley** was born in Fulton Twp., Lancaster Co., Pennsylvania, on April 29, 1921. He died in Peach Bottom Twp., York Co., Pennsylvania, on February 27, 1998. Elmer R. was buried in Quarryville Cemetery, Quarryville, Lancaster Co.., Pennsylvania.[150]

+ 444 m III. **Samuel Clayton**[9] **Wiley II** was born in Fulton Twp., Lancaster Co., Pennsylvania, on September 22, 1923. He was also known as **Pud**. Samuel Clayton died in Lancaster, Lancaster Co., Pennsylvania, on December 8, 2010. He was buried in Mount Zion United Methodist Church Cemetery, Peach Bottom, Fulton Twp., Lancaster Co., Pennsylvania.[151]

**297. Elmer Crawford**[8] **Wiley II** (*Sarah*[7] *Johnson, Martha Ann*[6] *Fulton, Sarah Jane*[5] *Miller, Margaret*[4] *Pegan, James*[3]*, Andrew*[2] *Pagan, James*[1]) was born on May 28, 1897, in Lower Chanceford Twp., York Co., Pennsylvania. He was the son of Elmer Ramsey Wiley and Sarah Johnson (137). Elmer Crawford died in Delta, Peach Bottom Twp., York Co., Pennsylvania, in September 1974 at age 77.

Elmer Crawford married **Nellie Stewart** before 1921. They had five children. Nellie Stewart was born in Lower Chanceford Twp., York Co., Pennsylvania, on October 15, 1900. Nellie reached age 80 and died in Delta, Peach Bottom Twp., York Co., Pennsylvania, in September 1981.

Children of Elmer Crawford Wiley II and Nellie Stewart:

+ 445  f   I.   **Sara E.[9] Wiley** was born in Lower Chanceford Twp., York Co., Pennsylvania, on April 8, 1921. She died in Glen Arm, Baltimore Co., Maryland on January 27, 2018. She was buried in Slateville Presbyterian Church Cemetery, Delta, Peach Bottom Twp., York Co., Pennsylvania.[49]

+ 446  f   II.  **Betty P.[9] Wiley** was born in Lower Chanceford Twp., York Co., Pennsylvania, on September 6, 1922.

+ 447  f   III. **Jeane Hawley[9] Wiley** was born in Lower Chanceford Twp., York Co., Pennsylvania, on August 21, 1924. She died in Delta, Peach Bottom Twp., York Co., Pennsylvania, on August 13, 1992.

+ 448  m  IV.  **Harold Kenneth[9] Wiley** was born in Lower Chanceford Twp., York Co., Pennsylvania, on February 28, 1926. He died in Delta, Peach Bottom Twp., York Co., Pennsylvania, on April 15, 2002. Harold Kenneth was buried in Slate Ridge Cemetery, Delta, Peach Bottom Twp., York Co., Pennsylvania.[20]

+ 449  m  V.   **John F.[9] Wiley** was born in Lower Chanceford Twp., York Co., Pennsylvania, on February 17, 1929. He was also known as **Jack**.

**298. Louise[8] Wiley** (*Sarah[7] Johnson, Martha Ann[6] Fulton, Sarah Jane[5] Miller, Margaret[4] Pegan, James[3], Andrew[2] Pagan, James[1]*) was born on November 2, 1900, in Lower Chanceford Twp., York Co., Pennsylvania. She was the daughter of Elmer Ramsey Wiley and Sarah Johnson (137). Louise died in Airville, Lower Chanceford Twp., York Co., Pennsylvania, in November 1985 at age 84.

She married **Samuel D. Manifold**. They had four children. Samuel D. Manifold was born in Lower Chanceford Twp., York Co., Pennsylvania, on September 17, 1902. Samuel D. reached age 83 and died in Brogue, Chanceford Twp., York Co., Pennsylvania, in March 1986.

Children of Louise Wiley and Samuel D. Manifold:

+ 450  m  I.   **Howard Hughes[9] Manifold** was born in Lower Chanceford Twp., York Co., Pennsylvania, on January 15, 1922. He died in York, York Co., Pennsylvania, on June 17, 1990. Howard Hughes was buried in Stewartstown Cemetery, Stewartstown, Hopewell Twp., York Co., Pennsylvania.[76]

+ 451  f   II.  **Sara Louise[9] Manifold** was born in Lower Chanceford Twp., York Co., Pennsylvania, on September 13, 1923. She died in a hospital in York, York Co., Pennsylvania, on October 22, 1996. Sara Louise was buried in Susquehanna Memorial Gardens Cemetery, York, York Co., Pennsylvania.[96]

+ 452  f   III. **Jane E.[9] Manifold** was born in Lower Chanceford Twp., York Co., Pennsylvania, in 1927.

+ 453  m  IV.  **Dale W.[9] Manifold** was born in Lower Chanceford Twp., York Co., Pennsylvania, on January 8, 1930.

**299. Robert Fulton[8] Dinsmore** (*Grace Anna[7] Johnson, Martha Ann[6] Fulton, Sarah Jane[5] Miller, Margaret[4] Pegan, James[3], Andrew[2] Pagan, James[1]*) was born on February 1, 1909, in Peach Bottom Twp., York Co., Pennsylvania. He was the son of Nelson Caldwell Dinsmore and Grace Anna Johnson (139). Robert Fulton died in Dade Co., Florida, in November 1967 at age 58.

Robert Fulton married **Elizabeth Gustene Barton** after 1940. They had one son. Elizabeth Gustene Barton was born in Peach Bottom Twp., York Co., Pennsylvania, on October 5, 1907. She was the daughter of Ross Barton and Alice Mabel Gemmill. Elizabeth Gustene reached age 67 and died in Delta, Peach Bottom Twp., York Co., Pennsylvania, in December 1974.

**300. Samuel Nelson⁸ Dinsmore** (*Grace Anna⁷ Johnson, Martha Ann⁶ Fulton, Sarah Jane⁵ Miller, Margaret⁴ Pegan, James³, Andrew² Pagan, James¹*) was born in 1910 in Peach Bottom Twp., York Co., Pennsylvania. He was the son of Nelson Caldwell Dinsmore and Grace Anna Johnson (139). Samuel Nelson died in 1955 at age 45. He was buried in Slate Ridge Cemetery, Delta, Peach Bottom Twp., York Co., Pennsylvania.[20]

Never married.

**301. Minna Marie⁸ Dinsmore** (*Grace Anna⁷ Johnson, Martha Ann⁶ Fulton, Sarah Jane⁵ Miller, Margaret⁴ Pegan, James³, Andrew² Pagan, James¹*) was born in 1912 in Peach Bottom Twp., York Co., Pennsylvania. She was also known as **Marie**. She was the daughter of Nelson Caldwell Dinsmore and Grace Anna Johnson (139). Minna Marie lived in 1940 in Wilmington, New Castle Co., Delaware. She died in Wilmington, New Castle, Delaware? in 1973 at age 61. Minna Marie was buried in Slate Ridge Cemetery, Delta, Peach Bottom Twp., York Co., Pennsylvania.[20]

Buried under the name Marie D. Burton.

Minna Marie married **Andrew John Burton** on October 11, 1939, in New Castle Co., Delaware. Andrew John Burton was born in Wilmington, New Castle Co., Delaware, on August 4, 1904. He was also known as **John Andrew Burton**. Andrew John died after 1940.

**302. James Alexander⁸ Dinsmore** (*Grace Anna⁷ Johnson, Martha Ann⁶ Fulton, Sarah Jane⁵ Miller, Margaret⁴ Pegan, James³, Andrew² Pagan, James¹*) was born on December 20, 1915, in Peach Bottom Twp., York Co., Pennsylvania. He was the son of Nelson Caldwell Dinsmore and Grace Anna Johnson (139). James Alexander died in Peach Bottom Twp., York Co., Pennsylvania, on September 1, 1973, at age 57. He was buried in Slate Ridge Cemetery, Delta, Peach Bottom Twp., York Co., Pennsylvania.[8]

James Alexander married **Anna M. Unknown** after 1940. Anna M. Unknown was born on April 15, 1913. Anna M. reached age 86 and died in Mesa, Maricopa Co., Arizona, on December 27, 1999. She was buried in Slate Ridge Cemetery, Delta, Peach Bottom Twp., York Co., Pennsylvania.[20]

**303. Lewis Price⁸ Fulton** (*David Edgar⁷, John Henry⁶, Sarah Jane⁵ Miller, Margaret⁴ Pegan, James³, Andrew² Pagan, James¹*) was born on July 12, 1906, in Peach Bottom Twp., York Co., Pennsylvania. He was the son of David Edgar Fulton (141) and Lena Kohlbus. Lewis Price died in Peach Bottom Twp., York Co., Pennsylvania, on December 25, 1914, at age eight. He was buried in Slate Ridge Cemetery, Delta, Peach Bottom Twp., York Co., Pennsylvania.[20]

**304. John F.⁸ Wise** (*Mary Janetta⁷ Fulton, John Henry⁶, Sarah Jane⁵ Miller, Margaret⁴ Pegan, James³, Andrew² Pagan, James¹*) was born on May 12, 1907, in Peach Bottom Twp., York Co., Pennsylvania. He was the son of Bunyan Hess Wise and Mary Janetta Fulton (142). John F. died in York, York Co., Pennsylvania, on September 24, 1990, at age 83. He was buried in Slate Ridge Cemetery, Delta, Peach Bottom Twp., York Co., Pennsylvania.[20]

John F. married **Thelma Williams** in 1930. They had one son. Thelma Williams was born in Maryland on January 26, 1904. Thelma reached age 67 and died in York, York Co., Pennsylvania, in July 1971. She was buried in Slate Ridge Cemetery, Delta, Peach Bottom Twp., York Co., Pennsylvania.[20]

Son of John F. Wise and Thelma Williams:

+ 454 m I.    **Donald David⁹ Wise** was born in Delta, Peach Bottom Twp., York Co., Pennsylvania, in 1931.

**305. Samuel A.⁸ Wise** (*Mary Janetta⁷ Fulton, John Henry⁶, Sarah Jane⁵ Miller, Margaret⁴ Pegan, James³, Andrew² Pagan, James¹*) was born on September 21, 1910, in Peach Bottom Twp., York Co., Pennsylvania. He was the son of Bunyan Hess Wise and Mary Janetta Fulton (142). Samuel A. died in York, York Co., Pennsylvania, on May 11, 1999, at age 88. He was buried in Slate Ridge

Cemetery, Delta, Peach Bottom Twp., York Co., Pennsylvania.[20]

Samuel A. married **Mary Catherine Ford** before 1938. They had one son. Mary Catherine Ford was born in Harford Co., Maryland? on July 26, 1909. She was also known as **Catherine**. Mary Catherine reached age 90 and died in York, York Co., Pennsylvania, on February 29, 2000. She was buried in Slate Ridge Cemetery, Delta, Peach Bottom Twp., York Co., Pennsylvania.[20]

Son of Samuel A. Wise and Mary Catherine Ford:

+ 455  m  I.    **Dale Ford⁹ Wise** was born in York, York Co., Pennsylvania, on January 13, 1938.

**306. Ralph Anderson⁸ Wise** (*Mary Janetta⁷ Fulton, John Henry⁶, Sarah Jane⁵ Miller, Margaret⁴ Pegan, James³, Andrew² Pagan, James¹*) was born on March 25, 1913, in Peach Bottom Twp., York Co., Pennsylvania. He was the son of Bunyan Hess Wise and Mary Janetta Fulton (142). Ralph Anderson lived in 1940 in Fairlawn-Dundalk-St. Helena, Baltimore Co., Maryland. He died in Delta, Peach Bottom Twp., York Co., Pennsylvania, 115on April 15, 1995, at age 82. Ralph Anderson was buried in Bryansville Cemetery, Bryansville, Peach Bottom Twp., York Co., Pennsylvania.[90]

Ralph Anderson married **Ethel Lavenia Smith** before 1935. They had two sons. Ethel Lavenia Smith was born in Peach Bottom Twp., York Co., Pennsylvania, on April 28, 1913. Ethel Lavenia reached age 92 and died in Delta, Peach Bottom Twp., York Co., Pennsylvania, on March 4, 2006. She was buried in Bryansville Cemetery, Bryansville, Peach Bottom Twp., York Co., Pennsylvania.[115]

Sons of Ralph Anderson Wise and Ethel Lavenia Smith:

+ 456  m  I.    **Ralph⁹ Wise II** was born in Peach Bottom Twp., York Co., Pennsylvania, on February 23, 1936.

+ 457  m  II.   **Roy⁹ Wise** was born in Peach Bottom Twp., York Co., Pennsylvania, on February 23, 1936.

**307. Mary Eleanor⁸ Wise** (*Mary Janetta⁷ Fulton, John Henry⁶, Sarah Jane⁵ Miller, Margaret⁴ Pegan, James³, Andrew² Pagan, James¹*) was born on June 2, 1915, in Peach Bottom Twp., York Co., Pennsylvania. She was the daughter of Bunyan Hess Wise and Mary Janetta Fulton (142). Mary Eleanor died in York, York Co., Pennsylvania, on December 10, 2001, at age 86. She was buried in Fawn Grove Methodist Church Cemetery, Fawn Grove, Fawn Grove Twp., York Co., Pennsylvania.[91]

Mary Eleanor married **William Clifton Matson** about 1939. They had two children. William Clifton Matson was born in Fawn Grove Twp., York Co., Pennsylvania, on February 12, 1918. He was also known as **Clifton**. William Clifton reached age 91 and died in York, York Co., Pennsylvania, on September 2, 2009. He was buried in Fawn Grove Methodist Church Cemetery, Fawn Grove, Fawn Grove Twp., York Co., Pennsylvania.[91]

**308. Grace Anna⁸ Wise** (*Mary Janetta⁷ Fulton, John Henry⁶, Sarah Jane⁵ Miller, Margaret⁴ Pegan, James³, Andrew² Pagan, James¹*) was born on September 16, 1917, in Peach Bottom Twp., York Co., Pennsylvania. She is the daughter of Bunyan Hess Wise and Mary Janetta Fulton (142).

Grace Anna married **Edwin Wilson Ailes** on May 30, 1952. They had two daughters. Edwin Wilson Ailes was born in Peach Bottom, Fulton Twp., Lancaster Co., Pennsylvania, on December 27, 1925. Edwin Wilson reached age 88 and died in York, York Co., Pennsylvania, on May 30, 2014. He was buried in Paddletown Cemetery, Newberrytown, Newberry Twp., York Co., Pennsylvania.[152]

Grace Anna Wise and Edwin Wilson Ailes had two daughters, including:

+ 458  f  II.   **Daughter⁹ Ailes.**

**309. Infant Daughter⁸ Wise** (*Mary Janetta⁷ Fulton, John Henry⁶, Sarah Jane⁵ Miller, Margaret⁴ Pegan, James³, Andrew² Pagan, James¹*) was born on January 15, 1922, in Peach Bottom Twp., York Co., Pennsylvania. She was the daughter of Bunyan Hess Wise and Mary Janetta Fulton (142). Infant Daughter died in Peach Bottom Twp., York Co.,

Pennsylvania, on January 15, 1922. Probably buried in Slate Ridge Cemetery, Delta, Peach Bottom Twp., York Co., Pennsylvania.

310. **Bertha M.⁸ Wise** (*Mary Janetta⁷ Fulton, John Henry⁶, Sarah Jane⁵ Miller, Margaret⁴ Pegan, James³, Andrew² Pagan, James¹*) was born on February 7, 1923, in Peach Bottom Twp., York Co., Pennsylvania. She is the daughter of Bunyan Hess Wise and Mary Janetta Fulton (142).

Bertha M. married **Frederick Meredith Evans** after 1940. Frederick Meredith Evans was born in Delta, Peach Bottom Twp., York Co., Pennsylvania, on November 19, 1924. Frederick Meredith reached age 78 and died in Delta, Peach Bottom Twp., York Co., Pennsylvania, on January 26, 2003. He was buried in Slate Ridge Cemetery, Delta, Peach Bottom Twp., York Co., Pennsylvania.[20]

311. **Daughter⁸ Fulton** (*James Anderson⁷, John Henry⁶, Sarah Jane⁵ Miller, Margaret⁴ Pegan, James³, Andrew² Pagan, James¹*) was born on October 19, 1912, in Peach Bottom Twp., York Co., Pennsylvania. She was the daughter of James Anderson Fulton (143) and Elizabeth Jane Parry. Daughter died in Peach Bottom Twp., York Co., Pennsylvania, on October 19, 1912. She was buried in Slate Ridge Cemetery, Delta, Peach Bottom Twp., York Co., Pennsylvania.[20]

312. **Margaret Eleanora⁸ Fulton** (*James Anderson⁷, John Henry⁶, Sarah Jane⁵ Miller, Margaret⁴ Pegan, James³, Andrew² Pagan, James¹*) was born on July 24, 1914, in Peach Bottom Twp., York Co., Pennsylvania. She was the daughter of James Anderson Fulton (143) and Elizabeth Jane Parry. Margaret Eleanora died in Peach Bottom Twp., York Co., Pennsylvania, on June 23, 1920, at age five. She was buried in Slate Ridge Cemetery, Delta, Peach Bottom Twp., York Co., Pennsylvania.[20]

313. **James Anderson⁸ Fulton II** (*James Anderson⁷, John Henry⁶, Sarah Jane⁵ Miller, Margaret⁴ Pegan, James³, Andrew² Pagan, James¹*) was born on October 16, 1918, in Peach Bottom Twp., York Co., Pennsylvania. He was the son of James Anderson Fulton (143) and Elizabeth Jane Parry. James Anderson died in Stevens, Ephrata Twp., Lancaster Co., Pennsylvania, on December 17, 1998, at age 80. He was buried

in Memory Gardens Cemetery, East Cocalico Twp., Lancaster Co., Pennsylvania.[116]

314. **John Henry⁸ Fulton** (*Samuel J.⁷, John Henry⁶, Sarah Jane⁵ Miller, Margaret⁴ Pegan, James³, Andrew² Pagan, James¹*) was born on July 17, 1912, in Peach Bottom Twp., York Co., Pennsylvania. He was the son of Samuel J. Fulton (144) and Grace W. Hughes. John Henry died in York, York Co., Pennsylvania, on January 1, 1991, at age 78. He was buried in Mount Rose Cemetery, Spring Garden Twp., York Co., Pennsylvania.[40]

He married **Cleo Smith** after 1940. They had one daughter. Cleo Smith was born in York, York Co., Pennsylvania, on September 21, 1915. Cleo reached age 100 and died in a facility in Wellsboro, Tioga Co., Pennsylvania, on May 27, 2016. She was buried in Mount Rose Cemetery, Spring Garden Twp., York Co., Pennsylvania.[40]

315. **Mildred⁸ Gregg** (*William Fulton⁷, Margaret A.⁶ Fulton, Sarah Jane⁵ Miller, Margaret⁴ Pegan, James³, Andrew² Pagan, James¹*) was born on June 4, 1909, in Astoria, Clatsop Co., Oregon. She was the daughter of William Fulton Gregg (146) and Euretta Irwin. Mildred died in Astoria, Clatsop Co., Oregon, on June 5, 1909. She was buried in Astoria, Clatsop Co., Oregon.

According to the Roy D. Pegan genealogy of James and Sarah Brannon Pegan descendants, Mildred Gregg is buried in an Astoria, Oregon cemetery.[2]

316. **William Terrell⁸ Fulton II** (*William Davis⁷, Robert Allen⁶, Sarah Jane⁵ Miller, Margaret⁴ Pegan, James³, Andrew² Pagan, James¹*) was born on May 9, 1921, in Baltimore, Baltimore Co., Maryland. He was the son of William Davis Fulton (150) and Grace Terrell. William Terrell died in Lutherville, Timonium Twp., Baltimore Co., Maryland, on April 14, 2008, at age 86.

317. **James Clarence⁸ Kilgore II** (*James Mitchell⁷, Margaret Rosa⁶ Mitchell, Martha Ellen⁵ Miller, Margaret⁴ Pegan, James³, Andrew² Pagan, James¹*) was born on March 17, 1915, in Lower Chanceford Twp., York Co., Pennsylvania. He was the son of James Mitchell Kilgore (156) and Hannah Jane McNeil. James Clarence died in Mansfield,

Madison Twp., Richland Co., Ohio, on February 6, 1998, at age 82. He was buried in Mansfield Memorial Park Cemetery, Ontario, Madison Twp., Richland Co., Ohio.[67]

James Clarence married **Bernice Day** before 1937. They had three children. Bernice Day was born in England on January 3, 1921. Bernice reached age 91 and died in Mansfield, Madison Twp., Richland Co., Ohio, on August 12, 2012. She was buried in Mansfield Memorial Park Cemetery, Ontario, Madison Twp., Richland Co., Ohio.[118]

Children of James Clarence Kilgore II and Bernice Day:

+ 459 f I. **Mary Jane[9] Kilgore** was born in Mansfield, Madison Twp., Richland Co., Ohio, in 1938.

+ 460 m II. **James L.[9] Kilgore II** was born in Mansfield, Madison Twp., Richland Co., Ohio, on March 25, 1940. He died in Mansfield, Madison Twp., Richland Co., Ohio, on July 22, 2012. James L. was buried in Mansfield Memorial Park Cemetery, Ontario, Madison Twp., Richland Co., Ohio.[118]

+ 461 m III. **William Harry[9] Kilgore** was born in Mansfield, Madison Twp., Richland Co., Ohio, on August 23, 1941. He died in Port Richey, Pasco Co., Florida, on November 24, 1998. William Harry was buried in Florida National Cemetery, Bushnell, Sumter Co., Florida.[153]

**318. Willis Leroy[8] Kilgore** (*James Mitchell[7]*, *Margaret Rosa[6] Mitchell*, *Martha Ellen[5] Miller*, *Margaret[4] Pegan*, *James[3]*, *Andrew[2] Pagan*, *James[1]*) was born on April 20, 1917, in Mansfield, Madison Twp., Richland Co., Ohio. He was the son of James Mitchell Kilgore (156) and Hannah Jane McNeil. Willis Leroy died in San Antonio, Bexar Co., Texas, on July 10, 1963, at age 46. He was buried in Fort Sam Houston National Cemetery, San Antonio, Bexar Co., Texas.[119]

Willis Leroy married **Helen Mae West** about 1936. They divorced. They had one daughter. Helen Mae West was born in Kokomo, Center Twp., Howard Co., Indiana, on November 5, 1920. She reached age 78 and died in Norwalk, Norwalk Twp., Huron Co., Ohio, on May 23, 1999. Helen Mae was buried in Grove Street Cemetery, New London, New London Twp., Huron Co., Ohio.[154]

Died under the name Helen M. Iceman.

Willis Leroy Kilgore married Mrs. **Doris Towberman** Robbins on August 6, 1952, in Richland Co., Ohio. They divorced. Doris Towberman was born in Boston, Suffolk Co., Massachusetts, about 1924.

Willis Leroy Kilgore married **Marsha Unknown** before 1963.

Daughter of Willis Leroy Kilgore and Helen Mae West:

+ 462 f I. **Patricia Ann[9] Kilgore** was born in Mansfield, Madison Twp., Richland Co., Ohio, on June 22, 1938. She died in New London, New London Twp., Huron Co., Ohio, on October 26, 2003. Patricia Ann was buried in Grove Street Cemetery, New London, New London Twp., Huron Co., Ohio.[154]

**319. George Franklin[8] Kilgore** (*James Mitchell[7]*, *Margaret Rosa[6] Mitchell*, *Martha Ellen[5] Miller*, *Margaret[4] Pegan*, *James[3]*, *Andrew[2] Pagan*, *James[1]*) was born on October 1, 1918, in Mansfield, Madison Twp., Richland Co., Ohio. He was the son of James Mitchell Kilgore (156) and Hannah Jane McNeil. George Franklin died in Mansfield, Madison Twp., Richland Co., Ohio, on February 13, 1985, at age 66. He was buried in Windsor Park Cemetery, Mansfield, Madison Twp., Richland Co., Ohio.[120]

George Franklin married **Mabel Turner** on February 6, 1948, in Ashland Co., Ohio. Mabel Turner was born in Uniontown, Fayette Co., Pennsylvania, on November 25, 1916. Mabel reached age 91 and died in Mansfield, Madison Twp., Richland Co., Ohio, on March 20, 2008. She was buried in Windsor Park Cemetery, Mansfield, Madison Twp., Richland Co., Ohio.[120]

**320. John Harvey⁸ Kilgore** (*James Mitchell⁷, Margaret Rosa⁶ Mitchell, Martha Ellen⁵ Miller, Margaret⁴ Pegan, James³, Andrew² Pagan, James¹*) was born on June 24, 1921, in Mansfield, Madison Twp., Richland Co., Ohio. He was the son of James Mitchell Kilgore (156) and Hannah Jane McNeil. John Harvey died in Mansfield, Madison Twp., Richland Co., Ohio, on July 8, 2010, at age 89. He was buried in Mansfield Memorial Park Cemetery, Ontario, Madison Twp., Richland Co., Ohio.[118]

He married **Doloris Marie Lesser**. They had two children. Doloris Marie Lesser was born in Odessa, Lincoln Co., Washington, on December 5, 1923. Doloris Marie lived in 1930 in Batum Precinct, Adams Co., Washington. She reached age 69 and died in Mansfield, Madison Twp., Richland Co., Ohio, on February 17, 1993. Doloris Marie was buried in Mansfield Memorial Park Cemetery, Ontario, Madison Twp., Richland Co., Ohio.[118]

John Harvey Kilgore and Doloris Marie Lesser had two children, including:

+ 463 f I. **Janie Marie⁹ Kilgore** was born in Mansfield, Madison Twp., Richland Co., Ohio, on April 22, 1948. She died in Cranberry Twp., Butler Co., Pennsylvania? on November 27, 2009. Janie Marie was buried in Plains United Presbyterian Church Cemetery, Cranberry Twp., Butler Co., Pennsylvania.[155]

**321. Joseph Raymond⁸ Kilgore** (*James Mitchell⁷, Margaret Rosa⁶ Mitchell, Martha Ellen⁵ Miller, Margaret⁴ Pegan, James³, Andrew² Pagan, James¹*) was born on September 18, 1927, in Mansfield, Madison Twp., Richland Co., Ohio. He was the son of James Mitchell Kilgore (156) and Hannah Jane McNeil. Joseph Raymond died in Fort Myers, Lee Co., Florida, on February 17, 1989, at age 61.

**322. Charles B.⁸ Burkins** (*Ula Agnes Ellen⁷ Kilgore, Margaret Rosa⁶ Mitchell, Martha Ellen⁵ Miller, Margaret⁴ Pegan, James³, Andrew² Pagan, James¹*) was born on January 9, 1913, in Peach Bottom Twp., York Co., Pennsylvania. He was the son of David Elwood Burkins and Ula Agnes Ellen

Kilgore (157). Charles B. died in York Springs, Adams Co., Pennsylvania, on April 6, 1998, at age 85. He was buried in Salem Union Cemetery, Jacobus, York Co., Pennsylvania.[121]

Charles B. married **Anna Burger** before 1940. They had one daughter. Anna Burger was born in York, York Co., Pennsylvania, on August 31, 1913. Anna reached age 91 and died in New Oxford Twp., Adams Co., Pennsylvania, on October 16, 2004. She was buried in Salem Union Cemetery, Jacobus, York Co., Pennsylvania.[121]

Daughter of Charles B. Burkins and Anna Burger:

+ 464 f I. **Marian V.⁹ Burkins** was born on September 21, 1940.

**323. Ida R.⁸ Burkins** (*Ula Agnes Ellen⁷ Kilgore, Margaret Rosa⁶ Mitchell, Martha Ellen⁵ Miller, Margaret⁴ Pegan, James³, Andrew² Pagan, James¹*) was born on August 28, 1914, in Peach Bottom Twp., York Co., Pennsylvania. She was the daughter of David Elwood Burkins and Ula Agnes Ellen Kilgore (157). Ida R. died in York, York Co., Pennsylvania, on September 8, 1941, at age 27. She was buried in Bethany United Methodist Church Cemetery, Felton, Chanceford Twp., York Co., Pennsylvania.[122]

Ida R. married **Kenneth Free Grove** before 1933. They had two children. Kenneth Free Grove was born in East Hopewell Twp., York Co., Pennsylvania, on July 24, 1911. Kenneth Free reached age 82 and died in Dallastown, Windsor Twp., York Co., Pennsylvania, on November 19, 1993. He was buried in Susquehanna Memorial Gardens Cemetery, York, York Co., Pennsylvania.[96]

Children of Ida R. Burkins and Kenneth Free Grove:

+ 465 f I. **Betty L.⁹ Grove** was born in Windsor Twp., York Co., Pennsylvania, on December 23, 1933.

+ 466 m II. **Charles Kenneth⁹ Grove** was born in Felton, Chanceford Twp., York Co., Pennsylvania, on July

17, 1935. He was also known as **Snowball**. Charles Kenneth died in York, York Co., Pennsylvania, on May 16, 1967. He was buried in Susquehanna Memorial Gardens Cemetery, York, York Co., Pennsylvania.[96]

**324. Ross**[8] **Burkins** (*Ula Agnes Ellen*[7] *Kilgore, Margaret Rosa*[6] *Mitchell, Martha Ellen*[5] *Miller, Margaret*[4] *Pegan, James*[3]*, Andrew*[2] *Pagan, James*[1]) was born on August 11, 1916, in Peach Bottom Twp., York Co., Pennsylvania. He was the son of David Elwood Burkins and Ula Agnes Ellen Kilgore (157). Ross died in Red Lion, York Twp., York Co., Pennsylvania, on November 1, 2005, at age 89. He was buried in Zion United Methodist Church Cemetery, Red Lion, York Twp., York Co., Pennsylvania.[123]

Ross married **Mabel Grove** after 1940. They had two children. Mabel Grove was born in Felton, Chanceford Twp., York Co., Pennsylvania, on May 9, 1912. Mabel reached age 85 and died in Red Lion, York Twp., York Co., Pennsylvania, on February 19, 1998. She was buried in Zion United Methodist Church Cemetery, Red Lion, York Twp., York Co., Pennsylvania.[123]

**325. Infant Son**[8] **Burkins** (*Ula Agnes Ellen*[7] *Kilgore, Margaret Rosa*[6] *Mitchell, Martha Ellen*[5] *Miller, Margaret*[4] *Pegan, James*[3]*, Andrew*[2] *Pagan, James*[1]) was born on November 19, 1928, in Peach Bottom Twp., York Co., Pennsylvania. He was the son of David Elwood Burkins and Ula Agnes Ellen Kilgore (157). Infant Son died in Peach Bottom Twp., York Co., Pennsylvania, on November 19, 1928. He was buried in Pine Grove Presbyterian Church Cemetery, Lower Chanceford Twp., York Co., Pennsylvania.[35]

**326. George William**[8] **Burns** (*Nora Eliza*[7] *Kilgore, Margaret Rosa*[6] *Mitchell, Martha Ellen*[5] *Miller, Margaret*[4] *Pegan, James*[3]*, Andrew*[2] *Pagan, James*[1]) was born on September 22, 1922, in Peach Bottom Twp., York Co., Pennsylvania. He was the son of Harry Wilson Burns and Nora Eliza Kilgore (158). George William died in Lower Chanceford Twp., York Co., Pennsylvania, on October 7, 1927, at

age five. He was buried in Mount Olivet United Methodist Church Cemetery, Fawn Grove, Fawn Twp., York Co., Pennsylvania.[68]

**327. Maggie Ruth**[8] **Burns** (*Nora Eliza*[7] *Kilgore, Margaret Rosa*[6] *Mitchell, Martha Ellen*[5] *Miller, Margaret*[4] *Pegan, James*[3]*, Andrew*[2] *Pagan, James*[1]) was born on March 14, 1924, in Goram, Lower Chanceford Twp., York Co., Pennsylvania. She was the daughter of Harry Wilson Burns and Nora Eliza Kilgore (158). Maggie Ruth died in Dallastown, Windsor Twp., York Co., Pennsylvania, on August 30, 2006, at age 82. She was buried in Saint Luke's Evangelical Lutheran Cemetery, New Bridgeville, Chanceford Twp., York Co., Pennsylvania.[124]

She married **James L. Uffelman**. They had three children. James L. Uffelman was born in Chanceford Twp., York Co., Pennsylvania, on December 2, 1922. James L. reached age 42 and died in York, York Co., Pennsylvania, on December 9, 1964. He was buried in Saint Luke's Evangelical Lutheran Cemetery, New Bridgeville, Chanceford Twp., York Co., Pennsylvania.[124]

**328. Harry Wilson**[8] **Burns II** (*Nora Eliza*[7] *Kilgore, Margaret Rosa*[6] *Mitchell, Martha Ellen*[5] *Miller, Margaret*[4] *Pegan, James*[3]*, Andrew*[2] *Pagan, James*[1]) was born on August 15, 1926, in Peach Bottom Twp., York Co., Pennsylvania. He was the son of Harry Wilson Burns and Nora Eliza Kilgore (158). Harry Wilson died in Lower Chanceford Twp., York Co., Pennsylvania, on August 27, 1929, at age three. He was buried in Mount Olivet United Methodist Church Cemetery, Fawn Grove, Fawn Twp., York Co., Pennsylvania.[68]

**329. Joseph Milton**[8] **Burns** (*Nora Eliza*[7] *Kilgore, Margaret Rosa*[6] *Mitchell, Martha Ellen*[5] *Miller, Margaret*[4] *Pegan, James*[3]*, Andrew*[2] *Pagan, James*[1]) was born on September 26, 1928, in Lower Chanceford Twp., York Co., Pennsylvania. He was also known as **Milton**. He was the son of Harry Wilson Burns and Nora Eliza Kilgore (158). Joseph Milton died in Dallastown, Windsor Twp., York Co., Pennsylvania, on July 15, 2015, at age 86.

He married **Mary E. Unknown**. They divorced. They had seven children. Mary E. Unknown was born on June 15, 1936.

Children of Joseph Milton Burns and Mary E. Unknown:

+ 467 m I. **Wilson⁹ Burns** was born in Brogue, Chanceford Twp., York Co., Pennsylvania, on August 23, 1955. He was also known as **Tyke**. Wilson died in Brogue, Chanceford Twp., York Co., Pennsylvania, on December 20, 2014.

**330. Charles W.⁸ Burns** (*Nora Eliza⁷ Kilgore, Margaret Rosa⁶ Mitchell, Martha Ellen⁵ Miller, Margaret⁴ Pegan, James³, Andrew² Pagan, James¹*) was born on August 16, 1960, in Lower Chanceford Twp., York Co., Pennsylvania. He was the son of Harry Wilson Burns and Nora Eliza Kilgore (158). Charles W. died in Columbia, Lancaster Co., Pennsylvania, on October 21, 2016, at age 56. He was buried in Mount Zion Baptist Church Cemetery, Brogue, Chanceford Twp., York Co., Pennsylvania.[125]

He married **Ellen Rebecca Tome**. They had three sons. Ellen Rebecca Tome was born in York, York Co., Pennsylvania, on December 4, 1934. Ellen Rebecca reached age 47 and died in York, York Co., Pennsylvania? on December 22, 1981. She was buried in Mount Zion Baptist Church Cemetery, Brogue, Chanceford Twp., York Co., Pennsylvania.[125]

Charles W. Burns and Ellen Rebecca Tome had three sons, including:

+ 468 m I. **Mark C.⁹ Burns** was born in Chanceford Twp., York Co., Pennsylvania, in 1966. He died in Chanceford Twp., York Co., Pennsylvania, in 1966. Mark C. was buried in Mount Zion Baptist Church Cemetery, Brogue, Chanceford Twp., York Co., Pennsylvania.[125]

+ 469 m II. **Robert E.⁹ Burns** was born in Chanceford Twp., York Co.,

Pennsylvania, in 1968. He died in Chanceford Twp., York Co., Pennsylvania, in 1968. Robert E. was buried in Mount Zion Baptist Church Cemetery, Brogue, Chanceford Twp., York Co., Pennsylvania.[125]

**331. Clyde⁸ Burns** (*Nora Eliza⁷ Kilgore, Margaret Rosa⁶ Mitchell, Martha Ellen⁵ Miller, Margaret⁴ Pegan, James³, Andrew² Pagan, James¹*) was born in 1933 in Lower Chanceford Twp., York Co., Pennsylvania. He is the son of Harry Wilson Burns and Nora Eliza Kilgore (158).

**332. J. Harold⁸ Burns** (*Nora Eliza⁷ Kilgore, Margaret Rosa⁶ Mitchell, Martha Ellen⁵ Miller, Margaret⁴ Pegan, James³, Andrew² Pagan, James¹*) was born in 1935 in Lower Chanceford Twp., York Co., Pennsylvania. He is the son of Harry Wilson Burns and Nora Eliza Kilgore (158).

**333. Marian E.⁸ Grove** (*Francis Henry⁷, Ida Melissa⁶ Pegan, Henry⁵, James⁴, James³, Andrew² Pagan, James¹*) was born on May 15, 1905, in Peach Bottom Twp., York Co., Pennsylvania. She was the daughter of Francis Henry Grove (161) and Mary P. McLaughlin. Marian E. died in Delta, Peach Bottom Twp., York Co., Pennsylvania, on June 4, 1991, at age 86. She was buried in Slate Ridge Cemetery, Delta, Peach Bottom Twp., York Co., Pennsylvania.[20]

Childless.

Marian E. married **William Henry Mobley** about 1928. William Henry Mobley was born in Peach Bottom Twp., York Co., Pennsylvania, on December 7, 1903. He was also known as **Henry**. William Henry reached age 97 and died in Oxford, Chester Co., Pennsylvania, on April 9, 2001. He was buried in Slate Ridge Cemetery, Delta, Peach Bottom Twp., York Co., Pennsylvania.[20]

**334. Mary Evelyn⁸ Grove** (*Francis Henry⁷, Ida Melissa⁶ Pegan, Henry⁵, James⁴, James³, Andrew² Pagan, James¹*) was born on February 24, 1909, in Bryansville, Peach Bottom Twp., York Co., Pennsylvania. She was also known as **Evelyn**. She was the daughter of Francis Henry Grove (161) and Mary P. McLaughlin. Mary Evelyn died in York, York Co., Pennsylvania, on August 5, 1984, at age 75. She was buried in Prospect Hill Cemetery, York Twp., York Co., Pennsylvania.[43]

Mary Evelyn Grove Herman is buried under her preferred name, Evelyn G. Herman.

Mary Evelyn married **Harris Milton Herman** before 1938. They had one son. Harris Milton Herman was born in Manchester Twp., York Co., Pennsylvania, on May 30, 1891. Harris Milton reached age 85 and died in York, York Co., Pennsylvania, on November 20, 1976. He was buried in Prospect Hill Cemetery, York Twp., York Co., Pennsylvania.[43]

Son of Mary Evelyn Grove and Harris Milton Herman:

+ 470 m I. **Frank Edward⁹ Herman** was born in York, York Co., Pennsylvania, on May 30, 1938. He died in York, York Co., Pennsylvania, on September 29, 2006. Frank Edward was buried in Prospect Hill Cemetery, York Twp., York Co., Pennsylvania.[43]

335. **Samuel Francis⁸ Grove** (*Francis Henry⁷, Ida Melissa⁶ Pegan, Henry⁵, James⁴, James³, Andrew² Pagan, James¹*) was born in 1912 in Peach Bottom Twp., York Co., Pennsylvania. He was the son of Francis Henry Grove (161) and Mary P. McLaughlin. Samuel Francis died in Peach Bottom Twp., York Co., Pennsylvania, in 1913 at age one. He was buried in Slate Ridge Cemetery, Delta, Peach Bottom Twp., York Co., Pennsylvania.[20]

336. **Wayne Kenneth⁸ Grove II** (*Wayne Penny⁷, Ida Melissa⁶ Pegan, Henry⁵, James⁴, James³, Andrew² Pagan, James¹*) was born on March 26, 1913, in York Twp., York Co., Pennsylvania. He was the son of Wayne Penny Grove (162) and Hanna M. McCleary. Wayne Kenneth died in York Twp., York Co., Pennsylvania, on August 17, 1978, at age 65. He was buried in Prospect Hill Cemetery, York Twp., York Co., Pennsylvania.[43]

Wayne Kenneth married **Pauline Dorothy Henry** on September 18, 1937, in Norfolk Co., Virginia. They had one son. Pauline Dorothy Henry was born in York, York Co., Pennsylvania, on October 8, 1912. Pauline Dorothy reached age 58 and died in York, York Co., Pennsylvania? on September 4, 1971. Probably buried in Prospect Hill Cemetery, York, York Co., Pennsylvania.

Wayne Kenneth Grove II married **Jean A. Gibbs** after 1971. Jean A. Gibbs was born in Jackson Twp., York Co., Pennsylvania, on August 12, 1922. Jean A. reached age 77 and died in York, York Co., Pennsylvania, on September 26, 1999.

Son of Wayne Kenneth Grove II and Pauline Dorothy Henry:

+ 471 m I. **Wayne Kenneth⁹ Grove III** was born in 1939.

337. **Anita Mae⁸ Grove** (*Wayne Penny⁷, Ida Melissa⁶ Pegan, Henry⁵, James⁴, James³, Andrew² Pagan, James¹*) was born on August 8, 1915, in York Twp., York Co., Pennsylvania. She was the daughter of Wayne Penny Grove (162) and Hanna M. McCleary. Anita Mae died in York Twp., York Co., Pennsylvania, on April 6, 2001, at age 85. She was buried in Mount Rose Cemetery, Spring Garden Twp., York Co., Pennsylvania.[40]

Never married.

338. **Louise E.⁸ Grove** (*Wayne Penny⁷, Ida Melissa⁶ Pegan, Henry⁵, James⁴, James³, Andrew² Pagan, James¹*) was born on September 18, 1917, in York Twp., York Co., Pennsylvania. She was the daughter of Wayne Penny Grove (162) and Hanna M. McCleary. Louise E. died in Thomasville, Jackson Twp., York Co., Pennsylvania, on December 6, 2000, at age 83. She was buried in Rest Haven Cemetery, Hanover Twp., York Co., Pennsylvania.[127]

She married **Edwin Albright Allewatt**. They had one son. Edwin Albright Allewatt was born in Hanover Twp., York Co., Pennsylvania, on January 19, 1916. Edwin Albright reached age 75 and died in Thomasville, Jackson Twp., York Co., Pennsylvania? on January 26, 1991. He was buried in Rest Haven Cemetery, Hanover Twp., York Co., Pennsylvania.[127]

**339. Dale W.[8] Grove** (*Wayne Penny[7], Ida Melissa[6] Pegan, Henry[5], James[4], James[3], Andrew[2] Pagan, James[1]*) was born on April 28, 1919, in York Twp., York Co., Pennsylvania. He was the son of Wayne Penny Grove (162) and Hanna M. McCleary. Dale W. died in York, York Co., Pennsylvania, on January 9, 2015, at age 95. He was buried in Susquehanna Memorial Gardens Cemetery, York, York Co., Pennsylvania.[96]

Dale W. married **Lois M. Gilbert** on May 9, 1959. They had two sons. Lois M. Gilbert was born in York, York Co., Pennsylvania, on January 31, 1925.

**340. Herbert Adams[8] Grove** (*Wayne Penny[7], Ida Melissa[6] Pegan, Henry[5], James[4], James[3], Andrew[2] Pagan, James[1]*) was born on September 24, 1920, in York Twp., York Co., Pennsylvania. He was the son of Wayne Penny Grove (162) and Hanna M. McCleary. Herbert Adams died in Long Beach, Los Angeles Co., California, on January 5, 2011, at age 90.

Seems to have never married.

**341. Carl Warren[8] Grove** (*Wayne Penny[7], Ida Melissa[6] Pegan, Henry[5], James[4], James[3], Andrew[2] Pagan, James[1]*) was born on August 19, 1922, in York Twp., York Co., Pennsylvania. He was also known as **Grovie**. He was the son of Wayne Penny Grove (162) and Hanna M. McCleary. Carl Warren died in York, York Co., Pennsylvania, on October 3, 2013, at age 91. He was buried in Prospect Hill Cemetery, York Twp., York Co., Pennsylvania.[43]

Carl Warren married **Fay C. Avila**. They had four children. Fay C. Avila was born in Muncy Twp., Lycoming Co., Pennsylvania on April 14, 1929.

**342. Leonard Allison[8] Grove** (*Wayne Penny[7], Ida Melissa[6] Pegan, Henry[5], James[4], James[3], Andrew[2] Pagan, James[1]*) was born on August 20, 1927, in York Twp., York Co., Pennsylvania. He was the son of Wayne Penny Grove (162) and Hanna M. McCleary. Leonard Allison died in York, York Co., Pennsylvania, on January 10, 2017, at age 89. He

was buried in Prospect Hill Cemetery, York Twp., York Co., Pennsylvania.[43]

Leonard Allison married **Miss Price** on January 27, 1950. They have three children.

**343. Alexander Allison[8] Grove** (*William Allison[7], Ida Melissa[6] Pegan, Henry[5], James[4], James[3], Andrew[2] Pagan, James[1]*) was born in 1911 in Detroit, Wayne Co., Michigan. He was also known as **Alex**. He was the son of William Allison Grove (163) and Fannie Irene Alexander. Alexander Allison died after 1930.

May have been adopted out after he was orphaned in 1933.

**344. Gertrude Melissa[8] Grove** (*Claire Jamison[7], Ida Melissa[6] Pegan, Henry[5], James[4], James[3], Andrew[2] Pagan, James[1]*) was born on September 20, 1917, in York, York Co., Pennsylvania. She was the daughter of Claire Jamison Grove (164) and Blanche Gertrude Gable. Gertrude Melissa died in Monterey, Monterey Co., California, on November 1, 1972, at age 55.

Gertrude Melissa married **Ernest James Houseberg** on November 26, 1942, in York Co., Pennsylvania. They divorced. They had one daughter. Ernest James Houseberg was born in Bangor, Washington Twp., Northampton Co., Pennsylvania, on August 7, 1920. He reached age 78 and died in Tuolumne City, Tuolumne Co., California, on August 18, 1998.

Daughter of Gertrude Melissa Grove and Ernest James Houseberg:

+ 472 f I. **Linda Gail[9] Houseberg** was born in San Francisco, San Francisco Co., California, on May 10, 1950. She died in Houston, Harris Co., Texas, on March 12, 2012.

**345. Earnest Benjamin[8] Horn** (*Anna Matilda[7] Grove, Ida Melissa[6] Pegan, Henry[5], James[4], James[3], Andrew[2] Pagan, James[1]*) was born on March 12, 1915, in Springettsbury Twp., York Co., Pennsylvania. He was the son of Melvin Benjamin Franklin Horn and Anna Matilda Grove (165). Earnest Benjamin died in Springettsbury Twp., York Co., Pennsylvania, on March 12, 1915. He was buried in Longstown

United Methodist Cemetery, York Twp., York Co., Pennsylvania.[71]

346. **Sarah Esther**[8] **Horn** (*Anna Matilda*[7] *Grove, Ida Melissa*[6] *Pegan, Henry*[5], *James*[4], *James*[3], *Andrew*[2] *Pagan, James*[1]) was born on May 22, 1916, in Springettsbury Twp., York Co., Pennsylvania. She was also known as **Esther**. She was the daughter of Melvin Benjamin Franklin Horn and Anna Matilda Grove (165). Sarah Esther died in York Twp., York Co., Pennsylvania, on January 22, 1994, at age 77. She was buried in Longstown United Methodist Cemetery, York Twp., York Co., Pennsylvania.[71]

Sarah Esther married **George Elmer Dietz** after 1940. They had two daughters. George Elmer Dietz was born in Lower Windsor Twp., York Co., Pennsylvania, on April 1, 1915. George Elmer reached age 80 and died in York Twp., York Co., Pennsylvania, on February 29, 1996. He was buried in Longstown United Methodist Cemetery, York Twp., York Co., Pennsylvania.[71]

347. **Rodger Melvin**[8] **Horn** (*Anna Matilda*[7] *Grove, Ida Melissa*[6] *Pegan, Henry*[5], *James*[4], *James*[3], *Andrew*[2] *Pagan, James*[1]) was born on October 26, 1919, in Springettsbury Twp., York Co., Pennsylvania. He was the son of Melvin Benjamin Franklin Horn and Anna Matilda Grove (165). Rodger Melvin died in Dallastown, Windsor Twp., York Co., Pennsylvania, on July 10, 2009, at age 89. He was buried in Mount Rose Cemetery, Spring Garden Twp., York Co., Pennsylvania.[40]

Rodger Melvin married **Margaret Prall Grove** about 1940. They divorced. They had two children. Margaret Prall Grove was born in York, York Co., Pennsylvania, on December 27, 1916. She was also known as **Peg**. Margaret Prall reached age 80 and died in Red Lion, York Twp., York Co., Pennsylvania, on October 24, 1997. She was buried in Mount Rose Cemetery, Spring Garden Twp., York Co., Pennsylvania.[40]

Rodger Melvin Horn and Margaret Prall Grove had two children, including:

+ 473 m II. **Barry Rodger Horn** was born in York Co., Pennsylvania, on May 3,

1944. He died in Red Lion, York Twp., York Co., Pennsylvania, on September 4, 1998. Barry Rodger was buried in Susquehanna Memorial Gardens Cemetery, York, York Co., Pennsylvania.[96]

348. **Romaine Grove**[8] **Horn** (*Anna Matilda*[7] *Grove, Ida Melissa*[6] *Pegan, Henry*[5], *James*[4], *James*[3], *Andrew*[2] *Pagan, James*[1]) was born on October 31, 1921, in Springettsbury Twp., York Co., Pennsylvania. She was the daughter of Melvin Benjamin Franklin Horn and Anna Matilda Grove (165). Romaine Grove died in York Twp., York Co., Pennsylvania, on May 3, 2004, at age 82. She was buried in Prospect Hill Cemetery, York Twp., York Co., Pennsylvania.[43]

Romaine Grove married **William Arthur McClure** before 1949. They had three children. William Arthur McClure was born in York Twp., York Co., Pennsylvania, on April 14, 1924. William Arthur reached age 75 and died in York Twp., York Co., Pennsylvania, on February 23, 2000. He was buried in Prospect Hill Cemetery, York Twp., York Co., Pennsylvania.[43]

Children of Romaine Grove Horn and William Arthur McClure:

+ 474 f I. **Cynthia Ann**[9] **McClure** was born in York Twp., York Co., Pennsylvania, on September 25, 1949. She died in York Twp., York Co., Pennsylvania, on February 28, 2010. Cynthia Ann was buried in Prospect Hill Cemetery, York Twp., York Co., Pennsylvania.[43]

349. **Donald W.**[8] **Grove** (*Samuel Gail*[7], *Ida Melissa*[6] *Pegan, Henry*[5], *James*[4], *James*[3], *Andrew*[2] *Pagan, James*[1]) was born on October 11, 1923 in Windsor Twp., York Co., Pennsylvania. He was the son of Samuel Gail Grove II (169) and Ada Irene Witmer. Donald W. Grove died in Mesa, Maricopa Co., Arizona on April 2, 1973. He is buried in Stony Brook Mennonite Cemetery, York, York Co., Pennsylvania.[73]

He married **Jane Agnes Goodman**. They had one daughter. Jane Agnes Goodman was born in New Freedom, Shrewsbury Twp., York Co., Pennsylvania, in 1927. She is also known as **Agnes**.

**350. E. Jean⁸ Grove** (*John Paul⁷, Alice Eva⁶ Pegan, Henry⁵, James⁴, James³, Andrew² Pagan, James¹*) was born on November 27, 1920, in High Rock, Lower Chanceford Twp., York Co., Pennsylvania. She was also known as **Jean**. She was the daughter of John Paul Grove (170) and Ida Mae Workinger. E. Jean died in Windsor Twp., York Co., Pennsylvania, on June 30, 2016, at age 95.

E. Jean married **John H. Morton** on July 12, 1941. They had two daughters. John H. Morton was born in Lower Chanceford Twp., York Co., Pennsylvania, on November 7, 1919. John H. reached age 94 and died in Windsor Twp., York Co., Pennsylvania, on April 9, 2014.

E. Jean Grove and John H. Morton had two daughters, including:

+ 475 f I. **Daughter⁹ Morton**.

**351. Bernice Elanora⁸ Grove** (*John Paul⁷, Alice Eva⁶ Pegan, Henry⁵, James⁴, James³, Andrew² Pagan, James¹*) was born on July 21, 1927, in High Rock, Lower Chanceford Twp., York Co., Pennsylvania. She was the daughter of John Paul Grove (170) and Ida Mae Workinger. Bernice Elanora died in Norristown, Montgomery Co., Pennsylvania, on November 15, 1998, at age 71.

She married **William Flaharty**(?). They had one daughter.

**352. Robert Wayne⁸ Miller** (*Mary Adelaide⁷ Wickersham, Mary Lena⁶ Pegan, Henry⁵, James⁴, James³, Andrew² Pagan, James¹*) was born on September 23, 1933, in Coatesville, Valley Twp., Chester Co., Pennsylvania. He was also known as **Wayne; R. Wayne Miller**. He was the son of Edgar Drew Miller and Mary Adelaide Wickersham (172). Robert Wayne died in Hopkinton, Merrimack Co., New Hampshire, on February 7, 1994, at age 60. He was buried in Upper Octarara Church Cemetery, Parkesburg, Sadbury Twp., Chester Co., Pennsylvania.[74]

He married **Miss Martin**. They had six children.

**353. Evelyn R.⁸ Pegan** (*Nathan Neil⁷, Harry Hutton⁶, Henry⁵, James⁴, James³, Andrew² Pagan, James¹*) was born on August 30, 1919, in Spring Grove, Jackson Twp., York Co., Pennsylvania. She was the daughter of Nathan Neil Pegan (175) and Bessie Sue Gunnet. Evelyn R. died in Spring Grove, Jackson Twp., York Co., Pennsylvania, on May 19, 1972, at age 52.

Evelyn R. married **Ross Shemwell Leonard** on December 30, 1944, in York Co., Pennsylvania. They had three children. Ross Shemwell Leonard was born in Ironton, Upper Twp., Lawrence Co., Ohio, on April 23, 1921.[156] Ross Shemwell reached age 85 and died in Vienna, Fairfax Co., Virginia, on June 7, 2006.[157] He was buried in Spring Grove Cemetery, Jackson Twp., York Co., Pennsylvania.[24]

**354. Ethel Virginia⁸ Pegan** (*Nathan Neil⁷, Harry Hutton⁶, Henry⁵, James⁴, James³, Andrew² Pagan, James¹*) was born in 1926 in Spring Grove, Jackson Twp., York Co., Pennsylvania. She was also known as **Etts**. She was the daughter of Nathan Neil Pegan (175) and Bessie Sue Gunnet.

Ethel Virginia married **Richard Eugene Messinger** on August 10, 1946.

Ethel Virginia Pegan and Richard Eugene Messinger had two sons, including:

+ 476 m I. **Richard Eugene⁹ Messinger II** was born in York, York Co., Pennsylvania, on July 20, 1947.[158] He died in York, York Co., Pennsylvania, on July 20, 1947.[159] Richard Eugene was buried in Spring Grove Cemetery, Jackson Twp., York Co., Pennsylvania.[24, 159]

**355. Karen Marie⁸ Trout** (*Jessie Eliza⁷ Manifold, Jennie Elizabeth⁶ Adams, Sarah Eliza⁵ Pegan, James⁴, James³, Andrew² Pagan, James¹*) was born in 1938 in East Hopewell Twp., York Co., Pennsylvania. She is the daughter of Harold Manifold Trout and Jessie Eliza Manifold (174).

**356. Son⁸ Trout** (*Jessie Eliza⁷ Manifold, Jennie Elizabeth⁶ Adams, Sarah Eliza⁵ Pegan, James⁴, James³, Andrew² Pagan, James¹*) was born on September 5, 1941, in

East Hopewell Twp., York Co., Pennsylvania. He was the son of Harold Manifold Trout and Jessie Eliza Manifold (175). Son died in East Hopewell Twp., York Co., Pennsylvania, on September 5, 1941. Son was buried in Round Hill Presbyterian Church Cemetery, Cross Roads, East Hopewell Twp., York Co., Pennsylvania.[39]

**357. Grace Elaine**[8] **Manifold** (*Samuel Benjamin*[7], *Jennie Elizabeth*[6] *Adams, Sarah Eliza*[5] *Pegan, James*[4]*, James*[3]*, Andrew*[2] *Pagan, James*[1]) was born in 1930 in East Hopewell Twp., York Co., Pennsylvania. She is also known as **Elaine**. She was the daughter of Samuel Benjamin Manifold (177) and Grace Veach.

Grace Elaine married **Dale Wiley Manifold** on April 7, 1950, in San Diego Co., California. They had three sons. Dale W. Manifold was born in Lower Chanceford Twp., York Co., Pennsylvania, on January 8, 1930. He was the son of Samuel D. Manifold and Louise Wiley (298). He reached age 88 and died in Yuma, Yuma Co., Arizona on February 3, 2018. He was buried in Eternal Hills Memorial Park Cemetery, Oceanside, San Diego Co., California.[159]

**358. Benjamin Eugene**[8] **Manifold** (*Samuel Benjamin*[7]*, Jennie Elizabeth*[6] *Adams, Sarah Eliza*[5] *Pegan, James*[4]*, James*[3]*, Andrew*[2] *Pagan, James*[1]) was born on February 28, 1933, in East Hopewell Twp., York Co., Pennsylvania. He was also known as **Eugene**. He was the son of Samuel Benjamin Manifold (177) and Grace Veach. Benjamin Eugene died in Stewartstown, Hopewell Twp., York Co., Pennsylvania, on July 28, 1997, at age 64. He was buried in Round Hill Presbyterian Church Cemetery, Cross Roads, East Hopewell Twp., York Co., Pennsylvania.[39]

Benjamin Eugene married **Lydia Mae Wolfe**. They had one son. Lydia Mae Wolfe was born in Hopewell Twp., York Co., Pennsylvania, on June 27, 1935.

Son of Benjamin Eugene Manifold and Lydia Mae Wolfe:

+ 477   m   I.   **Bret E.**[9] **Manifold** was born on November 19, 1965. He was buried in Round Hill Presbyterian Church Cemetery, Cross Roads, East Hopewell Twp., York Co., Pennsylvania.[39]

**359. Betty Lou**[8] **Manifold** (*Samuel Benjamin*[7]*, Jennie Elizabeth*[6] *Adams, Sarah Eliza*[5] *Pegan, James*[4]*, James*[3]*, Andrew*[2] *Pagan, James*[1]) was born in 1938 in Chanceford Twp., York Co., Pennsylvania. She is the daughter of Samuel Benjamin Manifold (177) and Grace Veach.

**360. Daughter**[8] **Manifold** (*Samuel Benjamin*[7]*, Jennie Elizabeth*[6] *Adams, Sarah Eliza*[5] *Pegan, James*[4]*, James*[3]*, Andrew*[2] *Pagan, James*[1]) was born in Chanceford Twp., York Co., Pennsylvania. She is the daughter of Samuel Benjamin Manifold (177) and Grace Veach.

Linda married **Larry F. Neal**. They had one son. Larry F. Neal was born in York, York Co., Pennsylvania, on September 1, 1943. Larry F. reached age 72 and died in New Park, Fawn Twp., York Co., Pennsylvania, on October 2, 2015. He was buried in Centre Presbyterian Cemetery, Fawn Twp., York Co., Pennsylvania.[160]

**361. Richard Weist**[8] **Lanius** (*Margaret Eleanor*[7] *Manifold, Jennie Elizabeth*[6] *Adams, Sarah Eliza*[5] *Pegan, James*[4]*, James*[3]*, Andrew*[2] *Pagan, James*[1]) was born on August 29, 1935, in Hopewell Twp., York Co., Pennsylvania. He was also known as **Zeke**. He was the son of Gemmill Weist Lanius and Margaret Eleanor Manifold (178). Richard Weist lived in Stewartstown, Hopewell Twp., York Co., Pennsylvania. He died in a hospital in Lebanon, North Lebanon Twp., Lebanon Co., Pennsylvania, on November 22, 1983, at age 48. Richard Weist was buried in Stewartstown Cemetery, Stewartstown, Hopewell Twp., York Co., Pennsylvania.[76]

Richard Weist married **Carolyn Ruth Vaught** They had one son. Carolyn Ruth Vaught was born on June 20, 1940. She is also known as **Ruth**.

Son of Richard Weist Lanius and Carolyn Ruth Vaught:

+ 478 m I. **Dirk Michael⁹ Lanius** was born on February 20, 1964. He died in a hospital in Baltimore, Baltimore Co., Maryland, on March 14, 1984.

362. **Son⁸ Lanius** (*Margaret Eleanor⁷ Manifold, Jennie Elizabeth⁶ Adams, Sarah Eliza⁵ Pegan, James⁴, James³, Andrew² Pagan, James¹*) was born after 1940. He is the son of Gemmill Weist Lanius and Margaret Eleanor Manifold (178). Probably died in infancy.

363. **Daughter⁸ Lanius** (*Margaret Eleanor⁷ Manifold, Jennie Elizabeth⁶ Adams, Sarah Eliza⁵ Pegan, James⁴, James³, Andrew² Pagan, James¹*) was born after 1940. She is the daughter of Gemmill Weist Lanius and Margaret Eleanor Manifold (178). Probably died in infancy.

364. **Gerard⁸ Baxter** (*Gladys Grove⁷ Adams, Samuel Jamieson⁶, Sarah Eliza⁵ Pegan, James⁴, James³, Andrew² Pagan, James¹*) was born in 1934 in Cardiff, Harford Co., Maryland. He is the son of McClellan F. Baxter and Gladys Grove Adams (181).

365. **Dennis⁸ Baxter** (*Gladys Grove⁷ Adams, Samuel Jamieson⁶, Sarah Eliza⁵ Pegan, James⁴, James³, Andrew² Pagan, James¹*) was born in 1939 in Baltimore, Baltimore Co., Maryland. He is the son of McClellan F. Baxter and Gladys Grove Adams (181).

366. **Carolyn⁸ Grove** (*David Earl⁷, James Pegan⁶, Margaret Jane⁵ Pegan, James⁴, James³, Andrew² Pagan, James¹*) was born in 1931 in York Co., Pennsylvania. She is the daughter of David Earl Grove (183) and Margaret Arlene Boring.

# 9th Generation

**367. Margaret[9] Walton** (*Luther Maurice[8], Elmer[7], Hannah Margaret[6] Nimlow, Margaret[5] Pegan, Andrew[4], James[3], Andrew[2] Pagan, James[1]*) was born on April 7, 1920, in Philadelphia, Philadelphia Co., Pennsylvania. She was the daughter of Luther Maurice Walton (186) and Katherine Mae Hutchinson. Margaret died in Alexandria, Porter Twp., Huntingdon Co., Pennsylvania, on May 25, 2002, at age 82. She was buried in Morris Cemetery, Phoenixville, Schuylkill Twp., Chester Co., Pennsylvania.[81]

Margaret married **Elwood Duane Faddis** on February 13, 1940, in Loudoun Co., Virginia. They had three children. Elwood Duane Faddis was born in Schuylkill Twp., Chester Co., Pennsylvania, on November 9, 1918. Elwood Duane reached age 82 and died in Tyrone, Blair Co., Pennsylvania, on October 27, 2002. He was buried in Morris Cemetery, Phoenixville, Schuylkill Twp., Chester Co., Pennsylvania.[81]

**368. Rebecca Walton[9] Douts** (*Mary Margaret[8] Walton, Elmer[7], Hannah Margaret[6] Nimlow, Margaret[5] Pegan, Andrew[4], James[3], Andrew[2] Pagan, James[1]*) was born on May 1, 1917, in Martic Twp., Lancaster Co., Pennsylvania. She was the daughter of Emerson Douts and Mary Margaret Walton (187). Rebecca Walton died in Quarryville, East Drumore Twp., Lancaster Co., Pennsylvania, on August 4, 2006, at age 89. She was buried in Mount Nebo United Methodist Church Cemetery, Pequea, Pequea Twp., Lancaster Co., Pennsylvania.[82]

Rebecca Walton married **Elias Benjamin Miller** about 1935. They had four children. Elias Benjamin Miller was born in Drumore Twp., Lancaster Co., Pennsylvania, on May 25, 1912. Elias Benjamin reached age 79 and died in Drumore Twp., Lancaster Co., Pennsylvania, on May 27, 1991. He was buried in Mount Nebo United Methodist Church Cemetery, Pequea, Pequea Twp., Lancaster Co., Pennsylvania.[82]

Children of Rebecca Walton Douts and Elias Benjamin Miller:

+ 479   f   I.   **Lucretia Mae[10] Miller** was born in Martic Twp., Lancaster Co., Pennsylvania, on May 28, 1936.

+ 480   m   II.   **David D.[10] Miller** was born in Martic Twp., Lancaster Co., Pennsylvania, on July 3, 1938.

+ 481   m   III.   **Donald Emerson[10] Miller** was born in Martic Twp., Lancaster Co., Pennsylvania, on August 27, 1939. He died in Martic Twp., Lancaster Co., Pennsylvania, on June 4, 1952. He was buried in Mount Nebo United Methodist Church Cemetery, Pequea, Pequea Twp., Lancaster Co., Pennsylvania.[82]

**369. John Luther[9] Douts** (*Mary Margaret[8] Walton, Elmer[7], Hannah Margaret[6] Nimlow, Margaret[5] Pegan, Andrew[4], James[3], Andrew[2] Pagan, James[1]*) was born on March 15, 1920, in Martic Twp., Lancaster Co., Pennsylvania. He was the son of Emerson Douts and Mary Margaret Walton (187). John Luther lived in Powers Lake, Burke Co., North Dakota. He died in Minot, Ward Co., North Dakota, on March 23, 2006, at age 86. John Luther was buried in Bethel Cemetery, Battleview, Burke Co., North Dakota.[131]

John Luther married **Verna Blomquist** after 1940. They had three children. Verna Blomquist was born in Lancaster Co., Pennsylvania? on February 25, 1919. Verna reached age 87 and died in Powers Lake, Burke Co., North Dakota, on October 30, 2006. She was buried in Bethel Cemetery, Battleview, Burke Co., North Dakota.[131]

John Luther Douts and Verna Blomquist had three children, including:

+ 482   f   I.   **Daughter[10] Douts**.

+ 483 f III. **Judy Kay**[10] **Douts** was born Powers Lake, Burke Co., North Dakota on February 6, 1952. She died in Powers Lake, Burke Co., North Dakota on December 30, 1989. Judy Kay was buried in Bethel Cemetery, Battleview, Burke Co., North Dakota.[131]

**370. Henry Elmer**[9] **Douts** (*Mary Margaret*[8] *Walton, Elmer*[7], *Hannah Margaret*[6] *Nimlow, Margaret*[5] *Pegan, Andrew*[4], *James*[3], *Andrew*[2] *Pagan, James*[1]) was born on January 19, 1922, in Martic Twp., Lancaster Co., Pennsylvania. He was also known as **Elmer**. He was the son of Emerson Douts and Mary Margaret Walton (187). Henry Elmer died in Saint Thomas, Franklin Co., Pennsylvania, on September 25, 2001, at age 79. He was buried in Mount Nebo United Methodist Church Cemetery, Pequea, Pequea Twp., Lancaster Co., Pennsylvania.[82]

**371. Anna Jane**[9] **Douts** (*Mary Margaret*[8] *Walton, Elmer*[7], *Hannah Margaret*[6] *Nimlow, Margaret*[5] *Pegan, Andrew*[4], *James*[3], *Andrew*[2] *Pagan, James*[1]) was born on June 7, 1923, in Martic Twp., Lancaster Co., Pennsylvania. She is also known as **Jane**. She is the daughter of Emerson Douts and Mary Margaret Walton (187).

She married **Willard Gerlach Tomlinson** after 1940. Willard Tomlinson was born in Martic Twp., Lancaster Co., Pennsylvania, on July 10, 1921. He was also known as **Tubby**. Willard reached age 85 and died in Pequea, Pequea Twp., Lancaster Co., Pennsylvania, on June 16, 2007. He is buried in Mount Nebo United Methodist Church Cemetery, Pequea, Pequea Twp., Lancaster Co., Pennsylvania.[82]

**372. Charles Emerson**[9] **Douts** (*Mary Margaret*[8] *Walton, Elmer*[7], *Hannah Margaret*[6] *Nimlow, Margaret*[5] *Pegan, Andrew*[4], *James*[3], *Andrew*[2] *Pagan, James*[1]) was born on November 4, 1926, in Martic Twp., Lancaster Co., Pennsylvania. He was the son of Emerson Douts and Mary Margaret Walton (187). Charles Emerson died in Washington Boro, Manor Twp., Lancaster Co., Pennsylvania, on November 2, 2016, at age 89. He was buried in Washington Boro Cemetery, Manor Twp., Lancaster Co., Pennsylvania.[42]

Charles Emerson married **Lottie E. Duke**. They had five children. Lottie E. Duke was born in Manor Twp., Lancaster Co., Pennsylvania on February 14, 1926.

**373. James Lawrence**[9] **Norris II** (*Luella A.*[8] *Walton, Elmer*[7], *Hannah Margaret*[6] *Nimlow, Margaret*[5] *Pegan, Andrew*[4], *James*[3], *Andrew*[2] *Pagan, James*[1]) was born on December 12, 1918, in Lancaster, Lancaster Co., Pennsylvania. He was the son of James Arthur Norris and Luella A. Walton (188). James Lawrence died in Boothbay Harbor, Lincoln Co., Maine, on July 15, 1988, at age 69. He was buried in Bergstrasse Cemetery, Ephrata, Ephrata Twp., Lancaster Co., Pennsylvania.[132]

He married **Gertrude Weaver**. Gertrude Weaver was born in Lancaster, Lancaster Co., Pennsylvania, on June 23, 1920. Gertrude reached age 77 and died in Boothbay Harbor, Lincoln Co., Maine, on August 27, 1997. She was buried in Bergstrasse Cemetery, Ephrata, Ephrata Twp., Lancaster Co., Pennsylvania.[132]

**374. Alberta**[9] **Grimm** (*Minerva Mae*[8] *Ortman, Ida*[7] *Akins, Anna Mary*[6] *Nimlow, Margaret*[5] *Pegan, Andrew*[4], *James*[3], *Andrew*[2] *Pagan, James*[1]) was born in 1928 in Paradise Twp., York Co., Pennsylvania. She is the daughter of Norman Lloyd Grimm and Minerva Mae Ortman (190).

**375. Norma Jean**[9] **Grimm** (*Minerva Mae*[8] *Ortman, Ida*[7] *Akins, Anna Mary*[6] *Nimlow, Margaret*[5] *Pegan, Andrew*[4], *James*[3], *Andrew*[2] *Pagan, James*[1]) was born in 1933 in York, York Co., Pennsylvania. She is the daughter of Norman Lloyd Grimm and Minerva Mae Ortman (190).

**376. Earl D.**[9] **Grimm** (*Minerva Mae*[8] *Ortman, Ida*[7] *Akins, Anna Mary*[6] *Nimlow, Margaret*[5] *Pegan, Andrew*[4], *James*[3], *Andrew*[2] *Pagan, James*[1]) was born on July 13, 1940, in Pennsylvania. He is the son of Norman Lloyd Grimm and Minerva Mae Ortman (190).

**377. Phillip Lee**[9] **Grimm** (*Minerva Mae*[8] *Ortman, Ida*[7] *Akins, Anna Mary*[6] *Nimlow, Margaret*[5] *Pegan, Andrew*[4], *James*[3], *Andrew*[2] *Pagan, James*[1]) was born on January 27, 1943, in McSherrystown, Adams Co., Pennsylvania. He was the son of Norman Lloyd Grimm and Minerva Mae Ortman (190). Phillip Lee died in West Manheim Twp., York Co., Pennsylvania, on July 15, 1961, at age 18. He was buried in Rest Haven Cemetery, Hanover Twp., York Co., Pennsylvania.[127]

**378. Dorothy V.⁹ Reisinger** (*Dorothy Everda⁸ Niblock, Clarence Watson⁷, George Niblock⁶ (Nimlow II), Margaret⁵ Pegan, Andrew⁴, James³, Andrew² Pagan, James¹*) was born on May 28, 1928, in Bainbridge, Conoy Twp., Lancaster Co., Pennsylvania. She is the daughter of James S. Reisinger and Dorothy Everda Niblock (193).

She married **Robert Marlin Singer**. Robert M. Singer was born in West Donegal Twp., Lancaster Co., Pennsylvania on July 18, 1925.

**379. Natalie Arlene⁹ Reisinger** (*Dorothy Everda⁸ Niblock, Clarence Watson⁷, George Niblock⁶ (Nimlow II), Margaret⁵ Pegan, Andrew⁴, James³, Andrew² Pagan, James¹*) was born on July 3, 1930, in Bainbridge, Conoy Twp., Lancaster Co., Pennsylvania. She was also known as **Arlene**. She was the daughter of James S. Reisinger and Dorothy Everda Niblock (193). Natalie Arlene died in Mount Joy Twp., Lancaster Co., Pennsylvania, on June 20, 2001, at age 70.

Natalie Arlene married **Unknown Quickel** about 1955.

Natalie Arlene Reisinger Quickel married **Unknown Sweigert** about 1958.

Natalie Arlene Reisinger Quickel Sweigert married **Unknown Brandt** about 1961.

**380. James Elwood⁹ Reisinger** (*Dorothy Everda⁸ Niblock, Clarence Watson⁷, George Niblock⁶ (Nimlow II), Margaret⁵ Pegan, Andrew⁴, James³, Andrew² Pagan, James¹*) was born on January 5, 1933, in Bainbridge, Conoy Twp., Lancaster Co., Pennsylvania. He was the son of James S. Reisinger and Dorothy Everda Niblock (193). James Elwood lived in Mannheim Twp., Lancaster Co., Pennsylvania. He died in Lebanon, North Lebanon Twp., Lebanon Co., Pennsylvania, on November 10, 1998, at age 65. James Elwood was buried in Goods Mennonite

Church Cemetery, Elizabethtown, Mt. Joy Twp., Lancaster Co., Pennsylvania.[85]

**381. Hope⁹ Glenn** (*Purdy Lester⁸, Grace Anna⁷ Kilgore, Alvin Levi⁶, Sarah Jane⁵ Pegan, Andrew⁴, James³, Andrew² Pagan, James¹*) was born in 1921 in Lower Chanceford Twp., York Co., Pennsylvania. She is the daughter of Purdy Lester Glenn (199) and Ethel Kilgore.

**382. Grace⁹ Glenn** (*Purdy Lester⁸, Grace Anna⁷ Kilgore, Alvin Levi⁶, Sarah Jane⁵ Pegan, Andrew⁴, James³, Andrew² Pagan, James¹*) was born in 1923 in Lower Chanceford Twp., York Co., Pennsylvania. She is the daughter of Purdy Lester Glenn (199) and Ethel Kilgore.

**383. Mary Ellen⁹ Glenn** (*Purdy Lester⁸, Grace Anna⁷ Kilgore, Alvin Levi⁶, Sarah Jane⁵ Pegan, Andrew⁴, James³, Andrew² Pagan, James¹*) was born in 1927 in Lower Chanceford Twp., York Co., Pennsylvania. She is the daughter of Purdy Lester Glenn (199) and Ethel Kilgore.

**384. Alice Clair⁹ Glenn** (*Purdy Lester⁸, Grace Anna⁷ Kilgore, Alvin Levi⁶, Sarah Jane⁵ Pegan, Andrew⁴, James³, Andrew² Pagan, James¹*) was born on September 30, 1937, in Delta, Peach Bottom Twp., York Co., Pennsylvania. She was the daughter of Purdy Lester Glenn (199) and Ethel Kilgore. Alice Clair died in Fawn Grove Twp., York Co., Pennsylvania? on September 23, 1998, at age 60.

She married **Joseph Bruce Spencer II**. They had five children. Joseph Bruce Spencer II was born in Fulton Twp., Lancaster Co., Pennsylvania, on October 16, 1938.

Alice Clair Glenn and Joseph Bruce Spencer II had five children, including:

+ 484 f I. **Beverly Diane¹⁰ Spencer** was born in York, York Co., Pennsylvania, on October 17, 1957. She died in York, York Co., Pennsylvania, on January 11, 1997.

**385. Alice Jean⁹ Glenn** (*Alvin Huber⁸, Grace Anna⁷ Kilgore, Alvin Levi⁶, Sarah Jane⁵ Pegan, Andrew⁴, James³, Andrew² Pagan, James¹*) was born in 1929 in Lower Chanceford Twp., York Co., Pennsylvania.

She is the daughter of Alvin Huber Glenn (201) and Nellie Salome Almoney.

**386. Phyllis E.⁹ Glenn** (*Alvin Huber⁸, Grace Anna⁷ Kilgore, Alvin Levi⁶, Sarah Jane⁵ Pegan, Andrew⁴, James³, Andrew² Pagan, James¹*) was born on March 1, 1934, in Lower Chanceford Twp., York Co., Pennsylvania. She is the daughter of Alvin Huber Glenn (201) and Nellie Salome Almoney.

Phyllis E. married **James Collins McPherson** on October 16, 1953, in Spokane Co., Washington. James Collins McPherson was born in High Rock, Lower Chanceford Twp., York Co., Pennsylvania, on December 30, 1931. James Collins reached age 56 and died in Schaumburg, Cook Co., Illinois, on November 20, 1988.

**387. Alvin Huber⁹ Glenn II** (*Alvin Huber⁸, Grace Anna⁷ Kilgore, Alvin Levi⁶, Sarah Jane⁵ Pegan, Andrew⁴, James³, Andrew² Pagan, James¹*) was born on Saturday, November 6, 1937, in Lower Chanceford Twp., York Co., Pennsylvania. He is the son of Alvin Huber Glenn (201) and Nellie Salome Almoney.

**388. Gary Elmer⁹ Brown** (*Lida Maxwell⁸ Glenn, Grace Anna⁷ Kilgore, Alvin Levi⁶, Sarah Jane⁵ Pegan, Andrew⁴, James³, Andrew² Pagan, James¹*) was born on July 7, 1935, in Lower Chanceford Twp., York Co., Pennsylvania. He was the son of James Paul Brown and Lida Maxwell Glenn (202). Gary Elmer lived in Wrightsville, Hellam Twp., York Co., Pennsylvania. He died in a hospital in York, York Co., Pennsylvania, on June 15, 1998, at age 62. Gary Elmer was buried in Susquehanna Memorial Gardens Cemetery, York, York Co., Pennsylvania. [70]

He married **Shirley M. Knopp**. They had one son. Shirley M. Knopp was born about 1935.

**389. Leon⁹ Kilgore II** (*Nora⁸ Glenn, Grace Anna⁷ Kilgore, Alvin Levi⁶, Sarah Jane⁵ Pegan, Andrew⁴, James³, Andrew² Pagan, James¹*) was born in 1935 in Lower Chanceford Twp., York Co., Pennsylvania. He is the son of Ralph Leon Kilgore and Nora Glenn (203).

**390. Carl⁹ Kilgore** (*Nora⁸ Glenn, Grace Anna⁷ Kilgore, Alvin Levi⁶, Sarah Jane⁵ Pegan, Andrew⁴, James³,*

*Andrew² Pagan, James¹*) was born in 1937 in Lower Chanceford Twp., York Co., Pennsylvania. He is the son of Ralph Leon Kilgore and Nora Glenn (203).

**391. Hazel⁹ Kilgore** (*Nora⁸ Glenn, Grace Anna⁷ Kilgore, Alvin Levi⁶, Sarah Jane⁵ Pegan, Andrew⁴, James³, Andrew² Pagan, James¹*) was born in 1939 in Lower Chanceford Twp., York Co., Pennsylvania. She is the daughter of Ralph Leon Kilgore and Nora Glenn (203).

**392. Infant Son⁹ Kilgore** (*Nora⁸ Glenn, Grace Anna⁷ Kilgore, Alvin Levi⁶, Sarah Jane⁵ Pegan, Andrew⁴, James³, Andrew² Pagan, James¹*) was born in 1943 in Lower Chanceford Twp., York Co., Pennsylvania. He was the son of Ralph Leon Kilgore and Nora Glenn (203). Son died in Lower Chanceford Twp., York Co., Pennsylvania, in 1943. He was buried in Pine Grove Presbyterian Church Cemetery, Lower Chanceford Twp., York Co., Pennsylvania. [35]

**393. Edward B.⁹ Dietrich** (*Nina Amanda⁸ Kilgore, Samuel Ralph⁷, Alvin Levi⁶, Sarah Jane⁵ Pegan, Andrew⁴, James³, Andrew² Pagan, James¹*) was born on Tuesday, August 6, 1935, in Toledo, Lucas Co., Ohio. He is the son of Thurman Clarence Diethrich and Nina Amanda Kilgore (204).

**394. Victor Boyd⁹ Kilgore** (*Clarence H.⁸, Hugh Whiteford⁷, James Ankrim⁶, Sarah Jane⁵ Pegan, Andrew⁴, James³, Andrew² Pagan, James¹*) was born on January 4, 1932, in Peach Bottom Twp., York Co., Pennsylvania. He was the son of Clarence H. Kilgore (208) and Nellie Susan Pierson. Victor Boyd died in Broadway, Lee Co., North Carolina, on September 15, 2013, at age 81. He was buried in Pine Grove Presbyterian Church Cemetery, Lower Chanceford Twp., York Co., Pennsylvania. [35]

He married and had three daughters.

**395. Hugh F.⁹ Kilgore** (*Clarence H.⁸, Hugh Whiteford⁷, James Ankrim⁶, Sarah Jane⁵ Pegan, Andrew⁴, James³, Andrew² Pagan, James¹*) was born on February 18, 1933, in Peach Bottom Twp., York Co., Pennsylvania. He was the son of Clarence H. Kilgore (208) and Nellie Susan Pierson. Hugh F. died in Peach Bottom Twp., York Co., Pennsylvania, on August 6, 1933. He was buried in Slateville Presbyterian Church Cemetery, Delta, Peach Bottom Twp., York Co., Pennsylvania.[33]

**396. Harriet⁹ Kilgore** (*Clarence H.⁸, Hugh Whiteford⁷, James Ankrim⁶, Sarah Jane⁵ Pegan, Andrew⁴, James³, Andrew² Pagan, James¹*) was born on August 28, 1938, in Peach Bottom Twp., York Co., Pennsylvania. She is the daughter of Clarence H. Kilgore (208) and Nellie Susan Pierson.

**397. Frederick F.⁹ Boyd II** (*Sarah Angeline⁸ Kilgore, Hugh Whiteford⁷, James Ankrim⁶, Sarah Jane⁵ Pegan, Andrew⁴, James³, Andrew² Pagan, James¹*) was born in 1935 in East Nottingham Twp., Chester Co., Pennsylvania. He is the son of Frederick E. Boyd and Sarah Angeline Kilgore (209).

**398. Jane Yvonne⁹ Boyd** (*Sarah Angeline⁸ Kilgore, Hugh Whiteford⁷, James Ankrim⁶, Sarah Jane⁵ Pegan, Andrew⁴, James³, Andrew² Pagan, James¹*) was born in 1937 in East Nottingham Twp., Chester Co., Pennsylvania. She is the daughter of Frederick E. Boyd and Sarah Angeline Kilgore (209).

**399. James⁹ Kilgore** (*Kenneth Dunlap⁸, Hugh Whiteford⁷, James Ankrim⁶, Sarah Jane⁵ Pegan, Andrew⁴, James³, Andrew² Pagan, James¹*) was born in 1933 in Havre de Grace, Harford Co., Maryland. He is the son of Kenneth Dunlap Kilgore (210) and Kathryn Rebecca Drumond.

**400. Emma⁹ Kilgore** (*Kenneth Dunlap⁸, Hugh Whiteford⁷, James Ankrim⁶, Sarah Jane⁵ Pegan, Andrew⁴, James³, Andrew² Pagan, James¹*) was born in 1935 in Havre de Grace, Harford Co., Maryland. She is the daughter of Kenneth Dunlap Kilgore (210) and Kathryn Rebecca Drumond.

**401. Ronald⁹ Cochran** (*Mary E.⁸ Kilgore, Hugh Whiteford⁷, James Ankrim⁶, Sarah Jane⁵ Pegan, Andrew⁴, James³, Andrew² Pagan, James¹*) was born in 1936 in Martic Twp., Lancaster Co., Pennsylvania. He is the son of Ivan Ellsworth Cochran and Mary E. Kilgore (211).

**402. Robert K.⁹ Boyd** (*Eunice⁸ Kilgore, Hugh Whiteford⁷, James Ankrim⁶, Sarah Jane⁵ Pegan, Andrew⁴, James³, Andrew² Pagan, James¹*) was born in 1934 in West Nottingham Twp., Chester Co., Pennsylvania. He is the son of Charles Boyd and Eunice Kilgore (212).

**403. Samuel⁹ Boyd** (*Eunice⁸ Kilgore, Hugh Whiteford⁷, James Ankrim⁶, Sarah Jane⁵ Pegan, Andrew⁴, James³, Andrew² Pagan, James¹*) was born in 1938 in West Nottingham Twp., Chester Co., Pennsylvania. He is the son of Charles Boyd and Eunice Kilgore (212).

**404. Hughjene⁹ Boyd** (*Eunice⁸ Kilgore, Hugh Whiteford⁷, James Ankrim⁶, Sarah Jane⁵ Pegan, Andrew⁴, James³, Andrew² Pagan, James¹*). He is the son of Charles Boyd and Eunice Kilgore (212). Died in young, as did his father's brother for whom he was named. Listed in the Roy D. Pegan genealogy, but not shown in any census or other online data.

**405. Dale R.⁹ Scott** (*Harold Edwin⁸, Cora⁷ Martin, Anna Margaret⁶ Kilgore, Sarah Jane⁵ Pegan, Andrew⁴, James³, Andrew² Pagan, James¹*) was born on September 4, 1949, in York, York Co., Pennsylvania. He was the son of Harold Edwin Scott (227) and Louise Stough Heilman. Dale R. died in York, York Co., Pennsylvania, on August 1, 2005, at age 55. He was buried in Saint Paul's Wolf's Evangelical Covenant Cemetery, West York Twp., York Co., Pennsylvania.[67]

He married but divorced. He and his former wife had one daughter.

**406. Carol E.⁹ Krewson** (*Marian L.⁸ Anderson, Daisy Mae⁷ Hess, Luella Jane⁶ Kilgore, Sarah Jane⁵ Pegan, Andrew⁴, James³, Andrew² Pagan, James¹*) was born on October 13, 1941, in Chanceford Twp., York Co., Pennsylvania. She was the daughter of Clair William Krewson and Marian L. Anderson (237). Carol E. died in Windsor Twp., York Co., Pennsylvania, on January 2, 2012, at age 70. She was buried in Bethel United Methodist Church Cemetery, Shenks Ferry, Chanceford Twp., York Co., Pennsylvania.[95]

Carol E. married **Mr. Jamison**. They had two daughters.

Daughter of Carol E. Krewson and Rodney B. Jamison:

+ 485 f I. **Daughter¹⁰ Jamison**.

**407. Ida Ruth⁹ Carter** (*Ruth Emeline⁸ Stouch, Cora I.⁷ Pegan, Lewis Cass⁶, Alexander L.⁵, Andrew⁴, James³, Andrew² Pagan, James¹*) was born on June 3, 1920, in Varnville, Hampton Co., South Carolina. She was the daughter of Wingard Williams Carter and Ruth Emeline Stouch (250). Ida Ruth died in Seneca, Oconee Co., South Carolina, on December 5, 1984, at age 64. She was buried in Oconee Memorial Park Cemetery and Mausoleum, Seneca, Oconee Co., South Carolina.[136]

Ida Ruth married **Jacob Patrick Cromer** after 1940. They had three children. Jacob Patrick Cromer was born in Seneca, Oconee Co., South Carolina, on January 28, 1918. Jacob Patrick reached age 81 and died in Seneca, Oconee Co., South Carolina, on February 1, 1999. He was buried in Oconee Memorial Park Cemetery and Mausoleum, Seneca, Oconee Co., South Carolina.[136]

Jacob P. Cromer was a former mayor of Seneca, South Carolina.

408. **Wingard William⁹ Carter II** (*Ruth Emeline⁸ Stouch, Cora I.⁷ Pegan, Lewis Cass⁶, Alexander L.⁵, Andrew⁴, James³, Andrew² Pagan, James¹*) was born on August 22, 1922, in Varnville, Hampton Co., South Carolina. He was the son of Wingard Williams Carter and Ruth Emeline Stouch (250). Wingard William died in Rock Hill, York Co., South Carolina, on February 26, 1978, at age 55. He was buried in Grandview Memorial Park Cemetery, Rock Hill, York Co., South Carolina.[137]

Seems to have never married.

409. **Daughter⁹ Carter** (*Ruth Emeline⁸ Stouch, Cora I.⁷ Pegan, Lewis Cass⁶, Alexander L.⁵, Andrew⁴, James³, Andrew² Pagan, James¹*) was born in 1923 in Varnville, Hampton Co., South Carolina. She was the daughter of Wingard Williams Carter and Ruth Emeline Stouch (248). Daughter died in Varnville, Hampton Co., South Carolina, in 1923. She was buried in Church of the Holy Apostles Episcopal Cemetery, Barnwell, Barnwell Co., South Carolina.[99]

410. **Nancy⁹ Liller** (*Anna C.⁸ Stouch, Cora I.⁷ Pegan, Lewis Cass⁶, Alexander L.⁵, Andrew⁴, James³, Andrew² Pagan, James¹*) was born in 1930 in Lancaster, Lancaster Co., Pennsylvania. She is the daughter of Robert H. Liller and Anna C. Stouch (251).

411. **Gloria Ann⁹ Liller** (*Anna C.⁸ Stouch, Cora I.⁷ Pegan, Lewis Cass⁶, Alexander L.⁵, Andrew⁴, James³, Andrew² Pagan, James¹*) was born in 1934 in Lancaster, Lancaster Co., Pennsylvania. She is the daughter of Robert H. Liller and Anna C. Stouch (251).

412. **Helen Roberta⁹ Liller** (*Anna C.⁸ Stouch, Cora I.⁷ Pegan, Lewis Cass⁶, Alexander L.⁵, Andrew⁴, James³, Andrew² Pagan, James¹*) was born in 1938 in Lancaster, Lancaster Co., Pennsylvania. She is the daughter of Robert H. Liller and Anna C. Stouch (251).

413. **Phyllis⁹ Stouch** (*Lewis⁸ Stouch, Cora I.⁷ Pegan, Lewis Cass⁶, Alexander L.⁵, Andrew⁴, James³, Andrew² Pagan, James¹*) was born in 1933 in Lancaster, Lancaster Co., Pennsylvania. She is the daughter of Lewis Stouch (253) and Marion Ross.

414. **Lewis⁹ Stouch II** (*Lewis⁸ Stouch, Cora I.⁷ Pegan, Lewis Cass⁶, Alexander L.⁵, Andrew⁴, James³, Andrew² Pagan, James¹*) was born in 1936 in Mannheim Twp., Lancaster Co., Pennsylvania? He is the son of Lewis Stouch (253) and Marion Ross.

415. **Thomas⁹ Stouch** (*Lewis⁸ Stouch, Cora I.⁷ Pegan, Lewis Cass⁶, Alexander L.⁵, Andrew⁴, James³, Andrew² Pagan, James¹*) was born in 1937 in Mannheim Twp., Lancaster Co., Pennsylvania? He is the son of Lewis Stouch (253) and Marion Ross.

416. **Doris R.⁹ Roschel** (*Julia M.⁸ Stouch, Cora I.⁷ Pegan, Lewis Cass⁶, Alexander L.⁵, Andrew⁴, James³, Andrew² Pagan, James¹*) was born on October 19, 1930, in Lancaster, Lancaster Co., Pennsylvania. She is the daughter of Daniel L. Roschel and Julia M. Stouch (254).

Doris married **Daniel Harvey Cauffman** on June 2, 1949, in Alexandria Co., Virginia. Daniel Harvey Cauffman was born in Mont Alto, Franklin Co., Pennsylvania, on July 7, 1928. Daniel Harvey reached age 63 and died in Selbyville, Sussex Co., Delaware? on September 4, 1991.

417. **Daniel L.⁹ Roschel II** (*Julia M.⁸ Stouch, Cora I.⁷ Pegan, Lewis Cass⁶, Alexander L.⁵, Andrew⁴, James³, Andrew² Pagan, James¹*) was born on Saturday, August 4, 1934, in Lancaster, Lancaster Co., Pennsylvania. He is the son of Daniel L. Roschel

and Julia M. Stouch (254). Daniel L. lived in 2005 in Lancaster, Lancaster Co., Pennsylvania.

He married **Nancy Unknown**.

**418. Charles H.**[9] **Roschel** (*Julia M.*[8] *Stouch, Cora I.*[7] *Pegan, Lewis Cass*[6], *Alexander L.*[5], *Andrew*[4], *James*[3], *Andrew*[2] *Pagan, James*[1]) was born on Friday, April 12, 1940, in Lancaster, Lancaster Co., Pennsylvania. He is the son of Daniel L. Roschel and Julia M. Stouch (254).

He married **Kathryn Unknown.**

**419. Chester Irvin**[9] **Knight II** (*Elizabeth Frances*[8] *Stouch, Cora I.*[7] *Pegan, Lewis Cass*[6], *Alexander L.*[5], *Andrew*[4], *James*[3], *Andrew*[2] *Pagan, James*[1]) was born in 1934 in Mannheim Twp., Lancaster Co., Pennsylvania. He is the son of Chester Irvin Knight and Elizabeth Frances Stouch (255).

**420. James Leroy**[9] **Knight** (*Elizabeth Frances*[8] *Stouch, Cora I.*[7] *Pegan, Lewis Cass*[6], *Alexander L.*[5], *Andrew*[4], *James*[3], *Andrew*[2] *Pagan, James*[1]) was born in 1936 in Mannheim Twp., Lancaster Co., Pennsylvania. He is the son of Chester Irvin Knight and Elizabeth Frances Stouch (255).

**421. Joseph W.**[9] **Gilgore** (*William*[8], *Harriet Jane*[7] *Pegan, Lewis Cass*[6], *Alexander L.*[5], *Andrew*[4], *James*[3], *Andrew*[2] *Pagan, James*[1]) was born on September 6, 1941, in Lancaster, Lancaster Co., Pennsylvania. He was the son of William Gilgore (259) and Helen Raum. Joseph W. died in Lancaster, Lancaster Co., Pennsylvania, on October 27, 1941. He was buried in Riverview Burial Park Cemetery Cemetery, Lancaster, Lancaster Co., Pennsylvania.[29]

**422. Dana Laird**[9] **Dettling** (*George Henry*[8], *Ruth Ann*[7] *Pegan, James Calvin*[6], *Alexander L.*[5], *Andrew*[4], *James*[3], *Andrew*[2] *Pagan, James*[1]) was born on July 27, 1956, in Pittsburgh, Allegheny Co., Pennsylvania. She was the daughter of George Henry Dettling II (275) and Sellie Seiler Hemple. Dana Laird died in Pittsburgh, Allegheny Co., Pennsylvania, on July 28, 1956. She was buried in Jefferson Memorial Park Cemetery, Pleasant Hills, Allegheny Co., Pennsylvania.[55, 56]

**423. Dorothy**[9] **Gentry** (*Ellsworth James*[8], *Adelaide or Adeline*[7] *Pegan, Elmer Ellsworth James*[6], *Alexander L.*[5], *Andrew*[4], *James*[3], *Andrew*[2] *Pagan, James*[1]) was born in 1935 in Gordon Heights, New Castle Co., Delaware. She is the daughter of Ellsworth James Gentry (279) and Dorothy P. Pierce.

**424. Ellsworth James**[9] **Gentry II** (*Ellsworth James*[8], *Adelaide or Adeline*[7] *Pegan, Elmer Ellsworth James*[6], *Alexander L.*[5], *Andrew*[4], *James*[3], *Andrew*[2] *Pagan, James*[1]) was born on September 23, 1936, in Gordon Heights, New Castle Co., Delaware. He was the son of Ellsworth James Gentry (279) and Dorothy P. Pierce. Ellsworth James died in Wilmington, New Castle Co., Delaware, on November 15, 1992, at age 56.

Ellsworth James married **Unknown Unknown** before 1958. They had one son.

Son of Ellsworth James Gentry II and Unknown Unknown:

+ 486 m I. **Ellsworth James**[10] **Gentry III** was born in Wilmington, New Castle Co., Delaware, on August 20, 1958. He died in Wilmington, New Castle Co., Delaware, on December 7, 1997. Ellsworth James was buried in Silverbrook Cemetery, Wilmington, New Castle Co., Delaware.[32]

**425. John E.**[9] **Gentry** (*Ellsworth James*[8], *Adelaide or Adeline*[7] *Pegan, Elmer Ellsworth James*[6], *Alexander L.*[5], *Andrew*[4], *James*[3], *Andrew*[2] *Pagan, James*[1]) was born on November 23, 1939, in Gordon Heights, New Castle Co., Delaware. He was the son of Ellsworth James Gentry (279) and Dorothy P. Pierce. John E. died in July 1968 at age 28.

**426. Thomas Daniel**[9] **Gentry** (*Ellsworth James*[8], *Adelaide or Adeline*[7] *Pegan, Elmer Ellsworth James*[6], *Alexander L.*[5], *Andrew*[4], *James*[3], *Andrew*[2] *Pagan, James*[1]) was born in 1942 in Gordon Heights, New Castle Co., Delaware. He was the son of Ellsworth James Gentry (279) and Dorothy P. Pierce. Thomas Daniel died in Wilmington, New Castle Co., Delaware, on August 23, 1947, at age five.

**427. Douglas Gary**[9] **Gentry** (*Ellsworth James*[8], *Adelaide or Adeline*[7] *Pegan, Elmer Ellsworth James*[6], *Alexander L.*[5], *Andrew*[4], *James*[3], *Andrew*[2] *Pagan, James*[1]) was born in 1949 in Wilmington, New Castle Co.,

Delaware. He was the son of Ellsworth James Gentry (279) and Dorothy P. Pierce. Douglas Gary died in Wilmington, New Castle Co., Delaware, on December 11, 2014, at age 65. He was buried in Silverbrook Cemetery, Wilmington, New Castle Co., Delaware.[20]

**428. Frank Paul[9] Pedelini** (*Mildred Jennie[8] Pegan, Everett[7], Elmer Ellsworth James[6], Alexander L.[5], Andrew[4], James[3], Andrew[2] Pagan, James[1]*) was born on December 10, 1955, in Wilmington, New Castle Co., Delaware. He was the son of Francis Paul Pedelini and Mildred Jennie Pegan (286). Frank Paul died in Merlin, Josephine Co., Oregon, on April 2, 2006, at age 50.

Frank Paul married a first **Unknown Unknown** in Josephine Co., Oregon. They divorced. They had two daughters.

Frank Paul Pedelini married a second **Unknown Unknown** in Josephine Co., Oregon. They had two daughters.

**429. Infant Daughter[8] Underkoffler** (*Arthur Allen[7], Bertha[6] Pegan, Andrew A.[5], Andrew[4], James[3], Andrew[2] Pagan, James[1]*) was born in Lancaster, Lancaster Co., Pennsylvania, on March 27, 1948. She was the daughter of Erma Elizabeth Urban (288) and Clair Eugene Underkoffler. She died in Lancaster, Lancaster Co., Pennsylvania, on March 27, 1948.[143]

**430. Carol Ann[8] Underkoffler** (*Arthur Alllen[7], Bertha[6] Pegan, Andrew A.[5], Andrew[4], James[3], Andrew[2] Pagan, James[1]*) was born in Lancaster, Lancaster Co., Pennsylvania, on February 15, 1949. She was the daughter of Erma Elizabeth Urban (288) and Clair Eugene Underkoffler.She died in Leola Lancaster, Lancaster Co., Pennsylvania, on August 9, 2010 at age 61. Carol Ann was buried in Millersville Mennonite Cemetery, Millersville, Manor Twp., Lancaster Co., Pennsylvania.[61]

Carol Ann married **Mr. Campbell** and had three sons.

**431. William James[9] Wiley** (*James Howard[8], Sarah[7] Johnson, Martha Ann[6] Fulton, Sarah Jane[5] Miller, Margaret[4] Pegan, James[3], Andrew[2] Pagan, James[1]*) was born on September 4, 1913, in Fulton Twp.,

Lancaster Co., Pennsylvania. He was the son of James Howard Wiley (295) and Jessie Nancy Barnett. William James died in Paradise Twp., Lancaster Co., Pennsylvania, on January 8, 1978, at age 64. He was buried in Old Leacock Presbyterian Cemetery, Intercourse, Leacock Twp., Lancaster Co., Pennsylvania.[146]

William James married **Dorothy E. Brown** before 1936. They had two children. Dorothy E. Brown was born in Drumore Twp., Lancaster Co., Pennsylvania, in 1919. Dorothy E. reached age 43 and died in Fulton Twp., Lancaster Co., Pennsylvania, in 1962. She was buried in Penn Hill (Friends) Burial Ground, Penn Hill, Fulton Twp., Lancaster Co., Pennsylvania.[117]

William James Wiley married **Frances Rebecca Simpson** after 1940. They had two children. Frances Rebecca Simpson was born in Paradise Twp., Lancaster Co., Pennsylvania, on February 20, 1922. Frances Rebecca reached age 75 and died in Christiana, Sadsbury Twp., Lancaster Co., Pennsylvania, on November 13, 1997. She was buried in Old Leacock Presbyterian Cemetery, Intercourse, Leacock Twp., Lancaster Co., Pennsylvania.[146]

Children of William James Wiley and Dorothy E. Brown:

+ 487 f I. **RaeArlene[10] Wiley** was born in Lancaster, Lancaster Co., Pennsylvania, in 1936.

+ 488 m II. **James Ernest[10] Wiley** was born in Lancaster, Lancaster Co., Pennsylvania, in 1938.

**432. Emma Rae[9] Wiley** (*James Howard[8], Sarah[7] Johnson, Martha Ann[6] Fulton, Sarah Jane[5] Miller, Margaret[4] Pegan, James[3], Andrew[2] Pagan, James[1]*) was born on October 5, 1916, in Fulton Twp., Lancaster Co., Pennsylvania. She was the daughter of James Howard Wiley (295) and Jessie Nancy Barnett. Emma Rae died in Elkton, Cecil Co., Maryland, on March 25, 2003, at age 86.

Emma Rae Wiley married **Chester E. Wiley Eckman** before 1938. They divorced. They had three children. Chester E. Wiley Eckman was born in Conowingo, Cecil Co., Maryland, on July 1, 1916. He reached age 85 and died in a facility in Montoursville, Lycoming Co., Pennsylvania, on March 26, 2002.

Emma Ray Wiley Eckman married **Dean Murphy**.

Children of Emma Rae Wiley and Chester E. Wiley Eckman:

+ 489 f I. **Lora K.**[10] **Eckman** was born in Conowingo, Cecil Co., Maryland, in 1938.

**433. Joseph Howard**[9] **Wiley** (*James Howard*[8], *Sarah*[7] *Johnson, Martha Ann*[6] *Fulton, Sarah Jane*[5] *Miller, Margaret*[4] *Pegan, James*[3], *Andrew*[2] *Pagan, James*[1]) was born on August 8, 1918, in Fulton Twp., Lancaster Co., Pennsylvania. He was the son of James Howard Wiley (295) and Jessie Nancy Barnett. Joseph Howard died in Fulton Twp., Lancaster Co., Pennsylvania, on April 20, 1920, at age one. He was buried in Mt. Nebo Church Cemetery, Peach Bottom Twp., York Co., Pennsylvania.[147]

**434. Warren Dunlap**[9] **Wiley** (*James Howard*[8], *Sarah*[7] *Johnson, Martha Ann*[6] *Fulton, Sarah Jane*[5] *Miller, Margaret*[4] *Pegan, James*[3], *Andrew*[2] *Pagan, James*[1]) was born on August 3, 1920, in Fulton Twp., Lancaster Co., Pennsylvania. He was the son of James Howard Wiley (295) and Jessie Nancy Barnett. Warren Dunlap died in a hospital in Lancaster, Lancaster Co., Pennsylvania, on November 20, 1920. He was buried in Mt. Nebo Church Cemetery, Peach Bottom Twp., York Co., Pennsylvania.[147]

**435. Hazel Marion**[9] **Wiley** (*James Howard*[8], *Sarah*[7] *Johnson, Martha Ann*[6] *Fulton, Sarah Jane*[5] *Miller, Margaret*[4] *Pegan, James*[3], *Andrew*[2] *Pagan, James*[1]) was born on August 15, 1921, in Delta, Peach Bottom Twp., York Co., Pennsylvania. She was the daughter of James Howard Wiley (295) and Jessie Nancy Barnett. Hazel Marion lived in 1994 in Elkville, Elk Twp., Jackson Co., Illinois. She also resided before 2007 in Royalton, Osage Twp., Franklin Co., Illinois. Hazel Marion died in a hospital in Marion, Marion Twp., Willliamson Co., Illinois, on March 5, 2007, at age 85. She was bur-

ied in Saint Mary's Orthodox Cemetery, Royalton, Osage Twp., Franklin Co., Illinois.[148]

She married **Unknown Gaskill** before 1945.

Hazel Marion Wiley Gaskill married **Charles Krelo** in 1945 in Pennsylvania. They had one daughter. Charles Krelo was born in Elkville, Elk Twp., Jackson Co., Illinois, on June 5, 1925. Charles lived in 1994 in Elkville, Elk Twp., Jackson Co., Illinois. He also resided before 2006 in Royalton, Osage Twp., Franklin Co., Illinois. Charles reached age 81 and died in a facility in Marion, Marion Twp., Williamson Co., Illinois, on November 3, 2006. He was buried in Saint Mary's Orthodox Cemetery, Royalton, Osage Twp., Franklin Co., Illinois.[148]

**435. Mary Sue**[9] **Wiley** (*James Howard*[8], *Sarah*[7] *Johnson, Martha Ann*[6] *Fulton, Sarah Jane*[5] *Miller, Margaret*[4] *Pegan, James*[3], *Andrew*[2] *Pagan, James*[1]) was born on November 30, 1925, in Court House, Floyd Co., Virginia. She was the daughter of James Howard Wiley (295) and Pencie Miller Ridinger. Mary Sue died in Springvale, York Co., Maine, on February 17, 1991, at age 65. She was buried in Roselawn Memorial Gardens Cemetery, Christiansburg, Montgomery Co., Virginia.[145]

Seems to have been childless.

Mary Sue married **Harvey Raymond Brooks** on July 8, 1944, in Montgomery Co., Virginia. They divorced. Harvey Raymond Brooks was born in Anson, Somerset Co., Maine, on June 13, 1919. He reached age 79 and died in Anson, Somerset Co., Maine, on June 6, 1999. Harvey Raymond was buried in Sunset View Cemetery, Norridgewock, Somerset Co., Maine.[161]

Mary Sue Wiley Brooks married **Roy William Ahl** on March 17, 1963. They divorced. Roy William Ahl was born in Big Lick, Roanoke Co., Virginia, on August 11, 1919. He reached age 54 and died in Blacksburg, Montgomery Co., Virginia, on April 6, 1974. Roy William was buried in Westview Cemetery, Blacksburg, Montgomery Co., Virginia.[162]

**437. Lillian Howard**[9] **Wiley** (*James Howard*[8], *Sarah*[7] *Johnson, Martha Ann*[6] *Fulton, Sarah Jane*[5] *Miller, Margaret*[4] *Pegan, James*[3], *Andrew*[2] *Pagan, James*[1]) was born on November 2, 1926, in Floyd, Floyd Co., Virginia. She was also known as **Pat**. She was the daughter of James Howard Wiley (295) and Stella May Reid. Lillian Howard lived in Elkton, Cecil Co., Maryland. She died in a hospital in Newark, New Castle Co., Delaware, on November 28, 1997, at age 71. Lillian Howard was buried in Delaware Veterans Memorial Cemetery, Bear, New Castle Co., Delaware.[149]

Lillian Howard married **Sidney Lawrence Wingo** on September 11, 1942, in Montgomery Co., Virginia. They had six children. Sidney Lawrence Wingo was born in Blacksburg, Montgomery Co., Virginia, on July 19, 1923. Sidney Lawrence reached age 70 and died in Catawba. Roanoke Co., Virginia, on July 4, 1994. He was buried in Delaware Veterans Memorial Cemetery, Bear, New Castle Co., Delaware.[149]

Lillian Howard Wiley Wingo married **Paul Robert Goodchild** after 1994. Paul Robert Goodchild was born in Chateaugay, Franklin Co., New York, on April 13, 1930. Paul R. Goodchild reached age 87 and died in Elkton, Cecil Co., Maryland on September 21, 2017. He was buried in Delaware Veterans Memorial Cemetery, Bear, New Castle Co., Delaware..[149]

Children of Lillian Howard Wiley and Sidney Lawrence Wingo:

+ 490 m I. **James Lawrence¹⁰ Wingo** was born in Blacksburg, Montgomery Co., Virginia, on November 12, 1942. He died in Blacksburg, Montgomery Co., Virginia, on November 30, 1942. James Lawrence was buried in Wingo Family Cemetery, Blacksburg, Montgomery Co., Virginia.[163]

+ 491 f II. **Rosa May¹⁰ Wingo** was born in Blacksburg, Montgomery Co., Virginia, on June 30, 1944. She died in Blacksburg, Montgomery Co., Virginia, on June 30, 1944. Rosa May was buried in Wingo Family Cemetery, Blacksburg, Montgomery Co., Virginia.[163]

+ 492 m III. **James Thomas¹⁰ Wingo** was born in Radford, Virginia, on April 26, 1948. He died in Bear, New Castle Co., Delaware, on September 28, 1998. James Thomas was buried in Delaware Veterans Memorial Cemetery, Bear, New Castle Co., Delaware.[149]

+ 493 m IV. **Dale Lawrence¹⁰ Wingo** was born in Radford, Virginia, on April 13, 1949. He died in a hospital in New Castle, New Castle Co., Delaware, on June 9, 1999. Dale Lawrence was buried in Gracelawn Memorial Park Cemetery, Farmhurst, New Castle Co., Delaware.[59]

**438. James Howard⁹ Wiley II** (*James Howard⁸, Sarah⁷ Johnson, Martha Ann⁶ Fulton, Sarah Jane⁵ Miller, Margaret⁴ Pegan, James³, Andrew² Pagan, James¹*) was born on July 18, 1928, in Blacksburg, Montgomery Co., Virginia. He is the son of James Howard Wiley (295) and Stella May Reid. He died in Dayton, Montgomery Co., Ohio on October 4, 2012 at age 84.

Childless.

James Howard married **Jane Babb** on June 3, 1949, in Radford, Virginia.

James Howard Wiley II married **Carolyn Ruth Penrod** on August 7, 1951, in Richmond, Virginia. Carolyn Ruth Penrod was born in Dayton, Montgomery Co., Ohio, on December 26, 1929.

James Howard Wiley II married **Judith Ann Shaner** after 1962.

James Howard Wiley II married **Janet Izor** on June 6, 1962, in Montgomery Co., Ohio.

James Howard Wiley II married **Diana Lynn Dunn** on August 8, 1983, in Campbell Co., Tennessee.

James Howard Wiley II married **Sharon Jean Mobley** on November 21, 1987, in Montgomery Co., Ohio.

**439. Dorothy Louise⁹ Wiley** (*James Howard⁸, Sarah⁷ Johnson, Martha Ann⁶ Fulton, Sarah Jane⁵ Miller, Margaret⁴ Pegan, James³, Andrew² Pagan, James¹*) was born in Blacksburg, Montgomery Co., Virginia on June 25, 1930. She was the daughter of James Howard Wiley (295) and Stella May Reid. Dorothy Louise died in Newark, New Castle Co., Delaware? on July 15, 1989 at age 59.

Dorothy Louise married **Mr. Romero.**

**440. Rebecca Jean⁹ Wiley** (*James Howard⁸, Sarah⁷ Johnson, Martha Ann⁶ Fulton, Sarah Jane⁵ Miller, Margaret⁴ Pegan, James³, Andrew² Pagan, James¹*) was born in 1932 in Blacksburg, Montgomery Co., Virginia. She was the daughter of James Howard Wiley (295) and Stella May Reid. Rebecca Jean died before 1940.

**441. Agnes Caroline⁹ Wiley** (*James Howard⁸, Sarah⁷ Johnson, Martha Ann⁶ Fulton, Sarah Jane⁵ Miller, Margaret⁴ Pegan, James³, Andrew² Pagan, James¹*) was born in 1934 in Blacksburg, Montgomery Co., Virginia. She is the daughter of James Howard Wiley (295) and Stella May Reid.

**442. Infant Son⁹ Wiley** (*Samuel Johnson⁸, Sarah⁷ Johnson, Martha Ann⁶ Fulton, Sarah Jane⁵ Miller, Margaret⁴ Pegan, James³, Andrew² Pagan, James¹*) was born in 1919 in Fulton Twp., Lancaster Co., Pennsylvania. He was the son of Samuel Johnson Wiley (296) and Mabel Chambers. Infant Son died in Fulton Twp., Lancaster Co., Pennsylvania, in 1919.

**443. Elmer R.⁹ Wiley** (*Samuel Johnson⁸, Sarah⁷ Johnson, Martha Ann⁶ Fulton, Sarah Jane⁵ Miller, Margaret⁴ Pegan, James³, Andrew² Pagan, James¹*) was born on April 29, 1921, in Fulton Twp., Lancaster Co., Pennsylvania. He was the son of Samuel Johnson Wiley (296) and Mabel Chambers. Elmer R. died in Peach Bottom Twp., York Co., Pennsylvania, on February 27, 1998, at age 76. He was buried in Quarryville Cemetery, Quarryville, Lancaster Co.., Pennsylvania.[150]

Elmer R. married **Tressie Andrews** after 1940. They had one son. Tressie Andrews was born in Allegheny Co., North Carolina, on August 25, 1929. Tressie reached age 77 and died in Lancaster, Lancaster Co., Pennsylvania, on April 12, 2007. She was buried in Quarryville Cemetery, Quarryville, Lancaster Co.., Pennsylvania.[150]

**444. Samuel Clayton⁹ Wiley II** (*Samuel Johnson⁸, Sarah⁷ Johnson, Martha Ann⁶ Fulton, Sarah Jane⁵ Miller, Margaret⁴ Pegan, James³, Andrew² Pagan, James¹*) was born on September 22, 1923, in Fulton Twp., Lancaster Co., Pennsylvania. He was also known as **Pud**. He was the son of Samuel Johnson Wiley (296) and Mabel Chambers. Samuel Clayton lived in Peach Bottom, Fulton Twp., Lancaster Co., Pennsylvania. He died in Lancaster, Lancaster Co., Pennsylvania, on December 8, 2010, at age 87. Samuel Clayton was buried in Mount Zion United Methodist Church Cemetery, Peach Bottom, Fulton Twp., Lancaster Co., Pennsylvania.[151]

Samuel Clayton married **AnnaBell Booth** after 1940. They had four children. AnnaBell Booth was born in Drumore Twp., Lancaster Co., Pennsylvania, on May 2, 1927. AnnaBell reached age 84 and died in Lancaster, Lancaster Co., Pennsylvania, on August 31, 2011. She was buried in Mount Zion United Methodist Church Cemetery, Peach Bottom, Fulton Twp., Lancaster Co., Pennsylvania.[151]

**445. Sara E.⁹ Wiley** (*Elmer Crawford⁸, Sarah⁷ Johnson, Martha Ann⁶ Fulton, Sarah Jane⁵ Miller, Margaret⁴ Pegan, James³, Andrew² Pagan, James¹*) was born on April 8, 1921, in Lower Chanceford Twp., York Co., Pennsylvania. She was the daughter of Elmer Crawford Wiley II (297) and Nellie Stewart. Sara E. died in Glen Arm, Baltimore Co., Maryland on January 27, 1918 at age 96. She was buried in Slateville Presbyterian Church Cemetery, Delta, Peach Bottom Twp., York Co., Pennsylvania.[49]

Sara E. married **Charles Harry Robinson** after 1940. They had four children. Charles Harry Robinson was born in Cardiff, Harford Co., Maryland, on February 3, 1916. Charles Harry reached age 79 and died in Whiteford, Harford Co., Maryland, on January 11, 1996. He was buried in Slateville Presbyterian Church

Cemetery, Delta, Peach Bottom Twp., York Co., Pennsylvania.[49]

**446. Betty P.⁹ Wiley** (*Elmer Crawford⁸, Sarah⁷ Johnson, Martha Ann⁶ Fulton, Sarah Jane⁵ Miller, Margaret⁴ Pegan, James³, Andrew² Pagan, James¹*) was born on September 6, 1922, in Lower Chanceford Twp., York Co., Pennsylvania. She is the daughter of Elmer Crawford Wiley II (297) and Nellie Stewart.

She married **LeRoy Franklin Kohlbus**. They had one son. LeRoy Franklin Kohlbus was born in Harford Co., Maryland, on March 10, 1917. He was also known as **Roy**. LeRoy Franklin reached age 72 and died in Delta, Peach Bottom Twp., York Co., Pennsylvania, on March 26, 1989. He was buried in Pine Grove Presbyterian Church Cemetery, Lower Chanceford Twp., York Co., Pennsylvania.[51]

**447. Jeane Hawley⁹ Wiley** (*Elmer Crawford⁸, Sarah⁷ Johnson, Martha Ann⁶ Fulton, Sarah Jane⁵ Miller, Margaret⁴ Pegan, James³, Andrew² Pagan, James¹*) was born on August 21, 1924, in Lower Chanceford Twp., York Co., Pennsylvania. She was the daughter of Elmer Crawford Wiley II (297) and Nellie Stewart. Jeane Hawley died in Delta, Peach Bottom Twp., York Co., Pennsylvania, on August 13, 1992, at age 67.

Never married.

**448. Harold Kenneth⁹ Wiley** (*Elmer Crawford⁸, Sarah⁷ Johnson, Martha Ann⁶ Fulton, Sarah Jane⁵ Miller, Margaret⁴ Pegan, James³, Andrew² Pagan, James¹*) was born on February 28, 1926, in Lower Chanceford Twp., York Co., Pennsylvania. He was the son of Elmer Crawford Wiley II (297) and Nellie Stewart. Harold Kenneth died in Delta, Peach Bottom Twp., York Co., Pennsylvania, on April 15, 2002, at age 76. He was buried in Slate Ridge Cemetery, Delta, Peach Bottom Twp., York Co., Pennsylvania.[20]

Harold Kenneth married **Mary Corrine Ramsey** in February 1957 in York Co., Pennsylvania. Mary Corrine Ramsey was born in Delta, Peach Bottom Twp., York Co., Pennsylvania, on March 24, 1929. She was also known as **Corrine**. Mary Corrine reached age 64 and died in Delta, Peach Bottom Twp., York Co., Pennsylvania, on March 2, 1994.

She was buried in Slate Ridge Cemetery, Delta, Peach Bottom Twp., York Co., Pennsylvania.[20]

**449. John F.⁹ Wiley** (*Elmer Crawford⁸, Sarah⁷ Johnson, Martha Ann⁶ Fulton, Sarah Jane⁵ Miller, Margaret⁴ Pegan, James³, Andrew² Pagan, James¹*) was born on February 17, 1929, in Lower Chanceford Twp., York Co., Pennsylvania. He was also known as **Jack**. He was the son of Elmer Crawford Wiley II (297) and Nellie Stewart..

**450. Howard Hughes⁹ Manifold** (*Louise⁸ Wiley, Sarah⁷ Johnson, Martha Ann⁶ Fulton, Sarah Jane⁵ Miller, Margaret⁴ Pegan, James³, Andrew² Pagan, James¹*) was born on January 15, 1922, in Lower Chanceford Twp., York Co., Pennsylvania. He was the son of Samuel D. Manifold and Louise Wiley (298). Howard Hughes died in York, York Co., Pennsylvania, on June 17, 1990, at age 68. He was buried in Stewartstown Cemetery, Stewartstown, Hopewell Twp., York Co., Pennsylvania.[76]

He married **J. Sylvania Unknown**.

**451. Sara Louise⁹ Manifold** (*Louise⁸ Wiley, Sarah⁷ Johnson, Martha Ann⁶ Fulton, Sarah Jane⁵ Miller, Margaret⁴ Pegan, James³, Andrew² Pagan, James¹*) was born on September 13, 1923, in Lower Chanceford Twp., York Co., Pennsylvania. She was the daughter of Samuel D. Manifold and Louise Wiley (298). Sara Louise lived in Red Lion, York Twp., York Co., Pennsylvania. She died in a hospital in York, York Co., Pennsylvania, on October 22, 1996, at age 73. Sara Louise was buried in Susquehanna Memorial Gardens Cemetery, York, York Co., Pennsylvania.[96]

She married **George C. Flaharty**. They had five children. George C. Flaharty was born in York Co., Pennsylvania, on August 29, 1920. George C. reached age 74 and died in Red Lion, York Twp., York Co., Pennsylvania, on August 9, 1995. He was buried in Susquehanna Memorial Gardens Cemetery, York, York Co., Pennsylvania.[96]

**452. Jane E.⁹ Manifold** (*Louise⁸ Wiley, Sarah⁷ Johnson, Martha Ann⁶ Fulton, Sarah Jane⁵ Miller, Margaret⁴ Pegan, James³, Andrew² Pagan, James¹*) was born in 1927 in Lower Chanceford Twp., York Co., Pennsylvania. She was the daughter of Samuel D. Manifold and Louise Wiley (298).

Jane E. married **Dean L. Flaharty** in 1946. They had six children. Dean L. Flaharty was born in Woodbine, Peach Bottom Twp., York Co., Pennsylvania, on March 5, 1928. He was also known as **Pete**. Dean L. reached age 84 and died in Delta, Peach Bottom Twp., York Co., Pennsylvania, on September 28, 2012. He was buried in Salem United Methodist Church Cemetery, Delta, Peach Bottom Twp., York Co., Pennsylvania.[52]

Children of Jane E. Manifold and Dean L. Flaharty:

+ 494 m I. **Infant Edward Dale[10] Flaharty** was born in York Co., Pennsylvania, on November 2, 1946. He died in York Co., Pennsylvania, on November 3, 1946. Infant Edward Dale was buried in Salem United Methodist Church Cemetery, Delta, Peach Bottom Twp., York Co., Pennsylvania.[52]

**453. Dale Wiley[9] Manifold** (*Louise[8] Wiley, Sarah[7] Johnson, Martha Ann[6] Fulton, Sarah Jane[5] Miller, Margaret[4] Pegan, James[3], Andrew[2] Pagan, James[1]*) was born on January 8, 1930, in Lower Chanceford Twp., York Co., Pennsylvania. He was the son of Samuel D. Manifold and Louise Wiley (298). He reached age 88 and died in Yuma, Yuma Co., Arizona on February 3, 2018. He was buried in Eternal Hills Memorial Park Cemetery, Oceanside, San Diego Co., California.[159]

Dale W. married **Grace Elaine Manifold** on April 7, 1950, in San Diego Co., California. Grace Elaine was born in 1930 in East Hopewell Twp., York Co., Pennsylvania. She is also known as **Elaine**. She was the daughter of Samuel Benjamin Manifold (177) and Grace Veach.

**454. Donald David[9] Wise** (*John F.[8], Mary Janetta[7] Fulton, John Henry[6], Sarah Jane[5] Miller, Margaret[4] Pegan, James[3], Andrew[2] Pagan, James[1]*) was born in 1931 in Delta, Peach Bottom Twp., York Co., Pennsylvania. He is the son of John F. Wise (304) and Thelma Williams.

**455. Dale Ford[9] Wise** (*Samuel A.[8], Mary Janetta[7] Fulton, John Henry[6], Sarah Jane[5] Miller, Margaret[4] Pegan, James[3], Andrew[2] Pagan, James[1]*) was born on Thursday, January 13, 1938, in York, York Co., Pennsylvania. He is the son of Samuel A. Wise (305) and Mary Catherine Ford.

**456. Ralph[9] Wise II** (*Ralph Anderson[8], Mary Janetta[7] Fulton, John Henry[6], Sarah Jane[5] Miller, Margaret[4] Pegan, James[3], Andrew[2] Pagan, James[1]*) was born on Sunday, February 23, 1936, in Peach Bottom Twp., York Co., Pennsylvania. He is the son of Ralph Anderson Wise (306) and Ethel Lavenia Smith.

**457. Roy[9] Wise** (*Ralph Anderson[8], Mary Janetta[7] Fulton, John Henry[6], Sarah Jane[5] Miller, Margaret[4] Pegan, James[3], Andrew[2] Pagan, James[1]*) was born on Sunday, February 23, 1936, in Peach Bottom Twp., York Co., Pennsylvania. He is the son of Ralph Anderson Wise (306) and Ethel Lavenia Smith.

**458. Daughter[9] Ailes** (*Grace Anna[8] Wise, Mary Janetta[7] Fulton, John Henry[6], Sarah Jane[5] Miller, Margaret[4] Pegan, James[3], Andrew[2] Pagan, James[1]*) She is the daughter of Edwin Wilson Ailes and Grace Anna Wise (308).

Childless.

Daughter Ailes married **Mr. Rost.** They divorced.

Daughter Ailes Rost married **James Christopher Braselman** about 1985. James Christopher Braselman was born in Media, Delaware Co., Pennsylvania, on July 25, 1954. James Christopher lived in 2013 in York, York Co., Pennsylvania. He reached age 59 and died in a hospital in Philadelphia, Philadelphia Co., Pennsylvania, on October 27, 2013. James Christopher was buried in Slateville Presbyterian Church Cemetery, Delta, Peach Bottom Twp., York Co., Pennsylvania.[49]

**459. Mary Jane[9] Kilgore** (*James Clarence[8], James Mitchell[7], Margaret Rosa[6] Mitchell, Martha Ellen[5] Miller, Margaret[4] Pegan, James[3], Andrew[2] Pagan, James[1]*) was born in 1938 in Mansfield, Madison Twp., Richland Co., Ohio. She is the daughter of James Clarence Kilgore II (317) and Bernice Day.

She married **William K. Miller**.

**460. James L.[9] Kilgore II** (*James Clarence[8], James Mitchell[7], Margaret Rosa[6] Mitchell, Martha Ellen[5] Miller, Margaret[4] Pegan, James[3], Andrew[2] Pagan, James[1]*) was born on March 25, 1940, in Mansfield, Madison Twp., Richland Co., Ohio. He was the son of James Clarence Kilgore II (317) and Bernice Day. James L. died in Mansfield, Madison Twp., Richland Co., Ohio, on July 22, 2012, at age 72. He was buried in Mansfield Memorial Park Cemetery, Ontario, Madison Twp., Richland Co., Ohio.[118]

Never married.

461. **William Harry**[9] **Kilgore** (*James Clarence*[8], *James Mitchell*[7], *Margaret Rosa*[6] *Mitchell, Martha Ellen*[5] *Miller, Margaret*[4] *Pegan, James*[3], *Andrew*[2] *Pagan, James*[1]) was born on August 23, 1941, in Mansfield, Madison Twp., Richland Co., Ohio. He was the son of James Clarence Kilgore II (317) and Bernice Day. William Harry died in Port Richey, Pasco Co., Florida, on November 24, 1998, at age 57. He was buried in Florida National Cemetery, Bushnell, Sumter Co., Florida.[153]

He married **Roeana Jean Thompson**. Roeana Jean Thompson was born in Prenter, Boone Co., West Virginia, on September 5, 1927. Roeana Jean reached age 70 and died in Port Richey, Pasco Co., Florida, on April 13, 1998. She was buried in Florida National Cemetery, Bushnell, Sumter Co., Florida.[153]

462. **Patricia Ann**[9] **Kilgore** (*Willis Leroy*[8], *James Mitchell*[7], *Margaret Rosa*[6] *Mitchell, Martha Ellen*[5] *Miller, Margaret*[4] *Pegan, James*[3], *Andrew*[2] *Pagan, James*[1]) was born on June 22, 1938, in Mansfield, Madison Twp., Richland Co., Ohio. She was the daughter of Willis Leroy Kilgore (318) and Helen Mae West. Patricia Ann died in New London, New London Twp., Huron Co., Ohio, on October 26, 2003, at age 65. She was buried in Grove Street Cemetery, New London, New London Twp., Huron Co., Ohio.[154]

She married **William R. O'Connor**. William R. O'Connor was born in New York? on May 8, 1911. William R. reached age 78 and died in Norwalk, Norwalk Twp., Huron Co., Ohio, on October 5, 1989. He was buried in Grove Street Cemetery, New London, New London Twp., Huron Co., Ohio.[154]

463. **Janie Marie**[9] **Kilgore** (*John Harvey*[8], *James Mitchell*[7], *Margaret Rosa*[6] *Mitchell, Martha Ellen*[5] *Miller, Margaret*[4] *Pegan, James*[3], *Andrew*[2] *Pagan, James*[1]) was born on April 22, 1948, in Mansfield, Madison Twp., Richland Co., Ohio. She was the daughter of John Harvey Kilgore (320) and Doloris Marie Lesser. Janie Marie died in Cranberry Twp., Butler Co., Pennsylvania? on November 27, 2009, at age 61. She was buried in Plains United Presbyterian Church Cemetery, Cranberry Twp., Butler Co., Pennsylvania.[155]

Janie Marie married **Mr. Zeller**. They had one daughter.

464. **Marian V.**[9] **Burkins** (*Charles B.*[8], *Ula Agnes Ellen*[7] *Kilgore, Margaret Rosa*[6] *Mitchell, Martha Ellen*[5] *Miller, Margaret*[4] *Pegan, James*[3], *Andrew*[2] *Pagan, James*[1]) was born on Saturday, September 21, 1940. She is the daughter of Charles B. Burkins (322) and Anna Burger.

She married **Unknown Fletcher**.

465. **Betty L.**[9] **Grove** (*Ida R.*[8] *Burkins, Ula Agnes Ellen*[7] *Kilgore, Margaret Rosa*[6] *Mitchell, Martha Ellen*[5] *Miller, Margaret*[4] *Pegan, James*[3], *Andrew*[2] *Pagan, James*[1]) was born on Saturday, December 23, 1933, in Windsor Twp., York Co., Pennsylvania. She is the daughter of Kenneth Free Grove and Ida R. Burkins (323). Betty L. lived in Prescott, Yavapai Co., Arizona.

She married **Unknown Carns**.

466. **Charles Kenneth**[9] **Grove** (*Ida R.*[8] *Burkins, Ula Agnes Ellen*[7] *Kilgore, Margaret Rosa*[6] *Mitchell, Martha Ellen*[5] *Miller, Margaret*[4] *Pegan, James*[3], *Andrew*[2] *Pagan, James*[1]) was born on July 17, 1935, in Felton, Chanceford Twp., York Co., Pennsylvania. He was also known as **Snowball**. He was the son of Kenneth Free Grove and Ida R. Burkins (323). Charles Kenneth died in York, York Co., Pennsylvania, on May 16, 1967, at age 31. He was buried in Susquehanna Memorial Gardens Cemetery, York, York Co., Pennsylvania.[96]

He married **Yvonne Anette Hildebrand**. They had four sons. Yvonne Anette Hildebrand was born in York, York Co., Pennsylvania, on July 9, 1937. Yvonne Anette reached age 50 and died in York, York Co., Pennsylvania, on

July 28, 1987. She was buried in Susquehanna Memorial Gardens Cemetery, York, York Co., Pennsylvania.[96]

Charles Kenneth Grove and Yvonne Anette Hildebrand had four sons, including:

+ 495 m II. **Carl Kevin[10] Grove** was born in York, York Co., Pennsylvania, on January 1, 1961. He died in Felton, Chanceford Twp., York Co., Pennsylvania, on August 25, 2007. Carl Kevin was buried in Susquehanna Memorial Gardens Cemetery, York, York Co., Pennsylvania.[96]

+ 496 m III. **Curtis Kelly[10] Grove** was born in York, York Co., Pennsylvania, on April 4, 1962. He died in York, York Co., Pennsylvania, on April 14, 1962. Curtis Kelly was buried in Susquehanna Memorial Gardens Cemetery, York, York Co., Pennsylvania.[96]

**467. Wilson[9] Burns** (*Joseph Milton[8], Nora Eliza[7] Kilgore, Margaret Rosa[6] Mitchell, Martha Ellen[5] Miller, Margaret[4] Pegan, James[3], Andrew[2] Pagan, James[1]*) was born on August 23, 1955, in Brogue, Chanceford Twp., York Co., Pennsylvania. He was also known as **Tyke**. He was the son of Joseph Milton Burns (329) and Mary E. Unknown. Wilson died in Brogue, Chanceford Twp., York Co., Pennsylvania, on December 20, 2014, at age 59.

Wilson married **Miss Lease.** They had eight children.

Wilson Burns and his wife had eight children, including:

+ 497 m V. **Son[10] Burns.**

**468. Mark C.[9] Burns** (*Charles W.[8], Nora Eliza[7] Kilgore, Margaret Rosa[6] Mitchell, Martha Ellen[5] Miller, Margaret[4] Pegan, James[3], Andrew[2] Pagan, James[1]*) was born in 1966 in Chanceford Twp., York Co., Pennsylvania. He was the son of Charles W. Burns (330) and Ellen Rebecca Tome. Mark C. died

in Chanceford Twp., York Co., Pennsylvania, in 1966. He was buried in Mount Zion Baptist Church Cemetery, Brogue, Chanceford Twp., York Co., Pennsylvania.[125]

**469. Robert E.[9] Burns** (*Charles W.[8], Nora Eliza[7] Kilgore, Margaret Rosa[6] Mitchell, Martha Ellen[5] Miller, Margaret[4] Pegan, James[3], Andrew[2] Pagan, James[1]*) was born in 1968 in Chanceford Twp., York Co., Pennsylvania. He was the son of Charles W. Burns (330) and Ellen Rebecca Tome. Robert E. died in Chanceford Twp., York Co., Pennsylvania, in 1968. He was buried in Mount Zion Baptist Church Cemetery, Brogue, Chanceford Twp., York Co., Pennsylvania.[125]

**470. Frank Edward[9] Herman** (*Mary Evelyn[8] Grove, Francis Henry[7], Ida Melissa[6] Pegan, Henry[5], James[4], James[3], Andrew[2] Pagan, James[1]*) was born on May 30, 1938, in York, York Co., Pennsylvania. He was the son of Harris Milton Herman and Mary Evelyn Grove (336). Frank Edward died in York, York Co., Pennsylvania, on September 29, 2006, at age 68. He was buried in Prospect Hill Cemetery, York Twp., York Co., Pennsylvania.[43]

Frank Edward married and had three sons.

**471. Wayne Kenneth[9] Grove III** (*Wayne Kenneth[8], Wayne Penny[7], Ida Melissa[6] Pegan, Henry[5], James[4], James[3], Andrew[2] Pagan, James[1]*) was born in 1939. He is the son of Wayne Kenneth Grove II (336) and Pauline Dorothy Henry.

**472. Linda Gail[9] Houseberg** (*Gertrude Melissa[8] Grove, Claire Jamison[7], Ida Melissa[6] Pegan, Henry[5], James[4], James[3], Andrew[2] Pagan, James[1]*) was born on May 10, 1950, in San Francisco, San Francisco Co., California. She was the daughter of Ernest James Houseberg and Gertrude Melissa Grove (344). Linda Gail died in Houston, Harris Co., Texas, on March 12, 2012, at age 61.

She married **Warren Jay Sousa.** They had one daughter. Warren Jay Sousa was born in Salinas, Monterey Co., California, on December 24, 1949. Warren Jay reached age 51 and died in Seabrook, Harris Co., Texas, on November 24, 2001.

**473. Barry Rodger[9] Horn** (*Rodger Melvin[8], Anna Matilda[7] Grove, Ida Melissa[6] Pegan, Henry[5], James[4],*

*James[3], Andrew[2] Pagan, James[1]*) was born on May 3, 1944, in York Co., Pennsylvania. He was the son of Rodger Melvin Horn (347) and Margaret Prall Grove. Barry Rodger died in Red Lion, York Twp., York Co., Pennsylvania, on September 4, 1998, at age 54. He was buried in Susquehanna Memorial Gardens Cemetery, York, York Co., Pennsylvania.[96]

He married **Jane A. Unknown**.

**474. Cynthia Ann[9] McClure** (*Romaine Grove[8] Horn, Anna Matilda[7] Grove, Ida Melissa[6] Pegan, Henry[5], James[4], James[3], Andrew[2] Pagan, James[1]*) was born on September 25, 1949, in York Twp., York Co., Pennsylvania. She was the daughter of William Arthur McClure and Romaine Grove Horn (348). Cynthia Ann died in York Twp., York Co., Pennsylvania, on February 28, 2010, at age 60. She was buried in Prospect Hill Cemetery, York Twp., York Co., Pennsylvania.[43]

Never married. But her obituary states Mr. Myers is the father of her children.

She had a relationship with **Mr. Myers**. They had five children.

**475. Daughter[9] Morton** (*E. Jean[8] Grove, John Paul[7], Alice Eva[6] Pegan, Henry[5], James[4], James[3], Andrew[2] Pagan, James[1]*). She is the daughter of John H. Morton and E. Jean Grove (350).

She married **Mr. Warner**. They had one daughter.

Daughter of Daughter Morton and Mr. Warner:

+ 498 f I. **Jennifer[10] Warner**. Jennifer died before 2014.

**476. Richard Eugene[9] Messinger II** (*Ethel Virginia[8] Pegan, Nathan Neil[7], Harry Hutton[6], Henry[5], James[4], James[3], Andrew[2] Pagan, James[1]*) was born on July 20, 1947, in York, York Co., Pennsylvania.[136] He was the son of Richard Eugene Messinger and Ethel Virginia Pegan (354). Richard Eugene died in York, York Co., Pennsylvania, on July 20,1947.[136] He was buried in Spring Grove Cemetery, Jackson Twp., York Co., Pennsylvania.[24, 159] No name is given for him on his death certificate, but his gravestone reads "Richard E. Messinger Jr.".[24]

**477. Bret E.[9] Manifold** (*Benjamin Eugene[8], Samuel Benjamin[7], Jennie Elizabeth[6] Adams, Sarah Eliza[5] Pegan, James[4], James[3], Andrew[2] Pagan, James[1]*) was born on November 19, 1965. He is the son of Benjamin Eugene Manifold (358) and Lydia Mae Wolfe. Bret E. was buried in Round Hill Presbyterian Church Cemetery, Cross Roads, East Hopewell Twp., York Co., Pennsylvania.[39]

**478. Dirk Michael[9] Lanius** (*Richard Weist[8], Margaret Eleanor[7] Manifold, Jennie Elizabeth[6] Adams, Sarah Eliza[5] Pegan, James[4], James[3], Andrew[2] Pagan, James[1]*) was born on February 20, 1964. He was the son of Richard Weist Lanius (361) and Carolyn Ruth Vaught. Dirk Michael died in in a hospital in Baltimore, Baltimore Co., Maryland, on March 14, 1984, at age 20.

He married **Unknown Unknown**. They had one son.

# 10th Generation

**479. Lucretia Mae**[10] **Miller** (*Rebecca Walton*[9] *Douts, Mary Margaret*[8] *Walton, Elmer*[7], *Hannah Margaret*[6] *Nimlow, Margaret*[5] *Pegan, Andrew*[4], *James*[3], *Andrew*[2] *Pagan, James*[1]) was born on Thursday, May 28, 1936, in Martic Twp., Lancaster Co., Pennsylvania. She is the daughter of Elias Benjamin Miller and Rebecca Walton Douts (368).

She married **Harold Wright**.

**480. David D.**[10] **Miller** (*Rebecca Walton*[9] *Douts, Mary Margaret*[8] *Walton, Elmer*[7], *Hannah Margaret*[6] *Nimlow, Margaret*[5] *Pegan, Andrew*[4], *James*[3], *Andrew*[2] *Pagan, James*[1]) was born on Sunday, July 3, 1938, in Martic Twp., Lancaster Co., Pennsylvania. He is the son of Elias Benjamin Miller and Rebecca Walton Douts (368).

**481. Donald Emerson**[10] **Miller** (*Rebecca Walton*[9] *Douts, Mary Margaret*[8] *Walton, Elmer*[7], *Hannah Margaret*[6] *Nimlow, Margaret*[5] *Pegan, Andrew*[4], *James*[3], *Andrew*[2] *Pagan, James*[1]) was born on August 27, 1939, in Martic Twp., Lancaster Co., Pennsylvania. He was the son of Elias Benjamin Miller and Rebecca Walton Douts (368). Donald Emerson died in Martic Twp., Lancaster Co., Pennsylvania, on June 4, 1952, at age 12. He was buried in Mount Nebo United Methodist Church Cemetery, Pequea, Pequea Twp., Lancaster Co., Pennsylvania.[82]

**482. Daughter**[10] **Douts** (*John Luther*[9], *Mary Margaret*[8] *Walton, Elmer*[7], *Hannah Margaret*[6] *Nimlow, Margaret*[5] *Pegan, Andrew*[4], *James*[3], *Andrew*[2] *Pagan, James*[1]). She is the daughter of John Luther Douts (369) and Verna Blomquist.

She married **John Patrick McCarty** on June 18, 1983, in Burke Co., North Dakota. John Patrick McCarty was born in Rugby, Pierce Co., North Dakota, on December 10, 1947. He reached age 49 and died in Leeds, Benson Co., North Dakota, on October 7, 1997. He was buried in Leeds Cemetery, Benson Co., North Dakota.[164]

**483. Judy Kay**[10] **Douts** (*John Luther*[9], *Mary Margaret*[8] *Walton, Elmer*[7], *Hannah Margaret*[6] *Nimlow, Margaret*[5] *Pegan, Andrew*[4], *James*[3], *Andrew*[2] *Pagan, James*[1]) was born in Powers Lake, Burke Co., North Dakota on February 6, 1952. She was the daughter of John Luther Douts (369) and Verna Blomquist. Judy Kay died on December 30, 1989 in Powers Lake, Burke Co., North Dakota? She was buried in Bethel Cemetery, Battleview, Burke Co., North Dakota.[131]

She married **Unknown Anderson.**

**484. Beverly Diane**[10] **Spencer** (*Alice Clair*[9] *Glenn, Purdy Lester*[8], *Grace Anna*[7] *Kilgore, Alvin Levi*[6], *Sarah Jane*[5] *Pegan, Andrew*[4], *James*[3], *Andrew*[2] *Pagan, James*[1]) was born on October 17, 1957, in York, York Co., Pennsylvania. She was the daughter of Joseph Bruce Spencer II and Alice Clair Glenn (384). Beverly Diane died in York, York Co., Pennsylvania, on January 11, 1997, at age 39.

Never married.

**485. Daughter**[10] **Jamison** (*Carol E.*[9] *Krewson, Marian L.*[8] *Anderson, Daisy Mae*[7] *Hess, Luella Jane*[6] *Kilgore, Sarah Jane*[5] *Pegan, Andrew*[4], *James*[3], *Andrew*[2] *Pagan, James*[1]). She is the daughter of Rodney B. Jamison and Carol E. Krewson (406).

She married **Mr. Poff**. They had one daughter.

Daughter of Daughter Jamison and Mr. Poff:

+ 499 f I. **Stephanie N.**[11] **Poff**. Stephanie N. was born in 1982. She died in 1982. She was buried in Bethel United Methodist Cemetery, Shenks Ferry, Chanceford Twp., York Co., Pennsylvania.[95]

**486. Ellsworth James**[10] **Gentry III** (*Ellsworth James*[9], *Ellsworth James*[8], *Adelaide or Adeline*[7] *Pegan, Elmer Ellsworth James*[6], *Alexander L.*[5], *Andrew*[4], *James*[3], *Andrew*[2] *Pagan, James*[1]) was born on August 20, 1958, in Wilmington, New Castle Co., Delaware. He was the son of Ellsworth James Gentry II (424) and Unknown Unknown. Ellsworth James died in Wilmington, New Castle Co., Delaware, on December 7, 1997, at age 39. He was buried in Silverbrook Cemetery, Wilmington, New Castle Co., Delaware.[32]

**487. RaeArlene**[10] **Wiley** (*William James*[9], *James Howard*[8], *Sarah*[7] *Johnson*, *Martha Ann*[6] *Fulton*, *Sarah Jane*[5] *Miller*, *Margaret*[4] *Pegan*, *James*[3], *Andrew*[2] *Pagan*, *James*[1]) was born in 1936 in Lancaster, Lancaster Co., Pennsylvania. She is the daughter of William James Wiley (431) and Dorothy E. Brown.

**488. James Ernest**[10] **Wiley** (*William James*[9], *James Howard*[8], *Sarah*[7] *Johnson*, *Martha Ann*[6] *Fulton*, *Sarah Jane*[5] *Miller*, *Margaret*[4] *Pegan*, *James*[3], *Andrew*[2] *Pagan*, *James*[1]) was born in 1938 in Lancaster, Lancaster Co., Pennsylvania. He is the son of William James Wiley (429) and Dorothy E. Brown.

**489. Lora K.**[10] **Eckman** (*Emma Rae*[9] *Wiley*, *James Howard*[8], *Sarah*[7] *Johnson*, *Martha Ann*[6] *Fulton*, *Sarah Jane*[5] *Miller*, *Margaret*[4] *Pegan*, *James*[3], *Andrew*[2] *Pagan*, *James*[1]) was born in 1938 in Conowingo, Cecil Co., Maryland. She is the daughter of Chester E. Wiley Eckman and Emma Rae Wiley (432).

**490. James Lawrence**[10] **Wingo** (*Lillian Howard*[9] *Wiley*, *James Howard*[8], *Sarah*[7] *Johnson*, *Martha Ann*[6] *Fulton*, *Sarah Jane*[5] *Miller*, *Margaret*[4] *Pegan*, *James*[3], *Andrew*[2] *Pagan*, *James*[1]) was born on November 12, 1942, in Blacksburg, Montgomery Co., Virginia. He was the son of Sidney Lawrence Wingo and Lillian Howard Wiley (437). James Lawrence died in Blacksburg, Montgomery Co., Virginia, on November 30, 1942. He was buried in Wingo Family Cemetery, Blacksburg, Montgomery Co., Virginia.[163]

**491. Rosa May**[10] **Wingo** (*Lillian Howard*[9] *Wiley*, *James Howard*[8], *Sarah*[7] *Johnson*, *Martha Ann*[6] *Fulton*, *Sarah Jane*[5] *Miller*, *Margaret*[4] *Pegan*, *James*[3], *Andrew*[2] *Pagan*, *James*[1]) was born on June 30, 1944, in Blacksburg, Montgomery Co., Virginia. She was the daughter of Sidney Lawrence Wingo and Lillian Howard Wiley (437). Rosa May died in Blacksburg, Montgomery Co., Virginia, on June 30, 1944. She was buried in Wingo Family Cemetery, Blacksburg, Montgomery Co., Virginia.[163]

**492. James Thomas**[10] **Wingo** (*Lillian Howard*[9] *Wiley*, *James Howard*[8], *Sarah*[7] *Johnson*, *Martha Ann*[6]

*Fulton*, *Sarah Jane*[5] *Miller*, *Margaret*[4] *Pegan*, *James*[3], *Andrew*[2] *Pagan*, *James*[1]) was born on April 26, 1948, in Radford, Virginia. He was the son of Sidney Lawrence Wingo and Lillian Howard Wiley (437). James Thomas died in Bear, New Castle Co., Delaware, on September 28, 1998. He is buried in Delaware Veterans Memorial Cemetery, Bear, New Castle Co., Delaware.[149]

He married **Unknown Unknown**. They had one son.

**493. Dale Lawrence**[10] **Wingo** (*Lillian Howard*[9] *Wiley*, *James Howard*[8], *Sarah*[7] *Johnson*, *Martha Ann*[6] *Fulton*, *Sarah Jane*[5] *Miller*, *Margaret*[4] *Pegan*, *James*[3], *Andrew*[2] *Pagan*, *James*[1]) was born on April 13, 1949, in Radford, Virginia. He was the son of Sidney Lawrence Wingo and Lillian Howard Wiley (437). Dale Lawrence lived in Newark, New Castle Co., Delaware. He died in a hospital in New Castle, New Castle Co., Delaware, on June 9, 1999, at age 50. Dale Lawrence was buried in Gracelawn Memorial Park Cemetery, Farmhurst, New Castle Co., Delaware.[59]

Dale Lawrence married Sandra Ann Unknown. They had three children.

**494. Infant Edward Dale**[10] **Flaharty** (*Jane E.*[9] *Manifold*, *Louise*[8] *Wiley*, *Sarah*[7] *Johnson*, *Martha Ann*[6] *Fulton*, *Sarah Jane*[5] *Miller*, *Margaret*[4] *Pegan*, *James*[3], *Andrew*[2] *Pagan*, *James*[1]) was born on November 2, 1946, in York Co., Pennsylvania. He was the son of Dean L. Flaharty and Jane E. Manifold (452). Infant Edward Dale died in York Co., Pennsylvania, on November 3, 1946. He was buried in Salem United Methodist Church Cemetery, Delta, Peach Bottom Twp., York Co., Pennsylvania.[52]

**495. Carl Kevin**[10] **Grove** (*Charles Kenneth*[9], *Ida R.*[8] *Burkins*, *Ula Agnes Ellen*[7] *Kilgore*, *Margaret Rosa*[6] *Mitchell*, *Martha Ellen*[5] *Miller*, *Margaret*[4] *Pegan*, *James*[3], *Andrew*[2] *Pagan*, *James*[1]) was born on January 1, 1961, in York, York Co., Pennsylvania. He was the son of Charles Kenneth Grove (466) and Yvonne Anette Hildebrand. Carl Kevin died in Felton, Chanceford Twp., York Co., Pennsylvania, on August 25, 2007, at age 46. He was buried in Susquehanna Memorial Gardens Cemetery, York, York Co., Pennsylvania.[96]

Never married.

**496. Curtis Kelly**[10] **Grove** (*Charles Kenneth*[9], *Ida R.*[8] *Burkins, Ula Agnes Ellen*[7] *Kilgore, Margaret Rosa*[6] *Mitchell, Martha Ellen*[5] *Miller, Margaret*[4] *Pegan, James*[3], *Andrew*[2] *Pagan, James*[1]) was born on April 4, 1962, in York, York Co., Pennsylvania. He was the son of Charles Kenneth Grove (466) and Yvonne Anette Hildebrand. Curtis Kelly died in York, York Co., Pennsylvania, on April 14, 1962. He was buried in Susquehanna Memorial Gardens Cemetery, York, York Co., Pennsylvania.[96]

**497. Son**[10] **Burns** (*Wilson*[9], *Joseph Milton*[8], *Nora Eliza*[7] *Kilgore, Margaret Rosa*[6] *Mitchell, Martha Ellen*[5] *Miller, Margaret*[4] *Pegan, James*[3], *Andrew*[2] *Pagan, James*[1]). He is the son of Wilson Burns (467) and his wife.

He married. He and his wife had at least one son.

Son of Son Burns and his wife:

+ 500 m I. **Braden Edward Skylar**[11] **Burns** was born in York, York Co., Pennsylvania, on August 30, 2011. He died in York, York Co., Pennsylvania, on November 16, 2011.

**498. Jennifer**[10] **Warner** (*Daughter*[9] *Morton, E. Jean*[8] *Grove, John Paul*[7], *Alice Eva*[6] *Pegan, Henry*[5], *James*[4], *James*[3], *Andrew*[2] *Pagan, James*[1]). She was the daughter of Mr. Warner and Daughter Morton (475). Jennifer died before 2014.

# 11th Generation

**499. Stephanie N.**[11] **Poff** (*Son*[10] *Jamison, Carol E.*[9] *Krewson, Marian L.*[8] *Anderson, Daisy Mae*[7] *Hess, Luella Jane*[6] *Kilgore, Sarah Jane*[5] *Pegan, Andrew*[4], *James*[3], *Andrew*[2] *Pagan, James*[1]). Stephanie N. was born in 1982. She was the daughter of Mr. Poff and Daughter Jamison (485). She died in 1982. She was buried in Bethel United Methodist Church Cemetery, Shenks Ferry, Chanceford Twp., York Co., Pennsylvania.[95]

**500. Braden Edward Skylar**[11] **Burns** (*Son*[10], *Wilson*[9], *Joseph Milton*[8] *Burns, Nora Eliza*[7] *Kilgore, Margaret Rosa*[6] *Mitchell, Martha Ellen*[5] *Miller, Margaret*[4] *Pegan, James*[3], *Andrew*[2] *Pagan, James*[1]) was born on August 30, 2011, in York, York Co., Pennsylvania. He was the son of Son Burns (497) and his wife. Braden Edward Skylar Burns died in York, York Co., Pennsylvania, on November 16, 2011.

# Endnotes

1   Find A Grave—Old Chestnut Level Presbyterian Church Cemetery, Drumore Twp., Lancaster Co., Pennsylvania, Find A Grave.com.

2   Roy D. Pegan, Roy D. Pegan file—James and Sarah Brannon Pegan family genealogy and notes (, 1950s), Lancaster County Historical Society, 230 North President Avenue, Lancaster, PA.

3   Andrew Pegan will (1788), Lancaster County, Pennsylvania Will Book F: Vol. 1: 84-86. Lancaster County, Pennsylvania Archives, 150 North Queen Street, Lancaster, PA.

4   Pagan/Pegan entries, Lancaster County, Pennsylvania Tax Lists, 1751-1800, Microfilm, Roll #23, Genealogy Center, Allen County Public Library, Fort Wayne, IN.

5   Lancaster County, Pennsylvania Deeds, Hugh Long and others to Peter Baughman, Lancaster County Deed Book N: Vol. 3: 305. Lancaster County, Pennsylvania Archives, 150 North Queen Street, Lancaster, PA.

6   Letter, along with warrant survey documents and maps, from Aaron McWilliams, research historian at the Pennsylvania State Archives, Harrisburg, Pennsylvania, to author Ann Miller Carr on July 24, 2015. Commonwealth of Pennsylvania, Lancaster County, Patent Book H, No. 3, pg. 135, James Pegan, #323. Original document at the Pennsylvania State Archives, 350 North Street, Harrisburg, PA.

7   "Warrant Registers, 1733-1957", [series #17.88, RG-17], Records of the Land Office, Lancaster County, Pennsylvania, pg. 175, James Pegan, #323. Pennsylvania Historical and Museum Commission, Bureau of Archives and History, Pennsylvania State Archives, Harrisburg, PA; Online database: http://www.phmc.state.pa.us/bah/dam/rg/di/r17-88WarrantRegisters/Lancaster/175.pdf.

8   "Patent Indexes, 1684-[ca 1957] {series #17.147, 154 & 155}. RG-17, Records of the Land Office, Lancaster County, Pennsylvania, H series, Vol. 1, 1809-1823, pg. 270/273, James Pegan. Pennsylvania Historical and Museum Commission, Bureau of Archives and History, Pennsylvania State Archives, Harrisburg, PA; Online database: http://www.phmc.state.pa.us/bah/dam/rg/di/r17PatentIndexes/H1809-23PatentIndex273.pdf.

9   "Ellis, Franklin and Samuel Evans, *History of Lancaster County, Pennsylvania, with biographical sketches of many of the pioneers and prominent men*. Philadelphia: Everts & Peck; 1883, pg. 969. Note: Although the book cites the date as 1745, volunteers at the Southern Lancaster Historical Society told the author that this date is too late. The Scots-Irish came to southwestern Lancaster County around 1736-37. As James Pegan I, the father of Andrew I, serves on a jury in 1741, the 1745 date is incorrect. Mishawaka Heritage Center, Mishawaka Penn-Harris Library, 290 Lincolnway East, Mishawaka, IN.

10  Hess, Larry E., "The History of Martic Township", *Millersville-Penn Manor Community History*; ed. by Robert E. Coley, James A. Jolly and Carole L. Slotter. Millersville, Pennsylvania: Produced by the Millersville-Penn Bicentennial Committee, 1976, pg. 80. Conestoga Area Historical Society, 51 Kendig Road, Conestoga, PA.

11  Muddy Run Pumped Storage Facility, Wikipedia. n.d. Online database: https://en.wikipedia.org/wiki/Muddy_Run_Pumped_Storage_Facility

12  Phone interview with Robert Pegan, Rochester, New York, by phone, March 19, 2017.

13  James Pegan Sr. will (1834), Lancaster County, Pennsylvania Will Book Q-R: 506-507. Lancaster County, Pennsylvania Archives, 150 North Queen Street, Lancaster, PA.

14  Find A Grave—Chanceford Presbyterian Church Cemetery, Airville, Lower Chanceford Twp., York Co., Pennsylvania, Find A Grave.com.

15  Find A Grave—Muddy Run Presbyterian Cemetery, Martic Twp., Lancaster Co., Pennsylvania, Find A Grave.com.

16  Find A Grave—Mount Nebo Cemetery, Martic Twp., Lancaster Co., Pennsylvania, Fina A Grave.com.

17  Lancaster County Directory, 1869-1870, Martic Township, pg. 322, entry for Pegan, Jane. Lancaster County Historical Society, 230 North President Avenue, Lancaster, PA.

18  Find A Grave—Lancaster Cemetery, Lancaster, Lancaster Co., Pennsylvania, Find A Grave.com.

19  Find A Grave—Green Mount Cemetery, Highville, Manor Twp., Lancaster Co., Pennsylvania, Find A Grave.com.

20  Find A Grave—Slate Ridge Cemetery, Delta, Peach Bottom Twp., York Co., Pennsylvania.

21  Find A Grave—Old Guinston Church Cemetery, Airville, Chanceford Twp., York Co., Pennsylvania, Find A Grave.com.

22  Obituary of Mary A. Pegan (Delta, Pennsylvania, Delta Herald and Times, 10 Apr 1896), Newspapers and Periodicals, Ancestry.com.

23  Pennsylvania, Veteran's Burial Cards, 1777-1999, Ancestry.com, Henry Pegan.

24  Find A Grave—Spring Grove Cemetery, Jackson Twp., York Co., Pennsylvania, Find A Grave.com, Phillip Eugene Pegan, Find A Grave Memorial #25678670.

25  Find A Grave—Greenwood Cemetery, Lancaster, Lancaster Co., Pennsylvania, Find A Grave.com.

26  Idaho Deaths and Burials, 1907-1965, FamilySearch, database, familysearch.org, Leeber Nimlow.

27  U.S. Veteran's Gravesites, ca. 1775-2006, Ancestry.com, Leeper Nimlow.

28  Find A Grave— Mount Tunnel Cemetery, Elizabethtown, Mt. Joy Twp., Lancaster Co., Pennsylvania, Find A Grave.com.

29  Find A Grave—Riverview Burial Park Cemetery, Lancaster, Lancaster Co., Pennsylvania, Find A Grave.com.

30  Find A Grave—Chartiers Cemetery, Carnegie, Scott Twp., Allegheny Co., Pennsylvania, Find A Grave.com.

31  Find A Grave—Zion Lutheran Cemetery, Leola, Upper Leacock Twp., Lancaster Co., Pennsylvania, Find A Grave.com.

32  Find A Grave—Silverbrook Cemetery, Wilmington, New Castle Co., Delaware, Find A Grave.com.

33  Find A Grave—Grace United Methodist Church Cemetery, Millersville, Manor Twp., Lancaster Co., Pennsylvania, Find A Grave.com.

34  Find A Grave—Woodward Hill Cemetery, Lancaster, Lancaster Co., Pennsylvania, Find A Grave.com.

35  Find A Grave—Lexington Cemetery, Lexington, Troy Twp., Richland Co., Ohio, Find A Grave.com.

36  Find A Grave—New Chestnut Level Presbyterian Church Cemetery, Drumore Twp., Lancaster Co., Pennsylvania, Find A Grave.com.

37  Find A Grave—Oxford Cemetery, Oxford, Chester Co., Pennsylvania, Find A Grave.com.

38  Find A Grave—Prospect Hill Cemetery, Harrisburg, Dauphin Co., Pennsylvania, Find A Grave.com.

39  Find A Grave—Round Hill Presbyterian Church Cemetery, Cross Roads, East Hopewell Twp., York Co., Pennsylvania, Find A Grave.com.

40  Find A Grave—Mount Rose Cemetery, Spring Garden Twp., York Co., Pennsylvania, Find A Grave.com.

41  Find A Grave—Bethesda United Methodist Church Cemetery, Bethesda, Martic Twp., Lancaster Co., Pennsylvania, Find A Grave.com.

42  Find A Grave—Washington Boro Cemetery, Manor Twp., Lancaster Co., Pennsylvania, Find A Grave.com.

43  Find A Grave—Prospect Hill Cemetery, York Twp., York Co., Pennsylvania, Find A Grave.com.

44  Pennsylvania, Death Certificates, 1906-1966, Ancestry.com, George Niblock, death cert. #104977.

45  Find A Grave—Bainbridge Cemetery, Conoy Twp., Lancaster Co., Pennsylvania, Find A Grave.com.

46  Find A Grave—Memorial Park Mausoleum Cemetery, Lima, Ottawa Twp., Allen Co., Ohio, Find A Grave.com.

47  Illinois, Deaths and Stillbirths Index, 1916-1947, Ancestry.com, Caroline Kilgore.

48  Find A Grave—Portage Cemetery, Portage, Wood Co., Ohio, Find A Grave.com.

49  Find A Grave—Slateville Presbyterian Church Cemetery, Delta, Peach Bottom Twp., York Co., Pennsylvania, Find A Grave.com.

50  Find A Grave—Memorial Park Cemetery, Lawrence, Douglas Co., Kansas, Find A Grave.com.

51  Find A Grave—Pine Grove Presbyterian Church Cemetery, Lower Chanceford Twp., York Co., Pennsylvania, Find A Grave.com.

52  Find A Grave—Salem United Methodist Church Cemetery, Delta, Peach Bottom Twp., York Co., Pennsylvania, Find A Grave.com.

53  Find A Grave—Hamilton Memorial Gardens, Hixon, Hamilton Co., Tennessee, Find A Grave.com.

54  Find A Grave—Mount Calvary Cemetery, Roslindale, Suffolk Co., Massachusetts, Find A Grave.com.

55  Find A Grave—Jefferson Memorial Park Cemetery, Pleasant Hills, Allegheny Co., Pennsylvania, Find A Grave.com.

56  Jefferson Memorial Park Cemetery Records, Jefferson Memorial Park Cemetery (Pleasant Hills, Pennsylvania), Jefferson Memorial Park Cemetery, 3368 Churchview Avenue, Pittsburgh, PA.

57  Find A Grave—Saint Paul's Lutheran Cemetery, Ardmore, Lower Merion Twp., Montgomery Co., Pennsylvania, Find A Grave.com.

58  Find A Grave—All Saints Cemetery, Wilmington, New Castle Co., Delaware, Find A Grave.com.

59  Find A Grave—Gracelawn Memorial Park Cemetery, Farmhurst, New Castle Co., Delaware, Find A Grave.com.

60  Find A Grave—Byerland Mennonite Cemetery, Pequa Twp., Lancaster Co., Pennsylvania, Find A Grave.com.

61  Find A Grave—Millersville Mennonite Cemetery, Millersville, Manor Twp., Lancaster Co., Pennsylvania, Find A Grave.com.

62  Pennsylvania, Death Certificates, 1906-1966, Ancestry.com, John Thomas Gregg, death cert. #57548.

63  Pennsylvania Veteran's Burial Cards, 1777-1999, Ancestry.com, J. Thomas Gregg.

64  North America, Family Histories, 1500-2000, Ancestry.com, John Thomas Gregg.

65  Ohio, Births and Christenings Index, 1774-1973, Ancestry.com, Ada Mae Douglass.

66  Ohio, Death Records, 1908-1932, 1938-2007, Ancestry.com, A.M. Douglas, death cert. #040004.

67  Find A Grave—Mansfield Cemetery, Mansfield, Madison Twp., Richland Co., Ohio, Find A Grave.com.

68  Find A Grave—Mount Olivet United Methodist Church Cemetery, Fawn Grove, Fawn Twp., York Co., Pennsylvania, Find A Grave.com.

69  Michigan, Death Records, 1867-1950, Ancestry.com, William A. Grove, death cert. #168847.

70  Find A Grave—Woodmere Cemetery, Detroit, Wayne Co., Michigan, Find A Grave.com.

71  Find A Grave—Longstown United Methodist Cemetery, York Twp., York Co., Pennsylvania, Find A Grave.com.

72  Find A Grave—Freysville Cemetery, Windsor Twp., York Co., Pennsylvania, Find A Grave.com.

73  Find A Grave—Stony Brook Mennonite Cemetery, York, York Co., Pennsylvania, Find A Grave.com.

74 Find A Grave—-Upper Octarara Church Cemetery, Parkesburg, Sadbury Twp., Chester Co., Pennsylvania, Find A Grave.com.

75 Pennsylvania, Death Certificates, 1906-1966, Ancestry.com, Lizzie Ann Pegan, death cert. #53670.

76 Find A Grave—Stewartstown Cemetery, Stewartstown, Hopewell Twp., York Co., Pennsylvania, Find A Grave.com.

77 Find A Grave—Shenandoah Memorial Park Cemetery, Winchester, Frederick Co., Virginia, Find A Grave.com.

78 Find A Grave—Fairview Cemetery, York Twp., York Co., Pennsylvania, Find A Grave.com.

79 Pennsylvania Veteran's Burial Cards, 1777-1999, Ancestry.com, Emory Grove.

80 Find A Grave—Red Lion Cemetery, Red Lion, York Twp., York Co., Pennsylvania, Find A Grave.com.

81 Find A Grave—Morris Cemetery, Phoenixville, Schuylkill Twp., Chester Co., Pennsylvania, Find A Grave.com.

82 Find A Grave—Mount Nebo United Methodist Church Cemetery, Pequea, Pequea Twp., Lancaster Co., Pennsylvania, Find A Grave.com.

83 Aldersgate United Methodist Church Records, Ellen Rostetter, Aldersgate United Methodist Church, 397 Tyler Run Road, York, PA.

84 Pennsylvania, Death Certificates, 1906-1966, Ancestry.com, Ellen Akins, death cert. #2513S.

85 Find A Grave—Goods Mennonite Cemetery, Elizabethtown, Mt. Joy Twp., Lancaster Co., Pennsylvania, Find A Grave.com.

86 Pennsylvania, Marriages, 1852-1968, Ancestry.com, Benjamin F. Gilberg and Genevieve Mae Niblock.

87 Find A Grave—Arlington National Cemetery, Arlington, Virginia, Find A Grave.com.

88 Find A Grave—Greenlawn Cemetery, Wapakoneta, Duchonquet Twp., Auglaize Co., Ohio, Find A Grave.com.

89 Find A Grave—Nottingham Cemetery, East Nottingham Twp., Chester Co., Pennsylvania, Find A Grave.com.

90 Find A Grave—Conestoga Memorial Park Cemetery, Lancaster Twp., Lancaster Co., Pennsylvania, Find A Grave.com.

91 Find A Grave—Fawn Grove Methodist Church Cemetery, Fawn Grove, Fawn Grove Twp., York Co., Pennsylvania, Find A Grave.com.

92 Find A Grave—McKendree United Methodist Cemetery, Airville, Lower Chanceford Twp., York Co., Pennsylvania, Find A Grave.com.

93 Find A Grave—Saint Paul's Wolf's Evangelical Covenant Cemetery, West York Twp., York Co., Pennsylvania, Find A Grave.com.

94 Find A Grave—Woodlawn Cemetery, Elmira, Chemug Co., New York, Find A Grave.com.

95 Find A Grave—Bethel United Methodist Church Cemetery, Shenks Ferry, Chanceford Twp., York Co., Pennsylvania, Find A Grave.com.

96 Find A Grave—Susquehanna Memorial Gardens Cemetery, York, York County, Pennsylvania, Find A Grave.com.

97 Find A Grave—Greenwood Cemetery, Knoxville, Knox Co., Tennessee, Find A Grave.com.

98 Find A Grave—Lynnhurst Cemetery, Knoxville, Knox Co., Tennessee, Find A Grave.com.

99 Find A Grave—Church of the Holy Apostles Episcopal Cemetery, Barnwell, Barnwell Co., South Carolina, Find A Grave.com.

100 Find A Grave—Mountain View Cemetery, Tacoma, Pierce Co., Washington, Find A Grave.com.

101 Find A Grave—Rancks United Methodist Church Cemetery, New Holland, Earl Twp., Lancaster Co., Pennsylvania, Find A Grave.com.

102 Find A Grave—St. Joseph's New Catholic Cemetery, Bausman, Lancaster Twp., Lancaster Co., Pennsylvania, Find A Grave.com.

103 Find A Grave—Westminster Presbyterian Cemetery, Mifflintown, Juniata Co., Pennsylvania, Find A Grave.com.

104 U.S. Veteran's Gravesites, ca. 1775-2006, Ancestry.com, Lewis C. Pegan.

105 Find A Grave—Bay Pines National Cemetery, Bay Pines, Pinellas Co., Florida, Find A Grave.com.

106 Find A Grave—St. Anthony's Roman Catholic Cemetery, Lancaster, Lancaster Co., Pennsylvania, Find A Grave.com.

107 Find A Grave—Forest Dale Cemetery, Malden, Middlesex Co., Massachusetts, Find A Grave.com.

108 Find A Grave—Balcom Cemetery, Berlin Center, Berlin Twp., Ionia Co., Michigan, Find A Grave.com.

109 Find A Grave—National Cemetery of the Alleghenies, Cecil Twp., Washington Co., Pennsylvania, Find A Grave.com.

110 Pennsylvania Veteran's Burial Cards, 1777-1999, Ancestry.com, Charles Kirkwood Geiges.

111 Delaware, Marriage Records, 1806-1933, Ancestry.com, William H. Pegan and Alva M. Cavender.

112 Wilmington, Delaware, Catholic Diocese Cemetery Index, 1876-2012, Ancestry.com.

113 Find A Grave—Miami Valley Memorial Gardens Cemetery, Springboro, Clearcreek Twp., Warren Co., Ohio, Find A Grave.com.

114 Find A Grave—Little Britain Presbyterian Church Cemetery, Fulton Twp., Lancaster Co., Pennsylvania, Find A Grave.com.

115 Find A Grave—Bryansville Cemetery, Bryansville, Peach Bottom Twp., York Co., Pennsylvania, Find A Grave.com.

116 Find A Grave—Memory Gardens Cemetery, East Cocalico Twp., Lancaster Co., Pennsylvania, Find A Grave.com.

117 Find A Grave—Penn Hill (Friends) Burial Ground, Penn Hill, Fulton Twp., Lancaster Co., Pennsylvania, Find A Grave.com.

118 Find A Grave—Mansfield Memorial Park Cemetery, Ontario, Madison Twp., Richland Co., Ohio, Find A Grave.com.

119 Find A Grave—Fort Sam Houston Cemetery, San Antonio, Bexar Co., Texas, Find A Grave.com, John E. Pegan Sr., Find A Grave Memorial #3040824.

120 Find A Grave—Windsor Park Cemetery, Mansfield, Madison Twp., Richland Co., Ohio, Find A Grave.com.

121 Find A Grave—Salem Union Cemetery, Jacobus, York Co., Pennsylvania, Find A Grave.com.

122 Find A Grave—Bethany United Methodist Church Cemetery, Felton, Chanceford Twp., York Co., Pennsylvania, Find A Grave.com.

123 Find A Grave—Zion United Methodist Church Cemetery, Red Lion, York Twp., York Co., Pennsylvania, Find A Grave.com.

124 Find A Grave—Saint Luke's Evangelical Lutheran Cemetery, New Bridgeville, Chanceford Twp., York Co., Pennsylvania, Find A Grave.com.

125 Find A Grave—Mount Zion Baptist Church Cemetery, Brogue, Chanceford Twp., York Co., Pennsylvania, Find A Grave.com.

126 Find A Grave—Angel Hill Cemetery, Harve de Grace, Harford Co., Maryland, Find A Grave.com.

127 Find A Grave—Rest Haven Cemetery, Hanover Twp., York Co., Pennsylvania, Find A Grave.com.

128 Arizona Deaths, 1870-1951, FamilySearch.org, Fannie Irene Grove—Death cert: State Index# 210, County Registrar #1160, Local Registrar #11749.

129 Find A Grave—Saint Jacobs Stone Church Cemetery, Glenville, Codorus Twp., York Co., Pennsylvania, Find A Grave.com.

130 Find A Grave—Charles Evans Cemetery, Reading, Berks Co., Pennsylvania, Find A Grave.com.

131 Find A Grave—Bethel Cemetery, Battleview, Burke Co., North Dakota, Find A Grave.com.

132 Find A Grave—Bergstrasse Cemetery, Ephrata, Ephrata Twp., Lancaster Co., Pennsylvania, Find A Grave.com.

133 Find A Grave—Manor Church Cemetery, Lancaster, Lancaster Co., Pennsylvania, Find A Grave.com.

134 Find A Grave—Grace Memorial Gardens Cemetery, Hudson, Pasco Co., Florida, Find A Grave.com.

135 Find A Grave—Valley View Cemetery, Garden City, Finney Co., Kansas, Find A Grave.com.

136 Find A Grave—Oconee Memorial Park Cemetery and Mausoleum, Seneca, Oconee Co., South Carolina, Find A Grave.com.

137 Find A Grave—Grandview Memorial Park Cemetery, Rock Hill, York Co., South Carolina, Find A Grave.com.

138 Find A Grave—Riverview Cemetery, Lancaster, Lancaster Co., Pennsylvania, Find A Grave.com.

139 Find A Grave—Laurel Hill Memorial Gardens Cemetery, Columbia, West Hempfield Twp., Lancaster Co., Pennsylvania, Find A Grave.com.

140 Find A Grave—Holy Cross Cemetery, North Arlington, Bergen Co., New Jersey, Find A Grave.com.

141 Virginia, Marriage Records, 1936-2014, Ancestry.com.

142 Find A Grave—First Reformed Church Memorial Garden Cemetery, Lancaster, Lancaster Co., Pennsylvania, Find A Grave.com.

143 Pennsylvania, Death Certificates, 1906-1966, Ancestry.com, Baby Girl Underkoffler, death cert. #24510.

144 Find A Grave—Floyd Cemetery, Floyd, Floyd Co., Virginia, Find A Grave.com.

145 Find A Grave—Roselawn Memorial Gardens Cemetery, Christiansburg, Montgomery Co., Virginia, Find A Grave.com.

146 Find A Grave—Old Leacock Presbyterian Cemetery, Intercourse, Leacock Twp., Lancaster Co., Pennsylvania, Find A Grave.com.

147 Find A Grave—Mt. Nebo Church Cemetery, Peach Bottom Twp., York Co., Pennsylvania, Find A Grave.com.

148 Find A Grave—Saint Mary's Orthodox Cemetery, Royalton, Osage Twp., Franklin Co., Illinois, Find A Grave.com.

149 Find A Grave—Delaware Veterans Memorial Cemtery, Bear, New Castle Co., Delaware, Find A Grave.com.

150 Find A Grave—Quarryville Cemetery, Quarryville, Lancaster Co.., Pennsylvania, Find A Grave.com.

151 Find A Grave—Mount Zion United Methodist Church Cemetery, Peach Bottom, Fulton Twp., Lancaster Co., Pennsylvania, Find A Grave.com.

152 Find A Grave—Paddletown Cemetery, Newberrytown, Newberry Twp., York Co., Pennsylvania, Find A Grave.com.

153 Find A Grave—Florida National Cemetery, Bushnell, Sumter Co., Florida, Find A Grave.com, Betty L. Bogan, Find A Grave Memorial #49685814.

154 Find A Grave—Grove Street Cemetery, New London, New London Twp., Huron Co., Ohio, Find A Grave.com.

155 Find A Grave—Plains United Presbyterian Church Cemetery, Cranberry Twp., Butler Co., Pennsylvania, Find A Grave.com.

156 U.S., Social Security Applications and Claims Index, Ancestry.com, Ross S. Leonard.

157 Social Security Death Index, Ancestry.com.

158 Pennsylvania, Death Certificates, 1906-1954, Ancestry.com, Baby Messenger, death cert. #1947-65667.

159 Find A Grave—Eternal Hills Memorial Park Cemetery, Oceanside, San Diego Co., California, Find A Grave.com.

160 Find A Grave—Centre Presbyterian Cemetery, Fawn Twp., York Co., Pennsylvania, Find A Grave.com.

161 Find A Grave—Sunset View Cemetery, Norridgewock, Somerset Co., Maine, Find A Grave.com.

162 Find A Grave—Westview Cemetery, Blacksburg, Montgomery Co., Virginia, Find A Grave.com.

163 Find A Grave—Wingo Family Cemetery, Blacksburg, Montgomery Co., Virginia, Find A Grave.

164 Find A Grave—Leeds Cemetery, Benson Co., North Dakota, Find A Grave.

# Descendants of John Pagan, Son of Andrew I

1. **John[3] Pagan** (*Andrew[2]*, *James[1]*) was born about 1754 in Martic Twp., Lancaster Co., Pennsylvania. He was the son of Andrew Pagan and Ann McDowell?. He died in Gallipolis, Gallipolis Twp., Gallia Co., Ohio, between 1819 and 1820.

John married **Ann Cherry or Chory** on April 4, 1782, in Lancaster Co., Pennsylvania.[1] They had two daughters. Ann Cherry or Chory was born in Lancaster Co., Pennsylvania, about 1762. Ann Cherry or died in Martic Twp., Lancaster Co., Pennsylvania?, before 1797.

Although the marriage record at First Reformed Church, Lancaster, Pennsylvania, reads John Pegan and Ann "Chory". However, there are no "Chorys" in Lancaster Co. But there is a George Cherry who is a neighbor of Andrew Pegan/Pagan, John Pegan's father, in Martic Township in Lancaster Co., Pennsylvania.[2]

John Pagan is enumerated in Martic Twp., Lancaster Co., Pennsylvania in 1790 *(Census Place: Martick, Lancaster, Pennsylvania; Series: M637; Roll: 8; Page: 58; Image: 748).* There is a one in col. 1 and a 3 in col. 3 (one male more than age 16 and three females).

John Pagan/Pegan is found on the 1793 Martic Twp., tax list, but he moves to Philadelphia, Philadelphia Co., Pennsylvania between 1793-97.[2]

His first wife, Ann Cherry/Chory, dies before 1797.

John Pagan married **Mary Margaret Russell** on February 25, 1797, in Philadelphia, Philadelphia Co., Pennsylvania.[3] They had three children. Mary Margaret Russell was born in Philadelphia, Philadelphia Co., Pennsylvania?, in 1775. Mary Margaret died in Gallia Co., Ohio, after 1819.

He was said to be an innkeeper.

John Pagan/Pegan seems to be the man with the surname Pegan, with no given name, who is mentioned in Watson's *Annals of Philadelphia and Pennsylvania, Vol. 1*, written 1830-1850, in Chapter 25, "Superstitions and Popular Credulity":

It seems that "fifty or sixty years ago" (around 1782-1792) a Mrs. Green owned a tavern and inn in Philadelphia known as The Sign of the Cock. She sold it to a man named Pegan, who found $5000 in a pot in the cellar. Mrs. Green, apparently hearing of the discovery, claimed she was the rightful owner, as her husband had put the money there. Her contention was doubtful, as her husband was never affluent, but, to settle matters, Mr. Pegan and Mrs. Green agreed to split the money in half. Mr. Watson contends that the $5000 was pirate treasure, as pirates were known to have been in that area of Philadelphia before the city was founded, and other pirate booty had been uncovered through the years.[4]

According to some of his descendants, John Pegan migrated from Philadelphia to western Pennsylvania and/or the "panhandle" of Virginia (now Ohio and Brooke counties, West Virginia). He removed to Green Twp. Gallia Co., Ohio by 1811, and died there most likely between 1819-1820.

John Pagan is not found in the 1800 or 1810 U.S. Federal Censuses.

Daughters of John Pagan and Ann Cherry or Chory:

+ 2   f   I.   **Daughter One[4] Pagan** was born in Martic Twp., Lancaster Co., Pennsylvania, before 1790.

+ 3   f   II.   **Daughter Two[4] Pagan** was born in Martic Twp., Lancaster Co., Pennsylvania, before 1790.

Children of John Pagan and Mary Margaret Russell:

+ 4   f   I.   **Mary Margaret[4] Pagan** was born in Philadelphia, Philadelphia Co., Pennsylvania?, on May 26, 1801.

She died in Raccoon Twp., Gallia Co., Ohio, on January 4, 1891. Mary Margaret was buried in Fairfield Church Cemetery, Centenary, Green Twp., Gallia Co., Ohio.[5]

+ 5 m II. **John**[4] **Pagan II** was born in Philadelphia, Philadelphia Co., Pennsylvania?, about 1803. He died in Green Twp., Gallia Co., Ohio, between 1836 and 1840.

+ 6 f III. **Catherine**[4] **Pagan** was born in Green Twp., Gallia Co., Ohio in 1811. She died in Gallipolis, Gallipolis Twp., Gallia Co., Ohio, about 1844.

# 4th Generation

**2.** **Daughter One**[4] **Pagan** (*John*[3], *Andrew*[2], *James*[1]) was born before 1790 in Martic Twp., Lancaster Co., Pennsylvania. She was the daughter of John Pagan (1) and Ann Cherry or Chory.

**3.** **Daughter Two**[4] **Pagan** (*John*[3], *Andrew*[2], *James*[1]) was born before 1790 in Martic Twp., Lancaster Co., Pennsylvania. She was the daughter of John Pagan (1) and Ann Cherry or Chory.

**4.** **Mary Margaret**[4] **Pagan** (*John*[3], *Andrew*[2], *James*[1]) was born on May 26, 1801, in Philadelphia, Philadelphia Co., Pennsylvania? She was the daughter of John Pagan (1) and Mary Margaret Russell. Mary Margaret died in Raccoon Twp., Gallia Co., Ohio, on January 4, 1891, at age 89. She was buried in Fairfield Church Cemetery, Centenary, Green Twp., Gallia Co., Ohio.[5]

Mary Margaret married **William Palmer** on September 19, 1819, in Gallia Co., Ohio. They had two children. William Palmer was born in England between 1775 and 1780. William died in Raccoon Twp., Gallia Co., Ohio, in 1825.

According to family records, William Palmer died in a shipwreck, most likely on the Ohio River.

William J. and Mary Margaret Pegan Palmer are enumerated in Green Twp., Gallia Co., Ohio in 1820 (*Census Place: Green, Gallia, Ohio; Page: 44; NARA Roll: M33_88; Image: 73*). There is a one in col. 6; a one in col. 7, and a one in col. 9 (one male more than age 45, one female under age 10 and one female 16-25).

Mary Margaret Pagan Palmer married **John Cheney** about 1826. There is no marriage record for them in Gallia County or anywhere else in Ohio. They had five children. John Cheney was born in Monongalia Co, (West) Virginia, on December 16, 1801. John reached age 83 and died in Green Twp., Gallia Co., Ohio, on July 7, 1885. He was buried in Fairfield Church Cemetery, Centenary, Green Twp., Gallia Co., Ohio.[5]

Children of Mary Margaret Pagan and William Palmer:

+ 7   m   I.   **Charles Nelson**[5] **Palmer** was born in Raccoon Twp., Gallia Co., Ohio, on July 29, 1821. He died in Green Twp., Gallia Co., Ohio, on April 27, 1896. Charles Nelson was buried in Fairfield Church Cemetery, Centenary, Green Twp., Gallia Co., Ohio.[5]

+ 8   f   II.   **Mary Ann**[5] **Palmer** was born in Green Twp., Gallia Co., Ohio, on February 9, 1824. She died in Green Twp., Gallia Co., Ohio, on March 3, 1891. Mary Ann was buried in Old Pine Cemetery, Rio Grande, Raccoon Twp., Gallia Co., Ohio.[6]

Children of Mary Margaret Pagan and John Cheney:

+ 9   f   I.   **Frances Madeline**[5] **Cheney** was born in Green Twp., Gallia Co., Ohio, on January 7, 1828. She died in Perry Twp., Gallia Co., Ohio, on August 24, 1909. Frances Madeline was buried in Old Pine Cemetery, Rio Grande, Raccoon Twp., Gallia Co., Ohio.[6]

+ 10   m   II.   **Ezekiel**[5] **Cheney** was born in Green Twp., Gallia Co., Ohio, on May 27, 1835. He died in Independence, Inyo Co., California, on July 26, 1870. Ezekiel was buried in San Francisco National Cemetery, San Francisco, San Francisco Co., California.[7]

+ 11   m   III.   **John Watts**[5] **Cheney** was born in Green Twp., Gallia Co., Ohio, on August 1, 1838. He died in Plain Twp., Franklin Co., Ohio, on January 12, 1914. John Watts was buried in New Albany Cemetery/

Landon Cemetery (Old Burial Ground), New Albany, Plain Twp., Franklin Co., Ohio.[8, 9]

+ 12  f  IV.  **Emily⁵ Cheney** was born in Green Twp., Gallia Co., Ohio, on December 7, 1841. She died in Wellston Twp., Jackson Co., Ohio, on April 5, 1907. Emily was buried in Old Pine Cemetery, Rio Grande, Raccoon Twp., Gallia Co., Ohio.[6]

+ 13  m  V.  **Silas B.⁵ Cheney** was born in Green Twp., Gallia Co., Ohio, on December 10, 1845. He died in Gallipolis, Gallipolis Twp., Gallia Co., Ohio, on March 5, 1928. Silas B. was buried in Mound Hill Cemetery, Gallipolis, Gallipolis Twp., Gallia Co., Ohio.[10]

5.  **John⁴ Pagan II** (*John³, Andrew², James¹*) was born about 1803 in Philadelphia, Philadelphia Co., Pennsylvania? He was the son of John Pagan (1) and Mary Margaret Russell. John died in Green Twp., Gallia Co., Ohio, between 1836 and 1840.

John married **Hannah Pettijohn** on May 4, 1826, in Gallia Co., Ohio. They had five children. Hannah Pettijohn was born in Ohio in 1809.[11] Hannah died in Green Twp., Gallia Co., Ohio, between 1860 and 1870. Hannah Pettijohn Pagan is enumerated in 1840 in Green Twp., Gallia Co., Ohio *(Census Place: Gallia, Ohio; Roll: 395; Page: 60)*. There is a two in col. 15, a one in col. 16, and a one in col. 19 (two females age five-10, one female 10-15, and one female 30-40.

In 1830, John Pagan is enumerated in Green Twp., Gallia Co., Ohio *(Census Place: Green, Gallia, Ohio; Page: 119; NARA Series: M19; Roll Number: 131)*. There is a one in col. 4; a one in col. 14 and a one in col. 18 (one male age 20-30; one female less than five years old and one female age 20-30).

In 1850, Hannah Pettijohn Pagan, age 41, is living with her son-in-law and daughter, Henry and Mary Ann Pegan Kring, in Gallipolis, Gallipolis Twp., Gallia Co., Ohio *(Census Place: Gallipolis, Gallia, Ohio; Roll: M432_681; Page: 5B; Image: 424)*. Henry

T. Kring, age 23, a blacksmith, was born in New York and Mary Ann Pegan Kring is age 21. Also in the home is Hannah's daughter Madeline Pegan, age 16, and a Francis Loucks, 13. All but Henry Kring were born in Ohio.

Hannah Pettijohn Pagan, age 51, is residing in Green Twp., Gallia Co., Ohio in 1860 *(Census Place: Green, Gallia, Ohio; Roll: M653_966; Page: 320; Image: 324)*. She is listed as "Anna Pegins." Living with her is her daughter Madeline, 25; both were born in Ohio. Hannah says she is a farmer.

Children of John Pagan II and Hannah Pettijohn:

+ 14  f  I.  **Mary Ann⁵ Pagan** was born in Green Twp., Gallia Co., Ohio, in November 1828. She died in Sedalia, Sedalia Twp., Pettis Co., Missouri?, between 1900 and 1910.

+ 15  f  II.  **Madeline E.⁵ Pagan** was born in Gallipolis, Gallipolis Twp., Gallia Co., Ohio, in 1834. She was also known as **Maddie.** Madeline E. died in Raccoon Twp., Gallia Co., Ohio, on April 25, 1878. She was buried in Calvary Baptist Cemetery, Rio Grande, Raccoon Twp., Gallia Co., Ohio.[12]

+ 16  m  III.  **James⁵ Pagan** was born in Gallia Co., Ohio, in October 1836. He died in Gallia Co., Ohio, before 1840.

+ 17  m  IV.  **Henry⁵ Pagan** was born in Green Twp., Gallia Co., Ohio, between 1826 and 1840. He died in Green Twp., Gallia Co., Ohio, before 1840.

+ 18  f  V.  **Daughter⁵ Pagan** was born in Green Twp., Gallia Co., Ohio, between 1830 and 1840. She died in Green Twp., Gallia Co., Ohio, before 1850.

6.  **Catherine⁴ Pagan** (*John³, Andrew², James¹*) was born in 1811 in Green Twp., Gallia Co., Ohio or Virginia.

She was the daughter of John Pagan (1) and Mary Margaret Russell. Catherine died in Gallipolis, Gallipolis Twp., Gallia Co., Ohio, about 1844 at age 33. She is probably buried in Pine Street Cemetery, Gallipolis, Gallipolis Twp., Gallia Co., Ohio.

Catherine married **James Johnson** on September 1, 1831, in Gallia Co., Ohio. They had two children. James Johnson was born in North Carolina or West Virginia in 1812. James reached age 22 and died in Gallipolis, Gallipolis Twp., Gallia Co., Ohio, on November 30, 1834. He is probably buried in Pine Street Cemetery, Gallipolis, Gallipolis Twp., Gallia Co., Ohio.

Catherine Pagan married **Alexander (Boisvert) Greenwood** on September 14, 1840, in Gallia Co., Ohio. They had two children. Alexander (Boisvert) Greenwood was born in Canada on October 15, 1802. Alexander (Boisvert) reached age 60 and died in Gallipolis, Gallipolis Twp., Gallia Co., Ohio, on May 9, 1863. He was buried in Pine Street Cemetery, Gallipolis, Gallipolis Twp., Gallia Co., Ohio.[13]

Alexander Greenwood Sr. was born Alexander Boisvert in France. He is thought to have married Josephte Parent in Canada in about 1828 and they had two children, Alexander, later called Alex B., and Matilda Boisvert, whose married surname was Lereux. Around 1833, Alexander Boisvert abandoned his family in Canada and went to Gallipolis, Gallipolis Twp., Gallia Co., Ohio, where there was a large settlement of French natives. When he arrived, he anglicized his surname to its English meaning, Greenwood.

Alexander married Catherine Pagan Johnson, widow of James Johnson about 1840. Catherine Pagan Johnson Greenwood brought to her new home her two children by James Johnson, John J. Johnson and Emma "Emily" Johnson, later the wife of William Randolph Murrell. Alexander (Boisvert) and Catherine Pagan Johnson Greenwood Sr. had two children, Alexander Jr. and Frances "Fannie" Greenwood, who later married James V. Hover, before Catherine died in1844.

In 1845, Alexander (Boisvert) Greenwood Sr. married for a third time to Mary "Polly" Rhine, who became a loving stepmother to his children by Catherine, and also cared for the Johnson children, but had no children of her own.

In 1849, Josephte Parent Boisvert and her two children arrived in Gallia Co. and threatened to bring Alexander (Boisvert) Greenwood Sr. to court for bigamy and declare his children by Catherine Pegan illegitimate. An out-of-court settlement was reached, whereby Alexander (Boisvert) Greenwood Sr., through a trustee, relinquished to his first and technically still legal wife Josephte real estate and and to his children by this marriage personal property in Canada. In turn, Josephte and the children, one of whom, Matlida, was grown and married by that time, relinquished all future claims to his real estate and personal property in America. Josephte and Matilda returned to Canada, but Alex Boisvert, then 18, chose to stay in Gallipolis with his father. He also changed his surname to Greenwood, eventually marrying and settling in Kentucky.

Although this situation with his Canadian children was settled, all was not with his American children. Alexander (Boisvert) Greenwood wrote his will before his death in 1863. more than 30 years later, the wording of his will was contested in court by his grandchildren by Fannie Greenwood Hover, Frank Burdette Greenwood and Hattie Greenwood Wolfe (Mrs. Darius Wolfe). Alexander Sr., in providing for the welfare of his son Alexander Jr. (by Catherine Pagan Johnson Greenwood), who lost a leg at age seven, appointed his then wife Mary "Polly" Rhine Greenwood as guardian of Alexander Jr. and of the property.

But when Alexander Sr. died, Alexander Jr. was of age, yet Mary "Polly" Rhine sold some lots and mortgaged others, even though she had no right to do so. Also, the wording of the will technically disinherited his daughter Fannie and any of her heirs. Alexander Jr. later married Johanna Burdette and had Hattie and Frank. Fannie Greenwood had married James V. Hover by the time her father died, but wording in the will implies that the marriage was rocky and/or Alexander did not trust her husband. After Alexander Sr. died, Fannie had at least one child, Harry A. Hover, and possibly a daughter Mary, who seems to have died before Frank Greenwood and Hattie Greenwood Wolfe's lawsuit in 1895. By 1895, Harry A. Hover had claimed one of his grandfather Alexander (Boivert) Greenwood's many property lots in Gallipolis, but the wording of his grandfather's will seem to exclude any children Fannie had. The lawsuit was settled in Harry A. Hover's favor.[14]

Children of Catherine Pagan and James Johnson:

+ 19 m I. **John J.⁵ Johnson** was born in Gallia Co., Ohio, in July 1832. He died in Upton Twp., Texas Co., Missouri?, after 1900.

+ 20 f II. **Emma⁵ Johnson** was born in Gallipolis, Gallipolis Twp., Gallia Co., Ohio, in January 1835. She was also known as **Emily.** Emma died in Edgefield, Davidson Co., Tennessee, on September 30, 1873.

Children of Catherine Pagan and Alexander (Boisvert) Greenwood:

+ 21 m I. **Alexander⁵ Greenwood II** was born in Gallipolis, Gallipolis Twp., Gallia Co., Ohio, on July 4, 1841. He died in Knoxville, Knox Co., Tennessee, on June 10, 1895. Alexander was buried in Pine Street Cemetery, Gallipolis, Gallipolis Twp., Gallia Co., Ohio.[13]

+ 22 f II. **Fannie⁵ Greenwood** was born in Gallipolis, Gallipolis Twp., Gallia Co., Ohio, on August 14, 1843. She died in Gallipolis, Gallipolis Twp., Gallia Co., Ohio, on September 11, 1866. Fannie was buried in Pine Street Cemetery, Gallipolis, Gallipolis Twp., Gallia Co., Ohio.[13]

# 5th Generation

7. **Charles Nelson⁵ Palmer** (*Mary Margaret⁴ Pagan, John³, Andrew², James¹*) was born on July 29, 1821, in Raccoon Twp., Gallia Co., Ohio. He was the son of William Palmer and Mary Margaret Pagan (4). Charles Nelson died in Green Twp., Gallia Co., Ohio, on April 27, 1896, at age 74. He was buried in Fairfield Church Cemetery, Centenary, Green Twp., Gallia Co., Ohio.[5]

Charles Nelson married **Mary Ann Donnally** on October 2, 1844, in Gallia Co., Ohio.[15] They had seven children. Mary Ann Donnally was born in Green Twp., Gallia Co., Ohio, on December 22, 1823. Mary Ann reached age 66 and died in Green Twp., Gallia Co., Ohio, on February 14, 1890. She was buried in Fairfield Church Cemetery, Centenary, Green Twp., Gallia Co., Ohio.[5]

Children of Charles Nelson Palmer and Mary Ann Donnally:

+ 23 f I. **Mary Frances⁶ Palmer** was born in Green Twp., Gallia Co., Ohio, on October 19, 1845. She died in Charleston, Kanawha Co., West Virginia, on May 21, 1923. Mary Frances was buried in Fairfield Church Cemetery, Centenary, Green Twp., Gallia Co., Ohio.[5]

+ 24 m II. **Thomas M.⁶ Palmer** was born in Green Twp., Gallia Co., Ohio, on May 17, 1847. He died in Minneapolis, Hennepin Co., Minnesota, on April 6, 1921. Thomas M. was buried in Oak Hill Cemetery, Minneapolis, Hennepin Co., Minnesota.[16]

+ 25 m III. **Charles Augustus⁶ Palmer II** was born in Green Twp., Gallia Co., Ohio, on May 25, 1849. He died in Arkansas City, Cowley Co., Kansas, on March 8, 1925. Charles Augustus was buried in Riverside Cemetery, Arkansas City, Cowley Co., Kansas.[17]

+ 26 m IV. **Lewis William⁶ Palmer** was born in Green Twp., Gallia Co., Ohio, on March 6, 1851. He died in Columbus, Franklin Co., Ohio, on June 25, 1890. Lewis William was buried in Woodland Cemetery, Ironton, Upper Twp., Lawrence Co., Ohio.[18]

+ 27 f V. **Elizabeth Marie⁶ Palmer** was born in Green Twp., Gallia Co., Ohio, on April 9, 1853. She died in Oklahoma City, Oklahoma, on February 3, 1910. Elizabeth Marie was buried in Fairlawn Cemetery, Oklahoma City, Oklahoma Co., Oklahoma.[19]

+ 28 f VI. **Anna Emma⁶ Palmer** was born in Green Twp., Gallia Co., Ohio, on May 12, 1855. She was also known as **Annie** . Anna Emma died in Green Twp., Gallia Co., Ohio, on June 20, 1896. She was buried in Fairfield Church Cemetery, Centenary, Green Twp., Gallia Co., Ohio.[5]

+ 29 m VII. **James Buchanan⁶ Palmer** was born in Green Twp., Gallia Co., Ohio, on November 20, 1857. He died in Oceana, Pentwater Co., Michigan, on February 9, 1931. James Buchanan was buried in Riverview Cemetery, Arkansas City, Cowley Co., Kansas.[20]

8. **Mary Ann⁵ Palmer** (*Mary Margaret⁴ Pagan, John³, Andrew², James¹*) was born on February 9, 1824, in Green Twp., Gallia Co., Ohio. She was the daughter of William Palmer and Mary Margaret Pagan (4). Mary Ann died in Green Twp., Gallia Co., Ohio, on March 3, 1891, at age 67. She was buried in Old Pine Cemetery, Rio Grande, Raccoon Twp., Gallia Co., Ohio.[6]

Mary Ann married **Levi Hamilton Smith** on February 24, 1847, in Gallia Co., Ohio. They had eight children. Levi Hamilton Smith was born in Perry Twp., Gallia Co., Ohio, on September 21, 1822.[2] Levi Hamilton reached age 83 and died in Perry Twp., Gallia Co., Ohio, on October 27, 1905.[2] He was buried in Old Pine Cemetery, Rio Grande, Raccoon Twp., Gallia Co., Ohio.[6]

Children of Mary Ann Palmer and Levi Hamilton Smith:

+ 30 f I. **Emily Jane⁶ Smith** was born in Perry Twp., Gallia Co., Ohio, on November 18, 1847. She died in Perry Twp., Gallia Co., Ohio, on December 23, 1897. Emily Jane was buried in Old Pine Cemetery, Rio Grande, Raccoon Twp., Gallia Co., Ohio.[6]

+ 31 m II. **John Henry⁶ Smith** was born in Perry Twp., Gallia Co., Ohio, on September 6, 1849. He died in Springfield Twp., Gallia Co., Ohio, on October 6, 1908. John Henry was buried in Old Pine Cemetery, Rio Grande, Raccoon Twp., Gallia Co., Ohio.[6]

+ 32 f III. **Mary Frances⁶ Smith** was born in Perry Twp., Gallia Co., Ohio, on October 9, 1851. She died in San Diego, San Diego Co., California, on July 18, 1917.

+ 33 m IV. **Charles Augustus⁶ Smith** was born in Perry Twp., Gallia Co., Ohio, on December 25, 1853. He died in Rio Grande, Raccoon Twp., Gallia Co., Ohio, on June 19, 1893. Charles Augustus was buried in Calvary Baptist Cemetery, Rio Grande, Raccoon Twp., Gallia Co., Ohio.[12]

+ 34 f V. **Lydia Luella⁶ Smith** was born in Rio Grande, Raccoon Twp., Gallia Co., Ohio, on August 29, 1856. She died in Oakwood, Montgomery Co., Ohio, on January 2, 1933. Lydia Luella was buried in Old Pine Cemetery, Rio Grande, Raccoon Twp., Gallia Co., Ohio.[6]

+ 35 m VI. **Wesley Thomas⁶ Smith** was born in Perry Twp., Gallia Co., Ohio, on November 3, 1858. He died in Columbus, Franklin Co., Ohio, on March 24, 1927. Wesley Thomas was buried in Calvary Baptist Cemetery, Rio Grande, Raccoon Twp., Gallia Co., Ohio.[12]

+ 36 m VII. **Lawrence Benton⁶ Smith** was born in Perry Twp., Gallia Co., Ohio, on January 26, 1861. He died in Oakland, Alameda Co., California, on October 24, 1937. Lawrence Benton was buried in Evergreen Cemetery, Oakland, Alameda Co., California.[21]

+ 37 f VIII. **Annie Dell⁶ Smith** was born in Perry Twp., Gallia Co., Ohio, on May 15, 1863. She died in Perry Twp., Gallia Co., Ohio, on March 10, 1864. Annie Dell was buried in Old Pine Cemetery, Rio Grande, Raccoon Twp., Gallia Co., Ohio.[6]

9. **Frances Madeline⁵ Cheney** (*Mary Margaret⁴ Pagan, John³, Andrew², James¹*) was born on January 7, 1828, in Green Twp., Gallia Co., Ohio. She was the daughter of John Cheney and Mary Margaret Pagan (4). Frances Madeline died in Perry Twp., Gallia Co., Ohio, on August 24, 1909, at age 81. She was buried in Old Pine Cemetery, Rio Grande, Raccoon Twp., Gallia Co., Ohio.[6]

She married **Charles Augustus Smith.** They had seven children. Charles Augustus Smith was born in Perry Twp., Gallia Co., Ohio, on February 4, 1829. He was also known as **Augustus.** He reached age 70 and died in Perry Twp., Gallia Co., Ohio, on April 15, 1899. Charles Augustus was buried in Old Pine Cemetery, Rio Grande, Raccoon Twp., Gallia Co., Ohio.[6]

Children of Frances Madeline Cheney and Charles Augustus Smith:

+ 38  m  I.  **John E.⁶ Smith** was born in Perry Twp., Gallia Co., Ohio, in 1855. He died in Perry Twp., Gallia Co., Ohio, on June 6, 1860. John E. was buried in Old Pine Cemetery, Rio Grande, Raccoon Twp., Gallia Co., Ohio.[6]

+ 39  m  II.  **Son⁶ Smith** was born in Perry Twp., Gallia Co., Ohio, about February 8, 1858. He died in Perry Twp., Gallia Co., Ohio, on February 8, 1858. Son was buried in Old Pine Cemetery, Rio Grande, Raccoon Twp., Gallia Co., Ohio.[6]

+ 40  m  III.  **Ezekiel Barton⁶ Smith** was born in Perry Twp., Gallia Co., Ohio, on May 30, 1859. He died in Wichita, Sedgwick Co., Kansas, on November 3, 1937. Ezekiel Barton was buried in Highland Cemetery, Wichita, Sedgwick Co., Kansas.[22]

+ 41  m  IV.  **Charles Augustus⁶ Smith II** was born in Perry Twp., Gallia Co., Ohio, on June 28, 1861. He died in Perry Twp., Gallia Co., Ohio, on November 10, 1897. Charles Augustus was buried in Old Pine Cemetery, Rio Grande, Raccoon Twp., Gallia Co., Ohio.[6]

+ 42  f  V.  **Mary⁻ Elma⁶ Smith** was born in Perry Twp., Gallia Co., Ohio, on February 22, 1864. She died in Perry Twp., Gallia Co., Ohio, on February 9, 1945. Mary Elma was buried in Old Pine Cemetery, Rio Grande, Raccoon Twp., Gallia Co., Ohio.[6]

+ 43  f  VI.  **Anna May⁶ Smith** was born in Perry Twp., Gallia Co., Ohio, on June 4, 1868. She died in Gallipolis, Gallipolis Twp., Gallia Co., Ohio, on March 5, 1954. Anna May was buried in Mound Hill Cemetery, Gallipolis, Gallipolis Twp., Gallia Co., Ohio.[10]

+ 44  m  VII.  **Frank⁶ Smith** was born in Cora, Perry Twp., Gallia Co., Ohio, on July 26, 1871. He died in Cora, Perry Twp., Gallia Co., Ohio, on December 13, 1902. Frank was buried in Old Pine Cemetery, Rio Grande, Raccoon Twp., Gallia Co., Ohio.[6]

**10. Ezekiel⁵ Cheney** (*Mary Margaret⁴ Pagan, John³, Andrew², James¹*) was born on May 27, 1835, in Green Twp., Gallia Co., Ohio. He was the son of John Cheney and Mary Margaret Pagan (4). Ezekiel died in Independence, Inyo Co., California, on July 26, 1870, at age 35. He was buried in San Francisco National Cemetery, San Francisco, San Francisco Co., California.[7]

It is not proven that this is the Ezekiel Cheney, son of John and Mary Pagan Cheney. But he seems to be. He went to California between 1850-1860 and served in two California regiments during the Civil War. He may have died of war injuries in a hospital in Independence, Inyo Co., California, and is buried in the San Francisco National Cemetery.

He seems to have never married.

**11. John Watts⁵ Cheney** (*Mary Margaret⁴ Pagan, John³, Andrew², James¹*) was born on August 1, 1838, in Green Twp., Gallia Co., Ohio. He was the son of John Cheney and Mary Margaret Pagan (4). John Watts died in Plain Twp., Franklin Co., Ohio, on January 12, 1914, at age 75. He was buried in New Albany Cemetery/Landon Cemetery (Old Burial Ground), New Albany, Plain Twp., Franklin Co., Ohio.[8, 9]

John Watts Cheney married **Helen Maria Soles** on December 24, 1878, in Gallia Co., Ohio. They had three children. Helen Maria Soles was born in Green Twp., Gallia Co., Ohio, on November 17, 1856. She was also known as **Ellen.** Helen Maria reached age 60 and died in Plain Twp., Franklin Co., Ohio, on January 27, 1917. She was buried in New Albany

Cemetery/Landon Cemetery (Old Burial Ground), New Albany, Plain Twp., Franklin Co., Ohio.[9, 23]

Children of John Watts Cheney and Helen Maria Soles:

+ 45 m I. **Charles Floyd[6] Cheney** was born in Springfield Twp., Gallia Co., Ohio, on September 4, 1879. He died in Gallipolis, Gallipolis Twp., Gallia Co., Ohio, on January 21, 1957. Charles Floyd was buried in New Albany Cemetery/Landon Cemetery (Old Burial Ground), New Albany, Plain Twp., Franklin Co., Ohio.[9]

+ 46 m II. **Clarence Dale[6] Cheney** was born in Springfield Twp., Gallia Co., Ohio, on August 28, 1881. He died in Detroit, Wayne Co., Michigan, on January 18, 1946.

+ 47 f III. **Mary A.[6] Cheney** was born in Springfield Twp., Gallia Co., Ohio, on August 26, 1883. She was also known as **Mamie.** Mary A. died in Columbus, Franklin Co., Ohio, on December 5, 1916. She was buried in New Albany Cemetery/Landon Cemetery (Old Burial Ground), New Albany, Plain Twp., Franklin Co., Ohio.[9]

**12. Emily[5] Cheney** (*Mary Margaret[4] Pagan, John[3], Andrew[2], James[1]*) was born on December 7, 1841, in Green Twp., Gallia Co., Ohio. She was the daughter of John Cheney and Mary Margaret Pagan (4). Emily died in Wellston Twp., Jackson Co., Ohio, on April 5, 1907, at age 65. She was buried in Old Pine Cemetery, Rio Grande, Raccoon Twp., Gallia Co., Ohio.[6]

Emily married **John J. Rickabaugh** on April 17, 1867, in Gallia Co., Ohio. They had three children. John J. Rickabaugh was born in Raccoon Twp., Gallia Co., Ohio, on September 20, 1829. John J. reached age 61 and died in Raccoon Twp., Gallia Co., Ohio, on August 10, 1891. He was buried in

Old Pine Cemetery, Rio Grande, Raccoon Twp., Gallia Co., Ohio.[6]

Children of Emily Cheney and John J. Rickabaugh:

+ 48 f I. **Lena[6] Rickabaugh** was born in Raccoon Twp., Gallia Co., Ohio, on January 17, 1868. She died in Lancaster, Fairfield Co., Ohio, on October 5, 1954. Lena was buried in Old Pine Cemetery, Rio Grande, Raccoon Twp., Gallia Co., Ohio.[6]

+ 49 f II. **Hattie[6] Rickabaugh** was born in Rio Grande, Raccoon Twp., Gallia Co., Ohio, on May 14, 1874. She died in Columbus, Franklin Co., Ohio, on December 22, 1953. Hattie was buried in Glen Rest Memorial Estate Cemetery, Reynoldsburg, Truro Twp., Franklin Co., Ohio.[24]

+ 50 m III. **Frank Benton[6] Rickabaugh** was born on August 1, 1880, in Raccoon Twp., Gallia Co., Ohio. He was the son of John J. Rickabaugh and Emily Cheney (12). Frank Benton lived in Chicago, Cook Co., Illinois in 1917. He resided in 1920 in Van Buren Twp., Montgomery Co., Ohio. He lived in 1976 in Dayton, Montgomery Co., Ohio. Frank Benton died in a facility in Columbus, Franklin Co., Ohio, on December 13, 1976, at age 96. He is buried in Dayton Memorial Park Cemetery, Dayton, Montgomery Co., Ohio.[25]

**13. Silas B.[5] Cheney** (*Mary Margaret[4] Pagan, John[3], Andrew[2], James[1]*) was born on December 10, 1845, in Green Twp., Gallia Co., Ohio. He was the son of John Cheney and Mary Margaret Pagan (4). Silas B. died in Gallipolis, Gallipolis Twp., Gallia Co., Ohio, on March 5, 1928, at age 82. He was buried in Mound Hill Cemetery, Gallipolis, Gallipolis Twp., Gallia Co., Ohio.[10]

Silas B. married **Elizabeth Beck** on December 16, 1874, in Gallia Co., Ohio. They had seven children. Elizabeth Beck was born in Gallipolis, Gallipolis Twp., Gallia Co., Ohio, in February 1856. She was also known as **Eliza.** Elizabeth reached age 67 and died in Gallipolis, Gallipolis Twp., Gallia Co., Ohio, on March 17, 1923. She was buried in Mound Hill Cemetery, Gallipolis, Gallipolis Twp., Gallia Co., Ohio.[10]

Children of Silas B. Cheney and Elizabeth Beck:

+ 51 m I. **John Leonard[6] Cheney** was born in Green Twp., Gallia Co., Ohio, on March 31, 1875. He died in Gallipolis, Gallipolis Twp., Gallia Co., Ohio, on July 7, 1951. John Leonard was buried in Mound Hill Cemetery, Gallipolis, Gallipolis Twp., Gallia Co., Ohio.[10]

+ 52 f II. **Pearl[6] Cheney** was born in Green Twp., Gallia Co., Ohio, on March 11, 1876. She died in Bay Village, Dover Twp., Cuyahoga Co., Ohio, on April 4, 1961. Pearl was buried in Cedar Hill Cemetery, Brownsville, Bowling Green Twp., Licking Co., Ohio.[26]

+ 53 m III. **Bert Ramsey[6] Cheney** was born in Green Twp., Gallia Co., Ohio, on October 2, 1879. He died in 1955. Bert Ramsey was buried in Germantown Cemetery, Germantown, German Twp., Montgomery Co., Ohio.[27]

+ 54 m IV. **Guy Bernard Johnson[6] Cheney** was born in Raccoon Twp., Gallia Co., Ohio, on November 12, 1881. He died between 1920 and 1927. Guy Bernard Johnson Cheney was buried in Mount Calvary Cemetery, Newark, Newark Twp., Licking Co., Ohio.[28]

+ 55 f V. **Carrie B.[6] Cheney** was born in Gallipolis, Gallipolis Twp., Gallia Co., Ohio, on December 21, 1884. She died in a facility in Somerset, Reading Twp., Perry Co., Ohio, on August 29, 1953. Carrie B. was buried in Cedar Hill Cemetery, Brownsville, Bowling Green Twp., Licking Co., Ohio.[26]

+ 56 f VI. **Margaret Genevieve[6] Cheney** was born in Gallipolis, Gallipolis Twp., Gallia Co., Ohio, in August 1887. She was also known as **Jennie** and **Jennie M..** Margaret Genevieve died in Lorain, Lorain Co., Ohio, on July 16, 1967. She was buried in St. Joseph Cemetery, Newark, Licking Co., Ohio.[29]

+ 57 m VII. **Carlton James[6] Cheney** was born in Gallipolis, Gallipolis Twp., Gallia Co., Ohio, on December 25, 1896. He was also known as **Carl.** Carleton James died in Gallipolis, Gallipolis Twp., Gallia Co., Ohio, on February 23, 1930. He was buried in Mound Hill Cemetery, Gallipolis, Gallipolis Twp., Gallia Co., Ohio.[10]

**14. Mary Ann[5] Pagan** (*John[4], John[3], Andrew[2], James[1]*) was born in November 1828 in Green Twp., Gallia Co., Ohio. She was the daughter of John Pagan II (5) and Hannah Pettijohn. Mary Ann died in Sedalia, Sedalia Twp., Pettis Co., Missouri?, between 1900 and 1910.

Mary Ann married **Henry T. King** on June 24, 1849, in Gallia Co., Ohio. They had five children. Henry T. King was born in New York in March 1826. Henry T. died in Sedalia, Sedalia Twp., Pettis Co., Missouri?, between 1906 and 1910.

In 1850, Henry and Mary Ann Pagan King are enumerated in Gallipolis, Gallipolis Twp., Gallia Co., Ohio *(Census Place: Gallipolis, Gallia, Ohio; Roll: M432_681; Page: 5B; Image: 424)*. Henry T. King, enumerated as Henry "Kring", age 23, a blacksmith, was born in New York and Mary Ann Pegan King is age 21. Also in the home is Mary Ann's mother,

Hannah Pettijohn Pegan (Pagan), age 41, Hannah's daughter Madeline Pegan, 16, and a Francis Loucks, 13. All but Henry King were born in Ohio

In 1860, Henry T. and Mary Ann Pagan King are found in Perry Twp., Gallia Co., Ohio. Henry King, age 32, born New York, is a watch repairer. Mary Ann Pagan King is 31 years old. Children in the home are Catherine, age nine, John, five and Effie, two.

Henry T. and Mary Ann Pagan King are residing in Beaver Twp., Pike Co., Ohio in 1880. In the home are Henry T. King, age 55, born New York, a farmer; Mary Ann Pagan King, 53, and daughter Cornelia, 16. Living with them are daughter Rosalie Catherine King Johnson, 29, and her children Eva, 10, Lulu, six and an unnamed son, one month.

By 1900, Henry T. and Mary Ann Pagan King have removed to Sedalia, Pettis Co., Missouri. Henry T. King, is age 74, born Mar 1826 in New York, and Mary Ann Pagan King is 71, born in Ohio in Nov 1828.

Henry T. King had one arm and still played the harp.

Children of Mary Ann Pagan and Henry T. King:

+ 58 f I. **Rosalie or Roselia Catherine[6] King** was born in Perry Twp., Gallia Co., Ohio, in 1850. She died after 1900.

+ 59 m II. **John A.[6] King** was born in Perry Twp., Gallia Co., Ohio, in January 1855. He died in Sedalia, Sedalia Twp., Pettis Co., Missouri, on February 16, 1923. John A. was buried in Crown Hill Cemetery, Sedalia, Pettis Co., Missouri.

+ 60 f III. **Effie Virginia[6] King** was born in Perry Twp., Gallia Co., Ohio, on October 6, 1857. She died in Los Angeles, Los Angeles Co., California, on December 5, 1941. Effie Virginia was buried in Forest Lawn Memorial Park Cemetery, Glendale, Los Angeles Co., California.[30]

+ 61 f IV. **Cornelia[6] King** was born in Perry Twp., Gallia Co., Ohio, in 1863. She died after 1900.

+ 62 V. **Child[6] King** was born in Ohio between 1849 and 1880. He or she died in Ohio between 1849 and 1880.

**15. Madeline E.[5] Pagan** (*John[4], John[3], Andrew[2], James[1]*) was born in 1834 in Gallipolis, Gallipolis Twp., Gallia Co., Ohio. She was also known as **Maddie.** She was the daughter of John Pagan II (5) and Hannah Pettijohn. Madeline E. died in Raccoon Twp., Gallia Co., Ohio, on April 25, 1878, at age 44.[8] She was buried in Calvary Baptist Cemetery, Rio Grande, Raccoon Twp., Gallia Co., Ohio.[12]

Buried under the name Maddie E. Troth.

Madeline E. married **Amos Troth** on February 13, 1862, in Gallia Co., Ohio. They had three children. Amos Troth was born in Raccoon Twp., Gallia Co., Ohio, in 1836. Amos reached age 80 and died in Centralia, Lewis Co., Washington, on July 1, 1916. He was buried in Pioneer Cemetery, Centralia, Lewis Co., Washington.[31]

By 1880, Amos Troth is married to his second wife, Emily Lewis.

Children of Madeline E. Pagan and Amos Troth:

+ 63 m I. **Marion[6] Troth** was born in Raccoon Twp., Gallia Co., Ohio, on October 9, 1864.[32] He died in Raccoon Twp., Gallia Co., Ohio, on November 21, 1882.[32] Marion was buried in Calvary Baptist Cemetery, Rio Grande, Raccoon Twp., Gallia Co., Ohio.[12]

+ 64 f II. **Daughter[6] Troth** was born in Raccoon Twp., Gallia Co., Ohio, on September 28, 1866. She died in Raccoon Twp., Gallia Co., Ohio, on October 1, 1866. Daughter was buried in Calvary Baptist Cemetery, Rio Grande, Raccoon Twp., Gallia Co., Ohio.[12]

+ 65    m    III.    **Harrison Wood[6] Troth** was born in Raccoon Twp., Gallia Co., Ohio, on July 2, 1873.[33] He was also known as **Harry.** Harrison Wood died in Akron, Summit Co., Ohio, on January 6, 1938.[34] He was buried in Mount Peace Cemetery, Akron, Summit Co., Ohio.[34, 35]

**16. James[5] Pegan** (*John[4] Pagan II, John[3], Andrew[2], James[1]*) was born in October 1836 in Gallia Co., Ohio. He was the son of John Pagan II (5) and Hannah Pettijohn. James died in Gallia Co., Ohio, before 1840.

**17. Henry[5] Pegan** (*John[4] Pagan II, John[3], Andrew[2], James[1]*) was born between 1826 and 1840 in Green Twp., Gallia Co., Ohio. He was the son of John Pagan II (5) and Hannah Pettijohn. Henry died in Green Twp., Gallia Co., Ohio, before 1840.

**18. Daughter[5] Pegan** (*John[4] Pagan II, John[3], Andrew[2], James[1]*) was born between 1830 and 1840 in Green Twp., Gallia Co., Ohio. She was the daughter of John Pagan II (5) and Hannah Pettijohn. Daughter died in Green Twp., Gallia Co., Ohio, before 1850.

**19. John J.[5] Johnson** (*Catherine[4] Pagan, John[3], Andrew[2], James[1]*) was born in July 1832 in Gallia Co., Ohio. He was the son of James Johnson and Catherine Pagan (6). John J. lived in Perry Twp., Gallia Co., Ohio in 1860. He resided in 1870 in Jackson Twp., Jackson Co., Ohio. John J. was living in Vinton Twp., Vinton Co., Ohio in 1880. He was located in 1900 in Upton Twp., Texas Co., Missouri. John J. died in Upton Twp., Texas Co., Missouri?, after 1900.

John Johnson and his sister Emma ("Emily"), with their surname listed as "Janson", are found in their stepfather Alexander Greenwood Sr.'s home in Gallipolis, Gallipolis Twp., Gallia Co., Ohio in 1850..

John J. married **Mary Jones** on June 19, 1855, in Gallia Co., Ohio. They had seven children. Mary

Jones was born in Wales in February 1837. Mary died in Upton Twp., Texas Co., Missouri?, after 1900.

Children of John J. Johnson and Mary Jones:

+ 66    m    I.    **William Roosevelt[6] Johnson** was born in Perry Twp., Gallia Co., Ohio, on March 25, 1856. He died in Monument, Grant Co., Oregon, on May 6, 1929. William Roosevelt was buried in Monument Cemetery, Monument, Grant Co., Oregon.[36]

+ 67    f    II.    **Mary[6] Johnson** was born in Perry Twp., Gallia Co., Ohio, in 1857. She died in Gallia Co. or Jackson Co., Ohio, between 1860 and 1870.

+ 68    m    III.    **John[6] Johnson II** was born in Perry Twp., Gallia Co., Ohio, in 1859. He died in Gallia Co. or Jackson Co., Ohio, between 1860 and 1870.

+ 69    f    IV.    **Margaret Catherine[6] Johnson** was born in Gallia Co. or Jackson Co., Ohio, in 1866. She died after 1880.

+ 70    m    V.    **James Edward[6] Johnson** was born in Jackson Twp., Jackson Co., Ohio, on September 13, 1870. He died in St Louis, St. Louis Co., Missouri, on February 17, 1936

+ 71    m    VI.    **David[6] Johnson** was born in Vinton Twp., Vinton Co., Ohio?, in 1872. He died after 1880.

+ 72    f    VII.    **Rebecca[6] Johnson** was born in Vinton Twp., Vinton Co., Ohio?, in 1875. She died after 1880.

**20. Emma[5] Johnson** (*Catherine[4] Pagan, John[3], Andrew[2], James[1]*) was born in January 1835 in Gallipolis, Gallipolis Twp., Gallia Co., Ohio. She was also known as **Emily.** She was the daughter of James Johnson and Catherine Pagan (6). Emma died in

Edgefield, Davidson Co., Tennessee, on September 30, 1873, at age 38.

Emma ("Emily") Johnson and her brother John, with their surname listed as "Janson", are found in their step-father's, Alexander Greenwood Sr.'s, home in Gallipolis, Gallipolis Twp., Gallia Co., Ohio in 1850.

Emma married **William Randolph Murrell** on July 4, 1855, in Gallia Co., Ohio. They had three children. William Randolph Murrell was born in Lynchburg, Campbell Co., Virginia, in September 1832. He reached age 71 and died in Dayton, Campbell Co., Kentucky, on November 27, 1903. William Randolph was buried in Evergreen Cemetery, Southgate, Campbell Co., Kentucky.[37]

William and Emma Johnson Randolph lived in Edgefield, Davidson Co., Tennessee in 1870 (enumerated as R.H. Mullen), and in Banister, Halifax Co., Virginia in 1880.

Children of Emma Johnson and William Randolph Murrell:

+ 73   f   I.   **Ella Matilda⁶ Murrell** was born in Lynchburg, Campbell Co., Virginia, on April 13, 1856. She died in Dayton, Campbell Co., Kentucky, on December 24, 1917. Ella Matilda was buried in Evergreen Cemetery, Southgate, Campbell Co., Kentucky.[37]

+ 74   f   II.   **Kate⁶ Murrell** was born in Gallipolis, Gallipolis Twp., Gallia Co., Ohio, in 1857. She died in Gallipolis, Gallipolis Twp., Gallia Co., Ohio, on May 4, 1858.

+ 75   m   III.   **Samuel⁶ Murrell** was born in Edgefield, Davidson Co., Tennessee?, in 1858. He died in Edgefield, Davidson Co., Tennessee?, before 1880.

**21. Alexander⁵ Greenwood II** (*Catherine⁴ Pagan, John³, Andrew², James¹*) was born on July 4, 1841, in Gallipolis, Gallipolis Twp., Gallia Co., Ohio. He was the son of Alexander (Boisvert) Greenwood and Catherine Pagan (6). Alexander died in Knoxville,

Knox Co., Tennessee, on June 10, 1895, at age 53. He was buried in Pine Street Cemetery, Gallipolis, Gallipolis Twp., Gallia Co., Ohio.[13]

Alexander Greenwood Jr. lost a leg in an accident when he was seven years old. According to his census information, Alexander was a painter in 1870 and a circus performer in 1880.

Alexander married **Joanna Burdette** on July 14, 1863, in Gallia Co., Ohio. They had two children. Joanna Burdette was born in Green Twp., Gallia Co., Ohio, on April 30, 1844. Joanna reached age 69 and died in Gallipolis, Gallipolis Twp., Gallia Co., Ohio, on July 19, 1913. She was buried in Pine Street Cemetery, Gallipolis, Gallipolis Twp., Gallia Co., Ohio.[9]

Children of Alexander Greenwood II and Joanna Burdette:

+ 76   f   I.   **Hattie⁶ Greenwood** was born in Gallipolis, Gallipolis Twp., Gallia Co., Ohio, on February 12, 1864. She died in Pittsburgh, Allegheny Co., Pennsylvania, on September 28, 1938. Hattie was buried in Pine Street Cemetery, Gallipolis, Gallipolis Twp., Gallia Co., Ohio.[12]

+ 77   m   II.   **Frank Burdette⁶ Greenwood** was born in Gallipolis, Gallipolis Twp., Gallia Co., Ohio, on January 21, 1866. He died in Edgewood, Perry Twp., Marion Co., Indiana, on May 28, 1944. Frank Burdette was buried in Round Hill Cemetery, Indianapolis, Perry Twp., Marion Co., Indiana.[38]

**22. Fannie⁵ Greenwood** (*Catherine⁴ Pagan, John³, Andrew², James¹*) was born on August 14, 1843, in Gallipolis, Gallipolis Twp., Gallia Co., Ohio. She was the daughter of Alexander (Boisvert) Greenwood and Catherine Pagan (6). Fannie died in Gallipolis, Gallipolis Twp., Gallia Co., Ohio, on September 11, 1866, at age 23. She was buried in Pine Street Cemetery, Gallipolis, Gallipolis Twp., Gallia Co., Ohio.[12]

Fannie married **James V. Hover** on February 7, 1863, in Gallia Co., Ohio. They had two children. James V. Hover was born in Mercer Co., Pennsylvania, in 1838. He lived in 1880 in Pana Twp., Christian Co., Illinois. James V. reached age 57 and died in Humboldt Twp., Richardson Co., Nebraska, on March 6, 1895. He was buried in Humboldt Cemetery, Humboldt, Humboldt Twp., Richardson Co., Nebraska.[39]

Children of Fannie Greenwood and James V. Hover:

+ 78 m I. **Harry A.**⁶ **Hover** or **Hoover** was born in Gallipolis, Gallipolis Twp., Gallia Co., Ohio, in 1863. He was also known as **Burt.** Harry A. Hover or died after 1920.

+ 79 f II. **Mary E.**⁶ **Hover** was born in Gallipolis, Gallipolis Twp., Gallia Co., Ohio, in 1866. She was also known as **May.** Mary E. died in Pana Twp., Christian Co., Illinois?, between 1880 and 1895.

# 6th Generation

**23. Mary Frances⁶ Palmer** (*Charles Nelson⁵, Mary Margaret⁴ Pagan, John³, Andrew², James¹*) was born on October 19, 1845, in Green Twp., Gallia Co., Ohio. She was the daughter of Charles Nelson Palmer (7) and Mary Ann Donnally. Mary Frances died in Charleston, Kanawha Co., West Virginia, on May 21, 1923, at age 77. She was buried in Fairfield Church Cemetery, Centenary, Green Twp., Gallia Co., Ohio.[5]

Mary Frances married **Veto Farrar** on September 12, 1882, in Gallia Co., Ohio. They had two children. Veto Farrar was born in Mason Co., (West) Virginia, on July 30, 1843. Veto lived in 1900 in Union Twp., Putnam Co., West Virginia. He resided in 1910 in London Twp., Kanawha Co., West Virginia. Veto reached age 82 and died in Charleston, Kanawha Co., West Virginia, on July 17, 1926. He was buried in Teays Hill Cemetery, Saint Albans, Kanawha Co., West Virginia.[40]

Children of Mary Frances Palmer and Veto Farrar:

+ 80　I.　**Child One⁷ Farrar** was born between 1882 and 1900. He or she died between 1882 and 1900.

+ 81　II.　**Child Two⁷ Farrar** was born between 1882 and 1900. He or she died between 1882 and 1900.

**24. Thomas M.⁶ Palmer** (*Charles Nelson⁵, Mary Margaret⁴ Pagan, John³, Andrew², James¹*) was born on May 17, 1847, in Green Twp., Gallia Co., Ohio. He was the son of Charles Nelson Palmer (7) and Mary Ann Donnally. Thomas M. lived in Green Twp., Gallia Co., Ohio in 1900. He also resided in 1910 in Springfield Twp., Gallia Co., Ohio. Thomas M. was living in 1920 in Minneapolis, Hennepin Co., Minnesota. He died in Minneapolis, Hennepin Co., Minnesota, on April 6, 1921, at age 73. Thomas M. was buried in Oak Hill Cemetery, Minneapolis, Hennepin Co., Minnesota.[16]

Thomas M. married **Alice McGath** on December 25, 1878, in Gallia Co., Ohio. They had six children. Alice McGath was born in Green Twp., Gallia Co., Ohio, in April 1855. Alice reached age 68 and died in Minneapolis, Hennepin Co., Minnesota, on August 18, 1923. She was buried in Oak Hill Cemetery, Minneapolis, Hennepin Co., Minnesota.[16]

Children of Thomas M. Palmer and Alice McGath:

+ 82　f　I.　**Bennora A.⁷ Palmer** was born in Crook, Boone Co., West Virginia, on February 27, 1880. She died in Riverside Co., California, on November 23, 1964.

+ 83　m　II.　**Charles Clyde⁷ Palmer** was born in Marmet, Kanawha Co., West Virginia, on June 15, 1884. He was also known as **Clyde.** Charles Clyde died in Ozark, Franklin Co., Arkansas, about May 10, 1962. He was buried in Oak Hill Cemetery, Minneapolis, Hennepin Co., Minnesota.[16]

+ 84　f　III.　**Maud Marie⁷ Palmer** was born in Green Twp., Gallia Co., Ohio, on September 13, 1887. She was also known as **Marie.** Maud Marie died in Fort Worth, Tarrant Co., Texas, on February 5, 1967. She was buried in Grapevine Cemetery, Grapevine, Tarrant Co., Texas.[41]

+ 85　m　IV.　**Roy Donnally⁷ Palmer** was born in Green Twp., Gallia Co., Ohio, on April 30, 1890. He died in Grandville, Wyoming Twp., Kent Co., Michigan, on April 24, 1957.

+ 86　m　V.　**George Merrill⁷ Palmer** was born in Green Twp., Gallia Co., Ohio, on June 24, 1892. He died in San Antonio, Bexar Co., Texas, on January 20, 1955. George Merrill was buried in Fort Sam Houston National Cemetery, San Antonio, Bexar Co., Texas.[42]

+ 87　VI.　**Child⁷ Palmer** was born in Crook, Boone Co., West Virginia or Green Twp., Gallia Co., Ohio, between

1880 and 1900. He or she died in Crook, Boone Co., West Virginia or Green Twp., Gallia Co., Ohio, between 1880 and 1900.

25. **Charles Augustus**[6] **Palmer II** (*Charles Nelson*[5], *Mary Margaret*[4] *Pagan*, *John*[3], *Andrew*[2], *James*[1]) was born on May 25, 1849, in Green Twp., Gallia Co., Ohio. He was the son of Charles Nelson Palmer (7) and Mary Ann Donnally. He died in Arkansas City, Cowley Co., Kansas, on March 8, 1925, at age 75. Charles Augustus was buried in Riverside Cemetery, Arkansas City, Cowley Co., Kansas.[17]

Childless.

Charles Augustus married **Mary E. Lively** in 1883. Mary E. Lively was born in Jackson Twp., Jackson Co., Ohio, on August 22, 1855. Mary E. reached age 77 and died in Arkansas City, Cowley Co., Kansas, in November 1932. She was buried in Riverside Cemetery, Arkansas City, Cowley Co., Kansas.[17]

26. **Lewis William**[6] **Palmer** (*Charles Nelson*[5], *Mary Margaret*[4] *Pagan*, *John*[3], *Andrew*[2], *James*[1]) was born on March 6, 1851, in Green Twp., Gallia Co., Ohio. He was the son of Charles Nelson Palmer (7) and Mary Ann Donnally. He died in Columbus, Franklin Co., Ohio, on June 25, 1890, at age 39. Lewis William was buried in Woodland Cemetery, Ironton, Upper Twp., Lawrence Co., Ohio.[18]

Lewis William Palmer was a physician. His tombstone reads, "Dr. Lewis Palmer".

Lewis William married **Amanda Jane Woods** on December 25, 1878, in Lawrence Co., Ohio. They had two children. Amanda Jane Woods was born in Lawrence Co., Kentucky, on April 18, 1858. Amanda Jane reached age 83 and died in Chicago, Cook Co., Illinois, on December 2, 1941. She was buried in Cedar Park Cemetery, Calumet Park, Cook Co., Illinois.[43]

She died under the name Amanda Jane Keye.

Children of Lewis William Palmer and Amanda Jane Woods:

+ 88 m I. **Charles Grover**[7] **Palmer** was born in Ironton, Upper Twp., Lawrence

Co., Ohio, on March 26, 1886. He died in Acacia, Cook Co., Illinois, on September 10, 1937. Charles Grover was buried in Cedar Park Cemetery, Calumet Park, Cook Co., Illinois.[43]

+ 89 f II. **Frances Mary**[7] **Palmer** was born in Ironton, Upper Twp., Lawrence Co., Ohio, on January 21, 1888. She was also known as **Frankie.** Frances Mary died in Columbus, Franklin Co., Ohio, in 1892.

27. **Elizabeth Marie**[6] **Palmer** (*Charles Nelson*[5], *Mary Margaret*[4] *Pagan*, *John*[3], *Andrew*[2], *James*[1]) was born on April 9, 1853, in Green Twp., Gallia Co., Ohio. She was the daughter of Charles Nelson Palmer (7) and Mary Ann Donnally. Elizabeth Marie died in Oklahoma City, Oklahoma, on February 3, 1910, at age 56. She was buried in Fairlawn Cemetery, Oklahoma City, Oklahoma Co., Oklahoma.[19]

Childless.

Elizabeth Marie married **James Andrew Bouy** on May 15, 1904, in Oklahoma Co., Oklahoma. James Andrew Bouy was born in Pennsylvania on November 8, 1845. James Andrew reached age 76 and died in Sulphur, Murray Co., Oklahoma, on August 5, 1922. He was buried in Fairlawn Cemetery, Oklahoma City, Oklahoma Co., Oklahoma.[19]

28. **Anna Emma**[6] **Palmer** (*Charles Nelson*[5], *Mary Margaret*[4] *Pagan*, *John*[3], *Andrew*[2], *James*[1]) was born on May 12, 1855, in Green Twp., Gallia Co., Ohio. She was also known as **Annie.** She was the daughter of Charles Nelson Palmer (7) and Mary Ann Donnally. Anna Emma died in Green Twp., Gallia Co., Ohio, on June 20, 1896, at age 41. She was buried in Fairfield Church Cemetery, Centenary, Green Twp., Gallia Co., Ohio.[5]

She is buried as Annie Palmer.

Never married.

29. **James Buchanan**[6] **Palmer** (*Charles Nelson*[5], *Mary Margaret*[4] *Pagan*, *John*[3], *Andrew*[2], *James*[1]) was born on November 20, 1857, in Green Twp., Gallia Co., Ohio. He was the son of Charles Nelson Palmer

(7) and Mary Ann Donnally. James Buchanan died in Oceana, Pentwater Co., Michigan, on February 9, 1931, at age 73. He was buried in Riverview Cemetery, Arkansas City, Cowley Co., Kansas.[20]

Oddly, Dr. James Buchanan Palmer dies under his brother Dr. Lewis William Palmer's name, only he changed the "Lewis" to "Louis". He is buried under the name "Louis W. Palmer". Did he assume his brother's identity?

James Buchanan married **Mary Jane Keiser** on November 12, 1902, in Kiowa Co., Oklahoma. They had three daughters. Mary Jane Keiser was born in Moline, Elk Co., Kansas, on December 7, 1875. Mary Jane reached age 55 and died in Oceana, Pentwater Co., Michigan, on March 14, 1931. She was buried in Riverview Cemetery, Arkansas City, Cowley Co., Kansas.[14]

Daughters of James Buchanan Palmer and Mary Jane Keiser:

+ 90  f  I.  **Iris Marie**⁷ **Palmer.**

+ 91  f  II.  **Gladys Marie**⁷ **Palmer**. was born in Guyman Twp., Texas Co., Oklahoma, on March 31, 1910.

+ 92  f  III.  **Ruth Beatrice**⁷ **Palmer**. was born in Missouri on March 25, 1913. She was adopted. Ruth Beatrice died in Garfield Twp., Grand Traverse Co., Michigan, on September 15, 1996. She was buried in Oak Grove Cemetery, Montague, Montague Twp., Muskegon Co., Michigan.[44]

**30. Emily Jane**⁶ **Smith** (*Mary Ann*⁵ *Palmer, Mary Margaret*⁴ *Pagan, John*³, *Andrew*², *James*¹) was born on November 18, 1847, in Perry Twp., Gallia Co., Ohio. She was the daughter of Levi Hamilton Smith and Mary Ann Palmer (8). Emily Jane died in Perry Twp., Gallia Co., Ohio, on December 23, 1897, at age 50. She was buried in Old Pine Cemetery, Rio Grande, Raccoon Twp., Gallia Co., Ohio.[6]

Emily Jane married **David Richard Davis** on May 29, 1867, in Gallia Co., Ohio. They had six children. David Richard Davis was born in Wales on August 28, 1840. David Richard reached age 65 and died in Perry Twp., Gallia Co., Ohio, on March 7, 1906. He was buried in Old Pine Cemetery, Rio Grande, Raccoon Twp., Gallia Co., Ohio.[6]

Children of Emily Jane Smith and David Richard Davis:

+ 93  m  I.  **Daniel L.**⁷ **Davis** was born in Perry Twp., Gallia Co., Ohio, on March 24, 1868. He died in Rio Grande, Raccoon Twp., Gallia Co., Ohio, on January 1, 1936. Daniel L. was buried in Old Pine Cemetery, Rio Grande, Raccoon Twp., Gallia Co., Ohio.[6]

+ 94  m  II.  **John W.**⁷ **Davis** was born in Perry Twp., Gallia Co., Ohio, on September 21, 1869. He died after 1880. John W. was buried in Old Pine Cemetery, Rio Grande, Raccoon Twp., Gallia Co., Ohio?

+ 95  f  III.  **Mary Ann**⁷ **Davis** was born in Perry Twp., Gallia Co., Ohio, on September 26, 1871. She was also known as **Marrianna.** Mary Ann died in Detroit, Wayne Co., Michigan, on October 24, 1952.

+ 96  f  IV.  **Elizabeth E.**⁷ **Davis** was born in Perry Twp., Gallia Co., Ohio, on December 15, 1873. She was also known as **Lizzie.** Elizabeth E. died in Udall, Ninnescah Twp., Cowley Co., Kansas, on August 28, 1965. She was buried in Mulvane Cemetery, Mulvane, Sumner Co., Kansas.[45]

+ 97  f  V.  **Emma J.**⁷ **Davis** was born in Perry Twp., Gallia Co., Ohio, in 1875. She died in Portsmouth, Scioto Co., Ohio, on March 6, 1958. Emma J. was buried in Old Pine Cemetery, Rio Grande, Raccoon Twp., Gallia Co., Ohio.[6]

+ 98  m  VI.  **David Benton**⁷ **Davis** was born in Perry Twp., Gallia Co., Ohio, on

September 16, 1877. He was also known as **Benton** and **D. Benton.** David Benton died in Poplar Bluff, Ash Hill Twp., Butler Co., Missouri, on October 3, 1949. He was buried in Rombauer Cemetery, Rombauer, St. Francis Twp., Butler Co., Missouri.[46]

**31. John Henry**[6] **Smith** (*Mary Ann*[5] *Palmer, Mary Margaret*[4] *Pagan, John*[3]*, Andrew*[2]*, James*[1]) was born on September 6, 1849, in Perry Twp., Gallia Co., Ohio. He was the son of Levi Hamilton Smith and Mary Ann Palmer (8). John Henry lived in 1880 in Wellston Twp., Jackson Co., Ohio. He died in Springfield Twp., Gallia Co., Ohio, on October 6, 1908, at age 59. John Henry was buried in Old Pine Cemetery, Rio Grande, Raccoon Twp., Gallia Co., Ohio.[6]

John Henry married **Mary Ella Norman** on March 25, 1875, in Gallia Co., Ohio. They had six children. Mary Ella Norman was born in Greenfield Twp., Gallia Co., Ohio, on July 24, 1855. Mary Ella reached age 40 and died in Springfield Twp., Gallia Co., Ohio, on March 28, 1896. She was buried in Old Pine Cemetery, Rio Grande, Raccoon Twp., Gallia Co., Ohio.[5]

John Henry Smith married **Mary Sofia Worman** on May 17, 1903, in Gallia Co., Ohio. They had one son. Mary Sofia Worman was born in Gallia Co., Ohio, on February 6, 1871. Mary Sofia reached age 56 and died in Springfield Twp., Gallia Co., Ohio, on April 13, 1927. She was buried in Old Pine Cemetery, Rio Grande, Raccoon Twp., Gallia Co., Ohio.[5]

Children of John 5Henry Smith and Mary Ella Norman:

+ 99 m I. **Lester H.**[7] **Smith** was born in Wellston Twp., Jackson Co., Ohio, on November 28, 1875. He died in Springfield Twp., Gallia Co., Ohio, on November 1, 1895. Lester H. was buried in Old Pine Cemetery, Rio Grande, Raccoon Twp., Gallia Co., Ohio.[2]

+ 100 f II. **Edna Grace**[7] **Smith** was born in Wellston Twp., Jackson Co., Ohio, on August 3, 1879. She died in San Diego, San Diego Co., California, on October 10, 1969.

+ 101 f III. **Anna Maude**[7] **Smith** was born in Rodney, Green Twp., Gallia Co., Ohio, on May 15, 1881. She was also known as **Maud.** Anna Maude died in Wilmington, Union Twp., Clinton Co., Ohio, on November 13, 1963. She was buried in Sunset Memorial Park Cemetery, Galloway, Franklin Co., Ohio.[47]

+ 102 f IV. **Auta May**[7] **Smith** was born in Rodney, Green Twp., Gallia Co., Ohio, on May 3, 1883. She died in Monroe Co., Florida, about May 7, 1969.

+ 103 m V. **Ernest Hamilton**[7] **Smith** was born in Rodney, Green Twp., Gallia Co., Ohio, on November 5, 1886. He died in San Diego, San Diego Co., California, on April 28, 1970. Ernest Hamilton was buried in Greenwood Memorial Park Cemetery, San Diego, San Diego Co., California.[48]

+ 104 m VI. **Raymond Howard**[7] **Smith** was born in Springfield Twp., Gallia Co., Ohio, on November 27, 1889. He died in Yucaipa, San Bernardino Co., California, on May 17, 1975. Raymond Howard was buried in Forest Lawn Memorial Park Cemetery, Glendale, Los Angeles Co., California.[30]

Son of John Henry Smith and Mary Sofia Worman:

+ 105 m I. **Orin Henry**[7] **Smith** was born in Springfield Twp., Gallia Co., Ohio, on September 19, 1904. He died in Pomeroy, Salisbury

Twp., Meigs Co., Ohio, on April 27, 1981. Orin Henry was buried in Gravel Hill Cemetery, Cheshire, Cheshire Twp., Gallia Co., Ohio.[49]

**32. Mary Frances⁶ Smith** (*Mary Ann⁵ Palmer, Mary Margaret⁴ Pagan, John³, Andrew², James¹*) was born on October 9, 1851, in Perry Twp., Gallia Co., Ohio. She was the daughter of Levi Hamilton Smith and Mary Ann Palmer (8). Mary Frances died in San Diego, San Diego Co., California, on July 18, 1917, at age 65.

Mary Frances married **David R. Wood** on November 1, 1870, in Gallia Co., Ohio. They had one daughter. David R. Wood was born in Raccoon Twp., Gallia Co., Ohio, on January 12, 1835. David R. reached age 36 and died in Raccoon Twp., Gallia Co., Ohio, on February 20, 1871. He was buried in Wood Cemetery, Raccoon Twp., Gallia Co., Ohio.[50]

Mary Frances Smith Wood married **Richard H. Gillispie** on December 25, 1873, in Gallia Co., Ohio. They had one son. Richard H. Gillispie was born in West Virginia in July 1843. Richard H. reached age 74 years and died in San Diego, San Diego Co., California, on September 1, 1917.

Daughter of Mary Frances Smith and David R. Wood:

+ 106 f I. **Cora Belle⁷ Wood** was born in Raccoon Twp., Gallia Co., Ohio, on September 12, 1871. She died in Howard, Fremont Co., Colorado in May 1956. She is buried Roselawn Cemetery, Pueblo, Pueblo Co., Colorado.[51]

Son of Mary Frances Smith and Richard H. Gillispie:

+ 107 m I. **Bleeker K.⁷ Gillispie** was born in Oak Hill Twp., Jackson Co., Ohio, on February 15, 1881. He died in Los Angeles, Los Angeles Co., California, on June 1, 1945.

**33. Charles Augustus⁶ Smith** (*Mary Ann⁵ Palmer, Mary Margaret⁴ Pagan, John³, Andrew², James¹*) was born on December 25, 1853, in Perry Twp., Gallia Co., Ohio. He was the son of Levi Hamilton Smith and Mary Ann Palmer (8). Charles Augustus died in Rio Grande, Raccoon Twp., Gallia Co., Ohio, on June 19, 1893, at age 39. He was buried in Calvary Baptist Cemetery, Rio Grande, Raccoon Twp., Gallia Co., Ohio.[12]

Charles Augustus married **Laura E. Gross** on June 6, 1877, in Gallia Co., Ohio. They had five children. Laura E. Gross was born in Rio Grande, Raccoon Twp., Gallia Co., Ohio, on July 23, 1857. Laura E. reached age 77 and died in South Charleston, Madison Twp., Clark Co., Ohio, on March 12, 1935. She was buried in Calvary Baptist Cemetery, Rio Grande, Raccoon Twp., Gallia Co., Ohio.[12]

Children of Charles Augustus Smith and Laura E. Gross:

+ 108 f I. **Ola Ethel⁷ Smith** was born in Raccoon Twp., Gallia Co., Ohio, on May 26, 1878. She died in a facility in Wilmington, Union Twp., Clinton Co., Ohio, on August 20, 1971. Ola Ethel was buried in Greenlawn Cemetery, South Charleston, Madison Twp., Clark Co., Ohio.[52]

+ 109 f II. **Maria Catherine⁷ Smith** was born in Rio Grande, Raccoon Twp., Gallia Co., Ohio, on May 5, 1880. She died in Athens, Athens Twp., Athens Co., Ohio, on March 2, 1963. Maria Catherine was buried in Gravel Hill Cemetery, Cheshire, Cheshire Twp., Gallia Co., Ohio.[49]

+ 110 f III. **Laura Luella⁷ Smith** was born in Rio Grande, Raccoon Twp., Gallia Co., Ohio, on April 20, 1884. She was also known as **Lou.** Laura Louella died in Rio Grande, Rac coon Twp., Gallia Co., Ohio, on February 2, 1954. She was buriedin Calvary Baptist Cemetery, Rio Grande,

Raccoon Twp., Gallia Co., Ohio.[8]

+ 111 m IV. **Charles Sidney[7] Smith** was born in Rio Grande, Raccoon Twp., Gallia Co., Ohio, on January 11, 1889. He died in Rio Grande, Raccoon Twp., Gallia Co., Ohio, on June 29, 1909. Charles Sidney was buried in Calvary Baptist Cemetery, Rio Grande, Raccoon Twp., Gallia Co., Ohio.[8]

+ 112 f V. **Cecile Gladys[7] Smith** was born in Rio Grande, Raccoon Twp., Gallia Co., Ohio, on May 21, 1893. She died in Syracuse, Onondaga Co., New York, about January 1963. Cecile Gladys was buried in Greenlawn Cemetery, South Charleston, Madison Twp., Clark Co., Ohio.[46]

**34. Lydia Luella[6] Smith** (*Mary Ann[5] Palmer, Mary Margaret[4] Pagan, John[3], Andrew[2], James[1]*) was born on August 29, 1856, in Rio Grande, Raccoon Twp., Gallia Co., Ohio. She was the daughter of Levi Hamilton Smith and Mary Ann Palmer (8). Lydia Luella died in Oakwood, Montgomery Co., Ohio, on January 2, 1933, at age 76. She was buried in Old Pine Cemetery, Rio Grande, Raccoon Twp., Gallia Co., Ohio.[2]

Lydia Luella married **Joseph Warren** on January 2, 1878. They had three children. Joseph Warren was born in Jefferson Twp., Jackson Co., Ohio?, in 1849. Joseph reached age 38 and died in Oak Hill, Madison Twp., Jackson Co., Ohio, on September 30, 1887.

Children of Lydia Luella Smith and Joseph Warren:

+ 113 f I. **Jessie O.[7] Warren** was born in Oak Hill, Jackson Co., Ohio, on December 21, 1878. She died in Orlando, Orange Co., Florida, on July 26, 1954. Jessie O. was buried in Woodlawn Cemetery,

Leslie, Leslie Twp., Ingham Co., Michigan.[53]

+ 114 f II. **Penelope Mary[7] Warren** was born in Oak Hill, Jackson Co., Ohio, on June 7, 1882. She was also known as **Nellie.** Penelope Mary died in Dayton, Montgomery Co., Ohio, on July 11, 1954. She was buried in Woodland Cemetery and Arboretum, Dayton, Montgomery Co., Ohio.[54]

+ 115 m III. **Parry Oberlin[7] Warren** was born in Oak Hill, Jackson Co., Ohio, on September 3, 1885. He died in Dayton, Montgomery Co., Ohio, on May 4, 1965. Parry Oberlin was buried in Woodland Cemetery and Arboretum, Dayton, Montgomery Co., Ohio.[48]

**35. Wesley Thomas[6] Smith** (*Mary Ann[5] Palmer, Mary Margaret[4] Pagan, John[3], Andrew[2], James[1]*) was born on November 3, 1858, in Perry Twp., Gallia Co., Ohio. He was the son of Levi Hamilton Smith and Mary Ann Palmer (8). Wesley Thomas lived in Perry Twp., Gallia Co., Ohio in 1900. He died in Columbus, Franklin Co., Ohio, on March 24, 1927, at age 68. Wesley Thomas was buried in Calvary Baptist Cemetery, Rio Grande, Raccoon Twp., Gallia Co., Ohio.[8]

Wesley Thomas married **Hannah Morgan** on September 20, 1883, in Gallia Co., Ohio. They had three children. Hannah Morgan was born in Perry Twp., Gallia Co., Ohio, in October 1858. Hannah reached age 45 and died in Perry Twp., Gallia Co., Ohio, in 1904. She was buried in Calvary Baptist Cemetery, Rio Grande, Raccoon Twp., Gallia Co., Ohio.[8] Her name was Hannah Womeldorff when she married Wesley Thomas Smith.

Children of Wesley Thomas Smith and Hannah Morgan:

+ 116 m I. **James Austin[7] Smith** was born in Perry Twp., Gallia Co., Ohio, on September 24, 1884.

He was also known as **Austin.** James Austin died in Pittsburgh, Allegheny Co., Pennsylvania, on January 3, 1906. He was buried in Calvary Baptist Cemetery, Rio Grande, Raccoon Twp., Gallia Co., Ohio..[8]

+ 117 m II. **Levi Morgan**[7] **Smith** was born in Perry Twp., Gallia Co., Ohio, on June 21, 1886. He died in Hammond, Lake Co., Indiana, on December 16, 1964. Levi Morgan was buried in Elmwood Cemetery, Hammond, Lake Co., Indiana.[55]

+ 118 f III. **Eva Marie**[7] **Smith** was born in Perry Twp., Gallia Co., Ohio, on August 20, 1889. She died in Los Angeles, Los Angeles Co., California, on July 31, 1980. Eva Marie was buried in Green Lawn Cemetery, Columbus, Franklin Co., Ohio.[56]

**36. Lawrence Benton**[6] **Smith** (*Mary Ann*[5] *Palmer, Mary Margaret*[4] *Pagan, John*[3]*, Andrew*[2]*, James*[1]) was born on January 26, 1861, in Perry Twp., Gallia Co., Ohio. He was the son of Levi Hamilton Smith and Mary Ann Palmer (8). Lawrence Benton lived in Mooresville Twp., Livingston Co., Missouri in 1900. He also resided in 1930 in Oakland, Alameda Co., California. Lawrence Benton was a physician. He died in Oakland, Alameda Co., California, on October 24, 1937, at age 76. Lawrence Benton was buried in Evergreen Cemetery, Oakland, Alameda Co., California.[15]

Lawrence Benton married **Stella Florence Moulton** on October 13, 1886, in Gallia Co., Ohio. They had one son. Stella Florence Moulton was born in Maine on December 18, 1865.[15] Stella Florence reached age 45 and died in Oakland, Alameda Co., California, on February 9, 1911. She was buried in Evergreen Cemetery, Oakland, Alameda Co., California.

Son of Lawrence Benton Smith and Stella Florence Moulton:

+ 119 m I. **Owen Benton**[7] **Smith** was born in Dayton, Montgomery Co., Ohio, on March 13, 1892.[57] He died in Oakland, Alameda Co., California, on September 6, 1935. Owen Benton was buried in Holy Cross Cemetery, Colma, San Mateo Co., California.[51]

**37. Annie Dell**[6] **Smith** (*Mary Ann*[5] *Palmer, Mary Margaret*[4] *Pagan, John*[3]*, Andrew*[2]*, James*[1]) was born on May 15, 1863, in Perry Twp., Gallia Co., Ohio. She was the daughter of Levi Hamilton Smith and Mary Ann Palmer (8). Annie Dell died in Perry Twp., Gallia Co., Ohio, on March 10, 1864. She was buried in Old Pine Cemetery, Rio Grande, Raccoon Twp., Gallia Co., Ohio.[2]

**38. John E.**[6] **Smith** (*Frances Madeline*[5] *Cheney, Mary Margaret*[4] *Pagan, John*[3]*, Andrew*[2]*, James*[1]) was born in 1855 in Perry Twp., Gallia Co., Ohio. He was the son of Charles Augustus Smith and Frances Madeline Cheney (9). John E. died in Perry Twp., Gallia Co., Ohio, on June 6, 1860, at age five. He was buried in Old Pine Cemetery, Rio Grande, Raccoon Twp., Gallia Co., Ohio.[2]

**39. Son**[6] **Smith** (*Frances Madeline*[5] *Cheney, Mary Margaret*[4] *Pagan, John*[3]*, Andrew*[2]*, James*[1]) was born about February 8, 1858 in Perry Twp., Gallia Co., Ohio. He was the son of Charles Augustus Smith and Frances Madeline Cheney (9). Son died in Perry Twp., Gallia Co., Ohio, on February 8, 1858. He was buried in Old Pine Cemetery, Rio Grande, Raccoon Twp., Gallia Co., Ohio.[2]

**40. Ezekiel Barton**[6] **Smith** (*Frances Madeline*[5] *Cheney, Mary Margaret*[4] *Pagan, John*[3]*, Andrew*[2]*, James*[1]) was born on May 30, 1859, in Perry Twp., Gallia Co., Ohio. He was the son of Charles Augustus Smith and Frances Madeline Cheney (9). He died in Wichita, Sedgwick Co., Kansas, on November 3, 1937, at age 78. Ezekiel Barton was buried in Highland Cemetery, Wichita, Sedgwick Co., Kansas.[16]

Ezekiel Barton married **Frances Allinson** before 1896. They had one son. Frances Allinson was born in Pleasant View Twp., Macon Co., Illinois, on February 17, 1866. Frances reached age 84 and died in Wichita, Sedgwick Co., Kansas, on June 18, 1950. She was buried in Highland Cemetery, Wichita, Sedgwick Co., Kansas.[16]

Son of Ezekiel Barton Smith and Frances Allinson:

+ 120 m  I.  **Edgar Barton**[7] **Smith** was born in Wichita, Sedgwick Co., Kansas, on August 28, 1896. He died in Wichita, Sedgwick Co., Kansas, on June 26, 1966. Edgar Barton was buried in Highland Cemetery, Wichita, Sedgwick Co., Kansas.[16]

41. **Charles Augustus**[6] **Smith II** (*Frances Madeline*[5] *Cheney, Mary Margaret*[4] *Pagan, John*[3]*, Andrew*[2]*, James*[1]) was born on June 28, 1861, in Perry Twp., Gallia Co., Ohio. He was the son of Charles Augustus Smith and Frances Madeline Cheney (9). Charles Augustus died in Perry Twp., Gallia Co., Ohio, on November 10, 1897, at age 36. He was buried in Old Pine Cemetery, Rio Grande, Raccoon Twp., Gallia Co., Ohio.[2]

Never married.

42. **Mary Elma**[6] **Smith** (*Frances Madeline*[5] *Cheney, Mary Margaret*[4] *Pagan, John*[3]*, Andrew*[2]*, James*[1]) was born on February 22, 1864, in Perry Twp., Gallia Co., Ohio. She was the daughter of Charles Augustus Smith and Frances Madeline Cheney (9). Mary Elma died in Perry Twp., Gallia Co., Ohio, on February 9, 1945, at age 80. She was buried in Old Pine Cemetery, Rio Grande, Raccoon Twp., Gallia Co., Ohio.[2]

Never married.

43. **Anna May**[6] **Smith** (*Frances Madeline*[5] *Cheney, Mary Margaret*[4] *Pagan, John*[3]*, Andrew*[2]*, James*[1]) was born on June 4, 1868, in Perry Twp., Gallia Co., Ohio. She was the daughter of Charles Augustus Smith and Frances Madeline Cheney (9). Anna May died in Gallipolis, Gallipolis Twp., Gallia Co., Ohio, on March 5, 1954, at age 85. She was buried in Mound Hill Cemetery, Gallipolis, Gallipolis Twp., Gallia Co., Ohio.[6]

Anna May married **Lorenzo Dow Watts** on September 18, 1889, in Gallia Co., Ohio. They had three children. Lorenzo Dow Watts was born in Green Twp., Gallia Co., Ohio, on November 16, 1862. Lorenzo Dow reached age 72 and died in Green Twp., Gallia Co., Ohio, on April 26, 1935. He was buried in Mound Hill Cemetery, Gallipolis, Gallipolis Twp., Gallia Co., Ohio.[6]

Children of Anna May Smith and Lorenzo Dow Watts:

+ 121 m  I.  **Ernest Augustus**[7] **Watts** was born in Green Twp., Gallia Co., Ohio, on June 30, 1890. He died in Gallipolis, Gallipolis Twp., Gallia Co., Ohio, on March 12, 1967. Ernest Augustus was buried in Mound Hill Cemetery, Gallipolis, Gallipolis Twp., Gallia Co., Ohio.[6]

+ 122 m  II.  **Heber Leslie**[7] **Watts** was born in Green Twp., Gallia Co., Ohio, on October 2, 1893. He died in Columbus, Franklin Co., Ohio, on July 18, 1960. Heber Leslie was buried in Mound Hill Cemetery, Gallipolis, Gallipolis Twp., Gallia Co., Ohio.[6]

+ 123 f  III.  **Marie**[7] **Watts** was born in Green Twp., Gallia Co., Ohio, on June 30, 1899. She died in Gallipolis, Gallipolis Twp., Gallia Co., Ohio, on January 21, 1977. Marie was buried in Mound Hill Cemetery, Gallipolis, Gallipolis Twp., Gallia Co., Ohio.[6]

44. **Frank**[6] **Smith** (*Frances Madeline*[5] *Cheney, Mary Margaret*[4] *Pagan, John*[3]*, Andrew*[2]*, James*[1]) was born on July 26, 1871, in Cora, Perry Twp., Gallia Co., Ohio. He was the son of Charles Augustus Smith and Frances Madeline Cheney (9). Frank died in Cora, Perry Twp., Gallia Co., Ohio, on December 13, 1902, at age 31. He was buried in Old Pine Cemetery, Rio Grande, Raccoon Twp., Gallia Co., Ohio.[2]

Seems to have never married.

**45. Charles Floyd[6] Cheney** (*John Watts[5], Mary Margaret[4] Pagan, John[3], Andrew[2], James[1]*) was born on September 4, 1879, in Springfield Twp., Gallia Co., Ohio. He was the son of John Watts Cheney (11) and Helen Maria Soles. Charles Floyd died in Gallipolis, Gallipolis Twp., Gallia Co., Ohio, on January 21, 1957, at age 77. He was buried in New Albany Cemetery/Landon Cemetery (Old Burial Ground), New Albany, Plain Twp., Franklin Co., Ohio.

Charles Floyd married **Stella May Ulrey** on August 31, 1912, in Franklin Co., Ohio. They had one daughter. Stella May Ulrey was born in Blendon Twp., Franklin Co., Ohio, on January 19, 1887. Stella May reached age 36 and died in Jefferson Twp., Franklin Co., Ohio, on November 16, 1923. She was buried in New Albany Cemetery/Landon Cemetery (Old Burial Ground), New Albany, Plain Twp., Franklin Co., Ohio.[58]

Stella May Ulrey Cheney's death certificate is erroneous. It says she is age 49, with a birthdate in 1874. But her birth certificate in Franklin Co., Ohio states a birthdate of 19 January 19, 1887. The death certificate also has her father as Whitehead and her mother as Ulrey, which is switched.

Daughter of Charles Floyd Cheney and Stella May Ulrey:

+ 124 f I. **Helen[7] Cheney** was born in Colulmbus, Franklin Co., Ohio, on July 13, 1918. She died in Newark, Newark Twp., Licking Co., Ohio, on March 29, 2002. Helen was buried in Maple Grove Cemetery, Granville, Granville Twp., Licking Co., Ohio.[59]

**46. Clarence Dale[6] Cheney** (*John Watts[5], Mary Margaret[4] Pagan, John[3], Andrew[2], James[1]*) was born on August 28, 1881, in Springfield Twp., Gallia Co., Ohio. He was the son of John Watts Cheney (11) and Helen Maria Soles. Clarence Dale died in Detroit, Wayne Co., Michigan, on January 18, 1946, at age 64.

Childless.

Clarence Dale married **Kathryn Sarah Bennett** on August 28, 1913, in Franklin Co., Ohio. Kathryn Sarah Bennett was born in Leesville, Orange Twp., Carroll Co., Ohio, on November 3, 1886. Kathryn Sarah reached age 28 and died in Plain Twp., Franklin Co., Ohio, on February 28, 1915. She was buried in New Albany Cemetery/Landon Cemetery (Old Burial Ground), New Albany, Plain Twp., Franklin Co., Ohio.[60]

Clarence Dale Cheney married **Unknown Unknown** between 1940 and 1946 in Michigan.

**47. Mary A.[6] Cheney** (*John Watts[5], Mary Margaret[4] Pagan, John[3], Andrew[2], James[1]*) was born on August 26, 1883, in Springfield Twp., Gallia Co., Ohio. She was also known as **Mamie.** She was the daughter of John Watts Cheney (11) and Helen Maria Soles. Mary A. died in Columbus, Franklin Co., Ohio, on December 5, 1916, at age 33. She was buried in New Albany Cemetery/Landon Cemetery (Old Burial Ground), New Albany, Plain Twp., Franklin Co., Ohio.[9]

Childless.

Mary A. married **Truman Orlando Warner** on October 1, 1901, in Gallia Co., Ohio. They divorced. Truman Orlando Warner was born in Wilson Twp., Clinton Co., Ohio, on February 1, 1880. He reached age 67 and died in Bennington Twp., Licking Co., Ohio, on December 1, 1947. Truman Orlando was buried in Maplewood Cemetery, New Albany, Plain Twp., Franklin Co., Ohio.[61]

**48. Lena[6] Rickabaugh** (*Emily[5] Cheney, Mary Margaret[4] Pagan, John[3], Andrew[2], James[1]*) was born on January 17, 1868, in Raccoon Twp., Gallia Co., Ohio. She was the daughter of John J. Rickabaugh and Emily Cheney (12). Lena died in Lancaster, Fairfield Co., Ohio, on October 5, 1954, at age 86. She was buried in Old Pine Cemetery, Rio Grande, Raccoon Twp., Gallia Co., Ohio.[2]

Lena married **David C. Wood** on December 25, 1889, in Gallia Co., Ohio. They had seven children. David C. Wood was born in Perry Twp., Gallia Co., Ohio, on September 30, 1866. David C. reached age 65 and died in Twin Twp., Ross Co., Ohio, on October 16, 1931. He was buried in Old Pine Cemetery, Rio Grande, Raccoon Twp., Gallia Co., Ohio.[2]

Children of Lena Rickabaugh and David C. Wood:

+ 125  m  I.  **Everett Marion**[7] **Wood** was born in Perry Twp., Gallia Co., Ohio, on February 1, 1891. He died in Gallipolis, Gallipolis Twp., Gallia Co., Ohio, on September 11, 1962. Everett Marion was buried in Mound Hill Cemetery, Gallipolis, Gallipolis Twp., Gallia Co., Ohio.[6]

+ 126  m  II.  **Oscar Sanford**[7] **Wood** was born in Perry Twp., Gallia Co., Ohio, on December 24, 1892. He died in Lancaster, Fairfield Co., Ohio, on November 21, 1978. Oscar Sanford was buried in Mound Hill Cemetery, Gallipolis, Gallipolis Twp., Gallia Co., Ohio.[6]

+ 127  m  III.  **Stanley D.**[7] **Wood** was born in Perry Twp., Gallia Co., Ohio, on December 10, 1894. He died in Gallipolis, Gallipolis Twp., Gallia Co., Ohio, on November 7, 1978. Stanley D. was buried in Mound Hill Cemetery, Gallipolis, Gallipolis Twp., Gallia Co., Ohio.[6]

+ 128  f  IV.  **Rita Pearl**[7] **Wood** was born in Perry Twp., Gallia Co., Ohio, on November 24, 1897. She died in a facility in Circleville, Pickaway Co., Ohio, on April 17, 1974. Rita Pearl was buried in Twin Township Cemetery, Bourneville, Twin Twp., Ross Co., Ohio.[62]

+ 129  f  V.  **Lillian May**[7] **Wood** was born in Perry Twp., Gallia Co., Ohio, on September 19, 1899. She died in a hospital in Columbus, Franklin Co., Ohio, on November 13, 1981.

+ 130  f  VI.  **Ethel Emily**[7] **Wood** was born in Perry Twp., Gallia Co., Ohio, on May 22, 1902. She died in Westerville, Blendon Twp., Franklin Co., Ohio, on March 10, 2000. Ethel Emily was buried in Harrison Township Cemetery, South Bloomfield, Harrison Twp., Pickaway Co., Ohio.[63]

+ 131  f  VII.  **Evelyn Odessa**[7] **Wood** was born in Perry Twp., Gallia Co., Ohio, on September 2, 1910. She died in Perry Twp., Gallia Co., Ohio, on May 16, 1913. Evelyn Odessa was buried in Old Pine Cemetery, Rio Grande, Raccoon Twp., Gallia Co., Ohio.[2]

**49. Hattie**[6] **Rickabaugh** (*Emily*[5] *Cheney, Mary Margaret*[4] *Pagan, John*[3], *Andrew*[2], *James*[1]) was born on May 14, 1874, in Rio Grande, Raccoon Twp., Gallia Co., Ohio. She was the daughter of John J. Rickabaugh and Emily Cheney (12). Hattie died in Columbus, Franklin Co., Ohio, on December 22, 1953, at age 79. She was buried in Glen Rest Memorial Estate Cemetery, Reynoldsburg, Truro Twp., Franklin Co., Ohio.[19]

Hattie married **Benjamin Massie** on October 5, 1893, in Gallia Co., Ohio. They had six children. Benjamin Massie was born in Perry Twp., Gallia Co., Ohio, on June 11, 1870. Benjamin reached age 79 and died in Columbus, Franklin Co., Ohio, on December 14, 1949. He was buried in Glen Rest Memorial Estate Cemetery, Reynoldsburg, Truro Twp., Franklin Co., Ohio.[19]

Children of Hattie Rickabaugh and Benjamin Massie:

+ 132  f  I.  **Medrith Marie**[7] **Massie** was born in Perry Twp., Gallia Co., Ohio, on February 18, 1895. She died in Columbus, Franklin Co., Ohio, on November 24, 1979. Medrith Marie was buried in Green Lawn Cemetery, Columbus, Franklin Co., Ohio.[50]

+ 133  m  II.  **Alfred Delver**[7] **Massie** was born in Perry Twp., Gallia Co., Ohio, on December 12, 1896. He died in Waterford, Waterford Twp., Washington Co., Ohio, on May

16, 1975. Alfred Delver was buried in Beverly Cemetery, Beverly, Center Twp., Washington Co., Ohio.[64]

+ 134  m  III.  **John Orville**[7] **Massie** was born in Perry Twp., Gallia Co., Ohio, on November 9, 1898. He died in Buffalo, Erie Co., New York, on November 6, 1958.

+ 135  m  IV.  **Raymond Neil**[7] **Massie** was born in Perry Twp., Gallia Co., Ohio, on March 21, 1901. He died in Birmingham, Jefferson Co., Alabama?, on December 12, 1954.

+ 136  f  V.  **Golden Odessa**[7] **Massie** was born in Wellston, Wellston Twp., Jackson Co., Ohio, on November 21, 1904. She died in Columbus, Franklin Co., Ohio, on December 30, 1987.

+ 137  m  VI.  **Ben Edgar**[7] **Massie** was born in Wellston, Wellston Twp., Jackson Co., Ohio, on March 6, 1908. He was also known as **Edgar B..** Ben Edgar died in Toledo, Lucas Co., Ohio, on March 11, 1947. He was buried in Glen Rest Memorial Estate Cemetery, Reynoldsburg, Truro Twp., Franklin Co., Ohio.[19]

**50. Frank Benton**[6] **Rickabaugh** (*Emily*[5] *Cheney, Mary Margaret*[4] *Pagan, John*[3], *Andrew*[2], *James*[1]) was born on August 1, 1880, in Raccoon Twp., Gallia Co., Ohio. He was the son of John J. Rickabaugh and Emily Cheney (12). Frank Benton lived in Chicago, Cook Co., Illinois in 1917. He resided in 1920 in Van Buren Twp., Montgomery Co., Ohio. He lived in 1976 in Dayton, Montgomery Co., Ohio. Frank Benton died in a facility in Columbus, Franklin Co., Ohio, on December 13, 1976, at age 96. He is buried in Dayton Memorial Park Cemetery, Dayton, Montgomery Co., Ohio..[25]

Childless.

Frank Benton married **Odessa Dean Page** on April 15, 1906, in Tuscarawas Co., Ohio. Odessa Dean Page was born in Tuscarawas Co., Ohio, on January 17, 1881. Odessa Dean reached age 82 and died in Dayton, Montgomery Co., Ohio, on December 26, 1963. She is buried in Dayton Memorial Park Cemetery, Dayton, Montgomery Co., Ohio.[25]

**51. John Leonard**[6] **Cheney** (*Silas B.*[5], *Mary Margaret*[4] *Pagan, John*[3], *Andrew*[2], *James*[1]) was born on March 31, 1875, in Green Twp., Gallia Co., Ohio. He was the son of Silas B. Cheney (13) and Elizabeth Beck. John Leonard died in Gallipolis, Gallipolis Twp., Gallia Co., Ohio, on July 7, 1951, at age 76. He was buried in Mound Hill Cemetery, Gallipolis, Gallipolis Twp., Gallia Co., Ohio.[6]

John Leonard married **Ella Malinda May (Eugenia) Day** on July 5, 1905, in Gallia Co., Ohio. They divorced. They had four children. Ella Malinda May Day (Eugenia) was born in Harrison Twp., Gallia Co., Ohio, on February 8, 1885. She was also known as **Linnie.** She reached age 54 and died in Evansville, Vanderburgh Co., Indiana, on July 24, 1939. Ella Malinda May Day was buried in Park Lawn Cemetery, Evansville, Vanderburgh Co., Indiana.[65]

After her divorce from John L. Cheney, Ella Malinda May "Linny" Day Cheney changed her given name to Eugenia. She married James Stovall and moved to Evansville, Vanderburgh Co., Indiana. On Eugenia Stovall's death certificate, her parents' names are given as Orlando Day and "Fannie" Lousher (Lusher), who were the parents of Ella Malinda May Day Cheney. As Ella Malinda May "Linny" Day had only one sibling, a sister who died in 1910, Ella is the "Eugenia". Her birthdate on the death certificate is February 8, 1895 instead of February 8, 1885, probably because she adjusted her age to be a contemporary with her second husband, James Stovall, who was born in 1895. She is buried under the name of Eugenia Stovall.

In 1930, two of her children by John L. Cheney, Marlin and Frances, are living with James and "Eugenia" Stovall in Evansville, Vanderburgh Co., Indiana.

John Leonard Cheney married **Georgia Hylton** before 1920. They had six children. Georgia Hylton was born in Pike Co., Kentucky, on June 5, 1900. Georgia reached age 93 and died in Gallipolis, Gallipolis Twp., Gallia Co., Ohio, on November 16, 1993. She was buried in Mound Hill Cemetery, Gallipolis, Gallipolis Twp., Gallia Co., Ohio.[6]

Children of John Leonard Cheney and Ella Malinda May Day (Eugenia):

+ 138 m  I.  **Marguerite[7] Elder** was born in Guyan Twp., Gallia Co., Ohio, on April 19, 1908. He died in Dayton, Montgomery Co., Ohio, on September 21, 1966. Marguerite was buried in Dayton National Cemetery, Dayton, Montgomery Co., Ohio.[66]

+ 139 f  II.  **Mary Virginia[7] Cheney** was born in Gallipolis, Gallipolis Twp., Gallia Co., Ohio, on January 21, 1909. She died in Gallipolis, Gallipolis Twp., Gallia Co., Ohio, on May 16, 1909. Mary Virginia was buried in Mound Hill Cemetery, Gallipolis, Gallipolis Twp., Gallia Co., Ohio.[6]

+ 140 f  III.  **Frances[7] Cheney** was born in Guyan Twp., Gallia Co., Ohio, on October 1, 1910. She died after 1939.

+ 141 m  IV.  **James C.[7] Cheney** was born in Guyan Twp., Gallia Co., Ohio, on January 7, 1915. He died in Evansville, Vanderburgh Co., Indiana, on July 13, 1937. James C. was buried in Mound Hill Cemetery, Gallipolis, Gallipolis Twp., Gallia Co., Ohio.[6]

Children of John Leonard Cheney and Georgia Hylton:

+ 142 f  I.  **Lillie May[7] Cheney** was born in Pikeville, Pike Co., Kentucky, on May 6, 1920. She died in Point Pleasant, Mason Co., West Vir-ginia, on August 3, 1996. Lillie Mae was buried in Mound Hill Cemetery, Gallipolis, Gallipolis Twp., Gallia Co., Ohio.[6]

+ 143 m  II.  **John[7] Cheney II** was born in Gallipolis, Gallipolis Twp., Gallia Co., Ohio, on January 28, 1922. He was also known as **Junior.** John died in Gallipolis, Gallipolis Twp., Gallia Co., Ohio, on January 18, 2004.

+ 144 f  III.  **Enabelle[7] Cheney** was born in Gallipolis, Gallipolis Twp., Gallia Co., Ohio, on July 20, 1924. She died in Point Pleasant, Mason Co., West Virginia, on December 7, 2008. Enabelle was buried in Lone Oak Cemetery, Point Pleasant, Mason Co., West Virginia.[67]

+ 145 f  IV.  **Jennie Ellen[7] Cheney** was born in Gallipolis, Gallipolis Twp., Gallia Co., Ohio, on July 6, 1927. She is also known as **Dottie.**

+ 146 m  V.  **Ray Leonard[7] Cheney** was born in Gallipolis, Gallipolis Twp., Gallia Co., Ohio, on September 29, 1929. He died in Gallipolis, Gallipolis Twp., Gallia Co., Ohio, on September 29, 1997. Ray Leonard was buried in Campaign Cemetery, Addison Twp., Gallia Co., Ohio.[68]

+ 147 m  VI.  **Carl Safford[7] Cheney** was born in Gallipolis, Gallipolis Twp., Gallia Co., Ohio, on November 1, 1931. He died in Gallipolis, Gallipolis Twp., Gallia Co., Ohio, on January 30, 2017. Carl Safford was buried in Mound Hill Cemetery, Gallipolis, Gallipolis Twp., Gallia Co., Ohio.[6]

**52. Pearl[6] Cheney** (*Silas B.[5], Mary Margaret[4] Pagan, John[3], Andrew[2], James[1]*) was born on March 11, 1876, in Green Twp., Gallia Co., Ohio. She was the daughter of Silas B. Cheney (13) and Elizabeth Beck.

Pearl died in Bay Village, Dover Twp., Cuyahoga Co., Ohio, on April 4, 1961, at age 85. She was buried in Cedar Hill Cemetery, Brownsville, Bowling Green Twp., Licking Co., Ohio.[20]

Pearl married **Harry Elder** on April 13, 1900, in Gallia Co., Ohio. They had two children. Harry Elder was born in Washington Twp., Fayette Co., Pennsylvania, on January 7, 1874. Harry reached age 68 and died in Zanesville, Muskingham Co., Ohio, on June 29, 1942. He was buried in Cedar Hill Cemetery, Brownsville, Bowling Green Twp., Licking Co., Ohio.[20]

Children of Pearl Cheney and Harry Elder:

+ 148 f I. **Marlin L.**[7] **Cheney** was born in Gallipolis, Gallipolis Twp., Gallia Co., Ohio, on April 27, 1901. She died in Lakeland, Polk Co., Florida, on February 4, 1985.

+ 149 m II. **Harley Lawrence**[7] **Elder** was born in Gallipolis, Gallipolis Twp., Gallia Co., Ohio, on July 31, 1906. He died in a hospital in Tampa, Hillsborough Co., Florida, on October 7, 1977.

53. **Bert Ramsey**[6] **Cheney** (*Silas B.*[5], *Mary Margaret*[4] *Pagan, John*[3], *Andrew*[2], *James*[1]) was born on October 2, 1879, in Green Twp., Gallia Co., Ohio. He was the son of Silas B. Cheney (13) and Elizabeth Beck. Bert Ramsey died in 1955 at age 75. He was buried in Germantown Cemetery, Germantown, German Twp., Montgomery Co., Ohio.[21]

Childless.

No death certificate is found for him in Ohio or any other state which has an online death certificate database.

Bert Ramsey married **Daisy S. Pressler** on December 23, 1905, in Montgomery Co., Ohio. Daisy S. Pressler was born in Germantown, German Twp., Montgomery Co., Ohio, on December 17, 1884. Daisy S. reached age 90 and died in Kettering, Miami Twp., Montgomery Co., Ohio, on May 22, 1975. She was buried in Germantown Cemetery,

Germantown, German Twp., Montgomery Co., Ohio.[21]

54. **Guy Bernard Johnson**[6] **Cheney** (*Silas B.*[5], *Mary Margaret*[4] *Pagan, John*[3], *Andrew*[2], *James*[1]) was born on November 12, 1881, in Raccoon Twp., Gallia Co., Ohio. He was the son of Silas B. Cheney (13) and Elizabeth Beck. Guy Bernard Johnson died in Madison Twp., Licking Co., Ohio?, between 1920 and 1927. He was buried in Mount Calvary Cemetery, Newark, Newark Twp., Licking Co., Ohio.[22]

Childless.

No death certificate is found for him in Ohio or any other state which has an online death certificate database.

Guy Bernard Johnson married **Florence Mary Davy** on September 24, 1913, in Licking Co., Ohio. Florence Mary Davy was born in Shawnee, Salt Lick Twp., Perry Co., Ohio, on March 7, 1887. Florence Mary reached age 93 and died in Madison Twp., Licking Co., Ohio, on March 6, 1981. She was buried in Mount Calvary Cemetery, Newark, Newark Twp., Licking Co., Ohio.[22]

She died under the name Florence Gundlach.

55. **Carrie B.**[6] **Cheney** (*Silas B.*[5], *Mary Margaret*[4] *Pagan, John*[3], *Andrew*[2], *James*[1]) was born on December 21, 1884, in Gallipolis, Gallipolis Twp., Gallia Co., Ohio. She was the daughter of Silas B. Cheney (13) and Elizabeth Beck. Carrie B. lived in Newark, Newark Twp., Licking Co., Ohio in 1952. She died in a facility in Somerset, Reading Twp., Perry Co., Ohio, on August 29, 1953, at age 68. Carrie B. was buried in Cedar Hill Cemetery, Brownsville, Bowling Green Twp., Licking Co., Ohio.[20]

Childless.

Carrie B. married **William H. Brooks** on May 31, 1910, in Darke Co., Ohio. They divorced. William H. Brooks was born in Athens Co., Ohio, on February 17, 1872.

Carrie B. Cheney Brooks married **Robert Hayes Jewell** on October 19, 1919, in Franklin Co., Ohio. Robert Hayes Jewell was born in Virginia Twp., Coshocton Co., Ohio, on May 1, 1878. Robert Hayes reached age 72 and died in Newark, Newark

Twp., Licking Co., Ohio, on December 21, 1950. He was buried in Cedar Hill Cemetery, Brownsville, Bowling Green Twp., Licking Co., Ohio.[20]

**56. Margaret Genevieve**[6] **Cheney** (*Silas B.*[5], *Mary Margaret*[4] *Pagan, John*[3], *Andrew*[2], *James*[1]) was born in August 1887 in Gallipolis, Gallipolis Twp., Gallia Co., Ohio. She was also known as **Jennie** and **Jennie M.**. She was the daughter of Silas B. Cheney (13) and Elizabeth Beck. Margaret Genevieve died in Lorain, Lorain Co., Ohio, on July 16, 1967, at age 79. She was buried in St. Joseph Cemetery, Newark, Licking Co., Ohio.[23] Margaret Genevieve Cheney Kiely always used her nickname, Jennie, as her preferred given name. Her death certificate is under Jennie M. Kiely and she is also buried under that name.

Margaret Genevieve married **Jerome Michael Kiely** on June 18, 1913, in Licking Co., Ohio. They had one son. Jerome Michael Kiely was born in Sandusky, Erie Co., Ohio, on January 26, 1888. Jerome Michael reached age 73 and died in Newark, Newark Twp., Licking Co., Ohio, on July 1, 1961. He was buried in St. Joseph Cemetery, Newark, Licking Co., Ohio.[23]

Son of Margaret Genevieve Cheney and Jerome Michael Kiely:

+ 150 m I. **Michael J. McKay**[7] **Kiely** was born in Ohio on April 11, 1919. He was adopted. Michael J. McKay died in Newark, Newark Twp., Licking Co., Ohio, on December 2, 1964. He was buried in St. Joseph Cemetery, Newark, Licking Co., Ohio.[23]

**57. Carleton James**[6] **Cheney** (*Silas B.*[5], *Mary Margaret*[4] *Pagan, John*[3], *Andrew*[2], *James*[1]) was born on December 25, 1896, in Gallipolis, Gallipolis Twp., Gallia Co., Ohio. He was also known as **Carl**. He was the son of Silas B. Cheney (13) and Elizabeth Beck. Carleton James died in Gallipolis, Gallipolis Twp., Gallia Co., Ohio, on February 23, 1930, at age 33. He was buried in Mound Hill Cemetery, Gallipolis, Gallipolis Twp., Gallia Co., Ohio.[6]

Never married.

**58. Rosalie or Roselia Catherine**[6] **King** (*Mary Ann*[5] *Pagan, John*[4], *John*[3], *Andrew*[2], *James*[1]) was born in 1850 in Perry Twp., Gallia Co., Ohio. She was the daughter of Henry T. King and Mary Ann Pagan (14). Rosalie or Roselia Catherine died after 1900.

Rosalie or Roselia Catherine married **William T. Johnson** on December 23, 1869, in Gallia Co., Ohio. They had four children. William T. Johnson was born in North Carolina.

Children of Rosalie or Roselia Catherine King and William T. Johnson:

+ 151 f I. **Eva**[7] **Johnson** was born in Ohio in 1870.

+ 152 f II. **Lulu**[7] **Johnson** was born in Ohio in 1874.

+ 153 m III. **Son**[7] **Johnson** was born in Beaver Twp., Pike Co., Ohio, in 1880.

+ 154 f IV. **Bessie M.**[7] **Johnson** was born in Sedalia, Sedalia Twp., Pettis Co., Missouri, in July 1890.

**59. John A.**[6] **King** (*Mary Ann*[5] *Pagan, John*[4], *John*[3], *Andrew*[2], *James*[1]) was born in January 1855 in Perry Twp., Gallia Co., Ohio. He was the son of Henry T. King and Mary Ann Pagan (14). John A. died in Sedalia, Sedalia Twp., Pettis Co., Missouri, on February 16, 1923, at age 68. He was buried in Crown Hill Cemetery, Sedalia, Pettis Co., Missouri. Mistakenly listed as only 58 years old on his death certificate, but his father is listed as Henry King.

He married **Frances Louise Robinson**. They divorced. They had five children. Frances Louise Robinson was born in Sedalia, Sedalia Twp., Pettis Co., Missouri, on December 13, 1863. She reached age 97 and died in Sedalia, Sedalia Twp., Pettis Co., Missouri, on January 10, 1961. Frances Louise was buried in Crown Hill Cemetery, Sedalia, Pettis Co., Missouri.[69] Oddly, Frances Louise Robinson King states on the 1900 census form that she has borne four children, all still alive, but two are missing from the home, Claud and another unknown one. Neither is found elsewhere in the census. In

1910, she says she has five children, all still surviving. Claud is in the home this time, but Bob A., listed in 1900 as born in Sep 1894, is not and either is the other unknown one.

John A. King married **Anna Unknown** after 1910.

Children of John A. King and Frances Louise Robinson:

+ 155 m I. **Charles Freimel**[7] **King** was born in Kansas City, Jackson Co., Missouri, on September 28, 1891. He died in Sedalia, Sedalia Twp., Pettis Co., Missouri, on January 24, 1985. Charles Freimel was buried in Crown Hill Cemetery, Sedalia, Pettis Co., Missouri.[63]

+ 156 m II. **Claude Amil**[7] **King** was born in Kansas City, Jackson Co., Missouri?, on September 27, 1893. He died in Los Angeles, Los Angeles Co., California, on December 18, 1971. Claude Amil was buried in Los Angeles National Cemetery, Los Angeles, Los Angeles Co., California.[70]

+ 157 m III. **Bob A.**[7] **King** was born in Kansas City, Jackson Co., Missouri, in September 1894. He died in Kansas City, Jackson Co., Missouri, before 1910.

+ 158 f IV. **Mary Ima**[7] **King** was born in Texas on June 3, 1901. She died in Laguna Hills, Orange Co., California, on February 17, 1996.

+ 159 V. **Child**[7] **King** was born in Kansas City, Jackson Co., Missouri, between 1900 and 1910. He or she died in Kansas City, Jackson Co., Missouri, between 1900 and 1910.

**60. Effie Virginia**[6] **King** (*Mary Ann*[5] *Pagan, John*[4]*, John*[3]*, Andrew*[2]*, James*[1]) was born on October 6, 1857, in Perry Twp., Gallia Co., Ohio. She was the daughter of Henry T. King and Mary Ann Pagan (14). Effie Virginia died in Los Angeles, Los Angeles Co., California, on December 5, 1941, at age 84. She was

buried in Forest Lawn Memorial Park Cemetery, Glendale, Los Angeles Co., California.[24]

Effie Virginia married **Arlington P. Ballard** on September 3, 1879, in Pike Co., Ohio. They had four children. Arlington P. Ballard was born in Wayne Twp., Noble Co., Ohio, in 1858. He was also known as **Arlie**. Arlington P. reached age 49 and died in a hospital in Columbus, Franklin Co., Ohio, on December 1, 1907. He was buried in Fairview Cemetery, Jeffersonville, Fayette Co., Ohio.[71]

Children of Effie Virginia King and Arlington P. Ballard:

+ 160 f I. **Inez Edith**[7] **Ballard** was born in Beaver Twp., Pike Co., Ohio, on March 30, 1881. She died in Los Angeles, Los Angeles Co., California, on February 11, 1936. Inez Edith was buried in Forest Lawn Memorial Park Cemetery, Glendale, Los Angeles Co., California.[24]

+ 161 f II. **Anna Mae**[7] **Ballard** was born in Beaver Twp., Pike Co., Ohio, on March 14, 1882. She died in Mechanicsburg, Goshen Twp., Champaign Co., Ohio, on May 2, 1918. Anna Mae was buried in Maple Grove Cemetery, Mechanicsburg, Goshen Twp., Champaign Co., Ohio.[72]

+ 162 f III. **Edna Opal**[7] **Ballard** was born in Jeffersonville, Jefferson Twp., Fayette Co., Ohio, on November 12, 1888. She died in Los Angeles, Los Angeles Co., California, on July 3, 1926.

+ 163 m IV. **Ronald**[7] **Ballard** was born in Jeffersonville, Jefferson Twp., Fayette Co., Ohio, on April 9, 1893. He died after 1917.

**61. Cornelia**[6] **King** (*Mary Ann*[5] *Pagan, John*[4]*, John*[3]*, Andrew*[2]*, James*[1]) was born in 1863 in Perry Twp., Gallia Co., Ohio. She was the daughter of Henry T.

King and Mary Ann Pagan (14). Cornelia died after 1900.

62. **Child[6] King** (*Mary Ann[5] Pagan, John[4], John[3], Andrew[2], James[1]*) was born between 1849 and 1880 in Ohio. He or she was a child of Henry T. King and Mary Ann Pagan (14). Child died in Ohio between 1849 and 1880.

63. **Marion[6] Troth** (*Madeline E.[5] Pagan, John[4], John[3], Andrew[2], James[1]*) was born on October 9, 1864, in Raccoon Twp., Gallia Co., Ohio.[26] He was the son of Amos Troth and Madeline E. Pagan (15). Marion died in Raccoon Twp., Gallia Co., Ohio, on November 21, 1882, at age 18.[26] He was buried in Calvary Baptist Cemetery, Rio Grande, Raccoon Twp., Gallia Co., Ohio.[8]

64. **Daughter[6] Troth** (*Madeline E.[5] Pagan, John[4], John[3], Andrew[2], James[1]*) was born on September 28, 1866, in Raccoon Twp., Gallia Co., Ohio.[8] She was the daughter of Amos Troth and Madeline E. Pagan (15). Daughter died in Raccoon Twp., Gallia Co., Ohio, on October 1, 1866.[8] She was buried in Calvary Baptist Cemetery, Rio Grande, Raccoon Twp., Gallia Co., Ohio.[8]

65. **Harrison Wood[6] Troth** (*Madeline E.[5] Pagan, John[4], John[3], Andrew[2], James[1]*) was born on July 2, 1873, in Raccoon Twp., Gallia Co., Ohio.[27] He was also known as **Harry.** He was the son of Amos Troth and Madeline E. Pagan (15). He lived in 1900 in Marietta, Marietta Twp., Washington Co., Ohio. Harrison Wood died in Akron, Summit Co., Ohio, on January 6, 1938, at age 64.[28, 29] He was buried in Mount Peace Cemetery, Akron, Summit Co., Ohio. [28, 30]

Never married.

66. **William Roosevelt[6] Johnson** (*John J.[5], Catherine[4] Pagan, John[3], Andrew[2], James[1]*) was born on March 25, 1856, in Perry Twp., Gallia Co., Ohio. He was the son of John J. Johnson (19) and Mary Jones. William Roosevelt lived in Joplin, Joplin Twp., Jasper Co., Missouri in 1900. He also resided in 1910 in Ward, Wheeler Co., Oregon. William Roosevelt was living in 1920 in Harper, Roanne Co., West Virginia. He died in Monument, Grant Co., Oregon, on May 6, 1929, at age 73. William

Roosevelt was buried in Monument Cemetery, Monument, Grant Co., Oregon.[31]

William Roosevelt married **Julia Linda Paxton** on February 15, 1880, in Roane Co., West Virginia. They had eight children. Julia Linda Paxton was born in Walton, Roane Co., West Virginia, in June 1863. Julia Linda reached age 76 and died in Bend, Deschutes Co., Oregon, on November 23, 1939. She was buried in Monument Cemetery, Monument, Grant Co., Oregon.[31]

Children of William Roosevelt Johnson and Julia Linda Paxton:

+ 164    I.    **Child One[7] Johnson** was born between 1880 and 1900. He or she died between 1880 and 1900.

+ 165    II.    **Child Two[7] Johnson** was born between 1880 and 1900. He or she died between 1880 and 1900.

+ 166    III.    **Child Three[7] Johnson** was born between 1880 and 1900. He or she died between 1880 and 1900.

+ 167 m IV.    **John Edward[7] Johnson** was born in Charleston, Kanawha Co., West Virginia, on February 27, 1881. He was also known as **Edd.** John Edward died in Monument, Grant Co., Oregon, on October 4, 1952.

+ 168 f V.    **Viola[7] Johnson** was born in Sioux City, Sioux City Twp., Woodbury Co., Iowa, on September 18, 1884. She died after 1900.

+ 169 m VI.    **Memphis Mason[7] Johnson** was born in Union Twp., Madison Co., Ohio, on April 1, 1889. He was also known as **Mason.** Memphis Mason died in Yarnell, Yavapai Co., Arizona, on May 31, 1965. He was buried in Genung Memorial Park Cemetery, Peeples Valley, Yavapai Co., Arizona.[73]

+ 170 f VII. **Luessia Marie**[7] **Johnson** was born in Little Rock, Pulaski Co.,

Arkansas, on July 15, 1898. She was also known as **Susie.** Luessia Marie died in Bend, Deschutes Co., Oregon, on October 5, 1996. She was buried in IOOF Cemetery, Roseburg, Douglas Co., Oregon.[74]

+ 171 m VIII. **Walter Cecil**[7] **Johnson** was born in Oklahoma on October 23, 1901. He died in Deschutes Co., Oregon, on November 19, 1980.

**67. Mary**[6] **Johnson** (*John J.*[5], *Catherine*[4] *Pagan, John*[3], *Andrew*[2], *James*[1]) was born in 1857 in Perry Twp., Gallia Co., Ohio. She was the daughter of John J. Johnson (19) and Mary Jones. Mary died in Gallia Co. or Jackson Co., Ohio, between 1860 and 1870.

**68. John**[6] **Johnson II** (*John J.*[5], *Catherine*[4] *Pagan, John*[3], *Andrew*[2], *James*[1]) was born in 1859 in Perry Twp., Gallia Co., Ohio. He was the son of John J. Johnson (19) and Mary Jones. John died in Gallia Co. or Jackson Co., Ohio, between 1860 and 1870.

**69. Margaret Catherine**[6] **Johnson** (*John J.*[5], *Catherine*[4] *Pagan, John*[3], *Andrew*[2], *James*[1]) was born in 1866 in Gallia Co. or Jackson Co., Ohio. She was the daughter of John J. Johnson (19) and Mary Jones. Margaret Catherine died after 1880.

**70. James Edward**[6] **Johnson** (*John J.*[5], *Catherine*[4] *Pagan, John*[3], *Andrew*[2], *James*[1]) was born on September 13, 1870, in Jackson Twp., Jackson Co., Ohio. He was the son of John J. Johnson (19) and Mary Jones. James Edward died in St Louis, Missouri, on February 17, 1936, at age 65. He was probably buried in Calvary Cemetery and Mausoleum, St. Louis, Missouri.

James Edward married **Nancy Elizabeth Lowery** on June 19, 1900, in Crawford Co., Arkansas. They were separated before 1936. They had five children. Nancy Elizabeth Lowery was born in Jasper Twp., Crawford Co., Arkansas, on October 14, 1880. She was also known as **Lizzie.** Nancy Elizabeth

reached age 59 and died in Berkeley, St. Louis Co., Missouri, on August 22, 1940. She was buried in Calvary Cemetery and Mausoleum, St. Louis, Missouri.[75]

Children of James Edward Johnson and Nancy Elizabeth Lowery:

+ 172 f I. **Alma L.**[7] **Johnson** was born in Muskogee Co., Oklahoma?, on December 3, 1904. She died in Montgomery City, Montgomery Twp., Montgomery Twp., Montgomery Co., Missouri, on September 17, 1998. Alma L. was buried in Saint Mary's Cemetery, Montgomery City, Montgomery Twp., Montgomery Co., Missouri.[76]

+ 173 m II. **Heber Clay**[7] **Johnson** was born in Muskogee Co., Oklahoma, on July 29, 1907. He was also known as **Johnny.** Heber Clay died in Cole County, Missouri, on July 20, 1990. He was buried in Bethany Memorial Gardens Cemetery, Crocker, Tavern Twp., Pulaski Co., Missouri.[77]

+ 174 f III. **Cloei**[7] **Johnson** was born in Wagoner, Wagoner Co., Oklahoma, on July 15, 1909. She died in Joplin, Joplin Twp., Jasper Co., Missouri, on August 9, 1910. Cloei was buried in Forest Park Cemetery, Joplin, Joplin Twp., Jasper Co., Missouri.[78]

+ 175 m IV. **Jesse**[7] **Johnson** was born in Oklahoma in 1913. He died after 1920.

+ 176 f V. **Bonnie Beatrice**[7] **Johnson** was born on December 24, 1915. She died on December 12, 1918.

**71. David**[6] **Johnson** (*John J.*[5], *Catherine*[4] *Pagan, John*[3], *Andrew*[2], *James*[1]) was born in 1872 in Vinton Twp., Vinton Co., Ohio? He was the son of John J. Johnson (19) and Mary Jones. David died after 1880.

**72. Rebecca**[6] **Johnson** (*John J.*[5], *Catherine*[4] *Pagan, John*[3], *Andrew*[2], *James*[1]) was born in 1875 in Vinton Twp., Vinton Co., Ohio? She was the daughter of John J. Johnson (19) and Mary Jones. Rebecca died after 1880.

**73. Ella Matilda**[6] **Murrell** (*Emma*[5] *Johnson, Catherine*[4] *Pagan, John*[3], *Andrew*[2], *James*[1]) was born on April 13, 1856, in Lynchburg, Campbell Co., Virginia. She was the daughter of William Randolph Murrell and Emma Johnson (20). Ella Matilda lived in Banister, Halifax Co., Virginia in 1880. She died in Dayton, Campbell Co., Kentucky, on December 24, 1917, at age 61. Ella Matilda was buried in Evergreen Cemetery, Southgate, Campbell Co., Kentucky.[32]

She had a child but may not have been married.

Son of Ella Matilda Murrell and Unknown Unknown:

+ 177 m I. **James W.**[7] **Murrell** was born in Lynchburg, Campbell Co., Virginia, on April 1, 1881. He died in a hospital in Mt. Vernon, Knox Co., Ohio, on January 16, 1952. James W. was buried in New Salem Methodist Episcopal Cemetery, Thorn Twp., Perry Co., Ohio.[79]

**74. Kate**[6] **Murrell** (*Emma*[5] *Johnson, Catherine*[4] *Pagan, John*[3], *Andrew*[2], *James*[1]) was born in 1857 in Gallipolis, Gallipolis Twp., Gallia Co., Ohio. She was the daughter of William Randolph Murrell and Emma Johnson (20). Kate died in Gallipolis, Gallipolis Twp., Gallia Co., Ohio, on May 4, 1858, at age one.

**75. Samuel**[6] **Murrell** (*Emma*[5] *Johnson, Catherine*[4] *Pagan, John*[3], *Andrew*[2], *James*[1]) was born in 1858 in Edgefield, Davidson Co., Tennessee? He was the son of William Randolph Murrell and Emma Johnson (20). Samuel died in Edgefield, Davidson Co., Tennessee?, before 1880.

**76. Hattie**[6] **Greenwood** (*Alexander*[5], *Catherine*[4] *Pagan, John*[3], *Andrew*[2], *James*[1]) was born on February 12, 1864, in Gallipolis, Gallipolis Twp., Gallia Co., Ohio. She was the daughter of Alexander Greenwood II (21) and Joanna Burdette. Hattie died in Pittsburgh, Allegheny Co., Pennsylvania, on September 28, 1938, at age 74. She was buried in Pine Street Cemetery, Gallipolis, Gallipolis Twp., Gallia Co., Ohio.[9]

Hattie married **Darius Wolfe** on November 9, 1881, in Gallia Co., Ohio. They had one son. Darius Wolfe was born in Gallipolis, Gallipolis Twp., Gallia Co., Ohio, on September 17, 1858. He resided in 1910 in Knoxville, Allegheny Co., Pennsylvania. Darius was living in 1920 in Pittsburgh, Allegheny Co., Pennsylvania. Darius reached age 81 and died in Pittsburgh, Allegheny Co., Pennsylvania, on February 6, 1940. He was buried in Pine Street Cemetery, Gallipolis, Gallipolis Twp., Gallia Co., Ohio.[9]

Although his son, Harry Wolfe, states on his father's Darius Wolfe's death certificate that Darius was born on September 17, 1860, census and other data indicate that he was born September 17, 1858.

Son of Hattie Greenwood and Darius Wolfe:

+ 178 m I. **Harry**[7] **Wolfe** was born in Gallipolis, Gallipolis Twp., Gallia Co., Ohio, in February 1883.[9] He died in Newark, Newark Twp., Licking Co., Ohio, on October 6, 1956. Harry was buried in Pine Street Cemetery, Gallipolis, Gallipolis Twp., Gallia Co., Ohio.[9]

**77. Frank Burdette**[6] **Greenwood** (*Alexander*[5], *Catherine*[4] *Pagan, John*[3], *Andrew*[2], *James*[1]) was born on January 21, 1866, in Gallipolis, Gallipolis Twp., Gallia Co., Ohio. He was the son of Alexander Greenwood II (21) and Joanna Burdette. Frank Burdette lived in Springfield, Springfield Twp., Clark Co., Ohio in 1900. He resided in 1910 in Indianapolis, Marion Co., Indiana. Frank Burdette died in Edgewood, Perry Twp., Marion Co., Indiana, on May 28, 1944, at age 78. He was buried in Round Hill Cemetery, Indianapolis, Perry Twp., Marion Co., Indiana.[33]

Frank Burdette married **Lena Meister** on September 1, 1887, in Gallia Co., Ohio. They had two children. Lena Meister was born in Zanesville, Muskingham Co., Ohio, on April 16, 1867. Lena reached age 80 and died in Indianapolis, Marion Co., Indiana, on

November 21, 1947. She was buried in Round Hill Cemetery, Indianapolis, Perry Twp., Marion Co., Indiana.[33]

Children of Frank Burdette Greenwood and Lena Meister:

+ 179 m   I.   **Frank Burdette[7] Greenwood II** was born in Springfield, Springfield Twp., Sangamon Co., Illinois, on August 18, 1888. He died in Indianapolis, Marion Co., Indiana, on April 28, 1946. Frank Burdette was buried in Round Hill Cemetery, Indianapolis, Perry Twp., Marion Co., Indiana.[33]

+ 180 f   II.   **Nelle[7] Greenwood** was born in Springfield, Springfield Twp., Sangamon Co., Illinois, on November 12, 1889. She died in Indianapolis, Marion Co., Indiana, on June 16, 1970. Nelle was buried in Round Hill Cemetery, Indianapolis, Perry Twp., Marion Co., Indiana.[33]

**78. Harry A.[6] Hover** or **Hoover** (*Fannie[5] Greenwood, Catherine[4] Pagan, John[3], Andrew[2], James[1]*) was born in 1863 in Gallipolis, Gallipolis Twp., Gallia Co., Ohio. He was also known as **Burt.** Harry A. Hover or Hoover was living in 1900 in Barboursville, Cabell Co., West Virginia. Harry A. Hover or Hoover lived in 1920 in Cincinnati, Hamilton Co., Ohio. He died after 1920.

In 1870, Harry A. Hover/Hoover and Mary E. Hover/Hoover, siblings, were living with their step-grandmother, Mary Rhine Greenwood, in Gallipolis, Gallipolis Twp., Gallia Co., Ohio. He continued to live with his step-grandmother in 1880, while his father and sister were living in Pana Twp., Christian Co., Illinois. On the 1880 census, he is listed as adopted by Mary Rhine Greenwood.

Harry A. Hover/Hoover married **Mary E. Harrison** on November 19, 1884, in Gallia Co., Ohio. They seem to have divorced. Mary E. Harrison was born in 1861.

Harry A. Hover/Hoover married **Nettie Catherine Diggens** on on December 1, 1890, in Gallia Co., Ohio. They divorced before 1900. Nettie Catherine Diggens was born in Harrison Twp., Gallia Co., Ohio on July 10, 1876. She reached age 73 and died in Cincinnati, Hamilton Co., Ohio, on April 20, 1950.

Harry A. Hover married his first wife Mary E. Harrison in 1884, but by 1890, he marries 14-year-old Nettie Catherine Diggins. Their marriage is allegedly sanctioned by her parents, but this permission is conveyed through a third party. Harry and Nettie have a daughter, Frances "Fannie" Virginia Hover, in 1895. But by 1900, Nettie C. Diggins Hover, listed as single, is living with her sister in Cincinnati, Hamilton Co., Ohio, while their daughter Fannie V. Hover is found in the Gallia County children's home.

About 1901, Nettie marries Fred Stradtman. In the 1910 census, they are living with their own two children in Cincinnati. But Frances "Fannie" Virginia Hover is not with them. Nettie, for some reason, says that she has borne four children, but only two were still alive. However, her daughter Fannie was still alive, and later marries.

She is buried under the name Nettie Stradtman.

Harry A. Hover or Hoover married **Alice Cooper** on November 18, 1907, in Scioto Co., Ohio. Alice Cooper was born in Greenup Co., Kentucky, in 1882.

Daughter of Harry A. Hover or Hoover and Nettie Catherine Diggens:

+ 181 f   I.   **Frances Virginia[7] Hover** was born in Gallipolis, Gallipolis Twp., Gallia Co., Ohio, on November 9, 1895. She was also known as **Fannie.** Frances Virginia died in Lower Lake, Lake Co., California, on April 28, 1973. She was buried in Lower Lake Cemetery, Lower Lake, Lake Co., California.[80]

**79. Mary E.[6] Hover** (*Fannie[5] Greenwood, Catherine[4] Pagan, John[3], Andrew[2], James[1]*) was born in 1866 in Gallipolis, Gallipolis Twp., Gallia Co., Ohio. She was also known as **May.** She was the daughter of James V. Hover and Fannie Greenwood (22). Mary E. died in Pana Twp., Christian Co., Illinois?, between 1880 and 1895.

In 1870, Harry A. Hover or Hoover and Mary E. Hover/Hoover, siblings, were living with their step-grandmother, Mary Rhine Greenwood, in Gallipolis, Gallipolis Twp., Gallia Co., Ohio.

In 1880, Mary E. Hover, age 14, is living with her father, James V. Hover, and his second wife in Pana Twp., Christian Co., Illinois, while her brother Harry A. Hover, 16, is listed as the adopted child of their step-grandmother, Mary "Polly" Rhine Greenwood, in Gallipolis, Gallia Co., Ohio.

No other records are found for Mary E. Hover. In 1895 in Gallia County court, Alexander (Boisvert) Greenwood Sr.'s two grandchildren by his first wife's son Alexander (Boisvert) Greenwood Jr., Hattie Greenwood Wolfe and Frank B. Greenwood, sue his other grandson Harry A. Hover, the son of his daughter Fannie Greenwood Hover by his second wife Catherine Pagan Johnson Greenwood. The lawsuit, over who should inherit Alexander Sr.'s property, does not mention Mary E. Hover, Fannie's daughter and Harry's sister, nor any children she may have had. It seems that she died before adulthood and without issue, but no record of her death exists. [14, 153]

# 7th Generation

**80. Child One**[7] **Farrar** (*Mary Frances*[6] *Palmer, Charles Nelson*[5], *Mary Margaret*[4] *Pagan, John*[3], *Andrew*[2], *James*[1]) was born between 1882 and 1900. He or she was a child of Veto Farrar and Mary Frances Palmer (23). Child One died between 1882 and 1900.

**81. Child Two**[7] **Farrar** (*Mary Frances*[6] *Palmer, Charles Nelson*[5], *Mary Margaret*[4] *Pagan, John*[3], *Andrew*[2], *James*[1]) was born between 1882 and 1900. He or she was a child of Veto Farrar and Mary Frances Palmer (23). Child Two died between 1882 and 1900.

**82. Bennora A.**[7] **Palmer** (*Thomas M.*[6], *Charles Nelson*[5], *Mary Margaret*[4] *Pagan, John*[3], *Andrew*[2], *James*[1]) was born on February 27, 1880, in Crook, Boone Co., West Virginia. She was the daughter of Thomas M. Palmer (24) and Alice McGath. Bennora A. died in Riverside Co., California, on November 23, 1964, at age 84.

Bennora A. married **Everett Robinson** on September 15, 1907, in Gallia Co., Ohio. They had three children. Everett Robinson was born in Ohio Twp., Gallia Co., Ohio, on December 3, 1878. Everett lived in Roy Twp., Potter Co., South Dakota in 1910. Everett resided in 1930 in Lebanon, Lebanon Twp., Potter Co., South Dakota. Everett was living in Gettysburg, Gettysburg Twp., Potter Co., South Dakota in 1940. He reached age 66 and died in Los Angeles Co., California, on May 31, 1945.

Children of Bennora A. Palmer and Everett Robinson:

+ 182 m I. **Palmer T.**[8] **Robinson** was born in Roy Twp., Potter Co., South Dakota, on May 19, 1908. He died in Riverside Co., California, on April 14, 1972.

+ 183 f II. **Pauline Everett**[8] **Robinson** was born in Roy Twp., Potter Co., South Dakota, on September 8, 1909. She was also known as **Pauline.** Pauline Everette died in San Diego, San Diego Co., California, on November 13, 1984.

+ 184 f III. **Allys or Alice**[8] **Robinson** was born in Lebanon, Lebanon Twp., Potter Co., South Dakota, on March 8, 1922.[81]

**83. Charles Clyde**[7] **Palmer** (*Thomas M.*[6], *Charles Nelson*[5], *Mary Margaret*[4] *Pagan, John*[3], *Andrew*[2], *James*[1]) was born on June 15, 1884, in Marmet, Kanawha Co., West Virginia. He was also known as **Clyde.** He was the son of Thomas M. Palmer (24) and Alice McGath. Charles Clyde lived in Minneapolis, Hennepin Co., Minnesota in 1920. He also resided in 1935 in Waupaca, Waupaca Co., Wisconsin. Charles Clyde was living in Port Townsend, Jefferson Co., Washington in 1940. He died in Ozark, Franklin Co., Arkansas, about May 10, 1962 at age 77. Charles Clyde was buried in Oak Hill Cemetery, Minneapolis, Hennepin Co., Minnesota.[11] Unmarried in 1920.

Childless.

Charles Clyde married **Gertrude Jensen** before 1940 in Wisconsin? Gertrude Jensen was born in Denmark in 1891. Gertrude lived in Minneapolis, Hennepin Co., Minnesota in 1920. She died in Port Townsend, Jefferson Co., Washington?, after 1940.

**84. Maud Marie**[7] **Palmer** (*Thomas M.*[6], *Charles Nelson*[5], *Mary Margaret*[4] *Pagan, John*[3], *Andrew*[2], *James*[1]) was born on September 13, 1887, in Green Twp., Gallia Co., Ohio. She was also known as **Marie.** She was the daughter of Thomas M. Palmer (24) and Alice McGath. Maud Marie died in Fort Worth, Tarrant Co., Texas, on February 5, 1967, at age 79. She was buried in Grapevine Cemetery, Grapevine, Tarrant Co., Texas.[36]

Childless.

Maud Marie married **Clarence Beaumont Phillips** after 1942. Clarence Beaumont Phillips was born in Grapevine, Tarrant Co., Texas, on October 6, 1882. Clarence Beaumont reached age 84 and died in Houston, Harris Co., Texas, on October 14, 1966. He was buried in Grapevine Cemetery, Grapevine, Tarrant Co., Texas.[36]

**85. Roy Donnally[7] Palmer** (*Thomas M.[6], Charles Nelson[5], Mary Margaret[4] Pagan, John[3], Andrew[2], James[1]*) was born on April 30, 1890, in Green Twp., Gallia Co., Ohio. He was the son of Thomas M. Palmer (24) and Alice McGath. He resided in 1920 in Avon Springs Twp., Potter Co., South Dakota. Roy Donnally was living in 1930 in Madison, Dane Co., Wisconsin. He died in Grandville, Wyoming Twp., Kent Co., Michigan, on April 24, 1957, at age 66.

Roy Donnally married **Ada Elenora Woodruff** on June 27, 1917, in Spink Co., South Dakota. They had three children. Ada Elenora Woodruff was born in Laurel Twp., Cedar Co., Nebraska?, on July 24, 1892. Ada Elenora reached age 83 and died in Grand Rapids, Grand Rapids Twp., Kent Co., Michigan, on June 27, 1976.

Children of Roy Donnally Palmer and Ada Elenora Woodruff:

+ 185 m I. **Donnally Woodruff[8] Palmer** was born in Avon Springs Twp., Potter Co., South Dakota, on June 6, 1918.

+ 186 m II. **Darwin Howard[8] Palmer** was born in Avon Springs Twp., Potter Co., South Dakota, on September 10, 1921. He died in Norton Shores, Muskegon Twp., Muskegon Co., Michigan, on May 10, 1989. Darwin Howard was buried in Mona View Cemetery, Muskegon Heights, Muskegon Co., Michigan.[82]

+ 187 f III. **Gloria E.[8] Palmer** was born in Gettysburg., Potter Co., South Dakota, on January 15, 1926. She died in Grand Rapids, Grand Rapids Twp., Kent Co., Michigan, on October 4, 2009. Gloria E. was buried in Grandville Cemetery, Grand Rapids Twp., Kent Co., Michigan.[83]

**86. George Merrill[7] Palmer** (*Thomas M.[6], Charles Nelson[5], Mary Margaret[4] Pagan, John[3], Andrew[2], James[1]*) was born on June 24, 1892, in Green Twp., Gallia Co., Ohio. He was the son of Thomas M. Palmer (24) and Alice McGath. He died in San Antonio, Bexar Co., Texas, on January 20, 1955, at age 62. George Merrill was buried in Fort Sam Houston National Cemetery, San Antonio, Bexar Co., Texas.[37]

George Merrill's career was in the U.S. Air Corps/Air Force. George Merrill lived in Kelly Field, Bexar Co., Texas in 1920. He resided in 1930 in Minneapolis, Hennepin Co., Minnesota. George Merrill was living in 1935 in Leavenworth, Leavenworth Co., Kansas. He was back living in Randolph Field, Bexar Co., Texas in 1940. .[37]

George Merrill married **Susan E. Gains** on May 18, 1918, in Bexar Co., Texas. They had one son. Susan E. Gains was born in Lyons, Rice Co., Kansas, on April 16, 1896. Susan E. reached age 89 and died in San Antonio, Bexar Co., Texas, on August 14, 1985. She was buried in Fort Sam Houston National Cemetery, San Antonio, Bexar Co., Texas.[37]

Son of George Merrill Palmer and Susan E. Gains:

+ 188 m I. **Jack Merrill[8] Palmer** was born in Fort Mills, Corregidor, Phillipine Islands, on March 5, 1922. He died in San Antonio, Bexar Co., Texas, on July 6, 2005. Jack Merrill was buried in Fort Sam Houston National Cemetery, San Antonio, Bexar Co., Texas.[37]

**87. Child[7] Palmer** (*Thomas M.[6], Charles Nelson[5], Mary Margaret[4] Pagan, John[3], Andrew[2], James[1]*) was born between 1880 and 1900 in Crook, Boone Co., West Virginia or Green Twp., Gallia Co., Ohio. He or she was a child of Thomas M. Palmer (24) and Alice McGath. Child died in Crook, Boone Co., West Virginia or Green Twp., Gallia Co., Ohio, between 1880 and 1900.

**88. Charles Grover[7] Palmer** (*Lewis William[6], Charles Nelson[5], Mary Margaret[4] Pagan, John[3], Andrew[2], James[1]*) was born on March 26, 1886, in Ironton, Upper Twp., Lawrence Co., Ohio. He was the son of Lewis William Palmer (26) and Amanda Jane Woods. Charles Grover died in Acacia, Cook Co.,

Illinois, on September 10, 1937, at age 51. He was buried in Cedar Park Cemetery, Calumet Park, Cook Co., Illinois.[38]

Charles Grover married **Eugenia Maria Sundquist** on June 17, 1908, in Cook Co., Illinois. They divorced. They had four children. Eugenia Maria Sundquist was born in Russia on October 26, 1886. She was also known as **Jenny.** Eugenia Maria lived in Plymouth, Center Twp., Marshall Co., Indiana in 1957. She reached age 70 and died in a hospital in South Bend, St. Joseph Co., Indiana, on February 28, 1957. Eugenia Maria was buried in New Oak Cemetery, Plymouth, Center Twp., Marshall Co., Indiana.[84]

Charles Grover Palmer married **Signa Adele Johnson** on June 22, 1919, in Cook Co., Illinois. Signa Adele Johnson was born in Sweden on August 3, 1886. Signa Adele reached age 47 and died in Chicago, Cook Co., Illinois, on July 30, 1934.

Charles Grover Palmer married **Mary Maurer** between 1934 and 1937. Mary Maurer was born in Chicago, Cook Co., Illinois?, on June 26, 1895. She was also known as **Mayme.** Mary died after 1937.

Children of Charles Grover Palmer and Eugenia Maria Sundquist:

+ 189 m I. **Charles Ethan**[8] **Palmer** was born in Chicago, Cook Co., Illinois, on April 19, 1909. He died in Mississauga, Peel, Ontario, Canada, in October 1979.

+ 190 f II. **Alice Eugenia**[8] **Palmer** was born in Chicago, Cook Co., Illinois, on February 5, 1910. She died in Chicago, Cook Co., Illinois, on March 10, 1975.

+ 191 f III. **Doris Jane**[8] **Palmer** was born in Chicago, Cook Co., Illinois, on August 29, 1912. She died in Traverse City, Grand Traverse Co., Michigan, on February 14, 1998 Doris Jane was buried in Ogdensburg Cemetery, Mapleton, Pen-

insula Twp., Grand Traverse Co., Michigan.[85]

+ 192 m IV. **Gaius Mattias**[8] **Palmer** was born in Chicago, Cook Co., Illinois, on July 1, 1915. He died in Phoenix, Maricopa Co., Arizona, on December 16, 1997. He was cremated.

89. **Frances Mary**[7] **Palmer** (*Lewis William*[6], *Charles Nelson*[5], *Mary Margaret*[4] *Pagan, John*[3], *Andrew*[2], *James*[1]) was born on January 21, 1888, in Ironton, Upper Twp., Lawrence Co., Ohio. She was also known as **Frankie.** She was the daughter of Lewis William Palmer (26) and Amanda Jane Woods. Frances Mary died in Columbus, Franklin Co., Ohio, in 1892 at age three.

90. **Iris Marie**[7] **Palmer** (*James Buchanan*[6], *Charles Nelson*[5], *Mary Margaret*[4] *Pagan, John*[3], *Andrew*[2], *James*[1]). She is the daughter of James Buchanan Palmer (29) and Mary Jane Keiser. Seems to have died in infancy or childhood.

91. **Gladys Marie**[7] **Palmer** (*James Buchanan*[6], *Charles Nelson*[5], *Mary Margaret*[4] *Pagan, John*[3], *Andrew*[2], *James*[1]) was born on March 31, 1910, in Guyman Twp., Texas Co., Oklahoma. She is the daughter of James Buchanan Palmer (29) and Mary Jane Keiser. Seems to have died young.

92. **Ruth Beatrice**[7] **Palmer** (*James Buchanan*[6], *Charles Nelson*[5], *Mary Margaret*[4] *Pagan, John*[3], *Andrew*[2], *James*[1]) was born on March 25, 1913, in Missouri. She was the daughter of James Buchanan Palmer (29) and Mary Jane Keiser. Ruth Beatrice was adopted. She died in Garfield Twp., Grand Traverse Co., Michigan, on September 15, 1996, at age 83. Ruth Beatrice was buried in Oak Grove Cemetery, Montague, Montague Twp., Muskegon Co., Michigan.[39]

Ruth Beatrice married **Monroe William Long** on October 7, 1934, in Lake Co., Indiana. They had four children. Monroe William Long was born in Glen Arbor Twp., Leelanau Co., Michigan, on May 23, 1913. Monroe William reached age 47 and died in Montague, Montague Twp., Muskegon Co., Michigan, on December 27, 1960. He was buried in

Oak Grove Cemetery, Montague, Montague Twp., Muskegon Co., Michigan.[39]

Ruth Beatrice Palmer and Monroe William Long:

+ 193 f I. **Mary Elizabeth⁸ Long** was born in Michigan City, Michigan Twp., LaPorte Co., Indiana, on May 3, 1936.

+ 194 f II. **Beatrice Ruth⁸ Long** was born in Cool Spring Twp., LaPorte Co., Indiana, on July 25, 1938. She died in Michigan City, Michigan Twp., LaPorte Co., Indiana, on July 25, 1938. Beatrice Ruth was buried in Greenwood Cemetery, Michigan City, Michigan Twp., LaPorte Co., Indiana.[86]

+ 195 III. **Child One⁸ Long**

+ 196 IV. **Child Two⁸ Long**

**93. Daniel L.⁷ Davis** (*Emily Jane⁶ Smith, Mary Ann⁵ Palmer, Mary Margaret⁴ Pagan, John³, Andrew², James¹*) was born on March 24, 1868, in Perry Twp., Gallia Co., Ohio. He was the son of David Richard Davis and Emily Jane Smith (30). Daniel L. died in Rio Grande, Raccoon Twp., Gallia Co., Ohio, on January 1, 1936, at age 67. He was buried in Old Pine Cemetery, Rio Grande, Raccoon Twp., Gallia Co., Ohio.[2]

Daniel L. married **Rozellma Tanner** on April 27, 1893, in Gallia Co., Ohio. They had five children. Rozellma Tanner was born in Perry Twp., Gallia Co., Ohio, on February 21, 1869. She was also known as **Zella.** Rozellma reached age 74 and died in Rio Grande, Raccoon Twp., Gallia Co., Ohio, on October 19, 1943. She was buried in Old Pine Cemetery, Rio Grande, Raccoon Twp., Gallia Co., Ohio.[2]

Children of Daniel L. Davis and Rozellma Tanner:

+ 197 m I. **Harold Warner⁸ Davis** was born in Cora, Perry Twp., Gallia Co., Ohio, on June 3, 1894. He died in Columbus, Franklin Co., Ohio, on January 8, 1971. Harold Warner was buried in Ashley Union Cemetery, Ashley, Ashley Twp., Delaware Co., Ohio.[87]

+ 198 f II. **Edith Wilma⁸ Davis** was born in Cora, Perry Twp., Gallia Co., Ohio, on June 13, 1896. She died in Hamden Twp., Vinton Co., Ohio, on September 26, 1977. Edith Wilma was buried in Calvary Baptist Cemetery, Rio Grande, Raccoon Twp., Gallia Co., Ohio.[8]

+ 199 f III. **Nelle Emily⁸ Davis** was born in Cora, Perry Twp., Gallia Co., Ohio, on June 7, 1898. She died in Clearwater, Pinellas Co., Florida, on March 22, 1994.

+ 200 m IV. **Roy A.⁸ Davis** was born in Cora, Perry Twp., Gallia Co., Ohio, on June 2, 1900. He died in Cora, Perry Twp., Gallia Co., Ohio, on January 11, 1907. Roy A. was buried in Old Pine Cemetery, Rio Grande, Raccoon Twp., Gallia Co., Ohio.[2]

+ 201 m V. **David Orville⁸ Davis** was born in Cora, Perry Twp., Gallia Co., Ohio, on January 23, 1904. He died in Lancaster, Fairfield Co., Ohio, on April 5, 1974.

**94. John W.⁷ Davis** (*Emily Jane⁶ Smith, Mary Ann⁵ Palmer, Mary Margaret⁴ Pagan, John³, Andrew², James¹*) was born on September 21, 1869, in Perry Twp., Gallia Co., Ohio. He was the son of David Richard Davis and Emily Jane Smith (30). John W. died after 1880. He was buried in Old Pine Cemetery, Rio Grande, Raccoon Twp., Gallia Co., Ohio? May be buried in Old Pine Cemetery, Rio Grande, Raccoon Twp., Gallia Co., Ohio.

**95. Mary Ann⁷ Davis** (*Emily Jane⁶ Smith, Mary Ann⁵ Palmer, Mary Margaret⁴ Pagan, John³, Andrew², James¹*) was born on September 26, 1871, in Perry

Twp., Gallia Co., Ohio. She was also known as **Marrianna.** She was the daughter of David Richard Davis and Emily Jane Smith (30). Mary Ann lived in Los Angeles, Los Angeles Co., California in 1920. She died in Detroit, Wayne Co., Michigan, on October 24, 1952, at age 81.

Mary Ann married **Charles K. Buckle** on May 24, 1898, in Gallia Co., Ohio. They had two daughters. Charles K. Buckle was born in Harrison Twp., Gallia Co., Ohio, in October 1872. Charles K. lived between 1902 and 1905 in South Dakota. He resided in 1910 in Laramie, Albany Co., Wyoming. Charles K. reached age 46 and died in Los Angeles, Los Angeles Co., California, on January 27, 1919.

Mary Ann Davis Buckle married **Unknown Johneke** before 1930 in Los Angeles Co., California?

Mary Ann Davis Buckle Johneke married **Unknown Carter** before 1940 in Los Angeles Co., California? Unknown Carter died before 1940.

Daughters of Mary Ann Davis and Charles K. Buckle:

+ 202 f I. **Gladys⁸ Buckle** was born in Perry Twp., Gallia Co., Ohio, on July 27, 1899. She died in Umatilla Co., Oregon, on December 7, 1963.

+ 203 f II. **Ruth Violet⁸ Buckle** was born in Bon Homme Co., South Dakota, on September 23, 1905. She died in Detroit, Wayne Co., Michigan, on February 1, 1963.

**96. Elizabeth E.⁷ Davis** (*Emily Jane⁶ Smith, Mary Ann⁵ Palmer, Mary Margaret⁴ Pagan, John³, Andrew², James¹*) was born on December 15, 1873, in Perry Twp., Gallia Co., Ohio. She was also known as **Lizzie.** She was the daughter of David Richard Davis and Emily Jane Smith (30). Elizabeth E. died in Udall, Ninnescah Twp., Cowley Co., Kansas, on August 28, 1965, at age 91. She was buried in Mulvane Cemetery, Mulvane, Sumner Co., Kansas.[45]

Elizabeth E. married **Sherman Russell Morton** on December 25, 1895, in Gallia Co., Ohio. They had two children. Sherman Russell Morton was born in Green Twp., Gallia Co., Ohio, on December 26,

1866. Sherman Russell reached age 88 and died in Udall, Ninnescah Twp., Cowley Co., Kansas, on July 30, 1955. He was buried in Mulvane Cemetery, Mulvane, Sumner Co., Kansas.[45]

Children of Elizabeth E. Davis and Sherman Russell Morton:

+ 204 m I. **Earl Davis⁸ Morton** was born in Green Twp., Gallia Co., Ohio, on September 13, 1899. He died in Udall, Ninnescah Twp., Cowley Co., Kansas, on October 2, 1995. Earl Davis was buried in Mulvane Cemetery, Mulvane, Sumner Co., Kansas.[45]

+ 205 f II. **Ruth⁸ Morton** was born in Maple Twp., Cowley Co., Kansas, in 1908. She died after 1920.

**97. Emma J.⁷ Davis** (*Emily Jane⁶ Smith, Mary Ann⁵ Palmer, Mary Margaret⁴ Pagan, John³, Andrew², James¹*) was born in 1875 in Perry Twp., Gallia Co., Ohio. She was the daughter of David Richard Davis and Emily Jane Smith (30). Emma J. died in Portsmouth, Scioto Co., Ohio, on March 6, 1958, at age 83. She was buried in Old Pine Cemetery, Rio Grande, Raccoon Twp., Gallia Co., Ohio.[2]

Emma J. married **Charles Shelby Tanner** on December 28, 1898, in Gallia Co., Ohio. They had four children. Charles Shelby Tanner was born in Perry Twp., Gallia Co., Ohio, on October 2, 1875. Charles Shelby reached age 77 and died in Portsmouth, Scioto Co., Ohio, on February 6, 1953. He was buried in Old Pine Cemetery, Rio Grande, Raccoon Twp., Gallia Co., Ohio.[2]

Children of Emma J. Davis and Charles Shelby Tanner:

+ 206 f I. **Ida Ethelyn⁸ Tanner** was born in Greenfield Twp., Gallia Co., Ohio, on August 12, 1900. She died after 1920.

+ 207 f II. **Sarah Emily⁸ Tanner** was born in Greenfield Twp., Gallia Co., Ohio, on September 27, 1903. She died in Ann Arbor, Ann Arbor Twp., Washtenaw Co., Michigan, on January 28, 1997. Sarah Emily was buried in Olive Methodist Church Cemetery, Cadmus, Walnut Twp., Gallia Co., Ohio.[88]

+ 208 m III. **Parry Benjamin**[8] **Tanner** was born in Greenfield Twp., Gallia Co., Ohio, on September 8, 1907. He was also known as **Bennie.** Parry Benjamin died in Arcanum, Twin Twp., Darke Co., Ohio, on December 6, 1987. He was buried in Old Pine Cemetery, Rio Grande, Raccoon Twp., Gallia Co., Ohio.[2]

+ 209 f IV. **Mary E.**[8] **Tanner** was born in Greenfield Twp., Gallia Co., Ohio, on March 10, 1912. She died in Bluffton, Richland Co., Allen Co., Ohio, on May 13, 1996. Mary E. was buried in Truro Cemetery, Columbus Grove, Pleasant Twp., Putnam Co., Ohio.[89]

**98. David Benton**[7] **Davis** (*Emily Jane*[6] *Smith, Mary Ann*[5] *Palmer, Mary Margaret*[4] *Pagan, John*[3], *Andrew*[2], *James*[1]) was born on September 16, 1877, in Perry Twp., Gallia Co., Ohio. He was also known as **Benton** and **D. Benton.** He was the son of David Richard Davis and Emily Jane Smith (30). David Benton lived in Perry Twp., Gallia Co., Ohio in 1910. He resided in 1918 in Ashland, Boyd Co., Kentucky. David Benton was living in 1920 in Wayne Co., Mississippi. David Benton died in Poplar Bluff, Ash Hill Twp., Butler Co., Missouri, on October 3, 1949, at age 72. He was buried in Rombauer Cemetery, Rombauer, St. Francis Twp., Butler Co., Missouri.[41]

David Benton married **Elizabeth Meek Wickline** on August 3, 1903, in Gallia Co., Ohio. They divorced. They had four children. Elizabeth Meek Wickline was born in Raccoon Twp., Gallia Co., Ohio, on January 16, 1880. She reached age 89 and died in Indianapolis, Marion Co., Indiana, on September 25, 1969. Elizabeth Meek was buried in Anderson

Cemetery, Warren Park, Warren Twp., Marion Co., Indiana.[90]

David Benton Davis married **Agnes Unknown** before 1940. Agnes Unknown was born in Missouri in 1891.

Children of David Benton Davis and Elizabeth Meek Wickline:

+ 210 m I. **David Walter**[8] **Davis** was born in Liberty Twp., Jackson Co., Ohio, on November 9, 1904. He was also known as **Walter.** David Walter died in East Ely, White Pine Co., Nevada, on May 18, 1981.

+ 211 m II. **Laurin Ernest**[8] **Davis** was born in Perry Twp., Gallia Co., Ohio, on May 21, 1907. He died in Hudson, Pasco Co., Florida, on March 16, 1989. Laurin Ernest was buried in Washington Park East Cemetery, Indianapolis, Warren Twp., Marion Co., Indiana.[91]

+ 212 f III. **Beatrice Emily**[8] **Davis** was born in Gallipolis, Gallipolis Twp., Gallia Co., Ohio, on September 5, 1911. She died in Indianapolis, Marion Co., Indiana, on January 16, 1986. Beatrice Emily was buried in Anderson Cemetery, Warren Park, Warren Twp., Marion Co., Indiana.[84]

+ 213 f IV. **Catherine Mae**[8] **Davis** was born in Perry Twp., Gallia Co., Ohio, on September 8, 1913. She died in Tujunga, Los Angeles Co., California, on April 15, 1984.

**99. Lester H.**[7] **Smith** (*John Henry*[6], *Mary Ann*[5] *Palmer, Mary Margaret*[4] *Pagan, John*[3], *Andrew*[2], *James*[1]) was born on November 28, 1875, in Wellston Twp., Jackson Co., Ohio. He was the son of John Henry Smith (31) and Mary Ella Norman. Lester H. died in Springfield Twp., Gallia Co., Ohio, on November 1, 1895, at age 19. He was buried in Old Pine Cemetery, Rio Grande, Raccoon Twp., Gallia Co., Ohio.[2]

Never married.

**100. Edna Grace⁷ Smith** (*John Henry⁶, Mary Ann⁵ Palmer, Mary Margaret⁴ Pagan, John³, Andrew², James¹*) was born on August 3, 1879, in Wellston Twp., Jackson Co., Ohio. She was the daughter of John Henry Smith (31) and Mary Ella Norman. Edna Grace died in San Diego, San Diego Co., California, on October 10, 1969, at age 90.

Childless.

Edna Grace married **Harry Maultby Skinner** on September 4, 1901, in Gallia Co., Ohio. They divorced. Harry Maultby Skinner was born in Norwich, Norfolk, England, on April 24, 1869. He reached age 84 and died in San Diego, San Diego Co., California, on August 14, 1953.

Edna Grace Smith Skinner married **William Fayette Warren** before 1920. William Fayette Warren was born in Waukechon, Shawano Co., Wisconsin?, on July 19, 1865. William Fayette reached age 75 and died in San Diego, San Diego Co., California, on August 18, 1940.

**101. Anna Maude⁷ Smith** (*John Henry⁶, Mary Ann⁵ Palmer, Mary Margaret⁴ Pagan, John³, Andrew², James¹*) was born on May 15, 1881, in Rodney, Green Twp., Gallia Co., Ohio. She was also known as **Maud.** She was the daughter of John Henry Smith (31) and Mary Ella Norman. Anna Maude died in Wilmington, Union Twp., Clinton Co., Ohio, on November 13, 1963, at age 82. She was buried in Sunset Memorial Park Cemetery, Galloway, Franklin Co., Ohio.[42]

Anna Maude married **John Hunter Williams** on January 28, 1903, in Gallia Co., Ohio. They had two children. John Hunter Williams was born in Walnut Twp., Gallia Co., Ohio, on July 4, 1878. John Hunter lived in Redlands, San Bernardino Co., California in 1948. He reached age 84 and died in Wilmington, Union Twp., Clinton Co., Ohio, on April 10, 1963. John Hunter was buried in Sunset Memorial Park Cemetery, Galloway, Franklin Co., Ohio.

Children of Anna Maude Smith and John Hunter Williams:

+ 214 f I. **Edith Norman⁸ Williams** was born in Columbus, Franklin Co., Ohio, on August 8, 1909. She died in Lansing, Lansing Twp., Ingham Co., Michigan, on July 1, 1941. Edith Norman was buried in Sunset Memorial Park Cemetery, Galloway, Franklin Co., Ohio.[42]

+ 215 m II. **John Kimber⁸ Williams** was born in Columbus, Franklin Co., Ohio, on September 28, 1913. He died in Wilmington, Union Twp., Clinton Co., Ohio, on August 1, 1974. John Kimber was buried in Sugar Grove Cemetery, Wilmington, Union Twp., Clinton Co., Ohio.[92]

**102. Auta Mae⁷ Smith** (*John Henry⁶, Mary Ann⁵ Palmer, Mary Margaret⁴ Pagan, John³, Andrew², James¹*) was born on May 3, 1883, in Rodney, Green Twp., Gallia Co., Ohio. She was the daughter of John Henry Smith (31) and Mary Ella Norman. Auta Mae died in Monroe Co., Florida, about May 7, 1969 at age 86.

Childless.

Auta Mae married **James Harold Campbell** on May 3, 1904, in Gallia Co., Ohio. They had one son. James Harold Campbell was born in Green Twp., Gallia Co., Ohio, on March 17, 1875. He was also known as **Harry.** James Harold reached age 32 and died in Green Twp., Gallia Co., Ohio?, on November 14, 1907. He was buried in Mount Zion Cemetery, Green Twp., Gallia Co., Ohio.[93]

Auta Mae Smith Campbell married **Otto Karl Eisennecher** on February 22, 1911, in Franklin Co., Ohio. Otto Karl Eisennecher was born in Germany on February 10, 1882. Otto Karl reached age 75 and died in Monroe Co., Florida, about June 10, 1957. He was buried in Sunset Memorial Park Cemetery, Galloway, Franklin Co., Ohio.[42]

Son of Auta Mae Smith and James Harold Campbell:

+ 216 m  I.  **Laurence Harold⁸ Campbell** was born in Green Twp., Gallia Co., Ohio, on November 10, 1904. He died in Dade Co., Florida, on September 7, 1970.

**103. Ernest Hamilton⁷ Smith** (*John Henry⁶, Mary Ann⁵ Palmer, Mary Margaret⁴ Pagan, John³, Andrew², James¹*) was born on November 5, 1886, in Rodney, Green Twp., Gallia Co., Ohio. He was the son of John Henry Smith (31) and Mary Ella Norman. Ernest Hamilton died in San Diego, San Diego Co., California, on April 28, 1970, at age 83. He was buried in Greenwood Memorial Park Cemetery, San Diego, San Diego Co., California.[43]

He married **Louise Ecker**. They had one son. Louise Ecker was born in Gallipolis, Gallipolis Twp., Gallia Co., Ohio, on January 9, 1891. Louise reached age 73 and died in San Diego, San Diego Co., California, on September 22, 1964.

Son of Ernest Hamilton Smith and Louise Ecker:

+ 217 m  I.  **Howard E.⁸ Smith** was born in San Diego, San Diego Co., California, on December 1, 1922. He died in San Diego, San Diego Co., California, on January 31, 2013.

**104. Raymond Howard⁷ Smith** (*John Henry⁶, Mary Ann⁵ Palmer, Mary Margaret⁴ Pagan, John³, Andrew², James¹*) was born on November 27, 1889, in Springfield Twp., Gallia Co., Ohio. He was the son of John Henry Smith (31) and Mary Ella Norman. Raymond Howard died in Yucaipa, San Bernardino Co., California, on May 17, 1975, at age 85. He was buried in Forest Lawn Memorial Park Cemetery, Glendale, Los Angeles Co., California.[24]

Seems to have never married.

**105. Orin Henry⁷ Smith** (*John Henry⁶, Mary Ann⁵ Palmer, Mary Margaret⁴ Pagan, John³, Andrew², James¹*) was born on September 19, 1904, in Springfield Twp., Gallia Co., Ohio. He was the

son of John Henry Smith (31) and Mary Sofia Worman. Orin Henry died in Pomeroy, Salisbury Twp., Meigs Co., Ohio, on April 27, 1981, at age 76. He was buried in Gravel Hill Cemetery, Cheshire, Cheshire Twp., Gallia Co., Ohio.[44]

Orin Henry married **Lillian Gertrude McAllister** on April 9, 1930, in Gallia Co., Ohio. They had two daughters. Lillian Gertrude McAllister was born in Middleport, Salisbury Twp., Meigs Co., Ohio, on October 20, 1907. Lillian Gertrude reached age 77 and died in Charleston, Kanawha Co., West Virginia, on June 9, 1985. She was buried in Gravel Hill Cemetery, Cheshire, Cheshire Twp., Gallia Co., Ohio.[44]

Daughters of Orin Henry Smith and Lillian Gertrude McAllister:

+ 218 f  I.  **Mary Lou⁸ Smith** was born in Rio Grande, Raccoon Twp., Gallia Co., Ohio, on May 18, 1931. She died in Myrtle Beach, Horry Co., South Carolina, on February 13, 2011.

+ 219 f  II.  **Lois Ann⁸ Smith** was born in Athens, Athens Twp., Athens Co., Ohio on January 28, 1936. She died in Groveland, Tuolumne Co., California, on May 29, 2013.

**106. Cora Belle⁷ Wood** (*Mary Frances⁶ Smith, Mary Ann⁵ Palmer, Mary Margaret⁴ Pagan, John³, Andrew², James¹*) was born on September 12, 1871, in Raccoon Twp., Gallia Co., Ohio. She was the daughter of David R. Wood and Mary Frances Smith (32). Cora Belle died in Howard, Fremont Co., Colorado in May 1956. She is buried in Roselawn Cemetery, Pueblo, Pueblo Co., Colorado.[51]

Cora Belle Wood is living with her maternal grandparents, Levi and Mary Ann Palmer Smith in Racoon Twp., Gallia Co., Ohio. She may have moved with some of her Smith relatives to Missouri.

Cora Belle married **Jacob Arthur Shore** on April 3, 1895 in Linn Co., Missouri.[94] They had two sons. Jacob A. Shore was born in (Lake) Carlton, Whiteside Co., Illinois? on January 28, 1867. Jacob died in October 1951 in Pueblo, Pueblo Co.,

Colorado. He is buried in Roselawn Cemetery, Pueblo, Pueblo Co., Colorado.[51]

Sons of Cora Belle Wood and Jacob Arthur Shore:

+ 220 f I. **Floyd Merle[8] Shore** was born in Marceline, Linn Co., Missouri on January 23, 1896. He died in Howard, Fremont Co., Colorado? on November 1, 1976. Floyd Merle was buried in Roselawn Cemetery, Pueblo, Pueblo, Colorado.[51]

+ 221 m II. **Lawrence Howard[8] Shore** was born in Las Animas, Bent Co., Colorado on January 25, 1906. He was adopted. He died after 1942.

**107. Bleeker K.[7] Gillispie** (*Mary Frances[6] Smith, Mary Ann[5] Palmer, Mary Margaret[4] Pagan, John[3], Andrew[2], James[1]*) was born on February 15, 1881, in Oak Hill Twp., Jackson Co., Ohio. He was the son of Richard H. Gillispie and Mary Frances Smith (32). Bleeker K. died in Los Angeles, Los Angeles Co., California, on June 1, 1945, at age 64.

Childless.

Bleeker K. married **Bessie Laura Northrup** on October 24, 1906, in Orange Co., California. Bessie Laura Northrup was born in San Francisco, San Francisco Co., California, on April 30, 1890. Bessie Laura reached age 82 and died in Newport Beach, Orange Co., California, on September 12, 1972.

**108. Ola Ethel[7] Smith** (*Charles Augustus[6], Mary Ann[5] Palmer, Mary Margaret[4] Pagan, John[3], Andrew[2], James[1]*) was born on May 26, 1878, in Raccoon Twp., Gallia Co., Ohio. She was the daughter of Charles Augustus Smith (33) and Laura E. Gross. Ola Ethel lived in 1971 in South Charleston, Madison Twp., Clark Co., Ohio. She died in a facility in Wilmington, Union Twp., Clinton Co., Ohio, on August 20, 1971, at age 93. Ola Ethel was buried in Greenlawn Cemetery, South Charleston, Madison Twp., Clark Co., Ohio.[52]

Childless.

Ola Ethel married **Charles Kemp** on July 7, 1905, in Gallia Co., Ohio. Charles Kemp was born in Union Twp., Madison Co., Ohio, on December 5, 1876. Charles lived in South Charleston, Madison Twp., Clark Co., Ohio in 1971. Charles reached age 95 and died in Memphis, Shelby Co., Tennessee, on January 9, 1972. He was buried in Greenlawn Cemetery, South Charleston, Madison Twp., Clark Co., Ohio.[52]

**109. Maria Catherine[7] Smith** (*Charles Augustus[6], Mary Ann[5] Palmer, Mary Margaret[4] Pagan, John[3], Andrew[2], James[1]*) was born on May 5, 1880, in Rio Grande, Raccoon Twp., Gallia Co., Ohio. She was the daughter of Charles Augustus Smith (33) and Laura E. Gross. Maria Catherine died in Athens, Athens Twp., Athens Co., Ohio, on March 2, 1963, at age 82. She was buried in Gravel Hill Cemetery, Cheshire, Cheshire Twp., Gallia Co., Ohio.[49]

Childless.

Maria Catherine married **Virgil Jacob Coughenour** on January 1, 1906, in Gallia Co., Ohio. Virgil Jacob Coughenour was born in Carlton, Cheshire Twp., Gallia Co., Ohio, on January 15, 1882. Virgil Jacob reached age 54 and died in Springfield, Springfield Twp., Clark Co., Ohio, on December 7, 1936. He was buried in Gravel Hill Cemetery, Cheshire, Cheshire Twp., Gallia Co., Ohio.[49]

**110. Laura Louella[7] Smith** (*Charles Augustus[6], Mary Ann[5] Palmer, Mary Margaret[4] Pagan, John[3], Andrew[2], James[1]*) was born on April 20, 1884, in Rio Grande, Raccoon Twp., Gallia Co., Ohio. She was also known as **Lou.** She was the daughter of Charles Augustus Smith (33) and Laura E. Gross. Laura Louella died in Rio Grande, Raccoon Twp., Gallia Co., Ohio, on February 2, 1954, at age 69. She was buried in Calvary Baptist Cemetery, Rio Grande, Raccoon Twp., Gallia Co., Ohio.[12]

Childless.

Laura Louella married **Otho Frederick Shiers** on April 18, 1908, in Gallia Co., Ohio. Otho Frederick Shiers was born in Rio Grande, Raccoon Twp., Gallia Co., Ohio, on March 9, 1884. Otho Frederick reached age 73 and died in Rio Grande,

Raccoon Twp., Gallia Co., Ohio, on September 12, 1957. He was buried in Calvary Baptist Cemetery, Rio Grande, Raccoon Twp., Gallia Co., Ohio.[12]

**111. Charles Sidney⁷ Smith** (*Charles Augustus⁶, Mary Ann⁵ Palmer, Mary Margaret⁴ Pagan, John³, Andrew², James¹*) was born on January 11, 1889, in Rio Grande, Raccoon Twp., Gallia Co., Ohio. He was the son of Charles Augustus Smith (33) and Laura E. Gross. Charles Sidney died in Rio Grande, Raccoon Twp., Gallia Co., Ohio, on June 29, 1909, at age 20. He was buried in Calvary Baptist Cemetery, Rio Grande, Raccoon Twp., Gallia Co., Ohio.[12]

Never married.

**112. Cecile Gladys⁷ Smith** (*Charles Augustus⁶, Mary Ann⁵ Palmer, Mary Margaret⁴ Pagan, John³, Andrew², James¹*) was born on May 21, 1893, in Rio Grande, Raccoon Twp., Gallia Co., Ohio. She was the daughter of Charles Augustus Smith (33) and Laura E. Gross. Cecile Gladys died in Syracuse, Onondaga Co., New York, about January 1963 at age 69. She was buried in Greenlawn Cemetery, South Charleston, Madison Twp., Clark Co., Ohio.[52]

Childless.

Cecile Gladys married **Isaac Clayton Wright** after 1930. Isaac Clayton Wright was born in Hollidaysburg, Blair Co., Pennsylvania, on September 18, 1895. Isaac Clayton reached age 80 and died in Syracuse, Onondaga, New York, in December 1975. He was buried in Greenlawn Cemetery, South Charleston, Madison Twp., Clark Co., Ohio.[52]

**113. Jessie O.⁷ Warren** (*Lydia Luella⁶ Smith, Mary Ann⁵ Palmer, Mary Margaret⁴ Pagan, John³, Andrew², James¹*) was born on December 21, 1878, in Oak Hill, Jackson Co., Ohio. She was the daughter of Joseph Warren and Lydia Luella Smith (34). Jessie O. died in Orlando, Orange Co., Florida, on July 26, 1954, at age 75. She was buried in Woodlawn Cemetery, Leslie, Leslie Twp., Ingham Co., Michigan.[53]

Childless.

Jessie O. married **Milo Coldren Jones** on August 11, 1908, in Essex, Ontario, Canada. Milo Coldren Jones was born in Leslie, Leslie Twp., Ingham Co., Michigan, on September 1, 1879. Milo Coldren lived in Washington, District of Columbia in 1917. He lived in 1940 in Newark, Essex Co., New Jersey. He reached age 76 and died in Orlando, Orange Co., Florida, on January 26, 1956. Milo Coldren was buried in Woodlawn Cemetery, Leslie, Leslie Twp., Ingham Co., Michigan.[53]

**114. Penelope Mary⁷ Warren** (*Lydia Luella⁶ Smith, Mary Ann⁵ Palmer, Mary Margaret⁴ Pagan, John³, Andrew², James¹*) was born on June 7, 1882, in Oak Hill, Jackson Co., Ohio. She was also known as **Nellie.** She was the daughter of Joseph Warren and Lydia Luella Smith (34). Penelope Mary died in Dayton, Montgomery Co., Ohio, on July 11, 1954, at age 72. She was buried in Woodland Cemetery and Arboretum, Dayton, Montgomery Co., Ohio.[54]

Childless.

Penelope Mary married **James Henry Adoue** on July 17, 1952, in Montgomery Co., Ohio. James Henry Adoue was born in Calvert, Robertson Co., Texas, on March 20, 1888. James Henry was living in 1952 in Dayton, Montgomery Co., Ohio. He resided in 1956 in Calvert, Robertson Co., Texas. James Henry reached age 68 and died in a hospital in Marlin, Falls Co., Texas, on June 21, 1956. He was buried in Calvert City Cemetery, Calvert, Robertson Co., Texas.[95]

**115. Parry Oberlin⁷ Warren** (*Lydia Luella⁶ Smith, Mary Ann⁵ Palmer, Mary Margaret⁴ Pagan, John³, Andrew², James¹*) was born on September 3, 1885, in Oak Hill, Jackson Co., Ohio. He was the son of Joseph Warren and Lydia Luella Smith (34). Parry Oberlin died in Dayton, Montgomery Co., Ohio, on May 4, 1965, at age 79. He was buried in Woodland Cemetery and Arboretum, Dayton, Montgomery Co., Ohio.[54]

Parry Oberlin married **Mabel M. Schnebly** about 1916. They had three sons. Mabel M. Schnebly was born in Dayton, Montgomery Co., Ohio, on February 18, 1892. Mabel M. reached age 82 and died in Dayton, Montgomery Co., Ohio, on

November 20, 1974. She was buried in Woodland Cemetery and Arboretum, Dayton, Montgomery Co., Ohio.[54]

Sons of Parry Oberlin Warren and Mabel M. Schnebly:

+ 222 m I. **Joseph Parry**[8] **Warren** was born in Dayton, Montgomery Co., Ohio, on February 8, 1917. He died in Vero Beach, Indiana River Co., Florida, on June 5, 1987. Joseph Parry was buried in Shiloh Park Cemetery, Shiloh, Harrison Twp., Montgomery Co., Ohio.[96]

+ 223 m II. **James William**[8] **Warren** was born in Dayton, Montgomery Co., Ohio, on July 13, 1920. He died in Columbus, Franklin Co., Ohio, on July 22, 2003. James William was buried in Glen Haven Memorial Gardens, Donnelsville, Bethel Twp., Clark Co., Ohio.[97]

+ 224 m III. **Jerry Schnebly**[8] **Warren** was born in Dayton, Montgomery Co., Ohio, on July 27, 1929. He was also known as **Jerry.** Jerry Schnebly died in Xenia, Xenia Twp., Greene Co., Ohio, on July 30, 1984. He was buried in Davids Cemetery, Kettering, Montgomery Co., Ohio.[98]

**116. James Austin**[7] **Smith** (*Wesley Thomas*[6], *Mary Ann*[5] *Palmer, Mary Margaret*[4] *Pagan, John*[3]*, Andrew*[2]*, James*[1]) was born on September 24, 1884, in Perry Twp., Gallia Co., Ohio. He was also known as **Austin.** He was the son of Wesley Thomas Smith (35) and Hannah Morgan. James Austin died in Pittsburgh, Allegheny Co., Pennsylvania, on January 3, 1906, at age 21. He was buried in Calvary Baptist Cemetery, Rio Grande, Raccoon Twp., Gallia Co., Ohio.[12]

Never married.

**117. Levi Morgan**[7] **Smith** (*Wesley Thomas*[6], *Mary Ann*[5] *Palmer, Mary Margaret*[4] *Pagan, John*[3]*, Andrew*[2]*, James*[1]) was born on June 21, 1886, in Perry

Twp., Gallia Co., Ohio. He was the son of Wesley Thomas Smith (35) and Hannah Morgan. Levi Morgan died in Hammond, Lake Co., Indiana, on December 16, 1964, at age 78. He was buried in Elmwood Cemetery, Hammond, Lake Co., Indiana.[55]

Levi Morgan married **Martha Abigail Watson** on November 8, 1911, in Gallia Co., Ohio. They had three children. Martha Abigail Watson was born in Addison Twp., Gallia Co., Ohio, on February 18, 1889. Martha Abigail reached age 94 and died in East Chicago, Lake Co., Indiana, on July 8, 1983. She was buried in Elmwood Cemetery, Hammond, Lake Co., Indiana.[55]

Children of Levi Morgan Smith and Martha Abigail Watson:

+ 225 m I. **Wesley Austin**[8] **Smith** was born in Hammond, Lake Co., Indiana, on January 31, 1916. He died in Bloomington, Monroe Co., Indiana, on February 6, 2001. Wesley Austin was buried in Valhalla Memorial Gardens, Bloomington, Monroe Co., Indiana.[99]

+ 226 f II. **Catherine Jane**[8] **Smith** was born in Hammond, Lake Co., Indiana, on January 19, 1918. She died in Hammond, Lake Co., Indiana, on February 24, 1920. Catherine Jane was buried in Elmwood Cemetery, Hammond, Lake Co., Indiana.[55]

+ 227 f III. **Doris Mary**[8] **Smith** was born in Hammond, Lake Co., Indiana, on June 8, 1922. She died in Dyer, Lake Co., Indiana, on April 14, 2014. Doris Mary was buried in Chapel Lawn Memorial Gardens Cemetery, Schererville, Lake Co., Indiana.[100]

**118. Eva Marie**[7] **Smith** (*Wesley Thomas*[6], *Mary Ann*[5] *Palmer, Mary Margaret*[4] *Pagan, John*[3]*, Andrew*[2]*, James*[1]) was born on August 20, 1889, in Perry Twp., Gallia Co., Ohio. She was the daughter of

Wesley Thomas Smith (35) and Hannah Morgan. Eva Marie died in Los Angeles, Los Angeles Co., California, on July 31, 1980, at age 90. She was buried in Green Lawn Cemetery, Columbus, Franklin Co., Ohio.[56]

Eva Marie married **Horace Hilburn Daugherty** on June 30, 1913, in Athens Co., Ohio. They had three children. Horace Hilburn Daugherty was born in Jackson, Lick Twp., Jackson Co., Ohio, on January 19, 1886. He was also known as **Doc.** Horace Hilburn reached age 69 and died in Columbus, Franklin Co., Ohio, on February 4, 1955. He was buried in Green Lawn Cemetery, Columbus, Franklin Co., Ohio.[56]

Children of Eva Marie Smith and Horace Hilburn Daugherty:

+ 228 f I. **Hannah Morgan**⁸ **Daugherty** was born in Columbus, Franklin Co., Ohio, on September 14, 1914. She died in Indio, Riverside Co., California, on August 22, 1989.

+ 229 m II. **Sam Pershing**⁸ **Daugherty** was born in Columbus, Franklin Co., Ohio, on October 3, 1917. He died in Hilton Head Island, Beaufort Co., South Carolina, on December 11, 2002. Sam Pershing was buried in Beaufort National Cemetery, Beaufort, Beaufort Co., South Carolina.[101]

+ 230 f III. **Merry Kay**⁸ **Daugherty** was born in Columbus, Franklin Co., Ohio, on March 5, 1921. She died in Hilton Head Island, Beaufort Co., South Carolina, on March 7, 2000. Merry Kay was buried in Six Oaks Cemetery, Sea Pines Plantation, Beaufort Co., South Carolina.[102]

**119. Owen Benton**⁷ **Smith** (*Lawrence Benton*⁶, *Mary Ann*⁵ *Palmer, Mary Margaret*⁴ *Pagan, John*³, *Andrew*², *James*¹) was born on March 13, 1892, in Dayton, Montgomery Co., Ohio.[51] He was the son of Lawrence Benton Smith (36) and Stella Florence Moulton. Owen Benton died in Oakland, Alameda Co., California, on September 6, 1935, at age 43. He was buried in Holy Cross Cemetery, Colma, San Mateo Co., California.[57]

Owen Benton married **Erna Ann Furrer** on May 12, 1915, in Alameda Co., California. They had two sons. Erna Ann Furrer was born in San Francisco, San Francisco Co., California, on August 1, 1893. Erna Ann reached age 89 and died in Oakland, Alameda Co., California, on January 26, 1983. She was buried in Evergreen Cemetery, Oakland, Alameda Co., California.[21]

Sons of Owen Benton Smith and Erna Ann Furrer:

+ 231 m I. **Stanley Lawrence**⁸ **Smith** was born in San Diego, San Diego Co., California, on February 16, 1916. He died in Post Falls, Kootenai Co., Idaho, on October 10, 2003. Stanley Lawrence was buried in Coeur D'Alene Memorial Gardens Cemetery, Coeur D'Alene, Rural Co., Idaho.[103]

+ 232 m II. **Weldon Harrold**⁸ **Smith** was born in Oakland, Alameda Co., California, on September 20, 1918. He died in Westport, Mendocino Co., California, on January 20, 2007.

**120. Edgar Barton**⁷ **Smith** (*Ezekiel Barton*⁶, *Frances Madeline*⁵ *Cheney, Mary Margaret*⁴ *Pagan, John*³, *Andrew*², *James*¹) was born on August 28, 1896, in Wichita, Sedgwick Co., Kansas. He was the son of Ezekiel Barton Smith (40) and Frances Allinson. Edgar Barton died in Wichita, Sedgwick Co., Kansas, on June 26, 1966, at age 69. He was buried in Highland Cemetery, Wichita, Sedgwick Co., Kansas.[22]

Childless.

Edgar Barton married **Margaret Davis** in 1927 in Sedgwick Co., Kansas. They divorced. Margaret Davis was born in Oklahoma in 1906. She died after 1930.

**121. Ernest Augustus**[7] **Watts** (*Anna May*[6] *Smith, Frances Madeline*[5] *Cheney, Mary Margaret*[4] *Pagan, John*[3], *Andrew*[2], *James*[1]) was born on June 30, 1890, in Green Twp., Gallia Co., Ohio. He was the son of Lorenzo Dow Watts and Anna May Smith (43). Ernest Augustus died in Gallipolis, Gallipolis Twp., Gallia Co., Ohio, on March 12, 1967, at age 76. He was buried in Mound Hill Cemetery, Gallipolis, Gallipolis Twp., Gallia Co., Ohio.[10]

Ernest Augustus married **Elizabeth Gladys Mossbarger** on December 29, 1915, in Gallia Co., Ohio. They had two sons. Elizabeth Gladys Mossbarger was born in Perry Twp., Gallia Co., Ohio, on August 26, 1893. She was also known as **Gladys.** Elizabeth Gladys reached age 92 and died in Gallipolis, Gallipolis Twp., Gallia Co., Ohio, on February 4, 1986. She was buried in Mound Hill Cemetery, Gallipolis, Gallipolis Twp., Gallia Co., Ohio.[10]

Sons of Ernest Augustus Watts and Elizabeth Gladys Mossbarger:

+ 233 m I. **Harold**[8] **Watts** was born in Perry Twp., Gallia Co., Ohio, on February 4, 1917. He died in Los Angeles, Los Angeles Co., California, on September 22, 1992.

+ 234 m II. **Kenneth C.**[8] **Watts** was born in Perry Twp., Gallia Co., Ohio, on June 21, 1921. He died in Gallipolis, Gallipolis Twp., Gallia Co., Ohio, on November 20, 1995. Kenneth C. was buried in Mound Hill Cemetery, Gallipolis, Gallipolis Twp., Gallia Co., Ohio.[10]

**122. Heber Leslie**[7] **Watts** (*Anna May*[6] *Smith, Frances Madeline*[5] *Cheney, Mary Margaret*[4] *Pagan, John*[3], *Andrew*[2], *James*[1]) was born on October 2, 1893, in Green Twp., Gallia Co., Ohio. He was the son of Lorenzo Dow Watts and Anna May Smith (43). Heber Leslie died in Columbus, Franklin Co., Ohio, on July 18, 1960, at age 66. He was buried in Mound Hill Cemetery, Gallipolis, Gallipolis Twp., Gallia Co., Ohio.[10]

Childless.

Heber Leslie married **Ruth M. Wigner** on May 14, 1915, in Mason Co., West Virginia. Ruth M. Wigner was born in Green Twp., Gallia Co., Ohio, on November 15, 1896. Ruth M. reached age 72 and died in Columbus, Franklin Co., Ohio, on December 30, 1968. She was buried in Mound Hill Cemetery, Gallipolis, Gallipolis Twp., Gallia Co., Ohio.[10]

**123. Marie**[7] **Watts** (*Anna May*[6] *Smith, Frances Madeline*[5] *Cheney, Mary Margaret*[4] *Pagan, John*[3], *Andrew*[2], *James*[1]) was born on June 30, 1899, in Green Twp., Gallia Co., Ohio. She was the daughter of Lorenzo Dow Watts and Anna May Smith (43). Marie died in Gallipolis, Gallipolis Twp., Gallia Co., Ohio, on January 21, 1977, at age 77. She was buried in Mound Hill Cemetery, Gallipolis, Gallipolis Twp., Gallia Co., Ohio.[10]

Marie married **James Herman Northup** on January 2, 1917, in Boyd Co., Kentucky. They had two sons. James Herman Northup was born in Northup, Green Twp., Gallia Co., Ohio, on June 26, 1895. He was also known as **Herman.** James Herman reached age 67 and died in Gallipolis, Gallipolis Twp., Gallia Co., Ohio, on April 18, 1963. He was buried in Mound Hill Cemetery, Gallipolis, Gallipolis Twp., Gallia Co., Ohio.[10]

Sons of Marie Watts and James Herman Northup:

+ 235 m I. **Harlan Watts**[8] **Northup** was born in Northup, Green Twp., Gallia Co., Ohio, on October 3, 1926. He died in Vinton, Huntington Twp., Gallia Co., Ohio, on October 23, 2010.

+ 236 m II. **James Ansel**[8] **Northup II** was born in Northup, Green Twp., Gallia Co., Ohio, on December 23, 1927. He died in Gallipolis, Gallipolis Twp., Gallia Co., Ohio, on December 11, 2004. James Ansel was buried in Mound Hill Cemetery, Gallipolis, Gallipolis Twp., Gallia Co., Ohio.[10]

**124. Helen**[7] **Cheney** (*Charles Floyd*[6], *John Watts*[5], *Mary Margaret*[4] *Pagan*, *John*[3], *Andrew*[2], *James*[1]) was born on July 13, 1918, in Colulmbus, Franklin Co., Ohio. She was the daughter of Charles Floyd Cheney (45) and Stella May Ulrey. Helen died in Newark, Newark Twp., Licking Co., Ohio, on March 29, 2002, at age 83. She was buried in Maple Grove Cemetery, Granville, Granville Twp., Licking Co., Ohio.[59]

Childless.

Helen married **Robert W. Messick** after 1940. Robert W. Messick was born in Union Twp., Licking Co., Ohio, on March 23, 1920. Robert W. lived in Newark, Newark Twp., Licking Co., Ohio in 1958. He reached age 38 and died in a hospital in Columbus, Franklin Co., Ohio, on August 29, 1958. Robert W. was buried in Maple Grove Cemetery, Granville, Granville Twp., Licking Co., Ohio.[59]

**125. Everett Marion**[7] **Wood** (*Lena*[6] *Rickabaugh*, *Emily*[5] *Cheney*, *Mary Margaret*[4] *Pagan*, *John*[3], *Andrew*[2], *James*[1]) was born on February 1, 1891, in Perry Twp., Gallia Co., Ohio. He was the son of David C. Wood and Lena Rickabaugh (48). Everett Marion died in Gallipolis, Gallipolis Twp., Gallia Co., Ohio, on September 11, 1962, at age 71. He was buried in Mound Hill Cemetery, Gallipolis, Gallipolis Twp., Gallia Co., Ohio.[10]

Everett Marion married **Emma Alice Shadrach** on December 25, 1919. They had one daughter. Emma Alice Shadrach was born in Madison Twp., Jackson Co., Ohio, on March 29, 1892. Emma Alice reached age 73 and died in Odessa, Ector Co., Texas, on February 9, 1966. She was buried in Mound Hill Cemetery, Gallipolis, Gallipolis Twp., Gallia Co., Ohio.[10]

Daughter of Everett Marion Wood and Emma Alice Shadrach:

+ 237 f I. **Edith Louise**[8] **Wood** was born in Gallipolis, Gallipolis Twp., Gallia Co., Ohio, on October 25, 1920. She died in Austin, Travis Co., Texas, on June 21, 2002.

Edith Louise was buried in Texas State Cemetery, Austin, Travis Co., Texas.[104]

**126. Oscar Sanford**[7] **Wood** (*Lena*[6] *Rickabaugh*, *Emily*[5] *Cheney*, *Mary Margaret*[4] *Pagan*, *John*[3], *Andrew*[2], *James*[1]) was born on December 24, 1892, in Perry Twp., Gallia Co., Ohio. He was the son of David C. Wood and Lena Rickabaugh (48). Oscar Sanford died in Lancaster, Fairfield Co., Ohio, on November 21, 1978, at age 85. He was buried in Mound Hill Cemetery, Gallipolis, Gallipolis Twp., Gallia Co., Ohio.10]

Oscar Sanford married **Jessie Marie Wood** on March 1, 1921, in Gallia Co., Ohio. Jessie Marie Wood was born in Perry Twp., Gallia Co., Ohio, on September 30, 1900. Jessie Marie reached age 34 and died in Athens, Athens Twp., Athens Co., Ohio, on October 23, 1934. She was buried in Old Pine Cemetery, Rio Grande, Raccoon Twp., Gallia Co., Ohio.[6]

Oscar Sanford Wood married **Mary Ethel Harbour** on January 19, 1938, in Ross Co., Ohio. They had two sons. Mary Ethel Harbour was born in Gallipolis, Gallipolis Twp., Gallia Co., Ohio, on September 14, 1916. Mary Ethel reached age 85 and died in Lancaster, Fairfield Co., Ohio, on February 11, 2002. She was buried in Mound Hill Cemetery, Gallipolis, Gallipolis Twp., Gallia Co., Ohio.[10]

Oscar Sanford Wood and Mary Ethel Harbour had two sons, including:

+ 238 m I. **David**[8] **Wood** was born in Clay Twp., Gallia Co., Ohio, in 1940.

**127. Stanley D.**[7] **Wood** (*Lena*[6] *Rickabaugh*, *Emily*[5] *Cheney*, *Mary Margaret*[4] *Pagan*, *John*[3], *Andrew*[2], *James*[1]) was born on December 10, 1894, in Perry Twp., Gallia Co., Ohio. He was the son of David C. Wood and Lena Rickabaugh (48). Stanley D. died in Gallipolis, Gallipolis Twp., Gallia Co., Ohio, on November 7, 1978, at age 83. He was buried in Mound Hill Cemetery, Gallipolis, Gallipolis Twp., Gallia Co., Ohio.[10]

He married **Anise Jones.** They had one son. Anise Jones was born in Perry Twp., Gallia Co., Ohio, on November 12, 1900. Anise reached age 93 and died in Gallipolis, Gallipolis Twp., Gallia Co., Ohio?, on February 14, 1994. She was buried in Mound Hill Cemetery, Gallipolis, Gallipolis Twp., Gallia Co., Ohio.[10]

Son of Stanley D. Wood and Anise Jones:

+ 239  m  I.  **Ray D.[8] Wood** was born in Perry Twp., Gallia Co., Ohio, on March 10, 1936.

128. **Rita Pearl[7] Wood** (*Lena[6] Rickabaugh, Emily[5] Cheney, Mary Margaret[4] Pagan, John[3], Andrew[2], James[1]*) was born on November 24, 1897, in Perry Twp., Gallia Co., Ohio. She was the daughter of David C. Wood and Lena Rickabaugh (48). Rita Pearl resided in 1954 in Chillicothe, Scioto Twp., Ross Co., Ohio. She lived in Baumville, Twin Twp., Ross Co., Ohio in 1974. Rita Pearl died in a facility in Circleville, Pickaway Co., Ohio, on April 17, 1974, at age 76. She was buried in Twin Township Cemetery, Bourneville, Twin Twp., Ross Co., Ohio.[62]

May have been childless.

Rita Pearl married **Thomas Edward Baum** on December 25, 1929, at Vol. 16, pg. 536, #8645 in Gallia Co., Ohio. Thomas Edward Baum was born in Bourneville, Twin Twp., Ross Co., Ohio, on July 17, 1886. He was also known as **Edward.** Thomas Edward reached age 67 and died in Chillicothe, Scioto Twp., Ross Co., Ohio, on January 19, 1954. He was buried in Twin Township Cemetery, Bourneville, Twin Twp., Ross Co., Ohio.[62]

129. **Lillian May[7] Wood** (*Lena[6] Rickabaugh, Emily[5] Cheney, Mary Margaret[4] Pagan, John[3], Andrew[2], James[1]*) was born on September 19, 1899, in Perry Twp., Gallia Co., Ohio. She was the daughter of David C. Wood and Lena Rickabaugh (48). Lillian May lived in Logan, Falls Twp., Hocking Co., Ohio in 1981. She died in a hospital in Columbus, Franklin Co., Ohio, on November 13, 1981, at age 82.

Lillian May married **Hollis McMillin** on December 22, 1928, in Gallia Co., Ohio. They had three sons. Hollis McMillin was born in Ewington, Huntington Twp., Gallia Co., Ohio, on January 27, 1904. Hollis reached age 77 and died in Logan, Falls Twp., Hocking Co., Ohio, on February 14, 1981.

Sons of Lillian May Wood and Hollis McMillin:

+ 240  m  I.  **Earl Byron[8] McMillin** was born in Huntington Twp., Gallia Co., Ohio, on August 26, 1929. He died in Chillicothe, Scioto Twp., Ross Co., Ohio, on January 26, 2006. Earl Byron was buried in Twin Township Cemetery, Bourneville, Twin Twp., Ross Co., Ohio.[62]

+ 241  m  II.  **Carroll Dean[8] McMillin** was born in Huntington Twp., Gallia Co., Ohio, on December 26, 1930.

+ 242  m  III.  **Marvin Lee[8] McMillin** was born in Huntington Twp., Gallia Co., Ohio, on October 26, 1936. He died in Logan, Falls Twp., Hocking Co., Ohio, on May 20, 1987. Marvin Lee was buried in Fairview Methodist Cemetery, Good Hope Twp., Hocking Co., Ohio.[105]

130. **Ethel Emily[7] Wood** (*Lena[6] Rickabaugh, Emily[5] Cheney, Mary Margaret[4] Pagan, John[3], Andrew[2], James[1]*) was born on May 22, 1902, in Perry Twp., Gallia Co., Ohio. She was the daughter of David C. Wood and Lena Rickabaugh (48). Ethel Emily lived in Hilliard, Franklin Co., Ohio in 2000. She died in Westerville, Blendon Twp., Franklin Co., Ohio, on March 10, 2000, at age 97. Ethel Emily was buried in Harrison Township Cemetery, South Bloomfield, Harrison Twp., Pickaway Co., Ohio.[63]

Ethel Emily married **Alfred Frederick Axe** in Stark Co., Ohio? They had two daughters. Alfred Frederick Axe was born in Pennsylvania on April 30, 1900. Alfred Frederick lived in Hilliard,

Franklin Co., Ohio in 2000. He reached age 100 and died in Westerville, Blendon Twp., Franklin Co., Ohio, on August 10, 2000. Alfred Frederick was buried in Harrison Township Cemetery, South Bloomfield, Harrison Twp., Pickaway Co., Ohio.[63]

Daughters of Ethel Emily Wood and Alfred Frederick Axe:

+ 243 f I. **Shirley L.[8] Axe** was born in Perry Twp., Carroll Co., Ohio, on October 17, 1933. She died in a hospital in Columbus, Franklin Co., Ohio, on March 5, 1988. Shirley L. was buried in Harrison Township Cemetery, South Bloomfield, Harrison Twp., Pickaway Co., Ohio.[63]

+ 244 f II. **Doris E.[8] Axe** was born in Steubenville, Cross Creek Twp., Jefferson Co., Ohio, on October 29, 1937. She died in Columbus, Franklin Co., Ohio, on September 10, 2014. Doris E. was buried in Harrison Township Cemetery, South Bloomfield, Harrison Twp., Pickaway Co., Ohio.[63]

**131. Evelyn Odessa[7] Wood** (*Lena[6] Rickabaugh, Emily[5] Cheney, Mary Margaret[4] Pagan, John[3], Andrew[2], James[1]*) was born on September 2, 1910, in Perry Twp., Gallia Co., Ohio. She was the daughter of David C. Wood and Lena Rickabaugh (48). Evelyn Odessa died in Perry Twp., Gallia Co., Ohio, on May 16, 1913, at age two. She was buried in Old Pine Cemetery, Rio Grande, Raccoon Twp., Gallia Co., Ohio.[6]

**132. Medrith Marie[7] Massie** (*Hattie[6] Rickabaugh, Emily[5] Cheney, Mary Margaret[4] Pagan, John[3], Andrew[2], James[1]*) was born on February 18, 1895, in Perry Twp., Gallia Co., Ohio. She was the daughter of Benjamin Massie and Hattie Rickabaugh (49). Medrith Marie died in Columbus, Franklin Co., Ohio, on November 24, 1979, at age 84. She was buried in Green Lawn Cemetery, Columbus, Franklin Co., Ohio.[56]

Medrith Marie married **William Emmett Lewis** on June 18, 1919, in Jackson Co., Ohio. They had one son. William Emmett Lewis was born in Columbus, Franklin Co., Ohio, on September 27, 1894. William Emmett reached age 35 and died in Columbus, Franklin Co., Ohio, on January 2, 1930. He was buried in Green Lawn Cemetery, Columbus, Franklin Co., Ohio.[56]

Son of Medrith Marie Massie and William Emmett Lewis:

+ 245 m I. **William Emmett[8] Lewis II** was born in Columbus, Franklin Co., Ohio, on October 7, 1923.

**133. Alfred Delver[7] Massie** (*Hattie[6] Rickabaugh, Emily[5] Cheney, Mary Margaret[4] Pagan, John[3], Andrew[2], James[1]*) was born on December 12, 1896, in Perry Twp., Gallia Co., Ohio. He was the son of Benjamin Massie and Hattie Rickabaugh (49). Alfred Delver died in Waterford, Waterford Twp., Washington Co., Ohio, on May 16, 1975, at age 78. He was buried in Beverly Cemetery, Beverly, Center Twp., Washington Co., Ohio.[64]

May have been childless.

Alfred Delver married **Sara J. Bell** on December 22, 1945, in Washington Co., Ohio. Sara J. Bell was born in Waterford, Waterford Twp., Washington Co., Ohio, on February 10, 1910. Sara J. reached age 92 and died in Waterford, Waterford Twp., Washington Co., Ohio, on January 31, 2003. She was buried in Beverly Cemetery, Beverly, Center Twp., Washington Co., Ohio.[63]

**134. John Orville[7] Massie** (*Hattie[6] Rickabaugh, Emily[5] Cheney, Mary Margaret[4] Pagan, John[3], Andrew[2], James[1]*) was born on November 9, 1898, in Perry Twp., Gallia Co., Ohio. He was the son of Benjamin Massie and Hattie Rickabaugh (49). He resided in 1940 in Youngstown, Mahoning Co., Ohio. John Orville died in Buffalo, Erie Co., New York, on November 6, 1958, at age 59.

John Orville married **Vera Caroline Smith** on June 11, 1924, in Franklin Co., Ohio. They had one daughter. Vera Caroline Smith was born in

Bucyrus, Bucyrus Twp., Crawford Co., Ohio, on September 26, 1900. Vera Caroline reached age 51 and died in Pittsburgh, Allegheny Co., Pennsylvania, on September 9, 1952.

Daughter of John Orville Massie and Vera Caroline Smith:

+ 246　f　I.　**Marilyn S.**[8] **Massie** was born in Youngstown, Mahoning Co., Ohio, about 1938.

**135. Raymond Neil**[7] **Massie** (*Hattie*[6] *Rickabaugh, Emily*[5] *Cheney, Mary Margaret*[4] *Pagan, John*[3], *Andrew*[2], *James*[1]) was born on March 21, 1901, in Perry Twp., Gallia Co., Ohio. He was the son of Benjamin Massie and Hattie Rickabaugh (49). Raymond Neil lived in Indianapolis, Marion Co., Indiana in 1940. He resided in 1949 in Birmingham, Jefferson Co., Alabama. Raymond Neil died in Birmingham, Jefferson Co., Alabama?, on December 12, 1954, at age 53.

He married **Melba Fern Sievenpiper.** They had one son. Melba Fern Sievenpiper was born in Clinton Twp., Lincoln Co., Ontario, Canada, on May 30, 1909. Melba Fern reached age 97 and died in Prescott, Yavapai Co., Arizona, on February 21, 2007.

Her name was Melba Fern Mitchell when she died.

Son of Raymond Neil Massie and Melba Fern Sievenpiper:

+ 247　m　I.　**Ben**[8] **Massie** was born in Indianapolis, Marion Co., Indiana?, on February 24, 1938.

**136. Golden Odessa**[7] **Massie** (*Hattie*[6] *Rickabaugh, Emily*[5] *Cheney, Mary Margaret*[4] *Pagan, John*[3], *Andrew*[2], *James*[1]) was born on November 21, 1904, in Wellston, Wellston Twp., Jackson Co., Ohio. She was the daughter of Benjamin Massie and Hattie Rickabaugh (49). Golden Odessa died in Columbus, Franklin Co., Ohio, on December 30, 1987, at age 83.

Golden Odessa married **Earl J. Brothers** on July 16, 1927, in Franklin Co., Ohio. They had one

daughter. Earl J. Brothers was born in Princeton, Patoka Twp., Gibson Co., Indiana, on July 26, 1903. Earl J. reached age 63 and died in Columbus, Franklin Co., Ohio, on March 21, 1967.

Daughter of Golden Odessa Massie and Earl J. Brothers:

+ 248　f　I.　**Emily A.**[8] **Brothers** was born in Columbus, Franklin Co., Ohio, on January 8, 1928. She died on December 31, 1976 in Gahanna, Mifflin Twp., Franklin Co., Ohio.

**137. Ben Edgar**[7] **Massie** (*Hattie*[6] *Rickabaugh, Emily*[5] *Cheney, Mary Margaret*[4] *Pagan, John*[3], *Andrew*[2], *James*[1]) was born on March 6, 1908, in Wellston, Wellston Twp., Jackson Co., Ohio. He was also known as **Edgar B..** He was the son of Benjamin Massie and Hattie Rickabaugh (49). Ben Edgar died in Toledo, Lucas Co., Ohio, on March 11, 1947, at age 39. He was buried in Glen Rest Memorial Estate Cemetery, Reynoldsburg, Truro Twp., Franklin Co., Ohio.[24]

Childless.

Ben Edgar married **Doris Glick** on January 1, 1937. Doris Glick was born in Arlington, Madison Twp., Hancock Co., Ohio, on January 18, 1916. Doris reached age 89 and died in Toledo, Lucas Co., Ohio, on August 9, 2005. She was buried in Glen Rest Memorial Estate Cemetery, Reynoldsburg, Truro Twp., Franklin Co., Ohio.[24]

**138. Marlin L.**[7] **Cheney** (*John Leonard*[6], *Silas B.*[5], *Mary Margaret*[4] *Pagan, John*[3], *Andrew*[2], *James*[1]) was born on April 19, 1908, in Guyan Twp., Gallia Co., Ohio. He was the son of John Leonard Cheney (51) and Ella Malinda May Day (Eugenia). Marlin L. died in Dayton, Montgomery Co., Ohio, on September 21, 1966, at age 58. He was buried in Dayton National Cemetery, Dayton, Montgomery Co., Ohio.[66]

Seems to have never married.

Oddly, Marlin Cheney, unmarried, is listed as a female in the 1930 census; he is living with his stepfather James Stovall and mother Ella Malinda May "Linny"/Eugenia Day Cheney Stovall in Evansville, Indiana.

**139. Mary Virginia**[7] **Cheney** (*John Leonard*[6], *Silas B.*[5], *Mary Margaret*[4] *Pagan*, *John*[3], *Andrew*[2], *James*[1]) was born on January 21, 1909, in Gallipolis, Gallipolis Twp., Gallia Co., Ohio. She was the daughter of John Leonard Cheney (51) and Ella Malinda May Day (Eugenia). Mary Virginia died in Gallipolis, Gallipolis Twp., Gallia Co., Ohio, on May 16, 1909. She was buried in Mound Hill Cemetery, Gallipolis, Gallipolis Twp., Gallia Co., Ohio.[10]

**140. Frances**[7] **Cheney** (*John Leonard*[6], *Silas B.*[5], *Mary Margaret*[4] *Pagan*, *John*[3], *Andrew*[2], *James*[1]) was born on October 1, 1910, in Guyan Twp., Gallia Co., Ohio. She was the daughter of John Leonard Cheney (51) and Ella Malinda May Day (Eugenia). Frances lived in 1939 in Evansville, Vanderburgh Co., Indiana. She died after 1939.

Frances married **Otis Gentry** after 1930. They divorced. Otis Gentry was born in Skelton Twp. Warrick Co., Indiana, on May 19, 1904. He lived in Michigan City, Michigan Twp., LaPorte Co., Indiana in 1940. Otis reached age 66 and died in Evansville, Vanderburgh Co., Indiana, on March 29, 1971. He was buried in Oak Hill Cemetery, Evansville, Vanderburgh Co., Indiana.[106]

Otis Gentry was incarcerated in the Indiana State Prison in Michigan City, Indiana in 1940.

**141. James C.**[7] **Cheney** (*John Leonard*[6], *Silas B.*[5], *Mary Margaret*[4] *Pagan*, *John*[3], *Andrew*[2], *James*[1]) was born on January 7, 1915, in Guyan Twp., Gallia Co., Ohio. He was the son of John Leonard Cheney (51) and Ella Malinda May Day (Eugenia). James C. died in Evansville, Vanderburgh Co., Indiana, on July 13, 1937, at age 22. He was buried in Mound Hill Cemetery, Gallipolis, Gallipolis Twp., Gallia Co., Ohio.[10]

Never married.

**142. Lillie Mae**[7] **Cheney** (*John Leonard*[6], *Silas B.*[5], *Mary Margaret*[4] *Pagan*, *John*[3], *Andrew*[2], *James*[1]) was born on May 6, 1920, in Pikeville, Pike Co., Kentucky. She was the daughter of John Leonard Cheney (51) and Georgia Hylton. Lillie Mae lived before 1996 in Lancaster, Fairfield Co., Ohio. She died in Point Pleasant, Mason Co., West Virginia, on August 3, 1996, at age 76. Lillie Mae was buried in Mound Hill Cemetery, Gallipolis, Gallipolis Twp., Gallia Co., Ohio.[10]

Never married.

**143. John**[7] **Cheney II** (*John Leonard*[6], *Silas B.*[5], *Mary Margaret*[4] *Pagan*, *John*[3], *Andrew*[2], *James*[1]) was born on January 28, 1922, in Gallipolis, Gallipolis Twp., Gallia Co., Ohio. He was also known as **Junior.** He was the son of John Leonard Cheney (51) and Georgia Hylton. John died in Gallipolis, Gallipolis Twp., Gallia Co., Ohio, on January 18, 2004, at age 81.

Seems to have never married.

**144. Enabelle**[7] **Cheney** (*John Leonard*[6], *Silas B.*[5], *Mary Margaret*[4] *Pagan*, *John*[3], *Andrew*[2], *James*[1]) was born on July 20, 1924, in Gallipolis, Gallipolis Twp., Gallia Co., Ohio. She was the daughter of John Leonard Cheney (51) and Georgia Hylton. Enabelle died in Point Pleasant, Mason Co., West Virginia, on December 7, 2008, at age 84. She was buried in Lone Oak Cemetery, Point Pleasant, Mason Co., West Virginia.[67]

Enbelle Cheney See's birth record says her original given name was Georgia.

Enabelle married **Russell M. See** after 1940. They had four children. Russell M. See was born in Point Pleasant, Mason Co., West Virginia, on August 3, 1914. Russell M. reached age 71 and died in Point Pleasant, Mason Co., West Virginia, on April 23, 1986. He was buried in Lone Oak Cemetery, Point Pleasant, Mason Co., West Virginia.[67]

Enabelle Cheney and Russell M. See had four children, including:

+ 249 f I. **Sharon Lyn**[8] **See** was born in Gallipolis, Gallipolis Twp., Gallia Co., Ohio, on March 24, 1948. She died in Point Pleasant, Mason Co., West Virginia, on October 15, 2003. Sharon Lyn was buried in Kirkland Memorial Gardens Cemetery, Point Pleasant, Mason Co., West Virginia.[107]

**145. Jennie Ellen[7] Cheney** (*John Leonard[6], Silas B.[5], Mary Margaret[4] Pagan, John[3], Andrew[2], James[1]*) was born on July 6, 1927, in Gallipolis, Gallipolis Twp., Gallia Co., Ohio. She was also known as **Dottie.** She was the daughter of John Leonard Cheney (51) and Georgia Hylton.

She married **Freeman Paul Locke II.** Freeman Paul Locke II was born in Roxton, Lamar Co., Texas, on November 1, 1929. Freeman Paul reached age 65 and died in Gallipolis, Gallipolis Twp., Gallia Co., Ohio, on August 30, 1995. He was buried in Mound Hill Cemetery, Gallipolis, Gallipolis Twp., Gallia Co., Ohio.[10]

**146. Ray Leonard[7] Cheney** (*John Leonard[6], Silas B.[5], Mary Margaret[4] Pagan, John[3], Andrew[2], James[1]*) was born on September 29, 1929, in Gallipolis, Gallipolis Twp., Gallia Co., Ohio. He was the son of John Leonard Cheney (51) and Georgia Hylton. Ray Leonard died in Gallipolis, Gallipolis Twp., Gallia Co., Ohio, on September 29, 1997, at age 68. He was buried in Campaign Cemetery, Addison Twp., Gallia Co., Ohio.[68]

Ray Leonard married **Grace Irene Baird** on April 15, 1955, in Gallia Co., Ohio. They had five children. Grace Irene Baird was born in Addison Twp., Gallia Co., Ohio, on July 31, 1929. Grace Irene reached age 85 and died in Gallipolis, Gallipolis Twp., Gallia Co., Ohio, on January 1, 2015. She was buried in Campaign Cemetery, Addison Twp., Gallia Co., Ohio.[68]

Ray Leonard Cheney and Grace Irene Baird had five children, including:

+ 250  f  II.  **Nancy Sue[8] Cheney** was born in Gallipolis, Gallipolis Twp., Gallia Co., Ohio, on October 4, 1958. She died in Gallipolis, Gallipolis Twp., Gallia Co., Ohio, on January 4, 1959. Nancy Sue was buried in Campaign Cemetery, Addison Twp., Gallia Co., Ohio.[68]

**147. Carl Safford[7] Cheney** (*John Leonard[6], Silas B.[5], Mary Margaret[4] Pagan, John[3], Andrew[2], James[1]*) was born on November 1, 1931, in Gallipolis, Gallipolis Twp., Gallia Co., Ohio. He was the son of John Leonard Cheney (51) and Georgia Hylton. Carl Safford died in Gallipolis, Gallipolis Twp., Gallia Co., Ohio, on January 30, 2017, at age 85. He was buried in Mound Hill Cemetery, Gallipolis, Gallipolis Twp., Gallia Co., Ohio.[10]

He married **Sara L. Unknown.** They divorced. They had four sons. Sara L. Unknown was born on September 17, 1938.

**148. Marguerite[7] Elder** (*Pearl[6] Cheney, Silas B.[5], Mary Margaret[4] Pagan, John[3], Andrew[2], James[1]*) was born on April 27, 1901, in Gallipolis, Gallipolis Twp., Gallia Co., Ohio. She was the daughter of Harry Elder and Pearl Cheney (52). Marguerite died in Lakeland, Polk Co., Florida, on February 4, 1985, at age 83.

May have been childless.

Marguerite married **John M. Hewitt** on September 12, 1931, in Ohio Co., West Virginia. They may have divorced. John M. Hewitt was born in Baltimore, Baltimore Co., Maryland?, on November 18, 1903. John M. reached age 66 and died in Panama City, Bay Co., Florida?, on May 18, 1970.

**149. Harley Lawrence[7] Elder** (*Pearl[6] Cheney, Silas B.[5], Mary Margaret[4] Pagan, John[3], Andrew[2], James[1]*) was born on July 31, 1906, in Gallipolis, Gallipolis Twp., Gallia Co., Ohio. He was the son of Harry Elder and Pearl Cheney (52). Harley Lawrence lived in Lakeland, Polk Co., Florida in 1977. He died in a hospital in Tampa, Hillsborough Co., Florida, on October 7, 1977, at age 71.

Childless.

Harley Lawrence married **Bertha L. Harrington** on July 9, 1933, in Licking Co., Ohio. They divorced. Bertha L. Harrington was born in Newark, Newark Twp., Licking Co., Ohio, on January 9, 1909. She reached age 80 and died as Bertha Long in Newark, Newark Twp., Licking Co., Ohio, on August 5, 1989.

Harley Lawrence Elder married **Nell Frances Everett** on November 13, 1938, in Pleasants Co., West Virginia. They divorced. Nell Frances Everett was born in Zanesville, Muskingham Co., Ohio, on April 8, 1906. She was also known as **Dolly.**

Nell Frances reached age 73 and died under the name Dolly Everett in Zanesville, Muskingham Co., Ohio, on June 1, 1979. She was buried in Tod Homestead Cemetery, Youngstown, Mahoning Co., Ohio.[108]

**150. Michael J. McKay[7] Kiely** (*Margaret Genevieve[6] Cheney, Silas B.[5], Mary Margaret[4] Pagan, John[3], Andrew[2], James[1]*) was born on April 11, 1919, in Ohio. He was the son of Jerome Michael Kiely and Margaret Genevieve Cheney (56). Michael J. McKay was adopted. He died in Newark, Newark Twp., Licking Co., Ohio, on December 2, 1964, at age 45. Michael J. McKay was buried in St. Joseph Cemetery, Newark, Licking Co., Ohio.[29]

Never married.

**151. Eva[7] Johnson** (*Rosalie or Roselia Catherine[6] King, Mary Ann[5] Pagan, John[4], John[3], Andrew[2], James[1]*) was born in 1870 in Ohio. She was the daughter of William T. Johnson and Rosalie or Roselia Catherine King (58).

**152. Lulu[7] Johnson** (*Rosalie or Roselia Catherine[6] King, Mary Ann[5] Pagan, John[4], John[3], Andrew[2], James[1]*) was born in 1874 in Ohio. She was the daughter of William T. Johnson and Rosalie or Roselia Catherine King (58).

**153. Son[7] Johnson** (*Rosalie or Roselia Catherine[6] King, Mary Ann[5] Pagan, John[4], John[3], Andrew[2], James[1]*) was born in 1880 in Beaver Twp., Pike Co., Ohio. He was the son of William T. Johnson and Rosalie or Roselia Catherine King (58).

**154. Bessie M.[7] Johnson** (*Rosalie or Roselia Catherine[6] King, Mary Ann[5] Pagan, John[4], John[3], Andrew[2], James[1]*) was born in July 1890 in Sedalia, Sedalia Twp., Pettis Co., Missouri. She was the daughter of William T. Johnson and Rosalie or Roselia Catherine King (58).

**155. Charles Freimel[7] King** (*John A.[6], Mary Ann[5] Pagan, John[4], John[3], Andrew[2], James[1]*) was born on September 28, 1891, in Kansas City, Jackson Co., Missouri. He was the son of John A. King (59) and Frances Louise Robinson. Charles Freimel died in Sedalia, Sedalia Twp., Pettis Co., Missouri, on January 24, 1985, at age 93. He was buried in Crown Hill Cemetery, Sedalia, Pettis Co., Missouri.[69]

Childless.

Charles Freimel married **Edna A. King** on May 29, 1919, in Johnson Co., Missouri. Edna A. King was born in Blackwater Twp., Saline Co., Missouri, on June 28, 1899. Edna A. reached age 74 and died in Sedalia, Sedalia Twp., Pettis Co., Missouri, on May 5, 1974. She was buried in Crown Hill Cemetery, Sedalia, Pettis Co., Missouri.[69]

**156. Claude Amil[7] King** (*John A.[6], Mary Ann[5] Pagan, John[4], John[3], Andrew[2], James[1]*) was born on September 27, 1893, in Kansas City, Jackson Co., Missouri? He was the son of John A. King (59) and Frances Louise Robinson. Claude Amil died in Los Angeles, Los Angeles Co., California, on December 18, 1971, at age 78. He was buried in Los Angeles National Cemetery, Los Angeles, Los Angeles Co., California.[70]

Claude Amil married **Blanche Ellen Wands** on March 11, 1925, in Jackson Co., Missouri. They divorced. They had one son. Blanche Ellen Wands was born in Camden, Ray Co., Missouri, on July 9, 1905. She reached age 86 and died in Los Angeles, Los Angeles Co., California, on August 6, 1991.

Son of Claude Amil King and Blanche Ellen Wands:

+ 251 m I.   **Claude Amil[8] King II** was born in Sedalia, Sedalia Twp., Pettis Co., Missouri, on January 3, 1931. He died in Burbank, Los Angeles Co., California, on November 5, 1987.

**157. Bob A.[7] King** (*John A.[6], Mary Ann[5] Pagan, John[4], John[3], Andrew[2], James[1]*) was born in September 1894 in Kansas City, Jackson Co., Missouri. He was the son of John A. King (59) and Frances Louise Robinson. Bob A. died in Kansas City, Jackson Co., Missouri, before 1910.

**158. Mary Ima[7] King** (*John A.[6], Mary Ann[5] Pagan, John[4], John[3], Andrew[2], James[1]*) was born on June 3, 1901, in Texas. She was the daughter of John A. King (59) and Frances Louise Robinson. Mary Ima died in Laguna Hills, Orange Co., California, on February 17, 1996, at age 94.

Mary Ima married **Daniel William Markham** on June 8, 1921, in Pettis Co., Missouri. They divorced. They had two children. Daniel William Markham was born in Grand Rapids, Grand Rapids Twp., Kent Co., Michigan, on April 17, 1890. He reached age 66 and died in Fulton, Callaway Co., Missouri, on April 24, 1956. Daniel William was buried in Jefferson City National Cemetery, Jefferson City, Cole Co., Missouri.[109]

Mary Ima King Markham married **Irwin Arthur Title** after 1956. Irwin Arthur Title was born in Cleveland Cuyahoga Co., Ohio, on June 2, 1901. Irwin Arthur reached age 77 and died in Poway, San Diego Co., California, on December 5, 1978.

Children of Mary Ima King and Daniel William Markham:

+ 252 m I. **Stephen L.[8] Markham** was born in Sedalia, Sedalia Twp., Pettis Co., Missouri, on July 10, 1922.

+ 253 f II. **Mary Frances Helen[8] Markham** was born in Sedalia, Sedalia Twp., Pettis Co., Missouri, on March 4, 1924. She died in Laguna Hills, Orange Co., California, on November 6, 2007.

**159. Child[7] King** (*John A.[6], Mary Ann[5] Pagan, John[4], John[3], Andrew[2], James[1]*) was born between 1900 and 1910 in Kansas City, Jackson Co., Missouri. He or she was a child of John A. King (59) and Frances Louise Robinson. Child One died in Kansas City, Jackson Co., Missouri, between 1900 and 1910.

**160. Inez Edith[7] Ballard** (*Effie Virginia[6] King, Mary Ann[5] Pagan, John[4], John[3], Andrew[2], James[1]*) was born on March 30, 1881, in Beaver Twp., Pike Co., Ohio. She was the daughter of Arlington P. Ballard and Effie Virginia King (60). Inez Edith died in Los Angeles, Los Angeles Co., California, on February 11, 1936, at age 54. She was buried in Forest Lawn Memorial Park Cemetery, Glendale, Los Angeles Co., California.[30]

Inez Edith married **Byron Chauncey Armstrong** on May 2, 1901, in Fayette Co., Ohio. They had two children. Byron Chauncey Armstrong was born in Union City, Branch Co., Michigan?, on December 30, 1871. Byron Chauncey reached age 91 and died in Ventura Co., California, on September 28, 1963. He was buried in Forest Lawn Memorial Park Cemetery, Glendale, Los Angeles Co., California.[30]

Children of Inez Edith Ballard and Byron Chauncey Armstrong:

+ 254 m I. **Arthur Wright[8] Armstrong** was born in Washington Court House, Union Twp., Fayette Co., Ohio, on December 7, 1906. He died in Los Angeles, Los Angeles Co., California, on August 11, 1978. Arthur Wright was buried in Los Angeles National Cemetery, Los Angeles, Los Angeles Co., California.[70]

+ 255 f II. **Mary Virginia[8] Armstrong** was born in Washington Court House, Union Twp., Fayette Co., Ohio, on July 26, 1908. She died in El Monte, Los Angeles Co., California?, on February 11, 1995. Mary Virginia was buried in Forest Lawn Memorial Park Cemetery, Glendale, Los Angeles Co., California.[30]

**161. Anna Mae[7] Ballard** (*Effie Virginia[6] King, Mary Ann[5] Pagan, John[4], John[3], Andrew[2], James[1]*) was born on March 14, 1882, in Beaver Twp., Pike Co., Ohio. She was the daughter of Arlington P. Ballard and Effie Virginia King (60). Anna Mae died in Mechanicsburg, Goshen Twp., Champaign Co., Ohio, on May 2, 1918, at age 36. She was buried in Maple Grove Cemetery, Mechanicsburg, Goshen Twp., Champaign Co., Ohio.[72]

Anna Mae married **Floyd Jobe** on June 8, 1904, in Fayette Co., Ohio. They had two children. Floyd Jobe was born in West Union, Tiffin Twp., Adams Co., Ohio, on December 10, 1884. Floyd reached age 71 and died in Mt. Vernon, Knox Co., Ohio, on October 2, 1956. He was buried in Maple Grove Cemetery, Mechanicsburg, Goshen Twp., Champaign Co., Ohio.[72]

In 1930, both of Floyd and Anna Mae Ballard Jobe's children, Charles and Helen, were living in The Pythian Home, an orphanage in Springfield, Ohio.

Children of Anna Mae Ballard and Floyd Jobe:

+ 256 m I. **Charles Edward⁸ Jobe** was born in Washington Court House, Union Twp., Fayette Co., Ohio, on October 13, 1906. He died in Dayton, Montgomery Co., Ohio, on December 25, 1943. Charles Edward was buried in Maple Grove Cemetery, Mechanicsburg, Goshen Twp., Champaign Co., Ohio.[72]

+ 257 f II. **Helen V.⁸ Jobe** was born in Springfield, Springfield Twp., Clark Co., Ohio, on April 22, 1908. She died in a hospital in Columbus, Franklin Co., Ohio, on June 29, 1992. She was buried in Washington Cemetery, Washington Court House, Fayette Co., Ohio.[110]

**162. Edna Opal⁷ Ballard** (*Effie Virginia⁶ King, Mary Ann⁵ Pagan, John⁴, John³, Andrew², James¹*) was born on November 12, 1888, in Jeffersonville, Jefferson Twp., Fayette Co., Ohio. She was the daughter of Arlington P. Ballard and Effie Virginia King (60). Edna Opal died on July 3, 1926, in Los Angeles, Los Angeles Co., California at age 37. She was buried in Forest Lawn Memorial Park Cemetery, Glendale, Los Angeles Co., California.[30]

Opal married **Edwin Byron Morehouse** on January 28, 1913, in Clark Co., Ohio. They had one son. Edwin B. Morehouse was born in Springfield, Springfield Twp., Clark Co., Ohio, on April 27, 1887. He reached age 69 and died on October 18, 1956 in Los Angeles, Los Angeles Co., California.

Son of Edna Opal Ballard and Edwin Byron Morehouse:

+ 258 m I. **John Franklin⁸ Morehouse** was born on August 13, 1917 in Springfield, Springfield Twp., Clark Co., Ohio. He died on June 11, 2004 in Los Alamitos, Orange Co., California. John Franklin was buried in Forest Lawn Memorial Park Cemetery, Cypress, Orange Co., California.[111]

**163. Ronald⁷ Ballard** (*Effie Virginia⁶ King, Mary Ann⁵ Pagan, John⁴, John³, Andrew², James¹*) was born on April 9, 1893, in Jeffersonville, Jefferson Twp., Fayette Co., Ohio. He was the son of Arlington P. Ballard and Effie Virginia King (60). Ronald died after 1917.

Ronald married **Minnie Miller** on May 30, 1914, in Clark Co., Ohio. They had at least one child. Minnie Miller was born in Springfield, Springfield Twp., Clark Co., Ohio, on December 6, 1897. She died after 1920.

When he registers for the WWI draft in 1917, Ronald A. Ballard is a prisoner in the Ohio State Penitentiary in Wittenburg, Clark Co., Ohio. He says he is married with two children.

Children of Ronald A. Ballard and Minnie Miller:

+ 259 m I. **Child⁸ Ballard** was born in Springfield, Springfield Twp., Clark Co., Ohio?, before 1917.

+ 260 m II. **Clint⁸ Ballard** was born in Springfield, Springfield Twp., Clark Co., Ohio, on February 15, 1917.

**164. Child One⁷ Johnson** (*William Roosevelt⁶, John J.⁵, Catherine⁴ Pagan, John³, Andrew², James¹*) was born between 1880 and 1900. He or she was a child of William Roosevelt Johnson (66) and Julia Linda Paxton. Child One died between 1880 and 1900.

**165. Child Two⁷ Johnson** (*William Roosevelt⁶, John J.⁵, Catherine⁴ Pagan, John³, Andrew², James¹*) was born between 1880 and 1900. He or she was a child of William Roosevelt Johnson (66) and Julia Linda Paxton. Child Two died between 1880 and 1900.

**166. Child Three**[7] **Johnson** (*William Roosevelt*[6], *John J.*[5], *Catherine*[4] *Pagan, John*[3], *Andrew*[2], *James*[1]) was born between 1880 and 1900. He or she was a child of William Roosevelt Johnson (66) and Julia Linda Paxton. Child Three died between 1880 and 1900.

**167. John Edward**[7] **Johnson** (*William Roosevelt*[6], *John J.*[5], *Catherine*[4] *Pagan, John*[3], *Andrew*[2], *James*[1]) was born on February 27, 1881, in Charleston, Kanawha Co., West Virginia. He was also known as **Edd.** He was the son of William Roosevelt Johnson (66) and Julia Linda Paxton. John Edward lived in Stevenson, Skamania Co., Washington in 1942. John E. died in Monument, Grant Co., Oregon, on October 4, 1952, at age 71. He was buried in Monument Cemetery, Monument, Grant Co., Oregon.[36]

He married **Ada Maud McNutt** on June 3, 1903 in Wood Co., Oklahoma. They had seven children. Ada Maud McNutt was born in Pratt Co., Kansas, on January 6, 1888. Ada Maud reached age 30 and died in Hamilton, Grant Co., Oregon, on December 16, 1918. She was buried in Monument Cemetery, Monument, Grant Co., Oregon.[36]

John Edward Johnson married **Estella May Copeland** on June 20, 1920, in Grant Co., Oregon. They had four children. Estella May Copeland was born in Redding, Shasta Co., California, on October 7, 1900. She was also known as **Stella May.** Estella May reached age 83 and died in Bend, Deschutes Co., Oregon, on April 11, 1984. She was buried in Pilot Butte Cemetery, Bend, Deschutes Co., Oregon.[112]

Children of John Edward Johnson and Ada Maud McNutt:

+ 261 m I. **Earnest Willard**[8] **Johnson** was born in Cleo, Wood Co., Oklahoma on October 10, 1904. He died in Crook Co., Oregon, on June 12, 1985. Earnest Willard was buried in Monument Cemetery, Monument, Grant Co., Oregon.[36]

+ 262 m II. **Everett E.**[8] **Johnson** was born in Ward, Wheeler Co., Oregon, on September 5, 1906. He died in Juneau, Juneau Bureau, Alaska, on September 4, 1971. Everett E. was buried in Monument Cemetery, Monument, Grant Co., Oregon.[36]

+ 263 m III. **Lawrence A.**[8] **Johnson** was born in Lone Rock Place, Klamath Co., Oregon, on September 29, 1908. He died in Klamath Co. Oregon on March 8, 2007. Lawrence A. was buried in Monument Cemetery, Monument, Grant Co., Oregon.[36]

+ 264 f IV. **Ethel**[8] **Johnson** was born in Ward, Wheeler Co., Oregon, in 1910. She died after 1920.

+ 265 m V. **Bertrim**[8] **Johnson** was born in Monument, Grant Co., Oregon, on January 5, 1912. He died in Grant Co., Oregon, on October 19, 1930. Bertrim was buried in Monument Cemetery, Monument, Grant Co., Oregon.[36]

+ 266 f VI. **Myrtle Grace**[8] **Johnson** was born in Monument, Grant Co., Oregon, on December 11, 1915. She was also known as **Grace.** Myrtle Grace died in Missoula, Missoula Co., Montana, on October 10, 1999.

+ 267 m VII. **Willard L.**[8] **Johnson** was born in Monument, Grant Co., Oregon, in September 1916. He died in Pine Forest, Deschutes Co., Oregon?, after 1940.

Children of John Edward Johnson and Estella May

Copeland:

+ 268 f I. **Ruthellen**[8] **Johnson** was born in Monument, Grant Co., Oregon, on January 7, 1922. She died in Portland, Multnomah Co., Oregon, on June 8, 1961. Ruthellen was buried in Lincoln Memorial Park Cemetery, Portland, Multnomah Co., Oregon.[113]

+ 269 f II. **Dorothy Viola**[8] **Johnson** was born in Mount Vernon, Grant Co., Oregon, on June 2, 1924. She died in Sandpoint, Bonner Co., Idaho, on March 6, 2001. Dorothy Viola was buried in Pilot Butte Cemetery, Bend, Deschutes Co., Oregon.[112]

+ 270 f III. **Isabelle Rosemary**[8] **Johnson** was born in Monument, Grant Co., Oregon, on April 9, 1927. She was also known as **Billie.** Isabelle Rose mary died in Bend, Deschutes Co., Oregon, on June 20, 2008. She was buried in Pilot Butte Cemetery, Bend, Deschutes Co., Oregon.[112]

+ 271 m IV. **Kenneth Eugene**[8] **Johnson** was born in Dayville, Grant Co., Oregon, on December 20, 1929. He died in Portland, Multnomah Co., Oregon, on February 21, 1995. Kenneth Eugene was buried in Pilot Butte Cemetery, Bend, Deschutes Co., Oregon.[112]

**168. Viola**[7] **Johnson** (*William Roosevelt*[6], *John J.*[5], *Catherine*[4] *Pagan, John*[3], *Andrew*[2], *James*[1]) was born on September 18, 1884, in Sioux City, Sioux City Twp., Woodbury Co., Iowa. She was the daughter of William Roosevelt Johnson (66) and Julia Linda Paxton. Viola died after 1900.

**169. Memphis Mason**[7] **Johnson** (*William Roosevelt*[6], *John J.*[5], *Catherine*[4] *Pagan, John*[3], *Andrew*[2], *James*[1]) was born on April 1, 1889, in Union Twp., Madison Co., Ohio. He was also known

as **Mason.** He was the son of William Roosevelt Johnson (66) and Julia Linda Paxton. Memphis Mason lived in North Bend, Coos Co., Oregon in 1920. He resided in 1930 in Laguna, Imperial Co., California. Memphis Mason died in Yarnell, Yavapai Co., Arizona, on May 31, 1965, at age 76. He was buried in Genung Memorial Park Cemetery, Peeples Valley, Yavapai Co., Arizona.[67]

Memphis Mason married **Ora Jane Caroline Wilson** on September 23, 1912, in Douglas Co., Oregon. They had three sons. Ora Jane Caroline Wilson was born in Delaware Co., Oklahoma, on September 12, 1894. Ora Jane Caroline reached age 89 and died in Prescott, Yavapai Co., Arizona, on November 2, 1983. She was buried in Genung Memorial Park Cemetery, Peeples Valley, Yavapai Co., Arizona.[73]

In 1900, Ora Wilson's family was living in Township 26, Cherokee Indian Territory, which is now Delaware Co., Oklahoma.

Sons of Memphis Mason Johnson and Ora Jane Caroline Wilson:

+ 272 m I. **Cecil Edward**[8] **Johnson** was born in Lone Rock, Gilliam Co., Oregon, on December 5, 1913. He was also known as **Shorty.** Cecil Edward died in Aztec, San Juan Co., New Mexico, on April 6, 1974. He was buried in Aztec Community Cemetery, Aztec, San Juan Co., New Mexico.[114]

+ 273 m II. **Marvin Earl**[8] **Johnson** was born in Roseburg, Douglas Co., Oregon, on August 1, 1915. He died in Paradise, Butte Co., California, on July 30, 1986.

+ 274 m III. **Teddy Eugene**[8] **Johnson** was born in Roseburg, Douglas Co., Oregon, on July 18, 1923. He died in near

Saipan, Northern Mariana Islands, on June 16, 1944. Teddy Eugene was buried in National Memorial Cemetery of the Pacific, Honolulu, Oahu Island, Hawaii.[115]

**170. Luessia Marie**[7] **Johnson** (*William Roosevelt*[6], *John J.*[5], *Catherine*[4] *Pagan, John*[3], *Andrew*[2], *James*[1]) was born on July 15, 1898, in Little Rock, Pulaski Co., Arkansas. She was also known as **Susie.** She was the daughter of William Roosevelt Johnson (66) and Julia Linda Paxton. Luessia Marie lived in Roseburg, Douglas Co., Oregon in 1965. She died in Bend, Deschutes Co., Oregon, on October 5, 1996, at age 98. Luessia Marie was buried in IOOF Cemetery, Roseburg, Douglas Co., Oregon.[74]

Luessia Marie married **Thomas F. Fletcher** on March 26, 1916, in Douglas Co., Oregon. They had three daughters. Thomas F. Fletcher was born in Roseburg, Douglas Co., Oregon, on February 24, 1891. Thomas F. reached age 53 and died in Civil Bend, Douglas Co., Oregon, on January 17, 1945. He was buried in Roseburg IOOF Cemetery, Roseburg, Douglas Co., Oregon.[74]

Luessia Marie Johnson Fletcher married **Paul Shanklin** about 1960. They divorced.

Luessia Marie Johnson Fletcher Shanklin married **Robert David McGhehey** about 1987. Robert David McGhehey was born in Roseburg, Douglas Co., Oregon, on August 1, 1897. Robert David reached age 95 and died in Burns, Harney Co., Oregon, on March 31, 1993. He was buried in Klamath Memorial Park Cemetery, Klamath Falls, Klamath Co., Oregon.[116]

Daughters of Luessia Marie Johnson and Thomas F. Fletcher:

+ 275 f I. **Neta Fern**[8] **Fletcher** was born in Civil Bend, Douglas Co., Oregon, on December 6, 1916.

+ 276 f II. **Frieda Nell**[8] **Fletcher** was born in Civil Bend, Douglas Co., Oregon, on June 23, 1919. She died in Roseburg, Douglas Co., Oregon, on September 25, 1981.

+ 277 f III. **Dora Mae**[8] **Fletcher** was born in Civil Bend, Douglas Co., Oregon, on January 1, 1924. She died in Bend, Deschutes Co., Oregon, on December 17, 2003. Dora Mae was buried in Evergreen Memorial Park Cemetery, McMinnville, Yamhill Co., Oregon.[117]

**171. Walter Cecil**[7] **Johnson** (*William Roosevelt*[6], *John J.*[5], *Catherine*[4] *Pagan, John*[3], *Andrew*[2], *James*[1]) was born on October 23, 1901, in Oklahoma. He was the son of William Roosevelt Johnson (66) and Julia Linda Paxton. Walter Cecil died in Deschutes Co., Oregon, on November 19, 1980, at age 79.

He married **Mildred Ethyl Cork.** They had three sons. Mildred Ethyl. Cork was born in Oregon on October 27, 1911. Mildred Ethyl. reached age 66 and died in Lane Co., Oregon, on August 7, 1978. She was buried in Monument Cemetery, Monument, Grant Co., Oregon.[36]

Sons of Walter Cecil Johnson and Mildred Ethyl. Cork:

+ 278 m I. **Loren Duane**[8] **Johnson** was born in North Fork, Grant Co., Oregon, on February 9, 1930.

+ 279 m II. **Donald Cecil**[8] **Johnson** was born in Monument, Grant Co., Oregon, on July 28, 1932. He died in Yucca Valley, San Bernardino Co., California, on November 17, 1996. Donald Cecil was buried in Greenwood Cemetery, Bend, Deschutes Co., Oregon.[118]

+ 280 m III. **Harold Gene⁸ Johnson** was born in Bend, Deschutes Co., Oregon, on November 25, 1939. He was also known as **Sandy.** Harold Gene died in Bend, Deschutes Co., Oregon, on June 17, 1991. He was buried in Deschutes Memorial Gardens Cemetery, Bend, Deschutes Co., Oregon.[119]

**172. Alma L.⁷ Johnson** (*James Edward⁶, John J.⁵, Catherine⁴ Pagan, John³, Andrew², James¹*) was born on December 3, 1904, in Muskogee Co., Oklahoma? She was the daughter of James Edward Johnson (70) and Nancy Elizabeth Lowery. Alma L. died in Montgomery City, Montgomery Twp., Montgomery Twp., Montgomery Co., Missouri, on September 17, 1998, at age 93. She was buried in Saint Mary's Cemetery, Montgomery City, Montgomery Twp., Montgomery Co., Missouri.[76]

She married **William B. Smith.** They had five children. William B. Smith was born in Missouri on October 27, 1906. William B. reached age 68 and died in Montgomery City, Montgomery Twp., Montgomery Twp., Montgomery Co., Missouri, on February 5, 1975. He was buried in Saint Mary's Cemetery, Montgomery City, Montgomery Twp., Montgomery Co., Missouri.[76]

Children of Alma L. Johnson and William B. Smith:

+ 281 m I. **William Donald⁸ Smith** was born in Central Twp., Perry Co., Missouri, on May 2, 1928. He died in Montgomery City, Montgomery Twp., Montgomery Twp., Montgomery Co., Missouri, on July 21, 2008. William Donald was buried in Fairmount Cemetery, Middletown, Prairie Twp., Montgomery Co., Missouri.[120]

+ 282 m II. **Norman Daniel⁸ Smith** was born in Central Twp., Perry Co., Mis-

souri, on December 31, 1929. He was also known as **Daniel Norman Smith.** Norman Daniel died in Montgomery City, Montgomery Twp., Montgomery Twp., Montgomery Co., Missouri, on November 13, 1955. He was buried in Saint Mary's Cemetery, Montgomery City, Montgomery Twp., Montgomery Co., Missouri.[76]

+ 283 m III. **Edward Dale⁸ Smith** was born in Central Twp., Perry Co., Missouri, on December 14, 1931. He was also known as **Dale.** Edward Dale died in Montgomery City, Montgomery Twp., Montgomery Twp., Montgomery Co., Missouri, on November 11, 2004. He was buried in Saint Mary's Cemetery, Montgomery City, Montgomery Twp., Montgomery Co., Missouri.[76]

+ 284 m IV. **Sherrill Dean⁸ Smith** was born in Missouri on October 8, 1933.

+ 285 f V. **Charlotte⁸ Smith** was born in Berkeley, St. Louis Co., Missouri?, in 1935.

**173. Heber Clay⁷ Johnson** (*James Edward⁶, John J.⁵, Catherine⁴ Pagan, John³, Andrew², James¹*) was born on July 29, 1907, in Muskogee Co., Oklahoma. He was also known as **Johnny.** He was the son of James Edward Johnson (70) and Nancy Elizabeth Lowery. Heber Clay died in Cole County, Missouri, on July 20, 1990, at age 82. He was buried in Bethany Memorial Gardens Cemetery, Crocker, Tavern Twp., Pulaski Co., Missouri.[77]

He married **Clarice Thelma Meiser.** They divorced. They had two sons. Clarice T. Meiser was born in Belleville, Belleville Twp., St. Clair Co., Illinois, on August 27, 1910. Clarice T. reached age age 48 and died in St Louis, St. Louis Co., Missouri, on March 17, 1959. She was buried in Snowdenville Cemetery, Cornwall, Madison Co., Missouri.[121]

She died under the name Clarice Bailey.

Heber Clay Johnson married **Alta E. Wilson** on September 18, 1946.

Sons of Heber Clay Johnson and Clarice T. Meiser:

+ 286 m I. **Heber[8] Johnson II** was born in Missouri on March 3, 1928. He died in Barnhart, Jefferson Co., Missouri?, on May 4, 1984.

+ 287 m II. **Raymond James[8] Johnson** was born in Independence, Independence Twp., Doniphan Co., Missouri, on August 6, 1930. He died in Iberia, Richwoods Twp., Miller Co., Missouri, on February 11, 2000. Raymond James was buried in Bethany Memorial Gardens

**174. Cloei[7] Johnson** (*James Edward[6], John J.[5], Catherine[4] Pagan, John[3], Andrew[2], James[1]*) was born on July 15, 1909, in Wagoner, Wagoner Co., Oklahoma. She was the daughter of James Edward Johnson (70) and Nancy Elizabeth Lowery. Cloei died in Joplin, Joplin Twp., Jasper Co., Missouri, on August 9, 1910, at age one. She was buried in Forest Park Cemetery, Joplin, Joplin Twp., Jasper Co., Missouri.[78]

**175. Jesse[7] Johnson** (*James Edward[6], John J.[5], Catherine[4] Pagan, John[3], Andrew[2], James[1]*) was born in 1913 in Oklahoma. He was the son of James Edward Johnson (70) and Nancy Elizabeth Lowery. Jesse died after 1920.

**176. Bonnie Beatrice[7] Johnson** (*James Edward[6], John J.[5], Catherine[4] Pagan, John[3], Andrew[2], James[1]*) was born on December 24, 1915. She was the daughter of James Edward Johnson (70) and Nancy Elizabeth Lowery. Bonnie Beatrice died on December 12, 1918, at age two.

**177. James W.[7] Murrell** (*Ella Matilda[6], Emma[5] Johnson, Catherine[4] Pagan, John[3], Andrew[2], James[1]*) was born on April 1, 1881, in Lynchburg, Campbell Co., Virginia. He was the son of Unknown Unknown and Ella Matilda Murrell (73). He was residing in Centerburg, Hilliar Twp., Knox Co., Ohio in 1952. He died in a hospital in Mt. Vernon, Knox

Co., Ohio, on January 16, 1952, at age 70. James W. was buried in New Salem Methodist Episcopal Cemetery, Thorn Twp., Perry Co., Ohio.[79]

James W. lived in 1920 in Chicago, Cook Co., Illinois. James W. is found in Clayton, Gloucester Co., New Jersey in 1930. He had moved by 1935 to Lynchburg, Campbell Co., Virginia before settling in Centerburg, Ohio.[79]

James Murrell's parents may have been William "Randolph" Murrell and Mary Bingham, as his death certificate in Ohio says, but Mary Bingham Murrell was past childbearing age when James Murrell was born. Also, his death certificate and gravestone say he was born in 1886, but he was born in 1881.

James W. Murrell married **Cordelia Mae Hand** on November 3, 1906, in Campbell Co., Kentucky. They divorced. They had two daughters. Cordelia Mae Hand was born in Cincinnati, Hamilton Co., Ohio, in June 1887. She reached age 79 and died in Dayton, Campbell Co., Kentucky, on July 6, 1966.

She died under the name Cordelia M. Lohr.

James W. married **Martha Katherine Rehmann** on August 25, 1915, in Cook Co., Illinois. They divorced. They had two daughters. Martha Katherine Rehmann was born in Grand Rapids, Wood Co., Wisconsin, in October 1888. Martha Katherine reached age 65 and died in Clayton, Gloucester Co., New Jersey, on January 7, 1954.

Her name was Martha Kuehl when she died.

James W. Murrell married **Leota Fay Bopes**. They had one daughter. Leota Fay Bopes was born in New Salem, Walnut Twp., Fairfield Co., Ohio, on August 21, 1895. Leota Fay lived in 1935 in Centerburg, Hilliar Twp., Knox Co., Ohio. She reached age 54 and died in a hospital in Mt. Vernon, Knox Co., Ohio, on May 5, 1950. Leota Fay was buried in New Salem Methodist Episcopal Cemetery, Thorn Twp., Perry Co., Ohio.[79]

Daughters of James W. Murrell and Cordelia Mae Hand:

+ 288 f I. **Ella Mae⁸ Murrell** was born in Dayton, Campbell Co., Kentucky, on November 12, 1907. She died in Alexandria, Alexandria Co., Virginia?, on December 29, 1999.

+ 289 f II. **Belinda⁸ Murrell** was born in Dayton, Campbell Co., Kentucky, on April 28, 1910. She died in Fort Thomas, Campbell Co., Kentucky, on January 29, 2001. She was buried in Evergreen Cemetery, Southgate, Campbell Co., Kentucky.[37]

Daughters of James W. Murrell and Martha Katherine Rehmann:

+ 290 f I. **Martha Jane⁸ Murrell** was born in Chicago, Cook Co., Illinois, on December 3, 1914. She was also known as **Dixie.** Martha Jane died in Fayetteville, Fayette Co., Georgia, on April 2, 1999.

+ 291 f II. **Mary Catherine8 Murrell** was born in Clayton, Gloucester Co., New Jersey, on August 23, 1927. She was also known as **Honey.** Mary Catherine died in Chula Vista, San Diego Co., California, on May 5, 2015. She was buried in Fort Rosecrans National Military Cemetery, San Diego, San Diego Co., California.[122]

Daughter of James W. Murrell and Leota Fay Bopes:

+ 292 f I. **Beatrix Lizbeth⁸ Murrell** was born in Lancaster, Fairfield Co., Ohio, on June 19, 1935. She was also known as **Betsy.** Beatrix Lizbeth died in Chula Vista, San Diego Co., California on April 8, 2014, at age 68.

**178. Harry⁷ Wolfe** (*Hattie⁶ Greenwood, Alexander⁵, Catherine⁴ Pagan, John³, Andrew², James¹*) was born in February 1883 in Gallipolis, Gallipolis Twp., Gallia Co., Ohio.[9] He was the son of Darius Wolfe and Hattie Greenwood (76). Harry lived in 1930 in Pittsburgh, Allegheny Co., Pennsylvania. He died in Newark, Newark Twp., Licking Co., Ohio, on October 6, 1956, at age 73. Harry was buried in Pine Street Cemetery, Gallipolis, Gallipolis Twp., Gallia Co., Ohio.[13]

Childless.

Harry married **Lottie Jane Ferguson** in 1908. Lottie Jane Ferguson was born in Gallipolis Twp., Gallia Co., Ohio, on March 30, 1882. Lottie Jane reached age 78 and died in Newark, Newark Twp., Licking Co., Ohio, on November 30, 1960. She was buried in Pine Street Cemetery, Gallipolis, Gallipolis Twp., Gallia Co., Ohio.[13]

**179. Frank Burdette⁷ Greenwood II** (*Frank Burdette⁶, Alexander⁵, Catherine⁴ Pagan, John³, Andrew², James¹*) was born on August 18, 1888, in Springfield, Springfield Twp., Sangamon Co., Illinois. He was the son of Frank Burdette Greenwood (77) and Lena Meister. Frank Burdette died in Indianapolis, Marion Co., Indiana, on April 28, 1946, at age 57. He was buried in Round Hill Cemetery, Indianapolis, Perry Twp., Marion Co., Indiana.[38]

**180. Nelle⁷ Greenwood** (*Frank Burdette⁶, Alexander⁵, Catherine⁴ Pagan, John³, Andrew², James¹*) was born on November 12, 1889, in Springfield, Springfield Twp., Sangamon Co., Illinois. She was the daughter of Frank Burdette Greenwood (77) and Lena Meister. Nelle died in Indianapolis, Marion Co., Indiana, on June 16, 1970, at age 80. She was buried in Round Hill Cemetery, Indianapolis, Perry Twp., Marion Co., Indiana.[38]

Nelle married **Calvin Walker Worrall II** on December 22, 1910, in Marion Co., Indiana. They divorced, but remarried on July 12, 1916, in Marion Co., Indiana. They had two children. Calvin Walker Worrall II was born in Bloomington, Monroe Co., Indiana, on August 31, 1885. Calvin Walker lived in Indianapolis, Marion Co., Indiana in 1940. He reached age 68 and died in Bloomington, Monroe Co., Indiana, on April 11, 1954. Calvin Walker was buried in Rose Hill Cemetery, Bloomington, Monroe Co., Indiana.[123]

Children of Nelle Greenwood and Calvin Walker Worrall II:

+ 293 m I. **Calvin Greenwood[8] Worrall III** was born in Des Moines, Polk Co., Iowa on September 22, 1912. He died in Indianapolis, Marion Co., Indiana, on July 28, 1956. Calvin Greenwood was buried in Rose Hill Cemetery, Bloomington, Monroe Co., Indiana.[122]

+ 294 f II. **Joann Betty[8] Worrall** was born in Indianapolis, Marion Co., Indiana, on January 26, 1918. She died in Latana, Palm Beach Co., Florida, on July 3, 2007. Joann Betty was buried in Greenwood Cemetery, Greenwood, Johnson Co., Indiana.[124]

**181. Frances Virginia[7] Hover** (*Harry A. Hover or[6] Hoover, Fannie[5] Greenwood, Catherine[4] Pagan, John[3], Andrew[2], James[1]*) was born on November 9, 1895, in Gallipolis, Gallipolis Twp., Gallia Co., Ohio. She was also known as **Fannie.** She was the daughter of Harry A. Hover or Hoover (78) and Nettie Catherine Diggens. Frances Virginia lived in Springfield Twp., Gallia Co., Ohio in 1910. She died in Lower Lake, Lake Co., California, on April 28, 1973, at age 77. Frances Virginia was buried in Lower Lake Cemetery, Lower Lake, Lake Co., California.[80]

Frances Virginia Hover is found in 1910 in the Gallia County Children's home. Her father is not found in the 1900 or any subsequent census, but her mother, Nettie Diggins Hover (later Stradtman), is residing in Cincinnati, Hamilton Co., Ohio with her own sister and other family members.

Frances Virginia married **Danie Franklin Gould** in 1914. They divorced, but remarry on March 15, 1924 in Franklin Co., Ohio. They divorced again. They had one daughter. Danie Franklin Gould was born in Lewis, Mason Co., West Virginia, on October 2, 1890. Danie Frankl in Columbus, Franklin Co., Ohio lived in 1920. Danie Franklin reached age 81 and died in San Pedro, Los Angeles Co., California, on July 4, 1972.

Frances Virginia Hover married **Charles R. Baker** before 1938. They had one son. Charles R. Baker was born in Indiana on June 13, 1889. Charles R. reached age 71 and died in Lower Lake, Lake Co., California, on June 12, 1961. He was buried in Lower Lake Cemetery, Lower Lake, Lake Co., California.[80]

Daughter of Frances Virginia Hover and Danie Franklin Gould:

+ 295 f I. **Crystabell C.[8] Gould** was born in Cabell Co., West Virginia, on July 17, 1914. She died in San Diego, San Diego Co., California, on July 29, 1975.

Son of Frances Virginia Hover and Charles R. Baker:

+ 296 m I. **Charles[8] Baker II** was born in Alisal, Monterey Co., California, in 1938.

# 8th Generation

**182. Palmer T.⁸ Robinson** (*Bennora A.⁷ Palmer, Thomas M.⁶, Charles Nelson⁵, Mary Margaret⁴ Pagan, John³, Andrew², James¹*) was born on May 19, 1908, in Roy Twp., Potter Co., South Dakota. He was the son of Everett Robinson and Bennora A. Palmer (82). Palmer T. died in Riverside Co., California, on April 14, 1972, at age 63.

Childless.

Palmer T. married **Bracie Burdina Pace** on November 5, 1960, in Los Angeles Co., California. Bracie Burdina Pace was born in Laurel, Jones Co., Mississippi, on July 16, 1915. Bracie Burdina reached age 96 and died as Bracie Roodhouse in Stanwood, Snohomish Co., Washington, on May 31, 2012.

**183. Pauline Everette⁸ Robinson** (*Bennora A.⁷ Palmer, Thomas M.⁶, Charles Nelson⁵, Mary Margaret⁴ Pagan, John³, Andrew², James¹*) was born on September 8, 1909, in Roy Twp., Potter Co., South Dakota. She was also known as **Pauline.** She was the daughter of Everett Robinson and Bennora A. Palmer (82). Pauline Everette lived in Madison, Dane Co., Wiscons in 1930. She died in San Diego, San Diego Co., California, on November 13, 1984, at age 75.

Never married.

**184. Allys L.⁸ Robinson** (*Bennora A.⁷ Palmer, Thomas M.⁶, Charles Nelson⁵, Mary Margaret⁴ Pagan, John³, Andrew², James¹*) was born on March 8, 1922, in Lebanon, Lebanon Twp., Potter Co., South Dakota.[81] She was the daughter of Everett Robinson and Bennora A. Palmer (82).

Alice or Allys L. married **Gilbert Harry Smith** on December 1, 1951, in San Diego Co., California.[125] They divorced. Gilbert Harry Smith was born in Des Moines Twp., Boone Co., Iowa, on March 1, 1916. [126] He reached age 73 and died in San Diego, San Diego Co., California, on March 24, 1989.

**185. Donnally Woodruff⁸ Palmer** (*Roy Donnally⁷, Thomas M.⁶, Charles Nelson⁵, Mary Margaret⁴ Pagan, John³, Andrew², James¹*) was born on June

6, 1918, in Avon Springs Twp., Potter Co., South Dakota. He is the son of Roy Donnally Palmer (85) and Ada Elenora Woodruff.

Donnally Woodruff married **Louise Greiner** on May 1, 1945, in Wayne Co., Michigan. They had two sons. Louise Greiner was born in Charlevoix, Charlevoix Co., Michigan, on March 9, 1921. She died on May 10, 2013 in Grand Rapids, Kent Co., Michigan.

**186. Darwin Howard⁸ Palmer** (*Roy Donnally⁷, Thomas M.⁶, Charles Nelson⁵, Mary Margaret⁴ Pagan, John³, Andrew², James¹*) was born on September 10, 1921, in Avon Springs Twp., Potter Co., South Dakota. He was the son of Roy Donnally Palmer (85) and Ada Elenora Woodruff. Darwin Howard died in Norton Shores, Muskegon Co., Michigan, on May 10, 1989, at age 67. He was buried in Mona View Cemetery, Muskegon Heights, Muskegon Twp., Muskegon Co., Michigan.[82]

Darwin Howard married **Annabelle Bursma** on April 3, 1942. They had two sons. Annabelle Bursma was born in Union, Union Co., South Carolina, on October 6, 1924. Annabelle reached age 88 and died in Norton Shores, Muskegon Twp., Muskegon Co., Michigan, on August 24, 2013. She was buried in Mona View Cemetery, Muskegon Twp., Muskegon Heights, Muskegon Co., Michigan.[82]

Darwin Howard Palmer and Annabelle Bursma had two sons, including:

+ 297 m II. **Terry⁹ Palmer** was born in Grand Rapids, Grand Rapids Twp., Kent Co., Michigan, on June 25, 1947. He died in Crystal Falls, Iron Co., Michigan, on June 4, 2001. Terry was buried in Evergreen Memorial Cemetery, Crystal Falls, Iron Co., Michigan.[127]

**187. Gloria E.⁸ Palmer** (*Roy Donnally⁷, Thomas M.⁶, Charles Nelson⁵, Mary Margaret⁴ Pagan, John³, Andrew², James¹*) was born on January

15, 1926, in Gettysburg., Potter Co., South Dakota. She was the daughter of Roy Donnally Palmer (85) and Ada Elenora Woodruff. Gloria E. died in Grand Rapids, Grand Rapids Twp., Kent Co., Michigan, on October 4, 2009, at age 83. She was buried in Grandville Cemetery, Grand Rapids, Grand Rapids Twp., Kent Co., Michigan.[83]

Gloria E. married **Warren J. Sullivan** on December 20, 1942, in Kent Co., Michigan. They had two sons. Warren J. Sullivan was born in Byron Twp., Kent Co., Michigan, on July 2, 1921.

**188. Jack Merrill[8] Palmer** (*George Merrill[7], Thomas M.[6], Charles Nelson[5], Mary Margaret[4] Pagan, John[3], Andrew[2], James[1]*) was born on March 5, 1922, in Fort Mills, Corregidor, Phillippine Islands. He was the son of George Merrill Palmer (86) and Susan E. Gains. Jack Merrill died in San Antonio, Bexar Co., Texas, on July 6, 2005, at age 83. He was buried in Fort Sam Houston National Cemetery, San Antonio, Bexar Co., Texas.[42]

Jack Merrill married **Marion Van Zandt Browne** in 1948 in Bexar Co., Texas. They had one son. Marion Van Zandt Browne was born in Kansas City, Wyandotte Co., Kansas, on October 16, 1928. She was also known as **Bunty.** Marion Van Zandt reached age 86 and died in San Antonio, Bexar Co., Texas, on July 12, 2015. She was buried in Fort Sam Houston National Cemetery, San Antonio, Bexar Co., Texas.[42]

**189. Charles Ethan[8] Palmer** (*Charles Grover[7], Lewis William[6], Charles Nelson[5], Mary Margaret[4] Pagan, John[3], Andrew[2], James[1]*) was born on April 19, 1909, in Chicago, Cook Co., Illinois. He was the son of Charles Grover Palmer (88) and Eugenia Maria Sundquist. Charles Ethan died in Mississauga, Peel, Ontario, Canada, in October 1979 at age 70.

Charles Ethan married **Dorothy Caroline Freytag** on November 19, 1935, in Cook Co., Illinois. They divorced. They had one daughter. Dorothy Caroline Freytag was born in West Bend, Washington Co., Wisconsin, on May 25, 1915. She reached age 90 and died in Evanston, Cook Co., Illinois, on March 8, 2006.

Charles Ethan Palmer married **Dorothy Rosalie Crider** before 1948. They divorced. They had three daughters. Dorothy Rosalie Crider was born in Mexico, Jefferson Twp., Miami Co., Indiana, on May 21, 1924. She reached age 55 and died in Palm Beach, Palm Beach Co., Florida, on February 6, 1980.

She died under the name Dorothy Dixon.

Charles Ethan Palmer and Dorothy Rosalie Crider had three daughters, including:

+ 298 f I. **Carol Elaine[9] Palmer** was born in Plymouth, Center Twp., Marshall Co., Indiana, on February 24, 1948. She died in Palm Beach, Palm Beach Co., Florida, on December 15, 1994.

**190. Alice Eugenia[8] Palmer** (*Charles Grover[7], Lewis William[6], Charles Nelson[5], Mary Margaret[4] Pagan, John[3], Andrew[2], James[1]*) was born on February 5, 1910, in Chicago, Cook Co., Illinois. She was the daughter of Charles Grover Palmer (88) and Eugenia Maria Sundquist. Alice Eugenia died in Chicago, Cook Co., Illinois, on March 10, 1975, at age 65.

Alice Eugenia married **Clyde Kenneth Bowles** before 1935. Clyde Kenneth Bowles was born in Mount Pulaski, Mount Pulaski Twp., Logan Co., Illinois, on August 25, 1906. Clyde Kenneth reached age 85 and died in Sun City, Maricopa Co., Arizona, on November 25, 1991.

Alice Eugenia Palmer Bowles married **Lawrence Arthur Pratt** on September 3, 1935, in Cook Co., Illinois. They divorced. They had two daughters. Lawrence Arthur Pratt was born in Paris, Paris Twp., Edgar Co., Illinois, on December 20, 1907. He reached age 97 and died in Santa Ana, Orange Co., California, on July 23, 2005. Lawrence Arthur was buried in Arlington National Cemetery, Arlington, Virginia.[128]

Alice Eugenia Palmer and Lawrence Arthur Pratt had two daughters, including:

+ 299 f II. **Dorothy Jane[9] Pratt** was born in Detroit, Wayne Co., Michigan, on

**191. Doris Jane[8] Palmer** (*Charles Grover[7], Lewis William[6], Charles Nelson[5], Mary Margaret[4] Pagan, John[3], Andrew[2], James[1]*) was born on August 29, 1912, in Chicago, Cook Co., Illinois. She was the daughter of Charles Grover Palmer (88) and Eugenia Maria Sundquist. Doris Jane lived in Chicago, Cook Co., Illinois in 1957. She died in Traverse City, Grand Traverse Co., Michigan, on February 14, 1998, at age 85. Doris Jane was buried in Ogdensburg Cemetery, Mapleton, Peninsula Twp., Grand Traverse Co., Michigan.[85]

Doris Jane married **Norman Dean Nevinger** on May 4, 1935, in Lake Co., Illinois. They had four children. Norman Dean Nevinger was born in Long Island, Queens Co., New York, on July 6, 1910. Norman Dean reached age 80 and died in Garfield Twp., Grand Traverse Co., Michigan, on August 6, 1990. He was buried in Ogdensburg Cemetery, Mapleton, Peninsula Twp., Grand Traverse Co., Michigan.[79]

Doris Jane Palmer and Norman Dean Nevinger had four children, including:

+ 300 m I. **Norman Dean[9] Nevinger II** was born in Chicago, Cook Co., Illinois, on August 4, 1936. He died in Peotone, Peotone Twp., Will Co., Illinois, on February 3, 2005.

+ 301 f II. **Linette Marie[9] Nevinger** was born in Chicago, Cook Co., Illinois, in 1940.

**192. Gaius Mattias[8] Palmer** (*Charles Grover[7], Lewis William[6], Charles Nelson[5], Mary Margaret[4] Pagan, John[3], Andrew[2], James[1]*) was born on July 1, 1915, in Chicago, Cook Co., Illinois. He was the son of Charles Grover Palmer (88) and Eugenia Maria Sundquist. Gaius Mattias lived in 1957 in Buffalo, Erie Co., New York. He died in Phoenix, Maricopa Co., Arizona, on December 16, 1997, at age 82.

Gaius Mattias married **Helen-Louise Davenport** on November 26, 1942, in Mississippi Co.

Arkansas. They divorced. They had three children. Helen-Louise Davenport was born in Buffalo, Erie Co., New York, on January 30, 1923. She reached age 93 and died in Richmond, Madison Co., Kentucky, on February 11, 2016 as Helen-Louise Snyder.

**193. Mary Elizabeth[8] Long** (*Ruth Beatrice[7] Palmer, James Buchanan[6], Charles Nelson[5], Mary Margaret[4] Pagan, John[3], Andrew[2], James[1]*) was born on May 3, 1936, in Michigan City, Michigan Twp., LaPorte Co., Indiana. She is the daughter of Monroe William Long and Ruth Beatrice Palmer (92).

**194. Beatrice Ruth[8] Long** (*Ruth Beatrice[7] Palmer, James Buchanan[6], Charles Nelson[5], Mary Margaret[4] Pagan, John[3], Andrew[2], James[1]*) was born on July 25, 1938, in Cool Spring Twp., LaPorte Co., Indiana. She was the daughter of Monroe William Long and Ruth Beatrice Palmer (92). Beatrice Ruth died in Michigan City, Michigan Twp., LaPorte Co., Indiana, on July 25, 1938. She was buried in Greenwood Cemetery, Michigan City, Michigan Twp., LaPorte Co., Indiana.[86]

**197. Harold Warner[8] Davis** (*Daniel L.[7], Emily Jane[6] Smith, Mary Ann[5] Palmer, Mary Margaret[4] Pagan, John[3], Andrew[2], James[1]*) was born on June 3, 1894, in Cora, Perry Twp., Gallia Co., Ohio. He was the son of Daniel L. Davis (93) and Rozellma Tanner. Harold Warner died in Columbus, Franklin Co., Ohio, on January 8, 1971, at age 76. He was buried in Ashley Union Cemetery, Ashley, Ashley Twp., Delaware Co., Ohio.[887]

Harold Warner married **Esther Annamarie Deubner** on June 8, 1929, in Darke Co., Ohio. They had two children. Esther Annamarie Deubner was born in Greenville Twp., Darke Co., Ohio, on June 28, 1903. Esther Annamarie reached age 85 and died in Worthington, Sharon Twp., Franklin Co., Ohio, on March 3, 1989. She was buried in Ashley Union Cemetery, Ashley, Ashley Twp., Delaware Co., Ohio.[81]

Children of Harold Warner Davis and Esther Annamarie Deubner:

+ 302 f I. **Arleen Marie⁹ Davis** was born in Ashley Twp., Delaware Co., Ohio, on September 25, 1930. She died in Shelby Twp., Richland Co., Ohio, on January 22, 1998. Arleen Marie was buried in Shelby-Oakland Cemetery, Shelby, Shelby Twp., Richland Co., Ohio.[129]

+ 303 m II. **Harold William⁹ Davis II** was born in Ashley Twp., Delaware Co., Ohio, on March 12, 1932. He died in Columbus, Franklin Co., Ohio, on May 21, 2011.

**198. Edith Wilma⁸ Davis** (*Daniel L.⁷, Emily Jane⁶ Smith, Mary Ann⁵ Palmer, Mary Margaret⁴ Pagan, John³, Andrew², James¹*) was born on June 13, 1896, in Cora, Perry Twp., Gallia Co., Ohio. She was the daughter of Daniel L. Davis (93) and Rozellma Tanner. Edith Wilma died in Hamden Twp., Vinton Co., Ohio, on September 26, 1977, at age 81. She was buried in Calvary Baptist Cemetery, Rio Grande, Raccoon Twp., Gallia Co., Ohio.[12]

Edith Wilma married **Elmer Lackey McCarley** on April 17, 1919, in Gallia Co., Ohio. They had three daughters. Elmer Lackey McCarley was born in Perry Twp., Gallia Co., Ohio, on September 20, 1893. Elmer Lackey reached age 79 and died in Rio Grande, Raccoon Twp., Gallia Co., Ohio, on June 6, 1973. He was buried in Calvary Baptist Cemetery, Rio Grande, Raccoon Twp., Gallia Co., Ohio.[12]

Daughters of Edith Wilma Davis and Elmer Lackey McCarley:

+ 304 f I. **Infant Twin Daughter⁹ McCarley** was born in Raccoon Twp., Gallia Co., Ohio, on September 1, 1920. She died in Raccoon Twp., Gallia Co., Ohio, on September 1, 1920. Infant Twin Daughter was buried in Calvary Baptist Cemetery, Rio Grande, Raccoon Twp., Gallia Co., Ohio.[8]

+ 305 f II. **Robin Louise⁹ McCarley** was born in Raccoon Twp., Gallia Co., Ohio, on September 1, 1920. She died in Steubenville, Cross Creek Twp., Jefferson Co., Ohio, on December 15, 1995. Robin Louise was buried in Calvary Baptist Cemetery, Rio Grande, Raccoon Twp., Gallia Co., Ohio.[12]

+ 306 f III. **Norma Jean⁹ McCarley** was born in Raccoon Twp., Gallia Co., Ohio, on January 1, 1925.

**199. Nelle Emily⁸ Davis** (*Daniel L.⁷, Emily Jane⁶ Smith, Mary Ann⁵ Palmer, Mary Margaret⁴ Pagan, John³, Andrew², James¹*) was born on June 7, 1898, in Cora, Perry Twp., Gallia Co., Ohio. She was the daughter of Daniel L. Davis (93) and Rozellma Tanner. Nelle Emily died in Clearwater, Pinellas Co., Florida, on March 22, 1994, at age 95.

Nelle Emily married **Ernest Gordon Boster** on June 4, 1919, in Gallia Co., Ohio. They had one son. Ernest Gordon Boster was born in Gallipolis, Gallipolis Twp., Gallia Co., Ohio, on November 16, 1893. Ernest Gordon reached age 66 and died in Mantua, Mantua Twp., Portage Co., Ohio, on June 6, 1960. He was buried in Mount Nebo United Methodist Church Cemetery, Sewickley Twp., Allegheny Co., Pennsylvania.[130]

Son of Nelle Emily Davis and Ernest Gordon Boster:

+ 307 m I. **Davis Eugene⁹ Boster** was born in Rio Grande, Raccoon Twp., Gallia Co., Ohio, on September 14, 1920. He was also known as **Gene.** Davis Eugene died in Arlington, Virginia, on July 7, 2005. He was buried in was buried in Arlington National Cemetery, Arlington, Virginia.[128]

**200. Roy A.⁸ Davis** (*Daniel L.⁷, Emily Jane⁶ Smith, Mary Ann⁵ Palmer, Mary Margaret⁴ Pagan, John³, Andrew², James¹*) was born on June 2, 1900, in

Cora, Perry Twp., Gallia Co., Ohio. He was the son of Daniel L. Davis (93) and Rozellma Tanner. Roy A. died in Cora, Perry Twp., Gallia Co., Ohio, on January 11, 1907, at age six. He was buried in Old Pine Cemetery, Rio Grande, Raccoon Twp., Gallia Co., Ohio.[6]

**201. David Orville⁸ Davis** (*Daniel L.⁷, Emily Jane⁶ Smith, Mary Ann⁵ Palmer, Mary Margaret⁴ Pagan, John³, Andrew², James¹*) was born on January 23, 1904, in Cora, Perry Twp., Gallia Co., Ohio. He was the son of Daniel L. Davis (93) and Rozellma Tanner. David Orville lived in Logan, Falls Twp., Hocking Co., Ohio in 1940. He died in Lancaster, Fairfield Co., Ohio, on April 5, 1974, at age 70.

David Orville married **Corrina Clark** on December 30, 1930, in Gallia Co., Ohio. They had three children. Corrina Clark was born in Pasadena, Los Angeles Co., California, on February 16, 1906. Corrina reached age 60 and died in Lancaster, Fairfield Co., Ohio, on August 16, 1966.

David Orville Davis and Corrina Clark had three children, including:

+ 308 f I. **Patricia Ann⁹ Davis** was born in Rio Grande, Raccoon Twp., Gallia Co., Ohio, on July 3, 1934. She died in Rio Grande, Raccoon Twp., Gallia Co., Ohio, on March 7, 1935. She was buried in Calvary Baptist Cemetery, Rio Grande, Raccoon Twp., Gallia Co., Ohio.[12]

+ 309 f II. **Annette⁹ Davis** was born in Union Furnace, Starr Twp., Hocking Co., Ohio, in 1937.

**202. Gladys⁸ Buckle** (*Mary Ann⁷ Davis, Emily Jane⁶ Smith, Mary Ann⁵ Palmer, Mary Margaret⁴ Pagan, John³, Andrew², James¹*) was born on July 27, 1899, in Perry Twp., Gallia Co., Ohio. She was the daughter of Charles K. Buckle and Mary Ann Davis (95). Gladys died in Umatilla Co., Oregon, on December 7, 1963, at age 64.

Gladys married **John Cambell Haston** before 1920. They divorced. They had two daughters. John Cambell Haston was born in Galveston Co., Texas, on February 21, 1899. He reached age 62 and died in Los Angeles, Los Angeles Co., California, on September 12, 1961. John Cambell was buried in Downey District Cemetery, Downey, Los Angeles Co., California.[131]

Gladys Buckle Haston married **Frank Emil Grossman** after 1922. Frank Emil Grossman was born in Platteville, Mills Co., Iowa, on November 26, 1899. Frank Emil reached age 75 and died in Pasadena, Los Angeles Co., California, on June 3, 1975. He was buried in Live Oak Memorial Park Cemetery, Monrovia, Los Angeles Co., California.[132]

Daughters of Gladys Buckle and John Cambell Haston:

+ 310 f I. **Claire Louise⁹ Haston** was born in Los Angeles, Los Angeles Co., California, on July 27, 1920. She died in Ashland, Jackson Co., Oregon, on July 9, 2011.

+ 311 f II. **Nancy M.⁹ Haston** was born in Los Angeles, Los Angeles Co., California, on February 5, 1922.

**203. Ruth Violet⁸ Buckle** (*Mary Ann⁷ Davis, Emily Jane⁶ Smith, Mary Ann⁵ Palmer, Mary Margaret⁴ Pagan, John³, Andrew², James¹*) was born on September 23, 1905, in Bon Homme Co., South Dakota. She was the daughter of Charles K. Buckle and Mary Ann Davis (95). Ruth Violet died in Detroit, Wayne Co., Michigan, on February 1, 1963, at age 57.

Ruth Violet married **Donald Jackson Sublette** on September 25, 1925, in Los Angeles Co., California. They had three children. Donald Jackson Sublette was born in Kirksville, Benton Twp., Adair Co., Missouri, on August 19, 1903. Donald Jackson reached age 90 and died in Royal Oak, Oakland Co., Michigan, on March 28, 1994.

Children of Ruth Violet Buckle and Donald Jackson Sublette:

+ 312 f I. **Donna Davies⁹ Sublette** was born in Detroit, Wayne Co., Michigan, on October 16, 1932.

+ 313 m II. **Warren Jackson⁹ Sublette** was born in Royal Oak, Oakland Co., Michigan, on October 27, 1937.

+ 314 f III. **Daughter⁹ Sublette.**

**204. Earl Davis⁸ Morton** (*Elizabeth E.⁷ Davis, Emily Jane⁶ Smith, Mary Ann⁵ Palmer, Mary Margaret⁴ Pagan, John³, Andrew², James¹*) was born on September 13, 1899, in Green Twp., Gallia Co., Ohio. He was the son of Sherman Russell Morton and Elizabeth E. Davis (96). Earl Davis died in Udall, Ninnescah Twp., Cowley Co., Kansas, on October 2, 1995, at age 96. He was buried in Mulvane Cemetery, Mulvane, Sumner Co., Kansas. [45]

Earl Davis married **Iva Mae Shoup** about 1924 in Kansas? They had four children. Iva Mae Shoup was born in Gore Twp., Sumner Co., Kansas, on September 25, 1901. Iva Mae reached age 79 and died in Udall, Ninnescah Twp., Cowley Co., Kansas, on September 21, 1981. She was buried in Mulvane Cemetery, Mulvane, Sumner Co., Kansas. [45]

Children of Earl Davis Morton and Iva Mae Shoup:

+ 315 f I. **Florence Ellen⁹ Morton** was born in Maple Twp., Cowley Co., Kansas, on December 13, 1924. She died in Yukon, Canadian Co., Oklahoma, on July 12, 2001. Florence Ellen was buried in Yukon Cemetery, Yukon, Canadian Co., Oklahoma. [133]

+ 316 m II. **Clyde Russell⁹ Morton** was born in Maple Twp., Cowley Co., Kansas, on July 1, 1928. He died in Udall, Ninnescah Twp., Cowley Co., Kansas, on February 25, 2015. Clyde Russell was buried in Red Bud Catholic Cemetery, Cowley Co., Kansas. [134]

+ 317 m III. **Oscar Earl⁹ Morton** was born in Maple Twp., Cowley Co., Kansas, on December 19, 1929. He died in Udall, Ninnescah Twp., Cowley Co., Kansas, on January 1, 2003. Oscar Earl was buried in Star Cemetery, Udall, Cowley Co., Kansas. [135]

+ 318 f IV. **Cora⁹ Morton** was born in Maple Twp., Cowley Co., Kansas, on April 5, 1936.

**205. Ruth⁸ Morton** (*Elizabeth E.⁷ Davis, Emily Jane⁶ Smith, Mary Ann⁵ Palmer, Mary Margaret⁴ Pagan, John³, Andrew², James¹*) was born in 1908 in Maple Twp., Cowley Co., Kansas. She was the daughter of Sherman Russell Morton and Elizabeth E. Davis (96). Ruth died after 1920.

**206. Ida Ethelyn⁸ Tanner** (*Emma J.⁷ Davis, Emily Jane⁶ Smith, Mary Ann⁵ Palmer, Mary Margaret⁴ Pagan, John³, Andrew², James¹*) was born on August 12, 1900, in Greenfield Twp., Gallia Co., Ohio. She was the daughter of Charles Shelby Tanner and Emma J. Davis (97). Ida Ethelyn died after 1920.

**207. Sarah Emily⁸ Tanner** (*Emma J.⁷ Davis, Emily Jane⁶ Smith, Mary Ann⁵ Palmer, Mary Margaret⁴ Pagan, John³, Andrew², James¹*) was born on September 27, 1903, in Greenfield Twp., Gallia Co., Ohio. She was the daughter of Charles Shelby Tanner and Emma J. Davis (97). Sarah Emily died in Ann Arbor, Ann Arbor Twp., Washtenaw Co., Michigan, on January 28, 1997, at age 93. She was buried in Olive Methodist Church Cemetery, Cadmus, Walnut Twp., Gallia Co., Ohio. [82]

Sarah Emily married **Wallace Eldon Wiseman** on November 26, 1927, in Montgomery Co., Ohio. They had two sons. Wallace Eldon Wiseman was born in Cadmus, Walnut Twp., Gallia Co., Ohio, on August 4, 1904. Wallace Eldon reached age 92 and died in Ann Arbor, Ann Arbor Twp., Washtenaw Co., Michigan, on April 21, 1997. He was buried in Olive Methodist Church Cemetery, Cadmus, Walnut Twp., Gallia Co., Ohio. [88]

Sons of Sarah Emily Tanner and Wallace Eldon Wiseman:

+ 319 m I. **Charles Eldon⁹ Wiseman** was born in Perry Twp., Gallia Co.,

Ohio, on February 21, 1933. He died in Wichita, Sedgwick Co., Kansas, on May 25, 2015. Charles Eldon was buried in Lakeview Cemetery, Wichita, Sedgwick Co., Kansas.[136]

+ 320 m II. **John Robert⁹ Wiseman** was born in Perry Twp., Gallia Co., Ohio, on May 4, 1936.

**208. Parry Benjamin⁸ Tanner** (*Emma J.⁷ Davis, Emily Jane⁶ Smith, Mary Ann⁵ Palmer, Mary Margaret⁴ Pagan, John³, Andrew², James¹*) was born on September 8, 1907, in Greenfield Twp., Gallia Co., Ohio. He was also known as **Bennie**. He was the son of Charles Shelby Tanner and Emma J. Davis (97). Parry Benjamin died in Arcanum, Twin Twp., Darke Co., Ohio, on December 6, 1987, at age 80. He was buried in Old Pine Cemetery, Rio Grande, Raccoon Twp., Gallia Co., Ohio.[6]

He married **Mary Elizabeth Evans.** They had four children. Mary Elizabeth Evans was born in Peniel, Greenfield Twp., Gallia Co., Ohio, on December 27, 1913. Mary Elizabeth reached age 99 and died in Strongsville, Cuyahoga Co., Ohio, on October 8, 2013. She was buried in Old Pine Cemetery, Rio Grande, Raccoon Twp., Gallia Co., Ohio.[6]

Parry Benjamin Tanner and Mary Elizabeth Evans had four children, including:

+ 321 f I. **Barbara Jean⁹ Tanner** was born in Columbia, Richland Co., South Carolina, in 1936.

**209. Mary E.⁸ Tanner** (*Emma J.⁷ Davis, Emily Jane⁶ Smith, Mary Ann⁵ Palmer, Mary Margaret⁴ Pagan, John³, Andrew², James¹*) was born on March 10, 1912, in Greenfield Twp., Gallia Co., Ohio. She was the daughter of Charles Shelby Tanner and Emma J. Davis (97). Mary E. died in Bluffton, Richland Co., Allen Co., Ohio, on May 13, 1996, at age 84. She was buried in Truro Cemetery, Columbus Grove, Pleasant Twp., Putnam Co., Ohio.[89]

Mary E. married **George L. Parry** before 1948. They had two daughters. George L. Parry was born in Oak Hill Twp., Jackson Co., Ohio, on June 4, 1904. George L. reached age 59 and died in Columbus Grove, Pleasant Twp., Putnam Co., Ohio, on September 4, 1963. He was buried in Truro Cemetery, Columbus Grove, Pleasant Twp., Putnam Co., Ohio.[89]

Mary E. Tanner and George L. Parry had two daughters, including:

+ 322 f I. **Susan K.⁹ Parry** was born in Lima, Ottawa Twp., Allen Co., Ohio, on November 4, 1948. She died in Glandorf, Ottawa Twp., Putnam Co., Ohio, on October 27, 2013. Susan K. was buried in Truro Cemetery, Columbus Grove, Pleasant Twp., Putnam Co., Ohio.[89]

**210. David Walter⁸ Davis** (*David Benton⁷, Emily Jane⁶ Smith, Mary Ann⁵ Palmer, Mary Margaret⁴ Pagan, John³, Andrew², James¹*) was born on November 9, 1904, in Liberty Twp., Jackson Co., Ohio. He was also known as **Walter.** He was the son of David Benton Davis (98) and Elizabeth Meek Wickline. David Walter died in East Ely, White Pine Co., Nevada, on May 18, 1981, at age 76.

**211. Laurin Ernest⁸ Davis** (*David Benton⁷, Emily Jane⁶ Smith, Mary Ann⁵ Palmer, Mary Margaret⁴ Pagan, John³, Andrew², James¹*) was born on May 21, 1907, in Perry Twp., Gallia Co., Ohio. He was the son of David Benton Davis (98) and Elizabeth Meek Wickline. Laurin Ernest died in Hudson, Pasco Co., Florida, on March 16, 1989, at age 81. He was buried in Washington Park East Cemetery, Indianapolis, Warren Twp., Marion Co., Indiana.[91]

Childless.

Laurin Ernest married **Iris Juanita Everhart** on November 3, 1928, in Tippecanoe Co., Indiana. They divorced. Iris Juanita Everhart was born in Campbell, Union Twp., Dunklin Co., Missouri, on May 29, 1911. She was also known as **Iris.** Iris Juanita lived before 1991 in Worden, Omphghent Twp., Madison Co., Illinois. She reached age 79 and died in Greenville, Greenville Twp., Bond Co., Illinois, on April 27, 1991. Iris Juanita was buried.

Died under the name Juanita Everhart Younger.

Laurin Ernest Davis married **Claire M. Strange** on March 1, 1963, in Marion Co., Indiana. Claire M. Strange was born in Plainville, Steele Twp., Daviess Co., Indiana, on December 22, 1905. Claire M. reached age 78 and died in Indianapolis, Marion Co., Indiana, on August 2, 1984. She was buried in Washington Park East Cemetery, Indianapolis, Warren Twp., Marion Co., Indiana.[91]

212. **Beatrice Emily**[8] **Davis** (*David Benton*[7], *Emily Jane*[6] *Smith*, *Mary Ann*[5] *Palmer*, *Mary Margaret*[4] *Pagan*, *John*[3], *Andrew*[2], *James*[1]) was born on September 5, 1911, in Gallipolis, Gallipolis Twp., Gallia Co., Ohio. She was the daughter of David Benton Davis (98) and Elizabeth Meek Wickline. Beatrice Emily died in Indianapolis, Marion Co., Indiana, on January 16, 1986, at age 74. She was buried under the name Beatrice Duncan Galbo in Anderson Cemetery, Warren Park, Warren Twp., Marion Co., Indiana.[90]

Beatrice Emily married **Norval Theodore Duncan** in 1931. They divorced. They had one daughter. Norval Theodore Duncan was born in Quincy, Taylor Twp., Owen Co., Indiana, on May 13, 1879. He reached age 75 and died in Indianapolis, Marion Co., Indiana, on February 14, 1955. Norval Theodore was buried in Anderson Cemetery, Warren Park, Warren Twp., Marion Co., Indiana.[90]

Beatrice Emily Davis Duncan married **Henry Ashbelle Goebel II** about 1933. They divorced. They had three children. Henry Ashbelle Goebel II was born in Indianapolis, Marion Co., Indiana, on December 28, 1912. He resided in 2001 in Rockville, Adams Twp., Parke Co., Indiana. Henry Ashbelle reached age 88 and died in a hospital in Terre Haute, Vigo Co., Indiana, on August 27, 2001. He was buried in Memory Garden Cemetery, Rockville, Adams Twp., Parke Co., Indiana.[137]

Beatrice Emily Davis Duncan Goebel married **Peter Galbo** on May 25, 1974, in Marion Co., Indiana. Peter Galbo was born in Salerno, Italy,

on June 24, 1900. Peter reached age 90 and died in Sarasota, Sarasota Co., Florida, on August 23, 1990.

Daughter of Beatrice Emily Davis and Norval Theodore Duncan:

+ 323 f I. **Mary Elizabeth**[9] **Duncan** was born in 1933.

Children of Beatrice Emily Davis and Henry Ashbelle Goebel II:

+ 324 f I. **Lula**[9] **Goebel?** was born in Warren Park, Warren Twp., Marion Co., Indiana, about 1932.

+ 325 f II. **Florence Mae**[9] **Goebel** was born in Warren Park, Warren Twp., Marion Co., Indiana, on February 19, 1934. She died in Beech Grove, Perry Twp., Marion Co., Indiana, on November 9, 2011. Florence Mae was buried in Memorial Park Cemetery, Indianapolis, Warren Twp., Marion Co., Indiana.[138]

+ 326 m III. **Henry August**[9] **Goebel III** was born in Warren Park, Warren Twp., Marion Co., Indiana, on April 15, 1937.

213. **Catherine Mae**[8] **Davis** (*David Benton*[7], *Emily Jane*[6] *Smith*, *Mary Ann*[5] *Palmer*, *Mary Margaret*[4] *Pagan*, *John*[3], *Andrew*[2], *James*[1]) was born on September 8, 1913, in Perry Twp., Gallia Co., Ohio. She was the daughter of David Benton Davis (98) and Elizabeth Meek Wickline. Catherine Mae died in Tujunga, Los Angeles Co., California, on April 15, 1984, at age 70.

Catherine Mae married **Frank William Laney** about 1930. They divorced. They had two daughters. Frank William Laney was born in Newark, Essex Co., New Jersey, on April 28, 1909. He reached age 91 and died in Duarte, Los Angeles, California, on August 21, 2000.

Catherine Mae Davis Laney married **Unknown Curry** after 1940.

Daughters of Catherine Mae Davis and Frank William Laney:

+ 327 f I. **Imogene F.⁹ Laney** was born in Akron, Summit Co., Ohio, on January 8, 1931.

+ 328 f II. **Shirley Ann⁹ Laney** was born in Pasadena, Los Angeles Co., California, on October 5, 1936.

**214. Edith Norman⁸ Williams** (*Anna Maude⁷ Smith, John Henry⁶, Mary Ann⁵ Palmer, Mary Margaret⁴ Pagan, John³, Andrew², James¹*) was born on August 8, 1909, in Columbus, Franklin Co., Ohio. She was the daughter of John Hunter Williams and Anna Maude Smith (101). Edith Norman died in Lansing, Lansing Twp., Ingham Co., Michigan, on July 1, 1941, at age 31. She was buried in Sunset Memorial Park Cemetery, Galloway, Franklin Co., Ohio.[47]

Edith Norman married **Frank Emerson Mapel** on May 11, 1940, in Franklin Co., Ohio. Frank Emerson Mapel was born in Columbus Grove, Pleasant Twp., Putnam Co., Ohio, on February 18, 1912. Frank Emerson reached age 76 and died in Indianapolis, Marion Co., Indiana, on December 6, 1988. He was buried in Forest Lawn Memory Gardens Cemetery, Greenwood, Johnson Co., Indiana.[139]

**215. John Kimber⁸ Williams** (*Anna Maude⁷ Smith, John Henry⁶, Mary Ann⁵ Palmer, Mary Margaret⁴ Pagan, John³, Andrew², James¹*) was born on September 28, 1913, in Columbus, Franklin Co., Ohio. He was the son of John Hunter Williams and Anna Maude Smith (101). He died in Wilmington, Union Twp., Clinton Co., Ohio, on August 1, 1974, at age 60. John Kimber was buried in Sugar Grove Cemetery, Wilmington, Union Twp., Clinton Co., Ohio.[92]

John Kimber Williams, a physician, married **Unknown Unknown** after 1940.

**216. Laurence Harold⁸ Campbell** (*Auta Mae⁷ Smith, John Henry⁶, Mary Ann⁵ Palmer, Mary Margaret⁴ Pagan, John³, Andrew², James¹*) was born on November 10, 1904, in Green Twp., Gallia Co., Ohio. He was the son of James Harold Campbell and Auta Mae Smith (102). Laurence Harold died

in Dade Co., Florida, on September 7, 1970, at age 65.

**217. Howard E.⁸ Smith** (*Ernest Hamilton⁷, John Henry⁶, Mary Ann⁵ Palmer, Mary Margaret⁴ Pagan, John³, Andrew², James¹*) was born on December 1, 1922, in San Diego, San Diego Co., California. He was the son of Ernest Hamilton Smith (103) and Louise Ecker. Howard E. died in San Diego, San Diego Co., California, on January 31, 2013, at age 90.

Howard E. married **Lucy Jane Motter** on August 1, 1954, in Orange Co., California. They had two children. Lucy Jane Motter was born in Macomb, McDonough Co., Illinois, on June 15, 1925. Lucy Jane reached age 82 and died in San Diego, San Diego Co., California, on March 15, 2008.

**218. Mary Lou⁸ Smith** (*Orin Henry⁷, John Henry⁶, Mary Ann⁵ Palmer, Mary Margaret⁴ Pagan, John³, Andrew², James¹*) was born on May 18, 1931, in Rio Grande, Raccoon Twp., Gallia Co., Ohio. She was the daughter of Orin Henry Smith (105) and Lillian Gertrude McAllister. Mary Lou died in Myrtle Beach, Horry Co., South Carolina, on February 13, 2011, at age 79.

She married **Unknown Schwab.** They divorced. They had three daughters.

**219. Lois Ann⁸ Smith** (*Orin Henry⁷, John Henry⁶, Mary Ann⁵ Palmer, Mary Margaret⁴ Pagan, John³, Andrew², James¹*) was born on January 28, 1936, in Athens, Athens Twp., Athens Co., Ohio. She was the daughter of Orin Henry Smith (105) and Lillian Gertrude McAllister. Lois Ann died in Groveland, Tuolumne Co., California, on May 29, 2013, at age 77.

Lois Ann married **Richard Rosenbaum** in 1955 in Meigs Co., Ohio. They had four children. Richard Rosenbaum was born in Pomeroy, Salisbury Twp., Meigs Co., Ohio, on October 28, 1929. Richard reached age 86 and died in Groveland, Tuolumne Co., California, on February 28, 2016.

Lois Ann Smith and Richard Rosenbaum had four children, including:

+ 329 m I. **Douglas Allan⁹ Rosenbaum** was born in Pomeroy, Salisbury Twp.,

Meigs Co., Ohio, on December 2, 1957. He died in a hospital in Columbus, Franklin Co., Ohio, on July 15, 1985. Douglas Allan was buried in Beech Grove Cemetery, Pomeroy, Salisbury Twp., Meigs Co., Ohio.[140]

+ 330 f II. **Daughter⁹ Rosenbaum**

**220. Floyd Merle⁸ Shore** (*Cora Belle⁷ Wood, Mary Frances⁶ Smith, Mary Ann⁵ Palmer, Mary Margaret⁴ Pagan, John³, Andrew², James¹*) was born in Marceline, Linn Co., Missouri on January 23, 1896. He was the adopted son of Jacob Arthur Shore and and Cora Belle Wood (106). He died in Howard, Fremont Co., Colorado? on November 1, 1976 at age 80. Floyd Merle was buried in Roselawn Cemetery, Pueblo, Pueblo, Colorado.[51]

Childless.

Floyd Merle married Mrs. **Martha Catherine Wyndle** Gregg on October 9, 1922 in El Paso Co., Colorado. Martha Catherine Wyndle was born in Mount Sandels, Sebastian Co., Arkansas on July 6, 1889. She was also known as **Kate**. Martha Catherine reached age 54 and died in Howard, Fremont Co., Colorado, on January 6, 1978. She was buried in Roselawn Cemetery, Pueblo, Pueblo, Colorado.[51]

**221. Lawrence Howard⁸ Shore** (*Cora Belle⁷ Wood, Mary Frances⁶ Smith, Mary Ann⁵ Palmer, Mary Margaret⁴ Pagan, John³, Andrew², James¹*) was born in Las Animas, Bent Co., Colorado on January 26, 1906. He was the adopted son of Jacob Arthur Shore and and Cora Belle Wood (106). He died after 1942.

There are no records for Lawrence Howard Shore after his WWII draft registration in Denver, Colorado. May have died in WWII?

Lawrence Howard Shore married **Henrietta Olive Unknown**.

**222. Joseph Parry⁸ Warren** (*Parry Oberlin⁷, Lydia Luella⁶ Smith, Mary Ann⁵ Palmer, Mary Margaret⁴ Pagan, John³, Andrew², James¹*) was born on

February 8, 1917, in Dayton, Montgomery Co., Ohio. He was the son of Parry Oberlin Warren (115) and Mabel M. Schnebly. Joseph Parry died in Vero Beach, Indiana River Co., Florida, on June 5, 1987, at age 70. He was buried in Shiloh Park Cemetery, Shiloh, Harrison Twp., Montgomery Co., Ohio.[96]

May have been childless.

Joseph Parry married **Betty May Swedberg** before 1972. Betty May Swedberg was born in Chicago, Cook Co., Illinois, on September 30, 1918. Betty May reached age 54 and died in Dayton, Montgomery Co., Ohio, on October 26, 1972. She was buried in Shiloh Park Cemetery, Shiloh, Harrison Twp., Montgomery Co., Ohio.[96]

Joseph Parry Warren married **Phyllis Agnes Humphreys** about 1978. Phyllis Agnes Humphreys was born in London, England, on May 14, 1913. Phyllis Agnes reached age 91 and died in Vero Beach, Indiana River Co., Florida, on June 29, 2004.

**223. James William⁸ Warren** (*Parry Oberlin⁷, Lydia Luella⁶ Smith, Mary Ann⁵ Palmer, Mary Margaret⁴ Pagan, John³, Andrew², James¹*) was born on July 13, 1920, in Dayton, Montgomery Co., Ohio. He was the son of Parry Oberlin Warren (115) and Mabel M. Schnebly. James William died in Columbus, Franklin Co., Ohio, on July 22, 2003, at age 83. He was buried in Glen Haven Memorial Gardens, Donnelsville, Bethel Twp., Clark Co., Ohio.[90]

**224. Jerry Schnebly⁸ Warren** (*Parry Oberlin⁷, Lydia Luella⁶ Smith, Mary Ann⁵ Palmer, Mary Margaret⁴ Pagan, John³, Andrew², James¹*) was born on July 27, 1929, in Dayton, Montgomery Co., Ohio. He was also known as **Jerry.** He was the son of Parry Oberlin Warren (115) and Mabel M. Schnebly. Jerry Schnebly died in Xenia, Xenia Twp., Greene Co., Ohio, on July 30, 1984, at age 55. He was buried in Davids Cemetery, Kettering, Montgomery Co., Ohio.[98]

Jerry Schnebly married **M. Laverne Brown** on January 30, 1951, in Montgomery Co., Ohio. M.

Laverne Brown was born in Dayton, Montgomery Co., Ohio, on November 19, 1932.

**225. Wesley Austin**[8] **Smith** (*Levi Morgan*[7], *Wesley Thomas*[6], *Mary Ann*[5] *Palmer*, *Mary Margaret*[4] *Pagan*, *John*[3], *Andrew*[2], *James*[1]) was born on January 31, 1916, in Hammond, Lake Co., Indiana. He was the son of Levi Morgan Smith (117) and Martha Abigail Watson. Wesley Austin died in Bloomington, Monroe Co., Indiana, on February 6, 2001, at age 85. He was buried in Valhalla Memorial Gardens, Bloomington, Monroe Co., Indiana.[99]

Wesley Austin married **Jean Johnson** after 1940. They had one daughter. Jean Johnson was born on October 27, 1919.

**226. Catherine Jane**[8] **Smith** (*Levi Morgan*[7], *Wesley Thomas*[6], *Mary Ann*[5] *Palmer*, *Mary Margaret*[4] *Pagan*, *John*[3], *Andrew*[2], *James*[1]) was born on January 19, 1918, in Hammond, Lake Co., Indiana. She was the daughter of Levi Morgan Smith (117) and Martha Abigail Watson. Catherine Jane died in Hammond, Lake Co., Indiana, on February 24, 1920, at age two. She was buried in Elmwood Cemetery, Hammond, Lake Co., Indiana.[49]

**227. Doris Mary**[8] **Smith** (*Levi Morgan*[7], *Wesley Thomas*[6], *Mary Ann*[5] *Palmer*, *Mary Margaret*[4] *Pagan*, *John*[3], *Andrew*[2], *James*[1]) was born on June 8, 1922, in Hammond, Lake Co., Indiana. She was the daughter of Levi Morgan Smith (117) and Martha Abigail Watson. Doris Mary died in Dyer, Lake Co., Indiana, on April 14, 2014, at age 91. She was buried in Chapel Lawn Memorial Gardens Cemetery, Schererville, Lake Co., Indiana.[93]

Doris Mary married **Paul Alrie Overstreet** on October 19, 1940, in Lake Co., Indiana. They had four children. Paul Alrie Overstreet was born in Indianapolis, Marion Co., Indiana, on August 5, 1918. Paul Alrie reached age 44 and died in Hammond, Lake Co., Indiana, on August 3, 1963. He was buried in Chapel Lawn Memorial Gardens Cemetery, Schererville, Lake Co., Indiana.[100]

Doris Mary Smith and Paul Alrie Overstreet had four children, including:

+ 331 f I. **Karen Louise**[9] **Overstreet** was born in Hammond, Lake Co., Indiana, on January 2, 1945. She died in Hammond, Lake Co., Indiana, on September 22, 2003.

**228. Hannah Morgan**[8] **Daugherty** (*Eva Marie*[7] *Smith*, *Wesley Thomas*[6], *Mary Ann*[5] *Palmer*, *Mary Margaret*[4] *Pagan*, *John*[3], *Andrew*[2], *James*[1]) was born on September 14, 1914, in Columbus, Franklin Co., Ohio. She was the daughter of Horace Hilburn Daugherty and Eva Marie Smith (118). Hannah Morgan died in Indio, Riverside Co., California, on August 22, 1989, at age 74.

May have been childless.

Hannah Morgan married **William Lawrence Kumler** on November 6, 1937, in Franklin Co., Ohio. William Lawrence Kumler was born in Bellefontaine, Lake Twp., Logan Co., Ohio, on September 11, 1911. William Lawrence reached age 81 and died in Indio, Riverside Co., California, on September 13, 1992.

**229. Sam Pershing**[8] **Daugherty** (*Eva Marie*[7] *Smith*, *Wesley Thomas*[6], *Mary Ann*[5] *Palmer*, *Mary Margaret*[4] *Pagan*, *John*[3], *Andrew*[2], *James*[1]) was born on October 3, 1917, in Columbus, Franklin Co., Ohio. He was the son of Horace Hilburn Daugherty and Eva Marie Smith (118). Sam Pershing died in Hilton Head Island, Beaufort Co., South Carolina, on December 11, 2002, at age 85. He was buried in Beaufort National Cemetery, Beaufort, Beaufort Co., South Carolina.[101]

Sam Pershing married **Unknown Unknown** before 1971. Unknown died before 1971.

Sam Pershing Daugherty married **Unknown Two Unknown** before 1971.

Sam Pershing Daugherty married **Mary Jean Rademacher** on October 1, 1971, in Winchester Co., Virginia. Mary Jean Rademacher was born in Nebraska on December 9, 1928. Her name was Mary Jean Rademacher Stenika when she married Sam Pershing Daugherty.

**230. Merry Kay⁸ Daugherty** (*Eva Marie⁷ Smith, Wesley Thomas⁶, Mary Ann⁵ Palmer, Mary Margaret⁴ Pagan, John³, Andrew², James¹*) was born on March 5, 1921, in Columbus, Franklin Co., Ohio. She was the daughter of Horace Hilburn Daugherty and Eva Marie Smith (118). Merry Kay lived before 2000 in Pacific Palisades, Los Angeles Co., California. She also resided before 2000 in Seal Beach, Orange Co., California. Merry Kay died in Hilton Head Island, Beaufort Co., South Carolina, on March 7, 2000, at age 79. She was buried in Six Oaks Cemetery, Sea Pines Plantation, Beaufort Co., South Carolina.[95]

Merry Kay married **Bennett E. Nau** before 1942. They divorced. Bennett E. Nau was born in Collumbus, Franklin Co., Ohio, on July 30, 1919. He reached age 90 and died in Columbus, Franklin Co., Ohio, on February 4, 2010.

Merry Kay Daugherty Nau married **James R. Richards II** after 1946.

**231. Stanley Lawrence⁸ Smith** (*Owen Benton⁷, Lawrence Benton⁶, Mary Ann⁵ Palmer, Mary Margaret⁴ Pagan, John³, Andrew², James¹*) was born on February 16, 1916, in San Diego, San Diego Co., California. He was the son of Owen Benton Smith (119) and Erna Ann Furrer. Stanley Lawrence died in Post Falls, Kootenai Co., Idaho, on October 10, 2003, at age 87. He was buried in Coeur D'Alene Memorial Gardens Cemetery, Couer D'Alene, Rural Co., Idaho.[103]

Stanley Lawrence married Mrs. **Nita Pauline McDonald** McBride between 1946 and 1948 in Chihuahua, Mexico. They divorced.

Stanley Lawrence Smith married **Ruth M. Unknown** after 1948. They had one child. Ruth M. Unknown was born on August 9, 1922..

**232. Weldon Harrold⁸ Smith** (*Owen Benton⁷, Lawrence Benton⁶, Mary Ann⁵ Palmer, Mary Margaret⁴ Pagan, John³, Andrew², James¹*) was born on September 20, 1918, in Oakland, Alameda Co., California. He was the son of Owen Benton Smith (119) and Erna Ann Furrer. Weldon Harrold died in Westport, Mendocino Co., California, on January 20, 2007, at age 88.

Weldon Harrold married **Lois Llewellyn** on October 11, 1951, in Alameda Co., California. Lois Llewellyn was born in 1925.

**233. Harold⁸ Watts** (*Ernest Augustus⁷, Anna May⁶ Smith, Frances Madeline⁵ Cheney, Mary Margaret⁴ Pagan, John³, Andrew², James¹*) was born on February 4, 1917, in Perry Twp., Gallia Co., Ohio. He was the son of Ernest Augustus Watts (121) and Elizabeth Gladys Mossbarger. Harold died in Los Angeles, Los Angeles Co., California, on September 22, 1992, at age 75.

**234. Kenneth C.⁸ Watts** (*Ernest Augustus⁷, Anna May⁶ Smith, Frances Madeline⁵ Cheney, Mary Margaret⁴ Pagan, John³, Andrew², James¹*) was born on June 21, 1921, in Perry Twp., Gallia Co., Ohio. He was the son of Ernest Augustus Watts (121) and Elizabeth Gladys Mossbarger. Kenneth C. died in Gallipolis, Gallipolis Twp., Gallia Co., Ohio, on November 20, 1995, at age 74. He was buried in Mound Hill Cemetery, Gallipolis, Gallipolis Twp., Gallia Co., Ohio.[10]

He married **Sylvia M. Burchett.** Sylvia M. Burchett was born in Pike Co., Kentucky, on December 12, 1932. Sylvia M. reached age 75 and died in Huntington, Cabell Co., West Virginia, on January 13, 2008. She was buried in Mound Hill Cemetery, Gallipolis, Gallipolis Twp., Gallia Co., Ohio.[10]

**235. Harlan Watts⁸ Northup** (*Marie⁷ Watts, Anna May⁶ Smith, Frances Madeline⁵ Cheney, Mary Margaret⁴ Pagan, John³, Andrew², James¹*) was born on October 3, 1926, in Northup, Green Twp., Gallia Co., Ohio. He was the son of James Herman Northup and Marie Watts (123). Harlan Watts lived before 2010 Columbus, Franklin Co., Ohio. He died in Vinton, Huntington Twp., Gallia Co., Ohio, on October 23, 2010, at age 84.

Harlan Watts married **Ellen Marie Maddy** on February 25, 1947, in Franklin Co., Ohio. They divorced. Ellen Marie Maddy was born in Gallipolis, Gallipolis Twp., Gallia Co., Ohio, on October 17, 1924. She was also known as **Marie**.

After the divorce, Ellen Marie married Mr. Boggs.

Harlan Watts Northup married **Ella Mae Love** on February 9, 1952, in Greenup Co., Kentucky. They had two sons. Ella Mae Love was born in Plain City, Madison Co., Ohio, on December 12, 1929. Ella Mae reached age 83 and died in Huntington, Cabell Co., West Virginia, on January 14, 2013. She was buried in Mound Hill Cemetery, Gallipolis, Gallipolis Twp., Gallia Co., Ohio.

Harlan Watts Northup and Ella Mae Love had two sons, including:

+ 332 m  I.   **Gregory Allen⁹ Northup** was born in Gallipolis, Gallipolis Twp., Gallia Co., Ohio, on November 28, 1952. He died in Gallipolis, Gallipolis Twp., Gallia Co., Ohio, on September 3, 2008. He was cremated and his ashes buried in Mound Hill Cemetery, Gallipolis, Gallipolis Twp., Gallia Co., Ohio.[10]

**236. James Ansel⁸ Northup II** (*Marie⁷ Watts, Anna May⁶ Smith, Frances Madeline⁵ Cheney, Mary Margaret⁴ Pagan, John³, Andrew², James¹*) was born on December 23, 1927, in Northup, Green Twp., Gallia Co., Ohio. He was the son of James Herman Northup and Marie Watts (123). James Ansel died in Gallipolis, Gallipolis Twp., Gallia Co., Ohio, on December 11, 2004, at age 76. He was buried in Mound Hill Cemetery, Gallipolis, Gallipolis Twp., Gallia Co., Ohio.[10]

He married **Patricia Unknown.** They had one son.

**237. Edith Louise⁸ Wood** (*Everett Marion⁷, Lena⁶ Rickabaugh, Emily⁵ Cheney, Mary Margaret⁴ Pagan, John³, Andrew², James¹*) was born on October 25, 1920, in Gallipolis, Gallipolis Twp., Gallia Co., Ohio. She was the daughter of Everett Marion Wood (125) and Emma Alice Shadrach. Edith Louise died in Austin, Travis Co., Texas, on June 21, 2002, at age 81. She was buried in Texas State Cemetery, Austin, Travis Co., Texas.[104]

Edith Louise married **Donald Charles Klein** on December 31, 1944, in Franklin Co., Ohio. Donald Charles Klein was born in Chillicothe, Scioto Twp., Ross Co., Ohio, on September 30,

1917. Donald Charles reached age 80 and died in Austin, Travis Co., Texas, on October 1, 1997. He was buried in Texas State Cemetery, Austin, Travis Co., Texas.[96]

**238. David⁸ Wood** (*Oscar Sanford⁷, Lena⁶ Rickabaugh, Emily⁵ Cheney, Mary Margaret⁴ Pagan, John³, Andrew², James¹*) was born in 1940 in Clay Twp., Gallia Co., Ohio. He is the son of Oscar Sanford Wood (126) and Mary Ethel Harbour.

**239. Ray D.⁸ Wood** (*Stanley D.⁷, Lena⁶ Rickabaugh, Emily⁵ Cheney, Mary Margaret⁴ Pagan, John³, Andrew², James¹*) was born on March 10, 1936, in Perry Twp., Gallia Co., Ohio. He is the son of Stanley D. Wood (127) and Anise Jones.

**240. Earl Byron⁸ McMillin** (*Lillian May⁷ Wood, Lena⁶ Rickabaugh, Emily⁵ Cheney, Mary Margaret⁴ Pagan, John³, Andrew², James¹*) was born on August 26, 1929, in Huntington Twp., Gallia Co., Ohio. He was the son of Hollis McMillin and Lillian May Wood (129). Earl Byron died in Chillicothe, Scioto Twp., Ross Co., Ohio, on January 26, 2006, at age 76. He was buried in Twin Township Cemetery, Bourneville, Twin Twp., Ross Co., Ohio.[62]

**241. Carroll Dean⁸ McMillin** (*Lillian May⁷ Wood, Lena⁶ Rickabaugh, Emily⁵ Cheney, Mary Margaret⁴ Pagan, John³, Andrew², James¹*) was born on December 26, 1930, in Huntington Twp., Gallia Co., Ohio. He is the son of Hollis McMillin and Lillian May Wood (129).

Carroll Dean married **Betty Reliford** on June 23, 1980, in Dickenson Co., Virginia. Betty Reliford was born in Nelsonville, York Twp., Athens Co., Ohio, on June 12, 1935. Betty reached age 71 and died in Logan, Falls Twp., Hocking Co., Ohio, on November 11, 2006. She was buried in Knollwood Cemetery, Logan, Falls Twp., Hocking Co., Ohio.[141]

**242. Marvin Lee⁸ McMillin** (*Lillian May⁷ Wood, Lena⁶ Rickabaugh, Emily⁵ Cheney, Mary Margaret⁴ Pagan, John³, Andrew², James¹*) was born on October 26, 1936, in Huntington Twp., Gallia Co., Ohio. He was the son of Hollis McMillin and Lillian May Wood (129). Marvin Lee died in Logan, Falls Twp., Hocking Co., Ohio, on May 20, 1987, at age 50. He was buried in Fairview

Methodist Cemetery, Good Hope Twp., Hocking Co., Ohio.[97]

**243. Shirley L.[8] Axe** (*Ethel Emily[7] Wood, Lena[6] Rickabaugh, Emily[5] Cheney, Mary Margaret[4] Pagan, John[3], Andrew[2], James[1]*) was born on October 17, 1933, in Perry Twp., Carroll Co., Ohio. She was the daughter of Alfred Frederick Axe and Ethel Emily Wood (130). Shirley L. lived in Pickerington, Violet Twp., Fairfield Co., Ohio in 1988. She died in a hospital in Columbus, Franklin Co., Ohio, on March 5, 1988, at age 54. Shirley L. was buried in Harrison Township Cemetery, South Bloomfield, Harrison Twp., Pickaway Co., Ohio.[63]

She married **Robert Lee Swoyer.** They had two daughters. Robert Lee Swoyer was born in Circleville, Circleville Twp., Pickaway Co., Ohio, on September 11, 1933. Robert Lee lived in Pickerington, Violet Twp., Fairfield Co., Ohio in 2014. He reached age 80 and died in a hospital in Columbus, Franklin Co., Ohio, on May 20, 2014. Robert Lee was buried in Harrison Township Cemetery, South Bloomfield, Harrison Twp., Pickaway Co., Ohio.[63]

**244. Doris E.[8] Axe** (*Ethel Emily[7] Wood, Lena[6] Rickabaugh, Emily[5] Cheney, Mary Margaret[4] Pagan, John[3], Andrew[2], James[1]*) was born on October 29, 1937, in Steubenville, Cross Creek Twp., Jefferson Co., Ohio. She was the daughter of Alfred Frederick Axe and Ethel Emily Wood (130). Doris E. died in Columbus, Franklin Co., Ohio, on September 10, 2014, at age 76. She was buried in Harrison Township Cemetery, South Bloomfield, Harrison Twp., Pickaway Co., Ohio.[63]

Doris E. married **Kenneth L. Applegate** in 1963. They divorced. They had one daughter. Kenneth L. Applegate was born in Staten Island, Richmond Co., New York, on January 4, 1936. He reached age 79 and died in Upper Sandusky, Crane Twp., Wyandot Co., Ohio, on June 25, 2015. Kenneth L. was buried in Oak Hill Cemetery, Upper Sandusky, Crane Twp., Wyandot Co., Ohio.[142]

**245. William Emmett[8] Lewis II** (*Medrith Marie[7] Massie, Hattie[6] Rickabaugh, Emily[5] Cheney, Mary Margaret[4] Pagan, John[3], Andrew[2], James[1]*) was born on October 7, 1923, in Columbus, Franklin Co., Ohio. He was the son of William Emmett Lewis and Medrith Marie Massie (132).

**246. Marilyn S.[8] Massie** (*John Orville[7], Hattie[6] Rickabaugh, Emily[5] Cheney, Mary Margaret[4] Pagan, John[3], Andrew[2], James[1]*) was born about 1938 in Youngstown, Mahoning Co., Ohio. She was the daughter of John Orville Massie (134) and Vera Caroline Smith. Marilyn S. died after 1940.

**247. Ben[8] Massie** (*Raymond Neil[7], Hattie[6] Rickabaugh, Emily[5] Cheney, Mary Margaret[4] Pagan, John[3], Andrew[2], James[1]*) was born on February 24, 1938, in Indianapolis, Marion Co., Indiana? He is the son of Raymond Neil Massie (135) and Melba Fern Sievenpiper.

**248. Emily A.[8] Brothers** (*Golden Odessa[7] Massie, Hattie[6] Rickabaugh, Emily[5] Cheney, Mary Margaret[4] Pagan, John[3], Andrew[2], James[1]*) was born on January 8, 1928, in Columbus, Franklin Co., Ohio. She is the daughter of Earl J. Brothers and Golden Odessa Massie (136). She died in Gahanna, Mifflin Twp., Franklin Co., Ohio on December 31, 1976 at age 47.

Emily A. Brothers married **James O. Elledge** on July 8, 1950, in Franklin Co., Ohio. They had at least one son. James O. Elledge was born in Columbus, Franklin Co., Ohio, on January 29, 1926.

Son of Emily A. Brothers and James O. Elledge:

+ 333 m I. **James Cimmaron[9] Elledge II** was born in Columbus, Franklin Co., Ohio, on August 20, 1951. He died in Columbus, Franklin Co., Ohio, on May 25, 1997. He was buried in Dublin Cemetery, Dublin, Washington Twp., Franklin Co., Ohio.[143]

**249. Sharon Lyn[8] See** (*Enabelle[7] Cheney, John Leonard[6], Silas B.[5], Mary Margaret[4] Pagan, John[3], Andrew[2], James[1]*) was born on March 24, 1948, in Gallipolis, Gallipolis Twp., Gallia Co., Ohio. She was the daughter of Russell M. See and Enabelle Cheney (144). Sharon Lyn died in Point Pleasant, Mason

Co., West Virginia, on October 15, 2003, at age 55. She was buried in Kirkland Memorial Gardens Cemetery, Point Pleasant, Mason Co., West Virginia.[107]

Never married.

250. **Nancy Sue⁸ Cheney** (*Ray Leonard⁷, John Leonard⁶, Silas B.⁵, Mary Margaret⁴ Pagan, John³, Andrew², James¹*) was born on October 4, 1958, in Gallipolis, Gallipolis Twp., Gallia Co., Ohio. She was the daughter of Ray Leonard Cheney (146) and Grace Irene Baird. Nancy Sue died in Gallipolis, Gallipolis Twp., Gallia Co., Ohio, on January 4, 1959. She was buried in Campaign Cemetery, Addison Twp., Gallia Co., Ohio.[68]

251. **Claude Amil⁸ King II** (*Claude Amil⁷, John A.⁶, Mary Ann⁵ Pagan, John⁴, John³, Andrew², James¹*) was born on January 3, 1931, in Sedalia, Sedalia Twp., Pettis Co., Missouri. He was the son of Claude Amil King (156) and Blanche Ellen Wands. Claude Amil died in Burbank, Los Angeles Co., California, on November 5, 1987, at age 56.

Claude Amil married **Dora Alicia Roberta Anguiano** on July 17, 1960, in Los Angeles Co., California. Dora Alicia Roberta Anguiano was born in Corona, Riverside Co., California, on December 9, 1929. She is also known as **Roberta.**

252. **Stephen L.⁸ Markham** (*Mary Ima⁷ King, John A.⁶, Mary Ann⁵ Pagan, John⁴, John³, Andrew², James¹*) was born on July 10, 1922, in Sedalia, Sedalia Twp., Pettis Co., Missouri. He is the son of Daniel William Markham and Mary Ima King (158).

253. **Mary Frances Helen⁸ Markham** (*Mary Ima⁷ King, John A.⁶, Mary Ann⁵ Pagan, John⁴, John³, Andrew², James¹*) was born on March 4, 1924, in Sedalia, Sedalia Twp., Pettis Co., Missouri. She was the daughter of Daniel William Markham and Mary Ima King (158). Mary Frances Helen died in Laguna Hills, Orange Co., California, on November 6, 2007, at age 83.

Mary Frances Helen Markham married **Unknown Unknown.** They divorced. They had one son.

Mary Frances Helen Markham Unknown married **Lauritz Labrecht Hommell Melchior** in 1964. They divorced. Lauritz Labrecht Hommell

Melchior was born in Denmark on March 20, 1890. He reached age 82 and died in Santa Monica, Los Angeles Co., California, on March 18, 1973. Lauritz Labrecht Hommell was buried in Assistens Kirkegaard Cemetery, Copenhagen, Denmark.[144]

Lauritz Melchoir was a world-famous opera singer who is considered perhaps the finest Wagnerian tenor ever.

Mary Frances Helen Markham Unknown Hommell married **Gary Damsker** after 1966. Gary Damsker was born in Philadelphia, Philadelphia Co., Pennsylvania, on March 16, 1934.

254. **Arthur Wright⁸ Armstrong** (*Inez Edith⁷ Ballard, Effie Virginia⁶ King, Mary Ann⁵ Pagan, John⁴, John³, Andrew², James¹*) was born on December 7, 1906, in Washington Court House, Union Twp., Fayette Co., Ohio. He was the son of Byron Chauncey Armstrong and Inez Edith Ballard (160). Arthur Wright died in Los Angeles, Los Angeles Co., California, on August 11, 1978, at age 71. He was buried in Los Angeles National Cemetery, Los Angeles, Los Angeles Co., California.[70]

255. **Mary Virginia⁸ Armstrong** (*Inez Edith⁷ Ballard, Effie Virginia⁶ King, Mary Ann⁵ Pagan, John⁴, John³, Andrew², James¹*) was born on July 26, 1908, in Washington Court House, Union Twp., Fayette Co., Ohio. She was the daughter of Byron Chauncey Armstrong and Inez Edith Ballard (160). Mary Virginia died in El Monte, Los Angeles Co., California?, on February 11, 1995, at age 86. She was buried in Forest Lawn Memorial Park Cemetery, Glendale, Los Angeles Co., California.[30]

She married **Joseph Jennings Baggett.** They had two children. Joseph Jennings Baggett was born in San Augustine Co., Texas, on June 10, 1910. Joseph Jennings reached age 64 and died in El Monte, Los Angeles Co., California?, on July 15, 1974. He was buried in Forest Lawn Memorial Park Cemetery, Glendale, Los Angeles Co., California.[30]

Mary Virginia Armstrong and Joseph Jennings Baggett had two children, including:

+ 334 m I. **Bruce**[9] **Baggett** was born in Los Angeles, Los Angeles Co., California, in 1934.

**256. Charles Edward**[8] **Jobe** (*Anna Mae*[7] *Ballard, Effie Virginia*[6] *King, Mary Ann*[5] *Pagan, John*[4], *John*[3], *Andrew*[2], *James*[1]) was born on October 13, 1906, in Washington Court House, Union Twp., Fayette Co., Ohio. He was the son of Floyd Jobe and Anna Mae Ballard (161). Charles Edward died in Dayton, Montgomery Co., Ohio, on December 25, 1943, at age 37. He was buried in Maple Grove Cemetery, Mechanicsburg, Goshen Twp., Champaign Co., Ohio.[66]

In 1930, Charles Edward Jobe and Helen V. Jobe (later Dunton), were living in The Pythian Home, an orphanage in Springfield, Ohio.

Never married.

**257. Helen V.**[8] **Jobe** (*Anna Mae*[7] *Ballard, Effie Virginia*[6] *King, Mary Ann*[5] *Pagan, John*[4], *John*[3], *Andrew*[2], *James*[1]) was born on April 22, 1908, in Springfield, Springfield Twp., Clark Co., Ohio. She was the daughter of Floyd Jobe and Anna Mae Ballard (161). Helen V. died in a hospital in Columbus, Franklin Co., Ohio, on June 29, 1992, at age 84. She was buried in Washington Cemetery, Washington Court House, Fayette Co., Ohio. [110]

In 1930, Helen V. Jobe and her brother Charles Edward Jobe were living in The Pythian Home, an orphanage in Springfield, Ohio.

Helen V. married **Robert L. Dunton** in October 1931 in Hamilton Co., Ohio? They had one son. Robert L. Dunton was born in Washington Court House, Union Twp., Fayette Co., Ohio, on January 8, 1908. Robert L. reached age 44 and died in Washington Court House, Union Twp., Fayette Co., Ohio, on July 19, 1952. He was buried in Washington Cemetery, Washington Court House, Union Twp., Fayette Co., Ohio.[110]

Helen V. Jobe Dunton married **Cecil Raymond Vanzant** on November 23, 1957, in Fayette Co., Ohio. Cecil Raymond Vanzant was born in Marshall, Marshall Twp., Highland Co., Ohio, on October 11, 1904. Cecil Raymond reached age 61 and died in Washington Court House, Union Twp., Fayette Co., Ohio, on January 26, 1966. He was buried in Washington Cemetery, Washington Court House, Union Twp., Fayette Co., Ohio.[110]

Son of Helen V. Jobe and Robert L. Dunton:

+ 335 m I. **Robert Alan**[9] **Dunton II** was born in Washington Court House, Union Twp., Fayette Co., Ohio, on October 14, 1937.

**258. John Franklin**[8] **Morehouse** (*Edna Opal*[7] *Ballard, Effie Virginia*[6] *King, Mary Ann*[5] *Pagan, John*[4], *John*[3], *Andrew*[2], *James*[1]) was born on August 13, 1917, Springfield, Springfield Twp., Clark Co., Ohio. He was the son of Edna Opal Ballard (167) and Edwin Byron Morehouse. John Franklin died in Los Alamitos, Orange Co., California on June 11, 2004, at age 93. He was buried in Forest Lawn Memorial Park Cemetery, Cypress, Orange Co., California.[111]

He married **Winifred Clara Alexander** after 1940. She was born on December 18, 1917 in Los Angeles, Los Angeles Co., California. Winifred Clara reached the age of 56 and died on January 19, 1973 in Cypress, Orange Co., California. She was buried in Forest Lawn Memorial Park Cemetery, Cypress, Orange Co., California.[111]

**259. Child One**[8] **Ballard** (*Donald A.*[7] *Ballard, Effie Virginia*[6] *King, Mary Ann*[5] *Pagan, John*[4], *John*[3], *Andrew*[2], *James*[1]) was born before 1917 in Springfield, Springfield Twp., Clark Co., Ohio? And was the child of Donald A. (163) and Minnie Miller. He or she died after 1917.

**260. Clint**[8] **Ballard** (*Donald A.*[7] *Ballard, Effie Virginia*[6] *King, Mary Ann*[5] *Pagan, John*[4], *John*[3], *Andrew*[2], *James*[1]) was born on February 15, 1917, in Springfield, Springfield Twp., Clark Co., Ohio. He was the son of Donald A. Ballard (163) and Minnie Miller. He died after 1917.

**261. Earnest Willard**[8] **Johnson** (*John Edward*[7], *William Roosevelt*[6], *John J.*[5], *Catherine*[4] *Pagan, John*[3], *Andrew*[2], *James*[1]) was born on October 10, 1904, in Cleo, Wood Co., Oklahoma. He was the son of John Edward Johnson (167) and Ada Maud McNutt. Earnest Willard died in Crook Co., Oregon, on June 12, 1985, at age 80. He was buried in Monument Cemetery, Monument, Grant Co., Oregon.[36]

He married **Elizabeth Unknown.**

262. **Everett E.**[8] **Johnson** (*John Edward*[7], *William Roosevelt*[6], *John J.*[5], *Catherine*[4] *Pagan, John*[3], *Andrew*[2], *James*[1]) was born on September 5, 1906, in Ward, Wheeler Co., Oregon. He was the son of John Edward Johnson (167) and Ada Maud McNutt. Everett E. lived before 1971 in Bend, Deschutes Co., Oregon. He died in Juneau, Juneau Bureau, Alaska, on September 4, 1971, at age 64. Everett E. was buried in Monument Cemetery, Monument, Grant Co., Oregon.[36]

He married **Alise Anna Cork** on April 7, 1927. They had two children. Alise A. Cork was born in Monument, Grant Co., Oregon, on September 3, 1908. Alise A. reached age 63 and died in Juneau, Juneau Bureau, Alaska, on September 4, 1971. She was buried in Monument Cemetery, Monument, Grant Co., Oregon.[36]

Children of Everett E. Johnson and Alise Anna Cork:

+ 336 m I. **Lavern Clair**[9] **Johnson** was born in Hordman, Morrow Co., Oregon, on November 6, 1927. He died in Cordova, Valdez-Cordova Precinct, Alaska, on August 14, 2002. Lavern Clair was buried in Cordova Cemetery, Cordova, Valdez-Cordova Precinct, Alaska.[145]

+ 337 f II. **Jacqueline**[9] **Johnson** was born in North Fork, Grant Co., Oregon, in 1930.

263. **Lawrence A.**[8] **Johnson** (*John Edward*[7], *William Roosevelt*[6], *John J.*[5], *Catherine*[4] *Pagan, John*[3], *Andrew*[2], *James*[1]) was born on September 29, 1908, in Lone Rock Place, Klamath Co., Oregon. He was the son of John Edward Johnson (167) and Ada Maud McNutt. Lawrence A. died in Klamath Co. Oregon on March 8, 2007, at age 98. He was bur-

ied in Monument Cemetery, Monument, Grant Co., Oregon.[36]

Lawrence A. married **Iva Ellen Emry** on June 30, 1930, in Grant Co., Oregon. They had two daughters. Iva Ellen Emry was born in Heppner, Morrow Co., Oregon on June 30, 1911. Iva Ellen reached age 89 and died in Redmond, Deschutes Co., Oregon, on October 22, 2000. She was buried in Monument Cemetery, Monument, Grant Co., Oregon.[36]

Daughters of Lawrence A. Johnson and Iva Ellen Emry:

+ 338 f I. **Joanne G.**[9] **Johnson** was born on September 10, 1931 in Grant Co., Oregon. She died in Albany, Linn Co., Oregon?, on December 5, 2015. She was buried in Redmond Memorial Cemetery, Redmond, Deschutes Co., Oregon.[146]

+ 339 f II. **Florence Alice**[9] **Johnson** was born on April 25, 1933 in Grant Co., Oregon. She died on February 24, 2014 in Salem, Polk Co., Oregon. She was buried in Restlawn Memorial Gardens Cemetery, Salem, Polk Co., Oregon.[147]

264. **Ethel**[8] **Johnson** (*John Edward*[7], *William Roosevelt*[6], *John J.*[5], *Catherine*[4] *Pagan, John*[3], *Andrew*[2], *James*[1]) was born in 1910 in Ward, Wheeler Co., Oregon. She was the daughter of John Edward Johnson (167) and Ada Maud McNutt. Ethel died after 1920.

265. **Bertrim**[8] **Johnson** (*John Edward*[7], *William Roosevelt*[6], *John J.*[5], *Catherine*[4] *Pagan, John*[3], *Andrew*[2], *James*[1]) was born on January 5, 1912, in Monument, Grant Co., Oregon. He was the son of John Edward Johnson (167) and Ada Maud McNutt. Bertrim died in Grant Co., Oregon, on October 19, 1930, at age 18. He was buried in Monument Cemetery, Monument, Grant Co., Oregon.[36]

Childless.

Bertrim married **Ethel Miriam Cupper** about 1930. Ethel Miriam Cupper was born in

Monument, Grant Co., Oregon, on October 28, 1913. She was also known as **Dynamite.** Ethel Miriam reached age 95 and died in Auburn, Placer Co., California, on January 31, 2009. She was buried in Monument Cemetery, Monument, Grant Co., Oregon.[36]

Her name was Ethel Miriam Leathers when she died.

**266. Myrtle Grace⁸ Johnson** (*John Edward⁷, William Roosevelt⁶, John J.⁵, Catherine⁴ Pagan, John³, Andrew², James¹*) was born on December 11, 1915, in Monument, Grant Co., Oregon. She was also known as **Grace.** She was the daughter of John Edward Johnson (167) and Ada Maud McNutt. Myrtle Grace died in Missoula, Missoula Co., Montana, on October 10, 1999, at age 83.

She died under the name Myrtle G. Christensen.

Myrtle Grace married **Unknown Marchand** before 1958.

Myrtle Grace Johnson Marchand married **Unknown Christensen** about 1960.

Myrtle Grace Johnson Marchand Christensen married **Richard W. Roderick** on July 14, 1965, in Clark Co., Washington. Richard W. Roderick was born in Portland, Multnomah Co., Oregon, on November 22, 1924. He died in Portland, Multomah Co., Oregon on July 10, 1974. He was buried in Willamette National Cemetery, Portland, Multnomah Co., Oregon.[148]

**267. Willard L.⁸ Johnson** (*John Edward⁷, William Roosevelt⁶, John J.⁵, Catherine⁴ Pagan, John³, Andrew², James¹*) was born in September 1916 in Monument, Grant Co., Oregon. He was the son of John Edward Johnson (167) and Ada Maud McNutt. Willard L. died in Pine Forest, Deschutes Co., Oregon?, after 1940.

He married **Helen Unknown.** Helen Unknown was born in Oregon in 1922.

**268. Ruthellen⁸ Johnson** (*John Edward⁷, William Roosevelt⁶, John J.⁵, Catherine⁴ Pagan, John³, Andrew², James¹*) was born on January 7, 1922, in Monument, Grant Co., Oregon. She was the daughter of John Edward Johnson (167) and Estella May Copeland. Ruthellen died in Portland,

Multnomah Co., Oregon, on June 8, 1961, at age 39. She was buried in Lincoln Memorial Park Cemetery, Portland, Multnomah Co., Oregon.[113]

Ruthellen married **Elmer Eugene Henderson** after 1940. Elmer Eugene Henderson was born in Manford, Creek Co., Oklahoma, on December 28, 1920. Elmer Eugene reached age 56 and died in Vancouver, Clark Co., Washington, on November 8, 1977. He was buried in Redmond Memorial Cemetery, Redmond, Deschutes Co., Oregon.[145]

**269. Dorothy Viola⁸ Johnson** (*John Edward⁷, William Roosevelt⁶, John J.⁵, Catherine⁴ Pagan, John³, Andrew², James¹*) was born on June 2, 1924, in Mount Vernon, Grant Co., Oregon. She was the daughter of John Edward Johnson (167) and Estella May Copeland. Dorothy Viola died in Sandpoint, Bonner Co., Idaho, on March 6, 2001, at age 76. She was buried in Pilot Butte Cemetery, Bend, Deschutes Co., Oregon.[112]

Dorothy Viola married **Donald Alfred Dyer.** He was born on March 8, 1924 in Spokane, Spokane Co., Washington. Donald Alfred reached age 70 and died in Portland, Multnomah Co., Oregon, on December 19, 1994. He was buried in Pilot Butte Cemetery, Bend, Deschutes Co., Oregon.[112]

**270. Isabelle Rosemary⁸ Johnson** (*John Edward⁷, William Roosevelt⁶, John J.⁵, Catherine⁴ Pagan, John³, Andrew², James¹*) was born on April 9, 1927, in Monument, Grant Co., Oregon. She was also known as **Billie.** She was the daughter of John Edward Johnson (167) and Estella May Copeland. Isabelle Rosemary died in Bend, Deschutes Co., Oregon, on June 20, 2008, at age 81. She was buried in Pilot Butte Cemetery, Bend, Deschutes Co., Oregon.[112]

She married **Unknown Von Burgess.** Von Burgess was born on August 20, 1926.

**271. Kenneth Eugene⁸ Johnson** (*John Edward⁷, William Roosevelt⁶, John J.⁵, Catherine⁴ Pagan, John³, Andrew², James¹*) was born on December 20, 1929, in Dayville, Grant Co., Oregon. He was the son of John Edward Johnson (167) and Estella May Copeland. Kenneth Eugene lived before 1995 in Bend, Deschutes Co., Oregon. He died in Portland, Multnomah Co., Oregon, on February

21, 1995, at age 65. Kenneth Eugene was buried in Pilot Butte Cemetery, Bend, Deschutes Co., Oregon.[112]

Kenneth Eugene married **Roberta Jean Fredenhagen** on November 19, 1952, in Clark Co., Washington. Roberta Jean Fredenhagen was born in Emmett, Gem Co., Idaho, on August 25, 1933. Roberta Jean reached age 73 and died in Bend, Deschutes Co., Oregon, on April 14, 2007. She was buried in Pilot Butte Cemetery, Bend, Deschutes Co., Oregon.[112]

**272. Cecil Edward**[8] **Johnson** (*Memphis Mason*[7], *William Roosevelt*[6], *John J.*[5], *Catherine*[4] *Pagan*, *John*[3], *Andrew*[2], *James*[1]) was born on December 5, 1913, in Lone Rock, Gilliam Co., Oregon. He was also known as **Shorty.** He was the son of Memphis Mason Johnson (169) and Ora Jane Caroline Wilson. Cecil Edward lived in Cuervo, Guadalupe Co., New Mexico in 1940. He died in Aztec, San Juan Co., New Mexico, on April 6, 1974, at age 60. Cecil Edward was buried in Aztec Community Cemetery, Aztec, San Juan Co., New Mexico.[114]

He married **Cleo P. Ward.** They had six children. Cleo P. Ward was born in Hale Co., Texas?, on November 11, 1913. Cleo P. reached age 63 and died in Aztec, San Juan Co., New Mexico, on July 21, 1977. She was buried in Aztec Community Cemetery, Aztec, San Juan Co., New Mexico.[114]

Cecil Edward Johnson and Cleo P. Ward had six children, including:

+ 340 m I. **Teddy Jack**[9] **Johnson** was born in Lockney, Floyd Co., Texas, on June 11, 1934. He was also known as **Jack.** Teddy Jack died in Bloomfield, San Juan Co., New Mexico, on June 26, 2003. He was buried in Aztec Community Cemetery, Aztec, San Juan Co., New Mexico.[114]

+ 341 f II. **Emma Louise**[9] **Johnson** was born in Clovis, Curry Co., New Mexico?, in 1936. She is also known as **Louise.**

+ 342 f III. **Ora Darline**[9] **Johnson** was born in Clovis, Curry Co., New Mexico, on June 3, 1938. She died in Lubbock, Lubbock Co., Texas, on October 2, 1983. Ora Darline was buried in Mission Garden of Memories Cemetery, Clovis, Curry Co., New Mexico.[149]

+ 343 f VI **Daughter**[9] **Johnson.**

**273. Marvin Earl**[8] **Johnson** (*Memphis Mason*[7], *William Roosevelt*[6], *John J.*[5], *Catherine*[4] *Pagan*, *John*[3], *Andrew*[2], *James*[1]) was born on August 1, 1915, in Roseburg, Douglas Co., Oregon. He was the son of Memphis Mason Johnson (169) and Ora Jane Caroline Wilson. Marvin Earl died in Paradise, Butte Co., California, on July 30, 1986, at age 70.

He married **Phyllis G. Bice.** They had one daughter. Phyllis G. Bice was born in Chewalah, Stevens Co., Washington, on September 6, 1923. Phyllis G. reached age 22 and died in Yolo Co., California, on May 5, 1946. She was buried in East Lawn Memorial Park Cemetery, Sacramento, Sacramento Co., California.[150]

Marvin Earl Johnson married **Louise Unknown** before 1975.

Daughter of Marvin Earl Johnson and Phyllis G. Bice:

+ 344A f I. **Dorothy Ellen**[9] **Johnson** was born in Placerville, El Dorado Co., California, on April 10, 1940. She died in Placerville, El Dorado Co., California, on September 21, 2013.

**274. Teddy Eugene**[8] **Johnson** (*Memphis Mason*[7], *William Roosevelt*[6], *John J.*[5], *Catherine*[4] *Pagan*, *John*[3], *Andrew*[2], *James*[1]) was born on July 18, 1923, in Roseburg, Douglas Co., Oregon. He was the son of Memphis Mason Johnson (169) and Ora Jane Caroline Wilson. Teddy Eugene died in near Saipan, Northern Mariana Islands, on June 16, 1944, at age 20. He is memorialized at the National Memorial Cemetery of the Pacific, Honolulu, Oahu Island, Hawaii.[115]

Teddy E. Johnson, U.S. Marine Corps, was lost at sea at the Battle of Saipan, Northern Mariana Islands, now United States territory, during WWII. His body was never recovered.

Never married.

275. **Neta Fern⁸ Fletcher** (*Luessia Marie⁷ Johnson, William Roosevelt⁶, John J.⁵, Catherine⁴ Pagan, John³, Andrew², James¹*) was born on December 6, 1916, in Civil Bend, Douglas Co., Oregon. She is the daughter of Thomas F. Fletcher and Luessia Marie Johnson (170).

Neta Fern married **Fred August Martin** on August 30, 1936. They had one daughter. Fred August Martin was born in Casper, Natrona Co., Wyoming, on June 16, 1916. Fred August lived in Albany, Linn Co., Oregon in 1990. He reached age 73 and died in a hospital in Corvallis, Benton Co., Oregon, on April 11, 1990. Fred August was buried in Roseburg IOOF Cemetery, Roseburg, Douglas Co., Oregon.[43]

Neta Fern Fletcher Martin married **George Melvyn Couron** on September 12, 1997, in Linn Co., Oregon. George Melvyn Couron was born in Fort Dodge, Cooper Twp., Webster Co., Iowa, on July 5, 1916. George Melvyn lived in Albany, Linn Co., Oregon in 2004. He reached age 87 and died in a hospital in Corvallis, Benton Co., Oregon, on May 27, 2004.

Daughter of Neta Fern Fletcher and Fred August Martin:

+ 344B  f  I.   **Luessia May⁹ Martin** was born in Coquille, Coos Co., Oregon, in 1939.

276. **Frieda Nell⁸ Fletcher** (*Luessia Marie⁷ Johnson, William Roosevelt⁶, John J.⁵, Catherine⁴ Pagan, John³, Andrew², James¹*) was born on June 23, 1919, in Civil Bend, Douglas Co., Oregon. She was the daughter of Thomas F. Fletcher and Luessia Marie Johnson (170). Frieda Nell died in Roseburg, Douglas Co., Oregon, on September 25, 1981, at age 62.

Frieda Nell married **Russell Telford Steinhauer** about 1940. They had four children. Russell Telford Steinhauer was born in Roseburg, Douglas

Co., Oregon, on October 22, 1914. Russell Telford Steinhauer reached age 94 and died in Roseburg, Douglas Co., Oregon, on September 19, 2009. He was buried in Civil Bend Cemetery, Winston, Douglas Co., Oregon.[151]

277. **Dora Mae⁸ Fletcher** (*Luessia Marie⁷ Johnson, William Roosevelt⁶, John J.⁵, Catherine⁴ Pagan, John³, Andrew², James¹*) was born on January 1, 1924, in Civil Bend, Douglas Co., Oregon. She was the daughter of Thomas F. Fletcher and Luessia Marie Johnson (170). Dora Mae died in Bend, Deschutes Co., Oregon, on December 17, 2003, at age 79. She was buried in Evergreen Memorial Park Cemetery, McMinnville, Yamhill Co., Oregon.[117]

Dora Mae married **Unknown Moore** before 1963.

Dora Mae Fletcher married **Oscar John Murray** on August 16, 1963, in Washoe Co., Nevada. Oscar John Murray was born in McMinnville, Yamhill Co., Oregon, on February 11, 1918. Oscar John reached age 84 and died in Bend, Deschutes Co., Oregon, on June 30, 2002. He was buried in Evergreen Memorial Park Cemetery, McMinnville, Yamhill Co., Oregon.[117]

278. **Loren Duane⁸ Johnson** (*Walter Cecil⁷, William Roosevelt⁶, John J.⁵, Catherine⁴ Pagan, John³, Andrew², James¹*) was born on February 9, 1930, in North Fork, Grant Co., Oregon. He is the son of Walter Cecil Johnson (171) and Mildred Ethyl Cork.

He married **Joan Carol Price.** They have three children. Joan Carol Price was born in Aberdeen, Grays Harbor Co., Washington, on May 12, 1939. Joan Carol reached age 66 and died in Prineville, Crook Co., Oregon, on May 16, 2005. She was buried in Greenwood Cemetery, Bend, Deschutes Co., Oregon.[118]

Loren Duane Johnson and Joan Carol Price had three children, including:

+ 345  f  I.   **Stacey Jo⁹ Johnson** was born in Bend, Deschutes Co., Oregon, on May 13, 1965. She died in Bend,

Deschutes Co., Oregon, on October 7, 2009. Stacey Jo was buried under her maiden name in Greenwood Cemetery, Bend, Deschutes Co., Oregon.[118]

**279. Donald Cecil⁸ Johnson** (*Walter Cecil⁷, William Roosevelt⁶, John J.⁵, Catherine⁴ Pagan, John³, Andrew², James¹*) was born on July 28, 1932, in Monument, Grant Co., Oregon. He was the son of Walter Cecil Johnson (171) and Mildred Ethyl. Cork. Donald Cecil died in Yucca Valley, San Bernardino Co., California, on November 17, 1996, at age 64. He was buried in Greenwood Cemetery, Bend, Deschutes Co., Oregon.[118]

He married **Georgia Eileen Albrecht.** Georgia Eileen Albrecht was born in Newburgh, Ohio Twp., Warrick Co., Indiana, on April 4, 1934. Georgia Eileen reached age 74 and died in Yucca Valley, San Bernardino Co., California, on October 7, 2008. She was buried in Greenwood Cemetery, Bend, Deschutes Co., Oregon.[118]

**280. Harold Gene⁸ Johnson** (*Walter Cecil⁷, William Roosevelt⁶, John J.⁵, Catherine⁴ Pagan, John³, Andrew², James¹*) was born on November 25, 1939, in Bend, Deschutes Co., Oregon. He was also known as **Sandy.** He was the son of Walter Cecil Johnson (171) and Mildred Ethyl. Cork. Harold Gene died in Bend, Deschutes Co., Oregon, on June 17, 1991, at age 51. He was buried in Deschutes Memorial Gardens Cemetery, Bend, Deschutes Co., Oregon.[118]

Harold Gene married **Ms. Guenther.**

**281. William Donald⁸ Smith** (*Alma L.⁷ Johnson, James Edward⁶, John J.⁵, Catherine⁴ Pagan, John³, Andrew², James¹*) was born on May 2, 1928, in Central Twp., Perry Co., Missouri. He was the son of William B. Smith and Alma L. Johnson (172). William Donald died in Montgomery City, Montgomery Twp., Montgomery Twp., Montgomery Co., Missouri, on July 21, 2008, at age 80. He was buried in Fairmount Cemetery, Middletown, Prairie Twp., Montgomery Co., Missouri.[120]

He married **Myra Joan Maskey.** They had one daughter. Myra Joan Maskey was born in Cuivre Twp., Audrain Co., Missouri, on May 5, 1931.

Daughter of William Donald Smith and Myra Joan Maskey:

+ 346 f I. **Daughter⁹ Smith**

**282. Norman Daniel⁸ Smith** (*Alma L.⁷ Johnson, James Edward⁶, John J.⁵, Catherine⁴ Pagan, John³, Andrew², James¹*) was born on December 31, 1929, in Central Twp., Perry Co., Missouri. He was also known as **Daniel Norman Smith.** He was the son of William B. Smith and Alma L. Johnson (172). Norman Daniel died in Montgomery City, Montgomery Twp., Montgomery Twp., Montgomery Co., Missouri, on November 13, 1955, at age 25. He was buried in Saint Mary's Cemetery, Montgomery City, Montgomery Twp., Montgomery Co., Missouri.[76]

He married **Myrtle Carr.**

**283. Edward Dale⁸ Smith** (*Alma L.⁷ Johnson, James Edward⁶, John J.⁵, Catherine⁴ Pagan, John³, Andrew², James¹*) was born on December 14, 1931, in Central Twp., Perry Co., Missouri. He was also known as **Dale.** He was the son of William B. Smith and Alma L. Johnson (172). Edward Dale died in Montgomery City, Montgomery Twp., Montgomery Twp., Montgomery Co., Missouri, on November 11, 2004, at age 72. He was buried in Saint Mary's Cemetery, Montgomery City, Montgomery Twp., Montgomery Co., Missouri.[76]

**284. Sherrill Dean⁸ Smith** (*Alma L.⁷ Johnson, James Edward⁶, John J.⁵, Catherine⁴ Pagan, John³, Andrew², James¹*) was born on October 8, 1933, in Missouri. He is the son of William B. Smith and Alma L. Johnson (172).

**285. Charlotte⁸ Smith** (*Alma L.⁷ Johnson, James Edward⁶, John J.⁵, Catherine⁴ Pagan, John³, Andrew², James¹*) was born in 1935 in Berkeley, St. Louis Co., Missouri? She is the daughter of William B. Smith and Alma L. Johnson (172).

**286. Heber⁸ Johnson II** (*Herbert Clay⁷, James Edward⁶, John J.⁵, Catherine⁴ Pagan, John³, Andrew², James¹*) was born on March 3, 1928, in Missouri. He was the son of Herbert Clay Johnson (173) and Clarice T. Meiser. Heber died in Barnhart, Jefferson Co., Missouri?, on May 4, 1984, at age 56.

**287. Raymond James[8] Johnson** (*Herbert Clay[7], James Edward[6], John J.[5], Catherine[4] Pagan, John[3], Andrew[2], James[1]*) was born on August 6, 1930, in Independence, Independence Twp., Doniphan Co., Missouri. He was the son of Herbert Clay Johnson (173) and Clarice T. Meiser. Raymond James died in Iberia, Richwoods Twp., Miller Co., Missouri, on February 11, 2000, at age 69. He was buried in Bethany Memorial Gardens Cemetery, Crocker, Tavern Twp., Pulaski Co., Missouri.[77]

Raymond James married **Helen Watson** on December 8, 1948, in Albany Co., Wyoming. They had three children. Helen Watson was born in Cheyenne, Laramie Co., Wyoming, on August 2, 1932. Helen reached age 74 and died in Lebanon, Lebanon Twp., LaClede Co., Missouri, on April 27, 2007. She was buried in Bethany Memorial Gardens Cemetery, Crocker, Tavern Twp., Pulaski Co., Missouri.[77]

**288. Ella Mae[8] Murrell** (*James W.[7], Ella Matilda[6], Emma[5] Johnson, Catherine[4] Pagan, John[3], Andrew[2], James[1]*) was born on November 12, 1907, in Dayton, Campbell Co., Kentucky. She was the daughter of James W. Murrell (177) and Cordelia Mae Hand. Ella Mae lived in Fort Myers, Lee Co., Florida before 1999. She died in Alexandria, Alexandria Co., Virginia?, on December 29, 1999, at age 92.

Ella Mae married **Arthur Keim Iber** in 1929 in Essex Co., New Jersey? They had three sons. Arthur Keim Iber was born in Garwood, Union Co., New Jersey, on June 27, 1905. Arthur Keim reached age 90 and died in Fort Myers, Lee Co., Florida, on July 26, 1995.

Ella Mae Murrell and Arthur Keim Iber had three sons, including:

+ 347A m I. **Peter Keim[9] Iber** was born in Elizabeth, Union Co., New Jersey, on July 26, 1937. He died in Sun City, Maricopa Co., Arizona,

on September 16, 2009. Peter Keim was buried in Arlington National Cemetery, Arlington, Virginia.[128]

**289. Belinda[8] Murrell** (*James W.[7], Ella Matilda[6], Emma[5] Johnson, Catherine[4] Pagan, John[3], Andrew[2], James[1]*) was born on April 28, 1910, in Dayton, Campbell Co., Kentucky. She was the daughter of James W. Murrell (177) and Cordelia Mae Hand. Belinda died in Fort Thomas, Campbell Co., Kentucky, on January 29, 2001, at age 90. She was buried in Evergreen Cemetery, Southgate, Campbell Co., Kentucky.[37]

She married **Mentor E. Graves.** They had one son. Mentor E. Graves was born in Newport, Campbell Co., Kentucky, on March 27, 1909. Mentor E. reached age 94 and died in a hospital in Wooster, Wooster Twp., Wayne Co., Ohio, on June 2, 2003. He was buried in Evergreen Cemetery, Southgate, Campbell Co., Kentucky.[37]

Son of Belinda Murrell and Mentor E. Graves:

+ 347B m I. **Thomas[9] Graves** was born in Newport, Campbell Co., Kentucky, on September 12, 1936.

**290. Martha Jane[8] Murrell** (*James W.[7], Ella Matilda[6], Emma[5] Johnson, Catherine[4] Pagan, John[3], Andrew[2], James*1) was born on December 3, 1914, in Chicago, Cook Co., Illinois. She was also known as **Dixie.** She was the daughter of James W. Murrell (177) and Martha Katherine Rehmann. Martha Jane died in Fayetteville, Fayette Co., Georgia, on April 2, 1999, at age 84.

She married **James Barnette.** They divorced. They had one son.

Martha Jane Murrell Barnette married **Willis H. Cheeseman II.** Willis H. Cheeseman II was born in Aura, Gloucester Co., New Jersey, on October 22, 1914. He was also known as **Bill.** Willis H. reached age 65 and died in Vineland, Cumberland Co., New Jersey, on June 8, 1980. He was buried in Manahath Cemetery, Glassboro, Gloucester Co., New Jersey.[152]

**291. Mary Catherine[8] Murrell** (*James W.[7], Ella Matilda[6], Emma[5] Johnson, Catherine[4] Pagan, John[3], Andrew[2], James[1]*) was born on August 23, 1927, in Clayton, Gloucester Co., New Jersey. She was also known as **Honey.** She was the daughter of James W. Murrell (177) and Martha Katherine Rehmann. Mary Catherine died in Chula Vista,

San Diego Co., California, on May 5, 2015, at age 87. She was buried in Fort Rosencrans National Military Cemetery, San Diego, San Diego Co., California.[122]

She married **Frank Paul Kanta.** They had four children. Frank Paul Kanta was born in Sumatra, Rosebud Co., Montana, on January 23, 1922. Frank Paul reached age 67 and died in Chula Vista, San Diego Co., California, on September 14, 1989. He was buried in Fort Rosencrans National Military Cemetery, San Diego, San Diego Co., California.[122]

**292. Beatrix Lizbeth[8] Murrell** (*James W.[7], Ella Matilda[6], Emma[5] Johnson, Catherine[4] Pagan, John[3], Andrew[2], James[1]*) was born on June 19, 1935, in Lancaster, Fairfield Co., Ohio. She was also known as **Betsy.** She was the daughter of James W. Murrell (177) and Leota Fay Bopes. Beatrix Lizbeth died in Chula Vista, San Diego, California, USA, on April 8, 2014, at age 68.

Never married.

**293. Calvin Greenwood[8] Worrall III** (*Nelle[7] Greenwood, Frank Burdette[6], Alexander[5], Catherine[4] Pagan, John[3], Andrew[2], James[1]*) was born on September 22, 1912 in Des Moines, Polk Co., Iowa. He was the son of Calvin Walker Worrall II and Nelle Greenwood (180). Calvin Greenwood died in Indianapolis, Marion Co., Indiana, on July 28, 1956, at age 44. He was buried in Rose Hill Cemetery, Bloomington, Monroe Co., Indiana.[113]

Calvin Greenwood married **Elizabeth Jeanne Allen** before 1934 in Shelby Co., Ohio? They had three children. Elizabeth Jeanne Allen was born in Van Wert, Pleasant Twp., Van Wert Co., Ohio, on August 19, 1913. Elizabeth Jeanne reached age 49 and died in Clayton, Liberty Twp., Hendricks Co., Indiana, on August 10, 1963. She was buried in

Floral Park Cemetery, Indianapolis, Marion Co., Indiana.[153]

She died under the name Elizabeth Jeanne Hansen.

Calvin Greenwood Worrall III and Elizabeth Jeanne Allen had three children, including:

+ 348  f  I.  **Susan[9] Worrall** was born in Sidney, Clinton Twp., Shelby Co., Ohio, on January 1, 1936. She died in Stockton, Stockton Twp., Cedar Co. Missouri, on March 21, 2014.

+ 349  f  II.  **Charlene[9] Worrall** was born in Sidney, Clinton Twp., Shelby Co., Ohio, on August 11, 1939. She died in Greencastle, Greencastle Twp., Putnam Co., Indiana, on March 27, 2017.

+ 350  f  II.  **Son[9] Worrall**

**294. Joann Betty[8] Worrall** (*Nelle[7] Greenwood, Frank Burdette[6], Alexander[5], Catherine[4] Pagan, John[3], Andrew[2], James[1]*) was born on January 26, 1918, in Indianapolis, Marion Co., Indiana. She was the daughter of Calvin Walker Worrall II and Nelle Greenwood (180). Joann Betty died in Latana, Palm Beach Co., Florida, on July 3, 2007, at age 89. She was buried in Greenwood Cemetery, Greenwood, Johnson Co., Indiana.[124]

Joann Betty married **Joseph W. Langley** on November 26, 1937, in Marion Co., Indiana. They had two daughters. Joseph W. Langley was born in Indianapolis, Marion Co., Indiana, on July 31, 1918. Joseph W. reached age 55 and died in Beech Grove, Marion Co., Indiana, on December 7, 1973. He was buried in Greenwood Cemetery, Greenwood, Johnson Co., Indiana.[139]

Joann Betty Worrall Langley married **Jesse John Hunt** on September 9, 1975, in Marion Co., Indiana. Jesse John Hunt was born in Indianapolis, Marion Co., Indiana, on June 4, 1909. Jesse John reached age 93 and died in Latana, Palm Beach Co., Florida, on April 20, 2003. He was buried in Forest Lawn Memory Gardens Cemetery, Greenwood, Johnson Co., Indiana.[139]

**295. Crystabell C.⁸ Gould** (*Frances Virginia⁷ Hover, Harry A. Hover or⁶ Hoover, Fannie⁵ Greenwood, Catherine⁴ Pagan, John³, Andrew², James¹*) was born on July 17, 1914, in Cabell Co., West Virginia. She was the daughter of Danie Franklin Gould and Frances Virginia Hover (181). Crystabell C. died in San Diego, San Diego Co., California, on July 29, 1975, at age 61.

Childless.

Crystabell C. married **Louis Paul Hemsley** on April 20, 1972, in San Diego Co., California.

Louis Paul Hemsley was born in Sugar, Salt Lake Co., Utah, on July 19, 1902. Louis Paul reached age 71 and died in San Diego, San Diego Co., California, on December 25, 1973.

**296. Charles⁸ Baker II** (*Frances Virginia⁷ Hover, Harry A. Hover or⁶ Hoover, Fannie⁵ Greenwood, Catherine⁴ Pagan, John³, Andrew², James¹*) was born in 1938 in Alisal, Monterey Co., California. He is the son of Charles R. Baker and Frances Virginia Hover (181).

# 9th Generation

**297. Terry⁹ Palmer** (*Darwin Howard⁸, Roy Donnally⁷, Thomas M.⁶, Charles Nelson⁵, Mary Margaret⁴ Pagan, John³, Andrew², James¹*) was born on June 25, 1947, in Grand Rapids, Grand Rapids Twp., Kent Co., Michigan. He was the son of Darwin Howard Palmer (186) and Annabelle Bursma. Terry died in Crystal Falls, Iron Co., Michigan, on June 4, 2001, at age 53. He was buried in Evergreen Memorial Cemetery, Crystal Falls, Iron Co., Michigan.[127]

Terry Palmer married and had four children.

**298. Carol Elaine⁹ Palmer** (*Charles Ethan⁸, Charles Grover⁷, Lewis William⁶, Charles Nelson⁵, Mary Margaret⁴ Pagan, John³, Andrew², James¹*) was born on February 24, 1948, in Plymouth, Center Twp., Marshall Co., Indiana. She was the daughter of Charles Ethan Palmer (189) and Dorothy Rosalie Crider. Carol Elaine died in Palm Beach, Palm Beach Co., Florida, on December 15, 1994, at age 46.

She married **Unknown Guido.**

**299. Dorothy Jane⁹ Pratt** (*Alice Eugenia⁸ Palmer, Charles Grover⁷, Lewis William⁶, Charles Nelson⁵, Mary Margaret⁴ Pagan, John³, Andrew², James¹*) was born on February 17, 1943, in Detroit, Wayne Co., Michigan. She was also known as **Jane.** She was the daughter of Lawrence Arthur Pratt and Alice Eugenia Palmer (190). Dorothy Jane died in Purcellville, Loudoun Co., Virginia, on August 12, 2013, at age 70.

Dorothy Jane married **Mr. Schilling.** They had two daughters.

**300. Norman Dean⁹ Nevinger II** (*Doris Jane⁸ Palmer, Charles Grover⁷, Lewis William⁶, Charles Nelson⁵, Mary Margaret⁴ Pagan, John³, Andrew², James¹*) was born on August 4, 1936, in Chicago, Cook Co., Illinois. He was the son of Norman Dean Nevinger and Doris Jane Palmer (191). Norman Dean died in Peotone, Peotone Twp., Will Co., Illinois, on February 3, 2005, at age 68.

Norman Dean married **Ms. McWilliams.** They had nine children.

Norman Dean Nevinger II and Ms. McWilliams had nine children, including:

+ 350 m I. **Norman Dean¹⁰ Nevinger III** was born in Crete, Crete Twp., Will Co., Illinois?, on April 5, 1961. He died in Lafayette, Fairfield Twp., Tippecanoe Co., Indiana, on April 1, 2012.

**301. Linette Marie⁹ Nevinger** (*Doris Jane⁸ Palmer, Charles Grover⁷, Lewis William⁶, Charles Nelson⁵, Mary Margaret⁴ Pagan, John³, Andrew², James¹*) was born in 1940 in Chicago, Cook Co., Illinois. She is the daughter of Norman Dean Nevinger and Doris Jane Palmer (191).

**302. Arleen Marie⁹ Davis** (*Harold Warner⁸, Daniel L.⁷, Emily Jane⁶ Smith, Mary Ann⁵ Palmer, Mary Margaret⁴ Pagan, John³, Andrew², James¹*) was born on September 25, 1930, in Ashley Twp., Delaware Co., Ohio. She was the daughter of Harold Warner Davis (197) and Esther Annamarie Deubner. Arleen Marie died in Shelby Twp., Richland Co., Ohio, on January 22, 1998, at age 67. She was buried in Shelby-Oakland Cemetery, Shelby, Shelby Twp., Richland Co., Ohio.[129]

Arleen Marie married **Edward Grant Dowds** before 1965. They had four children. Edward Grant Dowds was born in Shelby Twp., Richland Co., Ohio, on August 15, 1930. Edward Grant reached age 75 and died in Shelby Twp., Richland Co., Ohio, on September 1, 2005. He was buried in Shelby-Oakland Cemetery, Shelby, Shelby Twp., Richland Co., Ohio.[1129]

Arleen Marie Davis and Edward Grant Dowds had four children, including:

+ 352 m II. **Robert Grant¹⁰ Dowds** was born in Shelby, Shelby Twp., Richland Co., Ohio, on August 8, 1965. He died in North Lewisburg, Rush Twp., Champaign Co., Ohio, on August 11, 2016, at age 51. Robert Grant was buried in Shelby-Oakland

Cemetery, Shelby, Shelby Twp., Richland Co., Ohio.[129]

**303. Harold William⁹ Davis II** (*Harold Warner⁸, Daniel L.⁷, Emily Jane⁶ Smith, Mary Ann⁵ Palmer, Mary Margaret⁴ Pagan, John³, Andrew², James¹*) was born on March 12, 1932, in Ashley Twp., Delaware Co., Ohio. He was the son of Harold Warner Davis (197) and Esther Annamarie Deubner. Harold William lived in Worthington, Sharon Twp, Franklin Co., Ohio in 2011. He died in a hospital in Columbus, Franklin Co., Ohio, on May 21, 2011, at age 79.

He married **Patricia Unknown.** They had two children.

**304. Infant Twin Daughter⁹ McCarley** (*Edith Wilma⁸ Davis, Daniel L.⁷, Emily Jane⁶ Smith, Mary Ann⁵ Palmer, Mary Margaret⁴ Pagan, John³, Andrew², James¹*) was born on September 1, 1920, in Raccoon Twp., Gallia Co., Ohio. She was the daughter of Elmer Lackey McCarley and Edith Wilma Davis (198). Infant Twin Daughter died in Raccoon Twp., Gallia Co., Ohio, on September 1, 1920. She was buried in Calvary Baptist Cemetery, Rio Grande, Raccoon Twp., Gallia Co., Ohio.[12]

**305. Robin Louise⁹ McCarley** (*Edith Wilma⁸ Davis, Daniel L.⁷, Emily Jane⁶ Smith, Mary Ann⁵ Palmer, Mary Margaret⁴ Pagan, John³, Andrew², James¹*) was born on September 1, 1920, in Raccoon Twp., Gallia Co., Ohio. She was the daughter of Elmer Lackey McCarley and Edith Wilma Davis (198). Robin Louise died in Steubenville, Cross Creek Twp., Jefferson Co., Ohio, on December 15, 1995, at age 75. She was buried in Calvary Baptist Cemetery, Rio Grande, Raccoon Twp., Gallia Co., Ohio.[12]

Never married.

**306. Norma Jean⁹ McCarley** (*Edith Wilma⁸ Davis, Daniel L.⁷, Emily Jane⁶ Smith, Mary Ann⁵ Palmer, Mary Margaret⁴ Pagan, John³, Andrew², James¹*) was born on January 1, 1925, in Raccoon Twp., Gallia Co., Ohio. She was the daughter of Elmer Lackey McCarley and Edith Wilma Davis (198).

Norma Jean married **Charles William Edwards II** in 1949. They had two children. Charles William

Edwards II was born in Amsterdam, Springfield Twp., Jefferson Co., Ohio, on November 22, 1923. Charles William reached age 92 and died in Wintersville, Cross Creek Twp., Jefferson Co., Ohio, on June 11, 2016.

**307. Davis Eugene⁹ Boster** (*Nelle Emily⁸ Davis, Daniel L.⁷, Emily Jane⁶ Smith, Mary Ann⁵ Palmer, Mary Margaret⁴ Pagan, John³, Andrew², James¹*) was born on Tuesday, September 14, 1920, in Rio Grande, Raccoon Twp., Gallia Co., Ohio. He was also known as **Gene.** He was the son of Ernest Gordon Boster and Nelle Emily Davis (199). Davis Eugene died in Arlington, Virginia, on July 7, 2005, at age 84. He was buried in Arlington National Cemetery, Arlington, Virginia.[128]

Davis Eugene "Gene" Boster was appointed U.S. ambassador to Bangladesh in 1974 and Guatamala in 1976.

Davis Eugene married **Mary Elizabeth Shilts** on December 26, 1942, in Summit Co., Ohio. They divorced. They have five children. Mary Elizabeth Shilts was born in Hudson, Hudson Twp., Summit Co., Ohio, on March 12, 1920.

Davis Eugene Boster married **Ms. Gamero.** They divorced. They have one daughter.

**308. Patricia Ann⁹ Davis** (*David Orville⁸, Daniel L.⁷, Emily Jane⁶ Smith, Mary Ann⁵ Palmer, Mary Margaret⁴ Pagan, John³, Andrew², James¹*) was born on July 3, 1934, in Rio Grande, Raccoon Twp., Gallia Co., Ohio. She was the daughter of David Orville Davis (201) and Corrina Clark. Patricia Ann died in Rio Grande, Raccoon Twp., Gallia Co., Ohio, on March 7, 1935. She was buried in Calvary Baptist Cemetery, Rio Grande, Raccoon Twp., Gallia Co., Ohio.[12]

**309. Annette⁹ Davis** (*David Orville⁸, Daniel L.⁷, Emily Jane⁶ Smith, Mary Ann⁵ Palmer, Mary Margaret⁴ Pagan, John³, Andrew², James¹*) was born in 1937 in Union Furnace, Starr Twp., Hocking Co., Ohio. She is the daughter of David Orville Davis (201) and Corrina Clark.

**310. Claire Louise⁹ Haston** (*Gladys⁸ Buckle, Mary Ann⁷ Davis, Emily Jane⁶ Smith, Mary Ann⁵ Palmer, Mary Margaret⁴ Pagan, John³, Andrew², James¹*) was born on July 27, 1920, in Los Angeles, Los Angeles Co., California. She was the daughter of John Cambell Haston and Gladys Buckle (202). Claire Louise died in Ashland, Jackson Co., Oregon, on July 9, 2011, at age 90.

Claire Louise married **William Kirk Reordan** in August 1941. They had four children. William Kirk Reordan was born in Glendale, Los Angeles Co., California, on December 11, 1919. William Kirk reached age 83 and died in Carmel, Monterey Co., California, on January 11, 2003.

**311. Nancy M.⁹ Haston** (*Gladys⁸ Buckle, Mary Ann⁷ Davis, Emily Jane⁶ Smith, Mary Ann⁵ Palmer, Mary Margaret⁴ Pagan, John³, Andrew², James¹*) was born on February 5, 1922, in Los Angeles, Los Angeles Co., California. She is the daughter of John Cambell Haston and Gladys Buckle (202). Nancy died on April 23, 2015 in Sweet Home, Linn Co., Oregon, at age 93.

She married **Alfred Gene Bock.** They had one daughter. Alfred Gene Bock was born in Sundance, Crook Co., Wyoming, on June 20, 1914. Alfred Gene reached age 88 and died in Lebanon, Linn Co., Oregon, on May 2, 2003.

**312. Donna Davies⁹ Sublette** (*Ruth Violet⁸ Buckle, Mary Ann⁷ Davis, Emily Jane⁶ Smith, Mary Ann⁵ Palmer, Mary Margaret⁴ Pagan, John³, Andrew², James¹*) was born on October 16, 1932, in Detroit, Wayne Co., Michigan. She was the daughter of Donald Jackson Sublette and Ruth Violet Buckle (203).

She married **Cecil Randolph Smith II.** They had three children. Cecil Randolph Smith II was born in Denver, Denver Co., Colorado, on May 31, 1924. He reached age 79 and died in Cockeysville, Baltimore Co., Maryland, on February 6, 2004. He was cremated and his ashes scattered in Gunpowder Friends Meeting House Cemetery, Sparks, Baltimore Co., Maryland.[154]

Cecil Randolph Smith Jr. was an internationally known organic chemist. He specialized in and published papers on non-toxic pest control compounds and anti-tumor agents.

**313. Warren Jackson⁹ Sublette** (*Ruth Violet⁸ Buckle, Mary Ann⁷ Davis, Emily Jane⁶ Smith, Mary Ann⁵ Palmer, Mary Margaret⁴ Pagan, John³, Andrew², James¹*) was born on October 27, 1937, in Royal Oak, Oakland Co., Michigan. He is the son of Donald Jackson Sublette and Ruth Violet Buckle (203).

Warren Jackson married **Ms. Yale** on April 6, 1974, in Clinton Co., Ohio. They divorced.

**314. Daughter⁹ Sublette** (*Ruth Violet⁸ Buckle, Mary Ann⁷ Davis, Emily Jane⁶ Smith, Mary Ann⁵ Palmer, Mary Margaret⁴ Pagan, John³, Andrew², James¹*) in 1942, in Detroit, Wayne Co., Michigan. She was the daughter of Donald Jackson Sublette and Ruth Violet Buckle (203).

Daughter Sublette married **Hershel Ploshnick** before 1959. They had two sons. Hershel Ploshnick was born in Highland Park, Wayne Co., Michigan, on December 4, 1933. Hershel reached age 73 and died in Franklin, Oakland Co., Michigan, on January 25, 2007. He was buried in Christian Memorial Cemetery and Mausoleum, Rochester Hills, Wayne Co., Michigan.[155]

Daughter Sublettte Ploshnick married **Unknown Fischer** after 1960.

Daughter Sublette and Hershel Ploshnick had two sons, including:

+ 353 m I.   **Marc Stewart¹⁰ Ploshnick** was born in Detroit, Wayne Co., Michigan, on August 22, 1959. He died in Detroit, Wayne Co., Michigan, on September 16, 1959. Marc Stewart was buried in Hebrew Memorial Cemetery, Clinton Twp., Macomb Co., Michigan.[155]

**315. Florence Ellen⁹ Morton** (*Earl Davis⁸, Elizabeth E.⁷ Davis, Emily Jane⁶ Smith, Mary Ann⁵ Palmer, Mary Margaret⁴ Pagan, John³, Andrew², James¹*) was born on December 13, 1924, in Maple Twp., Cowley Co., Kansas. She was the daughter of Earl Davis Morton (204) and Iva Mae Shoup. Florence Ellen died in Yukon, Canadian Co., Oklahoma, on

July 12, 2001, at age 76. She was buried in Yukon Cemetery, Yukon, Canadian Co., Oklahoma.[133]

May have been childless.

Florence Ellen married **Unknown Demieville** after 1940 in Cowley Co., Kansas? They divorced.

Florence Ellen Morton Demieville married **Robert Tiffen Stone.** Robert Tiffen Stone was born in Udall, Ninnescah Twp., Cowley Co., Kansas, on November 28, 1917. Robert Tiffen reached age 88 and died in Yukon, Canadian Co., Oklahoma, on October 3, 2006.

316. **Clyde Russell⁹ Morton** (*Earl Davis⁸, Elizabeth E.⁷ Davis, Emily Jane⁶ Smith, Mary Ann⁵ Palmer, Mary Margaret⁴ Pagan, John³, Andrew², James¹*) was born on July 1, 1928, in Maple Twp., Cowley Co., Kansas. He was the son of Earl Davis Morton (204) and Iva Mae Shoup. Clyde Russell died in Udall, Ninnescah Twp., Cowley Co., Kansas, on February 25, 2015, at age 86. He was buried in Red Bud Catholic Cemetery, Cowley Co., Kansas.[134]

Clyde Russell married **Lydia Zapeda** on March 12, 1954, in San Diego Co., California. They had three children. Lydia Zapeda was born in Tuscon, Pima Co., Arizona, on November 2, 1927. Lydia reached age 77 and died in Udall, Ninnescah Twp., Cowley Co., Kansas, on August 9, 2005. She was buried in Red Bud Catholic Cemetery, Cowley Co., Kansas.[1134]

317. **Oscar Earl⁹ Morton** (*Earl Davis⁸, Elizabeth E.⁷ Davis, Emily Jane⁶ Smith, Mary Ann⁵ Palmer, Mary Margaret⁴ Pagan, John³, Andrew², James¹*) was born on December 19, 1929, in Maple Twp., Cowley Co., Kansas. He was the son of Earl Davis Morton (204) and Iva Mae Shoup. Oscar Earl died in Udall, Ninnescah Twp., Cowley Co., Kansas, on January 1, 2003, at age 73. He was buried in Star Cemetery, Udall, Cowley Co., Kansas.[135]

He married **Maxine Abel.** Maxine Abel was born in Creswell Twp., Cowley Co., Kansas, on February 13, 1929. Maxine reached age 45 and died in Udall, Cowley Co., Kansas?, on November 27, 1974. She was buried in Pleasant Valley Cemetery, Winfield, Cowley Co., Kansas.[156]

318. **Cora⁹ Morton** (*Earl Davis⁸, Elizabeth E.⁷ Davis, Emily Jane⁶ Smith, Mary Ann⁵ Palmer, Mary Margaret⁴ Pagan, John³, Andrew², James¹*) was born on April 5, 1936, in Maple Twp., Cowley Co., Kansas. She was the daughter of Earl Davis Morton (204) and Iva Mae Shoup.

She married **Harold Alonzo Mettling.** They had three children. Harold Alonzo Mettling was born in Lewis, Edwards Co., Kansas, on February 11, 1919. Harold Alonzo reached age 71 and died in Udall, Cowley Co., Kansas, on January 29, 1991. He was buried in Mulvane Cemetery, Mulvane, Sumner Co., Kansas.[45]

319. **Charles Eldon⁹ Wiseman** (*Sarah Emily⁸ Tanner, Emma J.⁷ Davis, Emily Jane⁶ Smith, Mary Ann⁵ Palmer, Mary Margaret⁴ Pagan, John³, Andrew², James¹*) was born on February 21, 1933, in Perry Twp., Gallia Co., Ohio. He was the son of Wallace Eldon Wiseman and Sarah Emily Tanner (207). Charles Eldon died in Wichita, Sedgwick Co., Kansas, on May 25, 2015, at age 82. He was buried in Lakeview Cemetery, Wichita, Sedgwick Co., Kansas.[136]

Charles Eldon Wiseman married **Unknown Unknown** before 1956. They divorced. They have three sons.

Charles Eldon married **Juanita Bacon** on April 4, 1964, in Sedgwick Co., Kansas. They had one son. Juanita Bacon was born on April 28, 1937.

320. **John Robert⁹ Wiseman** (*Sarah Emily⁸ Tanner, Emma J.⁷ Davis, Emily Jane⁶ Smith, Mary Ann⁵ Palmer, Mary Margaret⁴ Pagan, John³, Andrew², James¹*) was born on May 4, 1936, in Perry Twp., Gallia Co., Ohio. He is the son of Wallace Eldon Wiseman and Sarah Emily Tanner (207).

321. **Barbara Jean⁹ Tanner** (*Parry Benjamin⁸ Tanner, Emma J.⁷ Davis, Emily Jane⁶ Smith, Mary Ann⁵ Palmer, Mary Margaret⁴ Pagan, John³, Andrew², James¹*) was born in Columbia, Richland Co., South Carolina in 1936. She was the daughter of Parry Benjamin Tanner (208) and Mary Elizabeth Evans.

322. **Susan K.⁹ Parry** (*Mary E.⁸ Tanner, Emma J.⁷ Davis, Emily Jane⁶ Smith, Mary Ann⁵ Palmer, Mary*

*Margaret⁴ Pagan, John³, Andrew², James¹)* was born on November 4, 1948, in Lima, Ottawa Twp., Allen Co., Ohio. She was the daughter of George L. Parry and Mary E. Tanner (209). Susan K. died in Glandorf, Ottawa Twp., Putnam Co., Ohio, on October 27, 2013, at age 64. She was buried in Truro Cemetery, Columbus Grove, Pleasant Twp., Putnam Co., Ohio.[89]

Susan K. married **Karl D. Salisbury** on August 24, 1969. They had three sons. Karl D. Salisbury was born in Lima, Ottawa Twp., Allen Co., Ohio, on August 8, 1949. Karl D. reached age 63 and died in Lima, Ottawa Twp., Allen Co., Ohio, on August 31, 2012. He was buried in Truro Cemetery, Columbus Grove, Pleasant Twp., Putnam Co., Ohio.[89]

323. **Mary Elizabeth⁹ Duncan** (*Beatrice Emily⁸ Davis, David Benton⁷, Emily Jane⁶ Smith, Mary Ann⁵ Palmer, Mary Margaret⁴ Pagan, John³, Andrew², James¹)* was born in 1933. She is the daughter of Norval Theodore Duncan and Beatrice Emily Davis (212). Was Mary Elizabeth Duncan the "Lulu Goebel" in the 1940 census?

She married **Mr. Ray.**

324. **Lula⁹ Goebel** (*Beatrice Emily⁸ Davis, David Benton⁷, Emily Jane⁶ Smith, Mary Ann⁵ Palmer, Mary Margaret⁴ Pagan, John³, Andrew², James¹)* was born about 1932 in Warren Park, Warren Twp., Marion Co., Indiana. She is the daughter of Henry Ashbelle Goebel II and Beatrice Emily Davis (212)?

"Lula Goebel" is enumerated in the 1940 census in Henry and Beatrice Emily Davis Goebel's household. But her age matches that of Mary Elizabeth Duncan, Emily Davis' daughter from her first marriage. Was "Lula" actually Elizabeth?

325. **Florence Mae⁹ Goebel** (*Beatrice Emily⁸ Davis, David Benton⁷, Emily Jane⁶ Smith, Mary Ann⁵ Palmer, Mary Margaret⁴ Pagan, John³, Andrew², James¹)* was born on February 19, 1934, in Warren Park, Warren Twp., Marion Co., Indiana. She was the daughter of Henry Ashbelle Goebel II and Beatrice Emily Davis (212). Florence Mae died in Beech Grove, Perry Twp., Marion Co., Indiana, on November 9, 2011, at age 77. She was buried in

Memorial Park Cemetery, Indianapolis, Warren Twp., Marion Co., Indiana.[138]

She married **Robert L. Matthews.** They had two children. Robert L. Matthews was born in Indianapolis, Marion Co., Indiana, on April 14, 1931. Robert L. reached age 82 and died in Indianapolis, Marion Co., Indiana, on September 3, 2013. He was buried in Memorial Park Cemetery, Indianapolis, Warren Twp., Marion Co., Indiana.[1138]

Florence Mae Goebel and Robert L. Matthews had two children, including:

+ 354 m I. **Son¹⁰ Matthews.**

326. **Henry August Goebel III** (*Beatrice Emily⁸ Davis, David Benton⁷, Emily Jane⁶ Smith, Mary Ann⁵ Palmer, Mary Margaret⁴ Pagan, John³, Andrew², James¹)* was born on April 15, 1937, in Warren Park, Warren Twp., Marion Co., Indiana. He is the son of Henry Ashbelle Goebel II and Beatrice Emily Davis (212).

Henry August married **Ms. Henry.**

327. **Imogene F.⁹ Laney** (*Catherine Mae⁸ Davis, David Benton⁷, Emily Jane⁶ Smith, Mary Ann⁵ Palmer, Mary Margaret⁴ Pagan, John³, Andrew², James¹)* was born on January 8, 1931, in Akron, Summit Co., Ohio. She was the daughter of Frank William Laney and Catherine Mae Davis (213).

Imogene F. married **Leroy E. Schneider.** They divorced. Leroy E. Schneider was born in 1929.

Imogene F. Laney married **Larry Leroy Peets** on September 16, 1960, in Los Angeles Co., California. Larry Leroy Peets was born in Salina, Saline Co., Kansas, on December 20, 1937. Larry Leroy reached age 48 and died in Altadena, Los Angeles Co., California, on October 15, 1986.

328. **Shirley Ann⁹ Laney** (*Catherine Mae⁸ Davis, David Benton⁷, Emily Jane⁶ Smith, Mary Ann⁵ Palmer, Mary Margaret⁴ Pagan, John³, Andrew², James¹)* was born on October 5, 1936, in Pasadena, Los Angeles Co., California. She was the daughter of

Frank William Laney and Catherine Mae Davis (213).

Shirley Ann married **Walter Eugene Charboneau** on December 28, 1955, in San Diego Co., California. Walter Eugene Charboneau was born in Los Angeles, Los Angeles Co., California, on December 18, 1929. Walter Eugene reached age 82 and died in Los Angeles, Los Angeles Co., California, on July 5, 2012. He was buried in Forest Lawn Memorial Park Cemetery, Hollywood Hills, Los Angeles Co., California.[157]

329. **Douglas Allan[9] Rosenbaum** (*Lois Ann[8] Smith, Orin Henry[7], John Henry[6], Mary Ann[5] Palmer, Mary Margaret[4] Pagan, John[3], Andrew[2], James[1]*) was born on December 2, 1957, in Pomeroy, Salisbury Twp., Meigs Co., Ohio. He was the son of Richard Rosenbaum and Lois Ann Smith (219). Douglas Allan died in a hospital in Columbus, Franklin Co., Ohio, on July 15, 1985, at age 27. He was buried in Beech Grove Cemetery, Pomeroy, Salisbury Twp., Meigs Co., Ohio.[131]

Douglas Allan married **Ms. Smith.**

330. **Daughter[9] Rosenbaum** (*Lois Ann[8] Smith, Orin Henry[7], John Henry[6], Mary Ann[5] Palmer, Mary Margaret[4] Pagan, John[3], Andrew[2], James[1]*). She is the daughter of Richard Rosenbaum and Lois Ann Smith (219).

She married **Mr. Rhodes.** They had three sons.

Daughter Rosenbaum and Mr. Rhodes had three sons, including:

+ 355 m III. **Kyle Christopher[10] Rhodes** was born in Danville, Contra Costa Co., California, on July 17, 1994. He died in Danville, Contra Costa Co., California, on August 10, 2013.

331. **Karen Louise[9] Overstreet** (*Doris Mary[8] Smith, Levi Morgan[7], Wesley Thomas[6], Mary Ann[5] Palmer, Mary Margaret[4] Pagan, John[3], Andrew[2], James[1]*) was born on January 2, 1945, in Hammond, Lake Co., Indiana. She was the daughter of Paul Alrie Overstreet and Doris Mary Smith (227). Karen

Louise died in Hammond, Lake Co., Indiana, on September 22, 2003, at age 58.

Karen Louise married **Arthur Ronald Tibbets** on June 17, 1964, in Lake Co., Indiana. Arthur Ronald Tibbets was born in Manchester, Meriwether Co., Georgia, on March 15, 1947. Arthur Ronald reached age 59 and died in Melbourne, Brevard Co., Florida, on March 12, 2007.

332. **Gregory Allen[9] Northup** (*Harlan Watts[8], Marie[7] Watts, Anna May[6] Smith, Frances Madeline[5] Cheney, Mary Margaret[4] Pagan, John[3], Andrew[2], James[1]*) was born on November 28, 1952, in Gallipolis, Gallipolis Twp., Gallia Co., Ohio. He was the son of Harlan Watts Northup (235) and Ella Mae Love. Gregory Allen died in Gallipolis, Gallipolis Twp., Gallia Co., Ohio, on September 3, 2008, at age 55. He was cremated and his ashes buried in Mound Hill Cemetery, Gallipolis, Gallipolis Twp., Gallia Co., Ohio.[10]

Gregory Allen married **Ms. Shoots.** They divorced. They had two children.

333. **James Cimmaron[9] Elledge II** (*Emily A.[8] Brothers, Golden Odessa[7] Massie, Hattie[6] Rickabaugh, Emily[5] Cheney, Mary Margaret[4] Pagan, John[3], Andrew[2], James[1]*) was born on August 20, 1951, in Columbus, Franklin Co., Ohio. He was the son of James O. Elledge and Emily A. Brothers (248). Jame Cimmaron died in Columbus, Franklin Co., Ohio, on May 25, 1997 at age 45. He was buried in Dublin Cemetery, Dublin, Washington Twp., Franklin Co., Ohio.[143]

334. **Bruce[9] Baggett** (*Mary Virginia[8] Armstrong, Inez Edith[7] Ballard, Effie Virginia[6] King, Mary Ann[5] Pagan, John[4], John[3], Andrew[2], James[1]*) was born in Los Angeles, Los Angeles Co. California in 1934. He is the son of Joseph Jennings Baggett and Mary Virginia Armstrong (255).

335. **Robert Alan[9] Dunton II** (*Helen V.[8] Jobe, Anna Mae[7] Ballard, Effie Virginia[6] King, Mary Ann[5] Pagan, John[4], John[3], Andrew[2], James[1]*) was born on October 14, 1937, in Washington Court House, Union Twp., Fayette Co., Ohio. He is the son of Robert L. Dunton and Helen V. Jobe (257).

Robert Alan married **Vera Alena Safr.** They had two children. Vera Alena Safr was born in Czechoslovakia on August 7, 1940.

**336. Lavern Clair⁹ Johnson** (*Everett E.⁸, John Edward⁷, William Roosevelt⁶, John J.⁵, Catherine⁴ Pagan, John³, Andrew², James¹*) was born on November 6, 1927, in Hordman, Morrow Co., Oregon. He was the son of Everett E. Johnson (262) and Alise Anna Cork. Lavern Clair died in Cordova, Valdez-Cordova Precinct, Alaska, on August 14, 2002, at age 74. He was buried in Cordova Cemetery, Cordova, Valdez-Cordova Precinct, Alaska.[145]

Lavern Clair married **Alice Patricia Hodge** on September 29, 1949, in King Co., Washington. Alice Patricia Hodge was born in Seattle, King Co., Washington, on October 3, 1929. Alice Patricia reached age 76 and died in Cordova, Valdez-Cordova Precinct, Alaska, on August 1, 2006. She was buried in Cordova Cemetery, Cordova, Valdez-Cordova Precinct, Alaska.[137]

**337. Jacqueline⁹ Johnson** (*Everett E.⁸, John Edward⁷, William Roosevelt⁶, John J.⁵, Catherine⁴ Pagan, John³, Andrew², James¹*). She was the daughter of Everett E. Johnson (262) and Alise Anna Cork. She was born in 1930, in North Fork, Grant Co., Oregon.

**338. Joanne G.⁹ Johnson** (*Lawrence A.⁸, John Edward⁷, William Roosevelt⁶, John J.⁵, Catherine⁴ Pagan, John³, Andrew², James¹*). She was the daughter of Lawrence A. Johnson (263) and Iva Ellen Emry. She was born on September 10, 1931, in Grant Co., Oregon. Joanne G. died on December 5, 2015 in Albany, Linn Co., Oregon? She was buried in Redmond Memorial Cemetery, Redmond, Deschutes Co., Oregon.[146]

She married **Ernest Kuhn** on July 18, 1954, in Crook Co., Oregon. He was born on November 4, 1934 in Rosebud, Grant Co., Oregon.

**339. Florence Alice⁹ Johnson** (*Lawrence A.⁸, John Edward⁷, William Roosevelt⁶, John J.⁵, Catherine⁴ Pagan, John³, Andrew², James¹*). She is the daughter of Lawrence A. Johnson (263) and Iva Ellen Emry. Florence Alice was born on April 25, 1933 in Grant Co., Oregon. She died on February 24, 2014 in Salem, Polk Co., Oregon. Florence Alice is buried in Restlawn Memorial Gardens Cemetery, Salem, Polk Co., Oregon.[147]

She married **James Harvey Bones** on June 15, 1952, in Deschutes Co., Oregon. They had four children. He was also known as **Harvey**. He resided in Salem, Polk Co., Oregon in 2015. He died in a facility in Portland, Mulnomah Co., Oregon on December 25, 2015. James Harvey is buried in Restlawn Memorial Gardens Cemetery, Salem, Polk Co., Oregon.[147]

**340. Teddy Jack⁹ Johnson** (*Cecil Edward⁸, Memphis Mason⁷, William Roosevelt⁶, John J.⁵, Catherine⁴ Pagan, John³, Andrew², James¹*) was born on June 11, 1934, in Lockney, Floyd Co., Texas. He was also known as **Jack.** He was the son of Cecil Edward Johnson (272) and Cleo P. Ward. Teddy Jack died in Bloomfield, San Juan Co., New Mexico, on June 26, 2003, at age 69. He was buried in Aztec Community Cemetery, Aztec, San Juan Co., New Mexico.[114]

Teddy Jack married **Ruby Unknown** in 1956 in Roosevelt Co., New Mexico.

**341. Emma Louise⁹ Johnson** (*Cecil Edward⁸, Memphis Mason⁷, William Roosevelt⁶, John J.⁵, Catherine⁴ Pagan, John³, Andrew², James¹*) was born in 1936 in Clovis, Curry Co., New Mexico? She is also known as **Louise.** She is the daughter of Cecil Edward Johnson (272) and Cleo P. Ward.

She married **J.C. Johnson.**

**342. Ora Darline⁹ Johnson** (*Cecil Edward⁸, Memphis Mason⁷, William Roosevelt⁶, John J.⁵, Catherine⁴ Pagan, John³, Andrew², James¹*) was born on June 3, 1938, in Clovis, Curry Co., New Mexico. She was the daughter of Cecil Edward Johnson (272) and Cleo P. Ward. Ora Darline died in Lubbock, Lubbock Co., Texas, on October 2, 1983, at age 45. She was buried in Mission Garden of Memories Cemetery, Clovis, Curry Co., New Mexico.[149]

Ora Darline married **William P. Edwards II** on June 5, 1954, in Curry Co., New Mexico. They had three daughters. William P. Edwards II was born in Tuttle, Grady Co., Oklahoma, on

December 31, 1931. William P. reached age 81 and died in Clovis, Curry Co., New Mexico, on August 8, 2013. He was buried in Mission Garden of Memories Cemetery, Clovis, Curry Co., New Mexico.[149]

**343. Daughter**⁹ **Johnson** (*Cecil Edward*⁸, *Memphis Mason*⁷, *William Roosevelt*⁶, *John J.*⁵, *Catherine*⁴ *Pagan, John*³, *Andrew*², *James*¹). She is the daughter of Cecil Edward Johnson (272) and Cleo P. Ward.

She married **Elmer Emmitt Robinson II.** Elmer Emmitt Robinson II was born in Burlington, Burlington Twp., Coffey Co., Kansas, on August 7, 1939. Elmer Emmitt reached age 67 and died in Farmington, San Juan Co., New Mexico, on December 27, 2006. He was buried in Aztec Community Cemetery, Aztec, San Juan Co., New Mexico.[114]

**344A. Dorothy Ellen**⁹ **Johnson** (*Marvin Earl*⁸, *Memphis Mason*⁷, *William Roosevelt*⁶, *John J.*⁵, *Catherine*⁴ *Pagan, John*³, *Andrew*², *James*¹) was born on April 10, 1940, in Placerville, El Dorado Co., California. She was the daughter of Marvin Earl Johnson (273) and Phyllis G. Bice. Dorothy Ellen died in Placerville, El Dorado Co., California, on September 21, 2013, at age 73.

She married **Mr. Caruthers.** They divorced. They had one son.

Dorothy Ellen Johnson Caruthers married **Mr. Partain.** They had one daughter.

**344B. Luessia May**⁹ **Martin** (*Neta Fern*⁸ *Fletcher, Luessia Marie*⁷ *Johnson, William Roosevelt*⁶, *John J.*⁵, *Catherine*⁴ *Pagan, John*³, *Andrew*², *James*¹) was born in Coquille, Coos Co., Oregon in 1939. She is the daughter of Fred August Martin and Neta Fern Fletcher (275).

**345. Stacey Jo**⁹ **Johnson** (*Loren Duane*⁸, *Walter Cecil*⁷, *William Roosevelt*⁶, *John J.*⁵, *Catherine*⁴ *Pagan, John*³, *Andrew*², *James*¹) was born on May 13, 1965, in Bend, Deschutes Co., Oregon. She was the daughter of Loren Duane Johnson (278) and Joan Carol Price. Stacey Jo died in Bend, Deschutes Co., Oregon, on October 7, 2009, at age 44. She was buried in Greenwood Cemetery,

Bend, Deschutes Co., Oregon.[118] She used her maiden name even though married.

Stacey Jo married **Mr. Johnson.** They had three children.

Stacey Jo Johnson Johnson married **Mr. Lofte.** on June 30, 2001, in Bend Co., Oregon.

**346. Daughter**⁹ **Smith** (*William Donald*⁸, *Alma L.*⁷ *Johnson, James Edward*⁶, *John J.*⁵, *Catherine*⁴ *Pagan, John*³, *Andrew*², *James*¹). She is the daughter of William Donald Smith (281) and Myra Joan Maskey.

She married **Mr. Vogt.** They have two children.

Daughter Smith and Mr. Vogt had two children, including:

+ 356 m I.   **James Michael**¹⁰ **Vogt** was born in Kirksville, Benton Twp., Adair Co., Missouri, on November 10, 1995. He died in Kirksville, Benton Twp., Adair Co., Missouri, on January 27, 2017.

**347A. Peter Keim**⁹ **Iber** (*Ella Mae*⁸ *Murrell, James W.*⁷, *Ella Matilda*⁶, *Emma*⁵ *Johnson, Catherine*⁴ *Pagan, John*³, *Andrew*², *James*¹) was born on July 26, 1937, in Elizabeth, Union Co., New Jersey. He was the son of Arthur Keim Iber and Ella Mae Murrell (288). Peter Keim died in Sun City, Maricopa Co., Arizona, on September 16, 2009, at age 72. He was buried in Arlington National Cemetery, Arlington, Virginia.[128]

May have never married.

**347B. Thomas**⁹ **Graves** was born in Newport, Campbell Co., Kentucky, on September 12, 1936. He was the son of Mentor E. Graves and Belinda Murrell (289).

**348. Susan**⁹ **Worrall** (*Calvin*⁸ *Greenwood, Nelle*⁷ *Greenwood, Frank Burdette*⁶, *Alexander*⁵, *Catherine*⁴ *Pagan, John*³, *Andrew*², *James*¹) was born on January 1, 1936, in Sidney, Clinton Twp., Shelby Co., Ohio. She was the daughter of Calvin Greenwood Worrall III (293) and Elizabeth Jeanne Allen. Susan died in Stockton, Stockton Twp., Cedar Co. Missouri, on March 21, 2014, at age 78.

She married **Marvin Wayne Pope.** They had two children. Marvin Wayne Pope was born in Camby, Decatur Twp., Marion Co., Indiana, on February 10, 1933. Marvin Wayne reached age 68 and died in Oak Hill, Volusia Co., Florida?, on September 10, 2001.

Susan Worrall married **Oscar Raymond Winder.** Oscar Raymond Winder was born in Stockton, Stockton Twp., Cedar Co. Missouri, on November 24, 1934. He was also known as **Ray.** Oscar Raymond reached age 76 and died in Stockton, Stockton Twp., Cedar Co. Missouri, on February 3, 2011. He was buried in Pankey Cemetery, Stockton, Stockton Twp., Cedar Co., Missouri.[158]

Children of Susan Worrall and Marvin Wayne Pope:

+ 357 f I. **Michele Kay[10] Pope** was born in Indianapolis, Marion Co., Indiana, February 6, 1954. Michele Kay died in Stockton, Stockton Twp., Cedar Co. Missouri, on October 27, 2016.

**349. Charlene[9] Worrall** (*Calvin[8] Greenwood, Nelle[7] Greenwood, Frank Burdette[6], Alexander[5], Catherine[4] Pagan, John[3], Andrew[2], James[1]*) was born on August 11, 1939, in Sidney, Clinton Twp., Shelby Co., Ohio. She was the daughter of Calvin Greenwood Worrall III (293) and Elizabeth Jeanne Allen. Charlene died in Greencastle, Greencastle Twp., Putnam Co., Indiana, on March 27, 2017, at age 77.

Charlene married **John LeRoy Hasselburg** on April 27, 1956. They divorced. They had five children. John LeRoy Hasselburg was born in Indianapolis, Marion Co., Indiana, on July 9, 1937.

Charlene Worrall and John LeRoy Hasselburg had five children, including:

+ 358 m I. **Johnny Lee[10] Hasselburg** was born in Indianapolis, Marion Co., Indiana, on December 30, 1955. He died in Indianapolis, Marion Co., Indiana, on December 31, 1955. Johnny Lee was buried in Round Hill Cemetery, Indianapolis, Perry Twp., Marion Co., Indiana.[38]

**350. Son[9] Worrall** (*Calvin[8] Greenwood, Nelle[7] Greenwood, Frank Burdette[6], Alexander[5], Catherine[4] Pagan, John[3], Andrew[2], James[1]*) was born on September 1, 1946, in Indianapolis, Marion Co., Indiana. He is the son of Calvin Greenwood Worrall III (293) and Elizabeth Jeanne Allen.

Son Worrall married **Ms. Mohr.**

Son Worrall married **Bonnie Lee Johnson** on June 6, 1966, in Marion Co., Indiana. They divorced. They have one son. Bonnie Lee Johnson was born in Indianapolis, Marion Co., Indiana, on January 23, 1944. She reached age 44 and died in Stilesville, Franklin Twp., Hendricks Co., Indiana, on January 26, 1988.

She died under the name Bonnie Lee Sebanc.

Son Worrall married **Mrs. Unknown.**

# 10th Generation

**351. Norman Dean**[10] **Nevinger III** (*Norman Dean*[9], *Doris Jane*[8] *Palmer*, *Charles Grover*[7], *Lewis William*[6], *Charles Nelson*[5], *Mary Margaret*[4] *Pagan*, *John*[3], *Andrew*[2], *James*[1]) was born on April 5, 1961, in Crete, Crete Twp., Will Co., Illinois? He was the son of Norman Dean Nevinger II (300) and Victoria Jane McWilliams. Norman Dean died in Lafayette, Fairfield Twp., Tippecanoe Co., Indiana, on April 1, 2012, at age 50.

He married **Karen Unknown.** They divorced. They had three sons.

**352. Robert Grant**[10] **Dowds** (*Arleen Marie*[9] *Davis*, *Harold Warner*[8], *Daniel L.*[7], *Emily Jane*[6] *Smith*, *Mary Ann*[5] *Palmer*, *Mary Margaret*[4] *Pagan*, *John*[3], *Andrew*[2], *James*[1]) was born on August 8, 1965, in Shelby, Shelby Twp., Richland Co., Ohio. He was the son of Edward Grant Dowds and Arleen Marie Davis (302). Robert Grant died in North Lewisburg, Rush Twp., Champaign Co., Ohio, on August 11, 2016, at age 51. He was buried in Shelby-Oakland Cemetery, Shelby, Shelby Twp., Richland Co., Ohio.[129]

He married **Cindy Lee Morrow.** They divorced. They had four children. Cindy Lee Morrow was born in Springfield, Springfield Twp., Clark Co., Ohio, on October 9, 1958. She lived in Springfield, Springfield Twp., Clark Co., Ohio in 2012. Cindy Lee reached age 53 and died in a hospital in Columbus, Franklin Co., Ohio, on May 15, 2012. She was buried in Ferncliff Cemetery, Springfield, Springfield Twp., Clark Co., Ohio.[159]

She died under her maiden name, Cindy Lee Morrow.

**353. Marc Stewart**[10] **Ploshnick** (*Daughter*[9] *Sublette*, *Ruth Violet*[8] *Buckle*, *Mary Ann*[7] *Davis*, *Emily Jane*[6] *Smith*, *Mary Ann*[5] *Palmer*, *Mary Margaret*[4] *Pagan*, *John*[3], *Andrew*[2], *James*[1]) was born on August 22, 1959, in Detroit, Wayne Co., Michigan. He was the son of Hershel Ploshnick and Daughter Sublette (314). Marc Stewart died in Detroit, Wayne Co., Michigan, on September 16, 1959. He was buried in Hebrew Memorial Cemetery, Clinton Twp., Macomb Co., Michigan.[155]

**354. Son**[10] **Matthews** (*Florence Mae*[9] *Goebel*, *Beatrice Emily*[8] *Davis*, *David Benton*[7], *Emily Jane*[6] *Smith*, *Mary Ann*[5] *Palmer*, *Mary Margaret*[4] *Pagan*, *John*[3], *Andrew*[2], *James*[1]). He is the son of Robert L. Matthews and Florence Mae Goebel (325).

Son Matthews married **Patricia Unknown.** They had at least two children.

Son Matthews and Patricia Unknown had at least two children, including:

+ 359 m I. **Isaiah**[11] **Matthews** died before 2013.

+ 360 m II. **Casey**[11] **Matthews** died before 2013.

**355. Kyle Christopher**[10] **Rhodes** (*Daughter*[9] *Rosenbaum*, *Lois Ann*[8] *Smith*, *Orin Henry*[7], *John Henry*[6], *Mary Ann*[5] *Palmer*, *Mary Margaret*[4] *Pagan*, *John*[3], *Andrew*[2], *James*[1]) was born on July 17, 1994, in Danville, Contra Costa Co., California. He was the son of Mr. Rhodes and Rand Daughter Rosenbaum (366). Kyle Christopher died in Danville, Contra Costa Co., California, on August 10, 2013, at age 19.

**356. James Michael**[10] **Vogt** (*Daughter*[9] *Smith*, *William Donald*[8], *Alma L.*[7] *Johnson*, *James Edward*[6], *John J.*[5], *Catherine*[4] *Pagan*, *John*[3], *Andrew*[2], *James*[1]) was born on November 10, 1995, in Kirksville, Benton Twp., Adair Co., Missouri. He was the son of Mr. Vogt and Daughter Smith (346).. James Michael died in Kirksville, Benton Twp., Adair Co., Missouri, on January 27, 2017, at age 21.

He married **Unknown Unknown.** They had one son.

**357. Michele Kay**[10] **Pope** (*Susan*[9] *Worrall*, *Calvin Greenwood*[8], *Nelle*[7] *Greenwood*, *Frank Burdette*[6], *Alexander*[5], *Catherine*[4] *Pagan*, *John*[3], *Andrew*[2], *James*[1]) was born on February 6, 1954, in Indianapolis, Marion Co., Indiana. She was the daughter of Marvin Wayne Pope and Susan Worrall (348). Michele Kay died in Stockton, Stockton

Twp., Cedar Co. Missouri, on October 27, 2016, at age 62.

She married **Mr. Shepard.** They had three children.

**358. Johnny Lee**[10] **Hasselburg** (*Charlene*[9] *Worrall, Calvin Greenwood*[8]*, Nelle*[7] *Greenwood, Frank Burdette*[6]*, Alexander*[5]*, Catherine*[4] *Pagan, John*[3]*, Andrew*[2]*, James*[1]) was born on December 30, 1955, in Indianapolis, Marion Co., Indiana. He was the son of John LeRoy Hasselburg and Charlene Worrall (349). Johnny Lee died in Indianapolis, Marion Co., Indiana, on December 31, 1955. He was buried in Round Hill Cemetery, Indianapolis, Perry Twp., Marion Co., Indiana.[38]

# 11th Generation

**359. Isaiah**[11] **Matthews** (*Son*[10] *Matthews, Florence Mae*[9] *Goebel, Beatrice Emily*[8] *Davis, David Benton*[7], *Emily Jane*[6] *Smith, Mary Ann*[5] *Palmer, Mary Margaret*[4] *Pagan, John*[3], *Andrew*[2], *James*[1]). He was the son of Robert L. Matthews II (354) and Pamela Unknown. Isaiah died before 2013.

**360. Casey**[11] **Matthews** (*Son*[10] *Matthews, Florence Mae*[9] *Goebel, Beatrice Emily*[8] *Davis, David Benton*[7], *Emily Jane*[6] *Smith, Mary Ann*[5] *Palmer, Mary Margaret*[4] *Pagan, John*[3], *Andrew*[2], *James*[1]). He was the son of Robert L. Matthews II (354) and Pamela Unknown. Casey died before 2013.

# Endnotes

1   Pennsylvania, Church Records—Adams, Berks, and Lancaster Counties, 1729-1881, Ancestry.com; First Reformed Congregation at Lancaster, Pennsylvania, Marriage Records, John Pegan and Ann Chory, Martic Township.

2   Pagan/Pegan entries, Lancaster County, Pennsylvania Tax Lists, 1751-1800, Microfilm, Roll #23, Genealogy Center, Allen County Public Library, Fort Wayne, IN.

3   Pennsylvania, Compiled Marriage Records, 1700-1821, Ancestry.com, John Pagan and Mary Ann "Russel".

4   Watson, John Fanning, *Annals Of Philadelphia And Pennsylvania, Memoirs, Anecdotes, And Incidents Of the City And Its Inhabitants, And Of The Earliest Settlements Of The Inland Part of Pennsylvania; Intended To Preserve The Recollections Of Olden Time, And To Exhibit Society In Its Changes Of Manners and Customs, And The City And Country In Their Local Changes and Improvements, Member Of The Historical Societies of Pennsylvania, New York, And Massachusetts. Enlarged, With Many Revisions And Additions, Profusely Illustrated. In Three Volumes, Vol. 1*, Philadelphia: Edwin Stuart; 1844, pg. 272. (NOTE: Although written from 1830-1850, the bulk of the book was penned before 1842, and historians date any references from that year.) Genealogy Center, Allen County Public Library, Fort Wayne, IN.

5   Find A Grave—Fairfield Church Cemetery, Centenary, Green Twp., Gallia Co., Ohio, Find A Grave.com.

6   Find A Grave—Old Pine Cemetery, Rio Grande, Raccoon Twp., Gallia Co., Ohio, Find A Grave.com.

7   Find A Grave—San Francisco National Cemetery, San Francisco, San Francisco Co., California, Find A Grave.com.

8   Ohio Deaths, 1908-1953, FamilySearch.org, John W. "Chenny", death cert. #2303.

9   Find A Grave—New Albany Cemetery/Landon Cemetery (Old Burial Ground), New Albany, Plain Twp., Franklin Co., Ohio, Find A Grave.com.

10  Find A Grave—Mound Hill Cemetery, Gallipolis, Gallipolis Twp., Gallia Co., Ohio, Find A Grave.com.

11  1850 United States Federal Census, Ancestry.com, Year: 1850; Census Place: Galllipolis, Gallia, Ohio, Roll: M432_681; Page: 5B; Image: 424, entry for Hannah Pegan.

12  Find A Grave—Calvary Baptist Cemetery, Rio Grande, Raccoon Twp., Gallia Co., Ohio, Find A Grave.com.

13  Find A Grave—Pine Street Cemetery, Gallipolis, Gallipolis Twp., Gallia Co., Ohio, Find A Grave.com.

14  Tossell, William John, *Reports of Cases Argued and Determined in Ohio Courts of Record, Ohio Decisions, Vol. 14.* Norwalk, Ohio: The Laning Company; 1914, pg. 133. Chase Law Library, University of Northern Kentucky, 100 Louie B. Nunn Drive, Highland Heights, KY.

15  Ohio Marriages, 1800-1958, FamilySearch.org, familysearch.org.

16  Find A Grave—Oak Hill Cemetery, Minneapolis, Hennepin Co., Minnesota, Find A Grave.com.

17  Find A Grave—Riverside Cemetery, Arkansas City, Cowley Co., Kansas, Find A Grave.com.

18  Find A Grave—Woodland Cemetery, Ironton, Upper Twp., Lawrence Co., Ohio, Find A Grave.com.

19  Find A Grave—Fairlawn Cemetery, Oklahoma City, Oklahoma Co., Oklahoma, Find A Grave.com.

20  Find A Grave—Riverview Cemetery, Arkansas City, Cowley Co., Kansas, Find A Grave.com.

21  Find A Grave—Evergreen Cemetery, Oakland, Alameda Co., California, Find A Grave.com.

22  Find A Grave—Highland Cemetery, Wichita, Sedgwick Co., Kansas, Find A Grave.com.

23  Ohio Deaths, 1908-1953, FamilySearch.org, Helen Maria "Chenny", death cert. #2707.

24  Find A Grave—Glen Rest Memorial Estate Cemetery, Reynoldsburg, Truro Twp., Franklin Co., Ohio, Find A Grave.com.

25  Find A Grave—Dayton Memorial Park Cemetery, Dayton, Montgomery Co., Ohio, Find A Grave.com.

26  Find A Grave—Cedar Hill Cemetery, Brownsville, Bowling Green Twp., Licking Co., Ohio, Find A Grave.com.

27  Find A Grave—Germantown Cemetery, Germantown, German Twp., Montgomery Co., Ohio, Find A Grave.com.

28  Find A Grave—Mount Calvary Cemetery, Newark, Newark Twp., Licking Co., Ohio, Find A Grave.com.

29  Find A Grave—St. Joseph Cemetery, Newark, Licking Co., Ohio, Find A Grave.com.

30  Find A Grave—Forest Lawn Memorial Park Cemetery, Glendale, Los Angeles Co., California, Find A Grave.com.

31  Find A Grave—Pioneer Cemetery, Centralia, Lewis Co., Washington, Ancestry.com.

32  Obituary of Marion Troth (Gallipolis, Ohio, Gallipolis Journal, 30 Nov 1882), Dr. Samuel L. Bossard Memorial Library, 7 Spruce St., Gallipolis, OH. Gallipolis, OH 45631, Gallipolis (OH) Journal, pub. 30 Nov 1882.

33  Ohio, Births and Christenings Index, 1800-1962, Ancestry.com, "W.H. Troth", child of A. Troth and M.E. Peggans.

34  Ohio, Deaths, 1908-1932, 1938-2007, Ancestry.com, Harry Troth, death cert. #8686-6167.

35  Find A Grave—Mount Peace Cemetery, Akron, Summit Co., Ohio, Find A Grave.com.

36  Find A Grave—Monument Cemetery, Monument, Grant Co., Oregon, Find A Grave.com.

37  Find A Grave—Evergreen Cemetery, Southgate, Campbell Co., Kentucky, Find A Grave.com.

38 Find A Grave—Round Hill Cemetery, Indianapolis, Perry Twp., Marion Co., Indiana, Find A Grave.com.

39 Find A Grave—Humboldt Cemetery, Humboldt, Humboldt Twp., Richardson Co., Nebraska, Find A Grave.com.

40 Find A Grave—Teays Hill Cemetery, Saint Albans, Kanawha Co., West Virginia, Find A Grave.com.

41 Find A Grave—Grapevine Cemetery, Grapevine, Tarrant Co., Texas, Find A Grave.com.

42 Find A Grave—Fort Sam Houston Cemetery, San Antonio, Bexar Co., Texas, Find A Grave.com.

43 Find A Grave—Cedar Park Cemetery, Calumet Park, Cook Co., Illinois, Find A Grave.com.

44 Find A Grave—Oak Grove Cemetery, Montague, Montague Twp., Muskegon Co., Michigan, Find A Grave.com.

45 Find A Grave—Mulvane Cemetery, Mulvane, Sumner Co., Kansas, Find A Grave.com.

46 Find A Grave—Rombauer Cemetery, Rombauer, St. Francis Twp., Butler Co., Missouri, Find A Grave.com.

47 Find A Grave—Sunset Memorial Park Cemetery, Galloway, Franklin Co., Ohio, Find A Grave.com.

48 Find A Grave—Greenwood Memorial Park Cemetery, San Diego, San Diego Co., California, Find A Grave.com.

49 Find A Grave—Gravel Hill Cemetery, Cheshire, Cheshire Twp., Gallia Co., Ohio, Find A Grave.com.

50 Find A Grave—Wood Cemetery, Raccoon Twp., Gallia Co., Ohio, Find A Grave.com.

51 Find A Grave—Roselawn Cemetery, Pueblo, Pueblo Co., Colorado, Find A Grave.com.

52 Find A Grave—Greenlawn Cemetery, South Charleston, Madison Twp., Clark Co., Ohio, Find A Grave.com.

53 Find A Grave—Woodlawn Cemetery, Leslie, Leslie Twp., Ingham Co., Michigan, Find A Grave.com.

54 Find A Grave—Woodland Cemetery and Arboretum, Dayton, Montgomery Co., Ohio, Find A Grave.com.

55 Find A Grave—Elmwood Cemetery, Hammond, Lake Co., Indiana, Find A Grave.com.

56 Find A Grave—Green Lawn Cemetery, Columbus, Franklin Co., Ohio, Find A Grave.com.

57 Find A Grave—Holy Cross Cemetery, Colma, San Mateo Co., California, Find A Grave.com.

58 Ohio Deaths, 1908-1953, FamilySearch.org, Stella May Cheney.

59 Find A Grave—Maple Grove Cemetery, Granville, Granville Twp., Licking Co., Ohio, Find A Grave.com.

60 Ohio Deaths, 1908-1953, FamilySearch.org, "Kathryine Chenny".

61 Find A Grave—Maplewood Cemetery, New Albany, Plain Twp., Franklin Co., Ohio, Find A Grave.com.

62 Find A Grave—Twin Township Cemetery, Bourneville, Twin Twp., Ross Co., Ohio, Find A Grave.com.

63 Find A Grave—Harrison Township Cemetery, South Bloomfield, Harrison Twp., Pickaway Co., Ohio, Find A Grave.com.

64 Find A Grave—Beverly Cemetery, Beverly, Center Twp., Washington Co., Ohio, Find A Grave.com.

65 Find A Grave—Park Lawn Cemetery, Evansville, Vanderburgh Co., Indiana, Find A Grave.com.

66 Find A Grave—Dayton National Cemetery, Dayton, Montgomery Co., Ohio, Find A Grave.com.

67 Find A Grave—Lone Oak Cemetery, Point Pleasant, Mason Co., West Virginia, Find A Grave.com.

68 Find A Grave—Campaign Cemetery, Addison Twp., Gallia Co., Ohio, Find A Grave.com.

69 Find A Grave—Crown Hill Cemetery, Sedalia, Pettis Co., Missouri, Find A Grave.com.

70 Find A Grave—Los Angeles National Cemetery, Los Angeles, Los Angeles Co., California, Find A Grave.com.

71 Find A Grave—Fairview Cemetery, Jeffersonville, Fayette Co., Ohio, Find A Grave.com.

72 Find A Grave—Maple Grove Cemetery, Mechanicsburg, Goshen Twp., Champaign Co., Ohio, Find A Grave.com.

73 Find A Grave—Genung Memorial Park Cemetery, Peeples Valley, Yavapai Co., Arizona, Find A Grave.com.

74 Find A Grave—IOOF Cemetery, Roseburg, Douglas Co., Oregon, Find A Grave.com.

75 Find A Grave—Calvary Cemetery and Mausoleum, St. Louis, Missouri, Find A Grave.com.

76 Find A Grave—Saint Mary's Cemetery, Montgomery City, Montgomery Twp., Montgomery Co., Missouri, Find A Grave.com.

77 Find A Grave—Bethany Memorial Gardens Cemetery, Crocker, Tavern Twp., Pulaski Co., Missouri, Find A Grave.com.

78 Find A Grave—Forest Park Cemetery, Joplin, Joplin Twp., Jasper Co., Missouri, Find A Grave.com.

79 Find A Grave—New Salem Methodist Episcopal Cemetery, Thorn Twp., Perry Co., Ohio, Find A Grave.com.

80 Find A Grave—Lower Lake Cemetery, Lower Lake, Lake Co., California, Find A Grave.com.

81 South Dakota, School Records, 1879-1970, FamilySearch.org, Alice Robinson, fa. Everett, Gettysburg, Potter Co., South Dakota, Gettysburg Independent School Census, School District #1,1933; age 16, b. 08 Mar 1922.

82 Find A Grave—Mona View Cemetery, Muskegon Heights, Muskegon Twp., Muskegon Co., Michigan, Find A Grave.com.

83 Find A Grave—Grandville Cemetery, Grand Rapids, Grand Rapids Twp., Kent Co., Michigan, Find A Grave.com.

84 Find A Grave—New Oak Cemetery, Plymouth, Center Twp., Marshall Co., Indiana, Find A Grave.com.

85 Find A Grave—Ogdensburg Cemetery, Mapleton, Peninsula Twp., Grand Traverse Co., Michigan, Find A Grave.com.

86 Find A Grave—Greenwood Cemetery, Michigan City, Michigan Twp., LaPorte Co., Indiana, Find A Grave.com.

87 Find A Grave—Ashley Union Cemetery, Ashley, Ashley Twp., Delaware Co., Ohio, Find A Grave.com.

88 Find A Grave—Olive Methodist Church Cemetery, Cadmus, Walnut Twp., Gallia Co., Ohio, Find A Grave.com.

89 Find A Grave—Truro Cemetery, Columbus Grove, Putnam Co., Ohio, Find A Grave.com.

90 Find A Grave—Anderson Cemetery, Warren Park, Warren Twp., Marion Co., Indiana, Find A Grave.com.

91 Find A Grave—Washington Park East Cemetery, Indianapolis, Warren Twp., Marion Co., Indiana, Find A Grave.com.

92 Find A Grave—Sugar Grove Cemetery, Wilmington, Union Twp., Clinton Co., Ohio, Find A Grave.com.

93 Find A Grave—Mount Zion Cemetery, Green Twp., Gallia Co., Ohio, Find A Grave.com.

94 Missouri, Marriage Records, 1805-2002, Ancestry.com, Jacob A. Shore and Cora B. Wood.

95 Find A Grave—Calvert City Cemetery, Calvert, Robertson Co., Texas, Find A Grave.com.

96 Find A Grave—Shiloh Park Cemetery, Shiloh, Harrison Twp., Montgomery Co., Ohio, Find A Grave.com.

97 Find A Grave—Glen Haven Memorial Gardens Cemetery, Donnelsville, Bethel Twp., Clark Co., Ohio, Find A Grave.com.

98 Find A Grave—Davids Cemetery, Kettering, Montgomery Co., Ohio, Find A Grave.com.

99 Find A Grave—Valhalla Memorial Gardens, Bloomington, Monroe Co., Indiana, Find A Grave.com.

100 Find A Grave—Chapel Lawn Memorial Gardens Cemetery, Schererville, Lake Co., Indiana, Find A Grave.com.

101 Find A Grave—Beaufort National Cemetery, Beaufort, Beaufort Co., South Carolina, Find A Grave.com.

102 Find A Grave—Six Oaks Cemetery, Sea Pines Plantation, Beaufort Co., South Carolina, Find A Grave.com.

103 Find A Grave—Coeur D'Alene Memorial Gardens Cemetery, Coeur D'Alene, Rural Co., Idaho, Find A Grave.

104 Find A Grave—Texas State Cemetery, Austin, Travis Co., Texas, Find A Grave.com.

105 Find A Grave—Fairview Methodist Cemetery, Good Hope Twp., Hocking Co., Ohio, Find A Grave.com.

106 Find A Grave—Oak Hill Cemetery, Evansville, Vanderburgh Co., Indiana, Find A Grave.com.

107 Find A Grave—Kirkland Memorial Gardens Cemetery, Point Pleasant, Mason Co., West Virginia, Find A Grave.com.

108 Find A Grave—Tod Homestead Cemetery, Youngstown, Mahoning Co., Ohio, Find A Grave.com.

109 Find A Grave—Jefferson City National Cemetery, Jefferson City, Cole Co., Missouri, Find A Grave.com.

110 Find A Grave—Washington Cemetery, Washington Court House, Union Twp., Fayette Co., Ohio, Find A Grave.com.

111 Find A Grave—Forest Lawn Memorial Park Cemetery, Cypress, Orange Co., California, Find A Grave.com.

112 Find A Grave—Pilot Butte Cemetery, Bend, Deschutes Co., Oregon, Find A Grave.com.

113 Find A Grave—Lincoln Memorial Park Cemetery, Portland, Multnomah Co., Oregon, Find A Grave.com.

114 Find A Grave—Aztec Community Cemetery, Aztec, San Juan Co., New Mexico, Find A Grave.com.

115 Find A Grave—National Memorial Cemetery of the Pacific, Honolulu, Oahu Island, Hawaii, Find A Grave.com.

116 Find A Grave—Klamath Memorial Park Cemetery, Klamath Falls, Klamath Co., Oregon, Find A Grave.com.

117 Find A Grave—Evergreen Memorial Park Cemetery, McMinnville, Yamhill Co., Oregon, Find A Grave.com.

118 Find A Grave—Greenwood Cemetery, Bend, Deschutes Co., Oregon, Find A Grave.com.

119 Find A Grave—Deschutes Memorial Gardens Cemetery, Bend, Deschutes Co., Oregon, Find A Grave.com.

120 Find A Grave—Fairmount Cemetery, Middletown, Prairie Twp., Montgomery Co., Missouri, Find A Grave.com.

121 Find A Grave—Snowdenville Cemetery, Cornwall, Madison Co., Missouri, Find A Grave.com.

122 Find A Grave—Fort Rosecrans National Military Cemetery, San Diego, San Diego Co., California, Find A Grave.com.

123 Find A Grave—Rose Hill Cemetery, Bloomington, Monroe Co., Indiana, Find A Grave.com.

124 Find A Grave—Greenwood Cemetery, Greenwood, Johnson Co., Indiana, Find A Grave.com.

125 California, Marriage Index, 1949-1959, Ancestry.com, Gilbert H. Smith and Allys L. Robinson.

126 U.S., Social Security Applications and Claims Index, 1936-2014, Ancestry.com, Gilbert Harry Smith.

127 Find A Grave—Evergreen Memorial Cemetery, Crystal Falls, Iron Co., Michigan, Find A Grave.com.

128 Find A Grave—Arlington National Cemetery, Arlington, Virginia, Find A Grave.com.

129 Find A Grave—Shelby-Oakland Cemetery, Shelby, Shelby Twp., Richland Co., Ohio, Find A Grave.com.

130 Find A Grave—Mount Nebo United Methodist Church Cemetery, Sewickley Twp., Allegheny Co., Pennsylvania, Find A Grave.com.

131 Find A Grave—Downey District Cemetery, Downey, Los Angeles Co., California, Find A Grave.com.

132 Find A Grave—Live Oak Memorial Park Cemetery, Monrovia, Los Angeles Co., California, Find A Grave.com.

133 Find A Grave—Yukon Cemetery, Yukon, Canadian Co., Oklahoma, Find A Grave.com.

134 Find A Grave—Red Bud Catholic Cemetery, Cowley Co., Kansas, Find A Grave.com.

135 Find A Grave—Star Cemetery, Udall, Cowley Co., Kansas, Find A Grave.com.

136 Find A Grave—Lakeview Cemetery & Mausoleum, Wichita, Sedgwick Co., Kansas, Find A Grave.com.

137 Find A Grave—Memory Garden Cemetery, Rockville, Adams Twp., Parke Co., Indiana, Find A Grave.com.

138 Find A Grave—Memorial Park Cemetery, Indianapolis, Warren Twp., Marion Co., Indiana, Find A Grave.com.

139 Find A Grave—Forest Lawn Memory Gardens Cemetery, Greenwood, Johnson Co., Indiana, Find A Grave.com.

140 Find A Grave—Beech Grove Cemetery, Pomeroy, Salisbury Twp., Meigs Co., Ohio, Find A Grave.com.

141 Find A Grave—Knollwood Cemetery, Logan, Falls Twp., Hocking Co., Ohio, Find A Grave.com.

142 Find A Grave—Oak Hill Cemetery, Upper Sandusky, Crane Twp., Wyandot Co., Ohio, Find A Grave.com.

143 Find A Grave—Dublin Cemetery, Dublin, Washington Twp., Franklin Co., Ohio, Find A Grave.com.

144 Find A Grave—Assistens Kirkegaard Cemetery, Copenhagen, Denmark, Find A Grave.com.

145 Find A Grave—Cordova Cemetery, Cordova, Valdez-Cordova Precinct, Alaska, Find A Grave.com.

146 Find A Grave—Redmond Memorial Cemetery, Redmond, Deschutes Co., Oregon, Find A Grave.com.

147 Find A Grave—Restlawn Memorial Gardens Cemetery, Salem, Polk Co., Oregon, Find A Grave.com.

148 Find A Grave—Willamette National Cemetery, Portland, Multnomah Co., Oregon, Find A Grave.com.

149 Find A Grave—Mission Garden of Memories Cemetery, Clovis, Curry Co., New Mexico, Find A Grave.com.

150 Find A Grave—East Lawn Memorial Park Cemetery, Sacramento, Sacramento Co., California, Find A Grave.com.

151 Find A Grave—Civil Bend Cemetery, Winston, Douglas Co., Oregon, Find A Grave.com.

152 Find A Grave—Manahath Cemetery, Glassboro, Gloucester Co., New Jersey, Find A Grave.com.

153 Find A Grave—Floral Park Cemetery, Indianapolis, Marion Co., Indiana, Find A Grave.com.

154 Find A Grave—Gunpowder Friends Meeting House Cemetery, Sparks, Baltimore Co., Maryland, Find A Grave.com.

155 Find A Grave—Christian Memorial Cemetery, Rochester Hills, Wayne Co., Michigan, Find A Grave.com.

156 Find A Grave—Pleasant Valley Cemetery, Winfield, Cowley Co., Kansas, Find A Grave.com.

157 Find A Grave—Forest Lawn Memorial Park Cemetery, Hollywood Hills, Los Angeles Co., California, Find A Grave.com.

158 Find A Grave—Pankey Cemetery, Stockton, Stockton Twp., Cedar Co., Missouri, Find A Grave.com.

159 Find A Grave—Ferncliff Cemetery, Springfield, Springfield Twp., Clark Co., Ohio, Find A Grave.com.

# Descendants of Alexander Pagan, Son of Andrew Pegan II

1. **Alexander**[4] **Pagan** (*Andrew*[3] *Pegan II, Andrew*[2] *Pagan, James*[1]) was born about 1782 in Martic Twp., Lancaster Co., Pennsylvania. He was the son of Andrew Pegan II and Mary Ann Unknown. Alexander Pagan lived in 1810 in Brooke Co., (West) Virginia. He also resided in 1820 in Pleasant Twp., Brown Co., Ohio. Alexander Pagan died in Pleasant Twp., Brown Co., Ohio, between 1820 and 1830.

In his census enumerations, his name is given as "Alexander Pagan". But in the Brooke County (West) Virginia court records, his surname is "Pagen".

Alexander Pagan married Mrs. **Elizabeth McGrath?** Hamen in early 1810. They had one daughter. Elizabeth McGrath was born in Maryland on September 16, 1781. Elizabeth reached age 82 years and died in Levanna, Union Twp., Brown Co., Ohio, on April 10, 1864. She was buried in Pisgah Ridge Cemetery, Levanna, Union Twp., Brown Co., Ohio.[1]

Elizabeth was at least one year older than Alexander and was a widow with four children, a son and three daughters, when they wed. Her first husband, Steven Hamen, died in 1809, as her youngest child, Prudence Hamen, was a baby when she and Alexander married.[1] (They were married by the 1810 census. taken in August of that year.)

Alexander Pagan is enumerated in the 1810 census in Brooke Co., (West) Virginia (*Census Place: Brooke, Virginia; Roll: 66; Page: 680; Image: 0181426*) There is a one in col. 1 and a one in col. 3; a three in col. six, and a one in col. 9 (one male under age 10 and one male 16-25; three females under age 10 and a female 26-44. The census taker erred, as Alexander was 26-44 years old by then, according to Brooke Co. court records and tax roll documentation. The children were all Elizabeth McGrath Hamen Pagan/ Pagan's by her first marriage.

Alexander "Pagen" had two lawsuits filed for debts owed in Brooke Co., West Virginia.

Alexander Pagan (listed for some reason as "Absolom" [sic] in the index) and a Walter Cain, whose relationship to the Pagans is unknown, were sued in 1811 by Eli D. & "Cassander" (sic, probably Cassandra) Plummer. The Plummers contended that Alexander and Cain owed them $22.50, with interest of six cents per year, starting when the debt was assumed on August 8, 1810. Alexander and Cain failed to appear before the court. The court awarded the plaintiffs the debt and interest owed, plus costs.

It is unknown if Alexander Pagan paid his portion of this debt. (Although the index named him as "Absolom", a check of the actual court book confirms the given name as Alexander.[2, 3])

The Brooke County, West Virginia court again ruled against Alexander Pagan (who is somehow listed as his brother Robert) in John Iiams vs. "Robert Pagen" and Walter Cain on April 27, 1818. Alexander and Cain were sued by John Iiams for $4.00 and interest accrued until payment plus costs. As before, neither Alexander nor Cain appeared in court, and it is unknown whether the debt was ever settled. (This writer double-checked in a visit to Brooke County to confirm that Robert Pagan was indeed a defendant in this case, only to find that Alexander Pagan is the one that owed the debt.[4])

Although he was of age by 1804 and married by 1810, Alexander Pagan is only found on one tax list, the 1816 personal property tax list in Brooke County, West Virginia.[5]

Alexander Pagan does not appear in the Brooke County tax records after that date. He may have removed to Ohio, most likely to Brown County, by 1816. This may have been the reason Alexander never appeared in court for the 1818 lawsuit, and the suit seems to have never been settled.

In 1820 Alexander Pagan is living in Pleasant Twp., Brown Co., Ohio *(Census Place: Pleasant, Brown, Ohio; Page: 369; NARA Roll: M33_86; Image: 206).* There is a one in col. 5, a two in col. 7, a two in col. 9 and, it seems, a one in col. 11 (one male 26-44, two females under age 10, two females age 16-26, and one female more than age 45).

Alexander Pagan dies before 1830. His widow Elizabeth is not enumerated in the 1830 census.

On April 4, 1832, Elizabeth McGrath? Hamen Pagan married her third husband, James Sloane. After the wedding, neighbors visited their home, James and Elizabeth were walking their neighbors partway home. They were approaching the Pisgah Ridge Church when James Sloane suddenly fell over dead![1]

In 1850, Elizabeth McGrath? Hamen Pagan Sloane, age 59, a widow born in Maryland, is living with her son-in-law and daughter, William and Elizabeth Pagan McKee, in Union Twp., Brown Co., Ohio *(Census Place: Union, Brown, Ohio; Roll: M432_662; Page: 6B; Image: 453).* William McKee, the head of household, is enumerated as "William McKey". He is 33 years old and a laborer. Elizabeth Pagan/Pagen "McKey" is 31. William and Elizabeth have five sons: Josiah, 11, John, eight, Joseph, five, Jasper, four and "Lewis", one.

Elizabeth McGrath? Hamen Pagan/Pagan Sloane is not found in the 1860 census.

Daughter of Alexander Pagan and Elizabeth McGrath:

+ 2  f  I.  **Elizabeth[5] Pagan** was born in Brooke Co., (West) Virginia or Pleasant Twp., Brown Co., Ohio, on February 12, 1816. She died in St. Joseph, Washington Twp., Buchanan Co., Missouri, on May 23, 1903.

# 5th Generation

2. **Elizabeth**[5] **Pagan** (*Alexander*[4], *Andrew*[3] *Pegan II, Andrew*[2] *Pagan, James*[1]) was born on February 12, 1816, in Pleasant Twp., Brown Co., Ohio. She was the daughter of Alexander Pagan/Pagan (1) and Elizabeth McGrath. Elizabeth died in St. Joseph, Washington Twp., Buchanan Co., Missouri, on May 23, 1903, at age 87.

Elizabeth married **William Thomas McKee** on September 10, 1835, in Brown Co., Ohio.[6] They had eleven children. William Thomas McKee was born in East Franklin Twp., Armstrong Co., Pennsylvania, on November 9, 1813. William Thomas reached age 64 and died in St. Joseph, Buchanan Co., Missouri, on November 3, 1878.

Children of Elizabeth Pagan and William Thomas McKee:

+ 3   f   I.   **Martha Elizabeth**[6] **McKee** was born in Union Twp., Brown Co., Ohio, on August 2, 1836. She died in Union Twp., Brown Co., Ohio, on July 10, 1841.

+ 4   m   II.   **Josiah William**[6] **McKee** was born in Union Twp., Brown Co., Ohio, on September 20, 1838. He died in Brownwood, Brown Co., Texas, on March 12, 1886.

+ 5   m   III.   **James**[6] **McKee** was born in Union Twp., Brown Co., Ohio, on November 27, 1840. He died in Union Twp., Brown Co., Ohio, on September 16, 1841.

+ 6   m   IV.   **John**[6] **McKee** was born in Ripley Twp., Brown Co., Ohio, on June 29, 1842. He died in Billings, Yellowstone Co., Montana?, in 1892.

+ 7   m   V.   **Joseph**[6] **McKee** was born in Union Twp., Brown Co., Ohio, on January 13, 1845. He died about 1920.

+ 8   m   VI.   **Jasper Ervin**[6] **McKee** was born in Ripley Twp., Brown Co., Ohio, on November 20, 1846. He died in Soldier Twp., Jackson Co., Kansas, on January 26, 1925.

+ 9   m   VII.   **Jefferson Lewis**[6] **McKee** was born in Union Twp., Brown Co., Ohio, on March 15, 1849. He died in St. Joseph, Washington Twp., Buchanan Co., Missouri, on March 28, 1858.

+ 10   m   VIII.   **Amos Alfred**[6] **McKee** was born in Ripley Twp., Brown Co., Ohio, on April 4, 1851. He died in St. Joseph, Washington Twp., Buchanan Co., Missouri?, on January 18, 1880.

+ 11   f   IX.   **Mary Agli Matilda Jane**[6] **McKee** was born in Union Twp., Brown Co., Ohio, on February 23, 1853. She died in St. Joseph, Washington Twp., Buchanan Co., Missouri, after 1870.

+ 12   m   X.   **William Henry Harrison**[6] **McKee** was born in Ripley Twp., Brown Co., Ohio, on July 31, 1855. He was also known as **Henry.** William Henry Harrison died in St. Joseph, Washington Twp., Buchanan Co., Missouri, on August 17, 1932.[7]

+ 13   f   XI.   **Martha Amanda Elizabeth**[6] **McKee** was born in Union Twp., Brown Co., Ohio, on November 3, 1857. She died in St Joseph, Buchanan, Missouri, before 1870.

# 6th Generation

**3. Martha Elizabeth**[6] **McKee** (*Elizabeth*[5], *Alexander*[4], *Andrew*[3] *Pegan II*, *Andrew*[2] *Pagan*, *James*[1]) was born on August 2, 1836, in Union Twp., Brown Co., Ohio. She was the daughter of William Thomas McKee and Elizabeth Pagan (2). Martha Elizabeth died in Union Twp., Brown Co., Ohio, on July 10, 1841, at age four.

**4. Josiah William**[6] **McKee** (*Elizabeth*[5], *Alexander*[4], *Andrew*[3] *Pegan II*, *Andrew*[2] *Pagan*, *James*[1]) was born on September 20, 1838, in Union Twp., Brown Co., Ohio. He was the son of William Thomas McKee and Elizabeth Pagan (2). Josiah William lived in 1860 in Platte Twp., Clinton Co., Missouri. He also resided in 1870 in Platte Twp., Clinton Co., Missouri. Josiah William was living in 1880 in Brownwood, Brown Co., Texas. He died in Brownwood, Brown Co., Texas, on March 12, 1886, at age 47. Josiah William was buried in Indian Creek Cemetery, Brown Co., Texas.[8]

Josiah William married **Martha Amanda Gribble** on February 26, 1857, in Clinton Co., Missouri. They had eleven children. Martha Amanda Gribble was born in Haywood Co., North Carolina, on August 31, 1839. She was also known as **Maude.** Martha Amanda reached age 81 and died in Elmore City, Elmore Twp., Garvin Co., Oklahoma, on November 27, 1920. She was buried in Katie City Cemetery, Katie, Brady Twp., Garvin Co., Oklahoma.[9]

Children of Josiah William McKee and Martha Amanda Gribble:

+ 14    m    I.    **Samuel Stephen**[7] **McKee** was born in Platte Twp., Clinton Co., Missouri, on April 26, 1858. He died in Graham Twp., Carter Co., Oklahoma, on November 3, 1930.[9]

+ 15    f    II.    **Sarah Elvira Elizabeth Ann**[7] **McKee** was born in Platte Twp., Clinton Co., Missouri, on August 8, 1860. She died in Rotan, Fisher Co., Texas, on June 6, 1948.[10]

+ 16    m    III.    **William Robert**[7] **McKee** was born in Platte Twp., Clinton Co., Missouri, on January 8, 1863. He was also known as **Bob.** William Robert died in Brady Twp., Garvin Co., Oklahoma, on July 20, 1929.[9]

+ 17    m    IV.    **James L.**[7] **McKee** was born in Platte Twp., Clinton Co., Missouri, on October 8, 1865. He died in Pursley Twp., Grady Co., Oklahoma, on December 14, 1930.[11]

+ 18    f    V.    **Martha Louise Jane**[7] **McKee** was born in Platte Twp., Clinton Co., Missouri, on May 14, 1869. She died in Erin Springs, Lindsay Twp., Garvin Co., Oklahoma, on May 23, 1939.[12]

+ 19    m    VI.    **Josiah Andres**[7] **McKee II** was born in Platte Twp., Clinton Co., Missouri, on December 8, 1870. He died in Wilson, Hewitt Twp., Carter Co., Oklahoma, on July 29, 1945.[13]

+ 20    m    VII.    **Albert Milton**[7] **McKee** was born in Gentry Co., Missouri, on September 14, 1873. He died in Wirt, Hewitt Twp., Carter Co., Oklahoma, on December 1, 1920.[9]

+ 21    f    VIII.    **Mary Catherine**[7] **McKee** was born in Ellis Co., Texas, on August 29, 1876. She died in Shawnee, Rock Creek Twp., Pottawatomie Co., Oklahoma, on May 6, 1955.[14]

+ 22    m    IX.    **Charles Watson**[7] **McKee** was born in Brownwood, Brown Co., Texas, on March 15, 1879. He died in Lamesa, Dawson Co., Texas, on June 22, 1959.[10]

+ 23   m   X.   **Oliver Edwin**[7] **McKee** was born in Brownwood, Brown Co., Texas, on October 12, 1881. He died in Richland Hills, Tarrrant Co., Texas, on May 17, 1955.[10]

+ 24   f   XI.   **Rosa Lily**[7] **McKee** was born in Brownwood, Brown Co., Texas, on December 24, 1884. She died in Elmore City, Elmore Twp., Garvin Co., Oklahoma, on July 19, 1965.[9]

5.  **James**[6] **McKee** (*Elizabeth*[5], *Alexander Pagan*[4], *Andrew*[3] *Pegan II*, *Andrew*[2] *Pagan*, *James*[1]) was born on November 27, 1840, in Union Twp., Brown Co., Ohio. He was the son of William Thomas McKee and Elizabeth Pagan (2). James died in Union Twp., Brown Co., Ohio, on September 16, 1841.

6.  **John**[6] **McKee** (*Elizabeth*[5], *Alexander*[4], *Andrew*[3] *Pegan II*, *Andrew*[2] *Pagan*, *James*[1]) was born on June 29, 1842, in Ripley Twp., Brown Co., Ohio. He was the son of William Thomas McKee and Elizabeth Pagan (2). John died in Billings, Yellowstone Co., Montana?, in 1892 at age 49. Living in St. Joseph, Washington Twp., Buchanan Co., Missouri in 1880. He is not found in 1870 census. His wife and son William Henry McKee are not found after 1880.

John married **Susan Githens** on June 22, 1865, in Clinton Co., Missouri. They had four children. Susan Githens was born in Platte Twp., Clinton Co., Missouri, in 1845. Susan died in Billings, Yellowstone Co., Montana?, between September 14, 1893 and 1900. Susan Githens McKee is a witness to her daughter Sarah Elizabeth "Sadie" McKee's marriage to James Linsay Ralph on 14 Sep 1893 in Billings, Yellowstone Co., Montana.

Children of John McKee and Susan Githens:

+ 25   m   I.   **William Henry**[7] **McKee** was born in St. Joseph, Buchanan Co., Missouri, in 1866. He died after 1880.

+ 26   f   II.   **Agnes Belle**[7] **McKee** was born in St. Joseph, Buchanan Co., Missouri, in 1869.[15] She was also known as **Belle.** Agnes Belle died in Butte, Silver Bow, Montana?, after 1905.

+ 27   f   III.   **Sarah Elizabeth**[7] **McKee** was born in St. Joseph, Buchanan Co., Missouri, in 1871.[16] She was also known as **Sadie** and **Elizabeth.** Sarah Elizabeth died in Billings, Yellowstone Co., Montana?, between September 1893 and 1900.

+ 28   f   IV.   **Martha Jane**[7] **McKee** was born in St. Joseph, Buchanan Co., Missouri, in 1874. She died after 1880.

7.  **Joseph**[6] **McKee** (*Elizabeth*[5], *Alexander*[4], *Andrew*[3] *Pegan II*, *Andrew*[2] *Pagan*, *James*[1]) was born on January 13, 1845, in Union Twp., Brown Co., Ohio. He was the son of William Thomas McKee and Elizabeth Pagan (2). Joseph died about 1920 at age 74.

Childless?

Joseph married **Sarah Unknown** on July 16, 1871, in Missouri. Sarah died in Missouri before 1873.

Joseph McKee married **Mary Unknown** in 1873. Mary Unknown was born in 1850.

8.  **Jasper Ervin**[6] **McKee** (*Elizabeth*[5], *Alexander*[4], *Andrew*[3] *Pegan II*, *Andrew*[2] *Pagan*, *James*[1]) was born on November 20, 1846, in Ripley Twp., Brown Co., Ohio. He was the son of William Thomas McKee and Elizabeth Pagan (2). Jasper Ervin lived in 1880 in Washington Twp., Buchanan Co., Missouri. He died in Soldier Twp., Jackson Co., Kansas, on January 26, 1925, at age 78.

Jasper Ervin married **Hester Ann Cook** in 1867 in Missouri. They had six children. Hester Ann Cook was born in St. Joseph, Washington Twp., Buchanan Co., Missouri, on March 30, 1843. Hester Ann reached age 37 and died in St. Joseph, Washington Twp., Buchanan Co., Missouri, on June 9, 1880.

Children of Jasper Ervin McKee and Hester Ann Cook:

+ 29   f   I.   **Nancy Angeoline**[7] **McKee** was born in St. Joseph, Washington Twp., Buchanan Co., Missouri, on October 22, 1868. She died in St.

Joseph, Buchanan Co., Missouri, on January 30, 1942i.[17]

+ 30 f II. **Elizabeth**[7] **McKee** was born in St. Joseph, Washington Twp., Buchanan Co., Missouri, in 1870. She died in St. Joseph, Washington Twp., Buchanan Co., Missouri, in 1889.

+ 31 m III. **William Henry**[7] **McKee** was born in St. Joseph, Washington Twp., Buchanan Co., Missouri, on July 27, 1873. He died in Tulare Co., California, on July 18, 1950.

+ 32 f IV. **Etta May**[7] **McKee** was born in St. Joseph, Washington Twp., Buchanan Co., Missouri, in 1875. She died in St. Joseph, Washington Twp., Buchanan Co., Missouri, in 1892.

+ 33 f V. **Stella**[7] **McKee** was born in St. Joseph, Washington Twp., Buchanan Co., Missouri, in 1877. She died in St. Joseph, Washington Twp., Buchanan Co., Missouri, in 1880.

+ 34 f VI. **Martha**[7] **McKee** was born in St. Joseph, Washington Twp., Buchanan Co., Missouri, in 1879. She died in St. Joseph, Washington Twp., Buchanan Co., Missouri, after 1880.

9. **Jefferson Lewis**[6] **McKee** (*Elizabeth*[5], *Alexander*[4], *Andrew*[3] *Pegan II*, *Andrew*[2] *Pagan*, *James*[1]) was born on March 15, 1849, in Union Twp., Brown Co., Ohio. He was the son of William Thomas McKee and Elizabeth Pagan (2). Jefferson Lewis died in St. Joseph, Washington Twp., Buchanan Co., Missouri, on March 28, 1858, at age nine.

10. **Amos Alfred**[6] **McKee** (*Elizabeth*[5], *Alexander*[4], *Andrew*[3] *Pegan II*, *Andrew*[2] *Pagan*, *James*[1]) was born on April 4, 1851, in Ripley Twp., Brown Co., Ohio. He was the son of William Thomas McKee and Elizabeth Pagan (2). Amos Alfred died in St. Joseph,

Washington Twp., Buchanan Co., Missouri?, on January 18, 1880, at age 28.

11. **Mary Agli Matilda Jane**[6] **McKee** (*Elizabeth*[5], *Alexander*[4], *Andrew*[3] *Pegan II*, *Andrew*[2] *Pagan*, *James*[1]) was born on February 23, 1853, in Union Twp., Brown Co., Ohio. She was the daughter of William Thomas McKee and Elizabeth Pagan (2). Mary Agli Matilda Jane died in St. Joseph, Washington Twp., Buchanan Co., Missouri, after 1870.

12. **William Henry Harrison**[6] **McKee** (*Elizabeth*[5], *Alexander*[4], *Andrew*[3] *Pegan II*, *Andrew*[2] *Pagan*, *James*[1]) was born on July 31, 1855, in Ripley Twp., Brown Co., Ohio. He was also known as **Henry.** He was the son of William Thomas McKee and Elizabeth Pagan (2). William Henry Harrison lived in 1925 in Soldier, Jackson Co., Kansas. He died in St. Joseph, Washington Twp., Buchanan Co., Missouri, on August 17, 1932, at age 77. William Henry Harrison was buried in Ashland Cemetery, St. Joseph, Washington Twp., Buchanan Co., Missouri.[7]

William Henry Harrison married **Donna Belle Michael** on April 30, 1876, in Buchanan Co., Missouri. They had two daughters. Donna Belle Michael was born in Jackson Twp., Buchanan Co., Missouri, in 1859. Donna Belle died in St. Joseph, Washington Twp., Buchanan Co., Missouri, between 1880 and 1899.

William Henry Harrison McKee married **Thurza Ellen Prickett** on October 4, 1899, in Buchanan Co., Missouri. Thurza Ellen Prickett was born in Maryville, Polk Twp., Nodaway Co., Missouri, on December 18, 1863. Thurza Ellen reached age 66 years and died in St. Joseph, Washington Twp., Buchanan Co., Missouri, on February 4, 1930. She was buried in Ashland Cemetery, St. Joseph, Washington Twp., Buchanan Co., Missouri.[7]

Daughters of William Henry Harrison McKee and Donna Belle Michael:

+ 35    f    I.    **Cora Alvertie**[7] **McKee** was born in St. Joseph, Washington Twp., Buchanan Co., Missouri, on June 20, 1877. She died in St. Joseph, Washington Twp., Buchanan Co., Missouri, on April 9, 1953.[7]

+ 36    f    II.    **Gertrude**[7] **McKee** was born in St. Joseph, Washington Twp., Buchanan Co., Missouri, on December 17, 1879. She died in St. Joseph, Washington Twp., Buchanan Co., Missouri, on May 29, 1949.[7]

**13. Martha Amanda Elizabeth**[7] **McKee** (*Elizabeth*[5], *Alexander*[4], *Andrew*[3] *Pegan II, Andrew*[2] *Pagan, James*[1]) was born on November 3, 1857, in Union Twp., Brown Co., Ohio. She was the daughter of William Thomas McKee and Elizabeth Pagan (2). Martha Amanda Elizabeth died in St Joseph, Buchanan, Missouri, before 1870.

# 7th Generation

**14. Samuel Stephen[7] McKee** (*Josiah William[6], Elizabeth[5], Alexander[A], Andrew[3] Pegan II, Andrew[2] Pagan, James[1]*) was born on April 26, 1858, in Platte Twp., Clinton Co., Missouri. He was the son of Josiah William McKee (4) and Martha Amanda Gribble. Samuel Stephen died in Graham Twp., Carter Co., Oklahoma, on November 3, 1930, at age 72. He was buried in Katie City Cemetery, Katie, Brady Twp., Garvin Co., Oklahoma.[9]

Samuel Stephen married **Laura Ann Riley** on November 22, 1885, in Brown Co., Texas. They had six children. Laura Ann Riley was born in Burnet Co., Texas?, on February 17, 1865. Laura Ann reached age 53 and died in Katie, Brady Twp., Garvin Co., Oklahoma, on November 10, 1918. She was buried in Katie City Cemetery, Katie, Brady Twp., Garvin Co., Oklahoma.[9]

Children of Samuel Stephen McKee and Laura Ann Riley:

+ 37   f   I.   **Mary E.[8] McKee** was born in Burnet Co., Texas, on November 1, 1886. She was also known as **Mollie.** Mary E. died in Elmore Twp., Garvin Co., Oklahoma, on March 22, 1965.[9]

+ 38   f   II.   **Martha Ollie[8] McKee** was born in Brady Twp., Garvin Co., Oklahoma, on September 30, 1888. She was also known as **Ollie.** Martha Ollie died in Oklahoma City, Oklahoma, on March 11, 1974.[18]

+ 39   m   III.   **William H.[8] McKee** was born in Montague Co., Texas, on March 3, 1890. He died in Purcell, Moncrief Twp., McClain Co., Oklahoma, on December 13, 1970.[9]

+ 40   f   IV.   **Eva Alice[8] McKee** was born in Montague Co., Texas, on August 13, 1893. She died in Purcell, Moncrief Twp., McClain Co., Oklahoma, on July 13, 1988.[19]

+ 41   f   V.   **Fannie May[8] McKee** was born in Brady Twp., Garvin Co., Oklahoma, on March 10, 1900. She died in Bethany, Oklahoma Co., Oklahoma, on March 21, 1976.[20]

+ 42   f   VI.   **Margaret Ann[8] McKee** was born in Brady Twp., Garvin Co., Oklahoma, on April 1, 1904. She was also known as **Maggie.** Margaret Ann died in San Angelo, Tom Green Co., Texas, on September 19, 1958.[9]

**15. Sarah Elvira Elizabeth Ann[7] McKee** (*Josiah William[6], Elizabeth[5], Alexander[A], Andrew[3] Pegan II, Andrew[2] Pagan, James[1]*) was born on August 8, 1860, in Platte Twp., Clinton Co., Missouri. She was the daughter of Josiah William McKee (4) and Martha Amanda Gribble. Sarah Elvira Elizabeth Ann died in Rotan, Fisher Co., Texas, on June 6, 1948, at age 87. She was buried in Newman Cemetery, Sylvester, Fisher Co., Texas.[10]

Sarah Elvira Elizabeth Ann married **William Andrew Cross** on August 26, 1883, in Brown Co., Texas. They had nine children. William Andrew Cross was born in Bell Co., Texas, on June 27, 1862. He was also known as **Andy.** William Andrew reached age 88 and died in Rotan, Fisher Co., Texas, on August 14, 1950. He was buried in Newman Cemetery, Sylvester, Fisher Co., Texas.[10]

Children of Sarah Elvira Elizabeth Ann McKee and William Andrew Cross:

+ 43   m   I.   **Claud James[8] Cross** was born in Brownwood, Brown Co., Texas, on July 22, 1884. He died in Rotan, Fisher Co., Texas, on June 20, 1971.[10]

+ 44   f   II.   **Clara Jane[8] Cross** was born in Brownwood, Brown Co., Texas, on July 22, 1884. She died in Sylvester, Fisher Co., Texas, on May 27, 1982.[10]

+ 45   m   III.   **William Josiah Thomas[8] Cross** was born in Brownwood, Brown Co., Texas, on September 26, 1886. He was also known as **Thomas.** William Josiah Thomas died in Sylvester, Fisher Co., Texas, on April 17, 1920.[10]

+ 46   m   IV.   **Jesse Riley[8] Cross** was born in Brownwood, Brown Co., Texas, on December 18, 1887. He died in France on August 15, 1918.[10]

+ 47   f   V.   **Elizabeth Violet[8] Cross** was born in Brownwood, Brown Co., Texas, on December 18, 1887. She was also known as **Bessie.** Elizabeth Violet died in Sylvester, Fisher Co., Texas, on January 10, 1984.[10]

+ 48   m   VI.   **George Emmit[8] Cross** was born in Brownwood, Brown Co., Texas, on October 26, 1890. He died in McCaulley, Fisher Co., Texas, on January 16, 1974.[10]

+ 49   f   VII.   **Alice Emma[8] Cross** was born in Brownwood, Brown Co., Texas, on October 26, 1890. She died in Roby, Fisher Co., Texas, on November 16, 1982.[10]

+ 50   m   VIII.   **John Henry[8] Cross** was born in Brownwood, Brown Co., Texas, on June 27, 1894. He died in Rotan, Fisher Co., Texas, on June 22, 1978.[21]

+ 51   m   IX.   **Willie Franklin[8] Cross** was born in Brownwood, Brown Co., Texas, on May 19, 1896. He was also known as **Eddy.** Willie Franklin died in Abilene, Taylor Co., Texas, on July 18, 1921.[10]

**16. William Robert[7] McKee** (*Josiah William[6], Elizabeth[5], Alexander[4], Andrew[3] Pegan II, Andrew[2]*

*Pagan, James[1]*) was born on January 8, 1863, in Platte Twp., Clinton Co., Missouri. He was also known as **Bob.** He was the son of Josiah William McKee (4) and Martha Amanda Gribble. William Robert died in Brady Twp., Garvin Co., Oklahoma, on July 20, 1929, at age 66. He was buried in Katie City Cemetery, Katie, Brady Twp., Garvin Co., Oklahoma.[9]

William Robert married **Mary Elizabeth Fletcher** before 1891. They had eight children. Mary Elizabeth Fletcher was born in St. Jo, Montague Co., Texas, on September 29, 1867. Mary Elizabeth reached age 42 and died in Brady Twp., Garvin Co., Oklahoma, on February 13, 1910. She was buried in Katie City Cemetery, Katie, Brady Twp., Garvin Co., Oklahoma.[4]

Mary Elizabeth Fletcher McKee (Mrs. William Robert McKee) was a sister to Florence L. Fletcher McKee, wife of James L. McKee, William Robert McKee's brother.

Because his first wife, Mary Elizabeth Fletcher, was Choctaw, all of William Robert McKee's children were also considered Native American and were listed on Choctaw registers in Oklahoma.

Mary Elizabeth Fletcher McKee was a sister to Florence L. Fletcher McKee, wife of James L. McKee, William Robert's brother.

William Robert McKee married Mrs. **M.J. Charles** on June 18, 1910, in Garvin Co., Oklahoma. Either she died or they were divorced before 1915.

William Robert McKee married **Rhoda Perlina Hoggard** on August 20, 1915, in Garvin Co., Oklahoma. Rhoda Perlina Hoggard was born in Tarrant Co., Texas, on March 8, 1871. Rhoda Perlina reached age 82 and died in Lookeba, Caddo Co., Oklahoma, on November 27, 1953.

Children of William Robert McKee and Mary Elizabeth Fletcher:

+ 52   f   I.   **Mary Willie[8] McKee** was born in Brown Co., Texas, on June 23, 1892. She died in Rush Springs Twp., Grady Co., Oklahoma, on June 3, 1964.[22]

+ 53 m II. **James Andres⁸ McKee** was born in Montague Co., Texas, on May 5, 1894. He died in Chickasha, Chickasha Twp., Grady Co., Oklahoma, on July 21, 1967.[12]

+ 54 f III. **Clara Ida⁸ McKee** was born in Chagris Twp., Pickens Co., Oklahoma, on August 25, 1896. She died in Hatfield, Polk Co., Arkansas, on March 8, 1983.

+ 55 m IV. **George Washington⁸ McKee** was born in Chagris Twp., Pickens Co., Oklahoma, on September 26, 1898. He died in Brady Twp., Garvin Co., Oklahoma, on October 15, 1962.[9]

+ 56 f V. **Barbara⁸ McKee** was born in Brady Twp., Garvin Co., Oklahoma, on November 6, 1901. She died in Garvin Co., Oklahoma, on February 11, 1906.[9]

+ 57 f VI. **Martha Amanda⁸ McKee** was born in Indian City, Payne Co., Oklahoma, on May 7, 1904. She was also known as **Amanda** and **Manda.** Martha Amanda died in Norman, Norman Twp., Cleveland Co., Oklahoma, on September 16, 1952.[9]

+ 58 m VII. **Charles Albert⁸ McKee** was born in Indian City, Payne Co., Oklahoma, on December 2, 1906. He died in Oklahoma City, Oklahoma, in February 1986.[23]

+ 59 f VIII. **Anna Mae⁸ McKee** was born in Brady Twp., Garvin Co., Oklahoma, on September 9, 1909. She died in Hatfield, Polk Co., Arkansas, on March 16, 1986.

**17. James L.⁷ McKee** (*Josiah William⁶, Elizabeth⁵, Alexander⁴, Andrew³ Pegan II, Andrew² Pagan, James¹*) was born on October 8, 1865, in Platte Twp., Clinton Co., Missouri. He was the son of

Josiah William McKee (4) and Martha Amanda Gribble. James L. died in Pursley Twp., Grady Co., Oklahoma, on December 14, 1930, at age 65. He was buried in Bradley Cemetery, Bradley Twp., Grady Co., Oklahoma.[6] James L. McKee's wife, Florence L. Fletcher McKee, was a sister to Mary Elizabeth Fletcher McKee, wife of William Robert "Bob" McKee, James L.'s brother.

As Florence L. Fletcher McKee was Choctaw, all of James L. McKee's children were on the Choctaw tribal rolls.

James L. married **Florence Fletcher** about 1890. They had nine children. Florence Fletcher was born in St. Jo, Montague Co., Texas, on March 18, 1866. Florence reached age 43 and died in Dundee, Archer Co., Texas, on April 13, 1909. Florence L. Fletcher McKee (Mrs. James L.) was a sister to Mary Elizabeth Mckee, wife of William Robert "Bob" McKee, James L.'s brother

Children of James L. McKee and Florence Fletcher:

+ 60 f I. **Ella Florence⁸ McKee** was born in St. Jo, Montague Co., Texas, on June 13, 1891. She died in Enid, Garfield Co., Oklahoma, on August 12, 1938.[24]

+ 61 m II. **James George⁸ McKee** was born in Brown Co., Texas, on November 22, 1893. He was also known as **George.** James George died in Sulphur, Murray Co., Oklahoma, on April 4, 1973.[11]

+ 62 f III. **Laura Elvira⁸ McKee** was born in Brown Co., Texas, on September 25, 1895. She died in Garvin Co., Oklahoma, on October 31, 1970.[25]

+ 63 m IV. **Jasper Edmond⁸ McKee** was born in Chargis, Pickens Co. (now Carter Co.), Oklahoma, on December 20, 1897. He died in Garvin Co., Oklahoma, on December 16, 1918.

+ 64 m V. **Oliver Charleston⁸ McKee** was born in Chargis, Pickens Co. (now Carter Co.), Oklahoma, on March 2, 1899. He died in Lindsay, Lindsay Twp., Garvin Co., Oklahoma, on April 19, 1982.[11]

+ 65 f VI. **Mary Amanda⁸ McKee** was born in Chargis, Pickens Co. (now Carter Co.), Oklahoma, on January 20, 1902. She died in Vernon, Wilbarger Co., Texas, on March 22, 1987.[26]

+ 66 m VII. **Marvin Milton⁸ McKee** was born in Chargis, Pickens Co. (now Carter Co.), Oklahoma, on April 16, 1903. He died in Porterville, Tulare Co., California, on August 26, 1970.[27]

+ 67 m VIII. **Sie Andron⁸ McKee** was born in Chargis, Pickens Co. (now Carter Co.), Oklahoma, on November 15, 1906. He died in Chickasha, Chickasha Twp., Grady Co., Oklahoma, on August 12, 1983.[28]

+ 68 m IX. **Willie Fletcher⁸ McKee** was born in Archer Co., Texas, on April 12, 1909. He died in Rush Springs Twp., Grady Co., Oklahoma, on June 18, 1986.[11]

**18. Martha Louise Jane⁷ McKee** (*Josiah William⁶, Elizabeth⁵, Alexander⁴, Andrew³ Pegan II, Andrew² Pagan, James¹*) was born on May 14, 1869, in Platte Twp., Clinton Co., Missouri. She was the daughter of Josiah William McKee (4) and Martha Amanda Gribble. Martha Louise Jane died in Erin Springs, Lindsay Twp., Garvin Co., Oklahoma, on May 23, 1939, at age 70. She was buried in Erin Springs Cemetery, Erin Springs, Lindsay Twp., Garvin Co., Oklahoma.[7]

Martha Louise Jane married **Isaac H. Riley** on October 9, 1889, in Montague Co., Texas. They had seven children. Isaac H. Riley was born in Belton, Bell Co., Texas, on March 27, 1869. Isaac

H. reached age 47 and died in Harrison Twp., Grady Co., Oklahoma, on November 8, 1916. He was buried in Erin Springs Cemetery, Erin Springs, Lindsay Twp., Garvin Co., Oklahoma.[7]

Children of Martha Louise Jane McKee and Isaac H. Riley:

+ 69 m I. **Reuben Josiah⁸ Riley** was born in Montague Co., Texas, on August 12, 1890. He died in Lindsay, Lindsay Twp., Garvin Co., Oklahoma, on November 2, 1977.[12]

+ 70 f II. **Mary Malire⁸ Riley** was born in Montague Co., Texas, on May 13, 1892. She was also known as **Molly.** Mary Malire died in Erin Springs, Lindsay Twp., Garvin Co., Oklahoma, on September 4, 1945.[12]

+ 71 m III. **Isaac Russell⁸ Riley II** was born in Montague Co., Texas, on June 1, 1894. He was also known as **Russell.** Isaac Russell died in Luna Co., New Mexico, on January 24, 1962.[29]

+ 72 f IV. **Emma Neta⁸ Riley** was born in Montague Co., Texas, on December 20, 1895. She died in a hospital in Oklahoma City, Oklahoma Co., Oklahoma, on September 6, 1938.[28]

+ 73 f V. **Ada May⁸ Riley** was born in Township 3, Choctaw Nation, Indian Territory (now LaFlore or Caddo Co., Oklahoma), on February 14, 1898. She died in Harrison Twp., Grady Co., Oklahoma, on October 2, 1915.[12]

+ 74 f VI. **Janie Susan⁸ Riley** was born in Township 3, Choctaw Nation, Indian Territory (now LaFlore or Caddo Co., Oklahoma), on February 8, 1900. She died in Oklahoma City, Oklahoma, on April 20, 1968.[28]

+ 75   f   VII.   **Anna Martha⁸ Riley** was born in Harrison Twp., Grady Co., Oklahoma, on May 12, 1902. She died in Lindsay, Lindsay Twp., Garvin Co., Oklahoma, on March 7, 1975.[28]

**19. Josiah Andres⁷ McKee II** (*Josiah William⁶, Elizabeth⁵, Alexander⁴, Andrew³ Pegan II, Andrew² Pagan, James¹*) was born on December 8, 1870, in Platte Twp., Clinton Co., Missouri. He was the son of Josiah William McKee (4) and Martha Amanda Gribble. Josiah Andres died in Wilson, Hewitt Twp., Carter Co., Oklahoma, on July 29, 1945, at age 74. He was buried in Hewitt Cemetery, Wilson, Hewitt Twp., Carter Co., Oklahoma.[13]

Josiah Andres married **Lillie Alice Harrell** on August 5, 1894, in Cooke Co., Texas. They had nine children. Lillie Alice Harrell was born in Collin Co., Texas, on September 9, 1878. Lillie Alice reached age 70 and died in Wilson, Hewitt Twp., Carter Co., Oklahoma, on November 9, 1948. She was buried in Hewitt Cemetery, Wilson, Hewitt Twp., Carter Co., Oklahoma.[13]

Children of Josiah Andres McKee II and Lillie Alice Harrell:

+ 76   f   I.   **Willie Alice⁸ McKee** was born in Cooke Co., Texas or St. Jo, Montague Co., Texas, on September 4, 1895. She died in Wilson, Hewitt Twp., Carter Co., Oklahoma, on September 3, 1946.[13]

+ 77   m   II.   **Infant Twin Son⁸ McKee** was born in Hewitt Twp., Carter Co., Oklahoma, on May 2, 1897. He died in Brady Twp., Garvin Co., Oklahoma, on May 2, 1897.[30]

+ 78   m   III.   **George Washington Josiah⁸ McKee** was born in Hewitt Twp., Carter Co., Oklahoma, on May 2, 1897. He was also known as **Josiah** and **Joe.** George Washington Josiah died in Wilson, Hewitt Twp., Carter Co., Oklahoma, on August 9, 1971.[13]

+ 79   f   IV.   **Martha Ann⁸ McKee** was born in Brady Twp., Garvin Co., Oklahoma, on March 4, 1899. She was also known as **Anna** and **Annie.** Martha Anna died in Parks Twp., Stephens Co., Oklahoma?, on April 11, 1966.[31]

+ 80   f   V.   **Roxie Laurenda⁸ McKee** was born in Brady Twp., Garvin Co., Oklahoma, on February 10, 1902. She died in Wilson, Hewitt Twp., Carter Co., Oklahoma, on September 28, 1991.[13]

+ 81   f   VI.   **Sarah Lou⁸ McKee** was born in Brady Twp., Garvin Co., Oklahoma, on January 23, 1904. She died in Hewitt Twp., Carter Co., Oklahoma, on January 23, 1973.[13]

+ 82   m   VII.   **Henry William⁸ McKee** was born in Brady Twp., Garvin Co., Oklahoma, on April 23, 1907. He died in Wilson, Hewitt Twp., Carter Co., Oklahoma, on January 5, 1981.[13]

+ 83   m   VIII.   **Verdie Loyd⁸ McKee** was born in Brady Twp., Garvin Co., Oklahoma, on April 6, 1911. He died in Krotz Springs, Saint Landry Parish, Louisiana, on February 11, 1988.

+ 84   f   IX.   **Ruth Lea⁸ McKee** was born in Brady Twp., Garvin Co., Oklahoma, on September 9, 1913. She died in Ardmore, Morgan

Twp., Carter Co., Oklahoma, on April 16, 1997.[13]

**20. Albert Milton⁷ McKee** (*Josiah William⁶, Elizabeth⁵, Alexander⁴, Andrew³ Pegan II, Andrew² Pagan, James¹*) was born on September 14, 1873, in Gentry Co., Missouri. He was the son of Josiah William McKee (4) and Martha Amanda Gribble. Albert Milton died in Wirt, Hewitt Twp., Carter Co., Oklahoma, on December 1, 1920, at age 47. He was buried in Katie City Cemetery, Katie, Brady Twp., Garvin Co., Oklahoma.[9]

Albert Milton married **Juanita Roten** about 1893. They had two children. Juanita Roten was born in Nevada Co., Arkansas, on November 19, 1874. Juanita reached age 21 and died in Carter Co., Oklahoma, on August 25, 1896. She was buried in Chagger Cemetery, Carter Co., Oklahoma.[30]

Albert Milton McKee married **Nancy Anna Fletcher** on December 25, 1906, in Carter Co., Oklahoma. They had four children. Nancy Anna Fletcher was born in Montague Co., Texas, on December 18, 1874. She was also known as **Anna.** Nancy Anna reached age 81 and died in Pauls Valley, Whitebead Twp., Garvin Co., Oklahoma, on May 29, 1956.

Children of Albert Milton McKee and Juanita Roten:

+ 85 m I. **Josiah Milton⁸ McKee** was born in St. Jo, Montague Co., Texas, on August 8, 1894. He died in Oklahoma City, Oklahoma, on June 18, 1930.[9]

+ 86 f II. **Martha Amanda⁸ McKee** was born in Carter Co., Oklahoma, on July 31, 1896. She died in Garvin Co., Oklahoma, on September 8, 1896.

Children of Albert Milton McKee and Nancy Anna Fletcher:

+ 87 f I. **Vivian Violet⁸ McKee** was born in Brady Twp., Garvin Co., Oklahoma, on May 31, 1908. She was also known as **Violet.** Vivian Violet died in Norman, Cleveland

Co., Oklahoma, on February 15, 1994.[32]

+ 88 f II. **Rosa Lawana⁸ McKee** was born in Brady Twp., Garvin Co., Oklahoma, on April 27, 1910. She died in Oklahoma City, Oklahoma, on June 20, 1977.

+ 89 m III. **John James⁸ McKee** was born in Brady Twp., Garvin Co., Oklahoma, on October 21, 1911. He died in Paul's Valley, Whitebead Twp., Garvin Co., Oklahoma, on March 7, 1967.

+ 90 m IV. **Daniel⁸ McKee** was born in Hewitt Twp., Carter Co., Oklahoma, on February 11, 1913. He died in Paul's Valley, Whitebead Twp., Garvin Co., Oklahoma, on April 25, 1972.

**21. Mary Catherine⁷ McKee** (*Josiah William⁶, Elizabeth⁵, Alexander⁴, Andrew³ Pegan II, Andrew² Pagan, James¹*) was born on August 29, 1876, in Ellis Co., Texas. She was the daughter of Josiah William McKee (4) and Martha Amanda Gribble. Mary Catherine died in Shawnee, Rock Creek Twp., Pottawatomie Co., Oklahoma, on May 6, 1955, at age 78. She was buried in Tribbey Cemetery, Tribbey, Burnett Twp., Pottawatomie Co., Oklahoma.[14]

Mary Catherine married **John Dethridge Wright** on April 19, 1896, in Carter Co., Oklahoma. They had twelve children. John Dethridge Wright was born in Collin Co., Texas, on March 14, 1871. John Dethridge reached age 61 and died in Tribbey, Burnett Twp., Pottawatomie Co., Oklahoma, on January 25, 1933. He was buried in Tribbey Cemetery, Tribbey, Burnett Twp., Pottawatomie Co., Oklahoma.[14] Children of Mary Catherine McKee and John Dethridge Wright:

+ 91 f I. **Rosa Lillie⁸ Wright** was born in Johnsonville, McClain Co., Oklahoma, on March 11, 1897.

She died in Golden, Wood Co., Texas, on November 30, 1977.[33]

+ 92 f II. **Dedaunia Lucinda Amanda Jane**[8] **Wright** was born in Tribbey, Burnett Twp., Pottawatomie Co., Oklahoma, on November 12, 1898. She was also known as **Lucy Jane.** Dedaunia Lucinda Amanda Jane died in Macomb, Burnett Twp., Pottawatomie Co., Oklahoma, on March 1, 1981.

+ 93 f III. **Maemily Ann**[8] **Wright** was born in Tribbey, Burnett Twp., Pottawatomie Co., Oklahoma, on January 16, 1901. She was also known as **Emma.** Maemily Ann died in Tribbey, Burnett Twp., Pottawatomie Co., Oklahoma, on March 22, 1979.[14]

+ 94 m IV. **Infant Son**[8] **Wright** was born in Tribbey, Burnett Twp., Pottawatomie Co., Oklahoma, on January 5, 1903. He died in Tribbey, Burnett Twp., Pottawatomie Co., Oklahoma, on January 5, 1903.

+ 95 f V. **Mary Catherine**[8] **Wright** was born in Tribbey, Burnett Twp., Pottawatomie Co., Oklahoma, on July 11, 1904. She died in Checotah, McIntosh Co., Oklahoma, on August 7, 1992.[14]

+ 96 m VI. **John Martin**[8] **Wright** was born in Tribbey, Burnett Twp., Pottawatomie Co., Oklahoma, on August 24, 1907. He died in Shawnee, Rock Creek Twp., Pottawatomie Co., Oklahoma, on January 31, 1984.[34]

+ 97 f VII. **Sarah Elvara**[8] **Wright** was born in Tribbey, Burnett Twp., Pottawatomie Co., Oklahoma, on August 24, 1907. She was also known as **Eliz.** Sarah Elvara died

in Oklahoma City, Oklahoma, on April 14, 1981.[14]

+ 98 m VIII. **Willis Josiah**[8] **Wright** was born in Tribbey, Burnett Twp., Pottawatomie Co., Oklahoma, on September 12, 1910. He died in Newalla, Oklahoma Co., Oklahoma, on September 27, 1974. [35]

+ 99 m IX. **Charles Watson**[8] **Wright** was born in Tribbey, Burnett Twp., Pottawatomie Co., Oklahoma, on September 25, 1912. He died in Oklahoma City, Oklahoma, on April 28, 1990.[34]

+ 100 f X. **Violet Roberta**[8] **Wright** was born in Tribbey, Burnett Twp., Pottawatomie Co., Oklahoma, on January 30, 1915. She died in Sun City, Riverside Co., California, on October 29, 1992.[36]

+ 101 f XI. **Grace Aston**[8] **Wright** was born in Tribbey, Burnett Twp., Pottawatomie Co., Oklahoma, on February 4, 1917. She died in Eufala, McIntosh Co., Oklahoma, on November 15, 2007.

+ 102 m XII. **John Dethridge**[8] **Wright II** was born in Tribbey, Burnett Twp., Pottawatomie Co., Oklahoma, on July 10, 1921. He was also known as **J.D..** John Dethridge died in Shawnee, Rock Creek Twp., Pottawatomie Co., Oklahoma, on January 25, 1992.[34]

22. **Charles Watson**[7] **McKee** (*Josiah William*[6], *Elizabeth*[5], *Alexander*[4], *Andrew*[3] *Pegan II, Andrew*[2] *Pagan, James*[1]) was born on March 15, 1879, in Brownwood, Brown Co., Texas. He was the son of Josiah William McKee (4) and Martha Amanda Gribble. Charles Watson died in Lamesa, Dawson Co., Texas, on June 22, 1959, at age 80. He was buried in Newman Cemetery, Sylvester, Fisher

Co., Texas.[10] Charles Watson McKee's wife, Allie Lucene Rials, was a sister to Addie Laverne Rials, the wife of Charles' brother Oliver Edwin McKee. The couples had a double wedding.

Charles Watson married **Allie Lucine Rials** on August 19, 1906, in Pickens Co. (now Garvin Co.), Oklahoma. They had five children. Allie Lucine Rials was born in Dublin, Montgomery Co., Alabama, on August 31, 1888. Allie Lucine reached age 86 and died in Lamesa, Dawson Co., Texas, on April 10, 1975. She was buried in Newman Cemetery, Sylvester, Fisher Co., Texas.[10]

Children of Charles Watson McKee and Allie Lucine Rials:

+ 103 f I. **Martha Louisa Jane⁸ McKee** was born in Brady Twp., Garvin Co., Oklahoma, on September 21, 1907. She was also known as **Louisa.** Martha Louisa Jane died in Lamesa, Dawson Co., Texas, on December 19, 1993.[37]

+ 104 m II. **Albert Milton⁸ McKee** was born in Brady Twp., Garvin Co., Oklahoma, on June 16, 1909. He died in Fort Worth, Tarrant Co., Texas, on December 12, 1994.[38]

+ 105 f III. **Mary Katherine⁸ McKee** was born in Brady Twp., Garvin Co., Oklahoma, on May 18, 1912. She was also known as **Catherine.** Mary Katherine died in Lamont, Kern Co., California, on January 8, 1996.

+ 106 m IV. **Samuel Robert⁸ McKee** was born in Brady Twp., Garvin Co., Oklahoma, on July 6, 1915. He died in Fort Worth, Tarrant Co., Texas, on December 19, 1982.[10]

+ 107 m V. **Earnest L.⁸ McKee** was born in Brady Twp., Garvin Co., Oklahoma, on March 5, 1923. He died in Castroville, Medina Co., Texas, on January 10, 2013.[39]

**23. Oliver Edwin⁷ McKee** (*Josiah William⁶, Elizabeth⁵, Alexander⁴, Andrew³ Pegan II, Andrew² Pagan, James¹*) was born on October 12, 1881, in Brownwood, Brown Co., Texas. He was the son of Josiah William McKee (4) and Martha Amanda Gribble. Oliver Edwin died in Richland Hills, Tarrant Co., Texas, on May 17, 1955, at age 73. He was buried in Newman Cemetery, Sylvester, Fisher Co., Texas.[10] Oliver Edwin McKee's wife, Addie Laverne Rials, was a sister to Allie Lucene Rials, wife of Oliver's brother Charles Watson McKee. The couples had a double wedding.

Oliver Edwin married **Addie Laverne Rials** on August 19, 1906, in Pickens Co. (now Garvin Co.), Oklahoma. They had nine children. Addie Laverne Rials was born in Dublin, Montgomery Co., Alabama, on August 31, 1889. Addie Laverne reached age 47 and died in Brady Twp., Garvin Co., Oklahoma, on March 4, 1937. She was buried in Katie City Cemetery, Katie, Brady Twp., Garvin Co., Oklahoma.[9]

Children of Oliver Edwin McKee and Addie Laverne Rials:

+ 108 m I. **Samuel Robert⁸ McKee** was born in Brady Twp., Garvin Co., Oklahoma, on March 15, 1909. He died in Brady Twp., Garvin Co., Oklahoma, on January 27, 1910.[9]

+ 109 m II. **James Harvey⁸ McKee** was born in Brady Twp., Garvin Co., Oklahoma, on August 21, 1911. He was also known as **Harvey.** James Harvey died in Abilene, Taylor Co., Texas, on December 13, 1977.[10]

+ 110 f III. **Martha Rosa⁸ McKee** was born in Brady Twp., Garvin Co., Oklahoma, on March 14, 1916. She was also known as **Rosa.** Martha Rosa died in a hospital in Lubbock, Lubbock Co., Texas, on April 17, 2004.[10]

+ 111 f IV. **Meranda Ethel**[8] **McKee** was born in Brady Twp., Garvin Co., Oklahoma, on August 7, 1918. She was also known as **Ethel.** Meranda Ethel died in Norman, Norman Twp., Cleveland Co., Oklahoma, on March 23, 2004.[40]

+ 112 m V. **William Everett**[8] **McKee** was born in Brady Twp., Garvin Co., Oklahoma, on March 12, 1921. He was also known as **Everett.** William Everett died in Lovington, Lea Co., New Mexico, on December 7, 2000.[10]

+ 113 m VI. **Lee Roy**[8] **McKee** was born in Brady Twp., Garvin Co., Oklahoma, on June 19, 1924. He died in Everett, Snohomish Co., Washington, on August 16, 1962.

+ 114 f VII. **Mildred**[8] **McKee** was born in Brady Twp., Garvin Co., Oklahoma, on November 13, 1926.

+ 115 f VIII. **Sara Louise**[8] **McKee** was born in Brady Twp., Garvin Co., Oklahoma, on February 16, 1929. She died in Fort Worth, Tarrant Co., Texas, on January 31, 1988.[10]

+ 116 f IX. **Mamie Jo**[8] **McKee** was born in Brady Twp., Garvin Co., Oklahoma, on March 14, 1934. She died in West Reading, Berks Co., Pennsylvania.

24. **Rosa Lily**[7] **McKee** (*Josiah William*[6], *Elizabeth*[5], *Alexander*[4], *Andrew*[3] *Pegan II*, *Andrew*[2] *Pagan, James*[1]) was born on December 24, 1884, in Brownwood, Brown Co., Texas. She was the daughter of Josiah William McKee (4) and Martha Amanda Gribble. Rosa Lily died in Elmore City, Elmore Twp., Garvin Co., Oklahoma, on July 19, 1965, at age 80. She was buried in Katie City Cemetery, Katie, Brady Twp., Garvin Co., Oklahoma.[9]

Rosa Lily married **William Henry Riley** on March 23, 1905, in Carter Co., Oklahoma. They had three children. William Henry Riley was born in Burnet Co., Texas?, on May 4, 1874. William Henry reached age 74 and died in Brady Twp., Garvin Co., Oklahoma, on June 15, 1948. He was buried in Katie City Cemetery, Katie, Brady Twp., Garvin Co., Oklahoma.[9]

Children of Rosa Lily McKee and William Henry Riley:

+ 117 m I. **James Irwin**[8] **Riley** was born in Brady Twp., Garvin Co., Oklahoma, on May 25, 1906. He died in Oklahoma City, Oklahoma, on August 12, 1978.[41]

+ 118 m II. **Isaac Edwin**[8] **Riley** was born in Brady Twp., Garvin Co., Oklahoma, on December 14, 1907. He died in Oklahoma City, Oklahoma, on November 11, 1993.[9]

+ 119 f III. **Roberta Mae**[8] **Riley** was born in Brady Twp., Garvin Co., Oklahoma, on June 26, 1910. She died in Wynnewood, Brady Twp., Garvin Co., Oklahoma, on July 21, 2003.[42]

25. **William Henry**[7] **McKee** (*John*[6], *Elizabeth*[5], *Alexander*[4], *Andrew*[3] *Pegan II, Andrew*[2] *Pagan, James*[1]) was born in 1866 in St. Joseph, Buchanan Co., Missouri. He was the son of John McKee (6) and Susan Githens. William Henry died after 1880.

26. **Agnes Belle**[7] **McKee** (*John*[6], *Elizabeth*[5], *Alexander*[4], *Andrew*[3] *Pegan II, Andrew*[2] *Pagan, James*[1]) was born in 1869 in St. Joseph, Buchanan Co., Missouri.[15] She was also known as **Belle.** She was the daughter of John McKee (6) and Susan Githens. Agnes Belle died in Butte, Silver Bow, Montana?, after 1905.

Agnes Belle married **Charles Demars** on September 5, 1905, in Silver Bow Co., Montana.[15] Charles Demars was born in Buffalo, Erie Co., New York, in 1852.[15] Charles died after 1905.

When she married in 1905, Agnes Belle "Belle" McKee says her mother's Susan Githins maiden name was Kelley, but other sources refute this.

27. **Sarah Elizabeth**[7] **McKee** (*John*[6], *Elizabeth*[5], *Alexander*[4], *Andrew*[3] *Pegan II*, *Andrew*[2] *Pagan*, *James*[1]) was born in 1871 in St. Joseph, Buchanan Co., Missouri.[11] She was also known as **Sadie** and **Elizabeth.** She was the daughter of John McKee (6) and Susan Githens. Sarah Elizabeth died in Billings, Yellowstone Co., Montana?, between September 1893 and 1900.

Sarah Elizabeth married **James Lindsay Ralph** on September 14, 1893, in Yellowstone Co., Montana. [11] James Lindsay Ralph was born in Cynthiana, Perry Twp., Pike Co., Ohio, in July 1859.[11] James Lindsay died in Tuscarora, Elko Co., Nevada?, after 1900.

In the 1900 census, James Lindsay Ralph, a widower and a transient farmhand, is enumerated in Tuscarora, Elko Co., Nevada.

28. **Martha Jane**[7] **McKee** (*John*[6], *Elizabeth*[5], *Alexander*[4], *Andrew*[3] *Pegan II*, *Andrew*[2] *Pagan*, *James*[1]) was born in 1874 in St. Joseph, Buchanan Co., Missouri. She was the daughter of John McKee (6) and Susan Githens. Martha Jane died after 1880.

29. **Nancy Angeoline**[7] **McKee** (*Jasper Ervin*[6], *Elizabeth*[5], *Alexander*[4], *Andrew*[3] *Pegan II Pegan II*, *Andrew*[2] *Pagan*, *James*[1]) was born on October 22, 1868, in St. Joseph, Washington Twp., Buchanan Co., Missouri. She was the daughter of Jasper Ervin McKee (8) and Hester Ann Cook. Nancy Angeoline died in St. Joseph, Buchanan Co., Missouri, on January 30, 1942, at age 73. She was buried in Green Cemetery, Country Club Village, Jefferson Twp., Andrew Co., Missouri.[17]

Nancy Angeoline married **Washington Scott Tindle** on February 9, 1888, in Buchanan Co., Missouri. They had eleven children. Washington Scott Tindle was born in Wathena, Washington Twp., Doniphan Co., Kansas, on February 27, 1863. He was also known as **Scott.** Washington Scott reached age 85 and died in Industrial City, Washington Twp., Buchanan Co., Missouri, on December 26, 1948. He was buried in Green Cemetery, Country Club Village, Jefferson Twp., Andrew Co., Missouri.[17]

Children of Nancy Angeoline McKee and Washington Scott Tindle:

+ 120     I.     **Child One**[8] **Tindle** was born in Burr Oak Twp., Doniphan Co., Kansas, between 1888 and 1900. He or she died in Burr Oak Twp., Doniphan Co., Kansas, between 1888 and 1900.

+ 121     II.     **Child Two**[8] **Tindle** was born in Burr Oak Twp., Doniphan Co., Kansas, between 1888 and 1900. He or she died in Burr Oak Twp., Doniphan Co., Kansas, before 1900.

+ 122   m   III.     **Martin Van Buren**[8] **Tindle** was born in Burr Oak Twp., Doniphan Co., Kansas, between 1888 and 1900. He died in Burr Oak Twp., Doniphan Co., Kansas, before 1900.

+ 123   m   IV.     **Louis or Lewis**[8] **Tindle** was born in Burr Oak Twp., Doniphan Co., Kansas, on April 30, 1891. He died in Los Angeles, Los Angeles Co., California, on January 6, 1974.

+ 124   f    V.     **Lula Mae**[8] **Tindle** was born in Burr Oak Twp., Doniphan Co., Kansas, on September 17, 1893. She died after 1910.

+ 125   m   VI.     **James Ervin**[8] **Tindle** was born in Burr Oak Twp., Doniphan Co., Kansas, on November 19, 1894. He died in Valley Falls, Jefferson Co., Kansas, on November 11, 1970.[43]

+ 126   m   VII.     **Frank Scott**[8] **Tindle** was born in Burr Oak Twp., Doniphan Co.,Kansas, on July 15, 1896. He died in Kansas City, Jackson Co., Missouri, in August.[44]

+ 127   m   VIII.     **Charles William**[8] **Tindle** was born in Burr Oak Twp., Doniphan

Co., Kansas, on January 29, 1898. He died in St. Joseph, Buchanan Co., Missouri, in February 1970.

+ 128  f  IX.  **Rosa L.⁸ Tindle** was born in Burr Oak Twp., Doniphan Co., Kansas, on November 30, 1899. She was also known as **Rose.** Rosa L. died in St. Joseph, Buchanan Co., Missouri, in January.[45]

+ 129  f  X.  **Daisey Viola⁸ Tindle** was born in Burr Oak Twp., Doniphan Co., Kansas, on November 9, 1901. She died in Pattonsburg, Benton Twp., Daviess Co., Missouri, on December 7, 1965.[46]

+ 130     XI.  **Child Three⁸ Tindle** was born in Burr Oak Twp., Doniphan Co., Kansas, between 1900 and 1910. He or she died in Burr Oak Twp., Doniphan Co., Kansas, between 1900 and 1910.

**30. Elizabeth⁷ McKee** (*Jasper Ervin⁶, Elizabeth⁵, Alexander⁴, Andrew³ Pegan II, Andrew² Pagan, James¹*) was born in 1870 in St. Joseph, Washington Twp., Buchanan Co., Missouri. She was the daughter of Jasper Ervin McKee (8) and Hester Ann Cook. Elizabeth died in St. Joseph, Washington Twp., Buchanan Co., Missouri, in 1889 at age 19.

Never married.

**31. William Henry⁷ McKee** (*Jasper Ervin⁶, Elizabeth⁵, Alexander⁴, Andrew³ Pegan II, Andrew² Pagan, James¹*) was born on July 27, 1873, in St. Joseph, Washington Twp., Buchanan Co., Missouri. He was the son of Jasper Ervin McKee (8) and Hester Ann Cook. William Henry died in Tulare Co., California, on July 18, 1950, at age 76.

Childless.

William Henry married **Alta Newkirk** in 1917. Alta Newkirk was born in St. Joseph, Washington Twp., Buchanan Co., Missouri?, on May 25, 1884. Alta reached age 63 and died in Tulare Co., California, on July 8, 1947.

**32. Etta May⁷ McKee** (*Jasper Ervin⁶, Elizabeth⁵, Alexander⁴, Andrew³ Pegan II, Andrew² Pagan, James¹*) was born in 1875 in St. Joseph, Washington Twp., Buchanan Co., Missouri. She was the daughter of Jasper Ervin McKee (8) and Hester Ann Cook. Etta May died in St. Joseph, Washington Twp., Buchanan Co., Missouri, in 1892 at age 17.

Never married.

**33. Stella⁷ McKee** (*Jasper Ervin⁶, Elizabeth⁵, Alexander⁴, Andrew³ Pegan II, Andrew² Pagan, James¹*) was born in 1877 in St. Joseph, Washington Twp., Buchanan Co., Missouri. She was the daughter of Jasper Ervin McKee (8) and Hester Ann Cook. Stella died in St. Joseph, Washington Twp., Buchanan Co., Missouri, in 1880 at age three.

**34. Martha⁷ McKee** (*Jasper Ervin⁶, Elizabeth⁵, Alexander⁴, Andrew³ Pegan II, Andrew² Pagan, James¹*) was born in 1879 in St. Joseph, Washington Twp., Buchanan Co., Missouri. She was the daughter of Jasper Ervin McKee (8) and Hester Ann Cook. Martha died in St. Joseph, Washington Twp., Buchanan Co., Missouri, after 1880. In 1880, infant Martha McKee is enumerated in the home of her maternal grandmother, Ann Cook, in St. Joseph, Washington Twp., Buchanan Co., Missouri. She probably died in infancy.

**35. Cora Alvertie⁷ McKee** (*William Henry Harrison⁶, Elizabeth⁵, Alexander⁴, Andrew³ Pegan II, Andrew² Pagan, James¹*) was born on June 20, 1877, in St. Joseph, Washington Twp., Buchanan Co., Missouri. She was the daughter of William Henry Harrison McKee (12) and Donna Belle Michael. Cora Alvertie died in St. Joseph, Washington Twp., Buchanan Co., Missouri, on April 9, 1953, at age 75. She was buried in Ashland Cemetery, St. Joseph, Washington Twp., Buchanan Co., Missouri.[7]

Cora Alvertie married **William Richter** in 1897 in Buchanan Co., Missouri. They had three children. William Richter was born in Bethlehem, Lehigh Co., Pennsylvania, on January 11, 1877. William reached age 75 and died in St. Joseph, Washington Twp., Buchanan Co., Missouri, on March 28, 1952. He was buried in Ashland Cemetery, St. Joseph, Washington Twp., Buchanan Co., Missouri.[7]

Children of Cora Alvertie McKee and William Richter:

+ 131  m  I.  **William M.⁸ Richter II** was born in St. Joseph, Washington Twp., Buchanan Co., Missouri, in 1900. He died after 1920.

+ 132  m  II.  **Melvin Byron⁸ Richter** was born in St. Joseph, Washington Twp., Buchanan Co., Missouri, on July 10, 1903. He died in Montebello, Los Angeles Co., California, on July 18, 1978.

+ 133  f  III.  **Doris E.⁸ Richter** was born in St. Joseph, Washington Twp., Buchanan Co., Missouri, in 1912. She died after 1940.

**36. Gertrude⁷ McKee** (*William Henry Harrison⁶, Elizabeth⁵, Alexander⁴, Andrew³ Pegan II, Andrew²*

*Pagan, James¹*) was born on December 17, 1879, in St. Joseph, Washington Twp., Buchanan Co., Missouri. She was the daughter of William Henry Harrison McKee (12) and Donna Belle Michael. Gertrude died in St. Joseph, Washington Twp., Buchanan Co., Missouri, on May 29, 1949, at age 69. She was buried in Ashland Cemetery, St. Joseph, Washington Twp., Buchanan Co., Missouri.[7]

Childless.

She married **Joseph Wellenger.** Joseph Wellenger was born in Switzerland on October 4, 1874. Joseph reached age 76 and died in St. Joseph, Washington Twp., Buchanan Co., Missouri, on February 16, 1951. He was buried in Ashland Cemetery, St. Joseph, Washington Twp., Buchanan Co., Missouri.[7]

# 8th Generation

**37. Mary E.⁸ McKee** (*Samuel Stephen⁷, Josiah William⁶, Elizabeth⁵, Alexander⁴, Andrew³ Pegan II, Andrew² Pagan, James¹*) was born on November 1, 1886, in Burnet Co., Texas. She was also known as **Mollie.** She was the daughter of Samuel Stephen McKee (14) and Laura Ann Riley. Mary E. died in Elmore Twp., Garvin Co., Oklahoma, on March 22, 1965, at age 78. She was buried in Katie City Cemetery, Katie, Brady Twp., Garvin Co., Oklahoma.[9]

Mary E. married **Melvin H. Davis** before 1910. They had three children. Melvin H. Davis was born in Banks Co., Georgia, on July 29, 1879. Melvin H. reached age 106 and died in Purcell, Muncrief Twp., McClain Co., Oklahoma, on April 18, 1986. He was buried in Katie City Cemetery, Katie, Brady Twp., Garvin Co., Oklahoma.[9]

Children of Mary E. McKee and Melvin H. Davis:

+ 134 f I. **Mae Ophelia⁹ Davis** was born in Brady Twp., Garvin Co., Oklahoma, on May 24, 1910. She was also known as **Ophelia.** Mae Ophelia died in Oklahoma City, Oklahoma, on August 19, 2000.[19]

+ 135 m II. **Oscar⁹ Davis** was born in Brady Twp., Garvin Co., Oklahoma, on November 3, 1911. He died in Elmore Twp., Garvin Co., Oklahoma, on May 11, 1940.[9]

+ 136 m III. **DeWitt⁹ Davis** was born in Brady Twp., Garvin Co., Oklahoma, on October 28, 1916. DeWitt died in Dearborn, Wayne Co., Michigan, on January 31, 1976.

**38. Martha Ollie⁸ McKee** (*Samuel Stephen⁷, Josiah William⁶, Elizabeth⁵, Alexander⁴, Andrew³ Pegan II, Andrew² Pagan, James¹*) was born on September 30, 1888, in Brady Twp., Garvin Co., Oklahoma. She was also known as **Ollie.** She was the daughter of Samuel Stephen McKee (14) and Laura Ann Riley. Martha Ollie died in Oklahoma City, Oklahoma, on March 11, 1974, at age 85. She was buried in Fairlawn Cemetery, Elk City, Beckham Co., Oklahoma.[18]

Martha Ollie married **Andrew Martin Sims** on December 24, 1908, in Garvin Co., Oklahoma. They had one daughter. Andrew Martin Sims was born in Jackson, Pope Co., Arkansas, on September 27, 1883. Andrew Martin reached age 64 and died in Elk City, Beckham Co., Oklahoma, on June 10, 1948. He was buried in Fairlawn Cemetery, Elk City, Beckham Co., Oklahoma.[18]

Daughter of Martha Ollie McKee and Andrew Martin Sims:

+ 137 f I. **Ivy Jones⁹ Sims** was born in Brady Twp., Garvin Co., Oklahoma?, on February 25, 1911. She was adopted. Ivy Jones died in Elk City, Beckham Co., Oklahoma, on October 2, 2001.

**39. William H.⁸ McKee** (*Samuel Stephen⁷, Josiah William⁶, Elizabeth⁵, Alexander⁴, Andrew³ Pegan II, Andrew² Pagan, James¹*) was born on March 3, 1890, in Montague Co., Texas. He was the son of Samuel Stephen McKee (14) and Laura Ann Riley. William H. died in Purcell, Moncrief Twp., McClain Co., Oklahoma, on December 13, 1970, at age 80. He was buried in Katie City Cemetery, Katie, Brady Twp., Garvin Co., Oklahoma.[9] Alternate date of death: 03 Jan 1962

William H. married **Agnes Hunter** on March 3, 1922. They had three children. Agnes Hunter was born in Franklin Co., Arkansas?, on December 12, 1891. Agnes reached age 60 and died in Brady Twp., Garvin Co., Oklahoma, on January 2, 1952. She was buried in Katie City Cemetery, Katie, Brady Twp., Garvin Co., Oklahoma.[9]

Children of William H. McKee and Agnes Hunter:

+ 138 f I. **Floye Aleyne⁹ McKee** was born in Elmore City, Elmore Twp., Garvin Co., Oklahoma, on January 15,

1923. She died in Canyon, Randall Co., Texas, on December 28, 2011.[47]

+ 139 m II. **Lindsay Ellis⁹ McKee** was born in Elmore City, Elmore Twp., Garvin Co., Oklahoma, on June 13, 1924. He died in Purcell, Moncrief Twp., McClain Co., Oklahoma, on May 29, 2002.[9]

+ 140 m III. **Arlie Ardell⁹ McKee** was born in Elmore City, Elmore Twp., Garvin Co., Oklahoma, on May 26, 1926. He died in Purcell, Moncrief Twp., McClain Co., Oklahoma, on March 28, 2002.

**40. Eva Alice⁸ McKee** (*Samuel Stephen⁷, Josiah William⁶, Elizabeth⁵, Alexander⁴, Andrew³ Pegan II, Andrew² Pagan, James¹*) was born on August 13, 1893, in Montague Co., Texas. She was the daughter of Samuel Stephen McKee (14) and Laura Ann Riley. Eva Alice died in Purcell, Moncrief Twp., McClain Co., Oklahoma, on July 13, 1988, at age 94. She was buried in Hillside Cemetery, Purcell, Moncrief Twp., McClain Co., Oklahoma.[19]

Childless.

Eva Alice married **Harry Hines** on April 5, 1910, in Garvin Co., Oklahoma. Harry Hines was born in Kentucky on September 13, 1887. Harry reached age 69 and died in Purcell, Moncrief Twp., McClain Co., Oklahoma, on June 9, 1957. He was buried in Hillside Cemetery, Purcell, Moncrief Twp., McClain Co., Oklahoma.[19]

**41. Fannie May⁸ McKee** (*Samuel Stephen⁷, Josiah William⁶, Elizabeth⁵, Alexander⁴, Andrew³ Pegan II, Andrew² Pagan, James¹*) was born on March 10, 1900, in Brady Twp., Garvin Co., Oklahoma. She was the daughter of Samuel Stephen McKee (14) and Laura Ann Riley. Fannie May died in Bethany, Oklahoma Co., Oklahoma, on March 21, 1976, at age 76. She was buried in Bethany Cemetery, Bethany, Oklahoma Co., Oklahoma.[20]

She married **James W. Cross.** They had ten children. Reverend James W. Cross was born in Tarrant Co.,

Texas, on May 12, 1890. James W. lived in 1947 in Geary, Blaine Co., Oklahoma. He reached age 69 and died in Bethany, Oklahoma Co., Oklahoma, on November 6, 1959. James W. was buried in Bethany Cemetery, Bethany, Oklahoma Co., Oklahoma.

Fannie May McKee and James W. Cross had ten children, including:

+ 141 m I. **Charles Samuel⁹ Cross** was born in Hewitt Twp., Carter Co., Oklahoma, in 1917. He died in Hewitt Twp., Carter Co., Oklahoma, in 1919.[9]

+ 142 f II. **Louise⁹ Cross** was born in Hewitt Twp., Carter Co., Oklahoma, in 1920.

+ 143 m III. **Odis O.⁹ Cross** was born in Hewitt Twp., Carter Co., Oklahoma, on August 22, 1922. He died in Bethany, Oklahoma Co., Oklahoma, on September 9, 1987.[20]

+ 144 f IV. **Juanita Fern⁹ Cross** was born in Graham Twp., Carter Co., Oklahoma, on May 2, 1925. She died in Bethany, Oklahoma Co., Oklahoma, on March 29, 2011.[20]

+ 145 f V. **Loweta M.⁹ Cross** was born in Graham Twp., Carter Co., Oklahoma, on September 5, 1928.

+ 146 m VI. **James Austin⁹ Cross II** was born in Graham Twp., Carter Co., Oklahoma, on February 22, 1929. He died in Moore, Cleveland Co., Oklahoma, on September 30, 2002.

+ 147 f VII. **Artinea Voncell⁹ Cross** was born in Graham Twp., Carter Co., Oklahoma, on August 14, 1932. She died in Geary, Blaine Co., Oklahoma, on May 12, 2013.[48]

+ 148 m VIII. **Euin Theolas⁹ Cross** was born in Seminole Co., Oklahoma, on

November 21, 1934. He died in Kern Co., California, on March 22, 1987.

+ 149 m X. **Charles⁹ Cross** was born in King Co., Texas?, on May 16, 1944. He died in Bethany, Oklahoma Co., Oklahoma?, on July 15, 1992.[20]

**42. Margaret Ann⁸ McKee** (*Samuel Stephen⁷, Josiah William⁶, Elizabeth⁵, Alexander⁴, Andrew³ Pegan II, Andrew² Pagan, James¹*) was born on April 1, 1904, in Brady Twp., Garvin Co., Oklahoma. She was also known as **Maggie.** She was the daughter of Samuel Stephen McKee (14) and Laura Ann Riley. Margaret Ann died in San Angelo, Tom Green Co., Texas, on September 19, 1958, at age 54. She was buried in Katie City Cemetery, Katie, Brady Twp., Garvin Co., Oklahoma.[9]

She married **Charlie William Davis.** They had two children. Charlie William Davis was born in DeSoto, Sumter Co., Georgia, on March 4, 1896. Charlie William reached age 78 and died in San Angelo, Tom Green Co., Texas, on July 20, 1974. He was buried in Katie City Cemetery, Katie, Brady Twp., Garvin Co., Oklahoma.[9]

Children of Margaret Ann McKee and Charlie William Davis:

+ 150 m I. **Lenard Lee⁹ Davis** was born in Brady Twp., Garvin Co., Oklahoma, on October 12, 1920. He died in San Angelo, Tom Green Co., Texas, on March 4, 1993.

+ 151 f II. **Novis Marie⁹ Davis** was born in Elmore City, Elmore Twp., Garvin Co., Oklahoma, on July 12, 1923. She died in San Angelo, Tom Green Co., Texas, on January 25, 2002.

**43. Claud James⁸ Cross** (*Sarah Elvira Elizabeth Ann⁷ McKee, Josiah William⁶, Elizabeth⁵, Alexander⁴, Andrew³ Pegan II, Andrew² Pagan, James¹*) was born on July 22, 1884, in Brownwood, Brown Co., Texas. He was the son of William Andrew Cross and Sarah Elvira Elizabeth Ann McKee (15). Claud James died

in Rotan, Fisher Co., Texas, on June 20, 1971, at age 86. He was buried in Newman Cemetery, Sylvester, Fisher Co., Texas.[10]

Claud James married **Ada B. Tucker** about 1908. They had two sons. Ada B. Tucker was born in Texas on June 23, 1883. Ada B. reached age 72 and died in Sylvester, Fisher Co., Texas, on May 14, 1956. She was buried in Newman Cemetery, Sylvester, Fisher Co., Texas.[10]

Sons of Claud James Cross and Ada B. Tucker:

+ 152 m I. **James Rex⁹ Cross** was born in Sylvester, Fisher Co., Texas, on November 29, 1909. He died in Jones Co., Texas, on January 7, 2000.[10]

+ 153 m II. **Francis Elmo⁹ Cross** was born in Sylvester, Fisher Co., Texas, on December 28, 1911. He was also known as **Elmo.** Francis Elmo died in Denton, Denton Co., Texas, on March 20, 2000.[49]

**44. Clara Jane⁸ Cross** (*Sarah Elvira Elizabeth Ann⁷ McKee, Josiah William⁶, Elizabeth⁵, Alexander⁴, Andrew³ Pegan II, Andrew² Pagan, James¹*) was born on July 22, 1884, in Brownwood, Brown Co., Texas. She was the daughter of William Andrew Cross and Sarah Elvira Elizabeth Ann McKee (15). Clara Jane died in Sylvester, Fisher Co., Texas, on May 27, 1982, at age 97. She was buried in Newman Cemetery, Sylvester, Fisher Co., Texas.[10]

Clara Jane married **George Washington Ferrel** on February 3, 1907, in Fisher Co., Texas. They had three children. George Washington Ferrel was born in Fannin Co., Texas, on March 28, 1877. George Washington reached age 61 and died in Sylvester, Fisher Co., Texas, on June 5, 1938. He was buried in Newman Cemetery, Sylvester, Fisher Co., Texas.[10]

Children of Clara Jane Cross and George Washington Ferrel:

+ 154 f I. **Georgia Elizabeth⁹ Ferrel** was born in Sylvester, Fisher Co., Texas, on October 2, 1909. She died in Sylvester, Fisher Co., Texas, on November 26, 1985.[10]

+ 155 m II. **Frank C.**[9] **Ferrel** was born in Roby, Fisher Co., Texas, on February 1, 1912. He died in Ploesi, Romania, on August 1, 1943.

+ 156 f III. **Claudine**[9] **Ferrel** was born in Albuquerque, Bernalillo Co., New Mexico, on February 27, 1925. She died in Big Spring, Howard Co., Texas, on October 2, 1987.[10]

**45. William Josiah Thomas**[8] **Cross** (*Sarah Elvira Elizabeth Ann*[7] *McKee, Josiah William*[6]*, Elizabeth*[5]*, Alexander*[4]*, Andrew*[3] *Pegan II, Andrew*[2] *Pagan, James*[1]) was born on September 26, 1886, in Brownwood, Brown Co., Texas. He was also known as **Thomas.** He was the son of William Andrew Cross and Sarah Elvira Elizabeth Ann McKee (15). William Josiah Thomas died in Sylvester, Fisher Co., Texas, on April 17, 1920, at age 33. He was buried in Newman Cemetery, Sylvester, Fisher Co., Texas.[10]

Never married.

**46. Jesse Riley**[8] **Cross** (*Sarah Elvira Elizabeth Ann*[7] *McKee, Josiah William*[6]*, Elizabeth*[5]*, Alexander*[4]*, Andrew*[3] *Pegan II, Andrew*[2] *Pagan, James*[1]) was born on December 18, 1887, in Brownwood, Brown Co., Texas. He was the son of William Andrew Cross and Sarah Elvira Elizabeth Ann McKee (15). Jesse Riley died in France on August 15, 1918, at age 30. He was buried in Newman Cemetery, Sylvester, Fisher Co., Texas.[10] His residence on his WWI Draft application is Jenkins, Chavez Co., New Mexico.

Never married.

**47. Elizabeth Violet**[8] **Cross** (*Sarah Elvira Elizabeth Ann*[7] *McKee, Josiah William*[6]*, Elizabeth*[5]*, Alexander*[4]*, Andrew*[3] *Pegan II, Andrew*[2] *Pagan, James*[1]) was born on December 18, 1887, in Brownwood, Brown Co., Texas. She was also known as **Bessie.** She was the daughter of William Andrew Cross and Sarah Elvira Elizabeth Ann McKee (15). Elizabeth Violet died in Sylvester, Fisher Co., Texas, on January 10, 1984,

at age 96. She was buried in Newman Cemetery, Sylvester, Fisher Co., Texas.[10]

Elizabeth Violet married **Robert Seaborn Scott** on December 9, 1907, in Fisher Co., Texas. They had five children. Robert Seaborn Scott was born in Bryan, Brazos Co., Texas, on August 10, 1886. Robert Seaborn reached age 69 and died in Sylvester, Fisher Co., Texas, on July 24, 1956. He was buried in Newman Cemetery, Sylvester, Fisher Co., Texas.[10]

Children of Elizabeth Violet Cross and Robert Seaborn Scott:

+ 157 f I. **Roberta Jess**[9] **Scott** was born in Roby, Fisher Co., Texas, on September 4, 1911. She died in Rotan, Fisher Co., Texas, on March 28, 2012.[10]

+ 158 f II. **Thara Celeste**[9] **Scott** was born in Curry Co., New Mexico, on June 27, 1916. She died in Sylvester, Fisher Co., Texas, on September 6, 1941.[10]

+ 159 m III. **Robert N.**[9] **Scott II** was born in Lubbock, Lubbock Co., Texas, on December 4, 1920. He died in Abilene, Taylor Co., Texas, on October 25, 1991.[10]

+ 160 f IV. **Alice Lavern**[9] **Scott** was born in Tatum, Lea Co., New Mexico, on July 19, 1924. She died in Tatum, Lea Co., New Mexico, on January 9, 1925.[10]

+ 161 f V. **Willie Jolene**[9] **Scott** was born in Sylvester, Fisher Co., Texas, on September 15, 1926. She is also known as **Jolene.**

**48. George Emmit**[8] **Cross** (*Sarah Elvira Elizabeth Ann*[7] *McKee, Josiah William*[6]*, Elizabeth*[5]*, Alexander*[4]*, Andrew*[3] *Pegan II, Andrew*[2] *Pagan, James*[1]) was born on October 26, 1890, in Brownwood, Brown Co., Texas. He was the son of William Andrew Cross and Sarah Elvira Elizabeth Ann McKee (15). George

Emmit died in McCaulley, Fisher Co., Texas, on January 16, 1974, at age 83. He was buried in Newman Cemetery, Sylvester, Fisher Co., Texas.[10]

Never married.

49. **Alice Emma[8] Cross** (*Sarah Elvira Elizabeth Ann[7] McKee, Josiah William[6], Elizabeth[5], Alexander[4], Andrew[3] Pegan II, Andrew[2] Pagan, James[1]*) was born on October 26, 1890, in Brownwood, Brown Co., Texas. She was the daughter of William Andrew Cross and Sarah Elvira Elizabeth Ann McKee (15). Alice Emma died in Roby, Fisher Co., Texas, on November 16, 1982, at age 92. She was buried in Newman Cemetery, Sylvester, Fisher Co., Texas.[10]

Never married.

50. **John Henry[8] Cross** (*Sarah Elvira Elizabeth Ann[7] McKee, Josiah William[6], Elizabeth[5], Alexander[4], Andrew[3] Pegan II, Andrew[2] Pagan, James[1]*) was born on June 27, 1894, in Brownwood, Brown Co., Texas. He was the son of William Andrew Cross and Sarah Elvira Elizabeth Ann McKee (15). John Henry died in Rotan, Fisher Co., Texas, on June 22, 1978, at age 83. He was buried in Belvieu Cemetery, Rotan, Fisher Co., Texas.[21]

John Henry married **Gladys B. Reeves** on August 30, 1919, in Ford Co., Texas. They had one daughter. Gladys B. Reeves was born in Falls Co., Texas, on April 17, 1900. Gladys B. reached age 69 and died in Rotan, Fisher Co., Texas, on April 8, 1970. She was buried in Belvieu Cemetery, Rotan, Fisher Co., Texas.[21]

Daughter of John Henry Cross and Gladys B. Reeves:

+ 162 f I. **Ardell Colleen[9] Cross** was born in Newman, Fisher Co., Texas, on August 11, 1920. She died in Sylvester, Fisher Co., Texas, on August 9, 2012.[21]

51. **Willie Franklin[8] Cross** (*Sarah Elvira Elizabeth Ann[7] McKee, Josiah William[6], Elizabeth[5], Alexander[4], Andrew[3] Pegan II, Andrew[2] Pagan, James[1]*) was born on May 19, 1896, in Brownwood, Brown Co., Texas. He was also known as **Eddy**. He was the son of William Andrew Cross and Sarah Elvira Elizabeth Ann McKee (15). Willie Franklin died in Abilene,

Taylor Co., Texas, on July 18, 1921, at age 25. He was buried in Newman Cemetery, Sylvester, Fisher Co., Texas.[10]

He married **Dovie Mae Arnold.** They had three children. Dovie Mae Arnold was born in Burnet Co., Texas, on December 12, 1898. Dovie Mae reached age 92 and died in Sylvester, Fisher Co., Texas, on March 28, 1991. She was buried in Newman Cemetery, Sylvester, Fisher Co., Texas.[10]

Children of Willie Franklin Cross and Dovie Mae Arnold:

+ 163 f I. **Canevah Mae[9] Cross** was born in Sylvester, Fisher Co., Texas, on June 12, 1916. She died in a hospital in Abilene, Taylor Co., Texas, on April 9, 1989.[10]

+ 164 m II. **Jess Wiley[9] Cross** was born in Estancia, Torrance Co., New Mexico, on July 16, 1918. He died in Abilene, Taylor Co., Texas, on October 31, 2013.[10]

+ 165 m III. **William Arnold[9] Cross** was born in Estancia, Torrance Co., New Mexico, on June 6, 1920. He died in Midland, Midland Co., Texas, on August 11, 2011.[10]

52. **Mary Willie[8] McKee** (*William Robert[7], Josiah William[6], Elizabeth[5], Alexander[4], Andrew[3] Pegan II, Andrew[2] Pagan, James[1]*) was born on June 23, 1892, in Brown Co., Texas. She was the daughter of William Robert McKee (16) and Mary Elizabeth Fletcher. Mary Willie died in Rush Springs Twp., Grady Co., Oklahoma, on June 3, 1964, at age 71. She was buried in Rush Springs Cemetery, Rush Springs, Grady Co., Oklahoma.[22]

Mary Willie married **Albert Russell Riley** about 1908. They had seven children. Albert Russell Riley was born in Burnet Co., Texas, on July 9, 1877. Albert Russell reached age 81 and died in Rush Springs Twp., Grady Co., Oklahoma, on March 2, 1959. He was buried in Rush Springs Cemetery, Rush Springs, Grady Co., Oklahoma.[22]

Children of Mary Willie McKee and Albert Russell Riley:

+ 166 m I. **Reuben Russell⁹ Riley** was born in Coyle Twp., Murray Co., Oklahoma, on October 12, 1909. He died in Rush Springs Twp., Grady Co., Oklahoma, on March 4, 1993.[22]

+ 167 f II. **Bessie⁹ Riley** was born in Bradley Twp., Grady Co., Oklahoma, on December 23, 1911. She died in Bradley Twp., Grady Co., Oklahoma, on January 6, 1912.[25]

+ 168 f III. **Annie Laurie⁹ Riley** was born in Bradley Twp., Grady Co., Oklahoma, on August 19, 1913. She died in Bradley Twp., Grady Co., Oklahoma, on February 27, 1914.[25]

+ 169 m IV. **John William⁹ Riley** was born in Bradley Twp., Grady Co., Oklahoma, on May 8, 1916. He died in Sayre Twp., Bradford Co., Pennsylvania?, in January 1974.

+ 170 f V. **Sarah Jane⁹ Riley** was born in Bradley Twp., Grady Co., Oklahoma, on November 25, 1918. She died in Rush Springs Twp., Grady Co., Oklahoma, on December 2, 1984.

+ 171 m VI. **Robert Francis⁹ Riley** was born in Bradley Twp., Grady Co., Oklahoma, on November 7, 1920. He died in Odessa, Ector Co., Texas, on June 6, 1985.[50]

+ 172 m VII. **Walter Levi⁹ Riley** was born in Elmore City, Elmore Twp., Garvin Co., Oklahoma, on August 28, 1923. He was also known as **Buntin.** Walter Levi died in a hospital in Oklahoma City, Oklahoma Co., Oklahoma, on August 17, 2007.[51]

**53. James Andres⁸ McKee** (*William Robert⁷, Josiah William⁶, Elizabeth⁵, Alexander⁴, Andrew³ Pegan II, Andrew² Pagan, James¹*) was born on May 5, 1894, in Montague Co., Texas. He was the son of William Robert McKee (16) and Mary Elizabeth Fletcher. James Andres died in Chickasha, Chickasha Twp., Grady Co., Oklahoma, on July 21, 1967, at age 73. He was buried in Erin Springs Cemetery, Erin Springs, Lindsay Twp., Garvin Co., Oklahoma.[12]

James Andres married **Lydia May Pearce** on August 21, 1916, in Garvin Co., Oklahoma. They had nine children. Lydia May Pearce was born in Texas on November 28, 1896. Lydia May reached age 87 and died in Chickasha, Chickasha Twp., Grady Co., Oklahoma, on October 9, 1984. She was buried in Erin Springs Cemetery, Erin Springs, Lindsay Twp., Garvin Co., Oklahoma.[12]

Children of James Andres McKee and Lydia May Pearce:

+ 173 m I. **Marion⁹ McKee** was born in Wynnewood, Brady Twp., Garvin Co., Oklahoma, on February 23, 1919. He died in Panama Canal Zone on November 2, 1942.[12]

+ 174 m II. **Clyde Frank⁹ McKee** was born in Wynnewood, Brady Twp., Garvin Co., Oklahoma, on June 26, 1921. He died in Lindsay, Lindsay Twp., Garvin Co., Oklahoma, on January 28, 1999.[52]

+ 175 m III. **Lenard Carl⁹ McKee** was born in Wynnewood, Brady Twp., Garvin Co., Oklahoma, on February 14, 1923. He died in Chickasha, Chickasha Twp., Grady Co., Oklahoma, on March 28, 1997.[11]

+ 176 f IV. **Elzie Mae⁹ McKee** was born in Wynnewood, Brady Twp., Garvin Co., Oklahoma, on November 15, 1924. She died in Chickasha, Chickasha Twp., Grady Co., Oklahoma, on December 1, 1996.[52]

+ 177 f V. **Winnie Muril⁹ McKee** was born in Pursley Twp., Grady Co., Oklahoma, on April 18, 1926. She died in Chickasha, Chickasha Twp., Grady Co., Oklahoma, on July 20, 2005.[53]

+ 178 m VI. **William Henry⁹ McKee** was born in Pursley Twp., Grady Co., Oklahoma, on February 24, 1928. He was also known as **Henry.** William Henry died in Alex, Alex Twp., Grady Co. Oklahoma, on February 4, 2002.

+ 179 m VII. **James Orville⁹ McKee** was born in Pursley Twp., Grady Co., Oklahoma, on December 16, 1939. He was also known as **Orville.** James Orville died in Alex, Alex Twp., Grady Co. Oklahoma?, on March 27, 1983.[52]

+ 180 m VIII. **Wesley Dilbert⁹ McKee** was born in Alex, Alex Twp., Grady Co. Oklahoma, on April 9, 1933. He was also known as **Bill.** Wesley Dilbert died in Palmer, Matanuska-Susitna Borough, Alaska, on February 3, 1993.

+ 181 f IX. **Lena Mae⁹ McKee** was born in Alex, Alex Twp., Grady Co. Oklahoma, on March 8, 1937. She died in Alex, Alex Twp., Grady Co. Oklahoma, on March 13, 1937.[12]

**54. Clara Ida⁸ McKee** (*William Robert⁷, Josiah William⁶, Elizabeth⁵, Alexander⁴, Andrew³ Pegan II, Andrew² Pagan, James¹*) was born on August 25, 1896, in Chagris Twp., Pickens Co., Oklahoma. She was the daughter of William Robert McKee (16) and Mary Elizabeth Fletcher. Clara Ida died in Hatfield, Polk Co., Arkansas, on March 8, 1983, at age 86.

Clara Ida married **Pat Cearley** on March 11, 1914, in Garvin Co., Oklahoma. They had four children. Pat Cearley was born in Florence, Williamson Co.,

Texas, on March 12, 1892. Pat reached age 77 and died in Hatfield, Polk Co., Arkansas, on October 16, 1969.

Children of Clara Ida McKee and Pat Cearley:

+ 182 m I. **Clide⁹ Cearley** was born in Wynnewood, Brady Twp., Garvin Co., Oklahoma, on March 5, 1917. He died in Wynnewood, Brady Twp., Garvin Co., Oklahoma, on April 20, 1917.[54]

+ 183 f II. **Jessie⁹ Cearley** was born in Wynnewood, Brady Twp., Garvin Co., Oklahoma, on December 1, 1918. She died in Mount Ida, Montgomery Co., Arkansas, on November 25, 1998.

+ 184 f III. **Cora Edna⁹ Cearley** was born in Milburn, Johnston Co., Oklahoma, on September 2, 1921. She died in a hospital in Cove, Polk Co, Arkansas, on September 2, 2002.

+ 185 m IV. **James Albert⁹ Cearley** was born in Elmore City, Elmore Twp., Garvin Co., Oklahoma, on May 7, 1925. He died in Hatfield, Polk Co., Arkansas, on July 5, 1993.

**55. George Washington⁸ McKee** (*William Robert⁷, Josiah William⁶, Elizabeth⁵, Alexander⁴, Andrew³ Pegan II, Andrew² Pagan, James¹*) was born on September 26, 1898, in Chagris Twp., Pickens Co., Oklahoma. He was the son of William Robert McKee (16) and Mary Elizabeth Fletcher. George Washington died in Brady Twp., Garvin Co., Oklahoma, on October 15, 1962, at age 64. He was buried in Katie City Cemetery, Katie, Brady Twp., Garvin Co., Oklahoma.[9]

George Washington married **Mary Millie Rains** on September 15, 1921, in Garvin Co., Oklahoma. They had four sons. Mary Millie Rains was born in Brady Twp., Garvin Co., Oklahoma, on April 1, 1903. Mary Millie reached age 87 and died in Brady Twp., Garvin Co., Oklahoma?, on November 9,

1990. She was buried in Katie City Cemetery, Katie, Brady Twp., Garvin Co., Oklahoma.[9]

Sons of George Washington McKee and Mary Millie Rains:

+ 186 m I. **Earl Warren⁹ McKee** was born in Brady Twp., Garvin Co., Oklahoma, on June 24, 1922. He died in Elmore City, Elmore Twp., Garvin Co., Oklahoma, on February 4, 1998.[9]

+ 187 m II. **Troy E.⁹ McKee** was born in Brady Twp., Garvin Co., Oklahoma, on December 23, 1924.

+ 188 m III. **Harold Winfred⁹ McKee** was born in Eola, Brady Twp., Garvin Co., Oklahoma, on November 10, 1932. He died in a hospital in Lubbock, Lubbock Co., Texas, on September 9, 1989.[55]

+ 189 m IV. **Bobby Jean⁹ McKee** was born in Eola, Brady Twp., Garvin Co., Oklahoma, on November 15, 1936. He died in Norman, Norman Twp., Cleveland Co., Oklahoma, on January 28, 2001.[56]

56. **Barbara⁸ McKee** (*William Robert⁷, Josiah William⁶, Elizabeth⁵, Alexander⁴, Andrew³ Pegan II, Andrew² Pagan, James¹*) was born on November 6, 1901, in Brady Twp., Garvin Co., Oklahoma. She was the daughter of William Robert McKee (16) and Mary Elizabeth Fletcher. Barbara died in Garvin Co., Oklahoma, on February 11, 1906, at age four. She was buried in Katie City Cemetery, Katie, Brady Twp., Garvin Co., Oklahoma.[9]

57. **Martha Amanda⁸ McKee** (*William Robert⁷, Josiah William⁶, Elizabeth⁵, Alexander⁴, Andrew³ Pegan II, Andrew² Pagan, James¹*) was born on May 7, 1904, in Indian City, Payne Co., Oklahoma. She was also known as **Amanda** and **Manda**. She was the daughter of William Robert McKee (16) and Mary Elizabeth Fletcher. Martha Amanda died in Norman, Norman Twp., Cleveland Co., Oklahoma, on September 16, 1952, at age 48. She was buried in Katie City Cemetery, Katie, Brady Twp., Garvin Co., Oklahoma.[9] Martha Amanda "Manda" McKee was a patient at the Central Oklahoma State (Mental) Hospital for most of her adult life.

Martha Amanda married **Robert Phillips** on December 21, 1923, in Garvin Co., Oklahoma. They divorced. They had one daughter. Robert Phillips was born in Foster, Garvin Co., Oklahoma?, in 1894. He died in Washington, District of Columbia?, after 1940.

There is a Robert M. Phillips born about 1894 in Oklahoma, who is a patient at St. Elizabeth's (Mental Hospital) in Washington, DC in 1930 and 1940.

Daughter of Martha Amanda McKee and Robert Phillips:

+ 190 f I. **Daughter⁹ Phillips** was born about 1924. She died about 1924.

58. **Charles Albert⁸ McKee** (*William Robert⁷, Josiah William⁶, Elizabeth⁵, Alexander⁴, Andrew³ Pegan II, Andrew² Pagan, James¹*) was born on December 2, 1906, in Indian City, Payne Co., Oklahoma. He was the son of William Robert McKee (16) and Mary Elizabeth Fletcher. Charles Albert died in Oklahoma City, Oklahoma, in February 1986 at age 79. He was buried in Resthaven Gardens Cemetery, Oklahoma City, Cleveland Co., Oklahoma.[23]

Charles Albert married **Geneva L. Hocutt** on November 2, 1929, in Garvin Co., Oklahoma. They had two sons. Geneva L. Hocutt was born in Buley Springs, Fayette Co., Alabama, on May 29, 1914. Geneva L. reached age 78 and died in Oklahoma City, Oklahoma, in December 1992. She was buried in Resthaven Gardens Cemetery, Oklahoma City, Cleveland Co., Oklahoma.[23]

Sons of Charles Albert McKee and Geneva L. Hocutt:

+ 191 m I. **Charles Inman⁹ McKee II** was born on June 12, 1930.

+ 192 m II. **Billy Don⁹ McKee** was born in Oklahoma City, Oklahoma, on June 10, 1934.

**59. Anna Mae⁸ McKee** (*William Robert⁷, Josiah William⁶, Elizabeth⁵, Alexander⁴, Andrew³ Pegan II, Andrew² Pagan, James¹*) was born on September 9, 1909, in Brady Twp., Garvin Co., Oklahoma. She was the daughter of William Robert McKee (16) and Mary Elizabeth Fletcher. Anna Mae died in Hatfield, Polk Co., Arkansas, on March 16, 1986, at age 76.

May have been childless. Anna McKee Head was divorced and had resumed using her maiden surname, McKee, by 1940.

Anna Mae married **Charles Clayton Head** on November 11, 1929, in Garvin Co., Oklahoma. They divorced about 1930. Charles Clayton Head was born in Irwin Twp., Woodward Co., Oklahoma, on September 16, 1909. He was also known as **Clayton** and **Ted.** Charles Clayton reached age 61 and died in Shafter, Kern Co., California, on October 6, 1970. He was buried in Shafter Memorial Park Cemetery, Shafter, Kern Co., California.[57]

**60. Ella Florence⁸ McKee** (*James L.⁷, Josiah William⁶, Elizabeth⁵, Alexander⁴, Andrew³ Pegan II, Andrew² Pagan, James¹*) was born on June 13, 1891, in St. Jo, Montague Co., Texas. She was the daughter of James L. McKee (17) and Florence Fletcher. Ella Florence died in Enid, Garfield Co., Oklahoma, on August 12, 1938, at age 47. She was buried in Enid Cemetery, Enid, Garfield Co., Oklahoma.[24]

Ella Florence married **Luther L. Meyer** on March 11, 1917. They had five children. Luther L. Meyer was born in Middle Fork, Randolph Co., West Virginia, on July 10, 1891. Luther L. reached age 80 and died in Enid, Garfield Co., Oklahoma, on May 2, 1972. He was buried in Pleasant View Cemetery, Pine Ridge, Hale Twp., Caddo Co., Oklahoma.[58]

Children of Ella Florence McKee and Luther L. Meyer:

+ 193 m I. **Everett James⁹ Meyer** was born in Wynnewood, Brady Twp., Garvin Co., Oklahoma, on March 24, 1918. He died in Enid, Garfield Co., Oklahoma, on November 26, 1997.[59, 60]

+ 194 m II. **Edward Emil⁹ Meyer** was born in Wynnewood, Brady Twp., Garvin Co., Oklahoma, on March 25, 1919. He died in Enid, Garfield Co., Oklahoma, on June 2, 1978.

+ 195 m III. **Marvin Luther⁹ Meyer** was born in Wynnewood, Brady Twp., Garvin Co., Oklahoma, on May 15, 1921. He died in Perris, Riverside Co., California, on July 7, 1984.[61]

+ 196 f IV. **Iva Laura⁹ Meyer** was born in Wynnewood, Brady Twp., Garvin Co., Oklahoma, on January 25, 1923. She was also known as **Jeannie.** Iva Laura died in Haysville, Sedgwick Co., Kansas, on April 10, 2007.[62]

+ 197 f V. **Anola⁹ Meyer** was born in Wynnewood, Brady Twp., Garvin Co., Oklahoma, on December 2, 1924. She was also known as **Ola.** Anola died in Wichita, Sedgewick Co., Kansas, on July 23, 2012.[63]

**61. James George⁸ McKee** (*James L.⁷, Josiah William⁶, Elizabeth⁵, Alexander⁴, Andrew³ Pegan II, Andrew² Pagan, James¹*) was born on November 22, 1893, in Brown Co., Texas. He was also known as **George.** He was the son of James L. McKee (17) and Florence Fletcher. James George died in Sulphur, Murray Co., Oklahoma, on April 4, 1973, at age 79. He was buried in Bradley Cemetery, Bradley Twp., Grady Co., Oklahoma.[11] James George McKee usually used his middle name as his preferred name.

James George married **Hazel M. Worley** on November 3, 1926, in Garvin Co., Oklahoma. They were separated before 1940. They had one child. Hazel M. Worley was born in Lowrance, Murray Co., Oklahoma, on March 10, 1910. She reached age 84 and died in Sulphur, Murray Co., Oklahoma, on April 30, 1994.

**62. Laura Elvira⁸ McKee** (*James L.⁷, Josiah William⁶, Elizabeth⁵, Alexander⁴, Andrew³ Pegan II, Andrew² Pagan, James¹*) was born on September 25, 1895, in Brown Co., Texas. She was the daughter of

James L. McKee (17) and Florence Fletcher. Laura Elvira died in Garvin Co., Oklahoma, on October 31, 1970, at age 75. She was buried in Oaklawn Cemetery, Wynnewood, Brady Twp., Garvin Co., Oklahoma.[25]

Laura Elvira married **Lawson Harvey Meridth** before 1919. They had three children. Lawson Harvey Meridth was born in Carter Co., Oklahoma?, on March 12, 1888. He was also known as **Loss.** Lawson Harvey reached age 89 and died in Wynnewood, Brady Twp., Garvin Co., Oklahoma, on April 23, 1977. He was buried in Oaklawn Cemetery, Wynnewood, Brady Twp., Garvin Co., Oklahoma.[25]

Children of Laura Elvira McKee and Lawson Harvey Meridth:

+ 198 m I.   **Louis Harvey⁹ Meridth** was born in Wynnewood, Brady Twp., Garvin Co., Oklahoma, on September 7, 1919. He died in Wynnewood, Brady Twp., Garvin Co., Oklahoma, on March 10, 2007.[64]

+ 199 f II.   **Marie M.⁹ Meridth** was born in Wynnewood, Brady Twp., Garvin Co., Oklahoma, on June 16, 1924. She died in Purcell, Moncrief Twp., McClain Co., Oklahoma, on May 1, 2011.[25]

+ 200 f III.   **Emlie⁹ Meridth** was born in Brady Twp., Garvin Co., Oklahoma, on December 23, 1927.

**63. Jasper Edmond⁸ McKee** (*James L.⁷, Josiah William⁶, Elizabeth⁵, Alexander⁴, Andrew³ Pegan II, Andrew² Pagan, James¹*) was born on December 20, 1897, in Chargis, Pickens Co. (now Carter Co.), Oklahoma. He was the son of James L. McKee (17) and Florence Fletcher. Jasper Edmond died in Garvin Co., Oklahoma, on December 16, 1918, at age 20.

Never married.

**64. Oliver Charleston⁸ McKee** (*James L.⁷, Josiah William⁶, Elizabeth⁵, Alexander⁴, Andrew³ Pegan II, Andrew² Pagan, James¹*) was born on March 2, 1899, in Chargis, Pickens Co. (now Carter Co.),

Oklahoma. He was the son of James L. McKee (17) and Florence Fletcher. Oliver Charleston died in Lindsay, Lindsay Twp., Garvin Co., Oklahoma, on April 19, 1982, at age 83. He was buried in Bradley Twp., Grady Co., Oklahoma.[11]

Oliver Charleston married **Estella Smith** on March 22, 1927, in Garvin Co., Oklahoma. They had seven children. Estella Smith was born in Johnson Co., Texas, on August 30, 1905. Estella reached age 73 and died in Lindsay, Lindsay Twp., Garvin Co., Oklahoma, on November 1, 1978. She was buried in Bradley Cemetery, Bradley Twp., Grady Co., Oklahoma.[11]

Oliver Charleston McKee and Estella Smith had seven children, including:

+ 201 f I.   **Essie Mozelle⁹ McKee** was born in Elmore City, Elmore Twp., Garvin Co., Oklahoma, on April 6, 1928. She died in Chickasha, Chickasha Twp., Grady Co., Oklahoma, on January 3, 2007.[65]

+ 202 m II.   **Desie Andron⁹ McKee** was born in Pursley Twp., Grady Co., Oklahoma, on October 31, 1929. He died in Lindsay, Lindsay Twp., Garvin Co., Oklahoma, on November 16, 1991.[11]

+ 203 f III.   **Vida Marie⁹ McKee** was born in Pursley Twp., Grady Co., Oklahoma, on March 31, 1931. She died in Harrison Twp., Grady Co., Oklahoma, on August 12, 1939.[11]

+ 204 m IV.   **Milton William⁹ McKee** was born in Harrison Twp., Grady Co., Oklahoma, on August 22, 1934. He died in Wichita Falls, Wichita Co., Texas, on February 20, 2007.[66]

+ 205 m V.   **Elmer Ray⁹ McKee** was born in Harrison Twp., Grady Co., Oklahoma, on October 6, 1941. He died in Rock Springs, Sweetwater Co., Wyoming, on August 16, 1999.

+ 206 m VII. **Gale Raymond⁹ McKee** was born in Harrison Twp., Grady Co., Oklahoma, on December 18, 1947. He died in Lindsay, Lindsay Twp., Garvin Co., Oklahoma, on February 19, 2001.

**65. Mary Amanda⁸ McKee** (*James L.⁷, Josiah William⁶, Elizabeth⁵, Alexander⁴, Andrew³ Pegan II, Andrew² Pagan, James¹*) was born on January 20, 1902, in Chargis, Pickens Co. (now Carter Co.), Oklahoma. She was the daughter of James L. McKee (17) and Florence Fletcher. Mary Amanda died in Vernon, Wilbarger Co., Texas, on March 22, 1987, at age 85. She was buried in Roselawn Cemetery, Mangum, Greer Co., Oklahoma.[26]

Mary Amanda married **Stephen Andrew Raines** on August 25, 1922, in Garvin Co., Oklahoma. They had one daughter. Stephen Andrew Raines was born in Brady Twp., Garvin Co., Oklahoma, on January 13, 1892. Stephen Andrew reached age 92 and died in Altus, Jackson Co., Oklahoma, on January 3, 1985. He was buried in Roselawn Cemetery, Mangum, Greer Co., Oklahoma.[26]

Daughter of Mary Amanda McKee and Stephen Andrew Raines:

+ 207 f I. **Wanna Laflora⁹ Raines** was born in Brady Twp., Garvin Co., Oklahoma, on July 22, 1925. She died in Tipton, Tillman Co., Oklahoma, on December 1, 1980.[67]

**66. Marvin Milton⁸ McKee** (*James L.⁷, Josiah William⁶, Elizabeth⁵, Alexander⁴, Andrew³ Pegan II, Andrew² Pagan, James¹*) was born on April 16, 1903, in Chargis, Pickens Co. (now Carter Co.), Oklahoma. He was the son of James L. McKee (17) and Florence Fletcher. Marvin Milton died in Porterville, Tulare Co., California, on August 26, 1970, at age 67. He was buried in Hillcrest Cemetery, Porterville, Tulare Co., California.[27]

He married **Maud May Jones.** They had four children. Maud May Jones was born in Harrison Twp., Grady Co., Oklahoma, on February 20, 1904. Maud May reached age 62 and died in Porterville, Tulare Co., California, on June 7, 1966. She was buried in Hillcrest Cemetery, Porterville, Tulare Co., California.[27]

Children of Marvin Milton McKee and Maud May Jones:

+ 208 m I. **Henry Lee⁹ McKee** was born in Pursley Twp., Grady Co., Oklahoma, on August 16, 1930. He died in North Korea on November 22, 1951.[27]

+ 209 m II. **Carl Dean⁹ McKee** was born in Pursley Twp., Grady Co., Oklahoma, on February 5, 1936. He died in Porterville, Tulare Co., California, on February 3, 1995.

+ 210 f III. **Laverne Marie⁹ McKee** was born in Pursley Twp., Grady Co., Oklahoma, on May 1, 1940. She died in Porterville, Tulare Co., California, on March 25, 1996.

+ 211 m IV. **Baby⁹ McKee** was born in Pursley Twp., Grady Co., Oklahoma. He died in Pursley Twp., Grady Co., Oklahoma.

**67. Sie Adron⁸ McKee** (*James L.⁷, Josiah William⁶, Elizabeth⁵, Alexander⁴, Andrew³ Pegan II, Andrew² Pagan, James¹*) was born on November 15, 1906, in Chargis, Pickens Co. (now Carter Co.), Oklahoma. He was the son of James L. McKee (17) and Florence Fletcher. Sie Adron died in Chickasha, Chickasha Twp., Grady Co., Oklahoma, on August 12, 1983, at age 76. He was buried in Green Hill Cemetery, McClain Co., Oklahoma.[28]

Childless.

He married **Lela Leah Dutton.** Lela Leah Dutton was born in Cox City, Rush Springs Twp., Grady Co., Oklahoma, on March 14, 1918. Lela Leah reached age 88 and died in Lindsay, Lindsay Twp.,

Garvin Co., Oklahoma, on September 17, 2006. She was buried in Green Hill Cemetery, McClain Co., Oklahoma.[28]

**68. Willie Fletcher⁸ McKee** (*James L.⁷, Josiah William⁶, Elizabeth⁵, Alexander⁴, Andrew³ Pegan II, Andrew² Pagan, James¹*) was born on April 12, 1909, in Archer Co., Texas. He was the son of James L. McKee (17) and Florence Fletcher. Willie Fletcher died in Rush Springs Twp., Grady Co., Oklahoma, on June 18, 1986, at age 77. He was buried in Bradley Cemetery, Bradley Twp., Grady Co., Oklahoma.[11]

Willie Fletcher married **Edith May Heatley** in Hughes Co., Oklahoma? They had one son. Edith May Heatley was born in Hickman Co., Tennessee, on October 8, 1910. Edith May reached age 51 and died in Rush Springs Twp., Grady Co., Oklahoma, on April 10, 1962. She was buried in Bradley Cemetery, Bradley Twp., Grady Co., Oklahoma.

Son of Willie Fletcher McKee and Edith May Heatley:

+ 212 m I.   **Billie Roy⁹ McKee** was born in Rush Springs Twp., Grady Co., Oklahoma, on March 6, 1937. He died in Rush Springs Twp., Grady Co., Oklahoma, on March 6, 1937.

**69. Reuben Josiah⁸ Riley** (*Martha Louise Jane⁷ McKee, Josiah William⁶, Elizabeth⁵, Alexander⁴, Andrew³ Pegan II, Andrew² Pagan, James¹*) was born on August 12, 1890, in Montague Co., Texas. He was the son of Isaac H. Riley and Martha Louise Jane McKee (18). Reuben Josiah died in Lindsay, Lindsay Twp., Garvin Co., Oklahoma, on November 2, 1977, at age 87. He was buried in Erin Springs Cemetery, Erin Springs, Lindsay Twp., Garvin Co., Oklahoma.[12]

Reuben Josiah married **Sarah Julia Ann Dutton** on December 17, 1911, in Grady Co., Oklahoma. They had six children. Sarah Julia Ann Dutton was born in Coldwater, Chattooga Co., Georgia, on September 18, 1890. Sarah Julia Ann reached age 71 and died in Pursley Twp., Grady Co., Oklahoma, on October 23, 1961. She was buried in Erin Springs Cemetery, Erin Springs, Lindsay Twp., Garvin Co., Oklahoma.[12]

Children of Reuben Josiah Riley and Sarah Julia Ann Dutton:

+ 213 m I.   **Gussie Isaac⁹ Riley** was born in Bradley Twp., Grady Co., Oklahoma, on October 12, 1912. He was also known as **Isaac.** Gussie Isaac died in Justin, Denton Co., Texas, on March 15, 2006.

+ 214 f II.   **Lula Ann⁹ Riley** was born in Bradley Twp., Grady Co., Oklahoma, on August 8, 1914. She died in Oklahoma City, Oklahoma, on February 29, 2008.

+ 215 m III.   **Charles Russell⁹ Riley** was born in Bradley Twp., Grady Co., Oklahoma, on February 16, 1917. He was also known as **Bud.** Charles Russell died in Mustang, Canadian Co., Oklahoma, on April 13, 1981.[68]

+ 216 f IV.   **Lee Emma⁹ Riley** was born in Bradley Twp., Grady Co., Oklahoma, on July 22, 1921. She died in San Antonio, Bexar Co., Texas, on December 3, 2006.[12]

+ 217 f V.   **Ida Mae⁹ Riley** was born in Pursley Twp., Grady Co., Oklahoma, on June 20, 1924. She died in Lindsay, Lindsay Twp., Garvin Co., Oklahoma, on December 7, 1989.[12]

+ 218 f VI.   **Sarah Elvina⁹ Riley** was born in Pursley Twp., Grady Co., Oklahoma, on November 21, 1926.

**70. Mary Malire⁸ Riley** (*Martha Louise Jane⁷ McKee, Josiah William⁶, Elizabeth⁵, Alexander⁴, Andrew³ Pegan II, Andrew² Pagan, James¹*) was born on May 13, 1892, in Montague Co., Texas. She was also known as **Molly.** She was the daughter of Isaac H. Riley and Martha Louise Jane McKee (18). Mary Malire died in Erin Springs, Lindsay Twp., Garvin Co., Oklahoma, on September 4, 1945, at age 53. She was buried in Erin Springs Cemetery, Erin Springs, Lindsay Twp., Garvin Co., Oklahoma.[12]

Mary Malire married **Sampson Leroy Jones** on December 21, 1913, in Grady Co., Oklahoma. They had two children. Sampson Leroy Jones was born in Bryan Co., Oklahoma, on June 26, 1892. Sampson Leroy reached age 34 and died in Bradley Twp., Grady Co., Oklahoma, on March 14, 1927. He was buried in Erin Springs Cemetery, Erin Springs, Lindsay Twp., Garvin Co., Oklahoma.[12]

Mary Malire Riley Jones married **Jesse James Marker** after 1927. Jesse James Marker was born in Texas on January 28, 1886. Jesse James reached age 72 and died in Bradley Twp., Grady Co., Oklahoma, on February 23, 1958. He was buried in Erin Springs Cemetery, Erin Springs, Lindsay Twp., Garvin Co., Oklahoma.[12]

Children of Mary Malire Riley and Sampson Leroy Jones:

+ 219  f  I.  **Emma Mae**[9] **Jones** was born in Bradley Twp., Grady Co., Oklahoma, on January 30, 1915. She died in Oklahoma City, Oklahoma, on June 9, 1991.[23]

+ 220  m  II.  **Francis Horten**[9] **Jones** was born in Bradley Twp., Grady Co., Oklahoma, on September 28, 1922. He was also known as **Frank.** Francis Horten died in Odessa, Ector Co., Texas, on March 16, 1983.

**71. Isaac Russell**[8] **Riley II** (*Martha Louise Jane*[7] *McKee, Josiah William*[6]*, Elizabeth*[5]*, Alexander*[4]*, Andrew*[3] *Pegan II, Andrew*[2] *Pagan, James*[1]) was born on June 1, 1894, in Montague Co., Texas. He was also known as **Russell.** He was the son of Isaac H. Riley and Martha Louise Jane McKee (18). Isaac Russell died in Luna Co., New Mexico, on January 24, 1962, at age 67. He was buried in Mountain View Cemetery, Deming, Luna Co., New Mexico.[29]

Isaac Russell married **Edna Bassett** on June 9, 1915, in Garvin Co., Oklahoma. They had four children. Edna Bassett was born in McCurtain Co., Oklahoma, on October 27, 1900. Edna reached age 85 and died in Silver City, Grant Co., New Mexico,

in April 1986. She was buried in Mountain View Cemetery, Deming, Luna Co., New Mexico.[29]

Children of Isaac Russell Riley II and Edna Bassett:

+ 221  f  I.  **Bessie Elizabeth**[9] **Riley** was born in Bradley Twp., Grady Co., Oklahoma, on April 16, 1916. She died in Tucson, Pima Co., Arizona, on April 18, 1991.[69]

+ 222  f  II.  **Martha Lois**[9] **Riley** was born in Minco, Union Twp., Grady Co., Oklahoma, on November 9, 1924. She died in Pico Rivera, Los Angeles Co., California, on July 26, 1988.

+ 223  f  III.  **Betty Jean**[9] **Riley** was born in Skiatook, Tulsa Co., Oklahoma?, on November 24, 1931.

+ 224  m  IV.  **Billy Don**[9] **Riley** was born in Bradley Twp., Grady Co., Oklahoma, on December 16, 1934. He was also known as **Don.** Billy Don died in Albuquerque, Bernalillo Co., New Mexico, on July 19, 2003.

**72. Emma Neta**[8] **Riley** (*Martha Louise Jane*[7] *McKee, Josiah William*[6]*, Elizabeth*[5]*, Alexander*[4]*, Andrew*[3] *Pegan II, Andrew*[2] *Pagan, James*[1]) was born on December 20, 1895, in Montague Co., Texas. She was the daughter of Isaac H. Riley and Martha Louise Jane McKee (18). Emma Neta lived in 1938 in Bradley Twp., Grady Co., Oklahoma. She died in a hospital in Oklahoma City, Oklahoma Co., Oklahoma, on September 6, 1938, at age 42. Emma Neta was buried in Green Hill Cemetery, McClain Co., Oklahoma.[28]

Emma Neta Riley Gosnell's birthdate on the Social Security Death Index is July 17, 1893. Her Oklahoma death certificate says she was born on December 1895.

Emma Neta married **Charles William Gosnell** on June 29, 1915 in Grady Co., Oklahoma. They had two sons. Charles William Gosnell was born in Jacksboro, Jack Co., Texas, on December 18, 1892.

Charles William reached age 73 and died in Fresno, Fresno Co., California, on June 13, 1966.

Sons of Emma Neta Riley and Charles William Gosnell:

+ 225 m I. **Loyd Jesse⁹ Gosnell** was born in Bradley Twp., Grady Co., Oklahoma, on May 7, 1916. He died in Alex, Alex Twp., Grady Co. Oklahoma, on December 2, 1987.[52]

+ 226 m II. **William Isaac⁹ Gosnell** was born in Bradley Twp., Grady Co., Oklahoma, on November 22, 1922. He died in Marlow Twp., Stephens Co., Oklahoma, on March 13, 2003.[32]

**73. Ada May⁸ Riley** (*Martha Louise Jane⁷ McKee, Josiah William⁶, Elizabeth⁵, Alexander⁴, Andrew³ Pegan II, Andrew² Pagan, James¹*) was born on February 14, 1898, in Township 3, Choctaw Nation, Indian Territory (now LaFlore or Caddo Co., Oklahoma). She was the daughter of Isaac H. Riley and Martha Louise Jane McKee (18). Ada May died in Harrison Twp., Grady Co., Oklahoma, on October 2, 1915, at age 17. She was buried in Erin Springs Cemetery, Erin Springs, Lindsay Twp., Garvin Co., Oklahoma.[12]

Never married.

**74. Janie Susan⁸ Riley** (*Martha Louise Jane⁷ McKee, Josiah William⁶, Elizabeth⁵, Alexander⁴, Andrew³ Pegan II, Andrew² Pagan, James¹*) was born on February 8, 1900, in Township 3, Choctaw Nation, Indian Territory (now LaFlore or Caddo Co., Oklahoma). She was the daughter of Isaac H. Riley and Martha Louise Jane McKee (18). Janie Susan lived in Delaware, Nowata Co., Oklahoma? She died in Oklahoma City, Oklahoma, on April 20, 1968, at age 68. Janie Susan was buried in Green Hill Cemetery, McClain Co., Oklahoma.[28]

Janie Susan married **Marvin Wesley Groomes or Grooms** on June 14, 1918, in Grady Co., Oklahoma. They divorced about 1920. They had two children. Marvin Wesley Groomes or Grooms was born in Lincoln Co., Oklahoma, on May 5, 1900. He reached age 70 and died in Pawhuska, Osage Co.,

Oklahoma, about June 20, 1970. Marvin Wesley Groomes or was buried in Pawhuska Cemetery, Pawhuska, Osage Co., Oklahoma.[70]

Janie Susan Riley married **Scott Washington Dutton** on July 17, 1927. They had one daughter. Scott Washington Dutton was born in Coldwater, Chattooga Co., Georgia, on March 31, 1879. Scott Washington reached age 84 and died in Chickasha, Chickasha Twp., Grady Co., Oklahoma, on October 3, 1963. He was buried in Green Hill Cemetery, McClain Co., Oklahoma.[28]

Children of Janie Susan Riley and Marvin Wesley Groomes or Grooms:

+ 227 m I. **Leroy⁹ Grooms** was born in Brady Twp., Garvin Co., Oklahoma, on June 5, 1919. He was also known as **Buck.** Leroy died in Rush Springs Twp., Grady Co., Oklahoma, on June 18, 1993.[52]

+ 228 f II. **Ada Louise⁹ Grooms** was born in Brady Twp., Garvin Co., Oklahoma, in 1921. She died in Brady Twp., Garvin Co., Oklahoma, before 1930.

Daughter of Janie Susan Riley and Scott Washington Dutton:

+ 229 f I. **Anna Lee⁹ Dutton** was born in Cushing, Payne Co., Oklahoma, in 1928.

**75. Anna Martha⁸ Riley** (*Martha Louise Jane⁷ McKee, Josiah William⁶, Elizabeth⁵, Alexander⁴, Andrew³ Pegan II, Andrew² Pagan, James¹*) was born on May 12, 1902, in Harrison Twp., Grady Co., Oklahoma. She was the daughter of Isaac H. Riley and Martha Louise Jane McKee (18). Anna Martha died in Lindsay, Lindsay Twp., Garvin Co., Oklahoma, on March 7, 1975, at age 72. She was buried in Green Hill Cemetery, McClain Co., Oklahoma.[28]

Anna Martha married **Terry Everett Jones** on November 27, 1926, in Garvin Co., Oklahoma. They had four children. Terry Everett Jones was born in Harrison Twp., Grady Co., Oklahoma, on

July 2, 1897. Terry Everett reached age 82 and died in Lindsay, Lindsay Twp., Garvin Co., Oklahoma, on January 14, 1980. He was buried in Green Hill Cemetery, McClain Co., Oklahoma.[28]

Children of Anna Martha Riley and Terry Everett Jones:

+ 230 m I. **Kenneth Roy⁹ Jones** was born in Bradley Twp., Grady Co., Oklahoma, on September 12, 1930. He died in Bradley Twp., Grady Co., Oklahoma, on March 29, 1973.[28]

+ 231 f II. **Virginia⁹ Jones** was born in Bradley Twp., Grady Co., Oklahoma, in 1932.

+ 232 m III. **Terry Gene⁹ Jones II** was born in Pursley Twp., Grady Co., Oklahoma, in 1936.

+ 233 m IV. **Claud J.⁹ Jones** was born in Pursley Twp., Grady Co., Oklahoma, on January 17, 1939. He died in Lexington Twp., Cleveland Co., Oklahoma, on December 6, 2010.[28]

**76. Willie Alice⁸ McKee** (*Josiah Andres⁷, Josiah William⁶, Elizabeth⁵, Alexander⁴, Andrew³ Pegan II, Andrew² Pagan, James¹*) was born on September 4, 1895, in Cooke Co., Texas or St. Jo, Montague Co., Texas. She was the daughter of Josiah Andres McKee II (19) and Lillie Alice Harrell. Willie Alice died in Wilson, Hewitt Twp., Carter Co., Oklahoma, on September 3, 1946, at age 50. She was buried in Hewitt Cemetery, Wilson, Hewitt Twp., Carter Co., Oklahoma.[13]

Willie Alice married **Jesse Thomas Cross** on August 12, 1913, in Cooke Co., Texas. They had two children. Jesse Thomas Cross was born in Texas in 1894. Jesse Thomas reached age 22 and died in Katie, Brady Twp., Garvin Co., Oklahoma, on May 5, 1916. He was buried in Katie City Cemetery, Katie, Brady Twp., Garvin Co., Oklahoma.[9]

Willie Alice McKee Cross married **Frank Perry Alexander** on April 10, 1918, in Garvin Co., Oklahoma. They had three children. Frank Perry

Alexander was born in Mineral Twp., Jasper Co., Missouri, on January 15, 1876. Frank Perry reached age 59 and died in Wilson, Hewitt Twp., Carter Co., Oklahoma, on November 15, 1935. He was buried in Hewitt Cemetery, Wilson, Hewitt Twp., Carter Co., Oklahoma.[13]

Children of Willie Alice McKee and Jesse Thomas Cross:

+ 234 f I. **Christine Ellen⁹ Cross** was born in Elmore City, Elmore Twp., Garvin Co., Oklahoma, on July 2, 1914. She was also known as **Kitty.** Christine Ellen died in Bacliff, Galveston Co., Texas, on December 21, 1989.[71]

+ 235 m II. **Jesse Thomas⁹ Cross II** was born in Elmore City, Elmore Twp., Garvin Co., Oklahoma, on August 8, 1916. He died in Germany on March 13, 1945.[72]

Children of Willie Alice McKee and Frank Perry Alexander:

+ 236 f I. **Irene Dorothy⁹ Alexander** was born in Wirt, Hewitt Twp., Carter Co., Oklahoma, on March 31, 1919. She died in Hewitt Twp., Carter Co., Oklahoma, on October 2, 1972.[13]

+ 237 m II. **Frank Perry⁹ Alexander II** was born in Wirt, Hewitt Twp., Carter Co., Oklahoma, on March 19, 1921. He died in Prineville, Crook Co., Oregon, on September 17, 2006.[73]

+ 238 m III. **Bobby Joe⁹ Alexander** was born in Wirt, Hewitt Twp., Carter Co., Oklahoma, on April 5, 1925. He died in Wirt, Hewitt Twp., Carter Co., Oklahoma, on May 25, 1939.[13]

**77. Infant Twin Son⁸ McKee** (*Josiah Andres⁷, Josiah William⁶, Elizabeth⁵, Alexander⁴, Andrew³ Pegan II, Andrew² Pagan, James¹*) was born on May 2,

1897, in Hewitt Twp., Carter Co., Oklahoma. He was the son of Josiah Andres McKee II (19) and Lillie Alice Harrell. Infant Twin Son died in Brady Twp., Garvin Co., Oklahoma, on May 2, 1897. He was buried in Chagger Cemetery, Carter Co., Oklahoma.[30]

**78. George Washington Josiah[8] McKee** (*Josiah Andres[7], Josiah William[6], Elizabeth[5], Alexander[4], Andrew[3] Pegan II, Andrew[2] Pagan, James[1]*) was born on May 2, 1897, in Hewitt Twp., Carter Co., Oklahoma. He was also known as **Josiah** and **Joe.** He was the son of Josiah Andres McKee II (19) and Lillie Alice Harrell. George Washington Josiah died in Wilson, Hewitt Twp., Carter Co., Oklahoma, on August 9, 1971, at age 74. He was buried in Hewitt Cemetery, Wilson, Hewitt Twp., Carter Co., Oklahoma.[13]

George Washington Josiah married **Lucy Evelyn Ramsey** on March 12, 1919, in Garvin Co., Oklahoma. They had five children. Lucy Evelyn Ramsey was born in Oklahoma on August 30, 1901. She was also known as **Eva.** Lucy Evelyn reached age 62 and died in Wilson, Hewitt Twp., Carter Co., Oklahoma, on August 16, 1964. She was buried in Hewitt Cemetery, Wilson, Hewitt Twp., Carter Co., Oklahoma.[8]

Children of George Washington Josiah McKee III and Lucy Evelyn Ramsey:

+ 239 f I. **Opal Marie[9] McKee** was born in Wirt, Hewitt Twp., Carter Co., Oklahoma, on March 23, 1920. She died in Wilson, Hewitt Twp., Carter Co., Oklahoma, on November 27, 2002.[74]

+ 240 m II. **Jack[9] McKee** was born in Hewitt Twp., Carter Co., Oklahoma, on November 16, 1921. He died in Wilson, Hewitt Twp., Carter Co., Oklahoma, on July 15, 1962.[13]

+ 241 m III. **Richard Douglas[9] McKee** was born in Pernell, Elmore Twp., Garvin Co., Oklahoma, on May

18, 1924. He died in Peoria, Maricopa Co., Arizona, on April 12, 2012.[75]

+ 242 m IV. **Kenneth Gene[9] McKee** was born in Hewitt Twp., Carter Co., Oklahoma, on April 13, 1930.

+ 243 m V. **Jerry Ray[9] McKee** was born in Ratliff City, Graham Twp., Carter Co., Oklahoma, on August 24, 1934. He died in Ardmore, Morgan Twp., Carter Co., Oklahoma, on May 5, 2000.[31]

**79. Martha Anna[8] McKee** (*Josiah Andres[7], Josiah William[6], Elizabeth[5], Alexander[4], Andrew[3] Pegan II, Andrew[2] Pagan, James[1]*) was born on March 4, 1899, in Brady Twp., Garvin Co., Oklahoma. She was also known as **Anna** and **Annie.** She was the daughter of Josiah Andres McKee II (19) and Lillie Alice Harrell. Martha Anna died in Parks Twp., Stephens Co., Oklahoma?, on April 11, 1966, at age 67. She was buried in Green Hill Cemetery, Davis, Murray Co., Oklahoma.[31]

Martha Anna married **Charles Spurgeon Pierce** on August 8, 1914, in Garvin Co., Oklahoma. They had one daughter. Charles Spurgeon Pierce was born in Fannin Co., Texas, on August 11, 1892. Charles Spurgeon reached age 66 and died in Davis, Murray Co., Oklahoma, on January 7, 1959. He was buried in Green Hill Cemetery, Davis, Murray Co., Oklahoma.[31]

Daughter of Martha Anna McKee and Charles Spurgeon Pierce:

+ 244 f I. **Christine[9] Pierce** was born in Waurika, Jefferson Co., Oklahoma, on September 4, 1927. She was adopted after 1930. Christine died in a hospital in Ardmore, Morgan Twp., Carter Co., Oklahoma, on May 12, 1982. She is buried in Green Hill Cemetery, Davis, Murray Co., Oklahoma.[31]

**80. Roxie Laurenda⁸ McKee** (*Josiah Andres⁷, Josiah William⁶, Elizabeth⁵, Alexander⁴, Andrew³ Pegan II, Andrew² Pagan, James¹*) was born on February 10, 1902, in Brady Twp., Garvin Co., Oklahoma. She was the daughter of Josiah Andres McKee II (19) and Lillie Alice Harrell. Roxie Laurenda died in Wilson, Hewitt Twp., Carter Co., Oklahoma, on September 28, 1991, at age 89. She was buried in Hewitt Cemetery, Wilson, Hewitt Twp., Carter Co., Oklahoma.[13]

Roxie Laurenda married **Charles Raymond Wilson** on October 10, 1925, in Carter Co., Oklahoma. They had six children. Charles Raymond Wilson was born in Johnson Twp., Carter Co., Missouri?, on September 2, 1903. Charles Raymond reached age 68 and died in Oak Park, Cook Co., Illinois, on January 12, 1972.

Roxie Laurenda McKee and Charles Raymond Wilson had six children, including:

+ 245 m I.   **Ruel Pearce⁹ Wilson** was born in Fox, Graham Twp. Carter Co., Oklahoma, on August 13, 1926. He died in Ardmore, Morgan Twp., Carter Co., Oklahoma, on June 28, 1990.[13]

+ 246 f II.   **Betty Lou⁹ Wilson** was born in Maud, Oklahoma, on November 14, 1929. She died in Ardmore, Morgan Twp., Carter Co., Oklahoma, on September 13, 2012.[76]

+ 247 m III.  **Billy Gene⁹ Wilson** was born in Oklahoma in 1933.

+ 248 f IV.  **Virgie Mae⁹ Wilson** was born in Oklahoma on February 7, 1934. She died in Oklahoma City, Cleveland Co., Oklahoma, on January 1, 2008.[23]

+ 249 f V.   **Donna Raye⁹ Wilson** was born in Dillard, Wilson Twp., Carter Co., Okllahoma, on May 17, 1938. She died in Oklahoma City, Oklahoma, on February 28, 2004.

**81. Sarah Lou⁸ McKee** (*Josiah Andres⁷, Josiah William⁶, Elizabeth⁵, Alexander⁴, Andrew³ Pegan II, Andrew² Pagan, James¹*) was born on January 23, 1904, in Brady Twp., Garvin Co., Oklahoma. She was the daughter of Josiah Andres McKee II (19) and Lillie Alice Harrell. Sarah Lou died in Hewitt Twp., Carter Co., Oklahoma, on January 23, 1973, at age 69. She was buried in Hewitt Cemetery, Wilson, Hewitt Twp., Carter Co., Oklahoma.[13]

Sarah Lou married **Tilden Theodore Barrett** on April 16, 1927, in Jefferson Co., Oklahoma. They had five children. Tilden Theodore Barrett was born in Wright Twp., Jefferson Co., Oklahoma, on May 8, 1899. Tilden Theodore reached age 65 and died in Hewitt Twp., Carter Co., Oklahoma, on March 4, 1965. He was buried in Hewitt Cemetery, Wilson, Hewitt Twp., Carter Co., Oklahoma.[13]

Sarah Lou McKee and Tilden Theodore Barrett had five children, including:

+ 250 f I.   **Anna Marie⁹ Barrett** was born in Wilson, Hewitt Twp., Carter Co., Oklahoma, on January 7, 1928. She died in Sun City, Riverside Co., California, on September 5, 2000.

+ 251 m II.  **Mac Theodore⁹ Barrett** was born in Wilson, Hewitt Twp., Carter Co., Oklahoma, on September 6, 1933. He died in Wrightwood, San Bernardino Co., California, on April 7, 2001.

+ 252 f III.  **Barbara Jean⁹ Barrett** was born in Wilson, Hewitt Twp., Carter Co., Oklahoma, on January 25, 1938. She died in Kingston, Marshall Co., Oklahoma, on January 15, 2004.[13]

**82. Henry William⁸ McKee** (*Josiah Andres⁷, Josiah William⁶, Elizabeth⁵, Alexander⁴, Andrew³ Pegan II, Andrew² Pagan, James¹*) was born on April 23, 1907, in Brady Twp., Garvin Co., Oklahoma. He was the son of Josiah Andres McKee II (19) and Lillie Alice Harrell. Henry William died in

Wilson, Hewitt Twp., Carter Co., Oklahoma, on January 5, 1981, at age 73. He was buried in Hewitt Cemetery, Wilson, Hewitt Twp., Carter Co., Oklahoma.[13]

Henry William married **Willie Fay Odell** before 1946. They had six children. Willie Fay Odell was born in Elmore Twp., Garvin Co., Oklahoma, on June 11, 1907. Willie Fay reached age 84 and died in Wilson, Hewitt Twp., Carter Co., Oklahoma, on April 9, 1992. She was buried in Hewitt Cemetery, Wilson, Hewitt Twp., Carter Co., Oklahoma.[13]

Henry William McKee and Willie Fay Odell had six children, including:

+ 253 f I. **Nancy Marlene⁹ McKee** was born in Wilson, Hewitt Twp., Carter Co., Oklahoma, on February 1, 1946. She died in Oklahoma City, Oklahoma, on January 28, 2000.[13]

+ 254 m II. **Montie W.⁹ McKee** was born in Wilson, Hewitt Twp., Carter Co., Oklahoma, on September 13, 1947. He died in Healdton, Hewitt Twp., Carter Co., Oklahoma, on July 25, 2000.[13]

**83. Verdie Loyd⁸ McKee** (*Josiah Andres⁷, Josiah William⁶, Elizabeth⁵, Alexander⁴, Andrew³ Pegan II, Andrew² Pagan, James¹*) was born on April 6, 1911, in Brady Twp., Garvin Co., Oklahoma. He was the son of Josiah Andres McKee II (19) and Lillie Alice Harrell. Verdie Loyd died in Krotz Springs, Saint Landry Parish, Louisiana, on February 11, 1988, at age 76.

Verdie Loyd married **Julia Mae Shepherd** about 1940. They had one daughter. Julia Mae Shepherd was born in Wilson, Hewitt Twp., Carter Co., Oklahoma, on April 5, 1912. Julia Mae reached age 51 and died in Krotz Springs, Saint Landry Parish, Louisiana, on June 9, 1963.

Verdie Loyd McKee married **Unknown Unknown** on March 12, 1965.

Daughter of Verdie Loyd McKee and Julia Mae Shepherd:

+ 255 f I. **Rita Kaye⁹ McKee** was born in Wilson, Hewitt Twp., Carter Co., Oklahoma, on July 23, 1941. She died in Krotz Springs, Saint Landry Parish, Louisiana, on May 9, 1969.

**84. Ruth Lea⁸ McKee** (*Josiah Andres⁷, Josiah William⁶, Elizabeth⁵, Alexander⁴, Andrew³ Pegan II, Andrew² Pagan, James¹*) was born on September 9, 1913, in Brady Twp., Garvin Co., Oklahoma. She was the daughter of Josiah Andres McKee II (19) and Lillie Alice Harrell. Ruth Lea died in Ardmore, Morgan Twp., Carter Co., Oklahoma, on April 16, 1997, at age 83. She was buried in Hewitt Cemetery, Wilson, Hewitt Twp., Carter Co., Oklahoma.[13]

Ruth Lea married **Boyet V. Chance** on June 12, 1930, in Garvin Co., Oklahoma. They had four children. Boyet V. Chance was born in Fox, Graham Twp. Carter Co., Oklahoma, on December 27, 1909. Boyet V. reached age 44 and died in Hewitt Twp., Carter Co., Oklahoma, on April 16, 1954. He was buried in Hewitt Cemetery, Wilson, Hewitt Twp., Carter Co., Oklahoma.[13]

Ruth Lea McKee and Boyet V. Chance had four children, including:

+ 256 f I. **Delores Geraldine⁹ Chance** was born in Hewitt, Hewitt Twp., Carter Co., Oklahoma, on March 27, 1931. She died in Ardmore, Morgan Twp., Carter Co., Oklahoma, on August 2, 2006.[77]

+ 257 m II. **Gordon Henry⁹ Chance** was born in Hewitt, Hewitt Twp., Carter Co., Oklahoma, on November 18, 1933. He died in Ardmore, Morgan Twp., Carter Co., Oklahoma, on October 10, 2001.[13]

+ 258 m III. **Jimmie D.⁹ Chance** was born in Hewitt, Hewitt Twp., Carter Co., Oklahoma, on February 2, 1938.

**85. Josiah Milton⁸ McKee** (*Albert Milton⁷, Josiah William⁶, Elizabeth⁵, Alexander⁴, Andrew³ Pegan II, Andrew² Pagan, James¹*) was born on August 8, 1894, in St. Jo, Montague Co., Texas. He was the son of Albert Milton McKee (20) and Juanita Roten. Josiah Milton died in Oklahoma City, Oklahoma, on June 18, 1930, at age 35. He was buried in Katie City Cemetery, Katie, Brady Twp., Garvin Co., Oklahoma.[9]

Josiah Milton married **Mildred Valle Williams** on March 30, 1918, in Garvin Co., Oklahoma. They had two children. Mildred Valle Williams was born in Dunklin Co., Missouri, on March 10, 1901.[25] Mildred Valle reached age 59 and died in Walker Twp., Garvin Co., Oklahoma, on May 5, 1960. She was buried in Oaklawn Cemetery, Wynnewood, Brady Twp., Garvin Co., Oklahoma.[25]

Children of Josiah Milton McKee and Mildred Valle Williams:

+ 259 f I. **Juanita**[9] **McKee** was born in Hewitt Twp., Carter Co., Oklahoma, on March 17, 1920. She died in Hewitt Twp., Carter Co., Oklahoma, on November 6, 1923.[9]

+ 260 m II. **Pleas Milton**[9] **McKee** was born in Hewitt Twp., Carter Co., Oklahoma, on March 22, 1922. He was also known as **Pete.** Pleas Milton died in Abilene, Taylor Co., Texas, on August 21, 2007.[78]

86. **Martha Amanda**[8] **McKee** (*Albert Milton*[7], *Josiah William*[6], *Elizabeth*[5], *Alexander*[4], *Andrew*[3] *Pegan II, Andrew*[2] *Pagan, James*[1]) was born on July 31, 1896, in Carter Co., Oklahoma. She was the daughter of Albert Milton McKee (20) and Juanita Roten. Martha Amanda died in Garvin Co., Oklahoma, on September 8, 1896.

87. **Vivian Violet**[8] **McKee** (*Albert Milton*[7], *Josiah William*[6], *Elizabeth*[5], *Alexander*[4], *Andrew*[3] *Pegan II, Andrew*[2] *Pagan, James*[1]) was born on May 31, 1908, in Brady Twp., Garvin Co., Oklahoma. She was also known as **Violet.** She was the daughter of Albert Milton McKee (20) and Nancy Anna Fletcher. Vivian Violet died in Norman, Cleveland Co., Oklahoma, on February 15, 1994, at age 85.

She was buried in Marlow Cemetery, Marlow Twp., Stephens Co., Oklahoma.[32]

She married **William Wiley West.** They had one daughter. William Wiley West was born in Morrilton, Conway Co., Arkansas, on June 21, 1903. William Wiley reached age 62 and died in Oklahoma City, Oklahoma, on October 5, 1965. He was buried in Marlow Cemetery, Marlow Twp., Stephens Co., Oklahoma.

Daughter of Vivian Violet McKee and William Wiley West:

+ 261 f I. **Willene Violet**[9] **West** was born in McClain Co., Oklahoma?, on October 5, 1929.

88. **Rosa Lawana**[8] **McKee** (*Albert Milton*[7], *Josiah William*[6], *Elizabeth*[5], *Alexander*[4], *Andrew*[3] *Pegan II, Andrew*[2] *Pagan, James*[1]) was born on April 27, 1910, in Brady Twp., Garvin Co., Oklahoma. She was the daughter of Albert Milton McKee (20) and Nancy Anna Fletcher. Rosa Lawana died in Oklahoma City, Oklahoma, on June 20, 1977, at age 67.

Rosa Lawana married **George William Fox** on December 3, 1927, in Garvin Co., Oklahoma. They had three children. George William Fox was born in Clay Co., Texas, on July 26, 1903. George William reached age 88 and died in Oklahoma City, Oklahoma, on April 23, 1992.

Children of Rosa Lawana McKee and George William Fox:

+ 262 m I. **T.L.**[9] **Fox** was born in Marlow, Marlow Twp., Stephens Co., Oklahoma, on August 14, 1930. He died in Lubbock, Lubbock Co., Texas, on November 29, 1996.[79]

+ 263 m II. **Lyle Doan**[9] **Fox** was born in Wall Twp., Stephens Co., Oklahoma, on October 8, 1932. He died in Pueblo, Pueblo Co., Colorado, on November 1, 2003.[80]

+ 264 f III. **Cara Nome⁹ Fox** was born in Wall Twp., Stephens Co., Oklahoma, on October 6, 1935. She died in Oklahoma City, Oklahoma, on September 9, 1997.[81]

**89. John James⁸ McKee** (*Albert Milton⁷, Josiah William⁶, Elizabeth⁵, Alexander⁴, Andrew³ Pegan II, Andrew² Pagan, James¹*) was born on October 21, 1911, in Brady Twp., Garvin Co., Oklahoma. He was the son of Albert Milton McKee (20) and Nancy Anna Fletcher. John James died in Paul's Valley, Whitebead Twp., Garvin Co., Oklahoma, on March 7, 1967, at age 55.

John James married **Effie Emaline Crawford** on April 17, 1939. They had one son. Effie Emaline Crawford was born in Board Camp, Polk Co., Arkansas, on March 18, 1912. Effie Emaline reached age 89 and died in Norman, Cleveland Co., Oklahoma, on August 15, 2001.

Son of John James McKee and Effie Emaline Crawford:

+ 265 m I. **James Lowell⁹ McKee** was born in Elmore City, Elmore Twp., Garvin Co., Oklahoma, on April 9, 1940. He died in Paul's Valley, Whitebead Twp., Garvin Co., Oklahoma, on November 19, 1983.

**90. Daniel⁸ McKee** (*Albert Milton⁷, Josiah William⁶, Elizabeth⁵, Alexander⁴, Andrew³ Pegan II, Andrew² Pagan, James¹*) was born on February 11, 1913, in Hewitt Twp., Carter Co., Oklahoma. He was the son of Albert Milton McKee (20) and Nancy Anna Fletcher. Daniel died in Paul's Valley, Whitebead Twp., Garvin Co., Oklahoma, on April 25, 1972, at age 59.

**91. Rosa Lillie⁸ Wright** (*Mary Catherine⁷ McKee, Josiah William⁶, Elizabeth⁵, Alexander⁴, Andrew³ Pegan II, Andrew² Pagan, James¹*) was born on March 11, 1897, in Johnsonville, McClain Co., Oklahoma. She was the daughter of John Dethridge Wright and Mary Catherine McKee (21). Rosa Lillie died in Golden, Wood Co., Texas, on November 30, 1977, at age 80. She was buried in Pilgrim Rest Cemetery #2, Golden, Wood Co., Texas.[33]

Rosa Lillie married **Archie Aston Hughes** on January 11, 1917, in Carter Co., Oklahoma. They had twelve children. Archie Aston Hughes was born in Loco, Stephens Co., Oklahoma, on September 26, 1893. Archie Aston reached age 49 and died in Golden, Wood Co., Texas, on September 29, 1942. He was buried in Jamestown Cemetery, Jamestown, Smith Co., Texas.[82]

Rosa Lillie Wright married **Floyd Sellers** after 1942. Floyd Sellers was born on November 2, 1914. Floyd reached age 77 and died in Golden, Wood Co., Texas, on September 25, 1992. He was buried in Pilgrim Rest Cemetery #2, Golden, Wood Co., Texas.[33]

Children of Rosa Lillie Wright and Archie Aston Hughes:

+ 266 m I. **John Smith⁹ Hughes** was born in Tribbey, Burnett Twp., Pottawatomie Co., Oklahoma, on October 8, 1918. He died in Quinlan, Hunt Co., Texas, on March 7, 1977.[83]

+ 267 f II. **Mary Lillie⁹ Hughes**, was born in Tribbey, Burnett Twp., Pottawatomie Co., Oklahoma, on December 2, 1920. She died in Oklahoma City, Oklahoma Co., Oklahoma, on December 29, 1993.[84]

+ 268 m III. **Henry Aston⁹ Hughes** was born in Tribbey, Burnett Twp., Pottawatomie Co., Oklahoma, on August 1, 1922. He died in Phoenix, Maricopa Co., Arizona, on September 1, 1978.

+ 269 m IV. **Jimmie Lee⁹ Hughes** was born in Oklahoma City, Oklahoma, on December 1, 1924. He died between 1940 and 1977.

+ 270 f V. **Lola Lorene⁹ Hughes** was born in Oklahoma City, Oklahoma, on June 17, 1927. She died in Oklahoma City, Oklahoma, on September 29, 1996.[41]

+ 271 m VI. **Carl Shannon**[9] **Hughes** was born in Oklahoma City, Oklahoma, on April 8, 1929. He died in Bethany, Oklahoma Co., Oklahoma, on March 14, 1981.[85]

+ 272 f VII. **Betty Jene**[9] **Hughes** was born in Oklahoma City, Oklahoma, on March 18, 1931. She died in Odessa, Ector Co., Texas, on December 14, 2005.[86]

+ 273 f VIII. **Ima Jean**[9] **Hughes** was born in Oklahoma City, Oklahoma, in 1932. She died before 2005.

+ 274 f IX. **Dorothy Louise**[9] **Hughes** was born in Oklahoma City, Oklahoma, on May 17, 1936. She died in Oklahoma City, Oklahoma, on July 9, 2000.[87]

+ 275 m X. **Tommie S.**[9] **Hughes** was born in Oklahoma City, Oklahoma, on March 6, 1938. He died in Galveston, Galveston Co., Texas, on March 16, 1952.[82]

+ 276 m XI. **Paul Ray**[9] **Hughes** was born in Golden, Wood Co., Texas, in 1940.

+ 277 m XII. **Robert Vernon**[9] **Hughes** was born in Golden, Wood Co., Texas, on January 6, 1942. He died in Irving, Dallas Co., Texas, on June 27, 2010.[88]

**92. Dedaunia Lucinda Amanda Jane**[8] **Wright** (*Mary Catherine*[7] *McKee, Josiah William*[6]*, Elizabeth*[5]*, Alexander*[A]*, Andrew*[3] *Pegan II, Andrew*[2] *Pagan, James*[1]) was born on November 12, 1898, in Tribbey, Burnett Twp., Pottawatomie Co., Oklahoma. She was also known as **Lucy Jane.** She was the daughter of John Dethridge Wright and Mary Catherine McKee (21). Dedaunia Lucinda Amanda Jane died in Macomb, Burnett Twp., Pottawatomie Co., Oklahoma, on March 1, 1981, at age 82.

Dedaunia Lucinda Amanda Jane married **James William Hickey** on December 3, 1916, in Pottawatomie Co., Oklahoma. They had four children. James William Hickey was born in Burnett Twp., Pottawatomie Co., Oklahoma?, on September 13, 1897. He was also known as **Bud.** James William reached age 76 and died in Macomb, Burnett Twp., Pottawatomie Co., Oklahoma, on December 22, 1973. He was buried in Tecumseh Cemetery, Tecumseh, Brinton Twp., Pottawatomie Co., Oklahoma.[34]

Children of Dedaunia Lucinda Amanda Jane Wright and James William Hickey:

+ 278 f I. **Lucille Willie**[9] **Hickey** was born in Tribbey, Burnett Twp., Pottawatomie Co., Oklahoma, on September 27, 1917. She died in Clearwater, Sedgewick Co., Kansas, on January 2, 2009.[34]

+ 279 f II. **Maudie Mae**[9] **Hickey** was born in Tribbey, Burnett Twp., Pottawatomie Co., Oklahoma, on May 5, 1919. She died in Red Bluff, Tehama Co., California, on May 14, 1998.[89]

+ 280 f III. **Mary Almeda**[9] **Hickey** was born in Tribbey, Burnett Twp., Pottawatomie Co., Oklahoma, on July 13, 1920. She was also known as **Almeda.** Mary Almeda died in Macomb, Burnett Twp., Pottawatomie Co., Oklahoma, on October 17, 1999.[34]

+ 281 m IV. **Arlie Monroe**[9] **Hickey** was born in Tribbey, Burnett Twp., Pottawatomie Co., Oklahoma, on November 20, 1921. He died in Macomb, Burnett Twp., Pottawatomie Co., Oklahoma, on July 20, 2004.[90]

**93. Maemily Ann**[8] **Wright** (*Mary Catherine*[7] *McKee, Josiah William*[6]*, Elizabeth*[5]*, Alexander*[A]*, Andrew*[3] *Pegan II, Andrew*[2] *Pagan, James*[1]) was born on January 16, 1901, in Tribbey, Burnett Twp.,

Pottawatomie Co., Oklahoma. She was also known as **Emma.** She was the daughter of John Dethridge Wright and Mary Catherine McKee (21). Maemily Ann died in Tribbey, Burnett Twp., Pottawatomie Co., Oklahoma, on March 22, 1979, at age 78. She was buried in Tribbey Cemetery, Tribbey, Burnett Twp., Pottawatomie Co., Oklahoma.[14] Buried under the name Emma Wright Johnson.

Maemily Ann married **Jewell A. Berry** on August 29, 1920, in Garvin Co., Oklahoma. They had six children. Jewell A. Berry was born in Tribbey, Burnett Twp., Pottawatomie Co., Oklahoma, on April 13, 1903. Jewell A. reached age 71 and died in Wanette. Eason Twp., Pottawatomie Co., Oklahoma, on June 23, 1974. He was buried in Tribbey, Burnett Twp., Pottawatomie Co., Oklahoma.[14]

Maemily Ann Wright Berry married **Unknown Johnson** after 1974.

Children of Maemily Ann Wright and Jewell A. Berry:

+ 282 m I. **Thurman Andrew**[9] **Berry** was born in Tribbey, Burnett Twp., Pottawatomie Co., Oklahoma, on July 10, 1921. He died in Macomb, Burnett Twp., Pottawatomie Co., Oklahoma, on September 10, 1983.[14]

+ 283 f II. **Opal Ann**[9] **Berry** was born in Tribbey, Burnett Twp., Pottawatomie Co., Oklahoma, on April 1, 1923. She died in Creek Co., Oklahoma, on May 19, 1971.[14]

+ 284 f III. **Hazel**[9] **Berry** was born in Tribbey, Burnett Twp., Pottawatomie Co., Oklahoma, in 1924.

+ 285 m IV. **Joe**[9] **Berry** was born in Tribbey, Burnett Twp., Pottawatomie Co., Oklahoma, on September 12, 1926. He died in Norwalk, Los Angeles Co., California, on March 2, 1979, at age 52. Joe was buried in Tribbey Cemetery, Tribbey, Burnett Twp., Pottawatomie Co., Oklahoma.[14]

+ 286 f V. **Lorene**[9] **Berry** was born in Tribbey, Burnett Twp., Pottawatomie Co., Oklahoma, in 1928.

+ 287 m VI. **Newman**[9] **Berry** was born in Tribbey, Burnett Twp., Pottawatomie Co., Oklahoma, on October 6, 1930. He died in North Las Vegas, Clark Co., Nevada, on September 2, 2004.

94. **Infant Son**[8] **Wright** (*Mary Catherine*[7] *McKee, Josiah William*[6], *Elizabeth*[5], *Alexander*[4], *Andrew*[3] *Pegan II, Andrew*[2] *Pagan, James*[1]) was born on January 5, 1903, in Tribbey, Burnett Twp., Pottawatomie Co., Oklahoma. He was the son of John Dethridge Wright and Mary Catherine McKee (21). Infant Son died in Tribbey, Burnett Twp., Pottawatomie Co., Oklahoma, on January 5, 1903.

95. **Mary Catherine**[8] **Wright** (*Mary Catherine*[7] *McKee, Josiah William*[6], *Elizabeth*[5], *Alexander*[4], *Andrew*[3] *Pegan II, Andrew*[2] *Pagan, James*[1]) was born on July 11, 1904, in Tribbey, Burnett Twp., Pottawatomie Co., Oklahoma. She was the daughter of John Dethridge Wright and Mary Catherine McKee (21). Mary Catherine died in Checotah, McIntosh Co., Oklahoma, on August 7, 1992, at age 88. She was buried in Tribbey Cemetery, Tribbey, Burnett Twp., Pottawatomie Co., Oklahoma.[14]

Mary Catherine married **January Bryan Berry** on November 2, 1923, in McClain Co., Oklahoma. They had three sons. January Bryan Berry was born in Tribbey, Burnett Twp., Pottawatomie Co., Oklahoma, on January 3, 1897. He was also known as **Bryan** and **Jay.** January Bryan reached age 74 and died in Oklahoma City, Oklahoma, on May 22, 1971. He was buried in Tribbey Cemetery, Tribbey, Burnett Twp., Pottawatomie Co., Oklahoma.[14]

Sons of Mary Catherine Wright and January Bryan Berry:

+ 288 m I. **Guy Martin**[9] **Berry** was born in Tribbey, Burnett Twp., Pottawatomie Co., Oklahoma, on November 7, 1924. He died in Oklahoma

City, Oklahoma, on November 3, 2005.[9]

+ 289 m II. **John William**[9] **Berry** was born in Tribbey, Burnett Twp., Pottawatomie Co., Oklahoma, on April 18, 1928. He was also known as **Bill.** John William died in Moore, Cleveland Co., Oklahoma, on March 18, 1991.[14]

+ 290 m III. **Bobby Joe**[9] **Berry** was born in Tribbey, Burnett Twp., Pottawatomie Co., Oklahoma, on September 30, 1932. He died in Eufaula, McIntosh Co., Oklahoma, on May 2, 1995.[91]

96. **John Martin**[8] **Wright** (*Mary Catherine*[7] *McKee, Josiah William*[6], *Elizabeth*[5], *Alexander*[4], *Andrew*[3] *Pegan II, Andrew*[2] *Pagan, James*[1]) was born on August 24, 1907, in Tribbey, Burnett Twp., Pottawatomie Co., Oklahoma. He was the son of John Dethridge Wright and Mary Catherine McKee (21). John Martin died in Shawnee, Rock Creek Twp., Pottawatomie Co., Oklahoma, on January 31, 1984, at age 76. He was buried in Tecumseh Cemetery, Tecumseh, Brinton Twp., Pottawatomie Co., Oklahoma.[34]

John Martin married **Martha Ann James** on June 3, 1930, in Pottawatomie Co., Oklahoma. They had three children. Martha Ann James was born in Beckham Co., Oklahoma, on March 9, 1913. She was also known as **Annie.** Martha Ann reached age 88 and died in Shawnee, Rock Creek Twp., Pottawatomie Co., Oklahoma, on July 10, 2001. She was buried in Tecumseh Cemetery, Tecumseh, Brinton Twp., Pottawatomie Co., Oklahoma.[34]

Children of John Martin Wright and Martha Ann James:

+ 291 m I. **Edward Eugene**[9] **Wright** was born in Tribbey, Burnett Twp., Pottawatomie Co., Oklahoma, on April 30, 1930. He died in Norman, Cleveland Co., Oklahoma, on April 2, 2006.[34]

+ 292 f II. **Wanda Jo**[9] **Wright** was born in Tribbey, Burnett Twp., Pottawatomie Co., Oklahoma, on April 11, 1936.

+ 293 m III. **Terry W.**[9] **Wright** was born in Shawnee, Rock Creek Twp., Pottawatomie Co., Oklahoma, on November 2, 1948. He died in Shawnee, Rock Creek Twp., Pottawatomie Co., Oklahoma, on March 1, 2006.[34]

97. **Sarah Elvara**[8] **Wright** (*Mary Catherine*[7] *McKee, Josiah William*[6], *Elizabeth*[5], *Alexander*[4], *Andrew*[3] *Pegan II Pegan II, Andrew*[2] *Pagan, James*[1]) was born on August 24, 1907, in Tribbey, Burnett Twp., Pottawatomie Co., Oklahoma. She was also known as **Eliz.** She was the daughter of John Dethridge Wright and Mary Catherine McKee (21). Sarah Elvara died in Oklahoma City, Oklahoma, on April 14, 1981, at age 73. She was buried in Tribbey Cemetery, Tribbey, Burnett Twp., Pottawatomie Co., Oklahoma.[14]

Sarah Elvara married **Jack Ellis Bratton** on February 27, 1926, in Pottawatomie Co., Oklahoma. They had two sons. Jack Ellis Bratton was born in Voca, McCulloch Co., Texas, on April 6, 1900. Jack Ellis reached age 59 and died in Oklahoma City, Oklahoma, on November 29, 1959. He was buried in Tribbey Cemetery, Tribbey, Burnett Twp., Pottawatomie Co., Oklahoma.[14]

Sarah Elvara Wright Bratton married **Unknown White** after 1959.

Sons of Sarah Elvara Wright and Jack Ellis Bratton:

+ 294 m I. **Bobbie Stenson**[9] **Bratton** was born in Tribbey, Burnett Twp., Pottawatomie Co., Oklahoma, on December 20, 1926. He died in Oklahoma City, Oklahoma, on April 14, 1981.

+ 295 m II. **Jack Ellis**[9] **Bratton II** was born in Davis, Pottawatomie Co., Oklahoma, on February 26, 1931. He was also known as **Jacky.** Jack Ellis died in Oklahoma City, Oklahoma, on August 7, 1954.[14]

**98. Willis Josiah⁸ Wright** (*Mary Catherine⁷ McKee, Josiah William⁶, Elizabeth⁵, Alexander⁴, Andrew³ Pegan II, Andrew² Pagan, James¹*) was born on September 12, 1910, in Tribbey, Burnett Twp., Pottawatomie Co., Oklahoma. He was the son of John Dethridge Wright and Mary Catherine McKee (21). Willis Josiah died in Newalla, Oklahoma Co., Oklahoma, on September 27, 1974, at age 64. He was buried in Mars Hill Cemetery, St. Louis Twp., Pottawatomie Co., Oklahoma.[35]

Willis Josiah married **Chloe E. Ball** on December 29, 1934, in Pottawatomie Co., Oklahoma. They had four sons. Chloe E. Ball was born in Macomb, Burnett Twp., Pottawatomie Co., Oklahoma, on March 8, 1915. Chloe E. reached age 90 and died in Norman, Cleveland Co., Oklahoma, on February 15, 2006. She was buried in Tecumseh Cemetery, Tecumseh, Brinton Twp., Pottawatomie Co., Oklahoma.[29]

Sons of Willis Josiah Wright and Chloe E. Ball:

+ 296 m I. **Son One⁹ Wright** was born in Tribbey, Burnett Twp., Pottawatomie Co., Oklahoma, on January 5, 1936. He died in Tribbey, Burnett Twp., Pottawatomie Co., Oklahoma, on January 5, 1936.[14]

+ 297 m II. **Charles⁹ Wright** was born in Tribbey, Burnett Twp., Pottawatomie Co., Oklahoma, on March 5, 1937. He died in Tribbey, Burnett Twp., Pottawatomie Co., Oklahoma, on December 9, 1937.[14]

+ 298 m III. **Son Two⁹ Wright** was born in Norman, Cleveland Co., Oklahoma, on September 16, 1941. He died in Norman, Cleveland Co., Oklahoma, on September 16, 1941.[35]

**99. Charles Watson⁸ Wright** (*Mary Catherine⁷ McKee, Josiah William⁶, Elizabeth⁵, Alexander⁴, Andrew³ Pegan II, Andrew² Pagan, James¹*) was born on September 25, 1912, in Tribbey, Burnett Twp., Pottawatomie Co., Oklahoma. He was the son of John Dethridge Wright and Mary Catherine McKee (21). Charles Watson died in Oklahoma City, Oklahoma, on April 28, 1990, at age 77. He was buried in Tecumseh Cemetery, Tecumseh, Brinton Twp., Pottawatomie Co., Oklahoma.[34]

Charles Watson married **Loretta Knowles** on May 29, 1943, in Washoe Co., Nevada. They had one daughter. Loretta Knowles was born in Maud, Seminole Co., Oklahoma, on June 29, 1918. Loretta reached age 31 and died in Maywood, Los Angeles Co., California, on March 19, 1950. She was buried in Cummings Cemetery, Maud, Pottawatomie Co., Oklahoma.[92]

Charles Watson Wright married **Fannie Juanita Robinson** after 1950. Fannie Juanita Robinson was born in Tribbey, Burnett Twp., Pottawatomie Co., Oklahoma, on June 27, 1919. Fannie Juanita reached age 77 and died in Crescent Twp., Logan Co., Oklahoma, on June 5, 1997. She was buried in Tecumseh Cemetery, Tecumseh, Brinton Twp., Pottawatomie Co., Oklahoma.[34]

Daughter of Charles Watson Wright and Loretta Knowles:

+ 299 f I. **Loretta Charlene⁹ Wright** was born in Bell, Los Angeles Co., California, on April 9, 1945. She was also known as **Charlee Angel.** Loretta Charlene died in Springfield, Lane Co., Oregon, on April 5, 2007.

**100. Violet Roberta⁸ Wright** (*Mary Catherine⁷ McKee, Josiah William⁶, Elizabeth⁵, Alexander⁴, Andrew³ Pegan II, Andrew² Pagan, James¹*) was born on January 30, 1915, in Tribbey, Burnett Twp., Pottawatomie Co., Oklahoma. She was the daughter of John Dethridge Wright and Mary Catherine McKee (21). Violet Roberta died in Sun City, Riverside Co., California, on October 29, 1992, at age 77. She was buried in Desert Lawn Memorial Park Cemetery, Calimesa, Riverside Co., California.[36]

Violet Roberta married **Frank Kermit Thompson** on June 16, 1934, in Pottawatomie Co., Oklahoma. They had one son. Frank Kermit Thompson was born in Tecumseh, Brinton Twp., Pottawatomie Co., Oklahoma, on June 11, 1908. Frank Kermit reached age 91 and died in Tecumseh, Brinton Twp., Pottawatomie Co., Oklahoma, on July 31, 1999. He was buried in Council Creek Cemetery, Tribbey Twp., Pottawatomie Co., Oklahoma.[93]

Son of Violet Roberta Wright and Frank Kermit Thompson:

+ 300 m I. **Ray**[9] **Thompson** was born in Arkansas in 1934.

101. **Grace Aston**[8] **Wright** (*Mary Catherine*[7] *McKee, Josiah William*[6], *Elizabeth*[5], *Alexander*[4], *Andrew*[3] *Pegan II, Andrew*[2] *Pagan, James*[1]) was born on February 4, 1917, in Tribbey, Burnett Twp., Pottawatomie Co., Oklahoma. She was the daughter of John Dethridge Wright and Mary Catherine McKee (21). Grace Aston died under the name Grace A. Mooney in Eufala, McIntosh Co., Oklahoma, on November 15, 2007, at age 90.

May have been childless.

Grace Aston married **James Edward Byrd** on July 16, 1935, in Carter Co., Oklahoma. They divorced. James Edward Byrd was born in Wellborn, Conway Co., Arkansas, on July 30, 1915. James Edward reached age 54 and died in Ada, Pontotoc Co., Oklahoma, on November 15, 1969. He was buried in Valliant Cemetery, Valliant, McCurtain Co., Oklahoma.

Grace Aston Wright Byrd married **Albert Turner** before 1959.

Grace Aston Wright Byrd Turner married **Edward John O'Connell** on March 25, 1959, in Clark Co., Nevada. They divorced. Edward John O'Connell was born in Brooklyn, Kings Co., New York?, on January 24, 1913. Edward John reached age 93 and died in Phoenix, Maricopa Co., Arizona, on February 18, 2006.

Grace Aston Wright Byrd Turner O'Connell married **Unknown Mooney** in 1976.

102. **John Dethridge**[8] **Wright II** (*Mary Catherine*[7] *McKee, Josiah William*[6], *Elizabeth*[5], *Alexander*[4], *Andrew*[3] *Pegan II, Andrew*[2] *Pagan, James*[1]) was born on July 10, 1921, in Tribbey, Burnett Twp., Pottawatomie Co., Oklahoma. He was also known as **J.D..** He was the son of John Dethridge Wright and Mary Catherine McKee (21). John Dethridge died in Shawnee, Rock Creek Twp., Pottawatomie Co., Oklahoma, on January 25, 1992, at age 70. He was buried in Tecumseh Cemetery, Tecumseh, Brinton Twp., Pottawatomie Co., Oklahoma.[34]

John Dethridge married **Helen Ora White** on December 28, 1946. They had two sons. Helen Ora White was born in Shawnee, Rock Creek Twp., Pottawatomie Co., Oklahoma, on October 5, 1922. Helen Ora reached age 78 and died in Tecumseh, Brinton Twp., Pottawatomie Co., Oklahoma, on May 3, 2001. She was buried in Tecumseh Cemetery, Tecumseh, Brinton Twp., Pottawatomie Co., Oklahoma.[34]

103. **Martha Louisa Jane**[8] **McKee** (*Charles Watson*[7], *Josiah William*[6], *Elizabeth*[5], *Alexander*[4], *Andrew*[3], *Andrew*[2] *Pagan, James*[1]) was born on September 21, 1907, in Brady Twp., Garvin Co., Oklahoma. She was also known as **Louisa.** She was the daughter of Charles Watson McKee (22) and Allie Lucine Rials. Martha Louisa Jane died in Lamesa, Dawson Co., Texas, on December 19, 1993, at age 86. She was buried in Lamesa Memorial Park Cemetery, Lamesa, Dawson Co., Texas.[37]

Martha Louisa Jane married **Charlie Frank Raines** on December 19, 1922, in Cooke Co., Texas. They had four sons. Charlie Frank Raines was born in Brady Twp, Garvin Co., Oklahoma, on March 9, 1901. Charlie Frank reached age 80 and died in Lamesa, Dawson Co., Texas, on January 18, 1982. He was buried in Lamesa Memorial Park Cemetery, Lamesa, Dawson Co., Texas.[37]

Sons of Martha Louisa Jane McKee and Charlie Frank Raines:

+ 301 m I. **Herschel Edwin**[9] **Raines** was born in Elmore Twp., Garvin Co.,

Oklahoma, on January 17, 1924. He died in Lamesa, Dawson Co., Texas, on March 1, 2009.[94]

+ 302 m II. **Jewel Paul⁹ Raines** was born in Elmore Twp., Garvin Co., Oklahoma, on March 28, 1928. He was also known as **Paul.** Jewel Paul died in Hico, Hamilton Co., Texas, on June 16, 2002.[95]

+ 303 m III. **Herman Thomas⁹ Raines** was born in Elmore Twp., Garvin Co., Oklahoma, on October 12, 1930. He died in Lubbock, Lubbock Co., Texas, on August 23, 1990.[37]

+ 304 m IV. **Thurman Adolphus⁹ Raines** was born in Elmore Twp., Garvin Co., Oklahoma, on November 6, 1935. He died in Lamesa, Dawson Co., Texas, on January 8, 2009.[37]

**104. Albert Milton⁸ McKee** (*Charles Watson⁷, Josiah William⁶, Elizabeth⁵, Alexander⁴, Andrew³ Pegan II, Andrew² Pagan, James¹*) was born on June 16, 1909, in Brady Twp., Garvin Co., Oklahoma. He was the son of Charles Watson McKee (22) and Allie Lucine Rials. Albert Milton lived in 1940 in Sylvester, Fisher Co., Texas. He died in Fort Worth, Tarrant Co., Texas, on December 12, 1994, at age 85. Albert Milton was buried in Emerald Hills Cemetery, Kennedale, Tarrant Co., Texas.[38]

Albert Milton married **Bessie Mae Steele** on January 26, 1929, in Garvin Co., Oklahoma. They had four children. Bessie Mae Steele was born in Gowan Twp. Lattimer Co., Oklahoma, on August 27, 1912. Bessie Mae reached age 88 and died in Fort Worth, Tarrant Co., Texas, on July 23, 2001. She was buried in Emerald Hills Cemetery, Kennedale, Tarrant Co., Texas.[38]

Children of Albert Milton McKee and Bessie Mae Steele:

+ 305 f I. **Geraldine Faye⁹ McKee** was born in Garvin Co., Oklahoma, on November 28, 1932. She was also known as **Geri.** Geraldine Faye died in Everman, Tarrant Co., Texas, on December 16, 2011.[96]

+ 306 f II. **Nadine J.⁹ McKee** was born in Garvin Co., Oklahoma, on August 10, 1934.

+ 307 m III. **Charles F.⁹ McKee** was born in Garvin Co., Oklahoma, on February 23, 1936.

+ 308 f IV. **Ouida Gale⁹ McKee** was born in Ardmore, Morgan Twp., Carter Co., Oklahoma, on November 18, 1939. She was also known as **Mimi.** Ouida Gale died in Dallas, Dallas Co., Texas, on February 26, 2005.[39]

**105. Mary Katherine⁸ McKee** (*Charles Watson⁷, Josiah William⁶, Elizabeth⁵, Alexander⁴, Andrew³ Pegan II, Andrew² Pagan, James¹*) was born on May 18, 1912, in Brady Twp., Garvin Co., Oklahoma. She was also known as **Catherine.** She was the daughter of Charles Watson McKee (22) and Allie Lucine Rials. Mary Katherine died in Lamont, Kern Co., California, on January 8, 1996, at age 83.

Mary Katherine married **James Gordon Brown** on October 23, 1927. They had six children. James Gordon Brown was born in Paint Rock, Jackson Co., Alabama?, on December 21, 1906. James Gordon reached age 85 and died in Lamont, Kern Co., California, on June 8, 1992.

Children of Mary Katherine McKee and James Gordon Brown:

+ 309 f I. **Lois Ellen⁹ Brown** was born in Lindsay, Lindsay Twp., Garvin Co., Oklahoma, on September 23, 1929. She died in Porterville, Tulare Co., California, on February 17, 2006.[27]

+ 310 m II. **James Kenneth⁹ Brown** was born in Elmore City, Elmore Twp.,

Garvin Co., Oklahoma, on August 27, 1931. He died in Madison, Dane Co., Wisconsin, on March 18, 2002.[97]

+ 311 m IV. **Earl Edwin⁹ Brown** was born on September 22, 1933 in Elmore City, Elmore Twp., Garvin Co., Oklahoma. He died on December 5, 2016 in Rialto, San Bernardino Co., California?[61]

+ 312 m V. **Burl D.⁹ Brown** was born on March 18, 1937, in Elmore City, Elmore Twp., Garvin Co., Oklahoma.

+ 313 f III. **Lela Faye⁹ Brown** was born in Elmore City, Elmore Twp., Garvin Co., Oklahoma, on September 1, 1941. She died in Sanger, Fresno Co., California, on March 27, 2011.[98]

106. **Samuel Robert⁸ McKee** (*Charles Watson⁷, Josiah William⁶, Elizabeth⁵, Alexander⁴, Andrew³ Pegan II, Andrew² Pagan, James¹*) was born on July 6, 1915, in Brady Twp., Garvin Co., Oklahoma. He was the son of Charles Watson McKee (22) and Allie Lucine Rials. Samuel Robert died in Fort Worth, Tarrant Co., Texas, on December 19, 1982, at age 67. He was buried in Newman Cemetery, Sylvester, Fisher Co., Texas.[10] Samuel Robert and Martha Rose McKee McKee were double first cousins.

Samuel Robert married **Martha Rosa McKee** about 1940. They had four children. Martha Rosa McKee was born in Brady Twp., Garvin Co., Oklahoma, on March 14, 1916. She was also known as **Rosa.** Martha Rosa lived in Hobbs, Lea Co., New Mexico. Martha Rosa reached age 88 and died in a hospital in Lubbock, Lubbock Co., Texas, on April 17, 2004. She was buried in Newman Cemetery, Sylvester, Fisher Co., Texas.[10]

Samuel Robert and Martha Rose McKee McKee were double first cousins. She was the daughter of Oliver Edwin McKee (23) and Addie Laverne Rials.

Samuel Robert McKee and Martha Rosa McKee had four children, including:

+ 314 f I. **Doris⁹ McKee** was born in Eskota, Nolan Co., Texas, in 1940.

+ 315 m III. **Ralph Wayne⁹ McKee** was born in Eskota, Nolan Co., Texas, on November 18, 1946. He died in Sweetwater, Nolan Co., Texas, on December 15, 1946.[10]

107. **Earnest L.⁸ McKee** (*Charles Watson⁷, Josiah William⁶, Elizabeth⁵, Alexander⁴, Andrew³ Pegan II, Andrew² Pagan, James¹*) was born on March 5, 1923, in Brady Twp., Garvin Co., Oklahoma. He was the son of Charles Watson McKee (22) and Allie Lucine Rials. Earnest L. died in Castroville, Medina Co., Texas, on January 10, 2013, at age 89. He was buried in Castroville Community Cemetery, Castroville, Medina Co., Texas.[39]

Earnest L. married **Opal Ray Bullion** on February 7, 1944. They had three children. Opal Ray Bullion was born in Oak Hill, Fayette Co., West Virginia, on June 10, 1930. Opal Ray reached age 85 and died in San Antonio, Bexar Co., Texas, on August 10, 2015. She was buried in Castroville Community Cemetery, Castroville, Medina Co., Texas.[39]

Earnest L. McKee and Opal Ray Bullion had three children, including:

+ 316 f III. **Carol⁹ McKee** was born after 1940. Carol died before 2013.

108. **Samuel Robert⁸ McKee** (*Oliver Edwin⁷, Josiah William⁶, Elizabeth⁵, Alexander⁴, Andrew³ Pegan II, Andrew² Pagan, James¹*) was born on March 15, 1909, in Brady Twp., Garvin Co., Oklahoma. He was the son of Oliver Edwin McKee (23) and Addie Laverne Rials. Samuel Robert died in Brady Twp., Garvin Co., Oklahoma, on January 27, 1910. He was buried in Katie City Cemetery, Katie, Brady Twp., Garvin Co., Oklahoma.[9]

109. **James Harvey⁸ McKee** (*Oliver Edwin⁷, Josiah William⁶, Elizabeth⁵, Alexander⁴, Andrew³ Pegan II, Andrew² Pagan, James¹*) was born on August

21, 1911, in Brady Twp., Garvin Co., Oklahoma. He was also known as **Harvey.** He was the son of Oliver Edwin McKee (23) and Addie Laverne Rials. James Harvey died in Abilene, Taylor Co., Texas, on December 13, 1977, at age 66. He was buried in Newman Cemetery, Sylvester, Fisher Co., Texas.[9]

James Harvey McKee married **Zoal Dee Thompson.** They divorced. They had three children. Zoal Dee Thompson was born in Paul's Valley, Whitebead Twp., Garvin Co., Oklahoma, on September 8, 1922. She lived in 1988 in Ardmore, Morgan Twp., Carter Co., Oklahoma. Zoal Dee reached age 75 and died in a hospital in Duncan, Stephens Co., Oklahoma, on March 4, 1998. She was buried in Mount Olivet Cemetery, Paul's Valley, Whitebead Twp., Garvin Co., Oklahoma.[99]

James Harvey married **Mary Unknown** before 1977.

110. **Martha Rosa**[8] **McKee** (*Oliver Edwin*[7], *Josiah William*[6], *Elizabeth*[5], *Alexander*[4], *Andrew*[3] *Pegan II*, *Andrew*[2] *Pagan*, *James*[1]) was born on March 14, 1916, in Brady Twp., Garvin Co., Oklahoma. She was also known as **Rosa.** She was the daughter of Oliver Edwin McKee (23) and Addie Laverne Rials. Martha Rosa lived in Hobbs, Lea Co., New Mexico. She died in a hospital in Lubbock, Lubbock Co., Texas, on April 17, 2004, at age 88. Martha Rosa was buried in Newman Cemetery, Sylvester, Fisher Co., Texas.[10]

Martha Rosa married **Billy B. Neal** on March 6, 1938, in Garvin Co., Oklahoma. They divorced. Billy B. Neal was born in Chickasha, Chickasha Twp., Grady Co., Oklahoma, on August 15, 1908. He reached age 70 and died in Elmore City, Elmore Twp., Garvin Co., Oklahoma, on December 27, 1978. Billy B. was buried in Elmore City Cemetery, Elmore City, Elmore Twp., Garvin Co., Oklahoma.[42]

Martha Rosa McKee Neal married **Samuel Robert McKee** about 1940. They had four children. Samuel Robert McKee was born in Brady Twp., Garvin Co., Oklahoma, on July 6, 1915. Samuel

Robert reached age 67 and died in Fort Worth, Tarrant Co., Texas, on December 19, 1982.

Samuel Robert and Martha Rose McKee McKee were double first cousins. He was the son of Charles Watson McKee (22) and Allie Lucine Rials.

Children of Martha Rosa McKee and Samuel Robert McKee:

+ 314 f I. **Doris**[9] **McKee** was born in Eskota, Nolan Co., Texas, in 1940.

+ 315 m III. **Ralph Wayne**[9] **McKee** was born in Eskota, Nolan Co., Texas, on November 18, 1946. He died in Sweetwater, Nolan Co., Texas, on December 15, 1946.[10]

111. **Meranda Ethel**[8] **McKee** (*Oliver Edwin*[7], *Josiah William*[6], *Elizabeth*[5], *Alexander*[4], *Andrew*[3] *Pegan II*, *Andrew*[2] *Pagan*, *James*[1]) was born on August 7, 1918, in Brady Twp., Garvin Co., Oklahoma. She was also known as **Ethel.** She was the daughter of Oliver Edwin McKee (23) and Addie Laverne Rials. Meranda Ethel died in Norman, Norman Twp., Cleveland Co., Oklahoma, on March 23, 2004, at age 85. She was buried in Lakeview Cemetery, Marietta, Love Co., Oklahoma.[40] Buried under the name Ethel Bradley.

Meranda Ethel married **Ollie Bradley** in December 1934. They divorced about 1940. They had five children. Ollie Bradley was born in Washington Twp., Love Co., Oklahoma, on January 7, 1906. He reached age 61 and died in Marietta, Love Co., Oklahoma, on July 17, 1967. Ollie was buried in Lakeview Cemetery, Marietta, Love Co., Oklahoma.[40]

Meranda Ethel McKee Bradley married **Wayne Dillingham** on December 18, 1969, in Cooke Co., Texas. They divorced. Wayne Dillingham was born in Elmore Twp., Garvin Co., Oklahoma, on April 14, 1907. Wayne reached age 83 and died in Marietta, Love Co., Oklahoma, on October 30, 1990. He was buried in Lakeview Cemetery, Marietta, Love Co., Oklahoma.[35]

Meranda Ethel McKee and Ollie Bradley had five children, including:

+ 317 f I. **LaJune⁹ Bradley** was born in Elmore Twp., Garvin Co., Oklahoma, on January 15, 1937. She died in Elmore Twp., Garvin Co., Oklahoma, on January 15, 1937.[9]

**112. William Everett⁸ McKee** (*Oliver Edwin⁷, Josiah William⁶, Elizabeth⁵, Alexander⁴, Andrew³ Pegan II, Andrew² Pagan, James¹*) was born on March 12, 1921, in Brady Twp., Garvin Co., Oklahoma. He was also known as **Everett.** He was the son of Oliver Edwin McKee (23) and Addie Laverne Rials. William Everett died in Lovington, Lea Co., New Mexico, on December 7, 2000, at age 79. He was buried in Newman Cemetery, Sylvester, Fisher Co., Texas.[10]

William Everett married **Isadora Rials** on October 23, 1941, in Nolan Co., Texas. They had two daughters. Isadora Rials was born in Clay Co., Texas, on November 27, 1926. Isadora reached age 57 and died in Fort Worth, Tarrant Co., Texas, on April 28, 1984. She was buried in Newman Cemetery, Sylvester, Fisher Co., Texas.[10] Isadora Rials was William Everett McKee's first cousin.

Daughters of William Everett McKee and Isadora Rials:

+ 318 f I. **Sandra Arlene⁹ McKee** was born in Merkel, Taylor Co., Texas, on July 21, 1946. She died in Lovington, Lea Co., New Mexico, on November 24, 2009.[55]

+ 319 f II. **Janice Yvonne⁹ McKee** was born in Merkel, Taylor Co., Texas, on December 1, 1944. She died in Lubbock, Lubbock Co., Texas, on October 22, 1997.

**113. Lee Roy⁸ McKee** (*Oliver Edwin⁷, Josiah William⁶, Elizabeth⁵, Alexander⁴, Andrew³ Pegan II, Andrew² Pagan, James¹*) was born on June 19, 1924, in Brady Twp., Garvin Co., Oklahoma. He was the son of Oliver Edwin McKee (23) and Addie

Laverne Rials. Lee Roy died in Everett, Snohomish Co., Washington, on August 16, 1962, at age 38.

Lee Roy married **Carmen Marcia Brannan** on July 12, 1947, in Nolan Co., Texas. They had two sons. Carmen Marcia Brannan was born in Earlimart, Tulare Co., California, on June 14, 1932. Carmen Marcia reached age 66 and died in Sweetwater, Nolan Co., Texas, on May 30, 1999. Died under the name Carmen Marcia Taylor.

Roy McKee and Carmen Marcia Brannan had two sons, including:

+ 320 m I. **Alvin Edward⁹ McKee** was born in Nolan Co., Texas, on November 15, 1949. He died in Snohomish Co., Washington, on August 16, 1962.

**114. Mildred⁸ McKee** (*Oliver Edwin⁷, Josiah William⁶, Elizabeth⁵, Alexander⁴, Andrew³ Pegan II, Andrew² Pagan, James¹*) was born on November 13, 1926, in Brady Twp., Garvin Co., Oklahoma. She is the daughter of Oliver Edwin McKee (23) and Addie Laverne Rials.

Mildred married **Armous Milburn Downey** after 1940. They had one daughter. Armous Milburn Downey was born in Robberson, Elmore Twp., Garvin Co., Oklahoma, on March 28, 1925. He was also known as **Mib.** Armous Milburn reached age 81 and died in Ratliff City, Graham Twp., Carter Co., Oklahoma, on November 17, 2006. He was buried in Foster Cemetery, Foster, Elmore Twp., Garvin Co., Oklahoma.[100]

**115. Sara Louise⁸ McKee** (*Oliver Edwin⁷, Josiah William⁶, Elizabeth⁵, Alexander⁴, Andrew³ Pegan II, Andrew² Pagan, James¹*) was born on February 16, 1929, in Brady Twp., Garvin Co., Oklahoma. She was the daughter of Oliver Edwin McKee (23) and Addie Laverne Rials. Sara Louise died in Fort Worth, Tarrant Co., Texas, on January 31, 1988, at age 58. She was buried in Newman Cemetery, Sylvester, Fisher Co., Texas.[10]

Sara Louise married **George Junior Murphy II** on September 2, 1944, in Love Co., Oklahoma. They had four children. George Junior Murphy II was born in Monticello, Monticello Twp., Piatt Co.,

Illinois, on September 27, 1918. George Junior lived in 1996 in Seattle, King Co., Washington. He reached age 77 and died in Belleview, Clallam Co., Washington, on September 24, 1996. George Junior was buried in Willamette National Cemetery, Portland, Multnomah Co., Oregon.[101]

Sara Louise McKee and George Junior Murphy II had four children, including:

+ 321 m  I.  **George Arthur⁹ Murphy III** was born in Auburn, King Co., Washington, on October 4, 1946. He died in Cottage Grove, Lane Co., Oregon, on September 24, 1995.

+ 322 f  II.  **Carol Anne Murphy** was born in Sweetwater, Nolan Co., Texas, on August 18, 1947. She died in Roseburg, Douglas Co., Oregon, on March 14, 1991.[102]

116. **Mamie Jo⁸ McKee** (*Oliver Edwin⁷, Josiah William⁶, Elizabeth⁵, Alexander⁴, Andrew³ Pegan II, Andrew² Pagan, James¹*) was born on March 14, 1934, in Brady Twp., Garvin Co., Oklahoma. She was the daughter of Oliver Edwin McKee (23) and Addie Laverne Rials. Mamie Jo lived in 2000 in Laureldale, Berks Co., Pennsylvania. She died in West Reading, Berks Co., Pennsylvania, on March 25, 2002, at age 68.

She married **Mr. Gerhart.**

117. **James Irwin⁸ Riley** (*Rosa Lily⁷ McKee, Josiah William⁶, Elizabeth⁵, Alexander⁴, Andrew³ Pegan II, Andrew² Pagan, James¹*) was born on May 25, 1906, in Brady Twp., Garvin Co., Oklahoma. He was the son of William Henry Riley and Rosa Lily McKee (24). James Irwin died in Oklahoma City, Oklahoma, on August 12, 1978, at age 72. He was buried in Sunny Lane Cemetery, Del City, Oklahoma Co., Oklahoma.[41]

James Irwin married **Ethel M. Skaggs** on September 6, 1927, in Carter Co., Oklahoma. They had two children. Ethel M. Skaggs was born in Elmore City, Elmore Twp., Garvin Co., Oklahoma, on January 10, 1908. Ethel M. reached age 93 and

died in Oklahoma City, Oklahoma, on July 15, 2001. She was buried in Sunny Lane Cemetery, Del City, Oklahoma Co., Oklahoma.[41]

Children of James Irwin Riley and Ethel M. Skaggs:

+ 323 m  I.  **Jimmy K.⁹ Riley** was born in Elmore City, Elmore Twp., Garvin Co., Oklahoma, in 1934.

+ 324 f  II.  **Patricia Charline⁹ Riley II** was born in Grady Co., Oklahoma, on May 17, 1936. Patricia Charline died on May 17, 1936 in Grady Co., Oklahoma.[41]

118. **Isaac Edwin⁸ Riley** (*Rosa Lily⁷ McKee, Josiah William⁶, Elizabeth⁵, Alexander⁴, Andrew³ Pegan II, Andrew² Pagan, James¹*) was born on December 14, 1907, in Brady Twp., Garvin Co., Oklahoma. He was the son of William Henry Riley and Rosa Lily McKee (24). Isaac Edwin died in Oklahoma City, Oklahoma, on November 11, 1993, age 85. He was buried in Katie City Cemetery, Katie, Brady Twp., Garvin Co., Oklahoma.[9]

Isaac Edwin married **Stella Dunn Moore** on November 12, 1930, in Carter Co., Oklahoma. They had one daughter. Stella Dunn Moore was born in Foster Twp., Garvin Co., Oklahoma, on January 25, 1910. Stella Dunn reached age 78 and died in Oklahoma City, Oklahoma, on August 8, 1988. She was buried in Katie City Cemetery, Katie, Brady Twp., Garvin Co., Oklahoma.[9]

Daughter of Isaac Edwin Riley and Stella Dunn Moore:

+ 325 f  I.  **Elsie Fay⁹ Riley** was born in Brady Twp., Garvin Co., Oklahoma, in 1933.

119. **Roberta Mae⁸ Riley** (*Rosa Lily⁷ McKee, Josiah William⁶, Elizabeth⁵, Alexander⁴, Andrew³ Pegan II, Andrew² Pagan, James¹*) was born on June 26, 1910, in Brady Twp., Garvin Co., Oklahoma. She was the daughter of William Henry Riley and Rosa Lily McKee (24). Roberta Mae died in Wynnewood, Brady Twp., Garvin Co., Oklahoma, on July 21, 2003, at age 93. She was buried in Elmore City

Cemetery, Elmore City, Elmore Twp., Garvin Co., Oklahoma.[42]

Roberta Mae married **Ruben Melton Dutton** on July 18, 1928, in Garvin Co., Oklahoma. They had two children. Ruben Melton Dutton was born in Lindsay Twp., Garvin Co., Oklahoma, on October 17, 1907. Ruben Melton reached age 76 and died in Oklahoma City, Oklahoma, on October 26, 1983. He was buried in Elmore City Cemetery, Elmore City, Elmore Twp., Garvin Co., Oklahoma.[42]

Children of Roberta Mae Riley and Ruben Melton Dutton:

+ 326 f I. **Ida Mae⁹ Dutton** was born in Brady Twp., Garvin Co., Oklahoma, on June 21, 1929. She died in Moore, Cleveland Co., Oklahoma, on May 16, 2002.[42]

+ 327 m II. **Jerry Duane⁹ Dutton** was born in Brady Twp., Garvin Co., Oklahoma, in 1938.

120. **Child One⁸ Tindle** (*Nancy Angeoline⁷ McKee, Jasper Ervin⁶, Elizabeth⁵, Alexander⁴, Andrew³ Pegan II, Andrew² Pagan, James¹*) was born between 1888 and 1900 in Burr Oak Twp., Doniphan Co., Kansas. He or she was a child of Washington Scott Tindle and Nancy Angeoline McKee (29). Child One died in Burr Oak Twp., Doniphan Co., Kansas, between 1888 and 1900.

121. **Child Two⁸ Tindle** (*Nancy Angeoline⁷ McKee, Jasper Ervin⁶, Elizabeth⁵, Alexander⁴, Andrew³ Pegan II, Andrew² Pagan, James¹*) was born between 1888 and 1900 in Burr Oak Twp., Doniphan Co., Kansas. He or she was a child of Washington Scott Tindle and Nancy Angeoline McKee (29). Child Two died in Burr Oak Twp., Doniphan Co., Kansas, before 1900.

122. **Martin Van Buren⁸ Tindle** (*Nancy Angeoline⁷ McKee, Jasper Ervin⁶, Elizabeth⁵, Alexander⁴, Andrew³ Pegan II, Andrew² Pagan, James¹*) was born between 1888 and 1900 in Burr Oak Twp., Doniphan Co., Kansas. He was the son of Washington Scott Tindle and Nancy Angeoline McKee (29). Martin Van Buren died in Burr Oak Twp., Doniphan Co., Kansas, before 1900.

123. **Louis or Lewis Oliver⁸ Tindle** (*Nancy Angeoline⁷ McKee, Jasper Ervin⁶, Elizabeth⁵, Alexander⁴, Andrew³ Pegan II, Andrew² Pagan, James¹*) was born on April 30, 1891, in Burr Oak Twp., Doniphan Co., Kansas. He was the son of Washington Scott Tindle and Nancy Angeoline McKee (29). Louis or Lewis Oliver died in Los Angeles, Los Angeles Co., California, on January 6, 1974, at age 82.

Lewis Oliver Tindle preferred to spell his given name, "Louis".

He married **Sarah Unknown.** She is also known as **Sadie.**

124. **Lula Mae⁸ Tindle** (*Nancy Angeoline⁷ McKee, Jasper Ervin⁶, Elizabeth⁵, Alexander⁴, Andrew³ Pegan II, Andrew² Pagan, James¹*) was born on September 17, 1893, in Burr Oak Twp., Doniphan Co., Kansas. She was the daughter of Washington Scott Tindle and Nancy Angeoline McKee (29). Lula Mae died after 1910.

Never married.

125. **James Ervin⁸ Tindle** (*Nancy Angeoline⁷ McKee, Jasper Ervin⁶, Elizabeth⁵, Alexander⁴, Andrew³ Pegan II, Andrew² Pagan, James¹*) was born on November 19, 1894, in Burr Oak Twp., Doniphan Co., Kansas. He was the son of Washington Scott Tindle and Nancy Angeoline McKee (29). James Ervin died in Valley Falls, Jefferson Co., Kansas, on November 11, 1970, at age 75. He was buried in Ft. Leavenworth National Military Cemetery, Leavenworth, Leavenworth Twp., Leavenworth Co., Kansas.[43]

Probably childless.

He married **Unknown Unknown.** They divorced.

126. **Frank Scott⁸ Tindle** (*Nancy Angeoline⁷ McKee, Jasper Ervin⁶, Elizabeth⁵, Alexander⁴, Andrew³ Pegan II, Andrew² Pagan, James¹*) was born on July 15, 1896, in Burr Oak Twp., Doniphan Co., Kansas. He was the son of Washington Scott Tindle and Nancy Angeoline McKee (29). Frank Scott died in Kansas City, Jackson Co., Missouri, in August 1970 at age 74. He was buried in Elmwood Cemetery, Kansas City, Jackson Co., Missouri.[44]

He married **Anna Morris.** They had two children. Anna Morris was born in Missouri in 1896. Anna died after 1920.

Children of Frank Scott Tindle and Anna Morris:

+ 328 f I.     **Lillis Louise⁹ Tindle** was born in St. Joseph, Buchanan Co., Missouri, in 1916.

+ 329 m II.   **Dale Ervin⁹ Tindle** was born in St. Joseph, Buchanan Co., Missouri, on July 22, 1918. He died in Kansas City, Jackson Co., Missouri, on February 3, 2001.[103]

127. **Charles William⁸ Tindle** (*Nancy Angeoline⁷ McKee, Jasper Ervin⁶, Elizabeth⁵, Alexander⁴, Andrew³ Pegan II, Andrew² Pagan, James¹*) was born on January 29, 1898, in Burr Oak Twp., Doniphan Co., Kansas. He was the son of Washington Scott Tindle and Nancy Angeoline McKee (29). Charles William died in St. Joseph, Buchanan Co., Missouri, in February 1970 at age 72.

Charles William married **Pauline Unknown** in 1940 in Buchanan Co., Missouri.

128. **Rosa L.⁸ Tindle** (*Nancy Angeoline⁷ McKee, Jasper Ervin⁶, Elizabeth⁵, Alexander⁴, Andrew³ Pegan II, Andrew² Pagan, James¹*) was born on November 30, 1899, in Burr Oak Twp., Doniphan Co., Kansas. She was also known as **Rose.** She was the daughter of Washington Scott Tindle and Nancy Angeoline McKee (29). Rosa L. died in St. Joseph, Buchanan Co., Missouri, in January 1986 at age 86. She was buried in Saint Joseph Memorial Park Cemetery, St. Joseph, Buchanan Co., Missouri.[45]

She married **George Leroy Painter.** They had two sons. George Leroy Painter was born in Whiting, Whiting Twp., Jackson Co., Kansas?, on May 23, 1899. George Leroy reached age 72 and died in St. Joseph, Buchanan Co., Missouri, in December 1971. He was buried in Saint Joseph Memorial Park Cemetery, St. Joseph, Buchanan Co., Missouri.[45]

Sons of Rosa L. Tindle and George Leroy Painter:

+ 330 m I.     **Charles Leroy⁹ Painter** was born in Industrial City, Washington Twp., Buchanan Co., Missouri, in 1923.

+ 331 m II.   **Donald R.⁹ Painter** was born in Industrial City, Washington Twp., Buchanan Co., Missouri, in 1926.

129. **Daisey Viola⁸ Tindle** (*Nancy Angeoline⁷ McKee, Jasper Ervin⁶, Elizabeth⁵, Alexander⁴, Andrew³ Pegan II, Andrew² Pagan, James¹*) was born on November 9, 1901, in Burr Oak Twp., Doniphan Co., Kansas. She was the daughter of Washington Scott Tindle and Nancy Angeoline McKee (29). Daisey Viola died in Pattonsburg, Benton Twp., Daviess Co., Missouri, on December 7, 1965, at age 64. She was buried in Pattonsburg Memorial Gardens Cemetery, Pattonsburg, Benton Twp., Daviess Co., Misssouri.[46]

Daisey Viola married **Clyde Newman** before 1919. They had one daughter. Clyde Newman was born in Albany, Gentry Co., Missouri, on March 25, 1894. Clyde reached age 78 and died in Pattonsburg, Benton Twp., Daviess Co., Missouri, on October 20, 1972. He was buried in Pattonsburg Memorial Gardens Cemetery, Pattonsburg, Benton Twp., Daviess Co., Misssouri.[46]

Daughter of Daisey Viola Tindle and Clyde Newman:

+ 332 f I.     **Rosa Mae⁹ Newman** was born in Pattonsburg, Benton Twp., Daviess Co., Missouri, in 1919. She died in Pattonsburg, Benton Twp., Daviess Co., Missouri, in 1974.[46]

130. **Child Three⁸ Tindle** (*Nancy Angeoline⁷ McKee, Jasper Ervin⁶, Elizabeth⁵, Alexander⁴, Andrew³ Pegan II, Andrew² Pagan, James¹*) was born between 1900 and 1910 in Burr Oak Twp., Doniphan Co., Kansas. He or she was a child of Washington Scott Tindle and Nancy Angeoline McKee (29). Child Three died in Burr Oak Twp., Doniphan Co., Kansas, between 1900 and 1910.

131. **William M.⁸ Richter II** (*Cora Alvertie⁷ McKee, William Henry Harrison⁶, Elizabeth⁵, Alexander⁴,*

*Andrew³ Pegan II, Andrew² Pagan, James¹*) was born in 1900 in St. Joseph, Washington Twp., Buchanan Co., Missouri. He was the son of William Richter and Cora Alvertie McKee (35). William M. died after 1920.

132. **Melvin Byron⁸ Richter** (*Cora Alvertie⁷ McKee, William Henry Harrison⁶, Elizabeth⁵, Alexander⁴, Andrew³ Pegan II, Andrew² Pagan, James¹*) was born on July 10, 1903, in St. Joseph, Washington Twp., Buchanan Co., Missouri. He was the son of William Richter and Cora Alvertie McKee (35). Melvin Byron lived in Shamrock, Wheeler Co., Texas. He died in Montebello, Los Angeles Co., California, on July 18, 1978, at age 75.

He married **Roberta Unknown.** Roberta Unknown was born in Missouri in 1901. Roberta died in Montebello, Los Angeles Co., California?, after 1952.

133. **Doris E.⁸ Richter** (*Cora Alvertie⁷ McKee, William Henry Harrison⁶, Elizabeth⁵, Alexander⁴, Andrew³ Pegan II, Andrew² Pagan, James¹*) was born in 1912 in St. Joseph, Washington Twp., Buchanan Co., Missouri. She was the daughter of William Richter and Cora Alvertie McKee (35). Doris E. died after 1940.

# 9th Generation

**134. Mae Ophelia⁹ Davis** (*Mary E.⁸ McKee, Samuel Stephen⁷, Josiah William⁶, Elizabeth⁵, Alexander⁴, Andrew³ Pegan II, Andrew² Pagan, James¹*) was born on May 24, 1910, in Brady Twp., Garvin Co., Oklahoma. She was also known as **Ophelia.** She was the daughter of Melvin H. Davis and Mary E. McKee (37). Mae Ophelia died in Oklahoma City, Oklahoma, on August 19, 2000, at age 90. She was buried in Hillside Cemetery, Purcell, Moncrief Twp., McClain Co., Oklahoma.[19]

Mae Ophelia married **Charles Arthur Grimes** on April 3, 1927, in Garvin Co., Oklahoma. They had one son. Charles Arthur Grimes was born in Purdy, Madison Co., Arkansas?, on January 29, 1887. Charles Arthur reached age 41 and died in Brady Twp., Garvin Co., Oklahoma?, in 1929. He was buried in Katie City Cemetery, Katie, Brady Twp., Garvin Co., Oklahoma.[9]

Mae Ophelia Davis Grimes married **George Lewers Martindale.** They had one daughter. George Lewers Martindale was born in Hope, Hempstead Co., Arkansas, on November 3, 1896. He was also known as **Lew.** George Lewers reached age 68 and died in Oklahoma City, Oklahoma, on April 10, 1965. He was buried in Hillside Cemetery, Purcell, Moncrief Twp., McClain Co., Oklahoma.[19]

Mae Ophelia Davis Grimes Martindale married **Clyde Sisson.** They divorced. Clyde Sisson was born in Parkhill, Cherokee Co., Oklahoma, on January 18, 1907. Clyde reached age 92 and died in Oklahoma City, Oklahoma, on July 4, 1999. He was buried in Hillside Cemetery, Purcell, Moncrief Twp., McClain Co., Oklahoma.[19]

Son of Mae Ophelia Davis and Charles Arthur Grimes:

+ 333 m I.   **Charles Leroy¹⁰ Grimes II** was born in Elmore Twp., Garvin Co., Oklahoma, in 1928. He was also known as **Leroy.** Charles Leroy died in Purcell, Moncrief Twp., McClain Co., Oklahoma?, in 1931.[9]

Daughter of Mae Ophelia Davis and George Lewers Martindale:

+ 334 f I.   **Lametha Marniece¹⁰ Martindale** was born in Elmore City, Elmore Twp., Garvin Co., Oklahoma, on October 6, 1932. She died in Oklahoma City, Oklahoma, on January 12, 2011.[19]

**135. Oscar⁹ Davis** (*Mary E.⁸ McKee, Samuel Stephen⁷, Josiah William⁶, Elizabeth⁵, Alexander⁴, Andrew³ Pegan II, Andrew² Pagan, James¹*) was born on November 3, 1911, in Brady Twp., Garvin Co., Oklahoma. He was the son of Melvin H. Davis and Mary E. McKee (37). Oscar died in Elmore Twp., Garvin Co., Oklahoma, on May 11, 1940, at age 28. He was buried in Katie City Cemetery, Katie, Brady Twp., Garvin Co., Oklahoma.[9]

Never married.

**136. DeWitt⁹ Davis** (*Mary E.⁸ McKee, Samuel Stephen⁷, Josiah William⁶, Elizabeth⁵, Alexander⁴, Andrew³ Pegan II, Andrew² Pagan, James¹*) was born on October 28, 1916, in Brady Twp., Garvin Co., Oklahoma. He was the son of Melvin H. Davis and Mary E. McKee (37). DeWitt died in Dearborn, Wayne Co., Michigan, on January 31, 1976, at age 59.

May have never married.

**137. Ivy Jones⁹ Sims** (*Martha Ollie⁸ McKee, Samuel Stephen⁷, Josiah William⁶, Elizabeth⁵, Alexander⁴, Andrew³ Pegan II, Andrew² Pagan, James¹*) was born on February 25, 1911, in Brady Twp., Garvin Co., Oklahoma? She was the daughter of Andrew Martin Sims and Martha Ollie McKee (38). Ivy Jones was adopted. She died in Elk City, Beckham Co., Oklahoma, on October 2, 2001, at age 90. Ivy Jones was buried in Fairlawn Cemetery, Elk City, Beckham Co., Oklahoma.

Ivy Jones Sims married **Olvin Harold Auld** about 1928. They had one son. Olvin Harold Auld was born in Earl, Jefferson Co., Oklahoma, on January 4, 1910. Olvin Harold reached age 69 and died in Odessa, Ector Co., Texas, on April 4, 1979. He was buried in Resthaven Memorial Park Cemetery, Midland, Midland Co., Texas.

Ivy Jones Sims Auld married **George William Harness** in 1930. George William Harness was born in Wheeler Co., Texas, on May 29, 1908. George William reached age 67 and died in Elk City, Beckham Co., Oklahoma, in May 1976. He was buried in Fairlawn Cemetery, Elk City, Beckham Co., Oklahoma.[18]

Son of Ivy Jones Sims and Olvin Harold Auld:

+ 335 m I.    **Andrew Harold Auld**[10] **Harness** was born in Elk City, Beckham Co., Oklahoma, on December 4, 1928. He was adopted by his stepfather George William Harness after 1930. Andrew Harold Auld died in Oklahoma City, Oklahoma, on May 15, 1993.[104]

138. **Floye Aleyne**[9] **McKee** (*William H.*[8], *Samuel Stephen*[7], *Josiah William*[6], *Elizabeth*[5], *Alexander*[4], *Andrew*[3] *Pegan II*, *Andrew*[2] *Pagan*, *James*[1]) was born on January 15, 1923, in Elmore City, Elmore Twp., Garvin Co., Oklahoma. She was the daughter of William H. McKee (39) and Agnes Hunter. Floye Aleyne died in Canyon, Randall Co., Texas, on December 28, 2011, at age 88. She was buried in Memory Gardens Cemetery, Amarillo, Randall Co., Texas.[47]

Floye Aleyne married **William Earnest Hudson** on November 30, 1942, in Garvin Co., Oklahoma. They had one son. William Earnest Hudson was born in Turner Twp., Murray Co., Oklahoma, on March 2, 1922. William Earnest reached age 86 and died in Amarillo, Randall Co., Texas, on January 26, 2009. He was buried in Memory Gardens Cemetery, Amarillo, Randall Co., Texas.[47]

139. **Lindsay Ellis**[9] **McKee** (*William H.*[8], *Samuel Stephen*[7], *Josiah William*[6], *Elizabeth*[5], *Alexander*[4], *Andrew*[3] *Pegan II*, *Andrew*[2] *Pagan*, *James*[1]) was born on June 13, 1924, in Elmore City, Elmore Twp., Garvin Co., Oklahoma. He was the son of William H. McKee (39) and Agnes Hunter. Lindsay Ellis

died in Purcell, Moncrief Twp., McClain Co., Oklahoma, on May 29, 2002, at age 77. He was buried in Katie City Cemetery, Katie, Brady Twp., Garvin Co., Oklahoma.[9]

Lindsay Ellis married **Lola Beatrice Hilliard** on July 8, 1945, in McClain Co., Oklahoma. Lola Beatrice Hilliard was born in Ben Wheeler, Van Zandt Co., Texas, on June 21, 1926.

140. **Arlie Ardell**[9] **McKee** (*William H.*[8], *Samuel Stephen*[7], *Josiah William*[6], *Elizabeth*[5], *Alexander*[4], *Andrew*[3] *Pegan II*, *Andrew*[2] *Pagan*, *James*[1]) was born on May 26, 1926, in Elmore City, Elmore Twp., Garvin Co., Oklahoma. He was the son of William H. McKee (39) and Agnes Hunter. Arlie Ardell died in Purcell, Moncrief Twp., McClain Co., Oklahoma, on March 28, 2002, at age 75.

Arlie Ardell married **Betty Jewel Gossage** on June 3, 1947, in McClain Co., Oklahoma. Betty Jewel Gossage was born in 1931.

Arlie Ardell McKee married **Deborah Lennon?** on November 30, 1979, in Randall Co., Texas.

141. **Charles Samuel**[9] **Cross** (*Fannie May*[8] *McKee*, *Samuel Stephen*[7], *Josiah William*[6], *Elizabeth*[5], *Alexander*[4], *Andrew*[3] *Pegan II*, *Andrew*[2] *Pagan*, *James*[1]) was born in 1917 in Hewitt Twp., Carter Co., Oklahoma. He was the son of James W. Cross and Fannie May McKee (41). Charles Samuel died in Hewitt Twp., Carter Co., Oklahoma, in 1919 at age two. He was buried in Katie City Cemetery, Katie, Brady Twp., Garvin Co., Oklahoma.[9]

142. **Louise**[9] **Cross** (*Fannie May*[8] *McKee*, *Samuel Stephen*[7], *Josiah William*[6], *Elizabeth*[5], *Alexander*[4], *Andrew*[3] *Pegan II*, *Andrew*[2] *Pagan*, *James*[1]) was born in 1920 in Hewitt Twp., Carter Co., Oklahoma. She is the daughter of James W. Cross and Fannie May McKee (41).

Louise married **Leslie Lee Harrison** on April 25, 1936, in Seminole Co., Oklahoma. They divorced. They have one son. Leslie Lee Harrison was born in Lincoln, Seminole Co., Oklahoma?, on September 10, 1914. He reached age 61 and died in Vamoosa, Seminole Co., Oklahoma?, on August 28, 1976.

Leslie Lee was buried in Vamoosa Cemetery, Vamoosa, Seminole Co., Oklahoma.[105]

Son of Louise Cross and Leslie Lee Harrison:

+ 336 m I. **Jimmie Lee**[10] **Harrison** was born in Choctaw Co., Oklahoma?, on April 1, 1937.

**143. Odis O.**[9] **Cross** (*Fannie May*[8] *McKee, Samuel Stephen*[7], *Josiah William*[6], *Elizabeth*[5], *Alexander*[4], *Andrew*[3] *Pegan II, Andrew*[2] *Pagan, James*[1]) was born on August 22, 1922, in Hewitt Twp., Carter Co., Oklahoma. He was the son of James W. Cross and Fannie May McKee (41). Odis O. died in Bethany, Oklahoma Co., Oklahoma, on September 9, 1987, at age 65. He was buried in Bethany Cemetery, Bethany, Oklahoma Co., Oklahoma.[20]

Odis O. married **Lavern W. Marshall** after 1940. Lavern W. Marshall was born in Kemp, Bryan Co., Oklahoma, on April 15, 1924. Lavern W. reached age 65 and died in Bethany, Oklahoma Co., Oklahoma, on May 5, 1989. She was buried in Bethany Cemetery, Bethany, Oklahoma Co., Oklahoma.[20]

**144. Juanita Fern**[9] **Cross** (*Fannie May*[8] *McKee, Samuel Stephen*[7], *Josiah William*[6], *Elizabeth*[5], *Alexander*[4], *Andrew*[3] *Pegan II, Andrew*[2] *Pagan, James*[1]) was born on May 2, 1925, in Graham Twp., Carter Co., Oklahoma. She was the daughter of James W. Cross and Fannie May McKee (41). Juanita Fern died in Bethany, Oklahoma Co., Oklahoma, on March 29, 2011, at age 85. She was buried in Bethany Cemetery, Bethany, Oklahoma Co., Oklahoma.[20]

Juanita Fern married **Enex Daniel Ray** in January 1942 in Hardeman Co., Texas. They had three children. Enex Daniel Ray was born in Quanah, Hardeman Co., Texas, on December 4, 1921. Enex Daniel reached age 40 and died in Quanah, Hardeman Co., Texas, on January 31, 1962. He was buried in Quanah Memorial Park Cemetery, Quanah, Hardeman Co., Texas.[106]

Juanita Fern Cross Ray married **I. Murvin Kelley** on July 4, 1965. I. Murvin Kelley was born on June 8, 1916. I. Murvin reached age 84 and died in Bethany, Oklahoma Co., Oklahoma, on October 19, 2000. He was buried in Bethany Cemetery, Bethany, Oklahoma Co., Oklahoma.[20]

Juanita Fern Cross and Enex Daniel Ray had three children, including:

+ 337 m I. **Danny**[10] **Ray** was born in Quanah, Hardeman Co., Texas, on June 20, 1944. He died in Noble, Cleveland Co., Oklahoma, on April 28, 2001.

**145. Loweta M.**[9] **Cross** (*Fannie May*[8] *McKee, Samuel Stephen*[7], *Josiah William*[6], *Elizabeth*[5], *Alexander*[4], *Andrew*[3] *Pegan II, Andrew*[2] *Pagan, James*[1]) was born on September 5, 1928, in Graham Twp., Carter Co., Oklahoma. She is the daughter of James W. Cross and Fannie May McKee (41).

Loweta M. married **Cecil Ray Chesser** on June 23, 1946, in Hardeman Co., Texas. Cecil Ray Chesser was born in Eldorado, Jackson Co., Oklahoma, on May 7, 1926. Cecil Ray reached age 76 and died in Altus, Jackson Co., Oklahoma, on December 13, 2002. He was buried in Altus Cemetery, Altus, Jackson Co., Oklahoma.[107] Cecil Ray Chesser was a noted historian and educator who was dean of administration at Western Oklahoma State College.

**146. James Austin**[9] **Cross II** (*Fannie May*[8] *McKee, Samuel Stephen*[7], *Josiah William*[6], *Elizabeth*[5], *Alexander*[4], *Andrew*[3] *Pegan II, Andrew*[2] *Pagan, James*[1]) was born on February 22, 1929, in Graham Twp., Carter Co., Oklahoma. He was the son of James W. Cross and Fannie May McKee (41). James Austin lived in 2002 in Nicoma Park, Oklahoma Co., Oklahoma. He died in Moore, Cleveland Co., Oklahoma, on September 30, 2002, at age 73.

James Austin married **Imogene Kimery** on November 23, 1947, in Canadian Co., Oklahoma. They divorced. Imogene Kimery was born in Stella, Cleveland Co., Oklahoma, on June 15, 1930. She reached age 52 and died in Wichita Falls, Wichita Co., Texas, on February 15, 1983. Imogene was buried in Crestview Cemetery, Wichita Falls, Wichita Co., Texas.[108] Died under the name Imogene Cripps.

**147. Artinea Voncell⁹ Cross** (*Fannie May⁸ McKee, Samuel Stephen⁷, Josiah William⁶, Elizabeth⁵, Alexander⁴, Andrew³ Pegan II, Andrew² Pagan, James¹*) was born on August 14, 1932, in Graham Twp., Carter Co., Oklahoma. She was the daughter of James W. Cross and Fannie May McKee (41). Artinea Voncell died in Geary, Blaine Co., Oklahoma, on May 12, 2013, at age 80. She was buried in Geary Cemetery, Geary, Blaine Co., Oklahoma.[48]

Artinea Voncell married **Bobby Vernon Nance** on October 31, 1948, in Kiowa Co., Oklahoma. They had two daughters. Bobby Vernon Nance was born in Calumet, Canadian Co., Oklahoma, on December 5, 1928. Bobby Vernon reached age 84 and died in Geary, Blaine Co., Oklahoma, on October 3, 2013. He was buried in Geary Cemetery, Geary, Blaine Co., Oklahoma.[48]

**148. Euin Theolas⁹ Cross** (*Fannie May⁸ McKee, Samuel Stephen⁷, Josiah William⁶, Elizabeth⁵, Alexander⁴, Andrew³ Pegan II, Andrew² Pagan, James¹*) was born on November 21, 1934, in Seminole Co., Oklahoma. He was the son of James W. Cross and Fannie May McKee (41). Euin Theolas died in Kern Co., California, on March 22, 1987, at age 52.

Euin Theolas married **Velva Butler Riddle** on June 19, 1969, in Imperial Co., California. She was born about 1930. They seem to have divorced.

Euin Theolas Cross married **Barbara D. Tice** on May 18, 1971, in Johnson Co., Texas. Barbara D. Tice was born in 1938.

**149. Charles⁹ Cross** (*Fannie May⁸ McKee, Samuel Stephen⁷, Josiah William⁶, Elizabeth⁵, Alexander⁴, Andrew³ Pegan II, Andrew² Pagan, James¹*) was born on May 16, 1944, in King Co., Texas? He was the son of James W. Cross and Fannie May McKee (41). Charles died in Bethany, Oklahoma Co., Oklahoma?, on July 15, 1992, at age 48. He was buried in Bethany Cemetery, Bethany, Oklahoma Co., Oklahoma.[20]

**150. Lenard Lee⁹ Davis** (*Margaret Ann⁸ McKee, Samuel Stephen⁷, Josiah William⁶, Elizabeth⁵, Alexander⁴, Andrew³ Pegan II, Andrew² Pagan, James¹*) was born on October 12, 1920, in Brady Twp., Garvin Co.,

Oklahoma. He was the son of Charlie William Davis and Margaret Ann McKee (42). Lenard Lee died in San Angelo, Tom Green Co., Texas, on March 4, 1993, at age 92.

Lenard Lee married **Unknown Unknown** after 1940.

**151. Novis Marie⁹ Davis** (*Margaret Ann⁸ McKee, Samuel Stephen⁷, Josiah William⁶, Elizabeth⁵, Alexander⁴, Andrew³ Pegan II, Andrew² Pagan, James¹*) was born on July 12, 1923, in Elmore City, Elmore Twp., Garvin Co., Oklahoma. She was the daughter of Charlie William Davis and Margaret Ann McKee (42). Novis Marie died in San Angelo, Tom Green Co., Texas, on January 25, 2002, at age 78.

Novis Marie married **Robert Earl Fairchild** before 1950. They divorced. They had two children. Robert Earl Fairchild was born in Kenedy, Karnes Co., Texas, on March 24, 1924. He reached age 58 and died in San Angelo, Tom Green Co., Texas, on March 18, 1983. Robert Earl was buried in Lawnhaven Memorial Gardens Cemetery, San Angelo, Tom Green Co., Texas.[109]

**152. James Rex⁹ Cross** (*Claud James⁸, Sarah Elvira Elizabeth Ann⁷ McKee, Josiah William⁶, Elizabeth⁵, Alexander⁴, Andrew³ Pegan II, Andrew² Pagan, James¹*) was born on November 29, 1909, in Sylvester, Fisher Co., Texas. He was the son of Claud James Cross (43) and Ada B. Tucker. James Rex lived in Sylvester, Fisher Co., Texas. He died in Jones Co., Texas, on January 7, 2000, at age 90. James Rex was buried in Newman Cemetery, Sylvester, Fisher Co., Texas.[10]

James Rex married **Mozell Henson** on May 10, 1930, in Fisher Co., Texas. They had four children. Mozell Henson was born in Brown Co., Texas, on February 23, 1911. Mozell reached age 86 and died in Jones Co., Texas, on November 4, 1997.

Children of James Rex Cross and Mozell Henson:

+ 338  f  I.  **Wilma Fern¹⁰ Cross** was born in Sylvester, Fisher Co., Texas, on March 13, 1931.

+ 339 m II. **Riley Doyle**[10] **Cross** was born in Sylvester, Fisher Co., Texas, on December 2, 1932.

+ 340 f III. **Frances Juanita**[10] **Cross** was born in Longworth, Fisher Co., Texas, on April 30, 1936. She died in Longworth, Fisher Co., Texas, on April 30, 1936.[10]

+ 341 f IV. **Zenita**[10] **Cross** was born in Nolan Co., Texas, on October 30, 1937.

**153. Francis Elmo**[9] **Cross** (*Claud James*[8], *Sarah Elvira Elizabeth Ann*[7] *McKee, Josiah William*[6], *Elizabeth*[5], *Alexander*[4], *Andrew*[3] *Pegan II, Andrew*[2] *Pagan, James*[1]) was born on December 28, 1911, in Sylvester, Fisher Co., Texas. He was also known as **Elmo.** He was the son of Claud James Cross (43) and Ada B. Tucker. Francis Elmo died in Denton, Denton Co., Texas, on March 20, 2000, at age 88. He was buried in Restland Memorial Park Cemetery, Dallas, Tarrant Co., Texas.[49]

Francis Elmo married **Ruth Mae Burns** after 1940. They had one son. Ruth Mae Burns was born in Arkansas? on July 29, 1920. Ruth Mae reached age 80 and died in Denton, Denton Co., Texas, on August 10, 2000. She was buried in Restland Memorial Park Cemetery, Dallas, Tarrant Co., Texas.[49]

**154. Georgia Elizabeth**[9] **Ferrel** (*Clara Jane*[8] *Cross, Sarah Elvira Elizabeth Ann*[7] *McKee, Josiah William*[6], *Elizabeth*[5], *Alexander*[4], *Andrew*[3] *Pegan II, Andrew*[2] *Pagan, James*[1]) was born on October 2, 1909, in Sylvester, Fisher Co., Texas. She was the daughter of George Washington Ferrel and Clara Jane Cross (44). Georgia Elizabeth died in Sylvester, Fisher Co., Texas, on November 26, 1985, at age 76. She was buried in Newman Cemetery, Sylvester, Fisher Co., Texas.[10]

Georgia Elizabeth married **Orville Howard Cox** on September 1, 1951, in Fisher Co., Texas. They had two sons. Orville Howard Cox was born in Golan, Jones Co., Texas?, on August 27, 1907. Orville Howard reached age 67 and died in Rotan, Fisher Co., Texas, on September 29, 1974. He was

buried in Newman Cemetery, Sylvester, Fisher Co., Texas.[10]

Georgia Elizabeth Ferrel Cox married **Weldon Woodrow Powell** on January 16, 1976, in Jones Co., Texas. Weldon Woodrow Powell was born in Sylvester, Fisher Co., Texas, on April 24, 1912. He reached age 71 and died in Abilene, Taylor Co., Texas, on May 11, 1983. Weldon Woodrow was buried in Newman Cemetery, Sylvester, Fisher Co., Texas.[10]

Sons of Georgia Elizabeth Ferrel and Orville Howard Cox:

+ 342 m I. **Jackie Fred**[10] **Cox** was born in Rotan, Fisher Co., Texas, on February 25, 1952. He died in Rotan, Fisher Co., Texas, in February 1952. Jackie Fred was buried in Newman Cemetery, Sylvester, Fisher Co., Texas.[10]

+ 343 m II. **James Frank**[10] **Cox** was born in Rotan, Fisher Co., Texas, on February 25, 1952. He died in Rotan, Fisher Co., Texas, on February 27, 1952. James Frank was buried in Newman Cemetery, Sylvester, Fisher Co., Texas.[10]

**155. Frank C.**[9] **Ferrel** (*Clara Jane*[8] *Cross, Sarah Elvira Elizabeth Ann*[7] *McKee, Josiah William*[6], *Elizabeth*[5], *Alexander*[4], *Andrew*[3] *Pegan II, Andrew*[2] *Pagan, James*[1]) was born on February 1, 1912, in Roby, Fisher Co., Texas. He was the son of George Washington Ferrel and Clara Jane Cross (44). Frank C. died in Ploesi, Romania, on August 1, 1943, at age 31. He was buried in Florence American Cemetery and Memorial, Florence, Provincia di Firenze, Italy.[110] Died in WWII.

Frank C. married **Julia Maurese Putnam** in June 1941 in Jones Co., Texas. Julia Maurese Putnam was born in Lueders. Jones Co., Texas, on June 3, 1917. Julia Maurese reached age 81 and died in Austin, Travis Co., Texas, on December 12, 1998.

She was buried in Austin Memorial Park Cemetery, Austin, Travis Co., Texas.[111]

**156. Claudine**[9] **Ferrel** (*Clara Jane*[8] *Cross, Sarah Elvira Elizabeth Ann*[7] *McKee, Josiah William*[6], *Elizabeth*[5], *Alexander*[4], *Andrew*[3] *Pegan II, Andrew*[2] *Pagan, James*[1]) was born on February 27, 1925, in Albuquerque, Bernalillo Co., New Mexico. She was the daughter of George Washington Ferrel and Clara Jane Cross (44). Claudine died in Big Spring, Howard Co., Texas, on October 2, 1987, at age 62. She was buried in Newman Cemetery, Sylvester, Fisher Co., Texas.[10]

Claudine married **Simon F. Terrazas** on March 31, 1945. They had one son. Simon F. Terrazas was born in El Paso, El Paso Co., Texas, on July 12, 1899. Simon F. reached age 94 and died in Big Spring, Howard Co., Texas, on November 24, 1993. He was buried in Newman Cemetery, Sylvester, Fisher Co., Texas.[10]

**157. Roberta Jess**[9] **Scott** (*Elizabeth Violet*[8] *Cross, Sarah Elvira Elizabeth Ann*[7] *McKee, Josiah William*[6], *Elizabeth*[5], *Alexander*[4], *Andrew*[3] *Pegan II, Andrew*[2] *Pagan, James*[1]) was born on September 4, 1911, in Roby, Fisher Co., Texas. She was the daughter of Robert Seaborn Scott and Elizabeth Violet Cross (47). Roberta Jess died in Rotan, Fisher Co., Texas, on March 28, 2012, at age 100. She was buried in Newman Cemetery, Sylvester, Fisher Co., Texas.[10]

Childless.

Roberta Jess married **Roy Franklin Elliott** on August 28, 1933, in Taylor Co., Texas. Roy Franklin Elliott was born in Winnsboro, Wood Co., Texas, on August 5, 1905. Roy Franklin lived in 1954 in Quitman, Wood Co., Texas. He reached age 48 and died in a hospital in Gilmer, Upshur Co., Texas, on June 25, 1954. Roy Franklin was buried in Lee Cemetery, Winnsboro, Wood Co., Texas.[112]

Roberta Jess Scott Elliott married **Alton Jackson Hill** on August 8, 1959. Alton Jackson Hill was born in Essie, Jones Co., Texas, on September 17, 1908. Alton Jackson lived in 1975 in Sylvester, Fisher Co., Texas. He reached age 66 and died in a hospital in Abilene, Taylor Co., Texas, on May 12, 1975. He was buried in Rose Hill Cemetery, Merkel, Taylor Co., Texas.[113]

Roberta Jess Scott Elliott Hill married **Andrew J. Ford** on July 24, 1976, in Fisher Co., Texas. Andrew J. Ford was born in Cookville, Titus Co. Texas, on November 17, 1908. He was also known as **Blackie.** Andrew J. reached age 81 and died in Abilene, Taylor Co., Texas, on August 11, 1990. He was buried in Newman Cemetery, Sylvester, Fisher Co., Texas.[10]

**158. Thara Celeste**[9] **Scott** (*Elizabeth Violet*[8] *Cross, Sarah Elvira Elizabeth Ann*[7] *McKee, Josiah William*[6], *Elizabeth*[5], *Alexander*[4], *Andrew*[3] *Pegan II, Andrew*[2] *Pagan, James*[1]) was born on June 27, 1916, in Curry Co., New Mexico. She was the daughter of Robert Seaborn Scott and Elizabeth Violet Cross (47). Thara Celeste died in Sylvester, Fisher Co., Texas, on September 6, 1941, at age 25. She was buried in Newman Cemetery, Sylvester, Fisher Co., Texas.[10]

Never married.

**159. Robert N.**[9] **Scott II** (*Elizabeth Violet*[8] *Cross, Sarah Elvira Elizabeth Ann*[7] *McKee, Josiah William*[6], *Elizabeth*[5], *Alexander*[4], *Andrew*[3] *Pegan II, Andrew*[2] *Pagan, James*[1]) was born on December 4, 1920, in Lubbock, Lubbock Co., Texas. He was the son of Robert Seaborn Scott and Elizabeth Violet Cross (47). Robert N. died in Abilene, Taylor Co., Texas, on October 25, 1991, at age 70. He was buried in Newman Cemetery, Sylvester, Fisher Co., Texas.[10]

Robert N. married **Alma Doloris Niemier** after 1940. Alma Doloris Niemier was born in South Bend, St. Joseph Co., Indiana, on April 2, 1924. Alma Doloris lived in 1996 in Destrehan, St. Charles Parish, Louisiana. She reached age 72 and died in Midland, Midland Co., Texas, on December 10, 1996. Alma Doloris was buried in Newman Cemetery, Sylvester, Fisher Co., Texas.[10]

**160. Alice Lavern**[9] **Scott** (*Elizabeth Violet*[8] *Cross, Sarah Elvira Elizabeth Ann*[7] *McKee, Josiah William*[6], *Elizabeth*[5], *Alexander*[4], *Andrew*[3] *Pegan II, Andrew*[2] *Pagan, James*[1]) was born on July 19, 1924, in Tatum, Lea Co., New Mexico. She was the daughter of Robert Seaborn Scott and Elizabeth Violet Cross (47). Alice Lavern died in Tatum, Lea Co.,

New Mexico, on January 9, 1925. She was buried in Newman Cemetery, Sylvester, Fisher Co., Texas.[10]

161. **Willie Jolene⁹ Scott** (*Elizabeth Violet⁸ Cross, Sarah Elvira Elizabeth Ann⁷ McKee, Josiah William⁶, Elizabeth⁵, Alexander⁴, Andrew³ Pegan II, Andrew² Pagan, James¹*) was born on September 15, 1926, in Sylvester, Fisher Co., Texas. She was also known as **Jolene.** She was the daughter of Robert Seaborn Scott and Elizabeth Violet Cross (47).

Willie Jolene married **Frank L. Bracken** after 1940. Frank L. Bracken was born in Cleveland, Cuyahoga Co., Ohio, on April 16, 1922. Frank L. reached age 75 and died in Brandon, Hillsborough Co., Florida, on July 9, 1997. He was buried in Newman Cemetery, Sylvester, Fisher Co., Texas.[10]

162. **Ardell Colleen⁹ Cross** (*John Henry⁸, Sarah Elvira Elizabeth Ann⁷ McKee, Josiah William⁶, Elizabeth⁵, Alexander⁴, Andrew³ Pegan II, Andrew² Pagan, James¹*) was born on August 11, 1920, in Newman, Fisher Co., Texas. She was the daughter of John Henry Cross (50) and Gladys B. Reeves. Ardell Colleen died in Sylvester, Fisher Co., Texas, on August 9, 2012, at age 91. She was buried in Belvieu Cemetery, Rotan, Fisher Co., Texas.[21]

Ardell Colleen married **Richard Lavada Floyd** on December 5, 1936, in Fisher Co., Texas. They had three sons. Richard Lavada Floyd was born in Rotan, Fisher Co., Texas, on July 11, 1911. Richard Lavada reached age 96 and died in Sylvester, Fisher Co., Texas, on January 1, 2008. He was buried in Belvieu Cemetery, Rotan, Fisher Co., Texas.[21]

Ardell Colleen Cross and Richard Lavada Floyd had three sons, including:

+ 344 m I.   **Richard Lavada¹⁰ Floyd II** was born in Rotan, Fisher Co., Texas, on December 5, 1938. He died in Roscoe, Nolan Co., Texas, on August 17, 2010.[21]

+ 345 m III.   **Terry Lynn¹⁰ Floyd** was born in Sweetwater, Nolan Co., Texas, on March 28, 1949. He died in Fisher Co., Texas, on May 7, 1968.[21]

163. **Canevah Mae⁹ Cross** (*Willie Franklin⁸, Sarah Elvira Elizabeth Ann⁷ McKee, Josiah William⁶, Elizabeth⁵, Alexander⁴, Andrew³ Pegan II, Andrew² Pagan, James¹*) was born on June 12, 1916, in Sylvester, Fisher Co., Texas. She was the daughter of Willie Franklin Cross (51) and Dovie Mae Arnold. Canevah Mae lived in 1989 in Sweetwater, Nolan Co., Texas. She died in a hospital in Abilene, Taylor Co., Texas, on April 9, 1989, at age 72. Canevah Mae was buried in Newman Cemetery, Sylvester, Fisher Co., Texas.[10]

Canevah Mae married **William Mac Turner** on September 19, 1935. They had two sons. William Mac Turner was born in Lorraine, Mitchell Co., Texas, on March 2, 1914. He was also known as **Willie.** William Mac reached age 80 and died in Sweetwater, Nolan Co., Texas, on April 16, 1994. He was buried in Newman Cemetery, Sylvester, Fisher Co., Texas.[10]

Sons of Canevah Mae Cross and William Mac Turner:

+ 346 m I.   **Willie Jim¹⁰ Turner** was born in Sweetwater, Nolan Co., Texas, on July 31, 1936.

+ 347 m II.   **Jerry Cross¹⁰ Turner** was born in Sweetwater, Nolan Co., Texas, on March 3, 1940. He died in Potter Co., Texas, on November 2, 1992.[114]

164. **Jess Wiley⁹ Cross** (*Willie Franklin⁸, Sarah Elvira Elizabeth Ann⁷ McKee, Josiah William⁶, Elizabeth⁵, Alexander⁴, Andrew³ Pegan II, Andrew² Pagan, James¹*) was born on July 16, 1918, in Estancia, Torrance Co., New Mexico. He was the son of Willie Franklin Cross (51) and Dovie Mae Arnold. Jess Wiley died in Abilene, Taylor Co., Texas, on October 31, 2013, at age 95. He was buried in Newman Cemetery, Sylvester, Fisher Co., Texas.[10]

Jess Wiley married **Tempie Pearl Ham** on June 16, 1946, in Martin Co., Texas. They had one son. Tempie Pearl Ham was born in Lamesa, Dawson Co., Texas, on November 10, 1922. She was also known as **Pearl.** Tempie Pearl reached age 75 and died in Abilene, Taylor Co., Texas, on September

30, 1998. She was buried in Newman Cemetery, Sylvester, Fisher Co., Texas.[10]

**165. William Arnold⁹ Cross** (*Willie Franklin⁸, Sarah Elvira Elizabeth Ann⁷ McKee, Josiah William⁶, Elizabeth⁵, Alexander⁴, Andrew³ Pegan II, Andrew² Pagan, James¹*) was born on June 6, 1920, in Estancia, Torrance Co., New Mexico. He was the son of Willie Franklin Cross (51) and Dovie Mae Arnold. William Arnold died in Midland, Midland Co., Texas, on August 11, 2011, at age 91. He was buried in Newman Cemetery, Sylvester, Fisher Co., Texas.[10]

William Arnold married **Faye McHaney** on April 5, 1943, in Fisher Co., Texas. They had five children. Faye McHaney was born in Sweetwater, Nolan Co., Texas, on May 13, 1924. Faye reached age 86 and died in Midland, Midland Co., Texas, on January 22, 2011. She was buried in Newman Cemetery, Sylvester, Fisher Co., Texas.[10]

William Arnold Cross and Faye McHaney had five children, including:

+ 348 m I.   **Larry Jess¹⁰ Cross** was born in Lamesa, Dawson Co., Texas, on May 28, 1946. He died in Midland, Midland Co., Texas, on August 22, 2013.[10]

+ 349 m II.  **William W.¹⁰ Cross II** was born in Midland, Midland Co., Texas, on November 8, 1952. He was also known as **Bo.** William W. died on April 2, 1982.[10]

**166. Reuben Russell⁹ Riley** (*Mary Willie⁸ McKee, William Robert⁷, Josiah William⁶, Elizabeth⁵, Alexander⁴, Andrew³ Pegan II, Andrew² Pagan, James¹*) was born on October 12, 1909, in Coyle Twp., Murray Co., Oklahoma. He was the son of Albert Russell Riley and Mary Willie McKee (52). Reuben Russell died in Rush Springs Twp., Grady Co., Oklahoma, on March 4, 1993, at age 83. He was buried in Rush Springs Cemetery, Rush Springs, Grady Co., Oklahoma.[22]

Reuben Russell married **Gladys Snow** about 1931. They had four children. Gladys Snow

was born in Summerfield Twp., Le Flore Co., Oklahoma?, on May 16, 1912. Gladys reached age 84 and died in Marlow Twp., Stephens Co., Oklahoma, on March 12, 1997. She was buried in Rush Springs Cemetery, Rush Springs, Grady Co., Oklahoma.[22]

Children of Reuben Russell Riley and Gladys Snow:

+ 350 m I.   **William R.¹⁰ Riley** was born in Harrison Twp., Grady Co., Oklahoma, on February 7, 1932.

+ 351 f II.  **Gladys May¹⁰ Riley** was born in Harrison Twp., Grady Co., Oklahoma, in 1933.

+ 352 m III. **Lee Roy¹⁰ Riley** was born in Harrison Twp., Grady Co., Oklahoma, on March 10, 1936.

+ 353 m IV. **Luther Delbert¹⁰ Riley** was born in Harrison Twp., Grady Co., Oklahoma, on February 4, 1939. He died in Harrison Twp., Grady Co., Oklahoma, on November 4, 1940.[12]

**167. Bessie⁹ Riley** (*Mary Willie⁸ McKee, William Robert⁷, Josiah William⁶, Elizabeth⁵, Alexander⁴, Andrew³ Pegan II, Andrew² Pagan, James¹*) was born on December 23, 1911, in Bradley Twp., Grady Co., Oklahoma. She was the daughter of Albert Russell Riley and Mary Willie McKee (52). Bessie died in Bradley Twp., Grady Co., Oklahoma, on January 6, 1912. She was buried in Oaklawn Cemetery, Wynnewood, Brady Twp., Garvin Co., Oklahoma.[25]

**168. Annie Laurie⁹ Riley** (*Mary Willie⁸ McKee, William Robert⁷, Josiah William⁶, Elizabeth⁵, Alexander⁴, Andrew³ Pegan II, Andrew² Pagan, James¹*) was born on August 19, 1913, in Bradley Twp., Grady Co., Oklahoma. She was the daughter of Albert Russell Riley and Mary Willie McKee (52). Annie Laurie died in Bradley Twp., Grady Co., Oklahoma, on February 27, 1914. She was buried in Oaklawn Cemetery, Wynnewood, Brady Twp., Garvin Co., Oklahoma.[25]

**169. John William**[9] **Riley** (*Mary Willie*[8] *McKee, William Robert*[7], *Josiah William*[6], *Elizabeth*[5], *Alexander*[4], *Andrew*[3] *Pegan II, Andrew*[2] *Pagan, James*[1]) was born on May 8, 1916, in Bradley Twp., Grady Co., Oklahoma. He was the son of Albert Russell Riley and Mary Willie McKee (52). John William died in Sayre Twp., Bradford Co., Pennsylvania?, in January 1974 age 57.

He married **Lola Leslie Hamilton.** Lola Leslie Hamilton was born in Lindsay Twp., Garvin Co., Oklahoma, on June 27, 1912. Lola Leslie reached age 87 and died in Clovis, Fresno Co., California, on April 6, 2000. She was buried in Clovis Cemetery, Clovis, Fresno Co., California.[115]

She died under the name Lola L. Andrews.

**170. Sarah Jane**[9] **Riley** (*Mary Willie*[8] *McKee, William Robert*[7], *Josiah William*[6], *Elizabeth*[5], *Alexander*[4], *Andrew*[3] *Pegan II, Andrew*[2] *Pagan, James*[1]) was born on November 25, 1918, in Bradley Twp., Grady Co., Oklahoma. She was the daughter of Albert Russell Riley and Mary Willie McKee (52). Sarah Jane died in Rush Springs Twp., Grady Co., Oklahoma, on December 2, 1984, at age 66.

Sarah Jane married **Willie Walter Gamble** on August 4, 1934. They had three sons. Willie Walter Gamble was born in Franklin Co., Tennessee, on February 9, 1912. He was also known as **Puddin'.** Willie Walter reached age 73 and died in Lexington Twp., Cleveland Co., Oklahoma, in June 1985.

Sarah Jane Riley married Willie Walter Gamble. Her brother, Robert Francis Riley, married Willie's sister Annabelle Gamble.

Sons of Sarah Jane Riley and Willie Walter Gamble:

+ 354 m I. **James W.**[10] **Gamble** was born in Oklahoma on February 14, 1937. He died in Imperial Co., California, on March 17, 1964.[116]

+ 355 m II. **Albert D.**[10] **Gamble** was born in Oklahoma on February 15, 1939.

+ 356 m III. **Clarence Edward**[10] **Gamble** was born in Riverside, Riverside Co., California, on June 6, 1940. He died in Marysville, Yuba Co., California, on September 12, 2006.

**171. Robert Francis**[9] **Riley** (*Mary Willie*[8] *McKee, William Robert*[7], *Josiah William*[6], *Elizabeth*[5], *Alexander*[4], *Andrew*[3] *Pegan II, Andrew*[2] *Pagan, James*[1]) was born on November 7, 1920, in Bradley Twp., Grady Co., Oklahoma. He was the son of Albert Russell Riley and Mary Willie McKee (52). Robert Francis died in Odessa, Ector Co., Texas, on June 6, 1985, at age 64. He was buried in Sunset Memorial Gardens, Odessa, Ector Co., Texas.[50]

Robert Francis married **Annabelle Gamble** after 1940. They had one child. Annabelle Gamble was born in Colbert, McClain Co., Oklahoma, on June 6, 1924. Annabelle reached age 90 and died in Odessa, Ector Co., Texas, on October 25, 2014. She was buried in Sunset Memorial Gardens, Odessa, Ector Co., Texas.[50]

Robert Francis Riley married Annabelle Gambel. His sister Sarah Jane Riley married Annabelle's brother, Willie Walter Gamble.

**172. Walter Levi**[9] **Riley** (*Mary Willie*[8] *McKee, William Robert*[7], *Josiah William*[6], *Elizabeth*[5], *Alexander*[4], *Andrew*[3] *Pegan II, Andrew*[2] *Pagan, James*[1]) was born on August 28, 1923, in Elmore City, Elmore Twp., Garvin Co., Oklahoma. He was also known as **Buntin.** He was the son of Albert Russell Riley and Mary Willie McKee (52). Walter Levi lived in Amber, Grady Co., Oklahoma. He died in a hospital in Oklahoma City, Oklahoma Co., Oklahoma, on August 17, 2007, at age 83. Walter Levi was buried in Pocasset Cemetery, Pocasset Twp., Grady Co., Oklahoma.[51]

Childless.

Walter Levi Riley married **Wilma Ruth Covel.** They divorced. Wilma Ruth Covel was born in Pursley Twp., Grady Co., Oklahoma, on April 6, 1931. She reached age 46 years and died in Lindsay, Lindsay Twp., Garvin Co., Oklahoma, on December 18, 1977. Wilma Ruth was buried in

Green Hill Cemetery, McClain Co., Oklahoma.[28] Died under the name Wilma Ruth Thompson.

He married **Elsie Marie Alcorn.** Elsie Marie Alcorn was born in Ninnekah Twp., Grady Co., Oklahoma, on September 30, 1925. Elsie Marie reached age 79 and died in Pocasset, Grady Co., Oklahoma, on December 21, 2004. She was buried in Pocasset Cemetery, Pocasset, Grady Co., Oklahoma.[51]

**173. Marion⁹ McKee** (*James Andres⁸, William Robert⁷, Josiah William⁶, Elizabeth⁵, Alexander⁴, Andrew³ Pegan II, Andrew² Pagan, James¹*) was born on February 23, 1919, in Wynnewood, Brady Twp., Garvin Co., Oklahoma. He was the son of James Andres McKee (53) and Lydia May Pearce. Marion died in Panama Canal Zone on November 2, 1942, at age 23. He was buried in Erin Springs Cemetery, Erin Springs, Lindsay Twp., Garvin Co., Oklahoma.[12]

Never married.

**174. Clyde Frank⁹ McKee** (*James Andres⁸, William Robert⁷, Josiah William⁶, Elizabeth⁵, Alexander⁴, Andrew³ Pegan II, Andrew² Pagan, James¹*) was born on June 26, 1921, in Wynnewood, Brady Twp., Garvin Co., Oklahoma. He was the son of James Andres McKee (53) and Lydia May Pearce. Clyde Frank died in Lindsay, Lindsay Twp., Garvin Co., Oklahoma, on January 28, 1999, at age 77. He was buried in Alex Cemetery, Alex, Alex Twp., Grady Co., Oklahoma.[52]

He married **Nola Rosetta Fleming.** They have two daughters. Nola Rosetta Fleming was born in Middleberg, Grady Co., Oklahoma, on September 13, 1929.

Clyde Frank McKee and Nola Rosetta Fleming had two daughters, including

+ 357 f II. **Daughter¹⁰ McKee** was born on October 30, 1953.

**175. Lenard Carl⁹ McKee** (*James Andres⁸, William Robert⁷, Josiah William⁶, Elizabeth⁵, Alexander⁴, Andrew³ Pegan II, Andrew² Pagan, James¹*) was born on February 14, 1923, in Wynnewood, Brady Twp., Garvin Co., Oklahoma. He was the son of

James Andres McKee (53) and Lydia May Pearce. Lenard Carl died in Chickasha, Chickasha Twp., Grady Co., Oklahoma, on March 28, 1997, at age 74. He was buried in Bradley Cemetery, Bradley Twp., Grady Co., Oklahoma.[11]

Lenard Carl married **Margie Tollison** after 1940. They have four children. Margie Tollison was born in Bradley Twp., Grady Co., Oklahoma, in 1930.

Lenard Carl McKee and Margie Tollison had four children, including:

+ 358 m I. **Lenard Carl¹⁰ McKee II** was born in Grady Co., Oklahoma?, on July 2, 1952. He was also known as **Butch.** Lenard Carl died in Cleveland Co., Oklahoma, on January 1, 1978.[11]

**176. Elzie Mae⁹ McKee** (*James Andres⁸, William Robert⁷, Josiah William⁶, Elizabeth⁵, Alexander⁴, Andrew³ Pegan II, Andrew² Pagan, James¹*) was born on November 15, 1924, in Wynnewood, Brady Twp., Garvin Co., Oklahoma. She was the daughter of James Andres McKee (53) and Lydia May Pearce. Elzie Mae died in Chickasha, Chickasha Twp., Grady Co., Oklahoma, on December 1, 1996, at age 72. She was buried in Alex Cemetery, Alex, Alex Twp., Grady Co., Oklahoma.[52]

Elzie Mae married **Marion Willard Luther** on June 9, 1943, in Grady Co., Oklahoma. They had one son. Marion Willard Luther was born in Bonne Terre, Bonne Terre Twp., St. Francois Co., Missouri, on February 12, 1922. Marion Willard reached age 55 and died in St. Louis, Missouri, on June 23, 1977. He was buried in Jefferson Barracks National Cemetery, Lemay Twp., St. Louis Co., Missouri.[117]

Son of Elzie Mae McKee and Marion Willard Luther:

+ 359 m I. **Clyde Willard¹⁰ Luther** was born on January 5, 1959. He died on June 18, 1993.[52]

**177. Winnie Muril⁹ McKee** (*James Andres⁸, William Robert⁷, Josiah William⁶, Elizabeth⁵, Alexander⁴,*

*Andrew³ Pegan II, Andrew² Pagan, James¹*) was born on April 18, 1926, in Pursley Twp., Grady Co., Oklahoma. She was the daughter of James Andres McKee (53) and Lydia May Pearce. Winnie Muril died in Chickasha, Chickasha Twp., Grady Co., Oklahoma, on July 20, 2005, at age 79. She was buried in Fairlawn Cemetery, Chickasha, Grady Co., Oklahoma.[53]

Winnie Muril married **Arnett Homer Schoolfield** on March 1, 1947. They divorced. They had six children. Arnett Homer Schoolfield was born in Ninnekah Twp., Grady Co., Oklahoma, on April 2, 1923. He reached age 82 and died in Chickasha, Chickasha Twp., Grady Co., Oklahoma, on February 12, 2006. Arnett Homer was buried in Bradley Cemetery, Bradley Twp., Grady Co., Oklahoma.[11]

Winnie Muril McKee Schoolfield married **Leroy Vernon Ellis** on September 5, 1975. Leroy Vernon Ellis was born in Cyril, Caddo Co., Oklahoma, on March 12, 1922. He was also known as **Vernon.** Leroy Vernon reached age 73 and died in Chickasha, Chickasha Twp., Grady Co., Oklahoma, on April 6, 1995. He was buried in Fairlawn Cemetery, Chickasha, Grady Co., Oklahoma.[53]

178. **William Henry⁹ McKee** (*James Andres⁸, William Robert⁷, Josiah William⁶, Elizabeth⁵, Alexander⁴, Andrew³ Pegan II, Andrew² Pagan, James¹*) was born on February 24, 1928, in Pursley Twp., Grady Co., Oklahoma. He was also known as **Henry.** He was the son of James Andres McKee (53) and Lydia May Pearce. William Henry died in Alex, Alex Twp., Grady Co. Oklahoma, on February 4, 2002, at age 73.

William Henry married **Lena Fae Fleming** on December 7, 1948, in Maryland. They had six children. Lena Fae Fleming was born in Middleburg, Middleburg Twp., Grady Co., Oklahoma, on March 26, 1932.

William Henry McKee married Lena Fae Fleming. His brother, Clyde Frank McKee, married Lena's sister Nola Rosetta Fleming.

179. **James Orville⁹ McKee** (*James Andres⁸, William Robert⁷, Josiah William⁶, Elizabeth⁵, Alexander⁴, Andrew³ Pegan II, Andrew² Pagan, James¹*) was born on December 16, 1939, in Pursley Twp., Grady Co., Oklahoma. He was also known as **Orville.** He was the son of James Andres McKee (53) and Lydia May Pearce. James Orville died in Alex, Alex Twp., Grady Co. Oklahoma?, on March 27, 1983, at age 43. He was buried in Alex Cemetery, Alex, Alex Twp., Grady Co., Oklahoma.[52]

James Orville married **Charlene Patricia Hughes** in 1969. They had one daughter. Charlene Patricia Hughes was born in Ninnekah Twp., Grady Co., Oklahoma, on October 25, 1936. Charlene Patricia reached age 55 and died in Alex, Alex Twp., Grady Co. Oklahoma, on January 28, 1992. She was buried in Alex Cemetery, Alex, Alex Twp., Grady Co., Oklahoma.[52]

180. **Wesley Dilbert⁹ McKee** (*James Andres⁸, William Robert⁷, Josiah William⁶, Elizabeth⁵, Alexander⁴, Andrew³ Pegan II, Andrew² Pagan, James¹*) was born on April 9, 1933, in Alex, Alex Twp., Grady Co. Oklahoma. He was also known as **Bill.** He was the son of James Andres McKee (53) and Lydia May Pearce. Wesley Dilbert died in Palmer, Matanuska-Susitna Borough, Alaska, on February 3, 1993, at age 59.

Wesley Dilbert married **Mary Reta Unknown** before 1964. They had one daughter.

Wesley Dilbert McKee married **Clara Unknown** after 1964. They had one son.

181. **Lena Mae⁹ McKee** (*James Andres⁸, William Robert⁷, Josiah William⁶, Elizabeth⁵, Alexander⁴, Andrew³ Pegan II, Andrew² Pagan, James¹*) was born on March 8, 1937, in Alex, Alex Twp., Grady Co. Oklahoma. She was the daughter of James Andres McKee (53) and Lydia May Pearce. Lena Mae died in Alex, Alex Twp., Grady Co. Oklahoma, on March 13, 1937. She was buried in Erin Springs Cemetery, Erin Springs, Lindsay Twp., Garvin Co., Oklahoma.[12]

182. **Clide⁹ Cearley** (*Clara Ida⁸ McKee, William Robert⁷, Josiah William⁶, Elizabeth⁵, Alexander⁴, Andrew³ Pegan II, Andrew² Pagan, James¹*) was born on March 5, 1917, in Wynnewood, Brady Twp., Garvin Co., Oklahoma. He was the son of Pat Cearley and Clara Ida McKee (54). Clide died in Wynnewood, Brady Twp., Garvin Co., Oklahoma,

on April 20, 1917. He was buried in Wynnewood View Cemetery, Wynnewood, Brady Twp., Garvin Co., Oklahoma.[54]

**183. Jessie⁹ Cearley** (*Clara Ida⁸ McKee, William Robert⁷, Josiah William⁶, Elizabeth⁵, Alexander⁴, Andrew³ Pegan II, Andrew² Pagan, James¹*) was born on December 1, 1918, in Wynnewood, Brady Twp., Garvin Co., Oklahoma. She was the daughter of Pat Cearley and Clara Ida McKee (54). Jessie died in Mount Ida, Montgomery Co., Arkansas, on November 25, 1998, at age 79.

Seems to have been childless.

Jessie married **Arthur Gordon Dockery** on March 14, 1956. Arthur Gordon Dockery was born in Butler Co., Kentucky, on April 17, 1909. Arthur Gordon reached age 61 and died in Hensley, Pulaski Co., Arkansas, on November 15, 1970. He was buried in Hicks Cemetery, Little Rock, Pulaski Co., Arkansas.

**184. Cora Edna⁹ Cearley** (*Clara Ida⁸ McKee, William Robert⁷, Josiah William⁶, Elizabeth⁵, Alexander⁴, Andrew³ Pegan II, Andrew² Pagan, James¹*) was born on September 2, 1921, in Milburn, Johnston Co., Oklahoma. She was the daughter of Pat Cearley and Clara Ida McKee (54). Cora Edna lived in 2002 in Norman, Montgomery Co., Arkansas. She died in a hospital in Cove, Polk Co, Arkansas, on September 2, 2002, at age 81.

Cora Edna married **Lawrence Vernon Caughron** after 1940. They had one daughter. Lawrence Vernon Caughron was born in Whitney, Hill Co., Texas, on November 24, 1913. Lawrence Vernon reached age 79 and died in Mena, Polk Co., Arkansas, on October 17, 1993.

**185. James Albert⁹ Cearley** (*Clara Ida⁸ McKee, William Robert⁷, Josiah William⁶, Elizabeth⁵, Alexander⁴, Andrew³ Pegan II, Andrew² Pagan, James¹*) was born on May 7, 1925, in Elmore City, Elmore Twp., Garvin Co., Oklahoma. He was the son of Pat Cearley and Clara Ida McKee (54). James Albert died in Hatfield, Polk Co., Arkansas, on July 5, 1993, at age 68.

James Albert married **Edna Louise Simmons** after 1940. Edna Louise Simmons was born in Bradley Twp., Grady Co., Oklahoma, on June 17, 1929.

**186. Earl Warren⁹ McKee** (*George Washington⁸, William Robert⁷, Josiah William⁶, Elizabeth⁵, Alexander⁴, Andrew³ Pegan II, Andrew² Pagan, James¹*) was born on June 24, 1922, in Brady Twp., Garvin Co., Oklahoma. He was the son of George Washington McKee (55) and Mary Millie Rains. Earl Warren died in Elmore City, Elmore Twp., Garvin Co., Oklahoma, on February 4, 1998, at age 75. He was buried in Katie City Cemetery, Katie, Brady Twp., Garvin Co., Oklahoma.[9]

Earl Warren married **Roxie Morrison** after 1940. Roxie Morrison was born in Red Mound Twp., Seminole Co., Oklahoma, on May 29, 1931.

**187. Troy E.⁹ McKee** (*George Washington⁸, William Robert⁷, Josiah William⁶, Elizabeth⁵, Alexander⁴, Andrew³ Pegan II, Andrew² Pagan, James¹*) was born on December 23, 1924, in Brady Twp., Garvin Co., Oklahoma. He was the son of George Washington McKee (55) and Mary Millie Rains. Troy E. died in Elmore City, Elmore Twp., Garvin Co., Oklahoma, on December 11, 2017, at age 92.

Troy E. married **Willie Nell Cassell** before 1949. They had two children. Willie Nell Cassell was born in Colbert Twp., McClain Co., Oklahoma, on February 14, 1928. She reached age 90 and died in Elmore City, Elmore Twp., Garvin Co., Oklahoma, on January 6, 2019.

Troy E. McKee and Willie Nell Cassell had two children, including:

+ 360 f I. **Georgia Nelda Jean¹⁰ McKee** was born in Wynnewood, Brady Twp., Garvin Co., Oklahoma, on September 3, 1949. She was also known as **Nelda.** Georgia Nelda Jean died in Elmore City, Elmore Twp., Garvin Co., Oklahoma, on March 22, 2014.[42]

**188. Harold Winfred⁹ McKee** (*George Washington⁸, William Robert⁷, Josiah William⁶, Elizabeth⁵, Alexander⁴, Andrew³ Pegan II, Andrew² Pagan,*

James[1]) was born on November 10, 1932, in Eola, Brady Twp., Garvin Co., Oklahoma. He was the son of George Washington McKee (55) and Mary Millie Rains. Harold Winfred died in a hospital in Lubbock, Lubbock Co., Texas, on September 9, 1989, age 56. He was buried in Lovington Cemetery, Lovington, Lea Co., New Mexico.[55]

Harold Winfred married **Patsy Ann Courtney** before 1956. They had one son. Patsy Ann Courtney was born on September 1, 1937.

Son of Harold Winfred McKee and Patsy Ann Courtney:

+ 361 m I.   **Harold Dewayne[10] McKee II** was born on October 15, 1956. He died on October 16, 1956.

**189. Bobby Jean[9] McKee** (*George Washington[8]*, *William Robert[7]*, *Josiah William[6]*, *Elizabeth[5]*, *Alexander[4]*, *Andrew[3] Pegan II*, *Andrew[2] Pagan*, *James[1]*) was born on November 15, 1936, in Eola, Brady Twp., Garvin Co., Oklahoma. He was the son of George Washington McKee (55) and Mary Millie Rains. Bobby Jean died in Norman, Norman Twp., Cleveland Co., Oklahoma, on January 28, 2001, at age 64. He was buried in Warren Cemetery, Norman, Cleveland Co., Oklahoma.[56]

He married **Leona O. Unknown.** Leona O. Unknown was born on January 27, 1938.

**190. Daughter[9] Phillips** (*Martha Amanda[8] McKee*, *William Robert[7]*, *Josiah William[6]*, *Elizabeth[5]*, *Alexander[4]*, *Andrew[3] Pegan II*, *Andrew[2] Pagan*, *James[1]*) was born about 1924. She was the daughter of Robert Phillips and Martha Amanda McKee (57). Daughter died about 1924. Died in infancy.

**191. Charles Inman[9] McKee II** (*Charles Albert[8]*, *William Robert[7]*, *Josiah William[6]*, *Elizabeth[5]*, *Alexander[4]*, *Andrew[3] Pegan II*, *Andrew[2] Pagan*, *James[1]*) was born on June 12, 1930. He is the son of Charles Albert McKee (58) and Geneva L. Hocutt.

**192. Billy Don[9] McKee** (*Charles Albert[8]*, *William Robert[7]*, *Josiah William[6]*, *Elizabeth[5]*, *Alexander[4]*, *Andrew[3] Pegan II*, *Andrew[2] Pagan*, *James[1]*) was born on June 10, 1934, in Oklahoma City, Oklahoma. He is the son of Charles Albert McKee (58) and Geneva L. Hocutt.

**193. Everett James[9] Meyer** (*Ella Florence[8] McKee*, *James L.[7]*, *Josiah William[6]*, *Elizabeth[5]*, *Alexander[4]*, *Andrew[3] Pegan II*, *Andrew[2] Pagan*, *James[1]*) was born on March 24, 1918, in Wynnewood, Brady Twp., Garvin Co., Oklahoma. He was the son of Luther L. Meyer and Ella Florence McKee (60). Everett James died in Enid, Garfield Co., Oklahoma, on November 26, 1997, at age 79. He was buried in Memorial Park Cemetery, Enid, Garfield Co., Oklahoma.[59, 60]

**194. Edward Emil[9] Meyer** (*Ella Florence[8] McKee*, *James L.[7]*, *Josiah William[6]*, *Elizabeth[5]*, *Alexander[4]*, *Andrew[3] Pegan II*, *Andrew[2] Pagan*, *James[1]*) was born on March 25, 1919, in Wynnewood, Brady Twp., Garvin Co., Oklahoma. He was the son of Luther L. Meyer and Ella Florence McKee (60). Edward Emil died in Enid, Garfield Co., Oklahoma, on June 2, 1978, at age 59.

Edward Emil married **Celesta May Bealmear** after 1940. Celesta May Bealmear was born in Beaver, Beaver Co., Oklahoma, on December 11, 1913. Celesta May reached age 78 and died in Enid, Garfield Co., Oklahoma, on December 24, 1991. She was buried in Memorial Park Cemetery, Enid, Garfield Co., Oklahoma.[60]

**195. Marvin Luther[9] Meyer** (*Ella Florence[8] McKee*, *James L.[7]*, *Josiah William[6]*, *Elizabeth[5]*, *Alexander[4]*, *Andrew[3] Pegan II*, *Andrew[2] Pagan*, *James[1]*) was born on May 15, 1921, in Wynnewood, Brady Twp., Garvin Co., Oklahoma. He was the son of Luther L. Meyer and Ella Florence McKee (60). Marvin Luther died in Perris, Riverside Co., California, on July 7, 1984, at age 63. He was buried in Riverside National Cemetery, Riverside, Riverside Co., California.[61]

**196. Iva Laura[9] Meyer** (*Ella Florence[8] McKee*, *James L.[7]*, *Josiah William[6]*, *Elizabeth[5]*, *Alexander[4]*, *Andrew[3] Pegan II*, *Andrew[2] Pagan*, *James[1]*) was born on January 25, 1923, in Wynnewood, Brady Twp., Garvin Co., Oklahoma. She was also known as **Jeannie.** She was the daughter of Luther L. Meyer and Ella Florence McKee (60). Iva Laura died in Haysville, Sedgwick Co., Kansas, on April 10, 2007, at age 84. She was buried in Lakeview Cemetery & Mausoleum, Wichita, Sedgewick Co., Kansas.[62]

Iva Laura married **Edward Arthur John** after 1940. Edward Arthur John was born in Cinton, Rock Co., Wisconsin, on January 13, 1915. Edward Arthur reached age 86 and died in Wichita, Sedgewick Co., Kansas, on June 14, 2001. He was buried in Lakeview Cemetery & Mausoleum, Wichita, Sedgewick Co., Kansas.[62]

**197. Anola⁹ Meyer** (*Ella Florence⁸ McKee, James L.⁷, Josiah William⁶, Elizabeth⁵, Alexander⁴, Andrew³ Pegan II, Andrew² Pagan, James¹*) was born on December 2, 1924, in Wynnewood, Brady Twp., Garvin Co., Oklahoma. She was also known as **Ola.** She was the daughter of Luther L. Meyer and Ella Florence McKee (60). Anola died in Wichita, Sedgewick Co., Kansas, on July 23, 2012, at age 87. She was buried in Resthaven Gardens of Memory Cemetery, Wichita, Sedgewick Co., Kansas.[63]

Anola married **Harold William Krob** on August 10, 1945. They had two children. Harold William Krob was born in Loda, Reno Co., Kansas, on November 8, 1914. Harold William reached age 90 and died in Wichita, Sedgwick Co., Kansas, on November 28, 2004. He was buried in Resthaven Gardens of Memory Cemetery, Wichita, Sedgewick Co., Kansas.[63]

**198. Louis Harvey⁹ Meridth** (*Laura Elvira⁸ McKee, James L.⁷, Josiah William⁶, Elizabeth⁵, Alexander⁴, Andrew³ Pegan II, Andrew² Pagan, James¹*) was born on September 7, 1919, in Wynnewood, Brady Twp., Garvin Co., Oklahoma. He was the son of Lawson Harvey Meridth and Laura Elvira McKee (62). Louis Harvey died in Wynnewood, Brady Twp., Garvin Co., Oklahoma, on March 10, 2007, at age 87. He was buried in Oaklawn Cemetery, Sulphur, Murray Co., Oklahoma.[64]

Louis Harvey married **Lillie May Chronister** after 1940. They divorced. They had three children. Lillie May Chronister was born in Hennepin, Brady Twp., Garvin Co., Oklahoma, on November 3, 1925. Lillie May reached age 74 and died under the name Lillie Coster in Wynnewood, Brady Twp., Garvin Co., Oklahoma, on July 12, 2000.

Louis Harvey Meridth II married **Connie Doris Stevens** on December 18, 1973, in Cooke Co., Texas. Connie Doris Stevens was born in Comanche, Stephens Co., Oklahoma, on September 9, 1915. Connie Doris reached age 88 and died in Sulphur, Murray Co., Oklahoma, on October 12, 2003. She was buried in Oaklawn Cemetery, Sulphur, Murray Co., Oklahoma.[64]

**199. Marie M.⁹ Meridth** (*Laura Elvira⁸ McKee, James L.⁷, Josiah William⁶, Elizabeth⁵, Alexander⁴, Andrew³ Pegan II, Andrew² Pagan, James¹*) was born on June 16, 1924, in Wynnewood, Brady Twp., Garvin Co., Oklahoma. She was the daughter of Lawson Harvey Meridth and Laura Elvira McKee (62). Marie M. died in Purcell, Moncrief Twp., McClain Co., Oklahoma, on May 1, 2011, at age 86. She was buried in Oaklawn Cemetery, Wynnewood, Brady Twp., Garvin Co., Oklahoma.[25]

Marie M. married **William Carl Morris II** on October 20, 1945, in Garvin Co., Oklahoma. They had three children. William Carl Morris II was born in Davis, Murray Co., Oklahoma, on September 21, 1916. William Carl reached age 87 and died in Wynnewood, Brady Twp., Garvin Co., Oklahoma, on September 25, 2003. He was buried in Oaklawn Cemetery, Wynnewood, Brady Twp., Garvin Co., Oklahoma.[25]

Marie M. Meridth and William Carl Morris II had three children, including:

+ 362   f   I.   **Daughter¹⁰ Morris.**

**200. Emlie⁹ Meridth** (*Laura Elvira⁸ McKee, James L.⁷, Josiah William⁶, Elizabeth⁵, Alexander⁴, Andrew³ Pegan II, Andrew² Pagan, James¹*) was born on December 23, 1927, in Brady Twp., Garvin Co., Oklahoma. She is the daughter of Lawson Harvey Meridth and Laura Elvira McKee (62).

Emlie married **Carroll Edward Johnson** before 1951. They have three children. Carroll Edward Johnson was born in Hennepin, Brady Twp., Garvin Co., Oklahoma, on May 29, 1922. Carroll Edward reached age 69 and died in Wynnewood, Brady Twp., Garvin Co., Oklahoma, on March 14, 1992. He was buried in Hennepin Cemetery, Murray Co., Oklahoma.[118]

Emlie Meridth and Carroll Edward Johnson had three children, including:

+ 363 m I. **Carroll Ray**[10] **Johnson II** was born in Elmore City, Elmore Twp., Garvin Co., Oklahoma?, on March 3, 1951. He died in Ringwood, Major Co., Oklahoma, on March 28, 2009.[118]

**201. Essie Mozelle**[9] **McKee** (*Oliver Charleston*[8], *James L.*[7], *Josiah William*[6], *Elizabeth*[5], *Alexander*[4], *Andrew*[3] *Pegan II, Andrew*[2] *Pagan, James*[1]) was born on April 6, 1928, in Elmore City, Elmore Twp., Garvin Co., Oklahoma. She was the daughter of Oliver Charleston McKee (64) and Estella Smith. Essie Mozelle died in Chickasha, Chickasha Twp., Grady Co., Oklahoma, on January 3, 2007, at age 78. She was buried in Liberty Cemetery, near Chickasha, Grady Co., Oklahoma.[65]

Essie Mozelle married **Clyde Clifford Williams** on May 15, 1950, in Garvin Co., Oklahoma. They had one daughter. Clyde Clifford Williams was born in Lincoln Twp., Caddo Co., Oklahoma, on May 23, 1927. Clyde Clifford reached age 75 and died in Verden, Grady Co., Oklahoma, on June 14, 2002.

**202. Desie Adron**[9] **McKee** (*Oliver Charleston*[8], *James L.*[7], *Josiah William*[6], *Elizabeth*[5], *Alexander*[4], *Andrew*[3] *Pegan II, Andrew*[2] *Pagan, James*[1]) was born on October 31, 1929, in Pursley Twp., Grady Co., Oklahoma. He was the son of Oliver Charleston McKee (64) and Estella Smith. Desie Adron died in Lindsay, Lindsay Twp., Garvin Co., Oklahoma, on November 16, 1991, at age 62. He was buried in Bradley Cemetery, Bradley Twp., Grady Co., Oklahoma.[11]

Desie Adron married **Bertha Lee Stevens** after 1940. Bertha Lee Stevens was born on May 6, 1926.

**203. Vida Marie**[9] **McKee** (*Oliver Charleston*[8], *James L.*[7], *Josiah William*[6], *Elizabeth*[5], *Alexander*[4], *Andrew*[3] *Pegan II, Andrew*[2] *Pagan, James*[1]) was born on March 31, 1931, in Pursley Twp., Grady Co., Oklahoma. She was the daughter of Oliver Charleston McKee (64) and Estella Smith. Vida Marie died in Harrison Twp., Grady Co., Oklahoma, on August 12, 1939, at age eight. She was buried in Bradley Cemetery, Bradley Twp., Grady Co., Oklahoma.[11]

**204. Milton William**[9] **McKee** (*Oliver Charleston*[8], *James L.*[7], *Josiah William*[6], *Elizabeth*[5], *Alexander*[4], *Andrew*[3] *Pegan II, Andrew*[2] *Pagan, James*[1]) was born on August 22, 1934, in Harrison Twp., Grady Co., Oklahoma. He was the son of Oliver Charleston McKee (64) and Estella Smith. Milton William died in Wichita Falls, Wichita Co., Texas, on February 20, 2007, at age 72. He was buried in Crestview Memorial Park Cemetery, Wichita Falls, Wichita Co., Texas.[66]

Milton William married **Norma June Foster** after 1950. Norma June Foster was born in Alfalfa, Blaine Co., Oklahoma, on June 17, 1936.

**205. Elmer Ray**[9] **McKee** (*Oliver Charleston*[8], *James L.*[7], *Josiah William*[6], *Elizabeth*[5], *Alexander*[4], *Andrew*[3] *Pegan II, Andrew*[2] *Pagan, James*[1]) was born on October 6, 1941, in Harrison Twp., Grady Co., Oklahoma. He was the son of Oliver Charleston McKee (64) and Estella Smith. Elmer Ray died in Rock Springs, Sweetwater Co., Wyoming, on August 16, 1999, at age 57.

**206. Gale Raymond**[9] **McKee** (*Oliver Charleston*[8], *James L.*[7], *Josiah William*[6], *Elizabeth*[5], *Alexander*[4], *Andrew*[3] *Pegan II, Andrew*[2] *Pagan, James*[1]) was born on December 18, 1947, in Harrison Twp., Grady Co., Oklahoma. He was the son of Oliver Charleston McKee (64) and Estella Smith. Gale Raymond died in Lindsay, Lindsay Twp., Garvin Co., Oklahoma, on February 19, 2001, at age 53.

Gale Raymond married **Daisey Ruth Stevens** on December 23, 1974. They divorced in Tarrant Co., Texas, in August 1982. Daisey Ruth Stevens was born in Grandfield, Tillman Co., Oklahoma, on November 8, 1923. She reached age 72 and died in Lawton, Blaine Co., Oklahoma, on December 26, 1995.

**207. Wanna Laflora**[9] **Raines** (*Mary Amanda*[8] *McKee, James L.*[7], *Josiah William*[6], *Elizabeth*[5], *Alexander*[4], *Andrew*[3] *Pegan II, Andrew*[2] *Pagan, James*[1]) was born on July 22, 1925, in Brady Twp., Garvin Co., Oklahoma. She was the daughter of Stephen

Andrew Raines and Mary Amanda McKee (65). Wanna Laflora died in Tipton, Tillman Co., Oklahoma, on December 1, 1980, at age 55. She was buried in Tipton Cemetery, Tipton, Tillman Co., Oklahoma.[62]

She married **Carl Randall Burrows.** They had four children. Carl Randall Burrows was born in Maguire, Tillman Co., Oklahoma, on September 1, 1922. Carl Randall reached age 80 and died in Vernon, Wilbarger Co., Texas, on May 22, 2003. He was buried in Tipton Cemetery, Tipton, Tillman Co., Oklahoma.[67]

208. **Henry Lee[9] McKee** (*Marvin Milton[8], James L.[7], Josiah William[6], Elizabeth[5], Alexander[4], Andrew[3] Pegan II, Andrew[2] Pagan, James[1]*) was born on August 16, 1930, in Pursley Twp., Grady Co., Oklahoma. He was the son of Marvin Milton McKee (66) and Maud May Jones. Henry Lee died in North Korea on November 22, 1951, at age 21. He was buried in Hillcrest Cemetery, Porterville, Tulare Co., California.[27] Died in the Korean War.

Henry Lee married **Rosa Phillips** on August 11, 1951, in Tulare Co., California.

209. **Carl Dean[9] McKee** (*Marvin Milton[8], James L.[7], Josiah William[6], Elizabeth[5], Alexander[4], Andrew[3] Pegan II, Andrew[2] Pagan, James[1]*) was born on February 5, 1936, in Pursley Twp., Grady Co., Oklahoma. He was the son of Marvin Milton McKee (66) and Maud May Jones. Carl Dean died in Porterville, Tulare Co., California, on February 3, 1995, at age 58.

210. **Laverne Marie[9] McKee** (*Marvin Milton[8], James L.[7], Josiah William[6], Elizabeth[5], Alexander[4], Andrew[3] Pegan II, Andrew[2] Pagan, James[1]*) was born on May 1, 1940, in Pursley Twp., Grady Co., Oklahoma. She was the daughter of Marvin Milton McKee (66) and Maud May Jones. Laverne Marie died in Porterville, Tulare Co., California, on March 25, 1996, at age 55.

Laverne Marie married **Ivan A. Amos** on October 30, 1964, in Tulare Co., California. Ivan A. Amos was born in Prairie, Franklin Co., Arkansas, on December 30, 1907. Ivan A. reached age 78 and died in Porterville, Tulare Co., California, on October 7, 1986.

211. **Baby[9] McKee** (*Marvin Milton[8], James L.[7], Josiah William[6], Elizabeth[5], Alexander[4], Andrew[3] Pegan II, Andrew[2] Pagan, James[1]*) was born in Pursley Twp., Grady Co., Oklahoma. He was the son of Marvin Milton McKee (66) and Maud May Jones. Baby died in Pursley Twp., Grady Co., Oklahoma. He was buried in Bradley Cemetery, Bradley Twp., Grady Co., Oklahoma.[11]

212. **Billie Roy[9] McKee** (*Willie Fletcher[8], James L.[7], Josiah William[6], Elizabeth[5], Alexander[4], Andrew[3] Pegan II, Andrew[2] Pagan, James[1]*) was born on March 6, 1937, in Rush Springs Twp., Grady Co., Oklahoma. He was the son of Willie Fletcher McKee (68) and Edith May Heatley. Billie Roy died in Rush Springs Twp., Grady Co., Oklahoma, on March 6, 1937. He was buried in Bradley Cemetery, Bradley Twp., Grady Co., Oklahoma.

213. **Gussie Isaac[9] Riley** (*Reuben Josiah[8], Martha Louise Jane[7] McKee, Josiah William[6], Elizabeth[5], Alexander[4], Andrew[3] Pegan II, Andrew[2] Pagan, James[1]*) was born on October 12, 1912, in Bradley Twp., Grady Co., Oklahoma. He was also known as **Isaac.** He was the son of Reuben Josiah Riley (69) and Sarah Julia Ann Dutton. Gussie Isaac died in Justin, Denton Co., Texas, on March 15, 2006, at age 93.

Gussie Isaac married **Esther Faye Jeffcoat** before 1933. They had three daughters. Esther Faye Jeffcoat was born in Wade, Bryan Co., Texas, on June 30, 1912. Esther Faye reached age 63 and died in Pampa, Gray Co., Texas, on September 25, 1975.

Daughters of Gussie Isaac Riley and Esther Faye Jeffcoat:

+ 364 f I. **Ada Marie[10] Riley** was born in Pursley Twp., Grady Co., Oklahoma, on April 14, 1933.

+ 365 f II. **Joyce G.[10] Riley** was born in Pursley Twp., Grady Co., Oklahoma, in 1935.

+ 366 f III. **Ruby Esther[10] Riley** was born in Pursley Twp., Grady Co., Oklahoma, on November 9, 1939. She died in Pampa, Gray Co., Texas, on October 12, 1988.

**214. Lula Ann⁹ Riley** (*Reuben Josiah⁸, Martha Louise Jane⁷ McKee, Josiah William⁶, Elizabeth⁵, Alexander⁴, Andrew³ Pegan II, Andrew² Pagan, James¹*) was born on August 8, 1914, in Bradley Twp., Grady Co., Oklahoma. She was the daughter of Reuben Josiah Riley (69) and Sarah Julia Ann Dutton. Lula Ann died in Oklahoma City, Oklahoma, on February 29, 2008, at age 93.

She married **Harold McConnell** after 1940. They had one son.

**215. Charles Russell⁹ Riley** (*Reuben Josiah⁸, Martha Louise Jane⁷ McKee, Josiah William⁶, Elizabeth⁵, Alexander⁴, Andrew³ Pegan II, Andrew² Pagan, James¹*) was born on February 16, 1917, in Bradley Twp., Grady Co., Oklahoma. He was also known as **Bud.** He was the son of Reuben Josiah Riley (69) and Sarah Julia Ann Dutton. Charles Russell died in Mustang, Canadian Co., Oklahoma, on April 13, 1981, at age 64. He was buried in Evergreen Cemetery, Minco, Grady Co., Oklahoma.[68]

Charles Russell married **Velma Ione Anthony** before 1939. They had five children. Velma Ione Anthony was born in Cogar, Caddo Co., Oklahoma, on April 6, 1921. Velma Ione reached age 81 and died in Oklahoma City, Oklahoma, on September 6, 2002. She was buried in Evergreen Cemetery, Minco, Grady Co., Oklahoma.[68]

Children of Charles Russell Riley and Velma Ione Anthony had five children, including:

+ 367 f I. **Velma Charlene¹⁰ Riley** was born in Lone Rock Twp., Caddo Co., Oklahoma, in 1939.

+ 368 f II. **Virginia Carolyn¹⁰ Riley** was born in Lone Rock Twp., Caddo Co., Oklahoma, on October 3, 1942. She died in Choctaw, Oklahoma Co., Oklahoma, on April 14, 2013.[41]

**216. Lee Emma⁹ Riley** (*Reuben Josiah⁸, Martha Louise Jane⁷ McKee, Josiah William⁶, Elizabeth⁵, Alexander⁴, Andrew³ Pegan II, Andrew² Pagan, James¹*) was born on July 22, 1921, in Bradley Twp., Grady Co., Oklahoma. She was the daughter of Reuben Josiah Riley (69) and Sarah Julia Ann Dutton. Lee Emma died in San Antonio, Bexar Co., Texas, on December 3, 2006, at age 85. She was buried in Erin Springs Cemetery, Erin Springs, Lindsay Twp., Garvin Co., Oklahoma.[12]

Lee Emma married **Jay Lee Edgar** on August 9, 1938, in Stephens Co., Oklahoma. They had two sons. Jay Lee Edgar was born in Harrison Co., Texas?, on August 21, 1920. Jay Lee reached age 86 and died in Lindsay, Lindsay Twp., Garvin Co., Oklahoma, on October 26, 2006. He was buried in Erin Springs Cemetery, Erin Springs, Lindsay Twp., Garvin Co., Oklahoma.[12]

Sons of Lee Emma Riley and Jay Lee Edgar:

+ 369 m I. **Reuben Walter¹⁰ Edgar** was born in Lindsay, Lindsay Twp., Garvin Co., Oklahoma, on November 11, 1939. He died in Lindsay, Lindsay Twp., Garvin Co., Oklahoma, on July 26, 1992.

+ 370 m II. **Doyle Rayburn¹⁰ Edgar** was born in Lindsay, Lindsay Twp., Garvin Co., Oklahoma, on October 6, 1941. He died in Lindsay, Lindsay Twp., Garvin Co., Oklahoma, on February 24, 1988.

**217. Ida Mae⁹ Riley** (*Reuben Josiah⁸, Martha Louise Jane⁷ McKee, Josiah William⁶, Elizabeth⁵, Alexander⁴, Andrew³ Pegan II, Andrew² Pagan, James¹*) was born on June 20, 1924, in Pursley Twp., Grady Co., Oklahoma. She was the daughter of Reuben Josiah Riley (69) and Sarah Julia Ann Dutton. Ida Mae died in Lindsay, Lindsay Twp., Garvin Co., Oklahoma, on December 7, 1989, at age 65. She was buried in Erin Springs Cemetery, Erin Springs, Lindsay Twp., Garvin Co., Oklahoma.[12]

She married **Woodrow Caldwell** after 1940. They had one child. Woodrow Caldwell was born in Fowler Twp., McCurtain Co., Oklahoma, on February 22, 1925. Woodrow reached age 64 and died in Lindsay, Lindsay Twp., Garvin Co., Oklahoma, on July 6, 1989. He was buried in Erin

Springs Cemetery, Erin Springs, Lindsay Twp., Garvin Co., Oklahoma.[12]

**218. Sarah Elvina**[9] **Riley** (*Reuben Josiah*[8], *Martha Louise Jane*[7] *McKee, Josiah William*[6], *Elizabeth*[5], *Alexander*[A], *Andrew*[3] *Pegan II, Andrew*[2] *Pagan, James*[1]) was born on November 21, 1926, in Pursley Twp., Grady Co., Oklahoma. She is the daughter of Reuben Josiah Riley (69) and Sarah Julia Ann Dutton.

Sarah Elvina married **Leonard Gordon Simmons II** on November 6, 1947, in Cooke Co., Texas. They had four children. Leonard Gordon Simmons II was born in Texarkana, Miller Co., Arkansas, on September 3, 1924. He was also known as **June.** Leonard Gordon reached age 86 and died in Lindsay, Lindsay Twp., Garvin Co., Oklahoma, on October 20, 2010. He was buried in Green Hill Cemetery, McClain Co., Oklahoma.[28]

Sarah Elvina Riley and Leonard Gordon Simmons II had four children, including:

+ 371 f II. **Daughter**[10] **Simmons**

**219. Emma Mae**[9] **Jones** (*Mary Malire*[8] *Riley, Martha Louise Jane*[7] *McKee, Josiah William*[6], *Elizabeth*[5], *Alexander*[A], *Andrew*[3] *Pegan II, Andrew*[2] *Pagan, James*[1]) was born on January 30, 1915, in Bradley Twp., Grady Co., Oklahoma. She was the daughter of Sampson Leroy Jones and Mary Malire Riley (70). Emma Mae died in Oklahoma City, Oklahoma, on June 9, 1991, at age 76. She was buried in Resthaven Gardens Cemetery, Oklahoma City, Cleveland Co., Oklahoma.[23]

Childless.

Emma Mae married **Robert Leamon Adams** before 1940. Robert Leamon Adams was born in Harrison Twp., Grady Co., Oklahoma, on February 27, 1910. Robert Leamon reached age 31 and died in Palo Verde, Riverside Co., California, on November 9, 1941. He was buried in Green Hill Cemetery, McClain Co., Oklahoma.[28]

Emma Mae Jones Adams married **Roy Cecil Gatten** before 1991. Roy Cecil Gatten was born in Billings, Noble Co., Oklahoma, on January 5, 1919. Roy Cecil reached age 88 and died in Oklahoma City, Oklahoma, on March 2, 2007.

**220. Francis Horten**[9] **Jones** (*Mary Malire*[8] *Riley, Martha Louise Jane*[7] *McKee, Josiah William*[6], *Elizabeth*[5], *Alexander*[A], *Andrew*[3] *Pegan II, Andrew*[2] *Pagan, James*[1]) was born on September 28, 1922, in Bradley Twp., Grady Co., Oklahoma. He was also known as **Frank.** He was the son of Sampson Leroy Jones and Mary Malire Riley (70). Francis Horten died in Odessa, Ector Co., Texas, on March 16, 1983, at age 60.

Francis Horten married **Ruth Lucille Porter** after 1940. Ruth Lucille Porter was born on May 14, 1926.

**221. Bessie Elizabeth**[9] **Riley** (*Isaac Russell*[8], *Martha Louise Jane*[7] *McKee, Josiah William*[6], *Elizabeth*[5], *Alexander*[A], *Andrew*[3] *Pegan II, Andrew*[2] *Pagan, James*[1]) was born on April 16, 1916, in Bradley Twp., Grady Co., Oklahoma. She was the daughter of Isaac Russell Riley II (71) and Edna Bassett. Bessie Elizabeth died in Tucson, Pima Co., Arizona, on April 18, 1991, at age 75. She was buried in Green Valley Cemetery, Suhaurita, Pima Co., Arizona.[64]

Bessie Elizabeth married **Ralph Duane Swigert** on October 9, 1941, in San Miguel Co., New Mexico. They had two sons. Ralph Duane Swigert was born in Paruna, Harper Co., Oklahoma, on January 16, 1915. Ralph Duane reached age 87 and died in Sahuarita, Pima Co., Arizona, on October 21, 2002. He was buried in Green Valley Cemetery, Suhaurita, Pima Co., Arizona.[69]

**222. Martha Lois**[9] **Riley** (*Isaac Russell*[8], *Martha Louise Jane*[7] *McKee, Josiah William*[6], *Elizabeth*[5], *Alexander*[A], *Andrew*[3] *Pegan II, Andrew*[2] *Pagan, James*[1]) was born on November 9, 1924, in Minco, Union Twp., Grady Co., Oklahoma. She was the daughter of Isaac Russell Riley II (71) and Edna Bassett. Martha Lois died in Pico Rivera, Los Angeles Co., California, on July 26, 1988, at age 63.

She married **Mr. Greenwood.**

**223. Betty Jean**[9] **Riley** (*Isaac Russell*[8], *Martha Louise Jane*[7] *McKee, Josiah William*[6], *Elizabeth*[5], *Alexander*[A], *Andrew*[3] *Pegan II, Andrew*[2] *Pagan, James*[1]) was born on November 24, 1931, in Skiatook, Tulsa Co., Oklahoma? She is the daughter of Isaac Russell Riley II (71) and Edna Bassett.

Betty Jean married **David Moody Mayhon** before 1949. They had two daughters. David Moody Mayhon was born in Tolar, Roosevelt Co., New Mexico, on February 11, 1930. David Moody reached age 53 and died in Albuquerque, Bernalillo Co., New Mexico?, on December 18, 1983. He was buried in Sunset Memorial Park Cemetery, Albuquerque, Bernalillo Co., New Mexico.[119]

Betty Jean Riley and David Moody Mayhon had two children, including:

+ 372 f II. **Carolyn Sue**[10] **Mayhon** was born in Albuquerque, Bernalillo Co., New Mexico?, on November 19, 1949. She died in Calimesa, Riverside Co., California, on June 11, 2010.

**224. Billy Don**[9] **Riley** (*Isaac Russell*[8], *Martha Louise Jane*[7] *McKee, Josiah William*[6], *Elizabeth*[5], *Alexander*[4], *Andrew*[3] *Pegan II, Andrew*[2] *Pagan, James*[1]) was born on December 16, 1934, in Bradley Twp., Grady Co., Oklahoma. He was also known as **Don.** He was the son of Isaac Russell Riley II (71) and Edna Bassett. Billy Don died in Albuquerque, Bernalillo Co., New Mexico, on July 19, 2003, at age 68.

May have never married.

**225. Loyd Jesse**[9] **Gosnell** (*Emma Neta*[8] *Riley, Martha Louise Jane*[7] *McKee, Josiah William*[6], *Elizabeth*[5], *Alexander*[4], *Andrew*[3] *Pegan II, Andrew*[2] *Pagan, James*[1]) was born on May 7, 1916, in Bradley Twp., Grady Co., Oklahoma. He was the son of Charles William Gosnell and Emma Neta Riley (72). Loyd Jesse died in Alex, Alex Twp., Grady Co. Oklahoma, on December 2, 1987, at age 71. He was buried in Alex Cemetery, Alex, Alex Twp., Grady Co., Oklahoma.[52]

He married **Margaret Elizabeth Spencer.** They had two children. Margaret Elizabeth Spencer was born in Bradley Twp., Grady Co., Oklahoma, on December 2, 1915. She was also known as **Peggy.** Margaret Elizabeth reached age 67 and died in Chickasha, Chickasha Twp., Grady Co., Oklahoma, on September 23, 1983. She was buried in Alex Cemetery, Alex, Alex Twp., Grady Co., Oklahoma.[52]

Loyd Jesse Gosnell and Margaret Elizabeth Spencer had two children, including:

+ 373 m I. **Bobbie Allen**[10] **Gosnell** was born in Pursley Twp., Grady Co., Oklahoma, on November 17, 1934. He died in Alex, Alex Twp., Grady Co. Oklahoma, on May 12, 2001.[52]

**226. William Isaac**[9] **Gosnell** (*Emma Neta*[8] *Riley, Martha Louise Jane*[7] *McKee, Josiah William*[6], *Elizabeth*[5], *Alexander*[4], *Andrew*[3] *Pegan II, Andrew*[2] *Pagan, James*[1]) was born on November 22, 1922, in Bradley Twp., Grady Co., Oklahoma. He was the son of Charles William Gosnell and Emma Neta Riley (72). William Isaac died in Marlow Twp., Stephens Co., Oklahoma, on March 13, 2003, at age 80. He was buried in Marlow Cemetery, Marlow Twp., Stephens Co., Oklahoma.[32]

William Isaac married **Lucille Marie Kirkpatrick** on December 21, 1946. They had two children. Lucille Marie Kirkpatrick was born in Magnolia, Columbia Co., Arkansas, on December 3, 1913. Lucille Marie reached age 96 and died in Marlow Twp., Stephens Co., Oklahoma, on September 24, 2010. She was buried in Marlow Cemetery, Marlow Twp., Stephens Co., Oklahoma.[32]

William Isaac Gosnell and Lucille Marie Kirkpatrick had two children, including:

+ 374 m I. **Ben**[10] **Gosnell.** Ben died in Perth, Australia?, before 2003.

**227. Leroy**[9] **Grooms** (*Janie Susan*[8] *Riley, Martha Louise Jane*[7] *McKee, Josiah William*[6], *Elizabeth*[5], *Alexander*[4], *Andrew*[3] *Pegan II, Andrew*[2] *Pagan, James*[1]) was born on June 5, 1919, in Brady Twp., Garvin Co., Oklahoma. He was also known as **Buck.** He was the son of Marvin Wesley Groomes or Grooms and Janie Susan Riley (74). Leroy died in Rush Springs Twp., Grady Co., Oklahoma, on June 18, 1993, at age 74. He was buried in Alex Cemetery, Alex, Alex Twp., Grady Co., Oklahoma.[52]

Leroy married **Betty Lee Edgar** on July 23, 1938, in Grady Co., Oklahoma. They had two children. Betty Lee Edgar was born in Winnfield, Winn Parish, Louisiana, on April 9, 1919. Betty Lee reached age 85 and died in Rush Springs Twp., Grady Co., Oklahoma, on February 19, 2005. She was buried in Alex Cemetery, Alex, Alex Twp., Grady Co., Oklahoma.[52]

Leroy Grooms and Betty Lee Edgar had two children, including:

+ 375 m I. **Son**[10] **Grooms**

**228. Ada Louise**[9] **Grooms** (*Janie Susan*[8] *Riley, Martha Louise Jane*[7] *McKee, Josiah William*[6], *Elizabeth*[5], *Alexander*[4], *Andrew*[3] *Pegan II, Andrew*[2] *Pagan, James*[1]) was born in 1921 in Brady Twp., Garvin Co., Oklahoma. She was the daughter of Marvin Wesley Groomes or Grooms and Janie Susan Riley (74). Ada Louise died in Brady Twp., Garvin Co., Oklahoma, before 1930. May have died in infancy.

**229. Anna Lee**[9] **Dutton** (*Janie Susan*[8] *Riley, Martha Louise Jane*[7] *McKee, Josiah William*[6], *Elizabeth*[5], *Alexander*[4], *Andrew*[3] *Pegan II, Andrew*[2] *Pagan, James*[1]) was born in 1928 in Cushing, Payne Co., Oklahoma. She is the daughter of Scott Washington Dutton and Janie Susan Riley (74).

**230. Kenneth Roy**[9] **Jones** (*Anna Martha*[8] *Riley, Martha Louise Jane*[7] *McKee, Josiah William*[6], *Elizabeth*[5], *Alexander*[4], *Andrew*[3] *Pegan II, Andrew*[2] *Pagan, James*[1]) was born on September 12, 1930, in Bradley Twp., Grady Co., Oklahoma. He was the son of Terry Everett Jones and Anna Martha Riley (75). Kenneth Roy died in Bradley Twp., Grady Co., Oklahoma, on March 29, 1973, at age 42. He was buried in Green Hill Cemetery, McClain Co., Oklahoma.[28]

He married **Violet Crawford.**

**231. Virginia**[9] **Jones** (*Anna Martha*[8] *Riley, Martha Louise Jane*[7] *McKee, Josiah William*[6], *Elizabeth*[5], *Alexander*[4], *Andrew*[3] *Pegan II, Andrew*[2] *Pagan, James*[1]) was born in 1932 in Bradley Twp., Grady Co., Oklahoma. She is the daughter of Terry Everett Jones and Anna Martha Riley (75).

She married **Unknown Cunningham.**

**232. Terry Gene**[9] **Jones II** (*Anna Martha*[8] *Riley, Martha Louise Jane*[7] *McKee, Josiah William*[6], *Elizabeth*[5], *Alexander*[4], *Andrew*[3] *Pegan II, Andrew*[2] *Pagan, James*[1]) was born in 1936 in Pursley Twp., Grady Co., Oklahoma. He is also known as **Gene.** He is the son of Terry Everett Jones and Anna Martha Riley (75).

**233. Claud J.**[9] **Jones** (*Anna Martha*[8] *Riley, Martha Louise Jane*[7] *McKee, Josiah William*[6], *Elizabeth*[5], *Alexander*[4], *Andrew*[3] *Pegan II, Andrew*[2] *Pagan, James*[1]) was born on January 17, 1939, in Pursley Twp., Grady Co., Oklahoma. He was the son of Terry Everett Jones and Anna Martha Riley (75). Claud J. died in Lexington Twp., Cleveland Co., Oklahoma, on December 6, 2010, at age 71. He was buried in Green Hill Cemetery, McClain Co., Oklahoma.[28]

Claud J. married **Unknown Unknown.** They divorced. They had three daughters.

**234. Christine Ellen**[9] **Cross** (*Willie Alice*[8] *McKee, Josiah Andres*[7], *Josiah William*[6], *Elizabeth*[5], *Alexander*[4], *Andrew*[3] *Pegan II, Andrew*[2] *Pagan, James*[1]) was born on July 2, 1914, in Elmore City, Elmore Twp., Garvin Co., Oklahoma. She was also known as **Kitty.** She was the daughter of Jesse Thomas Cross and Willie Alice McKee (76). Christine Ellen died in Bacliff, Galveston Co., Texas, on December 21, 1989, at age 75. She was buried in Galveston Memorial Park Cemetery, Hitchcock, Galveston Co., Texas.[71]

Christine Ellen married **Eugene Dawson Alexander** about 1930. They had six children. Eugene Dawson Alexander was born in Bartlett, Williamson Co., Texas, on December 18, 1910. Eugene Dawson reached age 66 and died in Bacliff, Galveston Co., Texas, on October 10, 1977. He was buried in Galveston Memorial Park Cemetery, Hitchcock, Galveston Co., Texas.[71]

Christine Ellen Cross and Eugene Dawson Alexander had six children, including:

+ 376 m I. **Ledson Dawson**[10] **Alexander** was born in Hewitt Twp., Carter Co., Oklahoma, in 1931.

+ 377 m II. **Eugene Ulysses**[10] **Alexander II** was born in Wilson, Hewitt Twp., Carter Co., Oklahoma, on June 22, 1933. He died in Ardmore, Morgan Twp., Carter Co., Oklahoma, on December 21, 1994.[13]

+ 378 m III. **Jesse Lee**[10] **Alexander** was born in Hewitt, Hewitt Twp., Carter Co., Oklahoma, in 1937.

+ 379 f IV. **Oleta Joyce**[10] **Alexander** was born in Hewitt, Hewitt Twp., Carter Co., Oklahoma, in 1940.

+ 380 f VI. **Eugenia Dale**[10] **Alexander** was born in Hewitt, Hewitt Twp., Carter Co., Oklahoma, on April 9, 1954. She died in Hewitt, Hewitt Twp., Carter Co., Oklahoma, on July 25, 1954.[13]

**235. Jesse Thomas**[9] **Cross II** (*Willie Alice*[8] *McKee, Josiah Andres*[7], *Josiah William*[6], *Elizabeth*[5], *Alexander*[4], *Andrew*[3] *Pegan II, Andrew*[2] *Pagan, James*[1]) was born on August 8, 1916, in Elmore City, Elmore Twp., Garvin Co., Oklahoma. He was the son of Jesse Thomas Cross and Willie Alice McKee (76). Jesse Thomas died in Germany on March 13, 1945, at age 28. He was buried in Henri-Chapelle American Cemetery and Memorial, Henri-Chapelle, Liege, Belgium.[72] Died in WWII.

Never married.

**236. Irene Dorothy**[9] **Alexander** (*Willie Alice*[8] *McKee, Josiah Andres*[7], *Josiah William*[6], *Elizabeth*[5], *Alexander*[4], *Andrew*[3] *Pegan II, Andrew*[2] *Pagan, James*[1]) was born on March 31, 1919, in Wirt, Hewitt Twp., Carter Co., Oklahoma. She was the daughter of Frank Perry Alexander and Willie Alice McKee (76). Irene Dorothy died in Hewitt Twp., Carter Co., Oklahoma, on October 2, 1972, at age 53. She was buried in Hewitt Cemetery, Wilson, Hewitt Twp., Carter Co., Oklahoma.[13]

She married **Thomas Oscar Carriker.** They had two sons. Thomas Oscar Carriker was born in Hewitt Twp., Carter Co., Oklahoma, on September 16, 1919. Thomas Oscar reached age 25 and died

in The Netherlands on March 30, 1945. He was buried in Margraten Cemetery, Margraten, The Netherlands.[120] Died in WWII.

Irene Dorothy Alexander married **George Bailey.**

Sons of Irene Dorothy Alexander and Thomas Oscar Carriker:

+ 381 m I. **Frank Thomas**[10] **Carriker** was born in Wilson, Hewitt Twp., Carter Co., Oklahoma, in 1937.

+ 382 m II. **Lonnie Joe**[10] **Carriker** was born in Wilson, Hewitt Twp., Carter Co., Oklahoma, on September 6, 1940.

**237. Frank Perry**[9] **Alexander II** (*Willie Alice*[8] *McKee, Josiah Andres*[7], *Josiah William*[6], *Elizabeth*[5], *Alexander*[4], *Andrew*[3] *Pegan II, Andrew*[2] *Pagan, James*[1]) was born on March 19, 1921, in Wirt, Hewitt Twp., Carter Co., Oklahoma. He was the son of Frank Perry Alexander and Willie Alice McKee (76). Frank Perry died in Prineville, Crook Co., Oregon, on September 17, 2006, at age 85. He was buried in Juniper Haven Cemetery, Prineville, Crook Co., Oregon.[73]

Frank Perry married **Adrienne Leona See** on November 7, 1943, in Union Co., Oregon. They had three children. Adrienne Leona See was born in La Grande, Union Co., Oregon, on October 19, 1924. Adrienne Leona reached age 82 and died in Albany, Linn Co., Oregon, on February 20, 2007. She was buried in Juniper Haven Cemetery, Prineville, Crook Co., Oregon.[73]

Frank Perry Alexander II and Adrienne Leona See had three children, including:

+ 383 f I. **Carol Jeanne**[10] **Alexander** was born in La Grande, Union Co., Oregon, on September 20, 1945. She died in Prineville, Crook Co., Oregon, on June 5, 2000.

**238. Bobby Joe**[9] **Alexander** (*Willie Alice*[8] *McKee, Josiah Andres*[7], *Josiah William*[6], *Elizabeth*[5], *Alexander*[4], *Andrew*[3] *Pegan II, Andrew*[2] *Pagan, James*[1]) was born on April 5, 1925, in Wirt, Hewitt Twp., Carter

Co., Oklahoma. He was the son of Frank Perry Alexander and Willie Alice McKee (76). Bobby Joe died in Wirt, Hewitt Twp., Carter Co., Oklahoma, on May 25, 1939, at age 14. He was buried in Hewitt Cemetery, Wilson, Hewitt Twp., Carter Co., Oklahoma.[13]

**239. Opal Marie[9] McKee** (*George Washington Josiah[8], Josiah Andres[7], Josiah William[6], Elizabeth[5], Alexander[4], Andrew[3] Pegan II, Andrew[2] Pagan, James[1]*) was born on March 23, 1920, in Wirt, Hewitt Twp., Carter Co., Oklahoma. She was the daughter of George Washington Josiah McKee III (78) and Lucy Evelyn Ramsey. Opal Marie died in Wilson, Hewitt Twp., Carter Co., Oklahoma, on November 27, 2002, at age 82. She was buried in Lone Grove Cemetery, Lone Grove, Carter Co., Oklahoma.[74]

Opal Marie married **Frank James Gaston** on August 16, 1946. Frank James Gaston was born in Coal Co., Oklahoma, on June 26, 1911. Frank James reached age 81 and died in Ardmore, Morgan Twp., Carter Co., Oklahoma, on June 9, 1993. He was buried in Lone Grove Cemetery, Lone Grove, Carter Co., Oklahoma.[74]

**240. Jack[9] McKee** (*George Washington Josiah[8], Josiah Andres[7], Josiah William[6], Elizabeth[5], Alexander[4], Andrew[3] Pegan II, Andrew[2] Pagan, James[1]*) was born on November 16, 1921, in Hewitt Twp., Carter Co., Oklahoma. He was the son of George Washington Josiah McKee III (78) and Lucy Evelyn Ramsey. Jack died in Wilson, Hewitt Twp., Carter Co., Oklahoma, on July 15, 1962, at age 40. He was buried in Hewitt Cemetery, Wilson, Hewitt Twp., Carter Co., Oklahoma.[13]

Jack married **Valura Margaret Sides** after 1940. They had two children. Valura Margaret Sides was born in Wilson, Hewitt Twp., Carter Co., Oklahoma, on June 12, 1924. She was also known as **Meme.** Valura Margaret reached age 75 and died in Oklahoma City, Oklahoma, on December 10, 1999. She was buried in Green Hill Cemetery, Davis, Murray Co., Oklahoma.[31]

**241. Richard Douglas[9] McKee** (*George Washington Josiah[8], Josiah Andres[7], Josiah William[6], Elizabeth[5], Alexander[4], Andrew[3] Pegan II, Andrew[2] Pagan,*

*James[1]*) was born on May 18, 1924, in Pernell, Elmore Twp., Garvin Co., Oklahoma. He was the son of George Washington Josiah McKee III (78) and Lucy Evelyn Ramsey. Richard Douglas died in Peoria, Maricopa Co., Arizona, on April 12, 2012, at age 87. He was buried in Phoenix Memorial Park Cemetery, Phoenix, Maricopa Co., Arizona.[75]

Richard Douglas married **Thelma Jean Turner** after 1940. They had three children. Thelma Jean Turner was born in Ardmore, Morgan Twp., Carter Co., Oklahoma, on September 20, 1924. She was also known as **Jean.** Thelma Jean reached age 87 and died in Peoria, Maricopa Co., Arizona, on September 2, 2012. She was buried in Phoenix Memorial Park Cemetery, Phoenix, Maricopa Co., Arizona.[75]

**242. Kenneth Gene[9] McKee** (*George Washington Josiah[8], Josiah Andres[7], Josiah William[6], Elizabeth[5], Alexander[4], Andrew[3] Pegan II, Andrew[2] Pagan, James[1]*) was born on April 13, 1930, in Hewitt Twp., Carter Co., Oklahoma. He is the son of George Washington Josiah McKee III (78) and Lucy Evelyn Ramsey.

He married **Hazel Unknown.**

**243. Jerry Ray[9] McKee** (*George Washington Josiah[8], Josiah Andres[7], Josiah William[6], Elizabeth[5], Alexander[4], Andrew[3] Pegan II, Andrew[2] Pagan, James[1]*) was born on August 24, 1934, in Ratliff City, Graham Twp., Carter Co., Oklahoma. He was the son of George Washington Josiah McKee III (78) and Lucy Evelyn Ramsey. Jerry Ray died in Ardmore, Morgan Twp., Carter Co., Oklahoma, on May 5, 2000, at age 65. He was buried in Green Hill Cemetery, Davis, Murray Co., Oklahoma.[31]

Childless.

Jerry Ray married **Wanda Lee Lathum** in 1973. Wanda Lee Lathum was born in Springer, Berwyn Twp., Carter Co., Oklahoma, on January 29, 1932. She was also known as **Doodle.** Wanda Lee reached age 66 and died in Davis, Murray Co., Oklahoma, on January 21, 1999. She was buried in Green Hill Cemetery, Davis, Murray Co., Oklahoma.[31]

**244. Christine[9] Pierce** (*Martha Anna[8] McKee, Josiah Andres[7], Josiah William[6], Elizabeth[5], Alexander[4],*

*Andrew³ Pegan II, Andrew² Pagan, James¹*) was born on September 4, 1927, in Waurika, Jefferson Co., Oklahoma. She was the adopted daughter of Charles Spurgeon Pierce and Martha Anna McKee (79). Christine was adopted after 1930. She lived in 1982 in Ratliff City, Graham Twp., Carter Co., Oklahoma. Christine died in a hospital in Ardmore, Morgan Twp., Carter Co., Oklahoma, on May 12, 1982, at age 54. She was buried in Green Hill Cemetery, Davis, Murray Co., Oklahoma[31]

Childless.

She married **Mr. Matson.** They divorced.

Christine Pierce Matson married **Oscar Edward Williams** on May 6, 1970, in Murray Co., Oklahoma. Oscar Edward Williams was born in Milan, Gibson Co., Tennessee, on February 15, 1908. Oscar Edward reached age 76 and died in Ratliff City, Graham Twp., Carter Co., Oklahoma, on May 30, 1984. He was buried in Green Hill Cemetery, Davis, Murray Co., Oklahoma.[31]

245. **Ruel Pearce⁹ Wilson** (*Roxie Laurenda⁸ McKee, Josiah Andres⁷, Josiah William⁶, Elizabeth⁵, Alexander⁴, Andrew³ Pegan II, Andrew² Pagan, James¹*) was born on August 13, 1926, in Fox, Graham Twp. Carter Co., Oklahoma. He was the son of Charles Raymond Wilson and Roxie Laurenda McKee (80). Ruel Pearce died in Ardmore, Morgan Twp., Carter Co., Oklahoma, on June 28, 1990, at age 63. He was buried in Hewitt Cemetery, Wilson, Hewitt Twp., Carter Co., Oklahoma.[13]

Ruel Pearce married **Mary Margaret Jones** on January 25, 1947, in Cooke Co., Texas. They had four children. Mary Margaret Jones was born in Wheeler, Hewitt Twp., Carter Co., Oklahoma, on December 28, 1928. Mary Margaret reached age 87 and died in Ardmore, Morgan Twp., Carter Co., Oklahoma, on February 9, 2016.

Ruel Pearce Wilson and Mary Margaret Jones had four children, including:

+ 384 m III. **Billy Thomas¹⁰ Wilson** was born in Ardmore, Morgan Twp., Carter Co., Oklahoma, on November 24, 1951. He died in Healdton, Hewitt

Twp., Carter Co., Oklahoma, on November 12, 2016.[121]

246. **Betty Lou⁹ Wilson** (*Roxie Laurenda⁸ McKee, Josiah Andres⁷, Josiah William⁶, Elizabeth⁵, Alexander⁴, Andrew³ Pegan II, Andrew² Pagan, James¹*) was born on November 14, 1929, in Maud, Oklahoma. She was the daughter of Charles Raymond Wilson and Roxie Laurenda McKee (80). Betty Lou died in Ardmore, Morgan Twp., Carter Co., Oklahoma, on September 13, 2012, at age 82. She was buried in Reck Cemetery, Wilson, Hewitt Co., Oklahoma.[76]

Betty Lou married **Kirby Francis Aycox** on May 7, 1949, in Cooke Co., Texas. They had seven children. Kirby Francis Aycox was born in Wilson, Hewitt Twp., Carter Co., Oklahoma, on September 1, 1929. Kirby Francis reached age 71 and died in Ardmore, Morgan Twp., Carter Co., Oklahoma, on January 6, 2001. He was buried in Reck Cemetery, Wilson, Hewitt Co., Oklahoma.[76]

Children of Betty Lou Wilson and Kirby Francis Aycox:

+ 385 m I. **Donald Gene¹⁰ Aycox** was born in Ardmore, Morgan Twp., Carter Co., Oklahoma, on January 27, 1952. He died in Ardmore, Morgan Twp., Carter Co., Oklahoma, on January 25, 2015.[71]

+ 386 f III. **Loretta Ann¹⁰ Aycox** was born in 1962. She died between 2006 and 2012.

247. **Billy Gene⁹ Wilson** (*Roxie Laurenda⁸ McKee, Josiah Andres⁷, Josiah William⁶, Elizabeth⁵, Alexander⁴, Andrew³ Pegan II, Andrew² Pagan, James¹*) was born in 1933 in Oklahoma. He was the son of Charles Raymond Wilson and Roxie Laurenda McKee (80).

He married **Charlene Unknown.**

248. **Virgie Mae⁹ Wilson** (*Roxie Laurenda⁸ McKee, Josiah Andres⁷, Josiah William⁶, Elizabeth⁵, Alexander⁴, Andrew³ Pegan II, Andrew² Pagan, James¹*) was born on February 7, 1934, in Oklahoma. She was the

daughter of Charles Raymond Wilson and Roxie Laurenda McKee (80). Virgie Mae lived in Del City, Oklahoma Co., Oklahoma. She died in Oklahoma City, Cleveland Co., Oklahoma, on January 1, 2008, at age 73. Virgie Mae was buried in Resthaven Gardens Cemetery, Oklahoma City, Cleveland Co., Oklahoma.[23]

Virgie Mae married **Mr. Stewart** before 1953. They had four children.

Virgie Mae Wilson Stewart married **William Albion Roycroft** after 1958. William Albion Roycroft was born in Portland, Cumberland Co., Maine, on November 21, 1923. William Albion reached age 74 and died in Oklahoma City, Cleveland Co., Oklahoma, on December 1, 1997. He was buried in Resthaven Gardens Cemetery, Oklahoma City, Cleveland Co., Oklahoma.[23]

249. **Donna Raye⁹ Wilson** (*Roxie Laurenda⁸ McKee, Josiah Andres⁷, Josiah William⁶, Elizabeth⁵, Alexander⁴, Andrew³ Pegan II, Andrew² Pagan, James¹*) was born on May 17, 1938, in Dillard, Wilson Twp., Carter Co., Oklahoma. She was the daughter of Charles Raymond Wilson and Roxie Laurenda McKee (80). Donna Raye died in Oklahoma City, Oklahoma, on February 28, 2004, at age 65. She was buried in Hewitt Cemetery, Wilson, Hewitt Twp., Carter Co., Oklahoma.

Donna Raye married **Mr. Williams** about 1959. They divorced. They had one child.

Donna Raye Wilson Williams married **Mr. Potter** about 1974. They divorced.

250. **Anna Marie⁹ Barrett** (*Sarah Lou⁸ McKee, Josiah Andres⁷, Josiah William⁶, Elizabeth⁵, Alexander⁴, Andrew³ Pegan II, Andrew² Pagan, James¹*) was born on January 7, 1928, in Wilson, Hewitt Twp., Carter Co., Oklahoma. She was the daughter of Tilden Theodore Barrett and Sarah Lou McKee (81). Anna Marie died in Sun City, Riverside Co., California, on September 5, 2000, at age 72. She was buried in Green Hills Memorial Park Cemetery, Rancho Palos Verdes, Los Angeles Co., California.[122]

Anna Marie married **Franklin Thomas Thompson** after 1945. Franklin Thomas Thompson was born

in Wilson, Hewitt Twp., Carter Co., Oklahoma, on October 25, 1918. Franklin Thomas reached age 82 and died in Sun City, Riverside Co., California, on May 11, 2001. He was buried in Green Hills Memorial Park Cemetery, Rancho Palos Verdes, Los Angeles Co., California.[122]

251. **Mac Theodore⁹ Barrett** (*Sarah Lou⁸ McKee, Josiah Andres⁷, Josiah William⁶, Elizabeth⁵, Alexander⁴, Andrew³ Pegan II, Andrew² Pagan, James¹*) was born on September 6, 1933, in Wilson, Hewitt Twp., Carter Co., Oklahoma. He was the son of Tilden Theodore Barrett and Sarah Lou McKee (81). Mac Theodore died in Wrightwood, San Bernardino Co., California, on April 7, 2001, at age 67.

He married **Unknown Unknown.**

252. **Barbara Jean⁹ Barrett** (*Sarah Lou⁸ McKee, Josiah Andres⁷, Josiah William⁶, Elizabeth⁵, Alexander⁴, Andrew³ Pegan II, Andrew² Pagan, James¹*) was born on January 25, 1938, in Wilson, Hewitt Twp., Carter Co., Oklahoma. She was the daughter of Tilden Theodore Barrett and Sarah Lou McKee (81). Barbara Jean died in Kingston, Marshall Co., Oklahoma, on January 15, 2004, at age 65. She was buried in Hewitt Cemetery, Wilson, Hewitt Twp., Carter Co., Oklahoma.[13]

Barbara Jean married **Rodney Kendall Fitz** on May 4, 1957, in Los Angeles Co., California. They had four daughters. Rodney Kendall Fitz was born in Contra Costa Co., California, on March 8, 1937. Rodney Kendall reached age 78 and died in Healdton, Hewitt Twp., Carter Co., Oklahoma, on October 2, 2015.

253. **Nancy Marlene⁹ McKee** (*Henry William⁸, Josiah Andres⁷, Josiah William⁶, Elizabeth⁵, Alexander⁴, Andrew³ Pegan II, Andrew² Pagan, James¹*) was born on February 1, 1946, in Wilson, Hewitt Twp., Carter Co., Oklahoma. She was the daughter of Henry William McKee (82) and Willie Fay Odell. Nancy Marlene died in Oklahoma City, Oklahoma, on January 28, 2000, at age 53. She was buried in Hewitt Cemetery, Wilson, Hewitt Twp., Carter Co., Oklahoma.[13]

Never married.

**254. Montie W.**[9] **McKee** (*Henry William*[8], *Josiah Andres*[7], *Josiah William*[6], *Elizabeth*[5], *Alexander*[4], *Andrew*[3] *Pegan II, Andrew*[2] *Pagan, James*[1]) was born on September 13, 1947, in Wilson, Hewitt Twp., Carter Co., Oklahoma. He was the son of Henry William McKee (82) and Willie Fay Odell. Montie W. died in Healdton, Hewitt Twp., Carter Co., Oklahoma, on July 25, 2000, at age 52. He was buried in Hewitt Cemetery, Wilson, Hewitt Twp., Carter Co., Oklahoma.[13]

He married **Unknown Unknown.** They divorced. They have two daughters.

**255. Rita Kaye**[9] **McKee** (*Verdie Loyd*[8], *Josiah Andres*[7], *Josiah William*[6], *Elizabeth*[5], *Alexander*[4], *Andrew*[3] *Pegan II, Andrew*[2] *Pagan, James*[1]) was born on July 23, 1941, in Wilson, Hewitt Twp., Carter Co., Oklahoma. She was the daughter of Verdie Loyd McKee (83) and Julia Mae Shepherd. Rita Kaye died in Krotz Springs, Saint Landry Parish, Louisiana, on May 9, 1969, at age 27.

Never married.

**256. Delores Geraldine**[9] **Chance** (*Ruth Lea*[8] *McKee, Josiah Andres*[7], *Josiah William*[6], *Elizabeth*[5], *Alexander*[4], *Andrew*[3] *Pegan II, Andrew*[2] *Pagan, James*[1]) was born on March 27, 1931, in Hewitt, Hewitt Twp., Carter Co., Oklahoma. She was the daughter of Boyet V. Chance and Ruth Lea McKee (84). Delores Geraldine died in Ardmore, Morgan Twp., Carter Co., Oklahoma, on August 2, 2006, at age 75. She was buried in Hillcrest Memorial Park Cemetery, Ardmore, Morgan Twp., Carter Co., Oklahoma.[77]

She married **J. B. Means.** They have three children. J. B. Means was born in Oklahoma on September 30, 1930.

**257. Gordon Henry**[9] **Chance** (*Ruth Lea*[8] *McKee, Josiah Andres*[7], *Josiah William*[6], *Elizabeth*[5], *Alexander*[4], *Andrew*[3] *Pegan II, Andrew*[2] *Pagan, James*[1]) was born on November 18, 1933, in Hewitt, Hewitt Twp., Carter Co., Oklahoma. He was the son of Boyet V. Chance and Ruth Lea McKee (84). Gordon Henry died in Ardmore, Morgan Twp., Carter Co., Oklahoma, on October 10, 2001, at age 67. He was buried in Hewitt Cemetery, Wilson, Hewitt Twp., Carter Co., Oklahoma.[13]

He married **Unknown Unknown.** They divorced. They have two children.

**258. Jimmie D.**[9] **Chance** (*Ruth Lea*[8] *McKee, Josiah Andres*[7], *Josiah William*[6], *Elizabeth*[5], *Alexander*[4], *Andrew*[3] *Pegan II, Andrew*[2] *Pagan, James*[1]) was born on February 2, 1938, in Hewitt, Hewitt Twp., Carter Co., Oklahoma. He is the son of Boyet V. Chance and Ruth Lea McKee (84).

He married **Leah Unknown.**

**259. Juanita**[9] **McKee** (*Josiah Milton*[8], *Albert Milton*[7], *Josiah William*[6], *Elizabeth*[5], *Alexander*[4], *Andrew*[3] *Pegan II, Andrew*[2] *Pagan, James*[1]) was born on March 17, 1920, in Hewitt Twp., Carter Co., Oklahoma. She was the daughter of Josiah Milton McKee (85) and Mildred Valle Williams. Juanita died in Hewitt Twp., Carter Co., Oklahoma, on November 6, 1923, at age three. She was buried in Katie City Cemetery, Katie, Brady Twp., Garvin Co., Oklahoma.[9]

**260. Pleas Milton**[9] **McKee** (*Josiah Milton*[8], *Albert Milton*[7], *Josiah William*[6], *Elizabeth*[5], *Alexander*[4], *Andrew*[3] *Pegan II, Andrew*[2] *Pagan, James*[1]) was born on March 22, 1922, in Hewitt Twp., Carter Co., Oklahoma. He was also known as **Pete.** He was the son of Josiah Milton McKee (85) and Mildred Valle Williams. Pleas Milton died in Abilene, Taylor Co., Texas, on August 21, 2007, at age 85. He was buried in Elliott-Hamil Garden of Memories Cemetery, Abeline, Taylor Co., Texas.[78]

Pleas Milton married **Annabet Sargent** on February 11, 1951. They had seven children. Annabet Sargent was born in Hoisington, Barton Co., Kansas, on June 29, 1927. Annabet reached age 79 and died in Abilene, Taylor Co., Texas, on August 16, 2006. She was buried in Elliott-Hamil Garden of Memories Cemetery, Abeline, Taylor Co., Texas.[78]

**261. Willene Violet**[9] **West** (*Vivian Violet*[8] *McKee, Albert Milton*[7], *Josiah William*[6], *Elizabeth*[5], *Alexander*[4], *Andrew*[3] *Pegan II, Andrew*[2] *Pagan, James*[1]) was born on October 5, 1929, in McClain Co., Oklahoma? She is the daughter of William Wiley West and Vivian Violet McKee (87). Willene Violet lived in Lakewood, Pierce Co., Washington.

Willene Violet married **Ronald James Anderson** on February 23, 1950, in Oklahoma Co.,

Oklahoma. They had five children. Ronald James Anderson was born in Oklahoma City, Oklahoma, on January 16, 1931. Ronald James reached age 69 and died in Tacoma, Pierce Co., Washington, on November 1, 2000.

Willene Violet West and Ronald James Anderson had five children, including:

+ 387 f   I.   **Glenda Marie¹⁰ Anderson** was born in Oklahoma City, Oklahoma, on December 7, 1950. She died in San Antonio, Bexar Co., Texas, on July 22, 1956.[23]

+ 388 m   II.  **Douglas Martin¹⁰ Anderson** was born in San Mateo Co., California, on March 16, 1952. He died in Tacoma, Pierce Co., Washington, on April 15, 2002.

+ 389 f   IV.  **Wanda Teresa¹⁰ Anderson** was born in San Antonio, Bexar Co., Texas, on November 6, 1956. She was also known as **Terry.** Wanda Teresa died in Tacoma, Pierce Co., Washington or Summit, King Co., Washington, on October 1, 2007.

+ 390 m   V.   **Ralph William¹⁰ Anderson** was born in Lawton, Comanche Co., Oklahoma, on October 3, 1959. He died in Clackamas Co., Oregon, on January 30, 1995.

**262. T.L.⁹ Fox** (*Rosa Lawana⁸ McKee, Albert Milton⁷, Josiah William⁶, Elizabeth⁵, Alexander⁴, Andrew³ Pegan II, Andrew² Pagan, James¹*) was born on August 14, 1930, in Marlow, Marlow Twp., Stephens Co., Oklahoma. He was the son of George William Fox and Rosa Lawana McKee (88). T.L. died in Lubbock, Lubbock Co., Texas, on November 29, 1996, at age 66. He was buried in Resthaven Memorial Park Cemetery, Lubbock, Lubbock Co., Texas.[79]

T.L. married **Loretha Cristine Dill** on April 25, 1954, in Cooke Co., Texas. Loretha Cristine Dill was born in Elmore City, Elmore Twp., Garvin Co., Oklahoma, on January 29, 1938. She was also

known as **Cris.** Loretha Cristine reached age 73 and died in Lubbock, Lubbock Co., Texas, on June 30, 2011. She was buried in Resthaven Memorial Park Cemetery, Lubbock, Lubbock Co., Texas.[79]

**263. Lyle Doan⁹ Fox** (*Rosa Lawana⁸ McKee, Albert Milton⁷, Josiah William⁶, Elizabeth⁵, Alexander⁴, Andrew³ Pegan II, Andrew² Pagan, James¹*) was born on October 8, 1932, in Wall Twp., Stephens Co., Oklahoma. He was the son of George William Fox and Rosa Lawana McKee (88). Lyle Doan died in Pueblo, Pueblo Co., Colorado, on November 1, 2003, at age 71. He was buried in Fort Logan National Cemetery, Denver, Denver Co., Colorado.[80]

He and **Jane Joan Garner** had one daughter. Jane Joan Garner was born in Cross Timbers, Hickory Co., Missouri, on August 23, 1937.

Daughter of Lyle Doan Fox and Jane Joan Garner:

+ 391 f   I.   **Dorothy Joan Fox¹⁰ Garner** was born in San Juan, Puerto Rico, on September 16, 1956. She died in San Juan, Puerto Rico, on September 16, 1956.[123]

**264. Cara Nome⁹ Fox** (*Rosa Lawana⁸ McKee, Albert Milton⁷, Josiah William⁶, Elizabeth⁵, Alexander⁴, Andrew³ Pegan II, Andrew² Pagan, James¹*) was born on October 6, 1935, in Wall Twp., Stephens Co., Oklahoma. She was the daughter of George William Fox and Rosa Lawana McKee (88). Cara Nome died in Oklahoma City, Oklahoma, on September 9, 1997, at age 61. She was buried in San Marcos Cemetery, San Marcos, San Diego Co., California.[81]

She married **Kenneth Grant Ward.** Kenneth Grant Ward was born in Pauls Valley, Whitebead Twp., Garvin Co., Oklahoma, on September 28, 1923. Kenneth Grant reached age 75 and died in Oklahoma City, Oklahoma, on April 9, 1999. He was buried in Paoli Cemetery, Paoli, Whitebead Twp., Garvin Co., Oklahoma.[124]

**265. James Lowell⁹ McKee** (*John James⁸, Albert Milton⁷, Josiah William⁶, Elizabeth⁵, Alexander⁴, Andrew³ Pegan II, Andrew² Pagan, James¹*) was born on April

9, 1940, in Elmore City, Elmore Twp., Garvin Co., Oklahoma. He was the son of John James McKee (89) and Effie Emaline Crawford. James Lowell died in Paul's Valley, Whitebead Twp., Garvin Co., Oklahoma, on November 19, 1983, at age 43.

**266. John Smith⁹ Hughes** (*Rosa Lillie⁸ Wright, Mary Catherine⁷ McKee, Josiah William⁶, Elizabeth⁵, Alexander⁴, Andrew³ Pegan II, Andrew² Pagan, James¹*) was born on October 8, 1918, in Tribbey, Burnett Twp., Pottawatomie Co., Oklahoma. He was the son of Archie Aston Hughes and Rosa Lillie Wright (91). John Smith died in Quinlan, Hunt Co., Texas, on March 7, 1977, at age 58. He was buried in IOOF Cemetery, Quinlan, Hunt Co., Texas.[83]

John Smith married **Unknown Unknown** after 1940. They have three children.

John Smith Hughes married **Unknown Two Unknown.** They had one daughter.

**267. Mary Lillie⁹ Hughes** (*Rosa Lillie⁸ Wright, Mary Catherine⁷ McKee, Josiah William⁶, Elizabeth⁵, Alexander⁴, Andrew³ Pegan II, Andrew² Pagan, James¹*) was born on December 2, 1920, in Tribbey, Burnett Twp., Pottawatomie Co., Oklahoma. She was the daughter of Archie Aston Hughes and Rosa Lillie Wright (91). Mary Lillie died in Oklahoma City, Oklahoma Co., Oklahoma, on December 29, 1993, at age 73. She was buried in Sunset Memorial Park Cemetery, Norman, Cleveland Co., Oklahoma.[84]

Mary Lillie married **Arthur Homer Smith** on June 6, 1938, in Oklahoma Co., Oklahoma. They divorced. They had two sons. Arthur Homer Smith was born in Ardmore, Morgan Twp., Carter Co., Oklahoma, on February 18, 1919. He reached age 76 and died in Oklahoma City, Oklahoma, on April 5, 1995. Arthur Homer was buried in Sunny Lane Cemetery, Del City, Oklahoma Co., Oklahoma.[41]

Mary Lillie Hughes Smith married **Unknown Phillips** before 1994.

Sons of Mary Lillie Hughes and Arthur Homer Smith:

+ 392 m I. **Fred Arthur¹⁰ Smith** was born in Oklahoma City, Oklahoma, on

June 13, 1940. He died in Newalla, Oklahoma Co., Oklahoma, on March 11, 2008.

+ 393 m II. **Jimmie Gordon¹⁰ Smith** was born in Oklahoma City, Oklahoma, on February 5, 1942. He died in Moore, Cleveland Co., Oklahoma, on January 26, 2008.[84]

**268. Henry Aston⁹ Hughes** (*Rosa Lillie⁸ Wright, Mary Catherine⁷ McKee, Josiah William⁶, Elizabeth⁵, Alexander⁴, Andrew³ Pegan II, Andrew² Pagan, James¹*) was born on August 1, 1922, in Tribbey, Burnett Twp., Pottawatomie Co., Oklahoma. He was the son of Archie Aston Hughes and Rosa Lillie Wright (91). Henry Aston died in Phoenix, Maricopa Co., Arizona, on September 1, 1978, at age 56.

**269. Jimmie Lee⁹ Hughes** (*Rosa Lillie⁸ Wright, Mary Catherine⁷ McKee, Josiah William⁶, Elizabeth⁵, Alexander⁴, Andrew³ Pegan II, Andrew² Pagan, James¹*) was born on December 1, 1924, in Oklahoma City, Oklahoma. He was the son of Archie Aston Hughes and Rosa Lillie Wright (91). Jimmie Lee died between 1940 and 1977.

**270. Lola Lorene⁹ Hughes** (*Rosa Lillie⁸ Wright, Mary Catherine⁷ McKee, Josiah William⁶, Elizabeth⁵, Alexander⁴, Andrew³ Pegan II, Andrew² Pagan, James¹*) was born on June 17, 1927, in Oklahoma City, Oklahoma. She was the daughter of Archie Aston Hughes and Rosa Lillie Wright (91). Lola Lorene died in Oklahoma City, Oklahoma, on September 29, 1996, at age 69. She was buried in Sunny Lane Cemetery, Del City, Oklahoma Co., Oklahoma.[41]

Lola Lorene married **Gilbert Wayne Lewis** on February 22, 1946. Gilbert Wayne Lewis was born in Oklahoma City, Oklahoma, on February 20, 1921. Gilbert Wayne reached age 74 and died in Oklahoma City, Oklahoma, on March 17, 1995. He was buried in Sunny Lane Cemetery, Del City, Oklahoma Co., Oklahoma.[41]

**271. Carl Shannon⁹ Hughes** (*Rosa Lillie⁸ Wright, Mary Catherine⁷ McKee, Josiah William⁶, Elizabeth⁵,*

*Alexander⁴, Andrew³ Pegan II, Andrew² Pagan, James¹*) was born on April 8, 1929, in Oklahoma City, Oklahoma. He was the son of Archie Aston Hughes and Rosa Lillie Wright (91). Carl Shannon died in Bethany, Oklahoma Co., Oklahoma, on March 14, 1981, at age 51. He was buried in Resurrection Memorial Cemetery, Oklahoma City, Oklahoma Co., Oklahoma.[85]

May have never married.

**272. Betty Jene⁹ Hughes** (*Rosa Lillie⁸ Wright, Mary Catherine⁷ McKee, Josiah William⁶, Elizabeth⁵, Alexander⁴, Andrew³ Pegan II, Andrew² Pagan, James¹*) was born on March 18, 1931, in Oklahoma City, Oklahoma. She was the daughter of Archie Aston Hughes and Rosa Lillie Wright (91). Betty Jene died in Odessa, Ector Co., Texas, on December 14, 2005, at age 74. She was buried in Resthaven Memorial Park Cemetery, Midland, Midland Co., Texas.[86]

Betty Jene Hughes married **Leonard Edward Mills II.** They had one son.

Betty Jene Hughes Mills married **Charles Willis Harris** on July 10, 1967, in Winkler Co., Texas. They had three children. Charles Willis Harris was born in Pooleville, Graham Twp., Carter Co., Oklahoma, on April 17, 1928. Charles Willis reached age 82 and died in Odessa, Ector Co., Texas, on November 17, 2010. He was buried in Resthaven Memorial Park Cemetery, Midland, Midland Co., Texas.

Son of Betty Jene Hughes and Leonard Edward Mills II:

+ 394 m  I.  **Bennie Edward¹⁰ Mills.**

**273. Ima Jean⁹ Hughes** (*Rosa Lillie⁸ Wright, Mary Catherine⁷ McKee, Josiah William⁶, Elizabeth⁵, Alexander⁴, Andrew³ Pegan II, Andrew² Pagan, James¹*) was born in 1932 in Oklahoma City, Oklahoma. She was the daughter of Archie Aston Hughes and Rosa Lillie Wright (91). Ima Jean died before 2005.

**274. Dorothy Louise⁹ Hughes** (*Rosa Lillie⁸ Wright, Mary Catherine⁷ McKee, Josiah William⁶, Elizabeth⁵, Alexander⁴, Andrew³ Pegan II, Andrew² Pagan, James¹*) was born on May 17, 1936, in Oklahoma City, Oklahoma. She was the daughter of Archie Aston Hughes and Rosa Lillie Wright (91). Dorothy Louise died in Oklahoma City, Oklahoma, on July 9, 2000, at age 64. She was buried in Immaculate Conception Cemetery, Oklahoma City, Oklahoma Co., Oklahoma.[87]

She married **Leo Stewart McGinley II.** They had one known child. Leo Stewart McGinley II was born in Oklahoma City, Oklahoma, on November 17, 1927. Leo Stewart reached age 70 and died in Oklahoma City, Oklahoma, on March 7, 1998. He was buried in Immaculate Conception Cemetery, Oklahoma City, Oklahoma Co., Oklahoma.[87]

**275. Tommie S.⁹ Hughes** (*Rosa Lillie⁸ Wright, Mary Catherine⁷ McKee, Josiah William⁶, Elizabeth⁵, Alexander⁴, Andrew³ Pegan II, Andrew² Pagan, James¹*) was born on March 6, 1938, in Oklahoma City, Oklahoma. He was the son of Archie Aston Hughes and Rosa Lillie Wright (91). Tommie S. died in Galveston, Galveston Co., Texas, on March 16, 1952, at age 14. He was buried in Jamestown Cemetery, Jamestown, Smith Co., Texas.[82]

**276. Paul Ray⁹ Hughes** (*Rosa Lillie⁸ Wright, Mary Catherine⁷ McKee, Josiah William⁶, Elizabeth⁵, Alexander⁴, Andrew³ Pegan II, Andrew² Pagan, James¹*) was born in 1940 in Golden, Wood Co., Texas. He is the son of Archie Aston Hughes and Rosa Lillie Wright.[91]

He married **Mary Unknown.**

**277. Robert Vernon⁹ Hughes** (*Rosa Lillie⁸ Wright, Mary Catherine⁷ McKee, Josiah William⁶, Elizabeth⁵, Alexander⁴, Andrew³ Pegan II, Andrew² Pagan, James¹*) was born on January 6, 1942, in Golden, Wood Co., Texas. He was the son of Archie Aston Hughes and Rosa Lillie Wright (91). Robert Vernon lived in 2005 in Irving, Dallas Co., Texas. He died in Irving, Dallas Co., Texas, on June 27, 2010, at age 68. Robert Vernon was buried in Laurel Land Memorial Park Cemetery, Dallas, Dallas Co., Texas.[88]

Robert Vernon married **Donna Unknown** in 1959. They have five children.

**278. Lucille Willie**[9] **Hickey** (*Dedaunia Lucinda Amanda Jane*[8] *Wright, Mary Catherine*[7] *McKee, Josiah William*[6]*, Elizabeth*[5]*, Alexander*[4]*, Andrew*[3] *Pegan II, Andrew*[2] *Pagan, James*[1]) was born on September 27, 1917, in Tribbey, Burnett Twp., Pottawatomie Co., Oklahoma. She was the daughter of James William Hickey and Dedaunia Lucinda Amanda Jane Wright (92). Lucille Willie died in Clearwater, Sedgwick Co., Kansas, on January 2, 2009, at age 91. She was buried in Tecumseh Cemetery, Tecumseh, Brinton Twp., Pottawatomie Co., Oklahoma.[34]

Lucille Willie married **Carl Thompson** after 1940. They had two children. Carl Thompson was born in Tribbey, Burnett Twp., Pottawatomie Co., Oklahoma, on April 25, 1912. Carl reached age 97 and died in Viola, Sedwick Co., Kansas, on February 15, 2010. He was buried in Tecumseh Cemetery, Tecumseh, Brinton Twp., Pottawatomie Co., Oklahoma.[29]

**279. Maudie Mae**[9] **Hickey** (*Dedaunia Lucinda Amanda Jane*[8] *Wright, Mary Catherine*[7] *McKee, Josiah William*[6]*, Elizabeth*[5]*, Alexander*[4]*, Andrew*[3] *Pegan II, Andrew*[2] *Pagan, James*[1]) was born on May 5, 1919, in Tribbey, Burnett Twp., Pottawatomie Co., Oklahoma. She was the daughter of James William Hickey and Dedaunia Lucinda Amanda Jane Wright (92). Maudie Mae died in Red Bluff, Tehama Co., California, on May 14, 1998, at age 79. She was buried in Oak Hill Cemetery, Red Bluff, Tehama Co., California.[84]

Maudie Mae married **Woodrow Hoofard** on December 24, 1936, in Pottawatomie Co., Oklahoma. They have five children. Woodrow Hoofard was born in Eason Twp., Pottawatomie Co., Oklahoma, on October 4, 1918.

Maudie Mae Hickey and Woodrow Hoofard had five children, including:

+ 395 m I. **William E.**[10] **Hoofard** was born in Lexington Twp., Cleveland Co., Oklahoma, on January 5, 1939.

+ 396 f II. **Diana Kay**[10] **Hoofard** was born in Lexington Twp., Cleveland Co., Oklahoma, on October 1, 1940. She died in Lexington Twp., Cleveland Co., Oklahoma, on October 1, 1940.[125]

+ 397 f IV. **Loretta Lorene**[10] **Hoofard** was born in Oakland, Alameda Co., California, on December 15, 1943. She died in Shawnee, Rock Creek Twp., Pottawatomie Co., Oklahoma, on August 17, 1949.[126]

**280. Mary Almeda**[9] **Hickey** (*Dedaunia Lucinda Amanda Jane*[8] *Wright, Mary Catherine*[7] *McKee, Josiah William*[6]*, Elizabeth*[5]*, Alexander*[4]*, Andrew*[3] *Pegan II, Andrew*[2] *Pagan, James*[1]) was born on July 13, 1920, in Tribbey, Burnett Twp., Pottawatomie Co., Oklahoma. She was also known as **Almeda.** She was the daughter of James William Hickey and Dedaunia Lucinda Amanda Jane Wright (92). Mary Almeda died in Macomb, Burnett Twp., Pottawatomie Co., Oklahoma, on October 17, 1999, at age 79. She was buried in Tecumseh Cemetery, Tecumseh, Brinton Twp., Pottawatomie Co., Oklahoma.[34]

Mary Almeda married **Albert William French** after 1940. Albert William French was born in Tribbey, Burnett Twp., Pottawatomie Co., Oklahoma, on September 23, 1918. Albert William reached age 56 and died in Macomb, Burnett Twp., Pottawatomie Co., Oklahoma, on October 14, 1974. He was buried in Tecumseh Cemetery, Tecumseh, Brinton Twp., Pottawatomie Co., Oklahoma.[34]

**281. Arlie Monroe**[9] **Hickey** (*Dedaunia Lucinda Amanda Jane*[8] *Wright, Mary Catherine*[7] *McKee, Josiah William*[6]*, Elizabeth*[5]*, Alexander*[4]*, Andrew*[3] *Pegan II, Andrew*[2] *Pagan, James*[1]) was born on November 20, 1921, in Tribbey, Burnett Twp., Pottawatomie Co., Oklahoma. He was the son of James William Hickey and Dedaunia Lucinda Amanda Jane Wright (92). Arlie Monroe died in Macomb, Burnett Twp., Pottawatomie Co., Oklahoma, on July 20, 2004, at age 82. He was buried in Resthaven Memorial Park Cemetery, Shawnee, Pottawatomie Co., Oklahoma.[85]

Arlie Monroe married **Unknown Unknown** before 1965.

Arlie Monroe Hickey married **Billie Lora Chism** on January 23, 1965. Billie Lora Chism was born about 1939.

**282. Thurman Andrew⁹ Berry** (*Maemily Ann⁸ Wright, Mary Catherine⁷ McKee, Josiah William⁶, Elizabeth⁵, Alexander⁴, Andrew³ Pegan II, Andrew² Pagan, James¹*) was born on July 10, 1921, in Tribbey, Burnett Twp., Pottawatomie Co., Oklahoma. He was the son of Jewell A. Berry and Maemily Ann Wright (93). Thurman Andrew died in Macomb, Burnett Twp., Pottawatomie Co., Oklahoma, on September 10, 1983, at age 62. He was buried in Tribbey Cemetery, Burnett Twp., Pottawatomie Co., Oklahoma.[14]

He married **Venita Valentine Roselius.** They divorced. Venita Valentine Roselius was born in Alanreed, Gray Co., Texas, on February 23, 1923. She reached age 77 and died in Oroville, Okanogan Co., Washington, on June 19, 2000. Died under the name Venita Thrasher.

Thurman Andrew Berry married **Ruby Marie Mailcoat.** Ruby Marie Mailcoat was born in Turkey, Hall Co., Texas, on May 4, 1920. Ruby Marie reached age 88 and died in Valley, Chambers Co., Alabama, on August 23, 2008. She was buried in Wanette Cemetery, Wanette, Eason Twp., Pottawatomie Co., Oklahoma.[126]

**283. Opal Ann⁹ Berry** (*Maemily Ann⁸ Wright, Mary Catherine⁷ McKee, Josiah William⁶, Elizabeth⁵, Alexander⁴, Andrew³ Pegan II, Andrew² Pagan, James¹*) was born on April 1, 1923, in Tribbey, Burnett Twp., Pottawatomie Co., Oklahoma. She was the daughter of Jewell A. Berry and Maemily Ann Wright (93). Opal Ann died in Creek Co., Oklahoma, on May 19, 1971, at age 48. She was buried in Tribbey Cemetery, Tribbey, Burnett Twp., Pottawatomie Co., Oklahoma.[14]

Opal Ann married **Narvan B. Miller Chapman** after 1940. They had five children. Narvan B. Miller Chapman was born in Tishomingo, Johnston Co., Oklahoma, on May 29, 1918. He was also known as **Pete.** Narvan B. Miller reached age 78 and died in Tishomingo, Johnston Co., Oklahoma, on May 27, 1997.

Opal Ann Berry and Narvan B. Miller Chapman had five children, including:

+ 398 m I. **Narvin B.¹⁰ Chapman II.** Narvin B. died before 1997.

**284. Hazel⁹ Berry** (*Maemily Ann⁸ Wright, Mary Catherine⁷ McKee, Josiah William⁶, Elizabeth⁵, Alexander⁴, Andrew³ Pegan II, Andrew² Pagan, James¹*) was born in 1924 in Tribbey, Burnett Twp., Pottawatomie Co., Oklahoma. She is the daughter of Jewell A. Berry and Maemily Ann Wright (93).

**285. Joe⁹ Berry** (*Maemily Ann⁸ Wright, Mary Catherine⁷ McKee, Josiah William⁶, Elizabeth⁵, Alexander⁴, Andrew³ Pegan II, Andrew² Pagan, James¹*) was born on September 12, 1926, in Tribbey, Burnett Twp., Pottawatomie Co., Oklahoma. He was the son of Jewell A. Berry and Maemily Ann Wright (93). Joe died in Norwalk, Los Angeles Co., California, on March 2, 1979, at age 52. He was buried in Tribbey Cemetery, Tribbey, Burnett Twp., Pottawatomie Co., Oklahoma.[14]

He married **Mary Elizabeth Coppitt.** Mary Elizabeth Coppitt was born in Anniston, Calhoun Co., Alabama, on February 1, 1931. Mary Elizabeth reached age 71 and died in Artesia, Los Angeles Co., California, on June 27, 2002. She was buried in Riverside National Cemetery, Riverside, Riverside Co., California.[61]

**286. Lorene⁹ Berry** (*Maemily Ann⁸ Wright, Mary Catherine⁷ McKee, Josiah William⁶, Elizabeth⁵, Alexander⁴, Andrew³ Pegan II, Andrew² Pagan, James¹*) was born in 1928 in Tribbey, Burnett Twp., Pottawatomie Co., Oklahoma. She is the daughter of Jewell A. Berry and Maemily Ann Wright (93).

**287. Newman⁹ Berry** (*Maemily Ann⁸ Wright, Mary Catherine⁷ McKee, Josiah William⁶, Elizabeth⁵, Alexander⁴, Andrew³ Pegan II, Andrew² Pagan, James¹*) was born on October 6, 1930, in Tribbey, Burnett Twp., Pottawatomie Co., Oklahoma. He was the son of Jewell A. Berry and Maemily Ann Wright (93). He was also known as **Whitey.** Newman died in North Las Vegas, Clark Co.,

Nevada, on September 2, 2004, at age 73. He was buried in Wyoming.

Newman married **Twila Penfield** on August 31, 1957, in Los Angeles Co., California. They have two children. Twila Penfield was born in Lance Creek, Niobrara Co., Wyoming? on June 15, 1936.

Children of Newman Berry and Twila Penfield:

+ 399 f II. **Sondra Diana**<sup>10</sup> **Berry** was born in Downey, Los Angeles Co., California, on September 21, 1960. She died in Henderson, Clark Co., Nevada, on January 4, 2004.

**288. Guy Martin**<sup>9</sup> **Berry** (*Mary Catherine*<sup>8</sup> *Wright, Mary Catherine*<sup>7</sup> *McKee, Josiah William*<sup>6</sup>, *Elizabeth*<sup>5</sup>, *Alexander*<sup>4</sup>, *Andrew*<sup>3</sup> *Pegan II, Andrew*<sup>2</sup> *Pagan, James*<sup>1</sup>) was born on November 7, 1924, in Tribbey, Burnett Twp., Pottawatomie Co., Oklahoma. He was the son of January Bryan Berry and Mary Catherine Wright (95). Guy Martin died in Oklahoma City, Oklahoma, on November 3, 2005, at age 80. He was buried in Tribbey Cemetery, Tribbey, Burnett Twp., Pottawatomie Co., Oklahoma.[14]

Guy Martin married **Lavonia Juanita Rutledge** before 1948. They had one daughter. Lavonia Juanita Rutledge was born in Roosevelt Co., New Mexico, on July 12, 1928. Lavonia Juanita reached age 79 and died in Grove, Delaware Co., Oklahoma, on May 16, 2008. She was buried in Tribbey Cemetery, Tribbey, Burnett Twp., Pottawatomie Co., Oklahoma.[14]

Daughter of Guy Martin Berry and Lavonia Juanita Rutledge:

+ 400 f I. **Catherine Juanita**<sup>10</sup> **Berry** was born in Maywood, Los Angeles Co., California, on March 28, 1948. She died in Oklahoma City, Oklahoma, on February 1, 1962.[14]

**289. John William**<sup>9</sup> **Berry** (*Mary Catherine*<sup>8</sup> *Wright, Mary Catherine*<sup>7</sup> *McKee, Josiah William*<sup>6</sup>,

*Elizabeth*<sup>5</sup>, *Alexander*<sup>4</sup>, *Andrew*<sup>3</sup> *Pegan II, Andrew*<sup>2</sup> *Pagan, James*<sup>1</sup>) was born on April 18, 1928, in Tribbey, Burnett Twp., Pottawatomie Co., Oklahoma. He was also known as **Bill.** He was the son of January Bryan Berry and Mary Catherine Wright (95). John William died in Moore, Cleveland Co., Oklahoma, on March 18, 1991, at age 62. He was buried in Tribbey Cemetery, Tribbey, Burnett Twp., Pottawatomie Co., Oklahoma.[14]

John William married **Aline Unknown** before 1948. They have one son.

Son of John William Berry and Aline Unknown:

+ 401 m I. **Clarence William**<sup>10</sup> **Berry** was born in Shawnee, Rock Creek Twp., Pottawatomie Co., Oklahoma, on November 3, 1948. He died in Quincy, Grant Co., Washington, on June 7, 2007.

**290. Bobby Joe**<sup>9</sup> **Berry** (*Mary Catherine*<sup>8</sup> *Wright, Mary Catherine*<sup>7</sup> *McKee, Josiah William*<sup>6</sup>, *Elizabeth*<sup>5</sup>, *Alexander*<sup>4</sup>, *Andrew*<sup>3</sup> *Pegan II, Andrew*<sup>2</sup> *Pagan, James*<sup>1</sup>) was born on September 30, 1932, in Tribbey, Burnett Twp., Pottawatomie Co., Oklahoma. He was the son of January Bryan Berry and Mary Catherine Wright (95). Bobby Joe died in Eufaula, McIntosh Co., Oklahoma, on May 2, 1995, at age 62. He was buried in Celestial Gardens Cemetery, Cyril, Caddo Co. Oklahoma.[91]

Bobby Joe married **Unknown Unknown** before 1961. They divorced. They had one daughter.

Bobby Joe Berry married **Cherrl Dean Gilliam** on August 4, 1961, in Caddo Co., Oklahoma. Cherrl Dean Gilliam was born in Cyril, Caddo Co., Oklahoma, on December 13, 1933. Cherrl Dean reached age 80 and died in Cyril, Caddo Co., Oklahoma, on September 28, 2014. She was buried in Celestial Gardens Cemetery, Cyril, Caddo Co. Oklahoma.[91]

**291. Edward Eugene**<sup>9</sup> **Wright** (*John Martin*<sup>8</sup>, *Mary Catherine*<sup>7</sup> *McKee, Josiah William*<sup>6</sup>, *Elizabeth*<sup>5</sup>, *Alexander*<sup>4</sup>, *Andrew*<sup>3</sup> *Pegan II, Andrew*<sup>2</sup> *Pagan, James*<sup>1</sup>) was born on April 30, 1930, in Tribbey,

Burnett Twp., Pottawatomie Co., Oklahoma. He was the son of John Martin Wright (96) and Martha Ann James. Edward Eugene died in Norman, Cleveland Co., Oklahoma, on April 2, 2006, at age 75. He was buried in Tecumseh Cemetery, Tecumseh, Brinton Twp., Pottawatomie Co., Oklahoma.[34]

Edward Eugene married **Louise Chandler** on July 14, 1951, in Pottawatomie Co., Oklahoma. They had three children. Louise Chandler was born in Lexington, Cleveland Co., Oklahoma, on October 11, 1932. Louise reached age 67 and died in Tecumseh, Brinton Twp., Pottawatomie Co., Oklahoma, on November 10, 1999. She was buried in Tecumseh Cemetery, Tecumseh, Brinton Twp., Pottawatomie Co., Oklahoma.[34]

Edward Eugene Wright married **Onalee Kerley** on October 30, 2000. Onalee Kerley Cearley was born in 1924 in Lakeside Twp., Creek Co., Oklahoma?

**292. Wanda Jo⁹ Wright** (*John Martin⁸, Mary Catherine⁷ McKee, Josiah William⁶, Elizabeth⁵, Alexander⁴, Andrew³ Pegan II, Andrew² Pagan, James¹*) was born on April 11, 1936, in Tribbey, Burnett Twp., Pottawatomie Co., Oklahoma. She is the daughter of John Martin Wright (96) and Martha Ann James.

Wanda Jo married **Charles James Chapman** in October 1953 in Oklahoma City, Oklahoma. They have three children. Charles James Chapman was born in Binger, Fern Twp., Caddo Co., Oklahoma, on February 1, 1935. He was also known as **Jim.** Charles James reached age 73 and died in Chickasha, Chickasha Twp., Grady Co., Oklahoma, on February 13, 2008. He was buried in Fairview Cemetery, Tuttle, Tuttle Twp., Grady Co., Oklahoma.[127]

**293. Terry W.⁹ Wright** (*John Martin⁸, Mary Catherine⁷ McKee, Josiah William⁶, Elizabeth⁵, Alexander⁴, Andrew³ Pegan II, Andrew² Pagan, James¹*) was born on November 2, 1948, in Shawnee, Rock Creek Twp., Pottawatomie Co., Oklahoma. He was the son of John Martin Wright (96) and Martha Ann James. Terry W. died in Shawnee, Rock Creek Twp., Pottawatomie Co., Oklahoma, on March 1, 2006, at age 57. He was buried in Tecumseh

Cemetery, Tecumseh, Brinton Twp., Pottawatomie Co., Oklahoma.[34]

Terry W. married **Ms. Matthews.** They had five children.

**294. Bobbie Stenson⁹ Bratton** (*Sarah Elvara⁸ Wright, Mary Catherine⁷ McKee, Josiah William⁶, Elizabeth⁵, Alexander⁴, Andrew³ Pegan II, Andrew² Pagan, James¹*) was born on December 20, 1926, in Tribbey, Burnett Twp., Pottawatomie Co., Oklahoma. He was the son of Jack Ellis Bratton and Sarah Elvara Wright (97). Bobbie Stenson died in Oklahoma City, Oklahoma, on April 14, 1981, at age 54.

Bobbie Stenson married **Jean Analee Wilson** after 1940. They had two children. Jean Analee Wilson was born in Konawa, Seminole Co., Oklahoma, on June 14, 1923. Jean Analee reached age 89 and died in Oklahoma City, Oklahoma, on June 9, 2013. She was buried in Resthaven Gardens Cemetery, Oklahoma City, Cleveland Co., Oklahoma.[23] Died under the name Jean Castleberry.

**295. Jack Ellis⁹ Bratton II** (*Sarah Elvara⁸ Wright, Mary Catherine⁷ McKee, Josiah William⁶, Elizabeth⁵, Alexander⁴, Andrew³ Pegan II, Andrew² Pagan, James¹*) was born on February 26, 1931, in Davis, Pottawatomie Co., Oklahoma. He was also known as **Jacky.** He was the son of Jack Ellis Bratton and Sarah Elvara Wright (97). Jack Ellis died in Oklahoma City, Oklahoma, on August 7, 1954, at age. He was buried in Tribbey Cemetery, Tribbey, Burnett Twp., Pottawatomie Co., Oklahoma.[14]

Seems to have never married.

**296. Son One⁹ Wright** (*Willis Josiah⁸, Mary Catherine⁷ McKee, Josiah William⁶, Elizabeth⁵, Alexander⁴, Andrew³ Pegan II, Andrew² Pagan, James¹*) was born on January 5, 1936, in Tribbey, Burnett Twp., Pottawatomie Co., Oklahoma. He was the son of Willis Josiah Wright (98) and Chloe E. Ball. Son One died in Tribbey, Burnett Twp., Pottawatomie Co., Oklahoma, on January 5, 1936. He was buried in Tribbey Cemetery, Tribbey, Burnett Twp., Pottawatomie Co., Oklahoma.[14]

**297. Charles⁹ Wright** (*Willis Josiah⁸, Mary Catherine⁷ McKee, Josiah William⁶, Elizabeth⁵, Alexander⁴, Andrew³ Pegan II, Andrew² Pagan, James¹*) was born on March 5, 1937, in Tribbey, Burnett Twp., Pottawatomie Co., Oklahoma. He was the son of Willis Josiah Wright (98) and Chloe E. Ball. Charles died in Tribbey, Burnett Twp., Pottawatomie Co., Oklahoma, on December 9, 1937. He was buried in Tribbey Cemetery, Tribbey, Burnett Twp., Pottawatomie Co., Oklahoma.[14]

298. **Son Two⁹ Wright** (*Willis Josiah⁸, Mary Catherine⁷ McKee, Josiah William⁶, Elizabeth⁵, Alexander⁴, Andrew³ Pegan II, Andrew² Pagan, James¹*) was born on September 16, 1941, in Norman, Cleveland Co., Oklahoma. He was the son of Willis Josiah Wright (98) and Chloe E. Ball. Son Two died in Norman, Cleveland Co., Oklahoma, on September 16, 1941. He was buried in Mars Hill Cemetery, St. Louis Twp., Pottawatomie Co., Oklahoma.[35]

299. **Loretta Charlene⁹ Wright** (*Charles Watson⁸, Mary Catherine⁷ McKee, Josiah William⁶, Elizabeth⁵, Alexander⁴, Andrew³ Pegan II, Andrew² Pagan, James¹*) was born on April 9, 1945, in Bell, Los Angeles Co., California. She was also known as **Charlee Angel.** She was the daughter of Charles Watson Wright (99) and Loretta Knowles. Loretta Charlene died in Springfield, Lane Co., Oregon, on April 5, 2007, at age 61. Loretta Charlene Wright Robles died under the name Charlee Angel Wright. Her memorial service was held in Corsicana, Navarro Co., Texas.

She married **Gilbert E. Robles.** They divorced. They had one son. Gilbert E. Robles was born in Winterhaven, Imperial Co., California, on July 8, 1930. He reached age 46 and died in Los Angeles, Los Angeles Co., California, on August 12, 1976. Gilbert E. was buried in Yuma Pioneer Cemetery, Yuma, Yuma Co., Arizona.

Loretta Charlene Wright Robles married **Unknown Gonzales.** They divorced.

300. **Ray⁹ Thompson** (*Violet Roberta⁸ Wright, Mary Catherine⁷ McKee, Josiah William⁶, Elizabeth⁵, Alexander⁴, Andrew³ Pegan II, Andrew² Pagan, James¹*) was born in 1934 in Arkansas. He is the son of Frank Kermit Thompson and Violet Roberta Wright (100).

301. **Herschel Edwin⁹ Raines** (*Martha Louisa Jane⁸ McKee, Charles Watson⁷, Josiah William⁶, Elizabeth⁵,* *Alexander⁴, Andrew³ Pegan II, Andrew² Pagan, James¹*) was born on January 17, 1924, in Elmore Twp., Garvin Co., Oklahoma. He was the son of Charlie Frank Raines and Martha Louisa Jane McKee (103). Herschel Edwin died in Lamesa, Dawson Co., Texas, on March 1, 2009, at age 85. He was buried in Dawson County Cemetery, Lamesa, Dawson Co., Texas.[94]

Herschel Edwin married **Dorothy Louise Painter** after 1940. They had three children. Dorothy Louise Painter was born in Waco, McLennan Co., Texas, on September 5, 1925. Dorothy Louise reached age 84 and died in Lamesa, Dawson Co., Texas, on October 28, 2009. She was buried in Dawson County Cemetery, Lamesa, Dawson Co., Texas.[94]

302. **Jewel Paul⁹ Raines** (*Martha Louisa Jane⁸ McKee, Charles Watson⁷, Josiah William⁶, Elizabeth⁵, Alexander⁴, Andrew³ Pegan II, Andrew² Pagan, James¹*) was born on March 28, 1928, in Elmore Twp., Garvin Co., Oklahoma. He was also known as **Paul.** He was the son of Charlie Frank Raines and Martha Louisa Jane McKee (103). Jewel Paul died in Hico, Hamilton Co., Texas, on June 16, 2002, at age 74. He was buried in Hico Cemetery, Hico, Hamilton Co. Texas.[95]

Jewel Paul married **Joyce Jordan** on February 16, 1946, in Dawson Co., Texas. Joyce Jordan was born in Johnson Co., Texas, on August 18, 1931. Joyce reached age 40 and died in Mansfield, Tarrant Co., Texas, on August 14, 1972. She was buried in Emerald Hills Cemetery, Kennedale, Tarrant Co., Texas.[38]

303. **Herman Thomas⁹ Raines** (*Martha Louisa Jane⁸ McKee, Charles Watson⁷, Josiah William⁶, Elizabeth⁵, Alexander⁴, Andrew³ Pegan II, Andrew² Pagan, James¹*) was born on October 12, 1930, in Elmore Twp., Garvin Co., Oklahoma. He was the son of Charlie Frank Raines and Martha Louisa Jane McKee (103). Herman Thomas died in Lubbock, Lubbock Co., Texas, on August 23, 1990, at age 59. He was buried in Lamesa Memorial Park Cemetery, Lamesa, Dawson Co., Texas.[37]

Herman Thomas married **Doris Marie Hambrick** before 1960. They had one daughter. Doris Marie

Hambrick was born in Athens, Henderson Co., Texas, on March 6, 1937. Doris Marie lived in Lamesa, Dawson Co., Texas. She reached age 58 and died in a hospital in Midland, Midland Co., Texas, on June 9, 1995. Doris Marie was buried in Lamesa Memorial Park Cemetery, Lamesa, Dawson Co., Texas.[37]

Daughter of Herman Thomas Raines and Doris Marie Hambrick:

+ 402 f I. **Catherine Denise**[10] **Raines** was born in Lamesa, Dawson Co., Texas, on March 11, 1960. She died in Lamesa, Dawson Co., Texas, on June 24, 1964.[37]

**304. Thurman Adolphus**[9] **Raines** (*Martha Louisa Jane*[8] *McKee, Charles Watson*[7]*, Josiah William*[6]*, Elizabeth*[5]*, Alexander*[4]*, Andrew*[3] *Pegan II, Andrew*[2] *Pagan, James*[1]) was born on November 6, 1935, in Elmore Twp., Garvin Co., Oklahoma. He was the son of Charlie Frank Raines and Martha Louisa Jane McKee (103). Thurman Adolphus died in Lamesa, Dawson Co., Texas, on January 8, 2009, at age 73. He was buried in Lamesa Memorial Park Cemetery, Lamesa, Dawson Co., Texas.[37]

Thurman Adolphus married **Ruby Unknown** on June 2, 1958. They divorced. Ruby Unknown was born in 1940.

Thurman Adolphus Raines married **Sharon Ann Hudson** on October 1, 1970, in Dawson Co., Texas. They had two children. Sharon Ann Hudson was born in Lamesa, Dawson Co., Texas, on March 25, 1948. Sharon Ann reached age 63 and died in Lubbock, Lubbock Co., Texas, on October 1, 2011.

**305. Geraldine Faye**[9] **McKee** (*Albert Milton*[8]*, Charles Watson*[7]*, Josiah William*[6]*, Elizabeth*[5]*, Alexander*[4]*, Andrew*[3] *Pegan II, Andrew*[2] *Pagan, James*[1]) was born on November 28, 1932, in Garvin Co., Oklahoma. She was also known as **Geri**. She was the daughter of Albert Milton McKee (104) and Bessie Mae Steele. Geraldine Faye died in Everman, Tarrant Co., Texas, on December 16, 2011, at age 79. She was buried in Everman Cemetery, Everman, Tarrant Co., Texas.[96]

She married **James Henry Sikes.** They had five children. James Henry Sikes was born in Biardstown, Lamar Co., Texas, on December 23, 1930. James Henry reached age 57 and died in Fort Worth, Tarrant Co., Texas, on July 1, 1988. He was buried in Everman Cemetery, Everman, Tarrant Co., Texas.[96]

**306. Nadine J.**[9] **McKee** (*Albert Milton*[8]*, Charles Watson*[7]*, Josiah William*[6]*, Elizabeth*[5]*, Alexander*[4]*, Andrew*[3] *Pegan II, Andrew*[2] *Pagan, James*[1]) was born on August 10, 1934, in Garvin Co., Oklahoma. She is the daughter of Albert Milton McKee (104) and Bessie Mae Steele.

She married **Phillip Ray Pope.** Phillip Ray Pope was born in Denton Co., Texas, on March 6, 1935.

**307. Charles F.**[9] **McKee** (*Albert Milton*[8]*, Charles Watson*[7]*, Josiah William*[6]*, Elizabeth*[5]*, Alexander*[4]*, Andrew*[3] *Pegan II, Andrew*[2] *Pagan, James*[1]) was born on February 23, 1936, in Garvin Co., Oklahoma. He is the son of Albert Milton McKee (104) and Bessie Mae Steele.

He married **Juanita Unknown.**

**308. Ouida Gale**[9] **McKee** (*Albert Milton*[8]*, Charles Watson*[7]*, Josiah William*[6]*, Elizabeth*[5]*, Alexander*[4]*, Andrew*[3] *Pegan II, Andrew*[2] *Pagan, James*[1]) was born on November 18, 1939, in Ardmore, Morgan Twp., Carter Co., Oklahoma. She was also known as **Mimi.** She was the daughter of Albert Milton McKee (104) and Bessie Mae Steele. Ouida Gale died in Dallas, Dallas Co., Texas, on February 26, 2005, at age 65. She was buried in Emerald Hills Cemetery, Kennedale, Tarrant Co., Texas.[38]

She married **Emory O'Neal Brannon.** They divorced. They had two children. Emory O'Neal Brannon was born in Ellis Co., Texas, on March 21, 1934. He reached age 56 and died in Fort Worth, Tarrant Co., Texas, on June 15, 1990.

Ouida Gale McKee Brannon married **Bobby G. Lee** on July 19, 1958, in Tarrant Co., Texas. They divorced. They had five children. Bobby G. Lee was born in Ardmore West, Morgan Twp., Carter Co., Oklahoma, on October 18, 1932. He reached age 67 and died in Fort Worth, Tarrant Co., Texas, on June 1, 2000.

Children of Ouida Gale McKee and Emory O'Neal Brannon:

+ 403 f I. **Terry Elaine**[10] **Brannon** was born in Fort Worth, Tarrant Co., Texas, on May 5, 1955. She died in Fort Worth, Tarrant Co., Texas, on September 11, 2005.

+ 404 m II. **Jerry Keith**[10] **Brannon** was born in Fort Worth, Tarrant Co., Texas, on October 16, 1956. He died in a hospital in Fort Worth, Tarrant Co., Texas, on May 9, 1979.[38]

**309. Lois Ellen**[9] **Brown** (*Mary Katherine*[8] *McKee, Charles Watson*[7]*, Josiah William*[6]*, Elizabeth*[5]*, Alexander*[4]*, Andrew*[3] *Pegan II, Andrew*[2] *Pagan, James*[1]) was born on September 23, 1929, in Lindsay, Lindsay Twp., Garvin Co., Oklahoma. She was the daughter of James Gordon Brown and Mary Katherine McKee (105). Lois Ellen died in Porterville, Tulare Co., California, on February 17, 2006, at age 76. She was buried in Hillcrest Cemetery, Porterville, Tulare Co., California.[27]

She married **Floyd Edward Wallace.** They had four children. Floyd Edward Wallace was born in Tryon, Cimmaron Twp., Lincoln Co., Oklahoma, on June 24, 1922. Floyd Edward reached age 80 and died in Porterville, Tulare Co., California, on May 19, 2003.

Lois Ellen Brown and Floyd Edward Wallace had four children, including:

+ 405 m I. **Ronald Steven**[10] **Wallace** was born in Lindsay, Tulare Co., California, on April 30, 1958. He died in Crane Meadow Camp, near Ponderosa, Tulare Co., California, on September 2, 2007.

**310. James Kenneth**[9] **Brown** (*Mary Katherine*[8] *McKee, Charles Watson*[7]*, Josiah William*[6]*, Elizabeth*[5]*,

*Alexander*[4]*, Andrew*[3] *Pegan II, Andrew*[2] *Pagan, James*[1]) was born on August 27, 1931, in Elmore City, Elmore Twp., Garvin Co., Oklahoma. He was the son of James Gordon Brown and Mary Katherine McKee (105). James Kenneth died in Madison, Dane Co., Wisconsin, on March 18, 2002, at age 70. He was buried in Highland Memory Gardens Cemetery, Madison, Dane Co., Wisconsin.[97]

He married **Darlene A. Unknown.** Darlene A. Unknown was born in 1928.

**311. Earl Edwin Brown** (*Mary Katherine*[8] *McKee, Charles Watson*[7]*, Josiah William*[6]*, Elizabeth*[5]*, Alexander*[4]*, Andrew*[3] *Pegan II, Andrew*[2] *Pagan, James*[1]) was born on September 22, 1933 in Elmore City, Elmore Twp., Garvin Co., Oklahoma. He was the son of James Gordon Brown and Mary Katherine McKee (105). He died on December 5, 2016 in Rialto, San Bernardino Co., California? at age 83. Earl E. was buried in Riverside National Cemetery, Riverside, Riverside Co., California.[61]

Earl Edwin Brown married **Ms. Trull** on May 1, 1953 in Tulare Co., California.

**312. Burl D. Brown** (*Mary Katherine*[8] *McKee, Charles Watson*[7]*, Josiah William*[6]*, Elizabeth*[5]*, Alexander*[4]*, Andrew*[3] *Pegan II, Andrew*[2] *Pagan, James*[1]) was born on March 18, 1937, in Elmore City, Elmore Twp., Garvin Co., Oklahoma. He is the son of James Gordon Brown and Mary Katherine McKee (105).

**313. Lela Faye**[9] **Brown** (*Mary Katherine*[8] *McKee, Charles Watson*[7]*, Josiah William*[6]*, Elizabeth*[5]*, Alexander*[4]*, Andrew*[3] *Pegan II, Andrew*[2] *Pagan, James*[1]) was born on September 1, 1941, in Elmore City, Elmore Twp., Garvin Co., Oklahoma. She was the daughter of James Gordon Brown and Mary Katherine McKee (105). Lela Faye died in Sanger, Fresno Co., California, on March 27, 2011, at age 69. She was buried in Greenlawn Southwest Memorial Park Cemetery, Bakersfield, Kern Co., California.[98]

Lela Faye Brown married **Ira Richard Jones** on June 22, 1957 in Clark Co., Nevada. Ira Richard Jones was born in Muncie, Center Twp., Delaware Co., Indiana, on February 26, 1938. He was also known as **Sonny.** Ira Richard reached age 75 and died in Sanger, Fresno Co., California on February 27, 2013. He was buried in Southwest Memorial Park Cemetery, Bakersfield, Kern Co., California.[98]

**314. Doris[9] McKee** (*Samuel Robert[8], Charles Watson[7], Josiah William[6], Elizabeth[5], Alexander[4], Andrew[3] Pegan II, Andrew[2] Pagan, James[1]*) was born in 1940 in Eskola, Nolan Co., Texas. She is the daughter of Samuel Robert McKee (106) and Martha Rosa McKee (110).

**315. Ralph Wayne[9] McKee** (*Samuel Robert[8], Charles Watson[7], Josiah William[6], Elizabeth[5], Alexander[4], Andrew[3] Pegan II, Andrew[2] Pagan, James[1]*) was born on November 18, 1946, in Eskota, Nolan Co., Texas. He was the son of Samuel Robert McKee (106) and Martha Rosa McKee (110). Ralph Wayne died in Sweetwater, Nolan Co., Texas, on December 15, 1946. He was buried in Newman Cemetery, Sylvester, Fisher Co., Texas.[10]

**316. Carol[9] McKee** (*Earnest L.[8], Charles Watson[7], Josiah William[6], Elizabeth[5], Alexander[4], Andrew[3] Pegan II, Andrew[2] Pagan, James[1]*) was born after 1940. She was the daughter of Earnest L. and Opal Ray Bullion. She died before 2013.

**317. LaJune[9] Bradley** (*Meranda Ethel[8] McKee, Oliver Edwin[7], Josiah William[6], Elizabeth[5], Alexander[4], Andrew[3] Pegan II, Andrew[2] Pagan, James[1]*) was born on January 15, 1937, in Elmore Twp., Garvin Co., Oklahoma. She was the daughter of Ollie Bradley and Meranda Ethel McKee (111). LaJune died in Elmore Twp., Garvin Co., Oklahoma, on January 15, 1937. She was buried in Katie City Cemetery, Katie, Brady Twp., Garvin Co., Oklahoma.[9]

**318. Sandra Arlene[9] McKee** (*William Everett[8], Oliver Edwin[7], Josiah William[6], Elizabeth[5], Alexander[4], Andrew[3] Pegan II, Andrew[2] Pagan, James[1]*) was born on July 21, 1946, in Merkel, Taylor Co., Texas. She was the daughter of William Everett McKee (112) and Isadora Rials. Sandra Arlene died in Lovington, Lea Co., New Mexico, on November 24, 2009, at age 63. She was buried in Lovington Cemetery, Lovington, Lea Co., New Mexico.[55]

Sandra Arlene married **Mr. McMahon** on January 29, 1965. They had four children.

Sandra Arlene McKee and Ronald McMahon had four children, including:

+ 406 f I. **Toni Lynette[10] McMahon** was born in Lovington, Lea Co., New Mexico, on December 14, 1971. She died in Lovington, Lea Co., New Mexico, on March 15, 1974.[55]

**319. Janice Yvonne[9] McKee** (*William Everett[8], Oliver Edwin[7], Josiah William[6], Elizabeth[5], Alexander[4], Andrew[3] Pegan II, Andrew[2] Pagan, James[1]*) was born on December 1, 1944, in Merkel, Taylor Co., Texas. She was the daughter of William Everett McKee (112) and Isadora Rials. Janice Yvonne died in Lubbock, Lubbock Co., Texas, on October 22, 1997, at age 52.

Janice Yvonne married **Mr. Shadden.**

**320. Alvin Edward[9] McKee** (*Lee Roy[8], Oliver Edwin[7], Josiah William[6], Elizabeth[5], Alexander[4], Andrew[3] Pegan II, Andrew[2] Pagan, James[1]*) was born on November 15, 1949, in Nolan Co., Texas. He was the son of Lee Roy McKee (113) and Carmen Marcia Brannan. Alvin Edward died in Snohomish Co., Washington, on August 16, 1962, at age 12.

**321. George Arthur[9] Murphy III** (*Sara Louise[8] McKee, Oliver Edwin[7], Josiah William[6], Elizabeth[5], Alexander[4], Andrew[3] Pegan II, Andrew[2] Pagan, James[1]*) was born on October 4, 1946, in Auburn, King Co., Washington. He was the son of George Junior Murphy II and Sara Louise McKee (115). George Arthur died in Cottage Grove, Lane Co., Oregon, on September 24, 1995, at age 48.

George Arthur married **Sandra Unknown.**

**322. Carol Anne[9] Murphy** (*Sara Louise[8] McKee, Oliver Edwin[7], Josiah William[6], Elizabeth[5], Alexander[4], Andrew[3] Pegan II, Andrew[2] Pagan, James[1]*) was born on August 18, 1947, in Sweetwater, Nolan Co., Texas. She was the daughter of George Junior Murphy II and Sara Louise McKee (115). Carol Anne died in Roseburg, Douglas Co., Oregon, on March 14, 1991, at age 43. She was buried in Alford Cemetery, Harrisburg, Linn Co., Oregon.[102]

Carol Anne married **Unknown Fish.**

Carol Anne Murphy Fish married **Mr. Burns.**

323. **Jimmy K.⁹ Riley II** (*James Irwin⁸, Rosa Lily⁷ McKee, Josiah William⁶, Elizabeth⁵, Alexander⁴, Andrew³ Pegan II, Andrew² Pagan, James¹*) was born in 1934 in Elmore City, Elmore Twp., Garvin Co., Oklahoma. He is the son of James Irwin Riley (117) and Ethel M. Skaggs.

324. **Patricia Charline⁹ Riley** (*James Irwin⁸, Rosa Lily⁷ McKee, Josiah William⁶, Elizabeth⁵, Alexander⁴, Andrew³ Pegan II, Andrew² Pagan, James¹*) was born on May 17, 1936 in Grady Co., Oklahoma. She is the daughter of James Irwin Riley (117) and Ethel M. Skaggs. She died on May 17, 1936, in Grady Co., Oklahoma. Patricia Charline was buried in Sunny Lane Cemetery, Del City, Oklahoma Co., Oklahoma.[41]

325. **Elsie Fay⁹ Riley** (*Isaac Edwin⁸, Rosa Lily⁷ McKee, Josiah William⁶, Elizabeth⁵, Alexander⁴, Andrew³ Pegan II, Andrew² Pagan, James¹*) was born in 1933 in Brady Twp., Garvin Co., Oklahoma. She is the daughter of Isaac Edwin Riley (118) and Stella Dunn Moore.

326. **Ida Mae⁹ Dutton** (*Roberta Mae⁸ Riley, Rosa Lily⁷ McKee, Josiah William⁶, Elizabeth⁵, Alexander⁴, Andrew³ Pegan II, Andrew² Pagan, James¹*) was born on June 21, 1929, in Brady Twp., Garvin Co., Oklahoma. She was the daughter of Ruben Melton Dutton and Roberta Mae Riley (119). Ida Mae died in Moore, Cleveland Co., Oklahoma, on May 16, 2002, at age 72. She was buried in Elmore City Cemetery, Elmore City, Elmore Twp., Garvin Co., Oklahoma.[42]

Ida Mae married **Darvis Arthur Brown** after 1940. They had one daughter. Darvis Arthur Brown was born in Elmore City, Elmore Twp., Garvin Co., Oklahoma, on May 2, 1927. Darvis Arthur reached age 76 and died in Oklahoma City, Oklahoma, on August 9, 2003. He was buried in Elmore City Cemetery, Elmore City, Elmore Twp., Garvin Co., Oklahoma.[42]

327. **Jerry Duane⁹ Dutton** (*Roberta Mae⁸ Riley, Rosa Lily⁷ McKee, Josiah William⁶, Elizabeth⁵, Alexander⁴, Andrew³ Pegan II, Andrew² Pagan, James¹*) was born in 1938 in Brady Twp., Garvin Co., Oklahoma. He is the son of Ruben Melton Dutton and Roberta Mae Riley (119).

328. **Lillis Louise⁹ Tindle** (*Frank Scott⁸, Nancy Angeoline⁷ McKee, Jasper Ervin⁶, Elizabeth⁵, Alexander⁴, Andrew³ Pegan II, Andrew² Pagan, James¹*) was born in 1916 in St. Joseph, Buchanan Co., Missouri. She is the daughter of Frank Scott Tindle (126) and Anna Morris.

Lillis Louise married **Tong Joseph Spers** on December 18, 1941, in Clay Co., Missouri. Tong Joseph Spers was born in 1917.

329. **Dale Ervin⁹ Tindle** (*Frank Scott⁸, Nancy Angeoline⁷ McKee, Jasper Ervin⁶, Elizabeth⁵, Alexander⁴, Andrew³ Pegan II, Andrew² Pagan, James¹*) was born on July 22, 1918, in St. Joseph, Buchanan Co., Missouri. He was the son of Frank Scott Tindle (126) and Anna Morris. Dale Ervin died in Kansas City, Jackson Co., Missouri, on February 3, 2001, at age 82. He was buried in Forest Hill Cemetery, Kansas City, Jackson Co., Missouri.[103]

Dale Ervin married **Erma Sanders** after 1940. They had three daughters. Erma Sanders was born in Pardee, Atchison Co., Kansas, on July 9, 1920. Erma reached age 92 and died in Kansas City, Jackson Co., Missouri, on January 2, 2013. She was buried in Forest Hill Cemetery, Kansas City, Jackson Co., Missouri.[103]

330. **Charles Leroy⁹ Painter** (*Rosa L.⁸ Tindle, Nancy Angeoline⁷ McKee, Jasper Ervin⁶, Elizabeth⁵, Alexander⁴, Andrew³ Pegan II, Andrew² Pagan, James¹*) was born in 1923 in Industrial City, Washington Twp., Buchanan Co., Missouri. He is the son of George Leroy Painter and Rosa L. Tindle (128).

331. **Donald R.⁹ Painter** (*Rosa L.⁸ Tindle, Nancy Angeoline⁷ McKee, Jasper Ervin⁶, Elizabeth⁵, Alexander⁴, Andrew³ Pegan II, Andrew² Pagan, James¹*) was born in 1926 in Industrial City, Washington Twp., Buchanan Co., Missouri. He is the son of George Leroy Painter and Rosa L. Tindle (128).

332. **Rosa Mae⁹ Newman** (*Daisey Viola⁸ Tindle, Nancy Angeoline⁷ McKee, Jasper Ervin⁶, Elizabeth⁵,*

*Alexander⁴, Andrew³ Pegan II, Andrew² Pagan, James¹*) was born in 1919 in Pattonsburg, Benton Twp., Daviess Co., Missouri. She was the daughter of Clyde Newman and Daisey Viola Tindle (129). Rosa Mae died in Pattonsburg, Benton Twp., Daviess Co., Missouri, in 1974 at age 55. She was buried in Pattonsburg Memorial Gardens Cemetery, Pattonsburg, Benton Twp., Daviess Co., Misssouri.[46]

Rosa Mae married **Ray L. Shipers** on August 27, 1939, in Daviess Co., Missouri. They divorced. Ray L. Shipers was born in Benton Twp., Daviess Co., Missouri, on June 24, 1915. Ray L. reached age 57 and died in Pattonsburg, Benton Twp., Daviess Co., Missouri, on March 11, 1973.

Rosa Mae Newman Shippers married **Kenneth M. McColloch.** Kenneth M. McColloch was born in Miller Twp., Gentry Co., Missouri, on December 5, 1926. Kenneth M. reached age 49 and died in Pattonsburg, Benton Twp., Daviess Co., Missouri, on September 3, 1976. He was buried in Pattonsburg Memorial Gardens Cemetery, Pattonsburg, Benton Twp., Daviess Co., Misssouri.[46]

# 10th Generation

**333. Charles Leroy[10] Grimes II** (*Mae Ophelia[9] Davis, Mary E.[8] McKee, Samuel Stephen[7], Josiah William[6], Elizabeth[5], Alexander[4], Andrew[3] Pegan II, Andrew[2] Pagan, James[1]*) was born in 1928 in Elmore Twp., Garvin Co., Oklahoma. He was also known as **Leroy**. He was the son of Charles Arthur Grimes and Mae Ophelia Davis (134). Charles Leroy died in Purcell, Moncrief Twp., McClain Co., Oklahoma?, in 1931 at age three. He was buried in Katie City Cemetery, Katie, Brady Twp., Garvin Co., Oklahoma.[4]

In the 1930 census, his name is Charles L. Grimes. His gravestone says Leroy Grimes.

**334. Lametha Marniece[10] Martindale** (*Mae Ophelia[9] Davis, Mary E.[8] McKee, Samuel Stephen[7], Josiah William[6], Elizabeth[5], Alexander[4], Andrew[3] Pegan II, Andrew[2] Pagan, James[1]*) was born on October 6, 1932, in Elmore City, Elmore Twp., Garvin Co., Oklahoma. She was the daughter of George Lewers Martindale and Mae Ophelia Davis (134). Lametha Marniece died in Oklahoma City, Oklahoma, on January 12, 2011, at age 78. She was buried in Hillside Cemetery, Purcell, Moncrief Twp., McClain Co., Oklahoma.[19]

Lametha Marniece married **John Lee Brady** on April 10, 1953. They had one daughter. John Lee Brady was born on October 25, 1930.

**335. Andrew Harold Auld[10] Harness** (*Ivy Jones[9] Sims, Martha Ollie[8] McKee, Samuel Stephen[7], Josiah William[6], Elizabeth[5], Alexander[4], Andrew[3] Pegan II, Andrew[2] Pagan, James[1]*) was born on December 4, 1928, in Elk City, Beckham Co., Oklahoma. He was the son of Olvin Harold Auld and Ivy Jones Sims (137). Andrew Harold Auld was adopted after 1930. He died in Oklahoma City, Oklahoma, on May 15, 1993, at age 64. Andrew Harold Auld was buried in Chapel Hill Cemetery, Clinton, Custer Co., Oklahoma.[103]

Andrew Harold Auld was adopted by George William Harness, his stepfather, and he assumed the Harness surname.

Andrew Harold Auld Harness married **Valeria Fransen** on July 2, 1950. Valeria Fransen was born in Clinton, Washita Co., Oklahoma, on October 13, 1927. Valeria reached age 63 and died in Oklahoma City, Oklahoma, on March 21, 1991. Clinton, Oklahoma.

**336. Jimmie Lee[10] Harrison** (*Louise[9] Cross, Fannie May[8] McKee, Samuel Stephen[7], Josiah William[6], Elizabeth[5], Alexander[4], Andrew[3] Pegan II, Andrew[2] Pagan, James[1]*) was born on April 1, 1937, in Choctaw Co., Oklahoma? He is the son of Leslie Lee Harrison and Louise Cross (142).

**337. Danny[10] Ray** (*Juanita Fern[9] Cross, Fannie May[8] McKee, Samuel Stephen[7], Josiah William[6], Elizabeth[5], Alexander[4], Andrew[3] Pegan II, Andrew[2] Pagan, James[1]*) was born on June 20, 1944, in Quanah, Hardeman Co., Texas. He was the son of Enex Daniel Ray and Juanita Fern Cross (144). Danny died in Noble, Cleveland Co., Oklahoma, on April 28, 2001, at age 56. He was buried in Bethany Cemetery, Bethany, Oklahoma Co., Oklahoma.

He married **Ms. Satterfield.**

**338. Wilma Fern[10] Cross** (*James Rex[9], Claud James[8], Sarah Elvira Elizabeth Ann[7] McKee, Josiah William[6], Elizabeth[5], Alexander[4], Andrew[3] Pegan II, Andrew[2] Pagan, James[1]*) was born on March 13, 1931, in Sylvester, Fisher Co., Texas. She is the daughter of James Rex Cross (152) and Mozell Henson.

She married **Jack Irland Bland.** They had five children. Jack Irland Bland was born in Merkel, Taylor Co., Texas, on January 2, 1931. Jack Irland reached age 70 and died in Abilene, Taylor Co., Texas, on January 25, 2001. He was buried in Rose Hill Cemetery, Merkel, Taylor Co., Texas.[113]

Wilma Fern Cross and Jack Irland Bland had five children, including:

+ 407 m I.    **Timothy Lee[11] Bland** was born in Abilene, Taylor Co., Texas, on October 4, 1956. He died in Abilene, Taylor Co., Texas, on April 10, 1975.[113]

**339. Riley Doyle¹⁰ Cross** (*James Rex⁹, Claud James⁸, Sarah Elvira Elizabeth Ann⁷ McKee, Josiah William⁶, Elizabeth⁵, Alexander⁴, Andrew³ Pegan II, Andrew² Pagan, James¹*) was born on December 2, 1932, in Sylvester, Fisher Co., Texas. He is the son of James Rex Cross (152) and Mozell Henson.

**340. Frances Juanita¹⁰ Cross** (*James Rex⁹, Claud James⁸, Sarah Elvira Elizabeth Ann⁷ McKee, Josiah William⁶, Elizabeth⁵, Alexander⁴, Andrew³ Pegan II, Andrew² Pagan, James¹*) was born on April 30, 1936, in Longworth, Fisher Co., Texas. She was the daughter of James Rex Cross (152) and Mozell Henson. Frances Juanita died in Longworth, Fisher Co., Texas, on April 30, 1936. She was buried in Newman Cemetery, Sylvester, Fisher Co., Texas.[10]

**341. Zenita Lee¹⁰ Cross** (*James Rex⁹, Claud James⁸, Sarah Elvira Elizabeth Ann⁷ McKee, Josiah William⁶, Elizabeth⁵, Alexander⁴, Andrew³ Pegan II, Andrew² Pagan, James¹*) was born on October 30, 1937, in Nolan Co., Texas. She is the daughter of James Rex Cross (152) and Mozell Henson.

She married **Jackie Leon Gardner.** They had three children. Jackie Leon Gardner was born in Jones Co., Texas, on February 28, 1934.

Zenita Lee Cross and Jackie Leon Gardner had three children, including:

+ 408 m I. **Jimmy D.¹¹ Gardner** was born in Sylvester, Fisher Co., Texas, on May 1, 1955. He died in Choctaw, Oklahoma Co., Oklahoma, on February 15, 1987.

+ 409 m I. **Daughter¹¹ Gardner**

**342. Jackie Fred¹⁰ Cox** (*Georgia Elizabeth⁹ Ferrel, Clara Jane⁸ Cross, Sarah Elvira Elizabeth Ann⁷ McKee, Josiah William⁶, Elizabeth⁵, Alexander⁴, Andrew³ Pegan II, Andrew² Pagan, James¹*) was born on February 25, 1952, in Rotan, Fisher Co., Texas. He was the son of Orville Howard Cox and Georgia Elizabeth Ferrel (154). Jackie Fred died in Rotan, Fisher Co., Texas, in February 1952. He was buried in Newman Cemetery, Sylvester, Fisher Co., Texas.[10]

**343. James Frank¹⁰ Cox** (*Georgia Elizabeth⁹ Ferrel, Clara Jane⁸ Cross, Sarah Elvira Elizabeth Ann⁷ McKee, Josiah William⁶, Elizabeth⁵, Alexander⁴, Andrew³ Pegan II, Andrew² Pagan, James¹*) was born on February 25, 1952, in Rotan, Fisher Co., Texas. He was the son of Orville Howard Cox and Georgia Elizabeth Ferrel (154). James Frank died in Rotan, Fisher Co., Texas, on February 27, 1952. He was buried in Newman Cemetery, Sylvester, Fisher Co., Texas.[10]

**344. Richard Lavada¹⁰ Floyd II** (*Ardell Colleen⁹ Cross, John Henry⁸, Sarah Elvira Elizabeth Ann⁷ McKee, Josiah William⁶, Elizabeth⁵, Alexander⁴, Andrew³ Pegan II, Andrew² Pagan, James¹*) was born on December 5, 1938, in Rotan, Fisher Co., Texas. He was the son of Richard Lavada Floyd and Ardell Colleen Cross (162). Richard Lavada died in Roscoe, Nolan Co., Texas, on August 17, 2010, at age 71. He was buried in Belvieu Cemetery, Rotan, Fisher Co., Texas.[21]

He married **Carol Unknown.** They had two children.

**345. Terry Lynn¹⁰ Floyd** (*Ardell Colleen⁹ Cross, John Henry⁸, Sarah Elvira Elizabeth Ann⁷ McKee, Josiah William⁶, Elizabeth⁵, Alexander⁴, Andrew³ Pegan II, Andrew² Pagan, James¹*) was born on March 28, 1949, in Sweetwater, Nolan Co., Texas. He was the son of Richard Lavada Floyd and Ardell Colleen Cross (162). Terry Lynn died in Fisher Co., Texas, on May 7, 1968, at age 19. He was buried in Belvieu Cemetery, Rotan, Fisher Co., Texas.[21]

Never married.

**346. Willie Jim¹⁰ Turner** (*Canevah Mae⁹ Cross, Willie Franklin⁸, Sarah Elvira Elizabeth Ann⁷ McKee, Josiah William⁶, Elizabeth⁵, Alexander⁴, Andrew³ Pegan II, Andrew² Pagan, James¹*) was born on July 31, 1936, in Sweetwater, Nolan Co., Texas. He is the son of William Mac Turner and Canevah Mae Cross (163).

Willie Jim married **Mary Ann Nugent** on September 19, 1959, in Hockley Co., Texas. They have three daughters. Mary Ann Nugent was born in Palestine, Anderson Co., Texas, on September 26, 1938. Mary Ann reached age 76 and died in Sweetwater, Nolan Co., Texas, on July 12, 2015.

She was buried in Newman Cemetery, Sylvester, Fisher Co., Texas.[10]

**347. Jerry Cross[10] Turner** (*Canevah Mae[9] Cross, Willie Franklin[8], Sarah Elvira Elizabeth Ann[7] McKee, Josiah William[6], Elizabeth[5], Alexander[4], Andrew[3] Pegan II, Andrew[2] Pagan, James[1]*) was born on March 3, 1940, in Sweetwater, Nolan Co., Texas. He was the son of William Mac Turner and Canevah Mae Cross (163). Jerry Cross died in Potter Co., Texas, on November 2, 1992, at age 52. He was buried in Texline Cemetery, Texline, Dallam Co., Texas.[114]

He married **Unknown Unknown.** They had one son.

Son of Jerry Cross Turner and Unknown Unknown:

+ 410 m I.　**Bobby Mac[11] Turner** was born in Dalhart, Dallam Co., Texas, on October 11, 1971. He died in Tulsa, Tulsa Co., Oklahoma?, on January 15, 2004.[128]

**348. Larry Jess[10] Cross** (*William Arnold[9], Willie Franklin[8], Sarah Elvira Elizabeth Ann[7] McKee, Josiah William[6], Elizabeth[5], Alexander[4], Andrew[3] Pegan II, Andrew[2] Pagan, James[1]*) was born on May 28, 1946, in Lamesa, Dawson Co., Texas. He was the son of William Arnold Cross (165) and Faye McHaney. Larry Jess died in Midland, Midland Co., Texas, on August 22, 2013, at age 67. He was buried in Newman Cemetery, Sylvester, Fisher Co., Texas.[10]

He married **Monte Kay Unknown.** They have three children.

**349. William W.[10] Cross II** (*William Arnold[9], Willie Franklin[8], Sarah Elvira Elizabeth Ann[7] McKee, Josiah William[6], Elizabeth[5], Alexander[4], Andrew[3] Pegan II, Andrew[2] Pagan, James[1]*) was born on November 8, 1952, in Midland, Midland Co., Texas. He was also known as **Bo.** He was the son of William Arnold Cross (165) and Faye McHaney. William W. died on April 2, 1982, at age 29. He was buried in Newman Cemetery, Sylvester, Fisher Co., Texas.[10]

**350. William R.[10] Riley** (*Reuben Russell[9], Mary Willie[8] McKee, William Robert[7], Josiah William[6], Elizabeth[5] Pegan, Alexander[4] Pagan, Andrew[3] Pegan II, Andrew[2] Pagan, James[1]*) was born on February 7, 1932, in Harrison Twp., Grady Co., Oklahoma. He is the son of Reuben Russell Riley (166) and Gladys Snow.

**351. Gladys May[10] Riley** (*Reuben Russell[9], Mary Willie[8] McKee, William Robert[7], Josiah William[6], Elizabeth[5] Pegan, Alexander[4] Pagan, Andrew[3] Pegan II, Andrew[2] Pagan, James[1]*) was born in 1933 in Harrison Twp., Grady Co., Oklahoma. She is the daughter of Reuben Russell Riley (166) and Gladys Snow.

**352. Lee Roy[10] Riley** (*Reuben Russell[9], Mary Willie[8] McKee, William Robert[7], Josiah William[6], Elizabeth[5] Pegan, Alexander[4] Pagan, Andrew[3] Pegan II, Andrew[2] Pagan, James[1]*) was born on March 10, 1936, in Harrison Twp., Grady Co., Oklahoma. He is the son of Reuben Russell Riley (166) and Gladys Snow.

**353. Luther Delbert[10] Riley** (*Reuben Russell[9], Mary Willie[8] McKee, William Robert[7], Josiah William[6], Elizabeth[5], Alexander[4], Andrew[3] Pegan II, Andrew[2] Pagan, James[1]*) was born on February 4, 1939, in Harrison Twp., Grady Co., Oklahoma. He was the son of Reuben Russell Riley (166) and Gladys Snow. Luther Delbert died in Harrison Twp., Grady Co., Oklahoma, on November 4, 1940, at age one. He was buried in Erin Springs Cemetery, Erin Springs, Lindsay Twp., Garvin Co., Oklahoma.[12]

**354. James W.[10] Gamble** (*Sarah Jane[9] Riley, Mary Willie[8] McKee, William Robert[7], Josiah William[6], Elizabeth[5], Alexander[4], Andrew[3] Pegan II, Andrew[2] Pagan, James[1]*) was born on February 14, 1937, in Oklahoma. He was the son of Willie Walter Gamble and Sarah Jane Riley (170). James W. died in Imperial Co., California, on March 17, 1964, at age 27. He was buried in Evergreen Cemetery, El Centro, Imperial Co., California.[116]

James W. married **Ms. Peterson.**

**355. Albert D.[10] Gamble** (*Sarah Jane[9] Riley, Mary Willie[8] McKee, William Robert[7], Josiah William[6], Elizabeth[5] Pegan, Alexander[4] Pagan, Andrew[3] Pegan II, Andrew[2] Pagan, James[1]*) was born on February 15, 1939, in Oklahoma. He is the son of Willie Walter Gamble and Sarah Jane Riley (170).

He married **Frieda Unknown.**

**356. Clarence Edward**[10] **Gamble** (*Sarah Jane*[9] *Riley, Mary Willie*[8] *McKee, William Robert*[7]*, Josiah William*[6]*, Elizabeth*[5]*, Alexander*[4]*, Andrew*[3] *Pegan II, Andrew*[2] *Pagan, James*[1]) was born on June 6, 1940, in Riverside, Riverside Co., California. He was the son of Willie Walter Gamble and Sarah Jane Riley (170). Clarence Edward died in Marysville, Yuba Co., California, on September 12, 2006, at age 66.

Clarence Edward married **Ms. Cowdrey.**

**357. Daughter**[10] **McKee** (*Clyde Frank*[9]*, James Andres*[8]*, William Robert*[7]*, Josiah William*[6]*, Elizabeth*[5]*, Alexander*[4]*, Andrew*[3] *Pegan II, Andrew*[2] *Pagan, James*[1]) was born on October 30, 1953. She is the daughter of Clyde Frank McKee (174) and Nola Rosetta Fleming.

She married Mr. Young. They had three children.

Daughter McKee and **Mr. Young** had three children, including:

+ 411  m  I.  **Kyle Braden**[11] **Young** was born in Oklahoma City, Oklahoma, on June 5, 1985. He died in Chickasha, Chickasha Twp., Grady Co., Oklahoma, on November 2, 2013.[52]

**358. Lenard Carl**[10] **McKee II** (*Lenard Carl*[9]*, James Andres*[8]*, William Robert*[7]*, Josiah William*[6]*, Elizabeth*[5]*, Alexander*[4]*, Andrew*[3] *Pegan II, Andrew*[2] *Pagan, James*[1]) was born on July 2, 1952, in Grady Co., Oklahoma? He was also known as **Butch.** He was the son of Lenard Carl McKee (175) and Margie Tollison. Lenard Carl died in Cleveland Co., Oklahoma, on January 1, 1978, at age 25. He was buried in Bradley Cemetery, Bradley Twp., Grady Co., Oklahoma.[11]

He married **Barbara Arlene Haynes.** Barbara Arlene Haynes was born in Canadian Co., Oklahoma, on February 22, 1951. Barbara Arlene reached age 37 and died in Oklahoma Co., Oklahoma, on October 1, 1988. She was buried in Frisco Cemetery, Yukon, Canadian Co., Oklahoma.[129]

**359. Clyde Willard**[10] **Luther** (*Elzie Mae*[9] *McKee, James Andres*[8]*, William Robert*[7]*, Josiah William*[6]*, Elizabeth*[5]*, Alexander*[4]*, Andrew*[3] *Pegan II, Andrew*[2] *Pagan, James*[1]) was born on January 5, 1959. He was the son of Marion Willard Luther and Elzie Mae McKee (176). Clyde Willard died on June 18, 1993, at age 34. He was buried in Alex Cemetery, Alex, Alex Twp., Grady Co., Oklahoma.[52]

**360. Georgia Nelda Jean**[10] **McKee** (*Troy E.*[9]*, George Washington*[8]*, William Robert*[7]*, Josiah William*[6]*, Elizabeth*[5]*, Alexander*[4]*, Andrew*[3] *Pegan II, Andrew*[2] *Pagan, James*[1]) was born on September 3, 1949, in Wynnewood, Brady Twp., Garvin Co., Oklahoma. She was also known as **Nelda.** She was the daughter of Troy E. McKee (187) and Willie Nell Cassell. Georgia Nelda Jean died in Elmore City, Elmore Twp., Garvin Co., Oklahoma, on March 22, 2014, at age 64. She was buried in Elmore City Cemetery, Elmore City, Elmore Twp., Garvin Co., Oklahoma.[42]

Georgia Nelda Jean married **Francis Walter Shreve** on November 9, 1973, in Garvin Co., Oklahoma. They had one son. Francis Walter Shreve was born in Shattuck, Ellis Co., Oklahoma, on November 13, 1943. He was also known as **Frank.** Francis Walter reached age 52 and died in Elmore City, Elmore Twp., Garvin Co., Oklahoma, on May 5, 1996. He was buried in Elmore City Cemetery, Elmore City, Elmore Twp., Garvin Co., Oklahoma.[42]

**361. Harold Dewayne**[10] **McKee II** (*Harold Winfred*[9]*, George Washington*[8]*, William Robert*[7]*, Josiah William*[6]*, Elizabeth*[5] *Pegan, Alexander*[4] *Pagan, Andrew*[3] *Pegan II, Andrew*[2] *Pagan, James*[1]) was born on October 15, 1956. He was the son of Harold Winfred McKee (188) and Patsy Ann Courtney. Harold Dewayne died on October 16, 1956.

**362. Daughter**[10] **Morris** (*Marie M.*[9] *Meridth, Laura Elvira*[8] *McKee, James L.*[7]*, Josiah William*[6]*, Elizabeth*[5] *Pegan, Alexander*[4] *Pagan, Andrew*[3] *Pegan II, Andrew*[2] *Pagan, James*[1]). Daughter Morris was born after 1940. She is the daughter of William Carl Morris II and Marie M. Meridth (199).

She married **Mr. Parish.** They had one daughter.

Daughter of Daughter Morris and Mr. Parish:

+ 412 f    I.    **Daughter[11] Parish.**

**363. Carroll Ray[10] Johnson II** (*Emlie[9] Meridth, Laura Elvira[8] McKee, James L.[7], Josiah William[6], Elizabeth[5], Alexander[4], Andrew[3] Pegan II, Andrew[2] Pagan, James[1]*) was born on March 3, 1951, in Elmore City, Elmore Twp., Garvin Co., Oklahoma? He was the son of Carroll Edward Johnson and Emlie Meridth (200). Carroll Ray died in Ringwood, Major Co., Oklahoma, on March 28, 2009, at age 58. He was buried in Hennepin Cemetery, Murray Co., Oklahoma.[118]

Carroll Ray married **Ms. Pickett.** They had two children.

**364. Ada Marie[10] Riley** (*Gussie Isaac[9], Reuben Josiah[8], Martha Louise Jane[7] McKee, Josiah William[6], Elizabeth[5], Alexander[4], Andrew[3] Pegan II, Andrew[2] Pagan, James[1]*) was born on April 14, 1933, in Pursley Twp., Grady Co., Oklahoma. She is the daughter of Gussie Isaac Riley (213) and Esther Faye Jeffcoat.

She married **William R. Ince.** William R. Ince was born in Lafayette, Fairfield Twp., Tippecanoe Co., Indiana?, on December 19, 1931.

**365. Joyce G.[10] Riley** (*Gussie Isaac[9], Reuben Josiah[8], Martha Louise Jane[7] McKee, Josiah William[6], Elizabeth[5], Alexander[4], Andrew[3] Pegan II, Andrew[2] Pagan, James[1]*) was born in 1935 in Pursley Twp., Grady Co., Oklahoma. She is the daughter of Gussie Isaac Riley (213) and Esther Faye Jeffcoat.

**366. Ruby Esther[10] Riley** (*Gussie Isaac[9], Reuben Josiah[8], Martha Louise Jane[7] McKee, Josiah William[6], Elizabeth[5], Alexander[4], Andrew[3] Pegan II, Andrew[2] Pagan, James[1]*) was born on November 9, 1939, in Pursley Twp., Grady Co., Oklahoma. She was the daughter of Gussie Isaac Riley (213) and Esther Faye Jeffcoat. Ruby Esther died in Pampa, Gray Co., Texas, on October 12, 1988, at age 48.

Childless.

She married **Olin Dellis Lyons Harris.** Olin Dellis Lyons Harris was born in Pampa, Gray Co., Texas, on April 17, 1935. Olin Dellis Lyons reached

age 79 and died in Pampa, Gray Co., Texas, on September 23, 2014.

**367. Velma Charlene[10] Riley** (*Charles Russell[9], Reuben Josiah[8], Martha Louise Jane[7] McKee, Josiah William[6], Elizabeth[5] Pegan, Alexander[4] Pagan, Andrew[3] Pegan II, Andrew[2] Pagan, James[1]*) was born in 1939 in Lone Rock Twp., Caddo Co., Oklahoma. She is the daughter of Charles Russell Riley (215) and Velma Ione Anthony.

**368. Virginia Carolyn[10] Riley** (*Charles Russell[9], Reuben Josiah[8], Martha Louise Jane[7] McKee, Josiah William[6], Elizabeth[5], Alexander[4], Andrew[3] Pegan II, Andrew[2] Pagan, James[1]*) was born on October 3, 1942, in Lone Rock Twp., Caddo Co., Oklahoma. She was the daughter of Charles Russell Riley (215) and Velma Ione Anthony. Virginia Carolyn died in Choctaw, Oklahoma Co., Oklahoma, on April 14, 2013, at age 70. She was buried in Sunny Lane Cemetery, Del City, Oklahoma Co., Oklahoma.[41]

She married **Mr. Beningfield.** They had three daughters.

**369. Reuben Walter[10] Edgar** (*Lee Emma[9] Riley, Reuben Josiah[8], Martha Louise Jane[7] McKee, Josiah William[6], Elizabeth[5], Alexander[4], Andrew[3] Pegan II, Andrew[2] Pagan, James[1]*) was born on November 11, 1939, in Lindsay, Lindsay Twp., Garvin Co., Oklahoma. He was the son of Jay Lee Edgar and Lee Emma Riley (216). Reuben Walter died in Lindsay, Lindsay Twp., Garvin Co., Oklahoma, on July 26, 1992, at age 52.

He married **Unknown Unknown.** They had one son.

**370. Doyle Rayburn[10] Edgar** (*Lee Emma[9] Riley, Reuben Josiah[8], Martha Louise Jane[7] McKee, Josiah William[6], Elizabeth[5], Alexander[4], Andrew[3] Pegan II, Andrew[2] Pagan, James[1]*) was born on October 6, 1941, in Lindsay, Lindsay Twp., Garvin Co., Oklahoma. He was the son of Jay Lee Edgar and Lee Emma Riley (216). Doyle Rayburn died in Lindsay, Lindsay Twp., Garvin Co., Oklahoma, on February 24, 1988, at age 46.

**371. Daughter[10] Simmons** (*Sarah Elvina[9] Riley, Reuben Josiah[8], Martha Louise Jane[7] McKee, Josiah William[6], Elizabeth[5], Alexander[4], Andrew[3] Pegan II, Andrew[2]*

*Pagan, James[1]*). She is the daughter of Leonard Gordon Simmons II and Sarah Elvina Riley (218).

She married **Mr. McKee.** They had at least two children:

Daughters of Daughter Simmons and Mr. McKee:

+ 413 f I. **Julie Ann[11] McKee** was born in Lindsay, Lindsay Twp., Garvin Co., Oklahoma, on September 3, 1971. She died in Lindsay, Lindsay Twp., Garvin Co., Oklahoma, on January 12, 1984.[52]

+ 414 m II. **Kevin Kenneth[11] McKee** was born in Lindsay, Lindsay Twp., Garvin Co., Oklahoma, on January 17, 1980. He died in Oklahoma City, Oklahoma Co., Oklahoma, on May 25, 1989.[52]

**372. Carolyn Sue[10] Mayhon** (*Betty Jean[9] Riley, Isaac Russell[8], Martha Louise Jane[7] McKee, Josiah William[6], Elizabeth[5], Alexander[4], Andrew[3] Pegan II, Andrew[2] Pagan, James[1]*) was born on November 19, 1949, in Albuquerque, Bernalillo Co., New Mexico? She was the daughter of David Moody Mayhon and Betty Jean Riley (223). Carolyn Sue died in Calimesa, Riverside Co., California, on June 11, 2010, at age 60.

She married **Mr. Brewster.** They divorced.

**373. Bobbie Allen[10] Gosnell** (*Loyd Jesse[9], Emma Neta[8] Riley, Martha Louise Jane[7] McKee, Josiah William[6], Elizabeth[5], Alexander[4], Andrew[3] Pegan II, Andrew[2] Pagan, James[1]*) was born on November 17, 1934, in Pursley Twp., Grady Co., Oklahoma. He was the son of Loyd Jesse Gosnell (225) and Margaret Elizabeth Spencer. Bobbie Allen died in Alex, Alex Twp., Grady Co. Oklahoma, on May 12, 2001, at age 66. He was buried in Alex Cemetery, Alex, Alex Twp., Grady Co., Oklahoma.[52]

He married **Loretta Unknown.**

**374. Ben[10] Gosnell** (*William Isaac[9], Emma Neta[8] Riley, Martha Louise Jane[7] McKee, Josiah William[6], Elizabeth[5] Pegan, Alexander[4] Pagan, Andrew[3] Pegan II, Andrew[2] Pagan, James[1]*). He was the son of William Isaac Gosnell (226) and Lucille Marie Kirkpatrick. Ben died in Perth, Australia?, before 2003.

**375. Son[10] Grooms** (*Leroy[9], Janie Susan[8] Riley, Martha Louise Jane[7] McKee, Josiah William[6], Elizabeth[5], Alexander[4], Andrew[3] Pegan II, Andrew[2] Pagan, James[1]*). He is the son of Leroy Grooms (227) and Betty Lee Edgar.

He married **Viola Unknown.** They had at least one son.

Son of Son Grooms and Viola Unknown:

+ 415 m I. **Roy[11] Grooms** was born in Chickasha, Chickasha Twp., Grady Co., Oklahoma. He died in Chickasha, Chickasha Twp., Grady Co., Oklahoma, before 2005.

**376. Ledson Dawson[10] Alexander** (*Christine Ellen[9] Cross, Willie Alice[8] McKee, Josiah Andres[7], Josiah William[6], Elizabeth[5], Alexander[4], Andrew[3] Pegan II, Andrew[2] Pagan, James[1]*) was born in 1931 in Hewitt Twp., Carter Co., Oklahoma. He is the son of Eugene Dawson Alexander and Christine Ellen Cross (234).

**377. Eugene Ulysses[10] Alexander II** (*Christine Ellen[9] Cross, Willie Alice[8] McKee, Josiah Andres[7], Josiah William[6], Elizabeth[5], Alexander[4], Andrew[3] Pegan II, Andrew[2] Pagan, James[1]*) was born on June 22, 1933, in Wilson, Hewitt Twp., Carter Co., Oklahoma. He was the son of Eugene Dawson Alexander and Christine Ellen Cross (234). Eugene Ulysses died in Ardmore, Morgan Twp., Carter Co., Oklahoma, on December 21, 1994, at age 61. He was buried in Hewitt Cemetery, Wilson, Hewitt Twp., Carter Co., Oklahoma.[13]

**378. Jesse Lee[10] Alexander** (*Christine Ellen[9] Cross, Willie Alice[8] McKee, Josiah Andres[7], Josiah William[6], Elizabeth[5], Alexander[4], Andrew[3] Pegan II, Andrew[2] Pagan, James[1]*) was born in 1937 in Hewitt, Hewitt Twp., Carter Co., Oklahoma. He is the son of Eugene Dawson Alexander and Christine Ellen Cross (234).

**379. Oleta Joyce[10] Alexander** (*Christine Ellen[9] Cross, Willie Alice[8] McKee, Josiah Andres[7], Josiah William[6],*

*Elizabeth⁵, Alexander⁴, Andrew³ Pegan II, Andrew² Pagan, James¹*) was born in 1940 in Hewitt, Hewitt Twp., Carter Co., Oklahoma. She is the daughter of Eugene Dawson Alexander and Christine Ellen Cross (234).

380. **Eugenia Dale¹⁰ Alexander** (*Christine Ellen⁹ Cross, Willie Alice⁸ McKee, Josiah Andres⁷, Josiah William⁶, Elizabeth⁵, Alexander⁴, Andrew³ Pegan II, Andrew² Pagan, James¹*) was born on April 9, 1954, in Hewitt, Hewitt Twp., Carter Co., Oklahoma. She was the daughter of Eugene Dawson Alexander and Christine Ellen Cross (234). Eugenia Dale died in Hewitt, Hewitt Twp., Carter Co., Oklahoma, on July 25, 1954. She was buried in Hewitt Cemetery, Wilson, Hewitt Twp., Carter Co., Oklahoma.[13]

381. **Frank Thomas¹⁰ Carriker** (*Irene Dorothy⁹ Alexander, Willie Alice⁸ McKee, Josiah Andres⁷, Josiah William⁶, Elizabeth⁵, Alexander⁴, Andrew³ Pegan II, Andrew² Pagan, James¹*) was born on March 1, 1938 in Wilson, Hewitt Twp., Carter Co., Oklahoma. He is the son of Thomas Oscar Carriker and Irene Dorothy Alexander (236).

He married **Linda Faye Spencer.** They have five daughters. Linda Faye Spencer was born in Graham, Graham Twp., Carter Co., Oklahoma, on December 13, 1945. Linda Faye reached age 56 and died in Graham Twp., Carter Co., Oklahoma, on March 29, 2002. She was buried in Hewitt Cemetery, Wilson, Hewitt Twp., Carter Co., Oklahoma.[13]

382. **Lonnie Joe¹⁰ Carriker** (*Irene Dorothy⁹ Alexander, Willie Alice⁸ McKee, Josiah Andres⁷, Josiah William⁶, Elizabeth⁵ Pegan, Alexander⁴ Pagan, Andrew³ Pegan II, Andrew² Pagan, James¹*) was born on Friday, September 6, 1940, in Wilson, Hewitt Twp., Carter Co., Oklahoma. He is the son of Thomas Oscar Carriker and Irene Dorothy Alexander (236).

He married **Billy Jean Unknown.** Billy Jean Unknown was born in 1940.

383. **Carol Jeanne¹⁰ Alexander** (*Frank Perry⁹, Willie Alice⁸ McKee, Josiah Andres⁷, Josiah William⁶, Elizabeth⁵, Alexander⁴, Andrew³ Pegan II, Andrew² Pagan, James¹*) was born on September 20, 1945, in La Grande, Union Co., Oregon. She was the daughter of Frank Perry Alexander II (237)

and Adrienne Leona See. Carol Jeanne died in Prineville, Crook Co., Oregon, on June 5, 2000, at age 54.

She married **Jerry Lee Hensley.** Jerry Lee Hensley was born in 1940.

384. **Billy Thomas¹⁰ Wilson** (*Ruel Pearce⁹, Roxie Laurenda⁸ McKee, Josiah Andres⁷, Josiah William⁶, Elizabeth⁵, Alexander⁴, Andrew³ Pegan II, Andrew² Pagan, James¹*) was born on November 24, 1951, in Ardmore, Morgan Twp., Carter Co., Oklahoma. He was the son of Ruel Pearce Wilson (245) and Mary Margaret Jones. Billy Thomas died in Healdton, Hewitt Twp., Carter Co., Oklahoma, on November 12, 2016, at age 64. He was buried in Ringling Memorial Cemetery, Ringling, Jefferson Co., Oklahoma.[121]

He married **Ms. Henderson.**

385. **Donald Gene¹⁰ Aycox** (*Betty Lou⁹ Wilson, Roxie Laurenda⁸ McKee, Josiah Andres⁷, Josiah William⁶, Elizabeth⁵, Alexander⁴, Andrew³ Pegan II, Andrew² Pagan, James¹*) was born on January 27, 1952, in Ardmore, Morgan Twp., Carter Co., Oklahoma. He was the son of Kirby Francis Aycox and Betty Lou Wilson (246). Donald Gene died in Ardmore, Morgan Twp., Carter Co., Oklahoma, on January 25, 2015, at age 62. He was buried in Reck Cemetery, Wilson, Hewitt Co., Oklahoma.[76]

He married **Unknown Unknown.** They had one daughter.

386. **Loretta Ann¹⁰ Aycox** (*Betty Lou⁹ Wilson, Roxie Laurenda⁸ McKee, Josiah Andres⁷, Josiah William⁶, Elizabeth⁵, Alexander⁴, Andrew³ Pegan II, Andrew² Pagan, James¹*) was born in 1962. She was the daughter of Kirby Francis Aycox and Betty Lou Wilson (246). Loretta Ann died between 2006 and 2012.

Loretta Ann married **Mr. Owen.**

Loretta Ann Aycox Owen married **Roger Carlton Muse** on July 21, 2006, in Cooke Co., Texas. They divorced. Roger Carlton Muse was born in Ardmore, Morgan Twp., Carter Co., Oklahoma, on October 7, 1960. He reached age 54 and died in Lone Grove Twp., Carter Co., Oklahoma, on May 1, 2015.

**387. Glenda Marie**[10] **Anderson** (*Willene Violet*[9] *West, Vivian Violet*[8] *McKee, Albert Milton*[7] *, Josiah William*[6] *, Elizabeth*[5] *, Alexander*[4] *, Andrew*[3] *Pegan II, Andrew*[2] *Pagan, James*[1]) was born on December 7, 1950, in Oklahoma City, Oklahoma. She was the daughter of Ronald James Anderson and Willene Violet West (261). Glenda Marie died in San Antonio, Bexar Co., Texas, on July 22, 1956, at age five. She was buried in Resthaven Gardens Cemetery, Oklahoma City, Cleveland Co., Oklahoma.[23]

**388. Douglas Martin**[10] **Anderson** (*Willene Violet*[9] *West, Vivian Violet*[8] *McKee, Albert Milton*[7] *, Josiah William*[6] *, Elizabeth*[5] *, Alexander*[4] *, Andrew*[3] *Pegan II, Andrew*[2] *Pagan, James*[1]) was born on March 16, 1952, in San Mateo Co., California. He was the son of Ronald James Anderson and Willene Violet West (261). Douglas Martin died in Tacoma, Pierce Co., Washington, on April 15, 2002, at age 50.

**389. Wanda Teresa**[10] **Anderson** (*Willene Violet*[9] *West, Vivian Violet*[8] *McKee, Albert Milton*[7] *, Josiah William*[6] *, Elizabeth*[5] *, Alexander*[4] *, Andrew*[3] *Pegan II, Andrew*[2] *Pagan, James*[1]) was born on November 6, 1956, in San Antonio, Bexar Co., Texas. She was also known as **Terry.** She was the daughter of Ronald James Anderson and Willene Violet West (261). Wanda Teresa died in Tacoma, Pierce Co., Washington or Summit, King Co., Washington, on October 1, 2007, at age 50.

Wanda Teresa Anderson married **Mr. Smith.** They divorced.

Wanda Teresa Anderson Smith married **Mr. Foster.**

**390. Ralph William**[10] **Anderson** (*Willene Violet*[9] *West, Vivian Violet*[8] *McKee, Albert Milton*[7] *, Josiah William*[6] *, Elizabeth*[5] *, Alexander*[4] *, Andrew*[3] *Pegan II, Andrew*[2] *Pagan, James*[1]) was born on October 3, 1959, in Lawton, Comanche Co., Oklahoma. He was the son of Ronald James Anderson and Willene Violet West (261). Ralph William lived in Tacoma, Pierce Co., Washington. He died in Clackamas Co., Oregon, on January 30, 1995, at age 35.

**391. Dorothy Joan Fox**[10] **Garner** (*Lyle Doan*[9] *Fox, Rosa Lawana*[8] *McKee, Albert Milton*[7] *, Josiah William*[6] *,*

*Elizabeth*[5] *, Alexander*[4] *, Andrew*[3] *Pegan II, Andrew*[2] *Pagan, James*[1]) was born on September 16, 1956, in San Juan, Puerto Rico. She was the daughter of Lyle Doan Fox (263) and Jane Joan Garner. Dorothy Joan Fox died in San Juan, Puerto Rico, on September 16, 1956. She was buried in Puerto Rico National Cemetery, Bayamon, Puerto Rico.[123]

**392. Fred Arthur**[10] **Smith** (*Mary Lillie*[9] *Hughes, Rosa Lillie*[8] *Wright, Mary Catherine*[7] *McKee, Josiah William*[6] *, Elizabeth*[5] *, Alexander*[4] *, Andrew*[3] *Pegan II, Andrew*[2] *Pagan, James*[1]) was born on June 13, 1940, in Oklahoma City, Oklahoma. He was the son of Arthur Homer Smith and Mary Lillie Hughes (267). Fred Arthur died in Newalla, Oklahoma Co., Oklahoma, on March 11, 2008, at age 67.

He married **Billie Sue Unknown.**

**393. Jimmie Gordon**[10] **Smith** (*Mary Lillie*[9] *Hughes, Rosa Lillie*[8] *Wright, Mary Catherine*[7] *McKee, Josiah William*[6] *, Elizabeth*[5] *, Alexander*[4] *, Andrew*[3] *Pegan II, Andrew*[2] *Pagan, James*[1]) was born on February 5, 1942, in Oklahoma City, Oklahoma. He was the son of Arthur Homer Smith and Mary Lillie Hughes (267). Jimmie Gordon died in Moore, Cleveland Co., Oklahoma, on January 26, 2008, at age 65. He was buried in Sunset Memorial Park Cemetery, Norman, Cleveland Co., Oklahoma.[84]

Jimmie Gordon married **Unknown Unknown** on September 26, 1961, in Washoe Co., Nevada.

**394. Bennie Edward**[10] **Mills** (*Betty Jene*[8] *Hughes, Rosa Lillie*[8] *Wright, Mary Catherine*[7] *McKee, Josiah William*[6] *, Elizabeth*[5] *, Alexander*[4] *, Andrew*[3] *Pegan II, Andrew*[2] *Pagan, James*[1]) was born on October 28, 1946 in Wood Co., Texas. He was the son of Betty Jene Hughes (272) and Leonard Edward Mills II. He died on December 13, 2000.

**395. William E.**[10] **Hoofard** (*Maudie Mae*[9] *Hickey, Dedaunia Lucinda Amanda Jane*[8] *Wright, Mary Catherine*[7] *McKee, Josiah William*[6] *, Elizabeth*[5] *, Alexander*[4] *, Andrew*[3] *Pegan II, Andrew*[2] *Pagan, James*[1]) was born on January 5, 1939, in Lexington Twp., Cleveland Co., Oklahoma. He is the son of Woodrow Hoofard and Maudie Mae Hickey (279).

**396. Diana Kaye**[10] **Hoofard** (*Maudie Mae*[9] *Hickey, Dedaunia Lucinda Amanda Jane*[8] *Wright, Mary Catherine*[7] *McKee, Josiah William*[6]*, Elizabeth*[5]*, Alexander*[4]*, Andrew*[3] *Pegan II, Andrew*[2] *Pagan, James*[1]) was born on October 1, 1940, in Lexington Twp., Cleveland Co., Oklahoma. She was the daughter of Woodrow Hoofard and Maudie Mae Hickey (279). Diana Kaye died in Lexington Twp., Cleveland Co., Oklahoma, on October 1, 1940. She was buried in Lexington Cemetery, Lexington, Cleveland Co., Oklahoma.[125]

**397. Loretta Lorene**[10] **Hoofard** (*Maudie Mae*[9] *Hickey, Dedaunia Lucinda Amanda Jane*[8] *Wright, Mary Catherine*[7] *McKee, Josiah William*[6]*, Elizabeth*[5]*, Alexander*[4]*, Andrew*[3] *Pegan II, Andrew*[2] *Pagan, James*[1]) was born on December 15, 1943, in Oakland, Alameda Co., California. She was the daughter of Woodrow Hoofard and Maudie Mae Hickey (279). Loretta Lorene died in Shawnee, Rock Creek Twp., Pottawatomie Co., Oklahoma, on August 17, 1949, at age five. She was buried in Wanette Cemetery, Wanette, Eason Twp., Pottawatomie Co., Oklahoma.[126]

**398. Narvin B.**[10] **Chapman II** (*Opal Ann*[9] *Berry, Maemily Ann*[8] *Wright, Mary Catherine*[7] *McKee, Josiah William*[6]*, Elizabeth*[5] *Pegan, Alexander*[4] *Pagan, Andrew*[3] *Pegan II, Andrew*[2] *Pagan, James*[1]). Narvin B. Chapman II was born after 1940. He was the son of Narvan B. Miller Chapman and Opal Ann Berry (283). Narvin B. died before 1997. Seems to have died in infancy.

**399. Sondra Diana**[10] **Berry** (*Newman*[9]*, Maemily Ann*[8] *Wright, Mary Catherine*[7] *McKee, Josiah William*[6]*, Elizabeth*[5]*, Alexander*[4]*, Andrew*[3] *Pegan II, Andrew*[2] *Pagan, James*[1]) was born on September 21, 1960, in Downey, Los Angeles Co., California. She was the daughter of Newman Berry (287) and Twila Penfield. Sondra Diana died in Henderson, Clark Co., Nevada, on January 4, 2004, at age 43.

She married **Unknown Barros.** They had two sons.

Sondra Diana Berry Barros married **Mr. Williams** on May 14, 1994, in Clark Co., Nevada.

Sondra Diana Berry Barros Williams married **Mr. Kaleta** on November 27, 2003, in Clark Co., Nevada.

**400. Catherine Juanita**[10] **Berry** (*Guy Martin*[9]*, Mary Catherine*[8] *Wright, Mary Catherine*[7] *McKee, Josiah William*[6]*, Elizabeth*[5]*, Alexander*[4]*, Andrew*[3] *Pegan II, Andrew*[2] *Pagan, James*[1]) was born on March 28, 1948, in Maywood, Los Angeles Co., California. She was the daughter of Guy Martin Berry (288) and Lavonia Juanita Rutledge. Catherine Juanita died in Oklahoma City, Oklahoma, on February 1, 1962, at age 13. She was buried in Tribbey Cemetery, Tribbey, Burnett Twp., Pottawatomie Co., Oklahoma.[14]

**401. Clarence William**[10] **Berry** (*John William*[9]*, Mary Catherine*[8] *Wright, Mary Catherine*[7] *McKee, Josiah William*[6]*, Elizabeth*[5]*, Alexander*[4]*, Andrew*[3] *Pegan II, Andrew*[2] *Pagan, James*[1]) was born on November 3, 1948, in Shawnee, Rock Creek Twp., Pottawatomie Co., Oklahoma. He was the son of John William Berry (289) and Aline Unknown. Clarence William died in Quincy, Grant Co., Washington, on June 7, 2007, at age 58.

**402. Catherine Denise**[10] **Raines** (*Herman Thomas*[9]*, Martha Louisa Jane*[8] *McKee, Charles Watson*[7]*, Josiah William*[6]*, Elizabeth*[5]*, Alexander*[4]*, Andrew*[3] *Pegan II, Andrew*[2] *Pagan, James*[1]) was born on March 11, 1960, in Lamesa, Dawson Co., Texas. She was the daughter of Herman Thomas Raines (303) and Doris Marie Hambrick. Catherine Denise died in Lamesa, Dawson Co., Texas, on June 24, 1964, at age four. She was buried in Lamesa Memorial Park Cemetery, Lamesa, Dawson Co., Texas.[37]

**403. Terry Elaine**[10] **Brannon** (*Ouida Gale*[9] *McKee, Albert Milton*[8]*, Charles Watson*[7]*, Josiah William*[6]*, Elizabeth*[5]*, Alexander*[4]*, Andrew*[3] *Pegan II, Andrew*[2] *Pagan, James*[1]) was born on May 5, 1955, in Fort Worth, Tarrant Co., Texas. She was the daughter of Emory O'Neal Brannon and Ouida Gale McKee (308). Terry Elaine died in Fort Worth, Tarrant Co., Texas, on September 11, 2005, at age 50.

Terry Elaine married **Mr. Williams** on July 3, 1972, in Johnson Co., Texas.

Terry Elaine Brannon Williams married **Unknown Hale** before 2005.

**404. Jerry Keith**[10] **Brannon** (*Ouida Gale*[9] *McKee, Albert Milton*[8]*, Charles Watson*[7]*, Josiah William*[6]*, Elizabeth*[5]*, Alexander*[4]*, Andrew*[3] *Pegan II, Andrew*[2]

*Pagan, James*[1]) was born on October 16, 1956, in Fort Worth, Tarrant Co., Texas. He was the son of Emory O'Neal Brannon and Ouida Gale McKee (308). Jerry Keith lived in Forest Hill, Tarrant Co., Texas. He died in a hospital in Fort Worth, Tarrant Co., Texas, on May 9, 1979, at age 22. Jerry Keith was buried in Emerald Hills Cemetery, Kennedale, Tarrant Co., Texas.[38]

Never married.

**405. Ronald Steven**[10] **Wallace** (*Lois Ellen*[9] *Brown, Mary Katherine*[8] *McKee, Charles Watson*[7], *Josiah William*[6], *Elizabeth*[5], *Alexander*[4], *Andrew*[3] *Pegan II, Andrew*[2] *Pagan, James*[1]) was born on April 30, 1958, in Lindsay, Tulare Co., California. He was the son of Floyd Edward Wallace and Lois Ellen Brown (309).

Ronald Steven died in Crane Meadow Camp, near Ponderosa, Tulare Co., California, on September 2, 2007, at age 49.

He married **Carlene Unknown.** They had three children.

**406. Toni Lynette**[10] **McMahon** (*Sandra Arlene*[9] *McKee, William Everett*[8], *Oliver Edwin*[7], *Josiah William*[6], *Elizabeth*[5], *Alexander*[4], *Andrew*[3] *Pegan II, Andrew*[2] *Pagan, James*[1]) was born on December 14, 1971, in Lovington, Lea Co., New Mexico. She was the daughter of Ronald McMahon and Sandra Arlene McKee (318). Toni Lynette died in Lovington, Lea Co., New Mexico, on March 15, 1974, at age two. She was buried in Lovington Cemetery, Lovington, Lea Co., New Mexico.[55]

# 11th Generation

**407. Timothy Lee**[11] **Bland** (*Wilma Fern*[10] *Cross, James Rex*[9], *Claud James*[8], *Sarah Elvira Elizabeth Ann*[7] *McKee, Josiah William*[6], *Elizabeth*[5], *Alexander*[4], *Andrew*[3] *Pegan II, Andrew*[2] *Pagan, James*[1]) was born on October 4, 1956, in Abilene, Taylor Co., Texas. He was the son of Jack Irland Bland and Wilma Fern Cross (338). Timothy Lee died in Abilene, Taylor Co., Texas, on April 10, 1975, at age 18. He was buried in Rose Hill Cemetery, Merkel, Taylor Co., Texas.[113]

**408. Jimmy D.**[11] **Gardner** (*Zenita Lee*[10] *Cross, James Rex*[9], *Claud James*[8], *Sarah Elvira Elizabeth Ann*[7] *McKee, Josiah William*[6], *Elizabeth*[5], *Alexander*[4], *Andrew*[3] *Pegan II, Andrew*[2] *Pagan, James*[1]) was born on May 1, 1955, in Sylvester, Fisher Co., Texas. He was the son of Mr. Gardner and Living Cross (341). Jimmy D. died in Choctaw, Oklahoma Co., Oklahoma, on February 15, 1987, at age 31. He was buried in Newman Cemetery, Sylvester, Fisher Co., Texas.

May have never married.

**409. Daughter**[11] **Gardner** (*Zenita Lee*[10] *Cross, James Rex*[9], *Claud James*[8], *Sarah Elvira Elizabeth Ann*[7] *McKee, Josiah William*[6], *Elizabeth*[5], *Alexander*[4], *Andrew*[3] *Pegan II, Andrew*[2] *Pagan, James*[1]). She is the daughter of Jackie Leon Gardner and Zenita Lee Cross (341).

She married **Mr. Thomas.** They had two children.

Daughter Gardner and Mr. Thomas had two children, including:

+ 416 m I. **Son**[12] **Thomas**

**410. Bobby Mac**[11] **Turner** (*Jerry Cross*[10], *Canevah Mae*[9] *Cross, Willie Franklin*[8], *Sarah Elvira Elizabeth Ann*[7] *McKee, Josiah William*[6], *Elizabeth*[5], *Alexander*[4], *Andrew*[3] *Pegan II, Andrew*[2] *Pagan, James*[1]) was born on October 11, 1971, in Dalhart, Dallam Co., Texas. He was the son of Jerry Cross Turner (347) and Unknown Unknown. Bobby Mac died in Tulsa, Tulsa Co., Oklahoma?, on January 15, 2004, at age 32. He was buried in Odd Fellows Cemetery, Neosha, Newton Co., Missouri.[128]

**411. Kyle Braden**[11] **Young** (*Daughter*[10] *McKee, Clyde Frank*[9], *James Andres*[8], *William Robert*[7], *Josiah William*[6], *Elizabeth*[5], *Alexander*[4], *Andrew*[3] *Pegan II, Andrew*[2] *Pagan, James*[1]) was born on June 5,1985, in Oklahoma City, Oklahoma. He was the son of Mr. Young and Daughter McKee (357). Kyle Braden died in Chickasha, Chickasha Twp., Grady Co., Oklahoma, on November 2, 2013, at age 28. He was buried in Alex Cemetery, Alex, Alex Twp., Grady Co., Oklahoma.[52]

**412. Daughter**[11] **Parish** (*Daughter*[10] *Morris, Marie M.*[9] *Meridth, Laura Elvira*[8] *McKee, James L.*[7], *Josiah William*[6], *Elizabeth*[5], *Alexander*[4], *Andrew*[3] *Pegan II, Andrew*[2] *Pagan, James*[1]). She is the daughter of Mr. Parish and Daughter Morris (362).

She married **Mr. Thomason.** They had at least one daughter.

Daughter of Daughter Parish and Mr. Thomason:

+ 417 f I. **Kenley Alese**[12] **Thomason** was born in Oklahoma City, Oklahoma, on July 27, 2009. She died in Oklahoma City, Oklahoma, on July 27, 2009.[25]

**413. Julie Ann**[11] **McKee** (*Daughter*[10] *Simmons, Sarah Elvina*[9] *Riley, Reuben Josiah*[8], *Martha Louise Jane*[7] *McKee, Josiah William*[6], *Elizabeth*[5], *Alexander*[4], *Andrew*[3] *Pegan II, Andrew*[2] *Pagan, James*[1]) was born on September 3, 1971, in Lindsay, Lindsay Twp., Garvin Co., Oklahoma. She was the daughter of Mr. McKee and Daughter Simmons (371). Julie Ann died in Lindsay, Lindsay Twp., Garvin Co., Oklahoma, on January 12, 1984, at age 12. She was buried in Alex Cemetery, Alex, Alex Twp., Grady Co., Oklahoma.[52]

**414. Kevin Kenneth**[11] **McKee** (*Daughter*[10] *Simmons, Sarah Elvina*[9] *Riley, Reuben Josiah*[8], *Martha Louise Jane*[7] *McKee, Josiah William*[6], *Elizabeth*[5], *Alexander*[4], *Andrew*[3] *Pegan II, Andrew*[2] *Pagan, James*[1]) was born on January 17, 1980, in Lindsay, Lindsay Twp., Garvin Co., Oklahoma. He was the son of Mr. McKee and Daughter Simmons (371).

Kevin Kenneth died in Oklahoma City, Oklahoma Co., Oklahoma, on May 25, 1989, at age nine. He was buried in Alex Cemetery, Alex, Alex Twp., Grady Co., Oklahoma.[52]

415. **Roy**[11] **Grooms** (*Son*[10], *Leroy*[9], *Janie Susan*[8] *Riley*, *Martha Louise Jane*[7] *McKee*, *Josiah William*[6], *Elizabeth*[5], *Alexander*[4], *Andrew*[3] *Pegan II*, *Andrew*[2] *Pagan*, *James*[1]) He was the son of Son Grooms (375) and Viola Unknown. Roy died in Chickasha, Chickasha Twp., Grady Co., Oklahoma?, before 2005.

# 12th Generation

**416. Son[12] Thomas** (*Daughter[11] Gardner, Zenita Lee[10] Cross, James Rex[9], Claud James[8], Sarah Elvira Elizabeth Ann[7] McKee, Josiah William[6], Elizabeth[5], Alexander[4], Andrew[3] Pegan II, Andrew[2] Pagan, James[1]*) was born in 1972 in Odessa, Ector Co., Texas. He is the son of Mr. Thomas and Daughter Gardner (409).

He married **Erin Courtney Garmen** on April 4, 1999, in Fisher Co., Texas. They had two children. Erin Courtney Garmen was born on June 27, 1979, in Torrence, Los Angeles Co., California. She died on November 9, 2010 in Abeline, Taylor Co., Texas. Erin Courtney Garmen Thomas was buried in Elmwood Memorial Park Cemetery, Abeline, Taylor Co., Texas.[130]

Son Thomas married **Rebecca Unknown** after 2010.

Son Thomas and Erin Courtney Garmen had two children, including:

+ 418 m II. **Joseph[13] Thomas** was born in Abilene, Taylor Co., Texas, in 2001. He died in Abilene, Taylor Co., Texas, in 2007.

**417. Kenley Alese[12] Thomason** (*Daughter[11] Parish, Daughter[10] Morris, Marie M.[9] Meridth, Laura Elvira[8] McKee, James L.[7], Josiah William[6], Elizabeth[5], Alexander[4], Andrew[3] Pegan II, Andrew[2] Pagan, James[1]*) was born on July 27, 2009, in Oklahoma City, Oklahoma. She was the daughter of Living Thomason and Daughter Parish (412). Kenley Alese died in Oklahoma City, Oklahoma, on July 27, 2009. She was buried in Oaklawn Cemetery, Wynnewood, Brady Twp., Garvin Co., Oklahoma.[25]

# 13th Generation

**418. Joseph**[13] **Thomas** (*Son*[12] *Thomas, Daughter*[11] *Gardner, Roenna*[11] *Gardner, Zenita Lee*[10] *Cross, James Rex*[9], *Claud James*[8], *Sarah Elvira Elizabeth Ann*[7] *McKee, Josiah William*[6], *Elizabeth*[5], *Alexander*[4], *Andrew*[3] *Pegan II, Andrew*[2] *Pagan, James*[1]) was born in 2001 in Abilene, Taylor Co., Texas. He was the son of Son Thomas (416) and Erin Courtney Garmen. Joseph died in Abilene, Taylor Co., Texas, in 2007 at age six. He was buried in Elmwood Memorial Park Cemetery, Abeline, Taylor Co., Texas.[130]

# Endnotes

1 Find A Grave—Pisgah Ridge Cemetery, Levanna, Union Twp., Brown Co., Ohio, Find A Grave.com, Elizabeth Hamen, Find A Grave Memorial #92516148.

2 *Brooke County (WV) Index, Vol.12, Complete Transcription of the Final Third of County Court Order Book #6, November 1811-February 1813.* Compiled by Gwendolyn Mackey Hubbard and Bobbie Britt Elliott, Brooke County Genealogical Society, Beach Bottom, West Virginia; 2002, pg. 1219. Genealogy Center, Allen County Public Library, 900 Library Plaza, Fort Wayne, IN.

3 *Craft, Kenneth Fischer, Brooke County (WV) Index, card index to all Brooke Co. Courts' Case Files/Loose Papers from the West Virginia and Regional History Collection, West Virginia, Morgantown West Virginia, Vol. 56, Pt. 2, 1806-1817,* Wellsburg, West Virginia: B n G Books; 2003, pg. 5101. Genealogy Center, Allen County Public Library, 900 Library Plaza, Fort Wayne, IN.

4 *Brooke County (WV) Index, Vol.16, Complete Transcription of the First Third of County Court Order Book #8, December 1817-June 1819.* Compiled by Gwendolyn Mackey Hubbard and Bobbie Britt Elliott, Beach Bottom, West Virginia: Brooke County Genealogical Society; 2002, pg. 1597. Genealogy Center, Allen County Public Library, 900 Library Plaza, Fort Wayne, IN.

5 Hubbard, Gwendolyn Mackey. Elliott, Bobbie Britt. Craft, Kenneth Fischer. *Brooke County (WV) index: "Personal Time Line" Index to Vols. 1-63 with over 346, 000 entries; master cumulative index to pages 1-5662.* Beach Bottom, West Virginia: Brooke County Genealogical Society; c2008, pg. 1942. Genealogy Center, Allen County Public Library, 900 Library Plaza, Fort Wayne, IN.

6 Ohio, County Marriages, 1789-2013, FamilySearch.org, William McKee and Elizabeth Pagan, Brown County Marriage Records, Vol. E, No. 5, pg. 6, cert. #2, 481.

7 Find A Grave—Ashland Cemetery, St. Joseph, Washington Twp., Buchanan Co., Missouri, Find A Grave.com.

8 Find A Grave—Indian Creek Cemetery, Indian Creek, Brown Co., Texas, Find A Grave.com.

9 Find A Grave—Katie City Cemetery, Katie, Brady Twp., Garvin Co., Oklahoma, Find A Grave.com.

10 Find A Grave—Newman Cemetery, Sylvester, Fisher Co., Texas, Find A Grave.com.

11 Find A Grave—Bradley Cemetery, Bradley Twp., Grady Co., Oklahoma, Find A Grave.com.

12 Find A Grave—Erin Springs Cemetery, Erin Springs, Lindsay Twp., Garvin Co., Oklahoma, Find A Grave.com.

13 Find A Grave—Hewitt Cemetery, Wilson, Hewitt Twp., Carter Co., Oklahoma, Find A Grave.com.

14 Find A Grave—Tribbey Cemetery, Tribbey, Burnett Twp., Pottawatomie Co., Oklahoma, Find A Grave.com.

15 Montana, County Marriages, 1865-1950, FamilySearch.org, Charles Demars and Belle McKee.

16 Montana, County Marriages, 1865-1950, FamilySearch.org, James Ralph and "Saddie" McKee.

17 Find A Grave, Green Cemetery, Country Club Village, Jefferson Twp., Andrew Co., Missouri, Find A Grave.com, http://www.rootsweb.ancestry.com/~mobuchan/GreenCemeteryQ_Z.htm.

18 Find A Grave—Fairlawn Cemetery, Elk City, Beckham Co., Oklahoma, Find A Grave.com.

19 Find A Grave—Hillside Cemetery, Purcell, Moncrief Twp., McClain Co., Oklahoma, Find A Grave.com.

20 Find A Grave—Bethany Cemetery, Bethany, Oklahoma Co., Oklahoma, Find A Grave.com.

21 Find A Grave—Belvieu Cemetery, Rotan, Fisher Co., Texas, Find A Grave.com.

22 Find A Grave—Rush Springs Cemetery, Rush Springs, Grady Co., Oklahoma, Find A Grave.com.

23 Find A Grave—Resthaven Gardens Cemetery, Oklahoma City, Cleveland Co., Oklahoma, Find A Grave.com.

24 Find A Grave—Enid Cemetery, Enid, Garfield Co., Oklahoma, Find A Grave.com.

25 Find A Grave—Oaklawn Cemetery, Wynnewood, Brady Twp., Garvin Co., Oklahoma, Find A Grave.com.

26 Find A Grave—Roselawn Cemetery, Mangum, Greer Co., Oklahoma, Find A Grave.com.

27 Find A Grave—Hillcrest Cemetery, Porterville, Tulare Co., California, Find A Grave.com.

28 Find A Grave—Green Hill Cemetery, McClain Co., Oklahoma, Find A Grave.com.

29 Find A Grave—Mountain View Cemetery, Deming, Luna Co., New Mexico, Find A Grave.com.

30 Find A Grave—Chagger Cemetery, Carter Co., Oklahoma, Find A Grave.com.

31 Find A Grave—Green Hill Cemetery, Davis, Murray Co., Oklahoma, Find A Grave.com.

32 Find A Grave—Marlow Cemetery, Marlow Twp., Stephens Co., Oklahoma, Find A Grave.com.

33 Find A Grave—Pilgrim Rest Cemetery #2, Golden, Wood Co., Texas, Find A Grave.com.

34 Find A Grave—Tecumseh Cemetery, Brinton Twp., Tecumseh, Pottawatomie Co., Oklahoma, Find A Grave.com.

35 Find A Grave—Mars Hill Cemetery, St. Louis Twp., Pottawatomie Co., Oklahoma, Find A Grave.com.

36 Find A Grave—Desert Lawn Memorial Park Cemetery, Calimesa, Riverside Co., California, Find A Grave.com.

37 Find A Grave—Lamesa Memorial Park Cemetery, Lamesa, Dawson Co., Texas, Find A Grave.com.

38 Find A Grave—Emerald Hills Cemetery, Kennedale, Tarrant Co., Texas, Find A Grave.com.

39 Find A Grave—Castroville Community Cemetery, Castroville, Medina Co., Texas, Find A Grave.com.

40 Find A Grave—Lakeview Cemetery, Marietta, Love Co., Oklahoma, Find A Grave.com.

41 Find A Grave—Sunny Lane Cemetery, Del City, Oklahoma Co., Oklahoma, Find A Grave.com.

42 Find A Grave—Elmore City Cemetery, Elmore City, Elmore Twp., Garvin Co., Oklahoma, Find A Grave.com.

43 U.S. Veteran's Gravesites, ca. 1775-2006, Ancestry.com, James E. Tindle.

44 Find A Grave—Elmwood Cemetery, Kansas City, Jackson Co., Missouri, Find A Grave.com.

45 Find A Grave—Saint Joseph Memorial Park Cemetery, St. Joseph, Buchanan Co., Missouri, Find A Grave.com.

46 Find A Grave—Pattonsburg Memorial Gardens Cemetery, Pattonsburg, Benton Twp., Daviess Co., Misssouri, Find A Grave.com.

47 Find A Grave—Memory Gardens Cemetery, Amarillo, Randall Co., Texas, Find A Grave.com.

48 Find A Grave—Geary Cemetery, Geary, Blaine Co., Oklahoma, Find A Grave.com.

49 Find A Grave—Restland Memorial Park Cemetery, Dallas, Tarrant Co., Texas, Find A Grave.com.

50 Find A Grave—Sunset Memorial Gardens, Odessa, Ector Co., Texas, Find A Grave.com.

51 Find A Grave—Pocasset Cemetery, Pocasset, Grady Co., Oklahoma, Find A Grave.com.

52 Find A Grave—Alex Cemetery, Alex, Alex Twp., Grady Co., Oklahoma, Find A Grave.com.

53 Find A Grave—Fairlawn Cemetery, Chickasha, Grady Co., Oklahoma, Find A Grave.com.

54 Find A Grave—Wynnewood View Cemetery, Wynnewood, Brady Twp., Garvin Co., Oklahoma, Find A Grave.com.

55 Find A Grave—Lovington Cemetery, Lovington, Lea Co., New Mexico, Find A Grave.com.

56 Find A Grave—Warren Cemetery, Norman, Cleveland Co., Oklahoma, Find A Grave.com.

57 Find A Grave—Shafter Memorial Park Cemetery, Shafter, Kern Co., California, Find A Grave.com.

58 Find A Grave—Pleasant View Cemetery, Pine Ridge, Hale Twp., Caddo Co., Oklahoma, Find A Grave.com.

59 U.S. Veteran's Gravesites, ca. 1775-2006, Ancestry.com, Everett James Meyer.

60 Find A Grave—Memorial Park Cemetery, Enid, Garfield Co., Oklahoma, Find A Grave.com.

61 Find A Grave—Riverside National Cemetery, Riverside, Riverside Co., California, Find A Grave.com.

62 Find A Grave—Lakeview Cemetery & Mausoleum, Wichita, Sedgwick Co., Kansas, Find A Grave.com.

63 Find A Grave—Resthaven Gardens of Memory Cemetery, Wichita, Sedgewick Co., Kansas, Find A Grave.com.

64 Find A Grave—Oaklawn Cemetery, Sulphur, Murray Co., Oklahoma, Find A Grave.com.

65 Find A Grave—Liberty Cemetery, near Chickasha, Grady Co., Oklahoma, Find A Grave.com.

66 Find A Grave—Crestview Memorial Park Cemetery, Wichita Falls, Wichita Co., Texas, Find A Grave.com.

67 Find A Grave—Tipton Cemetery, Tipton, Tillman Co., Oklahoma, Find A Grave.com.

68 Find A Grave—Evergreen Cemetery, Minco, Grady Co., Oklahoma, Find A Grave.com.

69 Find A Grave—Green Valley Cemetery, Suhaurita, Pima Co., Arizona, Find A Grave.com.

70 Find A Grave—Pawhuska Cemetery, Pawhuska, Osage Co., Oklahoma, Find A Grave.com.

71 Find A Grave—Galveston Memorial Park Cemetery, Hitchcock, Galveston Co., Texas, Find A Grave.com.

72 Find A Grave—Henri-Chapelle American Cemetery and Memorial, Henri-Chapelle, Liege, Belgium, Find A Grave.com.

73 Find A Grave—Juniper Haven Cemetery, Prineville, Crook Co., Oregon, Find A Grave.com.

74 Find A Grave—Lone Grove Cemetery, Lone Grove, Carter Co., Oklahoma, Find A Grave.com.

75 Find A Grave—Phoenix Memorial Park Cemetery, Phoenix, Maricopa Co., Arizona, Find A Grave.com.

76 Find A Grave—Reck Cemetery, Wilson, Hewitt Co., Oklahoma, Find A Grave.com.

77 Find A Grave—Hillcrest Memorial Park Cemetery, Ardmore, Morgan Twp., Carter Co., Oklahoma, Find A Grave.com.

78 Find A Grave—Elliott-Hamil Garden of Memories Cemetery, Abeline, Taylor Co., Texas, Find A Grave.com.

79 Find A Grave—Resthaven Memorial Park Cemetery, Lubbock, Lubbock Co., Texas, Find A Grave.com.

80 Find A Grave—Fort Logan National Cemetery, Denver, Denver Co., Colorado, Find A Grave.com.

81 Find A Grave—San Marcos Cemetery, San Marcos, San Diego Co., California, Find A Grave.com.

82 Find A Grave—Jamestown Cemetery, Jamestown, Smith Co., Texas, Find A Grave.com.

83 Find A Grave—IOOF Cemetery, Quinlan, Hunt Co., Texas, Find A Grave.com.

84 Find A Grave—Sunset Memorial Park Cemetery, Norman, Cleveland Co., Oklahoma, Find A Grave.com.

85 Find A Grave—Resurrection Memorial Cemetery, Oklahoma City, Oklahoma Co., Oklahoma, Find A Grave.com.

86 Find A Grave—Resthaven Memorial Park Cemetery, Midland, Midland Co., Texas, Find A Grave.com.

87 Find A Grave—Immaculate Conception Cemetery, Oklahoma City, Oklahoma Co., Oklahoma, Find A Grave.com.

88  Find A Grave—Laurel Land Memorial Park Cemetery, Dallas, Dallas Co., Texas, Find A Grave.com.

89  Find A Grave—Oak Hill Cemetery, Red Bluff, Tehama Co., California, Find A Grave.com.

90  Find A Grave—Resthaven Memorial Park Cemetery, Shawnee, Pottawatomie Co., Oklahoma, Find A Grave.com.

91  Find A Grave—Celestial Gardens Cemetery, Cyril, Caddo Co. Oklahoma, Find A Grave.com.

92  Find A Grave—Cummings Cemetery, Maud, Pottawatomie Co., Oklahoma, Find A Grave.com.

93  Find A Grave—Council Creek Cemetery, Tribbey Twp., Pottawatomie Co., Oklahoma, Find A Grave.com.

94  Find A Grave—Dawson County Cemetery, Lamesa, Dawson Co., Texas, Find A Grave.com.

95  Find A Grave—Hico Cemetery, Hico, Hamilton Co. Texas, Find A Grave.com.

96  Find A Grave—Everman Cemetery, Everman, Tarrant Co., Texas, Find A Grave.com.

97  Find A Grave—Highland Memory Gardens Cemetery, Madison, Dane Co., Wisconsin, Find A Grave.com.

98  [98]    Find A Grave—Greenlawn Southwest Memorial Park Cemetery, Bakersfield, Kern Co., California, Find A Grave.com.

99  Find A Grave—Mount Olivet Cemetery, Paul's Valley, Whitebead Twp., Garvin Co., Oklahoma, Find A Grave.com.

100  Find A Grave—Foster Cemetery, Foster, Elmore Twp., Garvin Co., Oklahoma, Find A Grave.com.

101  Find A Grave—Willamette National Cemetery, Portland, Multnomah Co., Oregon, Find A Grave.com, Plot: L 5197.

102  Find A Grave—Alford Cemetery, Harrisburg, Linn Co., Oregon, Find A Grave.com.

103  Find A Grave—Forest Hill Cemetery, Kansas City, Jackson Co., Missouri, Find A Grave.com.

104  Find A Grave—Chapel Hill Cemetery, Clinton, Custer Co., Oklahoma, Find A Grave.com.

105  Find A Grave—Vamoosa Cemetery, Vamoosa, Seminole Co., Oklahoma, Find A Grave.com.

106  Find A Grave—Quanah Memorial Park Cemetery, Quanah, Hardeman Co., Texas, Find A Grave.com.

107  Find A Grave—Altus Cemetery, Altus, Jackson Co., Oklahoma, Find A Grave.com.

108  Find A Grave—Crestview Cemetery, Wichita Falls, Wichita Co., Texas, Find A Grave.com.

109  Find A Grave—Lawnhaven Memorial Gardens Cemetery, San Angelo, Tom Green Co., Texas, Find A Grave.com.

110  Find A Grave—Florence American Cemetery and Memorial, Florence, Provincia di Firenze, Italy, Find A Grave.com.

111  Find A Grave—Austin Memorial Park Cemetery, Austin, Travis Co., Texas, Find A Grave.com.

112  Find A Grave—Lee Cemetery, Winnsboro, Wood Co., Texas, Find A Grave.com.

113  Find A Grave—Rose Hill Cemetery, Merkel, Taylor Co., Texas, Find A Grave.com.

114  Find A Grave—Texline Cemetery, Texline, Dallam Co., Texas, Find A Grave.com.

115  Find A Grave—Clovis Cemetery, Clovis, Fresno Co., California, Find A Grave.com.

116  Find A Grave—Evergreen Cemetery, El Centro, Imperial Co., California, Find A Grave.com.

117  Find A Grave—Jefferson Barracks National Cemetery, Lemay Twp., St. Louis Co., Missouri, Find A Grave.com.

118  Find A Grave—Hennepin Cemetery, Murray Co., Oklahoma, Find A Grave.com.

119  Find A Grave—Sunset Memorial Park Cemetery, Albuquerque, Bernalillo Co., New Mexico, Find A Grave.com.

120  U.S. Rosters of WWII Dead, 1939-1945, Ancestry.com.

121  Find A Grave—Ringling Memorial Cemetery, Ringling, Jefferson Co., Oklahoma, Find A Grave.com.

122  Find A Grave—Green Hills Memorial Park Cemetery, Rancho Palos Verdes, Los Angeles Co., California, Find A Grave.com.

123  Find A Grave—Puerto Rico National Cemetery, Bayamon, Puerto Rico, Find A Grave.com.

124  Find A Grave—Paoli Cemetery, Paoli, Whitebead Twp., Garvin Co., Oklahoma, Find A Grave.

125  Find A Grave—Lexington Cemetery, Lexington, Cleveland Co., Oklahoma, Find A Grave.com.

126  Find A Grave—Wanette Cemetery, Wanette, Eason Twp., Pottawatomie Co., Oklahoma, Find A Grave.com.

127  Find A Grave—Fairview Cemetery, Tuttle, Tuttle Twp., Grady Co., Oklahoma, Find A Grave.com.

128  Find A Grave—Odd Fellows Cemetery, Neosha, Newton Co., Missouri, Find A Grave.com.

129  Find A Grave—Frisco Cemetery, Yukon, Canadian Co., Oklahoma, Find A Grave.com.

130  Find A Grave—Elmwood Memorial Park Cemetery, Abeline, Taylor Co., Texas, Find A Grave.com.

# Descendants of Elizabeth Jane Pegan Goudy

1. **Elizabeth Jane[4] Pegan** (*Andrew[3] Pegan II, Andrew[2] Pagan, James[1]*) was born in 1784 in Martic Twp., Lancaster Co., Pennsylvania. She was also known as **Jane.** She was the daughter of Andrew Pagan or Pegan II and Mary Unknown. Elizabeth Jane lived in 1850 in District 44, Ohio Co., West Virginia. She also resided in 1860 in Wheeling, Ohio Co., (West) Virginia. Elizabeth Jane died in Wheeling, Ohio Co., West Virginia, on March 8, 1864, at age 80.

Her surname is seen as Pegan or Pagan.

Elizabeth Jane married **Isaac Goudy** on August 16, 1803, in Washington Co., Pennsylvania. They had eight children. Isaac Goudy was born in Pennsylvania about 1781. He reached age 64 and died in Ohio Co., (West Virginia), on July 27, 1845.

Isaac and Elizabeth Jane Pegan Goudy are enumerated in the 1820 census in Wellsburg, Brooke Co., (West) Virginia (*Census Place: Wellsburg, Brooke, Virginia; Page: 84; NARA Roll: M33_132; Image: 61*). There is a three in col. 1, a two in col. 2, and a one in col. 5; a one in col. 7 and a one in col. 9 (three males under age 10, two males age 10-15, and one age 26-44; one female under age 10, and one 16-25).

In 1830, Isaac and Elizabeth Jane Pegan Goudy are still residing in Wellsburg, Brooke Co., (West) Virginia (*Census Place: Brooke, Virginia; Series: M19; Roll: 189; Page: 146*). There is a one in col. 1, a one in col. 2, a one in col. 4, a one in col. 5, and a one in col. 7; a one in col. 14, a one in col. 15, and a one in col. 20 (one male under five years old, one male age five-nine, one 15-19, one 20-29, and one 40-49; one female under five years old, one age five-nine, and one 40-49).

By 1840, Isaac and Elizabeth Jane Pegan "Goudey" have removed to Ohio Co., (West) Virginia and are most likely living in or near Wheeling (*Census Place: Ohio, Virginia; Page: 38*). There is a one in col. 3 and a one in col. 8; a one in col. 17, a one in col. 18, and a one in col. 21 (one male age 10-14, and one age 50-59; one female age 15-19, one 20-29, and one 50-59).

The widow Elizabeth Jane Pagan/Pegan Goudy, age 66, born Pennsylvania, is residing with her oldest son John Goudy and his family in District 44, Ohio Co., (West) Virginia in 1850 (*Census Place: District 44, Ohio, Virginia; Roll: M432_966; Page: 188B; Image: 382*). John Goudy, 46, is a carpenter and Rebecca Morgan Goudy is 41; both were also born in Pennsylvania. With them are children James H., 13, William M., 10, Mary E., eight and Rebecca J., five, all born in (West) Virginia. Also in the household is Eliza VanMeter, a servant, listed as age 27 and born in Ohio and her son Edward, one, born in (West) Virginia.

In 1860, Elizabeth Jane Pagan Goudy, enumerated as Jane, is still living with her son and his first wife, John and Rebecca Morgan Goudy, in Wheeling, Ohio Co., West Virginia (*Census Place: Wheeling Ward 5, Ohio, Virginia; Roll: M653_1368; Page: 388; Image: 400*). "Jane" Goudy is age 76, born in Pennsylvania. The head of the household, John Goudy, a carpenter, is age 56, also born in Pennsylvania. His wife, Rebecca Morgan Goudy, is 54, born in Virginia. Children in the home are James, 23, William ("Wm."), 19, and Mary E., 17. Also in the home are two domestic servants, Eliza VanMeter, 25, born Ohio, and 14-year-old Sarah Pender, born Virginia. Eliza VanMeter, who was 35 years old in this census, would later become the second wife of John Goudy.

Children of Elizabeth Jane Pegan and Isaac Goudy:

+ 2    m    I.    **John**[5] **Goudy** was born in Strabane Twp., Washington Co., Pennsylvania, between January 1, 1804 and June 26, 1804. He died in Washington Twp., Marshall Co., West Virginia, on June 26, 1887. John was buried in Wood Hill Cemetery, Marshall Co., West Virginia.[1]

+ 3    m    II.    **Andrew**[5] **Goudy** was born in Strabane Twp., Washington Co., Pennsylvania or Ohio, on February 7, 1807. He died in Bridgeport Twp., Belmont Co., Ohio, on October 23, 1891. Andrew was buried in Warrenton Cemetery, Rayland, Warren Twp., Jefferson Co., Ohio.[2]

+ 4    m    III.    **Robert**[5] **Goudy** was born in Brooke Co., (West) Virginia, in 1809. He died in Wellsburg Twp., Brooke Co., West Virginia, on December 20, 1875.

+ 5    m    IV.    **William**[5] **Goudy** was born in Brooke Co., (West) Virginia, in 1813. He died in St. Louis, Missouri, on July 15, 1879. William was buried in Holy Ghost Evangelical and Reformed/Old Pickers Cemetery, St. Louis, Missouri.[3]

+ 6    m    V.    **Isaac**[5] **Goudy II** was born in Brooke Co., (West) Virginia, on June 10, 1817. He died in Sherrard, Union Twp., Marshall Co., West Virginia, on October 14, 1890. Isaac was buried in Mount Olivet Cemetery, Wheeling, Ohio Co., West Virginia.[4]

+ 7    f    VI.    **Mary Jane**[5] **Goudy** was born in Brooke Co., (West) Virginia, in November 1819. She died in Triadelphia, Ohio Co., West Virginia? about 1905.

+ 8    f    VII.    **Eliza?**[5] **Goudy** was born in Brooke Co., (West) Virginia, between 1820 and 1825. She died after 1840.

+ 9    m    VIII.    **Son** [5] **Goudy** was born in Brooke Co. or Ohio Co., (West) Virginia, between 1825 and 1830. He died in Ohio Co., (West) Virginia, between 1840 and 1850.

# 5th Generation

**2. John⁵ Goudy** (*Elizabeth Jane⁴ Pegan, Andrew³ Pegan II, Andrew² Pagan, James¹*) was born between January 1, 1804 and June 26, 1804 in Strabane Twp., Washington Co., Pennsylvania. He was the son of Isaac Goudy and Elizabeth Jane Pegan (1). John died in Washington Twp., Marshall Co., West Virginia, on June 26, 1887. He was buried in Wood Hill Cemetery, Marshall Co., West Virginia.[1]

John married **Rebecca Morgan** on January 9, 1834, in Ohio Co., (West) Virginia.[5] They had four children. Rebecca Morgan was born in (West) Virginia in 1806. Rebecca reached age 66 and died in Limestone, Marshall Co., West Virginia, on June 19, 1872.

From the *History of the Panhandle, West Virginia:*

> "JOHN GOUDY, farmer, was born in Washington county, Pa., in Removed to Brooke county with his parents in 1807. In 1812, he married Rebecca Morgan, and had a family of three children. Moved to Wheeling in 1848. From the latter place he removed to Marshall county, in 1869. William M. Goudy, his son, served three years and three months in the rebellion. He was a member of the First West Virginia Infantry." [6]

John Goudy is enumerated in District 44, Ohio Co., (West) Virginia in 1850 *(Census Place: District 44, Ohio, Virginia; Roll: M432_966; Page: 188B; Image: 382)*. John Goudy, 46, is a carpenter and Rebecca Morgan Goudy is 41; both were also born in Pennsylvania. With them are children James H., 13, William M., 10, Mary E., eight and Rebecca J., five, all born in (West) Virginia. John Goudy's widowed mother, Elizabeth Jane Pagan/Pegan Goudy, age 66, born Pennsylvania, is residing with her oldest son. Also in the household is Eliza VanMeter, a servant, listed as age 27 and born in Ohio and her son Edward, one, born in (West)Virginia.

In 1860, John Goudy is found in Wheeling, Ohio Co., (West) Virginia *(Census Place: Wheeling Ward 5, Ohio, Virginia; Roll: M653_1368; Page: 388; Image: 400)*. The head of the household, John Goudy, a carpenter, is age 56, also born in Pennsylvania. His wife, Rebecca Morgan Goudy, is 54, born in (West) Virginia. Children in the home are James, 23, William ("Wm."), 19, and Mary E., 17. Elizabeth Jane Pagan Goudy, enumerated as Jane, 76, born Pennsylvania, is still living with her son John and his family. Also in the home are two domestic servants, Eliza VanMeter, 25, (really age 40 or so) born Ohio, and 14-year-old Sarah Pender, born Virginia.

John Goudy has removed to Washington Twp., Marshall Co., West Virginia by 1870 *(Census Place: Washington, Marshall, West Virginia; Roll: M593_1693; Page: 211B; Image: 14)*. John Goudy, age 66, born Pennsylvania, is now a farmer. Rebecca Morgan Goudy, 63, says she was born in West Virginia. William M. Goudy, 28, a farm hand, born (West) Virginia, is still living with his parents. Son Charles F. Goudy, 11, is also in the home, as is Elizabeth VanMeter, 47, a servant. There are two other children in the home, Ida M. Sudeker, 11 and Amanda V. Sudeker, nine, both born in Iowa; and a farmhand, William Bodoin, 24, born Pennsylvania.

In 1880, John Goudy continues to live in Washington Twp., Marshall Co., West Virginia *(Census Place: Washington, Marshall, West Virginia; Roll: 1407; Page: 155C; Enumeration District: 192)*. John Goudy, listed as age 66, but is 76, was born in Pennsylvania and is a farmer. Other household members include: John Goudy's son by Eliza VanMeter, Charles, 22, born West Virginia, parents born in Pennsylvania and Ohio, a farm hand; Eliza VanMeter, 60, born Ohio as were her parents, a housekeeper, James H. Goudy, 16, born West Virginia, whose relationship is listed as "___son" (grandson), born West Virginia as were his parents, a farm laborer. This "James H. Goudy" is really James Frank Goudy, the son of John Goudy's son James Hayson Goudy who died in the Civil War. Also in the household are Ida Snediker, 20, and Amanda V. Snediker, 17, both Iowa natives with their parents born in West Virginia, housekeepers; and Mollie Snediker, one, born West Virginia, listed as "illegitimate". In addition, there are boarders Mary E. Lossay, 35, born Kentucky as were her parents, a schoolteacher; and Richard Mooney, 16, born Virginia as were his parents, a farm laborer.

John Goudy may have married **Eliza Van Meter** after 1872. They had one son. Eliza Van Meter was born in Ohio about 1825. Eliza reached age 62 and died in Washington Twp., Marshall Co., West Virginia, on July 16, 1887.[1] She was buried in Wood Hill Cemetery, Marshall Co., West Virginia.[1]

John Goudy and Eliza VanMeter may have never officially married, but they did have a son, Charles T. Goudy.

Children of John Goudy and Rebecca Morgan:

+ 10 m I. **James Hayson⁶ Goudy** was born in Wellsburg Twp., Brooke Co., (West) Virginia, in November 1837. He died in Tennessee on June 7, 1864. James Hayson was buried in Nashville National Cemetery, Nashville, Davidson Co., Tennessee.[7]

+ 11 m II. **William M.⁶ Goudy** was born in Ohio Co., (West) Virginia, on October 6, 1840.[8] He died in Moundsville, Marshall Co., West Virginia, on July 28, 1921.[7] William M. was buried in Wood Hill Cemetery, Marshall Co., West Virginia.[1]

+ 12 f III. **Mary E.⁶ Goudy** was born in Wheeling, Ohio Co., (West) Virginia, on October 20, 1842. She died in Moundsville, Marshall Co., West Virginia, on May 23, 1927. Mary E. was buried in Mount Wood Cemetery, Wheeling, Ohio Co., West Virginia.[9]

+ 13 f IV. **Rebecca J.⁶ Goudy** was born in Wheeling, Ohio Co., (West) Virginia, in 1845. She died in Wheeling, Ohio Co., (West) Virginia, before 1860.

Son of John Goudy and Eliza Van Meter:

+ 14 m I. **Charles Thoburn⁶ Goudy** was born in Wheeling, Ohio Co.,

(West) Virginia, on February 11, 1858.[10] He died in Union Twp., Marshall Co., West Virginia, on May 9, 1926.[11] Charles Thoburn was buried in Allen Grove Cemetery, Sherrard, Union Twp., Marshall Co., West Virginia.[10]

3. **Andrew⁵ Goudy** (*Elizabeth Jane⁴ Pegan, Andrew³ Pegan II, Andrew² Pagan, James¹*) was born on February 7, 1807, in Strabane Twp., Washington Co., Pennsylvania or Ohio. He was the son of Isaac Goudy and Elizabeth Jane Pegan (1). Andrew worked as a Merchant, Grocer. He died in Bridgeport Twp., Belmont Co., Ohio, on October 23, 1891, at age 84. Andrew was buried in Warrenton Cemetery, Rayland, Warren Twp., Jefferson Co., Ohio.[2]

Andrew married **Nancy Goudy** about 1827 in Brooke Co., West Virginia? They had nine children. Nancy Goudy was born in Pennsylvania in 1807. Nancy reached age 53 and died in Warrenton, Warren Twp., Jefferson Co., Ohio, in 1860. She was the daughter of William Goudy. Nancy Goudy is probably buried in Warrenton Cemetery, Rayland, Warren Twp., Jefferson Co., Ohio.

A merchant, Andrew was enumerated in 1830 census in Warren Twp., Jefferson Co., Ohio. He moved by 1840 to Brooke Co., West Virginia, but returned to Andrew Warren Twp., Jefferson Co., Ohio by 1850. Andrew is not found in the 1860 census, but was residing in 1870 in Bridgeport Twp., Belmont Co., Ohio.

After Nancy's death, Andrew Goudy married **Amanda Hannah** on November 5, 1861, in Jefferson Co., Ohio. Amanda Hannah was born in Ohio Co., (West) Virginia, in 1819. Amanda reached age 85 and died in Bridgeport Twp., Belmont Co., Ohio, on January 13, 1904. She was buried in Mount Rose Cemetery, Moundsville, Marshall Co., West Virginia.12 [39]

Children of Andrew Goudy and Nancy Goudy:

+ 15 f I. **Nancy J.⁶ Goudy** was born in Warren Twp., Jefferson Co., Ohio, in 1829. She died in Uhrichsville, Mill Twp., Tuscarawas Co., Ohio, on October 20, 1881. Nancy J. was buried in Union Cemetery, Uhrichsville, Mill Twp., Tuscarawas Co., Ohio.[13]

+ 16    m    II.    **Isaac M.**[6] **Goudy** was born in Warren Twp., Jefferson Co., Ohio, on September 20, 1829. He died in Toronto, Knox Twp., Jefferson Co., Ohio, on August 28, 1895. Isaac M. was buried in Riverview Cemetery, Martins Ferry, Pease Twp., Belmont Co., Ohio.[14]

+ 17    f    III.    **Mary Ann**[6] **Goudy** was born in Warren Twp., Jefferson Co., Ohio, in 1831. She died after 1857.

+ 18    m    IV.    **John W. Samuel**[6] **Goudy** was born in Brooke Co., (West) Virginia, in 1833. He died in New Cumberland, Warren Twp., Tuscarawas Co., Ohio, on October 13, 1906. John W. Samuel was buried in East State Street Cemetery, Newcomerstown, Oxford Twp., Tuscarawas Co., Ohio.[15]

+ 19    f    V.    **Sarah Nancy**[6] **Goudy** was born in Warren Twp., Jefferson Co., Ohio, in 1834. She was also known as **Nannie.** Sarah Nancy died in Steubenville, Cross Creek Twp., Jefferson Co., Ohio, in 1874. She was buried in Union Cemetery, Steubenville, Cross Creek Twp., Jefferson Co., Ohio.[16]

+ 20    f    VI.    **Elizabeth Sophronia**[6] **Goudy** was born in Warren Twp., Jefferson Co., Ohio, on December 22, 1838. She died in Warwick Twp., Tuscarawas Co., Ohio, on July 21, 1926. Elizabeth Sophronia was buried in Dutch Valley Cemetery, Rush Twp., Tuscarawas Co., Ohio.[17]

+ 21    m    VII.    **William A.**[6] **Goudy** was born in Warren Twp., Jefferson Co., Ohio, in 1840. He died in Bridgeport Twp., Belmont Co., Ohio, on December 24, 1899. William A. was buried in Linwood Cemetery, Blaine, Pease Twp., Belmont Co., Ohio.[18]

+ 22    m    VIII.    **James M.**[6] **Goudy** was born in Warren Twp., Jefferson Co., Ohio, in 1846. He died between 1860 and 1865. James M. was buried in Warrenton Cemetery, Rayland, Warren Twp., Jefferson Co., Ohio.[2]

+ 23    f    IX.    **Hester**[6] **Goudy** was born in Warren Twp., Jefferson Co., Ohio, in 1854. She died in Warrenton, Warren Twp., Jefferson Co., Ohio? between 1860 and 1870.

4.    **Robert**[5] **Goudy** (*Elizabeth Jane*[4] *Pegan, Andrew*[3] *Pegan II, Andrew*[2] *Pagan, James*[1]) was born in 1809 in Brooke Co., (West) Virginia. He was the son of Isaac Goudy and Elizabeth Jane Pegan (1). Robert died in Wellsburg Twp., Brooke Co., West Virginia, on December 20, 1875, at age 66.

Robert married **Phrania Jones** in October 1833 in Brooke Co., (West) Virginia? They had four daughters. Phrania Jones was born in Baltimore, Baltimore Co., Maryland or Virginia, on January 19, 1810. Phrania reached age 85 and died in Wellsburg Twp., Brooke Co., West Virginia, on January 16, 1896.

He was a merchant and clothier who lived in Wellsburg Twp., Brooke Co., West Virginia.

Daughters of Robert Goudy and Phrania Jones:

+ 24    f    I.    **Lavinia**[6] **Goudy** was born in Wellsburg Twp., Brooke Co., (West) Virginia, in 1839. She died after 1860.

+ 25    f    II.    **Cordilla**[6] **Goudy** was born in Wellsburg Twp., Brooke Co., (West) Virginia, in 1843. She died in Buffalo, Brooke Co., West Virginia, on December 7, 1884. Cordilla was buried in Brooke Cemetery, Wellsburg, Brooke Co., West Virginia.[19]

+  26  f  III.  **Mary Rebecca[6] Goudy** was born in Wellsburg Twp., Brooke Co., (West) Virginia, in 1843. She was also known as **Rebecca** and **Dolly.** Mary Rebecca died after 1900.

+  27  f  IV.  **Phrania Elizabeth[6] Goudy** was born in Wellsburg Twp., Brooke Co., (West) Virginia, on September 20, 1846. She died in Norfolk, Norfolk City-Co., Virginia, on July 13, 1911. Phrania Elizabeth was buried in Forest Lawn Cemetery, Norfolk, Norfolk Co., Virginia.[20]

5.  **William[5] Goudy** (*Elizabeth Jane[4] Pegan, Andrew[3] Pegan II, Andrew[2] Pagan, James[1]*) was born in 1813 in Brooke Co., (West) Virginia. He was the son of Isaac Goudy and Elizabeth Jane Pegan (1). William lived in 1840 in Wheeling, Ohio Co., West Virginia. He died in St. Louis, Missouri, on July 15, 1879, at age 66. William was buried in Holy Ghost Evangelical and Reformed/Old Pickers Cemetery, St. Louis, Missouri.[3]

William married **Sarah Richman** on June 27, 1836, in Ohio Co., (West) Virginia? They had four children. Sarah Richman was born in Virginia in 1819. Sarah reached age 38 and died in Wheeling, Ohio Co., (West) Virginia, on May 30, 1857.

William Goudy married **Amelia Unknown** before 1860 in (West) Virginia. They had three children. Amelia Unknown was born in England in 1830. Amelia died in St. Louis, Missouri? between 1860 and 1870.

William Goudy married **Henrietta Unknown** before 1870. Henrietta Unknown was born in New York in 1830.

William Goudy is enumerated as "William Goady" in St. Louis, Missouri in 1870. He has a wife, Henrietta, listed as "Henry", and three children:

Herbert, Sarah and "Beny", all with his surname. (*Census Place: St Louis Ward 8, St Louis, Missouri; Roll: M593_818*; Page: *256A*).

A mystery surrounds this family, as there are no further records for Henrietta and the three children. William Goudy died in 1879, according to Missouri death records. But what happened to the youngest three "Goudy" children and William's third and last wife Henrietta is unknown.

Were these children William's by his second wife Amelia or by his last wife Henrietta? Or were some by Amelia and the rest by Henrietta? Herbert's and Sarah's birthplaces in the 1870 census say Virginia, like William's, but Henrietta is from New York. This does not preclude this possibility, but does indicate that William and his second wife, the late Amelia Unknown Goudy, could be their parents. (The youngest, "Beny" (Benjamin?) was born in Missouri.)

Or were the three children Henrietta's by a previous marriage, and the census taker erred by enumerating them under the "Goady" surname?

If the children were all Henrietta's, it is possible that William and Henrietta divorced before William died in 1879, and Henrietta remarried—and the children were adopted by, or just assumed, the surname of her next husband.

Or were some or all of the children Amelia's and were orphaned when William died? Then, unwanted by their step-siblings and their (probable) step-mother Henrietta, were they sent to an orphanage and adopted out? (William S. Goudy II, son of William Goudy and his first wife Sarah Richman, was living in St. Louis in 1880, and these children were not in his household.) However, searches for "Herbert" and "Benjamin/Barry" under other surnames, using their ages and birthplaces, yield no information in censuses or other documents.

Did a tragedy befall the family between 1870-1880 in which Henrietta and/or the children perished? Did they perish in an epidemic, fire or flood in St. Louis? A check of such major events as a massive fire, flood or epidemic reveals there wasn't any such catastrophe any in St. Louis in that time period.

This does not rule out an single event (house fire, sickness) however.

Children of William Goudy and Sarah Richman:

+ 28 f I. **Marianne Marilla<sup>6</sup> Goudy** was born in Wheeling, Ohio Co., (West) Virginia, in 1837. She died in Apple Grove, Hannon Dist., Mason Co., West Virginia, between 1864 and 1868.

+ 29 m II. **Martin Van Buren<sup>6</sup> Goudy** was born in Wheeling, Ohio Co., (West) Virginia, on January 30, 1840. He was also known as **Van Buren.** Martin Van Buren died in St. Louis, Missouri, on July 10, 1877. He was buried in Holy Ghost Evangelical and Reformed/ Old Pickers Cemetery, St. Louis, Missouri.[21]

+ 30 m III. **William S.<sup>6</sup> Goudy II** was born in Wheeling, Ohio Co., (West) Virginia, in 1842. He died in Medford, Jackson Co., Oregon, on December 30, 1916. William S. was buried in Eastwood IOOF Cemetery, Medford, Jackson Co., Oregon.[22]

+ 31 m IV. **John<sup>6</sup> Goudy** was born in Wheeling, Ohio Co., (West) Virginia, in 1848. He died after 1860.

Children (?) of William Goudy and Amelia Unknown:

+ 32 m I. **Herbert<sup>6</sup> Goudy** was born in Wheeling, Ohio Co., (West) Virginia, in 1861.

+ 33 f II. **Sarah<sup>6</sup> Goudy** was born in Wheeling, Ohio Co., West Virginia, in 1863.

+ 34 m III. **Benjamin or Barry<sup>6</sup> Goudy** was born in St. Louis, Missouri, in 1866.

**6. Isaac<sup>5</sup> Goudy II** (*Elizabeth Jane<sup>4</sup> Pegan, Andrew<sup>3</sup> Pegan II, Andrew<sup>2</sup> Pagan, James<sup>1</sup>*) was born on June 10, 1817, in Brooke Co., (West) Virginia. He was the son of Isaac Goudy and Elizabeth Jane Pegan (1). Isaac lived in 1840 and 1850 in Ohio Co., (West) Virginia. He resided in 1870 and 1880 in Union Twp., Marshall Co., West Virginia. He died in Sherrard, Union Twp., Marshall Co., West Virginia, on October 14, 1890, at age 73. Isaac was buried in Mount Olivet Cemetery, Wheeling, Ohio Co., West Virginia.[4]

Isaac married **Sarah Ann Stewart** on December 12, 1839, in Ohio Co., (West) Virginia. They had seven children. Sarah Ann Stewart was born in Virginia on June 13, 1819. Sarah Ann reached age 78 and died in Wheeling, Ohio Co., West Virginia, on March 19, 1898. She was buried in Mount Olivet Cemetery, Wheeling, Ohio Co., West Virginia.[4]

Children of Isaac Goudy II and Sarah Ann Stewart:

+ 35 m I. **James M.<sup>6</sup> Goudy** was born in Ohio Co., (West) Virginia, in 1839. He died after 1860.

+ 36 f II. **Elizabeth Jane<sup>6</sup> Goudy** was born in Ohio Co., (West) Virginia, on February 3, 1841.[23] She died in Wheeling, Ohio Co., West Virginia, on January 21, 1923. [23] Elizabeth Jane was buried in Greenwood Cemetery, Wheeling, Ohio Co., West Virginia.[24]

+ 37 m III. **Robert H.<sup>6</sup> Goudy** was born in Ohio Co., (West) Virginia, on August 5, 1844. He died in Wheeling, Ohio Co., West Virginia, on May 16, 1864.[25]

+ 38 m IV. **John William<sup>6</sup> Goudy** was born in Wheeling, Ohio Co., (West) Virginia, on June 30, 1845. He died in Wheeling, Ohio Co., West Virginia, on November 9, 1907. John William was buried in Mount Olivet Cemetery, Wheeling, Ohio Co., West Virginia.[4]

+ 39 f V. **Emmaliza<sup>6</sup> Goudy** was born in Ohio Co., (West) Virginia, on

March 30, 1848. She died in Ohio Co., West Virginia, on November 26, 1850.

+ 40 m VI. **Wilson Kenny⁶ Goudy** was born in Ohio Co., (West) Virginia, on September 7, 1851. He died in Ohio Co. or Marshall Co., West Virginia, on February 1, 1865.

+ 41 m VII. **Charles Dawson⁶ Goudy** was born in Ohio Co., (West) Virginia, on October 19, 1855. He died in Union Twp., Marshall Co., West Virginia, before 1870.

7. **Mary Jane⁵ Goudy** (*Elizabeth Jane⁴ Pegan, Andrew³ Pegan II, Andrew² Pagan, James¹*) was born in November 1819 in Brooke Co., (West) Virginia. She was the daughter of Isaac Goudy and Elizabeth Jane Pegan (1). Mary Jane died in Triadelphia, Ohio Co., West Virginia? about 1905 at age 85.

Mary Jane married **William Hill** on August 19, 1841, in Ohio Co., (West) Virginia. They had six children. William Hill was born in Pennsylvania in 1819. William reached age 41 and died in Wheeling, Ohio Co., (West) Virginia, about 1860.

Children of Mary Jane Goudy and William Hill:

+ 42 m I. **David Wellington⁶ Hill** was born in Ohio Co., (West) Virginia, on June 13, 1841. He died in Wheeling, Ohio Co., West Virginia, on March 1, 1919. He was buried in Peninsula Cemetery, Wheeling, Ohio Co., West Virginia.[26]

+ 43 m II. **William Hamilton⁶ Hill II** was born in McConnellsville, Morgan Twp., Morgan Co., Ohio, on July 2, 1842. He was also known as **Hamilton.** William Hamilton died in Wheeling, Ohio Co., West Virginia, on November 22, 1912. He-

was buried in Stone Church Cemetery, Elm Grove, Ohio Co., West Virginia.[27]

+ 44 m III. **John W.⁶ Hill** was born in McConnellsville, Morgan Twp., Morgan Co., Ohio, on July 22, 1846. He died in Wheeling, Ohio Co., West Virginia, on January 7, 1893. John W. was buried in Peninsula Cemetery, Wheeling, Ohio Co., West Virginia.[26]

+ 45 f IV. **Elizabeth Jane⁶ Hill** was born in McConnellsville, Morgan Twp., Morgan Co., Ohio, in November 1849. She was also known as **Jennie.** Elizabeth Jane died in a facility in Weston, Lewis Co., West Virginia, on November 24, 1928. She was buried in Mount Zion Cemetery, Wheeling, Ohio Co., West Virginia.[28]

+ 46 m V. **Robert E.⁶ Hill** was born in Wheeling, Ohio Co., (West) Virginia, in 1850. He died in Wheeling, Ohio Co., West Virginia, in 1855.

+ 47 f VI. **Emma⁶ Hill** was born in Wheeling, Ohio Co., (West) Virginia, in 1854. She died after 1870.

8. **Eliza?⁵ Goudy** (*Elizabeth Jane⁴ Pegan, Andrew³ Pegan II, Andrew² Pagan, James¹*) was born between 1820 and 1825 in Brooke Co., (West) Virginia. She was the daughter of Isaac Goudy and Elizabeth Jane Pegan (1). Eliza or Daughter died after 1840.

9. **Son⁵ Goudy** (*Elizabeth Jane⁴ Pegan, Andrew³ Pegan II, Andrew² Pagan, James¹*) was born between 1825 and 1830 in Brooke Co. or Ohio Co., (West) Virginia. He was the son of Isaac Goudy and Elizabeth Jane Pegan (1). Son died in Ohio Co., West Virginia, between 1840 and 1850.

# 6th Generation

**10. James Hayson[6] Goudy** (*John[5], Elizabeth Jane[4] Pegan, Andrew[3] Pegan II, Andrew[2] Pagan, James[1]*) was born in November 1837 in Wellsburg Twp., Brooke Co., (West) Virginia. He was the son of John Goudy (2) and Rebecca Morgan. James Hayson died in Tennessee on June 7, 1864, at age 26. He was buried in Nashville National Cemetery, Nashville, Davidson Co., Tennessee.[7]

James Hayson married **Samantha Faunce** on October 2, 1862, at Book 4, pg. 225 in Ohio Co., (West) Virginia.[29] They had one son. Samantha Faunce was born in Marshall Co., (West) Virginia, in December 1843.[27] She lived in 1870 and 1880 in Wheeling, Ohio Co., West Virginia. Samantha resided in 1900 in Donegal Twp., Washington Co., Pennsylvania. Samantha reached age 79 and died in Blaine Twp., Washington Co., Pennsylvania, in 1923. She was buried in Claysville Cemetery, Claysville, Washington Co., Pennsylvania.[30]

A captain in an Ohio regiment of the Union Army, James Hayson Goudy died in Tennessee (exact place unknown) of a gunshot wound.

Son of James Hayson Goudy and Samantha Faunce:

+ 48 m I. **James Frank[7] Goudy** was born in Wheeling, Ohio Co., West Virginia, on August 1, 1864.[31] He died in Chicago, Cook Co., Illinois, on October 24, 1929.[31, 32] James Frank was buried in Graceland Cemetery, Chicago, Cook Co., Illinois.[32]

**11. William M.[6] Goudy** (*John[5], Elizabeth Jane[4] Pegan, Andrew[3] Pegan II, Andrew[2] Pagan, James[1]*) was born on October 6, 1840, in Ohio Co., (West) Virginia.[8] He was the son of John Goudy (2) and Rebecca Morgan. He died in Moundsville, Marshall Co., West Virginia, on July 28, 1921, at age 80.[8] William M. was buried in Wood Hill Cemetery, Marshall Co., West Virginia.[1]

William M. married **Ann Rebecca Jones** on November 28, 1867.[8] They had three children.

Ann Rebecca Jones was born in (West) Virginia in 1842. Ann Rebecca reached age 62 and died in Moundsville, Marshall Co., West Virginia, on November 27, 1904.[1] She was buried in Wood Hill Cemetery, Marshall Co., West Virginia.[1] (Gravestone says Annie R. Goudy.)

William M. Goudy's Civil War 1886 pension file reveals much about his family.

Children of William M. Goudy and Ann Rebecca Jones:

+ 49 f I. **Effie[7] Goudy** was born in West Virginia on May 5, 1870.[8] She died in Marshall Co., West Virginia, on February 2, 1936.[1, 33] Effie was buried in Wood Hill Cemetery, Marshall Co., West Virginia.[1]

+ 50 m II. **Harry Home[7] Goudy** was born in Washington Twp., Marshall Co., West Virginia, on September 21, 1873.[34] He died in Fairmont, Marion Co., West Virginia, on November 4, 1957.[34] Harry Homer was buried in Woodlawn Cemetery, Fairmont, Marion Co., West Virginia.[34, 35]

+ 51 m III. **Edmond M.[7] Goudy** was born in Washington Twp., Marshall Co., West Virginia, on February 21, 1877.[8] He died in Washington Twp., Marshall Co., West Virginia, on May 20, 1877.[36]

**12. Mary E.[6] Goudy** (*John[5], Elizabeth Jane[4] Pegan, Andrew[3] Pegan II, Andrew[2] Pagan, James[1]*) was born on October 20, 1842, in Wheeling, Ohio Co., (West) Virginia. She was the daughter of John Goudy (2) and Rebecca Morgan. Mary E. died in Moundsville, Marshall Co., West Virginia, on May 23, 1927, at age 84. She was buried in Mount Wood Cemetery, Wheeling, Ohio Co., West Virginia.[9]

Mary E. married **Robert Harrison Blake** on November 2, 1869, in Marshall Co., West Virginia. They had one daughter. Robert Harrison Blake was born in Moundsville, Marshall Co., (West) Virginia, in 1839. Robert Harrison died in Wheeling, Ohio Co., West Virginia? after 1880.

Mary E. Goudy Blake married **George Kurtz Milligan** on October 23, 1901, in Ohio Co., West Virginia. George Kurtz Milligan was born in Claysville, Washington Co., Pennsylvania, on September 12, 1835. George Kurtz reached age 89 and died in Claysville, Washington Co., Pennsylvania, on December 26, 1924. He was buried in Claysville Cemetery, Claysville, Washington Co., Pennsylvania.[30]

Daughter of Mary E. Goudy and Robert Harrison Blake:

+ 52   f   I.     **Mary V.**[7] **Blake** was born in Wheeling, Ohio Co., West Virginia, in 1878. She died after 1880.

**13. Rebecca J.**[6] **Goudy** (*John*[5], *Elizabeth Jane*[4] *Pegan, Andrew*[3] *Pegan II, Andrew*[2] *Pagan, James*[1]) was born in 1845 in Wheeling, Ohio Co., (West) Virginia. She was the daughter of John Goudy (2) and Rebecca Morgan. Rebecca J. died in Wheeling, Ohio Co., (West) Virginia, before 1860.

**14. Charles Thoburn**[6] **Goudy** (*John*[5], *Elizabeth Jane*[4] *Pegan, Andrew*[3] *Pegan II, Andrew*[2] *Pagan, James*[1]) was born on February 11, 1858, in Wheeling, Ohio Co., (West) Virginia.[10] He was the son of John Goudy (2) and Eliza Van Meter. He died in Union Twp., Marshall Co., West Virginia, on May 9, 1926, at age 68.[11] Charles Thoburn was buried in Allen Grove Cemetery, Sherrard, Union Twp., Marshall Co., West Virginia.[10]

He married **Estella Elizabeth Kemple.** They had two children. Estella Elizabeth Kemple was born in West Virginia on June 20, 1869.[10] Estella Elizabeth reached age 103 and died in Union Twp., Marshall Co., West Virginia?, on February 27, 1973. She was buried in Allen Grove Cemetery, Sherrard, Union Twp., Marshall Co., West Virginia.[10]

Children of Charles Thoburn Goudy and Estella Elizabeth Kemple:

+ 53   m   I.     **Donald Reed**[7] **Goudy** was born in Union Twp., Marshall Co., West Virginia, on April 1, 1891. He died in Wheeling, Ohio Co., West Virginia, on August 13, 1917.[10] Donald Reed was buried in Allen Grove Cemetery, Sherrard, Union Twp., Marshall Co., West Virginia.[10]

+ 54   f   II.     **Mary A.**[7] **Goudy** was born in Union Twp., Marshall Co., West Virginia, on September 4, 1895.[37] She died in a hospital in Wheeling, Ohio Co., West Virginia, on July 1, 1969.[37] Mary A. was buried in Greenwood Cemetery, Wheeling, Ohio Co., West Virginia.[37]

**15. Nancy J.**[6] **Goudy** (*Andrew*[5], *Elizabeth Jane*[4] *Pegan, Andrew*[3] *Pegan II, Andrew*[2] *Pagan, James*[1]) was born in 1829 in Warren Twp., Jefferson Co., Ohio. She was the daughter of Andrew Goudy (3) and Nancy Goudy. Nancy J. died in Uhrichsville, Mill Twp., Tuscarawas Co., Ohio, on October 20, 1881, at age 52. She was buried in Union Cemetery, Uhrichsville, Mill Twp., Tuscarawas Co., Ohio.[13]

Nancy J. married **Samuel R. Thompson** on February 6, 1851, in Jefferson Co., Ohio. They had six children. Samuel R. Thompson was born in Harrison Co., (West) Virginia, in 1829. Samuel R. worked as a Physician. He reached age 75 and died in Uhrichsville, Mill Twp., Tuscarawas Co., Ohio, on November 14, 1904. Samuel R. was buried in Union Cemetery, Uhrichsville, Mill Twp., Tuscarawas Co., Ohio.[13]

Children of Nancy J. Goudy and Samuel R. Thompson:

+ 55   m   I.     **Lewis K.**[7] **Thompson** was born in Tippecanoe, Washington Twp., Harrison Co., Ohio, on December 12, 1851. He died in Uhrichsville, Mill Twp., Tuscarawas Co., Ohio, on January 16, 1929.

+ 56   f   II.     **Ella Nancy**[7] **Thompson** was born in Tippecanoe, Washington Twp., Harrison Co., Ohio, on February 28, 1855. She died in Uhrichsville,

Mill Twp., Tuscarawas Co., Ohio, on February 23, 1942. Ella Nancy was buried in Union Cemetery, Uhrichsville, Mill Twp., Tuscarawas Co., Ohio.[13]

+ 57 f III. **Sarah Virginia**[7] **Thompson** was born in Tippecanoe, Washington Twp., Harrison Co., Ohio, on June 21, 1856. She died in Mansfield, Madison Twp., Richland Co., Ohio, on September 7, 1945. Sarah Virginia was buried in Union Cemetery, Uhrichsville, Mill Twp., Tuscarawas Co., Ohio.[13]

+ 58 f IV. **Mary E.**[7] **Thompson** was born in Uhrichsville, Mill Twp., Tuscarawas Co., Ohio, on March 15, 1860. She died in Uhrichsville, Mill Twp., Tuscarawas Co., Ohio, on May 15, 1925. Mary E. was buried in Union Cemetery, Uhrichsville, Mill Twp., Tuscarawas Co., Ohio.[13]

+ 59 m V. **Harry**[7] **Thompson** was born in Uhrichsville, Mill Twp., Tuscarawas Co., Ohio, on November 21, 1867. He died in a facility in Massillon, Perry Twp., Stark Co., Ohio, on March 16, 1937. Harry was buried in Union Cemetery, Uhrichsville, Mill Twp., Tuscarawas Co., Ohio.

+ 60 m VI. **Robert**[7] **Thompson** was born in Uhrichsville, Mill Twp., Tuscarawas Co., Ohio, on September 10, 1870. He died in a facility in Cameron, Marshall Co., West Virginia, on August 22, 1963. Robert was buried in McMechen Cemetery, McMechen, Union Dist., Marshall Co., West Virginia.[38]

**16. Isaac M.**[6] **Goudy** (*Andrew*[5], *Elizabeth Jane*[4] *Pegan*, *Andrew3 Pegan II*, *Andrew*[2] *Pagan*, *James*[1]) was born on September 20, 1829, in Warren Twp., Jefferson Co., Ohio. He was the son of Andrew Goudy (3) and Nancy Goudy. Isaac M. died in Toronto, Knox Twp., Jefferson Co., Ohio, on August 28, 1895, at age 65. He was buried in Riverview Cemetery, Martins Ferry, Pease Twp., Belmont Co., Ohio.[14]

Isaac M. married **Margaret Brautner or Broughtner** on July 4, 1853, in Jefferson Co., Ohio? They had two daughters. Margaret Brautner or Broughtner was born in Moundsville, Marshall Co., West Virginia, in 1830. Margaret reached age 33 and died in Bridgeport Twp., Belmont Co., Ohio or Burlington, Burlington Twp., Des Moines Co., Iowa, about 1863. (Isaac Goudy lived in Burlington, Iowa from 1861-1864.)

Isaac M. Goudy married **Martha Brautner** or **Broughtner** on October 5, 1876, in Belmont Co., Ohio. Martha Brautner or Broughtner was born in Coraopolis, Allegheny Co., Pennsylvania, in 1827. Martha reached age 81 and died in Toronto, Knox Twp., Jefferson Co., Ohio, on February 10, 1908. She was buried in Riverview Cemetery, Martins Ferry, Pease Twp., Belmont Co., Ohio.[14]

Margaret and Martha Brautner or Broughtner seem to have been sisters.

Daughters of Isaac M. Goudy and Margaret Brautner or Broughtner:

+ 61 f I. **Laura Bell**[7] **Goudy** was born in Burlington, Burlington Twp., Des Moines Co., Iowa, on January 25, 1857. She died in Rush Twp., Tuscarawas Co., Ohio, on December 29, 1904, at age 47. Laura Bell was buried in Dutch Valley Cemetery, Rush Twp., Tuscarawas Co., Ohio.[17]

+ 62 f II. **Sarah**[7] **Goudy** was born in Burlington, Burlington Twp., Des Moines Co., Iowa, on January 5, 1859. She died in Martins Ferry, Pease Twp., Belmont Co., Ohio, on October 16, 1933, at age 74. Sarah was buried in Riverview Cemetery, Martins Ferry, Pease Twp., Belmont Co., Ohio.[14]

**17. Mary Ann**[6] **Goudy** (*Andrew*[5], *Elizabeth Jane*[4] *Pegan, Andrew*[3] *Pegan II, Andrew*[2] *Pagan, James*[1]) was born in 1831 in Warren Twp., Jefferson Co., Ohio. She was the daughter of Andrew Goudy (3) and Nancy Goudy. Mary Ann died after 1857.

Mary Ann married **Daniel Baughman** on May 17, 1857, in Jefferson Co., Ohio.

**18. John W. Samuel**[6] **Goudy** (*Andrew*[5], *Elizabeth Jane*[4] *Pegan, Andrew*[3] *Pegan II, Andrew*[2] *Pagan, James*[1]) was born in 1833 in Brooke Co., (West) Virginia. He was the son of Andrew Goudy (3) and Nancy Goudy. John W. Samuel lived in 1906 in Newcomerstown, Oxford Twp., Tuscarawas Co., Ohio. He died in New Cumberland, Warren Twp., Tuscarawas Co., Ohio, on October 13, 1906, at age 73. John W. Samuel was buried in East State Street Cemetery, Newcomerstown, Oxford Twp., Tuscarawas Co., Ohio.[15]

John W. Samuel married **Ann Eliza Huston** on February 28, 1858, in Tuscarawas Co., Ohio. They had two sons. Ann Eliza Huston was born in Moorfield Twp., Harrison Co., Ohio, in 1834. Ann Eliza reached age 47 and died in Newcomerstown, Oxford Twp., Tuscarawas Co., Ohio, on June 27, 1881. She was buried in East State Street Cemetery, Newcomerstown, Oxford Twp., Tuscarawas Co., Ohio.[15]

John W. Samuel Goudy married **Sarah Bethia Everhart.** Sarah Bethia Everhart was born in Salem Twp., Tuscarawas Co., Ohio, on December 8, 1854. Sarah Bethia reached age 70 and died in Coshocton, Coshocton Co., Ohio, on December 28, 1924. She was buried in East State Street Cemetery, Newcomerstown, Oxford Twp., Tuscarawas Co., Ohio.[15]

Sons of John W. Samuel Goudy and Ann Eliza Huston:

+ 63 m I. **John W. Huston**[7] **Goudy II** was born in Newcomerstown, Oxford Twp., Tuscarawas Co., Ohio, in November 1858. He died in Goshen Twp., Tuscarawas Co., Ohio, on April 10, 1938. John W. Huston was buried in East State Street Cem-etery, Newcomerstown, Oxford Twp., Tuscarawas Co., Ohio.[15]

+ 64 m II. **Rollin Andrew**[7] **Goudy** was born in Newcomerstown, Oxford Twp., Tuscarawas Co., Ohio, on October 30, 1863. He died in Newcomerstown, Oxford Twp., Tuscarawas Co., Ohio, on April 26, 1924. Rollin Andrew was buried in East State Street Cemetery, Newcomerstown, Oxford Twp., Tuscarawas Co., Ohio.[15]

**19. Sarah Nancy**[6] **Goudy** (*Andrew*[5], *Elizabeth Jane*[4] *Pegan, Andrew*[3] *Pegan II, Andrew*[2] *Pagan, James*[1]) was born in 1834 in Warren Twp., Jefferson Co., Ohio. She was also known as **Nannie.** She was the daughter of Andrew Goudy (3) and Nancy Goudy. Sarah Nancy died in Steubenville, Cross Creek Twp., Jefferson Co., Ohio, in 1874 at age 40. She was buried in Union Cemetery, Steubenville, Cross Creek Twp., Jefferson Co., Ohio.[14]

Never married.

**20. Elizabeth Sophronia**[6] **Goudy** (*Andrew*[5], *Elizabeth Jane*[4] *Pegan, Andrew*[3] *Pegan II, Andrew*[2] *Pagan, James*[1]) was born on December 22, 1838, in Warren Twp., Jefferson Co., Ohio. She was the daughter of Andrew Goudy (3) and Nancy Goudy. Elizabeth Sophronia died in Warwick Twp., Tuscarawas Co., Ohio, on July 21, 1926, at age 87. She was buried in Dutch Valley Cemetery, Rush Twp., Tuscarawas Co., Ohio.[17]

Elizabeth Sophronia married **Milton F. Wardell** on November 24, 1869, in Belmont Co., Ohio. They had four children. Milton F. Wardell was born in Tuscarawas Co., Ohio, on September 19, 1836. Milton F. reached age 76 and died in Rush Twp., Tuscarawas Co., Ohio, on November 10, 1912. He was buried in Dutch Valley Cemetery, Rush Twp., Tuscarawas Co., Ohio.[17]

Children of Elizabeth Sophronia Goudy and Milton F. Wardell:

+ 65 m I. **Andrew M.**[7] **Goudy** was born in Rush Twp., Tuscarawas Co., Ohio, on February 4, 1871. He died in

Uhrichsville, Mill Twp., Tuscarawas Co., Ohio, on April 6, 1952. Joseph A. was buried in Gnadenhutten-Clay Union Cemetery, Clay Twp., Tuscarawas Co., Ohio.[39]

+ 66   m   II.   **John Wesley**[7] **Wardell** was born in Rush Twp., Tuscarawas Co., Ohio, on August 1, 1873. He died in Los Angeles, Los Angeles Co., California, on December 7, 1951.

+ 67   f   III.   **Minnie Etta**[7] **Wardell** was born in Rush Twp., Tuscarawas Co., Ohio, on January 10, 1877. She died in South Gate, Los Angeles Co., California, on May 18,1957.

+ 68   f   IV.   **Gertrude Nan**[7] **Wardell** was born in Rush Twp., Tuscarawas Co., Ohio, on October 15, 1879. She was also known as **Nannie.** Gertrude Nan died in Los Angeles, Los Angeles Co., California, on November 5, 1965.

21. **William A.**[6] **Goudy** (*Andrew*[5], *Elizabeth Jane*[4] *Pegan, Andrew*[3] *Pegan II, Andrew*[2] *Pagan, James*[1]) was born in 1840 in Warren Twp., Jefferson Co., Ohio. He was the son of Andrew Goudy (3) and Nancy Goudy. William A. died in Bridgeport Twp., Belmont Co., Ohio, on December 24, 1899, at age 59. He was buried in Linwood Cemetery, Blaine, Pease Twp., Belmont Co., Ohio.[18]

William A. married **Sophia Geller** on October 3, 1867, in Belmont Co., Ohio. They had two children. Sophia Geller was born in St. Clairsville, Richland Twp., Belmont Co., Ohio, in April 1844. Sophia reached age 79 and died in Cleveland, Cuyahoga Co., Ohio, on January 19, 1924. She was buried in Linwood Cemetery, Blaine, Pease Twp., Belmont Co., Ohio.[18]

Children of William A. Goudy and Sophia Geller:

+ 69   m   I.   **Andrew M.**[7] **Goudy** was born in Bridgeport Twp., Belmont Co.,

Ohio, on January 10, 1869. He died in Wheeling, Ohio Co., West Virginia, on February 8, 1905. Andrew W. was buried in Linwood Cemetery, Blaine, Pease Twp., Belmont Co., Ohio.[18]

+ 70   f   II.   **Maud**[7] **Goudy** was born in Bridgeport Twp., Belmont Co., Ohio, on August 11, 1879. She died in Lakewood, Cuyahoga Co., Ohio, on July 20, 1960. Maud was buried in Western Reserve Mausoleum, Warren, Trumbull Co., Ohio.[40]

22. **James M.**[6] **Goudy** (*Andrew*[5], *Elizabeth Jane*[4] *Pegan, Andrew*[3] *Pegan II, Andrew*[2] *Pagan, James*[1]) was born in 1846 in Warren Twp., Jefferson Co., Ohio. He was the son of Andrew Goudy (3) and Nancy Goudy. James M. died between 1860 and 1865. He was buried in Warrenton Cemetery, Rayland, Warren Twp., Jefferson Co., Ohio.[2]

Never married.

James M. Goudy died in the Civil War.

23. **Hester**[6] **Goudy** (*Andrew*[5], *Elizabeth Jane*[4] *Pegan, Andrew*[3] *Pegan II, Andrew*[2] *Pagan, James*[1]) was born in 1854 in Warren Twp., Jefferson Co., Ohio. She was the daughter of Andrew Goudy (3) and Nancy Goudy. Hester died in Warrenton, Warren Twp., Jefferson Co., Ohio? between 1860 and 1870.

24. **Lavinia**[6] **Goudy** (*Robert*[5], *Elizabeth Jane*[4] *Pegan, Andrew*[3] *Pegan II, Andrew*[2] *Pagan, James*[1]) was born in 1839 in Wellsburg Twp., Brooke Co., (West) Virginia. She was the daughter of Robert Goudy (4) and Phrania Jones. Lavinia died after 1860.

25. **Cordilla**[6] **Goudy** (*Robert*[5], *Elizabeth Jane*[4] *Pegan, Andrew*[3] *Pegan II, Andrew*[2] *Pagan, James*[1]) was born in 1843 in Wellsburg Twp., Brooke Co., (West) Virginia. She was the daughter of Robert Goudy (4) and Phrania Jones. Cordilla died in Buffalo, Brooke Co., West Virginia, on December 7, 1884, at age 41. She was buried in Brooke Cemetery, Wellsburg, Brooke Co., West Virginia.[19]

Childless.

Cordilla married **John W. Lindsay** on October 14, 1884, in Brooke Co., West Virginia. John W. Lindsay was born in (West) Virginia on December 22, 1840. John W. reached age 64 and died in Cross Creek, Brooke Co., West Virginia, on July 23, 1905.

**26. Mary Rebecca**[6] **Goudy** (*Robert*[5], *Elizabeth Jane*[4] *Pegan*, *Andrew*[3] *Pegan II*, *Andrew*[2] *Pagan*, *James*[1]) was born in 1843 in Wellsburg Twp., Brooke Co., (West) Virginia. She was also known as **Rebecca** and **Dolly.** She was the daughter of Robert Goudy (4) and Phrania Jones. Mary Rebecca died after 1900.

Mary Rebecca married **John Blankensop** on October 24, 1867, in Brooke Co. West Virginia. They had three children. John Blankensop was born in (West) Virginia in 1834. John died after 1900.

Children of Mary Rebecca Goudy and John Blankensop:

+ 71   m   I.   **Robert Goudy**[7] **Blankensop** was born in Wellsburg, Brooke Co., West Virginia, on July 30, 1868. He died in Moundsville, Marshall Co., West Virginia, on November 2, 1936. Robert Goudy was buried in Mount Rose Cemetery, Moundsville, Marshall Co., West Virginia.[12]

+ 72   f   II.   **Phrenia**[7] **Blankensop** was born in Wellsburg, Brooke Co., West Virginia, in 1870. She died in Wellsburg, Brooke Co., West Virginia, on November 14, 1885. Phrenia was buried in Brooke Cemetery, Wellsburg, Brooke Co., West Virginia.[19]

+ 73   m   III.   **Markley**[7] **Blankensop** was born in Wellsburg, Brooke Co., West Virginia, in 1873. He died in Wellsburg, Brooke Co., West Virginia, on September 15, 1892.

**27. Phrania Elizabeth**[6] **Goudy** (*Robert*[5], *Elizabeth Jane*[4] *Pegan*, *Andrew*[3] *Pegan II*, *Andrew*[2] *Pagan*, *James*[1]) was born on September 20, 1846, in Wellsburg Twp., Brooke Co., (West) Virginia. She was the daughter of Robert Goudy (4) and Phrania Jones. Phrania

Elizabeth died in Norfolk, Norfolk City-Co., Virginia, on July 13, 1911, at age 64. She was buried in Forest Lawn Cemetery, Norfolk, Norfolk Co., Virginia.[20]

Phrania Elizabeth married **Fielding Whipp Pattie** on June 1, 1876, in Brooke Co., West Virginia. They had five children. Fielding Whipp Pattie was born in Franklin Co., Kentucky, on April 10, 1845. Fielding Whipp reached age 44 and died in Acton, Los Angeles Co., California, in 1890. He was buried in Evergreen Cemetery, Los Angeles, Los Angeles Co., California.[41]

Children of Phrania Elizabeth Goudy and Fielding Whipp Pattie:

+ 74   m   I.   **Paul Desha**[7] **Pattie** was born in Austin, Travis Co., Texas, on November 27, 1877. He died in Wheeling, Ohio Co., West Virginia, on March 8, 1952. Paul Desha was buried in Greenwood Cemetery, Wheeling, Ohio Co., West Virginia.[24]

+ 75   m   II.   **Shirley**[7] **Pattie** was born in Nova Scotia, Canada, on October 9, 1879. He died in Proviso, Cook Co., Illinois, on June 28, 1938. Shirley was buried in Forest Lawn Cemetery, Norfolk, Norfolk Co., Virginia.[20]

+ 76   f   III.   **Mary Phrania**[7] **Pattie** was born in Brooke Co., West Virginia, on March 8, 1883. She died in Berkeley, Alameda Co., California, on May 3, 1953. Mary Phrania was buried in Rochester, Oakland Co., Michigan, on May 5, 1953.

+ 77   f   IV.   **Creda**[7] **Pattie** was born in Acton, Los Angeles Co., California, on August 2, 1885. She died in Washington, District of Columbia, on May 10, 1962. Creda was buried in Rock Creek Cemetery, Washington, District of Columbia.[42]

+ 78  f  V.  **Abigail Louise**[7] **Pattie** was born in Acton, Los Angeles Co., California, on June 20, 1889. She died in Richmond, Henrico Co., Virginia, on November 8, 1913. Abigail Louise was buried in Forest Lawn Cemetery, Norfolk, Norfolk Co., Virginia.[20]

**28. Marianne Marilla**[6] **Goudy** (*William*[5], *Elizabeth Jane*[4] *Pegan*, *Andrew*[3] *Pegan II*, *Andrew*[2] *Pagan*, *James*[1]) was born in 1837 in Wheeling, Ohio Co., (West) Virginia. She was the daughter of William Goudy (5) and Sarah Richman. Marianne Marilla died in Apple Grove, Hannon Dist., Mason Co., West Virginia, between 1864 and 1868.

Marianne Marilla married **Robert Prentice Hereford** in 1861 in Mason Co., (West) Virginia. They had two children. Robert Prentice Hereford was born in Mercer's Bottom, Mason Co., (West) Virginia, on June 22, 1835. Robert Prentice reached age 47 and died in Los Angeles, Los Angeles Co., California, on March 8, 1883. He was buried in Oakhill Cemetery, Oakhurst, Madera Co., California.[43]

Children of Marianne Marilla Goudy and Robert Prentice Hereford:

+ 79  m  I.  **Worthington Wilson**[7] **Hereford** was born in Apple Grove, Hannon Dist., Mason Co., West Virginia, on May 12, 1862. He died in Flat, Yukon-Koyakuk, Alaska, on May 27, 1924.

+ 80  f  II.  **Sarah Sanson**[7] **Hereford** was born in Apple Grove, Hannon Dist., Mason Co., West Virginia, on March 6, 1864. She was also known as **Sadie.** Sarah Sanson died in Guadalupe or De Baca Co., New Mexico? on August 5, 1916. She was buried in Lone Oak Cemetery, Point Pleasant, Mason Co., West Virginia.[44]

**29. Martin Van Buren**[6] **Goudy** (*William*[5], *Elizabeth Jane*[4] *Pegan*, *Andrew*[3] *Pegan II*, *Andrew*[2] *Pagan*, *James*[1]) was born on January 30, 1840, in Wheeling, Ohio Co., (West) Virginia. He was also known as **Van Buren.** He was the son of William Goudy (5) and Sarah Richman. Martin Van Buren worked as a Carpenter. He died in St. Louis, Missouri, on July 10, 1877, at age 37. Martin Van Buren was buried in Holy Ghost Evangelical and Reformed/Old Pickers Cemetery, St. Louis, Missouri.[21]

Seems to have never married.

According to St. Louis burial records, Martin Van Buren Goudy was buried in "Old Picker's Cemetery". The actual name of this cemetery was Holy Ghost Evangelical and Reformed Church Cemetery. It was also commonly called just Picker's Cemetery and also Piccot's Cemetery. The cemetery was so nicknamed after the Rev. Franz Picker, pastor of German Evangelical Protestant Church of the Holy Ghost when the cemetery was founded in 1846.

In 1893, the St. Louis city government ordered burials in this cemetery stopped, but the mandate was ignored until around 1902. In 1917 the the city condemned the cemetery. Graves were removed to other cemeteries in St. Louis, including St. Marcus, Zion Evangelical, Bellefontaine, St. Peter's and Independent German Evangelical/New Picker's (now Gatewood Gardens) Cemeteries. Removal records are non-extent.

**30. William S.**[6] **Goudy II** (*William*[5], *Elizabeth Jane*[4] *Pegan*, *Andrew*[3] *Pegan II*, *Andrew*[2] *Pagan*, *James*[1]) was born in 1842 in Wheeling, Ohio Co., (West) Virginia. He was the son of William Goudy (5) and Sarah Richman. William S. lived in 1880 in St. Louis, Missouri. He died in Medford, Jackson Co., Oregon, on December 30, 1916, at age 74. William S. was buried in Eastwood IOOF Cemetery, Medford, Jackson Co., Oregon.[22]

Childless.

William S. Goudy fought for the Confederacy in the Civil War.

William S. married **Martha J. Unknown.** Martha J. Unknown was born in Tennessee in 1853. Martha J. reached age 28 and died in St. Louis, Missouri, on

November 24, 1881. She was buried in Holy Ghost Evangelical and Reformed/Old Pickers Cemetery, St. Louis, Missouri.[45]

William S. Goudy's will, written and proved in Jackson Co., Oregon, gives everything to his grand-niece, Nora Frances McNeill, granddaughter of his late sister, Marianne Marilla Goudy Hereford and daughter of Marianne's only child to have offspring, Sarah "Sadie" Hereford McNeill.

For some reason, William S. Goudy may have thought that his niece Sadie had only one child, Nora Frances McNeill. But Sarah "Sadie" Hereford McNeill had nine children, seven of whom were living when William died. Perhaps Nora was the one who wrote William and told him of Sadie's death Nora Frances "Frances" McNeill Bare Mitchell, her first husband Howard Clifford Bare and their two daughters later removed to Medford, Jackson Co., Oregon, where her Uncle William Goudy had lived. Perhaps she inherited some land from her uncle.

31. **John**[6] **Goudy** (*William*[5], *Elizabeth Jane*[4] *Pegan, Andrew*[3] *Pegan II, Andrew*[2] *Pagan, James*[1]) was born in 1848 in Wheeling, Ohio Co., (West) Virginia. He was the son of William Goudy (5) and Sarah Richman. John died after 1860. May have died in the Civil War.

32. **Herbert**[6] **Goudy** (*William*[5], *Elizabeth Jane*[4] *Pegan, Andrew*[3] *Pegan II, Andrew*[2] *Pagan, James*[1]) was born in 1861 in Wheeling, Ohio Co., (West) Virginia. He was the son of William Goudy (5) and Amelia Unknown ?

33. **Sarah**[6] **Goudy** (*William*[5], *Elizabeth Jane*[4] *Pegan, Andrew*[3] *Pegan II, Andrew*[2] *Pagan, James*[1]) was born in 1863 in Wheeling, Ohio Co., West Virginia. She was the daughter of William Goudy (5) and Amelia Unknown ?

34. **Benjamin or Barry**[6] **Goudy** (*William*[5], *Elizabeth Jane*[4] *Pegan, Andrew*[3] *Pegan II, Andrew*[2] *Pagan, James*[1]) was born in 1866 in St. Louis, Missouri. He was the son of William Goudy (5) and Amelia Unknown ?

35. **James M.**[6] **Goudy** (*Isaac*[5], *Elizabeth Jane*[4] *Pegan, Andrew*[3] *Pegan II, Andrew*[2] *Pagan, James*[1]) was born in 1839 in Ohio Co., (West) Virginia. He was the son of Isaac Goudy II (6) and Sarah Ann Stewart. James M. died after 1860. May have died in the Civil War.

He married **Jane Davis.**

36. **Elizabeth Jane**[6] **Goudy** (*Isaac*[5], *Elizabeth Jane*[4] *Pegan, Andrew*[3] *Pegan II, Andrew*[2] *Pagan, James*[1]) was born on February 3, 1841, in Ohio Co., (West) Virginia.[21] She was the daughter of Isaac Goudy II (6) and Sarah Ann Stewart. Elizabeth Jane died in Wheeling, Ohio Co., West Virginia, on January 21, 1923, at age 81.[23] She was buried in Greenwood Cemetery, Wheeling, Ohio Co., West Virginia.[24]

Elizabeth Jane married **Joseph Hawkins Cowl** on November 6, 1860, in Ohio Co., (West) Virginia. They had eight children. Joseph Hawkins Cowl was born in Wheeling, Ohio Co., (West) Virginia, on August 21, 1831. Joseph Hawkins reached age 63 and died in Wheeling, Ohio Co., West Virginia, on October 18, 1894.

Children of Elizabeth Jane Goudy and Joseph Hawkins Cowl:

+ 81   f   I.   **Sarah Jessie**[7] **Cowl** was born in Bethany, Brooke Co., (West) Virginia, on December 14, 1861. She died in a facility in Weston, Lewis Co., West Virginia, on September 21, 1941. Sarah Jessie was buried in Highland Cemetery, Cameron, Marshall Co., West Virginia.[46]

+ 82   f   II.   **Mary Elva**[7] **Cowl** was born in Bethany, Brooke Co., West Virginia, on October 11, 1864. She died in Wheeling, Ohio Co., West Virginia, on July 19, 1955. Mary Elva was buried in Mount Rose Cemetery, Moundsville, Marshall Co., West Virginia.[12]

+ 83   f   III.   **Elizabeth Jane**[7] **Cowl** was born in Bethany, Brooke Co., West Virginia, on February 22, 1867. She was also known as **Jennie.** Elizabeth Jane died in Glendale, Los Angeles Co., California, on

January 3, 1942. She was buried in Forest Lawn Memorial Park Cemetery, Glendale, Los Angeles Co., California.[47]

+ 84　f　IV.　**Emma Blanche**[7] **Cowl** was born in Putnam, Springfield Twp., Muskingum Co., Ohio, on May 5, 1869. She was also known as **Blanche.** Emma Blanche died in Sharon Twp., Franklin Co., Ohio, on March 2, 1951. She was buried in Sunset Memorial Park Cemetery, Galloway, Franklin Co., Ohio.[48]

+ 85　f　V.　**Nellie Augusta**[7] **Cowl** was born in Putnam, Springfield Twp., Muskingum Co., Ohio, on September 20, 1875. She died in Wheeling, Ohio Co., West Virginia, on October 1, 1968. Nellie Augusta was buried in Greenwood Cemetery, Wheeling, Ohio Co., West Virginia.[24]

+ 86　m　VI.　**Henry**[7] **Cowl** was born in Putnam, Springfield Twp., Muskingum Co., Ohio or LaSalle, LaSalle Twp., LaSalle Co., Illinois, on January 26, 1878. He was also known as **Harry.** Henry died in Wheeling, Ohio Co., West Virginia, on April 9, 1895. He was buried in Peninsula Cemetery, Wheeling, Ohio Co., West Virginia.[26]

+ 87　m　VII.　**Daniel Bird**[7] **Cowl** was born in LaSalle, LaSalle Twp., LaSalle Co., Illinois, on August 21, 1880. He died in Columbus, Franklin Co., Ohio, on January 22, 1960.

+ 88　f　VIII.　**Alice Louise**[7] **Cowl** was born in Wheeling, Ohio Co., West Virginia, on November 28, 1882. She died in Michigan? in 1965.

37. **Robert H.**[6] **Goudy** (*Isaac*[5], *Elizabeth Jane*[4] *Pegan*, *Andrew*[3] *Pegan II*, *Andrew*[2] *Pagan*, *James*[1]) was born on August 5, 1844, in Ohio Co., (West) Virginia. He was the son of Isaac Goudy II (6) and Sarah Ann Stewart. Robert H. died in Wheeling, Ohio Co., West Virginia, on May 16, 1864, at age 19.[25]

Never married.

38. **John William**[6] **Goudy** (*Isaac*[5], *Elizabeth Jane*[4] *Pegan*, *Andrew*[3] *Pegan II*, *Andrew*[2] *Pagan*, *James*[1]) was born on June 30, 1845, in Wheeling, Ohio Co., (West) Virginia. He was the son of Isaac Goudy II (6) and Sarah Ann Stewart. John William died in Wheeling, Ohio Co., West Virginia, on November 9, 1907, at age 62. He was buried in Mount Olivet Cemetery, Wheeling, Ohio Co., West Virginia.[4]

John William married **Melissa Rebecca Baldwin** on March 22, 1866. They had seven children. Melissa Rebecca Baldwin was born in Cameron, Marshall Co., West Virginia, on January 25, 1848. Melissa Rebecca reached age 67 and died in Wheeling, Ohio Co., West Virginia, on June 5, 1915. She was buried in Mount Olivet Cemetery, Wheeling, Ohio Co., West Virginia.[4]

Children of John William Goudy and Melissa Rebecca Baldwin:

+ 89　m　I.　**Edward Elmer**[7] **Goudy** was born in Wheeling, Ohio Co., West Virginia, on February 29, 1868. He died in Elyria, Elyria Twp., Lorain Co., Ohio, on May 21, 1948. Edward Elmer was buried in Ridge Hill Memorial Park Cemetery, Amherst, Amherst Twp., Lorraine Co., Ohio.[49]

+ 90　m　II.　**George C.**[7] **Goudy** was born in Wheeling, Ohio Co., West Virginia, on January 14, 1870. He died in Wheeling, Ohio Co., West Virginia, on August 6, 1910. George C. was buried in Mount Olivet Cemetery, Wheeling, Ohio Co., West Virginia.[4]

+ 91   f   III.   **Infant Daughter[7] Goudy** was born in Wheeling, Ohio Co., West Virginia, on November 18, 1872. She died in Wheeling, Ohio Co., West Virginia, on November 20, 1872.

+ 92   m   IV.   **Arthur Elwood[7] Goudy** was born in Wheeling, Ohio Co., West Virginia, on August 18, 1875. He died in Belmont, Goshen Twp., Belmont Co., Ohio, on February 8, 1964. Arthur Elwood was buried in Mount Olivet Cemetery, Wheeling, Ohio Co., West Virginia.[4]

+ 93   m   V.   **Robert Carl[7] Goudy** was born in Wheeling, Ohio Co., West Virginia, on January 16, 1880. He died in Sistersville, Tyler Co., West Virginia, on October 17, 1958. Robert Carl was buried in Mount Olivet Cemetery, Wheeling, Ohio Co., West Virginia.[4]

+ 94   m   VI.   **Howard Louis[7] Goudy** was born in Wheeling, Ohio Co., West Virginia, on June 9, 1883. He died in Wheeling, Ohio Co., West Virginia, on May 3, 1947. Howard Louis was buried in Mount Olivet Cemetery, Wheeling, Ohio Co., West Virginia.[4]

+ 95   f   VII.   **Minnie[7] Goudy** was born in Wheeling, Ohio Co., West Virginia, on July 7, 1888. She died in Wheeling, Ohio Co., West Virginia, on January 29, 1889.

**39. Emmaliza[6] Goudy** (*Isaac[5], Elizabeth Jane[4] Pegan, Andrew[3] Pegan II, Andrew[2] Pagan, James[1]*) was born on March 30, 1848, in Ohio Co., (West) Virginia. She was the daughter of Isaac Goudy II (6) and Sarah Ann Stewart. Emmaliza died in Ohio Co., West Virginia, on November 26, 1850, at age two.

**40. Wilson Kenny[6] Goudy** (*Isaac[5], Elizabeth Jane[4] Pegan, Andrew[3] Pegan II, Andrew[2] Pagan, James[1]*) was born on September 7, 1851, in Ohio Co., (West) Virginia. He was the son of Isaac Goudy II (6) and Sarah Ann Stewart. Wilson Kenny died in Ohio Co. or Marshall Co., West Virginia, on February 1, 1865, at age 13.

**41. Charles Dawson[6] Goudy** (*Isaac[5], Elizabeth Jane[4] Pegan, Andrew[3] Pegan II, Andrew[2] Pagan, James[1]*) was born on October 19, 1855, in Ohio Co., (West) Virginia. He was the son of Isaac Goudy II (6) and Sarah Ann Stewart. Charles Dawson died in Union Twp., Marshall Co., West Virginia, before 1870.

**42. David Wellington[6] Hill** (*Mary Jane[5] Goudy, Elizabeth Jane[4] Pegan, Andrew[3] Pegan II, Andrew[2] Pagan, James[1]*) was born on June 13, 1841, in Ohio Co., (West) Virginia. He was the son of William Hill and Mary Jane Goudy (7). David Wellington died in Wheeling, Ohio Co., West Virginia, on March 1, 1919, at age 77. He was buried in Peninsula Cemetery, Wheeling, Ohio Co., West Virginia.[26]

He married **Mary Emma Blackburn.** They had five children. Mary Emma Blackburn was born in Steubenville, Cross Creek Twp., Jefferson Co., Ohio, on April 13, 1849. She was also known as **Mamie.** Mary Emma reached age 86 and died in Wheeling, Ohio Co., West Virginia, on March 20, 1936. Mary Emma was buried in Peninsula Cemetery, Wheeling, Ohio Co., West Virginia.[26]

Children of David Wellington Hill and Mary Emma Blackburn:

+ 96   m   I.   **David Wellington[7] Hill II** was born in Wheeling, Ohio Co., West Virginia, on September 12, 1868. He died in Cambridge, Cambridge Twp., Guernsey Co., Ohio, on November 13, 1947. David Wellington was buried in Greenwood Cemetery, Bellaire, Pultney Twp., Belmont Co., Ohio.[50]

+ 97   f   II.   **Mary Emma[7] Hill** was born in Wheeling, Ohio Co., West Virginia, on October 18, 1870. She died in Wheeling, Ohio Co., West Virginia, on August 21, 1910.

Mary Emma was buried in Greenwood Cemetery, Wheeling, Ohio Co., West Virginia.[24]

+ 98 m III. **George Wellington**[7] **Hill** was born in Wheeling, Ohio Co., West Virginia, on May 24, 1873. He died in Wheeling, Ohio Co., West Virginia, on January 10, 1953. George Wellington was buried in Mount Zion Cemetery, Wheeling, Ohio Co., West Virginia.[28]

+ 99 f IV. **Beatrice Matilda**[7] **Hill** was born in Wheeling, Ohio Co., West Virginia, on May 29, 1975. She died after March 4, 1919.

+ 100 V. **Child**[7] **Hill** was born in Ohio Co., West Virginia, between 1868 and 1900. He or she died in Ohio Co., West Virginia, before 1900.

**43. William Hamilton**[6] **Hill II** (*Mary Jane*[5] *Goudy, Elizabeth Jane*[4] *Pegan, Andrew*[3] *Pegan II, Andrew*[2] *Pagan, James*[1]) was born on July 2, 1842, in McConnellsville, Morgan Twp., Morgan Co., Ohio. He was also known as **Hamilton.** He was the son of William Hill and Mary Jane Goudy (7). William Hamilton died in Wheeling, Ohio Co., West Virginia, on November 22, 1912, at age 70. He was buried in Stone Church Cemetery, Elm Grove, Ohio Co., West Virginia.[26]

William Hamilton married **Virginia Sarah Sage** on January 9, 1872, in Ohio Co., West Virginia. They had four children. Virginia Sarah Sage was born in Madison, Madison Twp., Jefferson Co., Indiana, in 1844. Virginia Sarah reached age 54 and died in Wheeling, Ohio Co., West Virginia, in 1898. She was buried in Stone Church Cemetery, Elm Grove, Ohio Co., West Virginia.[26]

Children of William Hamilton Hill and Virginia Sarah Sage:

+ 101 m I. **Charles L.**[7] **Hill** was born in Wheeling, Ohio Co., West Virginia, on June 10, 1873. He died

in Wheeling, Ohio Co., West Virginia, on July 15, 1938. Charles L. was buried in Stone Church Cemetery, Elm Grove, Ohio Co., West Virginia.[26]

+ 102 m II. **Howard Hamilton**[7] **Hill** was born in Wheeling, Ohio Co., West Virginia, on May 26, 1876. He died in Steubenville, Cross Creek Twp., Jefferson Co., Ohio, on February 27, 1946. Howard Hamilton was buried in Union Cemetery, Steubenville, Cross Creek Twp., Jefferson Co., Ohio.

+ 103 f III. **Ulina**[7] **Hill** was born in Wheeling, Ohio Co., West Virginia, in 1880.

+ 104 m IV. **Russell Sage**[7] **Hill** was born in Elm Grove, Ohio Co., West Virginia, on April 3, 1884. He died in New Martinsville, Wetzel Co., West Virginia, on September 26, 1953.

**44. John W.**[6] **Hill** (*Mary Jane*[5] *Goudy, Elizabeth Jane*[4] *Pegan, Andrew*[3] *Pegan II, Andrew*[2] *Pagan, James*[1]) was born on July 22, 1846, in McConnellsville, Morgan Twp., Morgan Co., Ohio. He was the son of William Hill and Mary Jane Goudy (7). John W. died in Wheeling, Ohio Co., West Virginia, on January 7, 1893, at age 46. He was buried in Peninsula Cemetery, Wheeling, Ohio Co., West Virginia.[26]

He married **Isabella Ellen McGill.** They had two children. Isabella Ellen McGill was born in Ohio Co., (West) Virginia, on July 18, 1845. She was also known as **Ella.** Isabella Ellen reached age 63 and died in Union Twp., Marshall Co., West Virginia? on August 23, 1908. She was buried in Peninsula Cemetery, Wheeling, Ohio Co., West Virginia.[26]

Children of John W. Hill and Isabella Ellen McGill:

+ 105 m I. **Charles Millard**[7] **Hill** was born in Wheeling, Ohio Co., West Virginia, on May 6, 1867. He died in Liberty, Ohio Co., West Virginia, on June 7, 1932. Charles Millard was buried in Greenwood Cemetery, Wheeling, Ohio Co., West Virginia.[24]

+ 106  f   II.   **Ella Allen**[7] **Hill** was born in Wheeling, Ohio Co., West Virginia, on September 26, 1869. She died in Steubenville, Cross Creek Twp., Jefferson Co., Ohio, on February 5, 1949. Ella Allen was buried in Union Cemetery, Steubenville, Cross Creek Twp., Jefferson Co., Ohio.[16]

**45. Elizabeth Jane**[6] **Hill** (*Mary Jane*[5] *Goudy, Elizabeth Jane*[4] *Pegan, Andrew*[3] *Pegan II, Andrew*[2] *Pagan, James*[1]) was born in November 1849 in McConnellsville, Morgan Twp., Morgan Co., Ohio. She was also known as **Jennie.** She was the daughter of William Hill and Mary Jane Goudy (7). Elizabeth Jane died in a facility in Weston, Lewis Co., West Virginia, on November 24, 1928, at age 79. She was buried in Mount Zion Cemetery, Wheeling, Ohio Co., West Virginia.[28]

Elizabeth Jane married **Arthur William Fox** on August 11, 1866, in Ohio Co., West Virginia. They had seven children. Arthur William Fox was born in Ireland on September 24, 1837. Arthur William reached age 78 and died in Wheeling, Ohio Co., West Virginia, on August 19, 1916. He was buried in Mount Zion Cemetery, Wheeling, Ohio Co., West Virginia.[28]

Children of Elizabeth Jane Hill and Arthur William Fox:

+ 107  m  I.    **Edward**[7] **Fox** was born in Hanging Rock Twp., Lawrence Co., Ohio, on April 21, 1868. He died in Wheeling, Ohio Co., West Virginia, on February 21, 1909. Edward was buried in Mount Zion Cemetery, Wheeling, Ohio Co., West Virginia.[28]

+ 108  f   II.   **Minnie Blanche**[7] **Fox** was born in Washington Co., Ohio, on August 2, 1871. She died in Buffalo, Erie Co., New York? about 1945. She was probably buried in Mt. Zion Cemetery, Wheeling, Ohio Co., West Virginia.

+ 109  f   III.  **Alice**[7] **Fox** was born in Washington Co., Ohio, on October 23, 1873. She died in Wheeling, Ohio Co., West Virginia, on August 23,1900. She was probably buried in Mt. Zion Cemetery, Wheeling, Ohio Co., West Virginia.

+ 110  f   IV.   **Stella**[7] **Fox** was born in Upper Ashland, Boyd Co., Kentucky, in March 1877. She died in Wheeling, Ohio Co., West Virginia, on April 1, 1898. She was probably buried in Mt. Zion Cemetery, Wheeling, Ohio Co., West Virginia

+ 111  m  V.    **Robert Arthur**[7] **Fox** was born in Wheeling, Ohio Co., West Virginia, on June 8, 1881. He died in Wheeling, Ohio Co., West Virginia, on March 8, 1922.

+ 112  f   VI.   **Jennie**[7] **Fox** was born in Wheeling, Ohio Co., West Virginia, on June 2, 1891. She died in Wheeling, Ohio Co., West Virginia, on January 2, 1935.

+ 113      VII.  **Ida**[7] **Fox** was born between 1866 and 1880. She died between 1866 and 1880.

**46. Robert E.**[6] **Hill** (*Mary Jane*[5] *Goudy, Elizabeth Jane*[4] *Pegan, Andrew*[3] *Pegan II, Andrew*[2] *Pagan, James*[1]) was born in 1850 in Wheeling, Ohio Co., (West) Virginia. He was the son of William Hill and Mary Jane Goudy (7). Robert E. died in Wheeling, Ohio Co., West Virginia, in 1855 at age five.

**47. Emma**[6] **Hill** (*Mary Jane*[5] *Goudy, Elizabeth Jane*[4] *Pegan, Andrew*[3] *Pegan II, Andrew*[2] *Pagan, James*[1]) was born in 1854 in Wheeling, Ohio Co., (West) Virginia. She was the daughter of William Hill and Mary Jane Goudy (7). Emma died after 1870.

# 7th Generation

**48. James Frank⁷ Goudy** (*James Hayson⁶, John⁵, Elizabeth Jane⁴ Pegan, Andrew³ Pegan II, Andrew² Pagan, James¹*) was born on August 1, 1864, in Wheeling, Ohio Co., West Virginia.[29] He was the son of James Hayson Goudy (10) and Samantha Faunce. James Frank died in Chicago, Cook Co., Illinois, on October 24, 1929, at age 65.[31, 32] He was buried in Graceland Cemetery, Chicago, Cook Co., Illinois.[32]

Childless.

James Frank married **Mary Jane Hudson** on April 20, 1891, in Cook Co., Illinois.[51] Mary Jane Hudson was born in Chicago, Cook Co., Illinois, in March 1871. She was also known as **Mamie.** Mary Jane reached age 86 and died in Chicago, Cook Co., Illinois, on August 14, 1957. [52] She was buried in Graceland Cemetery, Chicago, Cook Co., Illinois. [51] Mary Jane Hudson Goudy is listed as Mary Jane Goudy on her husband's, James Frank Goudy's, death certificate in 1929, but in the census records she is enumerated as Mamie/Mayme.

**49. Effie⁷ Goudy** (*William M.⁶, John⁵, Elizabeth Jane⁴ Pegan, Andrew³ Pegan II, Andrew² Pagan, James¹*) was born on May 5, 1870, in West Virginia.[7] She was the daughter of William M. Goudy (11) and Ann Rebecca Jones. Effie died in Marshall Co., West Virginia, on February 2, 1936, at age 65.[1, 33] She was buried in Wood Hill Cemetery, Marshall Co., West Virginia.[1]

Never married.

**50. Harry Homer⁷ Goudy** (*William M.⁶, John⁵, Elizabeth Jane⁴ Pegan, Andrew³ Pegan II, Andrew² Pagan, James¹*) was born on September 21, 1873, in Washington Twp., Marshall Co., West Virginia.[34] He was the son of William M. Goudy (11) and Ann Rebecca Jones. Harry Homer died in Fairmont, Marion Co., West Virginia, on November 4, 1957, at age 84.[34] He was buried in Woodlawn Cemetery, Fairmont, Marion Co., West Virginia.[34, 35]

Harry Homer married **Minnie Stillwill** on January 1, 1903, in Marshall Co., West Virginia.[53] They divorced before 1920. They had one daughter. Minnie Stillwill was born in Marshall Co., West Virginia? in 1878. She reached age 49 and died in Glendale, Marshall Co., West Virginia, on November 14, 1927.[54]

Harry Homer Goudy married **Esther Elizabeth Manley** on February 28, 1920, in Marion Co., West Virginia. Esther Elizabeth Manley was born in Marion Co., West Virginia, on March 26, 1880. Esther Elizabeth reached age 74 and died in Fairmont, Marion Co., West Virginia, on December 31, 1954. She was buried in Woodlawn Cemetery, Fairmont, Marion Co., West Virginia.[35]

Daughter of Harry Homer Goudy and Minnie Stillwill:

+ 114 f I. **Helen⁸ Goudy** was born in Moundsville, Marshall Co., West Virginia, on May 4, 1904.[55] She died in Moundsville, Marshall Co., West Virginia, on January 24, 1980. Helen was buried in Limestone Cemetery, Limestone, Marshall Co., West Virginia.[56]

**51. Edmund W.⁷ Goudy** (*William M.⁶, John⁵, Elizabeth Jane⁴ Pegan, Andrew³ Pegan II, Andrew² Pagan, James¹*) was born on February 21, 1877, in Washington Twp., Marshall Co., West Virginia.[8] He was the son of William M. Goudy (11) and Ann Rebecca Jones. Edmund W. died in Washington Twp., Marshall Co., West Virginia, on May 20, 1877.[36] Edmund Goudy is probably buried in Wood Hill Cemetery, Marshall Co., West Virginia.

**52. Mary V.⁷ Blake** (*Mary E.⁶ Goudy, John⁵, Elizabeth Jane⁴ Pegan, Andrew³ Pegan II, Andrew² Pagan, James¹*) was born in 1878 in Wheeling, Ohio Co., West Virginia. She was the daughter of Robert Harrison Blake and Mary E. Goudy (12). Mary V. died after 1880.

**53. Donald Reed⁷ Goudy** (*Charles Thoburn⁶, John⁵, Elizabeth Jane⁴ Pegan, Andrew³ Pegan II, Andrew² Pagan, James¹*) was born on April 1, 1891, in Union Twp., Marshall Co., West Virginia. He was the son of Charles Thoburn Goudy (14) and Estella Elizabeth Kemple. Donald Reed died in Wheeling, Ohio Co., West Virginia, on August 13, 1917, at age 26.[10] He was buried in Allen Grove Cemetery, Sherrard, Union Twp., Marshall Co., West Virginia.[10]

Never married.

**54. Mary A.[7] Goudy** (*Charles Thoburn[6], John[5], Elizabeth Jane[4] Pegan, Andrew[3] Pegan II, Andrew[2] Pagan, James[1]*) was born on September 4, 1895, in Union Twp., Marshall Co., West Virginia.[37] She was the daughter of Charles Thoburn Goudy (14) and Estella Elizabeth Kemple. Mary A. lived in 1969 in Sherrard, Union Twp., Marshall Co., West Virginia. She died in a hospital in Wheeling, Ohio Co., West Virginia, on July 1, 1969, at age 73.[37] Mary A. was buried in Greenwood Cemetery, Wheeling, Ohio Co., West Virginia.[24]

Childless.

Mary A. married **Robert White Reilly** on June 4, 1918, in Marshall Co., West Virginia. Robert White Reilly was born in Marshall Co., West Virginia, on December 21, 1890. Robert White reached age 30 and died in Benwood, Marshall Co., West Virginia, on April 21, 1921. He was buried in Allen Grove Cemetery, Sherrard, Union Twp., Marshall Co., West Virginia.[10]

Mary A. Goudy Reilly married **Charles Daly Bumgardner** on April 27, 1928, in Marshall Co., West Virginia. Charles Daly Bumgardner was born in Wheeling, Ohio Co., West Virginia, on February 15, 1896.[57] Charles Daly lived in 1958 in Sherrard, Union Twp., Marshall Co., West Virginia. He reached age 62 and died in a hospital in Wheeling, Ohio Co., West Virginia, on December 29, 1958. Charles Daly was buried in Greenwood Cemetery, Wheeling, Ohio Co., West Virginia.[24]

**55. Lewis K.[7] Thompson** (*Nancy J.[6] Goudy, Andrew[5], Elizabeth Jane[4] Pegan, Andrew[3] Pegan II, Andrew[2] Pagan, James[1]*) was born on December 12, 1851, in Tippecanoe, Washington Twp., Harrison Co., Ohio. He was the son of Samuel R. Thompson and Nancy J. Goudy (15). Lewis K. died in Uhrichsville, Mill Twp., Tuscarawas Co., Ohio, on January 16, 1929, at age 77.

He married **Rebecca A. Valentine.** They had one son. Rebecca A. Valentine was born in Rush Twp., Tuscarawas Co., Ohio, on April 14, 1856. Rebecca A. reached age 42 and died in Uhrichsville, Mill Twp., Tuscarawas Co., Ohio, on February 24, 1899.

Lewis K. Thompson married **Ida Harriet Evans.** They had one son. Ida Harriet Evans was born in Norwalk, Norwalk Twp., Huron Co., Ohio, in 1878. She was also known as **Hattie.** Ida Harriet reached age 45 and died in Akron, Summit Co., Ohio, on April 19, 1923.

Son of Lewis K. Thompson and Rebecca A. Valentine:

+ 115 m I. **Lewis or Louis MacAfee[8] Thompson II** was born in Cleveland, Cuyahoga Co., Ohio, on February 22, 1889. He died in O'Hara, Allegheny Co., Pennsylvania, on February 3, 1941.

Son of Lewis K. Thompson and Ida Harriet Evans:

+ 116 m I. **Samuel[8] Thompson** was born in Uhrichsville, Mill Twp., Tuscarawas Co., Ohio, on April 12, 1904. He died after 1930 in Contra Costa Co., California.

**56. Ella Nancy[7] Thompson** (*Nancy J.[6] Goudy, Andrew[5], Elizabeth Jane[4] Pegan, Andrew[3] Pegan II, Andrew[2] Pagan, James[1]*) was born on February 28, 1855, in Tippecanoe, Washington Twp., Harrison Co., Ohio. She was the daughter of Samuel R. Thompson and Nancy J. Goudy (15). Ella Nancy died in Uhrichsville, Mill Twp., Tuscarawas Co., Ohio, on February 23, 1942, at age 86. She was buried in Union Cemetery, Uhrichsville, Mill Twp., Tuscarawas Co., Ohio.[13]

She married **William Galbreath.** They had two children. William Galbreath was born in Oxford Twp., Guernsey Co., Ohio, in 1850. William reached age 35 and died in Fairview Valley Twp., Guernsey Co., Ohio, on February 20, 1885.

Children of Ella Nancy Thompson and William Galbreath:

+ 117 m I. **James Howard⁸ Galbreath** was born in Fairview Valley Twp., Guernsey Co., Ohio, on November 1, 1874. He was also known as **Howard.** James Howard died in Uhrichsville, Mill Twp., Tuscarawas Co., Ohio, on June 7, 1961. He was buried in Evergreen Burial Park, New Philadelphia, Tuscarawas Co., Ohio.[58]

+ 118 f II. **Clara E.⁸ Galbreath** was born in Fairview Valley Twp., Guernsey Co., Ohio, on June 30, 1880. She died in Uhrichsville, Mill Twp., Tuscarawas Co., Ohio, on September 14, 1906. Clara E. was buried in Union Cemetery, Uhrichsville, Mill Twp., Tuscarawas Co., Ohio.[13]

**57. Sarah Virginia⁷ Thompson** (*Nancy J.⁶ Goudy, Andrew⁵, Elizabeth Jane⁴ Pegan, Andrew³ Pegan II, Andrew² Pagan, James¹*) was born on June 21, 1856, in Tippecanoe, Washington Twp., Harrison Co., Ohio. She was the daughter of Samuel R. Thompson and Nancy J. Goudy (15). Sarah Virginia died in Mansfield, Madison Twp., Richland Co., Ohio, on September 7, 1945, at age 89. She was buried in Union Cemetery, Uhrichsville, Mill Twp., Tuscarawas Co., Ohio.[13]

Sarah Virginia married **John Pryor Cary** on March 4, 1881. They had two children. John Pryor Cary was born in Zanesville, Muskingham Co., Ohio, in February 1840. John Pryor reached age 61 and died in Uhrichsville, Mill Twp., Tuscarawas Co., Ohio, on June 4, 1901.

Sarah Virginia Thompson Cary married **Unknown Lee** before 1920.

Sarah Virginia Thompson Cary Lee married **Unknown Baxter** after 1920 in California? They may have divorced. Unknown Baxter died before 1930.

Sarah Virginia Thompson Cary Lee Baxter died under the name of Sarah Lee.

Children of Sarah Virginia Thompson and John Pryor Cary:

+ 119 f I. **Jessie A.⁸ Cary** was born in Uhrichsville, Mill Twp., Tuscarawas Co., Ohio, on September 14, 1883. She died in Sacramento, Sacramento Co., California, on March 25, 1922.

+ 120 m II. **Charles Stewart⁸ Cary** was born in Dennison, Mill Twp., Tuscarawas Co., Ohio, on April 14, 1887. He died in a hospital in Canton, Stark Co., Ohio, on February 1, 1974. Charles Stewart was buried in Saint Joseph Cemetery, Massillon, Perry Twp., Stark Co., Ohio.[59]

**58. Mary E.⁷ Thompson** (*Nancy J.⁶ Goudy, Andrew⁵, Elizabeth Jane⁴ Pegan, Andrew³ Pegan II, Andrew² Pagan, James¹*) was born on March 15, 1860, in Uhrichsville, Mill Twp., Tuscarawas Co., Ohio. She was the daughter of Samuel R. Thompson and Nancy J. Goudy (15). Mary E. died in Uhrichsville, Mill Twp., Tuscarawas Co., Ohio, on May 15, 1925, at age 65. She was buried in Union Cemetery, Uhrichsville, Mill Twp., Tuscarawas Co., Ohio.[13]

Mary E. married **Harry Artland Bovey** on March 25, 1880, in Tuscarawas Co., Ohio. They had two sons. Harry Artland Bovey was born in Uhrichsville, Mill Twp., Tuscarawas Co., Ohio, on March 25, 1860. Harry Artland reached age 74 and died in Uhrichsville, Mill Twp., Tuscarawas Co., Ohio, on March 27, 1934. He was buried in Union Cemetery, Uhrichsville, Mill Twp., Tuscarawas Co., Ohio.[13]

Sons of Mary E. Thompson and Harry Artland Bovey:

+ 121 m I. **Artland Robinson⁸ Bovey** was born in Conneaut, Conneaut Twp., Ashtabula Co., Ohio, on March 1, 1884. He died in Queens, Queens Co., New York? in August.

+ 122 m II. **Son⁸ Bovey** was born in Uhrichsville, Mill Twp., Tuscarawas Co., Ohio, on October 5, 1891. He died in Uhrichsville, Mill Twp., Tuscarawas Co., Ohio, on October 5, 1891.

59. **Harry⁷ Thompson** (*Nancy J.⁶ Goudy, Andrew⁵, Elizabeth Jane⁴ Pegan, Andrew³ Pegan II, Andrew² Pagan, James¹*) was born on November 21, 1867, in Uhrichsville, Mill Twp., Tuscarawas Co., Ohio. He was the son of Samuel R. Thompson and Nancy J. Goudy (15). Harry died in a facility in Massillon, Perry Twp., Stark Co., Ohio, on March 16, 1937, at age 69. He was buried in Union Cemetery, Uhrichsville, Mill Twp., Tuscarawas Co., Ohio.

Never married.

Harry Thompson lived at the Massillon State Hospital from before 1900 until he died.

60. **Robert⁷ Thompson** (*Nancy J.⁶ Goudy, Andrew⁵, Elizabeth Jane⁴ Pegan, Andrew³ Pegan II, Andrew² Pagan, James¹*) was born on September 10, 1870, in Uhrichsville, Mill Twp., Tuscarawas Co., Ohio. He was the son of Samuel R. Thompson and Nancy J. Goudy (15). Robert lived in 1963 in McMechen, Union Dist., Marshall Co., West Virginia. Robert died in a facility in Cameron, Marshall Co., West Virginia, on August 22, 1963, at age 92. He was buried in McMechen Cemetery, McMechen, Union Dist., Marshall Co., West Virginia.[38]

Robert married **Florence Elizabeth White** in 1900. They had one daughter. Florence Elizabeth White was born in Piedmont, Mineral Co., West Virginia, on October 12, 1870. Florence Elizabeth reached age 74 and died in McMechen, Union Dist., Marshall Co., West Virginia, on July 25, 1945. She was buried in McMechen Cemetery, McMechen, Union Dist., Marshall Co., West Virginia.[38]

Daughter of Robert Thompson and Florence Elizabeth White:

+ 123 f I. **Ellamae⁸ Thompson** was born in McMechen, Union Dist., Marshall Co., West Virginia, on November 2, 1905. She died in Uhrichsville, Mill Twp., Tuscarawas Co., Ohio? on April 9, 1954. Ellamae was buried in McMechen Cemetery, Union Dist., Marshall Co., West Virginia.[38].

61. **Laura Bell⁷ Goudy** (*Isaac M.⁶, Andrew⁵, Elizabeth Jane⁴ Pegan, Andrew³ Pegan II, Andrew² Pagan, James¹*) was born on January 25, 1857, in Burlington, Burlington Twp., Des Moines Co., Iowa. She was the daughter of Isaac M. Goudy (16) and Margaret Brautner or Broughtner. Laura Bell died in Rush Twp., Tuscarawas Co., Ohio, on December 29, 1904, at age 47. She was buried in Dutch Valley Cemetery, Rush Twp., Tuscarawas Co., Ohio.[17]

Laura Bell married **Benjamin Varner** on February 4, 1875, in Belmont Co., Ohio. They had two children. Benjamin Varner was born in Rush Twp., Tuscarawas Co., Ohio, on August 2, 1849. Benjamin lived in 1880 in Rush Twp., Tuscarawas Co., Ohio. He also resided in 1890 in Tuscarawas Co., Ohio. Benjamin reached age 83 and died in Mill Twp., Tuscarawas Co., Ohio, on February 13, 1933. He was buried in Dutch Valley Cemetery, Rush Twp., Tuscarawas Co., Ohio.[17]

Children of Laura Bell Goudy and Benjamin Varner:

+ 124 f I. **Nettie A.⁸ Varner** was born in Rush Twp., Tuscarawas Co., Ohio, on November 29, 1875. She died in Uhrichsville, Mill Twp., Tuscarawas Co., Ohio, on March 25, 1903. Nettie A. was buried in Dutch Valley Cemetery, Rush Twp., Tuscarawas Co., Ohio.[17]

+ 125 m II. **Charles W.⁸ Varner** was born in Rush Twp., Tuscarawas Co., Ohio, on August 11, 1877. He died in Rush Twp., Tuscarawas Co., Ohio, on August 20, 1894. Charles W. was buried in Dutch Valley Cemetery, Rush Twp., Tuscarawas Co., Ohio.[17]

**62. Sarah[7] Goudy** (*Isaac M.[6], Andrew[5], Elizabeth Jane[4] Pegan, Andrew[3] Pegan II, Andrew[2] Pagan, James[1]*) was born on January 5, 1859, in Burlington, Burlington Twp., Des Moines Co., Iowa. She was the daughter of Isaac M. Goudy (16) and Margaret Brautner or Broughtner. Sarah died in Martins Ferry, Pease Twp., Belmont Co., Ohio, on October 16, 1933, at age 74. She was buried in Riverview Cemetery, Martins Ferry, Pease Twp., Belmont Co., Ohio.[14]

Sarah married **Frank Neal Beazle** on April 13, 1876, in Belmont Co., Ohio. They had five children. Frank Neal Beazle was born in Pease Twp., Belmont Co., Ohio, on June 7, 1852. Frank Neal reached age 82 and died in Martins Ferry, Pease Twp., Belmont Co., Ohio, on August 1, 1934. He was buried in Riverview Cemetery, Martins Ferry, Pease Twp., Belmont Co., Ohio.[14]

Children of Sarah Goudy and Frank Neal Beazle:

+ 126 m I. **Guy Andrew[8] Beazle** was born in Pease Twp., Belmont Co., Ohio, on November 5, 1876. He died in Martins Ferry, Pease Twp., Belmont Co., Ohio, on June 10, 1947. Guy Andrew was buried in Riverview Cemetery, Martins Ferry, Pease Twp., Belmont Co., Ohio.[14]

+ 127 f II. **Bessie[8] Beazle** was born in Pease Twp., Belmont Co., Ohio, in 1879. She died in Pease Twp., Belmont Co., Ohio, between 1880 and 1881.

+ 128 f III. **May[8] Beazle** was born in Pittsburgh, Allegheny Co., Pennsylvania, in 1881. She died in Pittsburgh, Allegheny Co., Pennsylvania, on October 26, 1882.

+ 129 f IV. **Margaret[8] Beazle** was born in Pittsburgh, Allegheny Co., Pennsylvania, on April 12, 1883. She died in Martins Ferry, Pease Twp. Belmont Co., Ohio, on January 16, 1948. Margaret was buried in Riverview Cemetery, Martins Ferry, Pease Twp., Belmont Co., Ohio?

+ 130 f V. **Clara Janette[8] Beazle** was born in Martins Ferry, Pease Twp., Belmont Co., Ohio, on February 6, 1886. She died in a hospital in Canton, Stark Co., Ohio, on December 28, 1974. Clara Janette was buried in Riverview Cemetery, Martins Ferry, Pease Twp., Belmont Co., Ohio??

**63. John W. Huston[7] Goudy II** (*John W. Samuel[6], Andrew[5], Elizabeth Jane[4] Pegan, Andrew[3] Pegan II, Andrew[2] Pagan, James[1]*) was born in November 1858 in Newcomerstown, Oxford Twp., Tuscarawas Co., Ohio. He was the son of John W. Samuel Goudy (18) and Ann Eliza Huston. John W. Huston lived between 1900 and 1920 in Moorefield Twp., Clark Co., Ohio. He died in Goshen Twp., Tuscarawas Co., Ohio, on April 10, 1938, at age 79. John W. Huston was buried in East State Street Cemetery, Newcomerstown, Oxford Twp., Tuscarawas Co., Ohio.[15]

Childless.

John W. Huston married **Emma J. Fox** in 1881. They divorced. Emma J. Fox was born in Moorefield Twp., Clark Co., Ohio, on April 6, 1860. She reached age 83 and died in Springfield, Springfield Twp., Clark Co., Ohio, on May 2, 1943. Emma J. was buried in Ferncliff Cemetery, Springfield, Springfield Twp., Clark Co., Ohio.[60]

**64. Rollin Andrew[7] Goudy** (*John W. Samuel[6], Andrew[5], Elizabeth Jane[4] Pegan, Andrew[3] Pegan II, Andrew[2] Pagan, James[1]*) was born on October 30, 1863, in Newcomerstown, Oxford Twp., Tuscarawas Co., Ohio. He was the son of John W. Samuel Goudy (18) and Ann Eliza Huston. Rollin Andrew died in Newcomerstown, Oxford Twp., Tuscarawas Co., Ohio, on April 26, 1924, at age 60. He was buried in East State Street Cemetery, Newcomerstown, Oxford Twp., Tuscarawas Co., Ohio.[15]

Childless.

He married **Melvena Schneider.** Melvena Schneider was born in Oxford Twp., Tuscarawas Co., Ohio, in October 1879. Melvena reached age 76 and died in Newcomerstown, Oxford Twp., Tuscarawas Co., Ohio? on January 18, 1956. She was buried in East State Street Cemetery, Newcomerstown, Oxford Twp., Tuscarawas Co., Ohio.[15]

She remarried and died under the name Melvena Sparklin.

65. **Joseph A.**[7] **Wardell** (*Elizabeth Sophronia*[6] *Goudy, Andrew*[5]*, Elizabeth Jane*[4] *Pegan, Andrew*[3] *Pegan II, Andrew*[2] *Pagan, James*[1]) was born on February 4, 1871, in Rush Twp., Tuscarawas Co., Ohio. He was the son of Milton F. Wardell and Elizabeth Sophronia Goudy (20). Joseph A. died in Uhrichsville, Mill Twp., Tuscarawas Co., Ohio, on April 6, 1952, at age 81. He was buried in Gnadenhutten-Clay Union Cemetery, Clay Twp., Tuscarawas Co., Ohio.[39]

Joseph A. married **Elvina Ella Wolf** on November 10, 1894, in Tuscarawas Co., Ohio. They had two daughters. Elvina Ella Wolf was born in Warwick Twp., Tuscarawas Co., Ohio, on July 6, 1874. She was also known as **Ella.** Elvina Ella reached age 93 and died in Uhrichsville, Mill Twp., Tuscarawas Co., Ohio, on May 22, 1968. She was buried in Gnadenhutten-Clay Union Cemetery, Clay Twp., Tuscarawas Co., Ohio.[39]

Elvina Ella Wolf always used her middle name as her preferred name.

Daughters of Joseph A. Wardell and Elvina Ella Wolf:

+ 131 f I. **Mabel Estella**[8] **Wardell** was born in Mill Twp., Tuscarawas Co., Ohio, on June 9, 1895. She died in Dover, Dover Twp., Tuscarawas Co., Ohio, on January 3, 1992. Mabel Estella was buried in Gnadenhutten-Clay Union Cemetery, Clay Twp., Tuscarawas Co., Ohio.[39]

+ 132 f II. **Gladys Velma**[8] **Wardell** was born in Mill Twp., Tuscarawas Co., Ohio, on September 3, 1901. She died in Tuscarawas, Warwick Twp.,

Tuscarawas Co., Ohio, on December 15, 1975.

66. **John Wesley**[7] **Wardell** (*Elizabeth Sophronia*[6] *Goudy, Andrew*[5]*, Elizabeth Jane*[4] *Pegan, Andrew*[3] *Pegan II, Andrew*[2] *Pagan, James*[1]) was born on August 1, 1873, in Rush Twp., Tuscarawas Co., Ohio. He was the son of Milton F. Wardell and Elizabeth Sophronia Goudy (20). John Wesley died in Los Angeles, Los Angeles Co., California, on December 7, 1951.

Seems to have never married.

67. **Minnie Etta**[7] **Wardell** (*Elizabeth Sophronia*[6] *Goudy, Andrew*[5]*, Elizabeth Jane*[4] *Pegan, Andrew*[3] *Pegan II, Andrew*[2] *Pagan, James*[1]) was born on January 10, 1877, in Rush Twp., Tuscarawas Co., Ohio. She was the daughter of Milton F. Wardell and Elizabeth Sophronia Goudy (20). Minnie Etta died in South Gate, Los Angeles Co., California, on May 18, 1957.

Minnie Etta married **Simon Newton Toppin II** on August 2, 1892, in Tuscarawas Co., Ohio. They divorced before December 1893. Simon Newton Toppin II was born in Rush Twp., Tuscarawas Co., Ohio, on March 24, 1870. He was also known as **Newton.** Simon Newton reached age 82 and died in Rush Twp., Tuscarawas Co., Ohio, on February 23, 1953.

After her divorce, Minnie reclaimed her maiden name.

Minnie E. Wardell (Toppin) married **Charles H. Huff** on December 23, 1893, in Tuscarawas Co., Ohio. They divorced before 1915. They had two daughters. Charles H. Huff was born in Ohio in July 1863. He died after 1915.

Minnie Etta Wardell Toppin Huff married **Clyde Eugene Marshall** on July 28, 1915, in Cuyahoga Co., Ohio. Clyde Eugene Marshall was born in Uhrichsville, Mill Twp., Tuscarawas Co., Ohio, on August 13, 1885. Clyde Eugene reached age 65 and died in South Gate, Los Angeles Co., California, on December 25, 1950

Daughters of Minnie Etta Wardell and Charles H. Huff:

+ 133 f I. **Mildred Opal⁸ Huff** was born in Mill Twp., Tuscarawas Co., Ohio, on April 2, 1894. She died in Ramona, San Diego Co., California, on February 19, 1986.

+ 134 f II. **Beatrice LaVonne⁸ Huff** was born in Mill Twp., Tuscarawas Co., Ohio, on June 9, 1896. She died in South Gate, Los Angeles Co., California, on October 18, 1978.

**68. Gertrude Nan⁷ Wardell** (*Elizabeth Sophronia⁶ Goudy, Andrew⁵, Elizabeth Jane⁴ Pegan, Andrew³ Pegan II, Andrew² Pagan, James¹*) was born on October 15, 1879, in Rush Twp., Tuscarawas Co., Ohio. She was also known as **Nannie.** She was the daughter of Milton F. Wardell and Elizabeth Sophronia Goudy (20). Gertrude Nan died in Los Angeles, Los Angeles Co., California, on November 5, 1965, at age 86.

Childless.

Gertrude Nan Wardell Huff Gore Stein died under the name Gertrude Nan Huff.

Gertrude Nan married **Jesse Lawrence Huff** on August 1, 1896, in Tuscarawas Co., Ohio. They divorced before 1913. Jesse Lawrence Huff was born in Lafferty, Union Twp., Belmont Co., Ohio, on August 17, 1872. Jesse Lawrence reached age 87 and died in Uhrichsville, Mill Twp., Tuscarawas Co., Ohio, on January 4, 1960.

Gertrude Nan Wardell Huff married **Edward K. Gore** on December 29, 1913. They divorced. Edward K. Gore was born in Gallitzin Twp., Cambria Co., Pennsylvania, on September 19, 1883. He was also known as Eddie. Edward K. reached age 81 and died in Parma, Cuyahoga Co., Ohio, on August 14, 1965. He was buried in West Park Cemetery, Cleveland, Cuyahoga Co., Ohio.[61]

Gertrude Nan Wardell Huff Gore married **Samuel Stein** on April 29, 1921. They divorced. Samuel Stein was born in New York on March 15, 1886. He

died in Los Angeles, Los Angeles Co., California? after 1940.

**69. Andrew W.⁷ Goudy** (*William A.⁶, Andrew⁵, Elizabeth Jane⁴ Pegan, Andrew³ Pegan II, Andrew² Pagan, James¹*) was born on January 10, 1869, in Bridgeport Twp., Belmont Co., Ohio. He was the son of William A. Goudy (21) and Sophia Geller. Andrew W. died in Wheeling, Ohio Co., West Virginia, on February 8, 1905, at age 36. He was buried in Linwood Cemetery, Blaine, Pease Twp., Belmont Co., Ohio.[18]

Andrew W. married **Huldah Annie Pietz** on June 11, 1894, in Belmont Co., Ohio. They had two children. Huldah Annie Pietz was born in Wheeling, Ohio Co., West Virginia, on June 26, 1871. Huldah Annie reached age 74 and died in Weston, Lewis Co., West Virginia, on April 19, 1946.

Children of Andrew W. Goudy and Huldah Annie Pietz:

+ 135 f I. **Ada⁸ Goudy** was born in Bridgeport, Bellaire Twp., Belmont Co., Ohio, on August 14, 1894. She died in Bridgeport, Bellaire Twp., Belmont Co., Ohio, on September 1, 1894.

+ 136 m II. **Edwin Andrew⁸ Goudy** was born in Bridgeport, Bellaire Twp., Belmont Co., Ohio, on April 27, 1899. He died in Triadelphia, Ohio Co., West Virginia, on October 27, 1987. Edwin Andrew was buried in West Alexander Cemetery, West Alexander, Donegal Twp., Washington Co., Pennsylvania.[62]

**70. Maud⁷ Goudy** (*William A.⁶, Andrew⁵, Elizabeth Jane⁴ Pegan, Andrew³ Pegan II, Andrew² Pagan, James¹*) was born on August 11, 1879, in Bridgeport Twp., Belmont Co., Ohio. She was the daughter of William A. Goudy (21) and Sophia Geller. Maud died in Lakewood, Cuyahoga Co., Ohio, on July 20, 1960, at age 80. She was buried in Western Reserve Mausoleum, Warren, Trumbull Co., Ohio.[40]

She married **William Oliver Cooper.** They had two daughters. William Oliver Cooper was born in

Wellsville, Wellsville Twp., Columbiana Co., Ohio, on February 14, 1877. William Oliver reached age 61 and died in Cleveland, Cuyahoga Co., Ohio, on July 16, 1938. He was buried in Western Reserve Mausoleum, Warren, Trumbull Co., Ohio.[40]

Daughters of Maud Goudy and William Oliver Cooper:

+ 137 f I. **Irene⁸ Cooper** was born in Wellsville, Wellsville Twp., Columbiana Co., Ohio, on March 22, 1899. She died in Lakewood, Cuyahoga Co., Ohio, on April 17, 1980. Irene was buried in Western Reserve Mausoleum, Warren, Trumbull Co., Ohio.[40]

+ 138 f II. **Gwendolyn Lee⁸ Cooper** was born in Cleveland, Cuyahoga Co., Ohio, on November 7, 1916. She died in Eastlake, Lake Co., Ohio, on May 20, 2010. Gwendolyn Lee was buried in Western Reserve Mausoleum, Warren, Trumbull Co., Ohio.[40]

**71. Robert Goudy⁷ Blankensop** (*Mary Rebecca⁶ Goudy, Robert⁵, Elizabeth Jane⁴ Pegan, Andrew³ Pegan II, Andrew² Pagan, James¹*) was born on July 30, 1868, in Wellsburg, Brooke Co., West Virginia. He was the son of John Blankensop and Mary Rebecca Goudy (26). Robert Goudy died in Moundsville, Marshall Co., West Virginia, on November 2, 1936, at age 68. He was buried in Mount Rose Cemetery, Moundsville, Marshall Co., West Virginia.[12]

Robert Goudy married **Elizabeth Hunter** in 1890. They had three children. She was also known as **Bessie.** Elizabeth died in Moundsville, Marshall Co., West Virginia, in 1899. She was buried in Mount Rose Cemetery, Moundsville, Marshall Co., West Virginia.[12] May have died of childbirth complications after the birth of William Robert Blankensop.

Robert Goudy Blankensop married **Elizabeth Knight** in 1904 in Webster Co., West Virginia. Elizabeth Knight was born in Moundsville, Marshall Co., West Virginia, on February 20, 1881. Elizabeth reached age 74 and died in Marshall Co., West Virginia, on July 21, 1955. She was buried in

Mount Rose Cemetery, Moundsville, Marshall Co., West Virginia.[12]

Children of Robert Goudy Blankensop and Elizabeth Hunter:

+ 139 m I. **Robert Edwin⁸ Blankensop II** was born in Moundsville, Marshall Co., West Virginia, on May 23, 1893. He died in Berkeley Co., West Virginia, on July 6, 1957. Robert Edwin was buried in Arlington National Cemetery, Arlington, Virginia.[63]

+ 140 f II. **Anita⁸ Blankensop** was born in Moundsville, Marshall Co., West Virginia, on June 6, 1896.[39] She died in Alexandria, Fairfax Co., Virginia, on November 16, 1983. Anita was buried in Mount Rose Cemetery, Moundsville, Marshall Co., West Virginia.[12]

+ 141 m III. **William Rex⁸ Blankensop** was born in Moundsville, Marshall Co., West Virginia, on December 13, 1898. He died in Moundsville, Marshall Co., West Virginia, on April 6, 1953. William Rex was buried in Mount Rose Cemetery, Moundsville, Marshall Co., West Virginia.[12]

**72. Phrenia⁷ Blankensop** (*Mary Rebecca⁶ Goudy, Robert⁵, Elizabeth Jane⁴ Pegan, Andrew³ Pegan II, Andrew² Pagan, James¹*) was born in 1870 in Wellsburg, Brooke Co., West Virginia. She was the daughter of John Blankensop and Mary Rebecca Goudy (26). Phrenia died in Wellsburg, Brooke Co., West Virginia, on November 14, 1885, at age 15. She was buried in Brooke Cemetery, Wellsburg, Brooke Co., West Virginia.[19]

**73. Markley⁷ Blankensop** (*Mary Rebecca⁶ Goudy, Robert⁵, Elizabeth Jane⁴ Pegan, Andrew³ Pegan II, Andrew² Pagan, James¹*) was born in 1873 in Wellsburg, Brooke Co., West Virginia. He was the son of John Blankensop and Mary Rebecca Goudy

(26). Markley died in Wellsburg, Brooke Co., West Virginia, on September 15, 1892, at age 19. Probably buried in Brooke Cemetery, Wellsburg, Brooke Co., West Virginia.

**74. Paul Desha⁷ Pattie** (*Phrania Elizabeth⁶ Goudy, Robert⁵, Elizabeth Jane⁴ Pegan, Andrew³ Pegan II, Andrew² Pagan, James¹*) was born on November 27, 1877, in Austin, Travis Co., Texas. He was the son of Fielding Whipp Pattie and Phrania Elizabeth Goudy (27). Paul Desha died in Wheeling, Ohio Co., West Virginia, on March 8, 1952, at age 74. He was buried in Greenwood Cemetery, Wheeling, Ohio Co., West Virginia.[24]

Never married.

**75. Shirley⁷ Pattie** (*Phrania Elizabeth⁶ Goudy, Robert⁵, Elizabeth Jane⁴ Pegan, Andrew³ Pegan II, Andrew² Pagan, James¹*) was born on October 9, 1879, in Nova Scotia, Canada. He was the son of Fielding Whipp Pattie and Phrania Elizabeth Goudy (27). Shirley lived in 1938 in Copper Valley, Floyd Co., Virginia. He died in Proviso, Cook Co., Illinois, on June 28, 1938, at age 58. Shirley was buried in Forest Lawn Cemetery, Norfolk, Norfolk Co., Virginia.[20]

Shirley married **Ruth Gale Vaiden** about 1920 in Norfolk Co., Virginia? Ruth Gale Vaiden was born in Roanoke, Roanoke Co., Virginia, on July 21, 1894. Ruth Gale reached age 81 and died in Raleigh, Wake Co., North Carolina, on September 18, 1975. She was buried in Forest Lawn Cemetery, Norfolk, Norfolk Co., Virginia.[20]

**76. Mary Phrania⁷ Pattie** (*Phrania Elizabeth⁶ Goudy, Robert⁵, Elizabeth Jane⁴ Pegan, Andrew³ Pegan II, Andrew² Pagan, James¹*) was born on March 8, 1883, in Brooke Co., West Virginia. She was the daughter of Fielding Whipp Pattie and Phrania Elizabeth Goudy (27). Mary Phrania died in Berkeley, Alameda Co., California, on May 3, 1953, at age 70. She was buried in Rochester, Oakland Co., Michigan, on May 5, 1953.

Frank Li Roi and Mary Phrania Pattie Main were married in Stanford Chapel, Stanford University, Palo Alto, Santa Clara Co., California.

Mary Phrania married **Frank Le Roi Main** on December 4, 1916, in Palo Alto, Santa Clara Co.,

California. They had three children. Frank Le Roi Main was born in Bells, Grayson Co., Texas, on August 3, 1889. Frank Le Roi reached age 51 and died in Birmingham, Oakland Co., Michigan, on June 20, 1941. He was buried in White Chapel Memorial Park Cemetery, Troy, Oakland Co., Michigan.[64]

Children of Mary Phrania Pattie and Frank Le Roi Main:

+ 142 m I. **Donald Winston⁸ Main** was born in Providence, Providence Co., Rhode Island, on November 16, 1917. He died in Jackson, Jackson Co., Michigan, on March 3, 2006.

+ 143 f II. **Pattie⁸ Main** was born in Providence, Providence Co., Rhode Island, on May 17, 1919. She died in Van Nuys, Los Angeles Co., California, on November 20, 1999.

+ 144 m III. **John William⁸ Main** was born in Birmingham, Oakland Co., Michigan, in 1924.

**77. Creda⁷ Pattie** (*Phrania Elizabeth⁶ Goudy, Robert⁵, Elizabeth Jane⁴ Pegan, Andrew³ Pegan II, Andrew² Pagan, James¹*) was born on August 2, 1885, in Acton, Los Angeles Co., California. She was the daughter of Fielding Whipp Pattie and Phrania Elizabeth Goudy (27). Creda died in Washington, District of Columbia, on May 10, 1962, at age 76. She was buried in Rock Creek Cemetery, Washington, District of Columbia.[42]

Childless.

Creda Pattie married **Unknown Gates.**

Creda Pattie Gates married **Ernest Garfield Montrop** after 1930 in Washington, District of Columbia. Ernest Garfield Montrop was born in Washington, District of Columbia, on April 5, 1881. Ernest Garfield reached age 72 and died in Washington, District of Columbia? about 1954. He was buried in Rock Creek Cemetery, Washington, District of Columbia.[42]

**78. Abigail Louise⁷ Pattie** (*Phrania Elizabeth⁶ Goudy, Robert⁵, Elizabeth Jane⁴ Pegan, Andrew³ Pegan II,*

*Andrew[2] Pagan, James[1]*) was born on June 20, 1889, in Acton, Los Angeles Co., California. She was the daughter of Fielding Whipp Pattie and Phrania Elizabeth Goudy (27). Abigail Louise died in Richmond, Henrico Co., Virginia, on November 8, 1913, at age 24. She was buried in Forest Lawn Cemetery, Norfolk, Norfolk Co., Virginia.[20]

When Abigail Louise Pattie Crise was pregnant with her first child, the dress she was wearing caught fire. However, the baby, a little girl, was saved.

Abigail Louise married **Joseph Arthur Cruise** on November 4, 1911, in Norfolk Co., Virginia. They had one daughter. Joseph Arthur Cruise was born in Atkinson, Holt Co., Nebraska, on March 23, 1882. Joseph Arthur reached age 41 and died in Norfolk, Norfolk City-Co., Virginia, on March 3, 1924. He was buried in Forest Lawn Cemetery, Norfolk, Norfolk Co., Virginia.[18]

Daughter of Abigail Louise Pattie and Joseph Arthur Cruise:

+ 145  f  I.  **Mary Phrania[8] Cruise** was born in Norfolk, Norfolk City-Co., Virginia, on October 21, 1913. She died in Oak Lawn, Cook Co., Illinois, on May 19, 1996.

79. **Worthington Wilson[7] Hereford** (*Marianne Marilla[6] Goudy, William[5], Elizabeth Jane[4] Pegan, Andrew[3] Pegan II, Andrew[2] Pagan, James[1]*) was born on May 12, 1862, in Apple Grove, Hannon Dist., Mason Co., West Virginia. He was the son of Robert Prentice Hereford and Marianne Marilla Goudy (28). Worthington Wilson lived in 1877 in St. Louis Co., Missouri. He also resided in 1884 in Fresno, Fresno Co., California. Worthington Wilson was living in 1910 in Otter, Alaska. He died in Flat, Yukon-Koyakuk, Alaska, on May 27, 1924, at age 62.

Never married.

80. **Sarah Sanson[7] Hereford** (*Marianne Marilla[6] Goudy, William[5], Elizabeth Jane[4] Pegan, Andrew[3] Pegan II, Andrew[2] Pagan, James[1]*) was born on March 6, 1864, in Apple Grove, Hannon Dist., Mason Co.,

West Virginia. She was also known as **Sadie.** She was the daughter of Robert Prentice Hereford and Marianne Marilla Goudy (28). Sarah Sanson died in Guadalupe or De Baca Co., New Mexico? on August 5, 1916, at age 52. She was buried in Lone Oak Cemetery, Point Pleasant, Mason Co., West Virginia.[44]

Sarah Sanson married **Ashell Wesson Zale McNeill** on November 2, 1880, in Mason Co., West Virginia. They divorced before 1910. They had nine children. Ashell Wesson Zale McNeill was born in Mason, Deerfield Twp., Warren Co., Ohio, on July 31, 1849. He reached age 72 and died in Apple Grove, Hannon Dist., Mason Co., West Virginia, on March 27, 1922. Ashell Wesson Zale was buried in Beale Chapel Cemetery, Apple Grove, Hannon Dist., Mason Co., West Virginia.[65]

Children of Sarah Sanson Hereford and Ashell Wesson Zale McNeill:

+ 146  f  I.  **Mary Grace[8] McNeill** was born in Apple Grove, Hannon Dist., Mason Co., West Virginia, on September 25, 1881. She died in Huntington, Cabell Co., West Virginia, on January 24, 1964. Mary Grace was buried in Woodmere Memorial Park Cemetery, Huntington, Cabell Co., West Virginia.[66]

+ 147  f  II.  **Blanche Hereford[8] McNeill** was born in Apple Grove, Hannon Dist., Mason Co., West Virginia, on November 8, 1883. She died in Apple Grove, Hannon Dist., Mason Co., West Virginia, on October 2, 1897.

+ 148  f  III.  **Emma Pauline[8] McNeill** was born in Apple Grove, Hannon Dist., Mason Co., West Virginia, on March 9, 1886. She died in Apple Grove, Hannon Dist., Mason Co., West Virginia, on June 30, 1887.

+ 149 m IV. **Worthington Wilson⁸ McNeill** was born in Apple Grove, Hannon Dist., Mason Co., West Virginia, on April 24, 1888. He died in Goodland, Sherman Co., Kansas, on April 11, 1977. Worthington Wilson was buried in Goodland Cemetery, Goodland, Sherman Co., Kansas.[67]

+ 150 m V. **Frank Rhea⁸ McNeill** was born in Mercer's Bottom, Mason Co., West Virginia, on May 9, 1890. He died in Cortez, Montezuma Co., Colorado, on June 8, 1950.

+ 151 f VI. **Hallie Virginia⁸ McNeill** was born in Mercer's Bottom, Mason Co., West Virginia, on June 12, 1892. She died in Palo Alto, Santa Clara Co., California, on February 2, 1943. Hallie Richmond was buried in Golden Gate National Cemetery, San Bruno, San Mateo Co., California.[68]

+ 152 f VII. **Jessie Gertrude⁸ McNeill** was born in Mercer's Bottom, Mason Co., West Virginia, on February 21, 1894. She died in Buchanan, De Baca Co., New Mexico, on April 25, 1914. Jessie Gertrude was buried in Santa Rosa, Guadalupe Co., New Mexico.

+ 153 m VIII. **James Hereford⁸ McNeill** was born in Apple Grove, Hannon Dist., Mason Co., West Virginia, on December 11, 1897. He died in Raleigh, Wake Co., North Carolina, on August 19, 1984. He was cremated. His ashes were buried in Riverside Cemetery, Waterville, Marshall Co., Kansas. [69]

+ 154 f IX. **Nora Frances⁸ McNeill** was born in Apple Grove, Hannon Dist., Mason Co., West Virginia, on February 23, 1900. She was also known as **Frances.** Nora Frances died in Medford, Jackson Co., Oregon, on December 2, 1982. She was buried in Siskiyou Memorial Park Cemetery, Medford, Jackson Co., Oregon.[70]

**81. Sarah Jessie⁷ Cowl** (*Elizabeth Jane⁶ Goudy, Isaac⁵, Elizabeth Jane⁴ Pegan, Andrew³ Pegan II, Andrew² Pagan, James¹*) was born on December 14, 1861, in Bethany, Brooke Co., (West) Virginia. She was the daughter of Joseph Hawkins Cowl and Elizabeth Jane Goudy (36). Sarah Jessie died in a facility in Weston, Lewis Co., West Virginia, on September 21, 1941, at age 79. She was buried in Highland Cemetery, Cameron, Marshall Co., West Virginia.[46]

Sarah Jessie married **Henry Garner Fair** on October 16, 1892, in Brooke Co. West Virginia. They had five children. Henry Garner Fair was born in Wetzel Co., West Virginia, on July 4, 1861. Henry Garner reached age 69 and died in Ford City, Armstrong Co., Pennsylvania, on December 9, 1930. He was buried in Highland Cemetery, Cameron, Marshall Co., West Virginia.[46]

Children of Sarah Jessie Cowl and Henry Garner Fair:

+ 155 m I. **Louis Albert⁸ Fair** was born in Fish Creek Island, Marshall Co., West Virginia, on October 23, 1893. He died in Fish Creek Island, Marshall Co., West Virginia, on December 20, 1893.

+ 156 m II. **Harold Stewart⁸ Fair** was born in Adeline, Marshall Co., West Virginia, on November 23, 1894. He died in Kittanning, Kittanning Twp., Armstrong Co., Pennsylvania, on December 9, 1970. Harold Stewart was buried in Lawn Haven Burial Estates, Worthington, Armstrong Co., Pennsylvania.[71]

+ 157 f III. **Jane Augusta⁸ Fair** was born in Adeline, Marshall Co., West Virginia, on June 4, 1896. She was also known as **Jennie.** Jane Augusta died in a facility in Sistersville, Tyler Co., West Virginia, on August 4, 1970. She was buried in Halcyon Hills Memorial Park Cemetery, Sherrard, Marshall Co., West Virginia.[72]

+ 158 m IV. **Dewey Isaac⁸ Fair** was born in Adeline, Marshall Co., West Virginia, on November 30, 1898. He was also known as **Ike.** Dewey Isaac died in Ford City, Armstrong Co., Pennsylvania, on January 12, 1972. He was buried in Lawn Haven Burial Estates, Worthington, Armstrong Co., Pennsylvania.[71]

+ 159 m V. **Daniel Cowl⁸ Fair** was born in Liberty, Marshall Co., West Virginia, on November 23, 1903. He died in Butler, Butler Co., Pennsylvania? in March 1985.

**82. Mary Elva⁷ Cowl** (*Elizabeth Jane⁶ Goudy, Isaac⁵, Elizabeth Jane⁴ Pegan, Andrew³ Pegan II, Andrew² Pagan, James¹*) was born on October 11, 1864, in Bethany, Brooke Co., West Virginia. She was the daughter of Joseph Hawkins Cowl and Elizabeth Jane Goudy (36). Mary Elva died in Wheeling, Ohio Co., West Virginia, on July 19, 1955, at age 90. She was buried in Mount Rose Cemetery, Moundsville, Marshall Co., West Virginia.[12]

Childless.

Mary Elva married **William Edward Conner** on June 30, 1897, in Marshall Co., West Virginia. William Edward Conner was born in Moundsville, Marshall Co., West Virginia, on August 31, 1869. William Edward reached age 93 and died in Clarksburg, Harrison Co., West Virginia, on September 4, 1962. He was buried in Mount Rose Cemetery, Moundsville, Marshall Co., West Virginia.[12]

**83. Elizabeth Jane⁷ Cowl** (*Elizabeth Jane⁶ Goudy, Isaac⁵, Elizabeth Jane⁴ Pegan, Andrew³ Pegan II, Andrew²*

*Pagan, James¹*) was born on February 22, 1867, in Bethany, Brooke Co., West Virginia. She was also known as **Jennie.** She was the daughter of Joseph Hawkins Cowl and Elizabeth Jane Goudy (36). Elizabeth Jane died in Glendale, Los Angeles Co., California, on January 3, 1942, at age 74. She was buried in Forest Lawn Memorial Park Cemetery, Glendale, Los Angeles Co., California.[47]

Elizabeth Jane married **Lewis Albert Smith** on November 11, 1891, in Ohio Co., West Virginia. They had one son. Lewis Albert Smith was born in Wheeling, Ohio Co., West Virginia, on May 4, 1863. Lewis Albert reached age 47 and died in Wheeling, Ohio Co., West Virginia, on June 27, 1910. He was buried in Greenwood Cemetery, Wheeling, Ohio Co., West Virginia.[24]

Son of Elizabeth Jane Cowl and Lewis Albert Smith:

+ 160 m I. **Robert Cowl⁸ Smith** was born in Madison, Ohio Co., West Virginia, on May 6, 1894. He died in Glendale, Los Angeles Co., California, on November 6, 1935. Robert Cowl was buried in Forest Lawn Memorial Park Cemetery, Glendale, Los Angeles Co., California.[47]

**84. Emma Blanche⁷ Cowl** (*Elizabeth Jane⁶ Goudy, Isaac⁵, Elizabeth Jane⁴ Pegan, Andrew³ Pegan II, Andrew² Pagan, James¹*) was born on May 5, 1869, in Putnam, Springfield Twp., Muskingum Co., Ohio. She was also known as **Blanche.** She was the daughter of Joseph Hawkins Cowl and Elizabeth Jane Goudy (36). Emma Blanche died in Sharon Twp., Franklin Co., Ohio, on March 2, 1951, at age 81. She was buried in Sunset Memorial Park Cemetery, Galloway, Franklin Co., Ohio.[48]

Emma Blanche married **Edmund H. Redman** on November 19, 1890, in Ohio Co., West Virginia. They had four children. Edmund H. Redman was born in Wheeling, Ohio Co., West Virginia, on November 19, 1868. Edmund H. reached age 62 and died in Columbus, Franklin Co., Ohio, on April 19, 1931. He was buried in Sunset Memorial Park Cemetery, Galloway, Franklin Co., Ohio.[48]

Children of Emma Blanche Cowl and Edmund H. Redman:

+ 161 f I.   **Hazel**[8] **Redman** was born in Wheeling, Ohio Co., West Virginia, on September 9, 1891. She died in Columbus, Franklin Co., Ohio, in June 1967. Hazel was buried in Sunset Memorial Park Cemetery, Galloway, Franklin Co., Ohio.[48]

+ 162 m II.   **Harry E.**[8] **Redman** was born in Wheeling, Ohio Co., West Virginia, on January 10, 1898. He died in Mount Vernon, Knox Co., Ohio, on June 14, 1956.

+ 163 m III.   **Albert E.**[8] **Redman** was born in Columbus, Franklin Co., Ohio, on January 5, 1904. He died in Columbus, Franklin Co., Ohio, on December 30, 1975. Albert E. was buried in Green Lawn Cemetery, Columbus, Franklin Co., Ohio.[73]

+ 164 m IV.   **Edmond Cowl**[8] **Redman II** was born in Columbus, Franklin Co., Ohio, on May 24, 1906. He died in Columbus, Franklin Co., Ohio, on May 8, 2006. Edmond Cowl was buried in Sunset Memorial Park Cemetery, Galloway, Franklin Co., Ohio.[48]

**85. Nellie Augusta**[7] **Cowl** (*Elizabeth Jane*[6] *Goudy, Isaac*[5], *Elizabeth Jane*[4] *Pegan, Andrew*[3] *Pegan II, Andrew*[2] *Pagan, James*[1]) was born on September 20, 1875, in Putnam, Springfield Twp., Muskingum Co., Ohio. She was the daughter of Joseph Hawkins Cowl and Elizabeth Jane Goudy (36). Nellie Augusta died in Wheeling, Ohio Co., West Virginia, on October 1, 1968, at age 93. She was buried in Greenwood Cemetery, Wheeling, Ohio Co., West Virginia.[24]

Nellie Augusta married **Henry Jackson Stoller** on June 3, 1901, in Ohio Co., West Virginia. They had two daughters. Henry Jackson Stoller was born in East Finley Twp., Washington Co., Pennsylvania, on July 17, 1874. He was also known as **Harry.** Henry Jackson reached age 70 and died in Wheeling, Ohio Co., West Virginia, on June 6, 1945. He was buried in Greenwood Cemetery, Wheeling, Ohio Co., West Virginia.[24]

Daughters of Nellie Augusta Cowl and Henry Jackson Stoller:

+ 165 f I.   **Alice**[8] **Stoller** was born in Wheeling, Ohio Co., West Virginia, on October 23, 1903. She died in Bridgeport, Bellaire Twp., Belmont Co., Ohio, on March 6, 1997. Alice was buried in Greenwood Cemetery, Wheeling, Ohio Co., West Virginia.[24]

+ 166 f II.   **Elizabeth Jane**[8] **Stoller** was born in Wheeling, Ohio Co., West Virginia, on May 22, 1906. She was also known as **Jane.** Elizabeth Jane died in Elyria, Elyria Twp., Lorain Co., Ohio, on June 7, 1997.

**86. Henry**[7] **Cowl** (*Elizabeth Jane*[6] *Goudy, Isaac*[5], *Elizabeth Jane*[4] *Pegan, Andrew*[3] *Pegan II, Andrew*[2] *Pagan, James*[1]) was born on January 26, 1878, in Putnam, Springfield Twp., Muskingum Co., Ohio or LaSalle, LaSalle Twp., LaSalle Co., Illinois. He was also known as **Harry.** He was the son of Joseph Hawkins Cowl and Elizabeth Jane Goudy (36). Henry died in Wheeling, Ohio Co., West Virginia, on April 9, 1895, at age 17. He was buried in Peninsula Cemetery, Wheeling, Ohio Co., West Virginia.[26]

**87. Daniel Bird**[7] **Cowl** (*Elizabeth Jane*[6] *Goudy, Isaac*[5], *Elizabeth Jane*[4] *Pegan, Andrew*[3] *Pegan II, Andrew*[2] *Pagan, James*[1]) was born on August 21, 1880, in LaSalle, LaSalle Twp., LaSalle Co., Illinois. He was the son of Joseph Hawkins Cowl and Elizabeth Jane Goudy (36). Daniel Bird died in Columbus, Franklin Co., Ohio, on January 22, 1960, at age 79.

Never married.

**88. Alice Louise**[7] **Cowl** (*Elizabeth Jane*[6] *Goudy, Isaac*[5], *Elizabeth Jane*[4] *Pegan, Andrew*[3] *Pegan II, Andrew*[2] *Pagan, James*[1]) was born on November 28, 1882, in Wheeling, Ohio Co., West Virginia. She was the daughter of Joseph Hawkins Cowl and Elizabeth Jane Goudy (36). Alice Louise died in Michigan? in 1965 at age 82.

Alice Louise married **Edward Conrad McAllister** on November 25, 1903, in Ohio Co., West Virginia. They had one daughter. Edward Conrad McAllister was born in Wheeling, Ohio Co., West Virginia, on December 18, 1876. Edward Conrad reached age 86 and died in Wheeling, Ohio Co., West Virginia, on May 27, 1963. He was buried in Greenwood Cemetery, Wheeling, Ohio Co., West Virginia.[24]

Daughter of Alice Louise Cowl and Edward Conrad McAllister:

+ 167 f I. **Helen⁸ McAllister** was born in Wheeling, Ohio Co., West Virginia, on September 27, 1904. She died in Wheeling, Ohio Co., West Virginia, in August 1984.

**89. Edward Elmer⁷ Goudy** (*John William⁶, Isaac⁵, Elizabeth Jane⁴ Pegan, Andrew³ Pegan II, Andrew² Pagan, James¹*) was born on February 29, 1868, in Wheeling, Ohio Co., West Virginia. He was the son of John William Goudy (38) and Melissa Rebecca Baldwin. Edward Elmer died in Elyria, Elyria Twp., Lorain Co., Ohio, on May 21, 1948, at age 80. He was buried in Ridge Hill Memorial Park Cemetery, Amherst, Amherst Twp., Lorraine Co., Ohio.[49]

Edward Elmer married **Martha Brady** before 1890 in Marshall Co., West Virginia. They had three children. Martha Brady was born in Brady's Bend Twp., Armstrong Co., Pennsylvania, on December 19, 1873. Martha died in Elyria, Elyria Twp., Lorain Co., Ohio? after May 1948.

Children of Edward Elmer Goudy and Martha Brady:

+ 168 f I. **Elizabeth M.⁸ Goudy** was born in Wheeling, Ohio Co., West Virginia, in September 1891. She was also known as **Lizzie**. Elizabeth M. died after 1930.

+ 169 m II. **Edward Elmer⁸ Goudy II** was born in Wheeling, Ohio Co., West Vir-

ginia, on July 26, 1894. He died in Mesa, Maricopa Co., Arizona, on December 31, 1972. Edward Elmer was buried in Ridge Hill Memorial Park Cemetery, Amherst, Amherst Twp., Lorraine Co., Ohio.[49]

+ 170 m III. **James⁸ Goudy** was born in Wheeling, Ohio Co., West Virginia, on May 26, 1896. He died in Wheeling, Ohio Co., West Virginia, on May 27, 1896.

**90. George C.⁷ Goudy** (*John William⁶, Isaac⁵, Elizabeth Jane⁴ Pegan, Andrew³ Pegan II, Andrew² Pagan, James¹*) was born on January 14, 1870, in Wheeling, Ohio Co., West Virginia. He was the son of John William Goudy (38) and Melissa Rebecca Baldwin. George C. died in Wheeling, Ohio Co., West Virginia, on August 6, 1910, at age 40. He was buried in Mount Olivet Cemetery, Wheeling, Ohio Co., West Virginia.[4]

Childless.

George C. married **Jane Tappan** on September 20, 1903, in Ohio Co., West Virginia. Jane Tappan was born in Wheeling, Ohio Co., (West) Virginia, on May 6, 1856. She was also known as **Jennie**. Jane reached age 48 and died in Wheeling, Ohio Co., West Virginia, on March 4, 1905. She was buried in Peninsula Cemetery, Wheeling, Ohio Co., West Virginia.[26]

**91. Infant Daughter⁷ Goudy** (*John William⁶, Isaac⁵, Elizabeth Jane⁴ Pegan, Andrew³ Pegan II, Andrew² Pagan, James¹*) was born on November 18, 1872, in Wheeling, Ohio Co., West Virginia. She was the daughter of John William Goudy (38) and Melissa Rebecca Baldwin. Infant Daughter died in Wheeling, Ohio Co., West Virginia, on November 20, 1872.

**92. Arthur Elwood⁷ Goudy** (*John William⁶, Isaac⁵, Elizabeth Jane⁴ Pegan, Andrew³ Pegan II, Andrew² Pagan, James¹*) was born on August 18, 1875, in Wheeling, Ohio Co., West Virginia. He was the son of John William Goudy (38) and Melissa Rebecca Baldwin. Arthur Elwood died in Belmont, Goshen Twp., Belmont Co., Ohio, on February 8, 1964, at age 88. He was buried in Mount Olivet Cemetery, Wheeling, Ohio Co., West Virginia.[4]

Childless.

Arthur Elwood married **Lilly or Lulu Belle Holden** on September 28, 1896. They are divorced. Lilly or Lulu Belle Holden was born in Clarksburg, Harrison Co., West Virginia, in March 1877. She died after 1900.

Arthur Elwood Goudy married **Lenora Etheline Sutton** on January 29, 1916, in Ohio Co., West Virginia. They divorced before 1930. Lenora Etheline Sutton was born in Franklin, Franklin Twp., Jefferson Co., Ohio or Jefferson Co., Ohio, on December 29, 1887. She was also known as **Nora.** Lenora Etheline reached age 72 and died in Belmont, Goshen Twp., Belmont Co., Ohio, on February 14, 1960. She was buried in Mount Olivet Cemetery, Wheeling, Ohio Co., West Virginia.[4]

93. **Robert Carl⁷ Goudy** (*John William⁶, Isaac⁵, Elizabeth Jane⁴ Pegan, Andrew³ Pegan II, Andrew² Pagan, James¹*) was born on January 16, 1880, in Wheeling, Ohio Co., West Virginia. He was the son of John William Goudy (38) and Melissa Rebecca Baldwin. Robert Carl died in Sistersville, Tyler Co., West Virginia, on October 17, 1958, at age 78. He was buried in Mount Olivet Cemetery, Wheeling, Ohio Co., West Virginia.[4]

Robert Carl married **Anna Rust** on December 20, 1909, in Ohio Co., West Virginia. They had seven children. Anna Rust was born in Wheeling, Ohio Co., West Virginia, on April 4, 1881. Anna reached age 54 and died in Wheeling, Ohio Co., West Virginia, on April 2, 1936. She was buried in Our Lady of Seven Dolors Cemetery, Triadelphia, Ohio Co., West Virginia.[74]

By 1940, Robert Goudy's younger children were in orphanages or boy's correctional facilities.

Children of Robert Carl Goudy and Anna Rust:

+ 171 f I. **Alberta Anna⁸ Goudy** was born in Ritchie, Ohio Co., West Virginia, on August 22, 1910. She died in Girard, Trumbull Co., Ohio, on November 3, 2001. Alberta Anna was buried in Girard Liberty Union Cemetery, Girard, Trumbull Co., Ohio.[75]

+ 172 m II. **Robert Joseph⁸ Goudy II** was born in Ritchie, Ohio Co., West Virginia, on January 27, 1912. He died in Wheeling, Ohio Co., West Virginia, on July 25, 1973. Robert Joseph was buried in Mount Calvary Cemetery, Wheeling, Ohio Co., West Virginia.[76]

+ 173 f III. **Thelma Marie⁸ Goudy** was born in Triadelphia, Ohio Co., West Virginia, on August 20, 1913. She died in Bellaire, Pultney Twp., Belmont Co., Ohio, on October 7, 1974. Thelma Marie was buried in Davis Cemetery, Bellaire, Belmont Co., Ohio.[77]

+ 174 m IV. **Wilfred E.⁸ Goudy** was born in Triadelphia, Ohio Co., West Virginia, on August 27, 1917. He was also known as **Bud.** Wilfred E. died in West Terre Haute, Sugar Creek Twp., Vigo Co., Indiana, on May 6, 1999. He was buried in Roselawn Memorial Park Cemetery, Terre Haute, Vigo County, Indiana.[78]

+ 175 m V. **John Edward⁸ Goudy** was born in Wheeling, Ohio Co., West Virginia, on November 14, 1922. He died in Wheeling, Ohio Co., West Virginia, on November 15, 1922. John Edward was buried in Mount Olivet Cemetery, Wheeling, Ohio Co., West Virginia.[4]

+ 176 m VI. **Lawrence Henry⁸ Goudy** was born in Wheeling, Ohio Co., West Virginia, on December 24, 1923. He died in Jefferson, Jackson Co., Georgia, on December 16, 2000.

+ 177 m VII. **Henry J.⁸ Goudy** was born in Wheeling, Ohio Co., West Virginia, on April 28, 1928. He died in Austintown, Austintown Twp., Mahoning Co., Ohio, on October 12, 2006.

**94. Howard Louis⁷ Goudy** (*John William⁶, Isaac⁵, Elizabeth Jane⁴ Pegan, Andrew³ Pegan II, Andrew² Pagan, James¹*) was born on June 9, 1883, in Wheeling, Ohio Co., West Virginia. He was the son of John William Goudy (38) and Melissa Rebecca Baldwin. Howard Louis died in Wheeling, Ohio Co., West Virginia, on May 3, 1947, at age 63. He was buried in Mount Olivet Cemetery, Wheeling, Ohio Co., West Virginia.[4]

He married **Mary Jane Laheen.** They had four children. Mary Jane Laheen was born in Wheeling, Ohio Co., West Virginia, on February 12, 1888. Mary Jane reached age 56 and died in Wheeling, Ohio Co., West Virginia, on March 22, 1944. She was buried in Mount Olivet Cemetery, Wheeling, Ohio Co., West Virginia.[4]

Children of Howard Louis Goudy and Mary Jane Laheen:

+ 178 m I. **John Elwood⁸ Goudy** was born in Wheeling, Ohio Co., West Virginia, on November 13, 1906. He died in Wheeling, Ohio Co., West Virginia, on May 28, 1964. John Elwood was buried in Mount Olivet Cemetery, Wheeling, Ohio Co., West Virginia.[4]

+ 179 f II. **Clarice Melissa⁸ Goudy** was born in Wheeling, Ohio Co., West Virginia, on January 18, 1917. She died in Cadiz, Cadiz Twp., Harrison Co., Ohio, on April 16, 2000.

+ 180 f III. **Dorothy Elizabeth⁸ Goudy** was born in Wheeling, Ohio Co., West Virginia, on February 1, 1920. She died in Wheeling, Ohio Co., West Virginia, on November 10, 1999.

+ 181 m IV. **Howard Louis⁸ Goudy II** was born in Wheeling, Ohio Co., West Virginia, on September 5, 1922. He died in Wheeling, Ohio Co., West Virginia, in June 1981. Howard Louis was buried in Mount Olivet Cemetery, Wheeling, Ohio Co., West Virginia.[4]

**95. Minnie⁷ Goudy** (*John William⁶, Isaac⁵, Elizabeth Jane⁴ Pegan, Andrew³ Pegan II, Andrew² Pagan, James¹*) was born on July 7, 1888, in Wheeling, Ohio Co., West Virginia. She was the daughter of John William Goudy (38) and Melissa Rebecca Baldwin. Minnie died in Wheeling, Ohio Co., West Virginia, on January 29, 1889.

**96. David Wellington⁷ Hill II** (*David Wellington⁶, Mary Jane⁵ Goudy, Elizabeth Jane⁴ Pegan, Andrew³ Pegan II, Andrew² Pagan, James¹*) was born on September 12, 1868, in Wheeling, Ohio Co., West Virginia. He was the son of David Wellington Hill (42) and Mary Emma Blackburn. David Wellington died in Cambridge, Cambridge Twp., Guernsey Co., Ohio, on November 13, 1947, at age 79. He was buried in Greenwood Cemetery, Bellaire, Pultney Twp., Belmont Co., Ohio.[50]

He married **Lillie May Crider.** They had one daughter. Lillie May Crider was born in Ohio or Wheeling, Ohio Co., West Virginia, on October 30, 1869. Lillie May reached age 72 and died in Pultney Twp., Belmont Co., Ohio, on December 25, 1941. She was buried in Greenwood Cemetery, Bellaire, Pultney Twp., Belmont Co., Ohio.[50]

Daughter of David Wellington Hill II and Lillie May Crider:

+ 182 f I. **Mary E.⁸ Hill** was born in Ohio in 1904. She was adopted. Mary E. died after 1910.

**97. Mary Emma⁷ Hill** (*David Wellington⁶, Mary Jane⁵ Goudy, Elizabeth Jane⁴ Pegan, Andrew³ Pegan II, Andrew² Pagan, James¹*) was born on October 18,

1870, in Wheeling, Ohio Co., West Virginia. She was the daughter of David Wellington Hill (42) and Mary Emma Blackburn. Mary Emma died in Wheeling, Ohio Co., West Virginia, on August 21, 1910, at age 39. She was buried in Greenwood Cemetery, Wheeling, Ohio Co., West Virginia.[24]

She married **Francis M. Church.** They had one daughter. Francis M. Church was born in Pennsylvania on June 12, 1863. He was also known as **Frank.** Francis M. reached age 85 and died in Wheeling, Ohio Co., West Virginia, on April 14, 1949. He was buried in Greenwood Cemetery, Wheeling, Ohio Co., West Virginia.[24]

Daughter of Mary Emma Hill and Francis M. Church:

+ 183 f  I.  **Mabel B.⁸ Church** was born in Wheeling, Ohio Co., West Virginia, on February 10, 1890. She died in Jackson, Hinds Co., Mississippi, on October 24, 1981. Mabel B. was buried in Greenwood Cemetery, Wheeling, Ohio Co., West Virginia.[24]

**98. George Wellington⁷ Hill** (*David Wellington⁶, Mary Jane⁵ Goudy, Elizabeth Jane⁴ Pegan, Andrew³ Pegan II, Andrew² Pagan, James¹*) was born on May 24, 1873, in Wheeling, Ohio Co., West Virginia. He was the son of David Wellington Hill (42) and Mary Emma Blackburn. George Wellington died in Wheeling, Ohio Co., West Virginia, on January 10, 1953, at age 79. He was buried in Mount Zion Cemetery, Wheeling, Ohio Co., West Virginia.[28]

George Wellington married **Minnie Niedermeyer** in 1897. They had two sons. Minnie Niedermeyer was born in Wheeling, Ohio Co., West Virginia, on February 23, 1877. Minnie reached age 84 and died in Wheeling, Ohio Co., West Virginia, on December 22, 1961. She was buried in Mount Zion Cemetery, Wheeling, Ohio Co., West Virginia.[28]

Sons of George Wellington Hill and Minnie Niedermeyer:

+ 184 m  I.  **George Wellington⁸ Hill II** was born in Wheeling, Ohio Co., West Virginia, on December 1, 1898. He died in Ohio Co., West Virginia, on November 17, 1959. He was buried in Greenwood Cemetery, Wheeling, Ohio Co., West Virginia. [24]

+ 185 m  II.  **Harold Christian⁸ Hill** was born in Wheeling, Ohio Co., West Virginia, on November 5, 1900. He died in Wheeling, Ohio Co., West Virginia, on January 20, 1958. Harold Christian was buried in Greenwood Cemetery, Wheeling, Ohio Co., West Virginia.[24]

**99. Beatrice Matilda⁷ Hill** (*David Wellington⁶, Mary Jane⁵ Goudy, Elizabeth Jane⁴ Pegan, Andrew³ Pegan II, Andrew² Pagan, James¹*) was born on May 29, 1875, in Wheeling, Ohio Co., West Virginia. She was the daughter of David Wellington Hill (42) and Mary Emma Blackburn. Matilda B. died after March 1, 1919.

According to her father David's obituary in the March 4, 1919 *Wheeling (WV) Intelligencer*, her name was Mrs. Beatrice Mutter and she was living in Dayton, Ohio. No other records are found for her.

**100. Child⁷ Hill** (*David Wellington⁶, Mary Jane⁵ Goudy, Elizabeth Jane⁴ Pegan, Andrew³ Pegan II, Andrew² Pagan, James¹*) was born between 1868 and 1900 in Ohio Co., West Virginia. He or she was a child of David Wellington Hill (42) and Mary Emma Blackburn. Child died in Ohio Co., West Virginia, before 1900.

**101. Charles L.⁷ Hill** (*William Hamilton⁶, Mary Jane⁵ Goudy, Elizabeth Jane⁴ Pegan, Andrew³ Pegan II, Andrew² Pagan, James¹*) was born on June 10, 1873, in Wheeling, Ohio Co., West Virginia. He was the son of William Hamilton Hill (43) and Virginia Sarah Sage. Charles L. died in Wheeling, Ohio Co., West Virginia, on July 15, 1938, at age

65. He was buried in Stone Church Cemetery, Elm Grove, Ohio Co., West Virginia.[27]

Charles L. married **Barbara Ellen Murphy** in 1898 in Ohio Co., West Virginia. They had one child. Barbara Ellen Murphy was born in West Virginia in May 1879. Barbara Ellen reached age 79 and died in Lewis Co., West Virginia, on September 26, 1958.

Child of Charles L. Hill and Barbara Ellen Murphy:

+ 186    I.    **Child⁸ Hill** was born in West Virginia between 1900 and 1910. He or she died in West Virginia between 1900 and 1910.

102. **Howard Hamilton⁷ Hill** (*William Hamilton⁶, Mary Jane⁵ Goudy, Elizabeth Jane⁴ Pegan, Andrew³ Pegan II, Andrew² Pagan, James¹*) was born on May 26, 1876, in Wheeling, Ohio Co., West Virginia. He was the son of William Hamilton Hill (43) and Virginia Sarah Sage. Howard Hamilton died in Steubenville, Cross Creek Twp., Jefferson Co., Ohio, on February 27, 1946, at age 69. He was buried in Union Cemetery, Steubenville, Cross Creek Twp., Jefferson Co., Ohio.[16]

Howard Hamilton Hill married **Wilhelmina Sophia Maxwell** before 1906. They had one daughter. Wilhelmina Sophia Maxwell was born in Jefferson Co., Ohio, on October 12, 1875. She was also known as **Minnie.** Wilhelmina Sophia reached age 53 and died in Steubenville, Cross Creek Twp., Jefferson Co., Ohio, on August 29, 1929. She was buried in Union Cemetery, Steubenville, Cross Creek Twp., Jefferson Co., Ohio.[16]

He married **Cora Bell Hawley** after 1929. Cora Bell Hawley was born in West Virginia in 1880. Cora Bell died after 1946.

Daughter of Howard Hamilton Hill and Wilhelmina Sophia Maxwell:

+ 187   f   I.    **Emily Virginia⁸ Hill** was born in Steubenville, Cross Creek Twp., Jefferson Co., Ohio, on November 11, 1906. She died in Winchester,

Frederick Co., Virginia? on February 21, 1973, at age 66.

103. **Ulina⁷ Hill** (*William Hamilton⁶, Mary Jane⁵ Goudy, Elizabeth Jane⁴ Pegan, Andrew³ Pegan II, Andrew² Pagan, James¹*) was born in 1880 in Wheeling, Ohio Co., West Virginia. She was the daughter of William Hamilton Hill (43) and Virginia Sarah Sage. May have died in infancy.

104. **Russell Sage⁷ Hill** (*William Hamilton⁶, Mary Jane⁵ Goudy, Elizabeth Jane⁴ Pegan, Andrew³ Pegan II, Andrew² Pagan, James¹*) was born on April 3, 1884, in Elm Grove, Ohio Co., West Virginia. He was the son of William Hamilton Hill (43) and Virginia Sarah Sage. Russell Sage died in New Martinsville, Wetzel Co., West Virginia, on September 26, 1953, at age 69.

Russell Sage married **Carrie Etta Groves** in 1905 in Ohio Co., West Virginia. They had four children. Carrie Etta Groves was born in West Virginia on September 15, 1882. Carrie Etta reached age 47 and died in Wheeling, Ohio Co., West Virginia, on March 21, 1930. She was buried in Stone Church Cemetery, Elm Grove, Ohio Co., West Virginia.[27]

Russell Sage Hill married Mrs. **Bertha Louise Hammell** Vogel on February 1, 1951, in Harrison Co., West Virginia. Bertha Louise Hammell was born in New Martinsville, Wetzel Co., West Virginia, on January 6, 1890. Bertha Louise reached age 87 and died in Charleston, Kanawha Co., West Virginia, in January 1978. She was buried under the name Bertha L. Vogel in Northview Cemetery, New Martinsville, Wetzel Co., West Virginia.[79]

Children of Russell Sage Hill and Carrie Etta Groves:

+ 188   m   I.    **Russell G.⁸ Hill II** was born in Steubenville, Cross Creek Twp., Jefferson Co., Ohio, on June 6, 1908. He died in Thousand Oaks, Ventura Co., California, on March 18, 1985. Russell G. was buried in Pierce Brothers Valley Oaks Memorial Park Cemetery,

Westlake Village, Los Angeles Co., California.[80]

+ 189 m II. **William Harold**[8] **Hill** was born in Steubenville, Cross Creek Twp., Jefferson Co., Ohio, on June 26, 1910. He died in Crawley, Greenbrier Co., West Virginia? before 1969.

+ 190 f III. **Ethel Lillian**[8] **Hill** was born in Steubenville, Cross Creek Twp., Jefferson Co., Ohio, in 1916. She died after 1940.

+ 191 f IV. **Betty Jean**[8] **Hill** was born in Steubenville, Cross Creek Twp., Jefferson Co., Ohio, in 1918. She died after 1940.

**105. Charles Millard**[7] **Hill** (*John W.*[6], *Mary Jane*[5] *Goudy, Elizabeth Jane*[4] *Pegan, Andrew*[3] *Pegan II, Andrew*[2] *Pagan, James*[1]) was born on May 6, 1867, in Wheeling, Ohio Co., West Virginia. He was the son of John W. Hill (44) and Isabella Ellen McGill. Charles Millard died in Liberty, Ohio Co., West Virginia, on June 7, 1932, at age 65. He was buried in Greenwood Cemetery, Wheeling, Ohio Co., West Virginia.24]

He married **Josephine Kline.** They had six children. Josephine Kline was born in Wheeling, Ohio Co., West Virginia, on May 17, 1870. Josephine reached age 71 and died in Wheeling, Ohio Co., West Virginia, on February 7, 1942. She was buried in Greenwood Cemetery, Wheeling, Ohio Co., West Virginia.[24]

Children of Charles Millard Hill and Josephine Kline:

+ 192 f I. **Edna A.**[8] **Hill** was born in Wheeling, Ohio Co., West Virginia, on October 8, 1890. She died in Wheeling, Ohio Co., West Virginia, on April 5, 1892.

+ 193 m II. **Eugene Wilson**[8] **Hill** was born in Wheeling, Ohio Co., West Virginia, on June 3, 1893. He died

in East Liverpool, Liverpool Twp., Columbiana Co., Ohio, on June 12, 1962.

+ 194 f III. **Ella S.**[8] **Hill** was born in Wheeling, Ohio Co., West Virginia, on July 8, 1895. She died in Wheeling, Ohio Co., West Virginia, on March 8, 1898.

+ 195 f IV. **Nellie Caroline**[8] **Hill** was born in Ritchie, Ohio Co., West Virginia, on December 5, 1897. She died in Wheeling, Ohio Co., West Virginia, on July 9, 1979. Nellie Caroline was buried in Greenwood Cemetery, Wheeling, Ohio Co., West Virginia.[24]

+ 196 f V. **Dorretta Josephine**[8] **Hill** was born in Ritchie, Ohio Co., West Virginia, on February 5, 1900. She died in Belmont Co., Ohio, on January 6, 1998.

+ 197 f VI. **Harriet Ellen**[8] **Hill** was born in Ritchie, Ohio Co., West Virginia, on April 5, 1902. She died in Wheeling, Ohio Co., West Virginia, in February 1977. Harriet Ellen was buried in Greenwood Cemetery, Wheeling, Ohio Co., West Virginia.[24]

**106. Ella Allen**[7] **Hill** (*John W.*[6], *Mary Jane*[5] *Goudy, Elizabeth Jane*[4] *Pegan, Andrew*[3] *Pegan II, Andrew*[2] *Pagan, James*[1]) was born on September 26, 1869, in Wheeling, Ohio Co., West Virginia. She was the daughter of John W. Hill (44) and Isabella Ellen McGill. Ella Allen died in Steubenville, Cross Creek Twp., Jefferson Co., Ohio, on February 5, 1949, at age of 79. She was buried in Union Cemetery, Steubenville, Cross Creek Twp., Jefferson Co., Ohio.[16]

Ella Allen married **Charles William Hirth** in 1889 in Ohio Co., West Virginia. They are divorced. They had four children. Charles William Hirth was born in North Bloomfield Twp., Morrow Co., Ohio, on April 13, 1868. He reached age 86 and died in Wheeling, Ohio Co., West Virginia, on January 16, 1955.

Children of Ella Allen Hill and Charles William Hirth:

+ 198 f I. **Gertrude Isabella**[8] **Hirth** was born in Wheeling, Ohio Co., West Virginia, on June 4, 1890. She died in a facility in Cadiz, Cadiz Twp., Harrison Co., Ohio, on July 25, 1972. Gertrude Isabella was buried in Union Cemetery, Steubenville, Cross Creek Twp., Jefferson Co., Ohio.[16]

+ 199 f II. **Ada Roberts**[8] **Hirth** was born in Wheeling, Ohio Co., West Virginia, on July 26, 1892. She died in Peoria, Peoria Twp., Peoria Co., Illinois, on February 7, 1968. Ada Roberts was buried in Springdale Cemetery and Mausoleum, Peoria, Peoria Twp., Peoria Co., Illinois.[81]

+ 200 f III. **Della**[8] **Hirth** was born in Union Twp., Marshall Co. West Virginia, on June 12, 1898. She died in a hospital in Steubenville, Cross Creek Twp., Jefferson Co., Ohio, on February 8, 1988. Della was buried in Union Cemetery, Steubenville, Cross Creek Twp., Jefferson Co., Ohio.[16]

+ 201 m IV. **Charles William**[8] **Hirth II** was born in Wheeling, Ohio Co., West Virginia, on August 4, 1903. He was also known as **C. William Hirth**, **William** and **Bill.** Charles William died in a hospital in Wheeling, Ohio Co., West Virginia, on October 27, 1979. He was buried in Riverview Cemetery, Martins Ferry, Pease Twp., Belmont Co., Ohio.[14]

**107. Edward**[7] **Fox** (*Elizabeth Jane*[6] *Hill, Mary Jane*[5] *Goudy, Elizabeth Jane*[4] *Pegan, Andrew*[3] *Pegan II,*

*Andrew*[2] *Pagan, James*[1]) was born on April 21, 1868, in Hanging Rock Twp., Lawrence Co., Ohio. He was the son of Arthur William Fox and Elizabeth Jane Hill (45). Edward died in Wheeling, Ohio Co., West Virginia, on February 21, 1909, at age. He was buried in Mount Zion Cemetery, Wheeling, Ohio Co., West Virginia.[28]

Childless.

Edward married **Elizabeth Unknown** in 1891. Elizabeth Unknown was born in Ohio in October 1872. She was also known as **Lizzie.** Elizabeth died after 1909.

**108. Minnie Blanche**[7] **Fox** (*Elizabeth Jane*[6] *Hill, Mary Jane*[5] *Goudy, Elizabeth Jane*[4] *Pegan, Andrew*[3] *Pegan II, Andrew*[2] *Pagan, James*[1]) was born on August 2, 1871, in Washington Co., Ohio. She was the daughter of Arthur William Fox and Elizabeth Jane Hill (45). Minnie Blanche died in Buffalo, Erie Co., New York? about 1945 at age 73.

She was living in Buffalo, Erie Co., New York, with her son Benjamin, in the 1940 census. Undocumented family sources say she died there in 1945, but there is no death record for her in New York State or West Virginia online death records.

She married **John Howe Bridgeman.** They divorced. They had three sons. John Howe Bridgeman was born in Jackson Twp., Monroe Co., Ohio, on December 17, 1870. He reached age 60 and died in Shillington, Cumru Twp., Berks Co., Pennsylvania, on January 21, 1931. John Howe was buried in Charles Evans Cemetery, Reading, Berks Co., Pennsylvania.[82]

Sons of Minnie Blanche Fox and John Howe Bridgeman:

+ 202 m I. **Benjamin Cowen**[8] **Bridgeman** was born in New Martinsville, Wetzel Co., West Virginia, on November 21, 1894. He died in Buffalo, Erie Co., New York? after 1940.

+ 203 m II. **Arthur**[8] **Bridgeman** was born in New Martinsville, Wetzel Co., West Virginia, on November 21,

1899. He died in New Martins-ville, Wetzel Co., West Virginia, on July 13, 1904.

+ 204 m III. **John⁸ Bridgeman III** was born in New Martinsville, Wetzel Co. West Virginia, on March 21, 1906. He died in Lakeview, Erie Co., New York, in December 1970.,

**109. Alice⁷ Fox** (*Elizabeth Jane⁶ Hill, Mary Jane⁵ Goudy, Elizabeth Jane⁴ Pegan, Andrew³ Pegan II, Andrew² Pagan, James¹*) was born on October 23, 1873, in Washington Co., Ohio. She was the daughter of Arthur William Fox and Elizabeth Jane Hill (45). Alice died in Wheeling, Ohio Co., West Virginia, in August 23, 1900, at age 26. She was probably buried in Mount Zion Cemetery, Wheeling, Ohio Co., West Virginia.

Never married.

**110. Stella⁷ Fox** (*Elizabeth Jane⁶ Hill, Mary Jane⁵ Goudy, Elizabeth Jane⁴ Pegan, Andrew³ Pegan II, Andrew² Pagan, James¹*) was born in March 1877 in Washington Co., Ohio. She was the daughter of Arthur William Fox and Elizabeth Jane Hill (45). Stella died in Wheeling, Ohio Co., West Virginia, on April 1. 1900, at age 21. She was probably buried in Mount Zion Cemetery, Wheeling, Ohio Co., West Virginia.

Never married.

**111. Robert Arthur⁷ Fox** (*Elizabeth Jane⁶ Hill, Mary Jane⁵ Goudy, Elizabeth Jane⁴ Pegan, Andrew³ Pegan II, Andrew² Pagan, James¹*) was born on June 8, 1881, in Wheeling, Ohio Co., West Virginia. He was the son of Arthur William Fox and Elizabeth Jane Hill (45). Robert Arthur died in Wheeling, Ohio Co., West Virginia, on March 8, 1922, at age 40.

He married **Elizabeth Dichtenmuller.** They had two children. Elizabeth Dichtenmuller was born in Allegheny, Allegheny Co., Pennsylvania, on January 20, 1890. Elizabeth reached age 85 and died in Moundsville, Marshall Co., West Virginia, in September 1975.

Children of Robert Arthur Fox and Elizabeth Dichtenmuller:

+ 205 f I. **Roberta Elizabeth⁸ Fox** was born in Wheeling, Ohio Co., West Virginia, on February 3, 1911. She died in Glen Dale, Marshall Co., West Virginia, on October 20, 1983. Roberta Elizabeth was buried in Fairview Cemetery, Moundsville, Marshall Co., West Virginia.[83]

+ 206 m II. **Benjamin Harrison⁸ Fox** was born in Wheeling, Ohio Co., West Virginia, on July 25, 1918. He died in Wheeling, Ohio Co., West Virginia, on September 12, 1968. Benjamin Harrison was buried in Greenwood Cemetery, Wheeling, Ohio Co., West Virginia.[24]

**112. Jennie⁷ Fox** (*Elizabeth Jane⁶ Hill, Mary Jane⁵ Goudy, Elizabeth Jane⁴ Pegan, Andrew³ Pegan II, Andrew² Pagan, James¹*) was born on June 2, 1891, in Wheeling, Ohio Co., West Virginia. She was the daughter of Arthur William Fox and Elizabeth Jane Hill (45). Jennie died in Wheeling, Ohio Co., West Virginia, on January 2, 1935, at age 43.

Jennie married **John Edmond Flanegin** on August 1, 1908, in Ohio Co., West Virginia. They had three children. John Edmond Flanegin was born in New Cumberland, Hancock Co., West Virginia, on July 24, 1887. John Edmond reached age 56 and died in Jackson, Jackson Co., Michigan, on April 26, 1944. He was buried in Mount Zion Cemetery, Wheeling, Ohio Co., West Virginia.[28]

Children of Jennie Fox and John Edmond Flanegin:

+ 207 f I. **Marian Alice⁸ Flanegin** was born in Wheeling, Ohio Co., West Virginia, on August 2, 1909. She died in Wheeling, Ohio Co., West Virginia, on June 25, 1959. Marian Alice was buried in Greenwood

Cemetery, Wheeling, Ohio Co., West Virginia.[24]

+ 208 m II. **Edmund Arthur[8] Flanegin II** was born in Wheeling, Ohio Co., West Virginia, on April 28, 1912. He died in Wheeling, Ohio Co., West Virginia, on October 20, 1980. Edmund Arthur was buried in Greenwood Cemetery, Wheeling, Ohio Co., West Virginia.[24]

+ 209 f III. **Infant Daughter[8] Flanegin** was born in Wheeling, Ohio Co., West Virginia? on March 25, 1914. She died in Wheeling, Ohio Co., West Virginia, on March 25, 1914. Infant Daughter was buried in Mount Zion Cemetery, Wheeling, Ohio Co., West Virginia.[28]

**113. Ida[7] Fox** (*Elizabeth Jane[6] Hill, Mary Jane[5] Goudy, Elizabeth Jane[4] Pegan, Andrew[3] Pegan II, Andrew[2] Pagan, James[1]*) was born between 1866 and 1900. She was the daughter of Arthur William Fox and Elizabeth Jane Hill (45). Ida died between 1866 and 1900.

# 8th Generation

**114. Helen⁸ Goudy** (*Harry Homer⁷, William M.⁶, John⁵, Elizabeth Jane⁴ Pegan, Andrew³ Pegan II, Andrew² Pagan, James¹*) was born on May 4, 1904, in Moundsville, Marshall Co., West Virginia.[53] She was the daughter of Harry Homer Goudy (50) and Minnie Stillwill. Helen died in Moundsville, Marshall Co., West Virginia, on January 24, 1980, at age 75. She was buried in Limestone Cemetery, Limestone, Marshall Co., West Virginia.[56]

Helen married **Kirk Alexander Fisher** about 1926. They had one daughter. Kirk Alexander Fisher was born in Moundsville, Marshall Co., West Virginia, on January 25, 1898.[55] Kirk Alexander reached age 74 and died in Moundsville, Marshall Co., West Virginia, on November 18, 1972.[84] He was buried in Limestone Cemetery, Limestone, Marshall Co., West Virginia.[56]

Daughter of Helen Goudy and Kirk Alexander Fisher:

+ 210 f I. **Alice Eileen⁹ Fisher** was born in Sherrard, Union Twp., Marshall Co., West Virginia, on January 7, 1928. She is also known as **Eileen.**

**115. Lewis or Louis MacAfee⁸ Thompson II** (*Lewis K.⁷, Nancy J.⁶ Goudy, Andrew⁵, Elizabeth Jane⁴ Pegan, Andrew³ Pegan II, Andrew² Pagan, James¹*) was born on February 22, 1889, in Cleveland, Cuyahoga Co., Ohio. He was the son of Lewis K. Thompson (55) and Rebecca A. Valentine. Lewis or Louis MacAfee died in O'Hara, Allegheny Co., Pennsylvania, on February 3, 1941, at age 51.

Lewis or Louis MacAfee married **Susan Pearl Rikeard** or **Rickerd** on January 14, 1909, in Blakes Mills, Goshen Twp., Tuscarawas Co., Ohio. She was also known as Pearl. They had one son. Susan Pearl Rikeard or Rickerd was born in Blakes Mills, Goshen Twp., Tuscarawas Co., Ohio, on June 10, 1886. She reached age 26 and died on October 31, 1912 in Uhrichsville, Mill Twp., Tuscarawas Co., Ohio. Susan Pearl is buried under the name Pearl Susan Thompson in Union Cemetery, Uhrichsville, Mill Twp., Tuscarawas Co., Ohio.[13]

Lewis or Louis MacAfee Thompson II married **Ruth Sophia Metzger** on December 31, 1913, in Tuscarawas Co., Ohio. They divorced before 1920. Ruth Sophia Metzger was born in Warwick Twp., Tuscarawas Co., Ohio, on March 10, 1892.

Lewis or Louis MacAfee Thompson II married **Mary R. Unknown** before 1920. Mary R. Unknown was born in 1889.

Lewis or Louis MacAfee Thompson II married Mrs. **Margaret Donohue** Walton before 1930. Margaret Donohue was born in Ohio in 1889. Margaret died after 1941.

Son of Lewis or Louis MacAfee Thompson II and Pearl Rikeard:

+ 211 m I. **Son⁹ Thompson** was born in Uhrichsville, Mill Twp., Tuscarawas Co., Ohio, on April 8, 1909. He died in Uhrichsville, Mill Twp., Tuscarawas Co., Ohio, on April 9, 1909.

**116. Samuel⁸ Thompson** (*Lewis K.⁷, Nancy J.⁶ Goudy, Andrew⁵, Elizabeth Jane⁴ Pegan, Andrew³ Pegan II, Andrew² Pagan, James¹*) was born on April 12, 1904 in Uhrichsville, Mill Twp., Tuscarawas Co., Ohio. He died after 1930 in Contra Costa Co., California?

Samuel married **Gladys Maria Kadora** on July 27, 1923 in Brooke Co., West Virginia. They divorced. Gladys Maria Kadora was born in Pultney Twp., Belmont Co., Ohio on November 16, 1905. She reached age 64 and died as Gladys M. Huebner in Las Vegas, Clark Co., Nevada on January 30, 1970. Gladys is buried in Woodlawn Cemetery, Las Vegas, Clark Co., Nevada.[A]

**117. James Howard⁸ Galbreath** (*Ella Nancy⁷ Thompson, Nancy J.⁶ Goudy, Andrew⁵, Elizabeth Jane⁴ Pegan, Andrew³ Pegan II, Andrew² Pagan, James¹*) was born on November 1, 1874, in Fairview Valley Twp., Guernsey Co., Ohio. He was also known as **Howard.** He was the son of William Galbreath and Ella Nancy Thompson (56). James Howard died in Uhrichsville, Mill Twp., Tuscarawas Co., Ohio, on June 7, 1961, at age 86. He was buried in Evergreen Burial Park, New Philadelphia, Tuscarawas Co., Ohio.[58]

James Howard Galbreath always used his middle name, Howard, as his preferred name.

James Howard married **Eva E. Bratton** on May 16, 1894, in Guernsey Co., Ohio. They had three children. Eva E. Bratton was born in Kirkwood Twp., Belmont Co., Ohio, on October 12, 1877. Eva E. reached age 88 and died in Uhrichsville, Mill Twp., Tuscarawas Co., Ohio, on November 30, 1965. She was buried in Evergreen Burial Park, New Philadelphia, Tuscarawas Co., Ohio.[58]

Children of James Howard Galbreath and Eva E. Bratton:

+ 212 m I. **Guy Leroy⁹ Galbreath** was born in Uhrichsville, Mill Twp., Tuscarawas Co., Ohio, on July 27, 1895. He died in Uhrichsville, Mill Twp., Tuscarawas Co., Ohio, on October 18, 1956. Guy Leroy was buried in Longview Cemetery, Bowerston, Monroe Twp., Harrison Co., Ohio.[85]

+ 213 m II. **Raymond Arthur⁹ Galbreath** was born in Uhrichsville, Mill Twp., Tuscarawas Co., Ohio, on October 22, 1897. He died in Uhrichsville, Mill Twp., Tuscarawas Co., Ohio, on May 23, 1973. Raymond Arthur was buried in Evergreen Burial Park, New Philadelphia, Tuscarawas Co., Ohio.[58]

+ 214 f III. **Clara Irene⁹ Galbreath** was born in Uhrichsville, Mill Twp., Tuscarawas Co., Ohio, on June 24, 1905. She was also known as **Irene.** Clara Irene died in a hospital in Lancaster, Fairfield Co., Ohio, on December 12, 1998. She was buried in Evergreen Burial Park, New Philadelphia, Tuscarawas Co., Ohio.[58]

118. **Clara E.⁸ Galbreath** (*Ella Nancy⁷ Thompson, Nancy J.⁶ Goudy, Andrew⁵, Elizabeth Jane⁴ Pegan, Andrew³ Pegan II, Andrew² Pagan, James¹*) was born on June 30, 1880, in Fairview Valley Twp., Guernsey Co., Ohio. She was the daughter of William Galbreath and Ella Nancy Thompson˙ (56). Clara E. died in Uhrichsville, Mill Twp., Tuscarawas Co., Ohio, on September 14, 1906, at age 26. She was buried in Union Cemetery, Uhrichsville, Mill Twp., Tuscarawas Co., Ohio.[13]

Never married.

119. **Jessie A.⁸ Cary** (*Sarah Virginia⁷ Thompson, Nancy J.⁶ Goudy, Andrew⁵, Elizabeth Jane⁴ Pegan, Andrew³ Pegan II, Andrew² Pagan, James¹*) was born on September 14, 1883, in Uhrichsville, Mill Twp., Tuscarawas Co., Ohio. She was the daughter of John Pryor Cary and Sarah Virginia Thompson (57). Jessie A. died in Sacramento, Sacramento Co., California, on March 25, 1922, at age 38.

Childless.

Jessie A. married **Walter Renshaw** before 1918. Walter Renshaw was born in Chesterfield, Derby, England, on February 6, 1883. Walter reached age 62 and died in Los Angeles, Los Angeles Co., California, on March 25, 1945.

120. **Charles Stewart⁸ Cary** (*Sarah Virginia⁷ Thompson, Nancy J.⁶ Goudy, Andrew⁵, Elizabeth Jane⁴ Pegan, Andrew³ Pegan II, Andrew² Pagan, James¹*) was born on April 14, 1887, in Dennison, Mill Twp., Tuscarawas Co., Ohio. He was the son of John Pryor Cary and Sarah Virginia Thompson (57). He resided in 1974 in Massillon, Perry Twp., Stark Co., Ohio. Charles Stewart died in a hospital in Canton, Stark Co., Ohio, on February 1, 1974, at age 86. He was buried in Saint Joseph Cemetery, Massillon, Perry Twp., Stark Co., Ohio.[59]

Charles Stewart married **Mary Alice McCullough** on June 11, 1906. They had eight children. Mary Alice McCullough was born in Dennison, Mill Twp., Tuscarawas Co., Ohio, on February 14, 1888. Mary Alice reached age 54 and died in Massillon, Perry Twp., Stark Co., Ohio, on August 18, 1942. She was buried in Saint Joseph Cemetery, Massillon, Perry Twp., Stark Co., Ohio.[59]

Children of Charles Stewart Cary and Mary Alice McCullough:

+ 215 m I. **Charles Marshall⁹ Cary II** was born in Uhrichsville, Mill Twp., Tuscarawas Co., Ohio, on February 27, 1908. He died in Massillon, Perry Twp., Stark Co., Ohio, on July 6, 1981. Charles Marshall was buried in Saint Barbara Cemetery, Massillon, Perry Twp., Stark Co., Ohio.[86]

+ 216 f II. **Helen⁹ Cary** was born in Uhrichsville, Mill Twp., Tuscarawas Co., Ohio, in 1910. She died in Uhrichsville, Mill Twp., Tuscarawas Co., Ohio, in 1910.

+ 217 f III. **Betty J.⁹ Cary** was born in Uhrichsville, Mill Twp., Tuscarawas Co., Ohio, in 1912. She died after 1930.

+ 218 m IV. **Robert Glen⁹ Cary** was born in Uhrichsville, Mill Twp., Tuscarawas Co., Ohio, on January 23, 1914. He died on November 17, 2000, in Sun City, Maricopa Co., Arizona. He was buried in Sunland Memorial Park Cemetery, Sun City, Maricopa Co., Arizona.[87]

+ 219 f V. **Ruth Irene⁹ Cary** was born in Uhrichsville, Mill Twp., Tuscarawas Co., Ohio, on March 10, 1916. She died in Winnetka, Los Angeles Co., California, on December 23, 1997.

+ 220 f VI. **Margaret Jean⁹ Cary** was born in Uhrichsville, Mill Twp., Tuscarawas Co., Ohio, on August 7, 1918. She died in Louisvile, Jefferson Co., Kentucky, on January 27, 2001.

+ 221 m VII. **Thomas E.⁹ Cary** was born in Massillon, Perry Twp., Stark Co., Ohio, on November 24, 1925. He died in Massillon, Perry Twp., Stark Co., Ohio, on September 11, 2008.

+ 222 m VIII. **Edward⁹ Cary** was born in Massillon, Perry Twp., Stark Co., Ohio, in 1927. He died before 2001.

**121. Artland Robinson⁸ Bovey** (*Mary E.⁷ Thompson, Nancy J.⁶ Goudy, Andrew⁵, Elizabeth Jane⁴ Pegan, Andrew³ Pegan II, Andrew² Pagan, James¹*) was born on March 1, 1884, in Conneaut, Conneaut Twp., Ashtabula Co., Ohio. He was the son of Harry Artland Bovey and Mary E. Thompson (58). Artland Robinson died in Queens, Queens Co., New York? in August 1951 at age 67.

Artland Robinson married **Charlotte Olmsted** before 1905. They had five children. Charlotte Olmsted was born in Gates, Monroe Co., New York, on February 26, 1886. She was also known as **Lottie.** Charlotte reached age 31 and died in Cleveland, Cuyahoga Co., Ohio, on February 16, 1918. She was buried in Center Cemetery, Conneaut, Conneaut Twp., Ashtabula Co., Ohio.[88]

After his wife Charlotte Olmstead Bovey's death, Artland R. Bovey's children seemed to have been not in his care and may have been with foster families or adopted out.

Artland Robinson Bovey married **Margaret Unknown** after 1918. Margaret Unknown was born in Maryland in 1886. Margaret died in Queens, Queens Co., New York? after 1942.

Children of Artland Robinson Bovey and Charlotte Olmsted:

+ 223 f I. **Helen May⁹ Bovey (Seeley)** was born in Conneaut, Conneaut Twp., Ashtabula Co., Ohio, on April 5, 1905. She died in Federal Way, King Co., Washington, on September 25, 1987. Helen May was buried in Forest Lawn Memorial

Park Cemetery, Glendale, Los Angeles Co., California[47]

+ 224 m II. **Harry Olmstead[9] Bovey** was born in Massillon, Perry Twp., Stark Co., Ohio, on July 19, 1906. He died in Goleta, Santa Barbara Co., California, on November 20, 1988.

+ 225 f III. **Adeline May[9] Bovey** was born in Conneaut, Conneaut Twp., Ashtabula Co., Ohio, on November 20, 1908. She died in Yountville, Napa Co., California, on November 1, 2001. Adeline May was buried in Napa Valley Memorial Park Cemetery, Napa, Napa Co., California.[89]

+ 226 f IV. **Betty Maude[9] Bovey** was born in Conneaut, Conneaut Twp., Ashtabula Co., Ohio, on May 26, 1912. She died in Willis, Montgomery Co., Texas, on November 19, 1996. Betty Maude was buried in Willis Cemetery, Willis, Montgomery Co., Texas.[90]

+ 227 m V. **Frank[9] Bovey** was born in Cleveland, Cuyahoga Co., Ohio, on May 21, 1917. He died in Cleveland, Cuyahoga Co., Ohio, on September 25, 1917. Frank was buried in Harvard Grove Cemetery, Cleveland, Cuyahoga Co., Ohio.[91]

122. **Son[8] Bovey** (*Mary E.[7] Thompson, Nancy J.[6] Goudy, Andrew[5], Elizabeth Jane[4] Pegan, Andrew[3] Pegan II, Andrew[2] Pagan, James[1]*) was born on October 5, 1891, in Uhrichsville, Mill Twp., Tuscarawas Co., Ohio. He was the son of Harry Artland Bovey and Mary E. Thompson (58). Son died in Uhrichsville, Mill Twp., Tuscarawas Co., Ohio, on October 5, 1891.

123. **Ellamae[8] Thompson** (*Robert[7], Nancy J.[6] Goudy, Andrew[5], Elizabeth Jane[4] Pegan, Andrew[3] Pegan II, Andrew[2] Pagan, James[1]*) was born on November 2, 1905, in McMechen, Union Dist., Marshall Co., West Virginia. She was the daughter of Robert Thompson (60) and Florence Elizabeth White. Ellamae died in Uhrichsville, Mill Twp., Tuscarawas Co., Ohio?, on April 9, 1954, at age 48. She was buried in McMechen Cemetery, Union Dist., Marshall Co., West Virginia.[38]

Childless.

Ellamae married **Kermit Roosevelt Price** on October 16. 1942 in Marshall Co., West Virginia. They may have divorced. Kermit Roosevelt Price was born in Wayne, Wayne Co., West Virginia, on July 9, 1914. He reached age 71 and died in Tucson, Pima Co., Arizona, on December 26, 1985. Kermit is buried in East Lawn Palms Cemetery, Tucson, Pima Co., Arizona.[B]

124. **Nettie A.[8] Varner** (*Laura Bell[7] Goudy, Isaac M.[6], Andrew[5], Elizabeth Jane[4] Pegan, Andrew[3] Pegan II, Andrew[2] Pagan, James[1]*) was born on November 29, 1875, in Rush Twp., Tuscarawas Co., Ohio. She was the daughter of Benjamin Varner and Laura Bell Goudy (61). Nettie A. died in Uhrichsville, Mill Twp., Tuscarawas Co., Ohio, on March 25, 1903, at age 27. She was buried in Dutch Valley Cemetery, Rush Twp., Tuscarawas Co., Ohio.[17]

Childless.

Nettie A. married **Walter Edwin Crim** on February 25, 1900, in Tuscarawas Co., Ohio. They divorced. Walter Edwin Crim was born in Feed Springs, Franklin Twp., Harrison Co., Ohio, on August 10, 1873. He reached age 82 and died in Penn Hills, Allegheny Co., Pennsylvania, on May 29, 1956.

125. **Charles W.[8] Varner** (*Laura Bell[7] Goudy, Isaac M.[6], Andrew[5], Elizabeth Jane[4] Pegan, Andrew[3] Pegan II, Andrew[2] Pagan, James[1]*) was born on August 11, 1877, in Rush Twp., Tuscarawas Co., Ohio. Charles W. died in Rush Twp., Tuscarawas Co., Ohio, on August 20, 1894, at age 17. He was buried in Dutch Valley Cemetery, Rush Twp., Tuscarawas Co., Ohio.[17]

Never married.

126. **Guy Andrew[8] Beazle** (*Sarah[7] Goudy, Isaac M.[6], Andrew[5], Elizabeth Jane[4] Pegan, Andrew[3] Pegan II, Andrew[2] Pagan, James[1]*) was born on November 5, 1876, in Pease Twp., Belmont Co., Ohio. He was

the son of Frank Neal Beazle and Sarah Goudy (62). Guy Andrew died in Martins Ferry, Pease Twp., Belmont Co., Ohio, on June 10, 1947, at age 70. He was buried in Riverview Cemetery, Martins Ferry, Pease Twp., Belmont Co., Ohio.[14]

Guy Andrew married **Lucy Ann Gaughan** on April 1, 1899, in Jefferson Co., Ohio. They had two sons. Lucy Ann Gaughan was born in Goosetown, Harrison Co., West Virginia, on August 21, 1879. Lucy Ann reached age 60 and died in Martins Ferry, Pease Twp., Belmont Co., Ohio, on November 22, 1939. She was buried in Riverview Cemetery, Martins Ferry, Pease Twp., Belmont Co., Ohio.[14]

Guy Andrew Beazle married **Lissetta Sarah Carter** on August 28, 1940, in Jefferson Co., Ohio. Lissetta Sarah Carter was born in Mount Pleasant, Mount Pleasant Twp., Jefferson Co., Ohio, on January 6, 1886. She was also known as **Sarah.** Lissetta Sarah lived in 1968 in Martins Ferry, Pease Twp., Belmont Co., Ohio. She reached age 82 and died in a facility in New Philadelphia, Goshen Twp., Tuscarawas Co., Ohio, on May 10, 1968.

Lissetta Sarah Carter always used her middle name, Sarah, as her preferred name. She died under the name Sarah L. Berry.

Sons of Guy Andrew Beazle and Lucy Ann Gaughan:

+ 228 m I. **Harold Guy⁹ Beazle** was born in Hocking Co., Ohio, on February 4, 1901. He died in Martins Ferry, Pease Twp., Belmont Co., Ohio, on December 6, 1959. Harold Guy was buried in Piitsburgh, Allegheny Co., Pennsylvania.

+ 229 m II. **Frank⁹ Beazle** was born in Brilliant, Wells Twp., Jefferson Co., Ohio, on December 23, 1906. He died in Wheeling, Ohio Co., West Virginia, on October 19, 1964. Frank was buried in Riverview Cemetery, Martins Ferry, Pease Twp., Belmont Co., Ohio.[14]

**127. Bessie⁸ Beazle** (*Sarah⁷ Goudy, Isaac M.⁶, Andrew⁵, Elizabeth Jane⁴ Pegan, Andrew³ Pegan II, Andrew²*

*Pagan, James¹*) was born in 1879 in Pease Twp., Belmont Co., Ohio. She was the daughter of Frank Neal Beazle and Sarah Goudy (62). Bessie died in Pease Twp., Belmont Co., Ohio, between 1880 and 1881. Seems to have died in infancy.

**128. May⁸ Beazle** (*Sarah⁷ Goudy, Isaac M.⁶, Andrew⁵, Elizabeth Jane⁴ Pegan, Andrew³ Pegan II, Andrew² Pagan, James¹*) was born in 1881 in Pittsburgh, Allegheny Co., Pennsylvania. She was the daughter of Frank Neal Beazle and Sarah Goudy (62). May died in Pittsburgh, Allegheny Co., Pennsylvania, on October 26, 1882.

**129. Margaret⁸ Beazle** (*Sarah⁷ Goudy, Isaac M.⁶, Andrew⁵, Elizabeth Jane⁴ Pegan, Andrew³ Pegan II, Andrew² Pagan, James¹*) was born on April 12, 1883, in Pittsburgh, Allegheny Co., Pennsylvania. She was the daughter of Frank Neal Beazle and Sarah Goudy (62). Margaret died in Martins Ferry, Pease Twp., Belmont Co., Ohio, on January 16, 1948. She was buried in Riverview Cemetery, Martins Ferry, Pease Twp., Belmont Co., Ohio.[14]

Childless.

She married **William Edward Sizer.** William Edward Sizer was born in Alexandria, Virginia, on September 25, 1880. William Edward reached age 48 and died in Martins Ferry, Pease Twp., Belmont Co., Ohio, on April 15, 1929. He was buried in Riverview Cemetery, Martins Ferry, Pease Twp., Belmont Co., Ohio.[14]

**130. Clara Janette⁸ Beazle** (*Sarah⁷ Goudy, Isaac M.⁶, Andrew⁵, Elizabeth Jane⁴ Pegan, Andrew³ Pegan II, Andrew² Pagan, James¹*) was born on February 6, 1886, in Martins Ferry, Pease Twp., Belmont Co., Ohio. She was the daughter of Frank Neal Beazle and Sarah Goudy (62). Clara Janette lived in 1974 in Canton, Stark Co., Ohio. She died in a hospital in Canton, Stark Co., Ohio, on December 28, 1974. Clara Janette was buried in Riverview Cemetery, Martins Ferry, Pease Twp., Belmont Co., Ohio?

Clara Janette married **Harry Z. Galbraith** on March 25, 1913, in Ohio Co., West Virginia. They divorced. They had one daughter. Harry Z. Galbraith was born in New Jefferson Twp., Harrison Co., Ohio, on December 22, 1890. He reached age 54 and died in Akron, Summit Co.,

Ohio, on January 9, 1945. Harry Z. was buried in Germano Cemetery, Germano, German Twp., Harrison Co., Ohio.[92]

Daughter of Clara Janette Beazle and Harry Z. Galbraith:

+ 230  f  I.  **Dorothy Jean⁹ Galbraith** was born in Martins Ferry, Pease Twp., Belmont Co., Ohio, on June 13, 1914. She died in Herndon, Fairfax Co., Virginia, on August 25, 1996. Dorothy Jean was buried in Chestnut Grove Cemetery, Herndon, Fairfax Co., Virginia.[93]

131. **Mabel Estella⁸ Wardell** (*Joseph A.⁷, Elizabeth Sophronia⁶ Goudy, Andrew⁵, Elizabeth Jane⁴ Pegan, Andrew³ Pegan II, Andrew² Pagan, James¹*) was born on June 9, 1895, in Mill Twp., Tuscarawas Co., Ohio. She was the daughter of Joseph A. Wardell (65) and Elvina Ella Wolf. Mabel Estella died in Dover, Dover Twp., Tuscarawas Co., Ohio, on January 3, 1992, at age 96. She was buried in Gnadenhutten-Clay Union Cemetery, Clay Twp., Tuscarawas Co., Ohio.[39]

Never married.

132. **Gladys Velma⁸ Wardell** (*Joseph A.⁷, Elizabeth Sophronia⁶ Goudy, Andrew⁵, Elizabeth Jane⁴ Pegan, Andrew³ Pegan II, Andrew² Pagan, James¹*) was born on September 3, 1901, in Mill Twp., Tuscarawas Co., Ohio. She was the daughter of Joseph A. Wardell (65) and Elvina Ella Wolf. Gladys Velma died in Tuscarawas, Warwick Twp., Tuscarawas Co., Ohio, on December 15, 1975, at age 74.

Childless.

Gladys Velma married **Doyle Montford Baker** on December 1, 1945, in Tuscarawas Co., Ohio. Doyle Montford Baker was born in Uhrichsville, Mill Twp., Tuscarawas Co., Ohio, on May 8, 1898. Doyle Montford reached age 58 and died in Tuscarawas, Warwick Twp., Tuscarawas Co., Ohio, on April 15, 1957.

133. **Mildred Opal⁸ Huff** (*Minnie Etta⁷ Wardell, Elizabeth Sophronia⁶ Goudy, Andrew⁵, Elizabeth Jane⁴ Pegan, Andrew³ Pegan II, Andrew² Pagan, James¹*) was born on April 2, 1894, in Mill Twp.,

Tuscarawas Co., Ohio. She was the daughter of Charles H. Huff and Minnie Etta Wardell (67). Mildred Opal died in Ramona, San Diego Co., California, on February 19, 1986, at age 91.

Mildred Opal married **Judson Clarence Freeman** on August 22, 1912, in Cuyahoga Co., Ohio. They divorced. They had one son. Judson Clarence Freeman was born in Strongville, Cuyahoga Co., Ohio, on May 10, 1874. Judson Clarence died in Canada? after 1917.

Mildred Opal Huff Freeman married **Henry Edward Spilker** on June 22, 1915, in Cuyahoga Co., Ohio. They divorced. Henry Edward Spilker was born in Cleveland, Cuyahoga Co., Ohio, on February 27, 1891. Henry Edward reached age 60 and died in Cleveland, Cuyahoga Co., Ohio, on April 4, 1951. He was buried in Alger Cemetery, Cleveland, Cuyahoga Co., Ohio.[94]

Mildred Opal Huff Freeman Spilker married **Harry W. Frey** on October 27, 1917, in Cuyahoga Co., Ohio. Harry W. Frey was born in Germany in 1881. Harry W. died in Canada or Germany after 1917. They may have divorced.

Mildred Opal Huff Freeman Spilker Frey married **Daniel Harvey Getchell** on March 7, 1921, in Cuyahoga Co., Ohio. They divorced in Los Angeles Co., California, before 1928. Daniel Harvey Getchell was born in Akron, Summit Co., Ohio, on January 3, 1897. He reached age 76 and died in North Hollywood, Los Angeles Co., California, on December 29, 1973.

Mildred Opal Huff Freeman Spilker Frey Getchell married **John Milton Brunson** before 1940. John Milton Brunson was born in Riceville, Jenkins Twp., Mitchell Co., Iowa, on July 19, 1903. John Milton lived in 1940 in Long Valley, Mendocino Co., California. He reached age 82 and died in Ramona, San Diego Co., California, on December 26, 1985.

Son of Mildred Opal Huff and Judson Clarence Freeman:

+ 231  m  I.  **Judson Milton⁹ Freeman II** was born in Cleveland, Cuyahoga Co.,

Ohio, on July 11, 1913. He was also known as **Buckie.** Judson Milton died in Cleveland, Cuyahoga Co., Ohio, on February 22, 1921. He was buried in West Park Cemetery, Cleveland, Cuyahoga Co., Ohio.[61]

**134. Beatrice LaVonne[8] Huff** (*Minnie Etta[7] Wardell, Elizabeth Sophronia[6] Goudy, Andrew[5], Elizabeth Jane[4] Pegan, Andrew[3] Pegan II, Andrew[2] Pagan, James[1]*) was born on June 9, 1896, in Mill Twp., Tuscarawas Co., Ohio. She was the daughter of Charles H. Huff and Minnie Etta Wardell (67). Beatrice LaVonne died in South Gate, Los Angeles Co., California, on October 18, 1978, at age 82.

Childless.

Beatrice LaVonne married **Leo A. Crew** on December 26, 1919, in Cuyahoga Co., Ohio. They divorced. Leo A. Crew was born in Erie, Erie Co., Pennsylvania, on July 31, 1898. He reached age 65 and died in Manhattan Beach, Los Angeles Co., California, on December 22, 1963. Leo A. was buried in Pacific Crest Cemetery, Redondo Beach, Los Angeles Co., California.[95]

**135. Ada[8] Goudy** (*Andrew W.[7], William A.[6], Andrew[5], Elizabeth Jane[4] Pegan, Andrew[3] Pegan II, Andrew[2] Pagan, James[1]*) was born on August 14, 1894, in Bridgeport, Bellaire Twp., Belmont Co., Ohio. She was the daughter of Andrew W. Goudy (69) and Huldah Annie Pietz. Ada died in Bridgeport, Bellaire Twp., Belmont Co., Ohio, on September 1, 1894.

**136. Edwin Andrew[8] Goudy** (*Andrew W.[7], William A.[6], Andrew[5], Elizabeth Jane[4] Pegan, Andrew[3] Pegan II, Andrew[2] Pagan, James[1]*) was born on April 27, 1899, in Bridgeport, Bellaire Twp., Belmont Co., Ohio. He was the son of Andrew W. Goudy (69) and Huldah Annie Pietz. Edwin Andrew died in Triadelphia, Ohio Co., West Virginia, on October 27, 1987, at age 88. He was buried in West Alexander Cemetery, West Alexander, Donegal Twp., Washington Co., Pennsylvania.[62]

Edwin Andrew married **Elinor Weigelt** on March 23, 1925, in Ohio Co., West Virginia. They had one son. Elinor Weigelt was born in Wheeling, Ohio Co., West Virginia, on April 29, 1897. Elinor reached age 89 and died in Triadelphia, Ohio Co., West Virginia, in September 1986. She was buried in West Alexander Cemetery, West Alexander, Donegal Twp., Washington Co., Pennsylvania.[62]

Son of Edwin Andrew Goudy and Elinor Weigelt:

+ 232 m I. **Charles Andrew[9] Goudy** was born in Triadelphia, Ohio Co., West Virginia, on November 3, 1926. He died in a hospital in Wheeling, Ohio Co., West Virginia, on July 31, 2015.

**137. Irene[8] Cooper** (*Maud[7] Goudy, William A.[6], Andrew[5], Elizabeth Jane[4] Pegan, Andrew[3] Pegan II, Andrew[2] Pagan, James[1]*) was born on March 22, 1899, in Wellsville, Wellsville Twp., Columbiana Co., Ohio. She was the daughter of William Oliver Cooper and Maud Goudy (70). Irene died in Lakewood, Cuyahoga Co., Ohio, on April 17, 1980, at age 81. She was buried in Western Reserve Mausoleum, Warren, Trumbull Co., Ohio.[40]

Childless.

Irene married **Vance Surmo** on June 28, 1922, in Cuyahoga Co., Ohio. Vance Surmo was born in Holt, Marshall Co., Minnesota, on June 21, 1895. Vance reached age 53 and died in Flushing, Queens Co., New York, on December 28, 1948. He was buried in Long Island National Cemetery, Farmingdale, Suffolk Co., New York.[96]

**138. Gwendolyn Lee[8] Cooper** (*Maud[7] Goudy, William A.[6], Andrew[5], Elizabeth Jane[4] Pegan, Andrew[3] Pegan II, Andrew[2] Pagan, James[1]*) was born on November 7, 1916, in Cleveland, Cuyahoga Co., Ohio. She was the daughter of William Oliver Cooper and Maud Goudy (70). Gwendolyn Lee died in Eastlake, Lake Co., Ohio, on May 20, 2010, at age 93. She was buried in Western Reserve Mausoleum, Warren, Trumbull Co., Ohio.[40]

Childless.

Gwendolyn Lee married **Russell Edgar Gardner** on June 25, 1936, in Cuyahoga Co., Ohio. Russell

Edgar Gardner was born in Cleveland, Cuyahoga Co., Ohio, on January 23, 1913. Russell Edgar reached age 76 and died in Richmond Heights, Cuyahoga Co., Ohio, on October 18, 1989. He was buried in Western Reserve Mausoleum, Warren, Trumbull Co., Ohio.[40]

**139. Robert Edwin[8] Blankensop II** (*Robert Goudy[7], Mary Rebecca[6] Goudy, Robert[5], Elizabeth Jane[4] Pegan, Andrew[3] Pegan II, Andrew[2] Pagan, James[1]*) was born on May 23, 1893, in Moundsville, Marshall Co., West Virginia. He was the son of Robert Goudy Blankensop (71) and Elizabeth Hunter. Robert Edwin died in Berkeley Co., West Virginia, on July 6, 1957, at age 64. He was buried in Arlington National Cemetery, Arlington, Virginia.[63]

Robert Edwin married **Catherine Waldschmidt** in 1922 in Wood Co., West Virginia. They divorced between 1930 and 1940. They had one son. Catherine Waldschmidt was born in Turbotville, Northumberland Co., Pennsylvania, in 1900. She died after 1940.

Robert Edwin Blankensop II married **Marie Hall** in 1937 in Marshall Co., West Virginia. Marie Hall was born in Grandview Twp., Washington Co. Ohio, on November 27, 1900. Marie reached age 52 and died in Glen Dale, Marshall Co., West Virginia, on January 4, 1953. She was buried in Mount Rose Cemetery, Moundsville, Marshall Co., West Virginia.[41]

Son of Robert Edwin Blankensop II and Catherine Waldschmidt:

+ 233  m  I.  **Robert Edwin[9] Blankensop III** was born in Parkersburg, Wood Co., West Virginia, on November 19, 1926. He died in Beaufort, Beaufort Co., South Carolina, on April 17, 2011. Robert Edwin was buried in Good Shepherd Episcopal Church Columbarium, Parkersburg, Marshall Co., West Virginia.[97]

**140. Anita[8] Blankensop** (*Robert Goudy[7], Mary Rebecca[6] Goudy, Robert[5], Elizabeth Jane[4] Pegan,*

*Andrew[3] Pegan II, Andrew[2] Pagan, James[1]*) was born on June 6, 1896, in Moundsville, Marshall Co., West Virginia.[3912]She was the daughter of Robert Goudy Blankensop (71) and Elizabeth Hunter. Anita died in Alexandria, Fairfax Co., Virginia, on November 16, 1983, at age 87. She was buried in Mount Rose Cemetery, Moundsville, Marshall Co., West Virginia.[12]

Anita married **Clyde Lewis Lutes** in 1921 in Marshall Co., West Virginia. They had two children. Clyde Lewis Lutes was born in Moundsville, Marshall Co., West Virginia, on May 30, 1891. Clyde Lewis reached age 62 and died in Weston, Lewis Co., West Virginia, on October 4, 1953. He was buried in Mount Rose Cemetery, Moundsville, Marshall Co., West Virginia.[12]

Children of Anita Blankensop and Clyde Lewis Lutes:

+ 234  m  I.  **William Donald[9] Lutes** was born in Moundsville, Marshall Co., West Virginia, on March 18, 1922. He died in Alexandria, Alexandria Co., Virginia, on April 2, 1967.

+ 235  f  II.  **Elizabeth Ann[9] Lutes** was born in Moundsville, Marshall Co., West Virginia, in 1933.

**141. William Rex[8] Blankensop** (*Robert Goudy[7], Mary Rebecca[6] Goudy, Robert[5], Elizabeth Jane[4] Pegan, Andrew[3] Pegan II, Andrew[2] Pagan, James[1]*) was born on December 13, 1898, in Moundsville, Marshall Co., West Virginia. He was the son of Robert Goudy Blankensop (71) and Elizabeth Hunter. William Rex died in Moundsville, Marshall Co., West Virginia, on April 6, 1953, at age 54. He was buried in Mount Rose Cemetery, Moundsville, Marshall Co., West Virginia.[12]

William Rex married **Lucille Emma Wood** before 1930. They divorced. Lucille Emma Wood was born in Harrison Twp., Gallia Co., Ohio, on June 16, 1908. Lucille Emma reached age 83 and died in Trumbull Co., Ohio? on July 4, 1991.

She remarried several times and died under the name Lucille Emma Ault.

William Rex Blankensop married **Natalie Martin** after 1930. Natalie Martin was born in Moundsville, Marshall Co., West Virginia? on June 14, 1909. Natalie reached age 78 and died in Moundsville, Marshall Co., West Virginia, on April 16, 1988.

142. **Donald Winston⁸ Main** (*Mary Phrania⁷ Pattie, Phrania Elizabeth⁶ Goudy, Robert⁵, Elizabeth Jane⁴ Pegan, Andrew³ Pegan II, Andrew² Pagan, James¹*) was born on November 16, 1917, in Providence, Providence Co., Rhode Island. He was the son of Frank Le Roi Main and Mary Phrania Pattie (76). Donald Winston died in Jackson, Jackson Co., Michigan, on March 3, 2006, at age 88.

He married **Viola Grace Upper** on March 12, 1938 in Steuben Co., Indiana. They had at least two daughters. Viola Grace Upper was born in Pontiac, Wayne Co., Michigan on October 5, 1917. She reached age 69 and died in Jackson, Jackson Co., Michigan on February 16, 2008.

Daughters of Donald Winston Main and Viola Grace Upper:

+ 236 f I. **Marcia⁹ Main** was born in Birmingham, Oakland Co., Michigan, in 1938.

+ 237 f II. **Shirley⁹ Main** was born in Birmingham, Oakland Co., Michigan, in 1939.

143. **Pattie⁸ Main** (*Mary Phrania⁷ Pattie, Phrania Elizabeth⁶ Goudy, Robert⁵, Elizabeth Jane⁴ Pegan, Andrew³ Pegan II, Andrew² Pagan, James¹*) was born on May 17, 1919, in Providence, Providence Co., Rhode Island. She was the daughter of Frank Le Roi Main and Mary Phrania Pattie (76). Pattie died in Van Nuys, Los Angeles Co., California, on November 20, 1999, at age 80.

Seems to have been childless.

Pattie married **John Michael James Popovics** on June 29, 1959, in Los Angeles Co., California. John Michael James Popovics was born in Cleveland, Cuyahoga Co., Ohio, on July 14, 1916. John Michael James reached age 71 and died in Van Nuys, Los Angeles Co., California, on January 19, 1988.

144. **John William⁸ Main** (*Mary Phrania⁷ Pattie, Phrania Elizabeth⁶ Goudy, Robert⁵, Elizabeth Jane⁴ Pegan, Andrew³ Pegan II, Andrew² Pagan, James¹*) was born in 1924 in Birmingham, Oakland Co., Michigan. He was the son of Frank Le Roi Main and Mary Phrania Pattie (76).

John William married **Dorothy Mae Holden** on June 18, 1949, in Oakland Co., Michigan. They divorced in 1976. Dorothy Mae Holden was born in Berkley, Oakland Co., Michigan, on June 3, 1927. She was also known as **Dottie.** Dorothy Mae reached age 70 and died in Laguna Hills, Orange Co., California? in May 1998.

145. **Mary Phrania⁸ Cruise** (*Abigail Louise⁷ Pattie, Phrania Elizabeth⁶ Goudy, Robert⁵, Elizabeth Jane⁴ Pegan, Andrew³ Pegan II, Andrew² Pagan, James¹*) was born on October 21, 1913, in Norfolk, Norfolk City-Co., Virginia. She was the daughter of Joseph Arthur Cruise and Abigail Louise Pattie (78). Mary Phrania died in Oak Lawn, Cook Co., Illinois, on May 19, 1996, at age 82.

Mary Phrania Cruise's mother died when she was an infant, and when she was 14 months old, she was sent to her father's first cousins in Kankakee, Kankakee Co., Illinois, who reared her. She was orphaned when she was 10.

Mary Phrania married **Edward John Hunt** on November 26, 1936, in Kankakee Co., Illinois.[98] They had six children. Edward John Hunt was born in Cook Co., Illinois, on August 8, 1912. Edward John lived in 1940 in Omaha Co., Nebraska. He reached age 43 and died in Evergreen Park, Cook Co., Illinois, on November 18, 1955.

Child of Mary Phrania Cruise and Edward John Hunt born bef. 1940:

+ 238 f I. **Mary Kathleen⁹ Hunt** was born in Illinois in 1938.

146. **Mary Grace⁸ McNeill** (*Sarah Sanson⁷ Hereford, Marianne Marilla⁶ Goudy, William⁵, Elizabeth Jane⁴*

*Pegan, Andrew³ Pegan II, Andrew² Pagan, James¹)* was born on September 25, 1881, in Apple Grove, Hannon Dist., Mason Co., West Virginia. She was the daughter of Ashell Wesson Zale McNeill and Sarah Sanson Hereford (80). Mary Grace died in Huntington, Cabell Co., West Virginia, on January 24, 1964, at age 82. She was buried in Woodmere Memorial Park Cemetery, Huntington, Cabell Co., West Virginia.[66]

Mary Grace McNeill married **William Herbert Kanode** in 1899. They had one son. William Herbert Kanode was born in Hanon Dist., Mason Co., West Virginia, on September 20, 1876. William Herbert reached age 22 and died in Clendenin, Mason Co., West Virginia, on July 25, 1899. He was buried in Beale Chapel Cemetery, Apple Grove, Hannon Dist., Mason Co., West Virginia.[65]

Mary Grace McNeill Kanode married **Robert Curtis Withers.** They had two children. Robert Curtis Withers was born in Mason Co., West Virginia, on March 21, 1884. Robert Curtis reached age 52 and died in Hogsett, Mason Co., West Virginia, on June 19, 1936. He was buried in Beale Chapel Cemetery, Apple Grove, Hannon Dist., Mason Co., West Virginia.[65]

Son of Mary Grace McNeill and William Herbert Kanode:

+ 239 m I. **William Herbert⁹ Kanode II** was born in Clendenin, Mason Co., West Virginia, on March 9, 1900. He died in overseas? on November 1, 1918. William Herbert was buried in Beale Chapel Cemetery, Apple Grove, Hannon Dist., Mason Co., West Virginia.[65]

Children of Mary Grace McNeill and Robert Curtis Withers:

+ 240 f I. **Bernice Lucille⁹ Withers** was born in Huntington, Cabell Co., West Virginia, on November 24, 1902. She died in Huntington, Cabell Co., West Virginia, on July

7, 1994. Bernice Lucille was buried in Woodmere Memorial Park Cemetery, Huntington, Cabell Co., West Virginia.[66]

+ 241 m II. **Raymond Robert⁹ Withers** was born in Huntington, Cabell Co., West Virginia, on May 24, 1911. He died in Huntington, Cabell Co., West Virginia, on September 24, 1947. Raymond Robert was buried in Woodmere Memorial Park Cemetery, Huntington, Cabell Co., West Virginia[66]

147. **Blanche Hereford⁸ McNeill** *(Sarah Sanson⁷ Hereford, Marianne Marilla⁶ Goudy, William⁵, Elizabeth Jane⁴ Pegan, Andrew³ Pegan II, Andrew² Pagan, James¹)* was born on November 8, 1883, in Apple Grove, Hannon Dist., Mason Co., West Virginia. She was the daughter of Ashell Wesson Zale McNeill and Sarah Sanson Hereford (80). Blanche Hereford died in Apple Grove, Hannon Dist., Mason Co., West Virginia, on October 2, 1897.

148. **Emma Pauline⁸ McNeill** *(Sarah Sanson⁷ Hereford, Marianne Marilla⁶ Goudy, William⁵, Elizabeth Jane⁴ Pegan, Andrew³ Pegan II, Andrew² Pagan, James¹)* was born on March 9, 1886, in Apple Grove, Hannon Dist., Mason Co., West Virginia. She was the daughter of Ashell Wesson Zale McNeill and Sarah Sanson Hereford (80). Emma Pauline died in Apple Grove, Hannon Dist., Mason Co., West Virginia, on June 30, 1887.

149. **Worthington Wilson⁸ McNeill** *(Sarah Sanson⁷ Hereford, Marianne Marilla⁶ Goudy, William⁵, Elizabeth Jane⁴ Pegan, Andrew³ Pegan II, Andrew² Pagan, James¹)* was born on April 24, 1888, in Apple Grove, Hannon Dist., Mason Co., West Virginia. He was the son of Ashell Wesson Zale McNeill and Sarah Sanson Hereford (80). Worthington Wilson died in Goodland, Sherman Co., Kansas, on April 11, 1977, at age 88. He was buried in Goodland Cemetery, Goodland, Sherman Co., Kansas.[67]

Worthington Wilson married **Dora Marion Dean** on March 29, 1911, in Chaves Co., New Mexico.

They had three sons. Dora Marion Dean was born in Randolph, Riley Co., Kansas, on June 24, 1890. Dora Marion reached age 80 and died in Yakima, Yakima Co., Washington, on May 20, 1971. She was buried in Goodland Cemetery, Goodland, Sherman Co., Kansas.[67]

Sons of Worthington Wilson McNeill and Dora Marion Dean:

+ 242 m I. **Richard Hereford⁹ McNeill** was born in Dunlap, De Baca Co., New Mexico, on March 24, 1912. He died in Riggens, Idaho Co, Idaho, on April 18, 1948. Richard Hereford was buried in Canyon Hill Cemetery, Caldwell, Canyon Co., Idaho.[99]

+ 243 m II. **James Neill Worthington⁹ McNeill** was born in Dunlap, De Baca Co., New Mexico, on February 10, 1914. He was also known as **Jim.** James Neill Worthington died in Nampa, Canyon Co., Idaho, on December 1, 2009.

+ 244 m III. **George Dean⁹ McNeill** was born in Dunlap, De Baca Co., New Mexico, on October 6, 1915. He died in Goodland, Sherman Co., Kansas, on April 14, 1975. George Dean was buried in Goodland Cemetery, Goodland, Sherman Co., Kansas.[67]

**150. Frank Rhea⁸ McNeill** (*Sarah Sanson⁷ Hereford, Marianne Marilla⁶ Goudy, William⁵, Elizabeth Jane⁴ Pegan, Andrew³ Pegan II, Andrew² Pagan, James¹*) was born on May 9, 1890, in Mercer's Bottom, Mason Co., West Virginia. He was the son of Ashell Wesson Zale McNeill and Sarah Sanson Hereford (80). Frank Rhea died in Cortez, Montezuma Co., Colorado, on June 8, 1950, at age 60. Frank R. McNeill is probably buried in Cortez Cemetery, Cortez, Montezuma Co., Colorado.

Frank Rhea married **Emma H. Keisling** in Chaves Co., New Mexico. They divorced. They had seven children. Emma H. Keisling was born in Bracketville, Kinney Co., Texas, on October 6, 1892. She reached age 92 and died in Pueblo, Pueblo Co., Colorado, in March 1985. Emma H. was buried in Cortez Cemetery, Cortez, Montezuma Co., Colorado.[100]

Children of Frank Rhea McNeill and Emma H. Keisling:

+ 245 m I. **Stanley Ray⁹ McNeill** was born in Bisbee, Cochise Co., Arizona, on May 15, 1913. He died in Cortez, Montezuma Co., Colorado, on October 31, 1930. Stanley Ray was buried in Cortez Cemetery, Cortez, Montezuma Co., Colorado.[100]

+ 246 m II. **Clark Jeffrey⁹ McNeill** was born in Roswell, Chaves Co., New Mexico, on October 20, 1915. He was also known as **Jeff.** Clark Jeffrey died in Aurora, Arapahoe Co., Colorado, on November 28, 2011. He was buried in Fort Logan National Cemetery, Denver, Denver Co., Colorado.[101]

+ 247 m III. **David Monroe⁹ McNeill** was born in Roswell, Chaves Co., New Mexico, on September 21, 1918. He died in Cortez, Montezuma Co., Colorado, on November 26, 1983. David Monroe was buried in Cortez Cemetery, Cortez, Montezuma Co., Colorado.[100]

+ 248 m IV. **Frank Worthington⁹ McNeill II** was born in Cortez, Montezuma Co., Colorado, on January 14, 1921. He died in Hemet, Riverside Co., California, on October 14, 2011.

+ 249 f V. **Sadie Ann⁹ McNeill** was born in Dove Creek, Delores Co., Colorado, on August 9, 1924. She was also known as **Sadie.** Sadie Ann died in Moab, Grand Co., Utah, on December 31, 1996.

+ 250 m VI. **Howard Lee⁹ McNeill** was born in Cortez, Montezuma Co., Colorado, on May 23, 1927. He died in Long Beach, Los Angeles Co., California, on August 15, 2003.

+ 251 m VII. **James Merle⁹ McNeill** was born in Cortez, Montezuma Co., Colorado, on July 8, 1932.

**151. Hallie Virginia⁸ McNeill** (*Sarah Sanson⁷ Hereford, Marianne Marilla⁶ Goudy, William⁵, Elizabeth Jane⁴ Pegan, Andrew³ Pegan II, Andrew² Pagan, James¹*) was born on June 12, 1892, in Mercer's Bottom, Mason Co., West Virginia. She was the daughter of Ashell Wesson Zale McNeill and Sarah Sanson Hereford (80). Hallie Richmond died in Palo Alto, Santa Clara Co., California, on February 2, 1943, at age 50. She was buried in Golden Gate National Cemetery, San Bruno, San Mateo Co., California.[68]

She married **Oran or Orrin Johnson.** They had one son. Oran or Orrin Johnson was a carnival worker; little is known about him.

Hallie Virginia McNeill married **Unknown Reasoner** before 1926.

Hallie Virginia McNeill Reasoner married **Thomas Martin Hawkins** in 1926. Thomas Martin Hawkins was born in Wimberly, Hays Co., Texas, on March 22, 1889. Thomas Martin reached age 91 and died on June 27, 1980. He was buried in Golden Gate National Cemetery, San Bruno, San Mateo Co., California.[68]

Son of Hallie Virginia McNeill and Oran or Orrin Johnson:

+ 252 m I. **Delbert Lyle⁹ Johnson** was born in Washington Twp., Wapello Co., Iowa, on May 23, 1909. He died in Riverside, Riverside Co., California, on January 5, 1990, at age 80. Delbert Lyle was buried in Riverside National Cemetery, Riverside, Riverside Co., California.[102]

**152. Jessie Gertrude⁸ McNeill** (*Sarah Sanson⁷ Hereford, Marianne Marilla⁶ Goudy, William⁵, Elizabeth Jane⁴ Pegan, Andrew³ Pegan II, Andrew² Pagan, James¹*) was born on February 21, 1894, in Mercer's Bottom, Mason Co., West Virginia. She was the daughter of Ashell Wesson Zale McNeill and Sarah Sanson Hereford (80). Jessie Gertrude died in Buchanan, De Baca Co., New Mexico, on April 25, 1914, at age 20. She was buried in Santa Rosa, Guadalupe Co., New Mexico.

Jessie Gertrude McNeill committed suicide by swallowing strychnine on the day after she was jilted at the altar by H.L. Pride, a cattleman from Dunlap, De Baca Co., New Mexico. She was living at the home of a cousin, K.C. Gregg, where she died.

**153. James Hereford⁸ McNeill** (*Sarah Sanson⁷ Hereford, Marianne Marilla⁶ Goudy, William⁵, Elizabeth Jane⁴ Pegan, Andrew³ Pegan II, Andrew² Pagan, James¹*) was born on December 11, 1897, in Apple Grove, Hannon Dist., Mason Co., West Virginia. He was the son of Ashell Wesson Zale McNeill and Sarah Sanson Hereford (80). James Hereford died in Raleigh, Wake Co., North Carolina, on August 19, 1984, age 86. He was cremated and his ashes buried in Riverside Cemetery, Waterville, Marshall Co., Kansas.[69]

James Hereford married **Georgia Gertrude Dean** on September 16, 1936, in Thomas Co., Kansas. They had two children. Georgia Gertrude Dean was born in Dunlap, De Baca Co., New Mexico, on June 10, 1910. Georgia Gertrude reached age 86 and died in Euless, Tarrant Co., Texas, on February 26, 1997. She was buried in Riverside Cemetery, Waterville, Marshall Co., Kansas.[69]

James Hereford McNeill and Georgia Gertrude Dean had two children, including:

Children of James Hereford McNeill and Georgia Gertrude Dean:

+ 253 m I. **Donald James⁹ McNeill** was born in Goodland, Sherman Co., Kansas?, on April 16, 1942. He died in Goodland, Sherman Co., Kansas?, on April 16, 1942.

**154. Nora Frances⁸ McNeill** (*Sarah Sanson⁷ Hereford, Marianne Marilla⁶ Goudy, William⁵, Elizabeth Jane⁴ Pegan, Andrew³ Pegan II, Andrew² Pagan, James¹*) was born on February 23, 1900, in Apple Grove, Hannon Dist., Mason Co., West Virginia. She was also known as **Frances.** She was the daughter of Ashell Wesson Zale McNeill and Sarah Sanson Hereford (80). Nora Frances died in Medford, Jackson Co., Oregon, on December 2, 1982, at age 82. She was buried in Siskiyou Memorial Park Cemetery, Medford, Jackson Co., Oregon.[70]

The will of Nora Frances McNeill's uncle William S. Goudy, written and proven in Jackson County, Oregon, gives everything to his grand-niece, Nora, granddaughter of his late sister, Marianne Marilla Goudy Hereford and daughter of Marianne's only child to have offspring, Sarah "Sadie" Hereford McNeill. For some reason, William S. Goudy thought that his niece Sadie had only one child, Nora Frances McNeill. But Sarah "Sadie" Hereford McNeill had nine children, seven of whom were living when William died. Perhaps Nora was the one who wrote William and told him of Sadie's death.

Nora Frances "Frances" McNeill Bare Mitchell, her first husband Howard Clifford Bare and their two daughters later removed to Medford, Jackson Co., Oregon, where her Uncle William Goudy had lived. Perhaps she inherited some land from her uncle.

She married **Howard Clifford Bare.** They had two daughters. Howard Clifford Bare was born in Springfield, Monroe Co., West Virginia, on May 26, 1894. Howard Clifford reached age 39 and died in Medford, Jackson Co., Oregon, on February 1, 1934. He was buried in Siskiyou Memorial Park Cemetery, Medford, Jackson Co., Oregon.[70]

Nora Frances McNeill Bare married **Harold Utley Mitchell** after 1940 in Jackson Co., Oregon. Harold Utley Mitchell was born in Weiser, Washington Co., Idaho, on August 6, 1897. Harold Utley reached age 87 and died in Medford, Jackson Co., Oregon, on August 30, 1984. He was buried in Memory Gardens Memorial Park Cemetery, Medford, Jackson Co., Oregon.[103]

Daughters of Nora Frances McNeill and Howard Clifford Bare:

+ 254 f I. **Elinor Jean⁹ Bare** was born in Fort Spring, Greenbrier Co., West Virginia, on July 15, 1919. She was also known as **Jean.** Elinor Jean died in Medford, Jackson Co., Oregon, on November 24, 1997. She was buried in Siskiyou Memorial Park Cemetery, Medford, Jackson Co., Oregon.[70]

+ 255 f II. **Elizabeth Dickson⁹ Bare** was born in Fort Spring, Greenbrier Co., West Virginia, on September 4, 1921. She was also known as **Betty.** Elizabeth Dickson died in Las Vegas, Clark Co., Nevada, on September 17, 2008. She was buried in Davis Memorial Park Cemetery, Las Vegas, Clark Co., Nevada.[C]

**155. Louis Albert⁸ Fair** (*Sarah Jessie⁷ Cowl, Elizabeth Jane⁶ Goudy, Isaac⁵, Elizabeth Jane⁴ Pegan, Andrew³ Pegan II, Andrew² Pagan, James¹*) was born on October 23, 1893, in Fish Creek Island, Marshall Co., West Virginia. He was the son of Henry Garner Fair and Sarah Jessie Cowl (81). Louis Albert died in Fish Creek Island, Marshall Co., West Virginia, on December 20, 1893.

**156. Harold Stewart⁸ Fair** (*Sarah Jessie⁷ Cowl, Elizabeth Jane⁶ Goudy, Isaac⁵, Elizabeth Jane⁴ Pegan, Andrew³ Pegan II, Andrew² Pagan, James¹*) was born on November 23, 1894, in Adeline, Marshall Co., West Virginia. He was the son of Henry Garner Fair and Sarah Jessie Cowl (81). Harold Stewart lived in 1956 in Worthington, Armstrong Co., Pennsylvania. He died in Kittanning, Kittanning Twp., Armstrong Co., Pennsylvania, on December 9, 1970, at age 76. Harold Stewart was buried in Lawn Haven Burial Estates, Worthington, Armstrong Co., Pennsylvania.[71]

Harold Stewart married **Marie Isabelle Campbell** on November 21, 1923, in Armstrong Co., Pennsylvania? They had six children.

Marie Isabelle Campbell was born in Ford City, Armstrong Co., Pennsylvania, on August 16, 1895. Marie Isabelle lived in 1956 in Worthington, Armstrong Co., Pennsylvania. She reached age 60 and died in a hospital in Kittanning, Kittanning Twp., Armstrong Co., Pennsylvania, on August 2, 1956. Marie Isabelle was buried in Lawn Haven Burial Estates, Worthington, Armstrong Co., Pennsylvania.[71]

Children of Harold Stewart Fair and Marie Isabelle Campbell:

+ 256 m I. **Stewart Russell⁹ Fair** was born in New Buffalo Twp., Armstrong Co., Pennsylvania, on November 26, 1924. He died in West Kittanning Twp., Armstrong Co., Pennsylvania, on February 14, 1928. Stewart Russell was buried in Kittanning Cemetery, Kittanning Twp., Armstrong Co., Pennsylvania.[104]

+ 257 f II. **Helen⁹ Fair** was born in West Kittanning Twp., Armstrong Co., Pennsylvania, on November 2, 1926. She died in West Kittanning Twp., Armstrong Co., Pennsylvania, on November 4, 1926. Helen was buried in Kittanning Cemetery, Kittanning Twp., Armstrong Co., Pennsylvania.[104]

+ 258 m III. **Hugh Hartley⁹ Fair** was born in West Kittanning Twp., Armstrong Co., Pennsylvania, on January 17, 1928. He died in a hospital in Pittsburgh, Allegheny Co., Pennsylvania, on May 19, 2013. Hugh Hartley was buried in Slate Lick Cemetery, Kittanning Twp., Armstrong Co., Pennsylvania.[105]

+ 259 m IV. **Forest⁹ Fair** was born in Worthington, Armstrong Co., Pennsylvania, on June 15, 1930. He died in Kittanning, Armstrong Co., Pennsylvania on June 24, 2016. He was buried in Center Hill Church of the Brethren Cemetery, Kittanning, Armstrong Co., Pennsylvania.[106]

+ 260 f V. **Mary Louise⁹ Fair** was born in Worthington, Armstrong Co., Pennsylvania, on June 18, 1933. She died in Livingston, Polk Co., Texas, on June 7, 2009.

+ 261 f VI. **Ruth Harlene⁹ Fair** was born in Worthington, Armstrong Co., Pennsylvania, on August 3, 1938.

**157. Jane Augusta⁸ Fair** (*Sarah Jessie⁷ Cowl, Elizabeth Jane⁶ Goudy, Isaac⁵, Elizabeth Jane⁴ Pegan, Andrew³ Pegan II, Andrew² Pagan, James¹*) was born on June 4, 1896, in Adeline, Marshall Co., West Virginia. She was also known as **Jennie.** She was the daughter of Henry Garner Fair and Sarah Jessie Cowl (81). Jane Augusta lived in 1969 in Moundsville, Marshall Co., West Virginia. She died in a facility in Sistersville, Tyler Co., West Virginia, on August 4, 1970, at age 74. Jane Augusta was buried in Halcyon Hills Memorial Park Cemetery, Sherrard, Marshall Co., West Virginia.[72]

Jane Augusta married **John Wesley Crow** on May 29, 1920, in Marshall Co., West Virginia. They had six children. John Wesley Crow was born in North Dakota on May 29, 1892. John Wesley lived in 1963 in Moundsville, Marshall Co., West Virginia. He reached age 71 and died in a hospital in Glen Dale, Marshall Co., West Virginia, on September 27, 1963. John Wesley was buried in Halcyon Hills Memorial Park Cemetery, Sherrard, Marshall Co., West Virginia.[72]

Children of Jane Augusta Fair and John Wesley Crow:

+ 262 m I. **Dewey Edward⁹ Crow** was born in Moundsville, Marshall Co., West Virginia, on August 25, 1921. He died in Moundsville, Marshall Co., West Virginia, in March 1985. Dewey Edward was buried in Halcyon Hills Memorial Park Cemetery, Sherrard, Marshall Co., West Virginia.[72]

+ 263 f II. **Florence⁹ Crow** was born in Adeline, Marshall Co., West Virginia, on June 18, 1923.

+ 264 f III. **Frances J.⁹ Crow** was born in Dellslow, Monongalia Co., West Virginia, on February 26, 1926. She died in Canton, Stark Co., Ohio, on September 20, 2015. Frances J. was buried in Fairview Cemetery, New Albany, Floyd Co., Indiana.[107]

+ 265 f IV. **Margaret Anna⁹ Crow** was born in Moundsville, Marshall Co., West Virginia, on November 2, 1927. She died in Glen Easton, Marshall Co., West Virginia, on June 2, 1999. Margaret Anna was buried in Halcyon Hills Memorial Park Cemetery, Sherrard, Marshall Co., West Virginia.[72]

+ 266 m V. **Elmer Wayne⁹ Crow** was born in Moundsville, Marshall Co., West Virginia, on October 14, 1931. He was also known as **Wayne**. Elmer Wayne died in McMechen, Union Dist., Marshall Co., West Virginia, on May 20, 2009. He was buried in Halcyon Hills Memorial Park Cemetery, Sherrard, Marshall Co., West Virginia.[72]

+ 267 m VI. **Donal M⁹ Crow** was born in Moundsville, Marshall Co., West Virginia, on February 11, 1934.

**158. Dewey Isaac⁸ Fair** (*Sarah Jessie⁷ Cowl, Elizabeth Jane⁶ Goudy, Isaac⁵, Elizabeth Jane⁴ Pegan, Andrew³ Pegan II, Andrew² Pagan, James¹*) was born on November 30, 1898, in Adeline, Marshall Co., West Virginia. He was also known as **Ike.** He was the son of Henry Garner Fair and Sarah Jessie Cowl (81). Dewey Isaac died in Ford City, Armstrong Co., Pennsylvania, on January 12, 1972, at age 73. He was buried in Lawn Haven Burial Estates, Worthington, Armstrong Co., Pennsylvania.[71]

Dewey Isaac married **Rachel Miller** on August 30, 1924, in Marshall Co., West Virginia. They had three children. Rachel Miller was born in Bellefonte, Centre Co., Pennsylvania, on November 15, 1903. Rachel reached age 79 and died in Niagara Falls, Niagara Co., New York, in April 1983. She was buried in Lawn Haven Burial Estates, Worthington, Armstrong Co., Pennsylvania.[71]

Children of Dewey Isaac Fair and Rachel Miller:

+ 268 m I. **Frank V.⁹ Fair** was born in Ford City, Armstrong Co., Pennsylvania, on October 25, 1925. He died in Saint George, Washington Co., Utah, on January 15, 1995.

+ 269 m II. **Jack Edward⁹ Fair** was born in Ford City, Armstrong Co., Pennsylvania, on January 4, 1928. He died in Corrales, Sandoval Co., New Mexico, on December 30, 2009.

+ 270 f III. **Sally or Sallie Ann⁹ Fair** was born in Ford City, Armstrong Co., Pennsylvania, on March 13, 1934. She died in West Brandywine, Chester Co., Pennsylvania, on October 10, 2017.

**159. Daniel Cowl⁸ Fair** (*Sarah Jessie⁷ Cowl, Elizabeth Jane⁶ Goudy, Isaac⁵, Elizabeth Jane⁴ Pegan, Andrew³ Pegan II, Andrew² Pagan, James¹*) was born on November 23, 1903, in Liberty, Marshall Co., West Virginia. He was the son of Henry Garner Fair and Sarah Jessie Cowl (81). Daniel Cowl died in Butler, Butler Co., Pennsylvania? in March 1985 at age 81.

He married **Irene Mildred Jones** on December 2, 1933, in Marshall Co., West Virginia. They had three children. She was also known as **Gay**. Irene Mildred Jones was born in Cameron, Marshall Co., West Virginia, on July 5, 1911. She reached age 39 and died in Butler, Butler Twp., Butler Co., Pennsylvania? on March 21, 1951.

Daniel Cowl Fair and Irene Mildred Jones had three children, including:

+ 271 m I. **Charles Daniel⁹ Fair** was born in Cameron, Marshall Co., West Virginia, on March 29, 1935. Charles D. died in Butler, Butler Twp., Butler Co., Pennsylvania, on December 8, 1984. He was buried in Kittanning Cemetery, Kittanning, Kittanning Twp., Armstrong Co., Pennsylvania.[104]

+ 272 f II. **Virginia P.⁹ Fair** was born in Tri-adelphia Dist., Logan Co., West Virginia, in 1939.

**160. Robert Cowl⁸ Smith** (*Elizabeth Jane⁷ Cowl, Elizabeth Jane⁶ Goudy, Isaac⁵, Elizabeth Jane⁴ Pegan, Andrew³ Pegan II, Andrew² Pagan, James¹*) was born on May 6, 1894, in Madison, Ohio Co., West Virginia. He was the son of Lewis Albert Smith and Elizabeth Jane Cowl (83). Robert Cowl died in Glendale, Los Angeles Co., California, on November 6, 1935, at age 41. He was buried in Forest Lawn Memorial Park Cemetery, Glendale, Los Angeles Co., California.[47]

Never married.

**161. Hazel⁸ Redman** (*Emma Blanche⁷ Cowl, Elizabeth Jane⁶ Goudy, Isaac⁵, Elizabeth Jane⁴ Pegan, Andrew³ Pegan II, Andrew² Pagan, James¹*) was born on September 9, 1891, in Wheeling, Ohio Co., West Virginia. She was the daughter of Edmund H. Redman and Emma Blanche Cowl (84). Hazel died in Columbus, Franklin Co., Ohio, in June 1967 at age 75. She was buried in Sunset Memorial Park Cemetery, Galloway, Franklin Co., Ohio.[48]

Hazel married **Unknown Lair** between 1930 and 1940 in Franklin Co., Ohio? They divorced in Franklin Co., Ohio? before 1940.

**162. Harry E.⁸ Redman** (*Emma Blanche⁷ Cowl, Elizabeth Jane⁶ Goudy, Isaac⁵, Elizabeth Jane⁴ Pegan, Andrew³ Pegan II, Andrew² Pagan, James¹*) was born on January 10, 1898, in Wheeling, Ohio

Co., West Virginia. He was the son of Edmund H. Redman and Emma Blanche Cowl (84). Harry E. died in Mount Vernon, Knox Co., Ohio, on June 14, 1956, at age 58.

Harry E. married **E. Lavena Herboltzhelmer** on June 25, 1925, in Franklin Co., Ohio. They had three daughters. E. Lavena Herboltzhelmer was born in Perry Twp., Franklin Co., Ohio, on September 6, 1902. E. Lavena reached age 73 and died in Columbus, Franklin Co., Ohio, in December 1975.

Daughters of Harry E. Redman and E. Lavena Herboltzhelmer:

+ 273 f I. **Patricia R.⁹ Redman** was born in Columbus, Franklin Co., Ohio, on December 14, 1926. She died in Gettysburg, Cumberland Twp., Adams Co., Pennsylvania, on August 2, 2010.

+ 274 f II. **Janet Cowl⁹ Redman** was born in Columbus, Franklin Co., Ohio, on March 12, 1930.

+ 275 f III. **Jean⁹ Redman** was born in Columbus, Franklin Co., Ohio, about 1933.

**163. Albert E.⁸ Redman** (*Emma Blanche⁷ Cowl, Elizabeth Jane⁶ Goudy, Isaac⁵, Elizabeth Jane⁴ Pegan, Andrew³ Pegan II, Andrew² Pagan, James¹*) was born on January 5, 1904, in Columbus, Franklin Co., Ohio. He was the son of Edmund H. Redman and Emma Blanche Cowl (84). Albert E. died in Columbus, Franklin Co., Ohio, on December 30, 1975, at age 71. He was buried in Green Lawn Cemetery, Columbus, Franklin Co., Ohio.[73]

Albert E. married **Charlotte Demartini** on September 18, 1926, in Franklin Co., Ohio. Charlotte Demartini was born in Columbus, Franklin Co., Ohio, on January 26, 1905. Charlotte reached age 98 and died in Bradenton, Manatee Co., Florida, on April 24, 2003.

**164. Edmond Cowl⁸ Redman II** (*Emma Blanche⁷ Cowl, Elizabeth Jane⁶ Goudy, Isaac⁵, Elizabeth Jane⁴ Pegan, Andrew³ Pegan II, Andrew² Pagan, James¹*) was born on May 24, 1906, in Columbus, Franklin Co.,

Ohio. He was the son of Edmund H. Redman and Emma Blanche Cowl (84). Edmond Cowl died in Columbus, Franklin Co., Ohio, on May 8, 2006, at age 99. He was buried in Sunset Memorial Park Cemetery, Galloway, Franklin Co., Ohio.[48]

Edmond Cowl married **Vera Marie Adkison** on September 10, 1927, in Franklin Co., Ohio. They had two daughters. Vera Marie Adkison was born in Ipava, Pleasant Twp., Fulton Co., Illinois, on May 27, 1907. Vera Marie reached age 84 and died in Columbus, Franklin Co., Ohio, on April 25, 1992. She was buried in Sunset Memorial Park Cemetery, Galloway, Franklin Co., Ohio.[48]

Daughters of Edmond Cowl Redman II and Vera Marie Adkison:

+ 276 f I. **Nancy Lee⁹ Redman** was born in Upper Arlington, Franklin Co., Ohio, in 1931.

+ 277 f II. **Vera⁹ Redman** was born in Upper Arlington, Franklin Co., Ohio, on January 14, 1935.

165. **Alice⁸ Stoller** (*Nellie Augusta⁷ Cowl, Elizabeth Jane⁶ Goudy, Isaac⁵, Elizabeth Jane⁴ Pegan, Andrew³ Pegan II, Andrew² Pagan, James¹*) was born on October 23, 1903, in Wheeling, Ohio Co., West Virginia. She was the daughter of Henry Jackson Stoller and Nellie Augusta Cowl (85). Alice died in Bridgeport, Bellaire Twp., Belmont Co., Ohio, on March 6, 1997, at age 93. She was buried in Greenwood Cemetery, Wheeling, Ohio Co., West Virginia.[24]

Childless.

Alice married **John Robert Cowl** on August 23, 1941, in Ohio Co., West Virginia. John Robert Cowl was born in Bridgeport, Bellaire Twp., Belmont Co., Ohio, on August 5, 1909. John Robert lived in 1965 in Bridgeport, Bellaire Twp., Belmont Co., Ohio. He reached age 55 and died in a hospital in Wheeling, Ohio Co., West Virginia, on March 19, 1965. John Robert was buried in Greenwood Cemetery, Wheeling, Ohio Co., West Virginia.[24]

166. **Elizabeth Jane⁸ Stoller** (*Nellie Augusta⁷ Cowl, Elizabeth Jane⁶ Goudy, Isaac⁵, Elizabeth Jane⁴ Pegan, Andrew³ Pegan II, Andrew² Pagan, James¹*) was born on May 22, 1906, in Wheeling, Ohio Co., West Virginia. She was also known as **Jane.** She was the daughter of Henry Jackson Stoller and Nellie Augusta Cowl (85). Elizabeth Jane died in Elyria, Elyria Twp., Lorain Co., Ohio, on June 7, 1997, at age 91.

Elizabeth Jane married **Monroe Josiah Mechling** on September 13, 1929, in Ohio Co., West Virginia. They had four children. Monroe Josiah Mechling was born in Greensburg, Westmoreland Co., Pennsylvania, on October 22, 1895. Monroe Josiah reached age 87 and died in St. Clairsville, Richland Twp., Belmont Co., Ohio, on January 22, 1983.

Children of Elizabeth Jane Stoller and Monroe Josiah Mechling:

+ 278 m I. **Monroe Josiah⁹ Mechling II** was born in Wheeling, Ohio Co., West Virginia, on August 26, 1931.

+ 279 f II. **Elizabeth Jane⁹ Mechling** was born in Wheeling, Ohio Co., West Virginia, on June 12, 1934.

+ 280 f III. **Lois Jean⁹ Mechling** was born in Wheeling, Ohio Co., West Virginia, on August 12, 1937. She died in Elyria, Elyria Twp., Lorain Co., Ohio, on December 13, 2007. Lois Jean was buried in St. Clairsville Union Cemetery, St. Clairsville, Bellaire Twp., Belmont Co., Ohio.[108]

167. **Helen⁸ McAllister** (*Alice Louise⁷ Cowl, Elizabeth Jane⁶ Goudy, Isaac⁵, Elizabeth Jane⁴ Pegan, Andrew³ Pegan II, Andrew² Pagan, James¹*) was born on September 27, 1904, in Wheeling, Ohio Co., West Virginia. She was the daughter of Edward Conrad McAllister and Alice Louise Cowl (88). Helen died in Wheeling, Ohio Co., West Virginia, in August 1984 at age 79. Helen McAllister Griffin died under her maiden name.

Childless.

Helen married **Joe Rogers Griffin** on April 7, 1926, in Ohio Co., West Virginia. They divorced. Joe Rogers Griffin was born in Dola, Harrison Co., West Virginia, on September 25, 1903. He reached age 66 and died in Winchester, Middlesex Co., Massachusetts, in November 1969.

**168. Elizabeth M.⁸ Goudy** (*Edward Elmer⁷, John William⁶, Isaac⁵, Elizabeth Jane⁴ Pegan, Andrew³ Pegan II, Andrew² Pagan, James¹*) was born in September 1891 in Wheeling, Ohio Co., West Virginia. was born on September 15, 1891, in Wheeling, Ohio Co., West Virginia. She was also known as **Lizzie** when young and **Betty** as an adult. She was the daughter of Edward Elmer Goudy (89) and Martha Brady. Elizabeth M. died in Lincoln Park, Wayne Co., Michigan in December 1975 at age 84. She is buried in Halcyon Hills Memorial Park Cemetery, Sherrard, Marshall Co., West Virginia.[72]

Elizabeth M. married **Harry Earl Johnson** on April 25, 1910, in Ohio Co., West Virginia. They divorced. They had two daughters. Harry Earl Johnson was born in Oxford Twp., Guernsey Co., Ohio, on November 15, 1887. He reached age 94 and died in Lexington, Fayette Co., Kentucky, on April 12, 1982.

Elizabeth M. Goudy Johnson married **Lloyd Harmon** on March 13, 1930, in Brooke Co. West Virginia. Lloyd Harmon was born in Graysville, Washington Twp., Monroe Co., Ohio, on January 5, 1903. Lloyd reached age 79 and died in Coshocton, Jackson Twp., Coshocton Co., Ohio, on February 8, 1982. He was buried in Graysville Cemetery, Graysville, Washington Twp., Monroe Co., Ohio.[109]

Daughters of Elizabeth M. Goudy and Harry Earl Johnson:

+ 281 f I. **Martha⁹ Johnson** was born in Wheeling, Ohio Co., West Virginia, on February 10, 1911. She

died in Fort Myers, Lee Co., Florida, on January 9, 1985. Martha was buried in Halcyon Hills Memorial Park Cemetery, Sherrard, Marshall Co., West Virginia.[72]

+ 282 f II. **Harriet J.⁹ Johnson** was born in Wheeling, Ohio Co., West Virginia, on March 14, 1914. She died in Fort Myers, Lee Co., Florida, on February 25, 1987.

**169. Edward Elmer⁸ Goudy II** (*Edward Elmer⁷, John William⁶, Isaac⁵, Elizabeth Jane⁴ Pegan, Andrew³ Pegan II, Andrew² Pagan, James¹*) was born on July 26, 1894, in Wheeling, Ohio Co., West Virginia. He was the son of Edward Elmer Goudy (89) and Martha Brady. Edward Elmer died in Mesa, Maricopa Co., Arizona, on December 31, 1972, at age 78. He was buried in Ridge Hill Memorial Park Cemetery, Amherst, Amherst Twp., Lorraine Co., Ohio.[49]

Childless.

Edward Elmer married **Yolan Silverstein** on October 31, 1935, in Cuyahoga Co., Ohio. Yolan Silverstein was born in Cleveland, Cuyahoga Co., Ohio, in 1903. Yolan reached age 67 and died in Elyria, Elyria Twp., Lorain Co., Ohio, on August 5, 1970.

**170. James⁸ Goudy** (*Edward Elmer⁷, John William⁶, Isaac⁵, Elizabeth Jane⁴ Pegan, Andrew³ Pegan II, Andrew² Pagan, James¹*) was born on May 26, 1896, in Wheeling, Ohio Co., West Virginia. He was the son of Edward Elmer Goudy (89) and Martha Brady. James died in Wheeling, Ohio Co., West Virginia, on May 27, 1896.

**171. Alberta Anna⁸ Goudy** (*Robert Carl⁷, John William⁶, Isaac⁵, Elizabeth Jane⁴ Pegan, Andrew³ Pegan II, Andrew² Pagan, James¹*) was born on August 22, 1910, in Ritchie, Ohio Co., West Virginia. She was the daughter of Robert Carl Goudy (93) and Anna Rust. Alberta Anna died in Girard, Trumbull Co., Ohio, on November 3, 2001, at age 91. She was buried in Girard Liberty Union Cemetery, Girard, Trumbull Co., Ohio.[75]

Alberta Anna married **Frederick Charles Helmbrecht II** on October 5, 1929, in Ohio Co., West Virginia. They had four children. Frederick Charles Helmbrecht II was born in Wheeling, Ohio Co., West Virginia, on October 25, 1909. Frederick Charles reached age 57 and died in Girard, Trumbull Co., Ohio, on December 9, 1966. He was buried in Girard Liberty Union Cemetery, Girard, Trumbull Co., Ohio.[75]

Alberta Anna Goudy and Frederick Charles Helmbrecht II had four children, including:

+ 283 f I. **Betty Jane⁹ Helmbrecht** was born in Wheeling, Ohio Co., West Virginia, on August 27, 1930. She was also known as **Betty.** Betty Jane died in Youngstown, Mahoning Co., Ohio, on December 28, 2011.

+ 284 f II. **Mitzi L.⁹ Helmbrechtt** was born in Wheeling, Ohio Co., West Virginia, on June 10, 1933. She died in Youngstown, Mahoning Co., Ohio, on June 24, 2014. Mitzi L. was buried in Calvary Cemetery, Youngstown, Mahoning Co., Ohio.[110]

+ 285 m III. **Frederick C.⁹ Helmbrecht III** was born in Wheeling, Ohio Co., West Virginia, on November 9, 1935. He died in Fowler, Fowler Twp., Trumbull Co., Ohio, on March 20, 2015. Frederick C. was buried in Crown Hill Burial Park Cemetery, Vienna Twp., Trumbull Co., Ohio.[111]

172. **Robert Joseph⁸ Goudy II** (*Robert Carl⁷, John William⁶, Isaac⁵, Elizabeth Jane⁴ Pegan, Andrew³ Pegan II, Andrew² Pagan, James¹*) was born on January 27, 1912, in Ritchie, Ohio Co., West Virginia. He was the son of Robert Carl Goudy (93) and Anna Rust. Robert Joseph died in Wheeling, Ohio Co., West Virginia, on July 25, 1973, at age 61. He was buried in Mount Calvary Cemetery, Wheeling, Ohio Co., West Virginia.[76]

Robert Joseph married Mrs. **Sara Virginia Florio** Matheny on February 15, 1947, in Ohio Co., West Virginia. Sara Virginia Florio was born in Wheeling, Ohio Co., West Virginia, on March 4, 1920. She was also known as **Virginia.** Sara Virginia reached age 79 and died in Wheeling, Ohio Co., West Virginia, on September 30, 1999.

173. **Thelma Marie⁸ Goudy** (*Robert Carl⁷, John William⁶, Isaac⁵, Elizabeth Jane⁴ Pegan, Andrew³ Pegan II, Andrew² Pagan, James¹*) was born on August 20, 1913, in Triadelphia, Ohio Co., West Virginia. She was the daughter of Robert Carl Goudy (93) and Anna Rust. Thelma Marie died in Bellaire, Pultney Twp., Belmont Co., Ohio, on October 7, 1974, at age 61. She was buried in Davis Cemetery, Bellaire, Belmont Co., Ohio.[77]

Childless.

Thelma Marie married **William H. Gross** before 1942. They divorced before 1949. They remarried on January 20, 1949 in Ohio Co., West Virginia. William H. Gross was born in Short Creek, Brooke Co., West Virginia, on June 3, 1890. He died in October 1975 in either Bellaire, Pultney Twp., Belmont Co., Ohio or Wheeling, Ohio Co., West Virginia. He may be buried in Davis Cemetery, Bellaire, Pultney Twp., Belmont Co., Ohio with his second wife, Thelma Goudy Gross, or in Greenwood Cemetery, Wheeling, Ohio Co., West Virginia with his own family members.

Thelma's tombstone indicates William was to be buried next to her, but his birth date carved in the tombstone says "1886". There is no death date on the tombstone.

174. **Wilfred E.⁸ Goudy** (*Robert Carl⁷, John William⁶, Isaac⁵, Elizabeth Jane⁴ Pegan, Andrew³ Pegan II, Andrew² Pagan, James¹*) was born on August 27, 1917, in Triadelphia, Ohio Co., West Virginia. He was also known as **Bud.** He was the son of Robert Carl Goudy (93) and Anna Rust. Wilfred E. died in West Terre Haute, Sugar Creek Twp., Vigo Co., Indiana, on May 6, 1999, at age 81. He was buried in Roselawn Memorial Park Cemetery, Terre Haute, Vigo County, Indiana.[78]

Wilfred E. married **Sara Jane Lamb** on December 16, 1946, in Ohio Co., West Virginia. They divorced. They had three children. Sara Jane Lamb was born in Wheeling, Ohio Co., West Virginia, on October 23, 1915. She was also known as **Janie.** Sara Jane reached age 91 and died in West Terre Haute, Sugar Creek Twp., Vigo Co., Indiana, on March 28, 2007. She was buried in Roselawn Memorial Park Cemetery, Terre Haute, Vigo County, Indiana.[78]

Sarah Jane Lamb Goudy always used her middle name as her preferred name.

175. **John Edward[8] Goudy** (*Robert Carl[7], John William[6], Isaac[5], Elizabeth Jane[4] Pegan, Andrew[3] Pegan II, Andrew[2] Pagan, James[1]*) was born on November 14, 1922, in Wheeling, Ohio Co., West Virginia. He was the son of Robert Carl Goudy (93) and Anna Rust. John Edward died in Wheeling, Ohio Co., West Virginia, on November 15, 1922. He was buried in Mount Olivet Cemetery, Wheeling, Ohio Co., West Virginia.[4]

176. **Lawrence Henry[8] Goudy** (*Robert Carl[7], John William[6], Isaac[5], Elizabeth Jane[4] Pegan, Andrew[3] Pegan II, Andrew[2] Pagan, James[1]*) was born on December 24, 1923, in Wheeling, Ohio Co., West Virginia. He was the son of Robert Carl Goudy (93) and Anna Rust. Lawrence Henry died in Jefferson, Jackson Co., Georgia, on December 16, 2000, at age 76.

He married **Linda Unknown.**

177. **Henry J.[8] Goudy** (*Robert Carl[7], John William[6], Isaac[5], Elizabeth Jane[4] Pegan, Andrew[3] Pegan II, Andrew[2] Pagan, James[1]*) was born on April 28, 1928, in Wheeling, Ohio Co., West Virginia. He was the son of Robert Carl Goudy (93) and Anna Rust. Henry J. died in Austintown, Austintown Twp., Mahoning Co., Ohio, on October 12, 2006, at age 78.

He married **Barbara Ward.** They had two daughters. Barbara Ward was born on August 23, 1940.

178. **John Elwood[8] Goudy** (*Howard Louis[7], John William[6], Isaac[5], Elizabeth Jane[4] Pegan, Andrew[3] Pegan II, Andrew[2] Pagan, James[1]*) was born on November 13, 1906, in Wheeling, Ohio Co., West Virginia. He was the son of Howard Louis Goudy (94) and Mary Jane Laheen. John Elwood died in Wheeling, Ohio Co., West Virginia, on May 28, 1964, at age 57. He was buried in Mount Olivet Cemetery, Wheeling, Ohio Co., West Virginia.[4]

179. **Clarice Melissa[8] Goudy** (*Howard Louis[7], John William[6], Isaac[5], Elizabeth Jane[4] Pegan, Andrew[3] Pegan II, Andrew[2] Pagan, James[1]*) was born on January 18, 1917, in Wheeling, Ohio Co., West Virginia. She was the daughter of Howard Louis Goudy (94) and Mary Jane Laheen. Clarice Melissa died in Cadiz, Cadiz Twp., Harrison Co., Ohio, on April 16, 2000, at age 83.

Clarice Melissa married **Jacob Pershing Fonner** on April 5, 1941, in Belmont Co., Ohio. Jacob Pershing Fonner was born in Wheeling, Ohio Co., West Virginia, on January 24, 1918. Jacob Pershing reached age 51 and died in Export, Murrysville, Westmoreland Co., Pennsylvania? on March 17, 1969. He was buried in Woodlawn Cemetery, Export, Westmoreland Co., Pennsylvania.[112]

180. **Dorothy Elizabeth[8] Goudy** (*Howard Louis[7], John William[6], Isaac[5], Elizabeth Jane[4] Pegan, Andrew[3] Pegan II, Andrew[2] Pagan, James[1]*) was born on February 1, 1920, in Wheeling, Ohio Co., West Virginia. She was the daughter of Howard Louis Goudy (94) and Mary Jane Laheen. Dorothy Elizabeth died in Wheeling, Ohio Co., West Virginia, on November 10, 1999, at age 79.

Dorothy Elizabeth married **Robert Danford McAninch** on March 19, 1941, in Belmont Co., Ohio. They had one son. Robert Danford McAninch was born in Wheeling, Ohio Co., West Virginia, on October 13, 1918. Robert Danford reached age 59 and died in Wheeling, Ohio Co., West Virginia, on December 15, 1977.

181. **Howard Louis[8] Goudy II** (*Howard Louis[7], John William[6], Isaac[5], Elizabeth Jane[4] Pegan, Andrew[3] Pegan II, Andrew[2] Pagan, James[1]*) was born on September 5, 1922, in Wheeling, Ohio Co., West Virginia. He was the son of Howard Louis Goudy (94) and Mary Jane Laheen. Howard Louis died in Wheeling, Ohio Co., West Virginia, in June 1981 at age 58. He was buried in Mount

Olivet Cemetery, Wheeling, Ohio Co., West Virginia.[4]

**182. Mary E.⁸ Hill** (*David Wellington⁷, David Wellington II⁷, Mary Jane⁵ Goudy, Elizabeth Jane⁴ Pegan, Andrew³ Pegan II, Andrew² Pagan, James¹*) was born in 1904 in Ohio. She was the daughter of David Wellington Hill II (96) and Lillie May Crider. Mary E. was adopted. She died after 1910. Mary E. Hill was adopted by David and Lillie Crider Hill.

**183. Mabel B.⁸ Church** (*Mary Emma⁷ Hill, David Wellington⁶, Mary Jane⁵ Goudy, Elizabeth Jane⁴ Pegan, Andrew³ Pegan II, Andrew² Pagan, James¹*) was born on February 10, 1890, in Wheeling, Ohio Co., West Virginia. She was the daughter of Francis M. Church and Mary Emma Hill (97). Mabel B. died in Jackson, Hinds Co., Mississippi, on October 24, 1981, at age 91. She was buried in Greenwood Cemetery, Wheeling, Ohio Co., West Virginia.[24]

She married **Thomas Herbert Bachmann.** They had three children. Thomas Herbert Bachmann was born in Wheeling, Ohio Co., West Virginia, on October 19, 1889. He was also known as **Herbert.** Thomas Herbert reached age 28 and died in Albuquerque, Bernalillo Co., New Mexico, on May 25, 1918. He was buried in Greenwood Cemetery, Wheeling, Ohio Co., West Virginia.[24]

Thomas Herbert Bachmann always used his middle name as his preferred name.

Mabel B. Church Bachmann married **Louis Joseph Salena** on June 16, 1920, in Ohio Co., West Virginia. They divorced. Louis Joseph Salena was born in Coshocton, Coshocton Co., Ohio, on May 15, 1895. He reached age 73 and died in Wheeling, Ohio Co., West Virginia, on August 3, 1968. Louis Joseph was buried in Mount Calvary Cemetery, Wheeling, Ohio Co., West Virginia.[76]

Mabel B. Church Bachmann Salena married **Clifford Dearley Ullom** after 1920. Clifford Dearley Ullom was born in Marshall Co., West Virginia, on March 16, 1884. He reached age 58 and died in Dundalk, Baltimore Co., Maryland, on June 13, 1942.[76]

Children of Mabel B. Church and Thomas Herbert Bachmann:

+ 286 m I. **Kenneth C.⁹ Bachmann** was born in Wheeling, Ohio Co., West Virginia, on January 2, 1909. He died in Wheeling, Ohio Co., West Virginia, on May 9, 1922. Kenneth C. was buried in Greenwood Cemetery, Wheeling, Ohio Co., West Virginia.[24]

+ 287 f II. **Frances A.⁹ Bachmann** was born in Wheeling, Ohio Co., West Virginia, on July 19, 1911. She died in Jackson, Hinds Co., Mississippi, on October 26, 1982. Frances A. was buried in Greenwood Cemetery, Wheeling, Ohio Co., West Virginia.[24]

+ 288 m III. **Albert or Herbert⁹ Bachmann II** was born in Wheeling, Ohio Co., West Virginia, on September 18, 1915. He died in New York, New York, on July 30, 1987. Albert or Herbert was buried in Long Island National Cemetery, Farmingdale, Suffolk Co., New York.[96]

**184. George Wellington⁸ Hill II** (*George Wellington⁷, David Wellington⁶, Mary Jane⁵ Goudy, Elizabeth Jane⁴ Pegan, Andrew³ Pegan II, Andrew² Pagan, James¹*) was born on December 1, 1898, in Wheeling, Ohio Co., West Virginia. He was the son of George Wellington Hill (98) and Minnie Niedermeyer. George Wellington died in Ohio Co., West Virginia, on November 17, 1959, at age 60. He was buried in Greenwood Cemetery, Wheeling, Ohio Co., West Virginia.[24]

George Wellington Hill II married **Reba Smith.** They had one daughter. Reba Smith was born in Kirkwood Twp., Belmont Co., Ohio on January 14, 1902. She died in Wheeling, Ohio Co., West Virginia in January 1975. She was probably buried in Greenwood Cemetery, Wheeling, Ohio Co., West Virginia.

+ 289  f   I.   **Dorothy Virginia**[9] **Hill** was born in Bridgeport, Bellaire Twp., Belmont Co., Ohio on November 9, 1923. She died on November 16, 2014 in Wheeling, Ohio Co., West Virginia. She is buried in Greenwood Cemetery, Wheeling, Ohio Co., West Virginia.[24]

**185. Harold Christian**[8] **Hill** (*George Wellington*[7], *David Wellington*[6], *Mary Jane*[5] *Goudy, Elizabeth Jane*[4] *Pegan, Andrew*[3] *Pegan II, Andrew*[2] *Pagan, James*[1]) was born on November 5, 1900, in Wheeling, Ohio Co., West Virginia. He was the son of George Wellington Hill (98) and Minnie Niedermeyer. Harold Christian died in Wheeling, Ohio Co., West Virginia, on January 20, 1958, at age 57. He was buried in Greenwood Cemetery, Wheeling, Ohio Co., West Virginia.[24]

He married **Gertrude Katherine Hughes.** They had one son. Gertrude Katherine Hughes was born in Wheeling, Ohio Co., West Virginia, on August 10, 1905. Gertrude Katherine reached age 60 and died in Wheeling, Ohio Co., West Virginia, on October 2, 1965. She was buried in Greenwood Cemetery, Wheeling, Ohio Co., West Virginia.[24]

Son of Harold Christian Hill and Gertrude Katherine Hughes:

+ 290  m   I.   **Harold**[9] **Hill II** was born in Wheeling, Ohio Co., West Virginia, on July 2, 1923. He died in Wheeling, Ohio Co., West Virginia, on March 5, 1996.

**186. Child**[8] **Hill** (*Charles L.*[7], *William Hamilton*[6], *Mary Jane*[5] *Goudy, Elizabeth Jane*[4] *Pegan, Andrew*[3] *Pegan II, Andrew*[2] *Pagan, James*[1]) was born between 1900 and 1910 in West Virginia. He or she was a child of Charles L. Hill (101) and Barbara Ellen Murphy. Child died in West Virginia between 1900 and 1910.

**187. Emily Virginia**[8] **Hill** (*Howard Hamilton*[7], *William Hamilton*[6], *Mary Jane*[5] *Goudy, Elizabeth Jane*[4] *Pegan, Andrew*[3] *Pegan II, Andrew*[2] *Pagan, James*[1]) was born on November 11, 1906, in Steubenville, Cross Creek Twp., Jefferson Co., Ohio. She was the daughter of Howard Hamilton Hill (102) and Wilhelmina Sophia Maxwell. Emily Virginia died in Winchester, Frederick Co., Virginia? on February 21, 1973, at age 66.

She married **Ellis Elmer Harbaugh.** They had one son. Ellis Elmer Harbaugh was born in Hawvers, Frederick Co., Maryland, in 1903. Ellis Elmer worked as a Manager of a Coca-Cola bottling plant between 1941 and 1952. He reached age 49 and died in Winchester, Frederick Co., Virginia? in 1952.

Son of Emily Virginia Hill and Ellis Elmer Harbaugh:

+ 291  m   I.   **William Ellis**[9] **Harbaugh** was born in Winchester, Frederick Co., Virginia, on January 26, 1938.

**188. Russell G.**[8] **Hill II** (*Russell Sage*[7], *William Hamilton*[6], *Mary Jane*[5] *Goudy, Elizabeth Jane*[4] *Pegan, Andrew*[3] *Pegan II, Andrew*[2] *Pagan, James*[1]) was born on June 6, 1908, in Steubenville, Cross Creek Twp., Jefferson Co., Ohio. He was the son of Russell Sage Hill (104) and Carrie Etta Groves. Russell G. died in Thousand Oaks, Ventura Co., California, on March 18, 1985, at age 76. He was buried in Pierce Brothers Valley Oaks Memorial Park Cemetery, Westlake Village, Los Angeles Co., California.[80]

Russell G. married **Blanche Snyder** in 1929. They are divorced. They have one daughter. Blanche Snyder was born in Steubenville, Cross Creek Twp., Jefferson Co., Ohio, on January 21, 1908.

Russell G. Hill II married **Philomena Mitchell** after 1940. Philomena Mitchell was born in Rush Run, Warren Twp., Jefferson Co., Ohio, on March 18, 1913. She was also known as **Minnie.** Philomena reached age 89 and died in Thousand Oaks, Ventura Co., California, on June 10, 2002.

Daughter of Russell G. Hill II and Blanche Snyder:

+ 292  f   I.   **Audrey Jane**[9] **Hill** was born in Steubenville, Cross Creek Twp., Jefferson Co., Ohio, on November 28, 1930. She died in Steubenville, Cross Creek Twp., Jefferson Co.,

Ohio, on November 30, 1930. Audrey Jane was buried in Union Cemetery, Steubenville, Cross Creek Twp., Jefferson Co., Ohio.[16]

**189. William Harold⁸ Hill** (*Russell Sage⁷, William Hamilton⁶, Mary Jane⁵ Goudy, Elizabeth Jane⁴ Pegan, Andrew³ Pegan II, Andrew² Pagan, James¹*) was born on June 26, 1910, in Steubenville, Cross Creek Twp., Jefferson Co., Ohio. He was the son of Russell Sage Hill (104) and Carrie Etta Groves. William Harold died in Crawley, Greenbrier Co., West Virginia? before 1969.

William Harold married **Gertrude Margaret Mace** on June 26, 1931, in Jefferson Co., Ohio. They had two sons. Gertrude Margaret Mace was born in Richwood, Nicholas Co., West Virginia, on December 25, 1911. Gertrude Margaret reached age 73 and died in Rainelle, Greenbrier Co., West Virginia, on June 1, 1985. She was buried in Wallace Memorial Cemetery, Crawley, Greenbrier Co., West Virginia.[113]

Sons of William Harold Hill and Gertrude Margaret Mace:

+ 293 m I. **William Robert⁹ Hill II** was born in Steubenville, Cross Creek Twp., Jefferson Co., Ohio, on June 16, 1932. He died in Chattanooga, Hamilton Co., Tennessee, on April 15, 1991. William Robert was buried in Wallace Memorial Cemetery, Crawley, Greenbrier Co., West Virginia.[112]

+ 294 m II. **Earl Russell⁹ Hill** was born in Steubenville, Cross Creek Twp., Jefferson Co., Ohio, on June 20, 1937. He died in East Ridge, Hamilton Co., Tennessee, on December 2, 2015. Earl Russell was buried in Chattanooga National Cemetery, Chattanooga, Hamilton Co., Tennessee.[114]

**190. Ethel Lillian⁸ Hill** (*Russell Sage⁷, William Hamilton⁶, Mary Jane⁵ Goudy, Elizabeth Jane⁴ Pegan, Andrew³ Pegan II, Andrew² Pagan, James¹*) was born in 1916 in Steubenville, Cross Creek Twp., Jefferson Co., Ohio. She was the daughter of Russell Sage Hill (104) and Carrie Etta Groves. Ethel Lillian died after 1940.

**191. Betty Jean⁸ Hill** (*Russell Sage⁷, William Hamilton⁶, Mary Jane⁵ Goudy, Elizabeth Jane⁴ Pegan, Andrew³ Pegan II, Andrew² Pagan, James¹*) was born in 1918 in Steubenville, Cross Creek Twp., Jefferson Co., Ohio. She was the daughter of Russell Sage Hill (104) and Carrie Etta Groves. Betty Jean died after 1940.

**192. Edna A.⁸ Hill** (*Charles Millard⁷, John W.⁶, Mary Jane⁵ Goudy, Elizabeth Jane⁴ Pegan, Andrew³ Pegan II, Andrew² Pagan, James¹*) was born on October 8, 1890, in Wheeling, Ohio Co., West Virginia. She was the daughter of Charles Millard Hill (105) and Josephine Kline. Edna A. died in Wheeling, Ohio Co., West Virginia, on April 5, 1892, at age one.

**193. Eugene Wilson⁸ Hill** (*Charles Millard⁷, John W.⁶, Mary Jane⁵ Goudy, Elizabeth Jane⁴ Pegan, Andrew³ Pegan II, Andrew² Pagan, James¹*) was born on June 3, 1893, in Wheeling, Ohio Co., West Virginia. He was the son of Charles Millard Hill (105) and Josephine Kline. Eugene Wilson died in East Liverpool, Liverpool Twp., Columbiana Co., Ohio, on June 12, 1962, at age 69.

Childless.

Eugene Wilson married **Lizetta Cook** on June 18, 1919, in Ohio Co., West Virginia. Lizetta Cook was born in Wheeling, Ohio Co., West Virginia, in 1895. Lizetta reached age 70 and died in East Liverpool, Liverpool Twp., Columbiana Co., Ohio, on May 11, 1965.

**194. Ella S.⁸ Hill** (*Charles Millard⁷, John W.⁶, Mary Jane⁵ Goudy, Elizabeth Jane⁴ Pegan, Andrew³ Pegan II, Andrew² Pagan, James¹*) was born on July 8, 1895, in Wheeling, Ohio Co., West Virginia. She was the daughter of Charles Millard Hill (105) and Josephine Kline. Ella S. died in Wheeling, Ohio Co., West Virginia, on March 8, 1898, at age two.

**195. Nellie Caroline⁸ Hill** (*Charles Millard⁷, John W.⁶, Mary Jane⁵ Goudy, Elizabeth Jane⁴ Pegan, Andrew³ Pegan II, Andrew² Pagan, James¹*) was born on December 5, 1897, in Ritchie, Ohio Co., West Virginia. She was the daughter of Charles Millard Hill (105) and Josephine Kline. Nellie Caroline died in Wheeling, Ohio Co., West Virginia, on July 9, 1979, at age 81. She was buried in Greenwood Cemetery, Wheeling, Ohio Co., West Virginia.[24]

Nellie Caroline married **Alfred Raymond Howard** on March 29, 1919, in Ohio Co., West Virginia. They had two sons. Alfred Raymond Howard was born in Wheeling, Ohio Co., West Virginia, on December 24, 1897. Alfred Raymond lived in Wheeling, Ohio Co., West Virginia. He reached age 85 and died in a hospital in Cadiz, Cadiz Twp., Harrison Co., Ohio, on August 13, 1983. Alfred Raymond was buried in Greenwood Cemetery, Wheeling, Ohio Co., West Virginia.[24]

Sons of Nellie Caroline Hill and Alfred Raymond Howard:

+ 295 m I. **Wallace Raymond⁹ Howard** was born in Wheeling, Ohio Co., West Virginia, on November 8, 1919. He died in Wheeling, Ohio Co., West Virginia, on February 7, 1997. Wallace Raymond was buried in Greenwood Cemetery, Wheeling, Ohio Co., West Virginia.[24]

+ 296 m II. **Alfred Eugene⁹ Howard II** was born in Wheeling, Ohio Co., West Virginia, on November 28, 1921. He died in Wheeling, Ohio Co., West Virginia, on October 11, 1993. Alfred Eugene was buried in Greenwood Cemetery, Wheeling, Ohio Co., West Virginia.[24]

**196. Dorretta Josephine⁸ Hill** (*Charles Millard⁷, John W.⁶, Mary Jane⁵ Goudy, Elizabeth Jane⁴ Pegan, Andrew³ Pegan II, Andrew² Pagan, James¹*) was born on February 5, 1900, in Ritchie, Ohio Co., West Virginia. She was the daughter of Charles Millard Hill (105) and Josephine Kline. Dorretta Josephine died in Belmont Co., Ohio, on January 6, 1998, at age 97.

Dorretta Josephine married **Errett Clinton Mooney** on March 26, 1921, in Brooke Co. West Virginia. They had two daughters. Errett Clinton Mooney was born in Washington, Ohio Co., West Virginia, on December 10, 1899. Errett Clinton reached age 72 and died in Wheeling, Ohio Co., West Virginia, on March 26, 1972.

Daughters of Dorretta Josephine Hill and Errett Clinton Mooney:

+ 297 f I. **Helen⁹ Mooney** was born in Wheeling, Ohio Co., West Virginia, in 1923.

+ 298 f II. **Gloria Jean⁹ Mooney** was born in Wheeling, Ohio Co., West Virginia, in 1925.

**197. Harriet Ellen⁸ Hill** (*Charles Millard⁷, John W.⁶, Mary Jane⁵ Goudy, Elizabeth Jane⁴ Pegan, Andrew³ Pegan II, Andrew² Pagan, James¹*) was born on April 5, 1902, in Ritchie, Ohio Co., West Virginia. She was the daughter of Charles Millard Hill (105) and Josephine Kline. Harriet Ellen died in Wheeling, Ohio Co., West Virginia, in February 1977 at age 74. She was buried in Greenwood Cemetery, Wheeling, Ohio Co., West Virginia.[24]

Harriet Ellen married **Cecil Meril Clark** on December 27, 1922, in Brooke Co., West Virginia. They had two daughters. Cecil Meril Clark was born in Elm Grove, Ohio Co., West Virginia, on August 26, 1901. Cecil Meril reached age 62 and died in Ritchie, Ohio Co., West Virginia, on February 16, 1964. He was buried in Greenwood Cemetery, Wheeling, Ohio Co., West Virginia.[24]

Daughters of Harriet Ellen Hill and Cecil Meril Clark:

+ 299 f I. **June M.⁹ Clark** was born in Ritchie, Ohio Co., West Virginia, on June 19, 1925. She died in Ritchie, Ohio Co., West Virginia, on January 16, 1927. June M.

was buried in Greenwood Cemetery, Wheeling, Ohio Co., West Virginia.[24]

+ 300 f II. **Dorothy E.⁹ Clark** was born in Ritchie, Ohio Co., West Virginia, on November 29, 1927. She died in Wheeling, Ohio Co., West Virginia, on September 30, 1951. Dorothy E. was buried in Greenwood Cemetery, Wheeling, Ohio Co., West Virginia.[24]

**198. Gertrude Isabella⁸ Hirth** (*Ella Allen⁷ Hill, John W.⁶, Mary Jane⁵ Goudy, Elizabeth Jane⁴ Pegan, Andrew³ Pegan II, Andrew² Pagan, James¹*) was born on June 4, 1890, in Wheeling, Ohio Co., West Virginia. She was the daughter of Charles William Hirth and Ella Allen Hill (106). Gertrude Isabella died in a facility in Cadiz, Cadiz Twp., Harrison Co., Ohio, on July 25, 1972, at age 82. She was buried in Union Cemetery, Steubenville, Cross Creek Twp., Jefferson Co., Ohio.[16]

Gertrude Isabella married **George William Watters** on January 9, 1909, in Ohio Co., West Virginia. They had one son. George William Watters was born in Steubenville, Cross Creek Twp., Jefferson Co., Ohio, on August 17, 1884. George William reached age 77 and died in Steubenville, Cross Creek Twp., Jefferson Co., Ohio, on March 6, 1962.

Gertrude Isabella Hirth Watters married **Harry C. Howland** on June 15, 1910, in Jefferson Co., Ohio. They are divorced. They had one son. Harry C. Howland was born in Dover, Kent, England, in 1881. He died after 1912. Henry C. Howland may have returned to England.

Gertrude Isabella Hirth Watters Howland married **Luke Wallace Dunnan** about 1912. They had six children. Luke Wallace Dunnan was born in Leetonia, Salem Twp., Columbiana Co., Ohio, on May 15, 1880. He was also known as **Wallace.** Luke Wallace reached age 91 and died in Cadiz, Cadiz Twp., Harrison Co., Ohio, on September 1, 1971. He was buried in Union Cemetery,

Steubenville, Cross Creek Twp., Jefferson Co., Ohio.[16]

Son of Gertrude Isabella Hirth and George William Watters:

+ 301 m I. **George Allen⁹ Watters II** was born in Wheeling, Ohio Co., West Virginia, on March 24, 1909. He was also known as **Allen or Allyn.** George Allen died in Chicago, Cook Co., Illinois, on March 8, 1972.

Son of Gertrude Isabella Hirth and Harry C. Howland:

+ 302 m I. **Howard Clarke⁹ Howland** was born in Steubenville, Cross Creek Twp., Jefferson Co., Ohio, on November 7, 1912. He was also known as **Clarke.** Howard Clarke died in Steubenville, Cross Creek Twp., Jefferson Co., Ohio, on November 26, 1974. He was buried in Union Cemetery, Steubenville, Cross Creek Twp., Jefferson Co., Ohio.[16]

Children of Gertrude Isabella Hirth and Luke Wallace Dunnan:

+ 303 m I. **Norman Bruce⁹ Dunnan** was born in Pughtown (now New Manchester), Hancock Co., West Virginia, on August 23, 1915. He died in Fort Meade, Anne Arundel Co., Maryland, on December 5, 1951. Norman Bruce was buried in Arlington National Cemetery, Arlington, Virginia.[115]

+ 304 f II. **Ella Alice or Allys⁹ Dunnan** was born in Chester, Hancock Co., West Virginia, in 1916. She died after 1937.

+ 305 m III. **Hugh Ronald⁹ Dunnan** was born in Pughtown (now New Manchester), Hancock Co., West Virginia, on July 4, 1918. He was also known as **Ronald.** Hugh Ronald died in Charleston, Kanawha Co., West Virginia, on November 12, 1987.

+ 306 f IV. **Dorothy Ada[9] Dunnan** was born in Pughtown (now New Manchester), Hancock Co., West Virginia,on August 7, 1920. She died in Modesto, Stanislaus Co., Cali fornia, on June 27, 2015. Dorothy Ada was buried in Turlock Memorial Park Cemetery, Turlock, Stanislaus Co., California.[116]

+ 307 f V. **Marianne Frances[9] Dunnan** was born in Pughtown (now New Manchester), Hancock Co., West Virginia, on October 31, 1921. She died in a facility in Upper Arlington, Franklin Co., Ohio, on April 17, 2002.

+ 308 f VI. **Leah Gertrude[9] Dunnan** was born in Wayne Twp., Jefferson Co., Ohio, on September 26, 1923. She died in Richmond, Henrico Co., Virginia, on August 19, 2018. Leah Gertrude is buried in Westhampton Memorial Park Cemetery, Tuckahoe, Henrico Co., Virginia.[A]

**199. Ada Roberts[8] Hirth** (*Ella Allen[7] Hill, John W.[6], Mary Jane[5] Goudy, Elizabeth Jane[4] Pegan, Andrew[3] Pegan II, Andrew[2] Pagan, James[1]*) was born on July 26, 1892, in Wheeling, Ohio Co., West Virginia. She was the daughter of Charles William Hirth and Ella Allen Hill (106). Ada Roberts died in Peoria, Peoria Twp., Peoria Co., Illinois, on February 7, 1968, at age 75. She was buried in Springdale Cemetery and Mausoleum, Peoria, Peoria Twp., Peoria Co., Illinois.[81]

Ada Roberts married **Richard Andrew Mason** on May 18, 1909, in Ohio Co., West Virginia. They divorced. They had one son. Richard Andrew

Mason was born in Muldraugh, Kentucky, on May 25, 1887. He reached age 55 and died in Steubenville, Cross Creek Twp., Jefferson Co., Ohio, on February 23, 1943. Richard Andrew was buried in Union Cemetery, Steubenville, Cross Creek Twp., Jefferson Co., Ohio.[16]

Ada Roberts Hirth Mason married **Albert Liscoe Coleman** after 1943. Albert Liscoe Coleman was born in Chicago, Cook Co., Illinois, on August 24, 1884. Albert Liscoe reached age 72 and died in Peoria, Peoria Twp., Peoria Co., Illinois, on June 25, 1957. He was buried in Springdale Cemetery and Mausoleum, Peoria, Peoria Twp., Peoria Co., Illinois.[81]

Son of Ada Roberts Hirth and Richard Andrew Mason:

+ 309 m I. **Richard[9] Mason II** was born in West Virginia in 1910. He died before 1920.

**200. Della[8] Hirth** (*Ella Allen[7] Hill, John W.[6], Mary Jane[5] Goudy, Elizabeth Jane[4] Pegan, Andrew[3] Pegan II, Andrew[2] Pagan, James[1]*) was born on June 12, 1898, in Union Twp., Marshall Co. West Virginia. She was the daughter of Charles William Hirth and Ella Allen Hill (106). Della lived in 1988 in Mingo Junction, Steubenville Twp., Jefferson Co., Ohio. She died in a hospital in Steubenville, Cross Creek Twp., Jefferson Co., Ohio, on February 8, 1988, age 89. Della was buried in Union Cemetery, Steubenville, Cross Creek Twp., Jefferson Co., Ohio.[16]

She married **Harry Hawkins Moore.** They divorced. They had three children. Harry Hawkins Moore was born in Steubenville, Cross Creek Twp., Jefferson Co., Ohio, on June 7, 1893. He lived in 1980 in Mingo Junction, Steubenville Twp., Jefferson Co., Ohio. Harry Hawkins reached age 86 and died in a hospital in Steubenville, Cross Creek Twp., Jefferson Co., Ohio, on May 31, 1980. He was buried in Union Cemetery, Steubenville, Cross Creek Twp., Jefferson Co., Ohio.[16]

Children of Della Hirth and Harry Hawkins Moore:

+ 310 m I. **Robert Harold[9] Moore** was born in Steubenville, Cross Creek Twp.,

Jefferson Co., Ohio, on June 14, 1915. He died in Salinas, Monterey Co., California, on May 7, 1994. Robert Harold was buried in San Joaquin Valley National Cemetery, Santa Nella, Merced Co., California.[117]

+ 311 f II. **Ruth Eleanor**[9] **Moore** was born in Steubenville, Cross Creek Twp., Jefferson Co., Ohio, on March 2, 1917. She died in Steubenville, Cross Creek Twp., Jefferson Co., Ohio, on March 11, 1998. Ruth Eleanor was buried in New Alexandria Cemetery, New Alexandria, Ohio.[118]

+ 312 f III. **Jeanne**[9] **Moore** was born in Steubenville, Cross Creek Twp., Jefferson Co., Ohio, on October 6, 1919. She died in Washington, District of Columbia, on October 19, 2004. Jeanne was buried in Mount Calvary Cemetery, Steubenville, Cross Creek Twp., Jefferson Co., Ohio.[119]

**201. Charles William**[8] **Hirth II** (*Ella Allen*[7] *Hill, John W.*[6], *Mary Jane*[5] *Goudy, Elizabeth Jane*[4] *Pegan, Andrew*[3] *Pegan II, Andrew*[2] *Pagan, James*[1]) was born on August 4, 1903, in Wheeling, Ohio Co., West Virginia. He was also known as **C. William Hirth**, **William** and **Bill**. He was the son of Charles William Hirth and Ella Allen Hill (106). Charles William lived in 1979 in Martins Ferry, Pease Twp., Belmont Co., Ohio. He died in a hospital in Wheeling, Ohio Co., West Virginia, on October 27, 1979, at age 76. Charles William was buried in Riverview Cemetery, Martins Ferry, Pease Twp., Belmont Co., Ohio.[14]

Charles William married **Gladys Sarita Grey** on August 6, 1927, in Belmont Co., Ohio. They had one son. Gladys Sarita Grey was born in Martins Ferry, Pease Twp., Belmont Co., Ohio, on February 18, 1903. Gladys Sarita reached age 87 and died in Martins Ferry, Pease Twp., Belmont Co., Ohio, on October 24, 1990. She was buried in Riverview

Cemetery, Martins Ferry, Pease Twp., Belmont Co., Ohio.[14]

Son of Charles William Hirth II and Gladys Sarita Grey:

+ 313 m I. **Charles William**[9] **Hirth III** was born in Martins Ferry, Pease Twp., Belmont Co., Ohio, on August 9, 1934.

**202. Benjamin Cowen**[8] **Bridgeman** (*Minnie Blanche*[7] *Fox, Elizabeth Jane*[6] *Hill, Mary Jane*[5] *Goudy, Elizabeth Jane*[4] *Pegan, Andrew*[3] *Pegan II, Andrew*[2] *Pagan, James*[1]) was born on November 21, 1894, in New Martinsville, Wetzel Co., West Virginia. He was the son of John Howe Bridgeman and Minnie Blanche Fox (108). Benjamin Cowen died in Buffalo, Erie Co., New York? after 1940.

Benjamin Cowen married **Lulu May Whiteman** in 1918 in Marshall Co., West Virginia. They had three children. Lulu May Whiteman was born in Marshall Co., West Virginia, on December 22, 1893. Lulu May reached age 74 and died in Hope Twp., Bartholomew Co., Indiana, in October 1968.

Children of Benjamin Cowen Bridgeman and Lulu May Whiteman:

+ 314 m I. **Arthur William**[9] **Bridgeman** was born in Wheeling, Ohio Co., West Virginia, on October 25, 1918. He died in Wheeling, Ohio Co., West Virginia, on December 4, 1935. Arthur William was buried in Greenwood Cemetery, Wheeling, Ohio Co., West Virginia.[24]

+ 315 f II. **Betty Harriett**[9] **Bridgeman** was born in Wheeling, Ohio Co., West Virginia, on June 19, 1920. She died in Hope, Haw Creek Twp., Bartholomew Co., Indiana, on November 28, 2005. Betty Harriett was buried in Garland Brook Cemetery, Columbus, Bartholomew Co., Indiana.[120]

+ 316 m III. **Benjamin Cowen⁹ Bridgeman II** was born in Wheeling, Ohio Co., West Virginia, on June 23, 1921. He died in a hospital in Cuyahoga Falls, Cuyahoga Falls Twp., Summit Co., Ohio, on October 16, 1987.

**203. Arthur⁸ Bridgeman** (*Minnie Blanche⁷ Fox, Elizabeth Jane⁶ Hill, Mary Jane⁵ Goudy, Elizabeth Jane⁴ Pegan, Andrew³ Pegan II, Andrew² Pagan, James¹*) was born on November 21, 1899, in New Martinsville, Wetzel Co., West Virginia. He was the son of John Howe Bridgeman and Minnie Blanche Fox (108). Arthur died in New Martinsville, Wetzel Co., West Virginia, on July 13, 1904, at age four.

**204. John⁸ Bridgeman III** (*Minnie Blanche⁷ Fox, Elizabeth Jane⁶ Hill, Mary Jane⁵ Goudy, Elizabeth Jane⁴ Pegan, Andrew³ Pegan II, Andrew² Pagan, James¹*) was born on March 21, 1906, in New Martinsville, Wetzel Co., West Virginia. He was the son of John Howe Bridgeman and Minnie Blanche Fox (108). John died in Lakeview, Erie Co., New York, in December 1970 at age 64.

John married **Ruth Louise Grimm** on October 21, 1932, in Ohio Co., West Virginia. They had one son. Ruth Louise Grimm was born in Warwood, Wheeling, Ohio Co., West Virginia, on September 2, 1912. Ruth Louise reached age 66 and died in Buffalo, Erie Co., New York, on December 9, 1978. She was buried in Lakeside Memorial Park Cemetery, Hamburg, Erie Co., New York.[121]

Son of John Bridgeman III and Ruth Louise Grimm:

+ 317 m I. **John⁹ Bridgeman IV** was born in Wheeling, Ohio Co., West Virginia, in 1934.

**205. Roberta Elizabeth⁸ Fox** (*Robert Arthur⁷, Elizabeth Jane⁶ Hill, Mary Jane⁵ Goudy, Elizabeth Jane⁴ Pegan, Andrew³ Pegan II, Andrew² Pagan, James¹*) was born on February 3, 1911, in Wheeling, Ohio Co., West Virginia. She was the daughter of Robert Arthur Fox (111) and Elizabeth Dichtenmuller. Roberta Elizabeth died in Glen Dale, Marshall Co., West Virginia, on October 20, 1983, at age 72. She was buried in Fairview Cemetery, Moundsville, Marshall Co., West Virginia.[83]

Roberta Elizabeth married **James Dallas Ewing** on May 31, 1929, in Brooke Co. West Virginia. They had three sons. James Dallas Ewing was born in Pleasant Valley, Ohio Co., West Virginia, on August 26, 1901. James Dallas reached age 82 and died in Glen Dale, Marshall Co., West Virginia, on March 21, 1984. He was buried in Fairview Cemetery, Moundsville, Marshall Co., West Virginia.[83]

Sons of Roberta Elizabeth Fox and James Dallas Ewing:

+ 318 m I. **William Robert⁹ Ewing** was born in Sand Hill, Marshall Co., West Virginia, on July 6, 1930. He died in Glen Dale, Marshall Co., West Virginia, on November 17, 1992.

+ 319 m II. **James Addison⁹ Ewing II** was born in Marshall Co., West Virginia, on July 18, 1935. He died in Moundsville, Marshall Co., West Virginia, on June 15, 1991. James Addison was buried in Fairview Cemetery, Moundsville, Marshall Co., West Virginia.[83]

+ 320 m III. **Donald Gene⁹ Ewing** was born in Sand Hill., Marshall Co., West Virginia, on December 9, 1936. He died in Sand Hill, Marshall Co., West Virginia, on November 11, 1943.

**206. Benjamin Harrison⁸ Fox** (*Robert Arthur⁷, Elizabeth Jane⁶ Hill, Mary Jane⁵ Goudy, Elizabeth Jane⁴ Pegan, Andrew³ Pegan II, Andrew² Pagan, James¹*) was born on July 25, 1918, in Wheeling, Ohio Co., West Virginia. He was the son of Robert Arthur Fox (111) and Elizabeth Dichtenmuller. Benjamin Harrison died in Wheeling, Ohio Co., West Virginia, on September 12, 1968, at age 50. He was buried in Greenwood Cemetery, Wheeling, Ohio Co., West Virginia.[24]

Benjamin Harrison married **Fredaricka Schultz** in 1955 in Ohio Co., West Virginia. Fredaricka Schultz was born in Wheeling, Ohio Co., West Virginia, on March 7, 1925. Fredaricka reached age 80 and died in Wheeling, Ohio Co., West Virginia, on March 15, 2005.

207. **Marian Alice⁸ Flanegin** (*Jennie⁷ Fox, Elizabeth Jane⁶ Hill, Mary Jane⁵ Goudy, Elizabeth Jane⁴ Pegan, Andrew³ Pegan II, Andrew² Pagan, James¹*) was born on August 2, 1909, in Wheeling, Ohio Co., West Virginia. She was the daughter of John Edmond Flanegin and Jennie Fox (112). Marian Alice died in Wheeling, Ohio Co., West Virginia, on June 25, 1959, at age 49. She was buried in Greenwood Cemetery, Wheeling, Ohio Co., West Virginia.[24]

Marian Alice married **Walter Wilbur Hartman** on November 19, 1928, in Brooke Co., West Virginia. Walter Wilbur Hartman was born in Wheeling, Ohio Co., West Virginia, on September 11, 1906. Walter Wilbur reached age 64 and died in Wheeling, Ohio Co., West Virginia, on November 9, 1970. He was buried in Greenwood Cemetery, Wheeling, Ohio Co., West Virginia.[24]

208. **Edmund Arthur⁸ Flanegin II** (*Jennie⁷ Fox, Elizabeth Jane⁶ Hill, Mary Jane⁵ Goudy, Elizabeth Jane⁴ Pegan, Andrew³ Pegan II, Andrew² Pagan, James¹*) was born on April 28, 1912, in Wheeling, Ohio Co., West Virginia. He was the son of John Edmond Flanegin and Jennie Fox (112). Edmund Arthur died in Wheeling, Ohio Co., West Virginia, on October 20, 1980, at age 68. He was buried in Greenwood Cemetery, Wheeling, Ohio Co., West Virginia.[24]

Edmund Arthur married **Aliah Tennant** on September 8, 1932, in Ohio Co., West Virginia. They divorced. They had two children. Aliah Tennant was born in Ohio Co., West Virginia, on August 8, 1916. She reached age 86 and died in Belmont, Goshen Twp., Belmont Co., Ohio, on April 25, 2003.

Edmund Arthur Flanegin II married **Wilda Michaels** on April 26, 1946, in Ohio Co., West Virginia. They had two sons. Wilda Michaels was born in Wheeling, Ohio Co., West Virginia, on December 31, 1919. Wilda reached age 90 and died in Wheeling, Ohio Co., West Virginia, on August 10, 2010. She was buried in Parkview Memorial Gardens Cemetery, Wheeling, Ohio Co., West Virginia.[122]

Children of Edmund Arthur Flanegin II and Aliah Tennant:

+ 321 f I. **Marian Lee⁹ Flanegin** was born in Wheeling, Ohio Co., West Virginia, on February 11, 1933.

+ 322 m II. **Edmond Arthur⁹ Flanegin III** was born in Wheeling, Ohio Co., West Virginia, on February 18, 1935. He died in Wheeling, Ohio Co., West Virginia, on July 9, 1988. Edmund Arthur was buried in Greenwood Cemetery, Wheeling, Ohio Co., West Virginia.[24]

209. **Infant Daughter⁸ Flanegin** (*Jennie⁷ Fox, Elizabeth Jane⁶ Hill, Mary Jane⁵ Goudy, Elizabeth Jane⁴ Pegan, Andrew³ Pegan II, Andrew² Pagan, James¹*) was born on March 25, 1914, in Wheeling, Ohio Co., West Virginia? She was the daughter of John Edmond Flanegin and Jennie Fox (112). Infant Daughter died in Wheeling, Ohio Co., West Virginia, on March 25, 1914. She was buried in Mount Zion Cemetery, Wheeling, Ohio Co., West Virginia.[28]

# 9th Generation

**210. Alice Eileen[9] Fisher** (*Helen[8] Goudy, Harry Homer[7], William M.[6], John[5], Elizabeth Jane[4] Pegan, Andrew[3] Pegan II, Andrew[2] Pagan, James[1]*) was born on January 7, 1928, in Sherrard, Union Twp., Marshall Co., West Virginia. She was also known as **Eileen.** She was the daughter of Kirk Alexander Fisher and Helen Goudy (114).

Alice Eileen married **Joseph Nelson Wilson** on November 26, 1947, in Ohio Co., West Virginia. Joseph Nelson Wilson was born in Moundsville, Marshall Co., West Virginia, on December 4, 1918. Joseph Nelson reached age 86 and died in Moundsville, Marshall Co., West Virginia, on May 29, 2005. He was buried in Limestone Cemetery, Limestone, Marshall Co., West Virginia.[56]

**211. Son[9] Thompson** (*Lewis or Louis MacAfee[8], Lewis K.[7], Nancy J.[6] Goudy, Andrew[5], Elizabeth Jane[4] Pegan, Andrew[3] Pegan II, Andrew[2] Pagan, James[1]*) was born on April 8, 1909, in Uhrichsville, Mill Twp., Tuscarawas Co., Ohio. He was the son of Lewis or Louis MacAfee Thompson II (115) and Pearl Rikeard. Son died in Uhrichsville, Mill Twp., Tuscarawas Co., Ohio, on April 9, 1909.

**212. Guy Leroy[9] Galbreath** (*James Howard[8], Ella Nancy[7] Thompson, Nancy J.[6] Goudy, Andrew[5], Elizabeth Jane[4] Pegan, Andrew[3] Pegan II, Andrew[2] Pagan, James[1]*) was born on July 27, 1895, in Uhrichsville, Mill Twp., Tuscarawas Co., Ohio. He was the son of James Howard Galbreath (117) and Eva E. Bratton. Guy Leroy died in Knox Co., Ohio, on October 18, 1956, at age 61. He was buried in Longview Cemetery, Bowerston, Monroe Twp., Harrison Co., Ohio.[85]

Guy Leroy married **Mary E. Timmerman** in 1917 in Ohio Co., West Virginia. They had one son. Mary E. Timmerman was born in Bowerston, Monroe Twp., Harrison Co., Ohio, on October 9, 1890. Mary E. reached age 59 and died in Uhrichsville, Mill Twp., Tuscarawas Co., Ohio, on August 21, 1950. She was buried in Longview Cemetery, Bowerston, Monroe Twp., Harrison Co., Ohio.[85]

Son of Guy Leroy Galbreath and Mary E. Timmerman:

+ 323   m   I.   **Charles W.[10] Galbreath** was born in Uhrichsville, Mill Twp., Tuscarawas Co., Ohio, on February 25, 1917. He was also known as **Gilly.** Charles W. died in Santa Rosa, Sonoma Co., California, on December 20, 1984. He was buried in Longview Cemetery, Bowerston, Monroe Twp., Harrison Co., Ohio.[85]

**213. Raymond Arthur[9] Galbreath** (*James Howard[8], Ella Nancy[7] Thompson, Nancy J.[6] Goudy, Andrew[5], Elizabeth Jane[4] Pegan, Andrew[3] Pegan II, Andrew[2] Pagan, James[1]*) was born on October 22, 1897, in Uhrichsville, Mill Twp., Tuscarawas Co., Ohio. He was the son of James Howard Galbreath (117) and Eva E. Bratton. Raymond Arthur died in Uhrichsville, Mill Twp., Tuscarawas Co., Ohio, on May 23, 1973, at age 75. He was buried in Evergreen Burial Park, New Philadelphia, Tuscarawas Co., Ohio.[58]

Raymond Arthur married **Marjorie Marie Garrett** on July 14, 1918, in Brooke Co. West Virginia. They had five children. Marjorie Marie Garrett was born in Warwick Twp., Tuscarawas Co., Ohio, on February 4, 1901. Marjorie Marie lived in 1971 in Uhrichsville, Mill Twp., Tuscarawas Co., Ohio. She reached age 69 and died in a hospital in Columbus, Franklin Co., Ohio, on January 12, 1971. Marjorie Marie was buried in Evergreen Burial Park, New Philadelphia, Tuscarawas Co., Ohio.[58]

Children of Raymond Arthur Galbreath and Marjorie Marie Garrett:

+ 324   m   I.   **Howard Eugene[10] Galbreath** was born in Uhrichsville, Mill Twp., Tuscarawas Co., Ohio, on April 24, 1919. He died in Dennison, Mill Twp., Tuscarawas Co., Ohio, on February 27, 1970.

+ 325 f II. **Betty Jane**[10] **Galbreath** was born in Uhrichsville, Mill Twp., Tuscarawas Co., Ohio, on August 11, 1922. She died in Mansfield, Madison Twp., Richland Co., Ohio, on August 9, 2001. Betty Jane was buried in Ontario Cemetery, Ontario, Springfield Twp., Richland Co., Ohio.[123]

+ 326 m III. **Raymond J.**[10] **Galbreath II** was born in Uhrichsville, Mill Twp., Tuscarawas Co., Ohio, on September 4, 1925. He was also known as **Pete.** Raymond J. died in a hospital in Massillon, Perry Twp., Stark Co., Ohio, on November 29, 2014. He was buried in Berger (Brethren) Cemetery, Baltic, Clark Twp., Holmes Co., Ohio.[124]

+ 327 f IV. **Mary Margaret**[10] **Galbreath** was born in Uhrichsville, Mill Twp., Tuscarawas Co., Ohio, on February 3, 1931. She died in Uhrichsville, Mill Twp., Tuscarawas Co., Ohio, on February 22, 2015. Mary Margaret was buried in Evergreen Burial Park, New Philadelphia, Tuscarawas Co., Ohio.[58]

+ 328 m V. **Robert L.**[10] **Galbreath** was born in Uhrichsville, Mill Twp., Tuscarawas Co., Ohio, on January 18, 1934. He died in a hospital in Columbiana, Columbiana Co., Ohio, on April 26, 2007.

**214. Clara Irene**[9] **Galbreath** (*James Howard*[8], *Ella Nancy*[7] *Thompson, Nancy J.*[6] *Goudy, Andrew*[5], *Elizabeth Jane*[4] *Pegan, Andrew*[3] *Pegan II, Andrew*[2] *Pagan, James*[1]) was born on June 24, 1905, in Uhrichsville, Mill Twp., Tuscarawas Co., Ohio. She was also known as **Irene.** She was the daughter of James Howard Galbreath (117) and Eva E. Bratton. Clara Irene lived in Uhrichsville, Mill Twp., Tuscarawas Co., Ohio. She died in a hospital in Lancaster, Fairfield Co., Ohio, on December 12,

1998, at age 93. Clara Irene was buried in Evergreen Burial Park, New Philadelphia, Tuscarawas Co., Ohio.[58]

Clara Irene Galbreath Staley always used her middle name, Irene, as her preferred name.

Clara Irene married **Robert F. Staley** in 1925 in Ohio Co., West Virginia. They had two children. Robert F. Staley was born in Uhrichsville, Mill Twp., Tuscarawas Co., Ohio, on December 4, 1901. Robert F. reached age 61 and died in Uhrichsville, Mill Twp., Tuscarawas Co., Ohio, on March 4, 1963. He was buried in Evergreen Burial Park, New Philadelphia, Tuscarawas Co., Ohio.[58]

Children of Clara Irene Galbreath and Robert F. Staley:

+ 329 f I. **Virginia Lee**[10] **Staley** was born in Uhrichsville, Mill Twp., Tuscarawas Co., Ohio, on August 16, 1926.

+ 330 m II. **Don R.**[10] **Staley** was born in Uhrichsville, Mill Twp., Tuscarawas Co., Ohio, on July 4, 1928. He died in New Philadelphia, Goshen Twp., Tuscarawas Co., Ohio, on February 9, 1977. He was cremated and his ashes buried in Evergreen Burial Park, New Philadelphia, Tuscarawas Co., Ohio..[58]

**215. Charles Marshall**[9] **Cary II** (*Charles Stewart*[8], *Sarah Virginia*[7] *Thompson, Nancy J.*[6] *Goudy, Andrew*[5], *Elizabeth Jane*[4] *Pegan, Andrew*[3] *Pegan II, Andrew*[2] *Pagan, James*[1]) was born on February 27, 1908, in Uhrichsville, Mill Twp., Tuscarawas Co., Ohio. He was the son of Charles Stewart Cary (120) and Mary Alice McCullough. Charles Marshall died in Massillon, Perry Twp., Stark Co., Ohio, on July 6, 1981, at age 73. He was buried in Saint Barbara Cemetery, Massillon, Perry Twp., Stark Co., Ohio.[85]

Charles Marshall married **Zelma Z. Zimmer** on May 16, 1927, in Ohio Co., West Virginia. They divorced. They had one son. Zelma Z. Zimmer was born in Tuscarawas Twp., Stark Co., Ohio, on May 14, 1911. She reached age 20 and died in Massillon, Perry Twp., Stark Co., Ohio, on March 26, 1932.

Zelma Z. was buried in Massillon City Cemetery, Massillon, Perry Twp., Stark Co., Ohio.[125]

Charles Marshall Cary II and his first wife, Zelma Zimmer, divorced and Zelma died shortly thereafter. Afterwards, their son, Robert Glenn Cary, was raised by Zelma's parents who officially adopted him, and surname became Zimmer.

Charles Marshall Cary II married **Loretta Rosanna Wilhelm** in May 1932. They had two children. Loretta Rosanna Wilhelm was born in Massillon, Stark Co., Ohio, on December 3, 1908. Loretta Rosanna reached age 76 and died in Massillon, Perry Twp., Stark Co., Ohio, on January 28, 1985. She was buried in Saint Barbara Cemetery, Massillon, Perry Twp., Stark Co., Ohio.[86]

Son of Charles Marshall Cary II and Zelma Z. Zimmer:

+ 331 m I. **Robert Glenn[10] Cary (Zimmer)** was born in Massillon, Perry Twp., Stark Co., Ohio, on March 31, 1929. He died in Massillon, Perry Twp., Stark Co., Ohio, on February 13, 1997. Robert Glenn Cary was buried in Sunset Hills Burial Park Cemetery, Canton, Stark Co., Ohio.[126]

Charles Marshall Cary II and Loretta Rosanna Wilhelm had two children, including:

+ 332 m I. **Paul L.[10] Cary** was born in Massillon, Stark Co., Ohio? on January 14, 1927. He was adopted. Paul L. died in Cuyahoga Falls, Northampton Twp., Summit, Ohio, on September 9, 2010.

**216. Helen[9] Cary** (*Charles Stewart[8], Sarah Virginia[7] Thompson, Nancy J.[6] Goudy, Andrew[5], Elizabeth Jane[4] Pegan, Andrew[3] Pegan II, Andrew[2] Pagan, James[1]*) was born in 1910 in Uhrichsville, Mill Twp., Tuscarawas Co., Ohio. She was the daughter of Charles Stewart Cary (120) and Mary Alice McCullough. Helen died in Uhrichsville, Mill Twp., Tuscarawas Co., Ohio, in 1910.

**217. Betty J.[9] Cary** (*Charles Stewart[8], Sarah Virginia[7] Thompson, Nancy J.[6] Goudy, Andrew[5], Elizabeth Jane[4] Pegan, Andrew[3] Pegan II, Andrew[2] Pagan, James[1]*) was born in 1912 in Uhrichsville, Mill Twp., Tuscarawas Co., Ohio. She was the daughter of Charles Stewart Cary (120) and Mary Alice McCullough. Betty J. died after 1930.

**218. Robert Glen[9] Cary** (*Charles Stewart[8], Sarah Virginia[7] Thompson, Nancy J.[6] Goudy, Andrew[5], Elizabeth Jane[4] Pegan, Andrew[3] Pegan II, Andrew[2] Pagan, James[1]*) was born on January 23, 1914 in Uhrichsville, Mill Twp., Tuscarawas Co., Ohio. He was the son of Charles Stewart Cary (120) and Mary Alice McCullough. Robert Glen died on November 17, 2000 in Sun City, Maricopa Co., Arizona, at age 86. He was buried in Sunland Memorial Park Cemetery, Sun City, Maricopa Co., Arizona.[86]

Robert G. married **Virginia Louise Beardon** in Stark Co., Ohio? They had one son. Virginia Louise was born in Herman, Todd Co., Kentucky on September 19, 1918. She reached age 75 and died on November 25, 1993 in Sun City, Maricopa Co., Arizona. Virginia was buried in Sunland Memorial Park Cemetery, Sun City, Maricopa Co., Arizona.[87]

Son of Robert G. Cary and Virginia Louise Beardon:

+ 333 m I. **James[10] Cary** was born in Wyandotte, Wayne Co., Michigan, in 1939.

**219. Ruth Irene[9] Cary** (*Charles Stewart[8], Sarah Virginia[7] Thompson, Nancy J.[6] Goudy, Andrew[5], Elizabeth Jane[4] Pegan, Andrew[3] Pegan II, Andrew[2] Pagan, James[1]*) was born on March 10, 1916, in Uhrichsville, Mill Twp., Tuscarawas Co., Ohio. She was the daughter of Charles Stewart Cary (120) and Mary Alice McCullough. Ruth Irene died in Winnetka, Los Angeles Co., California, on December 23, 1997, at age 81.

Ruth Irene married **John Valentine Singer** before 1936. They had one son. John Valentine Singer was born in West Lebanon, Paint Twp., Wayne Co., Ohio, on February 14, 1914. John Valentine reached age 70 and died in Massillon, Perry Twp., Stark Co., Ohio, on May 4, 1984.

Ruth Irene Cary married **John William Teele** on November 25, 1951, in Los Angeles Co., California. John William Teele was born in Albia, Troy Twp., Monroe Co., Iowa, on November 30, 1923. John William reached age 49 and died in Los Angeles, Los Angeles Co., California, on October 15, 1973.

Son of Ruth Irene Cary and John Valentine Singer:

+ 334 m I. **John Beverly**[10] **Singer II** was born in Massillon, Perry Twp., Stark Co., Ohio, in 1936.

**220. Margaret Jean**[9] **Cary** (*Charles Stewart*[8], *Sarah Virginia*[7] *Thompson, Nancy J.*[6] *Goudy, Andrew*[5], *Elizabeth Jane*[4] *Pegan, Andrew*[3] *Pegan II, Andrew*[2] *Pagan, James*[1]) was born on August 7, 1918, in Uhrichsville, Mill Twp., Tuscarawas Co., Ohio. She was the daughter of Charles Stewart Cary (120) and Mary Alice McCullough. Margaret Jean died in Louisvile, Jefferson Co., Kentucky, on January 27, 2001, at age 82.

She married **Unknown Wetzel.** They had one daughter. She married **Unknown Lingrel.**

**221. Thomas E.**[9] **Cary** (*Charles Stewart*[8], *Sarah Virginia*[7] *Thompson, Nancy J.*[6] *Goudy, Andrew*[5], *Elizabeth Jane*[4] *Pegan, Andrew*[3] *Pegan II, Andrew*[2] *Pagan, James*[1]) was born on November 24, 1925, in Massillon, Perry Twp., Stark Co., Ohio. He was the son of Charles Stewart Cary (120) and Mary Alice McCullough. Thomas E. died in Massillon, Perry Twp., Stark Co., Ohio, on September 11, 2008, at age 82.

**222. Edward**[9] **Cary** (*Charles Stewart*[8], *Sarah Virginia*[7] *Thompson, Nancy J.*[6] *Goudy, Andrew*[5], *Elizabeth Jane*[4] *Pegan, Andrew*[3] *Pegan II, Andrew*[2] *Pagan, James*[1]) was born in 1927 in Massillon, Perry Twp., Stark Co., Ohio. He was the son of Charles Stewart Cary (120) and Mary Alice McCullough. Edward died before 2001. May have been adopted. Not in the Charles Stewart and Mary Alice McCullough Cary home in 1930.

**223. Helen May**[9] **Bovey (Seeley)** (*Artland Robinson*[8] *Bovey, Mary E.*[7] *Thompson, Nancy J.*[6] *Goudy, Andrew*[5], *Elizabeth Jane*[4] *Pegan, Andrew*[3] *Pegan II, Andrew*[2] *Pagan, James*[1]) was born on April 5, 1905, in Conneaut, Conneaut Twp., Ashtabula Co., Ohio. She was the daughter of Artland Robinson Bovey (121) and Charlotte Olmsted. Helen May died in Federal Way, King Co., Washington, on September 25, 1987, at age 82. She was buried in Forest Lawn Memorial Park Cemetery, Glendale, Los Angeles Co., California.[47]

She seems to have been adopted by Calvin and Charlotte Seeley of Los Angeles, Los Angeles Co., California.

Helen May Bovey (Seeley) married **Donald Fox McGaffey** on June 6, 1925, in Los Angeles Co., California. They had three children. Donald Fox McGaffey was born in Albuquerque, Bernalillo Co., New Mexico, on July 15, 1903. Donald Fox lived in 1930 in Beverly Hills, Los Angeles Co., California. He also resided in 1935 in Federal Way, King Co., Washington. Donald Fox reached age 49 and died in Los Angeles, Los Angeles Co., California, on November 18, 1952. He was buried in Forest Lawn Memorial Park Cemetery, Glendale, Los Angeles Co., California.[47]

Children of Helen May Bovey (Seeley) and Donald Fox McGaffey:

+ 335 m I. **Donald Seeley**[10] **McGaffey II** was born in Beverly Hills, Los Angeles Co., California, on July 1, 1926. He died in Puyallup, Pierce Co., Washington, on October 29, 2001. Donald Seeley was buried in Orting Cemetery, Orting, Pierce Co., Washington.[127]

+ 336 f II. **Marjorie**[10] **McGaffey** was born in Albuquerque, Bernalillo Co., New Mexico, on June 1, 1928.

+ 337 f III. **Katherine**[10] **McGaffey** was born in Beverly Hills, Los Angeles Co., California, on March 2, 1936.

**224. Harry Olmstead⁹ Bovey** (*Artland Robinson⁸, Mary E.⁷ Thompson, Nancy J.⁶ Goudy, Andrew⁵, Elizabeth Jane⁴ Pegan, Andrew³ Pegan II, Andrew² Pagan, James¹*) was born on July 19, 1906, in Massillon, Perry Twp., Stark Co., Ohio. He was the son of Artland Robinson Bovey (121) and Charlotte Olmsted. Harry Olmstead died in Goleta, Santa Barbara Co., California, on November 20, 1988, at age 82.

Childless.

Harry Olmstead Bovey submits an application for a delayed birth certificate on April 18, 1947 in the Ashtabula Co., Ohio probate court when he was a resident of Koloa, Kauai, Hawaii. He tells the court he was born in Lakeview Hospital in Conneaut, Ohio on 19 Jul 1906. However, the Stark Co., Ohio probate court has his birth registered on July 19, 1906 in Massillon, Perry Twp., Stark Co., Ohio.

Harry Olmstead married **Ida Ola Hall** on June 25, 1933, in Bernalillo Co., New Mexico. Ida Ola Hall was born in Garrison, Crouch Twp., Hamilton Co., Illinois, on March 5, 1903. Ida Ola reached age 74 and died in Los Angeles, Los Angeles Co., California, on September 21, 1977. She was buried in Westwood Memorial Park Cemetery, Los Angeles, Los Angeles Co., California.[128]

**225. Adeline May⁹ Bovey** (*Artland Robinson⁸, Mary E.⁷ Thompson, Nancy J.⁶ Goudy, Andrew⁵, Elizabeth Jane⁴ Pegan, Andrew³ Pegan II, Andrew² Pagan, James¹*) was born on November 20, 1908, in Conneaut, Conneaut Twp., Ashtabula Co., Ohio. She was the daughter of Artland Robinson Bovey (121) and Charlotte Olmsted. Adeline May died in Yountville, Napa Co., California, on November 1, 2001, at age 92. She was buried in Napa Valley Memorial Park Cemetery, Napa, Napa Co., California.[89]

Adeline May married **William Raymond Hard** on April 8, 1928, in Cleveland Co., Oklahoma. They divorced before 1960. They had four children. William Raymond Hard was born in Cleveland, Liberty Co., Texas, on August 4, 1904. He lived in 1935 in Tulsa, Tulsa Co., Oklahoma. William

Raymond also resided in 1940 in Harris Co., Texas. He was living in 1949 in Kennett, Dunklin Co., Missouri. William Raymond reached age 66 and died in Napa, Napa Co., California, on February 22, 1971.

Adeline May Bovey married **Frealin William Cummings** on July 26, 1960, in Lake Co., California. Frealin William Cummings was born in Jackson, Grant Co., Kansas, on June 16, 1902. He was also known as **Bill.** Frealin William reached age 78 and died in Vallejo, Solano Co., California, on September 27, 1980.

Children of Adeline May Bovey and William Raymond Hard:

+ 338   m   I.   **William Raymond¹⁰ Hard II** was born in Texas on July 10, 1930. He was also known as **Harry.** Willilam Raymond died in Napa, Napa Co., California, on August 19, 2003. He was buried in Napa Valley Memorial Park Cemetery, Napa, Napa Co., California.[89]

+ 339   m   II.   **Jimmy H.¹⁰ Hard** was born in Texas on June 16, 1933.

+ 340   f   III.   **Charlotte⁰ Hard** was born in Texas in 1935.

+ 341   m   IV.   **Robert H.¹⁰ Hard** was born in Harris Co., Texas, in 1937.

**226. Betty Maude⁹ Bovey** (*Artland Robinson⁸, Mary E.⁷ Thompson, Nancy J.⁶ Goudy, Andrew⁵, Elizabeth Jane⁴ Pegan, Andrew³ Pegan II, Andrew² Pagan, James¹*) was born on May 26, 1912, in Conneaut, Conneaut Twp., Ashtabula Co., Ohio. She was the daughter of Artland Robinson Bovey (121) and Charlotte Olmsted. Betty Maude died in Willis, Montgomery Co., Texas, on November 19, 1996, at age 84. She was buried in Willis Cemetery, Willis, Montgomery Co., Texas.[90]

Betty Maude married **Cecil Earl Doughtie** on March 24, 1937, in Montgomery Co., Texas. They had one son. Cecil Earl Doughtie was born in Willis, Montgomery Co., Texas, on April 23, 1913. Cecil Earl reached age 70 and died in Willis, Montgomery Co., Texas, on September 3, 1983. He was buried in Willis Cemetery, Willis, Montgomery Co., Texas.[90]

Son of Betty Maude Bovey and Cecil Earl Doughtie:

+ 342 m I. **Bobby Ray**[10] **Doughtie** was born in El Paso, El Paso Co., Texas, on May 28, 1932.

**227. Frank**[9] **Bovey** (*Artland Robinson*[8], *Mary E.*[7] *Thompson, Nancy J.*[6] *Goudy, Andrew*[5], *Elizabeth Jane*[4] *Pegan, Andrew*[3] *Pegan II, Andrew*[2] *Pagan, James*[1]) was born on May 21, 1917, in Cleveland, Cuyahoga Co., Ohio. He was the son of Artland Robinson Bovey (121) and Charlotte Olmsted. Frank died in Cleveland, Cuyahoga Co., Ohio, on September 25, 1917. He was buried in Harvard Grove Cemetery, Cleveland, Cuyahoga Co., Ohio.[91]

**228. Harold Guy**[9] **Beazle** (*Guy Andrew*[8], *Sarah*[7] *Goudy, Isaac M.*[6], *Andrew*[5], *Elizabeth Jane*[4] *Pegan, Andrew*[3] *Pegan II, Andrew*[2] *Pagan, James*[1]) was born on February 4, 1901, in Hocking Co., Ohio. He was the son of Guy Andrew Beazle (126) and Lucy Ann Gaughan. Harold Guy died in Martins Ferry, Pease Twp., Belmont Co., Ohio, on December 6, 1959, at age 58. His obituary says he was buried in Pittsburgh, Allegheny Co., Pennsylvania, but no cemetery is mentioned.

Harold Guy married **Elizabeth Jean McLaughlin** on April 3, 1926, in Brooke Co., West Virginia. They divorced. They had one son. Elizabeth Jean McLaughlin was born in Martins Ferry, Pease Twp., Belmont Co., Ohio, on February 13, 1909.[129] She reached age 90 and died in Reno, Washoe Co., Nevada, on July 28, 1999.

Elizabeth Jean remarried and died as Elizabeth J. Kelly.

Son of Harold Guy Beazle and Elizabeth McLaughlin:

+ 343 m I. **Owen Guy**[10] **Beazle** was born in Pease Twp., Belmont Co., Ohio, on

April 11, 1927. He died in Mahoning, Mahoning Co., Ohio, on November 18, 2005.

**229. Frank**[9] **Beazle** (*Guy Andrew*[8], *Sarah*[7] *Goudy, Isaac M.*[6], *Andrew*[5], *Elizabeth Jane*[4] *Pegan, Andrew*[3] *Pegan II, Andrew*[2] *Pagan, James*[1]) was born on December 23, 1906, in Brilliant, Wells Twp., Jefferson Co., Ohio. He was the son of Guy Andrew Beazle (126) and Lucy Ann Gaughan. Frank died in Wheeling, Ohio Co., West Virginia, on October 19, 1964, at age 57. He was buried in Riverview Cemetery, Martins Ferry, Pease Twp., Belmont Co., Ohio.[14]

Childless.

Frank married **Mary Lennon Thompson** on July 21, 1934, in Belmont Co., Ohio. Mary Lennon Thompson was born in Blaine, Pease Twp., Belmont Co., Ohio, on December 7, 1905. Mary Lennon reached age 81 and died in a hospital in Columbus, Franklin Co., Ohio, on August 6, 1987.

She remarried and died under the name Mary L. Moreland.

**230. Dorothy Jean**[9] **Galbraith** (*Clara Janette*[8] *Beazle, Sarah*[7] *Goudy, Isaac M.*[6], *Andrew*[5], *Elizabeth Jane*[4] *Pegan, Andrew*[3] *Pegan II, Andrew*[2] *Pagan, James*[1]) was born on June 13, 1914, in Martins Ferry, Pease Twp., Belmont Co., Ohio. She was the daughter of Harry Z. Galbraith and Clara Janette Beazle (130). Dorothy Jean died in Herndon, Fairfax Co., Virginia, on August 25, 1996, at age 82. She was buried in Chestnut Grove Cemetery, Herndon, Fairfax Co., Virginia.[93]

Dorothy Jean married **Charles H. Yoho** before 1940. They had one child. Charles H. Yoho was born in Martins Ferry, Pease Twp., Belmont Co., Ohio, on January 21, 1913. Charles H. reached age 80 and died in Canton, Stark Co., Ohio, on February 13, 1993. He was buried in Chestnut Grove Cemetery, Herndon, Fairfax Co., Virginia.[93]

**231. Judson Milton**[9] **Freeman II** (*Mildred Opal*[8] *Huff, Minnie Etta*[7] *Wardell, Elizabeth Sophronia*[6] *Goudy, Andrew*[5], *Elizabeth Jane*[4] *Pegan, Andrew*[3] *Pegan*

*II, Andrew² Pagan, James¹)* was born on July 11, 1913, in Cleveland, Cuyahoga Co., Ohio. He was also known as **Buckie.** He was the son of Judson Clarence Freeman and Mildred Opal Huff (133). Judson Milton died in Cleveland, Cuyahoga Co., Ohio, on February 22, 1921, at age seven. He was buried in West Park Cemetery, Cleveland, Cuyahoga Co., Ohio.[61]

232. **Charles Andrew⁹ Goudy** (*Edwin Andrew⁸, Andrew W.⁷, William A.⁶, Andrew⁵, Elizabeth Jane⁴ Pegan, Andrew³ Pegan II, Andrew² Pagan, James¹)* was born on November 3, 1926, in Triadelphia, Ohio Co., West Virginia. He was the son of Edwin Andrew Goudy (136) and Elinor Weigelt. Charles Andrew lived in 2015 in Triadelphia, Ohio Co., West Virginia. He died in a hospital in Wheeling, Ohio Co., West Virginia, on July 31, 2015, at age 88.

Charles Andrew married **Mabel Marie Philabaum** in 1951 in Ohio Co., West Virginia. They had five children. Mabel Marie Philabaum was born in Valley Grove, Liberty Dist., Ohio Co., West Virginia, on March 15, 1931.

Charles Andrew Goudy and Mabel Marie Philabaum had five children, including:

+ 344 m I. **Son¹⁰ Goudy**

+ 345 f IV. **Daughter¹⁰ Goudy.**

233. **Robert Edwin⁹ Blankensop III** (*Robert Edwin⁸, Robert Goudy⁷, Mary Rebecca⁶ Goudy, Robert⁵, Elizabeth Jane⁴ Pegan, Andrew³ Pegan II, Andrew² Pagan, James¹)* was born on November 19, 1926, in Parkersburg, Wood Co., West Virginia. He was the son of Robert Edwin Blankensop II (139) and Catherine Waldschmidt. Robert Edwin lived in 2011 in Parkersburg, Wood Co., West Virginia. He died in Beaufort, Beaufort Co., South Carolina, on April 17, 2011, at age 84. Robert Edwin was buried in Good Shepherd Episcopal Church Columbarium, Parkersburg, Marshall Co., West Virginia.[97]

Robert Edwin married **Ann Park Donnelly** in 1950. They had three children. Ann Park Donnelly was born in Marietta, Marietta Twp., Washington Co., Ohio, on December 8, 1930. Ann Park

reached age 82 and died in Beaufort, Beaufort Co., South Carolina, on February 7, 2013. She was buried in Good Shepherd Episcopal Church Colulmbarium, Parkersburg, Marshall Co., West Virginia.[97]

234. **William Donald⁹ Lutes** (*Anita⁸ Blankensop, Robert Goudy⁷, Mary Rebecca⁶ Goudy, Robert⁵, Elizabeth Jane⁴ Pegan, Andrew³ Pegan II, Andrew² Pagan, James¹)* was born on March 18, 1922, in Moundsville, Marshall Co., West Virginia. He was the son of Clyde Lewis Lutes and Anita Blankensop (140). William Donald died in Alexandria, Alexandria Co., Virginia, on April 2, 1967, at age 45.

William Donald married **Le Nore Unknown.** They had three children.

William Donald Lutes and Le Nore Unknown had three children, including:

+ 346 f II. **Gloria Ann Lutes** was born on February 19, 1949. Gloria Ann died in a hospital in Washington, District of Columbia, on June 22, 1962. She was buried in Mount Rose Cemetery, Moundsville, Marshall Co., West Virginia.[12]

235. **Elizabeth Ann⁹ Lutes** (*Anita⁸ Blankensop, Robert Goudy⁷, Mary Rebecca⁶ Goudy, Robert⁵, Elizabeth Jane⁴ Pegan, Andrew³ Pegan II, Andrew² Pagan, James¹)* was born in 1933 in Moundsville, Marshall Co., West Virginia. She is the daughter of Clyde Lewis Lutes and Anita Blankensop (140).

236. **Marcia⁹ Main** (*Donald Winston⁸, Mary Phrania⁷ Pattie, Phrania Elizabeth⁶ Goudy, Robert⁵, Elizabeth Jane⁴ Pegan, Andrew³ Pegan II, Andrew² Pagan, James¹)* was born in 1938 in Birmingham, Oakland Co., Michigan. She is the daughter of Donald Winston Main (142) and Viola Grace Upper.

237. **Shirley⁹ Main** (*Donald Winston⁸, Mary Phrania⁷ Pattie, Phrania Elizabeth⁶ Goudy, Robert⁵, Elizabeth Jane⁴ Pegan, Andrew³ Pegan II, Andrew² Pagan, James¹)* was born in 1939 in Birmingham, Oakland Co., Michigan. She is the daughter of Donald Winston Main (142) and Viola Grace Upper.

**238. Mary Kathleen⁹ Hunt** (*Mary Phrania⁸ Cruise, Abigail Louise⁷ Pattie, Phrania Elizabeth⁶ Goudy, Robert⁵, Elizabeth Jane⁴ Pegan, Andrew³ Pegan II, Andrew² Pagan, James¹*) was born in 1938 in Illinois. She is the daughter of Edward John Hunt and Mary Phrania Cruise (145).

**239. William Herbert⁹ Kanode II** (*Mary Grace⁸ McNeill, Sarah Sanson⁷ Hereford, Marianne Marilla⁶ Goudy, William⁵, Elizabeth Jane⁴ Pegan, Andrew³ Pegan II, Andrew² Pagan, James¹*) was born on March 9, 1900, in Clendenin, Mason Co., West Virginia. He was the son of William Herbert Kanode and Mary Grace McNeill (146). William Herbert lived in 1917 in Alliance, Stark Co., Ohio. He died overseas? on November 1, 1918, at age 18. William Herbert was buried in Beale Chapel Cemetery, Apple Grove, Hannon Dist., Mason Co., West Virginia.[65]

Never married.

William Herbert Kanode II was a U.S. soldier in WWI. His name is not found in any WWI Ohio casualty list, but he may have died in the influenza pandemic while overseas in the army.

**240. Bernice Lucille⁹ Withers** (*Mary Grace⁸ McNeill, Sarah Sanson⁷ Hereford, Marianne Marilla⁶ Goudy, William⁵, Elizabeth Jane⁴ Pegan, Andrew³ Pegan II, Andrew² Pagan, James¹*) was born on November 24, 1902, in Huntington, Cabell Co., West Virginia. She was the daughter of Robert Curtis Withers and Mary Grace McNeill (146). Bernice Lucille died in Huntington, Cabell Co., West Virginia, on July 7, 1994, at age 91. She was buried in Woodmere Memorial Park Cemetery, Huntington, Cabell Co., West Virginia.[66]

Bernice Lucille married **Roy Morris Sullivan** in 1928 in Kanawha Co., West Virginia. They had one daughter. Roy Morris Sullivan was born in Milton, Cabell Co., West Virginia, on January 24, 1903. Roy Morris lived in 1930 in Peytona, Boone Co., West Virginia. He reached age 27 and died in Logan, Logan Co., West Virginia, on June 30, 1930. Roy Morris was buried in Milton Cemetery, Milton, Cabell Co., West Virginia.[130]

Daughter of Bernice Lucille Withers and Roy Morris Sullivan:

+ 347  f  I.  **Joyce Withers¹⁰ Sullivan** was born in Peytona, Boone Co., West Virginia, on August 10, 1929.

**241. Raymond Robert⁹ Withers** (*Mary Grace⁸ McNeill, Sarah Sanson⁷ Hereford, Marianne Marilla⁶ Goudy, William⁵, Elizabeth Jane⁴ Pegan, Andrew³ Pegan II, Andrew² Pagan, James1*) was born on May 24, 1911, in Huntington, Cabell Co., West Virginia. He was the son of Robert Curtis Withers and Mary Grace McNeill (146). Raymond Robert died in Huntington, Cabell Co., West Virginia, on September 24, 1947, at age 36. He was buried in Woodmere Memorial Park Cemetery, Huntington, Cabell Co., West Virginia.[66]

Raymond Robert married **LeVeta Bradley** in 1936 in Cabell Co., West Virginia. They had at least two children. LeVeta Bradley was born in Huntington, Cabell Co., West Virginia, on July 3, 1915. LeVeta reached age 92 and died in Huntington, Cabell Co., West Virginia, on August 27, 2007. She was buried under the name LeVeta B. Rawn in Woodmere Memorial Park Cemetery, Huntington, Cabell Co., West Virginia.[66]

Children of Raymond Robert Withers and LeVeta Bradley:

+ 348  f  I.  **Carol Lynne¹⁰ Withers** was born in Huntington, Cabell Co., West Virginia, on March 15, 1938.

+ 349  m  II.  **Robert Kent¹⁰ Withers** was born in Huntington, Cabell Co., West Virginia, in 1939.

**242. Richard Hereford⁹ McNeill** (*Worthington Wilson⁸, Sarah Sanson⁷ Hereford, Marianne Marilla⁶ Goudy, William⁵, Elizabeth Jane⁴ Pegan, Andrew³ Pegan II, Andrew² Pagan, James¹*) was born on March 24, 1912, in Dunlap, De Baca Co., New Mexico. He was the son of Worthington Wilson McNeill (149) and Dora Marion Dean. Richard Hereford died in Riggens, Idaho Co, Idaho, on April 18, 1948, at age 36. He was buried in Canyon Hill Cemetery, Caldwell, Canyon Co., Idaho.[99]

Richard Hereford married **Virginia Arensburg** on June 18, 1936, in Red Willow Co., Nebraska. They had two sons. Virginia Arensburg was born in Atchison, Atchison Co., Kansas, on March 18, 1915. Virginia reached age 33 and died in Riggens, Idaho Co., Idaho, on April 18, 1948. She was buried in Canyon Hill Cemetery, Caldwell, Canyon Co., Idaho.[99]

Richard Hereford McNeill and Virginia Arensburg had two sons, including:

+ 350   m   II.   **Michael William**[10] **McNeill** was born in Caldwell, Canyon Co., Idaho, on December 8, 1942. He died in Tacoma, Pierce Co., Washington on December 25, 2012.[99]

**243. James Neill Worthington**[9] **McNeill** (*Worthington Wilson*[8], *Sarah Sanson*[7] *Hereford, Marianne Marilla*[6] *Goudy, William*[5], *Elizabeth Jane*[4] *Pegan, Andrew*[3] *Pegan II, Andrew*[2] *Pagan, James*[1]) was born on February 10, 1914, in Dunlap, De Baca Co., New Mexico. He was also known as **Jim.** He was the son of Worthington Wilson McNeill (149) and Dora Marion Dean. James Neill Worthington died in Nampa, Canyon Co., Idaho, on December 1, 2009, at age 95.

James Neill Worthington married **Dorothy Ellen Dimmett** on August 13, 1938, in McCook, Red Willow Co., Nebraska. They had at least two sons. Dorothy Ellen Dimmett was born in Goodland, Sherman Co., Kansas, on November 30, 1914. Dorothy Ellen reached age 94 and died in Nampa, Canyon Co., Idaho, on February 25, 2009.

Sons of James Neill Worthington McNeill and Dorothy Ellen Dimmett:

+ 351   m   I.   **Gary Richard**[10] **McNeill** was born in Denver, Denver Co., Colorado, in 1938.

+ 352   m   II.   **Steven Dimmett**[10] **McNeill** was born in Caldwell, Canyon Co., Idaho, in 1940.

**244. George Dean**[9] **McNeill** (*Worthington Wilson*[8], *Sarah Sanson*[7] *Hereford, Marianne Marilla*[6] *Goudy, William*[5], *Elizabeth Jane*[4] *Pegan, Andrew*[3] *Pegan II, Andrew*[2] *Pagan, James*[1]) was born on October 6, 1915, in Dunlap, De Baca Co., New Mexico. He was the son of Worthington Wilson McNeill (149) and Dora Marion Dean. George Dean died in Goodland, Sherman Co., Kansas, on April 14, 1975, at age 59. He was buried in Goodland Cemetery, Goodland, Sherman Co., Kansas.[67]

George Dean married **Janice M. Ellis** on March 21, 1936, in Kit Carson Co., Colorado. They had four children. Janice M. Ellis was born in Alma, Harlan Co., Nebraska, on June 30, 1915. Janice M. reached age 85 and died in Goodland, Sherman Co., Kansas, on December 23, 2000. She was buried in Goodland Cemetery, Goodland, Sherman Co., Kansas.[67] Died under the name Janice M. Poling but is buried under the name of Janice McNeill.

George Dean McNeill and Janice M. Ellis had four children, including:

+ 353   m   I.   **James Worthington**[10] **McNeill** was born in Goodland, Sherman Co., Kansas, on June 7, 1937. He died in Cedaredge, Delta Co., Colorado, on January 9, 2015. James Worthington was buried in Goodland Cemetery, Goodland, Sherman Co., Kansas.[67]

+ 354   f   II.   **Sharon Deanne McNeill** was born in Coquille, Coos Co., Oregon, on February 16, 1939.

+ 355   f   III.   **Georgia Ann McNeill** was born in Wilder, Canyon Co., Idaho, on September 15, 1940.

**245. Stanley Ray**[9] **McNeill** (*Frank Rhea*[8], *Sarah Sanson*[7] *Hereford, Marianne Marilla*[6] *Goudy, William*[5], *Elizabeth Jane*[4] *Pegan, Andrew*[3] *Pegan II, Andrew*[2]

*Pagan, James*[1]) was born on May 15, 1913, in Bisbee, Cochise Co., Arizona. He was the son of Frank Rhea McNeill (150) and Emma H. Keisling. Stanley Ray died in Cortez, Montezuma Co., Colorado, on October 31, 1930, at age 17. He was buried in Cortez Cemetery, Cortez, Montezuma Co., Colorado.[100]

246. **Clark Jeffrey**[9] **McNeill** (*Frank Rhea*[8], *Sarah Sanson*[7] *Hereford, Marianne Marilla*[6] *Goudy, William*[5], *Elizabeth Jane*[4] *Pegan, Andrew*[3] *Pegan II, Andrew*[2] *Pagan, James*[1]) was born on October 20, 1915, in Roswell, Chaves Co., New Mexico. He was also known as **Jeff.** He was the son of Frank Rhea McNeill (150) and Emma H. Keisling. Clark Jeffrey died in Aurora, Arapahoe Co., Colorado, on November 28, 2011, at age 96. He was buried in Fort Logan National Cemetery, Denver, Denver Co., Colorado.[101]

Clark Jeffrey married **Helen Augusta Hallbeck** in February 1942 in Denver Co., Colorado? They divorced. They had three children. Helen Augusta Hallbeck was born in Denver, Denver Co., Colorado, on April 22, 1919. She reached age 84 and died in Aurora, Arapahoe Co., Colorado, on September 28, 2003.

Clark "Jeff" McNeill, and his brother and sister-in-law, Frank Worthington McNeill and Janet Pauline Gohn McNeill, embarked on an around-the-world sailing trip on Frank and Janet's 40-foot sloop, *The Isle of Barra*, in 1996-7. "Jeff" helped crew most of the way. The had reached Sydney, New South Wales, Australia when Janet Gohn McNeill died.

247. **David Monroe**[9] **McNeill** (*Frank Rhea*[8], *Sarah Sanson*[7] *Hereford, Marianne Marilla*[6] *Goudy, William*[5], *Elizabeth Jane*[4] *Pegan, Andrew*[3] *Pegan II, Andrew*[2] *Pagan, James*[1]) was born on September 21, 1918, in Roswell, Chaves Co., New Mexico. He was the son of Frank Rhea McNeill (150) and Emma H. Keisling. David Monroe died in Cortez, Montezuma Co., Colorado, on November 26, 1983, at age 65. He was buried in Cortez Cemetery, Cortez, Montezuma Co., Colorado.[100]

David Monroe married **Muriel Catherine Sue Wheeler** on December 4, 1944, in San Juan Co.,

New Mexico. They had one daughter. Muriel Catherine Sue Wheeler was born in Cortez, Montezuma Co., Colorado, on June 29, 1923. She was also known as **Sue.** Muriel Catherine Sue reached age 81 and died in Cortez, Montezuma Co., Colorado, on March 10, 2005. She was buried in Cortez Cemetery, Cortez, Montezuma Co., Colorado.[99]

248. **Frank Worthington**[9] **McNeill II** (*Frank Rhea*[8], *Sarah Sanson*[7] *Hereford, Marianne Marilla*[6] *Goudy, William*[5], *Elizabeth Jane*[4] *Pegan, Andrew*[3] *Pegan II, Andrew*[2] *Pagan, James*[1]) was born on January 14, 1921, in Cortez, Montezuma Co., Colorado. He was the son of Frank Rhea McNeill (150) and Emma H. Keisling. Frank Worthington lived in 1994 in Amsterdam, Amsterdam, Noord-Holland, Netherlands. He died in Hemet, Riverside Co., California, on October 14, 2011, at age 90.

Frank Worthington married **Janet Pauline Gohn** on January 5, 1943, in San Diego Co., California. They had one son. Janet Pauline Gohn was born in Vernon, Vernon Twp., Jennings Co., Indiana, on September 1, 1926. Janet Pauline reached age 70 and died in Sydney, New South Wales, Australia, on March 27, 1997.

Janet Gohn McNeill died while on an around the world sailing trip with her husband Frank on their 40-foot sloop, *The Isle of Barra*. Her brother-in-law Clark "Jeff" McNeill, was also with them as a crew member.

249. **Sadie Ann**[9] **McNeill** (*Frank Rhea*[8], *Sarah Sanson*[7] *Hereford, Marianne Marilla*[6] *Goudy, William*[5], *Elizabeth Jane*[4] *Pegan, Andrew*[3] *Pegan II, Andrew*[2] *Pagan, James*[1]) was born on August 9, 1924, in Dove Creek, Delores Co., Colorado. She was also known as **Sadie.** She was the daughter of Frank Rhea McNeill (150) and Emma H. Keisling. Sadie Ann died in Moab, Grand Co., Utah, on December 31, 1996, at age 72.

Sadie Ann married **Unknown Graves** in 1944.

250. **Howard Lee**[9] **McNeill** (*Frank Rhea*[8], *Sarah Sanson*[7] *Hereford, Marianne Marilla*[6] *Goudy, William*[5], *Elizabeth Jane*[4] *Pegan, Andrew*[3] *Pegan II, Andrew*[2] *Pagan, James*[1]) was born on May 23, 1927, in

Cortez, Montezuma Co., Colorado. He was the son of Frank Rhea McNeill (150) and Emma H. Keisling. Howard Lee died in Long Beach, Los Angeles Co., California, on August 15, 2003, at age 76.

He married **Maurine Lois Haley.** They divorced in 1959. They had two children. Maurine Lois Haley was born in Texhoma, Texas Co., Oklahoma, on August 12, 1927. She reached age 87 and died in Dove Creek, Delores Co., Colorado, on March 26, 2015.

251. **James Merle⁹ McNeill** (*Frank Rhea⁸, Sarah Sanson⁷ Hereford, Marianne Marilla⁶ Goudy, William⁵, Elizabeth Jane⁴ Pegan, Andrew³ Pegan II, Andrew² Pagan, James¹*) was born on July 8, 1932, in Cortez, Montezuma Co., Colorado. He was the son of Frank Rhea McNeill (150) and Emma H. Keisling. James Merle lived in 2005 in Hot Lava Springs, Bannock Co., Idaho.

He married **Lori Unknown.**

252. **Delbert Lyle⁹ Johnson** (*Hallie Richmond⁸ McNeill, Sarah Sanson⁷ Hereford, Marianne Marilla⁶ Goudy, William⁵, Elizabeth Jane⁴ Pegan, Andrew³ Pegan II, Andrew² Pagan, James¹*) was born on May 23, 1909, in Washington Twp., Wapello Co., Iowa. He was the son of Oran or Orrin Johnson and Hallie Richmond McNeill (151). Delbert Lyle lived in Redlands, San Bernardino Co., California. He died in Riverside, Riverside Co., California, on January 5, 1990, at age 80. Delbert Lyle was buried in Riverside National Cemetery, Riverside, Riverside Co., California.[102]

Delbert Lyle married **Katherine Lucile Hawkins** in Washoe Co., Nevada. They had eight children. Katherine Lucile Hawkins was born in Chicago, Cook Co., Illinois, on January 31, 1920. Katherine Lucile reached age 75 and died in Woodstock, Cherokee Co., Georgia, on April 25, 1995. She was buried in Willamette National Cemetery, Portland, Multnomah Co., Oregon.[131]

Delbert Lyle Johnson married his step-sister, Katherine Hawkins Johnson.

Delbert Lyle Johnson and Katherine Lucile Hawkins had eight children, including:

+ 356 , f    V.    **Katherine Virginia¹⁰ Johnson** was born in San Diego, San Diego Co., California, on February 17, 1952. She died in Tacoma, Pierce Co., Washington, on July 22, 2007. Katherine Virginia was buried in Tahoma National Cemetery, Kent, King Co., Washington.[132]

253. **Donald James⁹ McNeill** (*James Hereford⁸, Sarah Sanson⁷ Hereford, Marianne Marilla⁶ Goudy, William⁵, Elizabeth Jane⁴ Pegan, Andrew³ Pegan II, Andrew² Pagan, James¹*) was born on April 16, 1942, in Goodland, Sherman Co., Kansas? He was the son of James Hereford McNeill (153) and Georgia Gertrude Dean. Donald James died in Goodland, Sherman Co., Kansas? on April 16, 1942.

254. **Elinor Jean⁹ Bare** (*Nora Frances⁸ McNeill, Sarah Sanson⁷ Hereford, Marianne Marilla⁶ Goudy, William⁵, Elizabeth Jane⁴ Pegan, Andrew³ Pegan II, Andrew² Pagan, James¹*) was born on July 15, 1919, in Fort Spring, Greenbrier Co., West Virginia. She was also known as **Jean.** She was the daughter of Howard Clifford Bare and Nora Frances McNeill (154). Elinor Jean died in Medford, Jackson Co., Oregon, on November 24, 1997, at age 78. She was buried in Siskiyou Memorial Park Cemetery, Medford, Jackson Co., Oregon.[70]

She married **Unknown Sadowsky.** They divorced.

255. **Elizabeth Dickson⁹ Bare** (*Nora Frances⁸ McNeill, Sarah Sanson⁷ Hereford, Marianne Marilla⁶ Goudy, William⁵, Elizabeth Jane⁴ Pegan, Andrew³ Pegan II, Andrew² Pagan, James¹*) was born on September 4, 1921, in Fort Spring, Greenbrier Co., West Virginia. She was also known as **Betty.** She is the daughter of Howard Clifford Bare and Nora Frances McNeill (154). Elizabeth Dickson died in Las Vegas, Clark Co., Nevada, on September 17, 2008, at age 87. She was buried in Davis Memorial Park Cemetery, Las Vegas, Clark Co., Nevada.[C]

Elizabeth married **Willis Harry Caples** in 1944 in Cameron Co., Texas. Willis Harry Caples was born in Fourth Plain (now Orchards), Clark Co., Washington, on January 24, 1919. He reached age 87 and died in Las Vegas, Clark Co., Nevada, on July 30, 2007. He was buried in Davis Memorial Park Cemetery, Las Vegas, Clark Co., Nevada.[C]

**256. Stewart Russell⁹ Fair** (*Harold Stewart⁸, Sarah Jessie⁷ Cowl, Elizabeth Jane⁶ Goudy, Isaac⁵, Elizabeth Jane⁴ Pegan, Andrew³ Pegan II, Andrew² Pagan, James¹*) was born on November 26, 1924, in New Buffalo Twp., Armstrong Co., Pennsylvania. He was the son of Harold Stewart Fair (156) and Marie Isabelle Campbell. Stewart Russell died in West Kittanning Twp., Armstrong Co., Pennsylvania, on February 14, 1928, at age three. He was buried in Kittanning Cemetery, Kittanning Twp., Armstrong Co., Pennsylvania.[104]

**257. Helen⁹ Fair** (*Harold Stewart⁸, Sarah Jessie⁷ Cowl, Elizabeth Jane⁶ Goudy, Isaac⁵, Elizabeth Jane⁴ Pegan, Andrew³ Pegan II, Andrew² Pagan, James¹*) was born on November 2, 1926, in West Kittanning Twp., Armstrong Co., Pennsylvania. She was the daughter of Harold Stewart Fair (156) and Marie Isabelle Campbell. Helen died in West Kittanning Twp., Armstrong Co., Pennsylvania, on November 4, 1926. She was buried in Kittanning Cemetery, Kittanning Twp., Armstrong Co., Pennsylvania.[104]

**258. Hugh Hartley⁹ Fair** (*Harold Stewart⁸, Sarah Jessie⁷ Cowl, Elizabeth Jane⁶ Goudy, Isaac⁵, Elizabeth Jane⁴ Pegan, Andrew³ Pegan II, Andrew² Pagan, James¹*) was born on January 17, 1928, in West Kittanning Twp., Armstrong Co., Pennsylvania. He was the son of Harold Stewart Fair (156) and Marie Isabelle Campbell. Hugh Hartley lived in Worthington, Armstrong Co., Pennsylvania. He died in a hospital in Pittsburgh, Allegheny Co., Pennsylvania, on May 19, 2013, at age 85. Hugh Hartley was buried in Slate Lick Cemetery, Kittanning Twp., Armstrong Co., Pennsylvania.[105]

Hugh Hartley married **Eyvette Rose Shearer** on June 17, 1950, in Armstrong Co., Pennsylvania. They had three children. Eyvette Rose Shearer was born in Herculaneum, Jefferson Co., Missouri, on January 25, 1930. Eyvette Rose reached age 77 and died in Cabot, Butler Co., Pennsylvania, on May 1, 2007. She was buried in Slate Lick

Cemetery, Kittanning Twp., Armstrong Co., Pennsylvania.[105]

Hugh Hartley Fair and Eyvette Rose Shearer had three children, including:

+ 357 m I. **Son¹⁰ Fair** was born on September 7, 1951.

+ 358 m III. **Michael H.¹⁰ Fair** was born in West Kittanning Twp., Armstrong Co., Pennsylvania, on October 30, 1957. He died in a hospital in Morgantown, Monongalia Co., West Virginia, on January 28, 2013.

**259. Forrest⁹ Fair** (*Harold Stewart⁸, Sarah Jessie⁷ Cowl, Elizabeth Jane⁶ Goudy, Isaac⁵, Elizabeth Jane⁴ Pegan, Andrew³ Pegan II, Andrew² Pagan, James¹*) was born on June 15, 1930, in Worthington, Armstrong Co., Pennsylvania. He was the son of Harold Stewart Fair (156) and Marie Isabelle Campbell. He died in Kittanning, Armstrong Co., Pennsylvania on June 24, 2016 at age 86. Forrest was buried in Center Hill Church of the Brethren Cemetery, Kittanning, Armstrong Co., Pennsylvania.[106]

He married **Jo Anne Bowser** on June 17, 1955. They had two children.

**260. Marie Louise⁹ Fair** (*Harold Stewart⁸, Sarah Jessie⁷ Cowl, Elizabeth Jane⁶ Goudy, Isaac⁵, Elizabeth Jane⁴ Pegan, Andrew³ Pegan II, Andrew² Pagan, James¹*) was born on June 18, 1933, in Worthington, Armstrong Co., Pennsylvania. She was the daughter of Harold Stewart Fair (156) and Marie Isabelle Campbell. Marie Louise lived in 1970 in Akron, Summit Co., Ohio. She died in Livingston, Polk Co., Texas, on June 7, 2009, at age 75.

She married **Charles Russell Crissman.** They had three children. Charles Russell Crissman was born in Manor Twp., Armstrong Co., Pennsylvania, on March 16, 1929. Charles Russell lived in 2006 in Circleville, Circleville Twp., Pickaway Co., Ohio. He reached age 77 and died in Dade City, Pasco Co., Florida, on December 12, 2006.

**261. Ruth Harlene⁹ Fair** (*Harold Stewart⁸, Sarah Jessie⁷ Cowl, Elizabeth Jane⁶ Goudy, Isaac⁵, Elizabeth Jane⁴ Pegan, Andrew³ Pegan II, Andrew² Pagan, James¹*) was born on August 3, 1938, in Worthington, Armstrong Co., Pennsylvania. She was the daughter of Harold Stewart Fair (156) and Marie Isabelle Campbell. Ruth lived in 1970 in Worthington, Armstrong Co., Pennsylvania.

She married **Lowell Bernard Reed.** They had one daughter. Lowell Bernard Reed was born on January 25, 1936.

262. **Dewey Edward⁹ Crow** (*Jane Augusta⁸ Fair, Sarah Jessie⁷ Cowl, Elizabeth Jane⁶ Goudy, Isaac⁵, Elizabeth Jane⁴ Pegan, Andrew³ Pegan II, Andrew² Pagan, James¹*) was born on August 25, 1921, in Moundsville, Marshall Co., West Virginia. He was the son of John Wesley Crow and Jane Augusta Fair (157). Dewey Edward died in Moundsville, Marshall Co., West Virginia, in March 1985 at age 63. He was buried in Halcyon Hills Memorial Park Cemetery, Sherrard, Marshall Co., West Virginia.[72]

263. **Florence⁹ Crow** (*Jane Augusta⁸ Fair, Sarah Jessie⁷ Cowl, Elizabeth Jane⁶ Goudy, Isaac⁵, Elizabeth Jane⁴ Pegan, Andrew³ Pegan II, Andrew² Pagan, James¹*) was born on June 18, 1923, in Adeline, Marshall Co., West Virginia. She was the daughter of John Wesley Crow and Jane Augusta Fair (157).

Florence married **James B. Schaffer II** on March 18, 1943, in Marshall Co., West Virginia. They had two daughters. James B. Schaffer II was born in Cresap, Marshall Co., West Virginia, on March 20, 1923. He was also known as **Buck.** James B. reached age 82 and died in Moundsville, Marshall Co., West Virginia?, on March 9, 2006.

264. **Frances J.⁹ Crow** (*Jane Augusta⁸ Fair, Sarah Jessie⁷ Cowl, Elizabeth Jane⁶ Goudy, Isaac⁵, Elizabeth Jane⁴ Pegan, Andrew³ Pegan II, Andrew² Pagan, James¹*) was born on February 26, 1926, in Dellslow, Monongalia Co., West Virginia. She was the daughter of John Wesley Crow and Jane Augusta Fair (157). Frances J. died in Canton, Stark Co., Ohio, on September 20, 2015, at age 89. She was buried in Fairview Cemetery, New Albany, Floyd Co., Indiana.[107]

She married **Harry Wilbert Cain.** They had three daughters. Harry Wilbert Cain was born in Cameron, Marshall Co., West Virginia, on March 26, 1925. Harry Wilbert reached age 65 and died in Canton, Stark Co., Ohio, on May 24, 1990. He was buried in Green View Cemetery, Powhatan Point, Marshall Co., West Virginia.[133]

265. **Margaret Anna⁹ Crow** (*Jane Augusta⁸ Fair, Sarah Jessie⁷ Cowl, Elizabeth Jane⁶ Goudy, Isaac⁵, Elizabeth Jane⁴ Pegan, Andrew³ Pegan II, Andrew² Pagan, James¹*) was born on November 2, 1927, in Moundsville, Marshall Co., West Virginia. She was the daughter of John Wesley Crow and Jane Augusta Fair (157). Margaret Anna died in Glen Easton, Marshall Co., West Virginia, on June 2, 1999, at age 71. She was buried in Halcyon Hills Memorial Park Cemetery, Sherrard, Marshall Co., West Virginia.[72]

She married **Floyd Allen Bungard.** They had three children. Floyd Allen Bungard was born in Cameron, Marshall Co., West Virginia, on January 7, 1919. Floyd Allen lived in 1989 in Glen Easton, Marshall Co., West Virginia. He reached age 70 and died in a hospital in Glen Dale, Marshall Co., West Virginia, on October 18, 1989. Floyd Allen was buried in Halcyon Hills Memorial Park Cemetery, Sherrard, Marshall Co., West Virginia.[72]

266. **Elmer Wayne⁹ Crow** (*Jane Augusta⁸ Fair, Sarah Jessie⁷ Cowl, Elizabeth Jane⁶ Goudy, Isaac⁵, Elizabeth Jane⁴ Pegan, Andrew³ Pegan II, Andrew² Pagan, James¹*) was born on October 14, 1931, in Moundsville, Marshall Co., West Virginia. He was also known as **Wayne.** He was the son of John Wesley Crow and Jane Augusta Fair (157). Elmer Wayne died in McMechen, Union Dist., Marshall Co., West Virginia, on May 20, 2009, at age 77. He was buried in Halcyon Hills Memorial Park Cemetery, Sherrard, Marshall Co., West Virginia.[72]

267. **Donal M.⁹ Crow** (*Jane Augusta⁸ Fair, Sarah Jessie⁷ Cowl, Elizabeth Jane⁶ Goudy, Isaac⁵, Elizabeth Jane⁴ Pegan, Andrew³ Pegan II, Andrew² Pagan, James¹*) was born on February 11, 1934, in Moundsville, Marshall Co., West Virginia. He was the son of John Wesley Crow and Jane Augusta Fair (157).

He married **Helen Unknown.** Helen Unknown was born on April 28, 1938.

**268. Frank V.⁹ Fair** (*Dewey Isaac⁸, Sarah Jessie⁷ Cowl, Elizabeth Jane⁶ Goudy, Isaac⁵, Elizabeth Jane⁴ Pegan, Andrew³ Pegan II, Andrew² Pagan, James¹*) was born on October 25, 1925, in Ford City, Armstrong Co., Pennsylvania. He was the son of Dewey Isaac Fair (158) and Rachel Miller. Frank V. lived in Niagara Falls, Niagara Co., New York. He died in Saint George, Washington Co., Utah, on January 15, 1995, at age 69.

**269. Jack Edward⁹ Fair** (*Dewey Isaac⁸, Sarah Jessie⁷ Cowl, Elizabeth Jane⁶ Goudy, Isaac⁵, Elizabeth Jane⁴ Pegan, Andrew³ Pegan II, Andrew² Pagan, James¹*) was born on January 4, 1928, in Ford City, Armstrong Co., Pennsylvania. He was the son of Dewey Isaac Fair (158) and Rachel Miller. Jack Edward lived in 1972 in Peoria, Peoria Co., Illinois. He died in Corrales, Sandoval Co., New Mexico, on December 30, 2009, at age 81.

**270. Sally Ann⁹ Fair** (*Dewey Isaac⁸, Sarah Jessie⁷ Cowl, Elizabeth Jane⁶ Goudy, Isaac⁵, Elizabeth Jane⁴ Pegan, Andrew³ Pegan II, Andrew² Pagan, James¹*) was born on March 13, 1934, in Ford City, Armstrong Co., Pennsylvania. She is the daughter of Dewey Isaac Fair (158) and Rachel Miller. She died in West Brandywine, Chester Co., Pennsylvania, on October 10, 2017, at age 83.

She married **Charles Davies II** in 1958. They divorced. They had four children.

**271. Charles Daniel⁹ Fair** (*Daniel Cowl⁸, Sarah Jessie⁷ Cowl, Elizabeth Jane⁴ Pegan, Andrew³ Pegan II, Andrew² Pagan, James¹*) was born on March 29, 1935, in Cameron, Marshall Co., West Virginia. He was the son of Daniel Crow Fair (159) and Mildred Irene Jones. Charles D. died in Butler, Butler Twp., Butler Co., Pennsylvania on December 8, 1984, at age 49. He was buried in Kittanning Cemetery, Kittanning, Kittanning Twp., Armstrong Co., Pennsylvania.[104]

Charles Daniel married **Norma Irene Mitchell**. They had at least two children. Norma Irene Mitchell was born in Kittanning, Kittanning Twp., Armstrong Co., Pennsylvania, on February 3, 1936. Norma Irene reached age 50 and died in Lydora, Butler Twp., Butler Co., Pennsylvania on January 20, 1997. She was buried in Kittanning Cemetery,

Kittanning, Kittanning Twp., Armstrong Co., Pennsylvania.[104]

Charles Daniel Fair and Norma Irene Mitchell had at least two children, including:

+ 359  f  I.  **Florence Louise¹⁰ Fair** was born in Kittanning, Kittanning Twp., Armstrong Co., Pennsylvania, on December 7, 1955. Florence died in Kittanning Twp., Armstrong Co., Pennsylvania, on December 7, 1955. She was buried in Kittanning Cemetery, Kittanning, Kittanning Twp., Armstrong Co., Pennsylvania.[104]

**272. Virginia P.⁹ Fair** (*Daniel Cowl⁸, Sarah Jessie⁷ Cowl, Elizabeth Jane⁶ Goudy, Isaac⁵, Elizabeth Jane⁴ Pegan, Andrew³ Pegan II, Andrew² Pagan, James¹*) was born in 1939 in Triadelphia Dist., Logan Co., West Virginia. She is the daughter of Daniel Cowl Fair (159) and Mildred Irene Jones.

**273. Patricia R.⁹ Redman** (*Harry E.⁸, Emma Blanche⁷ Cowl, Elizabeth Jane⁶ Goudy, Isaac⁵, Elizabeth Jane⁴ Pegan, Andrew³ Pegan II, Andrew² Pagan, James¹*) was born on December 14, 1926, in Columbus, Franklin Co., Ohio. She was the daughter of Harry E. Redman (162) and E. Lavena Herboltzhelmer. Patricia R. died in Gettysburg, Cumberland Twp., Adams Co., Pennsylvania, on August 2, 2010, at age 83.

Patricia R. married **Jerome David Keating** in December 1953. They had six children. Jerome David Keating was born in Bayonne, Hudson Co., New Jersey? on October 3, 1926.

**274. Janet Cowl⁹ Redman** (*Harry E.⁸, Emma Blanche⁷ Cowl, Elizabeth Jane⁶ Goudy, Isaac⁵, Elizabeth Jane⁴ Pegan, Andrew³ Pegan II, Andrew² Pagan, James¹*) was born on March 12, 1930, in Columbus, Franklin Co., Ohio. She is the daughter of Harry E. Redman (162) and E. Lavena Herboltzhelmer.

Janet Cowl married **Robert Louis Bartels** after 1940. Robert Louis Bartels was born in Gettysburg, Gettysburg Twp., Potter Co., South Dakota, on November 14, 1928. Robert reached age 88 and died in Columbus, Franklin Co., Ohio, about June 8, 2017.

Robert L. Bartels, Ph.D., was an All-America swimmer at Ohio State University. Dr. Bartels became head swimming coach at Kenyon College, Ohio University, and finally at Ohio State for many years.

**275. Jean⁹ Redman** (*Harry E.⁸, Emma Blanche⁷ Cowl, Elizabeth Jane⁶ Goudy, Isaac⁵, Elizabeth Jane⁴ Pegan, Andrew³ Pegan II, Andrew² Pagan, James¹*) was born about 1933 in Columbus, Franklin Co., Ohio. She is the daughter of Harry E. Redman (162) and E. Lavena Herboltzhelmer.

She married **Unknown Cunningham.**

**276. Nancy Lee⁹ Redman** (*Edmond Cowl⁸, Emma Blanche⁷ Cowl, Elizabeth Jane⁶ Goudy, Isaac⁵, Elizabeth Jane⁴ Pegan, Andrew³ Pegan II, Andrew² Pagan, James¹*) was born on September 11, 1931, in Upper Arlington, Franklin Co., Ohio. She is the daughter of Edmond Cowl Redman II (164) and Vera Marie Adkinson.

Nancy Lee married **Richard Barnes** on September 27, 1951 in Franklin Co., Ohio. Richard Barnes was born in Columbus, Franklin Co., Ohio on January 20, 1931.

**277. Vera⁹ Redman** (*Edmond Cowl⁸, Emma Blanche⁷ Cowl, Elizabeth Jane⁶ Goudy, Isaac⁵, Elizabeth Jane⁴ Pegan, Andrew³ Pegan II, Andrew² Pagan, James¹*) was born on January 14, 1935, in Upper Arlington, Franklin Co., Ohio. She is the daughter of Edmond Cowl Redman II (164) and Vera Marie Adkison.

She married **Unknown Blake.**

**278. Monroe Josiah⁹ Mechling II** (*Elizabeth Jane⁸ Stoller, Nellie Augusta⁷ Cowl, Elizabeth Jane⁶ Goudy, Isaac⁵, Elizabeth Jane⁴ Pegan, Andrew³ Pegan II, Andrew² Pagan, James¹*) was born on August 26, 1931, in Wheeling, Ohio Co., West Virginia. He is the son of Monroe Josiah Mechling and Elizabeth Jane Stoller (166).

Monroe Josiah II married **Barbara Jean Schoolcraft** before 1964. They divorced. They had three children. Barbara Jean Schoolcraft was born in Follansbee, Brooke Co., West Virginia, on October 7, 1934. She reached age 75 and died in Weirton, Brooke Co., West Virginia, on March 10, 2010. Barbara Jean was buried in New Cumberland Cemetery, New Cumberland, Hancock Co., West Virginia.[D]

She remarried and died under the name Barbara J. Williams.

Monroe Josiah Mechling II married **Gloria Hope McConnell** in 1964 in Brooke Co. West Virginia. They had one son. Gloria Hope McConnell was born in Weirton, Brooke Co., West Virginia, on May 21, 1939. Gloria Hope reached age 62 and died in Elkview, Kanawha Co., West Virginia? on August 17, 2001.

**279. Elizabeth Jane⁹ Mechling** (*Elizabeth Jane⁸ Stoller, Nellie Augusta⁷ Cowl, Elizabeth Jane⁶ Goudy, Isaac⁵, Elizabeth Jane⁴ Pegan, Andrew³ Pegan II, Andrew² Pagan, James¹*) was born on June 12, 1934, in Wheeling, Ohio Co., West Virginia. She is the daughter of Monroe Josiah Mechling and Elizabeth Jane Stoller (166).

She married **William Roger Melick.** They had two sons. William Roger Melick was born in Mt. Perry, Madison Twp., Perry Co., Ohio, on July 8, 1934. He was also known as **Roger.** William Roger reached age 67 and died in Sudbury, Middlesex Co., Massachusetts, on October 10, 2001.

**280. Lois Jean⁹ Mechling** (*Elizabeth Jane⁸ Stoller, Nellie Augusta⁷ Cowl, Elizabeth Jane⁶ Goudy, Isaac⁵, Elizabeth Jane⁴ Pegan, Andrew³ Pegan II, Andrew² Pagan, James¹*) was born on August 12, 1937, in Wheeling, Ohio Co., West Virginia. She was the daughter of Monroe Josiah Mechling and Elizabeth Jane Stoller (166). Lois Jean died in Elyria, Elyria Twp., Lorain Co., Ohio, on December 13, 2007, at age 70. She was buried in St. Clairsville Union Cemetery, St. Clairsville, Bellaire Twp., Belmont Co., Ohio.[108]

Childless.

She married **Daniel Eldon Edgar.** Daniel Eldon Edgar was born in Rittman, Wayne Co., Ohio, on February 23, 1938.

**281. Martha⁹ Johnson** (*Elizabeth M.⁸ Goudy, Edward Elmer⁷, John William⁶, Isaac⁵, Elizabeth Jane⁴ Pegan,*

*Andrew³ Pegan II, Andrew² Pagan, James¹*) was born on February 10, 1911, in Wheeling, Ohio Co., West Virginia. She was the daughter of Harry Earl Johnson and Elizabeth M. Goudy (168). Martha died in Fort Myers, Lee Co., Florida, on January 9, 1985, at age 73. She was buried in Halcyon Hills Memorial Park Cemetery, Sherrard, Marshall Co., West Virginia.[72]

Martha married **George Bruhn II** on August 17, 1929, in Brooke Co. West Virginia. They had two children. George Bruhn II was born in Richland, Ohio Co., West Virginia, on April 22, 1909.[70] George reached age 90 and died in Wheeling, Ohio Co., West Virginia, on October 26, 1999. He was buried in Halcyon Hills Memorial Park Cemetery, Sherrard, Marshall Co., West Virginia.[72]

Children of Martha Johnson and George Bruhn II:

+ 360 m I. **Gene¹⁰ Bruhn** was born in Wheeling, Ohio Co., West Virginia, in 1930.

+ 361 f II. **Dorothy¹⁰ Bruhn** was born in Wheeling, Ohio Co., West Virginia, in 1934.

**282. Harriet J.⁹ Johnson** (*Elizabeth M.⁸ Goudy, Edward Elmer⁷, John William⁶, Isaac⁵, Elizabeth Jane⁴ Pegan, Andrew³ Pegan II, Andrew² Pagan, James¹*) was born on March 14, 1914, in Wheeling, Ohio Co., West Virginia. She was the daughter of Harry Earl Johnson and Elizabeth M. Goudy (168). Harriet J. died in Fort Myers, Lee Co., Florida, on February 25, 1987, at age 72.

Harriet J. married **William Joseph Synan** on April 6, 1946, in Wayne Co., Michigan. William Joseph Synan was born in Zanesville, Muskingham Co., Ohio, on June 7, 1912. William Joseph reached age 83 and died in Fort Myers, Lee Co., Florida, on March 9, 1996.

**283. Betty Jane⁹ Helmbrecht** (*Alberta Anna⁸ Goudy, Robert Carl⁷, John William⁶, Isaac⁵, Elizabeth Jane⁴ Pegan, Andrew³ Pegan II, Andrew² Pagan, James¹*) was born on August 27, 1930, in Wheeling, Ohio Co., West Virginia. She was also known as **Betty.** She was the daughter of Frederick Charles

Helmbrecht II and Alberta Anna Goudy (171). Betty Jane died in Youngstown, Mahoning Co., Ohio, on December 28, 2011, at age 81.

Betty Jane married **Joseph Anthony Salus** on May 14, 1949. They have five children. Joseph Anthony Salus was born in Girard, Trumbull Co., Ohio, in 1930.

Betty Jane Helmbrecht and Joseph Anthony Salus had five children, including:

+ 362 f II. **Juanita Lee¹⁰ Salus** was born in Youngstown, Mahoning Co., Ohio, on May 9, 1956. She died in Youngstown, Mahoning Co., Ohio, on April 1, 2016.

+ 363 m V. **Timothy Lynn¹⁰ Salus** was born in Youngstown, Mahoning Co., Ohio, on May 26, 1959. He died in a hospital in Merrillville, Ross Twp., Lake Co., Indiana, on December 29, 2006.

**284. Mitzi L.⁹ Helmbrecht** (*Alberta Anna⁸ Goudy, Robert Carl⁷, John William⁶, Isaac⁵, Elizabeth Jane⁴ Pegan, Andrew³ Pegan II, Andrew² Pagan, James¹*) was born on June 10, 1933, in Wheeling, Ohio Co., West Virginia. She was the daughter of Frederick Charles Helmbrecht II and Alberta Anna Goudy (171). Mitzi L. died in Youngstown, Mahoning Co., Ohio, on June 24, 2014, at age 81. She was buried in Calvary Cemetery, Youngstown, Mahoning Co., Ohio.[110]

Mitzi L. married **Aloysius C. Carzoo II** on November 12, 1956. They had five children. Aloysius C. Carzoo II was born in Youngstown, Mahoning Co., Ohio, on September 21, 1932. Aloysius C. reached age 62 and died in Youngstown, Mahoning Co., Ohio, on February 19, 1995. He was buried in Calvary Cemetery, Youngstown, Mahoning Co., Ohio.[110]

**285. Frederick C.⁹ Helmbrecht III** (*Alberta Anna⁸ Goudy, Robert Carl⁷, John William⁶, Isaac⁵, Elizabeth Jane⁴ Pegan, Andrew³ Pegan II, Andrew² Pagan, James¹*) was born on November 9, 1935, in Wheeling, Ohio Co., West Virginia. He was the son of Frederick Charles Helmbrecht II and Alberta Anna Goudy (171). Frederick C. died in Fowler, Fowler Twp., Trumbull Co., Ohio, on March 20, 2015, at age 79. He was buried in Crown Hill Burial Park Cemetery, Vienna Twp., Trumbull Co., Ohio.[111]

Frederick C. married **Suzanne Kay Mackey** on February 13, 1960. They had two children. Suzanne Kay Mackey was born in Warren, Trumbull Co., Ohio, on November 8, 1937. She was also known as **Mimi.** Suzanne Kay reached age 59 and died in Warren, Trumbull Co., Ohio, on July 12, 1997.

286. **Kenneth C.⁹ Bachmann** (*Mabel B.⁸ Church, Mary Emma⁷ Hill, David Wellington⁶, Mary Jane⁵ Goudy, Elizabeth Jane⁴ Pegan, Andrew³ Pegan II, Andrew² Pagan, James¹*) was born on January 2, 1909, in Wheeling, Ohio Co., West Virginia. He was the son of Thomas Herbert Bachmann and Mabel B. Church (183). Kenneth C. died in Wheeling, Ohio Co., West Virginia, on May 9, 1922, at age 13. He was buried in Greenwood Cemetery, Wheeling, Ohio Co., West Virginia.[24]

287. **Frances A.⁹ Bachmann** (*Mabel B.⁸ Church, Mary Emma⁷ Hill, David Wellington⁶, Mary Jane⁵ Goudy, Elizabeth Jane⁴ Pegan, Andrew³ Pegan II, Andrew² Pagan, James¹*) was born on July 19, 1911, in Wheeling, Ohio Co., West Virginia. She was the daughter of Thomas Herbert Bachmann and Mabel B. Church (183). Frances A. died in Jackson, Hinds Co., Mississippi, on October 26, 1982, at age 71. She was buried in Greenwood Cemetery, Wheeling, Ohio Co., West Virginia.[24]

Frances A. married **Anson Charles Crockard** on May 20, 1933, in Ohio Co., West Virginia. They had one son. Anson Charles Crockard was born in Wheeling, Ohio Co., West Virginia, on October 12, 1902. Anson Charles reached age 44 and died in Wheeling, Ohio Co., West Virginia, on March 24, 1947. He was buried in Greenwood Cemetery, Wheeling, Ohio Co., West Virginia.[24]

Son of Frances A. Bachmann and Anson Charles Crockard:

+ 364 m I. **Charles H.¹⁰ Crockard** was born in Wheeling, Ohio Co., West Virginia, in 1933. He died in a hospital in Huntington, Cabell Co., West Virginia, on October 19, 1946. Charles H. was buried in Greenwood Cemetery, Wheeling, Ohio Co., West Virginia.[24]

288. **Albert or Herbert⁹ Bachmann II** (*Mabel B.⁸ Church, Mary Emma⁷ Hill, David Wellington⁶, Mary Jane⁵ Goudy, Elizabeth Jane⁴ Pegan, Andrew³ Pegan II, Andrew² Pagan, James¹*) was born on September 18, 1915, in Wheeling, Ohio Co., West Virginia. He was the son of Thomas Herbert Bachmann and Mabel B. Church (183). Albert or Herbert died in New York, New York, on July 30, 1987, at age 71. He was buried in Long Island National Cemetery, Farmingdale, Suffolk Co., New York.[96]

Never married.

This son seems to have been named Albert, not Herbert II, as he is enumerated in the 1920 census. There are no records for a Herbert Bachmann born in 1914-1916 after 1920. However, there are records for an Albert Bachman, born September 18, 1915, who lived in New York City.

289. **Dorothy Virginia Hill** (*George Wellington II⁸, George Wellington⁷, David Wellington⁶, Mary Jane⁵ Goudy, Elizabeth Jane⁴ Pegan, Andrew³ Pegan II, Andrew² Pagan, James¹*) was born on November 9, 1923, in Bridgeport, Bellaire Twp., Belmont Co., Ohio. She was the daughter of George Wellington Hill II (184) and Rheba Smith. Dorothy Virginia died in Wheeling, Ohio Co., West Virginia on November 16, 2014. She is buried in Greenwood Cemetery, Wheeling, Ohio Co., West Virginia.[24]

Dorothy Virginia married **Robert Carl Johnson.** They may have divorced. They had three children. Robert Carl Johnson was born in Uhrichsville, Mill Twp., Tuscarawas Co., Ohio on May 31, 1923. He died in Key West, Monroe Co., Florida on January 27, 1957. He is buried in Union Cemetery, Uhrichsville, Mill Twp., Tuscarawas Co., Ohio.[13]

**290. Harold⁹ Hill II** (*Harold Christian⁸, George Wellington⁷, David Wellington⁶, Mary Jane⁵ Goudy, Elizabeth Jane⁴ Pegan, Andrew³ Pegan II, Andrew² Pagan, James¹*) was born on July 2, 1923, in Wheeling, Ohio Co., West Virginia. He was the son of Harold Christian Hill (185) and Gertrude Katherine Hughes. Harold died in Wheeling, Ohio Co., West Virginia, on March 5, 1996, at age 72.

**291. William Ellis⁹ Harbaugh** (*Emily Virginia⁸ Hill, Howard Hamilton⁷, William Hamilton⁶, Mary Jane⁵ Goudy, Elizabeth Jane⁴ Pegan, Andrew³ Pegan II, Andrew² Pagan, James¹*) was born on January 26, 1938, in Winchester, Frederick Co., Virginia. He was the son of Ellis Elmer Harbaugh and Emily Virginia Hill (187). William Ellis lived in 1978 in Broad Run, Fauquier Co., Virginia. He also resided in 2010 in Cross Junction, Frederick Co., Virginia.

Childless.

William Ellis married **Barbara Ann Evans** on May 25, 1968, in Nelson Co., Virginia. They divorced in 1969. Barbara Ann Evans was born in Bloomfield, Stoddard Co., Missouri, on January 10, 1946.

William Ellis Harbaugh married **Diana Lee Johnson** on October 20, 1978, in Fauquier Co., Virginia. Diana Lee Johnson was born in Indianapolis, Marion Co., Indiana, on April 3, 1934. Diana Lee reached age 76 and died in a hospital in Charlottesville, Virginia, on April 11, 2010.

**292. Audrey Jane⁹ Hill** (*Russell G.⁸, Russell Sage⁷, William Hamilton⁶, Mary Jane⁵ Goudy, Elizabeth Jane⁴ Pegan, Andrew³ Pegan II, Andrew² Pagan, James¹*) was born on November 28, 1930, in Steubenville, Cross Creek Twp., Jefferson Co., Ohio. She was the daughter of Russell G. Hill II (188) and Blanche Snyder. Audrey Jane died in Steubenville, Cross Creek Twp., Jefferson Co., Ohio, on November 30, 1930. She was buried in Union Cemetery, Steubenville, Cross Creek Twp., Jefferson Co., Ohio.[16]

**293. William Robert⁹ Hill II** (*William Harold⁸, Russell Sage⁷, William Hamilton⁶, Mary Jane⁵ Goudy, Elizabeth Jane⁴ Pegan, Andrew³ Pegan II, Andrew² Pagan, James¹*) was born on June 16, 1932, in Steubenville, Cross Creek Twp., Jefferson Co.,

Ohio. He was the son of William Harold Hill (189) and Gertrude Margaret Mace. William Robert died in Chattanooga, Hamilton Co., Tennessee, on April 15, 1991, at age 58. He was buried in Wallace Memorial Cemetery, Crawley, Greenbrier Co., West Virginia.[113]

He married **Donnia Unknown.** Donnia Unknown was born on June 16, 1938. Donnia reached age 71 and died on April 26, 2010. She was buried in Wallace Memorial Cemetery, Crawley, Greenbrier Co., West Virginia.[113]

**294. Earl Russell⁹ Hill** (*William Harold⁸, Russell Sage⁷, William Hamilton⁶, Mary Jane⁵ Goudy, Elizabeth Jane⁴ Pegan, Andrew³ Pegan II, Andrew² Pagan, James¹*) was born on June 20, 1937, in Steubenville, Cross Creek Twp., Jefferson Co., Ohio. He was the son of William Harold Hill (189) and Gertrude Margaret Mace. Earl Russell died in East Ridge, Hamilton Co., Tennessee, on December 2, 2015, at age 78. He was buried in Chattanooga National Cemetery, Chattanooga, Hamilton Co., Tennessee.[114]

Earl Russell married **Nina May Barrows.** They had four children.

**295. Wallace Raymond⁹ Howard** (*Nellie Caroline⁸ Hill, Charles Millard⁷, John W.⁶, Mary Jane⁵ Goudy, Elizabeth Jane⁴ Pegan, Andrew³ Pegan II, Andrew² Pagan, James¹*) was born on November 8, 1919, in Wheeling, Ohio Co., West Virginia. He was the son of Alfred Raymond Howard and Nellie Caroline Hill (195). Wallace Raymond died in Wheeling, Ohio Co., West Virginia, on February 7, 1997, at age 77. He was buried in Greenwood Cemetery, Wheeling, Ohio Co., West Virginia.[24]

May have never married.

**296. Alfred Eugene⁹ Howard II** (*Nellie Caroline⁸ Hill, Charles Millard⁷, John W.⁶, Mary Jane⁵ Goudy, Elizabeth Jane⁴ Pegan, Andrew³ Pegan II, Andrew² Pagan, James¹*) was born on November 28, 1921, in Wheeling, Ohio Co., West Virginia. He was the son of Alfred Raymond Howard and Nellie Caroline Hill (195). Alfred Eugene died in Wheeling, Ohio Co., West Virginia, on October 11, 1993, at age 71. He was buried in Greenwood Cemetery, Wheeling, Ohio Co., West Virginia.[24]

Alfred Eugene married **Lena Katherine Sauders** in 1951 in Ohio Co., West Virginia. Lena Katherine Sauders was born in Wheeling, Ohio Co., West Virginia, on May 12, 1918. Lena Katherine lived in 1995 in Wheeling, Ohio Co., West Virginia. She reached age 77 and died in a facility in Belmont, Bellaire Twp., Belmont Co., Ohio, on July 25, 1995. Lena Katherine was buried in Greenwood Cemetery, Wheeling, Ohio Co., West Virginia.[24]

297. **Helen⁹ Mooney** (*Dorretta Josephine⁸ Hill, Charles Millard⁷, John W.⁶, Mary Jane⁵ Goudy, Elizabeth Jane⁴ Pegan, Andrew³ Pegan II, Andrew² Pagan, James¹*) was born in 1923 in Wheeling, Ohio Co., West Virginia. She is the daughter of Errett Clinton Mooney and Dorretta Josephine Hill (196).

298. **Gloria Jean⁹ Mooney** (*Dorretta Josephine⁸ Hill, Charles Millard⁷, John W.⁶, Mary Jane⁵ Goudy, Elizabeth Jane⁴ Pegan, Andrew³ Pegan II, Andrew² Pagan, James¹*) was born in 1925 in Wheeling, Ohio Co., West Virginia. She is the daughter of Errett Clinton Mooney and Dorretta Josephine Hill (196).

299. **June M.⁹ Clark** (*Harriet Ellen⁸ Hill, Charles Millard⁷, John W.⁶, Mary Jane⁵ Goudy, Elizabeth Jane⁴ Pegan, Andrew³ Pegan II, Andrew² Pagan, James¹*) was born on June 19, 1925, in Ritchie, Ohio Co., West Virginia. She was the daughter of Cecil Meril Clark and Harriet Ellen Hill (197). June M. died in Ritchie, Ohio Co., West Virginia, on January 16, 1927, at age one. She was buried in Greenwood Cemetery, Wheeling, Ohio Co., West Virginia.[24]

300. **Dorothy E.⁹ Clark** (*Harriet Ellen⁸ Hill, Charles Millard⁷, John W.⁶, Mary Jane⁵ Goudy, Elizabeth Jane⁴ Pegan, Andrew³ Pegan II, Andrew² Pagan, James¹*) was born on November 29, 1927, in Ritchie, Ohio Co., West Virginia. She was the daughter of Cecil Meril Clark and Harriet Ellen Hill (197). Dorothy E. died in Wheeling, Ohio Co., West Virginia, on September 30, 1951, at age 23. She was buried in Greenwood Cemetery, Wheeling, Ohio Co., West Virginia.[24]

Never married.

301. **George Allen⁹ Watters II** (*Gertrude Isabella⁸ Hirth, Ella Allen⁷ Hill, John W.⁶, Mary Jane⁵ Goudy,* *Elizabeth Jane⁴ Pegan, Andrew³ Pegan II, Andrew² Pagan, James¹*) was born on March 24, 1909, in Wheeling, Ohio Co., West Virginia. He was also known as **Allen or Allyn.** He was the son of George William Watters and Gertrude Isabella Hirth (198). George Allen lived in 1930 in Chicago, Cook Co., Illinois. He also resided in 1942 in Chicago, Cook Co., Illinois. George Allen died in Chicago, Cook Co., Illinois, on March 8, 1972, at age 62.

May have never married.

George Allyn Watters was legally adopted by his grandparents, Charles W. and Ella A. Hill Waters. His parents, George W. and Gertrude Isabella Hirth Watters, divorced shortly after his birth in 1909.

302. **Howard Clarke⁹ Howland** (*Gertrude Isabella⁸ Hirth, Ella Allen⁷ Hill, John W.⁶, Mary Jane⁵ Goudy, Elizabeth Jane⁴ Pegan, Andrew³ Pegan II, Andrew² Pagan, James¹*) was born on November 7, 1912, in Steubenville, Cross Creek Twp., Jefferson Co., Ohio. He was also known as **Clarke.** He was the son of Harry C. Howland and Gertrude Isabella Hirth (198). Howard Clarke died in Steubenville, Cross Creek Twp., Jefferson Co., Ohio, on November 26, 1974, at age 62. He was buried in Union Cemetery, Steubenville, Cross Creek Twp., Jefferson Co., Ohio.[16]

Childless.

Howard Clarke Howland was raised by his maternal grandmother, Ella May Hill Hirth.

He married **Unknown Unknown.** They divorced.

303. **Norman Bruce⁹ Dunnan** (*Gertrude Isabella⁸ Hirth, Ella Allen⁷ Hill, John W.⁶, Mary Jane⁵ Goudy, Elizabeth Jane⁴ Pegan, Andrew³ Pegan II, Andrew² Pagan, James¹*) was born on August 23, 1915, in Pughtown (now New Manchester), Hancock Co., West Virginia. He was the son of Luke Wallace Dunnan and Gertrude Isabella Hirth (198). Norman Bruce died in Fort Meade, Anne Arundel Co., Maryland, on December 5, 1951, at age 36. He was buried Arlington National Cemetery, Arlington, Virginia.[115]

Childless.

Norman Bruce married Mrs. **Louisa W. Unknown Masterson** after 1942. Louisa W. Unknown Masterson was born in Monaco or France on May 7, 1912. Louisa W. lived in 1944 in West Chester, Chester Co., Pennsylvania. She reached age 77 and died in West Chester, Chester Co., Pennsylvania? on April 28, 1990. Louisa W. was buried in Arlington National Cemetery, Arlington, Virginia.[115]

Louisa W. Unknown Masterson says on her Women's Army Corps enlistment form that she was born in Monaco or France.

304. **Ella Alice or Allys⁹ Dunnan** (*Gertrude Isabella⁸ Hirth, Ella Allen⁷ Hill, John W.⁶, Mary Jane⁵ Goudy, Elizabeth Jane⁴ Pegan, Andrew³ Pegan II, Andrew² Pagan, James¹*) was born in 1916 in Chester, Hancock Co., West Virginia. She was the daughter of Luke Wallace Dunnan and Gertrude Isabella Hirth (198). Ella Alice or Allys died after 1937.

Ella Alice or Allys married **Roy Oliver Leggett II** on January 18, 1937, in Ohio Co., West Virginia. Roy Oliver Leggett II was born in New Philadelphia, Goshen Twp., Tuscarawas Co., Ohio, on December 23, 1912. Roy Oliver lived in 1937 in Adena, Ohio. He reached age 70 and died in Canton, Stark Co., Ohio, on November 10, 1983.

305. **Hugh Ronald⁹ Dunnan** (*Gertrude Isabella⁸ Hirth, Ella Allen⁷ Hill, John W.⁶, Mary Jane⁵ Goudy, Elizabeth Jane⁴ Pegan, Andrew³ Pegan II, Andrew² Pagan, James¹*) was born on July 4, 1918, in Pughtown (now New Manchester), Hancock Co., West Virginia. He was also known as **Ronald**. He was the son of Luke Wallace Dunnan and Gertrude Isabella Hirth (198). Hugh Ronald died in Charleston, Kanawha Co., West Virginia, on November 12, 1987, at age 69.

Hugh Ronald married **Estelle Mills Livingston** on April 18, 1942, in Kanawha Co., West Virginia. Estelle Mills Livingston was born in Campbell Co., Virginia, on March 17, 1921. Estelle Mills reached age 53 and died in Charleston, Kanawha Co., West Virginia, in February 1975.

306. **Dorothy Ada⁹ Dunnan** (*Gertrude Isabella⁸ Hirth, Ella Allen⁷ Hill, John W.⁶, Mary Jane⁵ Goudy, Elizabeth Jane⁴ Pegan, Andrew³ Pegan II, Andrew²*

*Pagan, James¹*) was born on August 7, 1920, in Pughtown (now New Manchester), Hancock Co., West Virginia. She was the daughter of Luke Wallace Dunnan and Gertrude Isabella Hirth (198). Dorothy Ada died in Modesto, Stanislaus Co., California, on June 27, 2015, at age 94. She was buried in Turlock Memorial Park Cemetery, Turlock, Stanislaus Co., California.[116]

Dorothy Ada married **James Trevitt Jenkinson** on May 5, 1943. They had one daughter. James Trevitt Jenkinson was born in Cook Co., Illinois, on November 4, 1924. James Trevitt reached age 36 and died in Hilmer, Merced Co., California, on December 4, 1960. He was buried in Turlock Memorial Park Cemetery, Turlock, Stanislaus Co., California.[116]

307. **Marianne Frances⁹ Dunnan** (*Gertrude Isabella⁸ Hirth, Ella Allen⁷ Hill, John W.⁶, Mary Jane⁵ Goudy, Elizabeth Jane⁴ Pegan, Andrew³ Pegan II, Andrew² Pagan, James¹*) was born on October 31, 1921, in Pughtown (now New Manchester), Hancock Co., West Virginia. She was the daughter of Luke Wallace Dunnan and Gertrude Isabella Hirth (198). Marianne Frances lived in 2002 in Barnesville, Warren Twp., Belmont Co., Ohio. She died in a facility in Upper Arlington, Franklin Co., Ohio, on April 17, 2002, at age 80.

Marianne Frances married **Lawrence Emmett Wheeler** after 1940. Lawrence Emmett Wheeler was born in Hopedale, Green Twp., Harrison Co., Ohio, on April 4, 1914. Lawrence Emmett lived in 1993 in Barnesville, Warren Twp., Belmont Co., Ohio. He reached age 79 and died in a hospital in Wheeling, Ohio Co., West Virginia, on August 29, 1993.

308. **Leah Gertrude⁹ Dunnan** (*Gertrude Isabella⁸ Hirth, Ella Allen⁷ Hill, John W.⁶, Mary Jane⁵ Goudy, Elizabeth Jane⁴ Pegan, Andrew³, Andrew² Pagan, James¹*) was born on Wednesday, September 26, 1923, in Wayne Twp., Jefferson Co., Ohio. She was the daughter of Luke Wallace Dunnan and Gertrude Isabella Hirth (198). She died in Richmond, Henrico Co., Virginia, on August 19, 2018, at age 94. Leah Gertrude is buried in Westhampton Memorial Park Cemetery, Tuckahoe, Henrico Co., Virginia.[A]

Leah Gertrude married **Edward Rider Musser II** on February 11, 1955, in Miami Co., Ohio. They divorced. They had two sons. Edward Rider Musser II was born in Henrico Co., Virginia, on Thursday, December 20, 1928. He reached age 88 and died in Richmond, Henrico Co., Virginia, on September 30, 2017.

309. **Richard⁹ Mason II** (*Ada Roberts⁸ Hirth, Ella Allen⁷ Hill, John W.⁶, Mary Jane⁵ Goudy, Elizabeth Jane⁴ Pegan, Andrew³ Pegan II, Andrew² Pagan, James¹*) was born in 1910 in West Virginia. He was the son of Richard Andrew Mason and Ada Roberts Hirth (199). Richard died before 1920.

310. **Robert Harold⁹ Moore** (*Della⁸ Hirth, Ella Allen⁷ Hill, John W.⁶, Mary Jane⁵ Goudy, Elizabeth Jane⁴ Pegan, Andrew³ Pegan II, Andrew² Pagan, James¹*) was born on June 14, 1915, in Steubenville, Cross Creek Twp., Jefferson Co., Ohio. He was the son of Harry Hawkins Moore and Della Hirth (200). Robert Harold died in Salinas, Monterey Co., California, on May 7, 1994, at age 78. He was buried in San Joaquin Valley National Cemetery, Santa Nella, Merced Co., California.[117]

Robert Harold married **Betty Jane Ralston** on July 31, 1940, in Jefferson Co., Ohio. They divorced before 1947. Betty Jane Ralston was born in Steubenville, Cross Creek Twp., Jefferson Co., Ohio, on November 19, 1923. She reached age 56 and died in Steubenville, Cross Creek Twp., Jefferson Co., Ohio, on September 12, 1980. Betty Jane was buried under the name Betty Jean Zimmerman in Fort Steuben Burial Estates, Wintersville, Toronto Twp., Jefferson Co., Ohio.[134]

311. **Ruth Eleanor⁹ Moore** (*Della⁸ Hirth, Ella Allen⁷ Hill, John W.⁶, Mary Jane⁵ Goudy, Elizabeth Jane⁴ Pegan, Andrew³ Pegan II, Andrew² Pagan, James¹*) was born on March 2, 1917, in Steubenville, Cross Creek Twp., Jefferson Co., Ohio. She was the daughter of Harry Hawkins Moore and Della Hirth (200). Ruth Eleanor died in Steubenville, Cross Creek Twp., Jefferson Co., Ohio, on March 11, 1998, at age 81. She was buried in New Alexandria Cemetery, New Alexandria, Ohio.[118]

Ruth Eleanor married **Norman Wilson Boughner** on June 27, 1938, in Jefferson Co., Ohio. They had two children. Norman Wilson Boughner was born in Georges Run, Steubenville Twp., Jefferson Co., Ohio, on October 30, 1912. Norman Wilson lived in 1988 in Haines, Polk Co., Florida. He also resided in 1999 in Steubenville, Cross Creek Twp., Jefferson Co., Ohio. Norman Wilson reached age 86 and died in a hospital in Wheeling, Ohio Co., West Virginia, on March 22, 1999. He was buried in New Alexandria Cemetery, New Alexandria, Ohio.[118]

Children of Ruth Eleanor Moore and Norman Wilson Boughner:

+ 365 f I. **Nancy J.¹⁰ Boughner** was born in Steubenville, Cross Creek Twp., Jefferson Co., Ohio, on September 1, 1939.

312. **Jeanne⁹ Moore** (*Della⁸ Hirth, Ella Allen⁷ Hill, John W.⁶, Mary Jane⁵ Goudy, Elizabeth Jane⁴ Pegan, Andrew³ Pegan II, Andrew² Pagan, James¹*) was born on October 6, 1919, in Steubenville, Cross Creek Twp., Jefferson Co., Ohio. She was the daughter of Harry Hawkins Moore and Della Hirth (200). Jeanne died in Washington, District of Columbia, on October 19, 2004, at age 85. She was buried under the name Jeanne Hughes in Mount Calvary Cemetery, Steubenville, Cross Creek Twp., Jefferson Co., Ohio.[119]

Jeanne Moore married **Thomas J. Hughes** on August 31, 1940, in Jefferson Co., Ohio. Thomas J. Hughes was born in Mingo Junction, Steubenville Twp., Jefferson Co., Ohio, on July 8, 1906. Thomas J. lived in 1967 in Mingo Junction, Steubenville Twp., Jefferson Co., Ohio. He reached age 60 and died in a hospital in Steubenville, Cross Creek Twp., Jefferson Co., Ohio, on June 3, 1967. Thomas J. was buried in Mount Calvary Cemetery, Steubenville, Cross Creek Twp., Jefferson Co., Ohio.[119]

Jeanne Moore Hughes married **Jesse W. Jones** on January 20, 1973, in Jefferson Co., Ohio. Jesse W. Jones was born in Pennsylvania? on September 15, 1918. They may have divorced. Jesse W. lived in 1977 in Mingo Junction, Steubenville Twp., Jefferson Co., Ohio. He reached age 58 and died in a hospital in Steubenville, Cross Creek Twp., Jefferson Co., Ohio, on August 20, 1977.

**313. Charles William⁹ Hirth III** (*Charles William⁸, Ella Allen⁷ Hill, John W.⁶, Mary Jane⁵ Goudy, Elizabeth Jane⁴ Pegan, Andrew³ Pegan II, Andrew² Pagan, James¹*) was born on August 9, 1934, in Martins Ferry, Pease Twp., Belmont Co., Ohio. He is the son of Charles William Hirth II (201) and Gladys Sarita Grey.

He married **Joyce Unknown.** Joyce Unknown was born about 1936.

**314. Arthur William⁹ Bridgeman** (*Benjamin Cowen⁸, Minnie Blanche⁷ Fox, Elizabeth Jane⁶ Hill, Mary Jane⁵ Goudy, Elizabeth Jane⁴ Pegan, Andrew³ Pegan II, Andrew² Pagan, James¹*) was born on October 25, 1918, in Wheeling, Ohio Co., West Virginia. He was the son of Benjamin Cowen Bridgeman (202) and Lulu May Whiteman. Arthur William died in Wheeling, Ohio Co., West Virginia, on December 4, 1935, at age 17. He was buried in Greenwood Cemetery, Wheeling, Ohio Co., West Virginia.[24]

**315. Betty Harriett⁹ Bridgeman** (*Benjamin Cowen⁸, Minnie Blanche⁷ Fox, Elizabeth Jane⁶ Hill, Mary Jane⁵ Goudy, Elizabeth Jane⁴ Pegan, Andrew³ Pegan II, Andrew² Pagan, James¹*) was born on June 19, 1920, in Wheeling, Ohio Co., West Virginia. She was the daughter of Benjamin Cowen Bridgeman (202) and Lulu May Whiteman. Betty Harriett died in Hope, Haw Creek Twp., Bartholomew Co., Indiana, on November 28, 2005, at age 85. She was buried in Garland Brook Cemetery, Columbus, Bartholomew Co., Indiana.[120]

Betty Harriett married **William Arthur Johnson** on April 8, 1942, in Ohio Co., West Virginia. They had two children. William A. Johnson was born on July 18, 1918 in Bellaire, Pultney Twp., Belmont Co., Ohio. He was also known as **Squire.** William A. reached age 54 and died on July 11, 1973 in Columbus, Bartholomew Co., Indiana. He was buried in Garland Brook Cemetery, Columbus, Bartholomew Co., Indiana.[120]

**316. Benjamin Cowan⁹ Bridgeman II** (*Benjamin Cowen⁸, Minnie Blanche⁷ Fox, Elizabeth Jane⁶ Hill, Mary Jane⁵ Goudy, Elizabeth Jane⁴ Pegan, Andrew³ Pegan II, Andrew² Pagan, James¹*) was born on June 23, 1921, in Wheeling, Ohio Co., West Virginia. He was the son of Benjamin Cowen Bridgeman (202) and Lulu May Whiteman. Benjamin Cowan lived in 1987 in Akron, Summit Co., Ohio. He died in a hospital in Cuyahoga Falls, Cuyahoga Falls Twp., Summit Co., Ohio, on October 16, 1987, at age 66.

Benjamin Cowan married **Betty Lou Wardle** on October 23, 1947, in Ohio Co., West Virginia. Betty Lou Wardle was born in Bellaire, Pultney Twp., Belmont Co., Ohio, on May 26, 1928. Betty Lou reached age 66 and died in Akron, Summit Co., Ohio, on December 7, 1994.

**317. John⁹ Bridgeman IV** (*John⁸, Minnie Blanche⁷ Fox, Elizabeth Jane⁶ Hill, Mary Jane⁵ Goudy, Elizabeth Jane⁴ Pegan, Andrew³ Pegan II, Andrew² Pagan, James¹*) was born in 1934 in Wheeling, Ohio Co., West Virginia. He is the son of John Bridgeman III (204) and Ruth Louise Grimm.

**318. William Robert⁹ Ewing** (*Roberta Elizabeth⁸ Fox, Robert Arthur⁷, Elizabeth Jane⁶ Hill, Mary Jane⁵ Goudy, Elizabeth Jane⁴ Pegan, Andrew³ Pegan II, Andrew² Pagan, James¹*) was born on July 6, 1930, in Sand Hill, Marshall Co., West Virginia. He was the son of James Dallas Ewing and Roberta Elizabeth Fox (205). William Robert died in Glen Dale, Marshall Co., West Virginia, on November 17, 1992, at age 62.

William Robert married **Sandra Jean Gittings** in 1964 in Marshall Co., West Virginia. They divorced. They had two children. Sandra Jean Gittings was born in Moundsville, Marshall Co., West Virginia, on March 26, 1942. She reached age 71 and died in Moundsville, Marshall Co., West Virginia, on January 4, 2014.

William Robert Ewing married **Minnie Floy Wyckhoff.** They had one daughter. Minnie Floy Wyckhoff was born in Littleton, Wetzel Co., West Virginia., on September 5, 1935. Minnie Floy reached age 65 and died in Waynesburg, Greene Co., Pennsylvania, on October 10, 2000.

Daughter of William Robert Ewing and Minnie Floy Wyckhoff:

+ 366 f I. **Darlene Kay**[10] **Ewing** was born in Waynesburg, Greene Co., Pennsylvania, on April 15, 1956. She died in Waynesburg, Greene Co., Pennsylvania, on April 17, 1975.

319. **James Addison**[9] **Ewing II** (*Roberta Elizabeth*[8] *Fox, Robert Arthur*[7]*, Elizabeth Jane*[6] *Hill, Mary Jane*[5] *Goudy, Elizabeth Jane*[4] *Pegan, Andrew*[3] *Pegan II, Andrew*[2] *Pagan, James*[1]) was born on July 18, 1935, in Marshall Co., West Virginia. He was the son of James Dallas Ewing and Roberta Elizabeth Fox (205). James Addison died in Moundsville, Marshall Co., West Virginia, on June 15, 1991, at age 55. He was buried in Fairview Cemetery, Moundsville, Marshall Co., West Virginia.[83]

James Addison married **Anetta Cecil** in 1961 in Marshall Co., West Virginia. They had one child. Anetta Cecil was born in Moundsville, Marshall Co., West Virginia, on July 11, 1935.

320. **Donald Gene**[9] **Ewing** (*Roberta Elizabeth*[8] *Fox, Robert Arthur*[7]*, Elizabeth Jane*[6] *Hill, Mary Jane*[5] *Goudy, Elizabeth Jane*[4] *Pegan, Andrew*[3] *Pegan II, Andrew*[2] *Pagan, James*[1]) was born on December 9, 1936, in Sand Hill., Marshall Co., West Virginia. He was the son of James Dallas Ewing and Roberta Elizabeth Fox (205). Donald Gene died in Sand Hill, Marshall Co., West Virginia, on November 11, 1943, at age six.

321. **Marian Lee**[9] **Flanegin** (*Edmund Arthur*[8]*, Jennie*[7] *Fox, Elizabeth Jane*[6] *Hill, Mary Jane*[5] *Goudy, Elizabeth Jane*[4] *Pegan, Andrew*[3] *Pegan II, Andrew*[2] *Pagan, James*[1]) was born on February 11, 1933, in Wheeling, Ohio Co., West Virginia. She is the daughter of Edmund Arthur Flanegin II (208) and Aliah Tennant.

Marian Lee married **Herbert Eugene Smudski** in 1953 in Ohio Co., West Virginia. They have two sons. Herbert Eugene Smudski was born in Wheeling, Ohio Co., West Virginia, on September 5, 1930. Herbert Eugene reached age 47 and died in Wheeling, Ohio Co., West Virginia? on May 18, 1978.

322. **Edmund Arthur**[9] **Flanegin III** (*Edmund Arthur*[8]*, Jennie*[7] *Fox, Elizabeth Jane*[6] *Hill, Mary Jane*[5] *Goudy, Elizabeth Jane*[4] *Pegan, Andrew*[3] *Pegan II, Andrew*[2] *Pagan, James*[1]) was born on February 18, 1935, in Wheeling, Ohio Co., West Virginia. He was the son of Edmund Arthur Flanegin II (208) and Aliah Tennant. Edmund Arthur died in Wheeling, Ohio Co., West Virginia, on July 9, 1988, at age 53. He was buried in Greenwood Cemetery, Wheeling, Ohio Co., West Virginia.[24]

# 10th Generation

**323. Charles W.**[10] **Galbreath** (*Guy Leroy*[9], *James Howard*[8], *Ella Nancy*[7] *Thompson, Nancy J.*[6] *Goudy, Andrew*[5], *Elizabeth Jane*[4] *Pegan, Andrew*[3] *Pegan II, Andrew*[2] *Pagan, James*[1]) was born on February 25, 1917, in Uhrichsville, Mill Twp., Tuscarawas Co., Ohio. He was also known as **Gilly**. He was the son of Guy Leroy Galbreath (212) and Mary E. Timmerman. He died in Santa Rosa, Sonoma Co., California, on December 20, 1984, at age 67. Charles W. was buried in Longview Cemetery, Bowerston, Monroe Twp., Harrison Co., Ohio.[85]

Charles W. married **Charlotte Frances Heironimus** on August 4, 1950, in Washington, District of Columbia. They had two children. Charlotte Frances Heironimus was born in Washington, District of Columbia, on September 21, 1923. She was also known as **Frannie**. Charlotte Frances reached age 89 and died in Santa Rosa, Sonoma Co., California, on January 1, 2013. She was buried in Longview Cemetery, Bowerston, Monroe Twp., Harrison Co., Ohio.[85]

**324. Howard Eugene**[10] **Galbreath** (*Raymond Arthur*[9], *James Howard*[8], *Ella Nancy*[7] *Thompson, Nancy J.*[6] *Goudy, Andrew*[5], *Elizabeth Jane*[4] *Pegan, Andrew*[3] *Pegan II, Andrew*[2] *Pagan, James*[1]) was born on April 24, 1919, in Uhrichsville, Mill Twp., Tuscarawas Co., Ohio. He was the son of Raymond Arthur Galbreath (213) and Marjorie Marie Garrett. Howard Eugene died in Dennison, Mill Twp., Tuscarawas Co., Ohio, on February 27, 1970, at age 50.

Howard Eugene married **Maxine Amy Northam** in 1938 in Ohio Co., West Virginia. They had two sons. Maxine Amy Northam was born in Mill Twp., Tuscarawas Co., Ohio, on May 14, 1923. Maxine Amy reached age 59 and died in Canton, Stark Co., Ohio, on September 23, 1982. Maxine Amy Northam Galbreath Milhoan's birth record indicates her given name at birth was Leota M. Northam.

Sons of Howard Eugene Galbreath and Maxine Amy Northam:

+ 367 m I. **Howard Eugene**[11] **Galbreath II** was born in Dennison, Mill Twp., Tuscarawas Co., Ohio, on September 27, 1938. He died in Dennison, Mill Twp., Tuscarawas Co., Ohio, on June 8, 2002.

+ 368 m II. **Dennis Lynn**[11] **Galbreath** was born in Dennison, Mill Twp., Tuscarawas Co., Ohio, on May 2, 1944. He died in Akron, Summit Co., Ohio, on June 15, 1992.

**325. Betty Jane**[10] **Galbreath** (*Raymond Arthur*[9], *James Howard*[8], *Ella Nancy*[7] *Thompson, Nancy J.*[6] *Goudy, Andrew*[5], *Elizabeth Jane*[4] *Pegan, Andrew*[3] *Pegan II, Andrew*[2] *Pagan, James*[1]) was born on August 11, 1922, in Uhrichsville, Mill Twp., Tuscarawas Co., Ohio. She was the daughter of Raymond Arthur Galbreath (213) and Marjorie Marie Garrett. Betty Jane died in Mansfield, Madison Twp., Richland Co., Ohio, on August 9, 2001, at age 78. She was buried in Ontario Cemetery, Ontario, Springfield Twp., Richland Co., Ohio.[123]

She married **Kenneth Duane Gilmore.** They had four children. Kenneth Duane Gilmore was born in Gnadenhutten, Clay Twp., Tuscarawas Co., Ohio, on June 18, 1920. Kenneth Duane reached age 90 and died in a facility in Medina, Medina Co., Ohio, on December 29, 2010. He was buried in Ontario Cemetery, Ontario, Springfield Twp., Richland Co., Ohio.[123]

Betty Jane Galbreath and Kenneth Duane Gilmore had four children, including:

+ 369 m I. **Kenneth Duane**[11] **Gilmore II** was born in Dennison, Mill Twp., Tuscarawas Co., Ohio, on December 10, 1942. He died in San Jose, Santa Clara Co., California, on

January 24, 2004. Kenneth Duane was buried in Mission City Memorial Park Cemetery, San Jose, Santa Clara Co., California.[135]

+ 370　f　IV.　**Linda Kay[11] Gilmore** was born in Dennison, Mill Twp., Tuscarawas Co., Ohio, on June 3, 1949. She died in Dennison, Mill Twp., Tuscarawas Co., Ohio, on April 6, 1950. Linda Kay was buried in Evergreen Burial Park, New Philadelphia, Tuscarawas Co., Ohio.[58]

**326. Raymond J.[10] Galbreath II** (*Raymond Arthur[9], James Howard[8], Ella Nancy[7] Thompson, Nancy J.[6] Goudy, Andrew[5], Elizabeth Jane[4] Pegan, Andrew[3] Pegan II, Andrew[2] Pagan, James[1]*) was born on September 4, 1925, in Uhrichsville, Mill Twp., Tuscarawas Co., Ohio. He was also known as **Pete.** He was the son of Raymond Arthur Galbreath (213) and Marjorie Marie Garrett. Raymond J. lived in Baltic, Clark Twp., Holmes Co., Ohio. He died in a hospital in Massillon, Perry Twp., Stark Co., Ohio, on November 29, 2014, at age 89. Raymond J. was buried in Berger (Brethren) Cemetery, Baltic, Clark Twp., Holmes Co., Ohio.[124]

Raymond J. married **Kathryn A. Snyder** on September 9, 1955. They had three children. Kathryn A. Snyder was born in Baltic, Ohio, on June 14, 1927. She was also known as **Katy.** Kathryn A. reached age 81 and died in Baltic, Clark Twp., Holmes Co., Ohio, on February 2, 2009. She was buried in Berger (Brethren) Cemetery, Baltic, Clark Twp., Holmes Co., Ohio.[124]

**327. Mary Margaret[10] Galbreath** (*Raymond Arthur[9], James Howard[8], Ella Nancy[7] Thompson, Nancy J.[6] Goudy, Andrew[5], Elizabeth Jane[4] Pegan, Andrew[3] Pegan II, Andrew[2] Pagan, James[1]*) was born on February 3, 1931, in Uhrichsville, Mill Twp., Tuscarawas Co., Ohio. She was the daughter of Raymond Arthur Galbreath (213) and Marjorie Marie Garrett. Mary Margaret died in Uhrichsville, Mill Twp., Tuscarawas Co., Ohio, on February 22, 2015, at age 84. She was buried in Evergreen Burial Park, New Philadelphia, Tuscarawas Co., Ohio.[58]

Never married.

**328. Robert L.[10] Galbreath** (*Raymond Arthur[9], James Howard[8], Ella Nancy[7] Thompson, Nancy J.[6] Goudy, Andrew[5], Elizabeth Jane[4] Pegan, Andrew[3] Pegan II, Andrew[2] Pagan, James[1]*) was born on January 18, 1934, in Uhrichsville, Mill Twp., Tuscarawas Co., Ohio. He was the son of Raymond Arthur Galbreath (213) and Marjorie Marie Garrett. Robert L. lived in 2007 in Uhrichsville, Mill Twp., Tuscarawas Co., Ohio. He died in a hospital in Columbiana, Columbiana Co., Ohio, on April 26, 2007, at age 73.

He married **Lacie Unknown.** They divorced. They had one child.

**329. Virginia Lee[10] Staley** (*Clara Irene[9] Galbreath, James Howard[8], Ella Nancy[7] Thompson, Nancy J.[6] Goudy, Andrew[5], Elizabeth Jane[4] Pegan, Andrew[3] Pegan II, Andrew[2] Pagan, James[1]*) was born on August 16, 1926, in Uhrichsville, Mill Twp., Tuscarawas Co., Ohio. She was the daughter of Robert F. Staley and Clara Irene Galbreath (214). Virginia L. lived in Lancaster, Fairfield Co., Ohio.

She married **Louis Joseph Joos.** They had ten children. Louis Joseph Joos was born in Lancaster, Fairfield Co., Ohio, on June 11, 1927. Louis Joseph reached age 69 and died in Lancaster, Fairfield Co., Ohio, on January 6, 1997. He was buried in Saint Mary Cemetery, Lancaster, Fairfield Co., Ohio.[136]

Virginia Lee Staley and Louis Joseph Joos had 10 children, including:

+ 371　f　I.　**Carol Kaye[11] Joos** was born in Lancaster, Fairfield Co., Ohio, on March 23, 1950. She died in Fairfield, Lancaster Co., Ohio, on March 6, 1996. Carol Kaye was buried in Saint Mary Cemetery, Lancaster, Fairfield Co., Ohio..[136]

+ 372　f　II.　**Susan Diane[11] Joos** was born in Lancaster, Fairfield Co., Ohio, on March 28, 1951. She died in Waterford Twp., Oakland Co.,

Susan Dianne was buried in Farmer's Creek Cemetery, Metamora, Metamora Twp., Lapeer Co., Michigan.[E]

+ 373 m VII. **Christopher Brent¹¹ Joos** was was born in Lancaster, Fairfield Co., Ohio on January 22, 1959. He died in Columbus, Franklin Co., Ohio, on June 11, 2018.

**330. Don R.¹⁰ Staley** (*Clara Irene⁹ Galbreath, James Howard⁸, Ella Nancy⁷ Thompson, Nancy J.⁶ Goudy, Andrew⁵, Elizabeth Jane⁴ Pegan, Andrew³ Pegan II, Andrew² Pagan, James¹*) was born on July 4, 1928, in Uhrichsville, Mill Twp., Tuscarawas Co., Ohio. He was the son of Robert F. Staley and Clara Irene Galbreath (214). Don R. died in New Philadelphia, Goshen Twp., Tuscarawas Co., Ohio, on February 9, 1977, at age 48. He was cremated and his cremains buried in Evergreen Burial Park, New Philadelphia, Tuscarawas Co., Ohio.[58]

He married **Anna Mae Free.** They had four children. Anna Mae Free was born in Uhrichsville, Mill Twp., Tuscarawas Co., Ohio, on November 21, 1928. Anna Mae reached age 61 and died in Clearwater, Pinellas Co., Florida, on November 17, 1990. She was buried in Evergreen Burial Park, New Philadelphia, Tuscarawas Co., Ohio.[58]

Don R. Staley and Anna Mae Free had four children, including:

+ 374 m I. **Don R.¹¹ Staley II** was born in Dover, Dover Twp., Tuscarawas Co., Ohio, on January 18, 1957. He died in Dover, Dover Twp., Tuscarawas Co., Ohio, on October 14, 2012.

**331. Robert Glenn¹⁰ Cary (Zimmer)** (*Charles Marshall⁹ Cary II, Charles Stewart⁸, Sarah Virginia⁷ Thompson, Nancy J.⁶ Goudy, Andrew⁵, Elizabeth Jane⁴ Pegan, Andrew³ Pegan II, Andrew² Pagan, James¹*) was born on March 31, 1929, in Massillon, Perry Twp., Stark Co., Ohio. He was the son of Charles Marshall Cary II (215) and

Zelma Z. Zimmer. Robert Glenn (Cary) died in Massillon, Perry Twp., Stark Co., Ohio, on February 13, 1997, at age 67. He was buried in Sunset Hills Burial Park Cemetery, Canton, Stark Co., Ohio.[126]

Robert Glenn (Cary) Zimmer was officially adopted by his maternal grandparents Zimmer after his parents, Charles Marshall and Zelma Z. Zimmer Cary divorced and Zelma died months later. He used the surname Zimmer for the rest of his life.

**332. Paul L.¹⁰ Cary** (*Charles Marshall⁹, Charles Stewart⁸, Sarah Virginia⁷ Thompson, Nancy J.⁶ Goudy, Andrew⁵, Elizabeth Jane⁴ Pegan, Andrew³ Pegan II, Andrew² Pagan, James¹*) was born on January 14, 1927, in Massillon, Stark Co., Ohio? He was the son of Charles Marshall Cary II (215) and Loretta Rosanna Wilhelm. Paul L. lived in 1963 in Cuyahoga Falls, Northampton Twp., Summit, Ohio. He was adopted. Paul L. died in Cuyahoga Falls, Northampton Twp., Summit, Ohio, on September 9, 2010, at age 83.

Paul L. Cary may have been Loretta Wilhelm Cary's child by a previous marriage and was adopted by his stepfather, Charles M. Cary.

Paul L. married **Paula M. Quinn** on June 15, 1953, in Stark Co., Ohio. They had two daughters. Paula M. Quinn was born in 1928.

**333. James¹⁰ Cary** (*Robert G.⁹, Charles Stewart⁸, Sarah Virginia⁷ Thompson, Nancy J.⁶ Goudy, Andrew⁵, Elizabeth Jane⁴ Pegan, Andrew³ Pegan II, Andrew² Pagan, James¹*) was born in 1939 in Wyandotte, Wayne Co., Michigan. He is the son of Robert G. Cary (218) and Virginia Unknown.

**334. John Beverly¹⁰ Singer II** (*Ruth Irene⁹ Cary, Charles Stewart⁸, Sarah Virginia⁷ Thompson, Nancy J.⁶ Goudy, Andrew⁵, Elizabeth Jane⁴ Pegan, Andrew³ Pegan II, Andrew² Pagan, James¹*) was born in 1936 in Massillon, Perry Twp., Stark Co., Ohio. He is the son of John Valentine Singer and Ruth Irene Cary (219).

John Beverly married **Connie Marie Stamper** on May 25, 1995, in Tippecanoe Co., Indiana. Connie Marie Stamper was born in 1934.

**335. Donald Seeley[10] McGaffey II** (*Helen May[9] Bovey Seeley, Artland Robinson[8] Bovey [Seeley], Mary E.[7] Thompson, Nancy J.[6] Goudy, Andrew[5], Elizabeth Jane[4] Pegan, Andrew[3] Pegan II, Andrew[2] Pagan, James[1]*) was born on July 1, 1926, in Beverly Hills, Los Angeles Co., California. He was the son of Donald Fox McGaffey and Helen May Bovey (Seeley) (223). Donald Seeley died in Puyallup, Pierce Co., Washington, on October 29, 2001, at age 75. He was buried in Orting Cemetery, Orting, Pierce Co., Washington.[127]

He married **Elizabeth Unknown.**

**336. Marjorie[10] McGaffey** (*Helen May[9] Bovey [Seeley], Artland Robinson[8] Bovey, Mary E.[7] Thompson, Nancy J.[6] Goudy, Andrew[5], Elizabeth Jane[4] Pegan, Andrew[3] Pegan II, Andrew[2] Pagan, James[1]*) was born on June 1, 1928, in Albuquerque, Bernalillo Co., New Mexico. She is the daughter of Donald Fox McGaffey and Helen May Bovey (Seeley) (223).

She married **Joseph John Meyer.** Joseph John Meyer was born in Tacoma, Pierce Co., Washington, on May 24, 1924. Joseph John reached age 75 and died in Puyallup, Pierce Co., Washington, on December 14, 1999. He was buried in Orting Cemetery, Orting, Pierce Co., Washington.[127]

**337. Katherine[10] McGaffey** (*Helen May[9] Bovey [Seeley], Artland Robinson[8] Bovey, Mary E.[7] Thompson, Nancy J.[6] Goudy, Andrew[5], Elizabeth Jane[4] Pegan, Andrew[3] Pegan II, Andrew[2] Pagan, James[1]*) was born on March 2, 1936, in Beverly Hills, Los Angeles Co., California. She is the daughter of Donald Fox McGaffey and Helen May Bovey (Seeley) (223).

**338. William Raymond[10] Hard II** (*Adeline May[9] Bovey, Artland Robinson[8], Mary E.[7] Thompson, Nancy J.[6] Goudy, Andrew[5], Elizabeth Jane[4] Pegan, Andrew[3] Pegan II, Andrew[2] Pagan, James[1]*) was born on July 10, 1930, in Texas. He was also known as **Harry.** He was the son of William Raymond Hard and Adeline May Bovey (225). Wililam Raymond died in Napa, Napa Co., California, on August 19, 2003, at age 73. He was buried in Napa Valley Memorial Park Cemetery, Napa, Napa Co., California.[89]

He married **Mary Josephine JaKotich** in 1949. They had two daughters and adopted another.

Mary Josephine JaKotich was born in Crannell, Humboldt Co., California, on March 30, 1929. She reached age 89 and died in Napa, Napa Co., California, on August 19, 2018.

**339. Jimmy H.[10] Hard** (*Adeline May[9] Bovey, Artland Robinson[8], Mary E.[7] Thompson, Nancy J.[6] Goudy, Andrew[5], Elizabeth Jane[4] Pegan, Andrew[3] Pegan II, Andrew[2] Pagan, James[1]*) was born on June 16, 1933, in Texas. He is the son of William Raymond Hard and Adeline May Bovey (225).

**340. Charlotte[10] Hard** (*Adeline May[9] Bovey, Artland Robinson[8], Mary E.[7] Thompson, Nancy J.[6] Goudy, Andrew[5], Elizabeth Jane[4] Pegan, Andrew[3] Pegan II, Andrew[2] Pagan, James[1]*) was born in 1935 in Texas. She is the daughter of William Raymond Hard and Adeline May Bovey (225).

**341. Robert H.[10] Hard** (*Adeline May[9] Bovey, Artland Robinson[8], Mary E.[7] Thompson, Nancy J.[6] Goudy, Andrew[5], Elizabeth Jane[4] Pegan, Andrew[3] Pegan II, Andrew[2] Pagan, James[1]*) was born on February 14, 1937, in Harris Co., Texas. He is the son of William Raymond Hard and Adeline May Bovey (225).

**342. Bobby Ray[10] Doughtie** (*Betty Maude[9] Bovey, Artland Robinson[8], Mary E.[7] Thompson, Nancy J.[6] Goudy, Andrew[5], Elizabeth Jane[4] Pegan, Andrew[3] Pegan II, Andrew[2] Pagan, James[1]*) was born on May 28, 1932, in El Paso, El Paso Co., Texas. He is the son of Cecil Earl Doughtie and Betty Maude Bovey (226).

Bobby Ray married **Alyce Unknown Thurston** on December 31, 2005, in Montgomery Co., Texas. Alyce Unknown Thurston was born in 1941.

**343. Owen Guy[10] Beazle** (*Harold Guy[9], Guy Andrew[8], Sarah[7] Goudy, Isaac M.[6], Andrew[5], Elizabeth Jane[4] Pegan, Andrew[3] Pegan II, Andrew[2] Pagan, James[1]*) was born on April 11, 1927, in Pease Twp., Belmont Co., Ohio. He was the son of Harold Guy Beazle (228) and Elizabeth McLaughlin. Owen Guy died in Mahoning, Mahoning Co., Ohio, on November 18, 2005, at age 78.

**344. Son[10] Goudy** (*Charles Andrew[9], Edwin Andrew[8], Andrew W.[7], William A.[6], Andrew[5], Elizabeth Jane[4] Pegan, Andrew[3] Pegan II, Andrew[2] Pagan, James[1]*).

He is the son of Charles Andrew Goudy (232) and Mabel Marie Philabaum.

Son Gowdy has married twice. He and his first wife had one son:

Son of Son Goudy and his first wife:

+ 375 m I. **Kirt Edwin**[11] **Goudy** was born in Wheeling, Ohio Co., West Virginia, on September 25, 1975. He died in Wheeling, Ohio Co., West Virginia, on June 11, 2014.

**345. Daughter**[10] **Goudy** (*Charles Andrew*[9]*, Edwin Andrew*[8]*, Andrew W.*[7]*, William A.*[6]*, Andrew*[5]*, Elizabeth Jane*[4] *Pegan, Andrew*[3] *Pegan II, Andrew*[2] *Pagan, James*[1]). She is the daughter of Charles Andrew Goudy (232) and Mabel Marie Philabaum.

She married **Richard C. Forester.** Richard C. Forester was born on November 13, 1959 in Moundsville, Marshall Co., West Virginia. He died on April 1, 2010 in Sherrard, Marshall Co., West Virginia. He was buried in Halcyon Hills Memorial Park Cemetery, Sherrard, Marshall Co., West Virginia.[72]

**346. Gloria Ann**[10] **Lutes** (*William Donald*[9]*, Anita*[8] *Blankensop, Robert Goudy*[7]*, Mary Rebecca*[6] *Goudy, Robert*[5]*, Elizabeth Jane*[4] *Pegan, Andrew*[3] *Pegan II, Andrew*[2] *Pagan, James*[1]). She was the daughter of William Donald Lutes (234) and Le Nore Unknown. Gloria Ann died in a hospital in Washington, District of Columbia, on June 22, 1962. She was buried in Mount Rose Cemetery, Moundsville, Marshall Co., West Virginia.[39]

Gloria Ann died in infancy or childhood

**347. Joyce Withers**[10] **Sullivan** (*Bernice Lucille*[9] *Withers, Mary Grace*[8] *McNeill, Sarah Sanson*[7] *Hereford, Marianne Marilla*[6] *Goudy, William*[5]*, Elizabeth Jane*[4] *Pegan, Andrew*[3] *Pegan II, Andrew*[2] *Pagan, James*[1]) was born on August 10, 1929, in Peytona, Boone Co., West Virginia. She is the daughter of Roy Morris Sullivan and Bernice Lucille Withers (239).

Joyce Withers married **Douglas William Ey** in 1953 in Cabell Co., West Virginia. They had four children. Douglas William Ey was born in Fremont, Dickenson Co., Virginia, on August 17, 1927. He reached age 88 and died in Huntington, Cabell Co., West Virginia, on March 26, 2016. Douglas William was buried in Woodmere Memorial Park Cemetery, Huntington, Cabell Co., West Virginia.[66]

**348. Carol Lynne**[10] **Withers** (*Raymond Robert*[9]*, Mary Grace*[8] *McNeill, Sarah Sanson*[7] *Hereford, Marianne Marilla*[6] *Goudy, William*[5]*, Elizabeth Jane*[4] *Pegan, Andrew*[3] *Pegan II, Andrew*[2] *Pagan, James*[1]) was born on March 15, 1938, in Huntington, Cabell Co., West Virginia. She was the daughter of Raymond Robert Withers (240) and LeVeta Bradley.

Carol Lynne married **Linville Gregg Halloran** on September 15, 1962, in Richmond, Virginia. They divorced in 1988. They had two daughters. Linville Gregg Halloran was born in Beckley, Raleigh Co., West Virginia, on October 25, 1937. He reached age 64 and died in Richmond, Virginia, on April 1, 2002. Linville Gregg was buried in Hollywood Cemetery, Richmond, Virginia.[137]

**349. Robert Kent**[10] **Withers** (*Raymond Robert*[9]*, Mary Grace*[8] *McNeill, Sarah Sanson*[7] *Hereford, Marianne Marilla*[6] *Goudy, William*[5]*, Elizabeth Jane*[4] *Pegan, Andrew*[3] *Pegan II, Andrew*[2] *Pagan, James*[1]) was born on June 26, 1939, in Huntington, Cabell Co., West Virginia. He is the son of Raymond Robert Withers (241) and LeVeta Bradley.

He married **Ms. Penick.** They divorced. They had three children.

Robert Kent Withers and Ms. Penick had three children, including:

+ 376 m I. **Christopher Kent**[11] **Withers** was born in Huntington, Cabell Co., West Virginia, on May 4, 1989. He died in Huntington, Cabell Co., West Virginia, on June 10, 2007. Christopher Kent was buried in Woodmere Memorial Park Cemetery, Huntington, Cabell Co., West Virginia.[66]

**350. Michael William[10] McNeill** (*Richard Hereford[9], Worthington Wilson[8], Sarah Sanson[7] Hereford, Marianne Marilla[6] Goudy, William[5], Elizabeth Jane[4] Pegan, Andrew[3] Pegan II, Andrew[2] Pagan, James[1]*) was born in Caldwell, Canyon Co., Idaho, on December 8, 1942. He died in Tacoma, Pierce Co., Washington on December 25, 2012, at age 70.

Michael William McNeill married and had two children.

When he was five years old, William McNeill and his brother were orphaned when their parents Richard Hereford and Virginia Ruth Arensburg McNeill died in a plane crash. The boys were reared by their uncle and aunt, James Neill Worthington and Dorothy Ellen Dimmett McNeill.

**351. Gary Richard[10] McNeill** (*James Neill Worthington[9], Worthington Wilson[8], Sarah Sanson[7] Hereford, Marianne Marilla[6] Goudy, William[5], Elizabeth Jane[4] Pegan, Andrew[3], Andrew[2] Pagan, James[1]*) was born on Thursday, July 28, 1938, in Denver, Denver Co., Colorado. He is the son of James Neill Worthington McNeill (243) and Dorothy Ellen Dimmett.

Gary Richard married **Ms. Steele.** They have one son.

**352. Steven Dimmett[10] McNeill** (*James Neill Worthington[9], Worthington Wilson[8], Sarah Sanson[7] Hereford, Marianne Marilla[6] Goudy, William[5], Elizabeth Jane[4] Pegan, Andrew[3], Andrew[2] Pagan, James[1]*) was born on Friday, May 10, 1940, in Caldwell, Canyon Co., Idaho. He is the son of James Neill Worthington McNeill (243) and Dorothy Ellen Dimmett.

Steven Dimmett married **Ms. Lewis.**

**353. James Worthington[10] McNeill** (*George Dean[9], Worthington Wilson[8], Sarah Sanson[7] Hereford, Marianne Marilla[6] Goudy, William[5], Elizabeth Jane[4] Pegan, Andrew[3] Pegan II, Andrew[2] Pagan, James[1]*) was born on June 7, 1937, in Goodland, Sherman Co., Kansas. He was the son of George Dean McNeill (244) and Janice M. Ellis. James Worthington died in Cedaredge, Delta Co., Colorado, on January 9, 2015, at age 77. He was buried in Goodland Cemetery, Goodland, Sherman Co., Kansas.[67]

James Worthington married **Marilyn Grace House** on June 9, 1957, in Sherman Co., Kansasd. They had four children. Marilyn Grace House was born in Goodland, Sherman Co., Kansas, on September 6, 1936. Marilyn Grace reached age 76 and died in Cedaredge, Delta Co., Colorado, on November 9, 2012. She was buried in Goodland Cemetery, Goodland, Sherman Co., Kansas.[67]

James Worthington McNeill married **Ms. Willis** after 2012.

James Worthington McNeill and Marilyn Grace House had four children, including:

+ 377 m III. **John R.[11] McNeill** was born in Goodland, Sherman Co., Kansas, on December 25, 1961. He died in Goodland, Sherman Co., Kansas, on December 25, 1961. John R. was buried in Goodland Cemetery, Goodland, Sherman Co., Kansas.[67]

+ 378 m IV. **Bill Ryan[11] McNeill** was born in Goodland, Sherman Co., Kansas, on September 19, 1963. He died in Goodland, Sherman Co., Kansas, in December 1980. Bill Ryan was buried in Goodland Cemetery, Goodland, Sherman Co., Kansas.[67]

**354. Sharon Deanne[10] McNeill** (*George Dean[9], Worthington Wilson[8], Sarah Sanson[7] Hereford, Marianne Marilla[6] Goudy, William[5], Elizabeth Jane[4] Pegan, Andrew[3] Pegan II, Andrew[2] Pagan, James[1]*) was born on February 16, 1939, in Coquille, Coos Co., Oregon. She was the daughter of George Dean McNeill (244) and Janice M. Ellis.

Sharon Deanne married **Waldo Lynn Wickizer** on August 17, 1958. They divorced. They had two children. Waldo Lynn Wickizer was born in McCook, Red Willow Co., Nebraska, on Tuesday, July 5, 1938. He reached age 75 and died in Hays, Ellis Co., Kansas, on May 31, 2014. Waldo Lynn was buried in Mount Allen Cemetery, Hays, Ellis Co., Kansas.[138]

Sharon Deanne McNeill Wickizer married **Donald George Trulove** on May 22, 1982, in Cloud Co., Kansas. Donald George Trulove was born in Topeka, Shawnee Co., Kansas, on Tuesday, April 17, 1928. Donald George reached age 84 and died in Topeka, Shawnee Co., Kansas, on May 17, 2012. He was buried in Mount Hope Cemetery, Topeka, Shawnee Co., Kansas.[139]

355. **Georgia Ann¹⁰ McNeill** (*George Dean⁹, Worthington Wilson⁸, Sarah Sanson⁷ Hereford, Marianne Marilla⁶ Goudy, William⁵, Elizabeth Jane⁴ Pegan, Andrew³ Pegan II, Andrew² Pagan, James¹*) was born on September 15, 1940, in Wilder, Canyon Co., Idaho. She is the daughter of George Dean McNeill (244) and Janice M. Ellis.

Georgia Ann married **Robert Eugene Blackwelder** on January 31, 1960, in Sherman Co., Kansas. They had three children. Robert Eugene Blackwelder was born in Montezuma, Gray Co., Kansas, on December 6, 1937. Robert Eugene reached age 39 and died in Augusta, Columbia Co., Georgia, on February 13, 1977. He was buried in Fairview Cemetery, Montezuma, Gray Co., Kansas.[140]

Georgia Ann McNeill Blackwelder remarried.

356. **Katherine Virginia¹⁰ Johnson** (*Delbert Lyle⁹, Hallie Richmond⁸ McNeill, Sarah Sanson⁷ Hereford, Marianne Marilla⁶ Goudy, William⁵, Elizabeth Jane⁴ Pegan, Andrew³ Pegan II, Andrew² Pagan, James¹*) was born on February 17, 1952, in San Diego, San Diego Co., California. She was the daughter of Delbert Lyle Johnson (253) and Katherine Lucile Hawkins. Katherine Virginia died in Tacoma, Pierce Co., Washington, on July 22, 2007, at age 55. She was buried in Tahoma National Cemetery, Kent, King Co., Washington.[132]

Katherine Virginia Johnson married **Mr. Zuniga**. They divorced.

Katherine Virginia Johnson Zuniga married **Mr. Florek**. They divorced.

Katherine Virginia Johnson Zuniga Florek married **Mr. Moore**.

357. **Son¹⁰ Fair** (*Hugh Hartley⁹, Harold Stewart⁸, Sarah Jessie⁷ Cowl, Elizabeth Jane⁶ Goudy, Isaac⁵, Elizabeth Jane⁴ Pegan, Andrew³ Pegan II, Andrew² Pagan, James¹*) was born on September 7, 1951. He is the son of Hugh Hartley Fair (258) and Eyvette Rose Shearer.

Son Fair and his wife had children, including:

+ 379 m I. **Russell Wayne¹¹ Fair** was born in New Brighton, Beaver Co., Pennsylvania, on January 13, 1972. He died in New Brighton, Beaver Co., Pennsylvania, on January 14, 1972. Russell Wayne was buried in Lawn Haven Burial Estates, Worthington, Armstrong Co., Pennsylvania.[69]

358. **Michael H. Fair** (*Hugh Hartley⁹, Harold Stewart⁸, Sarah Jessie⁷ Cowl, Elizabeth Jane⁶ Goudy, Isaac⁵, Elizabeth Jane⁴ Pegan, Andrew³ Pegan II, Andrew² Pagan, James¹*) was born on October 30, 1957, in West Kittanning Twp., Armstrong Co., Pennsylvania. He was the son of Hugh Hartley Fair (258) and Eyvette Rose Shearer. Michael H. lived in 2013 in Yatesboro, Armstrong Co., Pennsylvania. He died in a hospital in Morgantown, Monongalia Co., West Virginia, on January 28, 2013, at age 55.

Michael H. married and had two children.

359. **Florence Louise¹⁰ Fair** (*Charles Daniel⁹, Daniel Cowl⁸, Sarah Jessie⁷ Cowl, Elizabeth Jane⁶ Goudy, Isaac⁵, Elizabeth Jane⁴ Pegan, Andrew³ Pegan II, Andrew² Pagan, James¹*) was born in Kittanning, Kittanning Twp., Armstrong Co., Pennsylvania, on December 7, 1955. She was the daughter of Charles Daniel (271) and Norma Irene Mitchell. Florence died in Kittanning Twp., Armstrong Co., Pennsylvania, on December 7, 1955. She was buried in Kittanning Cemetery, Kittanning, Kittanning Twp., Armstrong Co., Pennsylvania.[104]

360. **Gene¹⁰ Bruhn** (*Martha⁹ Johnson, Elizabeth M.⁸ Goudy, Edward Elmer⁷, John William⁶, Isaac⁵, Elizabeth Jane⁴ Pegan, Andrew³, Andrew² Pagan, James¹*) was born in 1930 in Wheeling, Ohio Co., West Virginia. He is the son of George Bruhn II and Martha Johnson (281).

**361. Dorothy¹⁰ Bruhn** (*Martha⁹ Johnson, Elizabeth M.⁸ Goudy, Edward Elmer⁷, John William⁶, Isaac⁵, Elizabeth Jane⁴ Pegan, Andrew³, Andrew² Pagan, James¹*) was born in 1934 in Wheeling, Ohio Co., West Virginia. She is the daughter of George Bruhn II and Martha Johnson (281).

**362. Juanita Lee¹⁰ Salus** (*Betty Jane⁹ Helmbrecht, Alberta Anna⁸ Goudy, Robert Carl⁷, John William⁶, Isaac⁵, Elizabeth Jane⁴ Pegan, Andrew³ Pegan II, Andrew² Pagan, James¹*) was born on May 9, 1956, in Youngstown, Mahoning Co., Ohio. She was the daughter of Joseph Anthony Salus and Betty Jane Helmbrecht (283). Juanita Lee died in Youngstown, Mahoning Co., Ohio, on April 1, 2016, at age 59.

Juanita Lee married **Mr. Hammond** on March 18, 1978, in Mahoning Co., Ohio. They divorced. They had four children.

Juanita Lee Salus Hammond married **Unknown Sims** after 1981. They divorced.

Juanita Lee Salus and Jeffery L. Hammond had four children, including:

+ 380 m IV. **Michael Allen⁶ Hammond** was born in Youngstown, Mahoning Co., Ohio, on June 20, 1981. He died on January 30, 2016, in Youngstown, Mahoning Co., Ohio.

**363. Timothy Lynn¹⁰ Salus** (*Betty Jane⁹ Helmbrecht, Alberta Anna⁸ Goudy, Robert Carl⁷, John William⁶, Isaac⁵, Elizabeth Jane⁴ Pegan, Andrew³ Pegan II, Andrew² Pagan, James¹*) was born on Tuesday, May 26, 1959, in Youngstown, Mahoning Co., Ohio. He was the son of Joseph Anthony Salus and Betty Jane Helmbrecht (283). Timothy Lynn lived in Griffith, Ross Twp., Lake Co., Indiana. He died in a hospital in Merrillville, Ross Twp., Lake Co., Indiana, on December 29, 2006, at age 47.

Childless.

Timothy Lynn Salus was married thrice.

**364. Charles H.¹⁰ Crockard** (*Frances A.⁹ Bachmann, Mabel B.⁸ Church, Mary Emma⁷ Hill, David Wellington⁶, Mary Jane⁵ Goudy, Elizabeth Jane⁴ Pegan, Andrew³ Pegan II, Andrew² Pagan, James¹*) was born in 1933 in Wheeling, Ohio Co., West Virginia. He was the son of Anson Charles Crockard and Frances A. Bachmann (287). Charles H. died in a hospital in Huntington, Cabell Co., West Virginia, on October 19, 1946, at age 13. He was buried in Greenwood Cemetery, Wheeling, Ohio Co., West Virginia.[24]

**365. Nancy J.¹⁰ Boughner** (*Ruth Eleanor⁹ Moore, Della⁸ Hirth, Ella Allen⁷ Hill, John W.⁶, Mary Jane⁵ Goudy, Elizabeth Jane⁴ Pegan, Andrew³ Pegan II, Andrew² Pagan, James¹*) was born on September 1, 1939, in Steubenville, Cross Creek Twp., Jefferson Co., Ohio. She is the daughter of Norman Wilson Boughner and Ruth Eleanor Moore (311).

**366. Darlene Kay¹⁰ Ewing** (*William Robert⁹, Roberta Elizabeth⁸ Fox, Robert Arthur⁷, Elizabeth Jane⁶ Hill, Mary Jane⁵ Goudy, Elizabeth Jane⁴ Pegan, Andrew³ Pegan II, Andrew² Pagan, James¹*) was born on Sunday, April 15, 1956, in Waynesburg, Greene Co., Pennsylvania. She was the daughter of William Robert Ewing (318) and Minnie Floy Wyckhoff. Darlene Kay died in Waynesburg, Greene Co., Pennsylvania, on April 17, 1975, at age 19.

Never married.

# 11th Generation

**367. Howard Eugene<sup>11</sup> Galbreath II** (*Howard Eugene<sup>10</sup>, Raymond Arthur<sup>9</sup>, James Howard<sup>8</sup>, Ella Nancy<sup>7</sup> Thompson, Nancy J.<sup>6</sup> Goudy, Andrew<sup>5</sup>, Elizabeth Jane<sup>4</sup> Pegan, Andrew<sup>3</sup> Pegan II, Andrew<sup>2</sup> Pagan, James<sup>1</sup>*) was born on September 27, 1938, in Dennison, Mill Twp., Tuscarawas Co., Ohio. He was the son of Howard Eugene Galbreath (324) and Maxine Amy Northam. Howard Eugene died in Dennison, Mill Twp., Tuscarawas Co., Ohio, on June 8, 2002, at age 63.

**368. Dennis Lynn<sup>11</sup> Galbreath** (*Howard Eugene<sup>10</sup>, Raymond Arthur<sup>9</sup>, James Howard<sup>8</sup>, Ella Nancy<sup>7</sup> Thompson, Nancy J.<sup>6</sup> Goudy, Andrew<sup>5</sup>, Elizabeth Jane<sup>4</sup> Pegan, Andrew<sup>3</sup> Pegan II, Andrew<sup>2</sup> Pagan, James<sup>1</sup>*) was born on May 2, 1944, in Dennison, Mill Twp., Tuscarawas Co., Ohio. He was the son of Howard Eugene Galbreath (324) and Maxine Amy Northam. Dennis Lynn died in Akron, Summit Co., Ohio, on June 15, 1992, at age 48.

He married **Jean Unknown.** They divorced. They have three children.

Dennis Lynn Galbreath married **Judith Ann Unknown.**

**369. Kenneth Duane<sup>11</sup> Gilmore II** (*Betty Jane<sup>10</sup> Galbreath, Raymond Arthur<sup>9</sup>, James Howard<sup>8</sup>, Ella Nancy<sup>7</sup> Thompson, Nancy J.<sup>6</sup> Goudy, Andrew<sup>5</sup>, Elizabeth Jane<sup>4</sup> Pegan, Andrew<sup>3</sup> Pegan II, Andrew<sup>2</sup> Pagan, James<sup>1</sup>*) was born on December 10, 1942, in Dennison, Mill Twp., Tuscarawas Co., Ohio. He was the son of Kenneth Duane Gilmore and Betty Jane Galbreath (325). Kenneth Duane lived in 2001 in San Jose, Santa Clara Co., California. He died in San Jose, Santa Clara Co., California, on January 24, 2004, at age 61. Kenneth Duane was buried in Mission City Memorial Park Cemetery, San Jose, Santa Clara Co., California.[135]

He married and had two sons.

**370. Linda Kay<sup>11</sup> Gilmore** (*Betty Jane<sup>10</sup> Galbreath, Raymond Arthur<sup>9</sup>, James Howard<sup>8</sup>, Ella Nancy<sup>7</sup> Thompson, Nancy J.<sup>6</sup> Goudy, Andrew<sup>5</sup>, Elizabeth Jane<sup>4</sup> Pegan, Andrew<sup>3</sup> Pegan II, Andrew<sup>2</sup> Pagan, James<sup>1</sup>*) was born in Dennison, Mill Twp.,

Tuscarawas Co., Ohio, on June 3, 1949. She was the daughter of Kenneth Duane Gilmore and Betty Jane Galbreath (325). She died in Dennison, Mill Twp., Tuscarawas Co., Ohio, on April 6, 1950. Linda Kay was buried in Evergreen Burial Park, New Philadelphia, Tuscarawas Co., Ohio.[58]

**371. Carol Kaye<sup>11</sup> Joos** was born in Lancaster, Fairfield Co., Ohio, on March 23, 1950. She was the daughter of Louis Joseph Joos and Virginia Lee Staley (329). She died in Fairfield, Lancaster Co., Ohio, on March 6, 1996. Carol Kaye was buried in Saint Mary Cemetery, Lancaster, Fairfield Co., Ohio.[136]

Never married.

**372. Susan Diane<sup>11</sup> Joos** (*Virginia L.<sup>10</sup> Staley, Clara Irene<sup>9</sup> Galbreath, James Howard<sup>8</sup>, Ella Nancy<sup>7</sup> Thompson, Nancy J.<sup>6</sup> Goudy, Andrew<sup>5</sup>, Elizabeth Jane<sup>4</sup> Pegan, Andrew<sup>3</sup> Pegan II, Andrew<sup>2</sup> Pagan, James<sup>1</sup>*) was born in Lancaster, Fairfield Co., Ohio on March 28, 1951. She was the daughter of Louis Joseph Joos and Virginia Lee Staley (329). She died in Waterford, Oakland Co., Michigan, on November 14, 1992, at age 41. Susan Diane was buried as Susan Salmond in Farmers Creek Cemetery, Metamora, Metamora Twp., Lapeer Co., Michigan.[E]

Susan Diane Joos married **Unknown Dionne.** They divorced.

Susan Diane Joos married **Mr. Salmond.** They divorced.

Susan Diane Joos Dionne Salmond married **Unknown Sharp** before 1992. They divorced.

**373. Christopher Brent<sup>11</sup> Joos** (*Virginia L.<sup>10</sup> Staley, Clara Irene<sup>9</sup> Galbreath, James Howard<sup>8</sup>, Ella Nancy<sup>7</sup> Thompson, Nancy J.<sup>6</sup> Goudy, Andrew<sup>5</sup>, Elizabeth Jane<sup>4</sup> Pegan, Andrew<sup>3</sup> Pegan II, Andrew<sup>2</sup> Pagan, James<sup>1</sup>*) was born in Lancaster, Fairfield Co., Ohio on January 22, 1959. He was the son of Louis Joseph Joos and Virginia Lee Staley (329). He died in Columbus, Franklin Co., Ohio, on June 11, 2018, at age 59.

Christopher Brent married **Gwendolyn S. Walker.** They divorced. They had one daughter.

Gwendolyn S. Walker was born in Columbus, Franklin Co., Ohio, on November 8, 1961. She reached age 56 and died in Wellston, Jackson Co., Ohio, on January 30, 2018.

**374. Don R.**[11] **Staley II** (*Don R.*[10], *Clara Irene*[9] *Galbreath, James Howard*[8], *Ella Nancy*[7] *Thompson, Nancy J.*[6] *Goudy, Andrew*[5], *Elizabeth Jane*[4] *Pegan, Andrew*[3] *Pegan II, Andrew*[2] *Pagan, James*[1]) was born on January 18, 1957, in Dover, Dover Twp., Tuscarawas Co., Ohio. He was the son of Don R. Staley (330) and Anna Mae Free. Don R. died in Dover, Dover Twp., Tuscarawas Co., Ohio, on October 14, 2012, at age 55.

He married and had one son, then divorced.

**375. Kirt Edwin**[11] **Goudy** (*Charles Andrew*[10], *Charles Andrew*[9], *Edwin Andrew*[8], *Andrew W.*[7], *William A.*[6], *Andrew*[5], *Elizabeth Jane*[4] *Pegan, Andrew*[3] *Pegan II, Andrew*[2] *Pagan, James*[1]) was born on September 25, 1975, in Wheeling, Ohio Co., West Virginia. He was the son of Son Goudy II (344) and his first wife. Kirt Edwin died in Wheeling, Ohio Co., West Virginia, on June 11, 2014, at age 38.

He married and had one son, then divorced.

**376. Christopher Kent**[11] **Withers** (*Robert Kent*[10], *Raymond Robert*[9], *Mary Grace*[8] *McNeill, Sarah Sanson*[7] *Hereford, Marianne Marilla*[6] *Goudy, William*[5], *Elizabeth Jane*[4] *Pegan, Andrew*[3] *Pegan II, Andrew*[2] *Pagan, James*[1]) was born on May 4, 1989, in Huntington, Cabell Co., West Virginia. He was the son of Robert Kent Withers (349) and Ms. Penick. Christopher Kent died in Huntington, Cabell Co., West Virginia, on June 10, 2007, at age 18. He was buried in Woodmere Memorial Park Cemetery, Huntington, Cabell Co., West Virginia.[66]

**377. John R.**[11] **McNeill** (*James Worthington*[10], *George Dean*[9], *Worthington Wilson*[8], *Sarah Sanson*[7] *Hereford, Marianne Marilla*[6] *Goudy, William*[5], *Elizabeth Jane*[4] *Pegan, Andrew*[3] *Pegan II, Andrew*[2] *Pagan, James*[1]) was born on December 25, 1961, in Goodland, Sherman Co., Kansas. He was the son of James Worthington McNeill (353) and Marilyn Grace House. John R. died in Goodland, Sherman Co., Kansas, on December 25, 1961. He was buried in Goodland Cemetery, Goodland, Sherman Co., Kansas.[67]

**378. Bill Ryan**[11] **McNeill** (*James Worthington*[10], *George Dean*[9], *Worthington Wilson*[8], *Sarah Sanson*[7] *Hereford, Marianne Marilla*[6] *Goudy, William*[5], *Elizabeth Jane*[4] *Pegan, Andrew*[3] *Pegan II, Andrew*[2] *Pagan, James*[1]) was born on September 19, 1963, in Goodland, Sherman Co., Kansas. He was the son of James Worthington McNeill (353) and Marilyn Grace House. Bill Ryan died in Goodland, Sherman Co., Kansas, in December 1980 at age. He was buried in Goodland Cemetery, Goodland, Sherman Co., Kansas.[67]

**379. Russell Wayne**[11] **Fair** (*Son*[10] *Fair, Hugh Hartley*[9], *Harold Stewart*[8], *Sarah Jessie*[7] *Cowl, Elizabeth Jane*[6] *Goudy, Isaac*[5], *Elizabeth Jane*[4] *Pegan, Andrew*[3] *Pegan II, Andrew*[2] *Pagan, James*[1]) was born on January 13, 1972, in New Brighton, Beaver Co., Pennsylvania. He was the son of Son Fair (357) and his wife. Russell Wayne died in New Brighton, Beaver Co., Pennsylvania, on January 14, 1972. He was buried in Lawn Haven Burial Estates, Worthington, Armstrong Co., Pennsylvania.[71]

**380. Michael Allen**[11] **Hammond II** (*Juanita Lee*[10] *Salus, Betty Jane*[9] *Helmbrecht, Alberta Anna*[8] *Goudy, Robert Carl*[7], *John William*[6], *Isaac*[5], *Elizabeth Jane*[4] *Pegan, Andrew*[3] *Pegan II, Andrew*[2] *Pagan, James*[1]) was born on June 20, 1981, in Youngstown, Mahoning Co., Ohio. He was the son of Mr. Hammond and Juanita Lee Salus (362). Michael Allen died in Youngstown, Mahoning Co., Ohio, on January 30, 2016, at age 34.

He married twice and had a child by each wife.

# Endnotes

1   Find A Grave—Wood Hill Cemetery, Marshall Co., West Virginia, Find A Grave.com.

2   Find A Grave—Warrenton Cemetery, Rayland, Warren Twp., Jefferson Co., Ohio, Find A Grave.com.

3   Missouri, Death Records 1834-1910, Ancestry.com, Wm. Goudy.

4   Find A Grave—Mount Olivet Cemetery, Wheeling, Ohio Co., West Virginia, Find A Grave.com.

5   West Virginia, Marriages Index, 1785-1971, Ancestry.com.

6   Newton, J.H., G.C. Nichols and A.G. Sprankle, *History of the Pan-Handle, West Virginia.* Wheeling, W.V.: J.A. Caldwell, pg. 410.

7   Find A Grave—Nashville National Cemetery, Nashville, Davidson Co., Tennessee., Find A Grave.com.

8   U.S. Veteran's Pension File, NARA—National Archives and Records Administration, 8601 Adelphi Road College Park, MD 20740-6001, William M. Goudy, Civil War Pension—Cert. # 333737, Application #537.162.

9   Find A Grave—Mount Wood Cemetery, Wheeling, Ohio Co., West Virginia, Find A Grave.com.

10  Find A Grave—Allen Grove Cemetery, Sherrard, Union Twp., Marshall Co., West Virginia, Find A Grave.com.

11  West Virginia, Deaths Index, 1853-1973, Ancestry.com, Charles Thoburn Goudy.

12  Find A Grave—Mount Rose Cemetery, Moundsville, Marshall Co., West Virginia, Find A Grave.com.

13  Find A Grave—Union Cemetery, Uhrichsville, Mill Twp., Tuscarawas Co., Ohio, Find A Grave.com.

14  Find A Grave—Riverview Cemetery, Martins Ferry, Pease Twp., Belmont Co., Ohio, Find A Grave.com.

15  Find A Grave—East State Street Cemetery, Newcomerstown, Oxford Twp., Tuscarawas Co., Ohio, Find A Grave.com.

16  Find A Grave—Union Cemetery, Steubenville, Cross Creek Twp., Jefferson Co., Ohio, Find A Grave.com.

17  Find A Grave—Dutch Valley Cemetery, Rush Twp., Tuscarawas Co., Ohio, Find A Grave.com.

18  Find A Grave—Linwood Cemetery, Blaine, Pease Twp., Belmont Co., Ohio, Find A Grave.com.

19  Find A Grave—Brooke Cemetery, Wellsburg, Brooke Co., West Virginia, Find A Grave.com.

20  Find A Grave—Forest Lawn Cemetery, Norfolk, Norfolk Co., Virginia, Find A Grave.com.

21  Missouri, Death Records 1834-1910, Ancestry.com, M. Van Buren Goudy.

22  Find A Grave—Eastwood IOOF Cemetery, Medford, Jackson Co., Oregon, Find A Grave.com.

23  West Virginia, Deaths Index, 1853-1973, Ancestry.com, Elizabeth Jane Cowl.

24  Find A Grave—Greenwood Cemetery, Wheeling, Ohio Co., West Virginia, Find A Grave.com.

25  West Virginia, Deaths Index, 1853-1973, Ancestry.com, Robert H. Goudy.

26  Find A Grave—Peninsula Cemetery, Wheeling, Ohio Co., West Virginia, Find A Grave.com.

27  Find A Grave—Stone Church Cemetery, Elm Grove, Ohio Co., West Virginia, Find A Grave.com.

28  Find A Grave—Mount Zion Cemetery, Wheeling, Ohio Co., West Virginia, Find A Grave.com.

29  West Virginia Marriages, 1853-1970, FamilySearch.org, James H. Goudy and Samantha Faunce.

30  Find A Grave—Claysville Cemetery, Claysville, Washington Co., Pennsylvania, Find A Grave.com.

31  Illinois, Deaths and Stillbirths Index, 1916-1947, Ancestry.com, J. Frank Goudy.

32  Graceland Cemetery Records, James Frank Goudy, Graceland Cemetery, 4001 North Clark Street Chicago, IL.

33  West Virginia, Deaths Index, 1853-1973, Ancestry.com, Effie May Goudy.

34  West Virginia, Deaths Index, 1853-1973, Ancestry.com, Harry Homer Goudy.

35  Find A Grave—Woodlawn Cemetery, Fairmont, Marion Co., West Virginia, Find A Grave.com.

36  West Virginia, Deaths Index, 1853-1973, Ancestry.com, Edmund Goudy.

37  West Virginia, Deaths Index, 1853-1973, Ancestry.com, Mary Bumgardner.

38  Find A Grave—McMechen Cemetery, McMechen, Union Dist., Marshall Co., West Virginia, Find A Grave.com.

39  Find A Grave—Gnadenhutten-Clay Union Cemetery, Clay Twp., Tuscarawas Co., Ohio, Find A Grave.com.

40  Find A Grave—Western Reserve Mausoleum, Warren, Trumbull Co., Ohio, Find A Grave.com.

41  Find A Grave—Evergreen Cemetery, Los Angeles, Los Angeles Co., California, Find A Grave.com.

42  Find A Grave—Rock Creek Cemetery, Washington, District of Columbia, Find A Grave.com.

43  Find A Grave—Oakhill Cemetery, Oakhurst, Madera Co., California, Find A Grave.com.

44  Find A Grave—Lone Oak Cemetery, Point Pleasant, Mason Co., West Virginia, Find A Grave.com.

45  Missouri, Death Records 1834-1910, Ancestry.com, Martha J. Goudy.

46  Find A Grave—Highland Cemetery, Cameron, Marshall Co., West Virginia, Find A Grave.com.

47  Find A Grave—Forest Lawn Memorial Park Cemetery, Glendale, Los Angeles Co., California, Find A Grave.com

48  Find A Grave—Sunset Memorial Park Cemetery, Galloway, Franklin Co., Ohio, Find A Grave.com.

49  Find A Grave—Ridge Hill Memorial Park Cemetery, Amherst, Amherst Twp., Lorraine Co., Ohio, Find A Grave.com.

50  Find A Grave—Greenwood Cemetery, Bellaire, Pultney Twp., Belmont Co., Ohio, Find A Grave.com.

51  Illinois Statewide Marriage Index 1763-1900, Illinois State Archives, Margaret Cross Norton Bldg. Capitol Complex, Springfield, Illinois 62756, James F. Goudy and Mary Jane Hudson, marriage cert. #00166278.

52  Graceland Cemetery Records, Mary Jane "Mamie" Goudy, Graceland Cemetery, 4001 North Clark Street Chicago, IL.

53  West Virginia, Marriages Index, 1785-1971, Ancestry.com, Harry Goudy and Minnie Stillwill.

54  West Virginia, Deaths Index, 1853-1973, Ancestry.com, Minnie Goudy.

55  Social Security Death Index, Ancestry.com.

56  Find A Grave—Limestone Cemetery, Limestone, Marshall Co., West Virginia, Find A Grave.com.

57  WW II Draft Registration Cards, 1942, Ancestry.com, Charles Daily Bumgardner.

58  Find A Grave—Evergreen Burial Park, New Philadelphia, Tuscarawas Co., Ohio, Find A Grave.com.

59  Find A Grave—Saint Joseph Cemetery, Massillon, Perry Twp., Stark Co., Ohio, Find A Grave.com.

60  Find A Grave—Ferncliff Cemetery, Springfield, Springfield Twp., Clark Co., Ohio, Find A Grave.com.

61  Find A Grave—West Park Cemetery, Cleveland, Cuyahoga Co., Ohio, Find A Grave.com.

62  Find A Grave—West Alexander Cemetery, West Alexander, Donegal Twp., Washington Co., Pennsylvania, Find A Grave.com.

63  U.S. Veteran's Gravesites, ca. 1775-2006, Ancestry.com, Robert Edwin Blankensop.

64  Find A Grave—White Chapel Memorial Park Cemetery, Troy, Oakland Co., Michigan, Find A Grave.com.

65  Find A Grave—Beale Chapel Cemetery, Apple Grove, Hannon Dist., Mason Co., West Virginia, Find A Grave.com.

66  Find A Grave—Woodmere Memorial Park Cemetery, Huntington, Cabell Co., West Virginia, Find A Grave.com.

67  Find A Grave—Goodland Cemetery, Goodland, Sherman Co., Kansas, Find A Grave.com.

68  Find A Grave—Golden Gate National Cemetery, San Bruno, San Mateo Co., California, Find A Grave.com.

69  Find A Grave—Riverside Cemetery, Waterville, Marshall Co., Kansas, Find A Grave.com.

70  Find A Grave—Siskiyou Memorial Park Cemetery, Medford, Jackson Co., Oregon, Find A Grave.com.

71  Find A Grave—Lawn Haven Burial Estates, Worthington, Armstrong Co., Pennsylvania, Find A Grave.com.

72  Find A Grave—Halcyon Hills Memorial Park Cemetery, Sherrard, Marshall Co., West Virginia, Find A Grave.com.

73  Find A Grave—Green Lawn Cemetery, Columbus, Franklin Co., Ohio, Find A Grave.com.

74  Find A Grave—Our Lady of Seven Dolors Cemetery, Triadelphia, Ohio Co., West Virginia, Find A Grave.com.

75  Find A Grave—Girard Liberty Union Cemetery, Girard, Trumbull Co., Ohio, Find A Grave.com.

76  Find A Grave—Mount Calvary Cemetery, Wheeling, Ohio Co., West Virginia, Find A Grave.com.

77  Find A Grave—Davis Cemetery, Bellaire, Pultney Twp., Belmont Co., Ohio, Find A Grave.com.

78  Find A Grave—Roselawn Memorial Park Cemetery, Terre Haute, Vigo County, Indiana, Find A Grave.com.

79  Find A Grave—Northview Cemetery, New Martinsville, Wetzel Co., West Virginia, Find A Grave.com.

80  Find A Grave—Pierce Brothers Valley Oaks Memorial Park Cemetery, Westlake Village, Los Angeles Co., California, Find A Grave.com.

81  Find A Grave—Springdale Cemetery and Mausoleum, Peoria, Peoria Twp., Peoria Co., Illinois, Find A Grave.com.

82  Find A Grave—Charles Evans Cemetery, Reading, Berks Co., Pennsylvania, Find A Grave.com.

83  Find A Grave—Fairview Cemetery, Moundsville, Marshall Co., West Virginia, Find A Grave.com.

84  West Virginia, Deaths Index, 1853-1973, Ancestry.com, Kirk Alexander Fisher.

85  Find A Grave—Longview Cemetery, Bowerston, Monroe Twp., Harrison Co., Ohio, Find A Grave.com.

86  Find A Grave—Saint Barbara Cemetery, Massillon, Perry Twp., Stark Co., Ohio, Find A Grave.com.

87  Find A Grave—Sunland Memorial Park Cemetery, Sun City, Maricopa Co., Arizona, Find A Grave.com.

88  Find A Grave—Center Cemetery, Conneaut, Conneaut Twp., Ashtabula Co., Ohio, Find A Grave.com.

89  Find A Grave—Napa Valley Memorial Park Cemetery, Napa, Napa Co., California, Find A Grave.com.

90  Find A Grave—Willis Cemetery, Willis, Montgomery Co., Texas, Find A Grave.com.

91  Find A Grave—Harvard Grove Cemetery, Cleveland, Cuyahoga Co., Ohio, Find A Grave.com.

92  Find A Grave—Germano Cemetery, Germano, German Twp., Harrison Co., Ohio, Find A Grave.com.

93  Find A Grave—Chestnut Grove Cemetery, Herndon, Fairfax Co., Virginia, Find A Grave.com.

94  Find A Grave—Alger Cemetery, Cleveland, Cuyahoga Co., Ohio, Find A Grave.com.

95  Find A Grave—Pacific Crest Cemetery, Redondo Beach, Los Angeles Co., California, Find A Grave.com.

96  Find A Grave—Long Island National Cemetery, Farmingdale, Suffolk Co., New York, Find A Grave.com.

97  Find A Grave—Good Shepherd Episcopal Church Columbarium, Parkersburg, Marshall Co., West Virginia, Find A Grave.com.

98  Kankakee County, Illinois Marriage Index, 1889-1962, Ancestry.com.

99  Find A Grave—Canyon Hill Cemetery, Caldwell, Canyon Co., Idaho, Find A Grave.com.

100 Find A Grave—Cortez Cemetery, Cortez, Montezuma Co., Colorado, Find A Grave.com.

101 Find A Grave—Fort Logan National Cemetery, Denver, Denver Co., Colorado, Find A Grave.com.

102 Find A Grave—Riverside National Cemetery, Riverside, Riverside Co., California, Find A Grave.com.

103 Find A Grave—Memory Gardens Memorial Park Cemetery, Medford, Jackson Co., Oregon, Find A Grave.com.

104 Find A Grave—Kittanning Cemetery, Kittanning Twp., Armstrong Co., Pennsylvania, Find A Grave.com.

105 Find A Grave—Slate Lick Cemetery, Kittanning Twp., Armstrong Co., Pennsylvania, Find A Grave.com.

106 Find A Grave—Center Hill Church of the Brethren Cemetery, Kittanning, Armstrong Co., Pennsylvania, Find A Grave.com.

107 Find A Grave—Fairview Cemetery, New Albany, Floyd Co., Indiana, Find A Grave.com.

108 Find A Grave—St. Clairsville Union Cemetery, St. Clairsville, Bellaire Twp., Belmont Co., Ohio, Find A Grave.com.

109 Find A Grave—Graysville Cemetery, Graysville, Washington Twp., Monroe Co., Ohio, Find A Grave.com.

110 Find A Grave—Calvary Cemetery, Youngstown, Mahoning Co., Ohio, Find A Grave.com.

111 Find A Grave—Crown Hill Burial Park Cemetery, Vienna Twp., Trumbull Co., Ohio, Find A Grave.com.

112 Find A Grave—Woodlawn Cemetery, Export, Westmoreland Co., Pennsylvania, Find A Grave.com.

113 Find A Grave—Wallace Memorial Cemetery, Crawley, Greenbrier Co., West Virginia, Find A Grave.com.

114 Find A Grave—Chattanooga National Cemetery, Chattanooga, Hamilton Co., Tennessee, Find A Grave.com.

115 Find A Grave—Arlington National Cemetery, Arlington, Virginia, Find A Grave.com.

116 Find A Grave—Turlock Memorial Park Cemetery, Turlock, Stanislaus Co., California, Find A Grave.com.

117 Find A Grave—San Joaquin Valley National Cemetery, Santa Nella, Merced Co., California, Find A Grave.com.

118 Find A Grave—New Alexandria Cemetery, New Alexandria, Ohio, Find A Grave.com.

119 Find A Grave—Mount Calvary Cemetery, Steubenville, Cross Creek Twp., Jefferson Co., Ohio, Find A Grave.com.

120 Find A Grave—Garland Brook Cemetery, Columbus, Bartholomew Co., Indiana., Find A Grave.com.

121 Find A Grave—Lakeside Memorial Park Cemetery, Hamburg, Erie Co., New York, Find A Grave.com.

122 Find A Grave—Parkview Memorial Gardens Cemetery, Wheeling, Ohio Co., West Virginia, Find A Grave.com.

123 Find A Grave—Ontario Cemetery, Ontario, Springfield Twp., Richland Co., Ohio, Find A Grave.com.

124 Find A Grave—Berger (Brethren) Cemetery, Baltic, Clark Twp., Holmes Co., Ohio, Find A Grave.com.

125 Find A Grave—Massillon City Cemetery, Massillon, Perry Twp., Stark Co., Ohio., Find A Grave.com.

126 Find A Grave—Sunset Hills Burial Park Cemetery, Canton, Stark Co., Ohio, Find A Grave.com.

127 Find A Grave—Orting Cemetery, Orting, Pierce Co., Washington, Find A Grave.com.

128 Find A Grave—Westwood Memorial Park Cemetery, Los Angeles, Los Angeles Co., California, Find A Grave.com.

129 Ohio, Birth Index, 1908-1964, Ancestry.com, Elizabeth H. McLaughlin, state file #1909011202.

130 Find A Grave—Milton Cemetery, Milton, Cabell Co., West Virginia, Find A Grave.com.

131 Find A Grave—Willamette National Cemetery, Portland, Multnomah Co., Oregon, Find A Grave.com.

132 Find A Grave—Tahoma National Cemetery, Kent, King Co., Washington, Find A Grave.com..

133 Find A Grave—Green View Cemetery, Powhatan Point, Marshall Co., West Virginia, Find A Grave.com.

134 Find A Grave—Fort Steuben Burial Estates, Wintersville, Toronto Twp., Jefferson Co., Ohio, Find A Grave.com.

135 Find A Grave—Mission City Memorial Park Cemetery, San Jose, Santa Clara Co., California, Find A Grave.com.

136 Find A Grave—Saint Mary Cemetery, Lancaster, Fairfield Co., Ohio, Find A Grave.com.

137 Find A Grave—Hollywood Cemetery, Richmond, Virginia, Find A Grave.com.

138 Find A Grave—Mount Allen Cemetery, Hays, Ellis Co., Kansas, Find A Grave.com.

139 Find A Grave—Mount Hope Cemetery, Topeka, Shawnee Co., Kansas, Find A Grave.com.

140 Find A Grave—Fairview Cemetery, Montezuma, Gray Co., Kansas, Find A Grave.com.

[A]  Find A Grave—Woodlawn Cemetery, Las Vegas, Clark Co., Nevada, Find A Grave.com.

[B]  Find A Grave—East Lawn Palms Cemetery, Tucson, Pima Co., Arizona, Find A Grave.com.

[C]  Find A Grave—Davis Memorial Park Cemetery, Las Vegas, Clark Co., Nevada, Find A Grave.com.

[D]  Find A Grave—Westhampton Memorial Park Cemetery, Tuckahoe, Henrico Co., Virginia, Find A Grave.com

[E]  Find A Grave—New Cumberland Cemetery, New Cumberland, Hancock Co., West Virginia, Find A Grave. com.

[F]  Find A Grave—Farmers Creek Cemetery, Metamora, Metamora Twp., Lapeer Co., Michigan, Find A Grave.com.

# Descendants of Mary Pegan VanAusdall

**1. Mary**[4] **Pegan** (*Andrew*[3] *Pegan, Andrew*[2] *Pagan, James*[1]) was born on June 3, 1795, in Strabane Twp., Washington Co., Pennsylvania. She was the daughter of Andrew Pegan II and Mary Unknown. Mary died in Otter Creek Twp., Jersey Co., Illinois, on April 17, 1872, at age 76. She was buried in Noble Cemetery, Otterville, Otter Creek Twp., Jersey Co., Illinois.[1]

Her surname is seen as Pegan and Pagan.

Mary married **John VanAusdall** about 1814 in Strabane Twp., Washington Co., Pennsylvania? They had at least eight children, probably more. John VanAusdall was born in York Co., Pennsylvania? on February 28, 1784. He reached age 81 and died in Otter Creek Twp., Jersey Co., Illinois, on November 6, 1865. John was buried in Noble Cemetery, Otterville, Otter Creek Twp., Jersey Co., Illinois.[1]

John worked as a cooper or barrel maker.

A biography of their youngest child Allen McCrary VanAusdall in *The History of Jersey County, Illinois*, says that John Vanausdall was from Pennsylvania and Mary Pegan VanAusdall hailed from Marietta, Ohio. This does not agree with census and other data. This book also says that John and Mary were married in Ohio, but no marriage record has been found for them in either Ohio or Virginia. They seem to have married in Pennsylvania, which did not keep civil marriage records in that era.[2]

In another biographical sketch of Allen M. Vanausdall, from the *History of Greene and Jersey Counties, Illinois*, states that John and Mary Pegan VanAusdall lived in Vincennes, Knox Co., Indiana in 1812 and "near Waterloo" in Monroe County, Illinois in 1824 before settling in Jersey County, Illinois in 1846.[3]

This is also erroneous. While John VanAusdall could have been stationed at Fort Vincennes in Vincennes, Indiana during the War of 1812, it is evident that after the war he returned to Washington Co., Pennsylvania or Brooke County (West) Virginia, where Mary Pegan VanAusdall was still living with her parents.

After their marriage, John and Mary Pegan VanAusdall did move to Ohio, as their eldest child, Margaret VanAusdall Hamilton, born in 1816, says on census records that her birthplace was that state. Was she born in Marietta, Marietta Twp., Washington Co., Ohio, and was that why her younger brother Allen thought their mother was from there?

By 1820, however, John and Mary Pegan VanAusdall were residing with or near Andrew and Mary Unknown Pegan II in the newly formed Salem Twp., Highland Co., Ohio. John VanAusdall (transcribed as "Vannossale?") signs the petition of May 15, 1820 in Salem Twp., Highland Co., Ohio asking for another justice of the peace for the new township. His signature is just below that of his father-in-law, Andrew Pegan II.[4]

Mary Pegan VanAusdall and her two children seem to be living with her parents, Andrew and Mary Unknown Pegan II, in Salem Twp., Highland County, Ohio in 1820 (*Census Place: Salem, Highland, Ohio; Roll: M33_92; Page: 37; Image: 44*). Andrew Pegan II is enumerated as "Andrew Pegans" in that census. In the household are one male under age 10, one male 26-45, one male more than age 45 (Andrew); one female under age 10, one female 16-26 and one female 26-45 (this is probably an error, as in Andrew's July 1821 court appearance for his pension hearing, he says his wife is 70 years old, and bible records prove that Mary Unknown Pegan is still alive).

The female 16-26 is most likely daughter Mary Pegan VanAusdall, as she is the only one of Andrew II's daughters in that age group. The two children under age 10 are Mary Pegan VanAusdall's daughter Margaret and a son, whose name is unknown and who seems to have died in childhood. Her husband, John VanAusdall, is not in the household. He may have been in Butler County, Ohio preparing for their move there.

Although the *History of Greene and Jersey Counties, Illinois* says John and Mary Pegan VanAusdall lived "near Waterloo" in Monroe County, Illinois in 1824 before settling in Jersey County, Illinois in 1846, this is also incorrect.[3] John and Mary's son Caleb VanAusdall's tombstone says he was born on March 29, 1827 in Butler County, Ohio, and the VanAusdall family is enumerated there in 1830.

In 1830, John and Mary Pegan VanAusdall are enumerated in Ross Twp., Butler Co., Ohio *(Census Place: Ross, Butler, Ohio; Series: M19; Roll: 127; Page: 154)*. There is a one in col. 1, a two in col. 2, a one in col. 3, and a one in col. 7; a one in col. 14, a one in col. 15, a one in col. 17, and a one in col. 19. (one male under age 5, two males age five to nine, one male age 10-14 and a male (age 40-50 (John); one female under age 5, one female age 5-9, and one female age 15-20, and one female age 30-40 (Mary). This would correspond with the 1820 data for John, Mary, and the two eldest children.

Two of John and Mary Pegan VanAusdall's sons are buried in Miles Cemetery in Miles Cemetery (also known as Eagle Cliffs Cemetery), in Bluff Twp., Monroe Co., Illinois. The first was interred in 1843, the second in 1845. It is probable that John and Mary Pegan VanAusdall moved from Butler County, Ohio to Monroe County, Illinois in 1834, not 1824, and to Jersey County, Illinois in 1846.

In 1840, John and Mary Pegan VanAusdall are found in Monroe Co., Illinois *(Census Place: Monroe, Illinois; Roll: 66; Page: 336)*. There is a one in col. 1, a one in col. 2, a 1 in col. 3, a one in col. 4, a one in col. 5, and a one in col. 8; a one in col. 15, a one in col. 17, and a one in col. 20. (one male under five years old, one male age five to nine, one male 10-14, one male 15-19, one male 20-29, and one male 50-59; one female age five-nine, one female 15-19, and one female 40-49.) Son Caleb's age seems to be wrong.

John and Mary Pegan VanAusdall are living in Township 7, Range 12 (later Jersey Twp.) in Jersey Co., Illinois in 1850 *(Census Place: Township 7 Range 12, Jersey, Illinois; Roll: M432_111; Page: 44B; Image: 96). In the home are John VanAusdall, age 65, a cooper; Mary VanAusdall, 55, and youngest son Allen, 11. John and Mary were born in Pennsylvania and Allen in Illinois.*

The John VanAusdalls are not enumerated in the 1860 census, but other sources indicate they are still living in Jersey Twp., Jersey Co., Illinois.

The widow Mary Pegan VanAusdall is residing with her son Allen's family in Township 7, Range 12 (Jersey Twp.), Jersey Co., Illinois in 1870 *(Census Place: Township 7 Range 12, Jersey, Illinois; Roll: M593_233; Page: 779B; Image: 362441). Mary, age 75, says she is a Pennsylvania native.*

The *History of Greene and Jersey Counties, Illinois* gives John VanAusdall's birth date as March 29, 1785 in Pennsylvania and his death date as November 6, 1865.[3] This corresponds with the inscription on his tombstone: died November 6, 1865, age 81 years, 7 months, 8 days. Mary Pegan VanAusdall's death date is stated as April 7, 1872, and that she was a Virginian by birth. This does not match with census data, as she says on her 1850 and 1860 census forms that she was born in Pennsylvania and her father Andrew Pegan II was living in Strabane Twp., Washington Co., Pennsylvania in 1800. Andrew did not move to Brooke Co., (West) Virginia until after that, where he is found in the 1810 census.

John and Mary VanAusdall's descendants use various spellings of the surname: Vanausdall and Vanausdoll are the most common.

Children of Mary Pegan and John VanAusdall:

+ 2   f   I.   **Margaret**[5] **VanAusdall** was born in Marietta, Marietta Twp., Washington Co., Ohio? in 1816. She died in Otter Creek Twp., Jersey Co., Illinois, on June 23, 1861. Margaret was buried in Noble Cemetery, Otterville, Otter Creek Twp., Jersey Co., Illinois.[1]

+ 3   m   II.   **Son One⁵ VanAusdall** was born in Union Twp., Highland Co., Ohio, in 1820. He died in Miles Twp., Monroe Co., Illinois, on August 22, 1843. Son One was buried in Miles Cemetery (Eagle Bluffs Cemetery), Bluff Twp., Monroe Co., Illinois.[5]

+ 4   m   III.   **Son Two⁵ VanAusdall** was born in Union Twp., Highland Co., Ohio or Ross Twp., Butler Co., Ohio, between 1820 and 1825. He died after 1840.

+ 5   m   IV.   **Mindred⁵ VanAusdall** was born in Union Twp., Highland Co., Ohio or Ross Twp., Butler Co., Ohio, between 1820 and 1825. He died in Bluff Twp., Monroe Co., Illinois?, in April 1845. Mindred was buried Miles Cemetery (Eagle Bluffs Cemetery), Bluff Twp., Monroe Co., Illinois.[5]

+ 6   f   V.   **Rachel C.⁵ VanAusdall** was born in Union Twp., Highland Co., Ohio or Ross Twp., Butler Co., Ohio, on May 17, 1825. She died in Otter Creek Twp., Jersey Co., Illinois, on December 17, 1878. Rachel C. was buried in Noble Cemetery, Otterville, Otter Creek Twp., Jersey Co., Illinois.[1]

+ 7   m   VI.   **Caleb⁵ VanAusdall** was born in Ross Twp., Butler Co., Ohio, on March 29, 1827. He died in Otter Creek Twp., Jersey Co., Illinois, on August 11, 1880. Caleb was buried in Noble Cemetery, Otterville, Otter Creek Twp., Jersey Co., Illinois.[1]

+ 8   f   VII.   **Mary Jane⁵ VanAusdall** was born in Ross Twp., Butler Co., Ohio on Jun 10, 1829. 1825 She died in Mississippi Twp. or Jersey Twp., Jersey Co., Illinois, on December 29, 1858. She was buried in Noble Cemetery, Otterville, Otter Creek Twp., Jersey Co., Illinois.[1]

+ 9   m   VIII.   **Allen McCreary⁵ VanAusdall** was born in Waterloo, Fountain Twp., Monroe Co., Illinois, on August 4, 1839. He died in Otterville, Otter Creek Twp., Jersey Co., Illinois, on November 19, 1932. Allen McCreary was buried in Noble Cemetery, Otterville, Otter Creek Twp., Jersey Co., Illinois.[1]

# 5<sup>th</sup> Generation

2. **Margaret<sup>5</sup> VanAusdall** (*Mary<sup>4</sup> Pegan, Andrew<sup>3</sup> Pegan II, Andrew<sup>2</sup> Pagan, James<sup>1</sup>*) was born in 1816 in in Marietta, Marietta Twp., Washington Co., Ohio? She was the daughter of John VanAusdall and Mary Pegan (1). Margaret died in Otter Creek Twp., Jersey Co., Illinois, on June 23, 1861, at age 45. She was buried in Noble Cemetery, Otterville, Otter Creek Twp., Jersey Co., Illinois.[1]

Margaret Vanausdoll Hamilton had four known children, but only the youngest lived to adulthood. Some undocumented internet sources have her death taking place in Vincennes, Vincennes Twp., Knox Co., Indiana, but all indications are she was living in Otter Creek Twp., Jersey Co., Illinois when she died.

She married **Jason H. Hamilton on** March 3, 1836 in Monroe Co., Illinois. They had four children. Jason H. Hamilton was born in Marietta, Marietta Twp., Washington Co., Ohio, on December 12, 1814. He reached age 83 and died on March 28, 1894 in Grafton, Quarry Twp., Jersey Co. Illinois. He may be buried in Noble Cemetery, Otterville, Otter Creek Twp., Jersey Co., Illinois.

Children of Margaret VanAusdall and Jason H. Hamilton:

+ 10   f   I.   **Henrietta<sup>6</sup> Hamilton** was born in Bluff Twp., Monroe Co., Illinois, on July 22, 1837. She died in Otter Creek Twp., Jersey Co., Illinois, on February 14, 1848. Henrietta was buried in Noble Cemetery, Otterville, Otter Creek Twp., Jersey Co., Illinois.[1]

+ 11   f   II.   **Melcinia<sup>6</sup> Hamilton** was born in Otter Creek Twp., Jersey Co., Illinois, on February 5, 1843. She died in Otter Creek Twp., Jersey Co., Illinois, on October 28, 1843. Melcinia was buried in Noble Cemetery, Otterville, Otter Creek Twp., Jersey Co., Illinois.[1]

+ 12   f   III.   **Emily<sup>6</sup> Hamilton** was born in Otter Creek Twp., Jersey Co., Illinois, in 1848. She died in Otter Creek Twp., Jersey Co., Illinois, on July 7, 1851.

+ 13   m   IV.   **Sylvester<sup>6</sup> Hamilton** was born in Otter Creek Twp., Jersey Co., Illinois, on July 20, 1854. He died in Chester, Chester Twp., Randolph Co., Illinois, on February 18, 1931. Sylvester was buried in Evergreen Cemetery, Chester, Chester Twp., Randolph Co., Illinois.[6]

3. **Son One<sup>5</sup> VanAusdoll** (*Mary<sup>4</sup> Pegan, Andrew<sup>3</sup> Pegan II, Andrew<sup>2</sup> Pagan, James<sup>1</sup>*) was born in 1820 in Union Twp., Highland Co., Ohio. He was the son of John VanAusdall and Mary Pegan (1). Son One died in Miles Twp., Monroe Co., Illinois, on August 22, 1843, at age 23. He was buried in Miles Cemetery (Eagle Bluffs Cemetery), Bluff Twp., Monroe Co., Illinois.[5]

4. **Son Two<sup>5</sup> VanAusdall** (*Mary<sup>4</sup> Pegan, Andrew<sup>3</sup> Pegan II, Andrew<sup>2</sup> Pagan, James<sup>1</sup>*) was born between 1820 and 1825 in Union Twp., Highland Co., Ohio or Ross Twp., Butler Co., Ohio. He was the son of John VanAusdall and Mary Pegan (1). Son Two died after 1830.

5. **Mindred<sup>5</sup> VanAusdall** (*Mary<sup>4</sup> Pegan, Andrew<sup>3</sup> Pegan II, Andrew<sup>2</sup> Pagan, James<sup>1</sup>*) was born between 1820 and 1825 in Union Twp., Highland Co., Ohio or Ross Twp., Butler Co., Ohio. He was the son of John VanAusdall and Mary Pegan (1). Mindred died in Bluff Twp., Monroe Co., Illinois, in April 1845. He was buried in Miles Cemetery (Eagle Bluffs Cemetery), Bluff Twp., Monroe Co., Illinois.[5]

6. **Rachel C.<sup>5</sup> VanAusdall** (*Mary<sup>4</sup> Pegan, Andrew<sup>3</sup> Pagan II, Andrew<sup>2</sup> Pagan, James<sup>1</sup>*) was born on May 17, 1825, in Union Twp., Highland Co., Ohio or Ross Twp., Butler Co., Ohio. She was the daughter of John VanAusdall and Mary Pegan (1). Rachel C. died in Otter Creek Twp., Jersey Co., Illinois,

on December 17, 1878, at age 53. She was buried in Noble Cemetery, Otterville, Otter Creek Twp., Jersey Co., Illinois.[1]

Rachel C. married **Henry Spangle Rogers** on November 14, 1844, in Monroe Co., Illinois. They had eight children. Henry Spangle Rogers was born in Jefferson Twp., Scioto Co., Ohio, on May 27, 1821. Henry Spangle reached age 76 and died in Oer Creek Twp., Jersey Co., Illinois, on November 19, 1897. He was buried in Noble Cemetery, Otterville, Otter Creek Twp., Jersey Co., Illinois.[1]

Henry S. Rogers had various occupations: He was a farmer, the owner and publisher of the *Franklin (IN) Jeffersonian* newspaper for two years, and a blacksmith.

Children of Rachel C. VanAusdall and Henry Spangle Rogers:

+ 14 m I. **Austin J.**[6] **Rogers** was born in Otter Creek Twp., Jersey Co., Illinois, on April 6, 1847. He died in Grafton, Quarry Twp., Jersey Co., Illinois, on November 13, 1878.

+ 15 f II. **Desdemona**[6] **Rogers** was born in Otter Creek Twp., Jersey Co., Illinois, on October 25, 1849. She died in Otter Creek Twp., Jersey Co., Illinois, on March 2, 1865.

+ 16 f III. **Mary E.**[6] **Rogers** was born in Otter Creek Twp., Jersey Co., Illinois, on December 18, 1851. She was also known as **Molly**. Mary E. died in Denver, Denver Co., Colorado, on April 17, 1915. She was buried in Crown Hill Cemetery, Wheat Ridge, Jefferson Co., Colorado.[7]

+ 17 m IV. **William Cornelius**[6] **Rogers** was born in Otter Creek Twp., Jersey Co., Illinois, on August 22, 1854. William Cornelius died in Otter Creek Twp., Jersey Co., Illinois, on May 18, 1892.

+ 18 m V. **John Vanausdoll**[6] **Rogers** was born in Otter Creek Twp., Jersey Co., Illinois, on February 11, 1857. He died in Alton, Alton Twp., Madison Co., Illinois, on June 6, 1937. John Vanausdoll. was buried in Oakwood Cemetery, Upper Alton, Alton Twp., Madison Co., Illinois.[8]

+ 19 f VI. **Margaret H.**[6] **Rogers** was born in Otter Creek Twp., Jersey Co., Illinois, on October 2, 1860. She died in Otter Creek Twp., Jersey Co., Illinois, on May 22, 1862.

+ 20 f VII. **Theresa C.**[6] **Rogers** was born in Otter Creek Twp., Jersey Co., Illinois, on March 6, 1863. She died in Frankfort Heights (now West Frankfort), Denning Twp., Franklin Co., Illinois, on December 8, 1919. Theresa C. was buried in OddFellows Cemetery, Benton Twp., Franklin Co., Illinois.[9]

+ 21 f VIII. **Rowena Maude**[6] **Rogers** was born in Otter Creek Twp., Jersey Co., Illinois, on August 13, 1865. She died in Santa Ana, Orange Co., California, on November 14, 1942. Rowena Maude was buried in Melrose Abbey Memorial Park Cemetery, Anaheim, Orange Co., California.[10]

7. **Caleb**[5] **Vanausdoll** (*Mary*[4] *Pegan, Andrew*[3] *Pegan II, Andrew*[2] *Pagan, James*[1]) was born on March 29, 1827, in Butler Co., Ohio. He was the son of John VanAusdall and Mary Pegan (1). Caleb lived in 1860 in Grafton Twp., (now Quarry Twp East), Jersey Co., Illinois. He also resided in 1870 in Township 7, Range 12, Jersey Co., Illinois. Caleb was living in 1880 in Otter Creek Twp., Jersey Co., Illinois. He died in Otter Creek Twp., Jersey Co., Illinois, on August 11, 1880, at age 53. Caleb was buried in Noble Cemetery, Otterville, Otter Creek Twp., Jersey Co., Illinois.[1]

Caleb married **Martha Hewitt** about 1852 in Christian Co., Illinois? They had twelve children. Martha Hewitt was born in Hamilton Co., Ohio, on February 20, 1835. Martha reached age 56 and died in Otter Creek Twp., Jersey Co., Illinois, on May 10, 1891. She was buried in Noble Cemetery, Otterville, Otter Creek Twp., Jersey Co., Illinois.[1]

Children of Caleb Vanausdoll and Martha Hewitt:

+ 22 m I. **Loring or Loren Earl[6] Vanausdoll** was born in Grafton Twp., (now Quarry Twp East), Jersey Co., Illinois, on February 24, 1853. He died in Wood River Twp., Madison Co., Illinois, on November 4, 1928. Loring or Loren Earl was buried in Noble Cemetery, Otterville, Otter Creek Twp., Jersey Co., Illinois.[1]

+ 23 m II. **Louis N.[6] Vanausdoll** was born in Grafton Twp., (now Quarry Twp East), Jersey Co., Illinois, on September 3, 1856. He died in English Twp., Jersey Co., Illinois, on October 17, 1931. Louis N. was buried in Noble Cemetery, Otterville, Otter Creek Twp., Jersey Co., Illinois.[1]

+ 24 f III. **Martha Jane[6] Vanausdoll** was born in Grafton Twp., (now Quarry Twp East), Jersey Co., Illinois, on September 12, 1857. She died in Dawson, Grant Twp., Richardson Co., Nebraska, on November 13, 1917. Martha Jane was buried in Humboldt Cemetery, Humboldt, Humboldt Twp., Richardson Co., Nebraska.[11]

+ 25 m IV. **John[6] Vanausdoll** was born in Grafton Twp., (now Quarry Twp East), Jersey Co., Illinois, in 1858. He died in Grafton Twp., (now Quarry Twp East), Jersey Co., Illinois, before 1860.

+ 26 f V. **Mary Ellen[6] Vanausdoll** was born in Grafton Twp., (now Quarry Twp East), Jersey Co., Illinois, on October 3, 1859. She died in Dawson, Grant Twp., Richardson Co., Nebraska, on March 2, 1943. Mary Ellen was buried in Table Rock Cemetery, Table Rock Twp., Pawnee Co., Nebraska.[12]

+ 27 m VI. **William Cornelius[6] Vanausdoll** was born in Montgomery Co., Illinois, on September 3, 1861. He died in Mississippi Twp., Jersey Co., Illinois, on June 2, 1943. William Cornelius was buried in Noble Cemetery, Otterville, Otter Creek Twp., Jersey Co., Illinois.[1]

+ 28 m VII. **Charles Wesley[6] Vanausdoll** was born in Grafton Twp., (now Quarry Twp East), Jersey Co., Illinois, on August 22, 1863. He died in Quarry Twp., Jersey Co., Illinois, on November 1, 1939. Charles Wesley was buried in Scenic Hill/Odd Fellows Cemetery, Quarry Twp., Jersey Co., Illinois.[13, 14]

+ 29 f VIII. **Cora Alice[6] Vanausdoll** was born in Grafton Twp., (now Quarry Twp East), Jersey Co., Illinois, in February 1867. She died in Lowell Twp., Cherokee Co., Kansas, on July 15, 1922. Cora Alice was buried in Oak Hill Cemetery, Galena, Cherokee Co., Kansas.[15]

+ 30 m IX. **Allen M.[6] Vanausdoll** was born in Grafton Twp., (now Quarry Twp East), Jersey Co., Illinois, on November 11, 1869. He died in Otter Creek Twp., Jersey Co., Illinois, on January 15, 1949. Allen M. was buried in Noble

Cemetery, Otterville, Otter Creek Twp., Jersey Co., Illinois.[1]

+ 31  f  X.  **Alice or Daughter⁶ Vanausdoll** was born in Grafton Twp., (now Quarry Twp East), Jersey Co., Illinois, in 1872. She died in Grafton Twp., (now Quarry Twp East), Jersey Co., Illinois, before 1880.

+ 32  m  XI.  **James Cornelius⁶ Vanausdoll** was born in Grafton Twp., (now Quarry Twp East), Jersey Co., Illinois, on October 21, 1874. He died in Dow, Mississippi Twp., Jersey Co., Illinois, on October 4, 1967. James Cornelius was buried in Noble Cemetery, Otterville, Otter Creek Twp., Jersey Co., Illinois.[1]

+ 33  f  XII.  **Ida B.⁶ Vanausdoll** was born in Grafton Twp., (now Quarry Twp East), Jersey Co., Illinois, in 1876. She died in Otter Creek Twp., Jersey Co., Illinois, on January 18, 1881. Ida B. was buried in Noble Cemetery, Otterville, Otter Creek Twp., Jersey Co., Illinois.[1]

8. **Mary Jane⁵ VanAusdall** (*Mary⁴ Pegan, Andrew³ Pegan II, Andrew² Pagan, James¹*) was born on June 10, 1829, in Ross Twp., Butler Co., Ohio. She was the daughter of John VanAusdall and Mary Pegan (1). She and died at age 29 in Mississippi Twp. or Jersey Twp., Jersey Co., Illinois on December 29, 1858. Mary Jane was buried in Noble Cemetery, Otterville, Otter Creek Twp., Jersey Co., Illinois.[1]

Mary Jane married **John Waggoner** on October 29, 1849, in Jersey Co., Illinois. John Waggoner was born in Greene Co., Illinois on August 16, 1828. John reached age 71 and died in Mississippi Twp. or Jersey Twp., Jersey Co., Illinois on May 5, 1859. John was buried in Noble Cemetery, Otterville, Otter Creek Twp., Jersey Co., Illinois.[1]

9. **Allen McCreary⁵ VanAusdall** (*Mary⁴ Pegan, Andrew³ Pegan II, Andrew² Pagan, James¹*) was

born on August 4, 1839, in Waterloo, Fountain Twp., Monroe Co., Illinois. He was the son of John VanAusdall and Mary Pegan (1). He died in Otterville, Otter Creek Twp., Jersey Co., Illinois, on November 19, 1932, at age 93. Allen McCreary was buried in Noble Cemetery, Otterville, Otter Creek Twp., Jersey Co., Illinois.[1]

Allen McCreary married **Agnes Ann Hillman** on May 6, 1860, in Jersey Co., Illinois. They had eleven children. Agnes Ann Hillman was born in Iowa on January 28, 1844. Agnes Ann reached age 71 and died in Otterville, Otter Creek Twp., Jersey Co., Illinois, on July 28, 1915. In 1900, Agnes Unknown Vanausdoll says she has born 11 children, but only three were still alive in 1900.

Allen M.'s surname is seen as VanAusdall and Vanausdoll. Allen "Vanausdoll", carpenter, has a biography in "The History of Jersey County" chapter of *The History of Greene and Jersey Counties, Illinois*.[3]

Children of Allen McCreary Vanausdoll and Agnes Ann Hillman:

+ 34  I.  **James⁶ Vanausdoll** was born in Jersey Co., Illinois, about 1862. He died in Jersey Co., Illinois, before 1870.

+ 35  f  II.  **Rachel Roseanna⁶ Vanausdoll** was born in Grafton Twp., (now Quarry Twp East), Jersey Co., Illinois, on December 11, 1864. She was also known as **Rosa** and **Rose**. Rachel Roseanna died in Alton, Alton Twp., Madison Co., Illinois, on December 28, 1940. She was buried in Oak Grove Cemetery, Jerseyville, Jersey Twp., Jersey Co., Illinois.[16]

+ 36  m  III.  **Edwin⁶ Vanausdoll** was born in Grafton Twp., (now Quarry Twp East), Jersey Co., Illinois, in 1866. He died in Otterville, Otter Creek Twp., Jersey Co., Illinois, before 1885.

+ 37   f   IV.   **Martha**[6] **Vanausdoll** was born in Grafton Twp., (now Quarry Twp East), Jersey Co., Illinois, on August 29, 1869. She was also known as **Mattie.** Martha died in Otterville, Otter Creek Twp., Jersey Co., Illinois, on March 8, 1888. She was buried in Noble Cemetery, Otterville, Otter Creek Twp., Jersey Co., Illinois.[1]

+ 38   m   V.   **John**[6] **Vanausdoll** was born in Grafton Twp., (now Quarry Twp East), Jersey Co., Illinois, about 1871. He died in Otterville, Otter Creek Twp., Jersey Co., Illinois, before 1880.

+ 39   f   VI.   **Millie Wyona**[6] **Vanausdoll** was born in Otterville, Otter Creek Twp., Jersey Co., Illinois, on September 6, 1874. She was also known as **Milly.** Millie Wyona died in Jerseyville, Jersey Twp., Jersey Co., Illinois, on July 13, 1957. She was buried in Valhalla Memorial Park and Mausoleum, Godfrey, Godfrey Twp., Madison Co., Illinois.[17]

+ 40   f   VII.   **Lillie**[6] **Vanausdoll** was born in Otterville, Otter Creek Twp., Jersey Co., Illinois, on September 6, 1874. She was also known as **Lilly.** Lillie died in Otterville, Otter Creek Twp., Jersey Co., Illinois, between 1885 and 1900.

+ 41   f   VIII.   **Mary or Mamie**[6] **Vanausdoll** was born in Otterville, Otter Creek Twp., Jersey Co., Illinois, in 1876. She was also known as **Mamie.** Mary or Mamie died in Otterville, Otter Creek Twp., Jersey Co., Illinois, in November 1881.

+ 42   f   IX.   **Sarah**[6] **Vanausdoll** was born in Otterville, Otter Creek Twp., Jersey Co., Illinois, about 1878. She died in Otterville, Otter Creek Twp., Jersey Co., Illinois, before 1880.

+ 43   m   X.   **Frederick**[6] **Vanausdoll** was born in Otterville, Otter Creek Twp., Jersey Co., Illinois, about 1880. He died in Otterville, Otter Creek Twp., Jersey Co., Illinois, before 1885.

+ 44   m   XI.   **Ebert Sylvester**[6] **Van Ausdall** was born in Otterville, Otter Creek Twp., Jersey Co., Illinois, on March 22, 1883. He died in Godfrey, Godfrey Twp., Madison Co., Illinois, on May 10, 1959. Ebert Sylvester was buried in Valhalla Memorial Park and Mausoleum, Godfrey, Godfrey Twp., Madison Co., Illinois.[14]

# 6th Generation

**10. Henrietta⁶ Hamilton** (*Margaret⁵ VanAusdall, Mary⁴ Pegan, Andrew³ Pegan II, Andrew² Pagan, James¹*) was born on July 22, 1837, in Bluff Twp., Monroe Co., Illinois. She was the daughter of Jason H. Hamilton and Margaret VanAusdall (2). Henrietta died in Otter Creek Twp., Jersey Co., Illinois, on February 14, 1848, at age 10. She was buried in Noble Cemetery, Otterville, Otter Creek Twp., Jersey Co., Illinois.[1]

**11. Melcinia⁶ Hamilton** (*Margaret⁵ VanAusdall, Mary⁴ Pegan, Andrew³ Pegan II, Andrew² Pagan, James¹*) was born on February 5, 1843, in Otter Creek Twp., Jersey Co., Illinois. She was the daughter of Jason H. Hamilton and Margaret VanAusdall (2). Melcinia died in Otter Creek Twp., Jersey Co., Illinois, on October 28, 1843. She was buried in Noble Cemetery, Otterville, Otter Creek Twp., Jersey Co., Illinois.[1]

**12. Emily⁶ Hamilton** (*Margaret⁵ VanAusdall, Mary⁴ Pegan, Andrew³ Pegan II, Andrew² Pagan, James¹*) was born in 1848 in Otter Creek Twp., Jersey Co., Illinois. She was the daughter of Jason H. Hamilton and Margaret VanAusdall (2). Emily died in Otter Creek Twp., Jersey Co., Illinois, on July 7, 1851, at age three.

**13. Sylvester⁶ Hamilton** (*Margaret⁵ VanAusdall, Mary⁴ Pegan, Andrew³ Pegan II, Andrew² Pagan, James¹*) was born on July 20, 1854, in Otter Creek Twp., Jersey Co., Illinois. He was the son of Jason H. Hamilton and Margaret VanAusdall (2). Sylvester died in Chester, Chester Twp., Randolph Co., Illinois, on February 18, 1931, at age 76. He was buried in Evergreen Cemetery, Chester, Chester Twp., Randolph Co., Illinois.[3]

Sylvester Hamilton, age 15, is not living with his father Jason H. Hamilton and Jason's second wife in the 1870 census. A fisherman, Sylvester lived in 1910 in South Fork, Fulton Co., Arkansas.

Sylvester married **Amy Talitha Carrico** on November 5, 1874, in Macoupin Co., Illinois. They had six children. Amy Talitha Carrico was born in Virden Twp., Macoupin Co., Illinois, on August 8, 1852. Amy Talitha reached age 60 and died in Camp, Fulton Co., Arkansas, on October 12, 1912.

Children of Sylvester Hamilton and Amy Talitha Carrico:

+ 45   m   I.   **Harry Leonard⁷ Hamilton** was born in Otterville, Otter Creek Twp., Jersey Co., Illinois, on May 14, 1875. He died in Los Angeles, Los Angeles Co., California, on August 9, 1960.

+ 46   m   II.  **Daniel Lester⁷ Hamilton** was born in Otterville, Otter Creek Twp., Jersey Co., Illinois, on September 6, 1879. He was also known as **Lester.** Daniel Lester died in Wickcliffe, Ballard Co., Kentucky, on January 25, 1949. He was buried in Evergreen Cemetery, Chester, Chester Twp., Randolph Co., Illinois.[3]

+ 47   f   III. **Jessie J.⁷ Hamilton** was born in Grafton, Quarry Twp., Jersey Co., Illinois, in January 1886. She died after 1911.

+ 48   f   IV.  **Doris Margaret⁷ Hamilton** was born in Grafton, Quarry Twp., Jersey Co., Illinois, on December 19, 1887. She died in Los Angeles, Los Angeles Co., California.

+ 49   m   V.   **Silas Vanculen⁷ Hamilton** was born in Grafton, Quarry Twp., Jersey Co., Illinois, on January 23, 1890. He died in a hospital in Kirkwood, St. Louis Co., Missouri, on January 27, 1965. Silas Vanculen was buried in Evergreen Cemetery, Chester, Chester Twp., Randolph Co., Illinois.[6]

+ 50   m   VI.  **Myron⁷ Hamilton** was born in Grafton, Quarry Twp., Jersey Co., Illinois, on April 19, 1892. He died in Grafton, Quarry Twp., Jersey Co., Illinois, on April 19, 1892.

**14. Austin J.**[6] **Rogers** (*Rachel C.*[5] *VanAusdall, Mary*[4] *Pegan, Andrew*[3] *Pegan II, Andrew*[2] *Pagan, James*[1]) was born on April 6, 1847, in Otter Creek Twp., Jersey Co., Illinois. He was the son of Henry Spangle Rogers and Rachel C. VanAusdall (6). Austin J. died in Grafton, Quarry Twp., Jersey Co., Illinois, on November 13, 1878, at age 31.

Austin J. married **Virginia Ann McCrory** on September 29, 1870, in Jersey Co., Illinois. They had two sons. Virginia Ann McCrory was born in Gordon Co., Tennessee, in 1852. She was also known as **Jenny or Ginny.** Virginia Ann reached age 70 and died in Osage City, Grant Twp., Osage Co., Kansas, on November 11, 1922. She was buried in Osage City Cemetery, Osage City, Grant Twp., Osage Co., Kansas.[18]

Died under the name Virginia Ann Burns.

Sons of Austin J. Rogers and Virginia Ann McCrory:

+ 51   m   I.   **Elmer Ellsworth**[7] **Rogers** was born in Grafton, Quarry Twp., Jersey Co., Illinois, on September 9, 1874. He died in Burlington, Burlington Twp., Coffey Co., Kansas, on March 8, 1951.He is buried in Osage Cemetery, Osage City, Grant Twp., Osage Co., Kansas.[18]

+ 52   m   II.   **Herbert Augusta**[7] **Rogers** was born in Grafton, Quarry Twp., Jersey Co., Illinois, on May 18, 1876. He died in Emporia, Emporia Twp., Lyon Co., Kansas, on August 14, 1964. Herbert Augusta was buried in Lincoln Cemetery, Lebo, Lincoln Twp., Coffey Co., Kansas.[19]

**15. Desdemona**[6] **Rogers** (*Rachel C.*[5] *VanAusdall, Mary*[4] *Pegan, Andrew*[3] *Pegan II, Andrew*[2] *Pagan, James*[1]) was born on October 25, 1849, in Otter Creek Twp., Jersey Co., Illinois. She was the daughter of Henry Spangle Rogers and Rachel C. VanAusdall (6).

Desdemona died in Otter Creek Twp., Jersey Co., Illinois, on March 2, 1865, at age 15.

**16. Mary E.**[6] **Rogers** (*Rachel C.*[5] *VanAusdall, Mary*[4] *Pegan, Andrew*[3] *Pegan II, Andrew*[2] *Pagan, James*[1]) was born on December 18, 1851, in Otter Creek Twp., Jersey Co., Illinois. She was also known as **Molly.** She was the daughter of Henry Spangle Rogers and Rachel C. VanAusdall (6). Mary E. died in Denver, Denver Co., Colorado, on April 17, 1915, at age 63. She was buried in Crown Hill Cemetery, Wheat Ridge, Jefferson Co., Colorado.[7]

Mary E. married **James Joab White** on October 2, 1870, in Jersey Co., Illinois. They divorced. They had two children. James Joab White was born in Otter Creek Twp., Jersey Co., Illinois, on October 28, 1845. He reached age 69 and died in Jacksonville, Jacksonville Twp., Morgan Co., Illinois, on October 21, 1915. James Joab was buried in Newbern Cemetery, East Newbern, Mississippi Twp., Jersey Co., Illinois.[20]

Mary E. Rogers White married **Thomas Allen Davis** on March 19, 1884, in Jersey Co., Illinois. They had one daughter. Thomas Allen Davis was born in Calloway Co., Missouri, on July 9, 1837. He reached age 77 and died in Jerseyville, Jersey Twp., Jersey Co., Illinois, on November 13, 1914. He was bried in Oak Grove Cemetery, Jerseyville, Jersey Twp., Jersey Co., Illinois.[16]

Thomas Allen Davis, a dentist, lived in 1887 in Winchester, Winchester Twp., Scott Co., Illinois. He also resided between 1888 and 1913 in Warsaw, Warsaw Twp., Hancock Co., Illinois. Later, Mary E. Rogers White Davis left Jerseyville, Illinois to reside with her daughters Myrtle White Ratterman and Viola Ruth Davis in Denver, Colorado.

Children of Mary E. Rogers and James Joab White:

+ 53   f   I.   **Myrtle Idona**[7] **White** was born in Dow, Mississippi Twp., Jersey Co., Illinois, on December 8, 1871. She died in Denver, Denver Co., Colorado, on January 25, 1946. Myrtle Idona was buried in Crown Hill Cemetery, Wheat Ridge, Jefferson Co., Colorado.[7]

+ 54 m II. **Walter Otis**[7] **White** was born in Dow, Mississippi Twp., Jersey Co., Illinois, on January 2, 1873. He died in Jerseyville, Jersey Twp., Jersey Co., Illinois, on August 12, 1941. Walter Otis was buried in Oak Grove Cemetery, Jerseyville, Jersey Twp., Jersey Co., Illinois.[16]

Daughter of Mary E. Rogers and Thomas Allen Davis:

+ 55 f I. **Viola Ruth**[7] **Davis** was born in Winchester, Winchester Twp., Scott Co., Illinois, on November 2, 1885. She died in Denver, Denver Co., Colorado, on July 18, 1949. Viola Ruth was buried in Crown Hill Cemetery, Wheat Ridge, Jefferson Co., Colorado.[7]

**17. William Cornelius**[6] **Rogers** (*Rachel C.*[5] *VanAusdall, Mary*[4] *Pegan, Andrew*[3] *Pegan II, Andrew*[2] *Pagan, James*[1]) was born on August 22, 1854, in Otter Creek Twp., Jersey Co., Illinois. He was also known as **William.** He was the son of Henry Spangle Rogers and Rachel C. VanAusdall (6). William Cornelius died in Otter Creek Twp., Jersey Co., Illinois, on May 18, 1892, at age 37.

Seems to have never married.

**18. John Vanausdoll**[6] **Rogers** (*Rachel C.*[5] *VanAusdall, Mary*[4] *Pegan, Andrew*[3] *Pegan II, Andrew*[2] *Pagan, James*[1]) was born on February 11, 1857, in Otter Creek Twp., Jersey Co., Illinois. He was the son of Henry Spangle Rogers and Rachel C. VanAusdall (6). John Vanausdoll. died in Alton, Alton Twp., Madison Co., Illinois, on June 6, 1937, at age 80. He was buried in Oakwood Cemetery, Upper Alton, Alton Twp., Madison Co., Illinois.[8]

John Vanausdoll married **Lulu J. Hobbs** on November 5, 1890, in Jersey Co., Illinois. They had nine children. Lulu J. Hobbs was born in Point Twp., Calhoun Co., Illinois, on October 28, 1871. Lulu J. reached age 95 and died in Alton, Alton Twp., Madison Co., Illinois, on June 19, 1967. She was buried in Oakwood Cemetery, Upper Alton, Alton Twp., Madison Co., Illinois.[5]

Children of John Vanausdoll. Rogers and Lulu J. Hobbs:

+ 56 m I. **Edwin Clifford**[7] **Rogers** was born in Otter Creek Twp., Jersey Co., Illinois, on January 6, 1893. He was also known as **Clifford.** Edwin Clifford died in Lakeland, Polk Co., Florida, on November 24, 1979. He was buried in Oak Grove Cemetery, Jerseyville, Jersey Twp., Jersey Co., Illinois.[16]

+ 57 f II. **Alta Mae**[7] **Rogers** was born in Otter Creek Twp., Jersey Co., Illinois, on December 25, 1894. She died in Glendora, Los Angeles Co., California, on January 4, 1982. Alta Mae was buried in Oakdale Memorial Park Cemetery, Glendora, Los Angeles Co., California.[21]

+ 58 m III. **George Warren**[7] **Rogers** was born in Otter Creek Twp., Jersey Co., Illinois, on June 8, 1897. He died in Alton, Alton Twp., Madison Co., Illinois, on May 5, 1990. George Warren was buried in Saint Patrick's Cemetery, Godfrey, Godfrey Twp., Madison Co., Illinois.[22]

+ 59 m IV. **John**[7] **Rogers II** was born in Otter Creek Twp., Jersey Co., Illinois, on March 1, 1900. He died in Otter Creek Twp., Jersey Co., Illinois, between March 1900 and December 1900.

+ 60 f V. **Helen M.**[7] **Rogers** was born in Otter Creek Twp., Jersey Co., Illinois, on March 1, 1900. She died in Jerseyville, Jersey Twp., Jersey Co., Illinois, on January 19, 1975. Helen M. was buried in Valhalla Memorial Park and Mausoleum, Godfrey, Godfrey Twp., Madison Co., Illinois.[17]

+ 61  f  VI.  **Imo Luella**[7] **Rogers** was born in Otter Creek Twp., Jersey Co., Illinois, on January 31, 1904. She died in Dallas, Dallas Co., Texas, on October 23, 1978. Imo Luella was buried in Calvary Cemetery and Mausoleum, Dallas, Dallas Co., Texas.[23]

+ 62  m  VII.  **Herbert**[7] **Rogers** was born in Otter Creek Twp., Jersey Co., Illinois, about 1906. He died in Otter Creek Twp., Jersey Co., Illinois, about 1906.

+ 63  m  VIII.  **William H.**[7] **Rogers** was born in Otter Creek Twp., Jersey Co., Illinois, on February 12, 1907. He died in Alton, Alton Twp., Madison Co., Illinois, on October 10, 1994. William H. was buried in Valhalla Memorial Park and Mausoleum, Godfrey, Godfrey Twp., Madison Co., Illinois.[14]

+ 64  f  IX.  **Dorothy Opal**[7] **Rogers** was born in Otter Creek Twp., Jersey Co., Illinois, on July 25, 1910. She died in a facility in Washington, Union Twp., Franklin Co., Missouri. Dorothy Opal was buried in Oak Grove Cemetery, Jerseyville, Jersey Twp., Jersey Co., Illinois.[16]

**19. Margaret H.**[6] **Rogers** (*Rachel C.*[5] *VanAusdall, Mary*[4] *Pegan, Andrew*[3] *Pegan II, Andrew*[2] *Pagan, James*[1]) was born on October 2, 1860, in Otter Creek Twp., Jersey Co., Illinois. She was the daughter of Henry Spangle Rogers and Rachel C. VanAusdall (6). Margaret H. died in Otter Creek Twp., Jersey Co., Illinois, on May 22, 1862, at age one.

**20. Theresa C.**[6] **Rogers** (*Rachel C.*[5] *VanAusdall, Mary*[4] *Pegan, Andrew*[3] *Pegan II, Andrew*[2] *Pagan, James*[1]) was born on March 6, 1863, in Otter Creek Twp., Jersey Co., Illinois. She was the daughter of Henry Spangle Rogers and Rachel C. VanAusdall (6).

Theresa C. died in Frankfort Heights (now West Frankfort), Denning Twp., Franklin Co., Illinois, on December 8, 1919, at age 56. She was buried in OddFellows Cemetery, Benton Twp., Franklin Co., Illinois.[9]

Theresa C. married **Seth Noah Fiske** on August 24, 1882, in Jersey Co., Illinois. They had two sons. Seth Noah Fiske was born in New Jersey on January 6, 1860. Seth Noah reached age 79 and died in West Frankfort, Denning Twp., Franklin Co., Illinois, on July 23, 1939. He was buried in OddFellows Cemetery, Benton Twp., Franklin Co., Illinois.[9]

Sons of Theresa C. Rogers and Seth Noah Fiske:

+ 65  m  I.  **Clinton W.**[7] **Fiske** was born in Quarry Twp., Jersey Co., Illinois, on August 9, 1891. He died in West Frankfort, Denning Twp., Franklin Co., Illinois, on November 8, 1918. Clinton W. was buried in OddFellows Cemetery, Benton Twp., Franklin Co., Illinois.9]

+ 66  m  II.  **Seth Raymond**[7] **Fiske II** was born in Quarry Twp., Jersey Co., Illinois, on February 1, 1900. He was also known as **Raymond.** Seth Raymond died after 1944.

**21. Rowena Maude**[6] **Rogers** (*Rachel C.*[5] *VanAusdall, Mary*[4] *Pegan, Andrew*[3] *Pegan II, Andrew*[2] *Pagan, James*[1]) was born on August 13, 1865, in Otter Creek Twp., Jersey Co., Illinois. She was the daughter of Henry Spangle Rogers and Rachel C. VanAusdall (6). Rowena Maude died in Santa Ana, Orange Co., California, on November 14, 1942, at age 77. She was buried in Melrose Abbey Memorial Park Cemetery, Anaheim, Orange Co., California.[10]

Rowena Maude married **Martin Asa Daniels** on October 24, 1889, in Hancock Co., Illinois. They had two children. Martin Asa Daniels was born in McDonough, Chenango Co., New York, on November 24, 1859. Martin Asa reached age 79 and died in Santa Ana, Orange Co., California, about September 16, 1939. He was buried in Melrose Abbey Memorial Park Cemetery, Anaheim, Orange Co., California.[10]

Children of Rowena Maude Rogers and Martin Asa Daniels:

+ 67  f  I.  **Faye Elisabeth**[7] **Daniels** was born in Hamilton, Monte Bello Twp., Hancock Co., Illinois, on October 9, 1888. She was also known as **Kitty.** Faye Elisabeth died in Santa Ana, Orange Co., California, on December 2, 1945.

+ 68  m  II.  **Robert Martin**[7] **Daniels** was born in Denver, Denver Co., Colorado, on August 9, 1890. He died in Laguna Hills, Orange Co., California, on August 15, 1980. Robert Martin was buried in Melrose Abbey Memorial Park Cemetery, Anaheim, Orange Co., California.[10]

**22. Loring or Loren Earl**[6] **Vanausdoll** (*Caleb*[5], *Mary*[4] *Pegan*, *Andrew*[3] *Pegan II*, *Andrew*[2] *Pagan*, *James*[1]) was born on February 24, 1853, in Grafton Twp., (now Quarry Twp East), Jersey Co., Illinois. He was the son of Caleb Vanausdoll (7) and Martha Hewitt. Loring or Loren Earl lived in 1928 in Jerseyville, Jersey Twp., Jersey Co., Illinois. He died in Wood River Twp., Madison Co., Illinois, on November 4, 1928, at age 75. Loring or Loren Earl was buried in Noble Cemetery, Otterville, Otter Creek Twp., Jersey Co., Illinois.[1]

Loring or Loren Earl married **Fannie Lane** on October 15, 1876, in Jersey Co., Illinois. They divorced. They had two children. Fannie Lane was born in Otterville, Otter Creek Twp., Jersey Co., Illinois, on October 7, 1860. She reached age 76 and died in Jerseyville, Jersey Twp., Jersey Co., Illinois, on December 28, 1936. Fannie was buried in McDow Cemetery, Otterville, Otter Creek Twp., Jersey Co., Illinois.[24]

Loring or Loren Earl Vanausdoll married **Martha Gillmore or Gilmore** on November 14, 1886, in Jersey Co., Illinois. They were separated before 1910. They had three children. Martha Gillmore or Gilmore was born in Otterville, Otter Creek Twp., Jersey Co., Illinois? in May 1861. She reached age 57 and died in Jerseyville, Jersey Twp., Jersey Co., Illinois, on April 10, 1919. Martha Gillmore or was buried in Oak Grove Cemetery, Jerseyville, Jersey Twp., Jersey Co., Illinois.[16]

Children of Loring or Loren Earl Vanausdoll and Fannie Lane:

+ 69  m  I.  **Clarence**[7] **Vanausdoll** was born in Otter Creek Twp., Jersey Co., Illinois, in December 1876. He died in Otter Creek Twp. or Mississippi Twp., Jersey Co., Illinois, on November 27, 1906. Clarence was buried in Oak Grove Cemetery, Jerseyville, Jersey Twp., Jersey Co., Illinois.[16]

+ 70  f  II.  **Bertha May**[7] **Vanausdoll** was born in Otter Creek Twp., Jersey Co., Illinois, on February 8, 1880. She died in Alton, Alton Twp., Madison Co., Illinois, on January 14, 1971. Bertha May was buried in Fieldon Cemetery, Fieldon, Richwoods Twp., Jersey Co., Illinois.[25]

Children of Loring or Loren Earl Vanausdoll and Martha Gillmore or Gilmore:

+ 71  m  I.  **Ermil**[7] **Vanausdoll** was born in Otter Creek Twp., Jersey Co., Illinois, in April 1888. He died in Jerseyville, Jersey Twp., Jersey Co., Illinois, in 1903.

+ 72  f  II.  **Blanche E.**[7] **Vanausdoll** was born in Otter Creek Twp., Jersey Co., Illinois, in September 1889. She died between 1910 and 1952.

+ 73  m  III.  **Raymond Loring**[7] **Vanausdoll** was born in Otter Creek

Twp., Jersey Jersey Co., Illinois, on June 23, 1893. He was also known as **Curley.** Raymond Loring died in a hospital in Alton, Alton Twp., Madison Co., Illinois, on October 17, 1952. He was buried in Oak Grove Cemetery, Jerseyville, Jersey Twp., Jersey Co., Illinois.[16]

**23. Louis N.[6] Vanausdoll** (*Caleb[5], Mary[4] Pegan, Andrew[3] Pegan II, Andrew[2] Pagan, James[1]*) was born on September 3, 1856, in Grafton Twp., (now Quarry Twp East), Jersey Co., Illinois. He was the son of Caleb Vanausdoll (7) and Martha Hewitt. Louis N. died in English Twp., Jersey Co., Illinois, on October 17, 1931, at age 75. He was buried in Noble Cemetery, Otterville, Otter Creek Twp., Jersey Co., Illinois.[1]

Never married.

**24. Martha Jane[6] Vanausdoll** (*Caleb[5], Mary[4] Pegan, Andrew[3] Pegan II, Andrew[2] Pagan, James[1]*) was born on September 12, 1857, in Grafton Twp., (now Quarry Twp East), Jersey Co., Illinois. She was the daughter of Caleb Vanausdoll (7) and Martha Hewitt. Martha Jane died in Dawson, Grant Twp., Richardson Co., Nebraska, on November 13, 1917, at age 60. She was buried in Humboldt Cemetery, Humboldt, Humboldt Twp., Richardson Co., Nebraska.[11]

Martha Jane married **Charles E. Gilmore** on April 12, 1876, in Jersey Co., Illinois. They had nine children. Charles E. Gilmore was born in Rock Island, Rock Island Co., Illinois, on April 8, 1854. Charles E. reached age 90 and died in Riverside, Riverside Co., California, on October 11, 1944. He was buried in Olivewood Cemetery, Riverside, Riverside Co., California.[26]

Children of Martha Jane Vanausdoll and Charles E. Gilmore:

+ 74 f I. **Laura Edith[7] Gilmore** was born in Otter Creek Twp., Jersey Co., Illinois, on May 17, 1878. She died in Riverside, Riverside Co., California, on October 4, 1954. Laura Edith was buried in Olivewood Cemetery, Riverside, Riverside Co., California.26]

+ 75 m II. **Harry Otis[7] Gilmore** was born in Otter Creek Twp., Jersey Co., Illinois, on December 13, 1879. He died in Pawnee City, Pawnee City Twp., Pawnee Co., Nebraska, on October 25, 1955. Harry Otis was buried in Pawnee City Cemetery, Pawnee City, Pawnee Twp., Pawnee Co., Nebraska.[27]

+ 76 m III. **Perl Edward[7] Gilmore** was born in Otter Creek Twp., Jersey Co., Illinois, on October 18, 1882. He died in San Bernardino Co., California, on May 22, 1947. Perl Edward was buried in Montecito Memorial Park Cemetery, Colton, San Bernardino Co., California.[28]

+ 77 m IV. **William C.[7] Gilmore** was born in Otter Creek Twp., Jersey Co., Illinois, on May 17, 1886. He died in Riverside, Riverside Co., California, on February 25, 1957. William C. was buried in Olivewood Cemetery, Riverside, Riverside Co., California.[26]

+ 78 f V. **Flossie[7] Gilmore** was born in Otter Creek Twp., Jersey Co., Illinois, on February 25, 1891. She died in Orange, Orange Co., California, on December 1, 1967. Flossie was buried in Olivewood Cemetery, Riverside, Riverside Co., California.[26]

+ 79 f VI. **Eva May[7] Gilmore** was born in Porter Twp., Richardson Co., Nebraska, on November 26, 1897. She was also known as **May** or **Mae**. She died in Neligh, Antelope Co., Nebraska on April 16, 1993. She was buried in Laurel Hill

Cemetery, Neligh, Antelope Co., Nebraska.[29]

+ 80    VII.    **Child One⁷ Gilmore** was born in Nebraska between 1900 and 1910. He or she died in Nebraska between 1900 and 1910.

+ 81    VIII.    **Child Two⁷ Gilmore** was born in Nebraska between 1900 and 1910. He or she died in Nebraska between 1900 and 1910.

+ 82    IX.    **Child Three⁷ Gilmore** was born in Nebraska between 1900 and 1910. He or she died in Nebraska between 1900 and 1910.

**25. John⁶ Vanausdoll** (*Caleb⁵, Mary⁴ Pegan, Andrew³ Pegan II, Andrew² Pagan, James¹*) was born in 1858 in Grafton Twp., (now Quarry Twp East), Jersey Co., Illinois. He was the son of Caleb Vanausdoll (7) and Martha Hewitt. John died in Grafton Twp., (now Quarry Twp East), Jersey Co., Illinois, before 1860.

**26. Mary Ellen⁶ Vanausdoll** (*Caleb⁵, Mary⁴ Pegan, Andrew³ Pegan II, Andrew² Pagan, James¹*) was born on October 3, 1859, in Grafton Twp., (now Quarry Twp East), Jersey Co., Illinois. She was the daughter of Caleb Vanausdoll (7) and Martha Hewitt. Mary Ellen died in Dawson, Grant Twp., Richardson Co., Nebraska, on March 2, 1943, at age 83. She was buried in Table Rock Cemetery, Table Rock Twp., Pawnee Co., Nebraska.[12]

Mary Ellen married **Silas Brant Day** on June 6, 1879, in Jersey Co., Illinois. They had twelve children. Silas Brant Day was born in New Orleans, New Orleans Parish, Louisiana, on April 5, 1851. Silas Brant reached age 85 and died in Humboldt Twp., Richardson Co., Nebraska, on December 11, 1936. He was buried in Table Rock Cemetery, Table Rock Twp., Pawnee Co., Nebraska.[12]

Children of Mary Ellen Vanausdoll and Silas Brant Day:

+ 83    f    I.    **Minnie⁷ Day** was born in Knights Prairie Twp., Hamilton Co., Illinois, in January 1880. She died in Knights Prairie Twp., Hamilton Co., Illinois, in February 1880.

+ 84    m    II.    **John William⁷ Day** was born in Otter Creek Twp., Jersey Co., Illinois, on November 12, 1881. He died in a hospital in Fort Scott, Bourbon Co., Kansas, on January 7, 1946. John William was buried in Moran Cemetery, Moran Twp., Allen Co., Kansas.[30]

+ 85    m    III.    **Charles Albert⁷ Day** was born in Grafton Twp., (now Quarry Twp East), Jersey Co., Illinois, on September 13, 1883. He died in a hospital in Pawnee, Pawnee Co., Nebraska, on December 20, 1966. Charles Albert was buried in Table Rock Cemetery, Table Rock Twp., Pawnee Co., Nebraska.[12]

+ 86    f    IV.    **Cora May Agnes⁷ Day** was born in Grafton Twp., (now Quarry Twp East), Jersey Co., Illinois, on August 8, 1885. She died in Dawson, Grant Twp., Richardson Co., Nebraska, on May 13, 1979. Cora May Agnes was buried in Heim Cemetery, Dawson, Grant Twp., Richardson Co., Nebraska.[31]

+ 87    m    V.    **Anthony Juduthan⁷ Day** was born in Grant Twp., Richardson Co., Nebraska, on July 9, 1888. He was also known as **Jum.** Anthony Juduthan died in Toppenish, Yakima Co., Washington, on March 3, 1970. He was buried in Table Rock Cemetery, Table Rock Twp., Pawnee Co., Nebraska.[12]

+ 88    f    VI.    **Mary Jane⁷ Day** was born in Grant Twp., Richardson Co. Nebraska, on October 20, 1890. She was also known as **Mayme.** Mary Jane died in Wapato, Yakima Co., Washington, on June 12, 1992.

+ 89   f    VII.   **Ruth Clara**[7] **Day** was born in Grant Twp., Richardson Co., Nebraska, on July 22, 1892. She died in Clear Creek Twp., Pawnee Co., Nebraska, on May 6, 1920. Ruth Clara was buried in Table Rock Cemetery, Table Rock Twp., Pawnee Co., Nebraska.[12]

+ 90   m    VIII.  **Silas Bryan**[7] **Day II** was born in Grant Twp., Richardson Co., Nebraska, on October 23, 1894. He was also known as **Bryan.** Silas Bryan died in Table Rock Twp., Pawnee Co., Nebraska, on January 5, 1919. He was buried in Table Rock Cemetery, Table Rock Twp., Pawnee Co., Nebraska.[12]

+ 91   f    IX.    **Hetty Pearl**[7] **Day** was born in Grant Twp., Richardson Co., Nebraska, on August 16, 1896. She died in Grant Twp., Richardson Co., Nebraska, in 1901.

+ 92   m    X.     **James Manahan**[7] **Day** was born in Grant Twp., Richardson Co., Nebraska, on November 6, 1898. He died in Yakima, Yakima Co., Washington, on January 3, 1975.

+ 93   m    XI.    **Lewis Allan**[7] **Day** was born in Grant Twp., Richardson Co., Nebraska, on September 6, 1900. He died in Table Rock Twp., Pawnee Co., Nebraska, on January 7, 1990. Lewis Allan was buried in Table Rock Cemetery, Table Rock Twp., Pawnee Co., Nebraska.[12]

+ 94   f    XII.   **Jessie Levern**[7] **Day** was born in Clear Creek Twp., Pawnee Co., Nebraska, on May 20, 1903. She was also known as **Bridget.** Jessie Levern died in Auburn, Douglas Twp., Nemaha Co., Nebraska, on April 1, 1995. She was buried

in Humboldt Cemetery, Humboldt, Humboldt Twp., Richardson Co., Nebraska.[11]

27. **William Cornelius**[6] **Vanausdoll** (*Caleb*[5], *Mary*[4] *Pegan*, *Andrew*[3] *Pegan II*, *Andrew*[2] *Pagan*, *James*[1]) was born on September 3, 1861, in Montgomery Co., Illinois. He was the son of Caleb Vanausdoll (7) and Martha Hewitt. William Cornelius lived in 1900 in Otter Creek Twp., Jersey Co., Illinois. He died in Mississippi Twp., Jersey Co., Illinois, on June 2, 1943, at age 81. William Cornelius was buried in Noble Cemetery, Otterville, Otter Creek Twp., Jersey Co., Illinois.[1]

William Cornelius married **Letitia Gillmore** on October 5, 1887, in Jersey Co., Illinois. They had nine children. Letitia Gillmore was born in Otter Creek Twp., Jersey Co., Illinois, on December 18, 1869. Letitia reached age 76 and died in Jerseyville, Jersey Twp., Jersey Co., Illinois, on January 2, 1946. She was buried in Noble Cemetery, Otterville, Otter Creek Twp., Jersey Co., Illinois.[1]

Children of William Cornelius Vanausdoll and Letitia Gillmore:

+ 95   m    I.     **Leonard R.**[7] **Vanausdoll** was born in Otter Creek Twp., Jersey Co., Illinois, on July 18, 1891. He died in San Diego, San Diego Co., California, on February 8, 1969.

+ 96   f    II.    **Theda**[7] **Vanausdoll** was born in Otter Creek Twp., Jersey Co., Illinois, in February 1894. She died in Otter Creek Twp., Jersey Co., Illinois, before 1910.

+ 97         III.   **Child One**[7] **Vanausdoll** was born in Otter Creek Twp., Jersey Co., Illinois, in 1896. He or she died in Otter Creek Twp., Jersey Co., Illinois, before 1900.

+ 98   f    IV.    **Ruby Frances**[7] **Vanausdoll** was born in Otter Creek Twp., Jersey Co., Illinois, on September 18, 1899. She died in Alton, Alton

Twp., Madison Co., Illinois, on August 19, 1931. Ruby Frances was buried in Noble Cemetery, Otterville, Otter Creek Twp., Jersey Co., Illinois.[1]

+ 99 f V. **Ora Lee[7] Vanausdoll** was born in Otter Creek Twp., Jersey Co., Illinois, on June 11, 1902. She died in Jerseyville, Jersey Twp., Jersey Co., Illinois, on February 25, 1978. Ora Lee was buried in Oak Grove Cemetery, Jerseyville, Jersey Twp., Jersey Co., Illinois.[16]

+ 100 f VI. **Ida Belle[7] Vanausdoll** was born in Otter Creek Twp., Jersey Co., Illinois, on December 22, 1904. She died in Cave Junction, Josephine Co., Oregon, on September 23, 1982. Ida Belle was buried in Laurel Cemetery, Cave Junction, Josephine Co., Oregon.[32]

+ 101 f VII. **Addie Rachel[7] Vanausdoll** was born in Jersey Twp., Jersey Co., Illinois, on November 13, 1906. She died in a hospital in Alton, Alton Twp., Madison Co., Illinois, on April 21, 1988. Addie Rachel was buried in Oakwood Cemetery, Upper Alton, Alton Twp., Madison Co., Illinois.[8]

+ 102 VIII. **Child Two[7] Vanausdoll** was born in Otter Creek Twp. or Mississippi Twp., Jersey Co., Illinois, between 1900 and 1910. He or she died in Otter Creek Twp. or Mississipp Twp., Jersey Co., Illinois, between 1900 and 1910.

+ 103 IX. **Child Three[7] Vanausdoll** was born in Otter Creek Twp. or Mississippi Twp., Jersey Co., Illinois, between 1900 and 1910. He or she died in Otter Creek Twp. or Mississippi Twp., Jersey Co., Illinois, between 1900 and 1910.

**28. Charles Wesley[6] Vanausdoll** (*Caleb[5]*, *Mary[4] Pegan*, *Andrew[3] Pegan II*, *Andrew[2] Pagan*, *James[1]*) was born on August 22, 1863, in Grafton Twp., (now Quarry Twp East), Jersey Co., Illinois. He was the son of Caleb Vanausdoll (7) and Martha Hewitt. Charles Wesley died in Quarry Twp., Jersey Co., Illinois, on November 1, 1939, at age 76. He was buried in Scenic Hill/Odd Fellows Cemetery, Quarry Twp., Jersey Co., Illinois.[13, 14]

Charles Wesley married **Syrenia/Rowena Helen Gowins** on November 29, 1885. They had three children. Rowena Helen Gowins was born in Otter Creek Twp., Jersey Co., Illinois, on November 7, 1866. She was also known as **Rena.** Syrenia Helen reached age 83 and died in Quarry Twp., Jersey Co., Illinois? on November 14, 1949. She was buried in Scenic Hill/Odd Fellows Cemetery, Quarry Twp., Jersey Co., Illinois.[13, 14]

She married Asbury Hart after Charles Wesley's death.

Was her given name Syrenia or Rowena? Census data are mixed. She preferred her nickname, Rena, to her given name. "Rena" is on her tombstone. Her Find A Grave entry is under Rowena Helen Gowins Vanausdoll Hart.

Children of Charles Wesley Vanausdoll and Syrenia/Rowena Helen Gowins:

+ 104 m I. **Otis Lafayette[7] Vanausdoll** was born in Quarry Twp., Jersey Co., Illinois, on March 20, 1887. He died in Grafton, Quarry Twp., Jersey Co., Illinois, on July 12, 1968. Otis Lafayette was buried in Scenic Hill/Odd Fellows Cemetery, Quarry Twp., Jersey Co., Illinois.[13, 14]

+ 105 m II. **Everett Charles[7] Vanausdoll** was born in Quarry Twp., Jersey Co., Illinois, on September 18, 1888. He died in Jerseyville, Jersey Twp., Jersey Co., Illinois, on November

2, 1963. Everett Charles was buried in Oak Grove Cemetery, Jerseyville, Jersey Twp., Jersey Co., Illinois.[16]

+ 106 f III. **Ada May**[7] **Vanausdoll** was born in Quarry Twp., Jersey Co., Illinois, on September 4, 1895. She died in Jerseyville, Jersey Twp., Jersey Co., Illinois, on December 31, 1979. Ada was buried in Valhalla Memorial Park and Mausoleum, Godfrey, Godfrey Twp., Madison Co., Illinois.[14]

**29. Cora Alice**[6] **Vanausdoll** (*Caleb*[5], *Mary*[4] *Pegan*, *Andrew*[3] *Pegan II*, *Andrew*[2] *Pagan*, *James*[1]) was born in February 1867 in Grafton Twp., (now Quarry Twp East), Jersey Co., Illinois. She was the daughter of Caleb Vanausdoll (7) and Martha Hewitt. Cora Alice died in Lowell Twp., Cherokee Co., Kansas, on July 15, 1922, at age 55. She was buried in Oak Hill Cemetery, Galena, Cherokee Co., Kansas.[15]

Cora Alice married **Allen D. Patton** on November 11, 1885, in Jersey Co., Illinois. They had nine children. Allen D. Patton was born in Illinois Twp., Jersey Co., Illinois? in July 1861. Allen D. reached age 49 and died in Lowell Twp., Cherokee Co., Kansas, on March 1, 1911. He was buried in Oak Hill Cemetery, Galena, Cherokee Co., Kansas.[15]

Cora Alice Vanausdoll married **Gilbert Dwight Wisner** after 1911. Gilbert Dwight Wisner was born in Leroy Twp., Calhoun Co., Michigan, on December 24, 1857. Gilbert Dwight reached age 77 and died in Garden Twp., Cherokee Co., Kansas, on August 22, 1935. He was buried in Oak Hill Cemetery, Galena, Cherokee Co., Kansas.[15]

Children of Cora Alice Vanausdoll and Allen D. Patton:

+ 107 I. **Child**[7] **Patton** was born between 1886 and 1900. He or she died between 1886 and 1900. **Olive**[7] **Patton** was born in Lowell Twp., Cherokee Co., Kansas, on

+ 108 f II. March 6, 1890. She died in Lowell Twp., Cherokee Co., Kansas, on October 3, 1890. Olive was buried in Oak Hill Cemetery, Galena, Cherokee Co., Kansas.[12]

+ 109 m III. **Charles Frederick**[7] **Patton** was born in Joplin, Joplin Twp., Jasper Co., Missouri, on April 1, 1892. He was also known as **Frederick** and **Fred.** Charles Frederick died in Wallace, Shoshone Co., Idaho, on October 8, 1937. He was buried in Nine Mile Cemetery, Wallace, Shoshone Co., Idaho.[33]

+ 110 f IV. **Zantha**[7] **Patton** was born in Nebraska in December 1894. She died after 1930.

+ 111 m V. **Louis Allan**[7] **Patton** was born in Lowell Twp., Cherokee Co., Kansas, on April 2, 1897. He died in Wallace, Shoshone Co., Idaho, on April 12, 1951. Louis Allan was buried in Forest Cemetery, Coeur d'Alene, Kootenai Co., Idaho.[34]

+ 112 m VI. **Ulis Everett**[7] **Patton** was born in Lowell Twp., Cherokee Co., Kansas, on December 19, 1899. He died in Newbury Park, Ventura Co., California, on July 2, 1977. Ulis Everett was buried in Victor Cemetery, Victor, Ravalli Co., Montana.[35]

+ 113 f VII. **Mary M.**[7] **Patton** was born in Lowell Twp., Cherokee Co., Kansas, on May 9, 1903. She died in Wallace, Shoshone Co., Idaho, on May 16, 1964. Mary M. was buried in Victor Cemetery, Victor, Ravalli Co., Montana.[34] ,

+ 114 m VIII. **Porter William**[7] **Patton** was born in Lowell Twp., Cherokee 1906. He died in Victor, Ravalli Co., Montana, on March 20, 1939. Porter William was buried in Victor Cemetery, Victor, Ravalli Co., Montana.[34]

+ 115 m IX. **Arthur M.**[7] **Patton** was born in Lowell Twp., Cherokee Co., Kansas, on May 31, 1908. He died in Missoula, Missoula Co., Montana, on May 31, 1978. Arthur M. was buried in Victor Cemetery, Victor, Ravalli Co., Montana.[34]

**30. Allen M.**[6] **Vanausdoll** (*Caleb*[5], *Mary*[4] *Pegan*, *Andrew*[3] *Pegan II*, *Andrew*[2] *Pagan*, *James*[1]) was born on November 11, 1869, in Grafton Twp., (now Quarry Twp East), Jersey Co., Illinois. He was the son of Caleb Vanausdoll (7) and Martha Hewitt. Allen M. died in Otter Creek Twp., Jersey Co., Illinois, on January 15, 1949, at age 79. He was buried in Noble Cemetery, Otterville, Otter Creek Twp., Jersey Co., Illinois.[1]

Allen M. married **Lenora Kirchner** on October 10, 1900, in Jersey Co., Illinois. They had two children. Lenora Kirchner was born in Otter Creek Twp., Jersey Co., Illinois, on October 1, 1880. Lenora reached age 97 and died in Carlinville, Macoupin Co., Illinois, on July 22, 1978. She was buried in Noble Cemetery, Otterville, Otter Creek Twp., Jersey Co., Illinois.[1]

Children of Allen M. Vanausdoll and Lenora Kirchner:

+ 116 f I. **Hallye Maude**[7] **Vanausdoll** was born in Otter Creek Twp., Jersey Co., Illinois, on April 23, 1901. She was also known as **Maude.** Hallye Maude died in Jerseyville, Jersey Twp., Jersey Co., Illinois, on February 23, 1982. She was buried in Oak Grove Cemetery, Jerseyville, Jersey Twp., Jersey Co., Illinois.[16]

+ 117 m II. **Allen Laverne**[7] **Vanausdoll** was born in Otter Creek Twp., Jersey Co., Illinois, on May 6, 1912. He died in Shipman, Shipman Twp., Macoupin Co., Illinois, on May 15, 2000. Allen Laverne was buried in Shipman Cemetery, Shipman, Shipman Twp., Macoupin Co., Illinois.[36]

**31. Alice**[6] **Vanausdoll** (*Caleb*[5], *Mary*[4] *Pegan*, *Andrew*[3] *Pegan II*, *Andrew*[2] *Pagan*, *James*[1]) was born in 1872 in Grafton Twp., (now Quarry Twp East), Jersey Co., Illinois. She was the daughter of Caleb Vanausdoll (7) and Martha Hewitt. Alice died in Grafton Twp., (now Quarry Twp East), Jersey Co., Illinois, before 1880.

**32. James Cornelius**[6] **Vanausdoll** (*Caleb*[5], *Mary*[4] *Pegan*, *Andrew*[3] *Pegan II*, *Andrew*[2] *Pagan*, *James*[1]) was born on October 21, 1874, in Grafton Twp., (now Quarry Twp East), Jersey Co., Illinois. He was the son of Caleb Vanausdoll (7) and Martha Hewitt. James Cornelius lived in 1900 in Otter Creek Twp., Jersey Co., Illinois. He died in Dow, Mississippi Twp., Jersey Co., Illinois, on October 4, 1967, at age 92. James Cornelius was buried in Noble Cemetery, Otterville, Otter Creek Twp., Jersey Co., Illinois.[1]

James Cornelius married **Rachael V. Gilmore** on November 25, 1897, in Jersey Co., Illinois. They had five children. Rachael V. Gilmore was born in Otter Creek Twp., Jersey Co., Illinois, in September 1876. Rachael V. reached age 31 and died in Mississippi Twp., Jersey Co., Illinois, about February 1908. She was buried in Noble Cemetery, Otterville, Otter Creek Twp., Jersey Co., Illinois.[1]

James Cornelius Vanausdoll married **Christena Schaaf** about 1910. They had eight children. Christena Schaaf was born in Richwood Twp., Jersey Co., Illinois, on March 18, 1888. Christina reached age 66 and died in Dow, Mississippi Twp., Jersey Co., Illinois, on November 22, 1954. She was buried in Noble Cemetery, Otterville, Otter Creek Twp., Jersey Co., Illinois.[1]

Children of James Cornelius Vanausdoll and Rachael V. Gilmore:

+ 118 m I. **Glenn Herbert**[7] **Vanausdoll** was born in Otter Creek Twp., Jersey

Co., Illinois, on May 14, 1898 He was also known as **Herbert.** Glenn Herbert died in St. Louis, Missouri, on September 27, 1939. He was buried in Memorial Park Cemetery, Jennings, St. Louis Co., Missouri.[37]

+ 119  f  II.  **Edna Marie**[7] **Vanausdoll** was born in Otter Creek Twp., Jersey Co., Illinois, on March 30, 1901. She died in Pine Lawn, St. Louis Co., Missouri, on February 24, 1936. Edna Marie was buried in Memorial Park Cemetery, Jennings, St. Louis Co., Missouri.[37]

+ 120  f  III.  **Florence G.**[7] **Vanausdoll** was born in Otter Creek Twp., Jersey Co., Illinois, on August 28, 1903. She died in Hazelwood, St. Louis Co., Missouri, on July 13, 1990.

+ 121  m  IV.  **Theodore**[7] **Vanausdoll** was born in Mississippi Twp., Jersey Co., Illinois, on May 26, 1905. He died in Lakewood, Jefferson Co., Colorado, on February 10, 1981. Theodore was buried in Memorial Park Cemetery, Jennings, St. Louis Co., Missouri.[36]

+ 122  f  V.  **Lucille Rachel**[7] **Vanausdoll** was born in Mississippi Twp., Jersey Co., Illinois, on February 14, 1908. She died in St. Ann, St. Louis Co.Missouri, on September 12, 1982. Lucille Rachel was buried in Calvary Cemetery and Mausoleum, St. Louis, Missouri.[38]                              ,

Children of James Cornelius Vanausdoll and Christena Schaaf:

+ 123  f  I.  **Hazel M.**[7] **Vanausdoll** was born in Mississippi Twp., Jersey

Co., Illinois, on December 26, 1911. She died in Bethalto, Fort Russell Twp., Madison Co., Illinois, on October 3, 1998. Hazel M. was buried in Oakwood Cemetery, Upper Alton, Alton Twp., Madison Co., Illinois.[8]

+ 124  f  II.  **Leah**[7] **Vanausdoll** was born in Mississippi Twp., Jersey Co., Illinois, on October 31, 1914. She died in Denver, Adams Co., Colorado, on February 6, 2000. Leah was buried in Crown Hill Cemetery, Wheat Ridge, Jefferson Co., Colorado.[7]

+ 125  f  III.  **Irene Ester**[7] **Vanausdoll** was born in Mississippi Twp., Jersey Co., Illinois, on April 15, 1917. She died in Heber Springs, Cleburne Co., Arkansas, on July 9, 2004. Irene Ester was buried in Cleburne County Memorial Gardens Cemetery, Heber Springs, Cleburne Co., Arkansas.[39]

+ 126  f  IV.  **Alice R.**[7] **Vanausdoll** was born in Mississippi Twp., Jersey Co., Illinois, on July 2, 1919. She died in Pacific, Union Twp., Franklin Co., Missouri, in December 1983. Alice R. was buried in Sunset Cemetery, Pacific, Boles Twp., Franklin Co., Missouri.[40]

+ 127  m  V.  **James Everett**[7] **Vanausdoll** was born in Mississippi Twp., Jersey Co., Illinois, on July 13, 1921.He died in Alton, Alton Twp., Madison Co., Illinois, on February 2, 1995. James Everett was buried in Oak Grove Cemetery, Jerseyville, Jersey Twp., Jersey Co., Illinois.[16]

+ 128  f  VI.  **Martha Ellen**[7] **Vanausdoll** born in Mississippi Twp., Jersey Co., Illinois, on August 9, 1923.

She died in Columbia, Monroe Co., Illinois or St. Louis, Missouri, on June 12, 2006. Martha Ellen was buried in Saint Paul's Evangelical Cemetery, Olivet, St. Louis Co., Missouri.[41]

+ 129 m VII. **Virgil Lee⁷ Vanausdoll** was born in Mississippi Twp., Jersey Co., Illinois, on August 9, 1927. He died in a hospital in Alton, Alton Twp., Madison Co., Illinois, on November 12, 1942. Virgil Lee was buried in Noble Cemetery, Otterville, Otter Creek Twp., Jersey Co., Illinois.[1]

+ 130 m VIII. **Herbert Eugene⁷ Vanausdoll** was born in Mississippi Twp., Jersey Co., Illinois, on April 6, 1930. He died in Affton, St. Louis Co., Missouri, on June 11, 2005. Herbert Eugene was buried in Sunset Memorial Park and Mausoleum, Affton, St. Louis Co., Missouri.[42]

**33. Ida B.⁶ Vanausdoll** (*Caleb⁵, Mary⁴ Pegan, Andrew³ Pegan II, Andrew² Pagan, James¹*) was born in 1876 in Grafton Twp., (now Quarry Twp East), Jersey Co., Illinois. She was the daughter of Caleb Vanausdoll (7) and Martha Hewitt. Ida B. died in Otter Creek Twp., Jersey Co., Illinois, on January 18, 1881, at age five. She was buried in Noble Cemetery, Otterville, Otter Creek Twp., Jersey Co., Illinois.[1]

**34. James⁶ Vanausdoll** (*Allen McCreary⁵, Mary⁴ Pegan, Andrew³ Pegan II, Andrew² Pagan, James¹*) was born about 1862 in Jersey Co., Illinois. He was a child of Allen McCreary Vanausdoll (9) and Agnes Ann Hillman. James died in Jersey Co., Illinois, before 1870.

**35. Rachel Roseanna⁶ Vanausdoll** (*Allen McCreary⁵, Mary⁴ Pegan, Andrew³ Pegan II, Andrew² Pagan, James¹*) was born on December 11, 1864, in Grafton Twp., (now Quarry Twp East), Jersey Co., Illinois. She was also known as **Rosa** and **Rose**. She was the daughter of Allen McCreary Vanausdoll (9) and Agnes Ann Hillman. Rachel Roseanna died

in Alton, Alton Twp., Madison Co., Illinois, on December 28, 1940, at age 76. She was buried in Oak Grove Cemetery, Jerseyville, Jersey Twp., Jersey Co., Illinois.[16]

Rachel Roseanna married **Bertram Dodson** on May 15, 1889, in Madison Co., Illinois. They had two daughters. Bertram Dodson was born in Otterville, Otter Creek Twp., Jersey Co., Illinois, on April 23, 1866. Bertram reached age 72 and died in Wood River, Wood River Twp., Madison Co., Illinois, on June 28, 1938. He was buried in Oak Grove Cemetery, Jerseyville, Jersey Twp., Jersey Co., Illinois.[16]

Daughters of Rachel Roseanna Vanausdoll and Bertram Dodson:

+ 131 f I. **Lillian Ethel⁷ Dodson** was born in Alton, Alton Twp., Madison Co., Illinois, on April 23, 1890. She died in Jerseyville, Jersey Twp., Jersey Co., Illinois, on November 8, 1949. Lillian Ethel was buried in Saint Patrick's Cemetery, Godfrey, Godfrey Twp., Madison Co., Illinois.[22]

+ 132 f II. **Lola⁷ Dodson** was born in Alton, Alton Twp., Madison Co., Illinois, on October 22, 1893. She died in Godfrey, Godfrey Twp., Madison Co., Illinois, on March 17, 1969. Lola was buried in Valhalla Memorial Park and Mausoleum, Godfrey, Godfrey Twp., Madison Co., Illinois.[17]

**36. Edwin⁶ Vanausdoll** (*Allen McCreary⁵, Mary⁴ Pegan, Andrew³ Pegan II, Andrew² Pagan, James¹*) was born in 1866 in Grafton Twp., (now Quarry Twp East), Jersey Co., Illinois. He was the son of Allen McCreary Vanausdoll (9) and Agnes Ann Hillman. Edwin died in Otterville, Otter Creek Twp., Jersey Co., Illinois, before 1885.

Never married.

**37. Martha⁶ Vanausdoll** (*Allen McCreary⁵, Mary⁴ Pegan, Andrew³ Pegan II, Andrew² Pagan, James¹*) was born on August 29, 1869, in Grafton Twp., (now

Quarry Twp East), Jersey Co., Illinois. She was also known as **Mattie.** She was the daughter of Allen McCreary Vanausdoll (9) and Agnes Ann Hillman. Martha died in Otterville, Otter Creek Twp., Jersey Co., Illinois, on March 8, 1888, at age 18. She was buried in Noble Cemetery, Otterville, Otter Creek Twp., Jersey Co., Illinois.[1]

Never married.

38. **John⁶ Vanausdoll** (*Allen McCreary⁵, Mary⁴ Pegan, Andrew³ Pegan II, Andrew² Pagan, James¹*) was born about 1871 in Grafton Twp., (now Quarry Twp East), Jersey Co., Illinois. He was the son of Allen McCreary Vanausdoll (9) and Agnes Ann Hillman. John died in Otterville, Otter Creek Twp., Jersey Co., Illinois, before 1880.

39. **Millie Wyona⁶ Vanausdoll** (*Allen McCreary⁵, Mary⁴ Pegan, Andrew³ Pegan II, Andrew² Pagan, James¹*) was born on September 6, 1874, in Otterville, Otter Creek Twp., Jersey Co., Illinois. She was also known as **Milly.** She was the daughter of Allen McCreary Vanausdoll (9) and Agnes Ann Hillman. Millie Wyona died in Jerseyville, Jersey Twp., Jersey Co., Illinois, on July 13, 1957, at age 82. She was buried in Valhalla Memorial Park and Mausoleum, Godfrey, Godfrey Twp., Madison Co., Illinois.[17]

Millie Wyona married **Richard Edsall** in 1891. They had three children. Richard Edsall was born in Mississippi Twp., Jersey Co., Illinois, on October 15, 1869. Richard lived in 1900 in Otterville, Otter Creek Twp., Jersey Co., Illinois. He reached age 63 and died in Jerseyville, Jersey Co., Illinois, on November 23, 1932. Richard was buried in Valhalla Memorial Park and Mausoleum, Godfrey, Godfrey Twp., Madison Co., Illinois.[17]

Millie Wyona Vanausdoll married **Robert Benton Beasley** on August 30, 1935, in Calhoun Co., Illinois. Robert Benton Beasley was born in Scott Co., Illinois, on March 7, 1877. Robert Benton lived in 1954 in Jerseyville, Jersey Twp., Jersey Co., Illinois. He reached age 77 and died in a facility in Alton, Alton Twp., Madison Co., Illinois, on December 22, 1954. Robert Benton was buried in Summit Grove Cemetery, Kampsville, Crater Twp., Calhoun Co., Illinois.[43]

Children of Millie Wyona Vanausdoll and Richard Edsall:

+ 133 f I. **Wyona Freelove⁷ Edsall** was born in Otterville, Otter Creek Twp., Jersey Co., Illinois, in June 1893. She was also known as **Freelove.** Wyona Freelove died in Jerseyville, Jersey Twp., Jersey Co., Illinois, on March 26, 1977. She was buried in Oak Grove Cemetery, Jerseyville, Jersey Twp., Jersey Co., Illinois.[16]

+ 134 m II. **Allen Richard Laverne⁷ Edsall** was born in Otterville, Otter Creek Twp., Jersey Co., Illinois, on March 23, 1895. He died in a hospital in Ann Arbor, Washtenaw Co., Michigan, on December 3, 1978.

+ 135 m III. **Clyde Hilman⁷ Edsall** was born in Otterville, Otter Creek Twp., Jersey Co., Illinois, on October 1, 1898. He died in a hospital in St. Louis, Missouri, on January 9, 1977. Clyde Hilman was buried in Valhalla Memorial Park and Mausoleum, Godfrey, Godfrey Twp., Madison Co., Illinois.[17]

40. **Lillie⁶ Vanausdoll** (*Allen McCreary⁵, Mary⁴ Pegan, Andrew³ Pegan II, Andrew² Pagan, James¹*) was born on September 6, 1874, in Otterville, Otter Creek Twp., Jersey Co., Illinois. She was also known as **Lilly.** She was the daughter of Allen McCreary Vanausdoll (9) and Agnes Ann Hillman. Lillie died in Otterville, Otter Creek Twp., Jersey Co., Illinois, between 1885 and 1900.

Seems to have never married.

41. **Mary or Mamie⁶ Vanausdoll** (*Allen McCreary⁵, Mary⁴ Pegan, Andrew³ Pegan II, Andrew² Pagan, James¹*) was born in 1876 in Otterville, Otter Creek Twp., Jersey Co., Illinois. She was also known as **Mamie.** She was the daughter of Allen McCreary Vanausdoll (9) and Agnes Ann Hillman. Mary or Mamie died in Otterville, Otter Creek Twp., Jersey Co., Illinois, in November 1881 at age five.

**42. Sarah⁶ Vanausdoll** (*Allen McCreary⁵, Mary⁴ Pegan, Andrew³ Pegan II, Andrew² Pagan, James¹*) was born about 1878 in Otterville, Otter Creek Twp., Jersey Co., Illinois. She was the daughter of Allen McCreary Vanausdoll (9) and Agnes Ann Hillman. Sarah died in Otterville, Otter Creek Twp., Jersey Co., Illinois, before 1880.

**43. Frederick⁶ Vanausdoll** (*Allen McCreary⁵, Mary⁴ Pegan, Andrew³ Pegan II, Andrew² Pagan, James¹*) was born about 1880 in Otterville, Otter Creek Twp., Jersey Co., Illinois. He was the son of Allen McCreary Vanausdoll (9) and Agnes Ann Hillman. Frederick died in Otterville, Otter Creek Twp., Jersey Co., Illinois, before 1885.

**44. Ebert Sylvester⁶ Van Ausdall** (*Allen McCreary⁵ Vanausdoll, Mary⁴ Pegan, Andrew³ Pegan II, Andrew² Pagan, James¹*) was born on March 22, 1883, in Otterville, Otter Creek Twp., Jersey Co., Illinois. He was the son of Allen McCreary Vanausdoll (9) and Agnes Ann Hillman. Ebert Sylvester died in Godfrey, Godfrey Twp., Madison Co., Illinois, on May 10, 1959, at age 76. He was buried in Valhalla Memorial Park and Mausoleum, Godfrey, Godfrey Twp., Madison Co., Illinois.[17]

Childless.

Ebert Sylvester married **Margaret May Lessner** before September 1929. Margaret May Lessner was born in Baltimore, Baltimore Co., Maryland, on December 15, 1883. Margaret May reached age 56 and died in Jerseyville, Jersey Twp., Jersey Co., Illinois, on June 21, 1940. She was buried in Valhalla Memorial Park and Mausoleum, Godfrey, Godfrey Twp., Madison Co., Illinois.[17]

Ebert Sylvester Van Ausdall married **Geneva Varble** before 1945. Geneva Varble was born in Woodville, Woodville Twp., Greene Co., Illinois, in October 1892. Geneva reached age 86 and died in Carrollton, Carrollton Twp., Greene Co., Illinois, on February 6, 1979. She was buried in Valhalla Memorial Park and Mausoleum, Godfrey, Godfrey Twp., Madison Co., Illinois.[17]

# 7th Generation

**45. Harry Leonard⁷ Hamilton** (*Sylvester⁶, Margaret⁵ VanAusdall, Mary⁴ Pegan, Andrew³ Pegan II, Andrew² Pagan, James¹*) was born on May 14, 1875, in Otterville, Otter Creek Twp., Jersey Co., Illinois. He was the son of Sylvester Hamilton (13) and Amy Talitha Carrico. Harry Leonard lived in 1910 in South Fork Twp., Fulton Co., Arkansas and in 1920 in Chester, Chester Twp., Randolph Co., Illinois. He died in Los Angeles, Los Angeles Co., California, on August 9, 1960, at age 85.

Harry Leonard married **Mabel M. Greenawalt** before 1896. They had six children. Mabel M. Greenawalt was born in Illinois on May 3, 1877. Mabel M. reached age 70 and died in Los Angeles, Los Angeles Co., California, on April 12, 1948.

Children of Harry Leonard Hamilton and Mabel M. Greenawalt:

+ 136  m  I.  **Harry Leonard⁸ Hamilton II** was born in Chester Twp., Randolph Co., Illinois, on June 23, 1896. He died in Long Beach, Los Angeles Co., California, on November 28, 1975.

+ 137  f  II.  **Theda V.⁸ Hamilton** was born in Chester, Chester Twp., Randolph Co., Illinois, on October 24, 1898. She died in Mount Vernon Twp., Jefferson Co., Illinois, on July 16, 1936. Theda V. was buried in Oakwood Cemetery, Mount Vernon, Mount Vernon Twp., Jefferson Co., Illinois.[44]

+ 138  m  III.  **Clark L.⁸ Hamilton** was born in Chester, Chester Twp., Randolph Co., Illinois, in 1901. He died after 1931.

+ 139  m  IV.  **Clyde Jesse⁸ Hamilton** was born in Chester, Chester Twp., Randolph Co., Illinois, on November 7, 1905. He was also known as **Jesse.** Clyde Jesse died in Chester, Chester Twp., Randolph Co., Illinois, on October 10, 1980. He was buried in St. Mary's Cemetery, Chester, Chester Twp., Randolph Co., Illinois.[45]

+ 140  m  V.  **Ray P.⁸ Hamilton** was born in Chester, Chester Twp., Randolph Co., Illinois, on September 19, 1908. He died in Murphysboro, Murphysboro Twp., Jackson Co., Illinois, on August 17, 1980. Ray P. was buried in Murdale Gardens of Memory, Murphysboro, Murphysboro Twp., Jackson Co., Illinois.[46]

+ 141  m  VI.  **Howard L.⁸ Hamilton** was born in South Fork, Fulton Co., Arkansas, on October 24, 1912. He died in Long Beach, Los Angeles Co., California, on May 1, 1986.

**46. Daniel Lester⁷ Hamilton** (*Sylvester⁶, Margaret⁵ VanAusdall, Mary⁴ Pegan, Andrew³ Pegan II, Andrew² Pagan, James¹*) was born on September 6, 1879, in Otterville, Otter Creek Twp., Jersey Co., Illinois. He was also known as **Lester.** He was the son of Sylvester Hamilton (13) and Amy Talitha Carrico. Daniel Lester died in Wickcliffe, Ballard Co., Kentucky, on January 25, 1949, at age 69. He was buried in Evergreen Cemetery, Chester, Chester Twp., Randolph Co., Illinois.[6]

Daniel Lester married **Warrene Fern Redd** on February 10, 1914, in Dyer Co., Tennessee. They divorced. They had three children. Warrene Fern Redd was born in Ohio Twp., Mississippi Co., Missouri, on February 27, 1898. She reached age 49 and died in Wickcliffe, Ballard Co., Kentucky, on June 4, 1947. Warrene Fern was buried in Wickcliffe Cemetery, Wickcliffe, Ballard Co., Kentucky.[47]

Buried under the name Warrene Fern Dennis.

Children of Daniel Lester Hamilton and Warrene Fern Redd:

+ 142 f I. **Amy Lucille[8] Hamilton** was born in Dyer Co., Tennessee? on November 21, 1914. She died in Wickcliffe, Ballard Co., Kentucky, on August 29, 1995. Amy Lucille was buried in Wickcliffe Cemetery, Wickcliffe, Ballard Co., Kentucky.[45]

+ 143 m II. **Chester Sylvester[8] Hamilton** was born in Dyer Co., Tennessee? on June 4, 1916. He died in a hospital in Memphis, Shelby Co., Tennessee, on May 6, 1943. Chester Sylvester was buried in Mound City National Cemetery, Mound City, Junction Twp., Pulaski Co., Illinois.[48]

+ 144 m III. **Charles Leonard[8] Hamilton** was born in Chester, Chester Twp., Randolph Co., Illinois, on October 12, 1919? He died in Cocoa, Brevard Co., Florida in August 1985?

**47. Jessie J.[7] Hamilton** (*Sylvester[6], Margaret[5] VanAusdall, Mary[4] Pegan, Andrew[3] Pegan II, Andrew[2] Pagan, James[1]*) was born in January 1886 in Grafton, Quarry Twp., Jersey Co., Illinois. She was the daughter of Sylvester Hamilton (13) and Amy Talitha Carrico. Jessie J. died after 1911.

Jessie J. married **Horace Greeley Garner** in Fulton Co., Arkansas before 1908. They had two children. Horace Greeley Garner was born in Perry Co., Tennessee, on January 22, 1881. He was also known as **Greeley.** Horace Greeley reached age 30 and died in Doniphan, Doniphan Twp., Ripley Co., Missouri, on February 21, 1911. He was buried in Camp Cemetery, Camp, Fulton Co., Arkansas.[49]

Children of Jessie J. Hamilton and Horace Greeley Garner:

+ 145 f I. **Dorothy[8] Garner** was born in Randolph Co., Illinois?, on December

14, 1907. She died in October 1980 in Newport, Jackson Co., Arkansas or Poplar Bluff, Poplar Bluff Twp., Butler Co., Missouri.

+ 146 m II. **Roy S.[8] Garner** was born in Camp, Fulton Co., Arkansas, on October 20, 1910. He died in Modesto, Stanislaus Co., California, on July 6, 1982.

**48. Doris Margaret[7] Hamilton** (*Sylvester[6], Margaret[5] VanAusdall, Mary[4] Pegan, Andrew[3] Pegan II, Andrew[2] Pagan, James[1]*) was born on December 19, 1887, in Grafton, Quarry Twp., Jersey Co., Illinois. She was the daughter of Sylvester Hamilton (13) and Amy Talitha Carrico. Doris Margaret died in Los Angeles, Los Angeles Co., California, on February 14, 1957, at age 69. Green Hills Memorial Park Cemetery, Rancho Pales Verdes, Los Angeles Co., California.[50]

Doris Margaret married **Lewis Blanchard Johnson** about 1909. They had six children. Lewis Blanchard Johnson was born in Scheller, Twp., Jefferson Co., Illinois, on January 22, 1876. Lewis Blanchard reached age 77 and died in Ste. Genevieve, Ste. Genevieve Twp., Ste. Genevieve Co., Missouri? on February 13, 1953. He was buried in Highland Memorial Cemetery, Mount Carmel, Mount Carmel Twp., Wabash Co., Illinois.[51]

Children of Doris Margaret Hamilton and Lewis Blanchard Johnson:

+ 147 f I. **Ruth E.[8] Johnson** was born in Chester, Chester Twp., Randolph Co., Illinois, on October 8, 1910. She died in Washington, Washington Twp. Daviess Co., Indiana, on December 29, 1999.

+ 148 f II. **Eva Grace[8] Johnson** was born in Wabash Twp., Wabash Co., Illinois, on September 22, 1922. She died in Los Angeles, Los Angeles Co., California, on June 10, 1965. Eva Grace was buried in Green Hills Memorial Park Cemetery,

Rancho Pales Verdes, Los Angeles Co., California.[48]

+ 149 f III. **Frances Louise⁸ Johnson** was born in Wabash Twp., Wabash Co., Illinois, on February 9, 1925. She died in St. Petersburg, Pinellas Co., Florida, on January 3, 2005.

+ 150 f IV. **Billie Rae⁸ Johnson** was born in Wabash Twp., Wabash Co., Illinois, on October 14, 1928. She died in Newbury Park, Ventura Co., California, on October 30, 2004.

+ 151 f V. **Daughter⁸ Johnson?** was born before 1940. She died before 1940.

+ 152 m VI. **Son⁸ Johnson?** was born before 1940. He died before 1940.

**49. Silas Vanculen⁷ Hamilton** (*Sylvester⁶, Margaret⁵ VanAusdall, Mary⁴ Pegan, Andrew³ Pegan II, Andrew² Pagan, James¹*) was born on January 23, 1890, in Grafton, Quarry Twp., Jersey Co., Illinois. He was the son of Sylvester Hamilton (13) and Amy Talitha Carrico. Silas Vanculen lived in 1965 in Fenton, St. Louis Co., Missouri. He died in a hospital in Kirkwood, St. Louis Co., Missouri, on January 27, 1965, at age 75. Silas Vanculen was buried in Evergreen Cemetery, Chester, Chester Twp., Randolph Co., Illinois.[6]

Silas Vanculen married **Cornelia Elizabeth Tiller** before 1913 in Fulton Co., Arkansas. They had ten children. Cornelia Elizabeth Tiller was born in Camp, Fulton Co., Arkansas, on August 4, 1895. Cornelia Elizabeth reached age 69 and died in Waterloo, Fountain Twp., Monroe Co., Illinois, on January 30, 1965. She was buried in Evergreen Cemetery, Chester, Chester Twp., Randolph Co., Illinois.[6]

Children of Silas Vanculen Hamilton and Cornelia Elizabeth Tiller:

+ 153 m I. **James Lyle⁸ Hamilton** was born in Camp, Fulton Co., Arkansas,

on August 3, 1913. He died in House Springs, Jefferson Co., Missouri, on November 29, 1988. James Lyle was buried in Evergreen Cemetery, Chester, Chester Twp., Randolph Co., Illinois.[6]

+ 154 f II. **Mary Hazel⁸ Hamilton** was born in Calvin, Hughes Co., Oklahoma, on January 25, 1916. She was also known as **Effie** and **Hazel.** Mary Hazel died in Portland, Multnomah Co., Oregon, on July 12, 2009. She was buried in Lincoln Memorial Park Cemetery, Portland, Multnomah Co., Oregon.[52]

+ 155 m III. **Oscar Myron⁸ Hamilton** was born in Chester, Chester Twp., Randolph Co., Illinois, on March 1, 1919. He was also known as **Myron.** Oscar Myron died in Charlotte, Mecklenburg Co., North Carolina, on January 30, 2011. He was buried in Evergreen Cemetery, Charlotte, Mecklenburg Co., North Carolina.[53]

+ 156 f IV. **Ola M.⁸ Hamilton** was born in Chester, Chester Twp., Randolph Co., Illinois, on November 9, 1921. She died in a hospital in Carbondale, Carbondale Twp., Jackson Co., Illinois, on November 15, 2000. Ola M. was buried in Evergreen Cemetery, Chester, Chester Twp., Randolph Co., Illinois.[6]

+ 157 f V. **Olga Fern⁸ Hamilton** was born in Chester, Chester Twp., Randolph Co., Illinois, on October 7, 1923.

+ 158 f VI. **Betty Mae⁸ Hamilton** was born in Chester, Chester Twp., Randolph Co., Illinois, on August 22, 1926. She died in Garden Grove,

Orange Co., California, on September 7, 1993. Bette May was buried in Melrose Abbey Memorial Park Cemetery, Anaheim, Orange Co., California.[10]

+ 159 f VII. **Norma Jean**[8] **Hamilton** was born in Chester, Chester Twp., Randolph Co., Illinois, on February 15, 1929. She died in Las Vegas, Clark Co., Nevada, on August 10, 2016. Norma Jean was buried in Palm Memorial Park Cemetery, Las Vegas, Clark Co., Nevada.[54]

+ 160 f VIII. **Wanda R.**[8] **Hamilton** was born in Chester, Chester Twp., Randolph Co., Illinois, on November 24, 1931. She died in Alton, Alton Twp., Madison Co., Illinois, on January 21, 2011. Wanda R. was buried in Evergreen Cemetery, Chester, Chester Twp., Randolph Co., Illinois.[6]

+ 161 f IX. **Barbara Ann**[8] **Hamilton** was born in Chester, Chester Twp., Randolph Co., Illinois, on June 3, 1934.

+ 162 f X. **Nedra L.**[8] **Hamilton** was born in Chester, Chester Twp., Randolph Co., Illinois, on January 13, 1937.

**50. Myron**[7] **Hamilton** (*Sylvester*[6], *Margaret*[5] *VanAusdall, Mary*[4] *Pegan, Andrew*[3] *Pegan II, Andrew*[2] *Pagan, James*[1]) was born on April 19, 1892, in Grafton, Quarry Twp., Jersey Co., Illinois. He was the son of Sylvester Hamilton (13) and Amy Talitha Carrico. Myron died in Grafton, Quarry Twp., Jersey Co., Illinois, on April 19, 1892.

**51. Elmer Ellsworth**[7] **Rogers** (*Austin J.*[6], *Rachel C.*[5] *VanAusdall, Mary*[4] *Pegan, Andrew*[3] *Pegan II, Andrew*[2] *Pagan, James*[1]) was born on September 9, 1874, in Grafton, Quarry Twp., Jersey Co., Illinois. He was the son of Austin J. Rogers (14) and Virginia Ann McCrory. Elmer Ellsworth lived in 1900 in Florence, Fremont Co., Colorado. He also resided in 1930 in South Gate, Los Angeles Co., California. Elmer Ellsworth died in Burlington, Burlington Twp., Coffey Co., Kansas, on March 8, 1951, at age 76. He is buried in Osage Cemetery, Osage City, Grant Twp. Osage Co., Kansas.[18]

Elmer Ellsworth married **Florence Martha Warner** in Osage Co., Kansas. They divorced. They had six children. Florence Martha Warner was born in Flint, Flint Twp., Genesee Co., Michigan, in August 1878. She reached age 59 and died in Great Bend, Liberty Twp., Barton Co., Kansas, on October 13, 1937. Florence Martha was buried in Hoisington Cemetery, Hoisington, Barton Co., Kansas.[55]

She is buried under the name F.M. Searing.

Elmer Ellsworth Rogers married **Mary Marguerite Smith** before 1925 in Kansas. They divorced. They had one daughter. Mary Marguerite Smith was born in Hartville, Wright Co., Missouri, in February 1889. Mary Marguerite reached age 69 and died in Vancouver, Clark Co., Washington, on April 11, 1958. She was buried in Park Hill Cemetery, Vancouver, Clark Co., Washington.[56]

Elmer Ellsworth Rogers married **Etta Mary Jernigan** on March 21, 1941, in Lyon Co., Kansas. Mary Etta Jernigan was born in Dixon Springs, Smith Co., Tennessee, on July 30, 1878. Mary Etta reached age 68 and died in Osage City, Grant Twp., Osage Co., Kansas, on June 2, 1947. e She is buried in Osage Cemetery, Osage City, Grant Twp. Osage Co., Kansas.[18]

Children of Elmer Ellsworth Rogers and Florence Martha Warner:

+ 163 m I. **Arthur Homer**[8] **Rogers** was born in Burlingame Twp., Osage Co., Kansas? on December 28, 1897. He died in Riverside, Riverside Co., California, on January 1, 1979. Arthur Homer was buried in Crestlawn Memorial Park Cemetery, Riverside, Riverside Co., California.[57]

+ 164 f II. **Esther Mabel⁸ Rogers** was born in Florence, Fremont Co., Colorado, on September 21, 1899. She died in a hospital in Iron Mountain, Dickinson Co., Michigan, on March 11, 1985. Esther Mabel was buried in Quinnesec Cemetery, Quinnesec, Dickinson Co., Michigan.[58]

+ 165 f III. **Evelyn Rowena⁸ Rogers** was born in Florence, Fremont Co., Colorado, on October 12, 1901. She died in Grand Junction, Mesa Co., Colorado, on February 1, 1929. Evelyn Rowena was buried in Calvary Cemetery, Orchard Mesa, Mesa Co., Colorado.[59]

+ 166 f IV. **Mildred Leona⁸ Rogers** was born in Burlingame Twp., Osage Co., Kansas, on June 9, 1905. She died in Burlingame Twp., Osage Co., Kansas, on November 5, 1905.

+ 167 f V. **Jessie Hazel⁸ Rogers** was born in Burlingame Twp., Osage Co., Kansas, on May 3, 1907. She died in La Junta, Otero Co., Colorado, on December 19, 1932. Jessie Hazel was buried in Fairview Cemetery, La Junta, Otero Co., Colorado.[60]

+ 168 m VI. **Charles Austin⁸ Rogers** was born in Burlingame Twp., Osage Co., Kansas, on May 26, 1908. He died in Burlingame Twp., Osage Co., Kansas, on May 26, 1908.

Daughter of Elmer Ellsworth Rogers and Mary Marguerite Smith:

+ 169 f I. **Mary C.⁸ Rogers** was born in Emporia, Emporia Twp., Lyon Co., Kansas, in 1929.

**52. Herbert Augusta⁷ Rogers** (*Austin J.⁶, Rachel C.⁵ VanAusdall, Mary⁴ Pegan, Andrew³ Pegan II, Andrew² Pagan, James¹*) was born on May 18, 1876, in Grafton,

Quarry Twp., Jersey Co., Illinois. He was the son of Austin J. Rogers (14) and Virginia Ann McCrory. Herbert Augusta died in Emporia, Emporia Twp., Lyon Co., Kansas, on August 14, 1964, at age 88. He was buried in Lincoln Cemetery, Lebo, Lincoln Twp., Coffey Co., Kansas.[19]

Herbert Augusta married **Margaret Ann Jones** on April 10, 1900, in Osage Co., Kansas. They had four sons. Margaret Ann Jones was born in Arvonia Twp., Osage Co., Kansas, on December 31, 1873. She was also known as **Maggie.** Margaret Ann reached age 80 and died in Arvonia Twp., Osage Co., Kansas, on September 23, 1954. She was buried in Lincoln Cemetery, Lebo, Lincoln Twp., Coffey Co., Kansas.[19]

Sons of Herbert Augusta Rogers and Margaret Ann Jones:

+ 170 m I. **William Harvey⁸ Rogers** was born in Arvonia Twp., Osage Co., Kansas, on May 10, 1905. He died in Huchinson, Reno Co., Kansas, on June 17, 1959. William Harvey was buried in Maplewood Memorial Lawn Cemetery, Emporia, Emporia Twp., Lyon Co., Kansas.[61]

+ 171 m II. **Sylvester LeRoy⁸ Rogers** was born in Arvonia Twp., Osage Co., Kansas, on November 5, 1906. He died in Emporia, Emporia Twp., Lyon Co., Kansas, on February 24, 1993. Sylvester LeRoy was buried in Lincoln Cemetery, Lebo, Lincoln Twp., Coffey Co., Kansas.[19]

+ 172 m III. **Ralph⁸ Rogers** was born in Arvonia Twp., Osage Co., Kansas, on August 11, 1909. He died in Emporia, Emporia Twp., Lyon Co., Kansas, on May 9, 1992. Ralph was buried in Lincoln Cemetery, Lebo, Lincoln Twp., Coffey Co., Kansas.[19]

+ 173 m IV. **Heber Austin⁸ Rogers** was born in Arvonia Twp., Osage Co., Kansas, on May 13, 1916. He died in Butler, Mount Pleasant Twp.,

Bates Co., Missouri, on August 13, 1983. Heber Austin was buried in Lincoln Cemetery, Lebo, Lincoln Twp., Coffey Co., Kansas.[19]

**53. Myrtle Idona[7] White** (*Mary E.[6] Rogers, Rachel C.[5] VanAusdall, Mary[4] Pegan, Andrew[3] Pegan II, Andrew[2] Pagan, James[1]*) was born on December 8, 1871, in Dow, Mississippi Twp., Jersey Co., Illinois. She was the daughter of James Joab White and Mary E. Rogers (16). Myrtle Idona lived in Colorado. She died in Denver, Denver Co., Colorado, on January 25, 1946, at age 74. Myrtle Idona was buried in Crown Hill Cemetery, Wheat Ridge, Jefferson Co., Colorado.[7]

Childless.

Myrtle Idona married **Bernard Frederick Schiller Rattermann** on October 30, 1894, in Hancock Co., Illinois. Bernard Frederick Schiller Rattermann was born in Cincinnati, Hamilton Co., Ohio, on November 10, 1859. He was also known as **Fred.** Bernard Frederick Schiller reached age 87 and died in Denver, Denver Co., Colorado, on March 24, 1947. He was buried in Crown Hill Cemetery, Wheat Ridge, Jefferson Co., Colorado.[4]

Bernard Frederick Schiller Rattermann always used the name Fred S. Rattermann.

**54. Walter Otis[7] White** (*Mary E.[6] Rogers, Rachel C.[5] VanAusdall, Mary[4] Pegan, Andrew[3] Pegan II, Andrew[2] Pagan, James[1]*) was born on January 2, 1873, in Dow, Mississippi Twp., Jersey Co., Illinois. He was the son of James Joab White and Mary E. Rogers (16). Walter Otis died in Jerseyville, Jersey Twp., Jersey Co., Illinois, on August 12, 1941, at age 68. He was buried in Oak Grove Cemetery, Jerseyville, Jersey Twp., Jersey Co., Illinois.[16]

Walter Otis married **Allie Johnson** on October 28, 1897, in Jersey Co., Illinois. Allie Johnson was born in Illinois in May 1880.

Walter Otis White married **Jessie Viola Balcom** on September 17, 1902, in Jersey Co., Illinois. They had five children. Jessie Viola Balcom was born in Otter Creek Twp., Jersey Co., Illinois, on December 17, 1886. Jessie Viola reached age 77 and died in Jerseyville, Jersey Twp., Jersey Co., Illinois, on

January 28, 1964. She was buried in Oak Grove Cemetery, Jerseyville, Jersey Twp., Jersey Co., Illinois.[16]

Walter Otis White's second wife, Jessie Viola Balcom, was the daughter of Fannie Lane Vanausdoll Balcom, the first wife of his first cousin, Loring Vanausdoll.

Children of Walter Otis White and Jessie Viola Balcom:

+ 174 m I. **Charles Otis[8] White** was born in Otterville, Otter Creek Twp., Jersey Co., Illinois, on April 29, 1904. He died in Jerseyville, Jersey Twp., Jersey Co., Illinois, on January 20, 1965. Charles Otis was buried in Oak Grove Cemetery, Jerseyville, Jersey Twp., Jersey Co., Illinois.[16]

+ 175 f II. **Ruth M.[8] White** was born in Otterville, Otter Creek Twp., Jersey Co., Illinois, on September 13, 1905. She died in Jerseyville, Jersey Twp., Jersey Co., Illinois, on March 29, 1930. Ruth M. was buried in Oak Grove Cemetery, Jerseyville, Jersey Twp., Jersey Co., Illinois.[16]

+ 176 m III. **Walter L.[8] White II** was born in Otterville, Otter Creek Twp., Jersey Co., Illinois, on October 8, 1907. He died in Jerseyville, Jersey Twp., Jersey Co., Illinois, on January 1, 1974. Walter L. was buried in Oak Grove Cemetery, Jerseyville, Jersey Twp., Jersey Co., Illinois.[16]

+ 177 m IV. **Lloyd Shively[8] White** was born in Rosedale Twp., Jersey Co., Illinois, on April 22, 1911. He died in Jerseyville, Jersey Twp., Jersey Co., Illinois, on November 18, 1974. Lloyd Shively was buried in Oak Grove Cemetery, Jerseyville, Jersey Twp., Jersey Co., Illinois.[16]

+ 178 f V. **Georgia Mae[8] White** was born in Rosedale Twp., Jersey Co., Illinois, on May 31, 1913. She died in Oklahoma City, Oklahoma, on February 13, 1996.

**55. Viola Ruth[7] Davis** (*Mary E.[6] Rogers, Rachel C.[5] VanAusdall, Mary[4] Pegan, Andrew[3] Pegan II, Andrew[2] Pagan, James[1]*) was born on November 2, 1885, in Winchester, Winchester Twp., Scott Co., Illinois. She was the daughter of Thomas Allen Davis and Mary E. Rogers (16). She died in Denver, Denver Co., Colorado, on July 18, 1949, at age 63. Viola Ruth was buried in Crown Hill Cemetery, Wheat Ridge, Jefferson Co., Colorado.[7]

Never married.

Viola R. Davis was living with her half-sister Myrtle White Rattermann and her husband Frederick Rattermann in 1930 and 1940 in Denver, Denver Co., Colorado. Her social security application index entry gives her date of birth as November 2, 1886, but census data indicate that it was November 2, 1885.

**56. Edwin Clifford[7] Rogers** (*John Vanausdoll.[6], Rachel C.[5] VanAusdall, Mary[4] Pegan, Andrew[3] Pegan II, Andrew[2] Pagan, James[1]*) was born on January 6, 1893, in Otter Creek Twp., Jersey Co., Illinois. He was also known as **Clifford.** He was the son of John Vanausdoll. Rogers (18) and Lulu J. Hobbs. Edwin Clifford died in Lakeland, Polk Co., Florida, on November 24, 1979, at age 86. He was buried in Oak Grove Cemetery, Jerseyville, Jersey Twp., Jersey Co., Illinois.[16]

Edwin Clifford Rogers married **Lola G. Whitley** on April 25, 1917, in Jersey Co., Illinois. They had one daughter. Lola G. Whitley was born in Norborne, Egypt Twp., Carroll Co., Missouri, on August 8, 1897. Lola G. lived in 1937 in Jerseyville, Jersey Twp., Jersey Co., Illinois. She reached age 40 and died in a hospital in St. Louis, Missouri, on September 16, 1937. Lola G. was buried in Oak Grove Cemetery, Jerseyville, Jersey Twp., Jersey Co., Illinois.[16]

Edwin Clifford married **Annie Jeannette Noble** on July 5, 1942, in Washtenaw Co., Michigan. Annie Jeannette Noble was born in Otterville, Otter Creek Twp., Jersey Co., Illinois, on March 28, 1895. Annie Jeannette reached age 84 and died on October 17, 1979. She was buried in Oak Grove Cemetery, Jerseyville, Jersey Twp., Jersey Co., Illinois.[13]

Edwin Clifford Rogers and Lola G. Whitley had one daughter:

+ 179 f I. **Dorothy Lorene[8] Rogers** was born in Jerseyville, Jersey Twp., Jersey Co., Illinois, on September 3, 1919. She died in a hospital in Normal, Normal Twp., McLean Co., Illinois, on December 6, 2005. Dorothy Lorene was buried in Oak Grove Cemetery, Jerseyville, Jersey Twp., Jersey Co., Illinois.[16]

**57. Alta Mae[7] Rogers** (*John Vanausdoll.[6], Rachel C.[5] VanAusdall, Mary[4] Pegan, Andrew[3] Pegan II, Andrew[2] Pagan, James[1]*) was born on December 25, 1894, in Otter Creek Twp., Jersey Co., Illinois. She was the daughter of John Vanausdoll. Rogers (18) and Lulu J. Hobbs. Alta Mae lived in 1978 in Glendora, Los Angeles Co., California. She died in Glendora, Los Angeles Co., California, on January 4, 1982, at age 87. Alta Mae was buried in Oakdale Memorial Park Cemetery, Glendora, Los Angeles Co., California.[21]

Alta Mae married **Joseph Mark Lowrance** on March 10, 1920, in Madison Co., Illinois. They had one daughter. Joseph Mark Lowrance was born in Bethalto, Fort Russell Twp., Madison Co., Illinois, on March 5, 1894. Joseph Mark reached age 32 and died in Alton, Alton Twp., Madison Co., Illinois, on June 23, 1926. He was buried in Oakwood Cemetery, Upper Alton, Alton Twp., Madison Co., Illinois.[8]

Alta Mae Rogers Lowrance married **Joseph Edward Campbell** before 1940 in Madison Co., Illinois? Joseph Edward Campbell was born in Huntsville, Salt Spring Twp., Randolph Co., Missouri, on March 5, 1887. He was also known as **Edward** and **J. Edward.** Joseph Edward reached age 60 and died in Alton, Alton Twp., Madison Co., Illinois, on May 22, 1947. He was buried in Oakwood Cemetery, Upper Alton, Alton Twp., Madison Co., Illinois.[8]

Daughter of Alta Mae Rogers and Joseph Mark Lowrance:

+ 180 f I. **Lois Jane[8] Lowrance** was born in Alton, Alton Twp., Madison Co.,

Illinois, on November 2, 1922. She died in Glendora, Los Angeles Co., California, on October 11, 1975. Lois Jane was buried in Oakdale Memorial Park Cemetery, Glendora, Los Angeles Co., California.[21]

**58. George Warren**[7] **Rogers** (*John Vanausdoll.*[6], *Rachel C.*[5] *VanAusdall, Mary*[4] *Pegan, Andrew*[3] *Pegan II, Andrew*[2] *Pagan, James*[1]) was born on June 8, 1897, in Otter Creek Twp., Jersey Co., Illinois. He was the son of John Vanausdoll. Rogers (18) and Lulu J. Hobbs. George Warren lived in 1978 in Alton, Alton Twp., Madison Co., Illinois. He died in Alton, Alton Twp., Madison Co., Illinois, on May 5, 1990, at age 92. George Warren was buried in Saint Patrick's Cemetery, Godfrey, Godfrey Twp., Madison Co., Illinois.[22]

Childless.

George Warren married **Marcella K. Collins** on September 30, 1967, in Madison Co., Illinois. Marcella K. Collins was born in Shrewsbury, St. Louis Co., Missouri, on June 10, 1912. Marcella K. lived before 1999 in Alton, Alton Twp., Madison Co., Illinois. She reached age 87 and died in a facililty in Madison, Granite City Twp., Madison Co., Illinois, on July 8, 1999. Marcella K. was buried in Saint Patrick's Cemetery, Godfrey, Godfrey Twp., Madison Co., Illinois.[22]

**59. John**[7] **Rogers II** (*John Vanausdoll.*[6], *Rachel C.*[5] *VanAusdall, Mary*[4] *Pegan, Andrew*[3] *Pegan II, Andrew*[2] *Pagan, James*[1]) was born on March 1, 1900, in Otter Creek Twp., Jersey Co., Illinois. He was the son of John Vanausdoll. Rogers (18) and Lulu J. Hobbs. John died in Otter Creek Twp., Jersey Co., Illinois, between March 1900 and December 1900.

**60. Helen M.**[7] **Rogers** (*John Vanausdoll.*[6], *Rachel C.*[5] *VanAusdall, Mary*[4] *Pegan, Andrew*[3] *Pegan II, Andrew*[2] *Pagan, James*[1]) was born on March 1, 1900, in Otter Creek Twp., Jersey Co., Illinois. She was the daughter of John Vanausdoll. Rogers (18) and Lulu J. Hobbs. Helen M. died

in Jerseyville, Jersey Twp., Jersey Co., Illinois, on January 19, 1975, at age 74. She was buried in Valhalla Memorial Park and Mausoleum, Godfrey, Godfrey Twp., Madison Co., Illinois.[17]

Helen M. married **Harmon Eugene Spaulding** on May 1, 1919, in Jersey Co., Illinois. They had one son. Harmon Eugene Spaulding was born in Mississippi Twp., Jersey Co., Illinois, on February 21, 1900. He was also known as **Eugene.** Harmon Eugene reached age 65 and died in Jerseyville, Jersey Twp., Jersey Co., Illinois, on January 27, 1966. He was buried in Valhalla Memorial Park and Mausoleum, Godfrey, Godfrey Twp., Madison Co., Illinois.[17]

Son of Helen M. Rogers and Harmon Eugene Spaulding:

+ 181 m I.   **Roger**[8] **Spaulding** was born in Jerseyville, Jersey Twp., Jersey Co., Illinois, on January 16, 1926. He died in a hospital in St. Louis, Missouri, on September 10, 2008. Roger was buried in Oak Grove Cemetery, Jerseyville, Jersey Twp., Jersey Co., Illinois.[16]

**61. Imo Luella**[7] **Rogers** (*John Vanausdoll.*[6], *Rachel C.*[5] *VanAusdall, Mary*[4] *Pegan, Andrew*[3] *Pegan II, Andrew*[2] *Pagan, James*[1]) was born on January 31, 1904, in Otter Creek Twp., Jersey Co., Illinois. She was the daughter of John Vanausdoll. Rogers (18) and Lulu J. Hobbs. Imo Luella died in Dallas, Dallas Co., Texas, on October 23, 1978, at age 74. She was buried in Calvary Cemetery and Mausoleum, Dallas, Dallas Co., Texas.[23]

She married **Gregory John Nordenbrock** before 1934. They had two daughters. Gregory John Nordenbrock was born in Burkettsville, Ohio, on September 10, 1905. Gregory John reached age 45 and died in University Park, Dallas Co., Texas, on April 20, 1951. He was buried in Calvary Cemetery and Mausoleum, Dallas, Dallas Co., Texas.[23]

Daughters of Imo Luella Rogers and Gregory John Nordenbrock:

+ 182 f I. **Shirley Ann⁸ Nordenbrock** was born in Dallas, Dallas Co., Texas, on April 22, 1934. She is also known as **Ann.**

+ 183 f II. **Elizabeth Lou⁸ Nordenbrock** was born in Dallas, Dallas Co., Texas, on July 22, 1937. She was also known as **Betty Lou.** Elizabeth Lou died in Amesbury, Essex Co., Massachusetts, on July 19, 2002.

**62. Herbert⁷ Rogers** (*John Vanausdoll.⁶, Rachel C.⁵ VanAusdall, Mary⁴ Pegan, Andrew³ Pegan II, Andrew² Pagan, James¹*) was born about 1906 in Otter Creek Twp., Jersey Co., Illinois. He was the son of John Vanausdoll. Rogers (18) and Lulu J. Hobbs. Herbert died in Otter Creek Twp., Jersey Co., Illinois, about 1906.

**63. William H.⁷ Rogers** (*John Vanausdoll.⁶, Rachel C.⁵ VanAusdall, Mary⁴ Pegan, Andrew³ Pegan II, Andrew² Pagan, James¹*) was born on February 12, 1907, in Otter Creek Twp., Jersey Co., Illinois. He was the son of John Vanausdoll. Rogers (18) and Lulu J. Hobbs. William H. lived in 1978 in Alton, Alton Twp., Madison Co., Illinois. He died in Alton, Alton Twp., Madison Co., Illinois, on October 10, 1994, at age 87. William H. was buried in Valhalla Memorial Park and Mausoleum, Godfrey, Godfrey Twp., Madison Co., Illinois.[17]

William H. Rogers married **Elizabeth Ward Stevens** before 1945. They divorced. They had one son. Elizabeth Ward Stevens was born in Ansonia, New Haven Co., Connecticut, on July 4, 1912. She reached age 72 and died in Pompano Beach, Broward Co., Florida, on March 20, 1985.

William H. married **Bernice Frey** on December 22, 1984, in Madison Co., Illinois. Bernice Frey was born in Alton, Alton Twp., Madison Co., Illinois, on October 30, 1909. She reached age age 87 and died in Alton, Alton Twp., Madison Co., Illinois, on August 13, 1997. Bernice was buried in Valhalla Memorial Park and Mausoleum, Godfrey, Godfrey Twp., Madison Co., Illinois.[17]

Son of William H. Rogers and Elizabeth Ward Stevens:

+ 184 m I. **John A.⁸ Rogers** was born in Alton, Alton Twp., Madison Co., Illinois, on August 13, 1945. He died in Edwardsville, Edwardsville Twp., Madison Co., Illinois? on August 25, 2013.

**64. Dorothy Opal⁷ Rogers** (*John Vanausdoll.⁶, Rachel C.⁵ VanAusdall, Mary⁴ Pegan, Andrew³ Pegan II, Andrew² Pagan, James¹*) was born on July 25, 1910, in Otter Creek Twp., Jersey Co., Illinois. She was the daughter of John Vanausdoll. Rogers (18) and Lulu J. Hobbs. Dorothy Opal lived in 1978 in Otterville, Otter Creek Twp., Jersey Co., Illinois. She also resided in 1992 in Jerseyville, Jersey Twp., Jersey Co., Illinois. Dorothy Opal died in a facility in Washington, Union Twp., Franklin Co., Missouri, on February 28, 1996, at age 85. She was buried in Oak Grove Cemetery, Jerseyville, Jersey Twp., Jersey Co., Illinois.[16]

Dorothy Opal married **Harold Leo Wahle** on November 5, 1930, in Jersey Co., Illinois. They had three sons. Harold Leo Wahle was born in Alton, Alton Twp., Madison Co., Illinois, on February 21, 1908. Harold Leo reached age 83 and died in Otterville, Otter Creek Twp., Jersey Co., Illinois, on July 12, 1991. He was buried in Oak Grove Cemetery, Jerseyville, Jersey Twp., Jersey Co., Illinois.[16]

Sons of Dorothy Opal Rogers and Harold Leo Wahle:

+ 185 m I. **William H.⁸ Wahle** was born in Piasa Twp., Jersey Co., Illinois, on February 4, 1933.

+ 186 m II. **Kenneth E.⁸ Wahle** was born in Piasa Twp., Jersey Co., Illinois, on June 24, 1938.

+ 187 m III. **Edwin D.⁸ Wahle** was born in Piasa Twp., Jersey Co., Illinois, on January 1, 1941.

**65. Clinton W.⁷ Fiske** (*Theresa C.⁶ Rogers, Rachel C.⁵ VanAusdall, Mary⁴ Pegan, Andrew³ Pegan II, Andrew² Pagan, James¹*) was born on August 9, 1891, in

Quarry Twp., Jersey Co., Illinois. He was the son of Seth Noah Fiske and Theresa C. Rogers (20). Clinton W. died in West Frankfort, Denning Twp., Franklin Co., Illinois, on November 8, 1918, at age 27. He was buried in OddFellows Cemetery, Benton Twp., Franklin Co., Illinois.[9]

Clinton W. married **Alpha Epperheimer** on September 4, 1916, in Marion Co., Illinois. Alpha Epperheimer was born in Eddyville, Eddyville Twp., Pope Co., Illinois, on April 19, 1895. She died in Detroit, Wayne Co., Michigan on July 6, 1979.

Alpha married twice more and died as Alpha Carden.

66. **Seth Raymond[7] Fiske II** (*Theresa C.[6] Rogers, Rachel C.[5] VanAusdall, Mary[4] Pegan, Andrew[3] Pegan II, Andrew[2] Pagan, James[1]*) was born on February 1, 1900, in Quarry Twp., Jersey Co., Illinois. He was also known as **Raymond.** He was the son of Seth Noah Fiske and Theresa C. Rogers (20). Seth Raymond died after 1944.

He married **Rapunzel Elizabeth Griffin** before 1920. They divorced. They had two sons. Rapunzel Elizabeth Griffin was born in Brandon, Lyon Co., Kentucky, on November 6, 1901. She was also known as **Elizabeth.** Rapunzel Elizabeth lived in 1970 in Wood River, Wood River Twp., Madison Co., Illinois. She reached age 68 and died in a hospital in Alton, Alton Twp., Madison Co., Illinois, on October 23, 1970. Rapunzel Elizabeth was buried in Oakwood Cemetery, Upper Alton, Alton Twp., Madison Co., Illinois.[8]

Sons of Seth Raymond Fiske II and Rapunzel Elizabeth Griffin:

+ 188 m I. **Douglas Ray[8] Fisk** was born in West Frankfort, Denning Twp., Franklin Co., Illinois, on February 12, 1920. He died in a hospital in St. Louis, Missouri, on February 15, 1977. Douglas Ray was buried in Oakwood Cemetery, Upper Alton, Alton Twp., Madison Co., Illinois.[8]

+ 189 m II. **Luther Alexander[8] Fisk** was born in West Frankfort, Denning Twp., Franklin, Illinois, on December 4, 1921. He was also known as **Jack.** Luther Alexander died in Alton, Alton Twp., Madison Co., Illinois, on March 24, 1944. He was buried in Oakwood Cemetery, Upper Alton, Alton Twp., Madison Co., Illinois.[8]

67. **Faye Elisabeth[7] Daniels** (*Rowena Maude[6] Rogers, Rachel C.[5] VanAusdall, Mary[4] Pegan, Andrew[3] Pegan II, Andrew[2] Pagan, James[1]*) was born on October 9, 1888, in Hamilton, Monte Bello Twp., Hancock Co., Illinois. She was also known as **Kitty.** She was the daughter of Martin Asa Daniels and Rowena Maude Rogers (21). Faye Elisabeth lived in 1920 in Denver, Denver Co., Colorado. She died in Santa Ana, Orange Co., California, on December 2, 1945, at age 57.

Chlldless.

Faye Elisabeth married **William S. Smith** before 1920. They divorced. William S. Smith was born in Canada in 1883. He lived in 1920 in Denver, Denver Co., Colorado. William S. died after 1920.

68. **Robert Martin[7] Daniels** (*Rowena Maude[6] Rogers, Rachel C.[5] VanAusdall, Mary[4] Pegan, Andrew[3] Pegan II, Andrew[2] Pagan, James[1]*) was born on August 9, 1890, in Denver, Denver Co., Colorado. He was the son of Martin Asa Daniels and Rowena Maude Rogers (21). Robert Martin lived in 1935 in Santa Adela, Camaguey, Cuba. He also resided in 1940 in Colorado Springs, El Paso Co., Colorado. Robert Martin died in Laguna Hills, Orange Co., California, on August 15, 1980, at age 90. He was buried in Melrose Abbey Memorial Park Cemetery, Anaheim, Orange Co., California.[10]

Robert Martin married **Edna V. Unknown** in 1916 in Denver Co., Colorado? She was born about 1893 in Colorado. They divorced. They had one son. Edna V. Unknown was born in Colorado in 1893. She died after 1922.

Robert Martin Daniels married **Veta Beatrice Ashby** about 1935 in Orange Co., California? Veta Beatrice

Ashby was born in Ogden, Weber Co., Utah, on September 3, 1893. Veta Beatrice reached age 88 and died in Laguna Hills, Orange Co., California, on March 17, 1982. She was buried in Melrose Abbey Memorial Park Cemetery, Anaheim, Orange Co., California.[10]

Son of Robert Martin Daniels and Edna V. Unknown:

+ 190 m I. **Edward Martin**[8] **Daniels** was born in Greeley, Weld Co., Colorado, on October 7, 1917. He died in Imperial Co., California, on February 12, 1970. Edward Martin was buried in Fairhaven Cemetery, Santa Ana, Orange Co., California.[62]

69. **Clarence**[7] **Vanausdoll** (*Loring or Loren Earl*[6], *Caleb*[5], *Mary*[4] *Pegan, Andrew*[3] *Pegan II, Andrew*[2] *Pagan, James*[1]) was born in December 1876 in Otter Creek Twp., Jersey Co., Illinois. He was the son of Loring or Loren Earl Vanausdoll (22) and Fannie Lane. Clarence died in Otter Creek Twp. or Mississippi Twp., Jersey Co., Illinois, on November 27, 1906, at age 29. He was buried in Oak Grove Cemetery, Jerseyville, Jersey Twp., Jersey Co., Illinois.[16]

Buried as "C. Vanausdoll".

70. **Bertha May**[7] **Vanausdoll** (*Loring or Loren Earl*[6], *Caleb*[5], *Mary*[4] *Pegan, Andrew*[3] *Pegan II, Andrew*[2] *Pagan, James*[1]) was born on February 8, 1880, in Otter Creek Twp., Jersey Co., Illinois. She was the daughter of Loring or Loren Earl Vanausdoll (22) and Fannie Lane. Bertha May died in Alton, Alton Twp., Madison Co., Illinois, on January 14, 1971, at age 90. She was buried in Fieldon Cemetery, Fieldon, Richwoods Twp., Jersey Co., Illinois.[25]

Bertha May married **Albert James Delp** on August 20, 1896, in Jersey Co., Illinois. They had six children. Albert James Delp was born in Dresden Twp., Pettis Co., Missouri, on February 24, 1874. Albert James reached age 62 and died in Clayton, St. Louis Co., Missouri, on April 8, 1936. He was buried in Fieldon Cemetery, Fieldon, Richwoods Twp., Jersey Co., Illinois.[25]

Children of Bertha May Vanausdoll and Albert James Delp:

+ 191 f I. **Freda Grace**[8] **Delp** was born in Grafton, Quarry Twp., Jersey Co., Illinois, on January 31, 1898. She died in Chester, Chester Twp., Randolph Co., Illinois, on October 14, 1935. Freda Grace was buried in Evergreen Cemetery, Chester, Chester Twp., Randolph Co., Illinois.[6]

+ 192 f II. **Leona Frances**[8] **Delp** was born in Jersey Co., Illinois, on July 4, 1900. She died in Alton, Alton Twp., Madison Co., Illinois, on September 27, 1962. Leona Frances was buried in Oakwood Cemetery, Upper Alton, Alton Twp., Madison Co., Illinois.[8]

+ 193 m III. **Roy Everett**[8] **Delp** was born in Valley Park, St. Louis Co., Missouri, on April 23, 1903. He died in Wood River, Wood River Twp., Madison Co., Illinois, on September 29, 1985. Roy Everett was buried in Valhalla Memorial Park and Mausoleum, Godfrey, Godfrey Twp., Madison Co., Illinois.[17]

+ 194 f IV. **Florence**[8] **Delp** was born in Elsah, Jersey Landing Twp., Jersey Co., Illinois, on March 11, 1906. She died in the Illinois River in Gilead Twp., Calhoun Co., Illinois, on July 16, 1931. Florence was buried in Fieldon Cemetery, Fieldon, Richwoods Twp., Jersey Co., Illinois.[25]

+ 195 m V. **Earl Leonard**[8] **Delp** was born in Greenfield, Greenfield Twp., Greene Co., Illinois, on July 17, 1910. He was also known as **Leonard.** Earl Leonard died in a hospital in St. Louis, Missouri Illinois, on January 11, 1969. He was buried in

Fieldon Cemetery, Fieldon, Richwoods Twp., Jersey Co., Illinois.[25]

+ 196  f  VI.  **Vera M.⁸ Delp** was born in Chapin, Bethel Twp., Morgan Co., Illinois, on April 23, 1913. She died in Oquawka, South Henderson Twp., Henderson Co., Illinois, on June 2, 1992. Vera M. was buried in Oquawka Cemetery, Oquawka, Oquawka Twp., Henderson Co., Illinois.[63]

71. **Ermil⁷ Vanausdoll** (*Loring or Loren Earl⁶, Caleb⁵, Mary⁴ Pegan, Andrew³ Pegan II, Andrew² Pagan, James¹*) was born in April 1888 in Otter Creek Twp., Jersey Co., Illinois. He was the son of Loring or Loren Earl Vanausdoll (22) and Martha Gillmore or Gilmore. Ermil died in Jerseyville, Jersey Twp., Jersey Co., Illinois, in 1903 at age 14.

72. **Blanche E.⁷ Vanausdoll** (*Loring or Loren Earl⁶, Caleb⁵, Mary⁴ Pegan, Andrew³ Pegan II, Andrew² Pagan, James¹*) was born in September 1889 in Otter Creek Twp., Jersey Co., Illinois. She was the daughter of Loring or Loren Earl Vanausdoll (22) and Martha Gillmore or Gilmore. Blanche E. died between 1910 and 1952.

Blanche E. married **Guy Thomas** on July 5, 1907, in Jersey Co., Illinois.

Blanche E. Vanausdoll Thomas married **Unknown Waisner** before 1910.

73. **Raymond Loring⁷ Vanausdoll II** (*Loring or Loren Earl⁶, Caleb⁵, Mary⁴ Pegan, Andrew³ Pegan II, Andrew² Pagan, James¹*) was born on June 23, 1893, in Otter Creek Twp., Jersey Co., Illinois. He was also known as **Curley**. He was the son of Loring or Loren Earl Vanausdoll (22) and Martha Gillmore or Gilmore. Raymond Loring lived in English Twp., Jersey Co., Illinois. He died in a hospital in Alton, Alton Twp., Madison Co., Illinois, on October 17, 1952, at age 59. Raymond Loring was buried in Oak Grove Cemetery, Jerseyville, Jersey Twp., Jersey Co., Illinois.[16]

Raymond Loring married **Leona Fanny Blay** on May 24, 1913, in Jersey Co., Illinois. They divorced before June 5, 1917. They had two sons. Leona

Fanny Blay was born in Mississippi Twp., Jersey Co., Illinois, on February 3, 1897. She was also known as **Fanny**. Leona Fanny reached age 62 and died in Jerseyville, Jersey Twp., Jersey Co., Illinois, on November 9, 1959. She was buried in Oakwood Cemetery, Upper Alton, Alton Twp., Madison Co., Illinois.[8]

On June 5, 1917, while incarcerated in the Illinois State Penitentiary in Pontiac, Illinois, Raymond Loring Vanausdall/Vanausdoll states on his WWI Draft Registration that he is single but has a dependent child (Harold).[64]

Raymond Loring Vanausdoll II married **Pauline E. Bush** on October 23, 1923, in Jersey Co., Illinois. Pauline E. Bush was born in Palmyra Twp., Lee Co., Illinois, on February 28, 1903. Pauline E. reached age 44 and died in English Twp., Jersey Co., Illinois, on August 17, 1947. She was buried in White Cemetery, Otter Creek Twp., Jersey Co., Illinois.[65]

Sons of Raymond Loring Vanausdoll II and Leona Fanny Blay:

+ 197  m  I.  **Harold A.⁸ Vanausdoll** was born in Jerseyville, Jersey Twp., Jersey Co., Illinois, on January 3, 1914. He died in Wickenburg, Maricopa Co., Arizona, on April 10, 1973.

+ 198  m  II.  **Theodore Willard⁸ Vanausdoll** was born in Jerseyville, Jersey Twp., Jersey Co., Illinois, on March 21, 1916. He died in Jerseyville, Jersey Twp., Jersey Co., Illinois, on October 5, 1916. He was buried in Oak Grove Cemetery, Jerseyville, Jersey Twp., Jersey Co., Illinois.[16]

74. **Laura Edith⁷ Gilmore** (*Martha Jane⁶ Vanausdoll, Caleb⁵, Mary⁴ Pegan, Andrew³ Pegan II, Andrew² Pagan, James¹*) was born on May 17, 1878, in Otter Creek Twp., Jersey Co., Illinois. She was the daughter of Charles E. Gilmore and Martha Jane Vanausdoll (24). Laura Edith died in Riverside, Riverside Co., California, on October 4, 1954, at age 76. She was buried in Olivewood Cemetery, Riverside, Riverside Co., California.[26]

Laura Edith married **Samuel Martin Babcock** in 1897 in Nebraska. They had four children. Samuel Martin Babcock was born in Humboldt, Humboldt Twp., Richardson Co., Nebraska, on March 6, 1875. He was also known as **Martin.** Samuel Martin reached age 78 and died in Riverside, Riverside Co., California, on May 8, 1953. He was buried in Olivewood Cemetery, Riverside, Riverside Co., California.[26]

Children of Laura Edith Gilmore and Samuel Martin Babcock:

+ 199 m I. **Charles Benjamin**[8] **Babcock** was born in Dawson, Richardson Co., Nebraska? on October 28, 1898. He died in Riverside, Riverside Co., California, on August 5, 1976.

+ 200 f II. **Ethel Mae**[8] **Babcock** was born in Riverside, Riverside Co., Cailfornia on July 11, 1903. She died in Riverside, Riverside Co., California on February 1, 2001.

+ 201 f III. **Ada E.**[8] **Babcock** was born in Dawson, Richardson Co., Nebraska? on March 30, 1907. She died in San Bernardino, San Bernardino Co., California, on April 28, 1976.

+ 202 m IV. **Lewis H.**[8] **Babcock** was born in Dawson, Richardson Co., Nebraska? on May 22, 1908. He died in Riverside, Riverside Co., California, on December 6, 1974.

**75. Harry Otis**[7] **Gilmore** (*Martha Jane*[6] *Vanausdoll, Caleb*[5]*, Mary*[4] *Pegan, Andrew*[3] *Pegan II, Andrew*[2] *Pagan, James*[1]) was born on December 13, 1879, in Otter Creek Twp., Jersey Co., Illinois. He was the son of Charles E. Gilmore and Martha Jane Vanausdoll (24). Harry Otis died in Pawnee City, Pawnee City Twp., Pawnee Co., Nebraska, on October 25, 1955, at age 75. He was buried in Pawnee City Cemetery, Pawnee City, Pawnee Twp., Pawnee Co., Nebraska.[27]

Harry Otis married **Charlotte Amelia Stafford** on September 24, 1901, in Jersey Co., Illinois.

They had five children. Charlotte Amelia Stafford was born in Rosedale Twp., Jersey Co., Illinois, on December 14, 1883. She was also known as **Lottie.** Charlotte Amelia reached age 77 and died in Pawnee City, Pawnee City Twp., Pawnee Co., Nebraska, on April 3, 1961. She was buried in Pawnee City Cemetery, Pawnee City, Pawnee Twp., Pawnee Co., Nebraska.[27]

Children of Harry Otis Gilmore and Charlotte Amelia Stafford:

+ 203 m I. **Albert LeRoy**[8] **Gilmore** was born in Broken Arrow, Tulsa Co., Oklahoma, on October 24, 1907. He was also known as **Roy.** Albert LeRoy died in Pawnee City, Pawnee City Twp., Pawnee Co., Nebraska, on September 8, 1982. He was buried in Pawnee City Cemetery, Pawnee City, Pawnee Twp., Pawnee Co., Nebraska.[27]

+ 204 f II. **Velma Rita**[8] **Gilmore** was born in Broken Arrow, Tulsa Co., Oklahoma, on June 30, 1909. She died in Pawnee City, Pawnee City Twp., Pawnee Co., Nebraska, on May 28, 1997. She was buried in Pawnee City Cemetery, Pawnee City, Pawnee Twp., Pawnee Co., Nebraska.[27]

+ 205 f III. **Juanita Muriel**[8] **Gilmore** was born in Sheridan Twp., Pawnee Co., Nebraska, on January 26, 1914. She was also known as **Cricket.** Juanita Muriel died in Pawnee City, Pawnee City Twp., Pawnee Co., Nebraska, on April 17, 2006. She was buried in Pawnee City Cemetery, Pawnee City, Pawnee Twp., Pawnee Co., Nebraska.[27]

+ 206 m IV. **Harry Eugene**[8] **Gilmore** was born in Sheridan Twp., Pawnee Co., Nebraska, on March 22, 1917. He died in Rock Port, Clay Twp., Atchison Co., Missouri, on May 4, 1989. Harry Eugene was buried in

London Cemetery, Peru, Peru Precinct, Nemaha Co., Nebraska.[66]

+ 207 m V. **Walter Laverne⁸ Gilmore** was born in Sheridan Twp., Pawnee Co., Nebraska, on May 9, 1919. He died in Pawnee City, Pawnee City Twp., Pawnee Co., Nebraska, on July 14, 1963. Walter Laverne was buried in Pawnee City Cemetery, Pawnee City, Pawnee Twp., Pawnee Co., Nebraska.[27]

**76. Perl Edward⁷ Gilmore** (*Martha Jane⁶ Vanausdoll, Caleb⁵, Mary⁴ Pegan, Andrew³ Pegan II, Andrew² Pagan, James¹*) was born on October 18, 1882, in Otter Creek Twp., Jersey Co., Illinois. He was the son of Charles E. Gilmore and Martha Jane Vanausdoll (24). Perl Edward died in San Bernardino Co., California, on May 22, 1947, at age 64. He was buried in Montecito Memorial Park Cemetery, Colton, San Bernardino Co., California.[28]

Perl Edward married **Mary Lou Spaulding** on November 15, 1905, in Pawnee Co., Nebraska. They had one son. Mary Lou Spaulding was born in Grant Twp., Richardson Co., Nebraska, in February 1888. Mary Lou died in Franklin Twp., Richardson Co., Nebraska, between 1910 and 1920.

Son of Perl Edward Gilmore and Mary Lou Spaulding:

+ 208 m I. **James Everett⁸ Gilmore** was born in Franklin Twp., Richardson Co., Nebraska, on March 16, 1907. He died in Los Angeles, Los Angeles Co., California, on April 8, 1955.

**77. William C.⁷ Gilmore** (*Martha Jane⁶ Vanausdoll, Caleb⁵, Mary⁴ Pegan, Andrew³ Pegan II, Andrew² Pagan, James¹*) was born on May 17, 1886, in Otter Creek Twp., Jersey Co., Illinois. He was the son of Charles E. Gilmore and Martha Jane Vanausdoll (24). William C. died in Riverside, Riverside Co., California, on February 25, 1957, at age 70. He was buried in Olivewood Cemetery, Riverside, Riverside Co., California.[26]

He married **Lillie B. Miller** before 1910. They had three daughters. Lillie B. Miller was born in Clay Twp., Pawnee Co., Nebraska, on October 6, 1889. Lillie B. reached age 82 and died in Riverside, Riverside Co., California, on May 2, 1972. She was buried in Olivewood Cemetery, Riverside, Riverside Co., California.[26]

Daughters of William C. Gilmore and Lillie B. Miller:

+ 209 f I. **Irma⁸ Gilmore** was born in Clear Creek Twp., Pawnee Co., Nebraska, in 1910.

+ 210 f II. **Viola⁸ Gilmore** was born in Clear Creek Twp., Pawnee Co., Nebraska, in 1912.

+ 211 f III. **Ila Mae⁸ Gilmore** was born in Clear Creek Twp., Pawnee Co., Nebraska, on September 25, 1915. She died in West Riverside, Riverside Co., California, on September 28, 1943. Ila Mae was buried in Olivewood Cemetery, Riverside, Riverside Co., California.[26]

**78. Flossie⁷ Gilmore** (*Martha Jane⁶ Vanausdoll, Caleb⁵, Mary⁴ Pegan, Andrew³ Pegan II, Andrew² Pagan, James¹*) was born on February 25, 1891, in Otter Creek Twp., Jersey Co., Illinois. She was the daughter of Charles E. Gilmore and Martha Jane Vanausdoll (24). Flossie died in Orange, Orange Co., California, on December 1, 1967, at age 76. She was buried in Olivewood Cemetery, Riverside, Riverside Co., California.[26]

She married **John William Miller** before 1910. They had five children. John William Miller was born in Marble Rock, Union Twp., Floyd Co., Iowa, on September 14, 1879. John William reached age 76 and died in Riverside, Riverside Co., California, on April 25, 1956. He was buried in Olivewood Cemetery, Riverside, Riverside Co., California.[26]

Children of Flossie Gilmore and John William Miller:

+ 212 f I. **Eva Fern⁸ Miller** was born in Miles Twp., Pawnee Co., Nebraska, on March 20, 1910. She died in Riverside, Riverside Co., California, on March 26, 1997. Eva Fern was buried in Riverside National Cemetery, Riverside, Riverside Co., California.[67]

+ 213 m II. **Homer L.[8] Miller** was born in Miles Twp., Pawnee Co., Nebraska, in 1912. He died between 1940 and 2014.

+ 214 m III. **Ray Richard[8] Miller** was born in Clay Twp., Pawnee Co., Nebraska, on March 7, 1916. He died in Yorba Linda, Orange Co., California, on January 18, 2007. Ray Richard was buried in Riverside National Cemetery, Riverside, Riverside Co., California.[66]

+ 215 f IV. **Doris[8] Miller** was born in Clay Twp., Pawnee Co., Nebraska, on October 11, 1919. She died in Orange, Orange Co., California, on October 13, 2014.

+ 216 f V. **Evelyn[8] Miller** was born in Mission Twp., San Bernardino Co., California, on July 22, 1924.

79. **Eva May[7] Gilmore** (*Martha Jane[6] Vanausdoll, Caleb[5], Mary[4] Pegan, Andrew[3] Pegan II, Andrew[2] Pagan, James[1]*) was born in Porter Twp., Richardson Co., Nebraska on November 26, 1897. She was the daughter of Charles E. Gilmore and Martha Jane Vanausdoll (24). She was also known as **May** or **Mae**. Eva May died in Neligh, Antelope Co., Nebraska on April 16, 1993 at age 95. She is buried in Laurel Hill Cemetery, Neligh, Antelope Co., Nebraska.[29]

Eva May married **John Lyle Perdew**. The had five children. John Lyle Perdew was born in Pawnee City, Pawnee City Twp., Pawnee Co., Nebraska on August 15, 1896. He died in Neligh, Antelope Co., Nebraska in Jan 1950. He is buried in Laurel Hill Cemetery, Neligh, Antelope Co., Nebraska.[29]

Children of Eva May Gilmore and John Lyle Perdew:

+ 217 m I. **John Lyle[8] Perdew II** was born in Lincoln, Lancaster Co., Nebraska,

on March 23, 1919. He died in Covina, Los Angeles Co., California, on August 19, 1993. He was buried in Oakdale Memorial Park Cemetery, Glendora, Los Angeles Co., California.[68]

+ 218 f II. **Lois Marie[8] Perdew** was born in Lincoln, Lancaster Co. Nebraska, on September 22, 1921. Lois Marie died in Pierre, Hughes Co., South Dakota on March 1, 2015. She is buried in Morningside Cemetery, Ree Heights, Hand Co., South Dakota.[69]

+ 219 f III. **Dorothy Ann[8] Perdew** was born in Lincoln, Lancaster Co., Nebraska, on September 26, 1923. She died in Neligh, Antelope Co., Nebraska? on January 31, 1999. Dorothy Ann was buried in Laurel Hill Cemetery, Neligh, Antelope Co., Nebraska.[29]

+ 220 f IV. **Phyllis[8] Perdew** was born was born in Blaine Twp., Antelope Co., Nebraska, in 1937.

+ 221 f V. **Rhea June[8] Perdew** was born in Blaine Twp., Antelope Co., Nebraska, on June 10, 1939. She died in a hospital in Aurora, Hamilton Co., Nebraska, on June 23, 2018.

80. **Child One[7] Gilmore** (*Martha Jane[6] Vanausdoll, Caleb[5], Mary[4] Pegan, Andrew[3] Pegan II, Andrew[2] Pagan, James[1]*) was born between 1900 and 1910 in Nebraska. He or she was a child of Charles E. Gilmore and Martha Jane Vanausdoll (24). Child Three died in Nebraska between 1900 and 1910.

81. **Child Two[7] Gilmore** (*Martha Jane[6] Vanausdoll, Caleb[5], Mary[4] Pegan, Andrew[3] Pegan II, Andrew[2] Pagan, James[1]*) was born between 1900 and 1910 in Nebraska. He or she was a child of Charles E. Gilmore and Martha Jane Vanausdoll (24). Child Four died in Nebraska between 1900 and 1910.

**82. Child Three⁷ Gilmore** (*Martha Jane⁶ Vanausdoll, Caleb⁵, Mary⁴ Pegan, Andrew³ Pegan II, Andrew² Pagan, James¹*) was born between 1900 and 1910 in Nebraska. He or she was a child of Charles E. Gilmore and Martha Jane Vanausdoll (24). Child Five died in Nebraska between 1900 and 1910.

**83. Minnie⁷ Day** (*Mary Ellen⁶ Vanausdoll, Caleb⁵, Mary⁴ Pegan, Andrew³ Pegan II, Andrew² Pagan, James¹*) was born in January 1880 in Knights Prairie Twp., Hamilton Co., Illinois. She was the daughter of Silas Brant Day and Mary Ellen Vanausdoll (26). Minnie died in Knights Prairie Twp., Hamilton Co., Illinois, in February 1880.

**84. John William⁷ Day** (*Mary Ellen⁶ Vanausdoll, Caleb⁵, Mary⁴ Pegan, Andrew³ Pegan II, Andrew² Pagan, James¹*) was born on November 12, 1881, in Otter Creek Twp., Jersey Co., Illinois. He was the son of Silas Brant Day and Mary Ellen Vanausdoll (26). John William lived in 1946 in Moran Twp., Allen Co., Kansas. He died in a hospital in Fort Scott, Bourbon Co., Kansas, on January 7, 1946, at age 64. John William was buried in Moran Cemetery, Moran Twp., Allen Co., Kansas.[26]

He married **Leoma Rose McClintock** before 1910. They had three children. Leoma Rose McClintock was born in Table Rock Twp., Pawnee Co., Nebraska, on December 18, 1888. Leoma Rose reached age 92 and died in Moran Twp., Allen Co., Kansas, on February 19, 1981. She was buried in Moran Cemetery, Moran Twp., Allen Co., Kansas.[26]

Children of John William Day and Leoma Rose McClintock:

+ 222 m I. **Randall M.⁸ Day** was born in Elm Twp., Allen Co., Kansas, on April 11, 1910. He died in Moran Twp., Allen Co., Kansas, on August 29, 1992. Randall M. was buried in Moran Cemetery, Moran Twp., Allen Co., Kansas.[26]

+ 223 f II. **Olive Marguerite⁸ Day** was born in Elm Twp., Allen Co., Kansas, on April 1, 1912. She died in Iola, Iola Twp., Allen Co., Kansas, on August 5, 2003. Olive Marguerite was buried in Highland Cemetery, Iola, Iola Twp., Allen Co., Kansas.[70]

+ 224 m III. **Glen Lee⁸ Day** was born in Elm Twp., Allen Co., Kansas, on January 12, 1914. He died in Gas, Elm Twp., Allen Co., Kansas, on April 22, 1999. Glen Lee was buried in Gas City Cemetery, Gas, Elm Twp., Allen Co., Kansas.[71]

**85. Charles Albert⁷ Day** (*Mary Ellen⁶ Vanausdoll, Caleb⁵, Mary⁴ Pegan, Andrew³ Pegan II, Andrew² Pagan, James¹*) was born on September 13, 1883, in Grafton Twp., (now Quarry Twp East), Jersey Co., Illinois. He was the son of Silas Brant Day and Mary Ellen Vanausdoll (26). Charles Albert lived in 1966 in Humboldt, Humboldt Twp., Richardson Co., Nebraska. He died in a hospital in Pawnee, Pawnee Co., Nebraska, on December 20, 1966, at age 83. Charles Albert was buried in Table Rock Cemetery, Table Rock Twp., Pawnee Co., Nebraska.[12]

He married **Blanche McLaughlin** before 1910. They had three children. Blanche McLaughlin was born in Table Rock Twp., Pawnee Co., Nebraska, on August 1, 1891. She was also known as **Kittie**. Blanche reached age 79 and died in Omaha, Douglas Co., Nebraska, on January 5, 1971. She was buried in Table Rock Cemetery, Table Rock Twp., Pawnee Co., Nebraska.[12]

Children of Charles Albert Day and Blanche McLaughlin:

+ 225 f I. **Mildred Lucille⁸ Day** was born in Table Rock Twp., Pawnee Co., Nebraska, on March 13, 1910. She died in Table Rock Twp., Pawnee Co., Nebraska, on June 28, 1919. Mildred Lucille was buried in Table Rock Cemetery, Table Rock Twp., Pawnee Co., Nebraska.[12]

+ 226  m  II.  **Forrest Harlan**[8] **Day** was born in Humboldt, Humboldt Twp., Richardson Co., Nebraska, on July 18, 1915. He was also known as **Frosty.** Forrest Harlan died in Humboldt, Humboldt Twp., Richardson Co., Nebraska, on February 27, 1994. He was buried in Humboldt Cemetery, Humboldt, Humboldt Twp., Richardson Co., Nebraska.[11]

+ 227  m  III.  **Lawrence Gerald**[8] **Day** was born in Franklin Twp., Richardson Co., Nebraska, on February 27, 1917. He died in De Soto, Dallas Co., Texas, on May 14, 1988.

**86. Cora May Agnes**[7] **Day** (*Mary Ellen*[6] *Vanausdoll, Caleb*[5]*, Mary*[4] *Pegan, Andrew*[3] *Pegan II, Andrew*[2] *Pagan, James*[1]) was born on August 8, 1885, in Grafton Twp., (now Quarry Twp East), Jersey Co., Illinois. She was the daughter of Silas Brant Day and Mary Ellen Vanausdoll (26). Cora May Agnes died in Dawson, Grant Twp., Richardson Co., Nebraska, on May 13, 1979, at age 93. She was buried in Heim Cemetery, Dawson, Grant Twp., Richardson Co., Nebraska.[31]

She married **John Elliot Spaulding** on November 11, 1902, in Richardson Co., Nebraska. They had nine children. John Elliot Spaulding was born in Grant Twp., Richardson Co., Nebraska, on September 29, 1882. John Elliot reached age 63 and died in Dawson, Grant Twp., Richardson Co., Nebraska, on March 1, 1946. He was buried in Heim Cemetery, Dawson, Grant Twp., Richardson Co., Nebraska.[31]

Children of Cora May Agnes Day and John Elliot Spaulding:

+ 228  f  I.  **Gladys Mae**[8] **Spaulding** was born in Grant Twp., Richardson Co., Nebraska, on October 10, 1904. She died in Humboldt, Humboldt Twp., Richardson Co., Nebraska, on March 17, 1997. Gladys Mae was buried in Heim Cemetery, Dawson, Grant Twp., Richardson Co., Nebraska.[27]

+ 229  m  II.  **John Raymond**[8] **Spaulding II** was born in Grant Twp., Richardson Co., Nebraska, on February 3, 1906. He died in Hiawatha, Hiawatha Twp., Brown Co., Kansas, on January 10, 1989. John Raymond was buried in Mount Hope Cemetery, Hiawatha, Hiawatha Twp., Brown Co., Kansas.[72]

+ 230  f  III.  **Thelma Ellen**[8] **Spaulding** was born in Grant Twp., Richardson Co., Nebraska, on December 16, 1907. She died in Marshall Co., Kansas, on July 1, 1982. Thelma Ellen was buried in Heim Cemetery, Dawson, Grant Twp., Richardson Co., Nebraska.[27]

+ 231  f  IV.  **Ruth Anna**[8] **Spaulding** was born in Grant Twp., Richardson Co., Nebraska, on August 17, 1909. She died in Palm Harbor, Pinellas Co., Florida, on December 24, 1993. Ruth Anna was buried in Heim Cemetery, Dawson, Grant Twp., Richardson Co., Nebraska.[31]

+ 232  m  V.  **Garl Vernon**[8] **Spaulding** was born in Grant Twp., Richardson Co., Nebraska, on December 19, 1911. He died in Paramount, Los Angeles Co., California, on September 25, 1984.

+ 233  m  VI.  **Carl Eldon**[8] **Spaulding** was born in Grant Twp., Richardson Co., Nebraska, on December 19, 1911. He died in Grant Twp., Richardson Co., Nebraska, on December 20, 1911.

+ 234  m  VII.  **Harold Woodrow**[8] **Spaulding** was born in Grant Twp., Richardson Co., Nebraska, on November 7, 1915. He died in Excelsior Springs, Clay Co., Missouri, on May 26, 2003. Harold Woodrow was buried in Floral Hills Cemetery, Kansas City, Jackson Co., Missouri.[73]

+ 235  f  VIII.  **Edith Ilene[8] Spaulding** was born in Grant Twp., Richardson Co., Nebraska, on September 19, 1917. She was also known as **Illene.** Edith Ilene died in Grant Twp., Richardson Co., Nebraska, on October 16, 1923. She was buried in Heim Cemetery, Dawson, Grant Twp., Richardson Co., Nebraska.[31]

+ 236  m  IX.  **Darrell Eugene[8] Spaulding** was born in Grant Twp., Richardson Co., Nebraska, on May 8, 1921. He died in Lincoln, Lancaster Co., Nebraska, on March 28, 1986. Darrell Eugene was buried in Heim Cemetery, Dawson, Grant Twp., Richardson Co., Nebraska.[27]

**87. Anthony Juduthan[7] Day** (*Mary Ellen[6] Vanausdoll, Caleb[5], Mary[4] Pegan, Andrew[3] Pegan II, Andrew[2] Pagan, James[1]*) was born on July 9, 1888, in Grant Twp., Richardson Co., Nebraska. He was also known as **Jum.** He was the son of Silas Brant Day and Mary Ellen Vanausdoll (26). Anthony Juduthan died in Toppenish, Yakima Co., Washington, on March 3, 1970, at age 81. He was buried in Table Rock Cemetery, Table Rock Twp., Pawnee Co., Nebraska.[12]

He married **Lillie M. Buckles** before 1913. They had three children. Lillie M. Buckles was born in Table Rock Twp., Pawnee Co., Nebraska, on May 20, 1893. Lillie M. reached age 77 and died in Yakima, Yakima Co., Washington, on March 20, 1971. She was buried in Table Rock Cemetery, Table Rock Twp., Pawnee Co., Nebraska.[12]

Children of Anthony Juduthan Day and Lillie M. Buckles:

+ 237  m  I.  **Howard Glen[8] Day** was born in Table Rock Twp., Pawnee Co., Nebraska, on April 25, 1913. He died in Selah, Yakima Co., Washington, on March 6, 1994.

+ 238  m  II.  **Lowrain Arthur[8] Day** was born in Pawnee City, Pawnee City Twp., Pawnee Co., Nebraska, on June 17, 1915. He was also known as **Laun** and **Rainey.** Lowrain Arthur died in a hospital in Wenatchee, Chelan Co., Washington, on September 4, 1983.

+ 239  f  III.  **Daughter[8] Day** was born in Table Rock Twp., Pawnee Co., Nebraska, on June 24, 1921. She died in Table Rock Twp., Pawnee Co., Nebraska, on June 24, 1924.

**88. Mary Jane[7] Day** (*Mary Ellen[6] Vanausdoll, Caleb[5], Mary[4] Pegan, Andrew[3] Pegan II, Andrew[2] Pagan, James[1]*) was born on October 20, 1890, in Grant Twp., Richardson Co., Nebraska. She was also known as **Mayme.** She was the daughter of Silas Brant Day and Mary Ellen Vanausdoll (26). Mary Jane lived in 1992 in Yakima, Yakima Co., Washington. She died in Wapato, Yakima Co., Washington, on June 12, 1992, at age 101.

She married **John Sherman Shiley** after 1934. They had one daughter, who may have been adopted after 1940. John Sherman Shiley was born in Liberty Twp., Richardson Co., Nebraska, on January 17, 1898. He was also known as **Jack.** John Sherman reached age 78 and died in Yakima, Yakima Co., Washington, on April 3, 1976.

Daughter of Anthony Juduthan Day and Lillie M. Buckles:

+ 240  f  I.  **Peggy[8] Shiley** was born after 1934. She may have been adopted.

**89. Ruth Clara[7] Day** (*Mary Ellen[6] Vanausdoll, Caleb[5], Mary[4] Pegan, Andrew[3] Pegan II, Andrew[2] Pagan,*

*James*[1]) was born on July 22, 1892, in Grant Twp., Richardson Co., Nebraska. She was the daughter of Silas Brant Day and Mary Ellen Vanausdoll (26). Ruth Clara died in Clear Creek Twp., Pawnee Co., Nebraska, on May 6, 1920, at age 27. She was buried in Table Rock Cemetery, Table Rock Twp., Pawnee Co., Nebraska.[12]

She married **Charles Raymond Phillips** before 1913. They had four children. Charles Raymond Phillips was born in Table Rock Twp., Pawnee Co., Nebraska, on September 24, 1892. Charles Raymond reached age 88 and died in McCool Junction, McFadden Twp., York Co., Nebraska, on December 16, 1980. He was buried in Waco Cemetery, Waco, Waco Twp., York Co., Nebraska.[74]

Children of Ruth Clara Day and Charles Raymond Phillips:

+ 241 m I. **Arnold Elvern[8] Phillips** was born in Table Rock Twp., Pawnee Co., Nebraska, on April 27, 1913. He died in Vallejo, Solano Co., California, on November 18, 1991.

+ 242 f II. **Zelma Leota[8] Phillips** was born in Clear Creek Twp., Pawnee Co., Nebraska, on July 16, 1915. She died in Medford, Jackson Co., Oregon, on October 17, 1968. Zelma Leota was buried in Hillcrest Memorial Park Cemetery, Medford, Jackson Co., Oregon.[75]

+ 243 f III. **Zethel Irene[8] Phillips** was born in Clear Creek Twp., Pawnee Co., Nebraska, on September 3, 1917. She died in Humboldt, Humboldt Twp., Richardson Co., Nebraska, on January 23, 2004. Zethel Irene was buried in Table Rock Cemetery, Table Rock Twp., Pawnee Co., Nebraska.[12]

+ 244 f IV. **Zeda Louise[8] Phillips** was born in Clear Creek Twp., Pawnee Co., Nebraska, on July 1, 1919. She

died in Seattle, King Co., Washington, on November 28, 2003.

90. **Silas Bryan[7] Day II** (*Mary Ellen[6] Vanausdoll, Caleb[5], Mary[4] Pegan, Andrew[3] Pegan II, Andrew[2] Pagan, James[1]*) was born on October 23, 1894, in Grant Twp., Richardson Co., Nebraska. He was also known as **Bryan.** He was the son of Silas Brant Day and Mary Ellen Vanausdoll (26). Silas Bryan died in Table Rock Twp., Pawnee Co., Nebraska, on January 5, 1919, at age 24. He was buried in Table Rock Cemetery, Table Rock Twp., Pawnee Co., Nebraska.[12]

Never married.

91. **Hetty Pearl[7] Day** (*Mary Ellen[6] Vanausdoll, Caleb[5], Mary[4] Pegan, Andrew[3] Pegan II, Andrew[2] Pagan, James[1]*) was born on August 16, 1896, in Grant Twp., Richardson Co., Nebraska. She was the daughter of Silas Brant Day and Mary Ellen Vanausdoll (26). Hetty Pearl died in Grant Twp., Richardson Co., Nebraska, in 1901 at age four. Hetty Pearl Day is probably buried in Table Rock Cemetery, Table Rock Twp., Richardson Co., Nebraska.

92. **James Manahan[7] Day** (*Mary Ellen[6] Vanausdoll, Caleb[5], Mary[4] Pegan, Andrew[3] Pegan II, Andrew[2] Pagan, James[1]*) was born on November 6, 1898, in Grant Twp., Richardson Co., Nebraska. He was the son of Silas Brant Day and Mary Ellen Vanausdoll (26). James Manahan died in Yakima, Yakima Co., Washington, on January 3, 1975, at age 76.

He married **Rosa Ella Holliger** before 1922. They had five children. Rosa Ella Holliger was born in Short Bend Twp., Dent Co., Missouri, on May 2, 1899. Rosa Ella reached age 74 and died in Yakima, Yakima Co., Washington, on July 8, 1973.

Children of James Manahan Day and Rosa Ella Holliger:

+ 245 m I. **Robert James[8] Day** was born in Clear Creek Twp., Richardson Co., Nebraska, on February 4, 1922. He died in Yakima, Yakima Co., Washington, on October 8, 1995. Robert James was buried in Tahoma

Cemetery, Yakima, Yakima Co., Washington.[76]

+ 246 f II. **Betty Irene⁸ Day** was born in Clear Creek Twp., Richardson Co., Nebraska, on July 29, 1924. She died in Kettle Falls, Stevens Co., Washington, on March 19, 2001. Betty Irene was buried in Meyers Falls Cemetery, Kettle Falls, Stevens Co., Washington.[77]

+ 247 m III. **Delmar Silas⁸ Day** was born in Pawnee City, Pawnee City Twp., Pawnee Co., Nebraska, on December 31, 1927. He was also known as **Del.** Delmar Silas died in Yakima, Yakima Co., Washington, on September 20, 2016. He was buried in Terrace Heights Memorial Park Cemetery, Yakima, Yakima Co., Washington.[78]

+ 248 m IV. **Raymond Edward⁸ Day** was born in St. Bridget Twp., Marshall Co., Kansas, on May 25, 1930.

+ 249 m V. **Donald Allan⁸ Day** was born in St. Bridget Twp., Marshall Co., Kansas, on May 13, 1933.

**93. Lewis Allan⁷ Day** (*Mary Ellen⁶ Vanausdoll, Caleb⁵, Mary⁴ Pegan, Andrew³ Pegan II, Andrew² Pagan, James¹*) was born on September 6, 1900, in Grant Twp., Richardson Co., Nebraska. He was the son of Silas Brant Day and Mary Ellen Vanausdoll (26). Lewis Allan died in Table Rock Twp., Pawnee Co., Nebraska, on January 7, 1990, at age 89. He was buried in Table Rock Cemetery, Table Rock Twp., Pawnee Co., Nebraska.[12]

He married **Laura Ellen Aylor** before 1927. They had two daughters. Laura Ellen Aylor was born in Table Rock Twp., Pawnee Co., Nebraska, on April 27, 1905. Laura Ellen reached age 72 and died in Beatrice, Gage Co., Nebraska, on December 19, 1977. She was buried in Table Rock Cemetery, Table Rock Twp., Pawnee Co., Nebraska.[12]

Daughters of Lewis Allan Day and Laura Ellen Aylor:

+ 250 f I. **Marian Lucille⁸ Day** was born in Table Rock Twp., Pawnee Co., Nebraska, on May 11, 1927.

+ 251 f II. **Janet Elaine⁸ Day** was born in Table Rock Twp., Pawnee Co., Nebraska, on July 4, 1931.

**94. Jessie Levern⁷ Day** (*Mary Ellen⁶ Vanausdoll, Caleb⁵, Mary⁴ Pegan, Andrew³ Pegan II, Andrew² Pagan, James¹*) was born on May 20, 1903, in Clear Creek Twp., Pawnee Co., Nebraska. She was also known as **Bridget.** She was the daughter of Silas Brant Day and Mary Ellen Vanausdoll (26). Jessie Levern died in Auburn, Douglas Twp., Nemaha Co., Nebraska, on April 1, 1995, at age 91. She was buried in Humboldt Cemetery, Humboldt, Humboldt Twp., Richardson Co., Nebraska.[11]

Jessie Levern married **Frank Edgar James** on August 8, 1923, in Pottawatomie Co., Iowa. They had three children. Frank Edgar James was born in Salem Twp., Richardson Co., Nebraska, on June 10, 1901. Frank Edgar reached age 67 and died in Auburn, Douglas Twp., Nemaha Co., Nebraska, on June 4, 1969. He was buried in Humboldt Cemetery, Humboldt, Humboldt Twp., Richardson Co., Nebraska.[11]

Jessie Levern Day and Frank Edgar James had three children, including:

+ 252 m I. **Dwaine Frank⁸ James** was born in Porter Twp., Richardson Co., Nebraska, on June 6, 1925. He died in Humboldt Twp., Richardson Co., Nebraska, on November 14, 1986. Dwaine Frank was buried in Humboldt Cemetery, Humboldt, Humboldt Twp., Richardson Co., Nebraska.[11]

+ 253 m II. **Dale Arthur⁸ James** was born in Porter Twp., Richardson Co., Nebraska, on May 13, 1928. He died in Pawnee City, Pawnee City Twp., Pawnee Co., Nebraska, on

March 21, 2000. Dale Arthur was buried in Humboldt Cemetery, Humboldt, Humboldt Twp., Richardson Co., Nebraska.

+ 254 f III. **Dorothy Arlene⁸ James** was born in Porter Twp., Richardson Co., Nebraska, on May 13, 1928.

**95. Leonard R.⁷ Vanausdoll** (*William Cornelius⁶, Caleb⁵, Mary⁴ Pegan, Andrew³ Pegan II, Andrew² Pagan, James¹*) was born on July 18, 1891, in Otter Creek Twp., Jersey Co., Illinois. He was the son of William Cornelius Vanausdoll (27) and Letitia Gillmore. Leonard R. lived in 1940 in Fort Russell Twp., Madison Co., Illinois. He died in San Diego, San Diego Co., California, on February 8, 1969, at age 77.

He married **Evelyn Rosina Waggoner** before 1916. They had three sons. Evelyn Rosina Waggoner was born in Quarry Twp., Jersey Co., Illinois, on July 22, 1892. Evelyn Rosina reached age 89 and died in San Diego, San Diego Co., California, on August 12, 1981.

Sons of Leonard R. Vanausdoll and Evelyn Rosina Waggoner:

+ 255 m I. **John W.⁸ Vanausdoll** was born in Mississippi Twp., Jersey Co., Illinois, on July 24, 1916. He died in San Diego, San Diego Co., California, on March 8, 2010.

+ 256 m II. **Willard Eldon⁸ Vanausdoll** was born in Mississippi Twp., Jersey Co., Illinois, on November 11, 1919. He died in San Diego, San Diego Co., California, on January 30, 1996.

+ 257 m III. **Robert Newell⁸ Vanausdoll** was born in Mississippi Twp., Jersey Co., Illinois, on November 7, 1921. He died in O'Fallon, O'Fallon Twp., St. Clair Co., Illinois, on February 17, 1998. Robert Newell was buried in Lake View

Memorial Gardens Cemetery, Fairview Heights, Caseyville Twp., St. Clair Co., Illinois.[79, 80]

**96. Theda⁷ Vanausdoll** (*William Cornelius⁶, Caleb⁵, Mary⁴ Pegan, Andrew³ Pegan II, Andrew² Pagan, James¹*) was born in February 1894 in Otter Creek Twp., Jersey Co., Illinois. She was the daughter of William Cornelius Vanausdoll (27) and Letitia Gillmore. Theda died in Otter Creek Twp., Jersey Co., Illinois, before 1910.

**97. Child One⁷ Vanausdoll** (*William Cornelius⁶, Caleb⁵, Mary⁴ Pegan, Andrew³ Pegan II, Andrew² Pagan, James¹*) was born in 1896 in Otter Creek Twp., Jersey Co., Illinois. He or she was a child of William Cornelius Vanausdoll (27) and Letitia Gillmore. Child One died in Otter Creek Twp., Jersey Co., Illinois, before 1900.

**98. Ruby Frances⁷ Vanausdoll** (*William Cornelius⁶, Caleb⁵, Mary⁴ Pegan, Andrew³ Pegan II, Andrew² Pagan, James¹*) was born on September 18, 1899, in Otter Creek Twp., Jersey Co., Illinois. She was the daughter of William Cornelius Vanausdoll (27) and Letitia Gillmore. Ruby Frances died in Alton, Alton Twp., Madison Co., Illinois, on August 19, 1931, at age 31. She was buried in Noble Cemetery, Otterville, Otter Creek Twp., Jersey Co., Illinois.[1]

Ruby Frances married **Parker Lafayette East** in 1922. They had four children. Parker Lafayette East was born in Kane Twp., Greene Co., Illinois, in 1901. He was also known as **Doe.** Parker Lafayette lived in 1964 in Jerseyville, Jersey Twp., Jersey Co., Illinois. He reached age 63 and died in a hospital in Alton, Alton Twp., Madison Co., Illinois, on April 9, 1964. Parker Lafayette was buried in Oak Grove Cemetery, Jerseyville, Jersey Twp., Jersey Co., Illinois.[16]

After Ruby Vanausdoll East's death, Park L. East married Helen Osborn and adopted her daughter, Dorothy.

Children of Ruby Frances Vanausdoll and Parker Lafayette East:

+ 258 m I. **Vernon Parker⁸ East** was born in Mississippi Twp., Jersey Co., Illinois, on July 10, 1923. He died in Tallahassee, Leon Co., Florida, on January 9, 1978. Vernon Parker was buried in Saint Mary's Cemetery, Fieldon, Richwoods Twp., Jersey Co., Illinois.[81]

+ 259 m II. **William Eldon[8] East** was born in Mississippi Twp., Jersey Co., Illinois, in 1926.

+ 260 f III. **Lillie Lois[8] East** was born in Mississippi Twp., Jersey Co., Illinois, on February 21, 1927. She died in Mississippi Twp., Jersey Co., Illinois, on February 21, 1927. Lillie Lois was buried in Oak Grove Cemetery, Jerseyville, Jersey Twp., Jersey Co., Illinois.[16]

+ 261 f IV. **Marjorie Jean[8] East** was born in Mississippi Twp., Jersey Co., Illinois, on December 20, 1929. She died in Lakeside, San Diego Co., California, on February 17, 1996. Marjorie Jean was buried in Alpine Cemetery, Alpine, San Diego Co., California.[82]

**99. Ora Lee[7] Vanausdoll** (*William Cornelius[6], Caleb[5], Mary[4] Pegan, Andrew[3] Pegan II, Andrew[2] Pagan, James[1]*) was born on June 11, 1902, in Otter Creek Twp., Jersey Co., Illinois. She was the daughter of William Cornelius Vanausdoll (27) and Letitia Gillmore. Ora Lee died in Jerseyville, Jersey Twp., Jersey Co., Illinois, on February 25, 1978, at age 75. She was buried in Oak Grove Cemetery, Jerseyville, Jersey Twp., Jersey Co., Illinois.[16]

Childless.

She married **Henry Wahle.** Henry Wahle was born in English Twp., Jersey Co., Illinois, on May 30, 1886. Henry reached age 91 and died in Jerseyville, Jersey Twp., Jersey Co., Illinois, on June 5, 1977. He was buried in Oak Grove Cemetery, Jerseyville, Jersey Twp., Jersey Co., Illinois.[13]

**100. Ida Belle[7] Vanausdoll** (*William Cornelius[6], Caleb[5], Mary[4] Pegan, Andrew[3] Pegan II, Andrew[2] Pagan,*

*James[1]*) was born on December 22, 1904, in Otter Creek Twp., Jersey Co., Illinois. She was the daughter of William Cornelius Vanausdoll (27) and Letitia Gillmore. Ida Belle died in Cave Junction, Josephine Co., Oregon, on September 23, 1982, at age 77. She was buried in Laurel Cemetery, Cave Junction, Josephine Co., Oregon.[32]

Ida Belle Vanausdoll married **Lawrence Kenneth Creswick.** They divorced after 1940. They had one daughter. Lawrence Kenneth Creswick was born in Quincy, Quincy Twp., Adams Co., Illinois, on May 28, 1905. He was also known as **Kenneth Lawrence Creswick.** Lawrence Kenneth reached age 78 and died in Davenport, Davenport Twp., Scott Co., Iowa, on October 12, 1983. Used both Lawrence Kenneth Creswick and Kenneth Lawrence Creswick as names. He donated his body to medical science.

Ida Bell married **Gerald Chapman Tillery** after 1962. Gerald Chapman Tillery was born in Amity, Polk Co., Oregon, on May 2, 1894. Gerald Chapman reached age 88 and died in Grants Pass, Josephine Co., Oregon, on September 23, 1982. He was buried in Laurel Cemetery, Cave Junction, Josephine Co., Oregon.[32]

Daughter of Ida Belle Vanausdoll and Lawrence Kenneth Creswick:

+ 262 f I. **Norma L.[8] Creswick** was born in Alton, Alton Twp., Madison Co., Illinois, on September 17, 1929. She died in Altoona, Clay Twp., Polk Co., Iowa, on December 7, 2011. Norma L. was buried in Laurel Cemetery, Cave Junction, Josephine Co., Oregon.[32]

**101. Addie Rachel[7] Vanausdoll** (*William Cornelius[6], Caleb[5], Mary[4] Pegan, Andrew[3] Pegan II, Andrew[2] Pagan, James[1]*) was born on November 13, 1906, in Jersey Twp., Jersey Co., Illinois. She was the daughter of William Cornelius Vanausdoll (27) and Letitia Gillmore. Addie Rachel lived in 1988 in East Alton, Wood River Twp., Madison Co., Illinois. She died in a hospital in Alton, Alton Twp., Madison Co., Illinois, on April 21, 1988, at age 81. Addie Rachel was buried in Oakwood Cemetery, Upper Alton, Alton Twp., Madison Co., Illinois.[8]

Addie Rachel married **William A. Clayton** on September 12, 1925, in Madison Co., Illinois. They divorced. They had one daughter. William A. Clayton was born in Foster Twp., Madison Co., Illinois, on August 16, 1905. He lived in 1974 in Bethalto, Fort Russell Twp., Madison Co., Illinois. William A. reached age 68 and died in a hospital in Alton, Alton Twp., Madison Co., Illinois, on July 5, 1974. He was buried in Valhalla Memorial Park and Mausoleum, Godfrey, Godfrey Twp., Madison Co., Illinois.[17]

Addie Rachel Vanausdoll married **Benjamin W. Woodson** on December 31, 1949, in Boone Co., Kentucky. Benjamin W. Woodson was born in Vandalia, Cuivre Twp., Audrain Co., Missouri, on February 12, 1902. Benjamin W. reached age 58 and died in Alton, Alton Twp., Madison Co., Illinois, on March 7, 1960. He was buried in Farber Cemetery, Farber, Cuivre Twp., Audrain Co., Missouri.[83]

Daughter of Addie Rachel Vanausdoll and William A. Clayton:

+ 263 f I. **Marcella June[8] Clayton** was born in Alton, Alton Twp., Madison Co., Illinois, on September 25, 1926. She died in a hospital in Alton, Alton Twp., Madison Co., Illinois, on July 2, 1985. Marcella June was buried in Oakwood Cemetery, Upper Alton, Alton Twp., Madison Co., Illinois.[8]

102. **Child Two[7] Vanausdoll** (*William Cornelius[6], Caleb[5], Mary[4] Pegan, Andrew[3] Pegan II, Andrew[2] Pagan, James[1]*) was born between 1900 and 1910 in Otter Creek Twp. or Mississippi Twp., Jersey Co., Illinois. He or she was a child of William Cornelius Vanausdoll (27) and Letitia Gillmore. Child Two died in Otter Creek Twp. or Mississippi Twp., Jersey Co., Illinois, between 1900 and 1910.

103. **Child Three[7] Vanausdoll** (*William Cornelius[6], Caleb[5], Mary[4] Pegan, Andrew[3] Pegan II, Andrew[2]*

*Pagan, James[1]*) was born between 1900 and 1910 in Otter Creek Twp. or Mississippi Twp., Jersey Co., Illinois. He or she was a child of William Cornelius Vanausdoll (27) and Letitia Gillmore. Child Three died in Otter Creek Twp. or Mississippi Twp., Jersey Co., Illinois, between 1900 and 1910.

104. **Otis Lafayette[7] Vanausdoll** (*Charles Wesley[6], Caleb[5], Mary[4] Pegan, Andrew[3] Pegan II, Andrew[2] Pagan, James[1]*) was born on March 20, 1887, in Quarry Twp., Jersey Co., Illinois. He was the son of Charles Wesley Vanausdoll (28) and Syrenia/Rowena Helen Gowins. Otis Lafayette died in Grafton, Quarry Twp., Jersey Co., Illinois, on July 12, 1968, at age 81. He was buried in Scenic Hill/Odd Fellows Cemetery, Quarry Twp., Jersey Co., Illinois.[13, 14]

Otis Lafayette married **Cassandra Ordealia Heath** on July 1, 1906, in Jersey Co., Illinois. They had nine children. Cassandra Ordealia Heath was born in Quarry Twp., Jersey Co., Illinois, on July 1, 1890. She was also known as **Cassie.** Cassandra Ordealia reached age 62 and died in Grafton, Quarry Twp., Jersey Co., Illinois, on February 3, 1953. She was buried in Scenic Hill/Odd Fellows Cemetery, Quarry Twp., Jersey Co., Illinois.[13, 14]

Children of Otis Lafayette Vanausdoll and Cassandra Ordealia Heath:

+ 264 m I. **Chester Heath[8] Van Ausdale** was born in Grafton, Quarry Twp., Jersey Co., Illinois, on May 10, 1907. He died in Grafton, Quarry Twp., Jersey Co., Illinois, on September 13, 1963. Chester Heath was buried in Scenic Hill/Odd Fellows Cemetery, Quarry Twp., Jersey Co., Illinois.[13, 14]

+ 265 m II. **Robert Clifton[8] Van Ausdale** was born in Grafton, Quarry Twp., Jersey Co., Illinois, on July 9, 1910. He died in a hospital in Florissant, St. Louis Co., Missouri, on May 29, 1988. Robert Clifton was buried in Scenic Hill/Odd

Fellows Cemetery, Quarry Twp., Jersey Co., Illinois.[13, 14]

+ 266 m III. **Jack Warren Kerrigan⁸ Van Ausdale** was born in Grafton, Quarry Twp., Jersey Co., Illinois, on September 14, 1914. He died in Carson, Los Angeles Co., California, on March 25, 1989. Jack Warren was buried in Scenic Hill/Odd Fellows Cemetery, Quarry Twp., Jersey Co., Illinois.[13, 14]

+ 267 f IV. **Ila Marie⁸ Vanausdoll** was born in Grafton, Quarry Twp., Jersey Co., Illinois, on August 14, 1918. She died in Grafton, Quarry Twp., Jersey Co., Illinois, on November 24, 2002. She was buried in Scenic Hill/Odd Fellows Cemetery, Quarry Twp., Jersey Co., Illinois.[14]

+ 268 m V. **Daniel Liberty⁸ Van Ausdale** was born in St. Louis, Missouri, on January 26, 1922. He died in Alton, Alton Twp., Madison Co., Illinois, on February 10, 1975. Daniel Liberty was buried in Scenic Hill/Odd Fellows Cemetery, Quarry Twp., Jersey Co., Illinois.[13, 14]

+ 269 m VI. **Otis Raymond⁸ Vanausdoll II** was born in St. Louis, Missouri, on August 12, 1924. He was also known as **Raymond** and **Ray.** Otis Raymond II died on October 4, 2017, in Shipman, Shipman Twp., Macoupin Co., Illinois. He was cremated and his cremains buried in Scenic Hill/Odd Fellows Cemetery, Grafton, Quarry Twp., Jersey Co., Illinois.[14]

+ 270 f VII. **Geraldine Yvonne⁸ Vanausdoll** was born in St. Louis, Missouri, on March 28, 1927. She was also known as **Gerry.** Geraldine Yvonne died in a hospital in Alton, Alton Twp., Madison Co., Illinois, on May 22, 1979. She was buried in Scenic Hill/Odd Fellows Cemetery, Quarry Twp., Jersey Co., Illinois.[13, 14]

+ 271 f VIII. **Cassie Maryanne⁸ Vanausdoll** was born in St. Louis, Missouri, on July 21, 1930. She died in Grafton, Quarry Twp., Jersey Co., Illinois, on May 24, 1956. Cassie Maryanne was buried in Hartford Cemetery, Grafton, Quarry Twp., Jersey Co., Illinois.[84]

+ 272 m IX. **Tim Ryan⁸ Vanausdoll** was born in St. Louis, Missouri, on November 29, 1932. He died in Cordell, Washita Co., Oklahoma, on August 6, 2013.

**105. Everett Charles⁷ Vanausdoll** (*Charles Wesley⁶, Caleb⁵, Mary⁴ Pegan, Andrew³ Pegan II, Andrew² Pagan, James¹*) was born on September 18, 1888, in Quarry Twp., Jersey Co., Illinois. He was the son of Charles Wesley Vanausdoll (28) and Syrenia/Rowena Helen Gowins. Everett Charles died in Jerseyville, Jersey Twp., Jersey Co., Illinois, on November 2, 1963, at age 75. He was buried in Oak Grove Cemetery, Jerseyville, Jersey Twp., Jersey Co., Illinois.[16]

Everett Charles married **Carolene Mary Quitt** on December 9, 1911, in Jersey Co., Illinois. They had seven children. Carolene Mary Quitt was born in Quarry Twp., Jersey Co., Illinois, on November 9, 1893. Carolene Mary reached age 89 and died in Jerseyville, Jersey Twp., Jersey Co., Illinois, on July 28, 1983. She was buried in Oak Grove Cemetery, Jerseyville, Jersey Twp., Jersey Co., Illinois.[13]

Children of Everett Charles Vanausdoll and Carolene Mary Quitt:

+ 273 m I. **Charles A.⁸ Vanausdoll** was born in Quarry Twp., Jersey Co., Illinois, on April 20, 1914. He died in Jerseyville, Jersey Twp., Jersey

Co., Illinois, on March 12, 1982. Charles A. was buried in Oak Grove Cemetery, Jerseyville, Jersey Twp., Jersey Co., Illinois.[16]

+ 274 m II. **Truman Everett⁸ Vanausdoll** was born in Quarry Twp., Jersey Co., Illinois, on January 5, 1920. He died in a hospital in Covina, Los Angeles Co., California, on November 28, 1996.

+ 275 m III. **Willie Warren⁸ Vanausdoll** was born in Quarry Twp., Jersey Co., Illinois, on February 13, 1923. He died in Eldred, Bluffdale Twp. Greene Co., Illinois, on October 7, 2004. Willie Warren was buried in Oak Grove Cemetery, Jerseyville, Jersey Twp., Jersey Co., Illinois.[16] ,

+ 276 f IV. **Pauline Irene⁸ Vanausdoll** was born in Quarry Twp., Jersey Co., Illinois, on February 13, 1923. He died in Eldred, Bluffdale Twp., Greene Co., Illinois, on October 7, 2004. Willie Warren was buried in Oak Grove Cemetery, Jerseyville, Jersey Twp., Jersey Co., Illinois.[16]

+ 277 m V. **Donald Lee⁸ Vanausdoll** was born in Quarry Twp., Jersey Co., Illinois, on August 9, 1931. He died in Jerseyville, Jersey Twp., Jersey Co., Illinois, on October 10, 2006. Donald Lee was buried in St. Francis Xavier Cemetery, Jerseyville, Jersey Twp., Jersey Co., Illinois.[85]

+ 278 m VI. **Darrel⁸ Vanausdoll** was born in Jersey Twp., Jersey Co., Illinois, on December 9, 1935.

+ 279 f VII. **Marlene Emma⁸ Vanausdoll** was born in Jersey Twp., Jersey Co., Illinois, in 1937.

**106. Ada May⁷ Vanausdoll** (*Charles Wesley⁶, Caleb⁵, Mary⁴ Pegan, Andrew³ Pegan II, Andrew² Pagan, James¹*) was born on September 4, 1895, in Quarry Twp., Jersey Co., Illinois. She was the daughter of Charles Wesley Vanausdoll (28) and Syrenia/Rowena Helen Gowins. Ada died in Jerseyville, Jersey Twp., Jersey Co., Illinois, on December 31, 1979, at age 84. She was buried in Valhalla Memorial Park and Mausoleum, Godfrey, Godfrey Twp., Madison Co., Illinois.[16]

Childless.

Ada married **William Jesse Hooper** on September 4, 1917, in Jersey Co., Illinois. William Jesse Hooper was born in Otter Creek Twp., Jersey Co., Illinois, on October 30, 1894. He was also known as **Jesse.** William Jesse reached age 56 and died in Otter Creek Twp., Jersey Co., Illinois, on September 29, 1951. He was buried in Valhalla Memorial Park and Mausoleum, Godfrey, Godfrey Twp., Madison Co., Illinois.[17]

**107. Child One⁷ Patton** (*Cora Alice⁶ Vanausdoll, Caleb⁵, Mary⁴ Pegan, Andrew³ Pegan II, Andrew² Pagan, James¹*) was born between 1886 and 1900. He or she was a child of Allen D. Patton and Cora Alice Vanausdoll (29). Child One died between 1886 and 1900.

**108. Olive⁷ Patton** (*Cora Alice⁶ Vanausdoll, Caleb⁵, Mary⁴ Pegan, Andrew³ Pegan II, Andrew² Pagan, James¹*) was born on March 6, 1890, in Lowell Twp., Cherokee Co., Kansas. She was the daughter of Allen D. Patton and Cora Alice Vanausdoll (29). Olive died in Lowell Twp., Cherokee Co., Kansas, on October 3, 1890. She was buried in Oak Hill Cemetery, Galena, Cherokee Co., Kansas.[16]

**109. Charles Frederick⁷ Patton** (*Cora Alice⁶ Vanausdoll, Caleb⁵, Mary⁴ Pegan, Andrew³ Pegan II, Andrew² Pagan, James¹*) was born on April 1, 1892, in Joplin, Joplin Twp., Jasper Co., Missouri. He was also known as **Frederick** and **Fred.** He was the son of Allen D. Patton and Cora Alice Vanausdoll (29). Charles Frederick died in Wallace, Shoshone Co., Idaho, on October 8, 1937, at age 45. He was buried in Nine Mile Cemetery, Wallace, Shoshone Co., Idaho.[33]

Charles Frederick married **Amelia Dorothy Young** on July 29, 1916, in Jasper Co., Missouri. They had three children. Amelia Dorothy Young was born in Baxter Springs, Spring Valley Twp., Cherokee Co., Kansas, on May 2, 1899. Amelia Dorothy reached age 56 and died in Oregon City, Clackamas Co., Oregon, on October 26, 1955. Amelia Young Patton is probably buried in Mountain View Cemetery, Oregon City, Clackamas Co., Oregon, where her son Gearald Pattton is buried.

Children of Charles Frederick Patton and Amelia Dorothy Young:

+ 280 m I. **Mortimer Revere**[8] **Patton** was born in Butler Co., Kansas, on September 4, 1919. He died in Kennesaw, Cobb Co., Georgia, on November 10, 2005. Mortimer Revere was buried in Georgia National Cemetery, Canton, Cherokee Co., Georgia.[86]

+ 281 m II. **Gearald E.**[8] **Patton** was born in Butler Co., Kansas, in 1922. He died in Wasco, Sherman Co., Oregon, on September 22, 1949. Gearald E. was buried in Mountain View Cemetery, Oregon City, Clackamas Co., Oregon.[87]

+ 282 f III. **Delores Evelyn**[8] **Patton** was born in Lowell Twp., Cherokee Co., Kansas, on March 22, 1924. She died in Milwaukie, Clackamas Co., Oregon, on January 22, 2008

**110. Zantha**[7] **Patton** (*Cora Alice*[6] *Vanausdoll, Caleb*[5], *Mary*[4] *Pegan, Andrew*[3] *Pegan II, Andrew*[2] *Pagan, James*[1]) was born in December 1894 in Nebraska. She was the daughter of Allen D. Patton and Cora Alice Vanausdoll (29). Zantha lived in 1930 in Aurora, Aurora Twp., Kane Co., Illinois. She died after 1930.

There is no Illinois death certificate for Zantha Patton Spencer in Illinois prior to 1947, and no obituary or burial records for her there either.

Zantha married **Charles E. Spencer** on November 8, 1913, in Barton Co., Missouri. They had two children. Charles E. Spencer was born in Webb City, Joplin Twp., Jasper Co., Missouri, on November 19, 1891. Charles E. died in Denver, Denver Co.., Colorado? between 1920 and 1929.

Charles E. and Zantha Patton Spencer were living in Columbus, Crawford Twp., Cherokee Co., Kansas in the 1920 U.S. Federal Census. Unsourced family records say he may have died there. After Charles' death, Zantha and her children seemed to have moved to Charles' hometown, Joplin, Missouri. The *Joplin (MO) Globe* reports on July 12, 1924 that Mrs. Zantha Spencer and her daughter Guila were leaving Joplin to live in Denver, Colorado to better Guila's health.

Zantha Spencer is listed as "Zan Spencer" in the Denver, Colorado city directory in 1929. A waitress, she is the widow of Charles E. By the 1930 census, Zantha, enumerated as "Zan" is residing in Aurora, Aurora, Kane Co., Illinois, and the Aurora city directory lists her in 1931. Her daughter Guila died in Aurora in 1932. There are no more records for Zantha.

Children of Zantha Patton and Charles E. Spencer:

+ 283 m I. **Albert J.**[8] **Spencer** was born in Barton Co., Missouri, in December 1914. He died in Aurora, Aurora Twp., Kane Co., Illinois, about September 18, 1995. Albert J. was buried in Mount Olivet Cemetery, Aurora, Aurora Twp., Kane Co., Illinois.[88]

+ 284 f II. **Guila Jean**[8] **Spencer** was born in Columbus, Crawford Twp., Cherokee Co., Kansas, in 1917. She died in Aurora, Aurora Twp., Kane Co., Illinois, on March 19, 1932.

**111. Louis Allan**[7] **Patton** (*Cora Alice*[6] *Vanausdoll, Caleb*[5], *Mary*[4] *Pegan, Andrew*[3] *Pegan II, Andrew*[2] *Pagan, James*[1]) was born on April 2, 1897, in Lowell Twp., Cherokee Co., Kansas. He was the son of Allen D. Patton and Cora Alice Vanausdoll

(29). Louis Allan died in Wallace, Shoshone Co., Idaho, on April 12, 1951, at age 54. He was buried in Forest Cemetery, Coeur d'Alene, Kootenai Co., Idaho.[34]

May have never married.

**112. Ulis Everett[7] Patton** (*Cora Alice[6] Vanausdoll, Caleb[5], Mary[4] Pegan, Andrew[3] Pegan II, Andrew[2] Pagan, James[1]*) was born on December 19, 1899, in Lowell Twp., Cherokee Co., Kansas. He was the son of Allen D. Patton and Cora Alice Vanausdoll (29). Ulis Everett died in Newbury Park, Ventura Co., California, on July 2, 1977, at age 77. He was buried in Victor Cemetery, Victor, Ravalli Co., Montana.[35]

**113. Mary M.[7] Patton** (*Cora Alice[6] Vanausdoll, Caleb[5], Mary[4] Pegan, Andrew[3] Pegan II, Andrew[2] Pagan, James[1]*) was born on May 9, 1903, in Lowell Twp., Cherokee Co., Kansas. She was the daughter of Allen D. Patton and Cora Alice Vanausdoll (29). Mary M. died in Wallace, Shoshone Co., Idaho, on May 16, 1964, at age 61. She was buried in Victor Cemetery, Victor, Ravalli Co., Montana.[35]

She married **Paul E. Hawkins.** They divorced. They had one son. Paul E. Hawkins was born in Indiana in 1899. Paul E. lived in 1930 in Columbus, Salamanca Twp., Cherokee Co., Kansas? He died in El Dorado, Butler Co., Kansas? after 1946.

Mary M. Patton married **Arthur Elmer Udstad** before 1940. Arthur Elmer Udstad was born in Aurora, Aurora Twp., Kane Co., Illinois, on February 20, 1907. Arthur Elmer reached age 72 and died in Silverton, Shoshone Co., Idaho, on June 29, 1979. He was buried in Victor Cemetery, Victor, Ravalli Co., Montana.[35]

Son of Mary M. Patton and Paul E. Hawkins:

+ 285 m I. **Paul Allen[8] Hawkins II** was born in Parsons, Walton Twp., Labette Co., Kansas, on March 20, 1922. He died in Silver Bow Co., Montana, on March 21, 1993. He was buried in New Hill Cemetery, Anaconda, Deer Lodge Co., Montana.[89]

**114. Porter William[7] Patton** (*Cora Alice[6] Vanausdoll, Caleb[5], Mary[4] Pegan, Andrew[3] Pegan II, Andrew[2] Pagan, James[1]*) was born on December 4, 1906, in Lowell Twp., Cherokee Co., Kansas. He was the son of Allen D. Patton and Cora Alice Vanausdoll (29). Porter William lived in 1930 in South Brown Twp., Edwards Co., Kansas. He died in Victor, Ravalli Co., Montana, on March 20, 1939, at age 32. Porter William was buried in Victor Cemetery, Victor, Ravalli Co., Montana.[35]

**115. Arthur M.[7] Patton** (*Cora Alice[6] Vanausdoll, Caleb[5], Mary[4] Pegan, Andrew[3] Pegan II, Andrew[2] Pagan, James[1]*) was born on May 31, 1908, in Lowell Twp., Cherokee Co., Kansas. He was the son of Allen D. Patton and Cora Alice Vanausdoll (29). Arthur M. lived in Stevensville, Ravalli Co., Montana. He died in Missoula, Missoula Co., Montana, on May 31, 1978, at age 70. Arthur M. was buried in Victor Cemetery, Victor, Ravalli Co., Montana.[35]

He married **Doris Esther Puyear** before 1930. They had one son. Doris Esther Puyear was born in Skalkaho, Ravalli Co., Montana, on February 20, 1909. Doris Esther reached age 88 and died in Missoula, Missoula Co., Montana, on November 21, 1997. She was buried in Victor Cemetery, Victor, Ravalli Co., Montana.[35]

Son of Arthur M. Patton and Doris Esther Puyear:

+ 286 m I. **Allen Marvin[8] Patton** was born in Stevensville, Ravalli Co., Montana, in 1930.

**116. Hallye Maude[7] Vanausdoll** (*Allen M.[6], Caleb[5], Mary[4] Pegan, Andrew[3] Pegan II, Andrew[2] Pagan, James[1]*) was born on April 23, 1901, in Otter Creek Twp., Jersey Co., Illinois. She was also known as **Maude.** She was the daughter of Allen M. Vanausdoll (30) and Lenora Kirchner. Hallye Maude died in Jerseyville, Jersey Twp., Jersey Co., Illinois, on February 23, 1982, at age 80. She was buried in Oak Grove Cemetery, Jerseyville, Jersey Twp., Jersey Co., Illinois.[16]

Hallye Maude married **Edward Ross Seago** on November 24, 1918, in Jersey Co., Illinois. They had five children. Edward Ross Seago was born in Jerseyville, Jersey Twp., Jersey Co., Illinois, on October 6, 1900. He was also known as **Ross**. Edward Ross reached age 81 and died in Jerseyville, Jersey Twp., Jersey Co., Illinois, on March 28, 1982. He was buried in Oak Grove Cemetery, Jerseyville, Jersey Twp., Jersey Co., Illinois.[16]

Hallye Maude Vanausdoll and Edward Ross Seago had four children, including:

+ 287 m I. **Wilbur Harold⁸ Seago** was born in Jerseyville, Jersey Twp., Jersey Co., Illinois, on November 21, 1919. He died in Jerseyville, Jersey Twp., Jersey Co., Illinois, on December 4, 1919.

+ 288 m II. **Carl Wayne⁸ Seago** was born in Otter Creek Twp., Jersey Co., Illinois, on July 28, 1921. He died in Phoenix, Maricopa Co., Arizona, on August 14, 2004. Carl Wayne was buried in National Memorial Cemetery of Arizona, Phoenix, Maricopa Co., Arizona.[90, 91]

+ 289 f III. **Dorothy Marie⁸ Seago** was born in Alton, Alton Twp., Madison Co., Illinois, on October 2, 1926. She died in a hospital in Chesterfield, Saint Louis Co., Missouri, on February 13, 1999. Dorothy Marie was buried in Hamburg Cemetery, Hamburg, Hamburg Twp., Calhoun Co., Illinois.[92]

+ 290 f IV. **Mildred I.⁸ Seago** was born in Mississippi Twp., Jersey Co., Illinois, on December 29, 1930.

**117. Allen Laverne⁷ Vanausdoll** (*Allen M.⁶, Caleb⁵, Mary⁴ Pegan, Andrew³ Pegan II, Andrew² Pagan, James¹*) was born on May 6, 1912, in Otter Creek Twp., Jersey Co., Illinois. He was the son of Allen M. Vanausdoll (30) and Lenora Kirchner. Allen Laverne died in Shipman, Shipman Twp., Macoupin Co., Illinois, on May 15, 2000, at age 88. He was buried in Shipman Cemetery, Shipman, Shipman Twp., Macoupin Co., Illinois.[36]

Allen Laverne married **Velma Ureta Hinman** on December 26, 1931, in Macoupin Co., Illinois. They had three children. Velma Ureta Hinman was born in Athensville Twp., Greene Co., Illinois, on February 25, 1910. Velma Ureta reached age 94 and died in Alton, Alton Twp., Madison Co., Illinois, on October 8, 2004. She was buried in Shipman Cemetery, Shipman, Shipman Twp., Macoupin Co., Illinois.[36]

Children of Allen Laverne Vanausdoll and Velma Ureta Hinman:

+ 291 m I. **Richard Anthony⁸ Vanausdoll** was born in Otterville, Otter Creek Twp., Jersey Co., Illinois, on March 24, 1932. He died in Denver, Denver Co., Colorado, on March 6, 1963. Richard Anthony was buried in Shipman Cemetery, Shipman, Shipman Twp., Macoupin Co., Illinois.[36]

+ 292 f II. **Vivian⁸ Vanausdoll** was born in Otterville, Otter Creek Twp., Jersey Co., Illinois, in 1936.

+ 293 m III. **Marvin Allen⁸ Vanausdoll** was born in Otterville, Otter Creek Twp., Jersey Co., Illinois, on September 7, 1938.

**118. Glenn Herbert⁷ Vanausdoll** (*James Cornelius⁶, Caleb⁵, Mary⁴ Pegan, Andrew³ Pegan II, Andrew² Pagan, James¹*) was born on May 14, 1898, in Otter Creek Twp., Jersey Co., Illinois. He was the son of James Cornelius Vanausdoll (32) and Rachael V. Gilmore. He was also known as **Herbert**. Glenn Herbert died in St. Louis, Missouri, on September 27, 1939, at age 41. He was buried in Memorial Park Cemetery, Jennings, St. Louis Co., Missouri.[32]

May have been childless.

He married **Mary June Schupp** before 1939. Mary was born in St. Louis, Missouri on December 12,

1898. She reached age 81 and died in Long Beach, Los Angeles Co., California, on April 6, 1980.

She died as Mary June Enokian.[32]

**119. Edna Marie[7] Vanausdoll** (*James Cornelius[6], Caleb[5], Mary[4] Pegan, Andrew[3] Pegan II, Andrew[2] Pagan, James[1]*) was born on March 30, 1901, in Otter Creek Twp., Jersey Co., Illinois. She was the daughter of James Cornelius Vanausdoll (32) and Rachael V. Gilmore. Edna Marie died in Pine Lawn, St. Louis Co., Missouri, on February 24, 1936, at age 34. She was buried in Memorial Park Cemetery, Jennings, St. Louis Co., Missouri.[32]

She married **Clyde McNair Ferguson** before 1926. They had two children. Clyde McNair Ferguson was born in Clinton, Clinton Twp., Clinton Co., Iowa, on March 10, 1899. Clyde McNair reached age 67 and died in Normandy, St. Louis Co., Missouri? about August 5, 1966.

Children of Edna Marie Vanausdoll and Clyde McNair Ferguson:

+ 294 m I. **Robert E.[8] Ferguson** was born in St. Louis, Missouri, on November 25, 1926.

+ 295 f II. **Arlene Estelyn[8] Ferguson** was born in St. Louis, Missouri, on September 20, 1928. She died in Ballwin, St. Louis Co., Missouri, on May 21, 2001.

**120. Florence G.[7] Vanausdoll** (*James Cornelius[6], Caleb[5], Mary[4] Pegan, Andrew[3] Pegan II, Andrew[2] Pagan, James[1]*) was born on August 28, 1903, in Otter Creek Twp., Jersey Co., Illinois. She was the daughter of James Cornelius Vanausdoll (32) and Rachael V. Gilmore. Florence G. died in Hazelwood, St. Louis Co., Missouri, on July 13, 1990, at age 86.

She married **Clarence L. Ferguson** before 1930. They had two children. Clarence L. Ferguson was born in St. Louis, Missouri, on April 9, 1903. Clarence L. reached age 84 and died in Hazelwood, St. Louis Co., Missouri, on August 6, 1987.

Children of Florence G. Vanausdoll and Clarence L. Ferguson:

+ 296 m I. **Kenneth Hunter[8] Ferguson** was born in Central Twp., St. Louis Co., Missouri, on July 5, 1930.

+ 297 f II. **Louise or Lois[8] Ferguson** was born in Normandy Twp., St. Louis Co., Missouri, on December 24, 1934. She died before 1990.

**121. Theodore[7] Vanausdoll** (*James Cornelius[6], Caleb[5], Mary[4] Pegan, Andrew[3] Pegan II, Andrew[2] Pagan, James[1]*) was born on May 26, 1905, in Mississippi Twp., Jersey Co., Illinois. He was the son of James Cornelius Vanausdoll (32) and Rachael V. Gilmore. Theodore lived in 1967 in Irondale, Washington Co., Missouri. He died in Lakewood, Jefferson Co., Colorado, on February 10, 1981, at age 75. Theodore was buried in Memorial Park Cemetery, Jennings, St. Louis Co., Missouri.[37]

Seems to have been childless.

Theodore married Mrs. **Melita H. Hudelston** Lyons on July 1, 1950, in Randolph Co., Arkansas. Melita H. Hudelston was born in Des Moines, Polk Co., Iowa, on October 21, 1904. Melita H. lived in 1961 in Jennings, St. Louis Co., Missouri. She reached age 57 and died in a hospital in Clayton, St. Louis Co., Missouri, on December 21, 1961. Melita was buried in Calvary Cemetery and Mausoleum, St. Louis, Missouri.[38]

**122. Lucille Rachel[7] Vanausdoll** (*James Cornelius[6], Caleb[5], Mary[4] Pegan, Andrew[3] Pegan II, Andrew[2] Pagan, James[1]*) was born on February 14, 1908, in Mississippi Twp., Jersey Co., Illinois. She was the daughter of James Cornelius Vanausdoll (32) and Rachael V. Gilmore. Lucille Rachel died in St. Ann, St. Louis Co., Missouri, on September 12, 1982, at age 74. She was buried in Calvary Cemetery and Mausoleum, St. Louis, Missouri.[38]

Childless.

Lucille Rachel married **Robert Arthur Josias** after 1930. Robert Arthur Josias was born in Chicago, Cook Co., Illinois, on October 17, 1885. Robert Arthur reached age 79 and died in Normandy

Twp., St. Louis Co., Missouri, on May 1, 1965. He was buried in Calvary Cemetery and Mausoleum, St. Louis, Missouri.[38]

**123. Hazel M.**[7] **Vanausdoll** (*James Cornelius*[6], *Caleb*[5], *Mary*[4] *Pegan, Andrew*[3] *Pegan II, Andrew*[2] *Pagan, James*[1]) was born on December 26, 1911, in Mississippi Twp., Jersey Co., Illinois. She was the daughter of James Cornelius Vanausdoll (32) and Christena Schaaf. Hazel M. died in Bethalto, Fort Russell Twp., Madison Co., Illinois, on October 3, 1998, at age 86. She was buried in Oakwood Cemetery, Upper Alton, Alton Twp., Madison Co., Illinois.[8]

She married **Harry J. Hunt** before 1930. They had two children. Harry J. Hunt was born in Jersey Twp., Jersey Co., Illinois, on March 16, 1907. Harry J. reached age 87 and died in Bethalto, Fort Russell Twp., Madison Co., Illinois, on August 29, 1994. He was buried in Oakwood Cemetery, Upper Alton, Alton Twp., Madison Co., Illinois.[5]

Children of Hazel M. Vanausdoll and Harry J. Hunt:

+ 298 m I. **Donald**[8] **Hunt** was born in Alton, Alton Twp., Madison Co., Illinois, in 1930.

+ 299 f II. **Shirley**[8] **Hunt** was born in Alton, Alton Twp., Madison Co., Illinois, in 1932.

**124. Leah**[7] **Vanausdoll** (*James Cornelius*[6], *Caleb*[5], *Mary*[4] *Pegan, Andrew*[3] *Pegan II, Andrew*[2] *Pagan, James*[1]) was born on October 31, 1914, in Mississippi Twp., Jersey Co., Illinois. She was the daughter of James Cornelius Vanausdoll (32) and Christena Schaaf. Leah died in Denver, Adams Co., Colorado, on February 6, 2000, at age 85. She was buried in Crown Hill Cemetery, Wheat Ridge, Jefferson Co., Colorado.[7]

She married **Robert Hinst** after 1940. They had one daughter. Robert Hinst was born in Denver, Adams Co., Colorado, on November 24, 1924. Robert reached age 81 and died in Denver, Adams Co., Colorado, on February 27, 2006. He was

buried in Crown Hill Cemetery, Wheat Ridge, Jefferson Co., Colorado.[7]

**125. Irene Ester**[7] **Vanausdoll** (*James Cornelius*[6], *Caleb*[5], *Mary*[4] *Pegan, Andrew*[3] *Pegan II, Andrew*[2] *Pagan, James*[1]) was born on April 15, 1917, in Mississippi Twp., Jersey Co., Illinois. She was the daughter of James Cornelius Vanausdoll (32) and Christena Schaaf. Irene Ester lived in 1995 in Heber Springs, Cleburne Co., Arkansas. She died in Heber Springs, Cleburne Co., Arkansas, on July 9, 2004, at age 87. Irene Ester was buried in Cleburne County Memorial Gardens Cemetery, Heber Springs, Cleburne Co., Arkansas.[39]

Childless.

She married **Ernie Onas Yates.** Ernie Onas Yates was born in Dixon, Union Twp., Pulaski Co., Missouri, on June 4, 1913. Ernie Onas reached age 84 and died in Heber Springs, Cleburne Co., Arkansas, on May 22, 1998. He was buried in Cleburne County Memorial Gardens Cemetery, Heber Springs, Cleburne Co., Arkansas.[39]

**126. Alice R.**[7] **Vanausdoll** (*James Cornelius*[6], *Caleb*[5], *Mary*[4] *Pegan, Andrew*[3] *Pegan II, Andrew*[2] *Pagan, James*[1]) was born on July 2, 1919, in Mississippi Twp., Jersey Co., Illinois. She was the daughter of James Cornelius Vanausdoll (32) and Christena Schaaf. Alice R. died in Pacific, Union Twp., Franklin Co., Missouri, in December 1983 at age 64. She was buried in Sunset Cemetery, Pacific, Boles Twp., Franklin Co., Missouri.[40]

Alice R. Vanausdoll married **Charles Adney** before 1939. They divorced about 1942. They had one son. Charles Adney was born in Chester Twp., Randolph Co., Illinois, on January 21, 1883. He reached age 59 and died in Alton, Alton Twp., Madison Co., Illinois, on March 7, 1942. Charles was buried in Alton National Cemetery, Alton, Alton Twp., Madison Co., Illinois.[93]

Alice R. Vanausdoll Adney married **James Inman Greer** about 1942? They divorced before 1950. They had one daughter. James Inman Greer? was born in Wood River Twp., Madison Co., Illinois, on July 26, 1920. He lived in Boulder, Boulder Co., Colorado. James Inman reached age 54 and died in Wisconsin on November 4, 1974. He was buried in Fort Logan National Cemetery, Denver, Denver Co., Colorado.[94]

Alice R. Vanausdoll Adney Greer married **Carl Hubert Kissel.** Carl Hubert Kissel was born in St. Louis, Missouri, on May 8, 1913. Carl Hubert reached age 78 and died in Pacific, Boles Twp., Franklin Co., Missouri, on February 23, 1992. He was buried in Sunset Cemetery, Pacific, Boles Twp., Franklin Co., Missouri.[40]

Son of Alice R. Vanausdoll and Charles Adney:

+ 300  m  I.  **Robert Eugene⁸ Adney** was born in Alton, Alton Twp., Madison Co., Illinois, on January 20, 1939. He died in Pacific, Boles Twp., Franklin Co., Missouri, on November 1, 2010.

Daughter of Alice R. Vanausdoll and James Inman Greer?:

+ 301  f  I.  **Roberta J.⁸ Greer** was born in Wood River Twp., Madison Co., Illinois, in 1943. She died in Bethalto, Fort Russell Twp., Madison Co., Illinois, on January 8, 1979. Roberta J. was buried in Oakwood Cemetery, Upper Alton, Alton Twp., Madison Co., Illinois.[8]

127. **James Everett⁷ Vanausdoll** (*James Cornelius⁶, Caleb⁵, Mary⁴ Pegan, Andrew³ Pegan II, Andrew² Pagan, James¹*) was born on July 13, 1921, in Mississippi Twp., Jersey Co., Illinois. He was the son of James Cornelius Vanausdoll (32) and Christena Schaaf. James Everett died in Alton, Alton Twp., Madison Co., Illinois, on February 2, 1995, at age 73. He was buried in Oak Grove Cemetery, Jerseyville, Jersey Twp., Jersey Co., Illinois.[16]

James Everett married **LaJune Gage** on March 3, 1946. They had two sons. LaJune Gage was born in Galesburg, Knox Co., Illinois? on August 9, 1922. She was also known as **June.** LaJune reached age 70 and died in Dow, Mississippi Twp., Jersey

Co., Illinois, on January 3, 1993. She was buried in Oak Grove Cemetery, Jerseyville, Jersey Twp., Jersey Co., Illinois.[16]

128. **Martha Ellen⁷ Vanausdoll** (*James Cornelius⁶, Caleb⁵, Mary⁴ Pegan, Andrew³ Pegan II, Andrew² Pagan, James¹*) was born on August 9, 1923, in Mississippi Twp., Jersey Co., Illinois. She was the daughter of James Cornelius Vanausdoll (32) and Christena Schaaf. Martha Ellen lived in 1995 in St. Louis, Missouri. She died in Columbia, Monroe Co., Illinois or St. Louis, Missouri, on June 13, 2006, at age 82. Martha Ellen was buried in Saint Paul's Evangelical Cemetery, Olivet, St. Louis Co., Missouri.[41]

Martha Ellen married **Armond Charles Maxeiner** on September 6, 1958, in St. Louis Co., Missouri. Armond Charles Maxeiner was born in St. Ferdinand, St. Louis Co., Missouri, on November 11, 1930. Armond Charles reached age 73 and died in Bradenton, Manatee Co., Florida, on April 1, 2004. He was buried in Saint Paul's Evangelical Cemetery, Olivet, St. Louis Co., Missouri.[41]

129. **Virgil Lee⁷ Vanausdoll** (*James Cornelius⁶, Caleb⁵, Mary⁴ Pegan, Andrew³ Pegan II, Andrew² Pagan, James¹*) was born on August 9, 1927, in Mississippi Twp., Jersey Co., Illinois. He was the son of James Cornelius Vanausdoll (32) and Christena Schaaf. Virgil Lee died in a hospital in Alton, Alton Twp., Madison Co., Illinois, on November 12, 1942, at age 15. He was buried in Noble Cemetery, Otterville, Otter Creek Twp., Jersey Co., Illinois.[1]

Virgil Lee Vanausdoll died several days after being hit by a car upon when he exited his school bus.

130. **Herbert Eugene⁷ Vanausdoll** (*James Cornelius⁶, Caleb⁵, Mary⁴ Pegan, Andrew³ Pegan II, Andrew² Pagan, James¹*) was born on April 6, 1930, in Mississippi Twp., Jersey Co., Illinois. He was the son of James Cornelius Vanausdoll (32) and Christena Schaaf. Herbert Eugene died in Affton, St. Louis Co., Missouri, on June 11, 2005, at age 75. He was buried in Sunset Memorial Park and Mausoleum, Affton, St. Louis Co., Missouri.[42]

Herbert Eugene married **Virginia Lee Bruegge** on March 24, 1951, in St. Louis, Missouri. Virginia

L. Bruegge was born in St. Louis, Missouri, on July 18, 1931. They had several children.

**131. Lillian Ethel**[7] **Dodson** (*Rachel Roseanna*[6] *Vanausdoll, Allen McCreary*[5]*, Mary*[4] *Pegan, Andrew*[3] *Pegan II, Andrew*[2] *Pagan, James*[1]) was born on April 23, 1890, in Alton, Alton Twp., Madison Co., Illinois. She was the daughter of Bertram Dodson and Rachel Roseanna Vanausdoll (35). Lillian Ethel died in Jerseyville, Jersey Twp., Jersey Co., Illinois, on November 8, 1949, at age 59. She was buried in Saint Patrick's Cemetery, Godfrey, Godfrey Twp., Madison Co., Illinois.[22]

Childless.

Lillian Ethel married **Clyde Earl Sunderland** after 1940. Clyde Earl Sunderland was born in Kane Twp., Greene Co., Illinois, on March 6, 1891. Clyde Earl reached age 75 and died in Pleasant Hill Twp., Pike Co., Illinois, on March 27, 1966. He was buried in Oak Grove Cemetery, Jerseyville, Jersey Twp., Jersey Co., Illinois.[16]

**132. Lola**[7] **Dodson** (*Rachel Roseanna*[6] *Vanausdoll, Allen McCreary*[5]*, Mary*[4] *Pegan, Andrew*[3] *Pegan II, Andrew*[2] *Pagan, James*[1]) was born on October 22, 1893, in Alton, Alton Twp., Madison Co., Illinois. She was the daughter of Bertram Dodson and Rachel Roseanna Vanausdoll (35). Lola died in Godfrey, Godfrey Twp., Madison Co., Illinois, on March 17, 1969, at age 75. She was buried in Valhalla Memorial Park and Mausoleum, Godfrey, Godfrey Twp., Madison Co., Illinois.[17]

Lola married **Charles Dilling** before 1914. They had five children. Charles Dilling was born in Alton, Alton Twp., Madison Co., Illinois, on July 31, 1892. Charles reached age 78 and died in Godfrey, Godfrey Twp., Madison Co., Illinois, on August 15, 1970. He was buried in Valhalla Memorial Park and Mausoleum, Godfrey, Godfrey Twp., Madison Co., Illinois.[17]

Children of Lola Dodson and Charles Dilling:

+ 302 f I. **Nordica Lind**[8] **Dilling** was born in Jerseyville, Jersey Twp., Jersey Co., Illinois, on January 26, 1914. She died in a facililty in Alton, Alton Twp., Madison Co., Illinois, on June 19, 2003. Nordica Lind was buried in Valhalla Memorial Park and Mausoleum, Godfrey, Godfrey Twp., Madison Co., Illinois.[17]

+ 303 m II. **Charles**[8] **Dilling II** was born in Alton, Alton Twp., Madison Co., Illinois, on July 25, 1915. He died in Godfrey, Godfrey Twp., Madison Co., Illinois, on September 15, 1988.

+ 304 m III. **Robert**[8] **Dilling** was born in Alton, Alton Twp., Madison Co., Illinois, on December 17, 1917. He died in Godfrey, Godfrey Twp., Madison Co., Illinois, on September 12, 1962. Robert was buried in Valhalla Memorial Park and Mausoleum, Godfrey, Godfrey Twp., Madison Co., Illinois.[17]

+ 305 f IV. **Nordell**[8] **Dilling** was born in Alton, Alton Twp., Madison Co., Illinois, on October 10, 1921. She died in Kankakee, Kankakee Twp., Kankakee Co., Illinois, on October 11, 1993. Nordell was buried in Saint Paul's Episcopal Columbarium, Kankakee, Kankakee Twp., Kankakee Co., Illinois.[95]

+ 306 f V. **Charlotte**[8] **Dilling** was born in Alton, Alton Twp., Madison Co., Illinois, on September 22, 1924. She was also known as **Shotie**. Charlotte died in Alton, Alton Twp., Madison Co., Illinois, on May 16, 2008. She was buried in Valhalla Memorial Park and Mausoleum, Godfrey, Godfrey Twp., Madison Co., Illinois.[17]

**133. Wyona Freelove**[7] **Edsall** (*Millie Wyona*[6] *Vanausdoll, Allen McCreary*[5]*, Mary*[4] *Pegan, Andrew*[3] *Pegan II, Andrew*[2] *Pagan, James*[1]) was born in June 1893 in Otterville, Otter Creek Twp., Jersey Co., Illinois. She was also known as **Freelove**. She was the daughter of Richard Edsall and Millie Wyona Vanausdoll (39). Wyona Freelove died in Jerseyville, Jersey Twp., Jersey Co., Illinois, on March 26, 1977, at age 83. She was buried in Oak Grove Cemetery, Jerseyville, Jersey Twp., Jersey Co., Illinois.[16]

Wyona Freelove married **Sylvester Leroy Moses** on December 20, 1920, in Jersey Co., Illinois. They had three children. Sylvester Leroy Moses was born in Rural Twp., Shelby Co., Illinois, on October 30, 1891. He was also known as **Leroy.** Sylvester Leroy reached age 75 and died in Jerseyville, Jersey Twp., Jersey Co., Illinois, on October 21, 1967. He was buried in Oak Grove Cemetery, Jerseyville, Jersey Twp., Jersey Co., Illinois.[16]

Children of Wyona Freelove Edsall and Sylvester Leroy Moses:

+ 307  f  I.  **Mary Agnes[8] Moses** was born in Jerseyville, Jersey Twp., Jersey Co., Illinois, on August 29, 1922. She died in Jerseyville, Jersey Twp., Jersey Co., Illinois, on August 29, 2008. Mary Agnes was buried in Oak Grove Cemetery, Jerseyville, Jersey Twp., Jersey Co., Illinois.[16]

+ 308  m  II.  **Darrell Laverne[8] Moses** was born in Jerseyville, Jersey Twp., Jersey Co., Illinois, on February 19, 1925. He died in Vermillion, Clay Co., South Dakota, on November 9, 2010. Darrell Laverne was buried in Bluff View Cemetery, Vermillion, Clay Co., South Dakota.[96]

+ 309  m  III.  **Charles Wesley[8] Moses** was born in Jerseyville, Jersey Twp., Jersey Co., Illinois, on January 29, 1928. He died in Jerseyville, Jersey Twp., Jersey Co., Illinois, on January 18, 1978. Charles Wesley was buried in Oak Grove Cemetery, Jerseyville, Jersey Twp., Jersey Co., Illinois.[16]

**134. Allen Richard Laverne[7] Edsall** (*Millie Wyona[6] Vanausdoll, Allen McCreary[5], Mary[4] Pegan, Andrew[3] Pegan II, Andrew[2] Pagan, James[1]*) was born on March 23, 1895, in Otterville, Otter Creek Twp., Jersey Co., Illinois. He was the son of Richard Edsall and Millie Wyona Vanausdoll (39). Allen Richard Laverne lived in Warren Twp., Macomb Co., Michigan. He died in a hospital in Ann Arbor, Washtenaw Co., Michigan, on December 3, 1978, at age 83.

Allen Richard Laverne married **Ethel Mae Viola Hart** before 1921. They had three children. Ethel Mae Viola Hart was born in Chandler Twp., Huron Co., Michigan, on July 11, 1898. Ethel Mae Viola reached age 91 and died in Port Angeles, Clallam Co., Washington, on February 8, 1990.

Children of Allen Richard Laverne Edsall and Ethel Mae Viola Hart:

+ 310  f  I.  **Loris Anita[8] Edsall** was born in Detroit, Wayne Co., Michigan, on August 28, 1921. She died in Detroit, Wayne Co., Michigan, on November 12, 2009.

+ 311  m  II.  **Richard Allen[8] Edsall** was born in Detroit, Wayne Co., Michigan, on March 23, 1923. He died in Klawak, Prince of Wales-Hyder, Alaska, on December 24, 2011.

+ 312  f  III.  **Maxine[8] Edsall** was born in Detroit, Wayne Co., Michigan, on January 17, 1925. She died in Columbus, Franklin Co., Ohio, on February 20, 2013. Maxine was buried in Green Lawn Cemetery, Columbus, Franklin Co., Ohio.[97]

**135. Clyde Hilman[7] Edsall** (*Millie Wyona[6] Vanausdoll, Allen McCreary[5], Mary[4] Pegan, Andrew[3] Pegan II, Andrew[2] Pagan, James[1]*) was born on October 1, 1898, in Otterville, Otter Creek Twp., Jersey Co., Illinois. He was the son of Richard Edsall and Millie Wyona Vanausdoll (39). Clyde Hilman lived in Jerseyville, Jersey Twp., Jersey Co., Illinois. He died in a hospital in St. Louis, Missouri, on January 9, 1977, at age 78. Clyde Hilman was buried in Valhalla Memorial Park and Mausoleum, Godfrey, Godfrey Twp., Madison Co., Illinois.[17]

Childless.

Clyde Hilman married **Anna Margaret Baker** on February 14, 1920, in Jersey Co., Illinois. They divorced. Anna Margaret Baker was born in Combs, Perry Co., Kentucky, on May 26, 1899. She reached age 65 and died in White Hall, White Hall Twp., Greene Co., Illinois, on September 13, 1964. Anna Margaret was buried in Oak Grove Cemetery, Jerseyville, Jersey Twp., Jersey Co., Illinois.[17]

Buried under the name Anna M. Whitlow.

# 8th Generation

**136. Harry Leonard[8] Hamilton II** (*Harry Leonard[7], Sylvester[6], Margaret[5] VanAusdall, Mary[4] Pegan, Andrew[3] Pegan II, Andrew[2] Pagan, James[1]*) was born on June 23, 1896, in Chester Twp., Randolph Co., Illinois. He was the son of Harry Leonard Hamilton (45) and Mabel M. Greenawalt. Harry Leonard died in Long Beach, Los Angeles Co., California, on November 28, 1975, at age 79.

**137. Theda V.[8] Hamilton** (*Harry Leonard[7], Sylvester[6], Margaret[5] VanAusdall, Mary[4] Pegan, Andrew[3] Pegan II, Andrew[2] Pagan, James[1]*) was born on October 24, 1898, in Chester, Chester Twp., Randolph Co., Illinois. She was the daughter of Harry Leonard Hamilton (45) and Mabel M. Greenawalt. Theda V. died in Mount Vernon Twp., Jefferson Co., Illinois, on July 16, 1936, at age 37. She was buried in Oakwood Cemetery, Mount Vernon, Mount Vernon Twp., Jefferson Co., Illinois.[44]

Theda Hamilton Demilt Mannen's two children by her first marriage, Virginia and James, used their stepfather's, Leslie Earl "Earl" Mannen's, surname in the 1930 census and other records. But they are not living with him, nor using his name, after their mother's death in 1936.

Theda V. Hamilton married **Unknown Demilt** before 1922. They had two children.

Theda V. Hamilton Demilt married **Leslie Earl Mannen II** in 1926. They had one daughter. Leslie Earl Mannen II was born in Waltonville, Jefferson Co., Illinois, on October 27, 1890. He was also known as **Earl.** Leslie Earl reached age 77 and died in Mount Vernon, Mount Vernon Twp., Jefferson Co., Illinois, on February 18, 1968. He was buried in Oakwood Cemetery, Mount Vernon, Mount Vernon Twp., Jefferson Co., Illinois.[44]

Children of Theda V. Hamilton and Unknown Demilt:

+ 313 f I. **Virginia[9] Demilt** was born in Illinois in 1922.

+ 314 m II. **James[9] Demilt** was born in Illinois in 1924.

Daughter of Theda V. Hamilton and Leslie Earl Mannen II:

+ 315 f I. **Shirley Ann[9] Mannen** was born in Mount Vernon, Mount Vernon Twp., Jefferson Co., Illinois, on August 27, 1929.

**138. Clark L.[8] Hamilton** (*Harry Leonard[7], Sylvester[6], Margaret[5] VanAusdall, Mary[4] Pegan, Andrew[3] Pegan II, Andrew[2] Pagan, James[1]*) was born in 1901 in Chester, Chester Twp., Randolph Co., Illinois. He was the son of Harry Leonard Hamilton (45) and Mabel M. Greenawalt. Clark L. died after 1931.

**139. Clyde Jesse[8] Hamilton** (*Harry Leonard[7], Sylvester[6], Margaret[5] VanAusdall, Mary[4] Pegan, Andrew[3] Pegan II, Andrew[2] Pagan, James[1]*) was born on November 7, 1905, in Chester, Chester Twp., Randolph Co., Illinois. He was also known as **Jesse** or **Chippy.** He was the son of Harry Leonard Hamilton (45) and Mabel M. Greenawalt. Clyde Jesse died in Chester, Chester Twp., Randolph Co., Illinois, on October 10, 1980, at age 74. He was buried in Saint Mary's Catholic Cemetery, Chester, Chester Twp., Randolph Co., Illinois.[45]

Clyde Jesse used the name Jesse Clyde or J. Clyde Hamilton.

Clyde Jesse married **Helen Wolshock** before 1940. They had three children. Helen Wolshock was born in Chester, Chester Twp., Randolph Co., Illinois on March 29, 1906. Helen died in Chester, Chester Twp.., Randolph Co., Illinois, in 1959.

Clyde Jesse married Mrs. **Edythe G. Kendrick** Unknown on September 30, 1960 in Alexander Co., Illinois. Edythe G. Kendrick was born on December 23, 1919 in Albion, Edwards Co., Illinois. She was also known as Gerry. Edythe reached age 93 and died on October 16, 2013 in Chester, Chester Twp., Randolph Co., Illinois. She was buried in Evergreen Cemetery, Chester, Chester Twp., Randolph Co., Illinois.[6]

**140. Ray P.[8] Hamilton** (*Harry Leonard[7], Sylvester[6], Margaret[5] VanAusdall, Mary[4] Pegan, Andrew[3] Pegan*

II, *Andrew² Pagan, James¹*) was born on September 19, 1908, in Chester, Chester Twp., Randolph Co., Illinois. He was the son of Harry Leonard Hamilton (45) and Mabel M. Greenawalt. Ray P. died in Murphysboro, Murphysboro Twp., Jackson Co., Illinois, on August 17, 1980, at age 71. He was buried in Murdale Gardens of Memory, Murphysboro, Murphysboro Twp., Jackson Co., Illinois.[46]

He married **Eileen G. Gordon** before 1933. They had three children. Eileen G. Gordon was born in Gilead Twp., Calhoun Co., Illinois, on April 29, 1915. Eileen G. reached age 68 and died in Murphysboro, Murphysboro Twp., Jackson Co., Illinois, on January 11, 1984. She was buried in Murdale Gardens of Memory, Murphysboro, Murphysboro Twp., Jackson Co., Illinois.[46]

Ray P. Hamilton and Eileen G. Gordon had three children, including:

+ 316 m I. **Thomas Ray⁹ Hamilton** was born in Hardin, Hardin Twp., Calhoun Co., Illinois, on January 27, 1933. He died in Korea on October 7, 1951. Thomas Ray was buried in Murdale Gardens of Memory, Murphysboro, Murphysboro Twp., Jackson Co., Illinois.[46]

+ 317 f II. **Theda E.⁹ Hamilton** was born in Chester, Chester Twp., Randolph Co., Illinois, on February 20, 1937. She died in a hospital in Houston, Harris Co., Texas, on November 6, 1989. Theda E. was buried in Murdale Gardens of Memory, Murphysboro, Murphysboro Twp., Jackson Co., Illinois.[46]

**141. Howard L.⁸ Hamilton** (*Harry Leonard⁷, Sylvester⁶, Margaret⁵ VanAusdall, Mary⁴ Pegan, Andrew³ Pegan II, Andrew² Pagan, James¹*) was born on October 24, 1912, in South Fork, Fulton Co., Arkansas. He was the son of Harry Leonard Hamilton (45) and Mabel M. Greenawalt. Howard L. died in Long Beach, Los Angeles Co., California, on May 1, 1986, at age 73.

Howard L. married **Elma N. Cooper** about 1933. They divorced. They had one daughter. Elma N. Cooper was born in Belleville, Belleville Twp., St. Clair Co., Illinois, on March 10, 1916. She reached age 83 and died in Springfield, Lane Co., Oregon, on September 25, 1999.

Daughter of Howard L. Hamilton and Elma N. Cooper:

+ 318 f I. **Janet⁹ Hamilton** was born in Chester, Chester Twp., Randolph Co., Illinois, in 1935.

**142. Amy Lucille⁸ Hamilton** (*Daniel Lester⁷, Sylvester⁶, Margaret⁵ VanAusdall, Mary⁴ Pegan, Andrew³ Pegan II, Andrew² Pagan, James¹*) was born on November 21, 1914, in Dyer Co., Tennessee? She was the daughter of Daniel Lester Hamilton (46) and Warrene Fern Redd. Amy Lucille died in Wickcliffe, Ballard Co., Kentucky, on August 29, 1995, at age 80. She was buried in Wickcliffe Cemetery, Wickcliffe, Ballard Co., Kentucky.[47]

Amy Lucille married **John Rogers Dennis** before 1934. They had six children. John Rogers Dennis was born in Wickcliffe, Ballard Co., Kentucky, on June 16, 1905. John Rogers lived in 1979 in Wickcliffe Cemetery, Wickcliffe, Ballard Co., Kentucky. He reached age 73 and died in Paducah, McCracken Co., Kentucky, on May 12, 1979. John Rogers was buried in Wickcliffe Cemetery, Wickcliffe, Ballard Co., Kentucky.[47]

Amy Lucille Hamilton and John Rogers Dennis had six chidren, including:

+ 319 m I. **Charles Rogers⁹ Dennis** was born in Wickcliffe, Ballard Co., Kentucky, on July 21, 1934. He was also known as **Bunky.** Charles Rogers died in Chicago, Cook Co., Illinois, on February 1, 1972. He was buried in Berkley Cemetery, Carlisle Co., Kentucky.[98]

+ 320 f II. **Rena June⁹ Dennis** was born in Wickcliffe, Ballard Co., Kentucky, in 1937.was born in Wickcliffe, Ballard Co., Kentucky, on February 6, 1937. She died in a hospital in Paducah, McCracken Co., Kentucky, on January 12, 2018.

+ 321 f III. **Sylvia Ann⁹ Dennis** was born in Wickcliffe, Ballard Co., Kentucky, on June 20, 1939.

**143. Chester Sylvester⁸ Hamilton** (*Daniel Lester⁷, Sylvester⁶, Margaret⁵ VanAusdall, Mary⁴ Pegan, Andrew³ Pegan II, Andrew² Pagan, James¹*) was born on June 4, 1916, in Dyer Co., Tennessee? He was the son of Daniel Lester Hamilton (46) and Warrene Fern Redd. Chester Sylvester lived in 1943 in Wickcliffe, Ballard Co., Kentucky. He died in a hospital in Memphis, Shelby Co., Tennessee, on May 6, 1943, at age 26. Chester Sylvester was buried in Mound City National Cemetery, Mound City, Junction Twp., Pulaski Co., Illinois.[48]

Chester Sylvester married **Mildred Harron** on October 19, 1942, in Mississippi Co., Missouri. Mildred Harron was born in Cincinnati, Hamilton Co., Ohio? in 1918. Mildred lived in 1942 in Canton, Stark Co., Ohio. She died after 1943.

**144. Charles Leonard⁸ Hamilton** (*Daniel Lester⁷, Sylvester⁶, Margaret⁵ VanAusdall, Mary⁴ Pegan, Andrew³ Pegan II, Andrew² Pagan, James¹*) was born on October 12, 1919?, in Chester, Chester Twp., Randolph Co., Illinois. He was the son of Daniel Lester Hamilton (46) and Warrene Fern Redd. He died in Cocoa, Brevard Co., Florida in August 1985?

Charles Leonard married **Alma Londean Hammonds** on April 10, 1943, in Mississippi Co., Missouri. They divorced. They had two children. Alma Londean Hammonds was born in Carlisle Co., Kentucky, on August 1, 1926. She was also known as **Londean**. She reached age 58 and died in Tehama, Tehama Co., California, on April 24, 1985. She was buried in Oak Hill Cemetery, Red Bluff, Tehama Co., California.[99]

She remarried and died under the name Alma L. Anderson.

Charles L. Hamilton retired from an Army career in 1959, but that is the last firm documentation on him.

**145. Dorothy⁸ Garner** (*Jessie J.⁷ Hamilton, Sylvester⁶, Margaret⁵ VanAusdall, Mary⁴ Pegan, Andrew³ Pegan II, Andrew² Pagan, James¹*) was born in Randolph Co., Illinois? on December 14, 1907. She was the daughter of Horace Greeley Garner and Jessie J. Hamilton (47). Dorothy died in Newport, Jackson Co., Arkansas, or Poplar Bluff, Poplar Bluff Twp., Butler Co., Missouri, on in Oct 1980 at age 72.

Dorothy married **Arthur Wilhelm Herman Wolters** on May 4, 1932 in Perry Co., Illinois. They had six children. Arthur Wilhelm Herman Wolters was born in Wine Hill, Wine Hill Twp., Randolph Co., Illinois, on June 14, 1906. Arthur reached age 50 and died in Chester, Chester Twp., Randolph Co., Illinois, on January 4, 1950. Arthur was buried in Saint Mark Lutheran Cemetery, Steeleville, Steeleville Twp., Randolph Co., Illinois.[A]

Dorothy Garner and Arthur Wilhelm Herman Wolters had six children, including:

+ 321A m I. **Arthur Vernon⁹ Wolters II** was born in Percy, Percy Twp., Randolph Co., Illinois, on August 23, 1932. He died in Poplar Bluff, Poplar Bluff Twp., Butler Co., Missouri, on June 23 1987. Arthur Vernon was buried in Brown Chapel Cemetery, Broseley, Ash Hill Twp., Butler Co., Missouri.[B]

+ 321B m II. **Ralph Albert⁹ Wolters** was born in Percy, Percy Twp., Randolph Co., Illinois, on March 4, 1905. He died in Poplar Bluff, Poplar Bluff Twp., Butler Co., Missouri on September 26, 1998.

+ 321C m III. **Charles Frederick⁹ Wolters** was born in Chester, Chester Twp.,

Randolph Co., Illinois, on July 18, 1938. He died in Natchez, Adams Co., Mississippi, on July 16, 1978.

+ 321D m IV. **Clyde Ray[9] Wolters** was born in Poplar Bluff, Poplar Bluff Twp., Butler Co., Missouri, on April 15, 1945. He died in Phoenix, Maricopa Co., Arizona, on June 9, 1998. Clyde Ray was buried in National Memorial Cemetery of Arizona, Phoenix, Maricopa Co., Arizona.[C]

+ 321E f V. **Linda Margaret[9] Wolters** was born in Poplar Bluff, Poplar Bluff Twp., Butler Co., Missouri, on May 19, 1947. She died in Jacksonport, Jackson Co., Arkansas, on January 20, 2009. Linda Margaret was buried in Ash Hill Cemetery, Fisk, Ash Hill Twp., Butler Co., Missouri.[D]

**146. Roy S.[8] Garner** (*Jessie J.[7] Hamilton, Sylvester[6], Margaret[5] VanAusdall, Mary[4] Pegan, Andrew[3] Pegan II, Andrew[2] Pagan, James[1]*) was born on October 20, 1910, in Camp, Fulton Co., Arkansas. He was the son of Horace Greeley Garner and Jessie J. Hamilton (47). Roy S. died in Modesto, Stanislaus Co., California, on July 6, 1982, at age 71.

**147. Ruth E.[8] Johnson** (*Doris Margaret[7] Hamilton, Sylvester[6], Margaret[5] VanAusdall, Mary[4] Pegan, Andrew[3] Pegan II, Andrew[2] Pagan, James[1]*) was born on October 8, 1910, in Chester, Chester Twp., Randolph Co., Illinois. She was the daughter of Lewis Blanchard Johnson and Doris Margaret Hamilton (48). Ruth E. died in Washington, Washington Twp. Daviess Co., Indiana, on December 29, 1999, at age 89.

She married **Oscar Vincent Harris.** They had two children. Oscar Vincent Harris was born in Beardstown, Cass Co., Illinois? on October 5, 1912. Oscar Vincent lived in 1920 in Fairfield, Fairfield Twp., Wayne Co., Illinois. He also resided in 1930 in Little Rock, Pulaski Co., Arkansas.

Oscar Vincent reached age 56 and died in New Orleans, Jefferson Parish, Louisiana, on January 30, 1969. He was buried in Port Hudson National Cemetery, Zachary, East Baton Rouge Parish, Lousiana.[100]

Ruth E. Johnson married **Everett Bresh** on April 5, 1957, in Clark Co., Nevada. Everett Bresh was born in South Washington Twp., Daviess Co., Indiana, on August 22, 1913. He was also known as **Bud.** Everett lived in 1977 in Washington, Washington Twp. Daviess Co., Indiana. He reached age 63 and died in a hospital in Evansville, Vanderburgh Co., Indiana, on August 7, 1977.

Children of Ruth E. Johnson and Oscar Vincent Harris:

+ 322 m I. **Max J.[9] Harris** was born in Illinois on December 22, 1933.

+ 323 f II. **Theda Lucille[9] Harris** was born in Detroit, Wayne Co., Michigan, on August 25, 1936.

**148. Eva Grace[8] Johnson** (*Doris Margaret[7] Hamilton, Sylvester[6], Margaret[5] VanAusdall, Mary[4] Pegan, Andrew[3] Pegan II, Andrew[2] Pagan, James[1]*) was born on September 22, 1922, in Wabash Twp., Wabash Co., Illinois. She was the daughter of Lewis Blanchard Johnson and Doris Margaret Hamilton (48). Eva Grace died in Los Angeles, Los Angeles Co., California, on June 10, 1965, at age 42. She was buried in Green Hills Memorial Park Cemetery, Rancho Pales Verdes, Los Angeles Co., California.[50]

Eva Grace Johnson had a relationship with **Unknown Unknown.** They had one daughter.

Eva Grace married **Unknown Cathcart.**

Daughter of Unknown Campbell and Eva Grace Johnson:

+ 324 f II. **Daughter[9] Johnson**

**149. Frances Louise[8] Johnson** (*Doris Margaret[7] Hamilton, Sylvester[6], Margaret[5] VanAusdall, Mary[4] Pegan, Andrew[3] Pegan II, Andrew[2] Pagan, James[1]*) was born on February 9, 1925, in Wabash Twp.,

Wabash Co., Illinois. She was the daughter of Lewis Blanchard Johnson and Doris Margaret Hamilton (48). Frances Louise died in St. Petersburg, Pinellas Co., Florida, on January 3, 2005, at age 79.

Never married.

150. **Billie Rae**[8] **Johnson** (*Doris Margaret*[7] *Hamilton, Sylvester*[6]*, Margaret*[5] *VanAusdall, Mary*[4] *Pegan, Andrew*[3] *Pegan II, Andrew*[2] *Pagan, James*[1]) was born on October 14, 1928, in Wabash Twp., Wabash Co., Illinois. She was the daughter of Lewis Blanchard Johnson and Doris Margaret Hamilton (48). Billie Rae died in Newbury Park, Ventura Co., California, on October 30, 2004, at age 76.

Billie Rae married **Daniel Stewart Dugger** on February 16, 1956, in Los Angeles Co., California. Daniel Stewart Dugger was born in Bay City, Bay Co., Michigan? on November 22, 1924. Daniel Stewart reached age 61 and died in Newbury Park, Ventura Co., California, on December 18, 1985.

151. **Daughter**[8] **Johnson?** (*Doris Margaret*[7] *Hamilton, Sylvester*[6]*, Margaret*[5] *VanAusdall, Mary*[4] *Pegan, Andrew*[3] *Pegan II, Andrew*[2] *Pagan, James*[1]) was born before 1940. She was the daughter of Lewis Blanchard Johnson and Doris Margaret Hamilton (48). Daughter died before 1940.

152. **Son**[8] **Johnson?** (*Doris Margaret*[7] *Hamilton, Sylvester*[6]*, Margaret*[5] *VanAusdall, Mary*[4] *Pegan, Andrew*[3] *Pegan II, Andrew*[2] *Pagan, James*[1]) was born before 1940. He was the son of Lewis Blanchard Johnson and Doris Margaret Hamilton (48). Son died before 1940.

153. **James Lyle**[8] **Hamilton** (*Silas Vanculen*[7]*, Sylvester*[6]*, Margaret*[5] *VanAusdall, Mary*[4] *Pegan, Andrew*[3] *Pegan II, Andrew*[2] *Pagan, James*[1]) was born on August 3, 1913, in Camp, Fulton Co., Arkansas. He was the son of Silas Vanculen Hamilton (49) and Cornelia Elizabeth Tiller. James Lyle died in House Springs, Jefferson Co., Missouri, on November 29, 1988, at age 75. He was buried in Evergreen Cemetery, Chester, Chester Twp., Randolph Co., Illinois.[6]

154. **Mary Hazel**[8] **Hamilton** (*Silas Vanculen*[7]*, Sylvester*[6]*, Margaret*[5] *VanAusdall, Mary*[4] *Pegan, Andrew*[3] *Pegan II, Andrew*[2] *Pagan, James*[1]) was born on January 25, 1916, in Calvin, Hughes Co., Oklahoma. She was

also known as **Effie** and **Hazel.** She was the daughter of Silas Vanculen Hamilton (49) and Cornelia Elizabeth Tiller. Mary Hazel died in Portland, Multnomah Co., Oregon, on July 12, 2009, at age 93. She was buried in Lincoln Memorial Park Cemetery, Portland, Multnomah Co., Oregon.[52]

She married **Marvin Douglas Chandler** about 1939 in St. Louis Co., Missouri ? They had four children. Marvin Douglas Chandler was born in St. Louis, Missouri, on December 10, 1914. Marvin Douglas lived in 1940 in St. Louis, Missouri. He reached age 62 and died in Miami, Dade Co., Florida, on May 9, 1977.

155. **Oscar Myron**[8] **Hamilton** (*Silas Vanculen*[7]*, Sylvester*[6]*, Margaret*[5] *VanAusdall, Mary*[4] *Pegan, Andrew*[3] *Pegan II, Andrew*[2] *Pagan, James*[1]) was born on March 1, 1919, in Chester, Chester Twp., Randolph Co., Illinois. He was also known as **Myron.** He was the son of Silas Vanculen Hamilton (49) and Cornelia Elizabeth Tiller. Oscar Myron lived in 2003 in Columbus, Muscogee Co., Georgia. He died in Charlotte, Mecklenburg Co., North Carolina, on January 30, 2011, at age 91. Oscar Myron was buried in Evergreen Cemetery, Charlotte, Mecklenburg Co., North Carolina.[53]

Oscar Myron married **Edna E. Waldrop** on April 24, 1946, in Muscogee Co., Georgia. They had two daughters. Edna E. Waldrop was born in LaGrange, Troup Co., Georgia, on April 8, 1921.

Oscar Myron Hamilton and Edna E. Waldrop had two daughters, including:

+ 325 f I. **Nancy Beth**[9] **Hamilton** was born in Columbus, Muscogee Co., Georgia, on July 22, 1947. She died in Columbia, Richland Co., South Carolina, on March 4, 2006. Nancy Beth was buried in McClellanville Methodist Church Cemetery, McClellanville, Charleston Co., South Carolina.[101]

156. **Ola M.**[8] **Hamilton** (*Silas Vanculen*[7]*, Sylvester*[6]*, Margaret*[5] *VanAusdall, Mary*[4] *Pegan, Andrew*[3] *Pegan II, Andrew*[2] *Pagan, James*[1]) was born on November 9, 1921, in Chester, Chester Twp.,

Randolph Co., Illinois. She was the daughter of Silas Vanculen Hamilton (49) and Cornelia Elizabeth Tiller. Ola M. lived in 2000 in McLeansboro, Town Twp., Hamilton Co., Illinois. She died in a hospital in Carbondale, Carbondale Twp., Jackson Co., Illinois, on November 15, 2000, at age 79. Ola M. was buried in Evergreen Cemetery, Chester, Chester Twp., Randolph Co., Illinois.[6]

Ola Hamilton Downen's sister Betty Mae Hamilton McGinnis Downen's second husband, Glenn F. Downen, was a twin brother to her own husband, George Downen.

Ola M. married **George Downen** on July 27, 1941, in Randolph Co., Illinois. They had four children. George Downen was born in Degonia Twp., Jackson Co., Illinois, on May 27, 1920. George reached age 89 and died in Perryville, Central Twp., Perry Co., Missouri, on December 1, 2009. He was buried in Evergreen Cemetery, Chester, Chester Twp., Randolph Co., Illinois.[6]

Ola M. Hamilton and George Downen had four children, including:

+ 326 m I. **James George**[9] **Downen** was born in Chester, Chester Twp., Randolph Co., Illinois, on June 21, 1942. He died in Garden Grove, Orange Co., California? on February 4, 1999.

+ 327 f II. **Son**[9] **Downen.**

**157. Olga Fern**[8] **Hamilton** (*Silas Vanculen*[7], *Sylvester*[6], *Margaret*[5] *VanAusdall, Mary*[4] *Pegan, Andrew*[3] *Pegan II, Andrew*[2] *Pagan, James*[1]) was born on October 7, 1923, in Chester, Chester Twp., Randolph Co., Illinois. She was the daughter of Silas Vanculen Hamilton (49) and Cornelia Elizabeth Tiller. Olga Fern lived in 2011 in Lancaster, Los Angeles Co., California.

Olga Fern married **John Frederick Hastings** in October 1942 in Perry Co., Missouri. They had three sons. John Frederick Hastings was born in Kincaid Twp., Jackson Co., Illinois, on August 24, 1921. John Frederick reached age 73 and died in Gainesville, Alachua Co., Florida, on October 25, 1994.

**158. Betty Mae**[8] **Hamilton** (*Silas Vanculen*[7], *Sylvester*[6], *Margaret*[5] *VanAusdall, Mary*[4] *Pegan, Andrew*[3] *Pegan II, Andrew*[2] *Pagan, James*[1]) was born on August 22, 1926, in Chester, Chester Twp., Randolph Co., Illinois. She was the daughter of Silas Vanculen Hamilton (49) and Cornelia Elizabeth Tiller. Betty Mae died in Garden Grove, Orange Co., California, on September 7, 1993, at age 67. She was buried in Melrose Abbey Memorial Park Cemetery, Anaheim, Orange Co., California.[10]

Betty Mae married **Gordon M. McGinnis** on November 25, 1949, in Arkansas. They divorced. They had one son. Gordon M. McGinnis was born in Carbondale, Carbondale Twp., Jackson Co., Illinois, on February 7, 1925.

Betty Mae Hamilton McGinnis married **Glenn F. Downen** in 1988. Glenn F. Downen was born in Degonia Twp., Jackson Co., Illinois, on May 27, 1920. Glenn F. reached age 88 and died in Garden Grove, Orange Co., California, on May 13, 2009. He was buried in either Evergreen Cemetery, Chester, Chester Twp., Randolph Co., Illinois or Melrose Abbey Memorial Park Cemetery, Anaheim, Orange Co., California [6, 10]

Glenn F. Downen has tombstones in both cemeteries.

Betty Mae Hamilton McGinnis Downen's second husband, Glenn F. Downen, was a twin brother to her sister Ola Hamilton Downen's husband George Downen.

**159. Norma Jean**[8] **Hamilton** (*Silas Vanculen*[7], *Sylvester*[6], *Margaret*[5] *VanAusdall, Mary*[4] *Pagan, Andrew*[3] *Pegan II, Andrew*[2] *Pagan, James*[1]) was born on February 15, 1929, in Chester, Chester Twp., Randolph Co., Illinois. She was the daughter of Silas Vanculen Hamilton (49) and Cornelia Elizabeth Tiller. Norma Jean lived in 1961 in Las Vegas, Clark Co., Nevada. Norma Jean died in Las Vegas, Clark Co., Nevada, on August 10, 2016, at age 87. She was buried under the name Norma Busch in Palm Memorial Park Cemetery, Las Vegas, Clark Co., Nevada.[54]

Norma Jean Hamilton married **Jake B. Rader II.** They had six children. Jake B. Rader II was born in Rockwood, Liberty Twp., Randolph Co., Illinois, on September 5, 1923. Jake B. reached age 52 and died in Chester, Chester Twp., Randolph Co., Illinois, on September 23, 1975. He was buried in Evergreen Cemetery, Chester, Chester Twp., Randolph Co., Illinois.[6]

Norma Jean Hamilton Rader married **Unknown Busch.**

Norma Jean Hamilton and Jake B. Rader II had six children, including:

+ 328 f I. **Mary Susan⁹ Rader** was born in Chester, Chester Twp., Randolph Co., Illinois, on June 10, 1947. She was also known as **Susan.** Mary Susan died in Las Vegas, Clark Co., Nevada, on March 5, 2003.

+ 329 m II. **Mark Steven⁹ Rader** was born in Red Bud, Union Twp., Randolph Co., Illinois, on December 6, 1952 He died in Las Vegas, Clark Co.,. Nevada, on June 14, 1992. Mark Steven was buried in Palm Memorial Park Cemetery, Las Vegas, Clark Co., Nevada.[54]

**160. Wanda R.⁸ Hamilton** (*Silas Vanculen⁷, Sylvester⁶, Margaret⁵ VanAusdall, Mary⁴ Pegan, Andrew³ Pegan II, Andrew² Pagan, James¹*) was born on November 24, 1931, in Chester, Chester Twp., Randolph Co., Illinois. She was the daughter of Silas Vanculen Hamilton (49) and Cornelia Elizabeth Tiller. Wanda R. died in Alton, Alton Twp., Madison Co., Illinois, on January 21, 2011, at age 79. She was buried in Evergreen Cemetery, Chester, Chester Twp., Randolph Co., Illinois.[6]

She married **Unknown Salmons.** They divorced. They have three children.

**161. Barbara Ann⁸ Hamilton** (*Silas Vanculen⁷, Sylvester⁶, Margaret⁵ VanAusdall, Mary⁴ Pegan, Andrew³ Pegan II, Andrew² Pagan, James¹*) was born on June 3, 1934, in Chester, Chester Twp., Randolph Co.,

Illinois. She was the daughter of Silas Vanculen Hamilton (49) and Cornelia Elizabeth Tiller.

Barbara Ann Hamilton married **Albert J. Gowan.** They divorced. They had four children. They divorced. Albert J. Gowan was born in East St. Louis, St. Clair Co., Illinois, on February 10, 1934.

Barbara Ann married **Brud Richard Meyer** on November 26, 1970, in Tippecanoe Co., Indiana. Brud Richard Meyer was born in Waukegan, Waukegan Twp., Lake Co., Illinois, on February 22, 1926. Brud Richard reached age 84 and died in Lafayette, Fairfield Twp., Tippecanoe Co., Indiana, on July 3, 2010. He was buried in Tippecanoe Memory Gardens, Lafayette, Fairfield Twp., Tippecanoe Co., Indiana.[102]

Daughter of Albert J. Gowan and Barbara Ann Hamilton:

+ 330 f I. **Daughter⁹ Gowan**

**162. Nedra L.⁸ Hamilton** (*Silas Vanculen⁷, Sylvester⁶, Margaret⁵ VanAusdall, Mary⁴ Pegan, Andrew³ Pegan II, Andrew² Pagan, James¹*) was born on January 13, 1937, in Chester, Chester Twp., Randolph Co., Illinois. She was the daughter of Silas Vanculen Hamilton (49) and Cornelia Elizabeth Tiller.

Nedra L. married **Joseph Zagorski** on July 7, 1956. They had four children. Joseph Zagorski was born in East St. Louis, St. Clair Co., Illinois, on January 19, 1934. Joseph reached age 82 and died in Rockford, Rockford Twp., Winnebago Co., Illinois, on February 20, 2016.

Nedra L. Hamilton and Joseph Zagorski had four children, including:

+ 331 m I. **David A.⁹ Zagorski** was born in East St. Louis, St. Clair Co., Illinois, on February 4, 1957. He died in Munster, Lake Co., Indiana, on October 5, 2008.

**163. Arthur Homer⁸ Rogers** (*Elmer Ellsworth⁷, Austin J.⁶, Rachel C.⁵ VanAusdall, Mary⁴ Pegan, Andrew³ Pegan II, Andrew² Pagan, James¹*) was born on December 28, 1897, in Burlingame Twp., Osage Co., Kansas? He was the son of Elmer Ellsworth

Rogers (51) and Florence Martha Warner. Arthur Homer died in Riverside, Riverside Co., California, on January 1, 1979, at age 81. He was buried in Crestlawn Memorial Park Cemetery, Riverside, Riverside Co., California.[50]

Arthur Homer Rogers married **Madge Meacher** before 1930. They divorced. Madge Meacher was born in Kansas in 1902. Madge died after 1930.

He married **Ella Elmira Sargent** after 1930. Ella Elmira Sargent was born in La Junta, Otero Co., Colorado, on April 13, 1908. Ella Elmira reached age 65 and died in Riverside, Riverside Co., California, on October 17, 1973. She was buried in Crestlawn Memorial Park Cemetery, Riverside, Riverside Co., California.[57]

**164. Esther Mabel⁸ Rogers** (*Elmer Ellsworth⁷, Austin J.⁶, Rachel C.⁵ VanAusdall, Mary⁴ Pegan, Andrew³ Pegan II, Andrew² Pagan, James¹*) was born on September 21, 1899, in Florence, Fremont Co., Colorado. She was the daughter of Elmer Ellsworth Rogers (51) and Florence Martha Warner. Esther Mabel lived in 1985 in Kingsford, Dickinson Co., Michigan. She died in a hospital in Iron Mountain, Dickinson Co., Michigan, on March 11, 1985, at age 85. Esther Mabel was buried in Quinnesec Cemetery, Quinnesec, Dickinson Co., Michigan.[58]

Esther Mabel married **Jasper Kay Ausmus** on September 4, 1919. They divorced. They had two children. Jasper Kay Ausmus was born in Brush, Morgan Co., Colorado, on March 19, 1899. He reached age 91 and died in Lamar, Prowers Co., Colorado, on May 15, 1990. Jasper Kay was buried in Fairmount Cemetery, Lamar, Prowers Co., Colorado.[103]

Esther Mabel Rogers Ausmus married **Otto William Neargarth** after 1940. Otto William Neargarth was born in Osceola, Osceola Co., Michigan, on April 4, 1909. Otto William lived in 1994 in Kingsford, Dickinson Co., Michigan. He reached age 84 and died in Breitung, Dickinson Co., Michigan, on March 3, 1994. Otto William was buried in Quinnesec Cemetery, Quinnesec, Dickinson Co., Michigan.[58]

Children of Esther Mabel Rogers and Jasper Kay Ausmus:

+ 332 m I. **Virgil Kay⁹ Ausmus** was born in Lamar, Prowers Co., Colorado, on October 22, 1920. He was also known as **Kay**. He died in Pueblo, Pueblo Co., Colorado, on March 19, 1983. He was buried in Mountain View Cemetery, Pueblo, Pueblo Co., Colorado.[104]

+ 333 f II. **Doris Leona⁹ Ausmus** was born in Lamar, Prowers Co., Colorado, on December 22, 1924. She died in Aberdeen, Grays Harbor Co., Washington, on May 10, 2013. Doris Leona was buried in Satsop Cemetery, Satsop, Grays Harbor Co., Washington.[105]

**165. Evelyn Rowena⁸ Rogers** (*Elmer Ellsworth⁷, Austin J.⁶, Rachel C.⁵ VanAusdall, Mary⁴ Pegan, Andrew³ Pegan II, Andrew² Pagan, James¹*) was born on October 12, 1901, in Florence, Fremont Co., Colorado. She was the daughter of Elmer Ellsworth Rogers (51) and Florence Martha Warner. Evelyn Rowena died in Grand Junction, Mesa Co., Colorado, on February 1, 1929, at age 27. She was buried in Calvary Cemetery, Orchard Mesa, Mesa Co., Colorado.[59]

Evelyn Rowena married **Archie Rogers** on March 7, 1920, in Prowers Co., Colorado. They had three children. Archie Rogers was born in Rich Hill, Osage Twp., Bates Co., Missouri, on April 25, 1899. Archie reached age 73 and died in Oroville, Butte Co., California, on August 15, 1972. He was buried in Memorial Park Cemetery, Oroville, Butte Co., California.[106]

Children of Evelyn Rowena Rogers and Archie Rogers:

+ 334 m I. **Floyd Cleo⁹ Rogers** was born in Granada, Powers Co., Colorado, on April 6, 1921. He died in San Francisco, San Francisco Co., California, on April 19, 1995. He was buried in San Joaquin Valley National Cemetery, Santa Nella, Merced Co., California.[107]

+ 335 f II. **Leona⁹ Rogers** was born in 1923.

+ 336 m III. **Ralph Wayne⁹ Rogers** was born in Cimmeron, Clark Co., Kansas, on May 2, 1925. He died in Fresno, Fresno Co., California, on April 23, 1972.

**166. Mildred Leona⁸ Rogers** (*Elmer Ellsworth⁷, Austin J.⁶, Rachel C.⁵ VanAusdall, Mary⁴ Pegan, Andrew³ Pegan II, Andrew² Pagan, James¹*) was born on June 9, 1905, in Burlingame Twp., Osage Co., Kansas. She was the daughter of Elmer Ellsworth Rogers (51) and Florence Martha Warner. Mildred Leona died in Burlingame Twp., Osage Co., Kansas, on November 5, 1905.

**167. Jessie Hazel⁸ Rogers** (*Elmer Ellsworth⁷, Austin J.⁶, Rachel C.⁵ VanAusdall, Mary⁴ Pegan, Andrew³ Pegan II, Andrew² Pagan, James¹*) was born on May 3, 1907, in Burlingame Twp., Osage Co., Kansas. She was the daughter of Elmer Ellsworth Rogers (51) and Florence Martha Warner. Jessie Hazel died in La Junta, Otero Co., Colorado, on December 19, 1932, at age 25. She was buried in Fairview Cemetery, La Junta, Otero Co., Colorado.[60]

Jessie Hazel married **Howard William Grimsley** on October 21, 1927. They had one daughter. Howard William Grimsley was born in Banner Elk, Watauga Co. (now Avery Co), North Carolina, on December 22, 1903. He was also known as **Fly**. Howard William reached age 57 and died in Rocky Ford, Otero Co., Colorado, in 1961. He was buried in Hillcrest Cemetery, Rocky Ford, Otero Co., Colorado.[108]

Daughter of Jessie Hazel Rogers and Howard William Grimsley:

+ 337 f I. **Evelyn⁹ Grimsley** was born in La Junta, Otero Co., Colorado, in 1931.

**168. Charles Austin⁸ Rogers** (*Elmer Ellsworth⁷, Austin J.⁶, Rachel C.⁵ VanAusdall, Mary⁴ Pegan, Andrew³*

*Pegan II, Andrew² Pagan, James¹*) was born on May 26, 1908, in Burlingame Twp., Osage Co., Kansas. He was the son of Elmer Ellsworth Rogers (51) and Florence Martha Warner. Charles Austin died in Burlingame Twp., Osage Co., Kansas, on May 26, 1908.

**169. Mary C.⁸ Rogers** (*Elmer Ellsworth⁷, Austin J.⁶, Rachel C.⁵ VanAusdall, Mary⁴ Pegan, Andrew³ Pegan II, Andrew² Pagan, James¹*) was born in 1929 in Emporia, Emporia Twp., Lyon Co., Kansas. She is the daughter of Elmer Ellsworth Rogers (51) and Mary Marguerite Smith.

**170. William Harvey⁸ Rogers** (*Herbert Augusta⁷, Austin J.⁶, Rachel C.⁵ VanAusdall, Mary⁴ Pegan, Andrew³ Pegan II, Andrew² Pagan, James¹*) was born on May 10, 1905, in Arvonia Twp., Osage Co., Kansas. He was the son of Herbert Augusta Rogers (52) and Margaret Ann Jones. William Harvey died in Huchinson, Reno Co., Kansas, on June 17, 1959, at age 54. He was buried in Maplewood Memorial Lawn Cemetery, Emporia, Emporia Twp., Lyon Co., Kansas.[61]

William Harvey married **Martha Marie Archer** on June 30, 1930, in Coffey Co., Kansas. They divorced. They had two children. Martha Marie Archer was born in Cottonwood Falls, Chase Co., Kansas, on March 18, 1912. Martha Marie reached age 67 and died in Hartford, Elmendaro Twp., Lyon Co., Kansas, on January 24, 1980. She was buried in Hartford Cemetery, Hartford, Elmendaro Twp., Lyon Co., Kansas.[109] Buried under the name Martha Marie Sutton.

William Harvey Rogers married **Evelyn Marx** after 1945.

Children of William Harvey Rogers and Martha Marie Archer:

+ 338 f I. **Ruth Catherine⁹ Rogers** was born in Arvonia Twp., Osage Co., Kansas, on August 18, 1931. She died in Longmont, Colorado? on December 7, 2005.

+ 339 m II. **William Herbert⁹ Rogers II** was born in Lebo, Lincoln Twp., Coffey Co., Kansas, on August 31, 1936. He died in Haysville, Sedgwick Co., Kansas, on July 15, 2005. William Herbert was buried in Greenwood Cemetery, Wichita, Sedgwick Co., Kansas.[110]

**171. Sylvester LeRoy⁸ Rogers** (*Herbert Augusta⁷, Austin J.⁶, Rachel C.⁵ VanAusdall, Mary⁴ Pegan, Andrew³ Pegan II, Andrew² Pagan, James¹*) was born on November 5, 1906, in Arvonia Twp., Osage Co., Kansas. He was the son of Herbert Augusta Rogers (52) and Margaret Ann Jones. Sylvester LeRoy died in Emporia, Emporia Twp., Lyon Co., Kansas, on February 24, 1993, at age 86. He was buried in Lincoln Cemetery, Lebo, Lincoln Twp., Coffey Co., Kansas.[19]

Sylvester LeRoy married **Leota Irene Crawford** on June 29, 1939, in Osage Co., Kansas. They had two sons. Leota Irene Crawford was born in Lebo, Lincoln Twp., Coffey Co., Kansas, on December 31, 1913. Leota Irene reached age 93 and died in Waverly, Rock Creek Twp., Coffey Co., Kansas, on November 17, 2007. She was buried in Lincoln Cemetery, Lebo, Lincoln Twp., Coffey Co., Kansas.[19]

**172. Ralph⁸ Rogers** (*Herbert Augusta⁷, Austin J.⁶, Rachel C.⁵ VanAusdall, Mary⁴ Pegan, Andrew³ Pegan II, Andrew² Pagan, James¹*) was born on August 11, 1909, in Arvonia Twp., Osage Co., Kansas. He was the son of Herbert Augusta Rogers (52) and Margaret Ann Jones. Ralph died in Emporia, Emporia Twp., Lyon Co., Kansas, on May 9, 1992, at age 82. He was buried in Lincoln Cemetery, Lebo, Lincoln Twp., Coffey Co., Kansas.[19]

Ralph married **Clara Bertha Jones** on May 22, 1940, in Coffey Co., Kansas. They had three children. Clara Bertha Jones was born in Lebo, Lincoln Twp., Coffey Co., Kansas, on April 16, 1920. Clara Bertha reached age 86 and died in Emporia, Emporia Twp., Lyon Co., Kansas, on September 18, 2006. She was buried in Lincoln Cemetery, Lebo, Lincoln Twp., Coffey Co., Kansas.[19]

Ralph Rogers and Clara Bertha Jones had three children, including:

+ 340 m I. **Robert Ralph⁹ Rogers** was born in Lebo, Lincoln Twp., Coffey Co., Kansas, on May 17, 1941. He died in a hospital in Wichita, Sedgwick Co., Kansas, on September 15, 2005. Robert Ralph was buried in Alexanderwhol Friedhof Cemetery, Goessel, West Branch Twp., Marion Co., Kansas.[111]

+ 341 f III. **Barbara Gail⁹ Rogers** was born in Emporia, Emporia Twp., Lyon Co., Kansas, on March 18, 1952. She died in Halstead, Halstead Twp., Harvey Co., Kansas, on October 25, 2014. Barbara Gail was buried in Lincoln Cemetery, Lebo, Lincoln Twp., Coffey Co., Kansas.[19]

**173. Heber Austin⁸ Rogers** (*Herbert Augusta⁷, Austin J.⁶, Rachel C.⁵ VanAusdall, Mary⁴ Pegan, Andrew³ Pegan II, Andrew² Pagan, James¹*) was born on May 13, 1916, in Arvonia Twp., Osage Co., Kansas. He was the son of Herbert Augusta Rogers (52) and Margaret Ann Jones. Heber Austin died in Butler, Mount Pleasant Twp., Bates Co., Missouri, on August 13, 1983, at age 67. He was buried in Lincoln Cemetery, Lebo, Lincoln Twp., Coffey Co., Kansas.[19]

Heber Austin married **Beatrice Bernice Schellenger** on May 19, 1940, in Coffey Co., Kansas. They had five children. Beatrice Bernice Schellenger was born in Ottumwa, Ottumwa Twp., Coffey Co., Kansas, on June 22, 1919. Beatrice Bernice reached age 60 and died in Rich Hill, Osage Twp., Bates Co., Missouri, on January 29, 1980. She was buried in Lincoln Cemetery, Lebo, Lincoln Twp., Coffey Co., Kansas.[19]

**174. Charles Otis⁸ White** (*Walter Otis⁷, Mary E.⁶ Rogers, Rachel C.⁵ VanAusdall, Mary⁴ Pegan, Andrew³ Pegan II, Andrew² Pagan, James¹*) was born on April 29, 1904, in Otterville, Otter Creek Twp., Jersey Co., Illinois. He was the son of Walter Otis White (54) and Jessie Viola Balcom. Charles Otis died in Jerseyville, Jersey Twp., Jersey Co., Illinois, on January 20, 1965, at age 60. He was buried in Oak Grove Cemetery, Jerseyville, Jersey Twp., Jersey Co., Illinois.[16]

Charles Otis White married **Cora Faye Simpson** on January 17, 1925, in Jersey Co., Illinois. They divorced about 1927. They had one child. Cora Faye Simpson was born in Piasa Twp., Jersey Co., Illinois, on April 1, 1905. She was also known as **Faye.** Cora Faye reached age 73 and died in Alton, Alton Twp., Madison Co., Illinois, on March 1, 1979. She was buried in Rose Lawn Memory Gardens Cemetery, Bethalto, Wood River Twp., Madison Co., Illinois.[112]

Charles Otis White married **Eva Esther Wayman** on April 28, 1933 in Jersey Co., Illinois They divorced. They had five sons. Eva Esther Wayman was born in Barr Twp., Macoupin Co., Illinois, on June 22, 1914. Eva Esther reached age 70 and died in Alton, Alton Twp., Madison Co., Illinois, on October 16, 1984. She was buried in Medora Cemetery, Ruyle Twp., Jersey Co., Illinois.[113]

Charles Otis White married **Unknown Unknown** after 1940. They had three daughters.

Child of Charles Otis White and Cora Faye Simpson:

+ 342    I.    **Ruth I.⁹ White** was born in Jerseyville, Jersey Twp., Jersey Co., Illinois, in 1926.

Sons of Charles Otis White and Eva Esther Wayman:

+ 343   m   I.    **Lloyd Cletus⁹ White** was born in Jerseyville, Jersey Twp., Jersey Co., Illinois, on August 6, 1934. He died in Kane, Kane Twp., Greene Co., Illinois, on March 23, 2009. Lloyd Cletus was buried in Kane Cemetery, Kane, Kane Twp., Greene Co., Illinois.[114]

+ 344   m   II.    **Charles Laverne⁹ White** was born in Jerseyville, Jersey Twp., Jersey Co., Illinois, on December 11, 1935. He died in Jerseyville, Jersey Twp., Jersey Co., Illinois, on February 7, 2015. Charles Laverne was buried in Oak Grove Cemetery, Jerseyville, Jersey Twp., Jersey Co., Illinois.[16]

+ 345   m   III.    **Walter Leonard⁹ White** was born in Jerseyville, Jersey Twp., Jersey Co., Illinois, on May 6, 1938. He was also known as **Leonard.** Walter Leonard died in Kane, Kane Twp., Greene Co., Illinois, on April 10, 2010. He was buried in Kane Cemetery, Kane, Kane Twp., Greene Co., Illinois.[114]

+ 346   m   IV.    **Robert Lee⁹ White** was born in Jerseyville, Jersey Twp., Jersey Co., Illinois, on January 18, 1940. He died in a hospital in Alton, Alton Twp., Madison Co., Illinois, on July 3, 1995. Robert Lee was buried in Medora Cemetery, Ruyle Twp., Jersey Co., Illinois.[113]

+ 347   m   V.    **Billy Gene⁹ White** was born in Carrollton, Carrollton Twp., Greene Co., Illinois, on August 6, 1942. He died in Grafton, Quarry Twp., Jersey Co., Illinois, on March 30, 2000. Billy Gene was buried in Medora Cemetery, Ruyle Twp., Jersey Co., Illinois.[113]

**175. Ruth M.⁸ White** (*Walter Otis⁷, Mary E.⁶ Rogers, Rachel C.⁵ VanAusdall, Mary⁴ Pegan, Andrew³ Pegan II, Andrew² Pagan, James¹*) was born on September 13, 1905, in Otterville, Otter Creek Twp., Jersey Co., Illinois. She was the daughter of Walter Otis White (54) and Jessie Viola Balcom. Ruth M. died in Jerseyville, Jersey Twp., Jersey Co., Illinois, on March 29, 1930, at age 24. She was buried in Oak Grove Cemetery, Jerseyville, Jersey Twp., Jersey Co., Illinois.[16]

Ruth M. married **Freddie F. Osborn** on May 29, 1926, in Jersey Co., Illinois. They had two sons. Freddie F. Osborn was born in Hardinsburg, Breckinridge Co., Kentucky, on January 27,

1906.[5] Freddie F. reached age 70 and died in Alton, Alton Twp., Madison Co., Illinois, on January 7, 1977. He was buried in Oakwood Cemetery, Upper Alton, Alton Twp., Madison Co., Illinois.[8]

Although originally spelled Osburn, Freddie Franklin Osburn's surname eventually was spelled Osborn.

Sons of Ruth M. White and Freddie F. Osborn:

+ 348 m I. **Ronald Ellsworth**[9] **Osborn** was born in Alton, Alton Twp., Madison Co., Illinois, on January 3, 1927. He died in Riverdale, Clayton Co., Georgia, on January 2, 2008.

+ 349 m II. **Freddie Franklin**[9] **Osborn II** was born in Alton, Alton Twp., Madison Co., Illinois, on February 16, 1929. He died in Alton, Alton Twp., Madison Co., Illinois, on May 18, 2003. Freddie Franklin was buried in Oak Grove Cemetery, Jerseyville, Jersey Twp., Jersey Co., Illinois.[16]

**176. Walter L.**[8] **White II** (*Walter Otis*[7], *Mary E.*[6] *Rogers*, *Rachel C.*[5] *VanAusdall*, *Mary*[4] *Pegan*, *Andrew*[3] *Pegan II*, *Andrew*[2] *Pagan*, *James*[1]) was born on October 8, 1907, in Otterville, Otter Creek Twp., Jersey Co., Illinois. He was the son of Walter Otis White (54) and Jessie Viola Balcom. Walter L. died in Jerseyville, Jersey Twp., Jersey Co., Illinois, on January 1, 1974, at age 66. He was buried in Oak Grove Cemetery, Jerseyville, Jersey Twp., Jersey Co., Illinois.[16]

He married **Golda M. Jaynes** before 1932. They had two children. Golda M. Jaynes was born on March 10, 1913. She was also known as **Goldie**. Golda M. reached age 60 and died on August 1, 1973. She was buried in Oak Grove Cemetery, Jerseyville, Jersey Twp., Jersey Co., Illinois.[16]

Children of Walter L. White II and Golda M. Jaynes:

+ 350 f I. **Dimple Mae**[9] **White** was born in Jerseyville, Jersey Twp., Jersey Co., Illinois, in 1932.

+ 351 m II. **James R.**[9] **White** was born in 1937.

**177. Lloyd Shively**[8] **White** (*Walter Otis*[7], *Mary E.*[6] *Rogers*, *Rachel C.*[5] *VanAusdall*, *Mary*[4] *Pegan*, *Andrew*[3] *Pegan II*, *Andrew*[2] *Pagan*, *James*[1]) was born on April 22, 1911, in Rosedale Twp., Jersey Co., Illinois. He was the son of Walter Otis White (54) and Jessie Viola Balcom. Lloyd Shively died in Jerseyville, Jersey Twp., Jersey Co., Illinois, on November 18, 1974, at age 63. He was buried in Oak Grove Cemetery, Jerseyville, Jersey Twp., Jersey Co., Illinois.[16]

Lloyd Shively married **Betty June Rampley** after 1940. They had one son. Betty June Rampley was born in Keokuk, Jackson Twp., Lee Co., Iowa, on September 14, 1928. Betty June reached age 76 and died in Jerseyville, Jersey Twp., Jersey Co., Illinois, on April 4, 2005. She was buried in Oak Grove Cemetery, Jerseyville, Jersey Twp., Jersey Co., Illinois.[16]

**178. Georgia Mae**[8] **White** (*Walter Otis*[7], *Mary E.*[6] *Rogers*, *Rachel C.*[5] *VanAusdall*, *Mary*[4] *Pegan*, *Andrew*[3] *Pegan II*, *Andrew*[2] *Pagan*, *James*[1]) was born on May 31, 1913, in Rosedale Twp., Jersey Co., Illinois. She was the daughter of Walter Otis White (54) and Jessie Viola Balcom. Georgia Mae lived in 1969 in Stephenville, Erath Co., Texas. She died in Oklahoma City, Oklahoma, on February 13, 1996, at age 82.

Georgia Mae White married **Lester Freeman Ludwig** on January 3, 1931, in Jersey Co., Illinois. They divorced. They had one daughter. Lester Freeman Ludwig was born in Dry Point Twp., Shelby Co., Illinois, on January 12, 1898. He reached age 42 and died in a hospital in Jacksonville, Jacksonville Twp., Morgan Co., Illinois, on December 25, 1940. Lester Freeman was buried in Oak Grove Cemetery, Jerseyville, Jersey Twp., Jersey Co., Illinois.[16]

Georgia Mae White Ludwig married **Preston Douglas Brown** on February 18, 1934, in Jersey Co., Illinois. They divorced. They had one son. Preston Douglas Brown was born in Woodville, Woodville Twp., Greene Co., Illinois, on August 2, 1912. He reached age 53 aand died in Kane, Kane Twp., Greene Co., Illinois, on December 14, 1965. Preston Douglas was buried in Kane Cemetery, Kane, Kane Twp., Greene Co., Illinois.[114]

Georgia Mae White Ludwig Brown married **William H. Abbott** after 1940. They had one son. William H. Abbott was born in English Twp., Jersey Co., Illinois, on September 18, 1911. William H. lived in 1982 in Fieldon, Richwoods Twp., Jersey Co., Illinois. He reached age 71 and died in a hospital in Florissant, St. Louis Co., Missouri, on November 10, 1982. William H. was buried in Oak Grove Cemetery, Jerseyville, Jersey Twp., Jersey Co., Illinois.[16]

Daughter of Georgia Mae White and Lester Freeman Ludwig:

+ 352 f I. **Garnetta Faye⁹ Ludwig** was born in Jerseyville, Jersey Twp., Jersey Co., Illinois, on July 8, 1931. She died in Oklahoma City, Oklahoma, on November 21, 1992. Garnetta Faye was buried in Flynn Cemetery, Agra, Lincoln Co., Oklahoma.[115]

Son of Georgia Mae White and Preston Douglas Brown:

+ 353 m I. **Preston Eugene⁹ Brown II** was born in Jerseyville, Jersey Twp., Jersey Co., Illinois, on April 19, 1934. He was also known as **Gene.** Preston Eugene died in a hospital in Glen Rose, Somervell Co., Texas, on January 23, 1979. He was buried in Oak Grove Cemetery, Jerseyville, Jersey Twp., Jersey Co., Illinois.[16]

Son of Georgia Mae White and William H. Abbott:

+ 354 m I. **Steven Wayne⁹ Abbott** was born in White Hall, White Hall Twp., Greene Co., Illinois, on July 14, 1949. He died in Jersey Twp., Jersey Co., Illinois, on October 27, 1978. Steven Wayne was buried in Oak Grove Cemetery, Jerseyville, Jersey Twp., Jersey Co., Illinois.[16]

**179. Dorothy Lorene⁸ Rogers** (*Edwin Clifford⁷, John Vanausdoll.⁶, Rachel C.⁵ VanAusdall, Mary⁴ Pegan, Andrew³ Pegan II, Andrew² Pagan, James¹*) was born on September 3, 1919, in Jerseyville, Jersey Twp., Jersey Co., Illinois. She was the daughter of Edwin Clifford Rogers (56) and Lola G. Whitley. Dorothy Lorene lived in 2005 in El Paso, Illinois. She died in a hospital in Normal, Normal Twp., McLean Co., Illinois, on December 6, 2005, at age 86. Dorothy Lorene was buried in Oak Grove Cemetery, Jerseyville, Jersey Twp., Jersey Co., Illinois.[16]

Dorothy Lorene married **John Arthur Penning** on February 27, 1942, in Madison Co., Illinois. They had two children. John Arthur Penning was born in Alton, Alton Twp., Madison Co., Illinois, on September 28, 1921. He was also known as **Jack.** John Arthur reached age 82 and died in Alton, Alton Twp., Madison Co., Illinois, on June 28, 2004. He was buried in Oak Grove Cemetery, Jerseyville, Jersey Twp., Jersey Co., Illinois.[16]

**180. Lois Jane⁸ Lowrance** (*Alta Mae⁷ Rogers, John Vanausdoll.⁶, Rachel C.⁵ VanAusdall, Mary⁴ Pegan, Andrew³ Pegan II, Andrew² Pagan, James¹*) was born on November 2, 1922, in Alton, Alton Twp., Madison Co., Illinois. She was the daughter of Joseph Mark Lowrance and Alta Mae Rogers (57). Lois Jane died in Glendora, Los Angeles Co., California, on October 11, 1975, at age 52. She was buried in Oakdale Memorial Park Cemetery, Glendora, Los Angeles Co., California.[21]

Lois Jane married **Bartlett Shappee** on September 18, 1943, in Madison Co., Illinois. They divorced. They had two sons. Bartlett Shappee was born in South Haven, South Haven Twp., Van Buren Co.,

Michigan, on September 3, 1912. He was also known as **Powerhouse.** Bartlett reached age 82 and died in a hospital in St. Louis, Missouri, on June 3, 1995. He was buried in McDowell Cemetery, South Haven Highlands, Casco Twp., Allegan Co., Michigan.[116]

Lois Jane Lowrance Shappee married **Hiram Robert Bratton** on December 16, 1961, in Los Angeles Co., California. They had one son. Hiram Robert Bratton was born in Edson Twp., Chippewa Co., Wisconsin, on June 2, 1924. He was also known as **Harm.** Hiram Robert reached age 89 and died in Glendora, Los Angeles Co., California, on December 13, 2013.

181. **Roger⁸ Spaulding** (*Helen M.⁷ Rogers, John Vanausdoll.⁶, Rachel C.⁵ VanAusdall, Mary⁴ Pegan, Andrew³ Pegan II, Andrew² Pagan, James¹*) was born on January 16, 1926, in Jerseyville, Jersey Twp., Jersey Co., Illinois. He was the son of Harmon Eugene Spaulding and Helen M. Rogers (60). Roger lived in 2008 in Edwardsville, Edwardsville Twp., Madison Co., Illinois. He died in a hospital in St. Louis, Missouri, on September 10, 2008, at age 82. Roger was buried in Oak Grove Cemetery, Jerseyville, Jersey Twp., Jersey Co., Illinois.[16]

He married **Jean Jennings** after 1940. They had two children. Jean Jennings was born in Delhi, Delhi Twp., Jersey Co., Illinois, on July 26, 1928. Jean reached age 87 and died in Glen Carbon, Edwardsville Twp., Madison Co., Illinois, on February 23, 2016. She was buried in Oak Grove Cemetery, Jerseyville, Jersey Twp., Jersey Co., Illinois.[16]

182. **Shirley Ann⁸ Nordenbrock** (*Imo Luella⁷ Rogers, John Vanausdoll.⁶, Rachel C.⁵ VanAusdall, Mary⁴ Pegan, Andrew³ Pegan II, Andrew² Pagan, James¹*) was born in Dallas, Dallas Co., Texas, on April 22, 1934. She is also known as **Ann.** She is the daughter of Gregory John Nordenbrock and Imo Luella Rogers (61).

Shirley Ann married **Duane Clifford Egan** on May 14, 1966 in Dallas, Dallas Co., Texas. Duane Clifford Egan was born on April 6, 1937.

183. **Elizabeth Lou⁸ Nordenbrock** (*Imo Luella⁷ Rogers, John Vanausdoll.⁶, Rachel C.⁵ VanAusdall, Mary⁴ Pegan, Andrew³ Pegan II, Andrew² Pagan, James¹*)

was born on July 22, 1937, in Dallas, Dallas Co., Texas. She was also known as **Betty Lou.** She was the daughter of Gregory John Nordenbrock and Imo Luella Rogers (61). Elizabeth Lou lived in 1978 in Austin, Travis Co., Texas. She died in Amesbury, Essex Co., Massachusetts, on July 19, 2002, at age 64.

Elizabeth Lou married **Leo Paul Mark Sullivan** on July 13, 1957. They had five children. Leo Paul Mark Sullivan was born in St. Paul, Ramsey Co., Minnesota, on July 2, 1921. He was also known as **Liam.** Leo Paul Mark reached age 82 and died in Amesbury, Essex Co., Massachusetts, on May 15, 2004.

Elizabeth Lou Nordenbrock and Leo Paul Mark Sullivan had five children, including:

+ 355 f I. **Paula Elizabeth⁹ Sullivan** was born in Dallas, Dallas Co., Texas, on July 13, 1962. She died in Poughkeepsie, Dutchess Co., New York, on October 12, 2010.

+ 356 m II. **Colin Gregory Nordenbrock⁹ Sullivan** was born in Scottsdale, Maricopa Co., Arizona, on November 10, 1963. He died in San Francisco, San Francisco Co., California, on February 25, 2010.

184. **John A.⁸ Rogers** (*William H.⁷, John Vanausdoll.⁶, Rachel C.⁵ VanAusdall, Mary⁴ Pegan, Andrew³ Pegan II, Andrew² Pagan, James¹*) was born on August 13, 1945, in Alton, Alton Twp., Madison Co., Illinois. He was the son of William H. Rogers (63) and Elizabeth Ward Stevens. John A. lived in 1994 in Edwardsville, Edwardsville Twp., Madison Co., Illinois. He died in Edwardsville, Edwardsville Twp., Madison Co., Illinois? on August 25, 2013, at age 68.

He married **Darlene Unknown.** They divorced.

185. **William H.⁸ Wahle** (*Dorothy Opal⁷ Rogers, John Vanausdoll.⁶, Rachel C.⁵ VanAusdall, Mary⁴ Pegan, Andrew³ Pegan II, Andrew² Pagan, James¹*) was born on February 4, 1933, in Piasa Twp., Jersey Co.,

Illinois. He is the son of Harold Leo Wahle and Dorothy Opal Rogers (64).

He married **Carol Unknown.**

**186. Kenneth E.⁸ Wahle** (*Dorothy Opal⁷ Rogers, John Vanausdoll.⁶, Rachel C.⁵ VanAusdall, Mary⁴ Pegan, Andrew³ Pegan II, Andrew² Pagan, James¹*) was born on June 24, 1938, in Piasa Twp., Jersey Co., Illinois. He is the son of Harold Leo Wahle and Dorothy Opal Rogers (64).

He married **Janet Unknown.**

**187. Edwin D.⁸ Wahle** (*Dorothy Opal⁷ Rogers, John Vanausdoll.⁶, Rachel C.⁵ VanAusdall, Mary⁴ Pegan, Andrew³ Pegan II, Andrew² Pagan, James¹*) was born on January 1, 1941, in Piasa Twp., Jersey Co., Illinois. He is the son of Harold Leo Wahle and Dorothy Opal Rogers (64).

He married **Mary Lou Marlow.** They have two children. Mary Lou Marlow was born in Rolla, Rolla Twp., Phelps Co., Missouri, on June 24, 1940. Mary Lou reached age 63 and died in Roach, Russell Twp., Camden Co., Missouri, on April 22, 2004. She was buried in Oak Grove Cemetery, St. Charles, St. Charles Twp., St. Charles Co., Missouri.[117]

Living Wahle and Mary Lou Marlow had two children, including:

+ 357 m I. **Scott Edwin⁹ Wahle** was born in Rolla, Rolla Twp., Phelps Co., Missouri, on August 2, 1963. He died in St. Charles, St. Charles Twp., St. Charles Co., Missouri, on March 12, 1988. Scott Edwin was buried in Oak Grove Cemetery, St. Charles, St. Charles Twp., St. Charles Co., Missouri[117]

**188. Douglas Ray⁸ Fisk** (*Seth Raymond⁷ Fiske II, Theresa C.⁶ Rogers, Rachel C.⁵ VanAusdall, Mary⁴ Pegan, Andrew³ Pegan II, Andrew² Pagan, James¹*) was born on February 12, 1920, in West Frankfort, Denning Twp., Franklin Co., Illinois. He was the son of Seth Raymond Fiske II (66) and Rapunzel Elizabeth Griffin. Douglas Ray lived in 1977 in Godfrey, Godfrey Twp.,

Madison Co., Illinois. He died in a hospital in St. Louis, Missouri, on February 15, 1977, at age 57. Douglas Ray was buried in Oakwood Cemetery, Upper Alton, Alton Twp., Madison Co., Illinois.[8]

Douglas Ray married **Evelyn Angell** on November 14, 1942, in Commanche Co., Oklahoma. They had three sons. Evelyn Angell was born in Washington, Union Twp., Franklin Co., Missouri, on April 18, 1920. Evelyn reached age 63 and died in Godfrey, Godfrey Twp., Madison Co., Illinois, on October 24, 1983. She was buried in Oakwood Cemetery, Upper Alton, Alton Twp., Madison Co., Illinois.[8]

**189. Luther Alexander⁸ Fiske** (*Seth Raymond⁷, Theresa C.⁶ Rogers, Rachel C.⁵ VanAusdall, Mary⁴ Pegan, Andrew³ Pegan II, Andrew² Pagan, James¹*) was born on December 4, 1921, in West Frankfort, Denning Twp., Franklin, Illinois, USA. He was also known as **Jack.** He was the son of Seth Raymond Fiske II (66) and Rapunzel Elizabeth Griffin. Luther Alexander died in Alton, Alton Twp., Madison Co., Illinois, on March 24, 1944, at age 22. He was buried in Oakwood Cemetery, Upper Alton, Alton Twp., Madison Co., Illinois.[8]

Luther Alexander married **Dorothy Jane Black** on August 4, 1942, in Madison Co., Illinois]. They had one daughter. Dorothy Jane Black was born in Eagle Creek Twp., Gallatin Co., Illinois, on March 13, 1925. Dorothy Jane lived in 1946 in San Pedro, Los Angeles Co., California. She also resided in 1979 in Sprio, LaFlore Co., Oklahoma. Dorothy Jane reached age 54 and died in a hospital in Poteau, LeFlore Co., Oklahoma, on September 30, 1979. She was buried in Valhalla Memorial Park and Mausoleum, Godfrey, Godfrey Twp., Madison Co., Illinois.[118]

She died under the name Dorothy J. Black.

**190. Edward Martin⁸ Daniels** (*Robert Martin⁷, Rowena Maude⁶ Rogers, Rachel C.⁵ VanAusdall, Mary⁴ Pegan, Andrew³ Pegan II, Andrew² Pagan, James¹*) was born on October 7, 1917, in Greeley, Weld Co., Colorado. He was the son of Robert Martin Daniels (68) and Edna V. Unknown. Edward Martin died in Imperial Co., California, on February 12, 1970, at age 52. He was buried in Fairhaven Cemetery, Santa Ana, Orange Co., California.[62]

**191. Freda Grace**[8] **Delp** (*Bertha May*[7] *Vanausdoll, Loring or Loren Earl*[6], *Caleb*[5], *Mary*[4] *Pegan, Andrew*[3] *Pegan II, Andrew*[2] *Pagan, James*[1]) was born on January 31, 1898, in Grafton, Quarry Twp., Jersey Co., Illinois. She was the daughter of Albert James Delp and Bertha May Vanausdoll (70). Freda Grace died in Chester, Chester Twp.., Randolph Co., Illinois, on October 14, 1935, at age 37. She was buried in Evergreen Cemetery, Chester, Chester Twp., Randolph Co., Illinois.[6]

Freda Grace married **Michael Clyde McIntyre** on August 24, 1915, in Jersey Co., Illinois. They had nine children. Michael Clyde McIntyre was born in Caledonia, Belview Twp., Washington Co., Missouri, on April 3, 1890. Michael Clyde reached age 87 and died in Tallulah, Madison Parish, Louisiana, in July 1977. He was buried in Evergreen Cemetery, Chester, Chester Twp., Randolph Co., Illinois.[6]

At least one source says that Michael Clyde McIntyre had 13 children. But only nine have been documented with his first wife, Freda Grace Delp. The other four may have been with his second wife, Bernice Unknown. Obituaries of most of his children indicate that Michael and Freda had nine children.

Michael Clyde lived in many places. By June 1917 he resided in Potosi, Breton Twp., Washington Co., Missouri, and Enid, Garfield Co., Oklahoma by that September. He'd moved to Snyder, Kiowa Co., Oklahoma by 1920. In 1930, Michael Clyde was in Lanagan, Lanagan Twp., McDonald Co., Missouri. He was a resident of Chester, Chester Twp., Randolph Co., Illinois in 1935, but removed to Bremen, Marys River Twp., Randolph Co., Illinois by 1940. In 1942, he settled in Tallulah, Madison Parish, Louisiana.

Children of Freda Grace Delp and Michael Clyde McIntyre:

+ 358 m I. **Clyde E.**[9] **McIntyre** was born in Jerseyville, Jersey Twp., Jersey Co., Illinois, on March 13, 1916. He died in Perryville, Central Twp., Perry Co., Missouri, on February 5, 1993. He was buried in Evergreen Cemetery, Chester, Chester Twp., Randolph Co., Illinois.[6]

+ 359 f II. **Hettie Mae**[9] **McIntyre** was born in Enid, Garfield Co., Oklahoma, on September 25, 1917. She died in Houston, Harris Co., Texas, on July 1, 2002. Hettie Mae was buried in Woodlawn Cemetery, Houston, Harris Co., Texas.[119]

+ 360 m III. **Elmer**[9] **McIntyre** was born in Snyder, Kiowa Co., Oklahoma, in 1920. He died in Snyder, Kiowa Co., Oklahoma or Neosho, Neosho Twp., Newton Co., Missouri, before 1930.

+ 361 f IV. **Nellie Nadine**[9] **McIntyre** was born in Neosho, Neosho Twp., Newton Co., Missouri, on June 15, 1921. She died in Houston, Harris Co., Texas, on December 7, 1992.

+ 362 f V. **Linnie Louise**[9] **McIntyre** was born in Neosho, Neosho Twp., Newton Co., Missouri, on June 22, 1923. She died in Houston, Harris Co., Texas, on October 8, 2001. Linnie Louise was buried in Memorial Oaks Cemetery, Houston, Harris Co., Texas.[120]

+ 363 m VI. **Charles Virgil**[9] **McIntyre** was born in Neosho, Neosho Twp., Newton Co., Missouri, on December 23, 1924. He died in Perryville, Central Twp., Perry Co., Missouri, on May 3, 2010. Charles Virgil was buried in Evergreen Cemetery, Chester, Chester Twp., Randolph Co., Illinois.[6]

+ 364 m VII. **Donald L.**[9] **McIntyre** was born in Lanagan, Lanagan Twp., McDonald Co., Missouri, in 1928. He died in Tallulah, Madison Parish, Louisiana? in 1948. Donald L. was buried in Evergreen Cemetery, Chester, Chester Twp., Randolph Co., Illinois.[6]

+ 365 m VIII. **Lester Roy[9] McIntyre** was born in Bremen, Marys River Twp., Randolph Co., Illinois, on November 27, 1930. He died in Tallulah, Madison Parish, Louisiana, on September 21, 2011. Lester Roy was buried in Memorial Park Cemetery, Tallulah, Madison Parish, Louisiana.[121]

+ 366 f IX. **Ruby Oleta[9] McIntyre** was born in Bremen, Marys River Twp., Randolph Co., Illinois, on March 4, 1933. She died in Conroe, Montgomery Co., Texas? in September 1981. Ruby Oleta was buried in Evergreen Cemetery, Chester, Chester Twp., Randolph Co., Illinois.[6]

**192. Leona Frances[8] Delp** (*Bertha May[7] Vanausdoll, Loring or Loren Earl[6], Caleb[5], Mary[4] Pegan, Andrew[3] Pegan II, Andrew[2] Pagan, James[1]*) was born on July 4, 1900, in Jersey Co., Illinois. She was the daughter of Albert James Delp and Bertha May Vanausdoll (70). Leona Frances died in Alton, Alton Twp., Madison Co., Illinois, on September 27, 1962, at age 62. She was buried in Oakwood Cemetery, Upper Alton, Alton Twp., Madison Co., Illinois.[8]

Frances married **Lester Roy Reed** on May 13, 1916, in Jersey Co., Illinois. They had one daughter. Lester Roy Reed was born in Jersey Co., Illinois, on December 17, 1887. Lester Roy lived in 1930 in Sulphur Springs, Benton Co., Arkansas. He reached age 96 and died in Jerseyville, Jersey Twp., Jersey Co., Illinois, on August 21, 1984. Lester Roy was buried in Oakwood Cemetery, Upper Alton, Alton Twp., Madison Co., Illinois.[8]

Daughter of Leona Frances Delp and Lester Roy Reed:

+ 367 f I. **Eileen R.[9] Reed** was born in Jerseyville, Jersey Twp., Jersey Co., Illinois, on September 20, 1917. She died in a hospital in Chester, Chester Twp.., Randolph Co., Illinois, on November 20, 1970. Eileen R. was buried in Oakwood Cemetery, Upper Alton, Alton Twp., Madison Co., Illinois.[8]

**193. Roy Everett[8] Delp** (*Bertha May[7] Vanausdoll, Loring or Loren Earl[6], Caleb[5], Mary[4] Pegan, Andrew[3] Pegan II, Andrew[2] Pagan, James[1]*) was born on April 23, 1903, in Valley Park, St. Louis Co., Missouri. He was the son of Albert James Delp and Bertha May Vanausdoll (70). Roy Everett died in Wood River, Wood River Twp., Madison Co., Illinois, on September 29, 1985, at age 82. He was buried in Valhalla Memorial Park and Mausoleum, Godfrey, Godfrey Twp., Madison Co., Illinois.[17]

Roy Everett married **Alice May Scoggins** on August 4, 1927, in Madison Co., Illinois. They had six children. Alice May Scoggins was born in Jerseyville, Jersey Twp., Jersey Co., Illinois, on May 5, 1909. Alice May reached age 93 and died in Alton, Alton Twp., Madison Co., Illinois, on August 11, 2002. She was buried in Valhalla Memorial Park and Mausoleum, Godfrey, Godfrey Twp., Madison Co., Illinois.[17]

Children of Roy Everett Delp and Alice May Scoggins:

+ 368 m I. **Roy W.[9] Delp II** was born in Jerseyville, Jersey Twp., Jersey Co., Illinois, on March 20, 1928. He died in Jerseyville, Jersey Twp., Jersey Co., Illinois, on July 7, 2009. Roy W. was buried in Rose Lawn Memory Gardens Cemetery, Bethalto, Wood River Twp., Madison Co., Illinois.[112]

+ 369 f II. **Betty J.[9] Delp** was born in Jerseyville, Jersey Twp., Jersey Co., Illinois, on June 18, 1929.

+ 370 m III. **Marvin**[9] **Delp** was born in Jerseyville, Jersey Twp., Jersey Co., Illinois, in 1931.

+ 371 m IV. **Damon Lavern**[9] **Delp** was born in Jerseyville, Jersey Twp., Jersey Co., Illinois? on November 18, 1932. He died in East Alton, Wood River Twp., Madison Co., Illinois, on August 13, 2001.

+ 372 f V. **Wynona Pearl**[9] **Delp** was born in Jerseyville, Jersey Twp., Jersey Co., Illinois, on December 10, 1937. She was also known as **Pearlie.** Wynona Pearl died in East Alton, Wood River Twp., Madison Co., Illinois, on April 7, 2015. She was buried in Valhalla Memorial Park and Mausoleum, Godfrey, Godfrey Twp., Madison Co., Illinois.[21]

+ 373 f VI. **Daughter Delp.**

**194. Florence**[8] **Delp** (*Bertha May*[7] *Vanausdoll, Loring or Loren Earl*[6]*, Caleb*[5]*, Mary*[4] *Pegan, Andrew*[3] *Pegan II, Andrew*[2] *Pagan, James*[1]) was born on March 11, 1906, in Elsah, Jersey Landing Twp., Jersey Co., Illinois. She was the daughter of Albert James Delp and Bertha May Vanausdoll (70). Florence lived in 1931 in Jerseyville, Jersey Twp., Jersey Co., Illinois. She died in the Illinois River in Gilead Twp., Calhoun Co., Illinois, on July 16, 1931. Florence was buried in Fieldon Cemetery, Fieldon, Richwoods Twp., Jersey Co., Illinois.[25]

Florence married **Ernest Briggs** about 1924. Ernest Briggs was born in Fieldon, Richwoods Twp., Jersey Co., Illinois? on March 10, 1900. Ernest lived in 1931 in Jerseyville, Jersey Twp., Jersey Co., Illinois. He reached age 31 and died in the Illinois River in Gilead Twp., Calhoun Co., Illinois, on July 16, 1931. Ernest was buried in Fieldon Cemetery, Fieldon, Richwoods Twp., Jersey Co., Illinois.[25]

Ernest and Florence Delp Briggs died in a boating accident on the Illinois River. They were walking along the river bank when a man came along in a boat. They asked him for a ride. Allegedly the man had told others earlier that, at some point, he intended to kill himself. In the middle of the river, it is believed he overturned the boat, drowning himself and the Briggs couple.

**195. Earl Leonard**[8] **Delp** (*Bertha May*[7] *Vanausdoll, Loring or Loren Earl*[6]*, Caleb*[5]*, Mary*[4] *Pegan, Andrew*[3] *Pegan II, Andrew*[2] *Pagan, James*[1]) was born on July 17, 1910, in Greenfield, Greenfield Twp., Greene Co., Illinois. He was also known as **Leonard.** He was the son of Albert James Delp and Bertha May Vanausdoll (70). Earl Leonard lived in 1969 in Jerseyville, Jersey Twp., Jersey Co., Illinois. He died in a hospital in St. Louis, Missouri, on January 11, 1969, at age 58. Earl Leonard was buried in Fieldon Cemetery, Fieldon, Richwoods Twp., Jersey Co., Illinois.[25]

Never married.

**196. Vera M.**[8] **Delp** (*Bertha May*[7] *Vanausdoll, Loring or Loren Earl*[6]*, Caleb*[5]*, Mary*[4] *Pegan, Andrew*[3] *Pegan II, Andrew*[2] *Pagan, James*[1]) was born on April 23, 1913, in Chapin, Bethel Twp., Morgan Co., Illinois. She was the daughter of Albert James Delp and Bertha May Vanausdoll (70). Vera M. lived in 1962 in Oquawka, South Henderson Twp., Henderson Co., Illinois. She died in Oquawka, South Henderson Twp., Henderson Co., Illinois, on June 2, 1992, at age 79. Vera M. was buried in Oquawka Cemetery, Oquawka, Oquawka Twp., Henderson Co., Illinois.[63]

Vera M. married **Russell R. Manning** in 1931. They divorced in 1954. They had three children. Russell R. Manning was born in Edwardsville, Edwardsville Twp., Madison Co., Illinois, in 1905. He reached age 63 and died in Oquawka, South Henderson Twp., Henderson Co., Illinois, on April 3, 1968. Russell R. was buried in Oquawka Cemetery, Oquawka, Oquawka Twp., Henderson Co., Illinois.[63]

Vera M. Delp married **Harry Leon Webb** on April 19, 1958, in Madison Co., Illinois. They divorced in 1959. Harry Leon Webb was born in Anna, Anna Twp., Union Twp., Illinois, on February 25, 1933. He reached age 61 and died in Peoria, Peoria Twp, Peoria Co., Illinois on August 23, 1994. He was buried in Biggsville Cemetery, Biggsville, Biggsville Twp., Henderson Co., Illinois.[122]

Vera M. Delp and Russell R. Manning had three children, including:

+ 374 m II. **Roger Ronald⁹ Manning** was born in Oquawka, South Henderson Twp., Henderson Co., Illinois, on February 10, 1937. He died in Oquawka, South Henderson Twp., Henderson Co., Illinois, on February 11, 1937. Roger Ronald was buried in Oquawka Cemetery, Oquawka, Oquawka Twp., Henderson Co., Illinois.[63]

+ 375 m III. **Keith Arthur⁹ Manning** was born in Oquawka, South Henderson Twp., Henderson Co., Illinois, on April 11, 1942. He died in a hospital in Monmouth, Monmouth Twp., Warren Co., Illinois, on July 28, 1942. Keith Arthur was buried in Oquawka Cemetery, Oquawka, Oquawka Twp., Henderson Co., Illinois.[63]

**197. Harold A.⁸ Vanausdoll** (*Raymond Loring⁷, Loring or Loren Earl⁶, Caleb⁵, Mary⁴ Pegan, Andrew³ Pegan II, Andrew² Pagan, James¹*) was born on January 3, 1914, in Jerseyville, Jersey Twp., Jersey Co., Illinois. He was the son of Raymond Loring Vanausdoll II (73) and Leona Fanny Blay. Harold A. died in Wickenburg, Maricopa Co., Arizona, on April 10, 1973, at age 59.

He married **Opal E. Plumb** before 1936. They divorced. They had one son. Opal E. Plumb was born in Fieldon, Richwoods Twp., Jersey Co., Illinois, on June 26, 1917. She reached age 83 and died in Jerseyville, Jersey Twp., Jersey Co., Illinois, on December 9, 2000. Opal E. was buried in Oak Grove Cemetery, Jerseyville, Jersey Twp., Jersey Co., Illinois.[16]

Died under the name Opal E. Gresham.

Son of Harold A. Vanausdoll and Opal E. Plumb:

+ 376 m I. **Robert Gene⁹ Vanausdoll** was born in Fieldon, Richwoods Twp.,

Jersey Co., Illinois, on November 23, 1936. He died in Florissant, St. Louis Co., Missouri, on May 1, 2003. Robert Gene was buried in Oak Grove Cemetery, Jerseyville, Jersey Twp., Jersey Co., Illinois.[16]

**198. Theodore Willard⁸ Vanausdoll** (*Raymond Loring⁷, Loring or Loren Earl⁶, Caleb⁵, Mary⁴ Pegan, Andrew³ Pegan II, Andrew² Pagan, James¹*) was born on March 21, 1916, in Jerseyville, Jersey Twp., Jersey Co., Illinois. He was the son of Raymond Loring Vanausdoll II (73) and Leona Fanny Blay. Theodore Willard died in Jerseyville, Jersey Twp., Jersey Co., Illinois, on October 5, 1916. He was buried in Oak Grove Cemetery, Jerseyville, Jersey Twp., Jersey Co., Illinois.[16]

**199. Charles Benjamin⁸ Babcock** (*Laura Edith⁷ Gilmore, Martha Jane⁶ Vanausdoll, Caleb⁵, Mary⁴ Pegan, Andrew³ Pegan II, Andrew² Pagan, James¹*) was born on October 28, 1898, in Dawson, Richardson Co., Nebraska? He was the son of Samuel Martin Babcock and Laura Edith Gilmore (74). Charles Benjamin died in Riverside, Riverside Co., California, on August 5, 1976, at age 77.

His birth name may have been Benjamin Charles Babcock, but he always used Charles Benjamin Babcock as his preferred name.

Charles Benjamin married **Viola Elizabeth Mackey** about 1921. They had two sons. Viola Elizabeth Mackey was born in Redlands, San Bernardino Co., California? on July 18, 1903. Viola Elizabeth reached age 79 and died in Riverside, Riverside Co., California, on July 8, 1983.

Sons of Charles Benjamin Babcock and Viola Elizabeth Mackey:

+ 377 m I. **Clarence E.⁹ Babcock** was born in Riverside, Riverside Co., California, on May 3, 1921. He died in Aurora, Adams Co., Colorado, on March 29, 1985.

+ 378 m II. **Harold Eugene⁹ Babcock** was born in Riverside, Riverside Co.,

California, on June 12, 1925. He died in Garden Grove, Orange Co., California, on October 3, 1999.

**200. Ethel Mae⁸ Babcock** (*Laura Edith⁷ Gilmore, Martha Jane⁶ Vanausdoll, Caleb⁵, Mary⁴ Pegan, Andrew³ Pegan II, Andrew² Pagan, James¹*) was born in Riverside, Riverside Co., California on July 11, 1903. She was the daughter of Samuel Martin Babcock and Laura Edith Gilmore (74). Ethel Mae died in Riverside, Riverside Co., California on February 1, 2001 at age 97.

May have been childless.

Ethel Mae married **Harry Ole Karstens** on November 6, 1931. Harry Ole Karstens was born in Blue Earth Co., Minnesota on January 14, 1903. Harry reached age 81 and died in Riverside, Riverside Co., California on April 6, 1984.

**201. Ada E.⁸ Babcock** (*Laura Edith⁷ Gilmore, Martha Jane⁶ Vanausdoll, Caleb⁵, Mary⁴ Pegan, Andrew³ Pegan II, Andrew² Pagan, James¹*) was born on March 30, 1907, in Dawson, Richardson Co., Nebraska? She was the daughter of Samuel Martin Babcock and Laura Edith Gilmore (74). Ada E. died in San Bernardino, San Bernardino Co., California, on April 28, 1976, at age 69.

She married **Francis Adolphus Sloan** before 1932. They had four children. Francis Adolphus Sloan was born in Ludlow, Ludlow Twp., Champaign Co., Illinois? on October 13, 1902. Francis Adolphus reached age 75 and died in San Bernardino, San Bernardino Co., California, on March 19, 1978.

Children of Ada E. Babcock and Francis Adolphus Sloan:

+ 379 m I. **Clyde Burdette⁹ Sloan** was born in Riverside, Riverside Co., California, on January 20, 1932. He died in Sierra Vista, Cochise Co., Arizona, on September 24, 1998.

+ 380 m II. **Martin Emmanuel⁹ Sloan** was born in Riverside, Riverside Co.,

California, on October 30, 1935. He died in Riverside, Riverside Co., California, on April 26, 2008. Martin Emmanuel was buried in Riverside National Cemetery, Riverside, Riverside Co., California.[67]

+ 381 f III. **Leona Evon⁹ Sloan** was born in Riverside, Riverside Co., California, on October 2, 1938.

+ 382 m IV. **Carl Francis⁹ Sloan** was born in Riverside, Riverside Co., California, on June 20, 1942. He died in Nuevo, Riverside Co., California, on March 19, 1999.

**202. Lewis H.⁸ Babcock** (*Laura Edith⁷ Gilmore, Martha Jane⁶ Vanausdoll, Caleb⁵, Mary⁴ Pegan, Andrew³ Pegan II, Andrew² Pagan, James¹*) was born on May 22, 1908, in Dawson, Richardson Co., Nebraska? He was the son of Samuel Martin Babcock and Laura Edith Gilmore (74). Lewis H. died in Riverside, Riverside Co., California, on December 6, 1974, at age 66.

He married **Eunice S. Lever** before 1934. They had three children. Eunice S. Lever was born in Riverside, Riverside Co., California, on February 24, 1912. Eunice S. reached age 73 and died in Riverside, Riverside Co., California, in December 1985.

Children of Lewis H. Babcock and Eunice S. Lever:

+ 383 f I. **June Laura⁹ Babcock** was born in Riverside, Riverside Co., California, on May 9, 1934. She died in San Bernardino, San Bernardino Co., California, on June 28, 1981.

+ 384 m II. **Richard Martin⁹ Babcock** was born in Riverside, Riverside Co., California, on June 13, 1935. He died in Anaheim, Orange Co., California? on December 11, 2011.

+ 385 m III. **Robert Lewis⁹ Babcock** was born in Riverside, Riverside Co., California, on June 13, 1935. He died in Las Vegas, Clark Co., Nevada, on March 22, 1995.

**203. Albert LeRoy[8] Gilmore** (*Harry Otis[7], Martha Jane[6] Vanausdoll, Caleb[5], Mary[4] Pegan, Andrew[3] Pegan II, Andrew[2] Pagan, James[1]*) was born on October 24, 1907, in Broken Arrow, Tulsa Co., Oklahoma. He was also known as **Roy.** He was the son of Harry Otis Gilmore (75) and Charlotte Amelia Stafford. Albert LeRoy died in Pawnee City, Pawnee City Twp., Pawnee Co., Nebraska, on September 8, 1982, at age 74. He was buried in Pawnee City Cemetery, Pawnee City, Pawnee Twp., Pawnee Co., Nebraska.[27]

Albert LeRoy married **Mary Grace Ireland** on October 14, 1923, in Pawnee Co., Nebraska. They had four children. Mary Grace Ireland was born in Pawnee City, Pawnee City Twp., Pawnee Co., Nebraska, on July 14, 1909. Mary Grace reached age 68 and died in Pawnee City, Pawnee City Twp., Pawnee Co., Nebraska, on May 5, 1978. She was buried in Pawnee City Cemetery, Pawnee City, Pawnee Twp., Pawnee Co., Nebraska.[24]

Children of Albert LeRoy Gilmore and Mary Grace Ireland:

+ 386 f I. **Dona Jean[9] Gilmore** was born in Sheridan Twp., Pawnee Co., Nebraska, on July 12, 1928. She died in Pawnee City, Pawnee City Twp., Pawnee Co., Nebraska, on March 22, 1987. Dona Jean was buried in Pawnee City Cemetery, Pawnee City, Pawnee Twp., Pawnee Co., Nebraska.[27]

+ 387 m II. **Richard[9] Gilmore** was born in Sheridan Twp., Pawnee Co., Nebraska, in January 1930.

+ 388 m III. **George Otis[9] Gilmore** was born in Sheridan Twp., Pawnee Co., Nebraska, on August 30, 1933 He died in Scurry, Kaufman Co., Texas, on May 15, 2013. George

Otis was buried in Rest Haven Memorial Park Cemetery, Rockwell, Rockwell Co., Texas.[123]

+ 389 m IV. **Ronald[9] Gilmore** was born in Sheridan Twp., Pawnee Co., Nebraska, on February 5, 1940. He died in Pawnee City, Pawnee City Twp., Pawnee Co., Nebraska? on December 26, 1989. Ronald was buried in Pawnee City Cemetery, Pawnee City, Pawnee Twp., Pawnee Co., Nebraska.[27]

**204. Velma Rita[8] Gilmore** (*Harry Otis[7], Martha Jane[6] Vanausdoll, Caleb[5], Mary[4] Pegan, Andrew[3] Pegan II, Andrew[2] Pagan, James[1]*) was born on June 30, 1909, in Broken Arrow, Tulsa Co., Oklahoma. She was the daughter of Harry Otis Gilmore (75) and Charlotte Amelia Stafford. Velma Rita died in Pawnee City, Pawnee City Twp., Pawnee Co., Nebraska, on May 28, 1997, at age 87. She was buried in Pawnee City Cemetery, Pawnee City, Pawnee Twp., Pawnee Co., Nebraska.[27]

Velma Rita married **Cleo George Koeneke** on September 11, 1928, in Pawnee Co., Nebraska. They had two sons. Cleo George Koeneke was born in Humboldt Twp., Richardson Co., Nebraska, on March 23, 1907. Cleo George reached age 88 and died in Pawnee City, Pawnee City Twp., Pawnee Co., Nebraska, on October 21, 1995. He was buried in Pawnee City Cemetery, Pawnee City, Pawnee Twp., Pawnee Co., Nebraska.[27]

Velma Rita Gilmore and Cleo George Koeneke had two sons, including:

+ 390 m II. **Larry Dwaine[9] Koeneke** was bor in Humboldt, Humboldt Twp., Richardson Co., Nebraska, on May 2, 1943. He died in Seneca, Richmond Twp., Nemaha Co., Kansas, on October 6, 2002. Larry Dwaine was buried in Pawnee City Cemetery, Pawnee City, Pawnee Twp., Pawnee Co., Nebraska.[27]

**205. Juanita Muriel⁸ Gilmore** (*Harry Otis⁷, Martha Jane⁶ Vanausdoll, Caleb⁵, Mary⁴ Pegan, Andrew³ Pegan II, Andrew² Pagan, James¹*) was born on January 26, 1914, in Sheridan Twp., Pawnee Co., Nebraska. She was also known as **Cricket.** She was the daughter of Harry Otis Gilmore (75) and Charlotte Amelia Stafford. Juanita Muriel died in Pawnee City, Pawnee City Twp., Pawnee Co., Nebraska, on April 17, 2006, at age 92. She was buried in Pawnee City Cemetery, Pawnee City, Pawnee Twp., Pawnee Co., Nebraska.[27]

Childless.

Juanita Muriel married **Owen Lee Gray** on May 17, 1941. Owen Lee Gray was born in South Palmyra Twp., Otoe Co., Nebraska, on January 26, 1917. Owen Lee reached age 62 and died in Pawnee City, Pawnee City Twp., Pawnee Co., Nebraska, on April 25, 1979. He was buried in Pawnee City Cemetery, Pawnee City, Pawnee Twp., Pawnee Co., Nebraska.[27]

**206. Harry Eugene⁸ Gilmore** (*Harry Otis⁷, Martha Jane⁶ Vanausdoll, Caleb⁵, Mary⁴ Pegan, Andrew³ Pegan II, Andrew² Pagan, James¹*) was born on March 22, 1917, in Sheridan Twp., Pawnee Co., Nebraska. He was the son of Harry Otis Gilmore (75) and Charlotte Amelia Stafford. Harry Eugene died in Rock Port, Clay Twp., Atchison Co., Missouri, on May 4, 1989, at age 72. He was buried in London Cemetery, Peru, Peru Precinct, Nemaha Co., Nebraska.[66]

Harry Eugene married **Dorothy Marie Groff** on November 20, 1937, in Page Co., Iowa. They had nine children. Dorothy Marie Groff was born in Peru Precinct., Nemaha Co., Nebraska, on August 6, 1920. Dorothy Marie reached age 94 and died in Tarkio, Tarkio Twp., Atchison Co., Missouri, on August 8, 2014. She was buried in London Cemetery, Peru, Peru Precinct, Nemaha Co., Nebraska.[66]

Harry Eugene Gilmore and Dorothy Marie Groff had nine children, including:

+ 391 f I. **Dorothy JoAnne⁹ Gilmore** was born in Peru, Peru Precinct, Nemaha Co., Nebraska, in 1938.

+ 392 m II. **Infant Son⁹ Gilmore** was born in Peru, Peru Precinct, Nemaha Co., Nebraska, in 1941. He died in Peru, Peru Precinct, Nemaha Co., Nebraska, in 1941. Infant Son was buried in London Cemetery, Peru, Peru Precinct, Nemaha Co., Nebraska.[66]

+ 393 m III. **Garland Eugene⁹ Gilmore** was born in Hamburg, Washington Twp., Fremont Co., Iowa, on August 18, 1942. He died in Anchorage, Anchorage Co., Alaska, on June 10, 2015. Garland Eugene was buried in Green Hill Cemetery, Rock Port, Clay Twp., Atchison Co., Missouri.[124]

+ 394 m IV. **Charles Junior⁹ Gilmore II** was born in Peru, Peru Precinct, Nemaha Co., Nebraska, on November 22, 1948. He died in a hospital in Omaha, Douglas Co., Nebraska, on March 12, 2011. Charles Junior was buried in Green Hill Cemetery, Rock Port, Clay Twp., Atchison Co., Missouri.[124]

+ 395 f V. **Linda J.⁹ Gilmore** was born in Pawnee City, Pawnee City Twp., Pawnee Co., Nebraska, on December 23, 1949. She died in Rock Port, Clay Twp., Atchison Co., Missouri, on November 2, 2012. Linda J. was buried in Green Hill Cemetery, Rock Port, Clay Twp., Atchison Co., Missouri.[124]

+ 396 f IX. **Sandra Arlene⁹ Gilmore** was born in Rock Port, Clay Twp., Atchison Co., Missouri, in 1959. She died in Anchorage, Anchorage Co., Alaska? in 1970. Sandra Arlene was buried in London Cemetery, Peru, Peru Precinct, Nemaha Co., Nebraska.[66]

**207. Walter Laverne⁸ Gilmore** (*Harry Otis⁷, Martha Jane⁶ Vanausdoll, Caleb⁵, Mary⁴ Pegan, Andrew3*

*Pegan II, Andrew[2] Pagan, James[1]*) was born on May 9, 1919, in Sheridan Twp., Pawnee Co., Nebraska. He was the son of Harry Otis Gilmore (75) and Charlotte Amelia Stafford. Walter Laverne died in Pawnee City, Pawnee City Twp., Pawnee Co., Nebraska, on July 14, 1963, at 44. He was buried in Pawnee City Cemetery, Pawnee City, Pawnee Twp., Pawnee Co., Nebraska.[27]

Walter Laverne married **Ruth Darlene Williams** on August 31, 1940, in Pawnee Co., Nebraska. They had one son. Ruth Darlene Williams was born in South Fork Twp., Pawnee Co., Nebraska, on January 26, 1924. Ruth Darlene reached age 59 and died in Pawnee City, Pawnee City Twp., Pawnee Co., Nebraska, on January 4, 1984. She was buried in Pawnee City Cemetery, Pawnee City, Pawnee Twp., Pawnee Co., Nebraska.[27]

Son of Walter Laverne Gilmore and Ruth Darlene Williams:

+ 397 m I. **Roger LaVerne[9] Gilmore** was born in Pawnee City, Pawnee City Twp., Pawnee Co., Nebraska, in 1941. He died in Pawnee City, Pawnee City Twp., Pawnee Co., Nebraska, in 1944. Roger LaVerne was buried in Pawnee City Cemetery, Pawnee City, Pawnee Twp., Pawnee Co., Nebraska.[27]

**208. James Everett[8] Gilmore** (*Perl Edward[7], Martha Jane[6] Vanausdoll, Caleb[5], Mary[4] Pegan, Andrew[3] Pegan II, Andrew[2] Pagan, James[1]*) was born on March 16, 1907, in Franklin Twp., Richardson Co., Nebraska. He was the son of Perl Edward Gilmore (76) and Mary Lou Spaulding. James Everett died in Los Angeles, Los Angeles Co., California, on April 8, 1955, at age 48.

**209. Irma[8] Gilmore** (*William C.[7], Martha Jane[6] Vanausdoll, Caleb[5], Mary[4] Pegan, Andrew[3] Pegan II, Andrew[2] Pagan, James[1]*) was born in 1910 in Clear Creek Twp., Pawnee Co., Nebraska. She is the daughter of William C. Gilmore (77) and Lillie B. Miller.

**210. Viola[8] Gilmore** (*William C.[7], Martha Jane[6] Vanausdoll, Caleb[5], Mary[4] Pegan, Andrew[3] Pegan II, Andrew[2] Pagan, James[1]*) was born in 1912 in Clear Creek Twp., Pawnee Co., Nebraska. She is the daughter of William C. Gilmore (77) and Lillie B. Miller.

**211. Ila Mae[8] Gilmore** (*William C.[7], Martha Jane[6] Vanausdoll, Caleb[5], Mary[4] Pegan, Andrew[3] Pegan II, Andrew[2] Pagan, James[1]*) was born on September 25, 1915, in Clear Creek Twp., Pawnee Co., Nebraska. She was the daughter of William C. Gilmore (77) and Lillie B. Miller. Ila Mae died in West Riverside, Riverside Co., California, on September 28, 1943, at age 28. She was buried in Olivewood Cemetery, Riverside, Riverside Co., California.[26]

She married **Earl Heril Timmons.** Earl Heril Timmons was born in Adrian, Deer Creek Twp., Bates Co., Missouri, on April 27, 1911. Earl Heril reached age 79 and died in Riverside, Riverside Co., California, on December 18, 1990. He was buried in Riverside National Cemetery, Riverside, Riverside Co., California.[67]

**212. Eva Fern[8] Miller** (*Flossie[7] Gilmore, Martha Jane[6] Vanausdoll, Caleb[5], Mary[4] Pegan, Andrew[3] Pegan II, Andrew[2] Pagan, James[1]*) was born on March 20, 1910, in Miles Twp., Pawnee Co., Nebraska. She was the daughter of John William Miller and Flossie Gilmore (78). Eva Fern died in Riverside, Riverside Co., California, on March 26, 1997, at age 87. She was buried in Riverside National Cemetery, Riverside, Riverside Co., California.[67]

Eva Fern married **Charles Lee Hood** after 1940 in Riverside Co., California? Charles Lee Hood was born in Shelby Co., Tennessee, on September 1, 1900. Charles Lee reached age 82 and died in Riverside, Riverside Co., California, on September 29, 1982. He was buried in Riverside National Cemetery, Riverside, Riverside Co., California.[67]

**213. Homer L.[8] Miller** (*Flossie[7] Gilmore, Martha Jane[6] Vanausdoll, Caleb[5], Mary[4] Pegan, Andrew[3] Pegan II, Andrew[2] Pagan, James[1]*) was born in 1912 in Miles Twp., Pawnee Co., Nebraska. He was the son of John William Miller and Flossie Gilmore (78). Homer L. died between 1940 and 2014.

**214. Ray Richard[8] Miller** (*Flossie[7] Gilmore, Martha Jane[6] Vanausdoll, Caleb[5], Mary[4] Pegan, Andrew[3] Pegan II, Andrew[2] Pagan, James[1]*) was born on March 7, 1916, in Clay Twp., Pawnee Co., Nebraska. He was the son of John William Miller and Flossie Gilmore (78). Ray Richard died in Yorba Linda, Orange Co., California, on January 18, 2007, at age 90. He was buried in Riverside National Cemetery, Riverside, Riverside Co., California.[67]

**215. Doris⁸ Miller** (*Flossie⁷ Gilmore, Martha Jane⁶ Vanausdoll, Caleb⁵, Mary⁴ Pegan, Andrew³ Pegan II, Andrew² Pagan, James¹*) was born on October 11, 1919, in Clay Twp., Pawnee Co., Nebraska. She was the daughter of John William Miller and Flossie Gilmore (78). Doris died in Orange, Orange Co., California, on October 13, 2014, at age 95.

She married **Willard Charles Gailey.** They had two children. Willard Charles Gailey was born in San Marcos, San Diego Co., California, on October 14, 1916. Willard Charles reached age 87 and died in Orange, Orange Co., California, on July 10, 2004.

**216. Evelyn⁸ Miller** (*Flossie⁷ Gilmore, Martha Jane⁶ Vanausdoll, Caleb⁵, Mary⁴ Pegan, Andrew³ Pegan II, Andrew² Pagan, James¹*) was born on July 22, 1924, in Mission Twp., San Bernardino Co., California. She is the daughter of John William Miller and Flossie Gilmore (78).

She married **Thomas Whitlock Hodson II** after 1940. They had one son. Thomas Whitlock Hodson II was born in Colton, San Bernardino Co., California, on February 27, 1922. Thomas Whitlock reached age 89 and died in Santa Barbara, Santa Barbara Co., California, on May 5, 2011. He was buried in Riverside National Cemetery, Riverside, Riverside Co., California.[67]

**217. John Lyle⁸ Purdew II** (*Eva May⁷ Gilmore, Martha Jane⁶ Vanausdoll, Caleb⁵, Mary⁴ Pegan, Andrew³ Pegan II, Andrew² Pagan, James¹*) was born in Lincoln, Lancaster Co., Nebraska on March 23, 1919. He was the son of John Lyle Perdew and Eva May Gilmore (79). John Lyle Jr. died in Covina, Los Angeles Co., California, on August 19, 1993, at age 74. He was buried in Oakdale Memorial Park Cemetery, Glendora, Los Angeles Co., California.[68]

John Lyle Perdew II married **Leona Ora Reutzel.** Leona Ora was born in Neligh, Antelope Co.,

Nebraska, on January 15, 1914. She reached age 93 and died in Camarillo, Ventura Co., California, on August 8, 2007. Leona was buried in Oakdale Memorial Park Cemetery, Glendora, Los Angeles Co., California.[68]

**218. Lois Marie⁸ Purdew** (*Eva May⁷ Gilmore, Martha Jane⁶ Vanausdoll, Caleb⁵, Mary⁴ Pegan, Andrew³ Pegan II, Andrew² Pagan, James¹*) was born in Lincoln, Lancaster Co., Nebraska on September 22, 1921. She is the daughter of John Lyle Perdew and Eva May Gilmore (79). Lois Marie died in Pierre, Hughes Co., South Dakota, on March 1, 2015 at age 93. She was buried in Morningside Cemetery, Ree Heights, Hand Co., South Dakota.[69]

Lois Marie married **James Arthur Blair.** They had five children. James was born in Coleridge, Cedar Co., Nebraska, on October 2, 1926.

Lois Marie Perdew and James Arthur Blair had five children, including:

+ 398 m IV. **Son⁹ Blair**

+ 399 m V. **Frank James⁹ Blair** was born in Miller, Hand Co., South Dakota on July 17, 1956. He died in Sioux Falls, Minnehaha Co., South Dakota on December 15, 2017. Frank James was buried in Morningside Cemetery, Ree Heights, Hand Co. South Dakota.[69]

**219. Dorothy Ann⁸ Purdew** (*Eva May⁷ Gilmore, Martha Jane⁶ Vanausdoll, Caleb⁵, Mary⁴ Pegan, Andrew³ Pegan II, Andrew² Pagan, James¹*) was born in Lincoln, Lancaster Co., Nebraska on September 26, 1923. She was the daughter of John Lyle Perdew and Eva May Gilmore (79). Dorothy Ann died in Neligh, Antelope Co., Nebraska, on January 31, 1999 at age 72. She was buried in Laurel Hill Cemetery, Neligh, Antelope Co., Nebraska.[29]

Never married.

**220. Phyllis⁸ Purdew** (*Eva May⁷ Gilmore, Martha Jane⁶ Vanausdoll, Caleb⁵, Mary⁴ Pegan, Andrew³ Pegan II, Andrew² Pagan, James¹*) was born in Blair, Antelope

Co., Nebraska in 1937. She is the daughter of John Lyle Perdew and Eva May Gilmore (79).

Never married.

**221. Rhea June[8] Purdew** (*Eva May[7] Gilmore, Martha Jane[6] Vanausdoll, Caleb[5], Mary[4] Pegan, Andrew[3] Pegan II, Andrew[2] Pagan, James[1]*) was born in Blaine Twp., Antelope Co., Nebraska, on June 10, 1939. She is the daughter of John Lyle Perdew and Eva May Gilmore (79). She lived in Tilden, Antelope Co., Nebraska. Rhea June died in a hospital in Aurora, Hamilton Co., Nebraska, on June 23, 2018, at age 79. She is buried in Laurel Hill Cemetery, Neligh, Antelope Co., Nebraska.[29]

Rhea June married **Richard D. Carstensen** on June 30, 1960. They had two sons. Richard D. Carstensen was born in Burwell, Garfield Co., Nebraska on June 30, 1937. Richard reached age 74 and died in Tilden, Antelope Co., Nebraska on July 13, 2011. He was buried in Laurel Hill Cemetery, Neligh, Antelope Co., Nebraska.[29]

**222. Randall M.[8] Day** (*John William[7], Mary Ellen[6] Vanausdoll, Caleb[5], Mary[4] Pegan, Andrew[3] Pegan II, Andrew[2] Pagan, James[1]*) was born on April 11, 1910, in Elm Twp., Allen Co., Kansas. He was the son of John William Day (84) and Leoma Rose McClintock. Randall M. died in Moran Twp., Allen Co., Kansas, on August 29, 1992, at age 82. He was buried in Moran Cemetery, Moran Twp., Allen Co., Kansas.[30]

Randall M. married **Meda A. Peebles** on May 10, 1930, in Independence Co., Missouri. They had two sons. Meda A. Peebles was born in Ayr Twp., Adams Co., Nebraska, on June 11, 1909. Meda A. reached age 83 and died in Moran Twp., Allen Co., Kansas, on August 5, 1992. She was buried in Moran Cemetery, Moran Twp., Allen Co., Kansas.[30]

Sons of Randall M. Day and Meda A. Peebles:

+ 400 m I. **Randall Keith[9] Day II** was born in Marmaton Twp., Allen Co., Kansas, in 1931. He died in Moran Twp., Allen Co., Kansas, in 1933.

Randall Keith was buried in Moran Cemetery, Moran Twp., Allen Co., Kansas.[30]

+ 401 m II. **John R.[9] Day** was born in 1937.

**223. Olive Marguerite[8] Day** (*John William[7], Mary Ellen[6] Vanausdoll, Caleb[5], Mary[4] Pegan, Andrew[3] Pegan II, Andrew[2] Pagan, James[1]*) was born on April 1, 1912, in Elm Twp., Allen Co., Kansas. She was the daughter of John William Day (84) and Leoma Rose McClintock. Olive Marguerite died in Iola, Iola Twp., Allen Co., Kansas, on August 5, 2003, at age 91. She was buried in Highland Cemetery, Iola, Iola Twp., Allen Co., Kansas.[70]

Olive Marguerite married **Archie Virgil Cuppy II** on May 5, 1936, in Cedar Co., Missouri. They had two children. Archie Virgil Cuppy II was born in Iola, Iola Twp., Allen Co., Kansas, on September 25, 1916. Archie Virgil reached age 74 and died in Muskogee, Muskogee Co., Oklahoma, on May 2, 1991. He was buried in Fort Gibson National Cemetery, Fort Gibson, Muskogee Co., Oklahoma.[125]

Children of Olive Marguerite Day and Archie Virgil Cuppy II:

+ 402 f I. **Diana Lea[9] Cuppy** was born in Moran Twp., Allen Co., Kansas, in 1937.

+ 403 m II. **Archie Gary[9] Cuppy III** was born in Moran Twp., Allen Co., Kansas, on June 20, 1939. He was also known as **Gary.** Archie Gary died in Moran Twp., Allen Co., Kansas, on October 25, 1989. He was buried in Moran Cemetery, Moran Twp., Allen Co., Kansas.[30]

**224. Glen Lee[8] Day** (*John William[7], Mary Ellen[6] Vanausdoll, Caleb[5], Mary[4] Pegan, Andrew[3] Pegan II, Andrew[2] Pagan, James[1]*) was born on January 12, 1914, in Elm Twp., Allen Co., Kansas. He was the son of John William Day (84) and Leoma Rose McClintock. Glen Lee died in Gas, Elm Twp., Allen Co., Kansas, on April 22, 1999, at age 85. He was buried in Gas City Cemetery, Gas, Elm Twp., Allen Co., Kansas.[71]

Glen Lee married **Laura May Yocham** after 1940. They divorced. Laura May Yocham was born in Nowata, Nowata Twp., Nowata Co., Oklahoma, on January 30, 1922. She reached age 71 and died in Gas, Elm Twp., Allen Co., Kansas, on January 6, 1994. Laura May was buried in Gas City Cemetery, Gas, Elm Twp., Allen Co., Kansas.[71]

Glen L. Day and Laura Mae Yocham Day seemed to have divorced. Laura married again but divorced once more. After Laura's divorce from her second marriage, Glen and Laura seemed to have remarried. They are buried together.

225. **Mildred Lucille⁸ Day** (*Charles Albert⁷, Mary Ellen⁶ Vanausdoll, Caleb⁵, Mary⁴ Pegan, Andrew³ Pegan II, Andrew² Pagan, James¹*) was born on March 13, 1910, in Table Rock Twp., Pawnee Co., Nebraska. She was the daughter of Charles Albert Day (85) and Blanche McLaughlin. Mildred Lucille died in Table Rock Twp., Pawnee Co., Nebraska, on June 28, 1919, at age nine. She was buried in Table Rock Cemetery, Table Rock Twp., Pawnee Co., Nebraska.[12]

226. **Forrest Harlan⁸ Day** (*Charles Albert⁷, Mary Ellen⁶ Vanausdoll, Caleb⁵, Mary⁴ Pegan, Andrew³ Pegan II, Andrew² Pagan, James¹*) was born on July 18, 1915, in Humboldt, Humboldt Twp., Richardson Co., Nebraska. He was also known as **Frosty.** He was the son of Charles Albert Day (85) and Blanche McLaughlin. Forrest Harlan died in Humboldt, Humboldt Twp., Richardson Co., Nebraska, on February 27, 1994, at age 78. He was buried in Humboldt Cemetery, Humboldt, Humboldt Twp., Richardson Co., Nebraska.[12]

Forrest Harlan married **Dorothy Lucille Rousch** on July 18, 1937, in Buena Vista Co., Iowa. They had one son. Dorothy Lucille Rousch was born in Humboldt, Humboldt Twp., Richardson Co., Nebraska, on October 17, 1916. Dorothy Lucille reached age 96 and died in Humboldt, Humboldt Twp., Richardson Co., Nebraska, on May 19, 2013. She was buried in Humboldt Cemetery, Humboldt, Humboldt Twp., Richardson Co., Nebraska.[12]

227. **Lawrence Gerald⁸ Day** (*Charles Albert⁷, Mary Ellen⁶ Vanausdoll, Caleb⁵, Mary⁴ Pegan, Andrew³ Pegan II, Andrew² Pagan, James¹*) was born on February 27, 1917, in Franklin Twp., Richardson Co., Nebraska. He was the son of Charles Albert Day (85) and Blanche McLaughlin. Lawrence Gerald died in De Soto, Dallas Co., Texas, on May 14, 1988, at age 71.

Lawrence Gerald married **Opal Mae Davis** before 1938. They divorced. They had two children. Opal Mae Davis was born in Morrill Twp., Brown Co., Kansas, on June 27, 1919. She reached age 59 and died in Mineral Wells, Palo Pinto Co., Texas, on February 10, 1979. Opal Mae was buried in Bethesda Cemetery, Garner, Parker Co., Texas.[126]

Died under the name Opal Gilbert.

Lawrence Gerald Day married **Flava Arlene McNown** on August 24, 1945, in Sedgwick Co., Kansas. They had one son. Flava Arlene McNown was born in Sedan, Sedan Twp., Chautauqua Co., Kansas, on February 4, 1924. She was also known as **Arlene.** Flava Arlene reached age 65 and died in Wichita, Sedgwick Co., Kansas, on February 4, 1989. She was buried in Moline Cemetery, Moline, Wildcat Twp., Elk Co., Kansas.[127]

Children of Lawrence Gerald Day and Opal Mae Davis:

+ 404 m I. **Larry Gale⁹ Day** was born in Highland, Iowa Twp., Doniphan Co., Kansas, on May 23, 1938. He died in Dallas, Dallas Co., Texas, on April 28, 1997. Larry Gale was buried in Table Rock Cemetery, Table Rock Twp., Pawnee Co., Nebraska.[12]

+ 405 f II. **Patricia Ann⁹ Day** was born in Wichita, Sedgwick Co., Kansas, on October 18, 1942. She died in Joplin, Joplin Twp., Jasper Co., Missouri, on July 12, 1986. Patricia Ann was buried in Lakeview Cemetery, Erie, Erie Twp., Neosho Co., Kansas.[128]

**228. Gladys Mae⁸ Spaulding** (*Cora May Agnes⁷ Day, Mary Ellen⁶ Vanausdoll, Caleb⁵, Mary⁴ Pegan, Andrew³ Pegan II, Andrew² Pagan, James¹*) was born on October 10, 1904, in Grant Twp., Richardson Co., Nebraska. She was the daughter of John Elliot Spaulding and Cora May Agnes Day (86). Gladys Mae died in Humboldt, Humboldt Twp., Richardson Co., Nebraska, on March 17, 1997, at age 92. She was buried in Heim Cemetery, Dawson, Grant Twp., Richardson Co., Nebraska.[31]

She married **Virgil Leroy Allen.** They had two children. Virgil Leroy Allen was born in Antelope Twp., Buffalo Co., Nebraska, on December 10, 1900. He was also known as **Happy.** Virgil Leroy reached age 29 and died in Dawson, Grant Twp., Richardson Co., Nebraska, on December 23, 1929. He was buried in Heim Cemetery, Dawson, Grant Twp., Richardson Co., Nebraska.[31]

Gladys Mae Spaulding married **Harry Gordon Fencil.** They had four children. Harry Gordon Fencil was born in Table Rock Twp., Pawnee Co., Nebraska, on June 25, 1905. Harry Gordon reached age 74 and died in Dawson, Grant Twp., Richardson Co., Nebraska, on February 16, 1980. He was buried in Heim Cemetery, Dawson, Grant Twp., Richardson Co., Nebraska.[27]

Children of Gladys Mae Spaulding and Virgil Leroy Allen:

+ 406 f I. **Yvonne Ailene⁹ Allen** was born in Dawson, Grant Twp., Richardson Co., Nebraska, on April 13, 1924. She was also known as **Bonnie.** Yvonne Ailene died in Brush Prairie, Clark Co., Washington, on February 23, 1986. She was buried in Camas Cemetery, Camas, Clark Co., Washington.[129]

+ 407 m II. **Carol Eldon⁹ Allen** was born in Dawson, Grant Twp., Richardson Co., Nebraska, on December 18, 1925. He died in Portland, Multnomah Co., Oregon, on August 9, 1995.

Children of Gladys Mae Spaulding and Harry Gordon Fencil:

+ 408 m I. **Harry Gordon⁹ Fencil II** was born in Humboldt, Humboldt Twp., Richardson Co., Nebraska, on March 23, 1901. He died in Ridgefield, Clark Co., Washington on March 12, 2018.

+ 409 f II. **Delverna⁹ Corrine Fencil** was born in Humboldt, Humboldt Twp., Richardson Co., Nebraska, on August 10, 1933. She died in La Center, Clark Co., Washington, on June 30, 2018.

+ 410 f III. **DeLauris C.⁹ Fencil** was born in Humboldt, Humboldt Twp., Richardson Co., Nebraska, on August 10, 1933.

+ 411 f IV. **Mary Ellyn⁹ Fencil** was born in Humboldt, Humboldt Twp., Richardson Co., Nebraska, on February 21, 1937. She died in a hospital in Lincoln, Lancaster Co., Nebraska, on April 29, 2010. Mary Ellyn was buried in Pleasant View Cemetery, Auburn, Douglas Twp., Nemaha Co., Nebraska.[130]

**229. John Raymond⁸ Spaulding II** (*Cora May Agnes⁷ Day, Mary Ellen⁶ Vanausdoll, Caleb⁵, Mary⁴ Pegan, Andrew³ Pegan II, Andrew² Pagan, James¹*) was born on February 3, 1906, in Grant Twp., Richardson Co., Nebraska. He was also known as **Raymond.** He was the son of John Elliot Spaulding and Cora May Agnes Day (86). John Raymond died in Hiawatha, Hiawatha Twp., Brown Co., Kansas, on January 10, 1989, at age 82. He was buried in Mount Hope Cemetery, Hiawatha, Hiawatha Twp., Brown Co., Kansas.[72]

John Raymond married **Ethel May Dougherty** on September 1, 1926, in Callaway Co., Missouri. They divorced. They had three sons. Ethel May Dougherty was born in Verdon, Liberty Twp., Richardson Co., Nebraska, on January 6, 1905. Ethel May reached age 76 and died in

Lincoln, Lancaster Co., Nebraska on October 16, 1981. She was buried in Lincoln Memorial Park Cemetery, Lincoln, Lancaster Co., Nebraska.[131]

She died under the name Ethel May Schultz.

John Raymond Spaulding II married **Mary Marie Schofield** on June 22, 1952, in Richardson Co., Nebraska. Mary Marie Schofield was born in Hiawatha, Hiawatha Twp., Brown Co., Kansas, on June 15, 1923. Mary Marie reached age 87 and died in Hiawatha, Hiawatha Twp., Brown Co., Kansas, on July 10, 2010. She was buried in Mount Hope Cemetery, Hiawatha, Hiawatha Twp., Brown Co., Kansas.[72]

Sons of John Raymond Spaulding II and Ethel May Dougherty:

+ 412 m I. **Ronald Raymond⁹ Spaulding** was born in Liberty Twp., Richardson Co., Nebraska, on March 31, 1927. He died in Lincoln, Lancaster Co., Nebraska, on January 12, 1988. Ronald Raymond was buried in Heim Cemetery, Dawson, Grant Twp., Richardson Co., Nebraska.[31]

+ 413 m II. **Donald Robert⁹ Spaulding** was born in Liberty Twp., Richardson Co., Nebraska, on April 23, 1929. He died in Goldendale, Klickitat Co., Washington, on October 28, 2013.

+ 414 m III. **Dale Elton⁹ Spaulding** was born in Liberty Twp., Richardson Co., Nebraska, on August 27, 1934. He was also known as **Spook.** Dale E. died in Lincoln, Lancaster Co., Nebraska, on January 3, 2012. He was buried in Lincoln Memorial Park Cemetery, Lincoln, Lancaster Co., Nebraska.[131]

**230. Thelma Ellen⁸ Spaulding** (*Cora May Agnes⁷ Day, Mary Ellen⁶ Vanausdoll, Caleb⁵, Mary⁴ Pegan, Andrew³ Pegan II, Andrew² Pagan, James¹*) was born on December 16, 1907, in Grant Twp., Richardson Co., Nebraska. She was the daughter of John Elliot Spaulding and Cora May Agnes Day (86). Thelma Ellen died in Marshall Co., Kansas, on July 1, 1982, at age 74. She was buried in Heim Cemetery, Dawson, Grant Twp., Richardson Co., Nebraska.[31]

Thelma Ellen married **Lyle William Brown** on December 3, 1925, in Richardson Co., Nebraska. He was also known as **Bud.** They divorced. They had two children. Lyle William Brown was born in Lost Creek Twp., Garden Co., Nebraska, on March 18, 1905. He reached age 68 and died in Omaha, Douglas Co., Nebraska, on August 2, 1973. He was buried in Heim Cemetery, Dawson, Grant Twp., Richardson Co., Nebraska.[31]

Thelma Ellen Spaulding married **Orvil H. Cudney** on July 6, 1937, in Richardson Co., Nebraska. Orvil H. Cudney was born in St. Joseph, Buchanan Co., Missouri? on January 22, 1906. Orvil H. reached age 78 and died in Marshall Co., Kansas, on March 17, 1984. He was buried in Heim Cemetery, Dawson, Grant Twp., Richardson Co., Nebraska.[31]

Children of Thelma Ellen Spaulding and Lyle William Brown:

+ 415 m I. **Lyle Raymond⁹ Brown II** was born in Humboldt, Humboldt Twp., Richardson Co., Nebraska, on July 28, 1926.

+ 416 f II. **Mary Lou⁹ Brown?** was born in Humboldt, Humboldt Twp., Richardson Co., Nebraska, on June 7, 1935.

**231. Ruth Anna⁸ Spaulding** (*Cora May Agnes⁷ Day, Mary Ellen⁶ Vanausdoll, Caleb⁵, Mary⁴ Pegan, Andrew³ Pegan II, Andrew² Pagan, James¹*) was born on August 17, 1909, in Grant Twp., Richardson Co., Nebraska. She was the daughter of John Elliot Spaulding and Cora May Agnes Day (86). Ruth Anna lived in Gresham, Stewart Twp., York Co., Nebraska. She died in Palm Harbor, Pinellas Co., Florida, on December 24, 1993, at age 84. Ruth Anna was buried in Heim Cemetery, Dawson, Grant Twp., Richardson Co., Nebraska.[31]

She married **Lawrence Brod.** They had one son. Lawrence Brod was born in Auburn, Douglas Twp., Nemaha Co., Nebraska, on September 21, 1907. Lawrence reached age 82 and died in Palm Harbor, Pinellas Co., Florida, on November 4, 1989. He was buried in Heim Cemetery, Dawson, Grant Twp., Richardson Co., Nebraska.[31]

Son of Ruth Anna Spaulding and Lawrence Brod:

+ 417 m I. **Larry J.⁹ Brod** was born in Goff, Harrison Twp., Nemaha Co., Nebraska, in 1933. He died in Goff, Harrison Twp., Nemaha Co., Nebraska, in 1933. Larry J. was buried in Heim Cemetery, Dawson, Grant Twp., Richardson Co., Nebraska.[31]

**232. Garl Vernon⁸ Spaulding** (*Cora May Agnes⁷ Day, Mary Ellen⁶ Vanausdoll, Caleb⁵, Mary⁴ Pegan, Andrew³ Pegan II, Andrew² Pagan, James¹*) was born on December 19, 1911, in Grant Twp., Richardson Co., Nebraska. He was the son of John Elliot Spaulding and Cora May Agnes Day (86). Garl Vernon died in Paramount, Los Angeles Co., California, on September 25, 1984, at age 72.

Garl Vernon married **Fernande Ada Belle Godfernon** on December 6, 1931, in Doniphan Co., Kansas. They had five children. Fernande Ada Belle Godfernon was born in Falls City, Falls City Twp., Richardson Co., Nebraska, on April 11, 1910. Fernande Ada Belle reached age 90 and died in Victorville, San Bernardino Co., California, on November 30, 2000.

Garl Vernon Spaulding and Fernande Ada Belle Godfernon had five children, including these and two more born after 1940:

+ 418 f I. **Edith May⁹ Spaulding** was born in Falls City Twp., Richardson Co., Nebraska, on June 2, 1932. She died in Murrieta, Riverside Co., California, on July 28, 2004. Edith May was buried in Riverside

National Cemetery, Riverside, Riverside Co., California.[67]

+ 419 m II. **Garl E.⁹ Spaulding II** was born in Falls City Twp., Richardson Co., Nebraska, on September 10, 1933. He is also known as **Bud.**

+ 420 f III. **Ruth A.⁹ Spaulding** was born in Walnut Twp., Brown Co., Kansas, on April 26, 1938.

+ 421 f IV. **Roberta L.⁹ Spaulding** was born in Walnut Twp., Brown Co., Kansas, on January 22, 1940.

**233. Carl Eldon⁸ Spaulding** (*Cora May Agnes⁷ Day, Mary Ellen⁶ Vanausdoll, Caleb⁵, Mary⁴ Pegan, Andrew³ Pegan II, Andrew² Pagan, James¹*) was born on December 19, 1911, in Grant Twp., Richardson Co., Nebraska. He was the son of John Elliot Spaulding and Cora May Agnes Day (86). Carl Eldon died in Grant Twp., Richardson Co., Nebraska, on December 20, 1911.

**234. Harold Woodrow⁸ Spaulding** (*Cora May Agnes⁷ Day, Mary Ellen⁶ Vanausdoll, Caleb⁵, Mary⁴ Pegan, Andrew³ Pegan II, Andrew² Pagan, James¹*) was born on November 7, 1915, in Grant Twp., Richardson Co., Nebraska. He was the son of John Elliot Spaulding and Cora May Agnes Day (86). Harold Woodrow died in Excelsior Springs, Clay Co., Missouri, on May 26, 2003, at age 88. He was buried in Floral Hills Cemetery, Kansas City, Jackson Co., Missouri.[73]

Harold Woodrow married **Jimmie Garnet McCulley** on October 27, 1937. They had four daughters. Jimmie Garnet McCulley was born in Jackson Twp., Camden Co., Missouri, on February 21, 1918. Jimmie Garnet reached age 52 and died in Kansas City, Jackson Co., Missouri, on August 23, 1970. She was buried in Floral Hills Cemetery, Kansas City, Jackson Co., Missouri.[73]

Harold Woodrow Spaulding married **Betty Jean Durnell** in February 1971. Betty Jean Durnell was born in Higgensville, Davis Twp., Lafayette Co., Missouri, on September 27, 1928. Betty Jean reached age 60 and died in Kansas City, Jackson Co., Missouri, on December 29, 1988.

Harold Woodrow Spaulding married **Laverne Cleda Card Davison** after 1988. Laverne Cleda Card Davison was born in Columbus, Salamanca Twp., Cherokee Co., Kansas, on August 23, 1919. Laverne Cleda Card reached age 85 and died in Columbus, Salamanca Twp., Cherokee Co., Kansas? on September 26, 2004. She was buried in Park Cemetery, Columbus, Salamanca Twp., Cherokee Co., Kansas.[132]

Daughters of Harold Woodrow Spaulding and Jimmie Garnet McCulley:

+ 422 f I. **Janet Kay**[9] **Spaulding** was born in Corning, Illinois Twp., Nemaha Co., Kansas, on August 3, 1938. She died in Auburn, Douglas Twp., Nemaha Co., Nebraska, on May 8, 2015.

+ 423 f II. **Brenda Lee**[9] **Spaulding** was born in Corning, Illinois Twp., Nemaha Co., Kansas, on January 15, 1940.

+ 424 f III. **Patricia Lynne**[9] **Spaulding** was born in Corning, Illinois Twp., Nemaha Co., Kansas, on July 19, 1942. She died in St. Joseph, Buchanan Co., Missouri, on December 14, 2012.

+ 425 f IV. **Constance Dee**[9] **Spaulding** was born in Sabetha, Creek Twp., Nemaha Co., Kansas, on June 29, 1946. She died in Hiawatha, Hiawatha Twp., Brown Co., Kansas, on July 16, 2003. Constance Dee was buried in Floral Hills Cemetery, Kansas City, Jackson Co., Missouri.[73]

235. **Edith Ilene**[8] **Spaulding** (*Cora May Agnes*[7] *Day, Mary Ellen*[6] *Vanausdoll, Caleb*[5]*, Mary*[4] *Pegan, Andrew*[3] *Pegan II, Andrew*[2] *Pagan, James*[1]) was born on September 19, 1917, in Grant Twp., Richardson Co., Nebraska. She was also known as **Illene.** She was the daughter of John Elliot Spaulding and Cora

May Agnes Day (86). Edith Ilene died in Grant Twp., Richardson Co., Nebraska, on October 16, 1923, at age six. She was buried in Heim Cemetery, Dawson, Grant Twp., Richardson Co., Nebraska.[27]

236. **Darrell Eugene**[8] **Spaulding** (*Cora May Agnes*[7] *Day, Mary Ellen*[6] *Vanausdoll, Caleb*[5]*, Mary*[4] *Pegan, Andrew*[3] *Pegan II, Andrew*[2] *Pagan, James*[1]) was born on May 8, 1921, in Grant Twp., Richardson Co., Nebraska. He was the son of John Elliot Spaulding and Cora May Agnes Day (86). Darrell Eugene died in Lincoln, Lancaster Co., Nebraska, on March 28, 1986, at age 64. He was buried in Heim Cemetery, Dawson, Grant Twp., Richardson Co., Nebraska.[27]

237. **Howard Glen**[8] **Day** (*Anthony Juduthan*[7]*, Mary Ellen*[6] *Vanausdoll, Caleb*[5]*, Mary*[4] *Pegan, Andrew*[3] *Pegan II, Andrew*[2] *Pagan, James*[1]) was born on April 25, 1913, in Table Rock Twp., Pawnee Co., Nebraska. He was the son of Anthony Juduthan Day (87) and Lillie M. Buckles. Howard Glen lived in Noti, Lane Co., Oregon. He died in Selah, Yakima Co., Washington, on March 6, 1994, at age 80.

Howard Glen married **Opal M. Frank** before 1940. Opal M. Frank was born in Broken Bow, Custer Co., Nebraska? in 1915. Opal M. died after 1940.

Howard Glen Day married **Minnie L. Weippert** on October 14, 1945. They had two sons. Minnie L. Weippert was born on June 17, 1929, in Toppenish, Yakima Co., Washington?

Howard Glen Day and Minnie L. Weippert had two sons, including:

+ 425A m **Tommy Glen**[9] **Day** was born in Yakima, Yakima Co., Washington, on January 1, 1948. Tommy Glen died in Moxee City, Yakima Co., Washington, on February 10, 2012.

238. **Lowrain Arthur**[8] **Day** (*Anthony Juduthan*[7]*, Mary Ellen*[6] *Vanausdoll, Caleb*[5]*, Mary*[4] *Pegan, Andrew*[3] *Pegan II, Andrew*[2] *Pagan, James*[1]) was born on June 17, 1915, in Pawnee City, Pawnee City Twp., Pawnee Co., Nebraska. He was also known as **Laun**

and **Rainey.** He was the son of Anthony Juduthan Day (87) and Lillie M. Buckles. Lowrain Arthur lived in 1983 in Quincy, Grant Co., Washington. He died in a hospital in Wenatchee, Chelan Co., Washington, on September 4, 1983, at age 68.

Lowrain Arthur Day married **Helen Judice Madden** on July 23, 1935. They divorced. They had seven children. Helen Judice Madden was born in Pawnee City, Pawnee City Twp., Pawnee Co., Nebraska, on October 9, 1915. She reached age 89 and died in Yakima, Yakima Co., Washington, on November 15, 2004. Helen Judice was buried in West Hills Memorial Park Cemetery, Yakima, Yakima Co., Washington.[133]

Died under the name Helen Shroll.

Lowrain married **Joanne Elaine Hendrickson.** Joanne Elaine Hendrickson was born in Spokane, Spokane Co., Washington, on June 17, 1938.

Lowrain Arthur Day and Helen Judice Madden had seven children, including:

+ 426   f   I.   **Jacqueline J.⁹ Day** was born in Pawnee City, Pawnee City Twp., Pawnee Co., Nebraska, on February 4, 1936. She died in a hospital in Olympia, Thurston Co., Washington, on September 23, 1973. Jacqueline J. was buried in Claquato Cemetery, Chehalis, Lewis Co., Washington.[134]

+ 427   f   II.   **Linda Lorraine⁹ Day** was born in Wapato, Yakima Co., Washington, on September 11, 1943. She was also known as **Blondie.** Linda Lorraine died in Yakima, Yakima Co., Washington, on October 25, 2015.

+ 428   m   V.   **Son⁹ Day.**

+ 429   m   IV.   **Darrell D.⁹ Day** was born in Wapato, Yakima Co., Washington, on June 13, 1950. He died in a hospital in Seattle, King Co. Washington, on December 31, 2009. Darrell D. was buried in Sil-

vercreek Cemetery, Randle, Lewis Co., Washington.[135]

+ 430   m   V.   **Garry Lee⁹ Day** was born in Wapato, Yakima Co., Washington, on January 30, 1953. He died in Yakima, Yakima Co., Washington, on January 27, 1980. Garry Lee was buried in Mabton Cemetery, Mabton, Yakima Co., Washington.[136]

239. **Daughter⁸ Day** (*Anthony Juduthan⁷, Mary Ellen⁶ Vanausdoll, Caleb⁵, Mary⁴ Pegan, Andrew³ Pegan II, Andrew² Pagan, James¹*) was born on June 24, 1921, in Table Rock Twp., Pawnee Co., Nebraska. She was the daughter of Anthony Juduthan Day (87) and Lillie M. Buckles. Daughter died in Table Rock Twp., Pawnee Co., Nebraska, on June 24, 1924, at age three. Probably buried in Table Rock Cemetery, Table Rock Twp., Pawnee Co., Nebraska.

240. **Peggy⁸ Shiley** (*Mary Jane⁷ Day, Mary Ellen⁶ Vanausdoll, Caleb⁵, Mary⁴ Pegan, Andrew³ Pegan II, Andrew² Pagan, James¹*). She is the daughter of John Sherman Shiley and Mary Jane Day (88). She either was born and died between 1934-1940 or was adopted after 1940.

241. **Arnold Elvern⁸ Phillips** (*Ruth Clara⁷ Day, Mary Ellen⁶ Vanausdoll, Caleb⁵, Mary⁴ Pegan, Andrew³ Pegan II, Andrew² Pagan, James¹*) was born on April 27, 1913, in Table Rock Twp., Pawnee Co., Nebraska. He was the son of Charles Raymond Phillips and Ruth Clara Day (89). Arnold Elvern died in Vallejo, Solano Co., California, on November 18, 1991, at age 78.

He married **Ann Kirkpatrick?** They divorced. Ann Kirkpatrick? was born in Nebraska in 1916. She died after 1940.

242. **Zelma Leota⁸ Phillips** (*Ruth Clara⁷ Day, Mary Ellen⁶ Vanausdoll, Caleb⁵, Mary⁴ Pegan, Andrew³ Pegan II, Andrew² Pagan, James¹*) was born on July 16, 1915, in Clear Creek Twp., Pawnee Co., Nebraska. She was the daughter of Charles Raymond Phillips and Ruth Clara Day (89). Zelma Leota died in Medford, Jackson Co., Oregon, on October 17, 1968, at age 53. She was buried in

Hillcrest Memorial Park Cemetery, Medford, Jackson Co., Oregon.[75]

Zelma Leota married **Dixon Earl Kenner** on August 29, 1934. They had two children. Dixon Earl Kenner was born in Galena, Jasper Co., Missouri, on February 9, 1915. Dixon Earl reached age 92 and died in Medford, Jackson Co., Oregon, on August 6, 2007. He was buried in Hillcrest Memorial Park Cemetery, Medford, Jackson Co., Oregon.[75]

Children of Zelma Leota Phillips and Dixon Earl Kenner:

+ 431 m I. **Richard Eugene⁹ Kenner** was born in Table Rock, Table Rock Twp., Pawnee Co., Nebraska, on August 10, 1936. He died in Medford, Jackson Co., Oregon, on June 11, 1980. Richard Eugene was buried in Hillcrest Memorial Park Cemetery, Medford, Jackson Co., Oregon.[75]

+ 432 f II. **Shirley Ruth⁹ Kenner** was born in Table Rock, Table Rock Twp., Pawnee Co., Nebraska, on December 4, 1938. She died in Medford, Jackson Co., Oregon, on September 9, 1997. Shirley Ruth was buried in Eagle Point National Cemetery, Eagle Point, Jackson Co., Oregon.[137]

**243. Zethel Irene⁸ Phillips** (*Ruth Clara⁷ Day, Mary Ellen⁶ Vanausdoll, Caleb⁵, Mary⁴ Pegan, Andrew³ Pegan II, Andrew² Pagan, James¹*) was born on September 3, 1917, in Clear Creek Twp., Pawnee Co., Nebraska. She was the daughter of Charles Raymond Phillips and Ruth Clara Day (89). Zethel Irene died in Humboldt, Humboldt Twp., Richardson Co., Nebraska, on January 23, 2004, at age 86. She was buried in Table Rock Cemetery, Table Rock Twp., Pawnee Co., Nebraska.[12]

She married **Robert Frederick Bowman**. They had four children. Robert Frederick Bowman was born in Fullerton Twp., Lance Co., Nebraska, on July 17, 1916. Robert Frederick reached age 48 and died in Humboldt, Humboldt Twp., Richardson Co., Nebraska, on August 4, 1964. He was buried

in Table Rock Cemetery, Table Rock Twp., Pawnee Co., Nebraska.[12]

Zethel Irene Phillips Bowman married **Lawrence Massey** after 1964.

Zethel Irene Phillips and Robert Frederick Bowman had four children, including:

+ 433 f I. **Beverly⁹ Bowman** was born in Table Rock Twp., Pawnee Co., Nebraska, in 1936.

+ 434 m II. **Robert⁹ Bowman II** was born in Table Rock Twp., Pawnee Co., Nebraska, on June 10, 1939.

+ 435 f III. **Judy⁹ Bowman** was born in Table Rock Twp., Pawnee Co., Nebraska, on March 29, 1941. She died in Grand Island, Hall Co., Nebraska, on March 20, 2009. Judy was buried in West Lawn Memorial Cemetery, Grand Island, Hall Co., Nebraska.[138]

**244. Zeda Louise⁸ Phillips** (*Ruth Clara⁷ Day, Mary Ellen⁶ Vanausdoll, Caleb⁵, Mary⁴ Pegan, Andrew³ Pegan II, Andrew² Pagan, James¹*) was born on July 1, 1919, in Clear Creek Twp., Pawnee Co., Nebraska. She was the daughter of Charles Raymond Phillips and Ruth Clara Day (89). Zeda Louise lived in Seatac, King Co., Washington. She died in Seattle, King Co., Washington, on November 28, 2003, at age 84.

She died under the name Zeda L. Lynch.

Zeda Louise married **Charles W. Power** before 1940. They divorced in 1940. They divorced. Charles W. Power was born in Humboldt, Humboldt Twp., Richardson Co., Nebraska, on March 12, 1915. Charles W. reached age 79 and died in Rathdrum, Kootenai Co., Idaho, on June 23, 1994. He was buried in Coeur D'Alene Memorial Gardens Cemetery, Coeur D'Alene, Rural Co., Idaho.[139]

Zeda Louise Phillips Power married **Vernon Arthur Lynch** on January 12, 1942. Vernon Arthur Lynch was born in Pomeroy, Garfield Co., Washington, on June 21, 1921. Vernon Arthur reached age 53 and died in Seattle, King Co., Washington, on March 31, 1975.

Zeda Louise Phillips Powers Lynch married **Samuel Leo Bailey** on May 23, 1980. They divorced. Samuel Leo Bailey was born in Seattle, King Co., Washington, on May 29, 1918. He was also known as **Sam Leo.** Samuel Leo reached age 78 and died in Seattle, King Co., Washington, on May 12, 1997. He was buried in Washington Memorial Park Cemetery, Seatac, King Co., Washington.[140]

245. **Robert James⁸ Day** (*James Manahan⁷, Mary Ellen⁶ Vanausdoll, Caleb⁵, Mary⁴ Pegan, Andrew³ Pegan II, Andrew² Pagan, James¹*) was born on February 4, 1922, in Clear Creek Twp., Richardson Co., Nebraska. He was the son of James Manahan Day (92) and Rosa Ella Holliger. Robert James died in Yakima, Yakima Co., Washington, on October 8, 1995, at age 73. He was buried in Tahoma Cemetery, Yakima, Yakima Co., Washington.[76]

He married **Doris Marie Collier.** Doris Marie Collier was born in Copeland, Boundary Co., Idaho, on June 23, 1926. Doris Marie reached age 84 and died in Yakima, Yakima Co., Washington, on December 3, 2010. She was buried in Tahoma Cemetery, Yakima, Yakima Co., Washington.[76]

246. **Betty Irene⁸ Day** (*James Manahan⁷, Mary Ellen⁶ Vanausdoll, Caleb⁵, Mary⁴ Pegan, Andrew³ Pegan II, Andrew² Pagan, James¹*) was born on July 29, 1924, in Clear Creek Twp., Richardson Co., Nebraska. She was the daughter of James Manahan Day (92) and Rosa Ella Holliger. Betty Irene died in Kettle Falls, Stevens Co., Washington, on March 19, 2001, at age 76. She was buried in Meyers Falls Cemetery, Kettle Falls, Stevens Co., Washington.[77]

Betty Irene married **Joseph Aloyzius Richartz II** on December 15, 1942, in Norfolk Co., Virginia. They divorced. They had six children. Joseph Aloyzius Richartz II was born in Yakima, Yakima Co., Washington, on October 17, 1919. He was also known as **Joseph Alfred.** Joseph Aloyzius reached age 85 and died in Yakima, Yakima Co., Washington, on March 20, 2005. He was bur-

ied in Terrace Heights Memorial Park Cemetery, Yakima, Yakima Co., Washington.[78]

Betty Irene Day married **Lyle Donnell Woodworth** on July 24, 1961. They had four children. Lyle Donnell Woodworth was born in Cochranton, Crawford Co., Pennsylvania, on April 3, 1928. He was also known as **Woody.** Lyle Donnell reached age 79 and died in Evans, Stevens Co., Washington, on May 18, 2007. He was buried in Bossberg Cemetery, Stevens Co., Washington.[141]

247. **Delmar Silas⁸ Day** (*James Manahan⁷, Mary Ellen⁶ Vanausdoll, Caleb⁵, Mary⁴ Pegan, Andrew³ Pegan II, Andrew² Pagan, James¹*) was born on December 31, 1927, in Pawnee City, Pawnee City Twp., Pawnee Co., Nebraska. He was also known as **Del.** He was the son of James Manahan Day (92) and Rosa Ella Holliger. He died in Yakima, Yakima Co., Washington, on September 20, 2016, at age 88. Delmar Silas was buried in Terrace Heights Memorial Park Cemetery, Yakima, Yakima Co., Washington.[78]

Delmar Silas married **Joyce Miflin Winters** on August 26, 1951, in Whitman Co., Washington. They had four children. Joyce Miflin Winters was born in Wheatland, Platte Co., Wyoming, on September 9, 1932.

Delmar Silas Day and Joyce Miflin Winters had four children, including:

+ 436 m IV. **David Warren⁹ Day** was born on September 21, 1954 in Yakima, Yakima Co., Washington. He died on September 10, 1977 in Yakima, Yakima Co., Washington. David Warren was buried in Terrace Heights Memorial Park Cemetery, Yakima, Yakima Co., Washington.[78]

248. **Raymond Edward⁸ Day** (*James Manahan⁷, Mary Ellen⁶ Vanausdoll, Caleb⁵, Mary⁴ Pegan, Andrew³ Pegan II, Andrew² Pagan, James¹*) was born on May 25, 1930, in St. Bridget Twp., Marshall Co., Kansas. He is the son of James Manahan Day (92) and Rosa Ella Holliger.

Raymond Edward married **Tola Rae Harris** on November 14, 1953, when. Tola Rae Harris was born in Highmore, Hyde Co., South Dakota, on May 24, 1936.

249. **Donald Allan⁸ Day** (*James Manahan⁷, Mary Ellen⁶ Vanausdoll, Caleb⁵, Mary⁴ Pegan, Andrew³ Pegan II, Andrew² Pagan, James¹*) was born on May 13, 1933, in St. Bridget Twp., Marshall Co., Kansas. He is the son of James Manahan Day (92) and Rosa Ella Holliger.

Donald Allan married **Rosalyn Lameire** on September 17, 1954. Rosalyn Lameire was born in Neshoba Co., Mississippi, on December 26, 1935.

250. **Marian Lucille⁸ Day** (*Lewis Allan⁷, Mary Ellen⁶ Vanausdoll, Caleb⁵, Mary⁴ Pegan, Andrew³ Pegan II, Andrew² Pagan, James¹*) was born on May 11, 1927, in Table Rock Twp., Pawnee Co., Nebraska. She is the daughter of Lewis Allan Day (93) and Laura Ellen Aylor.

Marian Lucille married **Arley Leonard Goodenkauf** on May 26, 1948. They had one child. Arley Leonard Goodenkauf was born in Table Rock Twp., Pawnee Co., Nebraska, on August 10, 1917. Arley Leonard lived in 1954 in Omaha, Douglas Co., Nebraska. He reached age 87 and died in Table Rock, Table Rock Twp., Pawnee Co., Nebraska, on October 22, 2004. Arley Leonard was buried in Table Rock Cemetery, Table Rock Twp., Pawnee Co., Nebraska.[12]

251. **Janet Elaine⁸ Day** (*Lewis Allan⁷, Mary Ellen⁶ Vanausdoll, Caleb⁵, Mary⁴ Pegan, Andrew³ Pegan II, Andrew² Pagan, James¹*) was born on July 4, 1931, in Table Rock Twp., Pawnee Co., Nebraska. She was the daughter of Lewis Allan Day (93) and Laura Ellen Aylor. She was also known as **Janie**. Janet Elaine died in Elk Creek, Johnson Co., Nebraska on November 5, 2016 at age 85. She was buried in Table Rock Cemetery, Table Rock Twp., Pawnee Co., Nebraska.[12]

Janet married **Christopher Harold Schuster** on April 21, 1956 in Johnson Co., Nebraska. They have three children. Christopher Harold Schuster was born in Ashland, Ashland Twp., Saunders Co., Nebraska, on January 15, 1929.

252. **Dwaine Frank⁸ James** (*Jessie Levern⁷ Day, Mary Ellen⁶ Vanausdoll, Caleb⁵, Mary⁴ Pegan, Andrew³ Pegan II, Andrew² Pagan, James¹*) was born on June 6, 1925, in Porter Twp., Richardson Co., Nebraska. He was the son of Frank Edgar James and Jessie Levern Day (94). Dwaine Frank died in Humboldt Twp., Richardson Co., Nebraska, on November 14, 1986, at age 61. He was buried in Humboldt Cemetery, Humboldt, Humboldt Twp., Richardson Co., Nebraska.[11]

Dwaine Frank married **Jacquelyn L. Frehse** on December 21, 1944. Jacquelyn L. Frehse was born in Falls City, Falls City Twp., Richardson Co., Nebraska, on October 2, 1925.

253. **Dale Arthur⁸ James** (*Jessie Levern⁷ Day, Mary Ellen⁶ Vanausdoll, Caleb⁵, Mary⁴ Pegan, Andrew³ Pegan II, Andrew² Pagan, James¹*) was born on May 13, 1928, in Porter Twp., Richardson Co., Nebraska. He was the son of Frank Edgar James and Jessie Levern Day (94). Dale Arthur died in Pawnee City, Pawnee City Twp., Pawnee Co., Nebraska, on March 21, 2000, at age 71. He was buried in Humboldt Cemetery, Humboldt, Humboldt Twp., Richardson Co., Nebraska.[11]

Dale Arthur married **Erma Jean Blecha** on September 5, 1948. Erma Jean Blecha was born in Spicer Twp., Richardson Co., Nebraska, on June 30, 1930.

254. **Dorothy Arlene⁸ James** (*Jessie Levern⁷ Day, Mary Ellen⁶ Vanausdoll, Caleb⁵, Mary⁴ Pegan, Andrew³ Pegan II, Andrew² Pagan, James¹*) was born on May 13, 1928, in Porter Twp., Richardson Co., Nebraska. She is the daughter of Frank Edgar James and Jessie Levern Day (94).

Dorothy Arlene married **Edwin Thomas Merwin** on June 12, 1948. They had one son. Edwin Thomas Merwin was born in Table Rock Twp., Pawnee Co., Nebraska, on April 8, 1926. Edwin Thomas reached age 78 and died in Humboldt, Humboldt Twp., Richardson Co., Nebraska, on February 13, 2005. He was buried in Humboldt Cemetery, Humboldt, Humboldt Twp., Richardson Co., Nebraska. He was buried in Humboldt Cemetery, Humboldt, Humboldt Twp., Richardson Co., Nebraska.[11]

Son of Dorothy Arlene James and Edwin Thomas Merwin:

+ 437  m  I.  **Son[9] Merwin.**

**255. John W.[8] Vanausdoll** (*Leonard R.[7], William Cornelius[6], Caleb[5], Mary[4] Pegan, Andrew[3] Pegan II, Andrew[2] Pagan, James[1]*) was born on July 24, 1916, in Mississippi Twp., Jersey Co., Illinois. He was the son of Leonard R. Vanausdoll (95) and Evelyn Rosina Waggoner. John W. died in San Diego, San Diego Co., California, on March 8, 2010, at age 93.

**256. Willard Eldon[8] Vanausdoll** (*Leonard R.[7], William Cornelius[6], Caleb[5], Mary[4] Pegan, Andrew[3] Pegan II, Andrew[2] Pagan, James[1]*) was born on November 11, 1919, in Mississippi Twp., Jersey Co., Illinois. He was the son of Leonard R. Vanausdoll (95) and Evelyn Rosina Waggoner. Willard Eldon died in San Diego, San Diego Co., California, on January 30, 1996, at age 76.

**257. Robert Newell[8] Vanausdoll** (*Leonard R.[7], William Cornelius[6], Caleb[5], Mary[4] Pegan, Andrew[3] Pegan II, Andrew[2] Pagan, James[1]*) was born on November 7, 1921, in Mississippi Twp., Jersey Co., Illinois. He was the son of Leonard R. Vanausdoll (95) and Evelyn Rosina Waggoner. Robert Newell died in O'Fallon, O'Fallon Twp., St. Clair Co., Illinois, on February 17, 1998, at age 76. He was buried in Lake View Memorial Gardens Cemetery, Fairview Heights, Caseyville Twp., St. Clair Co., Illinois. [79, 80]

**258. Vernon Parker[8] East** (*Ruby Frances[7] Vanausdoll, William Cornelius[6], Caleb[5], Mary[4] Pegan, Andrew[3] Pegan II, Andrew[2] Pagan, James[1]*) was born on July 10, 1923, in Mississippi Twp., Jersey Co., Illinois. He was the son of Parker Lafayette East and Ruby Frances Vanausdoll (98). Vernon Parker died in Tallahassee, Leon Co., Florida, on January 9, 1978, at age 54. He was buried in Saint Mary's Cemetery, Fieldon, Richwoods Twp., Jersey Co., Illinois.[81]

Vernon Parker married **Rosalie M. Narup** on July 2, 1949, in Jersey Co., Illinois. They had three children. Rosalie M. Narup was born in Batchtown, Calhoun Co., Illinois, on September 14, 1925. Rosalie M. reached age 90 and died in Jerseyville, Jersey Twp., Jersey Co., Illinois, on June 17, 2016. She was buried in Saint Mary's Cemetery, Fieldon, Richwoods Twp., Jersey Co., Illinois.[81]

Buried under the name Rosalie M. Narup Hughes.

Vernon Parker East and Rosalie M. Narup had three children, including:

+ 438  m  III.  **Daughter[9] East.**

**259. William Eldon[8] East** (*Ruby Frances[7] Vanausdoll, William Cornelius[6], Caleb[5], Mary[4] Pegan, Andrew[3] Pegan II, Andrew[2] Pagan, James[1]*) was born in 1926 in Mississippi Twp., Jersey Co., Illinois. He is the son of Parker Lafayette East and Ruby Frances Vanausdoll (98).

He married **Dorothy A. Harting.** They had six children. Dorothy A. Harting was born on September 7, 1928.

William Eldon East and Dorothy A. Harting had six children, including:

+ 439  m  III.  **William Randall[9] East II** was born in Fieldon, Richwoods Twp., Jersey Co., Illinois? in August 1949. He was also known as **Randy.** William Randall died in Fieldon, Richwoods Twp., Jersey Co., Illinois? about April 27, 1951. He was buried in Saint Mary's Cemetery, Fieldon, Richwoods Twp., Jersey Co., Illinois.[81]

+ 440  m  VI.  **Son[9] East.**

**260. Lillie Lois[8] East** (*Ruby Frances[7] Vanausdoll, William Cornelius[6], Caleb[5], Mary[4] Pegan, Andrew[3] Pegan II, Andrew[2] Pagan, James[1]*) was born on February 21, 1927, in Mississippi Twp., Jersey Co., Illinois. She was the daughter of Parker Lafayette East and Ruby Frances Vanausdoll (98). Lillie Lois died in Mississippi Twp., Jersey Co., Illinois, on February 21, 1927. She was buried in Oak Grove Cemetery, Jerseyville, Jersey Twp., Jersey Co., Illinois.[16]

**261. Marjorie Jean[8] East** (*Ruby Frances[7] Vanausdoll, William Cornelius[6], Caleb[5], Mary[4] Pegan, Andrew[3]*

*Pegan II, Andrew² Pagan, James¹)* was born on December 20, 1929, in Mississippi Twp., Jersey Co., Illinois. She was the daughter of Parker Lafayette East and Ruby Frances Vanausdoll (98). Marjorie Jean lived in 1964 in Lakeside, San Diego Co., California. She died in Lakeside, San Diego Co., California, on February 17, 1996, at age 66. Marjorie Jean was buried in Alpine Cemetery, Alpine, San Diego Co., California.[82]

She married **William C. Love.** William C. Love was born in Olive Twp., Decatur Co., Kansas? on August 27, 1915. William C. reached age 61 and died in Lakeside, San Diego Co., California, on May 22, 1977. He was buried in Alpine Cemetery, Alpine, San Diego Co., California.[82]

262. **Norma L.⁸ Creswick** (*Ida Belle⁷ Vanausdoll, William Cornelius⁶, Caleb⁵, Mary⁴ Pegan, Andrew³ Pegan II, Andrew² Pagan, James¹*) was born on September 17, 1929, in Alton, Alton Twp., Madison Co., Illinois. She was the daughter of Lawrence Kenneth Creswick and Ida Belle Vanausdoll (100). Norma L. died in Altoona, Clay Twp., Polk Co., Iowa, on December 7, 2011, at age 82. She was buried in Laurel Cemetery, Cave Junction, Josephine Co., Oregon.[32]

Norma L. married **Amos Yuel Vahrenwald** on December 4, 1958. They had two children. Amos Yuel Vahrenwald was born in Grants Pass, Josephine Co., Oregon, on December 19, 1929. Amos Yuel reached age 80 and died in Cave Junction, Josephine Co., Oregon, on October 3, 2010. He was buried in Laurel Cemetery, Cave Junction, Josephine Co., Oregon.[32]

263. **Marcella June⁸ Clayton** (*Addie Rachel⁷ Vanausdoll, William Cornelius⁶, Caleb⁵, Mary⁴ Pegan, Andrew³ Pegan II, Andrew² Pagan, James¹*) was born on September 25, 1926, in Alton, Alton Twp., Madison Co., Illinois. She was the daughter of William A. Clayton and Addie Rachel Vanausdoll (101). Marcella June lived in 1985 in East Alton, Wood River Twp., Madison Co., Illinois. She died in a hospital in Alton, Alton Twp., Madison Co., Illinois, on July 2, 1985, at age 58. Marcella June was buried in Oakwood Cemetery, Upper Alton, Alton Twp., Madison Co., Illinois.[8]

Marcella June Clayton married **Archibald Michael Halbach II.** They had two children. Archibald Michael Halbach II was born in Pacific, Missouri, on February 20, 1925. Archibald Michael lived in 1953 in Alton, Alton Twp., Madison Co., Illinois. He reached age 27 and died in a hospital in Jefferson Barracks, St. Louis Co., Missouri, on January 20, 1953. Archibald Michael was buried in Oakwood Cemetery, Upper Alton, Alton Twp., Madison Co., Illinois.[8]

Marcella June Clayton Hallbach married **Orville Russell Werts** after 1953. They divorced. They had one son. Orville Russell Werts was born in Fosterburg, Foster Twp., Madison Co., Illinois, on April 23, 1926. He lived in 1986 in Alton, Alton Twp., Madison Co., Illinois. Orville Russell reached age 60 and died in a hospital in Florissant, St. Louis Co., Missouri, on May 11, 1986. He was buried in Fosterburg Cemetery, Fosterburg, Foster Twp., Madison Co., Illinois.[142]

Marcella June Clayton and Archibald Michael Halbach II had two children, including:

+ 441 m I.    **Terry Lee⁹ Halbach** was born in Wood River, Wood River Twp., Madison Co., Illinois, on January 28, 1950. He died in a hospital in Wichita, Sedgwick Co., Kansas, on February 4, 1995. Terry Lee was buried in Attica Cemetery, Attica, Ruella Twp., Harper Co., Kansas.[143]

264. **Chester Heath⁸ Van Ausdale** (*Otis Lafayette⁷ Vanausdoll, Charles Wesley⁶, Caleb⁵, Mary⁴ Pegan, Andrew³ Pegan II, Andrew² Pagan, James¹*) was born on May 10, 1907, in Grafton, Quarry Twp., Jersey Co., Illinois. He was the son of Otis Lafayette Vanausdoll (104) and Cassandra Ordealia Heath. Chester Heath died in Grafton, Quarry Twp., Jersey Co., Illinois, on September 13, 1963, at age 56. He was buried in Scenic Hill/ Odd Fellows Cemetery, Quarry Twp., Jersey Co., Illinois.[13, 14]

He married **Edna G. Rupke or Rupkey.** They had three children. Edna G. Rupke or Rupkey was born in Valle Twp., Jefferson Co., Missouri, on February 26, 1910. Edna G. Rupke or reached age 76 and died in Kansas City, Jackson Co., Missouri, in July 1986.

Children of Chester Heath Van Ausdale and Edna G. Rupke or Rupkey:

+ 442 f I. **Lorraine**[9] **Van Ausdale** was born in St. Louis, Missouri, in 1927. She died between 1940 and 1954?

+ 443 f II. **Edna**[9] **Van Ausdale** was born in St. Louis, Missouri, in 1929. She died after 1954.

+ 444 m III. **Chester**[9] **Van Ausdale II** was born in St. Louis, Missouri, on August 11, 1930. He died in a hospital in Salina, Saline Co., Kansas, on July 14, 1954. Chester was buried in Scenic Hill/Odd Fellows Cemetery, Quarry Twp., Jersey Co., Illinois.[14]

**265. Robert Clifton**[8] **Van Ausdale** (*Otis Lafayette*[7] *Vanausdoll, Charles Wesley*[6]*, Caleb*[5]*, Mary*[4] *Pegan, Andrew*[3] *Pegan II, Andrew*[2] *Pagan, James*[1]) was born on July 9, 1910, in Grafton, Quarry Twp., Jersey Co., Illinois. He was the son of Otis Lafayette Vanausdoll (104) and Cassandra Ordealia Heath. Robert Clifton lived in 1988 in Grafton, Quarry Twp., Jersey Co., Illinois. He died in a hospital in Florissant, St. Louis Co., Missouri, on May 29, 1988, at age 77. Robert Clifton was buried in Scenic Hill/Odd Fellows Cemetery, Quarry Twp., Jersey Co., Illinois.[13, 14]

Childless.

Robert Clifton married **Margaret Hopkins** on September 13, 1941. Margaret Hopkins was born in Yancy Mills, Liberty Twp., Phelps Co., Missouri, on June 24, 1917. Margaret reached age 78 and died in Jerseyville, Jersey Twp., Jersey Co., Illinois, on February 13, 1996. She was buried in Scenic Hill/Odd Fellows Cemetery, Quarry Twp., Jersey Co., Illinois.[14]

**266. Jack Warren Kerrigan**[8] **Van Ausdale** (*Otis Lafayette*[7] *Vanausdoll, Charles Wesley*[6]*, Caleb*[5]*,*

*Mary*[4] *Pegan, Andrew*[3] *Pegan II, Andrew*[2] *Pagan, James*[1]) was born on September 14, 1914, in Grafton, Quarry Twp., Jersey Co., Illinois. He was the son of Otis Lafayette Vanausdoll (104) and Cassandra Ordealia Heath. Jack Warren Kerrigan died in Carson, Los Angeles Co., California, on March 25, 1989, at age 74. He was buried in Scenic Hill/Odd Fellows Cemetery, Quarry Twp., Jersey Co., Illinois.[10, 11]

Jack Warren Kerrigan Van Ausdale married **Hazel Leona Tyler** on September 12, 1934, in Jersey Co., Illinois. They had two daughters. Hazel Leona Tyler was born in Rolla, Rolla Twp., Phelps Co., Missouri, on June 16, 1917. Hazel Leona lived in Carson, Los Angeles Co., California. She reached age 92 and died in a hospital in Long Beach, Los Angeles Co., California, on October 5, 2009. Hazel Leona was buried in Scenic Hill/Odd Fellows Cemetery, Quarry Twp., Jersey Co., Illinois.[14]

Jack Warren Kerrigan Van Ausdale and Hazel Leona Tyler had two daughters, including:

+ 445 f I. **Pamela Sue**[9] **Van Ausdale** was born in St. Louis, Missouri? on January 17, 1948. She died in Carson, Los Angeles Co., California, on January 22, 2005. Pamela Sue was buried in Scenic Hill/Odd Fellows Cemetery, Quarry Twp., Jersey Co., Illinois.[14]

**267. Ila Marie**[8] **Vanausdoll** (*Otis Lafayette*[7]*, Charles Wesley*[6]*, Caleb*[5]*, Mary*[4] *Pegan, Andrew*[3] *Pegan II, Andrew*[2] *Pagan, James*[1]) was born on August 14, 1918, in Grafton, Quarry Twp., Jersey Co., Illinois. She was the daughter of Otis Lafayette Vanausdoll (104) and Cassandra Ordealia Heath. Ila Marie died in Grafton, Quarry Twp., Jersey Co., Illinois, on November 24, 2002, at age 84. She was buried in Scenic Hill/Odd Fellows Cemetery, Quarry Twp., Jersey Co., Illinois.[14]

Ila Marie Vanausdoll married **Freeman Hallie Hayes** on June 11, 1937, in Jersey Co., Illinois. They divorced. They had four children. Freeman Hallie Hayes was born in Grafton, Quarry Twp., Jersey Co., Illinois, on March 21, 1910. He reached age 88 and died in Jerseyville, Jersey Twp., Jersey Co., Illinois, on March 5, 1999. Freeman Hallie was buried in Scenic Hill/Odd Fellows Cemetery, Quarry Twp., Jersey Co., Illinois.[14]

Ila Marie Vanausdoll Hayes married **Harold Lee Laubscher** on August 24, 1962. They had one son. Harold Lee Laubscher was born in Piasa Twp., Jersey Co., Illinois, on December 15, 1936.

Marie Vanausdoll and Freeman Hallie Hayes had four children, including:

+ 446  m  I.  **Olney Freeman⁹ Hayes** was born in Grafton, Quarry Twp., Jersey Co., Illinois, on April 1, 1938. He died in Grafton, Quarry Twp., Jersey Co., Illinois, on April 7, 1938. Olney Freeman was buried in Scenic Hill/Odd Fellows Cemetery, Quarry Twp., Jersey Co., Illinois.[14].

+ 447  f  II.  **Enid Louise⁹ Hayes** was born in St. Louis, Missouri, on May 28, 1939. She was also known as **Louise.** Enid Louise died in Grafton, Quarry Twp., Jersey Co., Illinois, on January 17, 2005. She was buried in Scenic Hill/Odd Fellows Cemetery, Quarry Twp., Jersey Co., Illinois.[14]

+ 448  m  III.  **Robert Wayne⁹ Hayes** was born in Grafton, Quarry Twp., Jersey Co., Illinois, on May 31, 1941. He died in Grafton, Quarry Twp., Jersey Co., Illinois, on August 28, 2009.

**268. Daniel Liberty⁸ Van Ausdale** (*Otis Lafayette⁷ Vanausdoll, Charles Wesley⁶, Caleb⁵, Mary⁴ Pegan, Andrew³ Pegan II, Andrew² Pagan, James¹*) was born on January 26, 1922, in St. Louis, Missouri. He was the son of Otis Lafayette Vanausdoll (104) and Cassandra Ordealia Heath. Daniel Liberty died in Alton, Alton Twp., Madison Co., Illinois, on February 10, 1975, at age 53. He was buried in Scenic Hill/Odd Fellows Cemetery, Quarry Twp., Jersey Co., Illinois.[13, 14]

He married **Wanda Lee Ozment.** They had five children. Wanda Lee Ozment was born in Memphis, Shelby Co., Tennessee, on December 19, 1928. Wanda Lee lived in 1983 in Memphis, Shelby Co., Tennessee. She reached age 62 and died in Humphreys Co., Tennessee, on November 30, 1991. Wanda Lee was buried in Forest Hill Cemetery East, Memphis, Shelby Co., Tennessee.[144]

Daniel Liberty Van Ausdale and Wanda Lee Ozment had five children, including:

+ 449  m  I.  **Richard Dennis⁹ Van Ausdale** was born on December 6, 1940 in Grafton, Quarry Twp., Jersey Co., Illinois.

+ 450  m  II.  **Marc⁹ Van Ausdale** was born in Grafton, Quarry Twp., Jersey Co., Illinois, on August 19, 1952. He died in Joliet, Joliet Twp., Will Co., Illinois, on September 28, 1983. Marc was buried in Memphis National Cemetery, Memphis, Shelby Co., Tennessee.[145]

+ 451  m  III.  **Daniel Liberty⁹ Van Ausdale II** was born in Grafton, Quarry Twp., Jersey Co., Illinois, on September 10, 1954. He died in Joliet, Joliet Twp., Will Co., Illinois, on January 6, 2013.

**269. Otis Raymond⁸ Vanausdoll II** (*Otis Lafayette⁷, Charles Wesley⁶, Caleb⁵, Mary⁴ Pegan, Andrew³ Pegan II, Andrew² Pagan, James¹*) was born on August 12, 1924 in St. Louis, Missouri. He was also known as **Raymond** and **Ray.** He was the son of Otis Lafayette Vanausdoll (104) and Cassandra Ordealia Heath. Otis Raymond II died on October 4, 2017, in Shipman, Shipman Twp., Macoupin Co., Illinois at age 93. He was cremated and his cremains buried in Scenic Hill/Odd Fellows Cemetery, Grafton, Quarry Twp., Jersey Co., Illinois.[14]

Otis Raymond married **Sophie Grace Depasquale** in 1945 in Dade Co., Florida. They divorced. They had three sons. Sophie Grace Depasquale was born in Bronx, New York Co., New York, on May 22, 1927. She reached age 77 and died in Shipman, Shipman Twp., Macoupin Co., Illinois, on July 3, 2004. Sophie Grace was buried in Los Angeles National Cemetery, Los Angeles, Los Angeles Co., California.[146]

She is buried under the name Sophie Grace Van Bomel.

Otis Raymond Vanausdoll II married **Helen Reece** before 2005. Helen Reece was born in Hillview, Patterson Twp., Greene Co., Illinois, on July 6, 1919. Helen reached age 95 and died in Shipman, Shipman Twp., Macoupin Co., Illinois, on March 28, 2015.[36]

Otis Raymond Vanausdoll II and Sophie Grace Depasquale had three sons, including:

+ 452  m   I.   **Raymond J.[9] Vanausdoll II** was born in Grafton, Quarry Twp., Jersey Co., Illinois, on November 5, 1945. He died in San Pedro, Los Angeles Co., California, on April 26, 2007.

**270. Geraldine Yvonne[8] Vanausdoll** (*Otis Lafayette[7], Charles Wesley[6], Caleb[5], Mary[4] Pegan, Andrew[3] Pegan II, Andrew[2] Pagan, James[1]*) was born on March 28, 1927, in St. Louis, Missouri. She was also known as **Gerry.** She was the daughter of Otis Lafayette Vanausdoll (104) and Cassandra Ordealia Heath. Geraldine Yvonne lived in 1979 in Grafton, Quarry Twp., Jersey Co., Illinois. She died in a hospital in Alton, Alton Twp., Madison Co., Illinois, on May 22, 1979, at age 52. Geraldine Yvonne was buried in Scenic Hill/ Odd Fellows Cemetery, Quarry Twp., Jersey Co., Illinois.[13, 14]

Geraldine Yvonne married **Robert Wayne Rowling** on January 31, 1946. They had three children. Robert Wayne Rowling was born in Otter Creek Twp., Jersey Co., Illinois, on December 31, 1922. Robert Wayne reached age 61 and died in Dow, Mississippi Twp., Jersey Co., Illinois, on July 4, 1984. He was buried in Scenic Hill/Odd Fellows Cemetery, Quarry Twp., Jersey Co., Illinois.[13, 14]

Geraldine Yvonne Vanausdoll and Robert Wayne Rowling had three children, including:

+ 453  m   III.   **Jason Hal[9] Rowling** was born on April 1, 1975 in Alton, Alton Twp., Madison Co., Illinois. He died before 1979.

**271. Cassie Maryanne[8] Vanausdoll** (*Otis Lafayette[7], Charles Wesley[6], Caleb[5], Mary[4] Pegan, Andrew[3] Pegan II, Andrew[2] Pagan, James[1]*) was born on July 21, 1930, in St. Louis, Missouri. She was the daughter of Otis Lafayette Vanausdoll (104) and Cassandra Ordealia Heath. Cassie Maryanne died in Grafton, Quarry Twp., Jersey Co., Illinois, on May 24, 1956, at age 25. She was buried in Hartford Cemetery, Grafton, Quarry Twp., Jersey Co., Illinois.[84]

She married **Herbert Clark Watson.** They had two children. Herbert Clark Watson was born in Grafton, Quarry Twp., Jersey Co., Illinois, on November 1, 1929. He is also known as **Clark.**

**272. Tim Ryan[8] Vanausdoll** (*Otis Lafayette[7], Charles Wesley[6], Caleb[5], Mary[4] Pegan, Andrew[3] Pegan II, Andrew[2] Pagan, James[1]*) was born on November 29, 1932, in St. Louis, Missouri. He was the son of Otis Lafayette Vanausdoll (104) and Cassandra Ordealia Heath. Tim He died in Cordell, Washita Co., Oklahoma, on August 6, 2013, at age 80. Alternate date of birth: November 15, 1931

Tim Ryan married **Ruby C. Harmon** on May 22, 1954, in Jersey Co., Illinois. They divorced. They had one son. Ruby C. Harmon was born in Grafton, Quarry Twp., Jersey Co., Illinois, about 1937.

Son of Tim Ryan Vanausdoll and Ruby C. Harmon:

+ 454  m   I.   **Tim Ryan[9] Vanausdoll II** was born in Grafton, Quarry Twp., Jersey Co., Illinois, on November 21, 1954. He died in Hartford, Madison Co., Illinois, on December 20, 1993.

**273. Charles A.**[8] **Vanausdoll** (*Everett Charles*[7], *Charles Wesley*[6], *Caleb*[5], *Mary*[4] *Pegan, Andrew*[3] *Pegan II, Andrew*[2] *Pagan, James*[1]) was born on April 20, 1914, in Quarry Twp., Jersey Co., Illinois. He was the son of Everett Charles Vanausdoll (105) and Carolene Mary Quitt. Charles A. died in Jerseyville, Jersey Twp., Jersey Co., Illinois, on March 12, 1982, at age 67. He was buried in Oak Grove Cemetery, Jerseyville, Jersey Twp., Jersey Co., Illinois.[16]

Charles A. married **Lura Mourning** on December 14, 1940, in Jersey Co., Illinois. They had two daughters. Lura Mourning was born in Jersey Twp., Jersey Co., Illinois, on July 23, 1917. Lura reached age 78 and died in Jerseyville, Jersey Twp., Jersey Co., Illinois, on August 18, 1995. She was buried in Oak Grove Cemetery, Jerseyville, Jersey Twp., Jersey Co., Illinois.[16]

Daughters of Charles A. Vanausdoll and Lura Mourning:

+ 455A f I. **Mary Ellen**[9] **Vanausdoll** was born in Jerseyville, Jersey Twp., Jersey Co., Illinois, on October 14, 1946. She died in Jerseyville, Jersey Twp., Jersey Co., Illinois on October 14, 1946. Mary Ellen was buried in Oak Grove Cemetery, Jerseyville, Jersey Twp., Jersey Co., Illinois.[16]

+ 455B f II. **Janet**[9] **Vanausdoll** was born in Jerseyville, Jersey Twp., Jersey Co., Illinois, on September 5, 1947. She died in Jerseyville, Jersey Twp., Jersey Co., Illinois, on June 2, 2000. Janet was buried in Oak Grove Cemetery, Jerseyville, Jersey Twp., Jersey Co., Illinois.[16]

**274. Truman Everett**[8] **Vanausdoll** (*Everett Charles*[7], *Charles Wesley*[6], *Caleb*[5], *Mary*[4] *Pegan, Andrew*[3] *Pegan II, Andrew*[2] *Pagan, James*[1]) was born on January 5, 1920, in Quarry Twp., Jersey Co., Illinois. He was the son of Everett Charles Vanausdoll (105) and Carolene Mary Quitt. Truman Everett lived in 1996 in LaVerne, Los Angeles Co., California. He died in a hospi-

tal in Covina, Los Angeles Co., California, on November 28, 1996, at age 76.

He married **Audrey Patricia Moss.** They had two children. Audrey Patricia Moss was born in Newport, Monmouthshire, New South Wales, Australia, on October 21, 1926. Audrey Patricia reached age 74 age died in San Dimas, Los Angeles Co., California, on August 4, 2001.

**275. Willie Warren**[8] **Vanausdoll** (*Everett Charles*[7], *Charles Wesley*[6], *Caleb*[5], *Mary*[4] *Pegan, Andrew*[3] *Pegan II, Andrew*[2] *Pagan, James*[1]) was born on February 13, 1923, in Quarry Twp., Jersey Co., Illinois. He was the son of Everett Charles Vanausdoll (105) and Carolene Mary Quitt. He was also known as **Bill.** Willie Warren died in Eldred, Bluffdale Twp., Greene Co., Illinois, on October 7, 2004, at age 81. He was buried in Oak Grove Cemetery, Jerseyville, Jersey Twp., Jersey Co., Illinois.[16]

Willie Warren married **Lila M. Fraley** on April 18, 1947. They had two children. Lila Fraley was born in Jerseyville, Jersey Twp., Jersey Co., Illinois, on October 7, 1926. She was also known as **Sis.** Lila reached age 93 and died in Eldred, Bluffdale Twp., Greene Co., Illinois, on January 3, 2020. She was buried in Oak Grove Cemetery, Jerseyville, Jersey Twp., Jersey Co., Illinois.[16]

Willie Warren Vanausdoll and Lila M. Fraley had two children, including:

+ 455C m I. **Son**[9] **Vanausdoll.**

**276. Pauline Irene**[8] **Vanausdoll** (*Everett Charles*[7], *Charles Wesley*[6], *Caleb*[5], *Mary*[4] *Pegan, Andrew*[3] *Pegan II, Andrew*[2] *Pagan, James*[1]) was born on September 19, 1925, in Quarry Twp., Jersey Co., Illinois. She was the daughter of Everett Charles Vanausdoll (105) and Carolene Mary Quitt. Pauline Irene lived in Caulfield, Howell Co., Missouri. She died in Wabasha, Wabasha Co., Minnesota, on December 25, 1993, at age 68. Pauline Irene was buried in Oak Grove Cemetery, Jerseyville, Jersey Twp., Jersey Co., Illinois.[16]

Childless.

Pauline Irene married **James Edwards Abbott** before 1990. James Edwards Abbott was born in

Kane Twp., Greene Co., Illinois, on March 17, 1920. James Edwards reached age 70 and died in Caulfield, Howell Co., Missouri, on November 2, 1990. He was buried in Oak Grove Cemetery, Jerseyville, Jersey Twp., Jersey Co., Illinois.[16]

**277. Donald Lee**[8] **Vanausdoll** (*Everett Charles*[7], *Charles Wesley*[6], *Caleb*[5], *Mary*[4] *Pegan, Andrew*[3] *Pegan II, Andrew*[2] *Pagan, James*[1]) was born on August 9, 1931, in Quarry Twp., Jersey Co., Illinois. He was the son of Everett Charles Vanausdoll (105) and Carolene Mary Quitt. Donald Lee died in Jerseyville, Jersey Twp., Jersey Co., Illinois, on October 10, 2006, at age 75. He was buried in St. Francis Xavier Cemetery, Jerseyville, Jersey Twp., Jersey Co., Illinois.[73]

Donald Lee married **Josephine Joan Arter** on September 21, 1955, in Jersey Co., Illinois. They had four sons. Josephine Joan Arter was born in Jerseyville, Jersey Twp., Jersey Co., Illinois, on October 31, 1931. She is also known as **Joan.**

Donald Lee Vanausdoll and Josephine Joan Arter have four sons, including:

+ 456 m I. **Son One**[9] **Vanausdoll.**

+ 457 m II. **Son Two**[9] **Vanausdoll.**

**278. Darrel**[8] **Vanausdoll** (*Everett Charles*[7], *Charles Wesley*[6], *Caleb*[5], *Mary*[4] *Pegan, Andrew*[3] *Pegan II, Andrew*[2] *Pagan, James*[1]) was born on December 9, 1935, in Jersey Twp., Jersey Co., Illinois. He is the son of Everett Charles Vanausdoll (105) and Carolene Mary Quitt.

Darrel Dean married **Virginia M. Boner.** They divorced. They had two daughters. Virginia M. was born on July 14, 1937.

Darrel Dean married **Eva Nadine Bost.** Eva Nadine Bost was born in Bucoda, Salem Twp., Dunklin Co., Missouri, on July 19, 1928. She lived in Cardwell, Buffalo Twp., Dunklin Co., Missouri. She reached age 90 and died in a facility in Kennett, Independence Twp., Dunklin Co., Missouri, on May 26, 2019. She was buried in Dunklin Memorial Gardens Cemetery, Kennett, Independence Twp., Dunklin Co., Missouri.[H]

Darrel Vanausdoll and Virginia M. Boner had two daughters, including:

+ 458 f I. **Daughter**[9] **Vanausdoll.**

**279. Marlene Emma**[8] **Vanausdoll** (*Everett Charles*[7], *Charles Wesley*[6], *Caleb*[5], *Mary*[4] *Pegan, Andrew*[3] *Pegan II, Andrew*[2] *Pagan, James*[1]) was born in 1937 in Jersey Twp., Jersey Co., Illinois. She is the daughter of Everett Charles Vanausdoll (105) and Carolene Mary Quitt.

She married **William C. Schmidt** on May 17, 1958 in Jersey Co., Illinois. William Schmidt was born Wabasha, Wabasha Co., Minnesota, on September 15, 1930 in. He died on March 12, 1917, in Wabasha, Wabasha Co., Minnesota. William C. was buried in Saint Felix Cemetery, Wabasha, Wabasha Co., Minnesota.[146147]

Marlene Emma Vanausdoll and William C. Schmidt had three children, including:

+ 459 m I. **Gene Bernard**[9] **Schmidt** was born in Wabasha, Wabasha Co., Minnesota, on May 27, 1962. He died in Wabasha, Wabasha Co., Minnesota, on February 18, 1979. Gene Bernard was buried in Saint Felix Cemetery, Wabasha, Wabasha Co., Minnesota.[147]

**280. Mortimer Revere**[8] **Patton** (*Charles Frederick*[7], *Cora Alice*[6] *Vanausdoll, Caleb*[5], *Mary*[4] *Pegan, Andrew*[3] *Pegan II, Andrew*[2] *Pagan, James*[1]) was born on September 4, 1919, in Butler Co., Kansas. He was the son of Charles Frederick Patton (109) and Amelia Dorothy Young. Mortimer Revere died in Kennesaw, Cobb Co., Georgia, on November 10, 2005, at age 86. He was buried in Georgia National Cemetery, Canton, Cherokee Co., Georgia.[86]

**281. Gearald E.**[8] **Patton** (*Charles Frederick*[7], *Cora Alice*[6] *Vanausdoll, Caleb*[5], *Mary*[4] *Pegan, Andrew*[3] *Pegan II, Andrew*[2] *Pagan, James*[1]) was born in 1922 in Butler Co., Kansas. He was the son of Charles Frederick Patton (109) and Amelia Dorothy Young. Gearald E. died in Wasco, Sherman Co.,

Oregon, on September 22, 1949, at age 27. He was buried in Mountain View Cemetery, Oregon City, Clackamas Co., Oregon.[87]

**282. Delores Evelyn⁸ Patton** (*Charles Frederick⁷, Cora Alice⁶ Vanausdoll, Caleb⁵, Mary⁴ Pegan, Andrew³ Pegan II, Andrew² Pagan, James¹*) was born on March 22, 1924, in Lowell Twp., Cherokee Co., Kansas. She was the daughter of Charles Frederick Patton (109) and Amelia Dorothy Young. Delores Evelyn lived in Clackamas Co., Oregon. She died in Milwaukie, Clackamas Co., Oregon, on January 22, 2008, at age 83.

Delores Evelyn married **Lee Puckett?** in 1948.

**283. Albert J.⁸ Spencer** (*Zantha⁷ Patton, Cora Alice⁶ Vanausdoll, Caleb⁵, Mary⁴ Pegan, Andrew³ Pegan II, Andrew² Pagan, James¹*) was born in December 1914 in Barton Co., Missouri. He was the son of Charles E. Spencer and Zantha Patton (110). Albert J. died in Aurora, Aurora Twp., Kane Co., Illinois, about September 18, 1995 at age 80. He was buried in Mount Olivet Cemetery, Aurora, Aurora Twp., Kane Co., Illinois.[88]

He married **Marian Airoldi.** They had three children. Marian Airoldi was born in Aurora, Aurora Twp., Kane Co., Illinois, in 1917. Marian reached age 72 and died in Aurora, Aurora Twp., Kane Co., Illinois, about March 7, 1989. She was buried in Mount Olivet Cemetery, Aurora, Aurora Twp., Kane Co., Illinois.[76]

**284. Guila Jean⁸ Spencer** (*Zantha⁷ Patton, Cora Alice⁶ Vanausdoll, Caleb⁵, Mary⁴ Pegan, Andrew³ Pegan II, Andrew² Pagan, James¹*) was born in 1917 in Columbus, Crawford Twp., Cherokee Co., Kansas. She was the daughter of Charles E. Spencer and Zantha Patton (110). Guila Jean died in Aurora, Aurora Twp., Kane Co., Illinois, on March 19, 1932, at age 15.

**285. Paul Allen⁸ Hawkins II** (*Mary M.⁷ Patton, Cora Alice⁶ Vanausdoll, Caleb⁵, Mary⁴ Pegan, Andrew³ Pegan II, Andrew² Pagan, James¹*) was born on March 20, 1922, in Parsons, Walton Twp., Labette Co., Kansas. He was the son of Paul E. Hawkins and Mary M. Patton (113). Paul Allen lived in 1993 in Anaconda, Deer Lodge Co., Montana. He died in Silver Bow Co., Montana,

on March 21, 1993, at age 71. He was buried in New Hill Cemetery, Anaconda, Deer Lodge Co., Montana.[89]

Paul Allen Hawkins II married **Stella Ann Durkovich (Albright)** on April 2, 1949 in Silver Bow Co., Montana. They had three children. Stella Ann Durkovich (Albright) was born in St. Maries, Benewah Co., Idaho on April 6, 1927. She was also known as **Ann.** She either was adopted by or assumed the surname of her stepfather, Jesse Byron Albright. "Ann Albright" Hawkins reached age 87 and died in Anaconda, Deer Lodge Co., Montana on September 20, 2014. She is buried in New Hill Cemetery, Deer Lodge Co., Montana.[89]

She always used her middle name, Ann, as her preferred given name. Although her obituary and gravestone say her date of birth was April 26, 1927, her mother's U.S. naturalization application says (Stella) Ann was born on April 6, 1927.

**286. Allen Marvin⁸ Patton** (*Arthur M.⁷, Cora Alice⁶ Vanausdoll, Caleb⁵, Mary⁴ Pegan, Andrew³ Pegan II, Andrew² Pagan, James¹*) was born in 1930 in Stevensville, Ravalli Co., Montana. He is the son of Arthur M. Patton (115) and Doris Esther Puyear.

Allen Marvin married **Mary Jo Harrington.** They had one son.

Son of Allen Marvin Patton and Mary Jo Harrington:

+ 460 m I. **Eric Allen⁹ Patton** was born in Stevensville, Ravalli Co., Montana, on August 5, 1963. He died in Stevensville, Ravalli Co., Montana, on September 5, 1963. Eric Allen was buried in Victor Cemetery, Victor, Ravalli Co., Montana.[35]

**287. Wilbur Harold⁸ Seago** (*Hallye Maude⁷ Vanausdoll, Allen M.⁶, Caleb⁵, Mary⁴ Pegan, Andrew³ Pegan II, Andrew² Pagan, James¹*) was born on November 21, 1919, in Jerseyville, Jersey Twp., Jersey Co., Illinois. He was the son of Edward Ross Seago and Hallye Maude Vanausdoll (116). Wilbur Harold died in Jerseyville, Jersey Twp., Jersey Co., Illinois, on December 4, 1919.

**288. Carl Wayne[8] Seago** (*Hallye Maude[7] Vanausdoll, Allen M.[6], Caleb[5], Mary[4] Pegan, Andrew[3] Pegan II, Andrew[2] Pagan, James[1]*) was born on July 28, 1921, in Otter Creek Twp., Jersey Co., Illinois. He was the son of Edward Ross Seago and Hallye Maude Vanausdoll (116). Carl Wayne died in Phoenix, Maricopa Co., Arizona, on August 14, 2004, at age 83. He was buried in National Memorial Cemetery of Arizona, Phoenix, Maricopa Co., Arizona.[90, 91]

He married **Zella Louise Whitlow.** Zella Louise Whitlow was born in English Twp., Jersey Co., Illinois, in 1920. Zella Louise reached age 58 and died in Phoenix, Maricopa Co., Arizona, in 1978.

Carl Wayne Seago married **Marlene Evelyn Saunders** on June 22, 1979, in Clark Co., Nevada. Marlene Evelyn Saunders was born on May 7, 1936.

**289. Dorothy Marie[8] Seago** (*Hallye Maude[7] Vanausdoll, Allen M.[6], Caleb[5], Mary[4] Pegan, Andrew[3] Pegan II, Andrew[2] Pagan, James[1]*) was born on October 2, 1926, in Alton, Alton Twp., Madison Co., Illinois. She was the daughter of Edward Ross Seago and Hallye Maude Vanausdoll (116). Dorothy Marie lived in 1999 in Hamburg, Hamburg Twp., Calhoun Co., Illlinois. She died in a hospital in Chesterfield, Saint Louis Co., Missouri, on February 13, 1999, at age 72. Dorothy Marie was buried in Hamburg Cemetery, Hamburg, Hamburg Twp., Calhoun Co., Illinois.[92]

She married **James Franklin Gilbert.** They had eight children. James Franklin Gilbert was born in Eldred, Bluffdale Twp., Greene Co., Illinois, on February 2, 1917. James Franklin reached age 83 and died in Hamburg, Hamburg Twp., Calhoun Co., Illlinois, on August 1, 2000. He was buried in Hamburg Cemetery, Hamburg, Hamburg Twp., Calhoun Co., Illinois.[92]

Dorothy Marie Seago and James Franklin Gilbert had eight children, including:

+ 461 m I. **Arthur Edward[9] Gilbert** was born on March 17, 1946. He died on March 17, 1946.

+ 462 m II. **Son[9] Gilbert.**

+ 463 m III. **Daughter One[9] Gilbert.**

+ 464 m I. **Daughter Two[9] Gilbert.**

+ 465 m I. **Daughter Three[9] Gilbert.**

**290. Mildred I.[8] Seago** (*Hallye Maude[7] Vanausdoll, Allen M.[6], Caleb[5], Mary[4] Pegan, Andrew[3] Pegan II, Andrew[2] Pagan, James[1]*) was born on December 29, 1930, in Mississippi Twp., Jersey Co., Illinois. She is the daughter of Edward Ross Seago and Hallye Maude Vanausdoll (116).

She married **Thomas Philip Brewer.** They had two daughters. Thomas Philip Brewer was born in Vermontville, Vermontville Twp., Eaton Co., Michigan, on May 28, 1927. Thomas Philip reached age 88 and died in Phoenix, Maricopa Co., Arizona, on September 25, 2015.

**291. Richard Anthony[8] Vanausdoll** (*Allen Laverne[7], Allen M.[6], Caleb[5], Mary[4] Pegan, Andrew[3] Pegan II, Andrew[2] Pagan, James[1]*) was born on March 24, 1932, in Otterville, Otter Creek Twp., Jersey Co., Illinois. He was the son of Allen Laverne Vanausdoll (117) and Velma Ureta Hinman. Richard Anthony died in Denver, Denver Co., Colorado, on March 6, 1963, at age 30. He was buried in Shipman Cemetery, Shipman, Shipman Twp., Macoupin Co., Illinois.[36]

Richard Anthony Vanausdoll was murdered by his wife's paramour.

Richard Anthony married **Ms. Easter** on February 25, 1959. They had two children.

**292. Vivian[8] Vanausdoll** (*Allen Laverne[7], Allen M.[6], Caleb[5], Mary[4] Pegan, Andrew[3] Pegan II, Andrew[2] Pagan, James[1]*) was born in 1936 in Otterville, Otter Creek Twp., Jersey Co., Illinois. She is the daughter of Allen Laverne Vanausdoll (117) and Velma Ureta Hinman.

Vivian married **Unknown Mountain.** They had one son.

Vivian Vanausdoll Mountain married **Damon L. Helmantoler** on November 5, 1955. They divorced. They had three children. Damon L. Helmantoler was born in Wood River Twp.,

Madison Co., Illinois, on March 20, 1936. He died in Concord, Contra Costa Co., California on April 7, 2017.

**293. Marvin Allen⁸ Vanausdoll** (*Allen Laverne⁷, Allen M.⁶, Caleb⁵, Mary⁴ Pegan, Andrew³ Pegan II, Andrew² Pagan, James¹*) was born on September 7, 1938, in Otterville, Otter Creek Twp., Jersey Co., Illinois. He is the son of Allen Laverne Vanausdoll (117) and Velma Ureta Hinman.

He married **Loretta Unknown.**

**294. Robert E.⁸ Ferguson** (*Edna Marie⁷ Vanausdoll, James Cornelius⁶, Caleb⁵, Mary⁴ Pegan, Andrew³ Pegan II, Andrew² Pagan, James¹*) was born on November 25, 1926, in St. Louis, Missouri. He is the son of Clyde McNair Ferguson and Edna Marie Vanausdoll (119).

He married **Unknown Unknown.** They had one son.

**295. Arlene Estelyn⁸ Ferguson** (*Edna Marie⁷ Vanausdoll, James Cornelius⁶, Caleb⁵, Mary⁴ Pegan, Andrew³ Pegan II, Andrew² Pagan, James¹*) was born on September 20, 1928, in St. Louis, Missouri. She was the daughter of Clyde McNair Ferguson and Edna Marie Vanausdoll (119). Arlene Estelyn died in Ballwin, St. Louis Co., Missouri, on May 21, 2001, at age 72.

She married **William Lloyd.** They divorced. They had three children. William Lloyd was born in St. Louis, Missouri, on December 8, 1927. He reached age 83 and died in Horseshoe Bay, Llano Co., Texas, on June 1, 2011.

**296. Kenneth Hunter⁸ Ferguson** (*Florence G.⁷ Vanausdoll, James Cornelius⁶, Caleb⁵, Mary⁴ Pegan, Andrew³ Pegan II, Andrew² Pagan, James¹*) was born on July 5, 1930 in Central Twp., St. Louis Co., Missouri. He is the son of Clarence L. Ferguson and Florence G. Vanausdoll (120).

Kenneth married **Joye Jeane Casimiro** on December 15, 1950 in St. Louis, Missouri. She is also known as Jean. Joye Jeane Casimiro was born on December 3, 1930 in St. Louis, Missouri.

**297. Louise or Lois⁸ Ferguson** (*Florence G.⁷ Vanausdoll, James Cornelius⁶, Caleb⁵, Mary⁴ Pegan, Andrew³ Pegan II, Andrew² Pagan, James¹*) was born in 1934 in Normandy Twp., St. Louis Co., Missouri. She was the daughter of Clarence L. Ferguson and Florence G. Vanausdoll (120). Louise died before 1990.

**298. Donald⁸ Hunt** (*Hazel M.⁷ Vanausdoll, James Cornelius⁶, Caleb⁵, Mary⁴ Pegan, Andrew³ Pegan II, Andrew² Pagan, James¹*) was born in 1930 in Alton, Alton Twp., Madison Co., Illinois. He is the son of Harry J. Hunt and Hazel M. Vanausdoll (123).

**299. Shirley⁸ Hunt** (*Hazel M.⁷ Vanausdoll, James Cornelius⁶, Caleb⁵, Mary⁴ Pegan, Andrew³ Pegan II, Andrew² Pagan, James¹*) was born in 1932 in Alton, Alton Twp., Madison Co., Illinois. She is the daughter of Harry J. Hunt and Hazel M. Vanausdoll (123).

She married **Unknown Davis.**

**300. Robert Eugene⁸ Adney** (*Alice R.⁷ Vanausdoll, James Cornelius⁶, Caleb⁵, Mary⁴ Pegan, Andrew³ Pegan II, Andrew² Pagan, James¹*) was born on January 20, 1939, in Alton, Alton Twp., Madison Co., Illinois. He was the son of Charles Adney and Alice R. Vanausdoll (126). Robert Eugene lived in 1979 in Eureka, St. Louis Co., Missouri. He died in Pacific, Boles Twp., Franklin Co., Missouri, on November 1, 2010, at age 71.

Robert Eugene married **Ms. Skelton** in January 1959 in Union Co., Missouri.

**301. Roberta J.⁸ Greer** (*Alice R.⁷ Vanausdoll, James Cornelius⁶, Caleb⁵, Mary⁴ Pegan, Andrew³ Pegan II, Andrew² Pagan, James¹*) was born in 1943 in Wood River Twp., Madison Co., Illinois. She was the daughter of James Inman Greer? and Alice R. Vanausdoll (126). Roberta J. died in Bethalto, Fort Russell Twp., Madison Co., Illinois, on January 8, 1979, at age 36. She was buried in Oakwood Cemetery, Upper Alton, Alton Twp., Madison Co., Illinois.[8]

Never married.

**302. Nordica Lind⁸ Dilling** (*Lola⁷ Dodson, Rachel Roseanna⁶ Vanausdoll, Allen McCreary⁵, Mary⁴ Pegan, Andrew³ Pegan II, Andrew² Pagan, James¹*) was born on January 26, 1914, in Jerseyville, Jersey Twp., Jersey Co., Illinois. She was the daughter of Charles Dilling and Lola Dodson (132). Nordica

Lind lived in 2003 in Godfrey, Godfrey Twp., Madison Co., Illinois. She died in a facility in Alton, Alton Twp., Madison Co., Illinois, on June 19, 2003, at age 89.

She married **Wilber Austin Peters.** They had one daughter. Wilber Austin Peters was born in Frankfort, Franklin Co., Kentucky, on September 14, 1909. Wilber Austin reached age 95 and died in Godfrey, Godfrey Twp., Madison Co., Illinois, on April 2, 2005.

303. **Charles⁸ Dilling II** (*Lola⁷ Dodson, Rachel Roseanna⁶ Vanausdoll, Allen McCreary⁵, Mary⁴ Pegan, Andrew³ Pegan II, Andrew² Pagan, James¹*) was born on July 25, 1915, in Alton, Alton Twp., Madison Co., Illinois. He was the son of Charles Dilling and Lola Dodson (132). Charles died in Godfrey, Godfrey Twp., Madison Co., Illinois, on September 15, 1988, at age 73.

Charles married **Ruth Krepel** on September 10, 1937, in Crawford Co., Missouri. They had six children. Ruth Krepel was born in Lincoln, Logan Co., Illinois, on September 25, 1920. Ruth reached age 92 and died in Key Largo, Monroe Co., Florida? on December 15, 2012.

304. **Robert⁸ Dilling** (*Lola⁷ Dodson, Rachel Roseanna⁶ Vanausdoll, Allen McCreary⁵, Mary⁴ Pegan, Andrew³ Pegan II, Andrew² Pagan, James¹*) was born on December 17, 1917, in Alton, Alton Twp., Madison Co., Illinois. He was the son of Charles Dilling and Lola Dodson (132). Robert died in Godfrey, Godfrey Twp., Madison Co., Illinois, on September 12, 1962, at age 44. He was buried in Valhalla Memorial Park and Mausoleum, Godfrey, Godfrey Twp., Madison Co., Illinois.[17]

May have never married.

305. **Nordell⁸ Dilling** (*Lola⁷ Dodson, Rachel Roseanna⁶ Vanausdoll, Allen McCreary⁵, Mary⁴ Pegan, Andrew³ Pegan II, Andrew² Pagan, James¹*) was born on October 10, 1921, in Alton, Alton Twp., Madison Co., Illinois. She was the daughter of Charles Dilling and Lola Dodson (132). Nordell died in Kankakee, Kankakee Twp., Kankakee Co., Illinois, on October 11, 1993, at age 72. She was buried in Saint Paul's Episcopal Columbarium, Kankakee, Kankakee Twp., Kankakee Co., Illinois.[95]

She married **Wayne Kesinger.** They had four children. Wayne Kesinger was born in Rockbridge Twp., Greene Co., Illinois, on March 6, 1920. Wayne reached age 74 and died in Kankakee, Kankakee Twp., Kankakee Co., Illinois, on September 18, 1994. He was buried in Saint Paul's Episcopal Columbarium, Kankakee, Kankakee Twp., Kankakee Co., Illinois.[95]

Nordell Dilling and Wayne Kesinger had four children, including:

+ 466 m I. **Gregg⁹ Kesinger** was born in Madison or Kankakee Co., Illinois, on August 8, 1949. He died in Alexandria, Fairfax Co., Virginia, on April 27, 2004.

306. **Charlotte⁸ Dilling** (*Lola⁷ Dodson, Rachel Roseanna⁶ Vanausdoll, Allen McCreary⁵, Mary⁴ Pegan, Andrew³ Pegan II, Andrew² Pagan, James¹*) was born on September 22, 1924, in Alton, Alton Twp., Madison Co., Illinois. She was also known as **Shotie.** She was the daughter of Charles Dilling and Lola Dodson (132). Charlotte died in Alton, Alton Twp., Madison Co., Illinois, on May 16, 2008, at age 83. She was buried in Valhalla Memorial Park and Mausoleum, Godfrey, Godfrey Twp., Madison Co., Illinois.[17]

Charlotte married **Louis E. Landre** on March 17, 1952, in Madison Co., Illinois. They had two children. Louis E. Landre was born in Alton, Alton Twp., Madison Co., Illinois, on July 16, 1925. Louis E. reached age and died in Alton, Alton Twp., Madison Co., Illinois, on May 2, 2008. He was buried in Valhalla Memorial Park and Mausoleum, Godfrey, Godfrey Twp., Madison Co., Illinois.[17]

307. **Mary Agnes⁸ Moses** (*Wyona Freelove⁷ Edsall, Millie Wyona⁶ Vanausdoll, Allen McCreary⁵, Mary⁴ Pegan, Andrew³ Pegan II, Andrew² Pagan, James¹*) was born on August 29, 1922, in Jerseyville, Jersey Twp., Jersey Co., Illinois. She was the daughter of Sylvester Leroy Moses and Wyona Freelove Edsall (133). Mary Agnes died in Jerseyville, Jersey Twp., Jersey Co., Illinois, on August 29, 2008, at age 86.

She was buried in Oak Grove Cemetery, Jerseyville, Jersey Twp., Jersey Co., Illinois.[16]

Never married.

**308. Darrell Laverne[8] Moses** (*Wyona Freelove[7] Edsall, Millie Wyona[6] Vanausdoll, Allen McCreary[5], Mary[4] Pegan, Andrew[3] Pegan II, Andrew[2] Pagan, James[1]*) was born on February 19, 1925, in Jerseyville, Jersey Twp., Jersey Co., Illinois. He was the son of Sylvester Leroy Moses and Wyona Freelove Edsall (133). Darrell Laverne died in Vermillion, Clay Co., South Dakota, on November 9, 2010, at age 85. He was buried in Bluff View Cemetery, Vermillion, Clay Co., South Dakota.[96]

He married **Dorothy Unknown** after 1940. They have three children.

**309. Charles Wesley[8] Moses** (*Wyona Freelove[7] Edsall, Millie Wyona[6] Vanausdoll, Allen McCreary[5], Mary[4] Pegan, Andrew[3] Pegan II, Andrew[2] Pagan, James[1]*) was born on January 29, 1928, in Jerseyville, Jersey Twp., Jersey Co., Illinois. He was the son of Sylvester Leroy Moses and Wyona Freelove Edsall (133). Charles Wesley died in Jerseyville, Jersey Twp., Jersey Co., Illinois, on January 18, 1978, at age 49. He was buried in Oak Grove Cemetery, Jerseyville, Jersey Twp., Jersey Co., Illinois.[16]

Charles Wesley married **Barbara Ann Adams** on June 2, 1956. They have one daughter. Barbara Ann Adams was born on January 17, 1935.

After Charles' death, she married Mr. McGowan.

**310. Loris Anita[8] Edsall** (*Allen Richard Laverne[7], Millie Wyona[6] Vanausdoll, Allen McCreary[5], Mary[4] Pegan, Andrew[3] Pegan II, Andrew[2] Pagan, James[1]*) was born on August 28, 1921, in Detroit, Wayne Co., Michigan. She was the daughter of Allen Richard Laverne Edsall (134) and Ethel Mae Viola Hart. Loris Anita died in Detroit, Wayne Co., Michigan, on November 12, 2009, at age 88.

Loris Anita married **James Merlin Knight** on April 13, 1940, in Macomb Co., Michigan. They divorced before 1977. James Merlin Knight was born in Springhill, Cumberland, Nova Scotia, Canada, on July 4, 1920. He reached age 73 and died in Los Alamos, Santa Barbara Co., California, on July 12, 1993.

Loris Anita Edsall Knight married **Unknown Kerekes** before 1977.

**311. Richard Allen[8] Edsall** (*Allen Richard Laverne[7], Millie Wyona[6] Vanausdoll, Allen McCreary[5], Mary[4] Pegan, Andrew[3] Pegan II, Andrew[2] Pagan, James[1]*) was born on March 23, 1923, in Detroit, Wayne Co., Michigan. He was the son of Allen Richard Laverne Edsall (134) and Ethel Mae Viola Hart. Richard Allen died in Klawak, Prince of Wales-Hyder, Alaska, on December 24, 2011, at age 88.

He married **Esther Unknown** after 1940. They had one son.

**312. Maxine[8] Edsall** (*Allen Richard Laverne[7], Millie Wyona[6] Vanausdoll, Allen McCreary[5], Mary[4] Pegan, Andrew[3] Pegan II, Andrew[2] Pagan, James[1]*) was born on January 17, 1925, in Detroit, Wayne Co., Michigan. She was the daughter of Allen Richard Laverne Edsall (134) and Ethel Mae Viola Hart. Maxine died in Columbus, Franklin Co., Ohio, on February 20, 2013, at age 88. She was buried in Green Lawn Cemetery, Columbus, Franklin Co., Ohio.[97]

Maxine married **Billie E. Stamper** on May 17, 1941, in Wayne Co., West Virginia. They divorced. They had three children. Billie E. Stamper was born in Dunlow, Wayne Co., West Virginia, on November 22, 1921. He reached age 71 and died in Glendale, Maricopa Co., Arizona, on November 17, 1993. Billie E. was buried in Resthaven Park West Cemetery, Glendale, Maricopa Co., Arizona.[148]

Maxine Edsall Stamper married **Charles Secret Spetnagel** in 1967. Charles Secret Spetnagel was born in Chillicothe, Scioto Twp., Ross Co., Ohio, on December 12, 1922. Charles Secret lived in 1997 in Bonita Springs, Lee Co., Florida. He reached age 74 and died in a hospital in Fort Myers, Lee Co., Florida, on July 26, 1997. Charles Secret was buried in Green Lawn Cemetery, Columbus, Franklin Co., Ohio.[97]

Maxine Edsall and Billie E. Stamper had three children, including:

+ 467 m I. **Gary David[9] Stamper** was born in Detroit, Wayne Co., Michigan, on

July 17, 1943. He died in Columbus, Franklin Co., Ohio, on August 10, 1964. Gary David was buried in Green Lawn Cemetery, Columbus, Franklin Co., Ohio.[97]

+ 468 f II. **Bonnie Margaret**[9] **Stamper** was born in Crum, Wayne Co., West Virginia, on February 18, 1950. She died in Crum, Wayne Co., West Virginia, on March 2, 1950.

## 9th Generation

**313. Virginia⁹ Demilt** (*Theda V.⁸ Hamilton, Harry Leonard⁷, Sylvester⁶, Margaret⁵ VanAusdall, Mary⁴ Pegan, Andrew³ Pegan II, Andrew² Pagan, James¹*) was born in 1922 in Illinois. She is the daughter of Unknown Demilt and Theda V. Hamilton (137).

**314. James⁹ Demilt** (*Theda V.⁸ Hamilton, Harry Leonard⁷, Sylvester⁶, Margaret⁵ VanAusdall, Mary⁴ Pegan, Andrew³ Pegan II, Andrew² Pagan, James¹*) was born in 1924 in Illinois. He is the son of Unknown Demilt and Theda V. Hamilton (137). James Demilt is living with his uncle and aunt, Clyde Jesse and Helen Wolshock Hamilton, in 1940 in Chester, Chester Twp., Randolph Co., Illinois.

**315. Shirley Ann⁹ Mannen** (*Theda V.⁸ Hamilton, Harry Leonard⁷, Sylvester⁶, Margaret⁵ VanAusdall, Mary⁴ Pegan, Andrew³ Pegan II, Andrew² Pagan, James¹*) was born on August 27, 1929, in Mount Vernon, Mount Vernon Twp., Jefferson Co., Illinois. She was the daughter of Leslie Earl Mannen II and Theda V. Hamilton (137).

Shirley Ann married **Duane Wilbur Daniels** before 1953. They divorced. They had three children. Duane Wilbur Daniels was born in Springview, Keya Paha Co., Nebraska, on May 8, 1924. He was also known as **Danny.** Duane Wilbur reached age 76 and died in Brookings, Curry Co., Oregon, on December 9, 2000.

**316. Thomas Ray⁹ Hamilton** (*Ray P.⁸, Harry Leonard⁷, Sylvester⁶, Margaret⁵ VanAusdall, Mary⁴ Pegan, Andrew³ Pegan II, Andrew² Pagan, James¹*) was born on January 27, 1933, in Hardin, Hardin Twp., Calhoun Co., Illinois. He was the son of Ray P. Hamilton (140) and Eileen G. Gordon. Thomas Ray died in Korea on October 7, 1951, at age 18. He was buried in Murdale Gardens of Memory, Murphysboro, Murphysboro Twp., Jackson Co., Illinois.[40]

Thomas Ray Hamilton was killed in action during the Korean War.

Never married.

**317. Theda E.⁹ Hamilton** (*Ray P.⁸, Harry Leonard⁷, Sylvester⁶, Margaret⁵ VanAusdall, Mary⁴ Pegan, Andrew³ Pegan II, Andrew² Pagan, James¹*) was born on February 20, 1937, in Chester, Chester Twp., Randolph Co., Illinois. She was the daughter of Ray P. Hamilton (140) and Eileen G. Gordon. Theda E. lived in 1989 in Des Plaines, Cook Co., Illinois. She died in a hospital in Houston, Harris Co., Texas, on November 6, 1989, at age 52. Theda E. was buried in Murdale Gardens of Memory, Murphysboro, Murphysboro Twp., Jackson Co., Illinois.[46]

Never married.

**318. Janet⁹ Hamilton** (*Howard L.⁸, Harry Leonard⁷, Sylvester⁶, Margaret⁵ VanAusdall, Mary⁴ Pegan, Andrew³ Pegan II, Andrew² Pagan, James¹*) was born in 1935 in Chester, Chester Twp., Randolph Co., Illinois. She is the daughter of Howard L. Hamilton (141) and Elma N. Cooper.

**319. Charles Rogers⁹ Dennis** (*Amy Lucille⁸ Hamilton, Daniel Lester⁷, Sylvester⁶, Margaret⁵ VanAusdall, Mary⁴ Pegan, Andrew³ Pegan II, Andrew² Pagan, James¹*) was born on July 21, 1934, in Wickcliffe, Ballard Co., Kentucky. He was also known as **Bunky.** He was the son of John Rogers Dennis and Amy Lucille Hamilton (142). Charles Rogers died in Chicago, Cook Co., Illinois, on February 1, 1972, at age 37. He was buried in Berkley Cemetery, Carlisle Co., Kentucky.[98]

He married **Glenda Mae Blackburn.** They had three children. Glenda Mae Blackburn was born in Carlisle Co., Kentucky, on September 18, 1936. Glenda Mae lived in 2008 in Clinton, Hickman Co., Kentucky. She reached age 71 and died in a hospital in Fulton, Fulton Co., Kentucky, on June 9, 2008. Glenda Mae was buried in Berkley Cemetery, Carlisle Co., Kentucky.[98]

She is buried under the name Glenda Mae Blackburn Rucks.

Charles Rogers Dennis and Glenda Mae Blackburn had three children, including:

+ 469  f  I.  **Vickie Cheryl**[10] **Dennis** was born in Cairo, North Cairo Twp., Alexander Co., Illinois, on June 5, 1955. She died in Arlington, Carlisle Co., Kentucky, on August 1, 1978. Vickie Cheryl was buried in Berkley Cemetery, Carlisle Co., Kentucky.[98]

**320. Rena June**[9] **Dennis** (*Amy Lucille*[8] *Hamilton, Daniel Lester*[7], *Sylvester*[6], *Margaret*[5] *VanAusdall, Mary*[4] *Pegan, Andrew*[3] *Pegan II, Andrew*[2] *Pagan, James*[1]) was born in Wickcliffe, Ballard Co., Kentucky, on February 6, 1937. She was the daughter of John Rogers Dennis and Amy Lucille Hamilton (142). Rena June died in a hospital in Paducah, McCracken Co., Kentucky, on January 12, 2018, at age 80.

Rena June married **Jimmie L. Smith**. They had two daughters. Jimmie L. Smith was born on February 12, 1934.

**321. Sylvia Ann**[9] **Dennis** (*Amy Lucille*[8] *Hamilton, Daniel Lester*[7], *Sylvester*[6], *Margaret*[5] *VanAusdall, Mary*[4] *Pegan, Andrew*[3] *Pegan II, Andrew*[2] *Pagan, James*[1]) was born on June 20, 1939 in Wickcliffe, Ballard Co., Kentucky. She is the daughter of John Rogers Dennis and Amy Lucille Hamilton (142).

Sylvia Ann married **Guy Nickie Moore** before 1958. They had three children.

Sylvia Ann Dennis and Guy Nickie Moore had three children, including:

+ 469A  m  I.  **Guy Nickie**[10] **Moore II** was born in Albuquerque, Bernalillo Co., New Mexico, on May 11, 1958. He died in Paducah, McCracken Co., Kentucky, on May 11, 1986. Guy Nickie II is buried in Barlow Cemetery, Barlow, Ballard Co., Kentucky.[F]

+ 469B  m  II.  **Dennis Rogers**[10] **Moore** was born in Cairo, North Cairo Twp., Alex-

ander Co., Illinois, on July 3, 1960. He died in Paducah, McCracken Co., Kentucky, on July 23, 2001. Dennis Rogers is buried in Barlow Cemetery, Barlow, Ballard Co., Kentucky.[F]

**321A. Arthur Vernon**[9] **Wolters II** (*Dorothy*[8] *Garner, Jessie J.*[7] *Hamilton, Sylvester*[6], *Margaret*[5] *VanAusdall, Mary*[4] *Pegan, Andrew*[3] *Pegan II, Andrew*[2] *Pagan, James*[1]) was born in Percy, Percy Twp., Randolph Co., Illinois, on August 23, 1932. He was the son of Arthur Wilhelm Herman Dorothy Garner (145). He died in Poplar Bluff, Poplar Bluff Twp., Butler Co., Missouri, on June 23 1987, at age 54. Arthur Vernon was buried in Brown Chapel Cemetery, Broseley, Ash Hill Twp., Butler Co., Missouri.[B]

Never married.

**321B. Ralph Albert**[9] **Wolters** (*Dorothy*[8] *Garner, Jessie J.*[7] *Hamilton, Sylvester*[6], *Margaret*[5] *VanAusdall, Mary*[4] *Pegan, Andrew*[3] *Pegan II, Andrew*[2] *Pagan, James*[1]) was born in Percy, Percy Twp., Randolph Co., Illinois, on March 4, 1935. He was the son of Arthur Wilhelm Herman Dorothy Garner (145). Ralph Albert died in Poplar Bluff, Poplar Bluff Twp., Butler Co., Missouri on September 26, 1998, at age 63.

Never married.

**321C. Charles Frederick**[9] **Wolters** (*Dorothy*[8] *Garner, Jessie J.*[7] *Hamilton, Sylvester*[6], *Margaret*[5] *VanAusdall, Mary*[4] *Pegan, Andrew*[3] *Pegan II, Andrew*[2] *Pagan, James*[1]) was born in Chester, Chester Twp., Randolph Co., Illinois, on July 18, 1938. He was the son of Arthur Wilhelm Herman Dorothy Garner (145). Charles Frederick died in Natchez, Adams Co., Mississippi, on July 16, 1978, at age 39.

Charles Frederick married **Unknown Unknown**. They had one daughter.

**321D. Clyde Ray**[9] **Wolters** (*Dorothy*[8] *Garner, Jessie J.*[7] *Hamilton, Sylvester*[6], *Margaret*[5] *VanAusdall, Mary*[4] *Pegan, Andrew*[3] *Pegan II, Andrew*[2] *Pagan, James*[1]) was born in Poplar Bluff, Poplar Bluff Twp., Butler Co., Missouri, on April 15, 1945.

He was the son of Arthur Wilhelm Herman Dorothy Garner (145). Clyde Ray died in Phoenix, Maricopa Co., Arizona, on June 9, 1998, age 53. He was buried in National Memorial Cemetery of Arizona, Phoenix, Maricopa Co., Arizona.[C]

Clyde Ray married and he and his wife had three children.

321E. **Linda Margaret**[9] **Wolters** (*Dorothy*[8] *Garner, Jessie J.*[7] *Hamilton, Sylvester*[6], *Margaret*[5] *VanAusdall, Mary*[4] *Pegan, Andrew*[3] *Pegan II, Andrew*[2] *Pagan, James*[1]) was born in Poplar Bluff, Poplar Bluff Twp., Butler Co., Missouri, on May 19, 1947. She was the daughter of Arthur Wilhelm Herman Dorothy Garner (145). Linda Margaret died in Jacksonport, Jackson Co., Arkansas, on January 20, 2009, at age 61. She was buried in Ash Hill Cemetery, Fisk, Ash Hill Twp., Butler Co., Missouri.[D]

Linda Margaret married and had two children. Then she and her husband divorced.

322. **Max J.**[9] **Harris** (*Ruth E.*[8] *Johnson, Doris Margaret*[7] *Hamilton, Sylvester*[6], *Margaret*[5] *VanAusdall, Mary*[4] *Pegan, Andrew*[3] *Pegan II, Andrew*[2] *Pagan, James*[1]) was born on December 22, 1933, in Illinois. He is the son of Oscar Vincent Harris and Ruth E. Johnson (147).

323. **Theda Lucille**[9] **Harris** (*Ruth E.*[8] *Johnson, Doris Margaret*[7] *Hamilton, Sylvester*[6], *Margaret*[5] *VanAusdall, Mary*[4] *Pegan, Andrew*[3] *Pegan II, Andrew*[2] *Pagan, James*[1]) was born on August 25, 1936, in Detroit, Wayne Co., Michigan. She is the daughter of Oscar Vincent Harris and Ruth E. Johnson (147). She died in Lake Arrowhead, San Bernardino Co., California, on October 25, 2016.

Theda Lucille married **Jerry L. Wade** on July 4, 1958 in Los Angeles Co., California. They divorced.

Theda Lucille Harris Wade married **Irvin P. Koszewski** on November 30, 1963 in Clark Co., Nevada. They divorced. Irvin P. Koszewski was born in Camden, Camden Co., New Jersey, on August 30, 1934. He reached age 74 and died in Doylestown, Bucks Co., Pennsylvania on March 29, 2009.

Irvin P. Koszewski was a bodybuilder who is in the International Federation of Bodybuilders Hall of Fame in Madrid, Spain.

Theda Lucille Harris Wade Koszewski married **Unknown Romero**. They divorced. They had one daughter.

324. **Daughter**[9] **Johnson** (*Eva Grace*[8], *Doris Margaret*[7] *Hamilton, Sylvester*[6], *Margaret*[5] *VanAusdall, Mary*[4] *Pegan, Andrew*[3] *Pegan II, Andrew*[2] *Pagan, James*[1]) She is the daughter of Unknown Campbell and Eva Grace Johnson (148).

She married **Mr. Bieniasz.** Mr. Bieniasz was born in 1937. They had five children.

Mr. Bieniasz and Daughter Johnson had five children, including:

+ 470 m  II.  **Gregory Alan Bieniasz** was born in Westwood, Los Angeles Co., California, on January 18, 1964. He died in Santa Monica, Los Angeles Co., California? on July 12, 2003.

325. **Nancy Beth**[9] **Hamilton** (*Oscar Myron*[8], *Silas Vanculen*[7], *Sylvester*[6], *Margaret*[5] *VanAusdall, Mary*[4] *Pegan, Andrew*[3] *Pegan II, Andrew*[2] *Pagan, James*[1]) was born on July 22, 1947, in Columbus, Muscogee Co., Georgia. She was the daughter of Oscar Myron Hamilton (155) and Edna E. Waldrop. Nancy Beth died in Columbia, Richland Co., South Carolina, on March 4, 2006, at age 58. She was buried in McClellanville Methodist Church Cemetery, McClellanville, Charleston Co., South Carolina.[101]

She married **Mr. Holcombe II.** They had two sons.

326. **James George**[9] **Downen** (*Ola M.*[8] *Hamilton, Silas Vanculen*[7], *Sylvester*[6], *Margaret*[5] *VanAusdall, Mary*[4] *Pegan, Andrew*[3] *Pegan II, Andrew*[2] *Pagan, James*[1]) was born on June 21, 1942, in Chester, Chester Twp., Randolph Co., Illinois. He was the son of George Downen and Ola M. Hamilton (156). James George died in Garden Grove, Orange Co., California? on February 4, 1999, at age 56.

James George married **Ms. Rocha.**

327. **Son⁹ Downen** (*Ola M.⁸ Hamilton, Silas Vanculen⁷, Sylvester⁶, Margaret⁵ VanAusdall, Mary⁴ Pegan, Andrew³ Pegan II, Andrew² Pagan, James¹*) was born on February 16, 1944. He is the son of George Downen and Ola M. Hamilton (156). Thomas Glenn lived in 2009 in Jackson, Madison Co., Tennessee.

He married **Della Mae Patterson** in 1976. Della Mae Patterson was born in Cincinnati, Hamilton Co., Ohio, on March 17, 1941. Della Mae reached age 60 and died in Fallon, Churchill Co., Nevada, on January 3, 2002. She was buried in Ebenezer Memorial Cemetery, Rockwood, Liberty Twp., Randolph Co., Illinois.[149]

328. **Mary Susan⁹ Rader** (*Norma Jean⁸ Hamilton, Silas Vanculen⁷, Sylvester⁶, Margaret⁵ VanAusdall, Mary⁴ Pegan, Andrew³ Pegan II, Andrew² Pagan, James¹*) was born on June 10, 1947, in Chester, Chester Twp., Randolph Co., Illinois. She was also known as **Susan.** She was the daughter of Jake B. Rader II and Norma Jean Hamilton (159). Mary Susan died in Las Vegas, Clark Co., Nevada, on March 5, 2003.

She married **Unknown Stewart.**

329. **Mark Steven⁹ Rader** (*Norma Jean⁸ Hamilton, Silas Vanculen⁷, Sylvester⁶, Margaret⁵ VanAusdall, Mary⁴ Pegan, Andrew³ Pegan II, Andrew² Pagan, James¹*) was born on December 6, 1952, in Red Bud, Union Twp., Randolph Co., Illinois. He was the son of Jake B. Rader II and Norma Jean Hamilton (159). Mark Steven died in Las Vegas, Clark Co., Nevada, on June 14, 1992, at age 39. He was buried in Palm Memorial Park Cemetery, Las Vegas, Clark Co., Nevada.[54]

330. **Daughter⁹ Gowan** (*Barbara Ann⁸ Hamilton, Silas Vanculen⁷, Sylvester⁶, Margaret⁵ VanAusdall, Mary⁴ Pegan, Andrew³ Pegan II, Andrew² Pagan, James¹*). She is the daughter of Albert J. Gowan and Barbara Ann Hamilton (161).

Daughter Gowan married **Unknown Cornell.** They had one son.

Daughter Gowan Cornell married **Unknown Smith** before 2002.

Son of Daughter Gowan and Unknown Cornell:

+ 471 m I. **Lucas Ryan¹⁰ Cornell** was born in Lafayette, Fairfield Twp., Tippecanoe Co., Indiana, on August 12, 1980. He died in West Lafayette, Wabash Twp., Tippecanoe Co., Indiana, on May 27, 2002. Lucas Ryan was buried in Yorktown Cemetery, Stockwell, Lauramie Twp., Tippecanoe Co., Indiana.[150]

331. **David A.⁹ Zagorski** (*Nedra L.⁸ Hamilton, Silas Vanculen⁷, Sylvester⁶, Margaret⁵ VanAusdall, Mary⁴ Pegan, Andrew³ Pegan II, Andrew² Pagan, James¹*) was born on February 4, 1957, in East St. Louis, St. Clair Co., Illinois. He was the son of Joseph Zagorski and Nedra L. Hamilton (162). David A. died in Munster, Lake Co., Indiana, on October 5, 2008, at age 51.

He married **Angela Unknown.** They had four children.

332. **Virgil Kay⁹ Ausmus** (*Esther Mabel⁸ Rogers, Elmer Ellsworth⁷, Austin J.⁶, Rachel C.⁵ VanAusdall, Mary⁴ Pegan, Andrew³ Pegan II, Andrew² Pagan, James¹*) was born on October 22, 1920, in Lamar, Prowers Co., Colorado. He was the son of Jasper Kay Ausmus and Esther Mabel Rogers (164). Virgil Kay died in Pueblo, Pueblo Co., Colorado, on March 19, 1983, at age 62. He was buried in Mountain View Cemetery, Pueblo, Pueblo Co., Colorado.[104]

Virgil Kay Ausmus married **Ethel Fern Karr** after 1940. They had one daughter. Ethel Fern was born on September 9, 1925 in Pierceville Twp., Finney Co., Kansas. She died on April 20, 2009, in Pueblo, Pueblo Co., Colorado at age 83.

333. **Doris Leona⁹ Ausmus** (*Esther Mabel⁸ Rogers, Elmer Ellsworth⁷, Austin J.⁶, Rachel C.⁵ VanAusdall, Mary⁴ Pegan, Andrew³ Pegan II, Andrew² Pagan, James¹*) was born on December 22, 1924, in Lamar, Prowers Co., Colorado. She was the daughter of Jasper Kay Ausmus and Esther Mabel Rogers (164). Doris Leona died in Aberdeen, Grays Harbor Co., Washington, on May 10, 2013, at age 88. She was buried in Satsop Cemetery, Satsop, Grays Harbor Co., Washington.[105]

Doris Leona married **John Leno Prante** on October 23, 1948, in Lewis Co., Washington. They seem to have divorced. They had two children. John Leno Prante was born in Aberdeen, Grays Harbor Co., Washington, on November 28, 1918. John Leno reached age 51 and died in Elma, Grays Harbor Co., Washington, on May 30, 1970. He was buried in Satsop Cemetery, Satsop, Grays Harbor Co., Washington.[105]

Doris Leona Ausmus Prante married **Unknown Nielson**. They had one son.

334. **Floyd Cleo⁹ Rogers** (*Evelyn Rowena⁸, Elmer Ellsworth⁷, Austin J.⁶, Rachel C.⁵ VanAusdall, Mary⁴ Pegan, Andrew³ Pegan II, Andrew² Pagan, James¹*) was born on April 6, 1921, in Granada, Powers Co., Colorado. He was the son of Archie Rogers and Evelyn Rowena Rogers (165). Floyd Cleo died in San Francisco, San Francisco Co., California, on April 19, 1995, at age 74. He was buried in San Joaquin Valley National Cemetery, Santa Nella, Merced Co., California.[107]

335. **Leona⁹ Rogers** (*Evelyn Rowena⁸, Elmer Ellsworth⁷, Austin J.⁶, Rachel C.⁵ VanAusdall, Mary⁴ Pegan, Andrew³ Pegan II, Andrew² Pagan, James¹*) was born in 1923. She is the daughter of Archie Rogers and Evelyn Rowena Rogers (165).

336. **Ralph Wayne⁹ Rogers** (*Evelyn Rowena⁸, Elmer Ellsworth⁷, Austin J.⁶, Rachel C.⁵ VanAusdall, Mary⁴ Pegan, Andrew³ Pegan II, Andrew² Pagan, James¹*) was born on May 2, 1925, in Cimmeron, Clark Co., Kansas. He was the son of Archie Rogers and Evelyn Rowena Rogers (165). Ralph Wayne died in Fresno, Fresno Co., California, on April 23, 1972, at age 46.

He married **Grace May Spino.** They had four children. Grace May Spino was born in Newton Falls, Newton Twp., Trumbull Co., Ohio, on December 18, 1925. Grace May reached age 71 and died in Fresno, Fresno Co., California, on January 9, 1997.

337. **Evelyn⁹ Grimsley** (*Jessie Hazel⁸ Rogers, Elmer Ellsworth⁷, Austin J.⁶, Rachel C.⁵ VanAusdall, Mary⁴ Pegan, Andrew³ Pegan II, Andrew² Pagan, James¹*) was born in 1931 in La Junta, Otero Co., Colorado. She is the daughter of Howard William Grimsley and Jessie Hazel Rogers (167).

338. **Ruth Catherine⁹ Rogers** (*William Harvey⁸, Herbert Augusta⁷, Austin J.⁶, Rachel C.⁵ VanAusdall, Mary⁴ Pegan, Andrew³ Pegan II, Andrew² Pagan, James¹*) was born on August 18, 1931, in Arvonia Twp., Osage Co., Kansas. She was the daughter of William Harvey Rogers (170) and Martha Marie Archer. Ruth Catherine died in Longmont, Colorado? on December 7, 2005, at age 74.

Ruth Catherine married **Arthur Dale Weeks** in 1959. Arthur Dale Weeks was born in Grandview Twp., Morris Co., Kansas, on September 17, 1925. Arthur Dale reached age 74 and died in Grass Valley, Nevada Co., California, on April 22, 2000.

339. **William Herbert⁹ Rogers II** (*William Harvey⁸, Herbert Augusta⁷, Austin J.⁶, Rachel C.⁵ VanAusdall, Mary⁴ Pegan, Andrew³ Pegan II, Andrew² Pagan, James¹*) was born on August 31, 1936, in Lebo, Lincoln Twp., Coffey Co., Kansas. He was the son of William Harvey Rogers (170) and Martha Marie Archer. William Herbert died in Haysville, Sedgwick Co., Kansas, on July 15, 2005, at age 68. He was buried in Greenwood Cemetery, Wichita, Sedgwick Co., Kansas.[110]

340. **Robert Ralph⁹ Rogers** (*Ralph⁸, Herbert Augusta⁷, Austin J.⁶, Rachel C.⁵ VanAusdall, Mary⁴ Pegan, Andrew³ Pegan II, Andrew² Pagan, James¹*) was born on May 17, 1941, in Lebo, Lincoln Twp., Coffey Co., Kansas. He was the son of Ralph Rogers (172) and Clara Bertha Jones. Robert Ralph lived in 2005 in McPherson, McPherson Twp., McPherson Co. Kansas. He died in a hospital in Wichita, Sedgwick Co., Kansas, on September 15, 2005, at age 64. Robert Ralph was buried in Alexanderwhol Friedhof Cemetery, Goessel, West Branch Twp., Marion Co., Kansas.[111]

Robert Ralph married **Unknown Ratzlaff.** They had two children.

341. **Barbara Gail⁹ Rogers** (*Ralph⁸, Herbert Augusta⁷, Austin J.⁶, Rachel C.⁵ VanAusdall, Mary⁴ Pegan, Andrew³ Pegan II, Andrew² Pagan, James¹*) was born on March 18, 1952, in Emporia, Emporia Twp., Lyon Co., Kansas. She was the daughter of Ralph Rogers (172) and Clara Bertha Jones. Barbara Gail lived in 2005 in Newton, Kansas. She died in Halstead, Halstead Twp., Harvey Co., Kansas,

on October 25, 2014, at age 62. Barbara Gail was buried in Lincoln Cemetery, Lebo, Lincoln Twp., Coffey Co., Kansas.[19]

Never married.

**342. Ruth I.**[9] **White** (*Charles Otis*[8], *Walter Otis*[7], *Mary E.*[6] *Rogers, Rachel C.*[5] *VanAusdall, Mary*[4] *Pegan, Andrew*[3] *Pegan II, Andrew*[2] *Pagan, James*[1]) was born in 1926 in Jerseyville, Jersey Twp., Jersey Co., Illinois. She is the daughter of Charles Otis White (174) and Cora Faye Simpson.

**343. Lloyd Cletus**[9] **White** (*Charles Otis*[8], *Walter Otis*[7], *Mary E.*[6] *Rogers, Rachel C.*[5] *VanAusdall, Mary*[4] *Pegan, Andrew*[3] *Pegan II, Andrew*[2] *Pagan, James*[1]) was born on August 6, 1934, in Jerseyville, Jersey Twp., Jersey Co., Illinois. He was the son of Charles Otis White (174) and Eva Esther Wayman. Lloyd Cletus died in Kane, Kane Twp., Greene Co., Illinois, on March 23, 2009, at age 74. He was buried in Kane Cemetery, Kane, Kane Twp., Greene Co., Illinois.[114]

Lloyd Cletus married **Barbara Ellen Payne** on January 2, 1957. They had five children. Barbara Ellen Payne was born in South Pittsburg, Marion Co., Tennessee, on December 8, 1936. Barbara Ellen lived in 2003 in Kane, Kane Twp., Greene Co., Illinois. She reached age 66 and died in a hospital in St. Louis, Missouri, on September 29, 2003. Barbara Ellen was buried in Kane Cemetery, Kane, Kane Twp., Greene Co., Illinois.[114]

**344. Charles Laverne**[9] **White** (*Charles Otis*[8], *Walter Otis*[7], *Mary E.*[6] *Rogers, Rachel C.*[5] *VanAusdall, Mary*[4] *Pegan, Andrew*[3] *Pegan II, Andrew*[2] *Pagan, James*[1]) was born on December 11, 1935, in Jerseyville, Jersey Twp., Jersey Co., Illinois. He was the son of Charles Otis White (174) and Eva Esther Wayman. Charles Laverne died in Jerseyville, Jersey Twp., Jersey Co., Illinois, on February 7, 2015, at age 79. He was buried in Oak Grove Cemetery, Jerseyville, Jersey Twp., Jersey Co., Illinois.[16]

Charles Laverne married **Judith A. Purcell** in 1957. They had three children. Judith A. Purcell was born on May 4, 1939.

**345. Walter Leonard**[9] **White** (*Charles Otis*[8], *Walter Otis*[7], *Mary E.*[6] *Rogers, Rachel C.*[5] *VanAusdall,*

*Mary*[4] *Pegan, Andrew*[3] *Pegan II, Andrew*[2] *Pagan, James*[1]) was born on May 6, 1938, in Jerseyville, Jersey Twp., Jersey Co., Illinois. He was also known as **Leonard.** He was the son of Charles Otis White (174) and Eva Esther Wayman. Walter Leonard died in Kane, Kane Twp., Greene Co., Illinois, on April 10, 2010, at age 71. He was buried in Kane Cemetery, Kane, Kane Twp., Greene Co., Illinois.[114]

Walter Leonard married **Barbara Ann Kochersperger** on August 2, 1959. They had three children. Barbara Ann Kochersperger was born in Alton, Alton Twp., Madison Co., Illinois, on November 21, 1938. Barbara Ann reached age 77 and died in Carrollton, Carrollton Twp., Greene Co., Illinois, on January 6, 2016. She was buried in Kane Cemetery, Kane, Kane Twp., Greene Co., Illinois.[114]

**346. Robert Lee**[9] **White** (*Charles Otis*[8], *Walter Otis*[7], *Mary E.*[6] *Rogers, Rachel C.*[5] *VanAusdall, Mary*[4] *Pegan, Andrew*[3] *Pegan II, Andrew*[2] *Pagan, James*[1]) was born on January 18, 1940, in Jerseyville, Jersey Twp., Jersey Co., Illinois. He was the son of Charles Otis White (174) and Eva Esther Wayman. Robert Lee lived in 1995 in Brighton, Piasa Twp., Jersey Co., Illinois. He died in a hospital in Alton, Alton Twp., Madison Co., Illinois, on July 3, 1995, at age 55. Robert Lee was buried in Medora Cemetery, Ruyle Twp., Jersey Co., Illinois.[113]

Robert Lee married **Ms. Claxton**. They had four children.

Robert Lee White and Ms. Claxton had four children, including:

+ 472 f IV. **Joy Lynn**[10] **White** was born in Alton, Alton Twp., Madison Co., Illinois, on November 15, 1968. She died in a hospital in St. Louis, Missouri, on November 2, 1988. Joy Lynn was buried in Medora Cemetery, Ruyle Twp., Jersey Co., Illinois.[113]

**347. Billy Gene**[9] **White** (*Charles Otis*[8], *Walter Otis*[7], *Mary E.*[6] *Rogers, Rachel C.*[5] *VanAusdall, Mary*[4] *Pegan, Andrew*[3] *Pegan II, Andrew*[2] *Pagan, James*[1]) was born on August 6, 1942, in Carrollton, Carrollton Twp., Greene Co., Illinois. He was the son of Charles Otis White (174) and Eva Esther Wayman. Billy Gene died in Grafton, Quarry Twp., Jersey Co., Illinois, on March 30, 2000, at age 57. He was buried in Medora Cemetery, Ruyle Twp., Jersey Co., Illinois.[113]

Billy Gene White married **Ms. Maxheimer.** They divorced. They had two children.

Billy Gene married a second wife.

Billy Gene White and Ms. Maxheimer had two children, including:

+ 473  m  II.  **Rodney Maurice[10] White** was born in Jacksonville, Jacksonville Twp., Morgan Co., Illinois, on November 26, 1972. He died in Effingham, Douglas Twp., Effingham Co., Illinois, on April 13, 1998. Rodney Maurice was buried in Mount Pulaski Cemetery, Mount Pulaski. Mount Pulaski Twp., Logan Co., Illinois.[151]

348.  **Ronald Ellsworth[9] Osborn** (*Ruth M.[8] White, Walter Otis[7], Mary E.[6] Rogers, Rachel C.[5] VanAusdall, Mary[4] Pegan, Andrew[3] Pegan II, Andrew[2] Pagan, James[1]*) was born on January 3, 1927, in Alton, Alton Twp., Madison Co., Illinois. He was the son of Freddie F. Osborn and Ruth M. White (175). Ronald Ellsworth lived in 1977 in College Park, Clayton Co., Georgia. He died in Riverdale, Clayton Co., Georgia, on January 2, 2008, at age 80.

He married **Patricia Roth Goble** about 1946. They had five children. Patricia R. Goble was born on September 20, 1929.

Ronald Ellsworth Osborn and Patricia R. Goble have five children, including:

+ 474  m  I.  **James[10] Osborn.** James died before 2008.

349.  **Freddie Franklin[9] Osborn II** (*Ruth M.[8] White, Walter Otis[7], Mary E.[6] Rogers, Rachel C.[5] VanAusdall,*

*Mary[4] Pegan, Andrew[3] Pegan II, Andrew[2] Pagan, James[1]*) was born on February 16, 1929, in Alton, Alton Twp., Madison Co., Illinois. He was the son of Freddie F. Osborn and Ruth M. White (175). Freddie Franklin died in Alton, Alton Twp., Madison Co., Illinois, on May 18, 2003, at age 74. He was buried in Oak Grove Cemetery, Jerseyville, Jersey Twp., Jersey Co., Illinois.[16]

350.  **Dimple Mae[9] White** (*Walter L.[8], Walter Otis[7], Mary E.[6] Rogers, Rachel C.[5] VanAusdall, Mary[4] Pegan, Andrew[3] Pegan II, Andrew[2] Pagan, James[1]*) was born in 1932 in Jerseyville, Jersey Twp., Jersey Co., Illinois. She was the daughter of Walter L. White II (176) and Golda M. Jaynes.

Dimple Mae married **Norman Frederick Burch** on October 15, 1950, in Arkansas. They had three children. Norman Frederick Burch was born in Jerseyville, Jersey Twp., Jersey Co., Illinois, on April 8, 1932. Norman Frederick reached age 59 and died in Jerseyville, Jersey Twp., Jersey Co., Illinois, on June 11, 1991. He was buried in Oak Grove Cemetery, Jerseyville, Jersey Twp., Jersey Co., Illinois.[16]

351.  **James R.[9] White** (*Walter L.[8], Walter Otis[7], Mary E.[6] Rogers, Rachel C.[5] VanAusdall, Mary[4] Pegan, Andrew[3] Pegan II, Andrew[2] Pagan, James[1]*) was born in 1937. He is the son of Walter L. White II (176) and Golda M. Jaynes.

352.  **Garnetta Faye[9] Ludwig** (*Georgia Mae[8] White, Walter Otis[7], Mary E.[6] Rogers, Rachel C.[5] VanAusdall, Mary[4] Pegan, Andrew[3] Pegan II, Andrew[2] Pagan, James[1]*) was born on July 8, 1931, in Jerseyville, Jersey Twp., Jersey Co., Illinois. She was the daughter of Lester Freeman Ludwig and Georgia Mae White (178). Garnetta Faye lived in 1978 in Oklahoma City, Oklahoma. She died in Oklahoma City, Oklahoma, on November 21, 1992, at age 61. Garnetta Faye was buried in Flynn Cemetery, Agra, Lincoln Co., Oklahoma.[115]

Garnetta Faye married **James Howard Schumann** on October 19, 1947. They had six children. James Howard Schumann was born in Kampsville, Point Twp., Calhoun Co., Illinois, on October 16, 1930. James Howard reached age 75 and died in

Jerseyville, Jersey Twp., Jersey Co., Illinois, on June 10, 2006.

Garnetta Faye Ludwig and James Howard Schumann had six children, including:

+ 475 m III. **Michael James¹⁰ Schumann** was born in Carrollton, Carrollton Twp., Greene Co., Illinois, on March 2, 1955. He died in Oklahoma City, Oklahoma, on March 13, 2006. Michael James was buried in Flynn Cemetery, Agra, Lincoln Co., Oklahoma.[102]

353. **Preston Eugene⁹ Brown II** (*Georgia Mae⁸ White, Walter Otis⁷, Mary E.⁶ Rogers, Rachel C.⁵ VanAusdall, Mary⁴ Pegan, Andrew³ Pegan II, Andrew² Pagan, James¹*) was born on April 19, 1934, in Jerseyville, Jersey Twp., Jersey Co., Illinois. He was also known as **Gene.** He was the son of Preston Douglas Brown and Georgia Mae White (178). Preston Eugene lived in 1979 in Stephenville, Erath Co., Texas. He died in a hospital in Glen Rose, Somervell Co., Texas, on January 23, 1979, at age 44. Preston Eugene was buried in Oak Grove Cemetery, Jerseyville, Jersey Twp., Jersey Co., Illinois.[16]

Preston Eugene married **Patricia Pruitt.** They had four daughters. Patricia Pruitt was born about 1937.

354. **Steven Wayne⁹ Abbott** (*Georgia Mae⁸ White, Walter Otis⁷, Mary E.⁶ Rogers, Rachel C.⁵ VanAusdall, Mary⁴ Pegan, Andrew³ Pegan II, Andrew² Pagan, James¹*) was born on July 14, 1949, in White Hall, White Hall Twp., Greene Co., Illinois. He was the son of William H. Abbott and Georgia Mae White (178). Steven Wayne died in Jersey Twp., Jersey Co., Illinois, on October 27, 1978, at age 29. He was buried in Oak Grove Cemetery, Jerseyville, Jersey Twp., Jersey Co., Illinois.[13]

He married and had three daughters.

355. **Paula Elizabeth⁹ Sullivan** (*Elizabeth Lou⁸ Nordenbrock, Imo Luella⁷ Rogers, John Vanausdoll.⁶, Rachel C.⁵ VanAusdall, Mary⁴ Pegan, Andrew³ Pegan II, Andrew² Pagan, James¹*) was born on July 13, 1962, in Dallas, Dallas Co., Texas. She was the daughter of Leo Paul Mark Sullivan and Elizabeth Lou Nordenbrock (183). Paula Elizabeth died in Poughkeepsie, Dutchess Co., New York, on October 12, 2010, at age 48.

She married **Mr. Superti.** They divorced.

Paula Elizabeth Sullivan Superti married **Unknown Hocek.** They had one son.

356. **Colin Gregory Nordenbrock⁹ Sullivan** (*Elizabeth Lou⁸ Nordenbrock, Imo Luella⁷ Rogers, John Vanausdoll.⁶, Rachel C.⁵ VanAusdall, Mary⁴ Pegan, Andrew³ Pegan II, Andrew² Pagan, James¹*) was born on November 10, 1963, in Scottsdale, Maricopa Co., Arizona. He was the son of Leo Paul Mark Sullivan and Elizabeth Lou Nordenbrock (183). Colin Gregory Nordenbrock died in San Francisco, San Francisco Co., California, on February 25, 2010, at age 46.

Never married.

357. **Scott Edwin⁹ Wahle** (*Edwin D.⁸, Dorothy Opal⁷ Rogers, John Vanausdoll.⁶, Rachel C.⁵ VanAusdall, Mary⁴ Pegan, Andrew³ Pegan II, Andrew² Pagan, James¹*) was born on August 2, 1963, in Rolla, Rolla Twp., Phelps Co., Missouri. He was the son of Edwin D. Wahle (187) and Mary Lou Marlow. Scott Edwin died in St. Charles, St. Charles Twp., St. Charles Co., Missouri, on March 12, 1988, at age 24. He was buried in Oak Grove Cemetery, St. Charles, St. Charles Twp., St. Charles Co., Missouri.[117]

Scott Edwin married and had two sons.

358. **Clyde E.⁹ McIntyre** (*Freda Grace⁸ Delp, Bertha May⁷ Vanausdoll, Loring or Loren Earl⁶, Caleb⁵, Mary⁴ Pegan, Andrew³ Pegan II, Andrew² Pagan, James¹*) was born on March 13, 1916, in Jerseyville, Jersey Twp., Jersey Co., Illinois. He was the son of Michael Clyde McIntyre and Freda Grace Delp (191). Clyde E. died in Perryville, Central Twp., Perry Co., Missouri, on February 5, 1993, at age 76. He was buried in Evergreen Cemetery, Chester, Chester Twp., Randolph Co., Illinois.[6]

Clyde E. married **Beulah Unknown.** They had two children.

Children of Clyde E. McIntyre and Beulah Unknown:

+ 476 m I. **Larry¹⁰ McIntyre** was born in Brewerville Precinct, Randolph Co., Illinois, in 1937.

+ 477 f II. **Janet¹⁰ McIntyre** was born in Brewerville Precinct, Randolph Co., Illinois, in 1939.

**359. Hettie Mae⁹ McIntyre** (*Freda Grace⁸ Delp, Bertha May⁷ Vanausdoll, Loring or Loren Earl⁶, Caleb⁵, Mary⁴ Pegan, Andrew³ Pegan II, Andrew² Pagan, James¹*) was born on September 25, 1917, in Enid, Garfield Co., Oklahoma. She was the daughter of Michael Clyde McIntyre and Freda Grace Delp (191). Hettie Mae died in Houston, Harris Co., Texas, on July 1, 2002, at age 84. She was buried in Woodlawn Cemetery, Houston, Harris Co., Texas.[119]

Hettie Mae married **Unknown McCabe** before 1940. They divorced?

Hettie Mae McIntyre McCabe married **Walter Lee DeRieux.** Walter Lee DeRieux was born in Jayton, Kent Co., Texas, on September 17, 1916. He was also known as **Dub.** Walter Lee reached age 79 and died in Houston, Harris Co., Texas, on November 7, 1995. He was buried in Woodlawn Cemetery, Houston, Harris Co., Texas.[119]

**360. Elmer⁹ McIntyre** (*Freda Grace⁸ Delp, Bertha May⁷ Vanausdoll, Loring or Loren Earl⁶, Caleb⁵, Mary⁴ Pegan, Andrew³ Pegan II, Andrew² Pagan, James¹*) was born in 1920 in Snyder, Kiowa Co., Oklahoma. He was the son of Michael Clyde McIntyre and Freda Grace Delp (191). Elmer died in Snyder, Kiowa Co., Oklahoma or Neosho, Neosho Twp., Newton Co., Missouri, before 1930.

**361. Nellie Nadine⁹ McIntyre** (*Freda Grace⁸ Delp, Bertha May⁷ Vanausdoll, Loring or Loren Earl⁶, Caleb⁵, Mary⁴ Pegan, Andrew³ Pegan II, Andrew² Pagan, James¹*) was born on June 15, 1921, in Neosho, Neosho Twp., Newton Co., Missouri. She was the daughter of Michael Clyde McIntyre and Freda Grace Delp (191). Nellie Nadine lived in Callahan, Siskiyou Co., California. She died in Houston, Harris Co., Texas, on December 7, 1992, at age 71.

Nellie Nadine McIntyre married **Unknown McBride.** They divorced?

Nellie Nadine McIntyre McBride married **Unknown Simas.**

**362. Linnie Louise⁹ McIntyre** (*Freda Grace⁸ Delp, Bertha May⁷ Vanausdoll, Loring or Loren Earl⁶, Caleb⁵, Mary⁴ Pegan, Andrew³ Pegan II, Andrew² Pagan, James¹*) was born on June 22, 1923, in Neosho, Neosho Twp., Newton Co., Missouri. She was the daughter of Michael Clyde McIntyre and Freda Grace Delp (191). She was also known as **Louise.** Linnie Louise died in Houston, Harris Co., Texas, on October 8, 2001, at age 78. She was buried under the name Louise Dowell in Memorial Oaks Cemetery, Houston, Harris Co., Texas.[120]

Linnie Louise McIntyre married **Unknown Wallace.**

Linnie Louise McIntyre Wallace married **Unknown Faulk.** They divorced?

Linnie Louise McIntyre Wallace Faulk married **Unknown Walling.** They divorced?

Linnie Louise McIntyre Wallace Faulk Walling married **Edmond Carey Dowell**. Edmond Carey Dowell was born on February 8, 1929 in Ardmore, Morgan Twp., Carter Co., Oklahoma.

**363. Charles Virgil⁹ McIntyre** (*Freda Grace⁸ Delp, Bertha May⁷ Vanausdoll, Loring or Loren Earl⁶, Caleb⁵, Mary⁴ Pegan, Andrew³ Pegan II, Andrew² Pagan, James¹*) was born on December 23, 1924, in Neosho, Neosho Twp., Newton Co., Missouri. He was the son of Michael Clyde McIntyre and Freda Grace Delp (191). Charles Virgil died in Perryville, Central Twp., Perry Co., Missouri, on May 3, 2010, at age 85. He was buried in Evergreen Cemetery, Chester, Chester Twp., Randolph Co., Illinois.[6]

Charles Virgil married **Unknown Unknown.** They had one son.

**364. Donald L.⁹ McIntyre** (*Freda Grace⁸ Delp, Bertha May⁷ Vanausdoll, Loring or Loren Earl⁶, Caleb⁵, Mary⁴ Pegan, Andrew³ Pegan II, Andrew² Pagan, James¹*) was born in 1928 in Lanagan, Lanagan Twp., McDonald Co., Missouri. He was the son of Michael Clyde McIntyre and Freda Grace Delp (191). Donald L. died in Tallulah, Madison

Parish, Louisiana? in 1948 at age 20. He was buried in Evergreen Cemetery, Chester, Chester Twp., Randolph Co., Illinois.[3]

Never married.

365. **Lester Roy⁹ McIntyre** (*Freda Grace⁸ Delp, Bertha May⁷ Vanausdoll, Loring or Loren Earl⁶, Caleb⁵, Mary⁴ Pegan, Andrew³ Pegan II, Andrew² Pagan, James¹*) was born on November 27, 1930, in Bremen, Marys River Twp., Randolph Co., Illinois. He was the son of Michael Clyde McIntyre and Freda Grace Delp (191). Lester Roy lived in Tallulah, Madison Parish, Louisiana. He died in Tallulah, Madison Parish, Louisiana, on September 21, 2011, at age 80. Lester Roy was buried in Memorial Park Cemetery, Tallulah, Madison Parish, Louisiana.[121]

Lester Roy married **Bebe Louis** on August 3, 1950. They had three children. Bebe Louis was born on October 9, 1932.

366. **Ruby Oleta⁹ McIntyre** (*Freda Grace⁸ Delp, Bertha May⁷ Vanausdoll, Loring or Loren Earl⁶, Caleb⁵, Mary⁴ Pegan, Andrew³ Pegan II, Andrew² Pagan, James¹*) was born on March 4, 1933, in Bremen, Marys River Twp., Randolph Co., Illinois. She was the daughter of Michael Clyde McIntyre and Freda Grace Delp (191). Ruby Oleta lived before 1981 in Shreveport, Caddo Co., Louisiana. She died in Conroe, Montgomery Co., Texas? in September 1981 at age 48. Ruby Oleta was buried in Evergreen Cemetery, Chester, Chester Twp., Randolph Co., Illinois.[6]

She married **Unknown Smith.**

367. **Eileen R.⁹ Reed** (*Leona Frances⁸ Delp, Bertha May⁷ Vanausdoll, Loring or Loren Earl⁶, Caleb⁵, Mary⁴ Pegan, Andrew³ Pegan II, Andrew² Pagan, James¹*) was born on September 20, 1917, in Jerseyville, Jersey Twp., Jersey Co., Illinois. She was the daughter of Lester Roy Reed and Leona Frances Delp (192). Eileen R. lived in Steeleville, Georgetown Twp., Randolph Co., Illinois. She died in a hospital in Chester, Chester Twp.., Randolph Co., Illinois, on November 20, 1970, at age 53. Eileen R. was buried in Oakwood Cemetery, Upper Alton, Alton Twp., Madison Co., Illinois.[8]

She married **Edward Davenport.** They had one son.

Son of Edward Davenport and Eilen R. Reed:

+ 478 m I. **Roger Allen¹⁰ Davenport** was born in Alton, Alton Twp., Madison Co., Illinois, on October 22, 1951. He died in Alton, Alton Twp., Madison Co., Illinois, on October 27, 1951. Roger Allen was buried in Oakwood Cemetery, Upper Alton, Alton Twp., Madison Co., Illinois.[8]

368. **Roy W.⁹ Delp II** (*Roy Everett⁸, Bertha May⁷ Vanausdoll, Loring or Loren Earl⁶, Caleb⁵, Mary⁴ Pegan, Andrew³ Pegan II, Andrew² Pagan, James¹*) was born on March 20, 1928, in Jerseyville, Jersey Twp., Jersey Co., Illinois. He was the son of Roy Everett Delp (193) and Alice May Scoggins. Roy W. died in Jerseyville, Jersey Twp., Jersey Co., Illinois, on July 7, 2009, at age 81. He was buried in Rose Lawn Memory Gardens Cemetery, Bethalto, Wood River Twp., Madison Co., Illinois.[112]

Roy W. married **Erika Stegmann** on August 20, 1949. They had five children. Erika Stegmann was born in Ober-Ramstadt, Germany, on October 18, 1929. Erika reached age 81 and died in Alton, Alton Twp., Madison Co., Illinois, on August 12, 2011. She was buried in Rose Lawn Memory Gardens Cemetery, Bethalto, Wood River Twp., Madison Co., Illinois.[111]

Roy W. Delp II and Erika Stegmann had five children, including:

+ 479 m III. **Norman Edward Delp** was born in Alton, Alton Twp., Madison Co., Illinois, on October 30, 1955. He died in Brighton, Illinois, on July 26, 2013. Norman Edward was buried in Borlin Cemetery, Carrollton, Carrollton Twp., Greene Co., Illinois.[152]

**369. Betty J.⁹ Delp** (*Roy Everett⁸, Bertha May⁷ Vanausdoll, Loring or Loren Earl⁶, Caleb⁵, Mary⁴ Pegan, Andrew³ Pegan II, Andrew² Pagan, James¹*) was born on June 18, 1929, in Jerseyville, Jersey Twp., Jersey Co., Illinois. She was the daughter of Roy Everett Delp (193) and Alice May Scoggins.

She married **Dale Elwood Landers.** Dale Elwood Landers was born in Worden, Omphghent Twp., Madison Co., Illinois, on May 28, 1922. Dale Elwood reached age 75 and died in Wood River, Wood River Twp., Madison Co., Illinois, on April 15, 1998. He was buried in Valhalla Memorial Park and Mausoleum, Godfrey, Godfrey Twp., Madison Co., Illinois.[17]

Betty J. Delp Landers married **Unknown Sansone.**

**370. Marvin⁹ Delp** (*Roy Everett⁸, Bertha May⁷ Vanausdoll, Loring or Loren Earl⁶, Caleb⁵, Mary⁴ Pegan, Andrew³ Pegan II, Andrew² Pagan, James¹*) was born in 1931 in Jerseyville, Jersey Twp., Jersey Co., Illinois. He was the son of Roy Everett Delp (193) and Alice May Scoggins. Marvin lived in Alton, Alton Twp., Madison Co., Illinois.

He married **Gloria Unknown.** They had one son.

**371. Damon Lavern⁹ Delp** (*Roy Everett⁸, Bertha May⁷ Vanausdoll, Loring or Loren Earl⁶, Caleb⁵, Mary⁴ Pegan, Andrew³ Pegan II, Andrew² Pagan, James¹*) was born on November 18, 1932, in Jerseyville, Jersey Twp., Jersey Co., Illinois? He was the son of Roy Everett Delp (193) and Alice May Scoggins. Damon Lavern died in East Alton, Wood River Twp., Madison Co., Illinois, on August 13, 2001, at age 68.

**372. Wynona Pearl⁹ Delp** (*Roy Everett⁸, Bertha May⁷ Vanausdoll, Loring or Loren Earl⁶, Caleb⁵, Mary⁴ Pegan, Andrew³ Pegan II, Andrew² Pagan, James¹*) was born on December 10, 1937, in Jerseyville, Jersey Twp., Jersey Co., Illinois. She was also known as **Pearlie.** She is the daughter of Roy Everett Delp (193) and Alice May Scoggins. Wynona Pearl died in East Alton, Wood River Twp., Madison Co., Illinois, on April 7, 2015, at age 77. She was buried in Valhalla Memorial Park and Mausoleum, Godfrey, Godfrey Twp., Madison Co., Illinois.[17]

Wynona Pearl married **Donald R. Runion** on March 29, 1969. They had three sons. Donald R. Runion was born in East St. Louis, St. Clair Co., Illinois, on February 2, 1937. Donald R. reached age 74 and died in Worden, Omphghent Twp., Madison Co., Illinois, on February 6, 2011. He was buried in Valhalla Memorial Park and Mausoleum, Godfrey, Godfrey Twp., Madison Co., Illinois.[17]

**373. Daughter⁹ Delp** (*Roy Everett⁸, Bertha May⁷ Vanausdoll, Loring or Loren Earl⁶, Caleb⁵, Mary⁴ Pegan, Andrew³ Pegan II, Andrew² Pagan, James¹*) was born on January 31, 1941, in Jerseyville, Jersey Twp., Jersey Co., Illinois. She is the daughter of Roy Everett Delp (193) and Alice May Scoggins.

Daughter Delp married **Paul Dale Baldwin** 1957. They had six children. Paul Dale Baldwin was born in Alton, Alton Twp., Madison Co., Illinois, on July 20, 1938. Paul Dale lived in 2000 in East Alton, Wood River Twp., Madison Co., Illinois. He also resided in 2015 in Medora, Chesterfield Twp., Macoupin Co., Illinois. Paul Dale reached age 77 and died in a hospital in Florissant, St. Louis Co., Missouri, on October 20, 2015. He was buried in Valhalla Memorial Park and Mausoleum, Godfrey, Godfrey Twp., Madison Co., Illinois.[17]

**374. Roger Ronald⁹ Manning** (*Vera M.⁸ Delp, Bertha May⁷ Vanausdoll, Loring or Loren Earl⁶, Caleb⁵, Mary⁴ Pegan, Andrew³ Pegan II, Andrew² Pagan, James¹*) was born on February 10, 1937, in Oquawka, South Henderson Twp., Henderson Co., Illinois. He was the son of Russell R. Manning and Vera M. Delp (196). Roger Ronald died in Oquawka, South Henderson Twp., Henderson Co., Illinois, on February 11, 1937. He was buried in Oquawka Cemetery, Oquawka, Oquawka Twp., Henderson Co., Illinois.[63]

**375. Keith Arthur⁹ Manning** (*Vera M.⁸ Delp, Bertha May⁷ Vanausdoll, Loring or Loren Earl⁶, Caleb⁵, Mary⁴ Pegan, Andrew³ Pegan II, Andrew² Pagan, James¹*) was born on April 11, 1942, in Oquawka, South Henderson Twp., Henderson Co., Illinois. He was the son of Russell R. Manning and Vera M. Delp (196). Keith Arthur lived in 1942 in Oquawka, South Henderson Twp., Henderson Co., Illinois. He died in a hospital in Monmouth, Monmouth Twp., Warren Co., Illinois, on July

28, 1942. Keith Arthur was buried in Oquawka Cemetery, Oquawka, Oquawka Twp., Henderson Co., Illinois.[63]

376. **Robert Gene[9] Vanausdoll** (*Harold A.[8], Raymond Loring[7], Loring or Loren Earl[6], Caleb[5], Mary[4] Pegan, Andrew[3] Pegan II, Andrew[2] Pagan, James[1]*) was born on November 23, 1936, in Fieldon, Richwoods Twp., Jersey Co., Illinois. He was the son of Harold A. Vanausdoll (197) and Opal E. Plumb. Robert Gene died in Florissant, St. Louis Co., Missouri, on May 1, 2003, at age 66. He was buried in Oak Grove Cemetery, Jerseyville, Jersey Twp., Jersey Co., Illinois.[16]

Robert Gene married **Rebecca J. Mundy**. They had two daughters. Rebecca J. Mundy was born on January 27, 1939.

Robert Gene Vanausdoll and Rebecca J. Mundy had two daughters, including:

+ 479A   f   I.   **Daughter Vanausdoll.**

377. **Clarence E.[9] Babcock** (*Charles Benjamin[8], Laura Edith[7] Gilmore, Martha Jane[6] Vanausdoll, Caleb[5], Mary[4] Pegan, Andrew[3] Pegan II, Andrew[2] Pagan, James[1]*) was born on May 3, 1921, in Riverside, Riverside Co., California. He was the son of Charles Benjamin Babcock (199) and Viola Elizabeth Mackey. Clarence E. died in Aurora, Adams Co., Colorado, on March 29, 1985, at age 63.

378. **Harold Eugene[9] Babcock** (*Charles Benjamin[8], Laura Edith[7] Gilmore, Martha Jane[6] Vanausdoll, Caleb[5], Mary[4] Pegan, Andrew[3] Pegan II, Andrew[2] Pagan, James[1]*) was born on June 12, 1925, in Riverside, Riverside Co., California. He was the son of Charles Benjamin Babcock (199) and Viola Elizabeth Mackey. Harold Eugene died in Garden Grove, Orange Co., California, on October 3, 1999, at age 74.

379. **Clyde Burdette[9] Sloan** (*Ada E.[8] Babcock, Laura Edith[7] Gilmore, Martha Jane[6] Vanausdoll, Caleb[5], Mary[4] Pegan, Andrew[3] Pegan II, Andrew[2] Pagan, James[1]*) was born on January 20, 1932, in Riverside, Riverside Co., California. He was the son of Francis Adolphus Sloan and Ada E. Babcock (201). Clyde Burdette died in Sierra Vista, Cochise Co., Arizona, on September 24, 1998, at age 66.

380. **Martin Emmanuel[9] Sloan** (*Ada E.[8] Babcock, Laura Edith[7] Gilmore, Martha Jane[6] Vanausdoll, Caleb[5], Mary[4] Pegan, Andrew[3] Pegan II, Andrew[2] Pagan, James[1]*) was born on October 30, 1935, in Riverside, Riverside Co., California. He was the son of Francis Adolphus Sloan and Ada E. Babcock (201). Martin Emmanuel died in Riverside, Riverside Co., California, on April 26, 2008, at age 72. He was buried in Riverside National Cemetery, Riverside, Riverside Co., California.[67]

Martin Emmanuel married **Deanna Unknown** on April 6, 1957, in Tooele Co., Utah. They had two sons. Deanna Unknown was born on June 25, 1938.

381. **Leona Evon[9] Sloan** (*Ada E.[8] Babcock, Laura Edith[7] Gilmore, Martha Jane[6] Vanausdoll, Caleb[5], Mary[4] Pegan, Andrew[3] Pegan II, Andrew[2] Pagan, James[1]*) was born on October 2, 1938, in Riverside, Riverside Co., California. She is the daughter of Francis Adolphus Sloan and Ada E. Babcock (201).

Leona Evon married **Lawrence Frazer Mazzei** on December 5, 1994, in Clark Co., Nevada. Lawrence Frazer Mazzei was born in Merced, Merced Co., California? on December 13, 1936.

382. **Carl Francis[9] Sloan** (*Ada E.[8] Babcock, Laura Edith[7] Gilmore, Martha Jane[6] Vanausdoll, Caleb[5], Mary[4] Pegan, Andrew[3] Pegan II, Andrew[2] Pagan, James[1]*) was born on June 20, 1942, in Riverside, Riverside Co., California. He was the son of Francis Adolphus Sloan and Ada E. Babcock (201). Carl Francis died in Nuevo, Riverside Co., California, on March 19, 1999, at age 56.

Carl Francis married **Diana Teresa Hosack** on April 3, 1965, in Riverside Co., California. Diana Teresa Hosack was born in Fort Wayne, Allen Co., Indiana, on November 7, 1945. Diana Teresa reached age 51 and died in Nuevo, Riverside Co., California, on May 26, 1997.

383. **June Laura[9] Babcock** (*Lewis H.[8], Laura Edith[7] Gilmore, Martha Jane[6] Vanausdoll, Caleb[5], Mary[4] Pegan, Andrew[3] Pegan II, Andrew[2] Pagan, James[1]*) was born on May 9, 1934, in Riverside, Riverside

Co., California. She was the daughter of Lewis H. Babcock (202) and Eunice S. Lever. June Laura died in San Bernardino, San Bernardino Co., California, on June 28, 1981, at age 47.

June Laura married **Robert L. Bartz** on November 15, 1952, in Riverside Co., California. Robert L. Bartz was born in Nebraska in 1933.

384. **Richard Martin⁹ Babcock** (*Lewis H.⁸, Laura Edith⁷ Gilmore, Martha Jane⁶ Vanausdoll, Caleb⁵, Mary⁴ Pegan, Andrew³ Pegan II, Andrew² Pagan, James¹*) was born on June 13, 1935, in Riverside, Riverside Co., California. He was the son of Lewis H. Babcock (202) and Eunice S. Lever. Richard Martin died in Anaheim, Orange Co., California? on December 11, 2011, at age 76.

Richard Martin married **Carol Jessieflora Miller** on July 31, 1965, in Los Angeles Co., California. They divorced. Carol Jessieflora Miller was born in Los Angeles, Los Angeles Co., California, on January 8, 1938. She reached age 68 and died in Las Vegas, Clark Co., Nevada, on July 30, 2006.

Died under the name Carol J. Heacock.

Richard Martin Babcock married **Phyllis A. Unknown** after 1965. They divorced.

385. **Robert Lewis⁹ Babcock** (*Lewis H.⁸, Laura Edith⁷ Gilmore, Martha Jane⁶ Vanausdoll, Caleb⁵, Mary⁴ Pegan, Andrew³ Pegan II, Andrew² Pagan, James¹*) was born on June 13, 1935, in Riverside, Riverside Co., California. He was the son of Lewis H. Babcock (202) and Eunice S. Lever. Robert Lewis died in Las Vegas, Clark Co., Nevada, on March 22, 1995, at age 59.

Robert Lewis married **Linda Lee Dobbins** on March 23, 1957, in Riverside Co., California. They divorced. They had one son. Linda Lee Dobbins was born in Kansas City, Jackson Co., Missouri, on February 16, 1939. She reached age 52 and died in Riverside Co., California, on August 28, 1991.

Son of Robert Lewis Babcock and Linda Lee Dobbins:

+ 480 m I. **David Robert¹⁰ Babcock** was born in Riverside, Riverside Co., California, on June 25, 1959. He died

in Riverside, Riverside Co., California, on June 17, 1995.

386. **Dona Jean⁹ Gilmore** (*Albert LeRoy⁸, Harry Otis⁷, Martha Jane⁶ Vanausdoll, Caleb⁵, Mary⁴ Pegan, Andrew³ Pegan II, Andrew² Pagan, James¹*) was born on July 12, 1928, in Sheridan Twp., Pawnee Co., Nebraska. She was the daughter of Albert LeRoy Gilmore (203) and Mary Grace Ireland. Dona Jean died in Pawnee City, Pawnee City Twp., Pawnee Co., Nebraska, on March 22, 1987, at age 58. She was buried in Pawnee City Cemetery, Pawnee City, Pawnee Twp., Pawnee Co., Nebraska.[27]

Dona Jean married **Remmer Edward Menninga** on August 6, 1948, in Marshall Co., Kansas. Remmer Edward Menninga was born in Sterling Twp., Johnson Co., Nebraska, on April 12, 1913. Remmer Edward reached age 50 and died in Pawnee City, Pawnee City Twp., Pawnee Co., Nebraska, on March 28, 1964. He was buried in Pawnee City Cemetery, Pawnee City, Pawnee Twp., Pawnee Co., Nebraska.[27]

Dona Jean Gilmore Menninga married **Howard Eugene Byers** on October 14, 1973, in Richardson Co., Nebraska. Howard Eugene Byers was born in Pawnee City, Pawnee City Twp., Pawnee Co., Nebraska, on June 29, 1922. Howard Eugene reached age 69 years and died in Pawnee City, Pawnee City Twp., Pawnee Co., Nebraska, on March 28, 1992. He was buried in Pawnee City Cemetery, Pawnee City, Pawnee Twp., Pawnee Co., Nebraska.[27]

387. **Richard⁹ Gilmore** (*Albert LeRoy⁸, Harry Otis⁷, Martha Jane⁶ Vanausdoll, Caleb⁵, Mary⁴ Pegan, Andrew³ Pegan II, Andrew² Pagan, James¹*) was born in January 1930 in Sheridan Twp., Pawnee Co., Nebraska. He is the son of Albert LeRoy Gilmore (203) and Mary Grace Ireland.

He married **Bessie Unknown.**

388. **George Otis⁹ Gilmore** (*Albert LeRoy⁸, Harry Otis⁷, Martha Jane⁶ Vanausdoll, Caleb⁵, Mary⁴ Pegan, Andrew³ Pegan II, Andrew² Pagan, James¹*) was born on August 30, 1933, in Sheridan Twp., Pawnee Co., Nebraska. He was the son of Albert LeRoy Gilmore (203) and Mary Grace Ireland. George

Otis died in Scurry, Kaufman Co., Texas, on May 15, 2013, at age 79. He was buried in Rest Haven Memorial Park Cemetery, Rockwell, Rockwell Co., Texas.[123]

George Otis married **Delores Maxine Mason** in 1955. They divorced. They had five sons. Delores Maxine Mason was born on August 18, 1935, in Marshall Co., Kansas? She reached age 79 and died on October 8, 2014, in Buffalo, Brown Co., Nebraska. Delores Maxine is buried in Kilfoil Cemetery, Merna, Custer Co., Nebraska.[153]

George Otis Gilmore married **Unknown Unknown** in 1976.

George Otis Gilmore and Delores Maxine Mason had five sons, including:

+ 481 m I.    **Fred LeRoy¹⁰ Gilmore** was born on September 19, 1956, in Pawnee City, Pawnee City Twp., Pawnee Co., Nebraska. He died on May 31, 2001, in Kearney, Buffalo Co., Nebraska. He was buried in Kilfoil Cemetery, Merna, Custer Co., Nebraska.[153]

+ 482 m III.  **Dale Wayne¹⁰ Gilmore** was born on March 7, 1961, in Pawnee City, Pawnee City Twp., Pawnee Co., Nebraska. He died on January 30, 1982 in a U.S. military accident in Nebraska? He was buried in Kilfoil Cemetery, Merna, Custer Co., Nebraska.[153]

+ 483 m IV.   **Joel Glenn¹⁰ Gilmore** was born on October 1, 1962, in Pawnee City, Pawnee City Twp., Pawnee Co., Nebraska. He died on June 15, 2006, in Lexington, Dawson Co., Nebraska. He was buried in Immanuel Lutheran Cemetery, Amherst, Buffalo Co., Nebraska.[154]

+ 484 m V.    **Kurt Allen¹⁰ Gilmore** was born on January 4, 1969 in Pawnee City, Pawnee City Twp., Pawnee

Co., Nebraska? He died on October 8, 2010 in Kearney, Buffalo Co., Nebraska. He was buried in Immanuel Lutheran Cemetery, Amherst, Buffalo Co., Nebraska.[154]

389. **Ronald⁹ Gilmore** (*Albert LeRoy⁸, Harry Otis⁷, Martha Jane⁶ Vanausdoll, Caleb⁵, Mary⁴ Pegan, Andrew³ Pegan II, Andrew² Pagan, James¹*) was born on February 5, 1940, in Sheridan Twp., Pawnee Co., Nebraska. He was the son of Albert LeRoy Gilmore (203) and Mary Grace Ireland. Ronald died in Pawnee City, Pawnee City Twp., Pawnee Co., Nebraska? on December 26, 1989, at age 49. He was buried in Pawnee City Cemetery, Pawnee City, Pawnee Twp., Pawnee Co., Nebraska.[27]

390. **Larry Dwaine⁹ Koeneke** (*Velma Rita⁸ Gilmore, Harry Otis⁷, Martha Jane⁶ Vanausdoll, Caleb⁵, Mary⁴ Pegan, Andrew³ Pegan II, Andrew² Pagan, James¹*) was born on May 2, 1943, in Humboldt, Humboldt Twp., Richardson Co., Nebraska. He was the son of Cleo George Koeneke and Velma Rita Gilmore (204). Larry Dwaine died in Seneca, Richmond Twp., Nemaha Co., Kansas, on October 6, 2002, at age 59. He was buried in Pawnee City Cemetery, Pawnee City, Pawnee Twp., Pawnee Co., Nebraska.[27]

He married **Unknown Antholz.**

391. **Dorothy JoAnne⁹ Gilmore** (*Harry Eugene⁸, Harry Otis⁷, Martha Jane⁶ Vanausdoll, Caleb⁵, Mary⁴ Pegan, Andrew³ Pegan II, Andrew² Pagan, James¹*) was born in 1938 in Peru, Peru Precinct, Nemaha Co., Nebraska. She is the daughter of Harry Eugene Gilmore (206) and Dorothy Marie Groff.

392. **Infant Son⁹ Gilmore** (*Harry Eugene⁸, Harry Otis⁷, Martha Jane⁶ Vanausdoll, Caleb⁵, Mary⁴ Pegan, Andrew³ Pegan II, Andrew² Pagan, James¹*) was born in 1941 in Peru, Peru Precinct, Nemaha Co., Nebraska. He was the son of Harry Eugene Gilmore (206) and Dorothy Marie Groff. Infant Son died in Peru, Peru Precinct, Nemaha Co., Nebraska, in 1941. He was buried in London Cemetery, Peru, Peru Precinct, Nemaha Co., Nebraska.[66]

**393. Garland Eugene⁹ Gilmore** (*Harry Eugene⁸, Harry Otis⁷, Martha Jane⁶ Vanausdoll, Caleb⁵, Mary⁴ Pegan, Andrew³ Pegan II, Andrew² Pagan, James¹*) was born on August 18, 1942, in Hamburg, Washington Twp., Fremont Co., Iowa. He was the son of Harry Eugene Gilmore (206) and Dorothy Marie Groff. Garland Eugene lived in 2014 in Anchorage, Anchorage Co., Alaska. He died in Anchorage, Anchorage Co., Alaska, on June 10, 2015, at age 72. Garland Eugene was buried in Green Hill Cemetery, Rock Port, Clay Twp., Atchison Co., Missouri.[124]

Garland Eugene married **Ms. Bartles**. They divorced. They had two children.

**394. Charles Junior⁹ Gilmore II** (*Harry Eugene⁸, Harry Otis⁷, Martha Jane⁶ Vanausdoll, Caleb⁵, Mary⁴ Pegan, Andrew³ Pegan II, Andrew² Pagan, James¹*) was born on November 22, 1948, in Peru, Peru Precinct, Nemaha Co., Nebraska. He was the son of Harry Eugene Gilmore (206) and Dorothy Marie Groff. Charles Junior lived in 2011 in Rock Port, Clay Twp., Atchison Co., Missouri. He died in a hospital in Omaha, Douglas Co., Nebraska, on March 12, 2011, at age 62. Charles Junior was buried in Green Hill Cemetery, Rock Port, Clay Twp., Atchison Co., Missouri.[124]

Charles Junior married **Ms. Squires.**

**395. Linda J.⁹ Gilmore** (*Harry Eugene⁸, Harry Otis⁷, Martha Jane⁶ Vanausdoll, Caleb⁵, Mary⁴ Pegan, Andrew³ Pegan II, Andrew² Pagan, James¹*) was born on December 23, 1949, in Pawnee City, Pawnee City Twp., Pawnee Co., Nebraska. She was the daughter of Harry Eugene Gilmore (206) and Dorothy Marie Groff. Linda J. died in Rock Port, Clay Twp., Atchison Co., Missouri, on November 2, 2012, at age 62. She was buried in Green Hill Cemetery, Rock Port, Clay Twp., Atchison Co., Missouri.[124]

Linda J. Gilmore married **Unknown Jones** in 1967. They divorced. They have two daughters.

Linda J. Gilmore Jones married **Unknown Cooper.**

**396. Sandra Arlene⁹ Gilmore** (*Harry Eugene⁸, Harry Otis⁷, Martha Jane⁶ Vanausdoll, Caleb⁵, Mary⁴*

*Pegan, Andrew³ Pegan II, Andrew² Pagan, James¹*) was born in 1959 in Rock Port, Clay Twp., Atchison Co., Missouri. She was the daughter of Harry Eugene Gilmore (206) and Dorothy Marie Groff. Sandra Arlene died in Anchorage, Anchorage Co., Alaska? in 1970 at age 11. She was buried in London Cemetery, Peru, Peru Precinct, Nemaha Co., Nebraska.[66]

**397. Roger LaVerne⁹ Gilmore** (*Walter Laverne⁸, Harry Otis⁷, Martha Jane⁶ Vanausdoll, Caleb⁵, Mary⁴ Pegan, Andrew³ Pegan II, Andrew² Pagan, James¹*) was born in 1941 in Pawnee City, Pawnee City Twp., Pawnee Co., Nebraska. He was the son of Walter Laverne Gilmore (206) and Ruth Darlene Williams. Roger LaVerne died in Pawnee City, Pawnee City Twp., Pawnee Co., Nebraska, in 1944 at age three. He was buried in Pawnee City Cemetery, Pawnee City, Pawnee Twp., Pawnee Co., Nebraska.[27]

**398. Son⁹ Blair** (*Lois Marie⁸ Perdue, Eva May⁷ Gilmore, Martha Jane⁶ Vanausdoll, Caleb⁵, Mary⁴ Pegan, Andrew³ Pegan II, Andrew² Pagan, James¹*) was born in Miller, Hand Co., South Dakota. He is the son of James Arthur Blair and Lois Marie Perdew (218).

Son Blair married twice. He and his first wife had two daughters.

Son Blair and his first wife had two daughters, including:

+ 485 f I. **Heidi Suzanne¹⁰ Blair** was born in Huron, Beadle Co., South Dakota, on April 3, 1974. Heidi died in a hospital in Sioux Falls, Minnehaha Co., South Daktoa, on October 10, 2001. She was buried in Highmore City Cemetery, Highmore, Hyde Co., South Dakota.[155]

**399. Frank James⁹ Blair** (*Lois Marie⁸ Perdue, Eva May⁷ Gilmore, Martha Jane⁶ Vanausdoll, Caleb⁵, Mary⁴ Pegan, Andrew³ Pegan II, Andrew² Pagan, James¹*) was born in Miller, Hand Co., South Dakota on July 17, 1956. He was the son of James Arthur Blair and Lois Marie Perdew (218). He lived in 2017 in Miller, Hand Co., South Dakota. Frank James died in a hospital in Sioux Falls, Minnehaha Co., South Dakota, on December 15, 2017 at age

51. He was buried in Morningside Cemetery, Ree Heights, Hand Co., South Dakota.[69]

Frank James Blair married, but divorced. He and his wife had one daughter. He adopted his wife's son.

**400. Randall Keith[9] Day II** (*Randall M.*[8], *John William*[7], *Mary Ellen*[6] *Vanausdoll, Caleb*[5], *Mary*[4] *Pegan, Andrew*[3] *Pegan II, Andrew*[2] *Pagan, James*[1]) was born in 1931 in Marmaton Twp., Allen Co., Kansas. He was the son of Randall M. Day (222) and Meda A. Peebles. Randall Keith died in Moran Twp., Allen Co., Kansas, in 1933 at age two. He was buried in Moran Cemetery, Moran Twp., Allen Co., Kansas.[30]

**401. John R.[9] Day** (*Randall M.*[8], *John William*[7], *Mary Ellen*[6] *Vanausdoll, Caleb*[5], *Mary*[4] *Pegan, Andrew*[3] *Pegan II, Andrew*[2] *Pagan, James*[1]) was born in 1937 in Moran Twp., Allen Co., Kansas. He is the son of Randall M. Day (222) and Meda A. Peebles.

**402. Diana Lea[9] Cuppy** (*Olive Marguerite*[8] *Day, John William*[7], *Mary Ellen*[6] *Vanausdoll, Caleb*[5], *Mary*[4] *Pegan, Andrew*[3] *Pegan II, Andrew*[2] *Pagan, James*[1]) was born in 1937 in Moran Twp., Allen Co., Kansas. She is the daughter of Archie Virgil Cuppy II and Olive Marguerite Day (223).

**403. Archie Gary[9] Cuppy III** (*Olive Marguerite*[8] *Day, John William*[7], *Mary Ellen*[6] *Vanausdoll, Caleb*[5], *Mary*[4] *Pegan, Andrew*[3] *Pegan II, Andrew*[2] *Pagan, James*[1]) was born on June 20, 1939, in Moran Twp., Allen Co., Kansas. He was also known as **Gary.** He was the son of Archie Virgil Cuppy II and Olive Marguerite Day (223). Archie Gary died in Moran Twp., Allen Co., Kansas, on October 25, 1989, at age 50. He was buried in Moran Cemetery, Moran Twp., Allen Co., Kansas.[30]

Archie's death date on Social Security Death Index is October 15, 1989, but the death date on his tombstone is October 25, 1989.

**404. Larry Gale[9] Day** (*Lawrence Gerald*[8], *Charles Albert*[7], *Mary Ellen*[6] *Vanausdoll, Caleb*[5], *Mary*[4] *Pegan, Andrew*[3] *Pegan II, Andrew*[2] *Pagan, James*[1]) was born on May 23, 1938, in Highland, Iowa Twp., Doniphan Co., Kansas. He was the son of Lawrence Gerald Day (227) and Opal Mae Davis. Larry Gale died in Dallas, Dallas Co., Texas, on

April 28, 1997, at age 58. He was buried in Table Rock Cemetery, Table Rock Twp., Pawnee Co., Nebraska.[12]

**405. Patricia Ann[9] Day** (*Lawrence Gerald*[8], *Charles Albert*[7], *Mary Ellen*[6] *Vanausdoll, Caleb*[5], *Mary*[4] *Pegan, Andrew*[3] *Pegan II, Andrew*[2] *Pagan, James*[1]) was born on October 18, 1942, in Wichita, Sedgwick Co., Kansas. She was the daughter of Lawrence Gerald Day (227) and Opal Mae Davis. Patricia Ann died in Joplin, Joplin Twp., Jasper Co., Missouri, on July 12, 1986, at age 43. She was buried in Lakeview Cemetery, Erie, Erie Twp., Neosho Co., Kansas.[128]

Patricia Ann married **Unknown Nicholas** in 1961. They divorced. They had one daughter.

Patricia Ann Day married **Unknown Winans** in 1969. They hadtwo children.

**406. Yvonne Ailene[9] Allen** (*Gladys Mae*[8] *Spaulding, Cora May Agnes*[7] *Day, Mary Ellen*[6] *Vanausdoll, Caleb*[5], *Mary*[4] *Pegan, Andrew*[3] *Pegan II, Andrew*[2] *Pagan, James*[1]) was born on April 13, 1924, in Dawson, Grant Twp., Richardson Co., Nebraska. She was also known as **Bonnie.** She was the daughter of Virgil Leroy Allen and Gladys Mae Spaulding (228). Yvonne Ailene died in Brush Prairie, Clark Co., Washington, on February 23, 1986, at age 61. She was buried in Camas Cemetery, Camas, Clark Co., Washington.[129]

She married **Max Eugene Crawford.** They had one son. Max Eugene Crawford was born in Burr Oak, Jewell Co., Kansas, on May 3, 1922. Max Eugene reached age 66 and died in Portland, Multnomah Co., Oregon, on October 20, 1988. He was buried in Camas Cemetery, Camas, Clark Co., Washington.[129]

Yvonne Ailene Allen and Max Eugene Crawford had one son:

+ 486 m I. **Roger Allen[10] Crawford** was born in Humboldt, Humboldt Twp., Richardson Co., Nebraska, on December 1, 1942. He died in Vancouver, Clark Co., Washington, on October 12, 2010. Roger Allen was buried in Evergreen Memorial Gardens Cemetery, Vancouver, Clark Co., Washington.[156]

**407. Carol Eldon⁹ Allen** (*Gladys Mae⁸ Spaulding, Cora May Agnes⁷ Day, Mary Ellen⁶ Vanausdoll, Caleb⁵, Mary⁴ Pegan, Andrew³ Pegan II, Andrew² Pagan, James¹*) was born on December 18, 1925, in Dawson, Grant Twp., Richardson Co., Nebraska. He was the son of Virgil Leroy Allen and Gladys Mae Spaulding (228). Carol Eldon died in Portland, Multnomah Co., Oregon, on August 9, 1995, at age 69.

Carol Eldon married **Maria Joanne Coupe** in 1952. Maria Joanne Coupe was born in Portland, Multnomah Co., Oregon, on November 20, 1932. She was also known as **Joanne.** Maria Joanne reached age 69 and died in Vancouver, Clark Co., Washington, on March 10, 2002.

**408. Harry Gordon⁹ Fencil II** (*Gladys Mae⁸ Spaulding, Cora May Agnes⁷ Day, Mary Ellen⁶ Vanausdoll, Caleb⁵, Mary⁴ Pegan, Andrew³ Pegan II, Andrew² Pagan, James¹*) was born on March 26, 1931 in Humboldt, Humboldt Twp., Richardson Co., Nebraska. He is the son of Harry Gordon Fencil and Gladys Mae Spaulding (228). He is also known as **Gordon** or **Corky**. He died on March 12, 2018 in Ridgefield, Clark Co., Washington at age 86.

Harry Gordon Fencil II married Mrs. **Marion Breen** Peterson in 1963. They had one son.

**409. Delverna Corrine⁹ Fencil** (*Gladys Mae⁸ Spaulding, Cora May Agnes⁷ Day, Mary Ellen⁶ Vanausdoll, Caleb⁵, Mary⁴ Pegan, Andrew³ Pegan II, Andrew² Pagan, James¹*) was born on August 10, 1933 in Humboldt, Humboldt Twp., Richardson Co., Nebraska. She was the daughter of Harry Gordon Fencil and Gladys Mae Spaulding (228) and was a twin to DeLauris. Delverna Corrine died in La Center, Clark Co., Washington, on June 30, 2018, at age 84.

Delverna Corrine married **Dean D. Swanson** on March 21, 1953 in Clark Co., Washington. They had eight children. Dean Swanson was born in Rice Lake, Barron Co., Wisconsin on February 6, 1934.

Delverna Corrine Fencil and Dean D. Swanson had eight children, including:

+ 486A m I. **Infant Son¹⁰ Swanson** was born in Oregon on February 22, 1973. He died in Oregon on February 22, 1973. He is buried in Park Hill Cemetery, Vancouver, Clark Co., Washington.[56]

**410. DeLauris C.⁹ Fencil** (*Gladys Mae⁸ Spaulding, Cora May Agnes⁷ Day, Mary Ellen⁶ Vanausdoll, Caleb⁵, Mary⁴ Pegan, Andrew³ Pegan II, Andrew² Pagan, James¹*) was born on August 10, 1933 in Humboldt, Humboldt Twp., Richardson Co., Nebraska. She is the daughter of Harry Gordon Fencil and Gladys Mae Spaulding (228), and was a twin to Delverna.

DeLauris C. married **Paul Jerry Fankhauser.** They may have divorced. Paul J. Fankhauser was born about March 1930 in Humboldt Twp., Richardson Co., Nebraska. He is also known as **Jerry.**

**411. Mary Ellyn⁹ Fencil** (*Gladys Mae⁸ Spaulding, Cora May Agnes⁷ Day, Mary Ellen⁶ Vanausdoll, Caleb⁵, Mary⁴ Pegan, Andrew³ Pegan II, Andrew² Pagan, James¹*) was born on February 21, 1937, in Humboldt, Humboldt Twp., Richardson Co., Nebraska. She was the daughter of Harry Gordon Fencil and Gladys Mae Spaulding (228). Mary Ellyn died in a hospital in Lincoln, Lancaster Co., Nebraska, on April 29, 2010, at age 73. She was buried in Pleasant View Cemetery, Auburn, Douglas Twp., Nemaha Co., Nebraska.[130]

Mary Ellyn married **Claude Erisman II** on March 3, 1957, in Richardson Co., Nebraska. They had three daughters. Claude Erisman II was born on April 22, 1935, in Douglas Twp., Nemaha Co., Nebraska? He is also known as **Junior.**

**412. Ronald Raymond⁹ Spaulding** (*John Raymond⁸, Cora May Agnes⁷ Day, Mary Ellen⁶ Vanausdoll, Caleb⁵, Mary⁴ Pegan, Andrew³ Pegan II, Andrew² Pagan, James¹*) was born on March 31, 1927, in Liberty Twp., Richardson Co., Nebraska. He was the son of John Raymond Spaulding II (229) and Ethel May Dougherty. Ronald Raymond died in

Lincoln, Lancaster Co., Nebraska, on January 12, 1988, at age 70. He was buried in Heim Cemetery, Dawson, Grant Twp., Richardson Co., Nebraska.[31]

He married **Phyllis Anita Heim** on January 29, 1950. They had four children. Phyllis Anita Heim was born in Dawson, Grant Twp., Richardson Co., Nebraska, on June 1, 1931. Phyllis Anita reached age 67 and died in Lincoln, Lancaster Co., Nebraska, on February 9, 1999.

**413. Donald Robert⁹ Spaulding** (*John Raymond⁸, Cora May Agnes⁷ Day, Mary Ellen⁶ Vanausdoll, Caleb⁵, Mary⁴ Pegan, Andrew³ Pegan II, Andrew² Pagan, James¹*) was born on April 23, 1929, in Liberty Twp., Richardson Co., Nebraska. He was the son of John Raymond Spaulding II (229) and Ethel May Dougherty. Donald Robert lived in Northville, Oakland Co., Michigan. He died in Goldendale, Klickitat Co., Washington, on October 28, 2013, at age 84. Donald Robert Spaulding was married twice and had eight children.

Donald Robert married **Jacqueline Ann Harrison** on August 25, 1948, in Richardson Co., Nebraska. They had eight children. Jacqueline Ann Harrison was born in Falls City, Falls City Twp., Richardson Co., Nebraska, on November 24, 1930.

Donald Robert Spaulding and Jacqueline Ann Harrison had eight children, including:

+ 487 m I. **Thomas Michael¹⁰ Spaulding** was born in Sacramento, Sacramento Co., California, on January 3, 1949. He died in Sacramento, Sacramento Co., California, on January 4, 1949.

+ 488 m VIII. **Marc¹⁰ Spaulding** was born in Lincoln, Lancaster Co., Nebraska, on December 21, 1964. He died in Goldendale, Klickitat Co., Washington, on October 9, 1994.

**414. Dale Elton⁹ Spaulding** (*John Raymond⁸, Cora May Agnes⁷ Day, Mary Ellen⁶ Vanausdoll, Caleb⁵, Mary⁴ Pegan, Andrew³ Pegan II, Andrew² Pagan, James¹*) was born on August 27, 1934, in Liberty Twp.,

Richardson Co., Nebraska. He was also known as **Spook.** He was the son of John Raymond Spaulding II (229) and Ethel May Dougherty. Dale E. died in Lincoln, Lancaster Co., Nebraska, on January 3, 2012, at age 77. He was buried in Lincoln Memorial Park Cemetery, Lincoln, Lancaster Co., Nebraska.[131]

Dale E. married **Shirley Jane Pettit** on July 29, 1955, in Richardson Co., Nebraska. They have four children. Shirley Jane Pettit was born in Humboldt, Humboldt Twp., Richardson Co., Nebraska, on November 1, 1935.

**415. Lyle Raymond⁹ Brown II** (*Thelma Ellen⁸ Spaulding, Cora May Agnes⁷ Day, Mary Ellen⁶ Vanausdoll, Caleb⁵, Mary⁴ Pegan, Andrew³ Pegan II, Andrew² Pagan, James¹*) was born on July 28, 1926, in Humboldt, Humboldt Twp., Richardson Co., Nebraska. He was the son of Lyle William Brown and Thelma Ellen Spaulding (230).

**416. Mary Lou⁹ Brown?** (*Thelma Ellen⁸ Spaulding, Cora May Agnes⁷ Day, Mary Ellen⁶ Vanausdoll, Caleb⁵, Mary⁴ Pegan, Andrew³ Pegan II, Andrew² Pagan, James¹*) was born on June 7, 1935, in Humboldt, Humboldt Twp., Richardson Co., Nebraska. She is the daughter of Lyle William Brown and Thelma Ellen Spaulding (230).

**417. Larry J.⁹ Brod** (*Ruth Anna⁸ Spaulding, Cora May Agnes⁷ Day, Mary Ellen⁶ Vanausdoll, Caleb⁵, Mary⁴ Pegan, Andrew³ Pegan II, Andrew² Pagan, James¹*) was born in 1933 in Goff, Harrison Twp., Nemaha Co., Nebraska. He was the son of Lawrence Brod and Ruth Anna Spaulding (231). Larry J. died in Goff, Harrison Twp., Nemaha Co., Nebraska, in 1933. He was buried in Heim Cemetery, Dawson, Grant Twp., Richardson Co., Nebraska.[31]

**418. Edith May⁹ Spaulding** (*Garl Vernon⁸, Cora May Agnes⁷ Day, Mary Ellen⁶ Vanausdoll, Caleb⁵, Mary⁴ Pegan, Andrew³ Pegan II, Andrew² Pagan, James¹*) was born on June 2, 1932, in Falls City Twp., Richardson Co., Nebraska. She was the daughter of Garl Vernon Spaulding (232) and Fernande Ada Belle Godfernon. Edith May died in Murrieta, Riverside Co., California, on July 28, 2004, at age 72. She was buried in Riverside National Cemetery, Riverside, Riverside Co., California.[67]

Edith May married **Unknown House** in 1951. They divorced?

Edith May Spaulding House married **John Calcagno i**n 1952. John Calcagno was born in Pittsburgh, Allegheny Co., Pennsylvania, on December 5, 1925. John reached age 81 and died in Murrieta, Riverside Co., California, on November 2, 2007. He was buried in Riverside National Cemetery, Riverside, Riverside Co., California.[67]

**419. Garl E.**[9] **Spaulding II** (*Garl Vernon*[8], *Cora May Agnes*[7] *Day, Mary Ellen*[6] *Vanausdoll, Caleb*[5], *Mary*[4] *Pegan, Andrew*[3] *Pegan II, Andrew*[2] *Pagan, James*[1]) was born on September 10, 1933, in Falls City Twp., Richardson Co., Nebraska. He was also known as **Bud.** He is the son of Garl Vernon Spaulding (232) and Fernande Ada Belle Godfernon.

Garl E. II married **Geraldine Louise Giddens** on August 3, 1959 in King Co., Washington. They divorced. They had two children. Geraldine Louise Giddens was born in Bremerton, Kitsap Co., Washington, on September 19, 1936. She reached age 50 and died in Long Beach, Los Angeles Co., California, on April 15, 2010.

Geraldine remarried and died as Geraldine Fritts.

Garl E. married **Ms. McKay or McGinnis.**

Gale E. Spaulding II and Geraldine Louise Giddens had two children, including:

+ 489 m I.      **DeWayne Richard Garl**[10] **Spaulding** was born in San Diego, San Diego Co., California, on August 1, 1961. He died in Bellflower, Los Angeles Co., California, on March 12, 1969. He was also known as **Ricky**. He was buried in Forest Lawn Memorial Park Cemetery, Cypress, Orange Co., California.[G]

**420. Ruth A.**[9] **Spaulding** (*Garl Vernon*[8], *Cora May Agnes*[7] *Day, Mary Ellen*[6] *Vanausdoll, Caleb*[5], *Mary*[4] *Pegan, Andrew*[3] *Pegan II, Andrew*[2] *Pagan, James*[1]) was born on April 26, 1938, in Walnut Twp., Brown Co., Kansas. She is the daughter of Garl Vernon Spaulding (232) and Fernande Ada Belle Godfernon.

Ruth A. married **John Wilson Rumery.** They had five sons. John Wilson Rumery was born in Memphis, Shelby Co., Tennessee, on September 23, 1933. John Wilson reached age 67 and died in Gardena, Los Angeles Co., California, on June 5, 2001.

John Wilson Rumery and Ruth A. Spaulding had five children, including:

+ 490 m III.    **Son One**[10] **Rumery.**

+ 491 m IV.    **Son Two**[10] **Rumery**

**421. Roberta**[9] **Spaulding** (*Garl Vernon*[8], *Cora May Agnes*[7] *Day, Mary Ellen*[6] *Vanausdoll, Caleb*[5], *Mary*[4] *Pegan, Andrew*[3] *Pegan II, Andrew*[2] *Pagan, James*[1]) was born on January 22, 1940, in Walnut Twp., Brown Co., Kansas. She is the daughter of Garl Vernon Spaulding (232) and Fernande Ada Belle Godfernon.

**422. Janet Kay**[9] **Spaulding** (*Harold Woodrow*[8], *Cora May Agnes*[7] *Day, Mary Ellen*[6] *Vanausdoll, Caleb*[5], *Mary*[4] *Pegan, Andrew*[3] *Pegan II, Andrew*[2] *Pagan, James*[1]) was born on August 3, 1938, in Corning, Illinois Twp., Nemaha Co., Kansas. She was the daughter of Harold Woodrow Spaulding (234) and Jimmie Garnet McCulley. Janet Kay lived in 2003 in Hiawatha, Hiawatha Twp., Brown Co., Kansas. She died in Auburn, Douglas Twp., Nemaha Co., Nebraska, on May 8, 2015, at age 76.

Janet Kay married **Robert Dean Goodwin** on November 17, 1957. They had four children. Robert Dean Goodwin was born in Elmo, Lincoln Twp., Nodaway Co., Missouri, on March 21, 1933. Robert Dean reached age 71 and died in Hiawatha, Hiawatha Twp., Brown Co., Kansas, on June 21, 2004.

**423. Brenda Lee**[9] **Spaulding** (*Harold Woodrow*[8], *Cora May Agnes*[7] *Day, Mary Ellen*[6] *Vanausdoll, Caleb*[5], *Mary*[4] *Pegan, Andrew*[3] *Pegan II, Andrew*[2] *Pagan, James*[1]) was born on January 13, 1940, in Corning, Illinois Twp., Nemaha Co., Kansas. She is the daughter of Harold Woodrow Spaulding (234) and Jimmie Garnet McCulley.

**424. Patricia Lynne⁹ Spaulding** (*Harold Woodrow⁸, Cora May Agnes⁷ Day, Mary Ellen⁶ Vanausdoll, Caleb⁵, Mary⁴ Pegan, Andrew³ Pegan II, Andrew² Pagan, James¹*) was born on July 19, 1942, in Corning, Illinois Twp., Nemaha Co., Kansas. She was the daughter of Harold Woodrow Spaulding (234) and Jimmie Garnet McCulley. Patricia Lynne lived in 2003 in St. Joseph, Buchanan Co., Missouri. She died in St. Joseph, Buchanan Co., Missouri, on December 14, 2012, at age 70.

Patricia Lynne married **Mr. Quackenbush** in 1964. They had two children.

**425. Constance Dee⁹ Spaulding** (*Harold Woodrow⁸, Cora May Agnes⁷ Day, Mary Ellen⁶ Vanausdoll, Caleb⁵, Mary⁴ Pegan, Andrew³ Pegan II, Andrew² Pagan, James¹*) was born on June 29, 1946, in Sabetha, Creek Twp., Nemaha Co., Kansas. She was the daughter of Harold Woodrow Spaulding (234) and Jimmie Garnet McCulley. Constance Dee died in Hiawatha, Hiawatha Twp., Brown Co., Kansas, on July 16, 2003, at age 57. She was buried in Floral Hills Cemetery, Kansas City, Jackson Co., Missouri.[73]

Never married.

**425A. Tommy Glen⁹ Day** (*Howard Glen⁸, Anthony Juduthan⁷, Mary Ellen⁶ Vanausdoll, Caleb⁵, Mary⁴ Pegan, Andrew³ Pegan II, Andrew² Pagan, James¹*) was born on January 1, 1948, in Yakima, Yakima Co., Washington. He was the son of Howard Glen Day (237) and Minnie L. Weippert. Tommy Glen died in Moxee City, Yakima Co., Washington, on February 10, 2012.

Tommy Glen married **Unknown Unknown.** They divorced. They had three daughters.

**426. Jacqueline J.⁹ Day** (*Lowrain Arthur⁸, Anthony Juduthan⁷, Mary Ellen⁶ Vanausdoll, Caleb⁵, Mary⁴ Pegan, Andrew³ Pegan II, Andrew² Pagan, James¹*) was born on February 4, 1936, in Pawnee City, Pawnee City Twp., Pawnee Co., Nebraska. She was the daughter of Lowrain Arthur Day (238) and Helen Judice Madden. Jacqueline J. lived in 1973 in Chehalis, Lewis Co., Washington. She died in a hospital in Olympia, Thurston Co., Washington, on September 23, 1973, at age 37.

Jacqueline J. was buried in Claquato Cemetery, Chehalis, Lewis Co., Washington.[162]

Stanley Alfred Collier* and Jacqueline J. Day had four children, including:

+ 492 m I. **Robert J.¹⁰ Collier** was born in Portland, Multnomah Co., Oregon, on June 8, 1954. He died in Napavine, Lewis Co, Washington, on February 18, 2014.

+ 493 f II. **Cheryl J.¹⁰ Collier** was born in Ethel. Lewis Co., Washington, on March 4, 1963. She died in Napavine, Lewis Co, Washington, on February 18, 2014.

**427. Linda Lorraine⁹ Day** (*Lowrain Arthur⁸, Anthony Juduthan⁷, Mary Ellen⁶ Vanausdoll, Caleb⁵, Mary⁴ Pegan, Andrew³ Pegan II, Andrew² Pagan, James¹*) was born on September 11, 1943, in Wapato, Yakima Co., Washington. She was also known as **Blondie.** She was the daughter of Lowrain Arthur Day (238) and Helen Judice Madden. Linda Lorraine died in Yakima, Yakima Co., Washington, on October 25, 2015, at age 72.

She married **Mr. Ashbaugh.** They have three sons.

**428. Son⁹ Day** (*Lowrain Arthur⁸, Anthony Juduthan⁷, Mary Ellen⁶ Vanausdoll, Caleb⁵, Mary⁴ Pegan, Andrew³ Pegan II, Andrew² Pagan, James¹*) was born on August 18, 1948. He is the son of Lowrain Arthur Day (238) and Helen Judice Madden.

He married **Unknown Unknown.** They had at least one daughter.

Daughter of Son Day and his wife:

+ 494 f I. **Tammy D.¹⁰ Day** was born in Olympia, Thurston Co., Washington? about August 18, 1973. She died in a hospital in Chehalis, Lewis Co., Washington, on August 18, 1973. Tammy D. was buried in Claquato Cemetery, Chehalis, Lewis Co., Washington.[161]

**429. Darrell D.⁹ Day** (*Lowrain Arthur⁸, Anthony Juduthan⁷, Mary Ellen⁶ Vanausdoll, Caleb⁵, Mary⁴*

He married Susan K. Unknown. They had one son.

*Pegan, Andrew³ Pegan II, Andrew² Pagan, James¹*) was born on June 13, 1950, in Wapato, Yakima Co., Washington. He was the son of Lowrain Arthur Day (238) and Helen Judice Madden. Darrell D. lived in 2009 in Hoquiam, Grays Harbor Co., Washington. He also resided in 2009 in Chehalis, Lewis Co., Washington. Darrell D. died in a hospital in Seattle, King Co., Washington, on December 31, 2009, at age 59. He was buried in Silvercreek Cemetery, Randle, Lewis Co., Washington.[135]

He married **Susan K. Unknown.** They had one son.

430. **Garry Lee⁹ Day** (*Lowrain Arthur⁸, Anthony Juduthan⁷, Mary Ellen⁶ Vanausdoll, Caleb⁵, Mary⁴ Pegan, Andrew³ Pegan II, Andrew² Pagan, James¹*) was born on January 30, 1953, in Wapato, Yakima Co., Washington. He was the son of Lowrain Arthur Day (238) and Helen Judice Madden. Garry Lee died in Yakima, Yakima Co., Washington, on January 27, 1980, at age 26. He was buried in Mabton Cemetery, Mabton, Yakima Co., Washington.[136]

Garry Lee married **Ms. O'Connor** on September 30, 1967, in Chelen Co., Washington.

431. **Richard Eugene⁹ Kenner** (*Zelma Leota⁸ Phillips, Ruth Clara⁷ Day, Mary Ellen⁶ Vanausdoll, Caleb⁵, Mary⁴ Pegan, Andrew³ Pegan II, Andrew² Pagan, James¹*) was born on August 10, 1936, in Table Rock, Table Rock Twp., Pawnee Co., Nebraska. He was the son of Dixon Earl Kenner and Zelma Leota Phillips (242). Richard Eugene died in Medford, Jackson Co., Oregon, on June 11, 1980, at age 43. He was buried in Hillcrest Memorial Park Cemetery, Medford, Jackson Co., Oregon.[75]

Richard Eugene married **Misuko Unknown** before 1959 in Japan. They had three children. Misuko Unknown was born in Japan on February 3, 1934. Misuko reached age 81 and died in Sandy, Clackamas Co., Oregon, on November 26, 2015. She was buried in Cliffside Cemetery, Sandy, Clackamas Co., Oregon.[157]

432. **Shirley Ruth⁹ Kenner** (*Zelma Leota⁸ Phillips, Ruth Clara⁷ Day, Mary Ellen⁶ Vanausdoll, Caleb⁵, Mary⁴ Pegan, Andrew³ Pegan II, Andrew² Pagan, James¹*) was born on December 4, 1938, in Table Rock,

Table Rock Twp., Pawnee Co., Nebraska. She was the daughter of Dixon Earl Kenner and Zelma Leota Phillips (242). Shirley Ruth died in Medford, Jackson Co., Oregon, on September 9, 1997, at age 58. She was buried in Eagle Point National Cemetery, Eagle Point, Jackson Co., Oregon.[137]

Shirley Ruth married **Larry Dean McNealy** on February 14, 1957. They had two sons. Larry Dean McNealy was born in Medford, Jackson Co., Oregon? on April 27, 1936. Larry Dean reached age 71 and died in Medford, Jackson Co., Oregon, on May 17, 2007. He was buried in Eagle Point National Cemetery, Eagle Point, Jackson Co., Oregon.[137]

433. **Beverly⁹ Bowman** (*Zethel Irene⁸ Phillips, Ruth Clara⁷ Day, Mary Ellen⁶ Vanausdoll, Caleb⁵, Mary⁴ Pegan, Andrew³ Pegan II, Andrew² Pagan, James¹*) was born in 1936 in Table Rock Twp., Pawnee Co., Nebraska. She is the daughter of Robert Frederick Bowman and Zethel Irene Phillips (243).

434. **Robert⁹ Bowman II** (*Zethel Irene⁸ Phillips, Ruth Clara⁷ Day, Mary Ellen⁶ Vanausdoll, Caleb⁵, Mary⁴ Pegan, Andrew³ Pegan II, Andrew² Pagan, James¹*) was born in 1939 in Table Rock Twp., Pawnee Co., Nebraska. He is the daughter of Robert Frederick Bowman and Zethel Irene Phillips (243).

435. **Judy⁹ Bowman** (*Zethel Irene⁸ Phillips, Ruth Clara⁷ Day, Mary Ellen⁶ Vanausdoll, Caleb⁵, Mary⁴ Pegan, Andrew³ Pegan II, Andrew² Pagan, James¹*) was born on March 29, 1941, in Table Rock Twp., Pawnee Co., Nebraska. She was the daughter of Robert Frederick Bowman and Zethel Irene Phillips (243). Judy died in Grand Island, Hall Co., Nebraska, on March 20, 2009, at age 67. She was buried in West Lawn Memorial Cemetery, Grand Island, Hall Co., Nebraska.[138]

Judy married **Mr. Peterson** in 1958. They had two children.

Judy Bowman Peterson married **Mr. Graves** in 1969. They had one son.

Judy Bowman Peterson Graves married **George Edward Arnett** after 1969. George Edward Arnett was born on August 8, 1934, in Phillips, Hamilton Co., Nebraska. He reached age 49 and died on

January 24, 1984, in Grand Island, Hall Co., Nebraska. He was buried in West Lawn Memorial Cemetery, Grand Island, Hall Co., Nebraska.[138]

**436. David Warren⁹ Day** (*Delmar Silas,⁷ James Manahan,⁷ Mary Ellen⁶ Vanausdoll, Caleb⁵, Mary⁴ Pegan, Andrew³ Pegan II, Andrew² Pagan, James¹*) was born on September 21, 1954, in Yakima, Yakima Co., Washigton. He was the son of Delmar Silas Day (253) and Joyce Mifflin Winters. He died on September 10, 1977, in Yakima, Yakima Co., Washington. David Warren is buried in Terrace Heights Memorial Park Cemetery, Yakima, Yakima Co., Washington.[78]

**437. Son⁹ Merwin** (*Dorothy Arlene⁸ James, Jessie Levern⁷ Day, Mary Ellen⁶ Vanausdoll, Caleb⁵, Mary⁴ Pegan, Andrew³ Pegan II, Andrew² Pagan, James¹*) He is the son of Edwin Thomas Merwin and Dorothy Arlene James (254).

He married **Unknown Unknown.** They had at least one daughter.

Daughter of Son Merwin and Unknown Unknown:

+  495  f    I.    **Daughter¹⁰ Merwin.**

**438. Daughter⁹ East** (*Vernon Parker⁸, Ruby Frances⁷ Vanausdoll, William Cornelius⁶, Caleb⁵, Mary⁴ Pegan, Andrew³ Pegan II, Andrew² Pagan, James¹*). She is the daughter of Vernon Parker East (258) and Rosalie M. Narup.

Daughter East married **Robert Joseph Russell** on September 3, 1961, in Morgan Co., Illinois. They had one daughter. Robert Joseph Russell was born in Otterville, Otter Creek Twp., Jersey Co., Illinois, on June 18, 1937. Robert Joseph lived in 1997 in Jerseyville, Jersey Twp., Jersey Co., Illinois. He reached age 59 and died in a hospital in St. Louis, Missouri, on May 22, 1997. Robert Joseph was buried in Oak Grove Cemetery, Jerseyville, Jersey Twp., Jersey Co., Illinois.[16]

**439. William Randall⁹ East** (*William Eldon⁸, Ruby Frances⁷ Vanausdoll, William Cornelius⁶, Caleb⁵, Mary⁴ Pegan, Andrew³ Pegan II, Andrew² Pagan, James¹*) was born in August 1949 in Fieldon, Richwoods Twp., Jersey Co., Illinois? He was also known as **Randy.** He was the son of William Eldon East (259) and Dorothy A. Harting. William Randall died in Fieldon, Richwoods Twp., Jersey Co., Illinois? about April 27, 1951 at age one. He was buried in Saint Mary's Cemetery, Fieldon, Richwoods Twp., Jersey Co., Illinois.[81]

**440. Son⁹ East** (*William Eldon⁸, Ruby Frances⁷ Vanausdoll, William Cornelius⁶, Caleb⁵, Mary⁴ Pegan, Andrew³ Pegan II, Andrew² Pagan, James¹*) He is the son of William Eldon East (259) and Dorothy A. Harting. Son East married **Patricia Unknown.** They had at least one daughter.

Daughter of Son East and Patricia Unknown:

+  496  f    I.    **Daughter¹⁰ East.**

**441. Terry Lee⁹ Halbach** (*Marcella June⁸ Clayton, Addie Rachel⁷ Vanausdoll, William Cornelius⁶, Caleb⁵, Mary⁴ Pegan, Andrew³ Pegan II, Andrew² Pagan, James¹*) was born on January 28, 1950, in Wood River, Wood River Twp., Madison Co., Illinois. He was the son of Archibald Michael Halbach II and Marcella June Clayton (263). Terry Lee lived in 1995 in Attica, Ruella Twp., Harper Co., Kansas. He died in a hospital in Wichita, Sedgwick Co., Kansas, on February 4, 1995, at age 45. Terry Lee was buried in Attica Cemetery, Attica, Ruella Twp., Harper Co., Kansas.[143]

Terry Lee Halbach married **Unknown Unknown.** They divorced. They had two children.

Terry Lee married **Belinda Unknown.**

**442. Lorraine⁹ Van Ausdale** (*Chester Heath⁸, Otis Lafayette⁷ Vanausdoll, Charles Wesley⁶, Caleb⁵, Mary⁴ Pegan, Andrew³ Pegan II, Andrew² Pagan, James¹*) was born in 1927 in St. Louis, Missouri. She was the daughter of Chester Heath Van Ausdale (264) and Edna G. Rupke or Rupkey. Lorraine died between 1940 and 1954.

**443. Edna⁹ Van Ausdale** (*Chester Heath⁸, Otis Lafayette⁷ Vanausdoll, Charles Wesley⁶, Caleb⁵, Mary⁴ Pegan, Andrew³ Pegan II, Andrew² Pagan, James¹*) was born in 1929 in St. Louis, Missouri. She was the daughter of Chester Heath Van Ausdale (264) and Edna G. Rupke or Rupkey. Edna lived in 1954 in Kansas City, Jackson Co., Missouri. She died after 1954.

Edna Van Ausdale married **Unknown Scott** before 1954. They divorced.

Edna Van Ausdale Scott married **Unknown Fritico**.

444. **Chester[9] Van Ausdale II** (*Chester Heath[8], Otis Lafayette[7] Vanausdoll, Charles Wesley[6], Caleb[5], Mary[4] Pegan, Andrew[3] Pegan II, Andrew[2] Pagan, James[1]*) was born on August 11, 1930, in St. Louis, Missouri. He was the son of Chester Heath Van Ausdale (264) and Edna G. Rupke or Rupkey. Chester lived in 1934 in Golden, Jefferson Co., Colorado. He died in a hospital in Salina, Saline Co., Kansas, on July 14, 1954, at age 23. Chester was buried in Scenic Hill/Odd Fellows Cemetery, Quarry Twp., Jersey Co., Illinois.[14]

Chester married **Ms. Roff** before 1954.

445. **Pamela Sue[9] Van Ausdale** (*Jack Warren Kerrigan[8], Otis Lafayette[7] Vanausdoll, Charles Wesley[6], Caleb[5], Mary[4] Pegan, Andrew[3] Pegan II, Andrew[2] Pagan, James[1]*) was born on January 17, 1948, in St. Louis, Missouri? She was the daughter of Jack Warren Kerrigan Van Ausdale (266) and Hazel Leona Tyler. Pamela Sue died in Carson, Los Angeles Co., California, on January 22, 2005, at age 57. She was buried in Scenic Hill/Odd Fellows Cemetery, Quarry Twp., Jersey Co., Illinois.[14]

Never married.

446. **Olney Freeman[9] Hayes** (*Ila Marie[8] Vanausdoll, Otis Lafayette[7], Charles Wesley[6], Caleb[5], Mary[4] Pegan, Andrew[3] Pegan II, Andrew[2] Pagan, James[1]*) was born on April 1, 1938, in Grafton, Quarry Twp., Jersey Co., Illinois. He was the son of Freeman Hallie Hayes and Ila Marie Vanausdoll (267). Olney Freeman died in Grafton, Quarry Twp., Jersey Co., Illinois, on April 7, 1938. He was buried in Scenic Hill/Odd Fellows Cemetery, Quarry Twp., Jersey Co., Illinois.[14]

447. **Enid Louise[9] Hayes** (*Ila Marie[8] Vanausdoll, Otis Lafayette[7], Charles Wesley[6], Caleb[5], Mary[4] Pegan, Andrew[3] Pegan II, Andrew[2] Pagan, James[1]*) was born on May 28, 1939, in St. Louis, Missouri. She was also known as **Louise.** She was the daughter of Freeman Hallie Hayes and Ila Marie Vanausdoll (267). Enid Louise died in Grafton, Quarry Twp.,

Jersey Co., Illinois, on January 17, 2005, at age 65. She was buried in Scenic Hill/Odd Fellows Cemetery, Quarry Twp., Jersey Co., Illinois.[14]

Enid Louise married **Edward Joseph Baecht II** on May 3, 1958, in Jersey Co., Illinois. They had six children. Edward Joseph Baecht II was born in Grafton, Quarry Twp., Jersey Co., Illinois, on September 7, 1933. Edward Joseph reached age 64 and died in Grafton, Quarry Twp., Jersey Co., Illinois, on September 24, 1997. He was buried in Scenic Hill/Odd Fellows Cemetery, Quarry Twp., Jersey Co., Illinois.[14, 158]

Enid Louise Hayes and Edward Joseph Baecht II had six children, including:

+ 497 f I. **Lori[10] Baecht** was born in Grafton, Quarry Twp., Jersey Co., Illinois, in 1960. She died in Grafton, Quarry Twp., Jersey Co., Illinois, on October 28, 2011. Lori was buried in Scenic Hill/Odd Fellows Cemetery, Quarry Twp., Jersey Co., Illinois.[14]

+ 498 m IV. **Son[10] Baecht.**

448. **Robert Wayne[9] Hayes** (*Ila Marie[8] Vanausdoll, Otis Lafayette[7], Charles Wesley[6], Caleb[5], Mary[4] Pegan, Andrew[3] Pegan II, Andrew[2] Pagan, James[1]*) was born on May 31, 1941, in Grafton, Quarry Twp., Jersey Co., Illinois. He was the son of Freeman Hallie Hayes and Ila Marie Vanausdoll (267). Robert Wayne died in Grafton, Quarry Twp., Jersey Co., Illinois, on August 28, 2009, at age 68.

Robert Wayne married **Ms. Stewart.** They had three sons.

449. **Richard Dennis[9] Van Ausdale** (*Daniel Liberty[8], Otis Lafayette[7] Vanausdoll, Charles Wesley[6], Caleb[5], Mary[4] Pegan, Andrew[3] Pegan II, Andrew[2] Pagan, James[1]*) was born on December 6, 1940, in Grafton, Quarry Twp., Jersey Co., Illinois. He is the son of Daniel Liberty Van Ausdale (268) and Wanda Lee Ozment.

450. **Marc[9] Van Ausdale** (*Daniel Liberty[8], Otis Lafayette[7] Vanausdoll, Charles Wesley[6], Caleb[5], Mary[4] Pegan, Andrew[3] Pegan II, Andrew[2] Pagan, James[1]*) was born on August 19, 1952, in Grafton, Quarry Twp.,

Jersey Co., Illinois. He was the son of Daniel Liberty Van Ausdale (268) and Wanda Lee Ozment. Marc lived in 1983 in Lockport, Lockport Twp., Will Co., Illinois. He died in Joliet, Joliet Twp., Will Co., Illinois, on September 28, 1983, at age 31. Marc was buried in Memphis National Cemetery, Memphis, Shelby Co., Tennessee.[145]

Never married.

451. **Daniel Liberty⁹ Van Ausdale II** (*Daniel Liberty⁸ Van Ausdale, Otis Lafayette⁷ Vanausdoll, Charles Wesley⁶, Caleb⁵, Mary⁴ Pegan, Andrew³ Pegan II, Andrew² Pagan, James¹*) was born on September 10, 1954, in Grafton, Quarry Twp., Jersey Co., Illinois. He was the son of Daniel Liberty Van Ausdale (268) and Wanda Lee Ozment. Daniel Liberty died in Joliet, Joliet Twp., Will Co., Illinois, on January 6, 2013, at age 58.

He married **Donna Owens.** They had four children. Donna Owens was born in Evansville, Vanderburgh Co., Indiana, on January 1, 1954. Donna reached age 59 and died in Joliet, Joliet Twp., Will Co., Illinois, on March 18, 2013.

452. **Raymond J.⁹ Vanausdoll II** (*Otis Raymond⁸, Otis Lafayette⁷, Charles Wesley⁶, Caleb⁵, Mary⁴ Pegan, Andrew³ Pegan II, Andrew² Pagan, James¹*) was born on November 5, 1945, in Grafton, Quarry Twp., Jersey Co., Illinois. He was the son of Otis Raymond Vanausdoll II (269) and Sophie Grace Depasquale. Raymond J. died in San Pedro, Los Angeles Co., California, on April 26, 2007, at age 61.

453. **Jason Hal⁹ Rowling** (*Geraldine Yvonne⁸ Vanausdoll, Otis Lafayette⁷, Charles Wesley⁶, Caleb⁵, Mary⁴ Pegan, Andrew³ Pegan II, Andrew² Pagan, James¹*) was born on April 1, 1975, in Alton, Alton Twp., Madison Co., Illinos. He was the son of Robert Wayne Rowling and Geraldine Yvonne Vanausdoll (270). He died after 1999.

454. **Tim Ryan⁹ Vanausdoll II** (*Tim Ryan⁸, Otis Lafayette⁷, Charles Wesley⁶, Caleb⁵, Mary⁴ Pegan, Andrew³ Pegan II, Andrew² Pagan, James¹*) was born on November 21, 1954, in Grafton, Quarry Twp., Jersey Co., Illinois. He was the son of Tim Ryan Vanausdoll (272) and Ruby C. Harmon. Tim Ryan died in Hartford, Madison Co., Illinois, on December 20, 1993, at age 39.

455A. **Mary Ellen⁹ Vanausdoll** (*Charles A.⁸, Everett Charles⁷, Charles Wesley⁶, Caleb⁵, Mary⁴ Pegan, Andrew³ Pegan II, Andrew² Pagan, James¹*) was born on October 14, 1946, in Jerseyville, Jersey Twp., Jersey Co., Illinois. She was the daughter of Charles A. Vanausdoll (273) and Lura Mourning. She died on October 14, 1946, in Jerseyville, Jersey Twp., Jersey Co., Illinois. Mary Ellen is buried in Oak Grove Cemetery, Jerseyville, Jersey Twp., Jersey Co., Illinois.[16]

455B. **Janet⁹ Vanausdoll** (*Charles A.⁸, Everett Charles⁷, Charles Wesley⁶, Caleb⁵, Mary⁴ Pegan, Andrew³ Pegan II, Andrew² Pagan, James¹*) was born on September 5, 1947, in Jerseyville, Jersey Twp., Jersey Co., Illinois. She was the daughter of Charles A. Vanausdoll (273) and Lura Mourning. Janet died in Jerseyville, Jersey Twp., Jersey Co., Illinois, on June 2, 2000, at age 52. She was buried in Oak Grove Cemetery, Jerseyville, Jersey Twp., Jersey Co., Illinois.[16]

She married **Mr. Wiegand.**

455C. **Son⁹ Vanausdoll** (*Willie Warren⁸, Everett Charles⁷, Charles Wesley⁶, Caleb⁵, Mary⁴ Pegan, Andrew³ Pegan II, Andrew² Pagan, James¹*) He is the son of Willie Warren Vanausdoll (275) and Lila M. Fraley.

Son Vanausdale married **Kathryn Stephens.** They had four children. Kathryn Stephens was born in Gainesville, Hall Co., Georgia, on September 1, 1942. She reached age 76 and died in Clermont, Hall Co., Georgia, on August 2, 2019.

456. **Son One⁹ Vanausdoll** (*Donald Lee⁸, Everett Charles⁷, Charles Wesley⁶, Caleb⁵, Mary⁴ Pegan, Andrew³ Pegan II, Andrew² Pagan, James¹*). He is the son of Donald Lee Vanausdoll (277) and Josephine Joan Arter.

Son Vanausdoll married **Unknown Unknown.** They had four children.

Son Vanausdoll and Unknown Unknown had four children, including.

+ 499 f I. **Kara Lanae¹⁰ Vanausdoll** was born in Jerseyville, Jersey Twp., Jersey

Co., Illinois, on April 19, 1977. She died in a hospital in Florissant, St. Louis Co., Missouri, on July 18, 1989. Kara Lanae was buried in Arthur Cemetery, Arthur, Bourbon Twp., Douglas Co., Illinois.[159]

**457. Son Two**[9] **Vanausdoll** (*Donald Lee*[8], *Everett Charles*[7], *Charles Wesley*[6], *Caleb*[5], *Mary*[4] *Pegan, Andrew*[3] *Pegan II, Andrew*[2] *Pagan, James*[1]). He is the son of Donald Lee Vanausdoll (277) and Josephine Joan Arter.

Son II married **Unknown Unknown.** They had four children.

Son II Vanausdoll and Unknown Unknown had four children, including:

+ 500 m I. **Ryan Martin**[10] **Vanausdoll** was born in Jerseyville, Jersey Twp., Jersey Co., Illinois, on April 17, 1980. He died in Jerseyville, Jersey Twp., Jersey Co., Illinois, on July 20, 1980. Ryan Martin was buried in St. Francis Xavier Cemetery, Jerseyville, Jersey Twp., Jersey Co., Illinois.[85]

+ 501 m II. **Kyle Adam**[10] **Vanausdoll** was born in Jerseyville, Jersey Twp., Jersey Co., Illinois, on May 31, 1983. He died in Jersey Co., Illinois, on September 19, 2010. Kyle Adam was buried in St. Francis Xavier Cemetery, Jerseyville, Jersey Twp., Jersey Co., Illinois.[85]

**458. Daughter**[9] **Vanausdoll** (*Darrel*[8], *Everett Charles*[7], *Charles Wesley*[6], *Caleb*[5], *Mary*[4] *Pegan, Andrew*[3] *Pegan II, Andrew*[2] *Pagan, James*[1]). She is the daughter of Darrell Vanausdoll (278) and Virginia M Boner.

She had a relationship with **George Ronald Patterson.** They had one son. George Ronald Patterson was born in Carbondale, Carbondale Twp., Jackson Co., Illinois, on June 18, 1949. He reached age 63 and died in Herrin, Herrin Twp.,

Williamson Co., Illinois, on December 12, 2012. George Ronald was buried in Oakland Cemetery, Carbondale, Carbondale Twp., Jackson Co., Illinois.[H]

Daughter Vanausdoll had a relationship with **Unknown Pearson.** They had one son.

Daughter Vanausdoll married Mr. Cawthen. They had one daughter.

Son of Daughter Vanausdoll and George Ronald Patterson:

+ 502 m I. **Zachary Paul**[10] **Vanausdoll** was born in Carbondale, Carbondale Twp., Jackson Co., Illinois, on August 8, 1986. He died in a hospital in Anna, Anna Twp., Union Co., Illinois, on August 10, 2003.

**459. Gene Bernard**[9] **Schmidt** (*Marlene Emma*[8], *Everett Charles*[7], *Charles Wesley*[6], *Caleb*[5], *Mary*[4] *Pegan, Andrew Pagan or*[3], *Andrew*[2] *Pagan, James*[1]) was born on May 27, 1962, in Wabasha, Wabasha Co., Minnesota. He was the son of William C. Schmidt and Marlene Emma Vanausdoll (279). Gene Bernard died in Wabasha, Wabasha Co., Minnesota, on February 18, 1979, at age 16. He was buried in Saint Felix Cemetery, Wabasha, Wabasha Co., Minnesota.[147]

**460. Eric Allen**[9] **Patton** (*Allen Marvin*[8], *Arthur M.*[7] *Patton, Cora Alice*[6] *Vanausdoll, Caleb*[5], *Mary*[4] *Pegan, Andrew*[3] *Pegan II, Andrew*[2] *Pagan, James*[1]) was born on August 5, 1963, in Stevensville, Ravalli Co., Montana. He was the son of Allen Marvin Patton (286) and Mary Jo Harrington. Eric Allen died in Stevensville, Ravalli Co., Montana, on September 5, 1963. He was buried in Victor Cemetery, Victor, Ravalli Co., Montana.[35]

**461. Arthur Edward**[9] **Gilbert** (*Dorothy Marie*[8] *Seago, Hallye Maude*[7] *Vanausdoll, Allen M.*[6], *Caleb*[5], *Mary*[4] *Pegan, Andrew*[3] *Pegan II, Andrew*[2] *Pagan, James*[1]) was born on March 17, 1946. He was the son of James Franklin Gilbert and Dorothy Marie Seago (289). He died on March 17, 1946.

**462. Son**[9] **Gilbert** (*Dorothy Marie*[8] *Seago, Hallye Maude*[7] *Vanausdoll, Allen M.*[6], *Caleb*[5], *Mary*[4] *Pegan,*

*Andrew³ Pegan II, Andrew² Pagan, James¹*). He is the son of James Franklin Gilbert and Dorothy Marie Seago (289).

Son Gilbert seems to have married. He and his probable wife had at least one son.

Son of Son Gilbert and probable wife:

+ 503 m I. **Jeremiah¹⁰ Gilbert.** Jeremiah died before 1999.

**463. Daughter One⁹ Gilbert** (*Dorothy Marie⁸ Seago, Hallye Maude⁷ Vanausdoll, Allen M.⁶, Caleb⁵, Mary⁴ Pegan, Andrew Pagan or³, Andrew² Pagan, James¹*). She is the daughter of James Franklin Gilbert and Dorothy Marie Seago (289).

She married **Unknown Moore.** They had at least one son.

Son of Daughter One Gilbert and Unknown Moore:

+ 504 m I. **Son¹⁰ Moore.**

**464. Daughter Two⁹ Gilbert** (*Dorothy Marie⁸ Seago, Hallye Maude⁷ Vanausdoll, Allen M.⁶, Caleb⁵, Mary⁴ Pegan, Andrew Pagan or³, Andrew² Pagan, James¹*). She is the daughter of James Franklin Gilbert and Dorothy Marie Seago (289).

She married **Unknown Lynch.** They had at least one son.

Son of Daughter Two Gilbert and Unknown Lynch:

+ 505 m I. **Delbert¹⁰ Lynch** was born in 1967. He died in St Louis, St. Louis Co., Missouri, on May 24, 1984.

**465. Daughter Three⁹ Gilbert** (*Dorothy Marie⁸ Seago, Hallye Maude⁷ Vanausdoll, Allen M.⁶, Caleb⁵, Mary⁴ Pegan, Andrew Pagan or³, Andrew² Pagan, James¹*). She is the daughter of James Franklin Gilbert and Dorothy Marie Seago (289).

She married **Mr. Keefer.** They had one daughter.

Daughter of Daughter Three Gilbert and Mr. Keefer:

+ 506 f I. **Daughter¹⁰ Keefer.**

**466. Gregg⁹ Kesinger** (*Nordell⁸ Dilling, Lola⁷ Dodson, Rachel Roseanna⁶ Vanausdoll, Allen McCreary⁵, Mary⁴ Pegan, Andrew³ Pegan II, Andrew² Pagan, James¹*) was born on August 8, 1949, in Madison or Kankakee Co., Illinois. He was the son of Wayne Kesinger and Nordell Dilling (305). Gregg died in Alexandria, Fairfax Co., Virginia, on April 27, 2004, at age 54.

**467. Gary David⁹ Stamper** (*Maxine⁸ Edsall, Allen Richard Laverne⁷, Millie Wyond⁶ Vanausdoll, Allen McCreary⁵, Mary⁴ Pegan, Andrew³ Pegan II, Andrew² Pagan, James¹*) was born on July 17, 1943, in Detroit, Wayne Co., Michigan. He was the son of Billie E. Stamper and Maxine Edsall (312). Gary David died in Columbus, Franklin Co., Ohio, on August 10, 1964, at age 21. He was buried in Green Lawn Cemetery, Columbus, Franklin Co., Ohio.[97]

Never married.

**468. Bonnie Margaret⁹ Stamper** (*Maxine⁸ Edsall, Allen Richard Laverne⁷, Millie Wyond⁶ Vanausdoll, Allen McCreary⁵, Mary⁴ Pegan, Andrew³ Pegan II, Andrew² Pagan, James¹*) was born on February 18, 1950, in Crum, Wayne Co., West Virginia. She was the daughter of Billie E. Stamper and Maxine Edsall (312). Bonnie Margaret died in Crum, Wayne Co., West Virginia, on March 2, 1950.

\* (Addition to pg. 662, #426, Jacqueline J. Day: Jacqueline J. Day married **Stanley Alfred Collier.** They had four children. Stanley Alfred Collier was born in Spalding, Nez Perce Co., Idaho, on June 9, 1922. He reached age 82 and died in Yakima, Yakima Co. Washington, on January 8, 2005. Stanley Alfred was buried in Claquato Cemetery, Chehalis, Lewis Co., Washington.)

# 10th Generation

**469. Vickie Cheryl[10] Dennis** (*Charles Rogers[9], Amy Lucille[8] Hamilton, Daniel Lester[7], Sylvester[6], Margaret[5] VanAusdall, Mary[4] Pegan, Andrew[3] Pegan II, Andrew[2] Pagan, James[1]*) was born on June 5, 1955, in Cairo, North Cairo Twp., Alexander Co., Illinois. She was the daughter of Charles Rogers Dennis (319) and Glenda Mae Blackburn. Vickie Cheryl died in Arlington, Carlisle Co., Kentucky, on August 1, 1978, at age 23. She was buried in Berkley Cemetery, Carlisle Co., Kentucky.[87]

Vickie Cheryl Dennis married **Unknown Frizzell.** They had one daughter.

Vickie Cheryl Dennis Frizzell married **Unknown Gibson** in 1976.

**469A. Guy Nickie[10] Moore II** (*Sylvia Ann[9] Dennis, Amy Lucille[8] Hamilton, Daniel Lester[7], Sylvester[6], Margaret[5] VanAusdall, Mary[4] Pegan, Andrew[3] Pegan II, Andrew[2] Pagan, James[1]*) was born in Albuquerque, Bernalillo Co., New Mexico, on May 11, 1958. He was the son of Guy Nickie Moore and Sylvia Ann Dennis (321). Guy Nickie II died in Paducah, McCracken Co., Kentucky, on May 11, 1986, at age 30. He is buried in Barlow Cemetery, Barlow, Ballard Co., Kentucky.[F]

**469B. Dennis Rogers[10] Moore** (*Sylvia Ann[9] Dennis, Amy Lucille[8] Hamilton, Daniel Lester[7], Sylvester[6], Margaret[5] VanAusdall, Mary[4] Pegan, Andrew[3] Pegan II, Andrew[2] Pagan, James[1]*) was born in Cairo, North Cairo Twp., Alexander Co., Illinois, on July 3, 1960. He was the son of Guy Nickie Moore and Sylvia Ann Dennis (321). Dennis Rogers died in Paducah, McCracken Co., Kentucky, on July 23, 2001, at age 41. He is buried in Barlow Cemetery, Barlow, Ballard Co., Kentucky.[F]

**470. Gregory Alan[10] Bieniasz** (*Daughter[9] Johnson, Eva Grace[8], Doris Margaret[7] Hamilton, Sylvester[6], Margaret[5] VanAusdall, Mary[4] Pegan, Andrew[3] Pegan II, Andrew[2] Pagan, James[1]*) was born on January 18, 1964, in Westwood, Los Angeles Co., California. He was the son of Mr. Bieniasz

and Daughter Johnson (324). Gregory Alan died in Santa Monica, Los Angeles Co., California? on July 12, 2003, at age 39.

**471. Lucas Ryan[10] Cornell** (*Daughter[9] Gowan, Barbara Ann[8] Hamilton, Silas Vanculen[7], Sylvester[6], Margaret[5] VanAusdall, Mary[4] Pegan, Andrew[3] Pegan II, Andrew[2] Pagan, James[1]*) was born on August 12, 1980, in Lafayette, Fairfield Twp., Tippecanoe Co., Indiana. He was the son of Mr. Cornell and Living Gowan (330). Lucas Ryan died in West Lafayette, Wabash Twp., Tippecanoe Co., Indiana, on May 27, 2002, at age 21. He was buried in Yorktown Cemetery, Stockwell, Lauramie Twp., Tippecanoe Co., Indiana.[150]

Never married.

**472. Joy Lynn[10] White** (*Robert Lee[9], Charles Otis[8], Walter Otis[7], Mary E.[6] Rogers, Rachel C.[5] VanAusdall, Mary[4] Pegan, Andrew[3] Pegan II, Andrew[2] Pagan, James[1]*) was born on November 15, 1968, in Alton, Alton Twp., Madison Co., Illinois. She was the daughter of Robert Lee White (346) and Glenna J. Claxton. Joy Lynn died in a hospital in St. Louis, Missouri, on November 2, 1988, at age 19. She was buried in Medora Cemetery, Ruyle Twp., Jersey Co., Illinois.[113]

Never married.

**473. Rodney Maurice[10] White** (*Billy Gene[9], Charles Otis[8], Walter Otis[7], Mary E.[6] Rogers, Rachel C.[5] VanAusdall, Mary[4] Pegan, Andrew[3] Pegan II, Andrew[2] Pagan, James[1]*) was born on November 26, 1972, in Jacksonville, Jacksonville Twp., Morgan Co., Illinois. He was the son of Billy Gene White (347) and Judy Maxheimer. Rodney Maurice died in Effingham, Douglas Twp., Effingham Co., Illinois, on April 13, 1998, at age 25. He was buried in Mount Pulaski Cemetery, Mount Pulaski. Mount Pulaski Twp., Logan Co., Illinois.[151]

Never married.

**474. James[10] Osborn** (*Ronald Ellsworth[9], Ruth M.[8] White, Walter Otis[7], Mary E.[6] Rogers, Rachel C.[5] VanAusdall, Mary[4] Pegan, Andrew[3] Pegan II,*

*Andrew[2] Pagan, James[1]*). He was the son of Ronald Ellsworth Osborn (348) and Patricia R. Goble. James died before 2008.

475. **Michael James[10] Schumann** (*Garnetta Faye[9] Ludwig, Georgia Mae[8] White, Walter Otis[7], Mary E.[6] Rogers, Rachel C.[5] VanAusdall, Mary[4] Pegan, Andrew[3] Pegan II, Andrew[2] Pagan, James[1]*) was born on March 2, 1955, in Carrollton, Carrollton Twp., Greene Co., Illinois. He was the son of James Howard Schumann and Garnetta Faye Ludwig (352). Michael James died in Oklahoma City, Oklahoma, on March 13, 2006, at age 51. He was buried in Flynn Cemetery, Agra, Lincoln Co., Oklahoma.[115]

Along with two cohorts, Michael James Schumann gang- raped and sodomized a woman in an Oklahoma City motel room in 1982. Schumann held the woman at gunpoint while he helped bind her hands. The three assailants robbed the woman and her boyfriend, who was also bound, of money and jewelry and their car. Schumann and the others were later apprehended by police, While the other two men involved pleaded guilty, Schumann didn't and he went on trial. He was convicted and sentenced to 160 years in prison.

476. **Larry[10] McIntyre** (*Clyde E.[9] McIntyre, Freda Grace[8] Delp, Bertha May[7] Vanausdoll, Loring or Loren Earl[6], Caleb[5], Mary[4] Pegan, Andrew[3] Pegan II, Andrew[2] Pagan, James[1]*) was born about 1937. He is the son of Clyde E. McIntyre and (358) Beulah Unknown.

477. **Janet[10] McIntyre** (*Clyde E.[9] McIntyre, Freda Grace[8] Delp, Bertha May[7] Vanausdoll, Loring or Loren Earl[6], Caleb[5], Mary[4] Pegan, Andrew[3] Pegan II, Andrew[2] Pagan, James[1]*) was born about 1939. She is the daughter of Clyde E. McIntyre and (358) Beulah Unknown.

478. **Roger Allen[10] Davenport** (*Eileen R.[9] Reed, Leona Frances[8] Delp, Bertha May[7] Vanausdoll, Loring or Loren Earl[6], Caleb[5], Mary[4] Pegan, Andrew[3] Pegan II, Andrew[2] Pagan, James[1]*) was born on October 22, 1951, in Alton, Alton Twp., Madison Co., Illinois. He was the son of Edward Davenport and Eileen R. Reed (367). Roger Allen died in Alton, Alton Twp., Madison Co., Illinois, on October 27, 1951.

He was buried in Oakwood Cemetery, Upper Alton, Alton Twp., Madison Co., Illinois.[8]

479. **Norman Edward[10] Delp** (*Roy W.[9], Roy Everett[8], Bertha May[7] Vanausdoll, Loring or Loren Earl[6], Caleb[5], Mary[4] Pegan, Andrew[3] Pegan II, Andrew[2] Pagan, James[1]*) was born on October 30, 1955, in Alton, Alton Twp., Madison Co., Illinois. He was the son of Roy W. Delp II (368) and Erika Stegmann. He died in Brighton, Illinois, on July 26, 2013, at age 57. Norman Edward was buried in Borlin Cemetery, Carrollton, Carrollton Twp., Greene Co., Illinois.[152]

Norman Edward married **Unknown Unknown**.

479A. **Daughter[10] Vanausdoll** (*Robert Gene[9], Harold A.[8], Raymond Loring[7], Loring or Loren Earl[6], Caleb[5], Mary[4] Pegan, Andrew[3] Pegan II, Andrew[2] Pagan, James[1]*) She is the daughter of Robert Gene Vanausdoll and Rebecca J. Mundy.

Daughter Vanausdoll married **Randy Gene Newton.** They had one son. Randy Gene Newton was born in Fieldon, Richwoods Twp., Jersey Co., Illinois, on February 9, 1957. He reached age 33 and died in Brownsville, Fulton Co., Kentucky, on December 26, 1988. He is buried in Oak Grove Cemetery, Jerseyville, Jersey Twp., Jersey Co., Illinois.[16]

Daughter Vanausdoll Newton married **Travis Dee Farmer.** They had one daughter. Travis Dee Farmer was born in Alton, Alton Twp., Madison Co., Illinois, on September 28, 1955. He reached age 61 and died in Alton, Alton Twp., Madison Co., Illinois, on May 5, 2017. He was buried in Newbern Cemetery, East Newbern, Mississippi Twp., Jersey Co., Illinois.[I]

Daughter Vanausdoll Newton Farmer married **Unknown Sullivan.**

Son of Daughter Vanausdoll and Randy Gene Newton:

+ 507A  m  I.  **Joshua Cain[11] Newton** was born in Jerseyville, Jersey Twp., Jersey Co., Illinois on April 27, 1977. He died in a hospital in Richmond Heights, ,

St. Louis Co., Illinois, on February 13, 2018. Joshua Cain was buried in buried in Oak Grove Cemetery Jerseyville, Jersey Twp., Jersey Co., Illinois.[16]

Daughter of Daughter Vanausdoll and Travis Dee Farmer:

+ 507B f I. **Sarah Marie**[11] **Farmer** was born in Jerseyville, Jersey Twp., Jersey Co., Illinois, on November 22, 1990. She died in Jerseyville, Jersey Twp., Jersey Co., Illinois, on Octobern 12, 2006. Sarah Marie is buried in Oak Grove Cemetery, Jerseyville, Jersey Twp., Jersey Co., Illinois.[16]

**480. David Robert**[10] **Babcock** (*Robert Lewis*[9], *Lewis H.*[8], *Laura Edith*[7] *Gilmore, Martha Jane*[6] *Vanausdoll, Caleb*[5], *Mary*[4] *Pegan, Andrew*[3] *Pegan II, Andrew*[2] *Pagan, James*[1]) was born on June 25, 1959, in Riverside, Riverside Co., California. He was the son of Robert Lewis Babcock (385) and Linda Lee Dobbins. David Robert died in Riverside, Riverside Co., California, on June 17, 1995, at age 35.

**481. Fred LeRoy**[10] **Gilmore** (*George Otis*[9], *Albert LeRoy*[8], *Harry Otis*[7], *Martha Jane*[6] *Vanausdoll, Caleb*[5], *Mary*[4] *Pegan, Andrew*[3] *Pegan II, Andrew*[2] *Pagan, James*[1]) was born on September 19, 1956 in Pawnee City, Pawnee City Twp., Pawnee Co., Nebraska. He was the son of George Otis Gilmore (388) and Delores Maxine Mason. He was also known as **LeRoy**. He died on May 31, 2001, in Kearney, Buffalo Co., Nebraska at age 44. Fred LeRoy was buried in Kilfoil Cemetery, Merna, Custer Co., Nebraska.[153]

**482. Dale Wayne**[10] **Gilmore** (*George Otis*[9], *Albert LeRoy*[8], *Harry Otis*[7], *Martha Jane*[6] *Vanausdoll, Caleb*[5], *Mary*[4] *Pegan, Andrew*[3] *Pegan II, Andrew*[2] *Pagan, James*[1]) was born on March 7, 1961, in Pawnee City, Pawnee City Twp., Pawnee Co., Nebraska. He was the son of George Otis Gilmore (388) and Delores Maxine Mason. He died on January 30, 1982 at age 20 in a U.S. Military acci-

dent in Nebraska? Dale Wayne is buried in Kilfoil Cemetery, Merna, Custer Co., Nebraska.[144]

Dale married.

**483. Joel Glenn**[10] **Gilmore** (*George Otis*[9], *Albert LeRoy*[8], *Harry Otis*[7], *Martha Jane*[6] *Vanausdoll, Caleb*[5], *Mary*[4] *Pegan, Andrew*[3] *Pegan II, Andrew*[2] *Pagan, James*[1]) was born on October 7, 1962, in Pawnee City, Pawnee City Twp., Pawnee Co., Nebraska. He was the son of George Otis Gilmore (388) and Delores Maxine Mason. Joel Glenn died on June 15, 2006, in Lexington, Dawson Co., Nebraska at age 43. He is buried in Immanuel Lutheran Cemetery, Amherst, Buffalo Co., Nebraska.[154]

**484. Kurt Allen**[10] **Gilmore** (*George Otis*[9], *Albert LeRoy*[8], *Harry Otis*[7], *Martha Jane*[6] *Vanausdoll, Caleb*[5], *Mary*[4] *Pegan, Andrew*[3] *Pegan II, Andrew*[2] *Pagan, James*[1]) was born on January 4, 1969 in Pawnee City, Pawnee City Twp., Pawnee Co., Nebraska? He was the son of George Otis Gilmore (388) and Delores Maxine Mason. Kurt Allen died on November 6, 2010, in Kearney, Buffalo Co., Nebraska at age 41. He was buried in Immanuel Lutheran Cemetery, Amherst, Buffalo Co., Nebraska.[154]

**485. Heidi Suzanne**[10] **Blair** (*Son*[9] *Blair, Lois Marie*[8] *Perdue, Eva May*[7] *Gilmore, Martha Jane*[6] *Vanausdoll, Caleb*[5], *Mary*[4] *Pegan, Andrew*[3] *Pegan II, Andrew*[2] *Pagan, James*[1]) was born in Huron, Beadle Co., South Dakota on April 3, 1974. She was the daughter of Son Blair (398) and his first wife. Heidi Suzanne died in a hospital in Sioux Falls, Minnehaha Co., South Dakota on October 10, 2001. She was buried in Highmore City Cemetery, Highmore, Hyde Co., South Dakota.[155]

Childless.

Heidi Suzanne married **Mr. Kunz**. They divorced. She died under her maiden name.

**486. Roger Allen**[10] **Crawford** (*Yvonne Ailene*[9] *Allen, Gladys Mae*[8] *Spaulding, Cora May Agnes*[7] *Day, Mary Ellen*[6] *Vanausdoll, Caleb*[5], *Mary*[4] *Pegan, Andrew*[3] *Pegan II, Andrew*[2] *Pagan, James*[1]) was born on December 1, 1942, in Humboldt, Humboldt Twp., Richardson Co., Nebraska. He was the son of Max Eugene Crawford and Yvonne Ailene Allen (406). Roger Allen died in

Vancouver, Clark Co., Washington, on October 12, 2010, at age 67. He was buried in Evergreen Memorial Gardens Cemetery, Vancouver, Clark Co., Washington.[156]

Roger Allen Crawford married twice.

**486A. Infant Son**[10] **Swanson** (*Delverna Corrine*[9] *Swanson, Gladys Mae*[8] *Spaulding, Cora May Agnes*[7] *Day, Mary Ellen*[6] *Vanausdoll, Caleb*[5], *Mary*[4] *Pegan, Andrew*[3] *Pegan II, Andrew*[2] *Pagan, James*[1]) was born in Oregon on February 22, 1973. He was the son of Dean D. Swanson and Delverna Corrine Fencil (409). He died in Oregon on February 22, 1973. He is buried in Park Hill Cemetery, Vancouver, Clark Co., Washington.[56]

**487. Thomas Michael**[10] **Spaulding** (*Donald Robert*[9], *John Raymond*[8], *Cora May Agnes*[7] *Day, Mary Ellen*[6] *Vanausdoll, Caleb*[5], *Mary*[4] *Pegan, Andrew*[3] *Pegan II, Andrew*[2] *Pagan, James*[1]) was born on January 3, 1949, in Sacramento, Sacramento Co., California. He was the son of Donald Robert Spaulding (413) and Jacqueline Ann Harrison. Thomas Michael died in Sacramento, Sacramento Co., California, on January 4, 1949.

**488. Marc**[10] **Spaulding** (*Donald Robert*[9], *John Raymond*[8], *Cora May Agnes*[7] *Day, Mary Ellen*[6] *Vanausdoll, Caleb*[5], *Mary*[4] *Pegan, Andrew*[3] *Pegan II, Andrew*[2] *Pagan, James*[1]) was born on December 21, 1964, in Lincoln, Lancaster Co., Nebraska. He was the son of Donald Robert Spaulding (413) and Jacqueline Ann Harrison. Marc died in Goldendale, Klickitat Co., Washington, on October 9, 1994, at age 29.

**489. Dewayne Robert Garl**[10] **Spaulding** (*Garl E.*[9] *Spaulding, Garl Vernon*[8], *Cora May Agnes*[7] *Day, Mary Ellen*[6] *Vanausdoll, Caleb*[5], *Mary*[4] *Pegan, Andrew*[3] *Pegan II, Andrew*[2] *Pagan, James*[1]) was born on August 1, 1961, in San Diego, San Diego Co., California. He was the son of Garl E. Spaulding (419) and Geraldine Louise Giddens. He was also known as **Ricky**. DeWayne "Ricky" died in Bellflower, Los Angeles Co., California, on March 12, 1969, at age seven. He was buried in Forest Lawn Memorial Park Cemetery, Cypress, Orange Co., California.[G]

**490. Son One**[10] **Rumery** (*Ruth A.*[9] *Spaulding, Garl Vernon*8, *Cora May Agnes*[7] *Day, Mary Ellen*[6] *Vanausdoll, Caleb*[5], *Mary*[4] *Pegan, Andrew*[3] *Pegan II, Andrew*[2] *Pagan, James*[1]) was born on November 5, 1957, in Los Angeles Co., California. He is the son of John Wilson Rumery and Daughter Spaulding (420).

Son I married **Unknown Unknown**. They had two sons.

Son Rumery and his wife had two sons, including:

+ 507C m I. **Raymond Edward**[11] **Rumery** was born in Los Angeles, Los Angeles Co., California, on February 19, 1984. He died in Los Angeles, Los Angeles Co., California, on February 21, 1984. Raymond Edward was buried in Forest Lawn Memorial Park Cemetery, Glendale, Los Angeles Co., California.[160]

**491. Son Two**[10] **Rumery** (*Ruth A.*[9] *Spaulding, Garl Vernon*[8], *Cora May Agnes*[7] *Day, Mary Ellen*[6] *Vanausdoll, Caleb*[5], *Mary*[4] *Pegan, Andrew*[3] *Pegan II, Andrew*[2] *Pagan, James*[1]) was born on November 21, 1958, in Los Angeles Co., California. He is the son of John Wilson Rumery and Daughter Spaulding (420).

Son II married **Unknown Unknown**. They had five children.

Son Two Rumery and Unknown Unknown had five children, including:

+ 508 f III. **Kayla Elizabeth**[11] **Rumery** was born in Los Angeles Co., California, on March 21, 1989. She died in Los Angeles Co., California, on May 13, 1989. Kayla Elizabeth was buried in Green Hills Memorial Park Cemetery, Rancho Palos Verdes, Los Angeles Co., California.[50]

**492. Dewayne Robert Garl**[10] **Spaulding** (*Garl E.*[9] *Spaulding, Garl Vernon*[8], *Cora May Agnes*[7] *Day,*

*Mary Ellen⁶ Vanausdoll, Caleb⁵, Mary⁴ Pegan, Andrew³ Pegan II, Andrew² Pagan, James¹*) was born on August 1, 1961, in San Diego, San Diego Co., California. He was the son of Garl E. Spaulding (419) and Geraldine Louise Giddens. He was also known as **Ricky**. DeWayne "Ricky" died in Bellflower, Los Angeles Co., California, on March 12, 1969, at age seven. He was buried in Forest Lawn Memorial Park Cemetery, Cypress, Orange Co., California.[G]

**493. Robert J.¹⁰ Collier** (*Jacqueline J.⁹ Day, Lowrain Arthur⁸, Anthony Juduthan⁷, Mary Ellen⁶ Vanausdoll, Caleb⁵, Mary⁴ Pegan, Andrew³ Pegan II, Andrew² Pagan, James¹*) was born on June 8, 1954, in Portland, Multnomah Co., Oregon. He was the son of Stanley Alfred Collier and Jacqueline J. Day (426). Robert J. died in Napavine, Lewis Co, Washington, on February 18, 2014, at age 59.

Seems to have never married.

Robert Collier and his sister Cheryl J. Collier Ausland (Brannon) were found dead of unknown causes on February 18, 2014 in the home they shared together in Napervine, Washington. Later, toxicology reports revealed they died of prescription drug overdoses.

**494. Cheryl J.¹⁰ Collier** (*Jacqueline J.⁹ Day, Lowrain Arthur⁸, Anthony Juduthan⁷, Mary Ellen⁶ Vanausdoll, Caleb⁵, Mary⁴ Pegan, Andrew³ Pegan II, Andrew² Pagan, James¹*) was born on March 4, 1963, in Ethel. Lewis Co., Washington. She was the daughter of Stanley Alfred Collier and Jacqueline J. Day (426). Cheryl J. died in Napavine, Lewis Co, Washington, on February 18, 2014, at age 50.

She married **Mr. Ausland.**

Cheryl J. Collier Ausland married **Unknown Brannon.** They divorced. Cheryl resumed using the surname Ausland.

Cheryl J. Collier Ausland (Brannon) and her brother Robert Collier were found dead on February 18, 2014 of unknown causes in the home they shared together in Napervine, Washington. Later, toxicology reports revealed they died of prescription drug overdoses.

**495. Tammy D.¹⁰ Day** (*Son⁹, Lowrain Arthur⁸, Anthony Juduthan⁷, Mary Ellen⁶ Vanausdoll, Caleb⁵, Mary⁴ Pegan, Andrew³ Pegan II, Andrew² Pagan, James¹*) was born about August 18, 1973 in Olympia, Thurston Co., Washington? She was the daughter of Son Day (428) and his wife. Tammy D. died in a hospital in Chehalis, Lewis Co., Washington, on August 18, 1973. She was buried in Claquato Cemetery, Chehalis, Lewis Co., Washington.[161]

**496. Daughter¹⁰ Merwin** (*Son⁹ Merwin, Dorothy Arlene⁸ James, Jessie Levern⁷ Day, Mary Ellen⁶ Vanausdoll, Caleb⁵, Mary⁴ Pegan, Andrew³ Pegan II, Andrew² Pagan, James¹*). She is the daughter Son Merwin (437) and his wife.

Daughter Merwin married **Mr. Sherman.** They had at least one daughter.

Daughter of Daughter Merwin and Mr. Sherman:

+ 509    f    I.    **Emerson Grace¹¹ Sherman** was born in Tecumseh, Nemaha Twp., Johnson Co., Nebraska, on July 29, 2004. She was also known as **Emma.** Emerson Grace died in Pawnee City, Pawnee City Twp., Pawnee Co., Nebraska, on August 19, 2004. She was buried in Bohemian National Cemetery, Dodge, Webster Twp., Dodge Co., Nebraska.[162]

**497. Daughter¹⁰ East** (*Son⁹, William Eldon⁸, Ruby Frances⁷ Vanausdoll, William Cornelius⁶, Caleb⁵, Mary⁴ Pegan, Andrew³ Pegan II, Andrew² Pagan, James¹*). She is the daughter of Son East (440) and Patricia Unknown.

She married **Mr. Webster.** They divorced.

Daughter East Webster married **Mr. Short.** They had at least one son.

Son of Daughter East and Mr. Short:

+ 510 m I.  **Garrett Stephen**[11] **Short** was born in Jerseyville, Jersey Twp., Jersey Co., Illinois, on November 26, 1989. He died in Chicago, Cook Co., Illinois, on December 28, 2010. Garrett Stephen was buried in Oak Grove Cemetery, Jerseyville, Jersey Twp., Jersey Co., Illinois.[16]

498. **Lori**[10] **Baecht** (*Enid Louise*[9] *Hayes, Ila Marie*[8] *Vanausdoll, Otis Lafayette*[7], *Charles Wesley*[6], *Caleb*[5], *Mary*[4] *Pegan, Andrew*[3] *Pegan II, Andrew*[2] *Pagan, James*[1]) was born in 1960 in Grafton, Quarry Twp., Jersey Co., Illinois. She was the daughter of Edward Joseph Baecht II and Enid Louise Hayes (447). Lori died in Grafton, Quarry Twp., Jersey Co., Illinois, on October 28, 2011, age 51. She was buried in Scenic Hill/Odd Fellows Cemetery, Quarry Twp., Jersey Co., Illinois.[14]

She married **Mr. Griffin.**

499. **Son**[10] **Baecht** (*Enid Louise*[9] *Hayes, Ila Marie*[8] *Vanausdoll, Otis Lafayette*[7], *Charles Wesley*[6], *Caleb*[5], *Mary*[4] *Pegan, Andrew*[3] *Pegan II, Andrew*[2] *Pagan, James*[1]). He is the son of Edward Joseph Baecht II and Enid Louise Hayes (447).

He married **Unknown Unknown.** They had at least one son.

Son of Son Baecht and Unknown Unknown:

+ 511 m I.  **Zachary Alan**[11] **Baecht** was born in Alton, Alton Twp., Madison Co., Illinois, on July 12, 1990. He died in Alton, Alton Twp., Madison Co., Illinois, on July 12, 1990. Zachary Alan was buried in Grimes-Neeley Cemetery, English Twp., Jersey Co., Illinois.[163]

500. **Kara Lanae**[10] **Vanausdoll** (*Son*[9], *Donald Lee*[8], *Everett Charles*[7], *Charles Wesley*[6], *Caleb*[5], *Mary*[4] *Pegan, Andrew*[3] *Pegan II, Andrew*[2] *Pagan, James*[1]) was born on April 19, 1977, in Jerseyville, Jersey Twp., Jersey Co., Illinois. She was the daughter of Son Vanausdoll (456) and his wife. Kara Lanae died

in a hospital in Florissant, St. Louis Co., Missouri, on July 18, 1989, at age 12. She was buried in Arthur Cemetery, Arthur, Bourbon Twp., Douglas Co., Illinois.[159]

501. **Ryan Martin**[10] **Vanausdoll** (*Son II*[9], *Donald Lee*[8], *Everett Charles*[7], *Charles Wesley*[6], *Caleb*[5], *Mary*[4] *Pegan, Andrew*[3] *Pegan II, Andrew*[2] *Pagan, James*[1]) was born on April 17, 1980, in Jerseyville, Jersey Twp., Jersey Co., Illinois. He was the son of Son II Vanausdoll (457) and Unknown Unknown. Ryan Martin died in Jerseyville, Jersey Twp., Jersey Co., Illinois, on July 20, 1980. He was buried in St. Francis Xavier Cemetery, Jerseyville, Jersey Twp., Jersey Co., Illinois.[85]

502. **Kyle Adam**[10] **Vanausdoll** (*Son II*[9], *Donald Lee*[8], *Everett Charles*[7], *Charles Wesley*[6], *Caleb*[5], *Mary*[4] *Pegan, Andrew*[3] *Pegan II, Andrew*[2] *Pagan, James*[1]) was born on May 31, 1983, in Jerseyville, Jersey Twp., Jersey Co., Illinois. He was the son of Son II Vanausdoll (457) and his wife. Kyle Adam died in Jersey Co., Illinois, on September 19, 2010, at age 27. He was buried in St. Francis Xavier Cemetery, Jerseyville, Jersey Twp., Jersey Co., Illinois.[85]

Kyle Adam Vanausdoll was killed in an auto accident.

503. **Zachary Paul**[10] **Vanausdoll** (*Daughter*[9], *Darrell*[8], *Everett Charles*[7], *Charles Wesley*[6], *Caleb*[5], *Mary*[4] *Pegan, Andrew*[3] *Pegan II, Andrew*[2] *Pagan, James*[1]) was born on August 8, 1986, in Carbondale, Carbondale Twp., Jackson Co., Illinois. He was the son of George Ronald Patterson and Daughter Vanausdoll (458). Zachary Paul lived in 2003 in Goreville, Elvira Twp., Johnson Co., Illinois. He died in a hospital in Anna, Anna Twp., Union Co., Illinois, on August 10, 2003, at age 17.

504. **Jeremiah**[10] **Gilbert** (*Son*[9] *Gilbert, Dorothy Marie*[8] *Seago, Hallye Maude*[7] *Vanausdoll, Allen M.*[6], *Caleb*[5], *Mary*[4] *Pegan, Andrew*[3] *Pegan II, Andrew*[2] *Pagan, James*[1]). He was the son of Son Gilbert (462) and Unknown Unknown. Jeremiah died, probably young, before 1999.

505. **Son**[10] **Moore** (*Daughter*[9] *Gilbert, Dorothy Marie*[8] *Seago, Hallye Maude*[7] *Vanausdoll, Allen M.*[6], *Caleb*[5], *Mary*[4] *Pegan, Andrew Pagan or*[3], *Andrew*[2] *Pagan,*

*James[1]*). He is the son of Mr. Moore and Daughter Gilbert (463).

He married **Unknown Unknown.** They had at least one son.

Son of Son Moore and Unknown Unknown:

+ 512 m I. **Joshuae[11] Moore.** Joshuae died before 1999.

**506. Delbert[10] Lynch** (*Daughter II[9] Gilbert, Dorothy Marie[8] Seago, Hallye Maude[7] Vanausdoll, Allen M.[6], Caleb[5], Mary[4] Pegan, Andrew[3] Pegan II, Andrew[2] Pagan, James[1]*). He was the son of Unknown Lynch and Daughter II Gilbert (464). Delbert was born in 1967 and died on in St. Louis, Missouri, on May 28, 1984 at about age 17.

**507. Daughter[10] Keefer** (*Daughter III[9] Gilbert, Dorothy Marie[8] Seago, Hallye Maude[7] Vanausdoll, Allen M.[6], Caleb[5], Mary[4] Pegan, Andrew Pagan or[3], Andrew[2] Pagan, James[1]*). She is the daughter of Mr. Keefer and Daughter III Gilbert (465).

She married **Mr. Bartlett.** They had at least one daughter.

Daughter of Daughter Keefer and Mr. Bartlett:

+ 513 f I. **Shannon Marie[11] Bartlett** was born in Jerseyville, Jersey Twp., Jersey Co., Illinois, on April 25, 1991. She died in Jerseyville, Jersey Twp., Jersey Co., Illinois, on April 25, 1991. Shannon Marie was buried in Oak Grove Cemetery, Jerseyville, Jersey Twp., Jersey Co., Illinois.[16]

# 11th Generation

**507A. Joshua Cain[11] Newton** (*Daughter[10], Robert Gene[9], Harold A.[8], Raymond Loring[7], Loring or Loren Earl[6], Caleb[5], Mary[4] Pegan, Andrew[3] Pegan II, Andrew[2] Pagan, James[1]*) was born in Jerseyville, Jersey Twp., Jersey Co., Illinois on April 27, 1977. He died in a hospital in Richmond Heights, St. Louis Co., Illinois, on February 13, 2018, at age 33. Joshua Cain was buried in buried in Oak Grove Cemetery, Jerseyville, Jersey Twp., Jersey Co., Illinois.[16]

Joshua Cain may have married. He had three children.

**507B. Sarah Marie[11] Farmer** (*Daughter[10], Robert Gene[9], Harold A.[8], Raymond Loring[7], Loring or Loren Earl[6], Caleb[5], Mary[4] Pegan, Andrew[3] Pegan II, Andrew[2] Pagan, James[1]*) was born in Jerseyville, Jersey Twp., Jersey Co., Illinois, on November 22, 1990. She died in Jerseyville, Jersey Twp., Jersey Co., Illinois, on October 12, 2006, at age 15. Sarah Marie is buried in Oak Grove Cemetery, Jerseyville, Jersey Twp., Jersey Co., Illinois.[16]

**507C. Raymond Edward[11] Rumery** was born in Los Angeles, Los Angeles Co., California, on February 19, 1984. He died in Los Angeles, Los Angeles Co., California, on February 21, 1984. Raymond Edward was buried in Forest Lawn Memorial Park Cemetery, Glendale, Los Angeles Co., California.[160]

**508. Kayla Elizabeth[11] Rumery** (*Son II[10] Rumery, Ruth A.[9] Spaulding, Garl Vernon[8], Cora May Agnes[7] Day, Mary Ellen[6] Vanausdoll, Caleb[5], Mary[4] Pegan, Andrew[3] Pegan II, Andrew[2] Pagan, James[1]*) was born on March 21, 1989, in Los Angeles Co., California. She was the daughter of Son II Rumery (482) and his wife. Kayla Elizabeth died in Los Angeles Co., California, on May 13, 1989. She was buried in Green Hills Memorial Park Cemetery, Rancho Palos Verdes, Los Angeles Co., California.[50]

**509. Emerson Grace[11] Sherman** (*Living II[10] Merwin, Rodney[9], Dorothy Arlene[8] James, Jessie Levern[7] Day, Mary Ellen[6] Vanausdoll, Caleb[5], Mary[4] Pegan, Andrew[3] Pegan II, Andrew[2] Pagan, James[1]*) was born on July 29, 2004, in Tecumseh, Nemaha Twp., Johnson Co., Nebraska. She was also known as Emma. She was the daughter of Daughter Merwin (487) and her Mr. Sherman. Emerson Grace died in Pawnee City, Pawnee City Twp., Pawnee Co., Nebraska, on August 19, 2004. She was buried in Bohemian National Cemetery, Dodge, Webster Twp., Dodge Co., Nebraska.[162]

**510. Garrett Stephen[11] Short** (*Daughter[10] East, David[9], William Eldon[8], Ruby Frances[7] Vanausdoll, William Cornelius[6], Caleb[5], Mary[4] Pegan, Andrew[3] Pegan II, Andrew[2] Pagan, James[1]*) was born on November 26, 1989, in Jerseyville, Jersey Twp., Jersey Co., Illinois. He was the son of Daughter East (496) and Mr. Short. Garrett Stephen died in Chicago, Cook Co., Illinois, on December 28, 2010, at age 21. He was buried in Oak Grove Cemetery, Jerseyville, Jersey Twp., Jersey Co., Illinois.[16]

Never married.

**511. Zachary Alan[11] Baecht** (*Son[10] Hayes, Enid Louise[9] Hayes, Ila Marie[8] Vanausdoll, Otis Lafayette[7], Charles Wesley[6], Caleb[5], Mary[4] Pegan, Andrew[3] Pegan II, Andrew[2] Pagan, James[1]*) was born on July 12, 1990, in Alton, Alton Twp., Madison Co., Illinois. He was the son of Son Baecht (498) and his wife. Zachary Alan died in Alton, Alton Twp., Madison Co., Illinois, on July 12, 1990. He was buried in Grimes-Neeley Cemetery, English Twp., Jersey Co., Illinois.[163]

**512. Joshuae[11] Moore** (*Son[10] Moore, Daughter[9] Gilbert, Dorothy Marie[8] Seago, Hallye Maude[7] Vanausdoll, Allen M.[6], Caleb[5], Mary[4] Pegan, Andrew[3] Pegan II, Andrew[2] Pagan, James[1]*). He was the son of Son Moore (504) and his wife. Joshuae died before 1999.

**513. Shannon Marie[11] Bartlett** (*Daughter[10] Keefer, Daughter II[9] Gilbert, Dorothy Marie[8] Seago, Hallye Maude[7] Vanausdoll, Allen M.[6], Caleb[5], Mary[4] Pegan, Andrew[3] Pegan II, Andrew[2] Pagan, James[1]*) was born on April 25, 1991, in Jerseyville, Jersey Twp., Jersey Co., Illinois. She was the daughter of Daughter Keefer (506) and Mr. Bartlett. Shannon Marie died in Jerseyville, Jersey Twp., Jersey Co., Illinois, on April 25, 1991. She was buried in Oak Grove Cemetery, Jerseyville, Jersey Twp., Jersey Co., Illinois.[16]

# Endnotes

1  Find A Grave—Noble Cemetery, Otterville, Otter Creek Twp., Jersey Co., Illinois, Find A Grave.com.

2  *History of Jersey County, Illinois*; ed. by Oscar B. Hamilton, Jersey Co. Historical Society, Chicago: Munsell Publishing; 1919, pg. 641-2. Genealogy Center, Allen County Public Library, 900 Library Plaza, Fort Wayne, IN.

3  *History of Greene and Jersey Counties, Illinois: together with sketches of the towns, villages and townships, educational, civil, military, and political history; portraits of prominent individuals, and biographies of representative men.* Springfield, Illinois: Continental Historical Co.; 1885, pg. 297. Genealogy Center, Allen County Public Library, 900 Library Plaza, Fort Wayne, IN.

4  McBride, David N. and Jane N., *Highland County, Ohio Common Pleas Court Records, 1805-1860*, Hillsboro, Ohio, The Southern Ohio Genealogical Society, reprint ed. 1984; pg. 270-1. Highland County District Library, 10 Willettsville Pike, Hillsboro, OH.

5  Find A Grave—Miles Cemetery (Eagle Bluffs Cemetery), Bluff Twp., Monroe Co., Illinois, Find A Grave.com.

6  Find A Grave—Evergreen Cemetery, Chester, Chester Twp., Randolph Co., Illinois, Find A Grave.com.

7  Find A Grave—Crown Hill Cemetery, Wheat Ridge, Jefferson Co., Colorado, Find A Grave.com.

8  Find A Grave—Oakwood Cemetery, Upper Alton, Alton Twp., Madison Co., Illinois, Find A Grave.com.

9  Find A Grave—Oddfellows Cemetery, Benton Twp., Franklin Co., Illinois, Find A Grave.com.

10  Find A Grave—Melrose Abbey Memorial Park Cemetery, Anaheim, Orange Co., California, Find A Grave.com.

11  Find A Grave—Humboldt Cemetery, Humboldt, Humboldt Twp., Richardson Co., Nebraska, Find A Grave.com.

12  Find A Grave—Table Rock Cemetery, Table Rock Twp., Pawnee Co., Nebraska, Find A Grave.com.

13  USGENWEB—Jersey County Index of Burials, USGENWEB. org, www.usgenweb.com.

14  Find A Grave—Scenic Hill Cemetery, Grafton, Quarry Twp., Jersey Co., Illinois, Find A Grave.com.

15  Find A Grave—Oak Hill Cemetery, Galena, Cherokee Co., Kansas, Find A Grave.com.

16  Find A Grave—Oak Grove Cemetery, Jerseyville, Jersey Twp., Jersey Co., Illinois, Find A Grave.com.

17  Find A Grave—Valhalla Memorial Park and Mausoleum, Godfrey, Godfrey Twp., Madison Co., Illinois, Find A Grave. com.

18  Find A Grave—Osage City Cemetery, Osage City, Grant Twp., Osage Co., Kansas, Find A Grave.com.

19  Find A Grave—Lincoln Cemetery, Lebo, Lincoln Twp., Coffey Co., Kansas, Find A Grave.com.

20  Find A Grave—Newbern Cemetery, East Newbern, Mississippi Twp., Jersey Co., Illinois, Find A Grave.com.

21  Find A Grave—Oakdale Memorial Park Cemetery, Glendora, Los Angeles Co., California, Find A Grave.com.

22  Find A Grave—Saint Patrick's Cemetery, Godfrey, Godfrey Twp., Madison Co., Illinois, Find A Grave.com.

23  Find A Grave—Calvary Cemetery and Mausoleum, Dallas, Dallas Co., Texas, Find A Grave.com.

24  Find A Grave—McDow Cemetery, Otterville, Otter Creek Twp., Jersey Co., Illinois, Find A Grave.com.

25  Find A Grave—Fieldon Cemetery, Fieldon, Richwoods Twp., Jersey Co., Illinois, Find A Grave.com.

26  Find A Grave—Olivewood Cemetery, Riverside, Riverside Co., California, Find A Grave.com.

27  Find A Grave—Pawnee City Cemetery, Pawnee City, Pawnee Twp., Pawnee Co., Nebraska, Find A Grave.com.

28  Find A Grave—Montecito Memorial Park Cemetery, Colton, San Bernardino Co., California, Find A Grave.com.

29  Find A Grave—Laurel Hill Cemetery, Neligh, Antelope Co., Nebraska, Find A Grave.com.

30  Find A Grave—Moran Cemetery, Moran Twp., Allen Co., Kansas, Find A Grave.com.

31  Find A Grave—Heim Cemetery, Dawson, Grant Twp., Richardson Co., Nebraska, Find A Grave.com.

32  Find A Grave—Laurel Cemetery, Cave Junction, Josephine Co., Oregon, Find A Grave.com.

33  Find A Grave—Nine Mile Cemetery, Wallace, Shoshone Co., Idaho, Find A Grave.com.

34  Find A Grave—Forest Cemetery, Coeur d'Alene, Kootenai Co., Idaho, Find A Grave.com.

35  Find A Grave—Victor Cemetery, Victor, Ravalli Co., Montana, Find A Grave.com.

36  Find A Grave—Shipman Cemetery, Shipman, Shipman Twp., Macoupin Co., Illinois, Find A Grave.com.

37  Find A Grave—Memorial Park Cemetery, Jennings, St. Louis Co., Missouri, Find A Grave.com.

38  Find A Grave—Calvary Cemetery and Mausoleum, St. Louis, Missouri, Find A Grave.com.

39  Find A Grave—Cleburne County Memorial Gardens Cemetery, Heber Springs, Cleburne Co., Arkansas, Find A Grave.com.

40  Find A Grave—Sunset Cemetery, Pacific, Boles Twp., Franklin Co., Missouri, Find A Grave.com.

41  Find A Grave—Saint Paul's Evangelical Cemetery, Olivet, St. Louis Co., Missouri, Find A Grave.com.

42  Find A Grave—Sunset Memorial Park and Mausoleum, Affton, St. Louis Co., Missouri, Find A Grave.com.

43  Find A Grave—Summit Grove Cemetery, Kampsville, Crater Twp., Calhoun Co., Illinois, Find A Grave.com.

44  Find A Grave—Oakwood Cemetery, Mount Vernon, Mount Vernon Twp., Jefferson Co., Illinois, Find A Grave.com.

45  Find A Grave—Saint Mary's Catholic Cemetery, Chester, Chester Twp., Randolph Co., Illinois, Find A Grave.com.

46  Find A Grave—Murdale Gardens of Memory, Murphysboro, Murphysboro Twp., Jackson Co., Illinois, Find A Grave.com.

47  Find A Grave—Wickcliffe Cemetery, Wickcliffe, Ballard Co., Kentucky, Find A Grave.com.

48  Find A Grave—Mound City National Cemetery, Mound City, Junction Twp., Pulaski Co., Illinois, Find A Grave.com.

49  Find A Grave—Camp Cemetery, Camp, Fulton Co., Arkansas, Find A Grave.com.

50  Find A Grave—Green Hills Memorial Park Cemetery, Rancho Palos Verdes, Los Angeles Co., California, Find A Grave.com.

51  Find A Grave—Highland Memorial Cemetery, Mount Carmel, Mount Carmel Twp., Wabash Co., Illinois, Find A Grave.com.

52  Find A Grave—Lincoln Memorial Park Cemetery, Portland, Multnomah Co., Oregon, Find A Grave.com.

53  Find A Grave—Evergreen Cemetery, Charlotte, Mecklenburg Co., North Carolina, Find A Grave.com.

54  Find A Grave—Palm Memorial Park Cemetery, Las Vegas, Clark Co., Nevada, Find A Grave.com.

55  Find A Grave—Hoisington Cemetery, Hoisington, Barton Co., Kansas, Find A Grave.com.

56  Find A Grave—Park Hill Cemetery, Vancouver, Clark Co., Washington, Find A Grave.com.

57  Find A Grave—Crestlawn Memorial Park Cemetery, Riverside, Riverside Co., California, Find A Grave.com.

58  Find A Grave—Quinnesec Cemetery, Quinnesec, Dickinson Co., Michigan, Find A Grave.com.

59  Find A Grave—Calvary Cemetery, Orchard Mesa, Mesa Co., Colorado, Find A Grave.com.

60  Find A Grave—Fairview Cemetery, La Junta, Otero Co., Colorado, Find A Grave.com.

61  Find A Grave—Maplewood Memorial Lawn Cemetery, Emporia, Emporia Twp., Lyon Co., Kansas, Find A Grave.com.

62  Find A Grave—Fairhaven Cemetery, Santa Ana, Orange Co., California, Find A Grave.com.

63  Find A Grave—Oquawka Cemetery, Oquawka, Oquawka Twp., Henderson Co., Illinois, Find A Grave.com.

64  U.S., WWI Draft Registration Cards, 1917-1918, Raymond Loring Vanausdoll, Pontiac, Illinois.

65  Find A Grave—White Cemetery, Otter Creek Twp., Jersey Co., Illinois, Find A Grave.com.

66  Find A Grave—London Cemetery, Peru, Peru Precinct, Nemaha Co., Nebraska, Find A Grave.com.

67  Find A Grave—Riverside National Cemetery, Riverside, Riverside Co., California, Find A Grave.com.

68  Find A Grave—Oakdale Memorial Park Cemetery, Glendora, Los Angeles Co., California, Find A Grave.com.

69  Find A Grave—Morningside Cemetery, Ree Heights, Hand Co., South Dakota, Find A Grave.com.

70  Find A Grave—Highland Cemetery, Iola, Iola Twp., Allen Co., Kansas, Find A Grave.com.

71  Find A Grave—Gas City Cemetery, Gas, Elm Twp., Allen Co., Kansas, Find A Grave.com.

72  Find A Grave—Mount Hope Cemetery, Hiawatha, Hiawatha Twp., Brown Co., Kansas, Find A Grave.com.

73  Find A Grave—Floral Hills Cemetery, Kansas City, Jackson Co., Missouri, Find A Grave.com.

74  Find A Grave—Waco Cemetery, Waco, Waco Twp., York Co., Nebraska, Find A Grave.com.

75  Find A Grave—Hillcrest Memorial Park Cemetery, Medford, Jackson Co., Oregon, Find A Grave.com.

76  Find A Grave—Tahoma Cemetery, Yakima, Yakima Co., Washington, Find A Grave.com.

77  Find A Grave—Meyers Falls Cemetery, Kettle Falls, Stevens Co., Washington, Find A Grave.com.

78  Find A Grave—Terrace Heights Memorial Park Cemetery, Yakima, Yakima Co., Washington, Find A Grave.com.

79  U.S. Veteran's Gravesites, ca. 1775-2006, Ancestry.com, Robert Newell Vanausdoll.

80  Find A Grave—Lake View Memorial Gardens Cemetery, Fairview Heights, Caseyville Twp., St.Clair Co., Illinois, Find A Grave.com.

81  Find A Grave—Saint Mary's Cemetery, Fieldon, Richwoods Twp., Jersey Co., Illinois, Find A Grave.com.

82  Find A Grave—Alpine Cemetery, Alpine, San Diego Co., California, Find A Grave.com.

83  Find A Grave—Farber Cemetery, Farber, Cuivre Twp., Audrain Co., Missouri, Find A Grave.com.

84  Find A Grave—Hartford Cemetery, Grafton, Quarry Twp., Jersey Co., Illinois, Find A Grave.com.

85  Find A Grave—St. Francis Xavier Cemetery, Jerseyville, Jersey Twp., Jersey Co., Illinois, Find A Grave.com.

86  Find A Grave—Georgia National Cemetery, Canton, Cherokee Co., Georgia, Find A Grave.com.

87  Find A Grave—Mountain View Cemetery, Oregon City, Clackamas Co., Oregon, Find A Grave.com.

88  Find A Grave—Mount Olivet Cemetery, Aurora, Aurora Twp., Kane Co., Illinois, Find A Grave.com.

89  Find A Grave—New Hill Cemetery, Anaconda, Deer Lodge Co., Montana, Find A Grave.com.

90  U.S. Veteran's Gravesites, ca. 1775-2006, Ancestry.com, Carl Wayne Seago.

91  Find A Grave—National Memorial Cemetery of Arizona, Phoenix, Maricopa Co., Arizona, Find A Grave.com.

92 Find A Grave—Hamburg Cemetery, Hamburg, Hamburg Twp., Calhoun Co., Illinois, Find A Grave.com.

93 Find A Grave—Alton National Cemetery, Alton, Alton Twp., Madison Co., Illinois, Find A Grave.com.

94 Find A Grave—Fort Logan National Cemetery, Denver, Denver Co., Colorado, Find A Grave.com.

95 Find A Grave—Saint Paul's Episcopal Columbarium, Kankakee, Kankakee Tw p., Kankakee Co., Illinois, Find A Grave.com.

96 Find A Grave—Bluff View Cemetery, Vermillion, Clay Co., South Dakota, Find A Grave.com.

97 Find A Grave—Green Lawn Cemetery, Columbus, Franklin Co., Ohio, Find A Grave.com.

98 Find A Grave—Berkley Cemetery, Carlisle Co., Kentucky, Find A Grave.com.

99 Find A Grave—Oak Hill Cemetery, Red Bluff, Tehama Co., California, Find A Grave.com.

100 Find A Grave—Port Hudson National Cemetery, Zachary, East Baton Rouge Parish, Lousiana, Find A Grave.com.

101 Find A Grave—McClellanville Methodist Church Cemetery, McClellanville, Charleston Co., South Carolina, Find A Grave.com.

102 Find A Grave—Tippecanoe Memory Gardens, Lafayette, Fairfield Twp., Tippecanoe Co., Indiana, Find A Grave.com.

103 Find A Grave—Fairmount Cemetery, Lamar, Prowers Co., Colorado, Find A Grave.com.

104 Find A Grave—Mountain View Cemetery, Pueblo, Pueblo Co., Colorado, Find A Grave.com.

105 Find A Grave—Satsop Cemetery, Satsop, Grays Harbor Co., Washington, Find A Grave.com.

106 Find A Grave—Memorial Park Cemetery, Oroville, Butte Co., California, Find A Grave.com.

107 Find A Grave—San Joaquin Valley National Cemetery, Santa Nella, Merced Co., California, Find A Grave.com.

108 Find A Grave—Hillcrest Cemetery, Rocky Ford, Otero Co., Colorado, Find A Grave.com.

109 Find A Grave—Hartford Cemetery, Hartford, Elmendaro Twp., Lyon Co., Kansas, Find A Grave.com.

110 Find A Grave—Greenwood Cemetery, Wichita, Sedgwick Co., Kansas, Find A Grave.com.

111 Find A Grave—Alexanderwhol Friedhof Cemetery, Goessel, West Branch Twp., Marion Co., Kansas, Find A Grave.com.

112 Find A Grave—Rose Lawn Memory Gardens Cemetery, Bethalto, Wood River Twp., Madison Co., Illinois, Find A Grave.com.

113 Find A Grave—Medora Cemetery, Ruyle Twp., Jersey Co., Illinois, Find A Grave.com.

114 Find A Grave—Kane Cemetery, Kane, Kane Twp., Greene Co., Illinois, Find A Grave.com.

115 Find A Grave—Flynn Cemetery, Agra, Lincoln Co., Oklahoma, Find A Grave.com.

116 Find A Grave—McDowell Cemetery, South Haven Highlands, Casco Twp., Allegan Co., Michigan, Find A Grave.com.

117 Find A Grave—Oak Grove Cemetery, St. Charles, St. Charles Twp., St. Charles Co., Missouri, Find A Grave.com.

118 Find A Grave—Valhalla Memorial Gardens, Bloomington, Monroe Co., Indiana, Find A Grave.com.

119 Find A Grave—Woodlawn Cemetery, Houston, Harris Co., Texas, Find A Grave.com.

120 Find A Grave—Memorial Oaks Cemetery, Houston, Harris Co., Texas, Find A Grave.com.

121 Find A Grave—Memorial Park Cemetery, Tallulah, Madison Parish, Louisiana, Find A Grave.com.

122 Find A Grave—Biggsville Cemetery, Biggsville, Biggsville Twp., Henderson Co., Illinois, Find A Grave.com.

123 Find A Grave—Rest Haven Memorial Park Cemetery, Rockwell, Rockwell Co. Texas, Find A Grave.com.

124 Find A Grave—Green Hill Cemetery, Rock Port, Clay Twp., Atchison Co., Missouri, Find A Grave.com.

125 Find A Grave—Fort Gibson National Cemetery, Fort Gibson, Muskogee Co., Oklahoma, Find A Grave.com.

126 Find A Grave—Bethesda Cemetery, Garner, Parker Co., Texas, Find A Grave.com.

127 Find A Grave—Moline Cemetery, Moline, Wildcat Twp., Elk Co., Kansas, Find A Grave.com.

128 Find A Grave—Lakeview Cemetery, Erie, Erie Twp., Neosho Co., Kansas, Find A Grave.com.

129 Find A Grave—Camas Cemetery, Camas, Clark Co., Washington, Find A Grave.com.

130 Find A Grave—Pleasant View Cemetery, Auburn, Douglas Twp., Nemaha Co., Nebraska, Find A Grave.com.

131 Find A Grave—Lincoln Memorial Park Cemetery, Lincoln, Lancaster Co., Nebraska, Find A Grave.com.

132 Find A Grave—Park Cemetery, Columbus, Salamanca Twp., Cherokee Co., Kansas, Find A Grave.com.

133 Find A Grave—West Hills Memorial Park Cemetery, Yakima, Yakima Co., Washington, Find A Grave.com.

134 Find A Grave—Claquato Cemetery, Chehalis, Lewis Co., Washington, Find A Grave.com.

135 Find A Grave—Silvercreek Cemetery, Randle, Lewis Co., Washington, Find A Grave.com.

136 Find A Grave—Mabton Cemetery, Mabton, Yakima Co., Washington, Find A Grave.com.

137 Find A Grave—Eagle Point National Cemetery, Eagle Point, Jackson Co., Oregon, Find A Grave.com.

138 Find A Grave—West Lawn Memorial Cemetery, Grand Island, Hall Co., Nebraska, Find A Grave.com.

139 Find A Grave—Coeur D'Alene Memorial Gardens Cemetery, Coeur D'Alene, Rural Co., Idaho, Find A Grave.com.

140 Find A Grave—Washington Memorial Park Cemetery, Seatac, King Co., Washington, Find A Grave.com.

141 Find A Grave—Bossberg Cemetery, Stevens Co., Washington, Find A Grave.com.

142 Find A Grave—Fosterburg Cemetery, Fosterburg, Foster Twp., Madison Co., Illinois, Find A Grave.com.

143 Find A Grave—Attica Cemetery, Attica, Ruella Twp., Harper Co., Kansas, Find A Grave.com.

144 Find A Grave—Forest Hill Cemetery East, Memphis, Shelby Co., Tennessee, Find A Grave.com.

145 Find A Grave—Memphis National Cemetery, Memphis, Shelby Co., Tennessee, Find A Grave.com.

146 Find A Grave—Los Angeles National Cemetery, Los Angeles, Los Angeles Co., California, Find A Grave.com.

147 Find A Grave—Saint Felix Cemetery, Wabasha, Wabasha Co., Minnesota, Find A Grave.com.

148 Find A Grave—Resthaven Park West Cemetery, Glendale, Maricopa Co., Arizona, Find A Grave.com.

149 Find A Grave—Ebenezer Memorial Cemetery, Rockwood, Liberty Twp., Randolph Co., Illinois, Find A Grave.com.

150 Find A Grave—Yorktown Cemetery, Stockwell, Lauramie Twp., Tippecanoe Co., Indiana, Find A Grave.com.

151 Find A Grave—Mount Pulaski Cemetery, Mount Pulaski. Mount Pulaski Twp., Logan Co., Illinois, Find A Grave.com.

152 Find A Grave—Borlin Cemetery, Carrollton, Carrollton Twp., Greene Co., Illinois, Find A Grave.com.

153 Find A Grave—Kilfoil Cemetery, Merna, Custer Co., Nebraska, Find A Grave.com.

154 Find A Grave—Immanuel Lutheran Cemetery, Amherst, Buffalo Co., Nebraska, Find A Grave.com.

155 Find A Grave—Highmore City Cemetery, Highmore, Hyde Co., South Dakota, Find A Grave.com.

156 Find A Grave—Evergreen Memorial Gardens Cemetery, Vancouver, Clark Co., Washington, Find A Grave.com.

157 Find A Grave—Cliffside Cemetery, Sandy, Clackamas Co., Oregon, Find A Grave.com.

158 U.S. Veteran's Gravesites, ca. 1775-2006, Ancestry.com, Edward J. Baecht.

159 Find A Grave—Arthur Cemetery, Arthur, Bourbon Twp., Douglas Co., Illinois, Find A Grave.com.

160 Find A Grave—Forest Lawn Memorial Park Cemetery, Glendale, Los Angeles Co., California, Find A Grave.com.

161 Find A Grave—Claquato Cemetery, Chehalis, Lewis Co., Washington, Find A Grave.com.

162 Find A Grave—Bohemian National Cemetery, Dodge, Webster Twp., Dodge Co., Nebraska, Find A Grave.com.

163 Find A Grave—Grimes-Neeley Cemetery, English Twp., Jersey Co., Illinois, Find A Grave.com.

[A] Find A Grave—Saint Mark Lutheran Cemetery, Steeleville, Steeleville Twp., Randolph Co., Illinois, Find A Grave.com.

[B] Find A Grave—Brown Chapel Cemetery, Broseley, Ash Hill Twp., Butler Co., Missouri, Find A Grave.com.

[C] Find A Grave—National Memorial Cemetery of Arizona, Phoenix, Maricopa Co., Arizona, Find A Grave.com.

[D] Find A Grave—Ash Hill Cemetery, Fisk, Ash Hill Twp., Butler Co., Missouri, Find A Grave.com.

[E] Find A Grave—Dunklin Memorial Gardens Cemetery, Kennett, Independence Twp., Dunklin Co., Missouri, Find A Grave.com.

[F] Find A Grave—Barlow Cemetery, Barlow, Ballard Co., Kentucky, Find A Grave.com.

[G] Find A Grave—Forest Lawn Memorial Park Cemetery, Cypress, Orange Co., California, Find A Grave.com.

[H] Find A Grave—Oakland Cemetery, Carbondale, Carbondale Twp., Jackson Co., Illinois, Find A Grave.com.

[I] Find A Grave—Newbern Cemetery, East Newbern, Mississippi Twp., Jersey Co., Illinois, Find A Grave.com.

# Appendix

## LEGEND

| ~ About | < Before | > After |
|---------|----------|---------|

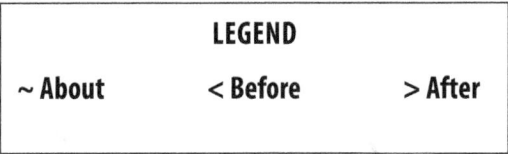

# Descendant Chart for James Pagan I

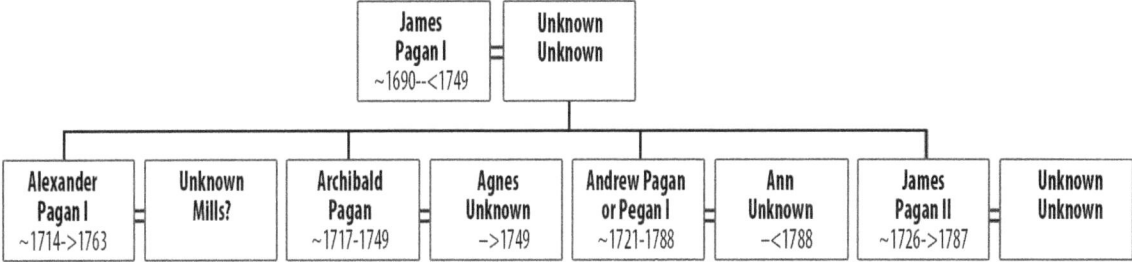

```
          ┌─────────────┬─────────────┐
          │   James     │   Unknown   │
          │   Pagan I   │=│ Unknown   │
          │ ~1690--<1749│             │
          └─────────────┴─────────────┘
```

| Alexander Pagan I | Unknown Mills? | Archibald Pagan | Agnes Unknown | Andrew Pagan or Pegan I | Ann Unknown | James Pagan II | Unknown Unknown |
|---|---|---|---|---|---|---|---|
| ~1714->1763 | | ~1717-1749 | ->1749 | ~1721-1788 | -<1788 | ~1726->1787 | |

# Descendant Chart for Alexander Pagan I

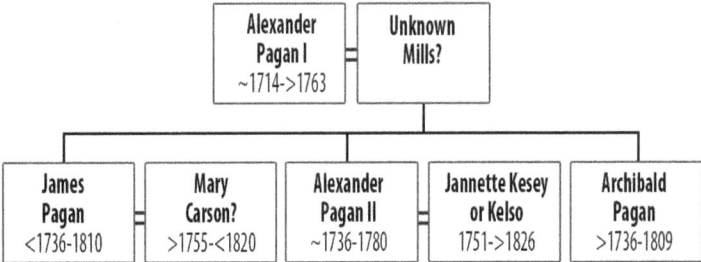

```
          ┌─────────────┬─────────────┐
          │  Alexander  │   Unknown   │
          │   Pagan I   │=│  Mills?   │
          │ ~1714->1763 │             │
          └─────────────┴─────────────┘
```

| James Pagan | Mary Carson? | Alexander Pagan II | Jannette Kesey or Kelso | Archibald Pagan |
|---|---|---|---|---|
| <1736-1810 | >1755-<1820 | ~1736-1780 | 1751->1826 | >1736-1809 |

# Descendant Chart for Archibald Pagan

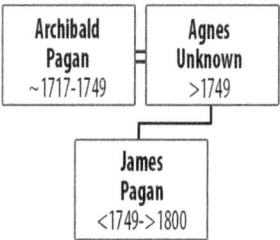

```
          ┌─────────────┬─────────────┐
          │  Archibald  │    Agnes    │
          │   Pagan     │=│  Unknown  │
          │ ~1717-1749  │    >1749    │
          └─────────────┴─────────────┘
                      │
              ┌─────────────┐
              │    James    │
              │    Pagan    │
              │  <1749->1800│
              └─────────────┘
```

# Descendant Chart for Andrew Pagan or Pegan I

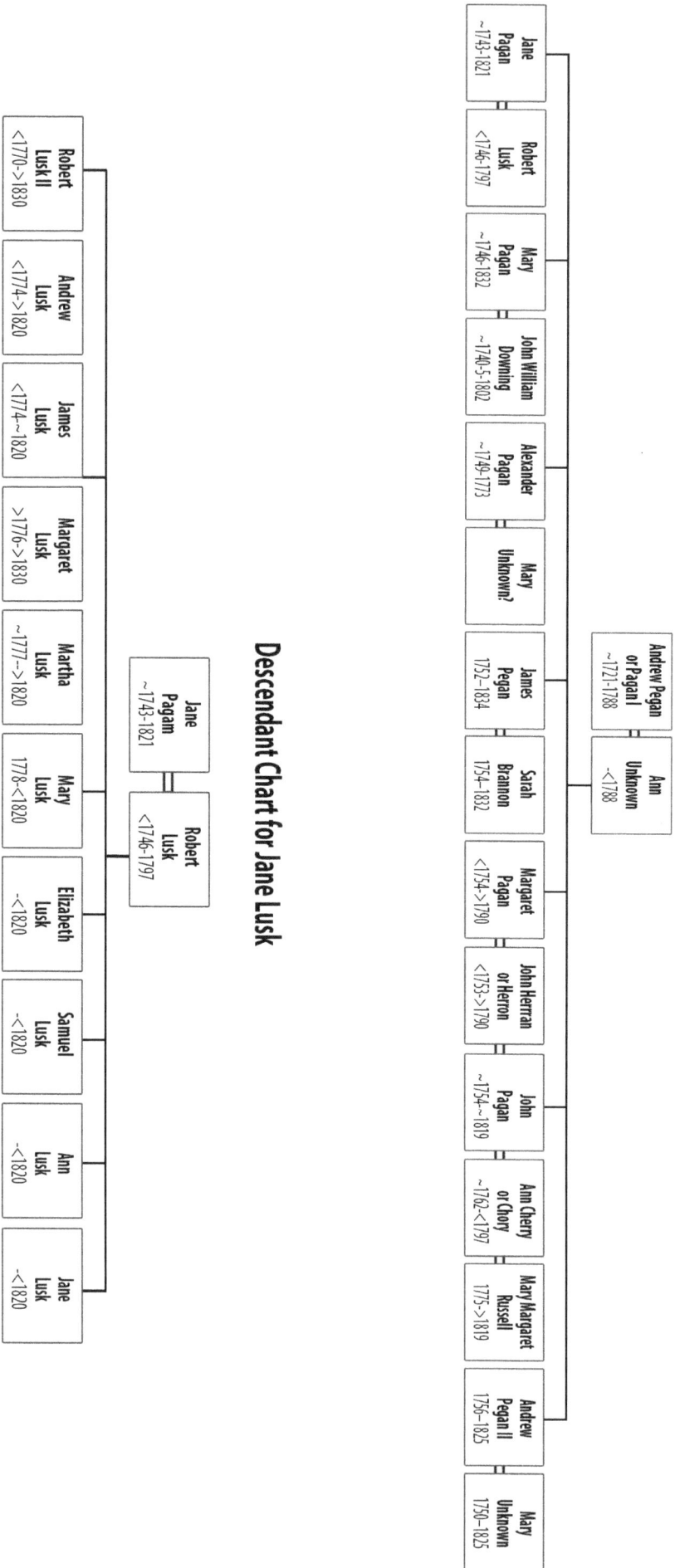

```
                                        Andrew Pegan
                                         or Pagan I
                                         ~1721-1788
                                            ==
                                            Ann
                                          Unknown
                                           -<1788
```

| Jane Pagan ~1743-1821 | Robert Lusk <1746-1797 | Mary Pagan ~1746-1832 | John William Downing ~1740-5-1802 | Alexander Pagan ~1749-1773 | Mary Unknown? | James Pegan 1752-1834 | Sarah Brannon 1754-1832 | Margaret Pagan <1754->1790 | John Herran or Herron <1753->1790 | John Pagan ~1754-~1819 | Ann Cherry or Chory ~1762-<1797 | Mary Margaret Russell 1775->1819 | Andrew Pegan II 1756-1825 | Mary Unknown 1750-1825 |
|---|---|---|---|---|---|---|---|---|---|---|---|---|---|---|

# Descendant Chart for Jane Lusk

```
        Jane
        Pagam
       ~1743-1821
          ==
        Robert
         Lusk
       <1746-1797
```

| Robert Lusk II <1770->1830 | Andrew Lusk <1774->1820 | James Lusk <1774-~1820 | Margaret Lusk >1776->1830 | Martha Lusk ~1777->1820 | Mary Lusk 1778-<1820 | Elizabeth Lusk -<1820 | Samuel Lusk -<1820 | Ann Lusk -<1820 | Jane Lusk -<1820 |
|---|---|---|---|---|---|---|---|---|---|

# Descendant Chart for Mary Pagan

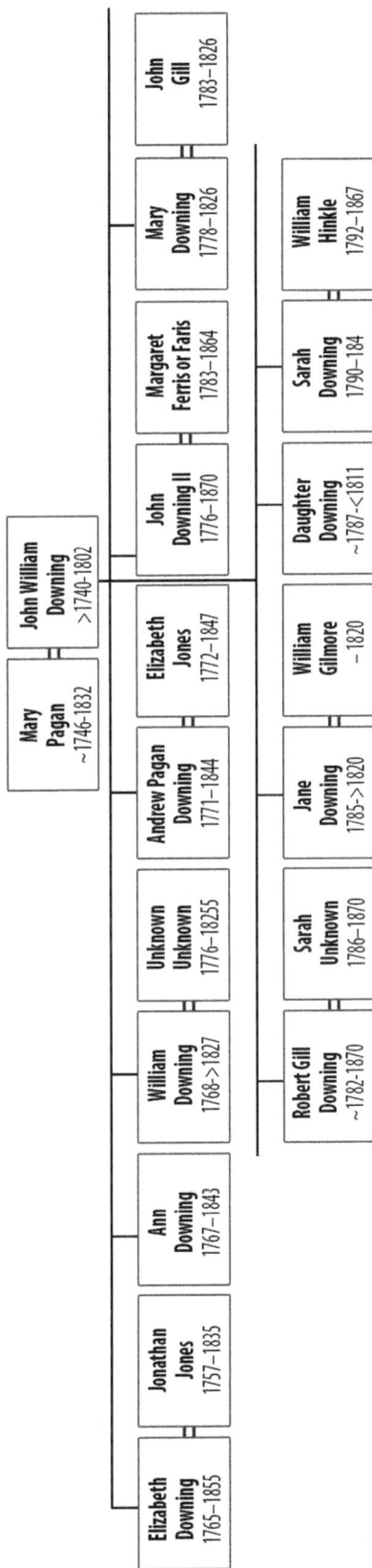

```
                                    Mary              John William
                                   Pagan      ══      Downing
                                 ~1746-1832          >1740-1802
```

| Elizabeth Downing 1765–1855 | Jonathan Jones 1757–1835 | Ann Downing 1767–1843 | William Downing 1768–>1827 | Unknown Unknown 1776–1855 | Andrew Pagan Downing 1771–1844 | Elizabeth Jones 1772–1847 | John Downing II 1776–1870 | Margaret Ferris or Faris 1783–1864 | Mary Downing 1778–1826 | John Gill 1783–1826 |

| Robert Gill Downing ~1782-1870 | Sarah Unknown 1786–1870 | Jane Downing 1785->1820 | William Gilmore –1820 | Daughter Downing ~1787-<1811 | Sarah Downing 1790–184 | William Hinkle 1792–1867 |

# Descendant Chart for James Pegan, Son of Andrew I

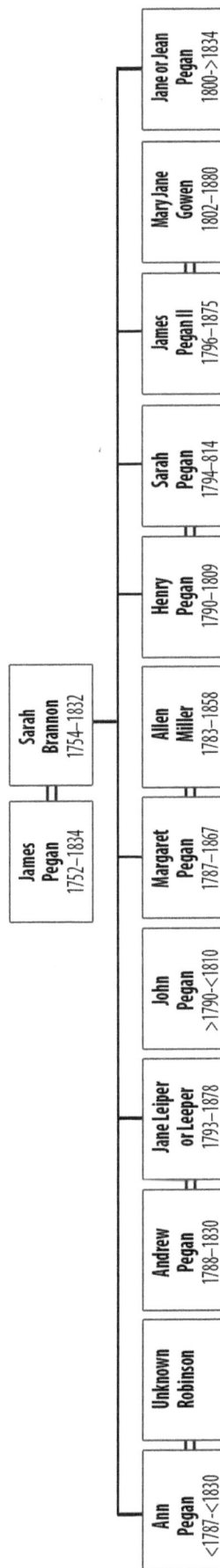

```
                    James                    Sarah
                    Pegan          ══        Brannon
                   1752–1834                1754–1832
```

| Ann Pegan <1787-<1830 | Unknown Robinson | Andrew Pegan 1788–1830 | Jane Leiper or Leeper 1793–1878 | John Pegan >1790-<1810 | Margaret Pegan 1787–1867 | Allen Miller 1783–1858 | Henry Pegan 1790–1809 | Sarah Pegan 1794–814 | James Pegan II 1796–1875 | Mary Jane Gowen 1802–1880 | Jane or Jean Pegan 1800->1834 |

## Descendant Chart for Margaret Pagan

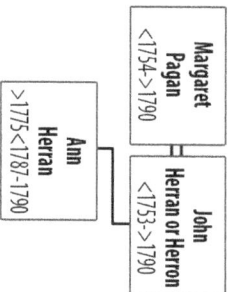

```
Margaret
Pagan
<1754->1790
    ==
John
Herran or Herron
<1753->1790
    |
Ann
Herran
>1775<1787-1790
```

## Descendant Chart for John Pagan

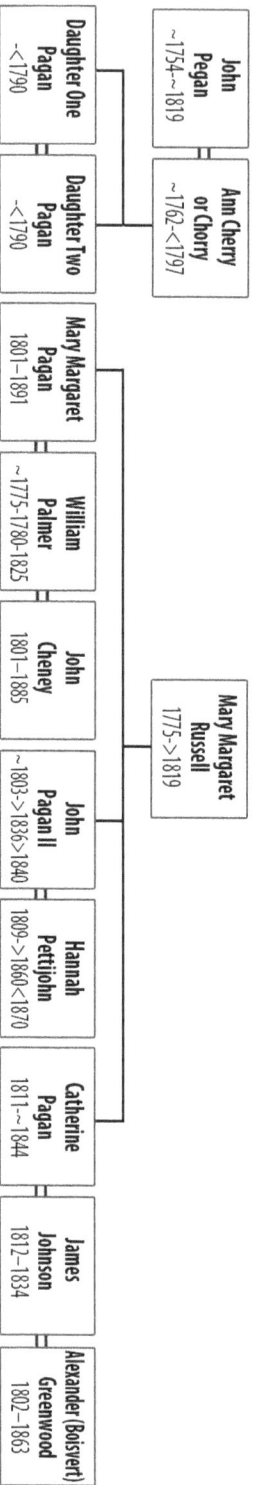

```
John
Pegan
~1754-~1819
    ==
Ann Cherry
or Chorry
~1762-<1797
    |
    +-- Daughter One
    |   Pagan
    |   -<1790
    |
    +-- Daughter Two
        Pagan
        -<1790

Mary Margaret
Pagan
1801-1891
    ==
William
Palmer
~1775-1780-1825

John
Cheney
1801-1885

Mary Margaret
Russell
1775->1819
    |
    +-- John
    |   Pagan II
    |   ~1803->1836>1840
    |       ==
    |   Hannah
    |   Pettijohn
    |   1809->1860<1870
    |
    +-- Catherine
    |   Pagan
    |   1811-~1844
    |       ==
    |   James
    |   Johnson
    |   1812-1834
    |
    +-- Alexander (Boisvert)
        Greenwood
        1802-1863
```

## Descendant Chart for Andrew Pegan II

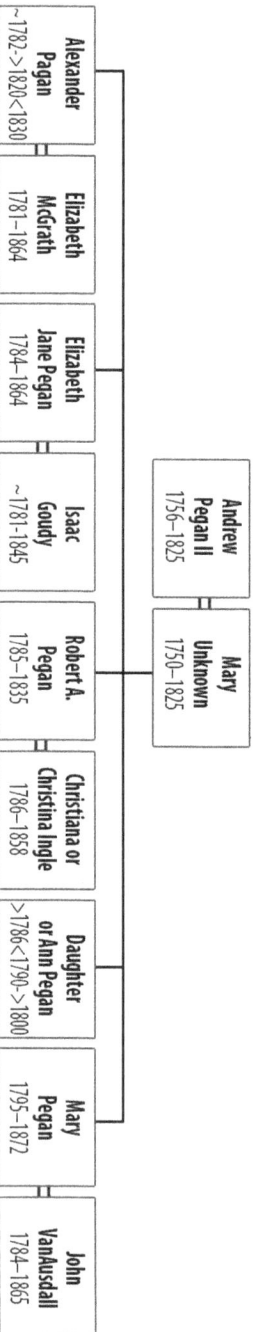

```
Andrew
Pegan II
1756-1825
    ==
Mary
Unknown
1750-1825
    |
    +-- Alexander
    |   Pagan
    |   ~1782->1820<1830
    |       ==
    |   Elizabeth
    |   McGrath
    |   1781-1864
    |
    +-- Elizabeth
    |   Jane Pegan
    |   1784-1864
    |       ==
    |   Isaac
    |   Goudy
    |   ~1781-1845
    |
    +-- Robert A.
    |   Pegan
    |   1785-1835
    |       ==
    |   Christiana or
    |   Christina Ingle
    |   1786-1858
    |
    +-- Daughter
    |   or Ann Pegan
    |   >1786<1790->1800
    |
    +-- Mary
        Pegan
        1795-1872
            ==
        John
        VanAusdall
        1784-1865
```

# Descendant Chart for James Pagan II

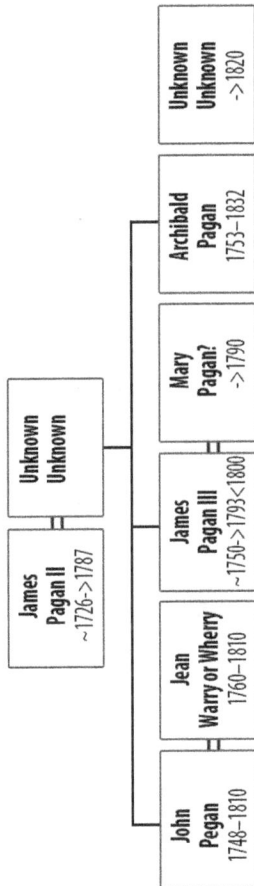

```
                    James                    Unknown
                  Pagan II                   Unknown
                  ~1726->1787

        John          Jean          James           Mary         Archibald      Unknown
       Pegan      Warry or Wherry  Pagan III       Pagan?         Pagan         Unknown
      1748-1810     1760-1810    ~1750->1793<1800   ->1790      1753-1832        ->1820
```

# Descendant Chart for Elizabeth Jane Pegan

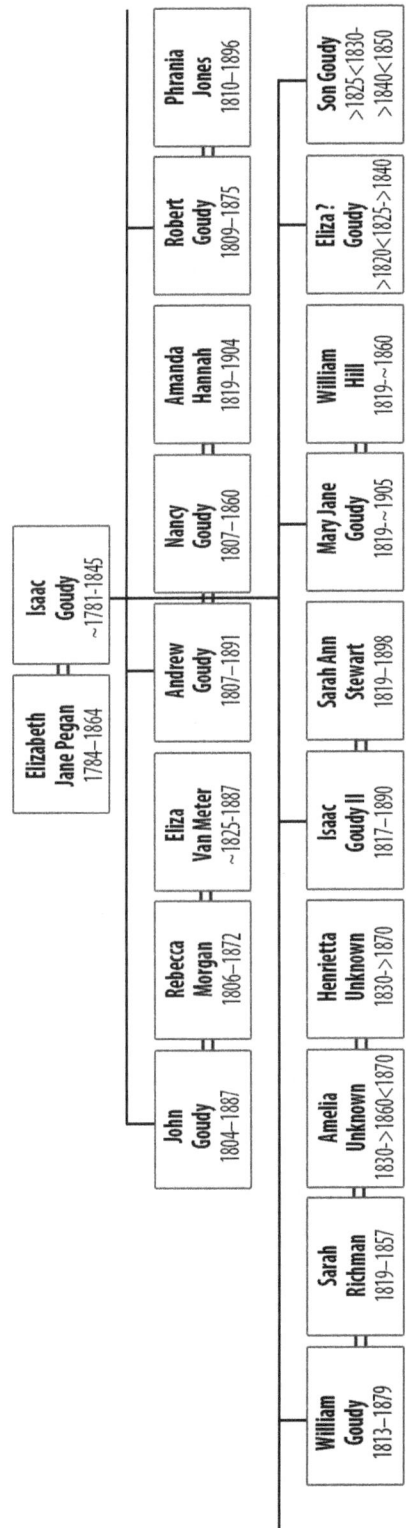

```
              Elizabeth                Isaac
             Jane Pegan                Goudy
              1784-1864             ~1781-1845

  John         Rebecca      Eliza       Andrew       Nancy        Amanda        Robert       Phrania
  Goudy        Morgan     Van Meter     Goudy        Goudy        Hannah        Goudy         Jones
 1804-1887   1806-1872    ~1825-1887  1807-1891    1807-1860    1819-1904    1809-1875     1810-1896

William     Sarah      Amelia         Henrietta      Isaac      Sarah Ann    Mary Jane    William      Eliza ?         Son Goudy
Goudy      Richman    Unknown         Unknown       Goudy II     Stewart      Goudy        Hill        Goudy          >1825<1830-
1813-1879  1819-1857  1830->1860<1870  1830->1870  1817-1890   1819-1898   1819-~1905   1819-~1860  >1820<1825->1840  >1840<1850
```

# Descendant Chart for Alexander Pagan, Son of Andrew Pegan II

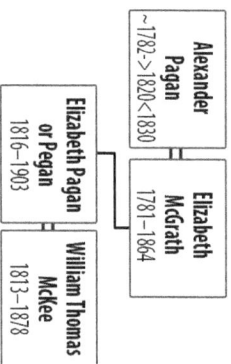

**Alexander Pagan** ~1782->1820<1830

**Elizabeth McGrath** 1781-1864

**Elizabeth Pagan or Pegan** 1816-1903

**William Thomas McKee** 1813-1878

# Descendant Chart for Mary Pegan

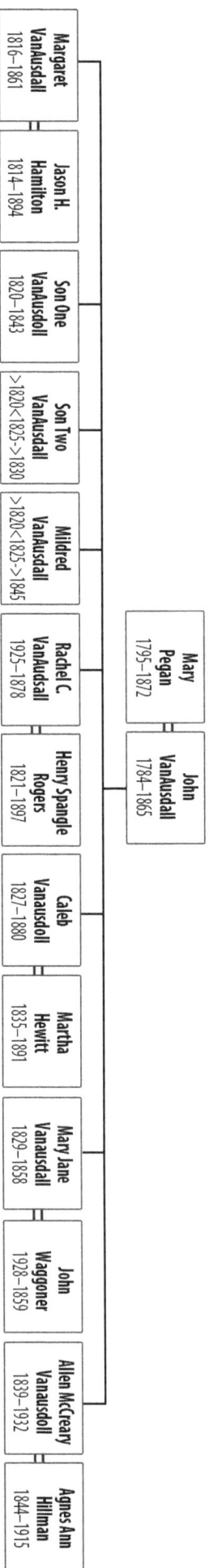

**Mary Pegan** 1795-1872

**John VanAusdall** 1784-1865

**Margaret VanAusdall** 1816-1861

**Jason H. Hamilton** 1814-1894

**Son One VanAusdoll** 1820-1843

**Son Two VanAusdall** >1820<1825->1830

**Mildred VanAusdall** >1820<1825->1845

**Rachel C VanAudsall** 1925-1878

**Henry Spangle Rogers** 1821-1897

**Caleb Vanausdoll** 1827-1880

**Martha Hewitt** 1835-1891

**Mary Jane Vanausdall** 1829-1858

**John Waggoner** 1928-1859

**Allen McCreary Vanausdoll** 1839-1932

**Agnes Ann Hillman** 1844-1915

# Descendant Chart for Robert A. Pegan

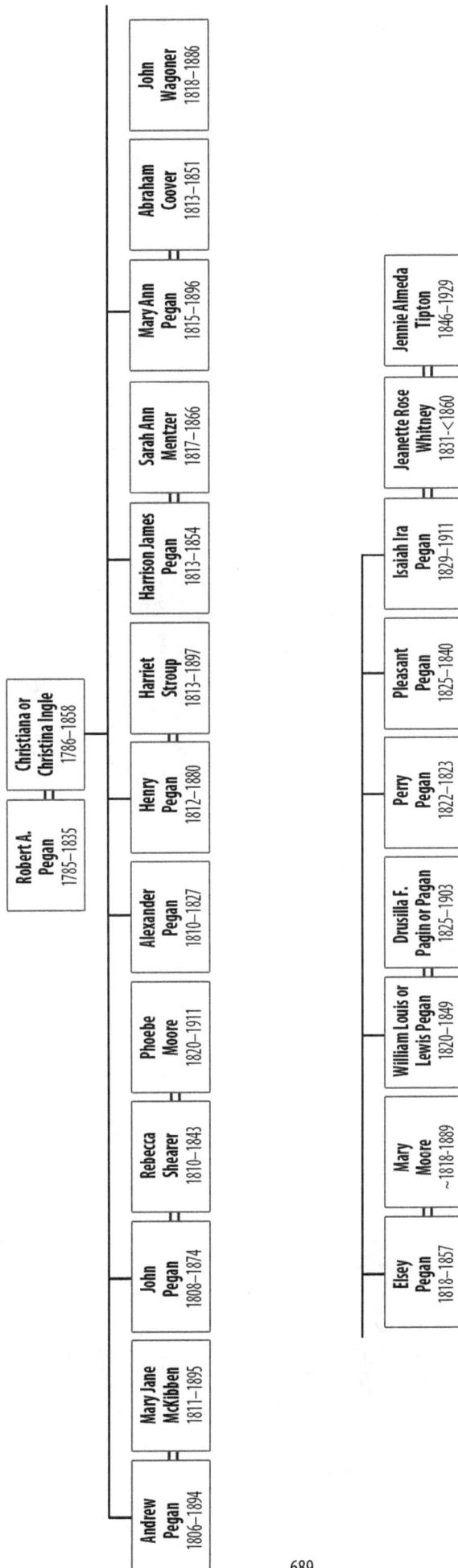

```
                    Robert A.          Christiana or
                    Pegan              Christina Ingle
                    1785–1835          1786–1858
```

**Generation 1 / children:**

| Andrew Pegan 1806–1894 | Mary Jane McKibben 1811–1895 | John Pegan 1808–1874 | Rebecca Shearer 1810–1843 | Phoebe Moore 1820–1911 | Alexander Pegan 1810–1827 | Henry Pegan 1812–1880 | Harriet Stroup 1813–1897 | Harrison James Pegan 1813–1854 | Sarah Ann Mentzer 1817–1866 | Mary Ann Pegan 1815–1896 | Abraham Coover 1813–1851 | John Wagoner 1818–1886 |

**Second group:**

| Elsey Pegan 1818–1857 | Mary Moore ~1818–1889 | William Louis or Lewis Pegan 1820–1849 | Drusilla F. Pagin or Pagan 1825–1903 | Perry Pegan 1822–1823 | Pleasant Pegan 1825–1840 | Isaiah Ira Pegan 1829–1911 | Jeanette Rose Whitney 1831–<1860 | Jennie Almeda Tipton 1846–1929 |

**OUTLINED IN VOLUME 1**

Oldest Pegan grave in America—Archibald Pagan, who died November 20, 1749, age 32. He is buried in Old Chestnut Level Presbyterian Church Lower Cemetery, Drumore Township, Lancaster County, Pennsylvania.

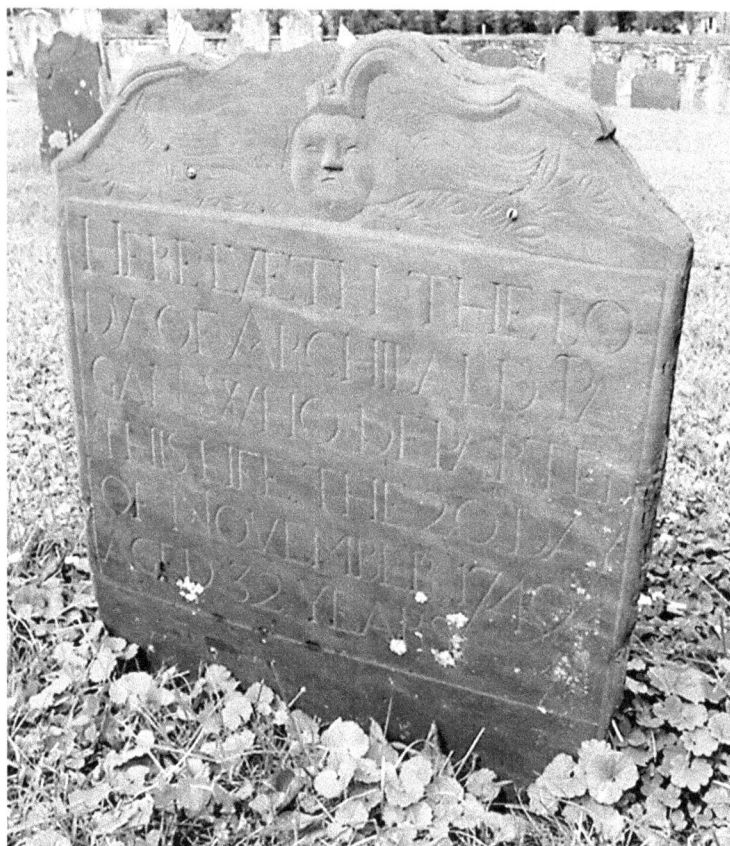

Near Archibald Pagan's grave are those of his nephew, James Pegan, son of Andrew Pegan I, who died January 20, 1834, and James' wife Sarah Brannon Pegan, who died March 3, 1832.

James Pagan/Pegan I selected as a juror for a 741 Lancaster County, Pennsylvania Court Case. This is the first evidence of our Pegan line in America.

### COURT HELD 4 AUGUST 1741

"Before Thomas Edwards Esqr and his Associates Justices".

Sheriff: Robert Buchanen Esqr.

Persons sworn on the Grand Inquest: Gabriel Davies, William Caldwell, James Stewart, Charles Vance, John Morgan, James McAffarson, Mathew Atkinson, Andrew Middleton, James McConnel, David Shields, David Mitchel, Chales [sic] Caldwell, John Dickson, Hugh Long, Samuel McCullough.

Recognizances Ret to this present Sessions

Henry Mosselman that Abraham Mier shall be of good behavior to ffelix Landus and appear at ye next Court. Cont.

John Atcheson to appear and prosecute William Bailey and Charles King for felony.

Mathew Atchison to appear and give evidence against said King.

William Steel: for commiting fornication with Elizabeth Miller. Says he is not guilty. Prosecutor: John Kinsey, Esqr.

Jury: Daniel McConnel, Andrew Allison, James Buchanen, James Rutherford, Theophelus Simonton, Andrew Hamilton, James McClelin, Samuel Leard, William McCloghlin, James Pegan, Samuel Dickson, and David Logan find him not guilty. Discharged on paying fees.

Andrew Pegan/Pagan I and his younger brother James Pagan II in the 1751 Martic Township, Lancaster County, Pennsylvania Tax List, the first extent for that county.

James Pagan/Pegan II buys land in Martic Township, Lancaster County, Pennsylvania on January 15, 1763. First known Pegan deed in this country. Note that this property is said to be adjacent to his brother, Andrew's ("Andrew Pagans") is mentioned, even though Andrew never legally owned his land. Their brother Archibald refers to "his land" in his will, but no deed is found for it.

BENJAMIN ARCHIBALD )    THIS INDENTURE Made the fifteenth day of January in the
        TO     )
              )·   Year of Our Lord One Thousand Seven Hundred and Sixty Three
JAMES PAGAN )

See
Satis-      BETWEEN Benjamin Archibald of the Township of Martock & County of Lancaster Cooper
faction
on          of the One Part  and James Pagan of the Same Place of the other Part,
Page
438
                            WITNESSETH

that the said Benjamin Archibald in Consideration of the Value of One Hundred and Eighty
Eight Pounds Pennsylvania Currency in Hand Payed by the said James Pagan the Receipt
Whereof the said Benjamin Archibald doth hereby acknowldege Hath granted bargained
and Sold and by these Presents Doth grant bargain and Sell unto the said James Pagan
his Heirs Executors Administrators or Assigns,

    ALL THAT Tract of Land Situate in Martock Township and in the said County
Joyning Widow Steels Plantation on the East side & Thomas Whites on the North Side
and Andrew Pagans on the West & South Sides, Containing Two hundred and Three Acres
of land with the Usual Allowance for Roads &c.

                        TOGETHER with all and Singular
the Buildings Improvements Rights Members Hereditaments and Appurtenances whatsoever
thereunto belonging and the Reversions and Remaindors & All Deeds Evidences  and
Writings whatsoever Concerning the same,

                  TO HAVE HOLD AND RETAIN to him the
said James Pagan his Heirs Executors Administrators or Assigns forever,

                          PROVIDED
allways that if the said Benjamin Archibald his Heirs Executors Administrators shall
well and truly pay unto the said James Pagan or to his Heirs Executors Administrators
the said Sum of one Hundred and Eighty Eight Pounds of Currant & Lawfull Money of
Pennsylvania and every Part thereof in manner following that is to say fourty Two
Pounds thereof upon the first day of November Next and fifteen Pounds more thereof
on the first Day of May in the Year of our Lord one Thousand seven Hundred and Sixty
five and fifteen Pounds more Part thereof on the first Day of May in the Year of
our Lord One Thousand Seven Hundred and Sixty six  and fifteen Pounds more Part thereof on the first day of May in the Year of our Lord One thousand seven Hundred and
Sixty Seven  and fifteen Pounds more Part thereof on the first day of May in the
Year of our Lord One thousand Seven Hundred and Sixty Eight and fifteen Pounds more
Part thereof on the first Day of May in the Year of our Lord One Thousand Seven
Hundred and Sixty Nine  and fifteen Pounds more on the first day of May which will
be in the Year of our Lord one Thousand Seven Hundred and Seventy  and fifteen Pounds
more part thereof on the first day of May which will be in the Year of our Lord One
Thousand Seven hundred and Seventy one  and fifteen Pounds more on the first Day of
May which will be in the Year of our Lord One Thousand Seven Hundred and Seventy Two
and Twenty Six Pounds more Part thereof on the first Day of May which will be in the
Year of our Lord One Thousand Seven Hundred and Seventy Three without fraud or further
Delay that then and from thenceforth This Indenture shall be Void and the Estate
hereby Granted shall cease and Determine,

Otherwise This Indenture shall be in

full force and the Land and Premises therein mentioned shall Remain and be in Sole

Right and Property of the said James Pagan his Heirs & Assigns forever without any

Equity of Redemption whatsoever,

IN WITNESS whereof the Parties to these

Presents have interchangeably set their Hands and Seals the Day and Year first above

Written.

Sealed and Delivered in the Presence of us    )   Benjamin Archibald  (SEAL)
   Archibald Ankriem  Ann Ankriem ( Isaac Sanders  )

LANCASTER COUNTY SS: The 15th Day of January A. D. 1763, Came the within named

Benjamin Archibald before me the Subscriber one of his Majesty's Justices of the

Peace for the said County and brought the within Instrument of Writing and Acknowled-

ged the same to be his Act and Deed and Desires that the same may be recorded.    IN

TESTIMONY whereof I have hereunto set my hand and Seal the Day and Year abovesaid.

Isaac Sanders    (SEAL)

RECORDED 4th February 1763.
Edwd. Shippen Recorder

I James Pagan the Mortgagee in this Mortgage named Acknowledge to have received

of Benjamin Archibald the Mortgagor full Satisfaction for this Mortgage.  IN WITNESS

Whereof I the said James Pagan have hereunto set my hand & Seal the Second Day of

October Anno. Domini 1769.

Acknowledged the same Day & Year before me        James Pagan  (SEAL)
      Edwd. Shippen Recorder

Pegans in Martic Township, Lancaster County, Pennsylvania, who signed "Memorials Against Calling a Convention" in 1779. Included are James Pegan II (Sr.), and his sons John, James III and Archibald; and Andrew Pegan I and his sons James and Andrew II (Andy). James Pegan, the miller, the son of Archibald Pagan, brother to Andrew I and James II, seems not to have signed it. Also signing was James Heron (Herran), husband of Margaret Pegan, daughter of Andrew I.

Memorials Against Calling a Convention, 1779

```
Martick's Township.
To the Honorable the Bepresentatives of the Freemen of the Slate
of Pennsylvania in this Memorial Humbly Skeweth :

That your memorialist are of opinion that frequent changes
in Government have a tendency to weaken it and to create di-
visions and contests among the people, & ought, as much as
possible, to be avoided.

Therefore, your taking up and passing a late resolve for tak-
ing ye sense of the people upon certain matters in the Consti-
tution of this Commonwealth before the people had sufficient
experience of it, has a tendency to produce the above men-
tioned bad effects, especially as said resolve appears to have
been grounded merely upon supposed inconveniences in the
present Constitution and form of Government, suggested by
Divers petitions to former assemblies of this Commonwealth,
and adopted without any call, of the community, without any
representation from the executive Branch specifying the in-
competency of the present Constitution for the purposes of
Good Government, without any concurrence of that honorable
Body that we know of, or any opposition or embarrassment in
the way obstructing the execution of your Laws that we have
heard of. We cannot help, therefore, being of opinion that
in passing the resolve in Question, especially in the manner
and circumstances above mentioned, you have exceeded the
powers Delegated to you, and treated that constitution, of
which you were the appointed Guardians, with Great neglect.

That, however, your memorialists, if just and weighty rea-
sons would be assigned, might not be against caUing a con-
vention, yet we cannot look upon the manner in which you
have appointed the votes to be taken to be fare and unexcep-
tionable ; the question is perplexed by your doubling it, and.
```

```
however, they, who arc for a convention, may vote on both
sides, we cannot see the propriety or consistency of voting
against one, and at the same time electing the members who
are to compose it.

There are Great Numbers of your constituents who have
taken a solemn oath to preserve the present Commonwealth,
who are apprehensive will not think themselves justifiable in
putting it into the hands of a Convention in any other way
than by the Constitution itself is directed, and who, we are
persuaded, cannot bring themselves to a compliance with the
resolve in question in its proposed mode of execution.

For these causes and before you put the good people of this
state to the great trouble and expense of a new convention,
your Memorialists presume that you will take the first opper-
tunity of revising your late resolve, and that your wisdom and
goodness and your regard to the peace & Tranquility of this
state will induce you either to drop it entirely, or to adopt it
and carry it into execution in a manner not liable to any great
and just exceptions.
```

JOHN BRANNON,
JAMES DUNCAN,
JOHN PAGAN,

ARCHIBALD PEGAN,

JAMES PAGAN,

JAMES WHARRY,
JOHN McCALSTER,
JOHN BARR,
SAMUEL DICKSON,
JAMES PEGAN,
JOHN BOYD,
THOS. BOYD,
JAS. MOORE,
SAMUEL McCOLLOUCH,
DAVID McCOLLOUGH,
ROBERT McCOLLOUGH,
PATRICK CAMPBELL,
JAMES MITCHEL,
VALENTINE GARTER,
JAMES ALEXANDER,
WILLIAM CLARK,
JOHN HART,
SAMUEL WILSON, Sen.,
JOHN McCREARY,
HUGH BIGHAM,

ANDY PEGAN,
ANDREW PEGAN,
JOHN BROWN,
JAMES BROWN,
JAMES PEGAN, Sen.,
JAMES HERON,
ADAM MOORE,
JAMES MOORE,
WILLIAM MOORE,
SAMUEL SIMPSON,
DAVID GIBSON,
PETER SIMPSON,
SAMUEL SIMPSON,
JAMES SAVAGE,
JOSEPH McCOLLAGH,
WILLIAM KENNEDY,
JAMES CALLAHAN,

In 1787, James Pegan II's property in Martic Township, Lancaster County, Pennsylvania was confiscated by Lancaster County for non-payment of property tax and sold at auction. At this time, James II and his sons John and Archibald removed to Mifflin Township, Allegheny County, Pennsylvania. His son James III, however, stayed in Martic Township.

11-533: Sheriff James Ross rel.to Paul Zantzinger, merchant, of Lancaster Borough
   200a Martic tp.: HISTORY: On 11 Aug 1787, the Court of Common Pleas ordered the sheriff to seize the real estate of James Pagan, yeoman, of Lancaster County, due to unpaid debts owing to George Hess & Margaret Graham [the executors of John Graham]. The sheriff duly seized 200a Martic tp., which he later sold at public vendue to Paul Zantzinger, the party hereto.
   3 June 1789: R.W. Ball & Jacob Graeff

Andrew Pegan II listed among the deserters from the Pennsylvania/Virginia navy ship Montgomery, June 25, 1776, *Philadelphia Gazette?*

# TWENTY DOLLARS REWARD,

RUN AWAY from the Province Ship (called the Montgomery) lying in the river Delaware, opposite the Fort-Island: Five Marines, belonging to William Brown's Company, viz. PETER ABLE, about 26 years of age, 5 feet 9 or 10 inches high, fair curly hair, large white eye brows, very light eyes, was born in Conogocheague, Cumberland county, speaks broken Dutch: had on when he went away, a new oznabrig shirt and trowsers.

WILLIAM TINLY, born in England, about 25 years of age, 5 feet 6 inches high, fresh complexion, curly hair, formerly lived in or near Leesbury, Virginia, but enlisted in Lancaster.

EDWARD THOMAS, born in England, about 26 years of age, 5 feet 6 inches high, red hair and much freckled, formerly lived in or near Harford, Maryland.

ANDREW PEGAN, country born, about 19 years of age, 5 feet 8 or 9 inches high, straight and well made, a weaver by trade, supposed to have gone to his father's in Martick township, Lancaster county.

JOSEPH KENMER, born in Ireland, about 5 feet 8 inches high, 24 years of age, well made, wears his hair tied; will, it is supposed, go towards Harford in Maryland, where he formerly lived.

Whoever takes up said Deserters and brings them on board said ship, or confines them in jail, shall have the above reward, or FOUR DOLLARS for each, paid by

8 w.     WILLIAM BROWN

Lancaster County, Pennsylvania

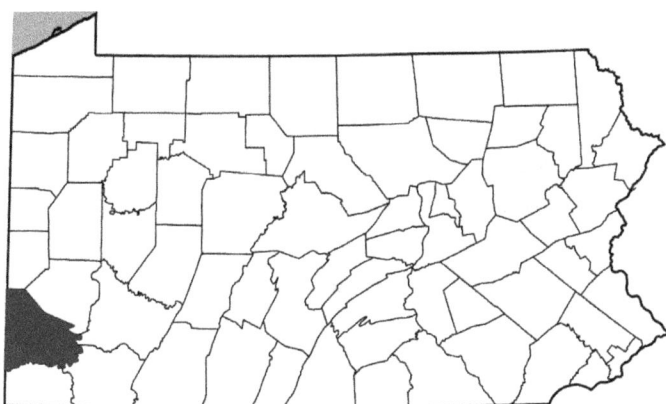

Washington County, Pennsylvania

Martic Township in Lancaster County, Pennsylvania

Around 1790, Andrew Pegan II and his sister, Margaret Pegan Herran, were residents of Strabane Township, Washington County, Pennsylvania. Later, as this modern-day map shows this township was split into two, Northern and Southern Strabane.

Will of Andrew Pegan I, written September 9, 1788, proved January 13, 1789, Lancaster County, Pennsylvania.

Recorded & Exam'd & James Jacks Reg'r

Andrew Pegan dec'd

# In the Name of God. Amen.

I Andrew Pegan Sen'r of Martick Township Lancaster County and state of Pennsylvania Yeoman being mindfull of Mortality and knowing that that it is appointed for all Men once to die do make this my last Will and Testament in the manner following that is to say recommending my Soul into the hands of God that gave it nothing doubting but that I shall receive the same again by the mighty power of God at the day of the general Resurrection and for my Body I recommend the same to the Earth to be buried in a christian and decent like manner at the discretion of my Executors and I do order that all my just debts and other my funeral charges be duly paid and for all my worldly Estate wherewith it hath pleased God to bless me in this Life I give and dispose of the same in the following manner. I give and bequeath to my well beloved Son John Pegan the one half of my part of the Stock such as cows sheep and Hogs likewise eight pounds lawfull Money to be paid of the Land one Year and half after my decease likewise my large Pott and little Walnut table. I give and bequeath to my well beloved Son James Pegan the whole Land I now live on with all the Horses and his half of the moveable Stock such as cows sheep and hogs now in his Possession. I give and bequeath to my well beloved Son Andrew Pegan the other half of my part of cows Sheep and hogs with all my wearing or Body cloaths. I give and bequeath to my well beloved daughter Jean Luck the Sum of seven shillings and six pence. I give and bequeath to my well beloved Daughter Margret Herron the one half of my puter and to my Grand daughter Ann Herron the other half of the puter; to wit four Dishes and twelve plates to be equaly devided between them both. I give and bequeath to my well beloved Daughter Mary donning the Sum of seven shilling and six pence. I give and bequeath to my Grand daughter Ann Pegan daughter to Son James Pegan my Father Bed and Bed cloaths such as Rug and Blankits. And I do hereby Nominate and appoint my two trusty Friends John Caldwell and James Pegan my son to be my Executors of this my last Will and Testament ratifying and confirming this and no other to be my last Will and Testament. In Witness whereof I have hereto set my hand and Seal this ninth day of Septem'r Anno Domini 1788.

Andrew A Pegan
his mark

Signed sealed published pronounced and declared by the said Andrew Pegan the Testator as his last Will & Testament in the presence of us the Subscribers

Hugh Penny. John Maffet.

Lancaster County ss. On the thirteenth day of January Anno Domini 1789 before me the subscriber personally appeared Hugh Penny and John Maffet the two subscribing Witnesses to the above and foregoing Will and their Solemn Oaths by uplifted hand respectively did depose and say that they were present and saw and heard Andrew Pegan the Testator therein named Sign Seal publish pronounce and declare the said above writing as and for his last Will and Testament and that at the doing thereof he was of sound and well disposing Mind Memory and Understanding to the best of their Knowledge Observation and belief.

James Jacks Reg'r

Be it Remembered that on the thirteenth day of January Anno Domini 1789

In 1795, James Pegan, son of Andrew Pegan I, applies for a land patent for property in Martic Township, Lancaster County, Pennsylvania. This is the land his father, and perhaps his grandfather James I, squatted on for decades. The land stayed in the hands of James' descendants until the mid-20th century.

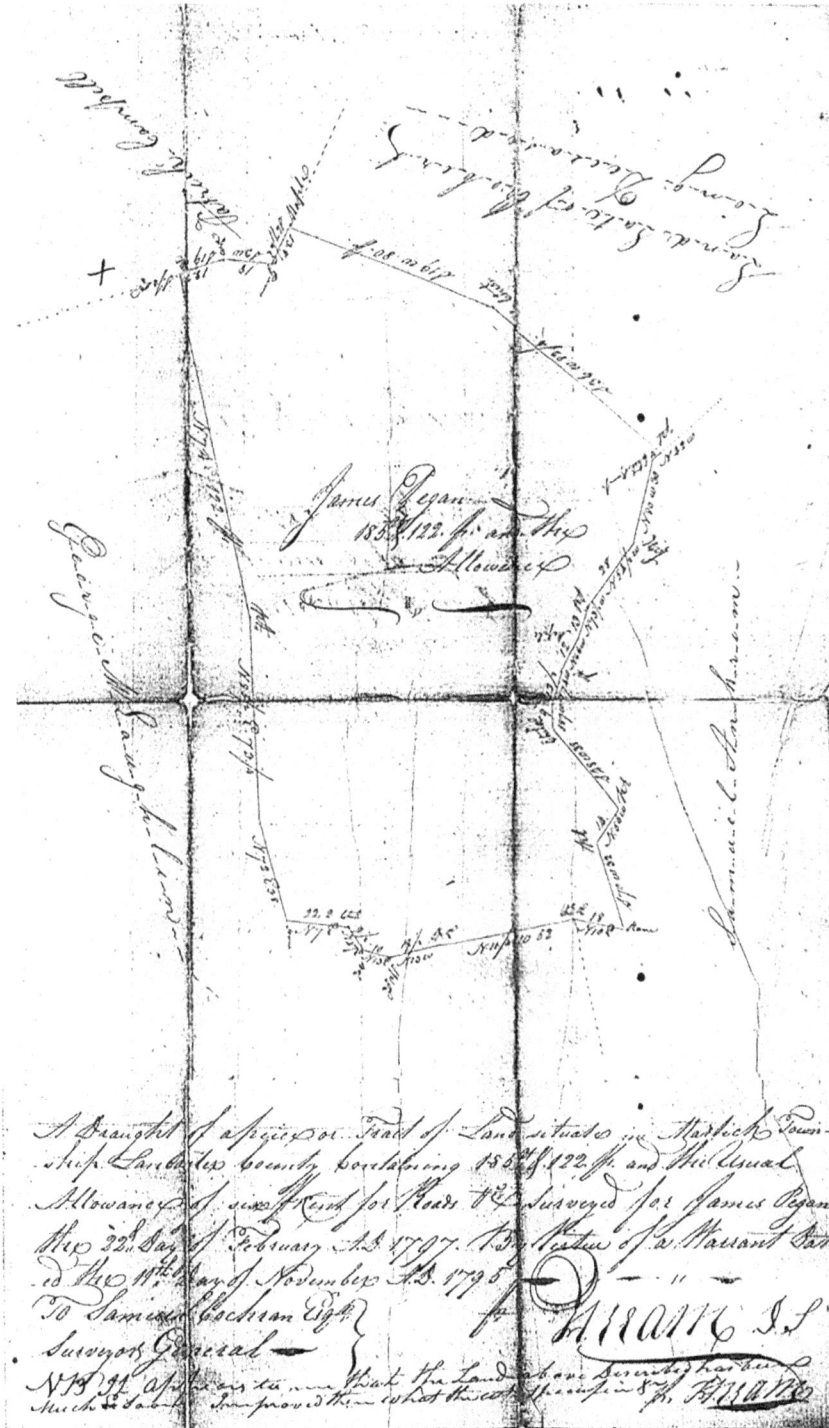

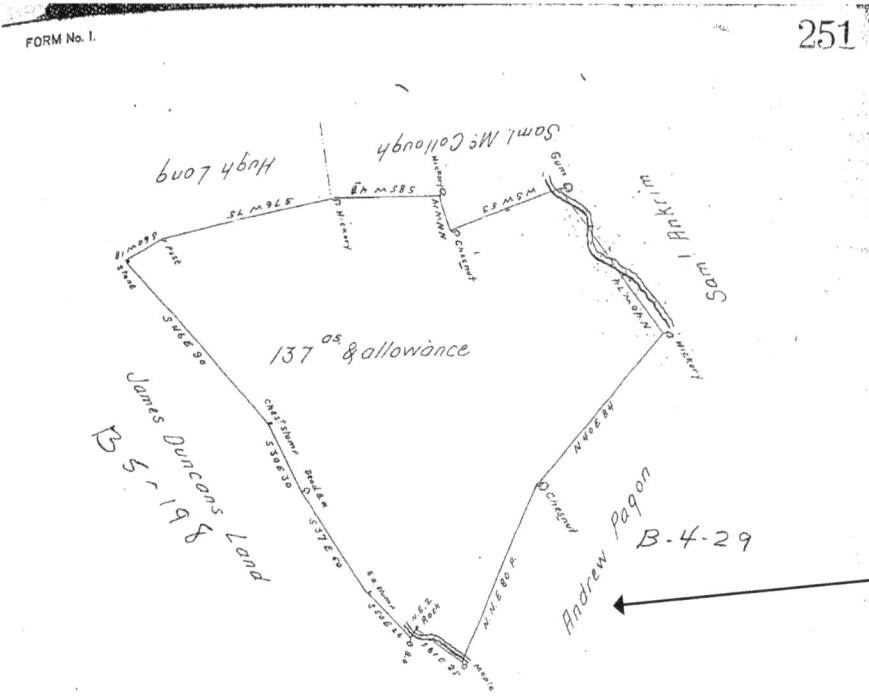

Andrew Pegan I squatted on land in Martic Township, Lancaster County, Pennsylvania. Even though he never legally owned the land, his name appears on others' surveys, like this one in 1769.

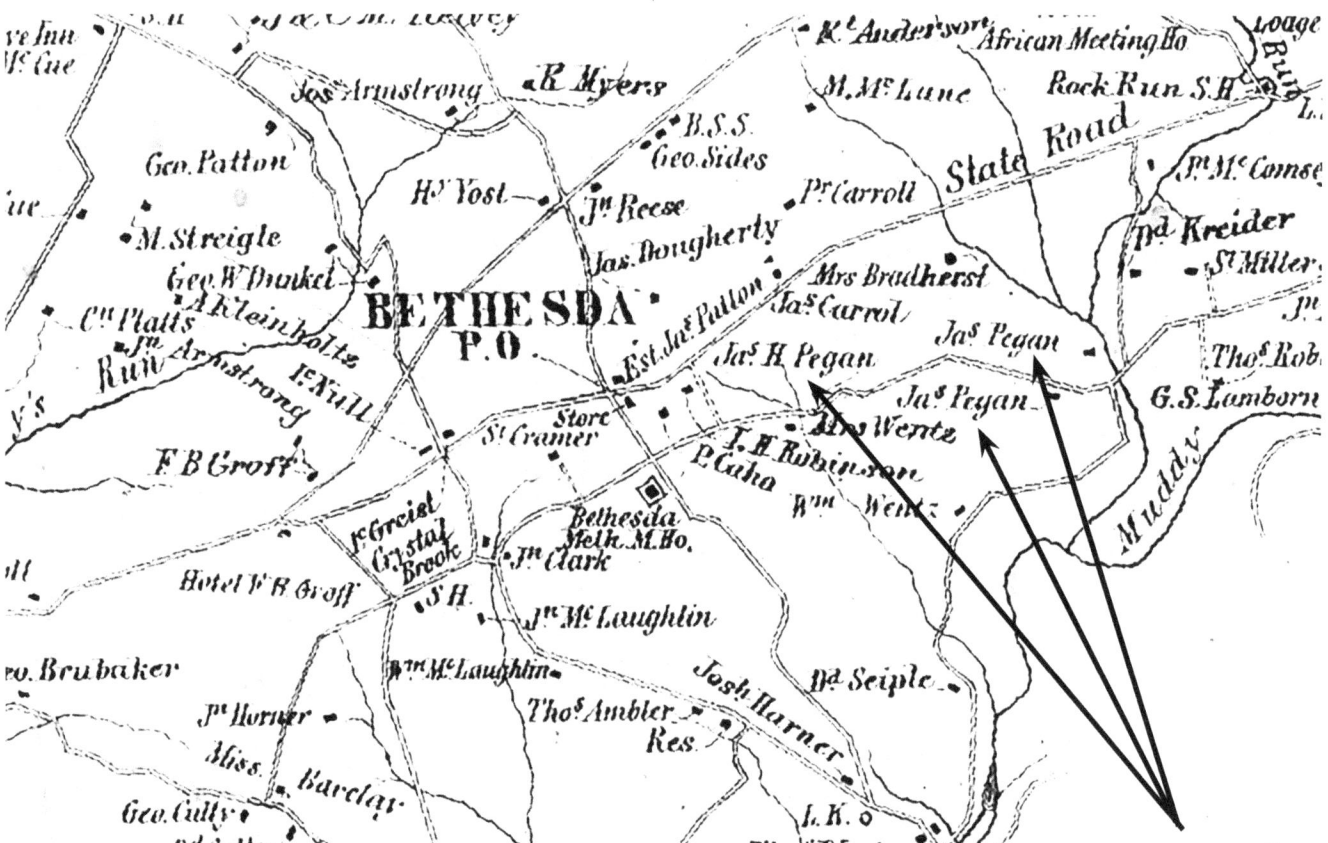

Andrew Pagan/Pegan I's son James Pegan inherited this land in Martic Township, Lancaster County, Pennsylvania from his father. James did apply for a patent to finally legally own the property, which he called "Pegan's Fancy". This map, from 1864, shows the land, which is now underwater in the Muddy Run Recreation Reservoir in Lancaster County, Pennsylvania. The two James Pegans listed on the map are James Pegan, are James Henry Pegan, a grandson of the James who obtained the patent, and James Pegan Jr., the son of the original patent holder and an uncle to James Henry Pegan.

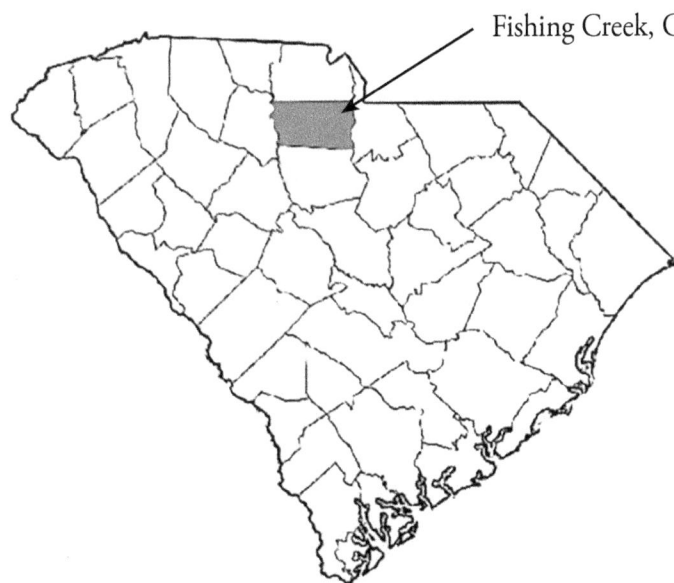

Allegheny County
Pennsylvania
Township Map

Beaver
County

Washington
County

Link to Allegheny
County Map ca. 1880

James Pagan II and sons John and Archibald relocated from Martic Township, Lancaster County, Pennsylvania about the time James II's land was seized by the Lancaster County Sheriff for non-payment of taxe In 1787. They settled in Mifflin and Versailles townships. His son James stayed in Martic Township.

Fishing Creek, Chester County, South Carolina

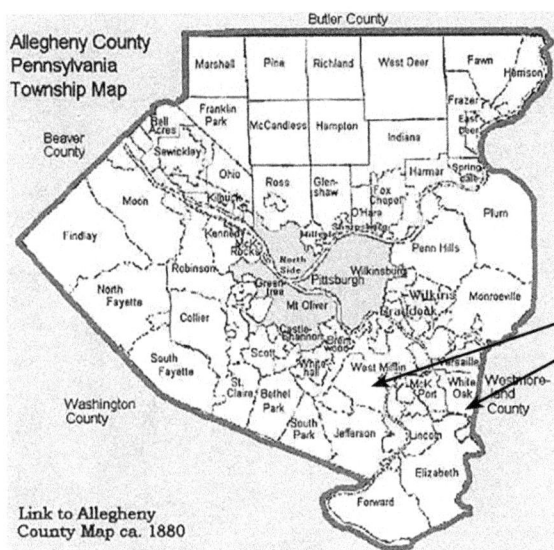

Alexander Pagan I , his sons James, Alexander II and Ambrose, moved from Martic Township, Lancaster County, Pennsylvania to Fishing Creek in what is now Chester County, South Carolina, around 1762-3. His nieces Jane Pagan and Mary Pagan Downing, daughters of Alexander I's brother Andrew Pegan I, also went with Alexander, his sons, and other congregants from Muddy Run Presbyterian Church in Martic Township because of Indian raids during the French and Indian War.

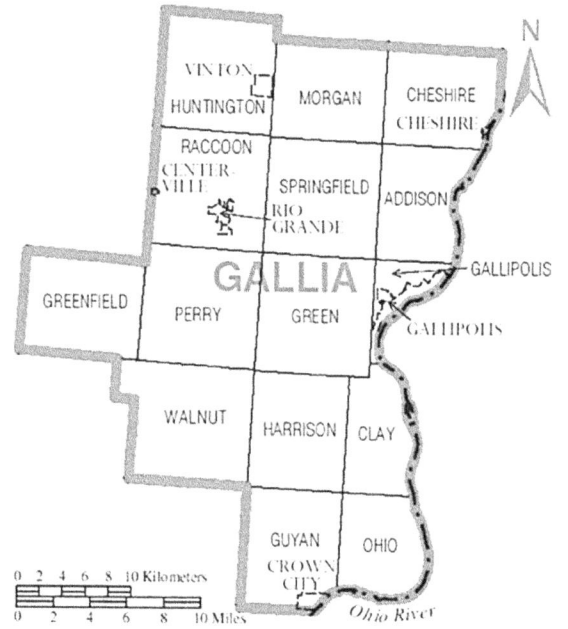

John Pagan removed to Gallipolis, Gallia Co., Ohio from Philadelphia, Pennsylvania.

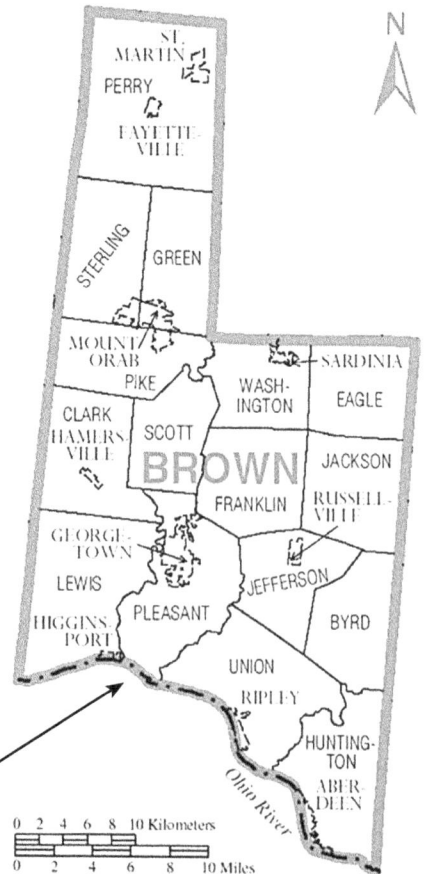

Alexander Pagan, son of Andrew Pegan II, settled in Pleasant Township, Brown County, Ohio.

Elizabeth Pegan Goudy lived in Wheeling, Ohio County, West Virginia, then still a part of Virginia. She died in Wheeling.

Mary Pegan VanAusdall settled in Jersey Township, Jersey County, Illinois.

# Index

Garner, Jane Joan—400

Garner, Roy S.—563, 599

Garrett, Marjorie Marie—502

Gaskill, Unknown—202

Gaston, Frank James—396

Gates, Unknown—459

Gatten, Roy Cecil—392

Gaughan, Lucy Ann—477

Geiger, George Fulton II—110, 142

Geiger, George--110

Geiger, Infant Daughter One—110, 142

Geiger, Infant Daughter Two—110, 142

Geiges, Charles Kirkwood—134, 174

Geiges, Harold Marcus—134

Geller, Sophia—443

Gemmel, Pearl—125

Gentry, Adaline Blair—135, 175

Gentry, Dorothy—175, 200

Gentry, Douglas Gary—175, 200

Gentry, Ellsworth James II—175, 200

Gentry, Ellsworth James III—200, 210

Gentry, Ellsworth James—135, 174

Gentry, John E.—175, 200

Gentry, Otis—271

Gentry, Thomas Daniel II—135, 175

Gentry, Thomas Daniel—135

Gentry, Thomas Daniel—175, 200

Gerhart, Mr.—371

Getchell, Daniel Harvey—478

Gibbs, Jean A.—188

Giberg/Gilbert, Benjamin F.—120

Gibson, Eleanor M.—104

Gibson, Unknown—669

Giddens, Geraldine Louise—661

Gilbert, Arthur Edward—638, 667

Gilbert, Daughter One (Moore)—638, 668

Gilbert, Daughter Three (Keefer)—638, 668

Gilbert, Daughter Two (Lynch)—638, 668

Gilbert, James Franklin—638

Gilbert, Jeremiah—668, 674

Gilbert, Lois M.—189

Gilbert, Melvin Benjamin—120, 157

Gilbert, Son--638, 667

Gilbert, Theo G.—120, 158

Gilgore, Dorothy (Pontz)—130, 170

Gilgore, Harlan Edgar—130, 170

Gilgore, John Wesley—130

Gilgore, Joseph W.—171, 200

Gilgore, Robert Claire—130, 171

Gilgore, William—130, 171

Gill, Elizabeth Eveline—11

Gill, John—47

Gilliam, Cherrl Dean—405

Gillispie, Bleeker K.—238, 262

Gillispie, Richard H.—238

Gillmore, Letitia—554

Gilmore or Gillmore, Martha—551

Gilmore, Albert LeRoy—574, 616

Gilmore, Charles E.—552

Gilmore, Charles Junior—617, 657

Gilmore, Child One—553, 576

Gilmore, Child Three—553, 577

Gilmore, Child Two—553, 576

Gilmore, Dale Wayne—656, 671

Gilmore, Dona Jean (Menninga Byers)—616, 655

Gilmore, Dorothy JoAnne (Slater)—617, 656

Gilmore, Eva May (Perdew)—552, 576

Gilmore, Flossie (Miller)—552, 575

Gilmore, Fred LeRoy—656, 671

Gilmore, Garland Eugene—617, 657

Gilmore, George Otis—616, 655

Gilmore, Harry Eugene—574, 617

Gilmore, Harry Otis—552, 574

Gilmore, Ila Mae (Timmons)—575, 618

Gilmore, Infant Son—617, 656

Gilmore, Irma—575, 618

Gilmore, James Everett—575, 618

Gilmore, Joel Glenn—656, 671

Gilmore, Juanita Muriel (Gray)—574, 617

Gilmore, Kenneth Duane II—525, 533

Gilmore, Kenneth Duane—525

Gilmore, Kurt Allen—656, 671

Gilmore, Laura Edith (Babcock)—552, 573

Gilmore, Linda J. (Jones, Cooper)—617, 657

Gilmore, Linda Kay—526, 533

Gilmore, Perl Edward—552, 575

Gilmore, Rachel V.—557

Gilmore, Richard—616, 655

Gilmore, Roger LaVerne—618, 657

Gilmore, Ronald—616, 656

Gilmore, Sandra Arlene—617, 657

Gilmore, Velma Rita (Koeneke)—574, 616

Gilmore, Viola—575, 618

Gilmore, Walter Laverne—575, 617

Gilmore, William C.—552, 575

Githens, Susan—327

Gittings, Sandra Jean—523

Glenn, Alice Clair (Spencer)—158, 196

Glenn, Alice Jean—159, 196

Glenn, Alvin Huber II—159, 197

Glenn, Alvin Huber—121, 159

Glenn, Grace—158, 196

Glenn, Hope—158, 196

Glenn, James Andrew—121

Glenn, James Earl—121, 158

Glenn, Lida Maxwell (Brown)—122, 159

Glenn, Mary Ellen—158, 196

Glenn, Nora (Kilgore)—122, 159

Glenn, Phyllis E. (McPherson)—159, 197

Glenn, Purdy Lester—121, 158

Glick, Doris—270

Goble, Patricia Roth—649

Godfernon, Fernande Ada Belle—624

Goebel, Florence May (Matthews)—290, 311

Goebel, Henry Ashbelle II—290

Goebel, Henry August III—290, 311

Goebel, Lula—290, 311

Gohn, Jane Pauline—511

Gonzales, Unknown—407

Goodchild, Paul Robert—203

Goodenkauf, Arlie Leonard—629

Goodling, Carrie—97

www.ingramcontent.com/pod-product-compliance
Lightning Source LLC
Chambersburg PA
CBHW080803300326

41914CB00056B/1167